Acknowledgments

As scholars engaged in the study of mergers and acquisitions (M&A), we have over the past years often been involved in conversations with our peers on the need for integration across disciplines studying M&A. It was listening to one such a discussion that prompted David Faulkner to kick start the project of editing a Handbook of M&A that would provide one answer to the state of affairs. Satu Teerikangas and Richard Joseph were added to the team to ensure the international and inter-disciplinary reach of the editing team.

The specific wish of our commissioning editor David Musson from Oxford University Press was to ensure the inclusion of prominent M&A scholars across disciplines into the Handbook. With this aim in mind, over the past years we approached M&A colleagues regarding their availability and willingness to contribute to the Handbook. For some themes and disciplines, this process was easy, given the few experts studying a particular facet of M&A. For other themes, the process required difficult choices, given the number of excellent scholars studying certain core themes on M&A. Further, there were themes for which it appeared more difficult to find seminal authors, in which case we authored the chapter ourselves.

Over the past years, we have been in active touch with Oxford University Press and the authors of the Handbook's chapters. We wish here to extend our sincere gratitude to Oxford University Press for their cooperation and support over the years. In particular, we wish to acknowledge David Musson, the Business and Management editor, for supporting the idea and taking it forward at Oxford University Press, as well as Emma Lambert, the Assistant Commissioning Editor, and Carol Carnegie, the Production editor for their supportive, prompt and caring helpfulness throughout the project until its final stages. We are particularly thankful for Virginia Williams for her meticulous precision and 24h/24 availability in copy-editing the Handbook's chapters.

No edited handbook would exist without its authors. In this respect, we extend our warmest gratitude to the involved authors for their excellent contributions and cooperation throughout the Handbook editing process. Book projects are always longer than expected, from idea to publication. For authors, participating in a Handbook project is an opportunity, yet does bear a lot of revision rounds and hard work. We are grateful for the patience and perseverance of our authors, as well as for the excellence of their scholarship visible in the quality and promptness of their work. As co-editors, Satu and Rick wish to thank David for initiating the project. Our gratitude goes to families and close ones for ongoing support to all those involved in making this Handbook happen. To the readers, we hope that the Handbook provides an informative, insightful, but also provocative read prompting greater integration across the disciplines engaged in the study and practice of M&A, thus ultimately leading to enhanced execution and value creation in M&A.

David Faulkner, Satu Teerikangas and Richard Joseph
In Oxford, London, and Boston,
December 6th 2011.

MERGERS AND ACQUISITIONS

THE HANDBOOK OF

MERGERS AND ACQUISITIONS

Edited by

DAVID FAULKNER, SATU TEERIKANGAS,
AND RICHARD J. JOSEPH

OXFORD
UNIVERSITY PRESS

UNIVERSITY PRESS

Great Clarendon Street, Oxford OX2 6DP
United Kingdom

Oxford University Press is a department of the University of Oxford.
It furthers the University's objective of excellence in research, scholarship,
and education by publishing worldwide. Oxford is a registered trade mark of
Oxford University Press in the UK and in certain other countries

© Oxford University Press 2012

The moral rights of the authors have been asserted

First Edition published in 2012

First published in paperback 2014

Impression: 1

Published in the United States of America by Oxford University Press
198 Madison Avenue, New York, NY 10016, United States of America

British Library Cataloguing in Publication Data

Data available

Library of Congress Cataloging in Publication Data

The handbook of mergers and acquisitions / edited by
David Faulkner, Satu Teerikangas, Richard J. Joseph.
1. Consolidation and merger of coporations.   I. Faulkner, David,
1938–   II. Teerikangas, Satu.   III. Joseph, Richard J.
HD2746.5.H363   2012
338.8'3—dc23
2012004254

ISBN 978–0–19–960146–2 (hbk.)
ISBN 978–0–19–870388–4 (pbk.)

Printed in Great Britain by
MPG Books Group, Bodmin and King's Lynn

Contents

PART I A STRATEGIC LENS FOR M&A

PART II A FINANCIAL LENS FOR M&A

PART III A SOCIOCULTURAL LENS FOR M&A

PART IV A SECTORIAL LENS FOR M&A

PART V SYNTHESIS

LIST OF FIGURES

List of Tables

ABBREVIATIONS

AA	Arthur Andersen
ABS	Asset-backed securities
AMACOM	American Management Association
AMC	Awareness-motivation-capability
APV	Adjusted present value
AY	Arthur Young
BATNA	Best alternative to no agreement
BBH	Baltic Beverages Holding
BCG	Boston Consulting Group
BCH	Banco Central Hispanomericano
BCI	Banca Commerciale Italiana
BHARs	Buy-and-hold abnormal returns
BHC	Bank Holding Company
BIS	Bank for International Settlements
BNP	Banque Nationale de Paris
BRIC	Brazil, Russia, India, and China
BSOPM	Black–Scholes Option Pricing Model
C&L	Coopers & Lybrand
CAP	Competitive advantage period
CAPM	Capital asset pricing model
CARs	Cumulative abnormal returns
CDO	Collaterized debt obligations
CEO	Chief executive officer
CFTC	Commodity Futures Trading Commission
CGT	Capital gains tax
CLO	Collaterized loan obligations
CMS	Critical management studies
CSR	Clean surplus relation
DBS	Development Bank of Singapore
DCF	Discounted cash flow
DHS	Deloitte Haskins & Sells
DTM	Decision tree model
EADS	European Aeronautic Defence and Space Company
E&W	Ernst and Whinney
E&Y	Ernst & Young

EBITDA	Earnings before interest, tax, depreciation, and amortization
ECLAC	Economic Commission on Latin America and the Caribbean
EGOS	European Group for Organizational Studies
EPS	Earnings per share
ER	Exchange ratio
ERP	Equity risk premium
EV/EBIT	Enterprise value/earnings before interest and tax
EV/EBITDA	Enterprise value/earnings before interest, tax, depreciation, and amortization
EVA	Economic value added
EVBV	Equity value to book value of equity
EVM	Enterprise value multiple
F-2-F	Face-to-face
FCFE	Free cash flow to equity holders
FCFF	Free cash flow to the firm
FCF	Free cash flow
FCIC	Financial Crisis Inquiry Commission
FDI	Foreign direct investment
FTC	Federal Trade Commission
GE	General Electric
HRM	Human resource management
IB	International business
ICR	Interest coverage ratio
IJV	International joint venture
ING	Internationale Nederlanden Group
IPO	Initial public offering
IRC	Internal revenue code
IRR	Internal rate of return
KM	Knowledge management
IRR	Internal rate of return
LBO	Leveraged buyout
IRR	Internal rate of return
LIBOR	London Interbank Offered Rate
LLCs	Limited liability companies
LOF	Liability of foreignness
LTIPS	Long-term incentive plans
M&A	Mergers and acquisitions
M/B	Market-to-book
MABs	Monoclonal antibodies
MBI	Management buy-in
MBO	Management buyout
MD	Managing director

MENA   Middle East and North Africa region
MNC   Multinational companies
MTBV   Market-to-book ratio
NRA   No rival acquisition
OC   Organizational culture
OLI   Ownership-location-internationalization
NC   National culture
PE   Private equity
PER   Price/earnings ratio
PM   Peat Marwick
PPP   Profits per partner
PSF   Professional service firm
PTBV   Price-to-book ratio
PTV   Pre-acquisition target
PW   Price Waterhouse
PwC   PricewaterhouseCoopers
R&D   Research and development
RA   Rival acquirers
RBS   Royal Bank of Scotland
RBV   Resource-based view
RI   Residual income
RLBO   Reverse LBO
ROA   Return on assets
ROCE   Return on capital employed
ROE   Return on equity
ROI   Return on investment
ROS   Return on sales
S&Ls   Savings and Loan associations
S&O   Spicer & Oppenheim
S&P   Standard & Poor's
SA   Serial acquirer
SDC   Securities Data Corporation
SEOs   Secondary equity offerings
SIA   Social identity approach
SOI   Spicer & Oppenheim International
SOP   Sum of parts
SOX   Sarbanes–Oxley
SWOT   Strengths, weaknesses, opportunities, and threats
TARP   Troubled asset relief program
TBTF   Too-big-to-fail
TCE   Transaction cost economics
TNC   Transnational corporation

TR	Touche Ross
TSR	Total shareholder return
TV	Terminal value
UNCTAD	United Nations Conference on Trade and Development
UOB	United Overseas Bank
VC	Venture capital
WACC	Weighted average cost of capital

Notes on Contributors

Professor Duncan Angwin is Professor of Strategy at Oxford Brookes University, ENPC, Paris and associate fellow of Warwick Business School. Prior to an academic career, he was a senior investment banker. He judges for the Management Consultancies Association awards for best consultancies, sits on the M&A Research Centre advisory board (Cass Business School, London), and has chaired the Strategic Management Society's awards panel for best practice paper. Duncan has authored over 40 articles on M&A, Strategy and Strategy Directors in leading journals including *California Management Review, Sloan Management Review, Organization Studies, European Management Journal, Journal of World Business* and is author of six books, including *The Strategy Pathfinder* (2011) (EURAM award for innovation) and *Mergers and Acquisitions* (2007), which aims to resolve core paradoxes in the field. He has recently won a three-year research grant from Saïd Business School, Oxford University to study M&A communications practices.

Maria Carapeto is Senior Lecturer in Finance, the Deputy Director of the M&A Research Centre, and Course Director of the BSc Banking and International Finance at Cass Business School, City University London. Her research focuses on corporate financing, particularly as related to mergers and acquisitions, corporate restructuring, bankruptcy, and investment banking, and she has published in well-regarded journals. She previously taught at the Portuguese Catholic University, ISCTE, Portuguese Naval College, and Maria Ulrich Higher Institute of Education. She has worked at the Center for Applied Studies of the Portuguese Catholic University and as a consultant to the Lisbon Stock Exchange and the Portuguese Association of Ceramics.

Professor Susan Cartwright is Professor of Organizational Psychology and Well-Being at Lancaster University, UK and Director of the Centre for Organizational Health and Well-Being. She previously held a personal chair in Organizational Psychology at Manchester Business School. Susan is a Chartered Psychologist, a Fellow of the British Psychological Society, a Fellow of the British Academy of Management, and a past Chair and President of the British Academy of Management. She has been conducting research into the human aspects of mergers and acquisitions for over 20 years and has published widely in this field. Her books on the topic—*Managing Mergers, Acquisitions and Strategic Alliances : Integrating People and Cultures* (1997) and *HR Know How in Mergers and Acquisitions* (2000) have been translated into several languages.

Professor John Child is Emeritus Professor at Birmingham Business School and Visiting Professor at the University of Hong Kong. He has been on the faculties at the London Business School, Aston University, Cambridge University, and the China-Europe Management Centre in Beijing. He was Editor in Chief of *Organization Studies*; is the author of 15 books and over 80 articles in refereed journals; and his works are widely cited. His major areas of interest are organizational studies, cooperative strategy, and international business and strategy.

Professor Viktoria Dalko, PhD is a Global Professor of Finance at Hult International Business School, and recipient of the Joanne Fussa Distinguished Teacher award from Harvard University Extension School. Viktoria has served as Advisor to the President of the National Bank of Hungary and was Chief of Staff of the Committee of Budget, Tax and Finances of the Hungarian Parliament. She provides executive training and consulting on financial markets, risk management, corporate strategy, corporate finance especially as related to mergers and acquisitions in the USA, East and Southeast Asia, MENA, and the EU. Viktoria holds an MA and PhD in Economics from the University of Pennsylvania.

Professor Gary A. Dymski has been Professor of Economics at the University of California, Riverside from 1991 to 2013. He is currently Chair in Applied Economics at the Leeds University Business School, University of Leeds. He received his PhD in economics from the University of Massachusetts, Amherst in 1987. From 2003 to 2009, Gary was the founding Executive Director of the University of California Center, Sacramento. Gary's most recent books are *Capture and Exclude: Developing Nations and the Poor in Global Finance* (New Delhi: Tulika Books, 2007), co-edited with Amiya Bagchi, and *The Crisis of 2008 and the Future of Capitalism* (Routledge, 2012), co-edited with Kiichiro Yagi, Nobuharu Yokokawa, and Shinjiro Hagiwara.

Nicholas Fairclough (LL.B (Hons); MBA) is a doctoral candidate in the Department of Strategic Management and Organization at the University of Alberta. He began his career as a capital markets lawyer for Allen and Overy in London in 1992, and then worked in banking and private equity for a major Japanese investment bank. He later spent several years in Paris and Geneva working as an internal consultant on strategy and organizational matters for a global professional services firm. His research interests include institution theory, professional service firms, and public policy and entrepreneurship.

Dr Samantha Fairclough (DPhil, University of Oxford) is Assistant Professor of Management at the University of Mississippi, USA, and an Associate Fellow with the Novak Druce Centre for Professional Service Firms at the Said Business School, University of Oxford. A former environmental lawyer in the UK and New Zealand, her research interests include the structure and management of international professional service firms, the reproduction of institutions, and the relationship between business and the environment.

Professor David Faulkner (BSc (ECON), MA (OXON) D Phil) is Emeritus of Strategy, University of London. He was formerly official Student (Fellow) of Christ Church, Oxford and Deputy Director of the Said Business School, Oxford University. He is an Oxford educated economist by background, who has spent much of his early career as a strategic management consultant with McKinsey and Co and Arthur D. Little. He gained a Doctorate from Oxford University (D Phil), researching into conditions for success in International Strategic Alliances. He has written and edited thirteen books including: *The Oxford Handbook of Strategy* (OUP).

Dr Steffen R. Giessner is Associate Professor at the Rotterdam School of Management, Erasmus University. He holds an MSc in Psychology from the University of Kent at Canterbury, UK and a PhD in Psychology from the Friedrich-Schiller-Universität Jena, Germany. His research is located at the intersection of organizational and social psychology and is focused on employee support during organizational merger, followers' perceptions of leadership, antecedents of leader behavior, and non-verbal communication of power. He has authored or co-authored papers in the areas of social psychology, organizational behavior, and management.

Dr Jerayr Haleblian is Associate Professor of Management at University of California—Riverside. He received his PhD from the University of Southern California. His research focuses on organizational learning, mergers and acquisitions, and corporate leadership and governance. His research has been published in leading management journals such as the *Academy of Management Journal, Administrative Science Quarterly, Strategic Management Journal*, and *Organization Science*. Dr Haleblian is currently serving on the editorial board of the *Academy of Management Journal*.

Elina Happonen, MSc. (Eng.) is Senior Associate in the Transactions and Restructuring team of KPMG, Helsinki. She holds previous work experience in Nordic banks. Her research centres on the management of pre-acquisition decision-making. She has an MSc degree in industrial engineering and management from Helsinki University of Technology.

Professor Michael A. Hitt is Distinguished Professor of Management at Texas A&M University and holds the Joe B. Foster Chair in Business Leadership. He received his PhD from the University of Colorado. A recent article in the *Journal of Management* listed him as one of the ten most cited authors in management over a 25-year period. Additionally, the *Times Higher Education* in 2010 listed him among the top scholars in economics, finance, and management based on the number of articles with a high citation rate on the Web of Science. His research focuses on international strategy, M&As, strategic alliances, and strategic entrepreneurship.

Dr Sajjad M. Jasimuddin is Associate Professor at the Euromed Management, France, and is visiting Professor at Dalian University of Foreign Languages (China), and Center for Advanced Studies in Management and Economics (Portugal). Previously, he taught at Aberystwyth University, Southampton University, King Abdulaziz University, and University of Dhaka. He received MPhil from Judge Business School at Cambridge University, and PhD from Southampton University. He has authored ten chapters, and 60 articles- appeared in *Information Systems Journal, Information Systems Management, Journal of Operational Research Society, Management Decision, Journal of Business and Industrial Marketing, Business Strategy, IJOA, IJIM, JIKM, JKM, K&PM*, and *KMR&P*. Recently he publishes a book *Knowledge Management- An Interdisciplinary Perspective* (World Scientific, 2012). His research interests are in knowledge management, international business, and strategic management.

Richard J. Joseph is former Provost and Vice President for Academic Affairs at Hult International Business School. Before joining Hult, he served on the faculty and administration of the McCombs School of Business at The University of Texas at Austin, where he taught Mergers and Acquisitions, International Taxation, Tax Research Methodology, and Business Law. Before embarking on his academic career, Provost Joseph worked as an investment banker at Lehman Brothers, a securities trader at Bear Stearns, an international banker at Citibank, and a mergers and acquisitions lawyer for the Bass Group, Fort Worth. A graduate *magna cum laude* of Harvard College (BA), Oxford University (MLitt), and the University of Texas at Austin School of Law (JD), he is co-author of Prentice Hall's Federal Taxation Series and has written numerous commentaries in the *Financial Times, Christian Science Monitor*, and *Tax Notes International*. His book, *The Origins of the American Income Tax* (Syracuse University Press, 2004), explores the original intent, rationale, and effect of the early American income tax.

Professor Prashant Kale is Professor of Strategic Management at the Jones School of Management, Rice University. He has also been a full-time faculty at the University of Michigan and visiting faculty at the Wharton School and Kellogg School of Management. His research focuses on management of acquisitions and alliances, firm-capabilities, and strategies for competing in emerging economies and he has received awards from the *Academy of Management* and the *Strategic Management Society*. He received his PhD at the Wharton School.

Professor Thomas Keil is Professor of International Management at the University of Zurich. His research focuses on corporate entrepreneurship and venturing, strategic renewal, mergers and acquisitions, and strategic management of multinational enterprises. His work has been published in leading European and North-American journals including *Harvard Business Review, Sloan Management Review, Academy of Management Review, Strategic Management Journal, Organization Science, Journal of Business Venturing, Entrepreneurship Theory & Practice, Journal of Management, Journal of Management Studies*, and others, and has won several international awards.

Dr David R. King earned his PhD in Strategy and Entrepreneurship from Indiana University's Kelley School of Business. After retiring from the US Air Force, he joined Marquette University as an Associate Professor in the College of Business Administration where he teaches undergraduate and graduate business strategy. His research focuses on merger and acquisition (M&A) integration and performance. His co-authored meta-analysis was published in *Strategic Management Journal*, and he also has articles appearing in *Academy of Management Journal, Organization Science*, and *Journal of Management*. A complete list of his publications can be found at www.drking.biz.

Dr Kalin Kolev is Assistant Professor of Management at California State University, Fullerton. He received his PhD in strategic management from Michigan State University. His research focuses on strategic decision making in organizations and its implications for risk taking and performance. In particular, Kalin's interests fall under two broad domains: 1) antecedents and outcomes of M&As, divestitures, and diversification; and 2) the intersection of strategic leadership and corporate governance. Dr. Kolev's research has been published in *Strategic Management Journal* and he is an ad-hoc reviewer for *Journal of Management* and *Journal of Management Studies*.

Professor Hema Krishnan is Associate Dean and Professor of Management & Entrepreneurship at Xavier University, Cincinnati. She obtained her MBA from the Indian Institute of Management (Bangalore) and her PhD in Strategic Management from the University of Tennessee, Knoxville. Her research on mergers & acquisitions and top management teams appears in *Strategic Management Journal, Academy of Management Best Papers, Business Horizons, Journal of Management Studies*, and *Journal of Business Research* among others. She worked for several years for a multi-billion dollar petroleum company, and was the first woman in sales in the petroleum industry in India.

Professor Tomi Laamanen is a Chaired Professor of Strategic Management and Director at the Institute of Management of the University of St. Gallen. His research focuses on strategic management with a special emphasis on acquisition programs, strategy processes and practices, capability dynamics, and management's cognition. Tomi is one of the associate editors of the *Strategic Management Journal* and an editorial board member in the *Journal of Management*. His work has appeared or is forthcoming in leading European and North-American journals, including *Strategic Management Journal, Journal of Management, Journal of International Business Studies, Journal of Management Studies, Strategic Organization, Research Policy, Harvard Business Review*, and *Research Policy*. Tomi has worked with a number of firms from different industries both as Member of the Board and strategy consultant.

Aino Mäkisalo has an LL.M. from the University of Helsinki and an MSc from the Helsinki University of Technology. Her Master's thesis for Helsinki University of Technology, finalized in the spring of 2009, focused on the development of acquisition program capabilities, while her Master's thesis for the Faculty of Law at the University of Helsinki in 2010 focused on direct corporate tax benefits and the concept of fiscal State aid in the European Union. Currently she works in a Nordic law firm with a focus on public and private M&A and capital markets.

Dr Marianna Makri is Associate Professor in the School of Business Administration at the University of Miami. She holds a Bachelor's and Master's Degrees in Mathematics from the University of South Florida and a Ph.D. degree in Business Administration from Arizona State University. Dr. Makri is interested in the effects of corporate governance and science-based research on strategy formulation. Her continued interest in these questions has led to publications in two main streams of research. The first stream examines why family firms approach strategic decisions differently than their non-family counterparts. The second stream examines the role of science in the innovation process and more specifically, the effect of knowledge relatedness in R&D collaborations and high technology M&As.

Professor Gerry McNamara is Professor of Management at Michigan State University. He received his Ph.D. from the University of Minnesota. His research focuses on how the dynamics of markets, competitive pressures, organizational characteristics, executive compensation, and top manager characteristics influence strategic decision making. His research has been published in numerous journals, including the *Academy of Management Journal*, the *Strategic Management Journal*, *Organization Science, Organizational Behavior and Human Decision Processes*, and the *Journal of International Business Studies*. Dr. McNamara's research on mergers and acquisitions has been abstracted in the *New York Times, Business Week,* the *Economist,* and *Financial Week*. He is currently an Associate Editor for the *Academy of Management Journal* and previously served on the editorial boards of the *Academy of Management Journal*, the *Academy of Management Review, Organization Science*, and the *Strategic Management Journal*.

Professor Brendan McSweeney (PhD LSE) is Professor of Management, Royal Holloway, University of London and a visiting professor at Stockholm Business School, University of Stockholm. He is a member of the advisory board of the Europe, Middle East and Africa division of a large globally located private Japanese company. Prior to becoming an academic he worked in a variety of fields including: central banking, commercial banking, and trade unions. His work has been published in major scholarly journals including *Accounting, Organizations & Society, Human Relations, International Marketing Review, Journal of International Business Studies, Organization Studies*, and *the Political Quarterly.*

Professor Scott Moeller is the Director and Founder of the M&A Research Centre at Cass Business School where he is a Professor in the Practice of Finance. Scott's most recent book was published in 2009 by John Wiley & Sons: *Surviving M&A: Making the Most of Your Company being Acquired.* Together with Professor Chris Brady, he also wrote the award-winning *Intelligent M&A: Navigating the Mergers and Acquisitions Minefield* (Wiley, 2007). Prior to teaching, Scott worked at Booz Allen & Hamilton management consultants for five years, Morgan Stanley for over 12 years in New York, Tokyo, and Frankfurt, and finally for Deutsche Bank in London for six years. Scott has three degrees from Yale University.

Professor Vassilis M. Papadakis is Professor and Chair of the Department of Business Administration at Athens University of Economics and Business (AUEB) in Greece. His research interests are related to strategic decision making and mergers and acquisitions. He has published in journals such as the *Strategic Management Journal, Organization Science, British Journal of Management, Technology Analysis & Strategic Management,* and the *European Management Journal.* His research has received two noted best paper awards from the Academy of Management (1996 and 2003) and a nomination for the 2010 Strategic Management Society best conference paper prize.

Dr Robert Pitkethly is a Fellow and Tutor in Management at St Peter's College, Oxford, a committee member of the Oxford IP Research Centre, and a member of Oxford University's faculty of management. He has worked as a management consultant in connection with a wide variety of technology and general management issues and holds degrees in chemistry, business administration, and Japanese studies. He is a qualified UK and European patent attorney and an honorary research fellow of the Intellectual Property Institute, London. Prior to moving to Oxford, he was a Research Fellow at the Judge Institute in Cambridge University.

Professor Annette L. Ranft (PhD, University of North Carolina, Chapel Hill) is the Jim Moran Professor of Management at Florida State University. She specializes in acquisition integration, knowledge-based perspectives, and strategic leadership. She has published in the *Academy of Management Review, Academy of Management Journal, Organization Science, Journal of International Business Studies,* and others. She serves on the editorial review boards of the *Academy of Management Review* and *Strategic Management Journal* and serves as Associate Editor of the *Journal of Management.* Professor Ranft received a BS in Mathematics from Appalachian State University and an MSM from the Georgia Institute of Technology.

Professor Bill Ryan is Professor of Accounting at Hult International Business School London and is part of their global faculty. He teaches across a range of accounting and finance courses that span accounting and strategy. His research is in the general area of management control spanning accounting and business strategy and he has published papers across these areas. He is a fellow of the Higher Education Academy and has been a regular contributor to external programs, including Mellon Financial Corporation. Before entering academic life, he held a number of senior management positions in accounting and change management in companies such as Chrysler and the 3M Corporation and was until recently a member of the Faculty at Royal Holloway, University of London.

Dr Mario Schijven is Assistant Professor of Management at Mays Business School, Texas A&M University. He received his Ph.D. from Tilburg University in the Netherlands. His research focuses primarily on corporate development activities, such as acquisitions, alliances, and organizational restructuring. In particular, he studies how capability development unfolds in such strategic settings, using theories of organizational learning, behavioral decision making, evolutionary economics, and cognitive psychology.

Professor Lars Schweizer has held the UBS-Endowed Professorship for Management at Goethe University Frankfurt since December 2007 and was Associate Professor for Organizational Behavior and Management at Grenoble Graduate School of Business in France. Moreover, he is Associate Dean of Goethe Business School (GBS) and the Academic Director of the Goethe Full Time MBA Program. His publications have appeared in journals such as the *Academy of Management Journal*, the *Journal of Engineering and Technology Management*, the *Journal of General Management*, *Scandinavian Journal of Management*, and *Industrial and Corporate Change*.

Jennifer C. Sexton (doctoral candidate, Florida State University) specializes in top management teams and innovation processes. Specifically, her research interests include innovation, knowledge-based perspectives, and merger and acquisition integration. Her work has been published in *Organizational Research Methods*. She is the recipient of the outstanding doctoral student research award.

Professor Katsuhiko (Katsu) Shimizu is Professor of Organization Theory and Strategic Management at the Graduate School of Business Administration, Keio University in Japan. Previously, he taught at University of Texas at San Antonio for ten years. He received his Ph.D. from Texas A&M University. He is serving the editorial review boards for multiple top journals. With a ten-year strategic management consulting background, he has actively researched such topics as organizational capabilities of decision change and decision implementation under uncertainty, learning from mistakes, and managing challenges in international contexts including international mergers and acquisitions.

Professor Harbir Singh is the William and Phyllis Mack Professor of Management and former Chair of the Management Department at the Wharton School of Business. He is also Co-Director of the Mack Center for Technological Innovation. His research interests include effective strategies for managing acquisitions and alliances, firm strategies for dealing with emerging technologies, and corporate restructuring. He has received awards for his work from the Academy of Management and the Strategic Management Society. He received his PhD at the University of Michigan.

Professor Sudi Sudarsanam is Emeritus Professor of Finance and Corporate Control at Cranfield School of Management. He is the author of *The Essence of Mergers and Acquisitions* (1995), and *Creating Value from Mergers and Acquisitions: The Challenges* (2003 and 2010). Sudi has published extensively in leading international academic journals. Sudi is a member of the UK Competition Commission, Honorary Senior Visiting Fellow at the Mergers and Acquisitions Research Centre (MARC) at Cass Business School, London, and an affiliate of the Centre for Management Buyouts at Nottingham University. He has been a visiting professor at several universities in the US, Austria, Greece, and Poland.

Dr Satu Teerikangas is Senior Lecturer in Management at University College London. She received her PhD from Helsinki University of Technology. Her research centres on the management of mergers & acquisitions and the methods involved in its study, and features in *Journal of Management, British Journal of Management* and *Human Resource Management*. She has co-edited Special Issues on M&As with *Scandinavian Journal of Management* and *European Journal of International Management*. She is co-chair of the M&A tracks at the *European Academy of Management* and *European Group of Organizational Studies* annual conferences. Prior to an academic career, Dr Teerikangas worked for Shell in the Netherlands and the UK. She is on the editorial review board of *International Journal of Cross-Cultural Management*.

Dr Ioannis C. Thanos is Lecturer in Strategy at the Adam Smith Business School, University of Glasgow, UK. He conducts research on strategic decision processes, mergers and acquisitions, and the internationalization processes of small and medium enterprises. His papers have been accepted for publication in the *British Journal of Management, International Business Review* and *International Journal of Human Resource Management*. In addition, he is a regular presenter and reviewer for top academic conferences, including the AOM, SMS, BAM, EURAM, and EIBA. Awards include nominations for the 2010 and 2012 Strategic Management Society best conference paper prizes.

Professor Janne Tienari is Professor of Organizations and Management at Aalto University, School of Economics, Finland. He was Editor-in-Chief of *Scandinavian Journal of Management*. He received his Ph.D. from Helsinki School of Economics. His research interests include managing multinational corporations, mergers and acquisitions, cross-cultural studies of gender and organizing, strategy, media representations, critical discourse analysis, and the language of global capitalism.

Professor Johannes Ullrich is Professor of Social Psychology in the Department of Psychology at the University of Zurich, Switzerland. He obtained a PhD in Social Psychology at Philipps-University, Marburg, Germany, and completed his Habilitation at Goethe University, Frankfurt, Germany. His research interests include attitudes and attitude strength, intergroup relations, and social identity processes in organizations. Mergers and acquisitions in particular have fascinated him since his diploma thesis, for which he transcribed hours of audiotaped interviews.

Professor Rolf van Dick is Professor of Social Psychology in the Department of Psychology at Goethe University, Frankfurt, Germany. After his PhD in Social Psychology (Philipps-University, Marburg), he worked at Aston Business School (Aston University, Birmingham). He has been Editor-in-chief of the *British Journal of Management* and is currently the Editor-in-chief of the *Journal of Personnel Psychology*. His research interests focus on social identity processes in organizational settings (e.g., M&As, diversity, leadership) and he has more than 100 publications in books and journals such as *Journal of Applied Psychology, Journal of Organizational Behavior, Journal of Marketing, Journal of Personality and Social Psychology.*

Professor Eero Vaara is Professor of Management and Organization at Hanken School of Economics in Helsinki, Finland, and permanent Visiting Professor at EM Lyon Business School, France. He also holds visiting professorships with Copenhagen Business School and Lancaster University. He is former President and current member of Board of *European Group of Organization Studies*, and member of the board of the *Academy of Management*. His research focuses on strategy implementation, organizational change, multinational enterprises and globalization. Professor Vaara's work features in the most prestigious outlets in management studies, including e.g. *Academy of Management Journal, Academy of Management Review, Strategic Management Journal, Journal of Management Studies, Human Relations, Organization Studies*, to name a few. He is well known for his discursive and narrative approach in the study of corporate strategy and organizational change.

Professor Philippe Véry is Professor of Strategic Management at EDHEC Business School, France. Professor Véry is the author of many articles published in Rank A journals and of several books. His main areas of research cover the management of M&A and the management of criminal risks.

Dr Adelaide Wilcox King is Associate Professor at the McIntire School of Commerce at the University of Virginia. She specializes in strategic management, with a particular interest in research linking top management cognition and motivation with firm outcomes. Her research has been published in the *Academy of Management Review*, the *Strategic Management Journal*, and the *Journal of Management*. She is currently an Associate Editor for the *Academy of Management Review*. Professor King received a BA from Davidson College and an MBA from the Darden Graduate School of Business at UVA.

Dr Hong Zhu is Assistant Professor in the management department at the Chinese University of Hong Kong. She received her PhD from Texas A&M University. Her research uses an institutional approach to advance the understanding of the interactions between institutions and organizations in the global era. This focused research agenda involves several logically connected research streams, including neo-institutional theory in economics and sociology, resource-based view (RBV), cross-border M&As, and emerging economies, particularly China. Hong's research has been published in *Business Horizon, Journal of International Management*, and *Journal of Small Business Strategy*. She has also presented her research at academic conferences and annual meetings, such as the Strategic Management Society, Academy of Management, and the Academy of International Business.

CHAPTER 1

··

INTRODUCTION

··

DAVID FAULKNER, SATU TEERIKANGAS,
AND RICHARD J. JOSEPH

A CALL FOR RE-ROOTING THE STUDY
AND PRACTICE OF M&A

··

With its inception at the end of the 19th century as a means of consolidation and reor-ganization, mergers and acquisitions (M&A) have since become quasi-institutionalized as one of the primary strategic options for organizations, as they seek to secure their posi-tion in an ever more competitive, and globalizing market place (see Chapter 2). M&A is often used as a vehicle for growth (Trautwein 1990). In such instances, within-sector hor-izontal or vertical integration, diversification to new sectors (Lynch 2006), gaining tech-nological know-how, or geographical roll out to cover more markets (Bower 2001) count among the sought aims. Alternatively, M&A can be regarded as a form of "co-operation strategy," with the aim of co-operating with other players within or outside one's industry (Lynch 2006); or of buying out a competitor. Over the years, M&A activity has shifted from the domain of corporations across industrial and professional sectors to also being practiced by public sector organizations, as in e.g. health care or higher education.

Despite the optimism surrounding M&A as strategic moves, research on post-merger company performance provides a bleaker image of the reality behind this phenomenon. A meta-analysis (King et al. 2004), as well as several recent studies (Schoenberg 2006; Zollo and Meier 2008; Papadakis and Thanos 2010; Chapters 4, 5, and 8), reconfirm that most firms engaging in M&A activity do not achieve the sought-after performance targets be it soon or in the years following the deal. The only winner would seem to be the selling side, i.e. the target firm and/or its shareholders (King et al. 2004; Chapters 2, 4 and 5). This leads one to ask—what is it that drives M&A activity when research results do not support the performance expectations of these undertakings? Alternatively, have M&A scholars got it all wrong in the way that M&A performance is measured? Is the topic too complex, enduring, and multifaceted to study? Or are M&A undertaken for reasons other than improved short-term performance?

Faced with this seeming conundrum, M&A scholars and practitioners have increasingly expressed the need to enhance the state of the art of M&A research. In this respect, calls for better methodologies for the study of M&A have been made (Cartwright et al. 2010; Meglio and Risberg 2010). The need for more theory-building in the study of M&A has been recognized (Greenwood et al. 1994; Schweiger and Goulet 2000). A social network analysis of the M&A research community highlighted the scarcity of collaboration not only amongst M&A researchers, but also between this research field and others, be they distant or related (Mirc et al. 2010). This might explain why a recent review of the literature highlighted the need for better integration between the various disciplines in its study (Haleblian et al. 2009). This *Handbook* constitutes a response to these calls.

We argue that the field of M&A is in need of a re-rooting. With this term, we mean patiently stepping back and critically reviewing what has been done, whilst withholding opportunities for seeing the field afresh, and revisiting some of the fundamental assumptions that the work has come to be based upon.

Beyond Disciplinary Silos: Bridging Strategic, Financial, and Sociocultural Approaches to M&A

In this section, we argue that a key issue that has prevented efforts in the practice and study of M&A from achieving dynamic synthesis has been the disciplinary gulf separating strategy, finance, and human relations schools.

The prevalence of this silo effect across decades, despite increasing M&A activity, deserves to be highlighted and questioned. Critically speaking, what the enduring and persisting presence of such human-created, discipline-based silos points toward is that there would seem to be either an innate tendency for individuals to position themselves in light of existing disciplinary and topical structures, i.e. to limit their focus to specific disciplines, without a priori questioning the existence and influence of the latter approach. This would seem to be paralleled by the tendency to disregard systemic, holistic treatment of phenomena, such as M&A, be it in the domain of practice or of science. It would seem that we join existing structures without a priori questioning their *"raison d'être."*

In the domain of M&A, whereas the strategic decision to acquire is made by some, finance's expertise lies primarily in addressing pre-acquisition deal- and finance-related activities, whereas sociocultural concerns relate particularly to the post-acquisition phase, and to some extent this role extends into the pre-acquisition phase. Roughly put, the making of the contractual deal in a merger or acquisition seems, still today, to mark a defining line in both scholarship and practice. This division of work would not matter, were it not for the fact that scholars and practicing managers find difficulty in addressing M&A in a way that would align both lenses.

As a result of this largely silo-based outlook on M&A, integrative views combining M&A–critical disciplines are lacking. The practice, teaching, and study of M&A would thus seem to be wrought with partial understandings owing to each side's viewing the phenomenon from a somewhat narrow focus, disregarding others. Critically speaking, it would seem that the present state of our understanding, knowledge, and practice on M&A rests on a collection of individual perspectives that at worst might not be relevant and moreover, fail to reflect the entire picture.

This is the gap that needs to be bridged if the practice and study of M&A are to move forward toward more meaningful results. Through this *Handbook*, we aim to help practitioners and academics break free of the existing silos as they approach the study and practice of M&A.

Toward this end, we have brought together a set of prominent and emerging scholars and practitioners engaged in the study of M&A. Throughout the *Handbook*, as we return to some of the basics in the study of M&A through a series of extensive, mostly conceptual review papers that explore M&A through a variety of lenses, our objectives are twofold: (1) to elaborate on the strategic, financial, and sociocultural dimensions of M&A, or more appropriately, summarize key findings in the current M&A literature, and (2) to explore ways in which these lenses can be reconciled or "synthesized"?

As perhaps one of the first books to combine the thus far unrelated disciplines of strategy, finance, and human relations in the study and practice of M&A, we provide both scholars and practitioners with an appreciation of the ways in which M&A is viewed across disciplines, as well as identifying linkages and gaps that have hitherto been invisible in siloed paradigm and practice structures. All the while, we adopt a systemic view of M&A, highlighting unexplored dimensions, unidentified assumptions relating to the study and practice of M&A, and in so doing, engage the reader in a deeper-reaching reflection and exploration of the phenomenon of M&A; in short, to break down the silo mentality.

As a means of launching this reflection, throughout the following sections, we proceed to critically expounding on four shortcomings in the current practical and academic approaches to M&A. These shortcomings are considered to result from the prevailing disconnect between the financial and managerial approaches to M&A. By way of a provocative style, we aim to initiate the reader's reflection process on the key issues facing M&A practitioners and academics at the dawn of the third millennium: what are M&A, actually? What makes M&A succeed? How to combine disciplines in such an effort? Why do M&A occur? What does successful M&A execution consist in?

THE SILO EFFECT AND THE RESULTING SHORTCOMINGS IN M&A ACTIVITY

The ongoing disconnect between the strategic, financial, and sociocultural views has led to a set of shortcomings marking the M&A literature. These shortcomings relate to: (1) egotistic drivers of M&A activity, (2) M&A as victims of myopic growth,

(3) a "Tayloristic" view that omits the human element, and (4) a prevailing short-term focus. It is our hope that, by bridging disciplinary silos, this *Handbook* will shed further light on these central concerns.

Egotistic Drivers of M&A Activity

The conduct of M&A results in the perceived growth of the acquiring firm in terms of assets, resources, people, and financial status. It has been argued that an underlying, or possibly *the* underlying, driver behind M&A activity is hubris and overconfidence, the ego of the involved senior managers or chief executives (see Chapter 8), i.e. the vainglory and overwhelming pride involved in undertaking corporate expansion through M&A. The size and competitive industry ranking of a corporation can be regarded as parallel-ing the importance of the involved managers.

We would further argue that an underlying reason behind the ego-boosting of corpo-rate managers engaged in active M&A activity is fear. Fear of losing out, fear of not being important. Fear of not daring to run one's company in a way different from other com-panies, and hence being lulled into a global craze for more and more deals. Has a machine been set that cannot be stopped?

M&A as Victims of Myopic Growth

Another flawed characteristic of M&A activity is a seeming "growth myopia" (see Chapter 13; also Levitt 1975 on "marketing myopia"). As a result of the increasing pres-sures to remain competitive on a global scale, the corporate arena can be regarded as having moved into a systemic state, wherein M&A transactions are ritualistically car-ried out, even to the extent of corporate myopia. Taking a critical stance, it can be argued that these transactions have become so commonplace that the corporate arena has come to believe in their effectiveness, despite strong evidence of potential adverse performance effects, not to mention the long-term managerial and organizational hurdles involved in operating merged organizations (King et al. 2004; Barkema and Schijven 2008). Critically speaking, is the recurring M&A activity a sign that corpora-tions have fallen victim to a self-fulfilling growth prophecy, partly unmatched by results?

A look at the numbers would seem to support this argument. The significance of M&A has increased dramatically over the last century, whether measured in terms of the number and value of deals conducted, the financial capital involved, the human toll, or the impact on surrounding societies. If we consider globalization as having begun its explosive growth since the 19th century following the industrial revolution and subse-quent speedy technological progress, the shift toward a capitalism-based economy, the increase in international, inter- and intra-continental trade (Burnes 2009), then M&A can be regarded as having become a vehicle that has paralleled, resulted from, and fed into this ongoing spiral and cycle of globalization (Chapter 2). M&A, in essence, can be regarded as both a cause and consequence of the fast-paced spiral of globalization.

Global change continued throughout the 20th century, fueled by the liberalization of trade and rapid spread of technology. In tune with this, M&A activity has occurred in "waves" since the end of the 19th century, the most recent wave having culminated in the financial crisis of late-2008 and constituting one of the most powerful M&A waves ever witnessed (see Chapter 10). Whether set in a historical, present, or forward-looking context, M&A represent an important, significant, and consequent societal and corporate phenomenon.

The trouble with the current literature is that despite the seeming popularity of M&A transactions in the minds of corporate managers, scientific evidence relating to the value-adding potential of M&A for the merging parties remains mixed (King et al. 2004). That there exists a positive rationale for M&A activity remains dubious (see Chapters 4 and 5). One key finding is that on average, M&A transactions tend to be more financially favorable for the selling vs. the buying firm (Porter 1987; King et al. 2004). Moreover, post-merger financial performance may improve the longer the time period of the study (Biggadike 1979; Quah and Young 2005: Chakrabarti et al. 2009). This would seem to point to the critical importance of patiently awaiting the long-term results of corporate integration measures and actions.

The ongoing focus on failed M&A transactions overlooks the 30–50% declared successes. Seen from this perspective, some acquirers seem to have developed core competences in acquisition management and some do not. We will explore the characteristics of serial acquirers, the impact of experience, and the emerging notion of M&A capability in Chapter 6 of this *Handbook* (see also Chapters 4, 5, and 8). Moreover, the notions of serendipity (Graebner 2004), pure luck, or of having the right persons involved in that particular deal are always important.

We wish to ask, then, what explains the frenzy of M&A activity, if many M&A transactions fail to produce the desired results; if, further, our scientific-reasoning-based research does not support the claim that M&A performance has been beneficial. Could it be argued that, at worst, M&A has become part of a global machine aimed at growth regardless of the costs involved, a story that we have all so well swallowed and internalized that we have forgotten to question its underlying assumptions (see Chapters 13, 23)? Are M&A transactions just a route to power? Or alternatively, have researchers got it all wrong—are researchers measuring M&A performance through an erroneous lens? Are M&A, actually, carried out for reasons, in ways, and with outcomes that have not been captured by academic research?

A "Tayloristic" View Omitting the Human Element

A third shortcoming characteristic of the M&A literature relates to an underlying underestimation of the human hurdles involved in the merging or acquiring of organizations (Napier 1989; Cartwright and Cooper 1990, 1992). This is a well-known argument (see e.g. Buono et al. 1985). Indeed, since the early 1980s, academic researchers and consultants have pointed to the human, cultural, and managerial challenges inherent in M&A (Marks 1982; Buono and Bowditch 1989).

Yet, a deep rift would still seem to divide corporate managers and financial analysts on the one hand, and consultants and human resource professionals on the other hand regarding the extent to which the human side of M&A should be weighted. Whilst the former seem to see only the good in M&A from strategic, rational, and financial standpoints, the latter are more skeptical. They have difficulties in having their voices heard as regards the hurdles in making M&A work. The "human element" of M&A activity is frequently neglected, an issue raised already in 1995 by Cartwright and Cooper in their article "Organizational marriage: hard vs. soft issues."

Examples of this gulf abound. Despite years of M&A activity, most pre-deal valuation activity conducted by bankers still does not account for the human side of these corporate encounters. Cultural fit is rarely thoroughly considered, if at all. The issue has been raised (Kissin and Herrera 1990; Greenwood et al. 1994; Cartwright 1998).

In addition to unimpressive financial performance records, M&A boast worrying human and societal effects as well. The amount of emotional stress and uncertainty caused by M&A to the employees of the firms involved, in the years immediately following the deal (Napier 1989; Cartwright and Cooper 1990), as well as in the corporate reorganizations that are likely to follow in the years thereafter, are substantial (Barkema and Schijven 2008). What is the link to ineffective time spent at work (see Chapter 15), unexplained absences from work, illnesses? What about the societal effects of cross-border M&A in particular, whereby the corporate governance of a previously locally run factory in the middle of France is shifted to a far-away country? Once the direct managerial link to a local site is lost, the burden of making difficult decisions vis-à-vis foreign sites becomes significantly lighter. As a vector of globalization, M&A has played a critical role in changing the modern societal landscape.

These examples lead us again to ask the question—why engage in M&A activity, if it is the long-term cause of such human and societal distress and, further, is questionable from a financial value-adding perspective? We find this underlying misalignment between the two perspectives to reflect a certain one-sidedness and deafness, even, toward the human challenges involved. In a worldwide business logic based on growth to increase shareholder returns (see Chapter 13), the capital-related human outcome in M&A would not seem to matter, nor be seriously entertained. Yet, an organizational change is ultimately about people willing to change and working toward making changes operational. It is as though nothing had changed in managerial thinking since the time of Taylor in the early 20th century. Are we running our businesses at the dawn of the third millennium with the same logic that was routinely applied in Fordist times? In an era that boasts of the significance of human capital and innovation-intensiveness (Kanter 1989, 1997; Nonaka 1991), critically speaking, the disregard of the human element in M&A is particularly troublesome. Is there an opportunity to view M&A activity afresh?

A Short-Term Focus

This leads us to the final and fourth shortcoming in the current M&A literature: the seemingly short-term outlook and responsibility vis-à-vis merging or acquiring.

This short-term focus materializes and is well exemplified in the way that performance is measured in scientific research: a lot of research captures changes in the market value of either the acquiring or the target firm in the days preceding vs. following the deal, whilst some research attempts to analyze the post-merger performance using accounting-based measures in the year, possibly years after the deal (for an overview, see Chapter 5). Rare is evidence of M&A performance beyond three years following a deal. Academics taking longer-term views increasingly note the need to discuss the time effect of M&A performance (Chapter 5).

Likewise, in the corporate arena, acquired businesses are expected to have been absorbed into the acquiring firm's operations at the end of the formal integration process, often set at a time between three months to a year following the deal. What both of these short-term measures ignore is the possibility that M&As have long-term effects and consequences. All the while, qualitative studies on M&A integration point to the long-term nature of integration, with figures between five to twelve years raised (Birkinshaw et al. 2000; Barkema and Schijven 2008). Would a study of M&A performance twenty years following a deal highlight results different than those produced by a short-term study? Moreover, would the former study enable us to better capture the long-term human and societal consequences of the deal on the organizations, people, and local communities involved? Likewise, in the corporate world, would a view to post-acquisition or post-merger integration spanning ten to twenty years following a deal allow for a different appreciation of the implementation challenges and the results?

It seems that the prevailing short-term horizon has severe shortcomings. It ignores the long-term consequences of M&A on those involved and affected by the deal. In so doing, it encourages managers to continue engaging in M&A activity in a seemingly short-sighted manner, disregarding the long-term consequences of their actions. If M&A is to remain a much-used strategy to thrive in a globalizing competitive landscape, then this strategy should take into consideration the longer-term financial, organizational, human, and societal consequences thereof. In a world facing sustainability crises, is a logic of continuous growth sustainable? Further, where does this logic draw from (Chapter 13)?

In this *Handbook*, we wish to raise the fundamental question—at the beginning of third millennium, in Western terms—is it time to rethink the prevailing approach and mindset with regard to M&A? Is it possible to move to a view of M&A that is long-term, sustainable, and takes into account the interests of relevant corporate, societal, local, and within-firm stakeholders? A view, moreover, wherein M&A is carried out on a responsible basis inspired by sound business strategy, as opposed to unconscious managerial hubris or set in a myopia of systemic growth and increasing shareholder returns? An approach to M&A where most of the value destroyed would not result from a mismanagement of the human capital therein. It is with these questions and this critical mindset that we reiterate our call for "re-rooting" the study of M&A by bridging the disciplines involved.

Overview of the Handbook: A Three-Dimensional Approach to M&A

In order to address the prevailing silo effect in the practice and study of M&A and to capture the multidimensionality of the M&A phenomenon, throughout the *Handbook* we approach M&A management from a three-dimensional perspective with the aim of linking the strategic, financial, and sociocultural dimensions of M&A activity (see Figure 1.1). This threefold approach provides the backdrop for the structure of the *Handbook*, as well as for the forthcoming syntheses (see Chapter 27).

Following this threefold approach, in the forthcoming chapters, eminent and emerging M&A academics and practitioners explore the M&A phenomenon. The *Handbook*'s first three parts explore the strategic, financial, and sociocultural dimensions of M&A. In an effort to broaden our understanding of the diversity in M&A execution, the fourth part presents M&A across sectors, industries, and countries. Part V concludes by critically reviewing the current state of the art of M&A, and by also proposing a set of dynamic syntheses of the hitherto separate disciplinary perspectives on M&A.

A Strategic Lens for M&A

The first part of the *Handbook* focuses on a strategic perspective to M&A. In Chapter 2, Kalin Kolev, Jerayr Haleblian, and Gerry McNamara provide an overview of the M&A phenomenon since the end of the 19th century. They attempt to explain what has led to the numerous M&A waves since the end of the 1890s, whilst also highlighting the differences in and rationales for the types of deals conducted over time, as well as their performance. In

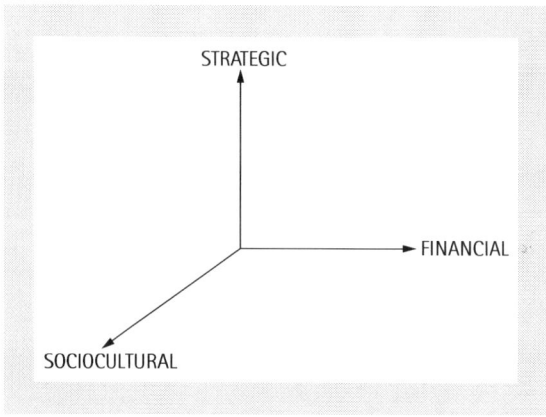

FIG. 1.1 Three-dimensional approach to M&A management

order to make sense of the array of approaches and frameworks to M&A since the 1960s, in Chapter 3 Duncan Angwin portrays the historical development of M&A strategy, pre-deal, and post-deal typologies. The chapter notes how each typology captures part of the M&A phenomenon, and deplores the fact that more recent typologies have not been empirically validated.

In order to understand why and how M&A deals are conducted, and to appreciate the complexity therein, in Chapter 4 Michael Hitt, David King, Hema Krishnan, Marianna Makri, Mario Schijven, Katsuhiko Shimizu, and Hong Zhu provide an extensive overview of value creation in M&A. Through their review of academic work on M&A performance from 1983 to 2008, the authors identify the "top five" most used independent variables to study M&A performance: diversification, relative size, experience, method of payment, and pre-deal performance. Whilst the variables have remained surprisingly consistent over the years, the latter two have more recently gained in importance. In a second part of the chapter, the authors discuss five distinct value creation mechanisms in M&A: premium paid, divesting acquired businesses, capability building in acquisitions, technological learning in acquisitions, and undertaking cross-border acquisitions. The authors call for research on M&A to use a common set of independent variables in order to gradually reach consensus on this manifold phenomenon.

Chapter 5 continues with an in-depth review of the ways in which performance has been measured in the management literature on M&A since 1980. In their review, Ioannis Thanos and Vassilis Papadakis identify seven approaches that have been used to measure M&A performance: short-term financial performance, accounting-based performance, long-term financial performance, key informants' retrospective assessments, divestiture, integration process performance, and innovation. The chapter thereafter proceeds to propose priorities that need to be addressed if we are to gain more rounded perspectives on M&A performance.

As most medium-to-large size firms today have grown through acquisitions, the notions of "acquisition experience" and "acquisition capability" have gained currency. Organizations frequently involved in M&A activity, so-called "serial acquirers," have adopted acquisition programs to manage this activity not only at the level of series of acquisitions, but at the level of acquisitions series. In Chapter 5, Thomas Keil, Tomi Laamanen, and Aino Mäkisalo provide an overview of this emerging perspective to the study and practice of M&A, calling for more research into this promising avenue.

A Financial Lens for M&A

The second part of the *Handbook* turns to the financial aspects of M&A activity. Its first three chapters discuss activities occurring in the pre-deal phase. In Chapter 7, Brendan McSweeney and Elina Happonen present an overview of pre-deal activities. They explain that M&A transactions proceed in successive phases—from systematic search and screening, to strategy formulation, company valuation, due diligence, preliminary and final negotiations, deal structuring, acquisition financing, documentation, and closing.

They emphasize that each of these phases is interrelated and interdependent. Pre-merger planning and execution invariably shape post-merger integration.

The following chapters delve further into pre-deal activities. In Chapter 8, Sudi Sudarsanam explores pre-acquisition valuation. Valuation needs to be driven by healthy strategic considerations regarding the deal. The author argues that creating value from an acquisition is a *necessary* condition for conferring shareholder benefits. It is not, however, a *sufficient* condition. For shareholders to benefit from the acquisition, the acquirer must effectively "appropriate" this value. Value appropriation, in turn, is influenced by e.g. the relative bargaining strengths of the acquirer and the target, bid strategies, acquisition tactics, and how the deal is structured. The author provides an extensive overview of the variety of available valuation models, whilst also highlighting their inherent weaknesses. Further, the behavioral dynamics shaping the pre-deal phase and the decision to acquire are critically discussed. We note the shaky ground upon which acquisition decisions can be based, despite the seemingly rational image of the pre-deal phase.

On deal structuring, in Chapter 9 Richard Joseph and Bill Ryan highlight factors that influence M&A transactional form, including tax law, securities regulations, target asset values, statutory procedures, target liabilities, and cultural synergies. They elaborate on a key principle that influences economic substance in the universe of US transactions: *continuity of interest*. They note that in the American market, deals structured with voting stock as consideration essentially "continue" stakeholder interests and are non-taxable. By contrast, deals structured with cash or other assets as consideration effectively liquidate stakeholder interests and are taxable. They further highlight the inherent limitations in the methods of accounting used in pre-deal valuation and pricing. In particular, the inability of current accounting practices to cater for the intangible or human element in M&A is highlighted, and more accurate means for accounting for intangibles are called for.

The following three chapters identify novel forms of M&A that have emerged since the 1980s.

In Chapter 10, Scott Moeller and Maria Carapeto explain that an acquisition is one of three routes to corporate restructuring, the others being reorganization and liquidation. They observe that acquisitions of distressed and bankrupt firms have become more frequent over the years, and such deals generally proceed at a pace faster than takeovers of financially healthy companies. They conclude that these types of acquisitions are counter-cyclical, in that distressed and bankrupt M&A activity generally coincides with downswings in financial markets; yet bankrupt deals are more numerous than distressed deals. The authors note the relative paucity of research on this deal type.

Within the pre-merger phase, the formulation and execution of strategy is critical to the post-merger outcome. In Chapter 11, Brendan McSweeney explores key aspects of this strategy: takeover approaches and defensive tactics. He notes that legal, institutional, and other factors have shaped the frequency, scale, and type of takeovers within and between countries. They have also influenced the variety and effectiveness of the defense tactics adopted by target-firm management. He concludes with the admonition that the contrast between pre-bid expectations and the often dull, and sometimes disastrous, outcomes demonstrates the importance of sober and effective pre-bid management.

In Chapter 12, Viktoria Dalko discusses the characteristics of a particular type of transaction: the leveraged buyout (LBO). She points out that the availability of acquisition financing has been a major catalyst in the cyclical surges of M&A activity over the past few decades. She observes that historically, LBO activity has been propelled by an abundance of credit, particularly in the form of bank loans and high yield bonds. In recent years, however, such activity has been fueled by an abundance of equity capital, particularly as regards amounts contributed by private equity firms (PE), hedge funds, and company managers. She predicts that this trend will accelerate in the future. The author explains the characteristics of LBO acquisitions and their performance consequences. More research efforts on this scarcely studied topic are called for.

On a rhetorical note, in Chapter 13 Bill Ryan questions whether growth through M&A creates significant shareholder value. The author provides a historical overview of the factors that have led to the prevailing shareholder value-driven business logic. He argues that maximizing growth does not necessarily maximize shareholder value; furthermore, that growth should not be the main objective of strategic planning, but rather an incidental outcome of a sound investment strategy. This is the context in which M&A activity needs to be placed, argues the author. Consequently, executives should beware of conducting M&A in a systemic growth logic; rather, M&A should be carefully considered as a possible strategic option.

A Sociocultural Lens for M&A

In the third part of the *Handbook,* the focus shifts to the sociocultural dimensions of M&A activity. In Chapter 14, Satu Teerikangas and Richard Joseph provide an overview of the state of the art of knowledge on post-acquisition integration management. Whilst early pointers to the difficulty of this phase in M&A date to the 1960s, it was only the 1980s that saw the advent of more concerted efforts to approach integration. The chapter provides an overview of this development toward a "process perspective" to M&A management (Haspeslagh and Jemison 1991). Aspects that have been identified as critical to M&A integration success are presented, ranging from integration management, involved individuals, best practices, integration strategy, organizational fit, and post-deal integration processes. The chapter ends with a case study of a recent university merger, and discusses recent insights on the ways in which integration might affect M&A performance. More research efforts on integration dynamics and its performance consequences are called for.

Together with the challenges of integrating the two firms post-deal, the human issues are considered as paramount in succeeding in M&A. In Chapter 15, Susan Cartwright explains how M&A research has been dominated by a finance discourse, the human side having emerged only in the 1980s. The chapter provides an overview of the behavioral and emotional causes that explain why M&A can be stressful to those involved. The people strain in M&A has been found to hold across personality types. The issues of M&A dynamics, executive turnover, as well as leadership and merger management are discussed. Successful M&A are ones where change management and leadership have been catered for, Cartwright concludes, and warns against the need to develop a single framework to approach M&A, as all deals have their unique aspects.

In Chapter 16, Satu Teerikangas and Philippe Véry provide a review of the literature on culture in M&A. The chapter provides a chronological overview of the study of culture in M&A since the 1980s, and in so doing, notes how most studies have approached culture only at the organizational and national levels of analysis, whilst our knowledge from organization theory and sociology, amongst others, point to the cultural encounter in M&A as being more complex. An overview of the effect of culture on performance is provided, together with an overview of the dynamics of the cultural encounter in M&A. Overall, organizational culture tends to have negative performance effects, regardless of the measures used, whereas the effect of national culture can be positive. More fine-tuned research efforts are called for that cope with the complexity of the cultural encounter and study its unfolding dynamics in cross-border settings.

The topic of culture continues in Chapter 17, where David Faulkner, Robert Pitkethly, and John Child present their empirical findings on country-specific integration strategies. Based on their study of multinational acquirers in the UK market, Chapter 17 identifies integration strategies as depending on the country of origin of the buying firm. All the while, in certain areas, all acquirers, regardless of nationality would seem to share similar integration characteristics, this pointing to a certain degree of "universality" in (Western) firms' integration approaches. Also, the integration approach of acquirers from some countries was not found to befit the country's stereotype, this pointing to the need for caution when adapting existing culture models to business situations as in M&A.

In Chapter 18, Sajjad Jasimuddin discusses the state of the art on knowledge management in M&A. Whilst knowledge enhancement rationales underlie an increasing number of M&A, Sajjad Jasimuddin notes that the domain of knowledge management in M&A has received, relatively speaking, lesser attention. Based on the available insights, the challenges and best practices in knowledge transfer following M&A are presented.

In Chapter 19, the focus shifts to identity formation following M&A, a more recent area of interest. Steffen Giessner, Johannes Ullrich, and Rolf van Dick apply a social identity theory lens to post-merger identification, discussing the challenges and opportunities therein. This approach shows that the adoption of a post-merger identity results in pro-merger behaviors. Yet, pre-merger identities tend to prevail post-deal, hindering the development of post-merger identities. All the while, members from acquiring and acquired organizations will follow differing identification processes depending on the relative pre- and post-merger status of both organizations. Post-merger identification can be furthered by establishing its distinctiveness, providing members with a sense of continuity, thorough communications, and a fair approach. Leaders with a background in the pre-merger organization tend to be most trustworthy in this process. The authors conclude by noting that, despite their significance, these human-related success factors are often neglected in M&A execution.

A discussion on power and politics in M&A follows in Chapter 20. Janne Tienari and Eero Vaara provide an overview of the approaches to power in the literature on organizations. Moving on to M&A, they note the seeming absence of an overt and active discussion on the power and political dimensions of M&A activity; both themes have been implicitly explored. They identify the implicit presence of these themes in M&A research as regards work on motives and performance, employee concerns, cultures and cultural politics, identities and identification, institutions, legitimation and discursive struggles, and marginalization and exclusion. As a result, the authors call for more critical studies on M&A.

In synthesis, the third part ends with a look at the "silent forces" shaping the performance of cross-border acquisitions, Chapter 21. Based on a large-scale qualitative case-based study, Satu Teerikangas provides an overview of the cross-border acquisition process, and the factors leading to its success. The chapter introduces the notion of "silent forces" to identify those managerial, human, and cultural dimensions of M&A activity that rarely make it to the practicing managers' attention span, in contrast to the strategic, structural, and financial ones that tend to dominate it. This would matter little were it not for the consequences that this lack of attention has on the outcome of M&A, as regards the extent to which strategic objectives have been met, the deal's financial performance, and the degrees of cultural change, and organizational identification achieved.

A Sectorial Lens for M&A

M&A differ in terms of characteristics, challenges, and execution from one industrial sector and geographical region to another. The fourth part in the *Handbook* focuses on the sectorial, geographical, and industrial differences with regard to M&A activity. The thrust of the section is to highlight the many ways in which M&A transactions can differ in terms of their nature, challenges, and management.

Chapter 22 deals with the characteristics of M&A activity by emerging market multinationals. Prashant Kale and Harbir Singh explain the difference in the integration approach adopted by firms from emerging markets; an approach that they term a "partnering" approach in contrast to a typical "takeover" or "integration" approach adopted by many Western firms. A partnering approach entails providing targets with autonomy, retaining target firm executives, whilst focusing on coordinating core activities, and aligning values and incentives. The authors point to the relative success that firms from emerging markets have enjoyed in their M&A activity, this contradicting results from M&A in more advanced markets. A partnering approach is recommended if the target has unique resources or capabilities, the primary goal of the deal is value creation, the acquiring firm's home market is growing, and the acquiring firm's organizational culture favors collaboration and inclusiveness.

In Chapter 23, the focus shifts to the characteristics of finance sector M&A. Gary Dymski presents the changing nature of M&A in the worldwide finance sector since the 1980s. The author positions M&A activity in the finance sector as having resulted from banking firm strategies and structural market conditions. For the latter, changes in microeconomic, macro-structural, and geo-economic factors over the years explain the rise in finance sector M&A. On a critical note, Dymski concludes with the questions surrounding capital markets as a result of the post-2008 financial crisis, and the position of M&A therein.

In Chapter 24, Nicholas and Samantha Fairclough introduce the distinctive features of professional service firms, as regards the nature of their task and resources, organizational form, and governance mode. They then explain the nature of M&A in this sector by providing an extensive overview of the merger wave that swept large-sized professional service firms in the 1990s and 2000s, using the example of a transnational professional industry: accounting. The reasons that led to the consolidation in the industry, "from the big eight to the big five" in the 1980s and 1990s are identified as resulting from regulatory changes that made merging possible, as well as the need to remain big enough to be able to provide products and services across the globe to ever more international customers. These professional suppliers thus followed their customers. Other rationales include bulwarking expanding competitors, remaining viable, spoiling other deals, and access to capital and insurance.

Annette Ranft, Adelaide Wilcox King, and Jennifer Sexton explore technology sector M&A in Chapter 25. Technology acquisitions have increased in prevalence since the 1980s, as companies have sought to gain access to a wider variety of technological expertise. The authors argue that a key challenge in making technology M&A work stems from the ambiguities therein. The chapter proposes a model on ambiguity management in the context of technology acquisitions.

Having introduced the evolution of the biotechnology industry, Lars Schweizer presents the characteristics and management challenges in acquisitions of biotechnology firms in Chapter 26. Acquisitions in this sector have been on the rise since the 1990s, paralleling the rapid emergence and developments in this industry. Two types of biotechnology acquisitions are identified: acquisitions between biotechnology firms, and acquisitions that link a biotechnology start-up with an established pharmaceutical company. Culture-wise, national culture is not an issue in this sector that describes itself as "global," yet organizational differences become salient in the merging of a small start-up by a larger pharmaceutical player. Whilst retention of talent is critical in these knowledge-based deals, most managers leave in the post-deal years; yet it is the engineers, not the managers, that are most critical in terms of their knowledge. A hybrid approach that simultaneously caters for distinct short- and long-term needs for the acquisition is recommended for the integration of biotechnology firms.

A Critical Overview and Dynamic Syntheses

The last part of the *Handbook* summarizes the various chapter findings and attempts to integrate the strategic, financial, sociocultural, and sectorial views into a critical overview and sets of dynamic syntheses. In the final Chapter 27, the editors Satu Teerikangas,

Richard Joseph and David Faulkner discuss the key insights emerging from the wide range of M&A-related topics reviewed throughout the *Handbook*. First, a critical overview of the study of M&A across disciplines and methodological lenses is provided. Thereafter, the chapter proceeds to synthesizing the emerging understanding as regards: (1) the changing nature of M&A activity over time, (2) the ways in which M&A differ, (3) a contextual framework for M&A management, and (4) a three-dimensional model combining the strategic, financial, and sociocultural lenses to M&A management. Throughout the discussion, the editors identify gaps in the current practice and academic study of M&A, and identify future research directions as means of addressing these gaps.

References

Barkema, H. G., & Schijven, M. (2008). "Toward Unlocking the Full Potential of Acquisitions: The Role of Organizational Restructuring." *Academy of Management Journal*, 51/4: 696–722.

Biggadike R. (1979). "The Risky Business of Diversification." *Harvard Business Review*, 57/3: 103–11.

Birkinshaw, J., Bresman, H., & Håkansson, L. (2000). "Managing the Post-Acquisition Integration Process: How the Human Integration and Task Integration Processes Interact to Foster Value Creation." *Journal of Management Studies*, 37/3: 395–425.

Bower, J. L. (2001). "Not All M&As Are Alike—And That Matters." *Harvard Business Review*, 79/3: 93–101.

Buono, A. F., & Bowditch, J. L. (1989). *The Human Side of Mergers and Acquisitions: Managing Collisions between People, Cultures and Organizations*. London: Jossey-Bass.

————& Lewis, J. W. (1985). "When Cultures Collide: The Anatomy of a Merger." *Human Relations*, 38/5: 477–500.

Burnes, B. (2009). *Managing Change* (4th ed.). Harlow: Pearson.

Cartwright, S. (1998). "International Mergers and Acquisitions: the Issues and Challenges," in M. Gertsen, A.-M. Söderberg, & J. E. Torp (eds.), *Cultural Dimensions of International Mergers and Acquisitions*. Berlin: De Gruyter, 5–16.

——& Cooper, C. L. (1992). *Managing Mergers, Acquisitions and Strategic Alliances: Integrating People and Cultures*. Oxford: Butterworth-Heinemann.

—— —— (1993). "The Role of Culture Compatibility in Successful Organizational Marriage." *Academy of Management Executive*, 7: 2: 57–70.

—— —— (1995). "Organizational Marriage: Hard vs. Soft Issues." *Personnel Review*, 24/3: 32–42.

—— Teerikangas, S., Rouzies, A., & Wilson-Evered, E. (2010). "The Study of Inter-Organizational Encounters: Initiating A Research Methodological Debate." *Scandinavian Journal of Management*, Special issue: Call for papers, September.

Chakrabarti, R., Gupta-Mukherjee, S., & Jayaraman, N. (2009). "Mars-Venus Marriages: Culture and Cross-Border M&A." *Journal of International Business Studies*, 40: 216–36.

Graebner, M. E. (2004). "Momentum and Serendipity: How Acquired Firm Leaders Create Value in the Integration of Technology Firms." *Strategic Management Journal*, 25/8–9: 751–77.

Greenwood, R., Hinings, C. R., & Brown, J. (1994). "Merging Professional Service Firms." *Organization Science*, 5/2: 239–57.

Haleblian, J., Devers, C. E., McNamara, G., Carpenter, M. A., & Davison, R. B. (2009). "Taking Stock of What We Know About Mergers and Acquisitions: A Review and Research Agenda." *Journal of Management*, 35: 469–502.

Haspeslagh, P. C., & Jemison, D. B. (1991). *Managing Acquisitions: Creating Value through Corporate Renewal*. New York: The Free Press.

Kanter, R. M. (1989). *When Giants Learn to Dance: Mastering the Challenges of Strategy, Management, and Careers in the 1990s*. London: Unwin.

—— (1997. *World Class: Thriving Locally in the Global Economy*. New York: Simon & Schuster.

King, D. R., Dalton, D. R., Daily, C. M., & Covin, J. G. (2004). "Meta-Analyses of Post-Acquisition Performance: Indications of Unidentified Moderators." *Strategic Management Journal*, 25/2: 187–200.

Kissin, W. D., & Herrera, J. (1990). "International Mergers and Acquisitions." *The Journal of Business Strategy*, 11, July/August: 51–4.

Levitt, T. (1975). "Marketing Myopia." *Harvard Business Review*, 4/4: 2–14.

Lynch, R. (2006). *Corporate Strategy* (4th ed.). Harlow: Prentice-Hall.

Marks, M. L. (1982). "Merging Human Resources: A Review of the Literature." *Mergers and Acquisitions*, 16, Summer: 38–44.

Meglio, O., & Risberg, A. (2010). "Mergers and Acquisitions – Time for a Methodological Rejuvenation of the Field?" *Scandinavian Journal of Management*, 26: 87–97.

Mirc, N., Rouzies, A., Teerikangas, S., & Tarba, S. (2010). "The M&A Community: Myth or Reality? A Social Network Analysis of M&A Scholars." Paper presented at the Annual Conference of the European Academy of Management, Rome, May 19–22.

Napier, N. K. (1989). "Mergers and Acquisitions, Human Resource Issues and Outcomes: A Review and Suggested Typology." *Journal of Management Studies*, 26/3: 271–89.

Nonaka, T. (1991). "The Knowledge-Creating Company." *Harvard Business Review*, 69, November–December: 96–104.

Papadakis, V., and Thanos, I. (2010). "Measuring the Performance of Acquisitions: An Empirical Investigation Using Multiple Criteria." *British Management Journal*, 21, 859–73.

Porter, M. (1987). "From Competitive Advantage to Corporate Strategy." *Harvard Business Review*, 65/3: 43–59.

Quah, P., & Young, S. (2005). "Post-Acquisition Management: A Phases Approach for Cross-border M&A." *European Management Journal*, 23/1: 65–75.

Schweiger, D. M., & Goulet, P. K. (2000). "Integrating Mergers and Acquisitions: An International Research Review," in C. Cooper and A. Gregory (eds.). *Advances in Mergers and Acquisitions*, 1. Amsterdam: JAI Press, 61–91.

Schoenberg, R. (2006). "Measuring the Performance of Corporate Acquisitions: An Empirical Comparison of Alternative Metrics." *British Management Journal*, 17(s1): 361–70.

Trautwein, F. (1990). "Merger Motives and Merger Prescriptions." *Strategic Management Journal*, 11: 283–95.

Zollo, M., and Meier, D. (2008). "What is M&A Performance?" *Academy of Management Perspectives*, 22/3, August, 55–77.

PART I

A STRATEGIC LENS FOR M&A

CHAPTER 2

A REVIEW OF THE MERGER AND ACQUISITION WAVE LITERATURE

History, Antecedents, Consequences, and Future Directions

KALIN KOLEV, JERAYR HALEBLIAN, AND GERRY McNAMARA

Mergers and acquisitions have been shown to occur in waves of intense activity in which the number of deals increases significantly over a prior period. This increased rate of activity is sustained for a certain time period before returning to the previous level of merger frequency. Over 50% of acquisitions that occurred over the last century took place in merger and acquisition waves (Stearns and Allan 1996). In fact, the observation that mergers and acquisitions often occur in waves is one of the "most consistent empirical features of merger activity" (Andrade et al. 2001: 104). Research on these waves has centered on three key topics: (a) the main characteristics of prior merger waves, (b) the antecedent conditions to these waves, and (c) their performance implications.

Perhaps surprisingly, while a sizable body of research about merger and acquisition waves has developed across a number of academic areas, there are no comprehensive overviews of the existing research. To fill this gap in the literature, we provide a detailed framework of what we currently know about these waves, drawing upon research in economics, finance, management, and sociology. In addition, we offer future direction and recommendations for researchers. The chapter proceeds as follows. First, we outline the five major merger and acquisition waves and explicate their key characteristics and features. Next, we follow with a categorization of the underlying antecedents that drive the emergence and development of waves in which we focus on exogenous factors, such as economic, technological and business factors that initiate waves and the underlying managerial motives for participating in such waves. We then provide evidence of the outcomes of merger and acquisition waves in which we describe not only the performance implications for firms, but also the overall effect of waves on value creation or value destruction. Finally, we conclude with discussion of the current findings in merger and acquisition wave research and outline potential areas that need further investigation and present an opportunity for scholars to better understand these waves.

DEFINITION OF MERGER AND ACQUISITION WAVES

Merger and acquisition waves are periods of intense merger and acquisition activity. The beginning of the wave is characterized by a dramatic increase in the number of executed acquisitions relative to the prior period. This intense period of activity reaches a plateau, which often continues for several years. Finally, there is a significant drop in the overall activity as acquisition activity tends to return back to pre-wave levels (see Carow et al. 2004; McNamara et al. 2008 for further definitions).

The fundamental characteristic of merger and acquisition waves is that the frequency of acquisitions varies systematically from a random walk process, with periods of significantly higher acquisition activity than typical periods. Early research provided inconsistent results regarding this assertion. For example, to test the general claim that mergers and acquisitions occur in waves, Shughart and Tollison (1984) examined whether mergers and acquisitions occur randomly, rather than in waves. Their data failed to reject the hypothesis that mergers and acquisitions are generated by a random walk, suggesting merger and acquisition activity could be random. However, later research supported the merger and acquisition wave hypothesis. Linn and Zhu (1997) and Town (1992) argued that waves are not a random walk process and provided evidence for a two-stage switching model in which for a period of time aggregate merger and acquisition activity is very intense and encompasses a large volume of transactions. This period is followed by relative inactivity with very few transactions. Later research supported this conclusion, finding that merger and acquisition waves represented periods of non-random spikes in acquisition activity (e.g. Harford 2005; McNamara et al. 2008). Thus, recent research has provided strong, compelling empirical evidence supporting the common belief that mergers and acquisitions occur in waves.

CHARACTERISTICS OF THE FIVE INTER-INDUSTRY MERGER WAVES

Since the turn of the 19th century five major inter-industry merger and acquisition waves have been identified and scholars from various disciplines have attempted to explain the nature of such waves (see Table 2.1 for a summary).

The First Merger and Acquisition Wave (1897–1903)   The first wave appeared in the United States at the turn of the 19th century and is referred to as the Great Merger Wave. This is the first time that intense acquisition activity was witnessed within a relatively short time period. The main participants in this wave were firms trying to achieve horizontal consolidations through the formation of trusts (Banerjee and Eckard 1998). In this first wave, firms were merging to form monopolies, which led to the creation of giant firms that controlled markets (Stigler 1950).

This first wave is viewed as a response to radical changes in technology, economic expansion, new state legislation, and the development of industrial stock exchanges (Martynova and Renneboog 2008; Stigler 1950). Additionally, a central factor that facilitated the rise of merger and acquisition activity was the lack of antitrust regulation. Thus, firms did not face legal constraints in acquiring other companies and consolidating particular industries. In addition, mergers and acquisitions were classified as friendly and relied on cash as the dominant source of financing. The end of this wave was marked by the crash of the equity market in 1903–5.

Since these mergers and acquisitions led to industry consolidation to the point of creating tight oligopolies in some industries, it is logical to conclude that market restructuring to create favorable industry conditions was the underlying motivation for undertaking mergers and acquisitions. However, existing evidence shows that competitors suffered value loss, which is contrary to the arguments of industry consolidation, where all competitors should benefit from the more favorable industry environment. Interestingly, empirical findings support the claim that realization of efficient operations was driving this merger wave. Participants in these consolidations were able to generate returns of 12% to 18% (measured as cumulative abnormal returns over one-month and two-month windows) which indicates that mergers and acquisitions during this period were a successful tool for increasing firm performance (Banerjee and Eckard 1998).

The Second Merger and Acquisition Wave (1920–1929)   The second merger and acquisition wave developed in the United States and was preceded by a period of economic recovery after the end of World War I. During this wave the main objective of merging firms was to create oligopolies. These mergers and acquisitions were initiated by smaller firms within industries as they attempted to increase their size, achieve economies of scale, and compete with the leading firm on a more equal basis (Stigler 1950). As a result, industry structures often changed from previous near-monopoly to oligopoly. Interestingly, this wave was not characterized by intense mergers by monopoly firms, as the enforcement of antitrust laws increased in this period. Moreover, the second merger wave was disproportionately characterized by petroleum and primary metals industries, which accounted for nearly 40% of total merger and acquisition value (Eis 1969). In contrast to the first merger wave at the beginning of the 20th century, the second merger wave featured more emphasis on stock as a means of financing acquisitions (Martynova and Renneboog 2008). The end of the second merger and acquisition wave was marked by the stock market crash and the beginning of the Great Depression.

Research has also been conducted on the consequences of takeovers on shareholder wealth during the second wave. In a detailed analysis of the performance effects of mergers, Leeth and Borg (2002) found evidence that while target firms enjoyed abnormal returns of 15% (measured over a one-month window), these positive effects were not mirrored by acquiring firms' shareholders, which did not achieve positive abnormal returns. In fact, the combined market value gains of target and bidding firms were insignificant. Furthermore, returns for target and acquiring firms were not affected by the mode of acquisition (tender offer vs. non-tender offer), means of financing (cash vs. stock), and degree of relatedness (Leeth and Borg 2002).

The Third Merger and Acquisition Wave (1960s)   The third merger and acquisition wave took place primarily in the 1960s, reached its peak in 1968, but collapsed in 1973 after the development of the oil crisis (Martynova and Renneboog 2008). In contrast to the first two waves, which were restricted to the United States, the third merger and acquisition wave took place not only in the US but also in the United Kingdom and Continental Europe. The wave was marked by the strategy of unrelated diversification and as such was known as the conglomerate merger wave. Participants in the wave engaged in friendly acquisitions through stock financing and typically large firms acquired small public or private firms outside of their main line of business (Shleifer and Vishny 1991).

Existing research outlines several major explanations underlying the motivation to engage in acquisitions during this period. While different, these explanations are not mutually exclusive, and may have worked together to spur intense merger activity among companies. First, agency problems were proposed as driving merger and acquisition activity. Driven by self-interest, managers increased firm size through diversification and thus gained private benefits, such as larger compensation (Jensen 1986; Tosi et al. 2000). In addition, diversifying acquisitions could reduce managerial employment risk, as managing a diversified company requires significant skills and may make managers more indispensable to the company (Amihud and Lev 1981; Shleifer and Vishny 1989). Second, conglomerate acquisitions were viewed as a means to enhance shareholder wealth. Managers making acquisitions grow the firm, and thus compensate for the slow growth of a firm's business in mature markets. Hence, diversification mergers allowed firms to buy growth in industries which were unrelated to their main lines of business. Evidence for improved shareholder wealth comes from Matsusaka (1993), who found that acquiring firms buying growing targets were perceived positively by the market. In addition, diversifying acquisitions allowed the maintenance of higher levels of debt and cross-subsidizing across divisions via efficient internal capital allocation processes. In other words, due to the imperfections and underdevelopment of the external capital markets at the time, managers used diversifying acquisitions to overcome asymmetric information problems and made better allocation decisions, and improved shareholder wealth (Servaes 1996). Third, legal constraints and enforced antitrust regulations have also been proposed as the major drivers of the conglomerate merger and acquisition wave. Antitrust laws did not allow mergers in the same industry and forced managers to seek alternative opportunities in unrelated lines of business.

Evidence on the consequences of diversifying mergers during this wave on firm performance is mixed. Some studies find the market reacted positively to announcement of conglomerate mergers. For instance, Hubbard and Palia (1999) show that bidder abnormal returns were positive, which may result from expectations that diversifying acquisitions create efficient capital allocation systems. In contrast, though, other empirical work is more skeptical about the benefit of diversifying acquisitions. Servaes (1996) showed that diversified firms traded at a discount compared to single-business companies, while Ravenscraft and Scherer (1987) documented that profitability of acquiring firms did not improve. Additionally, it has been shown that many of the previously acquired targets were subsequently divested (Porter 1987; Ravenscraft and Scherer 1987), which is consistent with the notion that conglomerate mergers are not efficient. A more nuanced view may be that the initial market reaction to diversifying mergers was positive, but this enthusiasm faded when mergers failed to generate significant operational improvements (Shleifer and Vishny 1989).

The Fourth Merger and Acquisition Wave (1980s)   The 1980s takeovers—which took place on an international scale across the United States, Europe, and Asia—reversed the process of the conglomerate acquisitions and brought corporations back to the strategy of greater specialization (Shleifer and Vishny 2003). The wave was characterized by target companies that were much bigger in size compared to targets in the 1960s. As Shleifer and Vishny (1991) report, around 28% of the Fortune 500 firms during 1981 were acquired by 1989. In addition, a new phenomenon emerged—hostile takeovers and new forms of control became very popular. "Bustup" takeovers were a common occurrence in which significant parts of the acquired company were subsequently divested. In addition, the leveraged buyout (LBO), in which a significant percentage of the purchase price was financed through borrowing, accounted for almost 15% of all acquisition value (Ravenscraft 1987). Finally, acquisitions were mainly financed with cash.

This merger and acquisition wave eliminated the conglomerate structure and its associated inefficiencies, as managers emphasized acquisitions in related industries (Bhagat et al. 1990). Another major driver of this fourth merger and acquisition wave was the relaxation of antitrust enforcement and increased emphasis on deregulation. Since authorities did not challenge acquisitions in the same industries, related acquisitions grew dramatically (Shleifer and Vishny 1991). Additional factors for this wave consisted of favorable economic conditions (e.g. recovery after the economic recession), permissive legal environment (e.g. relaxed antitrust policy, deregulation of financial markets), and financial innovations, such as junk bonds that were necessary conditions for the wave. In addition, fringe players in the market initiated acquisitions and due to their success, imitators started mimicking their behaviors, which ultimately led to the emergence of a wave (Stearns and Allan 1996).

The empirical findings about performance implications of this merger and acquisition wave are generally consistent across scholars. Morck, Shleifer, and Vishny (1990) found positive results for related acquisitions and negative results for unrelated ones. Similarly, other scholars also found profitability improvements for acquisitions in the 1980s (Healy et al. 1992; Kaplan 1989).

The Fifth Merger and Acquisition Wave (1990s)   The fifth merger and acquisition wave coincides with increased economic globalization and the technological revolution

Table 2.1 Summary of Waves

	First Merger Wave	Second Merger Wave	Third Merger Wave	Fourth Merger Wave	Fifth Merger Wave
Time period	1897–1903	1920–1929	1960s–1973	1980s	1990s–2001
Geographic scope	US	US	US, UK, Europe	US, UK, Europe, Asia	US, UK, Europe, Asia
Value (in $Billion)*	6.9	7.3	46	618	4,500
Number of deals**	3012	4828	NA	9617	31,152
Rationale	Creation of monopolies	Creation of oligopolies	Managerial self-interest; growth through diversification; exploiting efficiencies of internal capital allocation markets	Elimination of conglomerate structures and inefficiencies	International expansion
Drivers of wave	Changes in technology; economic expansion; introduction of new legislation and industrial stock exchanges; lack of antitrust regulation	Increase in antitrust laws; economic recovery after World War I	Increase in antitrust regulation; underdeveloped external capital markets	Relaxation of antitrust regulation; favorable economic conditions; financial innovations (e.g. junk bonds)	Globalization; deregulation; privatization
Acquisition types	Friendly acquisitions		Friendly and diversifying acquisitions	Related acquisitions; hostile takeovers; LBOs	Related acquisitions
Financing	Cash	Stock	Stock	Cash	Stock
Performance effects	Positive effects— merging firms gained 12–18% in cumulative abnormal returns	Positive effects only for target firms— 15% in abnormal returns	Mixed effects for acquiring firms— initial market reaction to mergers positive, but insignificant operational improvements. Positive effects for target firms	Acquiring firm effects depend on relatedness— related acquisitions generated value, unrelated acquisitions generated losses. Positive effects for target firms	Positive effects only for targets—16% in abnormal returns

* Merger activity in the US industry.
** Involving US companies.
Source: Ghauri and Buckley (2003).

of the 1990s (Martynova and Renneboog 2008). This was clearly a global wave involving intense acquisition activity in the United States, Europe, and Asia. Consistent with a global strategy, cross-border acquisitions increased significantly and helped domestic companies better compete against international rivals. In addition, these acquisitions were marked by a disappearance of hostility, as only 4% of mergers and acquisitions during the 1990s were hostile (Andrade et al. 2001). Consistent with the 1980s, this merger and acquisition wave continued with the dominant role of related acquisitions, which also involved stock swaps between the merging companies. However, in contrast to the 1980s merger and acquisition wave, acquirers relied primarily on stock to complete transactions—in 58% of cases the transactions were entirely financed with stock. Finally, the major driver of the fifth wave appears to be deregulation and privatization, which emerged as a major shock that particularly affected the acquisition activity of companies within some industries (e.g. communications, information technology).

The performance outcomes of the fifth merger and acquisition wave showed an asymmetric pattern for target and acquiring companies in which targets benefited with an average of 16% abnormal returns (measured over a several-day window), while the bidding companies tended not to benefit from these acquisitions (Martynova and Renneboog 2008).

Antecedents to Merger and Acquisition Waves

We now turn our attention to the antecedents of merger and acquisition waves and categorize the factors that underlie their emergence. There are two distinctive perspectives that have attempted to explain the emergence of waves—neoclassical theory and the market misvaluations framework. Below we present both theoretical and empirical justifications for these two perspectives, along with evidence supporting the notion that combining factors from various perspectives may yield a better description and explanation of merger wave drivers.

Neoclassical Hypothesis

The neoclassical hypothesis stipulates that merger and acquisition waves are driven by macro-environmental or industry shocks, leading to the reallocation of assets (Harford 2005). Because these shocks create different environmental conditions for firms, firms are forced to respond through increased acquisition of industry assets. Mergers and acquisitions cluster in time as managers "compete for the best combination of assets" (Harford 2005: 533). Furthermore, the idiosyncratic nature of shocks and their particular relevance to certain industries leads to uneven distribution of merger activity across industries, with the highest activity being observed in industries with significant disturbances (Mitchell and Mulherin 1996). Regardless of the nature of those shocks (e.g. economic, technological, or regulatory), they alter industry structure and foster collective acquisition actions targeted at accommodating industry change.

Gort (1969) proposed the initial industry shock theory of mergers and acquisitions in which he argued that an industry disturbance leads to valuation discrepancies in firm stock, changes in managers' expectations of future stock values, and lower predictability about the future. Such industry instability may be sufficient to trigger managerial efforts to buy other companies' stock, which generates increased merger activity, leading to an industry wave.

There are several major shocks that have received empirical attention and have been shown to affect the emergence of industry waves.

Economic shocks Economic shocks include changes in environmental conditions that affect the general economic and business environment of firms, such as sales growth, employment changes, market booms, and increased demand. In a comprehensive study of the 1980s merger and acquisition wave, Mitchell and Mulherin (1996) provide strong evidence for the role of economic factors and shocks on acquisition intensity. They show that sales growth and employment changes are major indicators of altering economic conditions and should have a positive effect on combined merger activity. They find that a 1% change in sales shocks[1] leads to a 4.6% increase in takeover industry activity. Similar results are reported for the relationship between employment shock and increased takeover industry activity. Industry product demand is another factor that has been shown to spur increased acquisition activity. Increased demand is positively associated with pursuit of synergies and economies of scale that may be achieved through mergers and acquisitions. Hence, when the economy is growing and the product demand is increasing, firms will seek mergers and acquisitions and those mergers and acquisitions are more likely to be seen across rising product markets (Lambrecht 2004). Support for the role of industry demand on mergers and acquisitions has also been shown in other studies. For example, general macroeconomic growth (GDP) has been shown to be positively associated with merger and acquisition activity (Becketti 1986). Qiu and Zhou (2007) also show that industry demand drives mergers and acquisitions. However, they show that negative demand shock motivates mergers and acquisition—under unfavorable business conditions in which demand is decreasing, merging firms improve production efficiencies.

Regulatory shocks Regulatory shocks are another factor that may create industry disturbance and motivate acquisition activity. Throughout the history of merger waves, laws and legal conditions have played a major role in spurring or constraining mergers. For example, antitrust regulations in the United States during the 1960s did not allow mergers in the same industries and thus firms oriented toward acquisitions in unrelated businesses (Shleifer and Vishny 1991). In contrast, during the 1980s antitrust enforcement was relaxed, which allowed firms to merge within their own industries and create related acquisitions (Shleifer and Vishny 1991). In other words, through legal regulations the government reduced the costs of mergers and acquisitions, legitimized certain acquisitions, and sent "corporate actors the message that they have carte blanche to act in their interests" (Stearns and Allan 1996: 702). Government regulatory reform in the 1980s was a major driver of intense merger and acquisition activity. Because of a laissez-faire position on market functioning and reduced emphasis on antitrust law enforcement, the government significantly altered the business environment and encouraged mergers on a massive scale (Stearns and Allan 1996). In a similar vein, changes in tax codes have been discussed as an additional driving factor in companies' motivation to engage in mergers and acquisitions (Ravenscraft 1987).

Deregulation is another underlying cause for the emergence of merger and acquisition waves. The impact of deregulations across banking, broadcasting, communications, transportation, and oil and gas industries was significant and created incentives for intense merger and acquisition activity during the 1980s. In a comprehensive study on the role of industry shocks on industry merger and acquisition activity, Mitchell and Mulherin (1996) outline the impact of deregulation and show empirical support for its positive influence on total takeover activity.

Technology shocks While technology shocks have received less attention in their role as causing industry disturbances, there is strong empirical evidence for their significance in this process. The underlying logic is that the arrival of new technology brings pressure on firms to adopt it and thus favorable conditions for merger and acquisition waves develop. New technology leads to reallocation of capital and mergers and acquisitions appear as an efficient way to redistribute corporate assets. The impact of new technology emergence is to increase the dispersion in Tobin's Q among firms in which high-Q firms (i.e. market value above the replacement cost of capital)—acquire low-Q ones (i.e. firms with market values below the replacement cost of capital). For example, Jovanovic and Rousseau (2008) test the argument that technological shocks during the 1900s, 1920s, 1980s, and 1990s led to the emergence of waves during those periods. They find that the arrival of electricity and the combustion engine during 1890–1930 and the advent of the microcomputer and information technology during 1980–90 were technological shocks that spurred merger and acquisition activity.

Financial innovations The emergence of financial innovations and their widespread recognition across markets have been shown to be an important factor that created industry disturbance and generated intensified merger and acquisition activities. Financial innovations created an alternative source of capital for companies and made it easier to borrow funds even for smaller and less-prominent players. Hence, a larger number of firms had access to financial resources and enjoyed the opportunity to undertake mergers. Some examples of financial innovations include the stock innovation during the first merger and acquisition wave (Navin and Sears 1955), marketing techniques during the 1920s merger and acquisition wave (Reid 1968), and "merger accounting" (Barmash 1971) during the 1960s mergers and acquisitions wave.

One of the most comprehensive accounts of the role of financial innovations in the emergence of merger and acquisition waves was given by Stearns and Allan (1996) in their discussion of the 1980s mergers and acquisition wave. One novelty of this wave period was the significant expansion of mutual funds and the easy access firms had to their capital. During the 1980s the resources of mutual funds in the US grew several times and offered new sources of capital available for undertaking acquisitions. In addition, the emergence of the junk bonds had a huge impact on companies willing to acquire but having reduced access to financial resources. This was particularly evident for small and fringe players that had previously been at a disadvantage in terms of securing capital. The invention of the junk bonds helped those players to get fast and easy access to capital and undertake a series of acquisitions. Mitchell and Mulherin (1996) provide additional evidence for the role of financial innovations during the 1980s merger and acquisition wave. They argue that the emergence of high-yield debt financing was a shock that enhanced firms' abilities to use leveraged financing for mergers. Overall, financial innovations have had a significant positive effect on the development of takeover activity.

The main findings consistent with the neoclassical hypothesis show that various types of shocks, such as economic, regulatory, technological, and financial innovations, have a positive association with industry merger waves. Emerging evidence, though, suggests that these shocks might be a necessary but insufficient condition for the emergence of industry waves. An additional factor that needs to be present is the availability of capital liquidity (Harford 2005), which reduces constraints and allows for an easier execution of transactions (Shleifer and Vishny 1992). Thus, it is not surprising that merger and acquisition waves occur in boom markets—times when capital is easily available and financial constraints are relatively low. This argument is further supported by Harford (2005), who shows that firms with cash reserves are more likely to acquire. In a similar vein, Polonchek and Sushka (1987) link increased merger and acquisition activity with a low cost of capital during the conglomerate boom of 1967–9. Therefore, the combination of industry shocks and capital liquidity positively affects the emergence of merger and acquisition waves (Harford 2005) in which liquidity leads to clustering in time of industry waves that result in aggregate-level merger and acquisition waves.

Market Misvaluation Framework

The market misevaluation framework argues that merger and acquisition waves appear during periods when the market overvalues firms (Rhodes-Kropf and Viswanathan 2004). Merger and acquisition waves are more likely to emerge during periods of high market valuations and high dispersion in those valuations. Thus, the misvaluation framework relies on the assumption that financial markets are inefficient and rational managers are trying to take advantage of market imperfections. When the bidding firm is overvalued, its managers are more likely to engage in acquisitions of undervalued assets with their stock. Rather than using cash, bidding firm managers rely on their overvalued stock to obtain other firms' assets at a lower price. This argument, when combined with the notion of a market misperception of merger and acquisition synergies, leads to a clustering of merger and acquisition activity (Shleifer and Vishny 2003). While the motivation of the acquiring firms' executives is obvious, there are different explanations for the motivation of target managers who accept the acquisition bid. Shleifer and Vishny (2003) argue that target managers are self-interested with short-run horizons and do not necessarily protect shareholder value. Instead, they are willing to accept the overvalued stock of the acquiring company and quickly cash out. In contrast, Rhodes-Kropf and Viswanathan (2004, 2005) defend the argument that target managers are led by imperfect information and assumptions about the potential synergies of mergers and acquisitions and overestimate future benefits. These arguments suggest that market overvaluation will lead to an increased number of merger and acquisition bids, creating merger waves.

Consistent with the misvaluation framework, the 1960s mergers and acquisitions might have been directed to unrelated industries in which targets were undervalued. Moreover, own-industry acquisitions may have been unattractive because of target overvaluations. Similarly, De Bondt and Thompson (1992) provide evidence that merger and acquisition waves since the 1930s are explained by target firm undervaluations. In this case, bidding firms could gain from the transaction by buying quality assets at a temporary low market price. The main implication of the misvaluation framework is that high market-to-book (M/B) value firms acquire low M/B firms. This is consistent with the Q-Theory of mergers where high-Q firms will buy low-Q firms (Jovanovic and Rousseau 2002). Thus, highly valued firms are the drivers of merger and acquisition activity and those firms account for almost 50% of all acquisitions (Rhodes-Kropf and Viswanathan 2005).

While the merits of the misvaluations framework should not be underestimated, it should not be seen as the ultimate explanation for industry merger and acquisition waves. Rhodes-Kropf and Viswanathan (2005) show evidence that sector-level misvaluation explains only 15% of merger waves' emergence. There appear to be other forces, such as industry shocks, that contribute to our understanding of waves. Yet, the misvaluation framework helps provide understanding of wave dynamics by outlining the major participants in waves and shows who has a tendency to acquire whom (Rhodes-Kropf and Viswanathan 2005; Shleifer and Vishny 2003).

Other Behavioral Foundations of Industry Merger and Acquisition Waves

While the neoclassical hypothesis and the misvaluation perspective are the most common frameworks used in studying merger waves, there are additional behavioral theories in which managerial motivations may help explain merger wave emergence. These theories underscore the importance of managers in the merger and acquisitions process and their key role in initiating and sustaining industry waves. Below we outline two such theories.

Imitation and bandwagon behavior Prior research suggests mergers and acquisitions are a means for fringe firms to improve on their market position and profitability. Prior work shows that "challengers" are firms that are "denied the social prestige and investment opportunities" (Stearns and Allan 1996: 702) and use mergers and acquisitions to break the status quo and better position themselves in the market. Since such firms are "outsiders" and have less to lose in terms of social prestige and legitimacy, they are more willing to experiment with strategic alternatives (Leblebici et al. 1991), such as mergers and acquisitions. However, if their acquisitions are successful and gain market legitimacy (Scott 2001; Suchman 1995), such "fringe" players may become trendsetters and enjoy a more central and beneficial position in the market. When existing players in the market see the success of challengers and start imitating them, merger waves become more likely. Forced by the existing institutional pressures and normative order (DiMaggio and Powell 1983), more firms become followers and engage in merger and acquisition behaviors.

Similar logic has been applied when presenting merger and acquisition waves as driven by bandwagon pressures (Abrahamson and Rosenkopf 1993; Fiol and O'Connor 2003; McNamara et al. 2008). While firms that initiate acquisitions are looking for first-mover advantages (Lieberman and Montgomery 1988), followers mimic others' acquisitions because of fears of being left out in the competitive field (McNamara et al. 2008). In other words, leaders in waves are primarily motivated by seeking competitive advantage, while followers join the merger and acquisition frenzy, seeking social and institutional legitimacy.

Merger and acquisition waves as outcome of managerial self-interest Goel and Thakor (2009) utilize the construct of CEO envy as a driving force of industry waves. Because firm size is a significant predictor of CEO compensation (Tosi et al. 2000), acquisitions appear to be an easy way to increase firm size and subsequent executive compensation. The existing dispersion in CEO compensation leaves some CEOs underpaid and envious of others' compensation packages. To reduce this gap and enhance their own pay, envious CEOs are willing to undertake "size-enhancing acquisitions, thereby starting a merger and acquisition wave" (Goel and Thakor 2009: 489). These arguments are consistent with "empire building," in which managers are willing to sacrifice corporate funds to fulfill personal ego motives.

Another emerging perspective is that merger and acquisition waves are driven by the defensive motivations of executives. One of the main objectives of managers is to stay in control of their firms and prevent takeover attempts by their rivals. Mergers and acquisitions allow the firm to grow larger and thus it becomes a more difficult target for others. If this motive is shared by a large number of executives, it may result in merger waves in which executives feel they need to "eat-or-be-eaten" (Gorton et al. 2009)—particularly in industries in which the majority of firms are of a similar size.

In summary, research has suggested that a range of factors at both the market and the firm level may work in combination to trigger or spur on acquisition waves. This includes environmental shocks, such as changes in demand conditions or technological discontinuities that necessitate the re-alignment of organizational assets to meet these changing environmental conditions. Additionally, there are other environmental shocks, such as industry deregulation and changes in antitrust enforcement, that trigger merger activity to pursue new opportunities to build scale efficiencies and market power. Increases in the availability of capital are also likely to facilitate heightened acquisition activity. At the firm level, high firm valuations are likely to spur acquisition actions as firms strive to use their overvalued stock to purchase underpriced assets. There are also managerial motives that may spur on acquisition waves. Driven by self-interest, such as self-enrichment through empire building, managers have the incentive to take acquisition actions that trigger or spur on merger waves. There are also defensive incentives, such as competitive and institutional bandwagon pressures, that lead managers to join a growing acquisition trend lest they be left behind by their competitors.

PERFORMANCE IMPLICATIONS OF MERGER AND ACQUISITION WAVES

Research has also focused on firm performance outcomes associated with merger and acquisition waves. Consistent with the general findings for mergers and acquisitions, research has shown that target shareholders benefit from an increased stock price from mergers and acquisitions within waves, and this result holds across various waves. Leeth and Borg (2002) show positive cumulative abnormal returns (CARs) for target firms during the 1920s merger and acquisition wave. Work shows CARs of around 30% during the conglomerate merger and acquisition wave (Bradley 1980; Bradley and Jarrell 1980). During the 1980s merger and acquisition wave, Servaes (1991) shows that target firms generated positive cumulative abnormal returns in the 20–30% range. During the last merger and acquisition wave of the 1990s, target companies were once again beneficiaries and experienced returns of 15–20% (Goergen and Renneboog 2004; Martynova and Renneboog 2008).[2] While the general trend is that targets within waves benefit, performance nuances have also been found. Servaes (1991) found that hostile bids result in almost 50% higher CARs than friendly bids. Cash transactions have been found to be more beneficial to target firms than equity-based transactions (Andrade et al. 2001; Franks et al. 1991).

In contrast to target firms, most studies find that bidders do not benefit from their mergers and acquisitions during waves, as negative or insignificant results have been found for acquiring companies across various merger and acquisition waves (Andrade et al. 2001). That said, however, evidence has been presented that during the conglomerate merger and acquisition wave, diversifying mergers and acquisitions were favored by the market due to the exploitation of efficient internal capital allocation markets (Hubbard and Palia 1999; Matsusaka 1993). However, the subsequent reversal from diversifying mergers and acquisitions and the emphasis on focus-enhancing mergers and acquisitions during the 1980s suggests that these bidder benefits were only temporary. When mergers and acquisitions during waves are evaluated in terms of accounting measures of performance, empirical results link acquisitions with a subsequent decrease in profitability, especially when earnings-based indicators are applied (Martynova and

Renneboog 2008). Thus, it appears that across waves, and across measures of perform-ance, the evidence shows that acquiring firms do not benefit from making mergers and acquisitions during waves.

Research has also been conducted on the performance implications for firms based on their position within the wave. Carow and colleagues (2004) draw on the first-mover advantage theory to argue that early mergers and acquisitions within waves will outper-form later ones. They found that acting early in a wave allows firms to benefit from infor-mation asymmetries and obtain valuable resources at a lower price. In addition, conducting strategic acquisitions in growing industries and paying with cash was found to be the optimal combination for realizing gains by early acquirers. Similar results were found by McNamara and colleagues (2008) who showed that acting early in a wave is beneficial as early movers experience positive abnormal returns, while those firms that initiate acquisitions at the peak of the wave experience very negative abnormal returns. As the wave begins to weaken, though, abnormal returns improved, suggesting the peak of waves is driven by bandwagon behavior, but when these effects diminish, the wave dies out and returns for bidders return to more normal levels. They also found this pat-tern of high acquisition returns for early movers and losses for firms acquiring at the height of the wave was stronger for firms in faster-growing and more dynamic industries and for firms that do not undertake acquisitions regularly or use stock to finance acquisitions.

Finally, research at the industry level of analysis has been conducted that compares whether differences exist between merger performance within and outside waves. Harford (2005) used various measures of performance and found that mergers in waves do not underperform other mergers. Interestingly, with some measures, such as sales growth and analyst forecasts of long-term growth, mergers in waves appear to perform better than mergers outside waves.

In summary, research findings indicate that the performance implications of merger and acquisition waves are asymmetric for target and acquiring companies. While target firms generate value from the merger and acquisition process, acquirers do not benefit. Furthermore, evidence exists that acting early in a wave is associated with positive returns, while acquiring at the peak of a wave is detrimental to performance. Finally, there is some indication that mergers and acquisitions in waves are at least as profitable as mergers and acquisitions outside waves.

FUTURE DIRECTIONS FOR MERGER AND ACQUISITIONS WAVE RESEARCH

While the research to date has given us insight into prior waves, triggers to waves, and their performance implications for acquirers and targets, there are a number of unex-plored issues related to merger waves.

First, we do not fully understand which firms choose to participate in merger and acquisition waves compared with those that do not. Although prevailing evidence exists that high market-to-book value firms buy lower market-to-book firms (see Rhodes-Kropf and Viswanathan 2004; Shleifer and Vishny 2003), research needs to further explore the distinctions between participating and non-participating firms. Organizational characteristics, such as the firm's generic strategy or their organization's goals, may influence their likelihood of participating in an acquisition wave. Additionally, their financial resources and access to capital and debt markets may influence their likelihood of participation. There could also be corporate governance drivers of merger wave participation. Since acquisitions have been associated with positive effects for CEO compensation (Kroll et al. 1997; Wright et al. 2002), self-serving CEOs and their compensation contracts may help explain why some firms are more likely to participate in waves. Relatedly, CEOs envious of their peers' compensation (Goel and Thakor 2009) may use acquisitions as a quick and relatively easy way to increase their compensation. It may even be that a sufficient number of envious CEOs within an industry could help trigger merger waves. In contrast, the existence of diligent boards of directors and appropriate incentive systems (Jensen and Meckling 1976) could deter self-serving CEOs from inappropriately entering merger and acquisition waves.

Second, research should examine particular firm characteristics that influence when firms choose to participate in merger and acquisition waves. For example, merger and acquisition experience is an important factor that has received less attention in the context of merger and acquisition waves. Having conducted prior acquisitions may help firms generate valuable knowledge and identify the right timing of joining a wave. However, the blind application of prior knowledge to current acquisition waves might also have some detrimental effects on acquisition performance (Haleblian and Finkelstein 1999). A competitive-dynamics framework focuses on the *causes* and *consequences* of the action and reaction of firms within industries (Smith et al. 2001), and has shown that firm characteristics are related to the timing of firm actions (Smith et al. 2001) that drive rival firm behavior. Based on this approach, we would suggest that firm age, size, slack resources, performance, structure, and research and development intensity might be important firm characteristics that distinguish leaders from followers in acquisition waves. Prior competitive-dynamics research has identified three underlying drivers of rival behavior: awareness of competitors' initiatives, the motivation to act (or respond), and the capability to do so (Smith et al. 2001). Future work could assess firm-level causes to determine whether early movers within industry merger and acquisition waves have greater awareness-motivation-capability (AMC) (Chen 1996) relative to followers.

Third, an open question is whether firms manage merger and acquisitions differently in wave periods than non-wave periods. For example, are there any significant differences in merger and acquisition planning (number of targets considered, degree of due diligence, time spent on pre-acquisition steps) across merger and acquisition wave periods and non-wave periods? Drawing on the evidence that large numbers of firms experience bandwagon pressures to engage in a wave (McNamara et al. 2008), it could be argued that those firms pay less attention to details, undermine due-diligence procedures, and skip important steps of the pre-acquisition examination of potential targets. On the contrary, firms that acquire during non-wave periods might have extra time to investigate potential targets, evaluate complementarities, and avoid surprises. In a similar vein, do differences exist in merger and acquisition implementation (degree of integration of acquired firm, premium paid, type of financing typically used, length of integration period, likelihood of divestiture of assets) between wave periods and non-wave periods? The degree and length of integration period for the acquired firm is closely related to the quality of the pre-acquisition planning. In other words, the better the planning phase, the faster the integration phase will be. Assuming that during merger and acquisition waves firms have to act fast and have less time to carefully select their targets, it could be expected that wave acquisitions are harder to implement and more likely to be divested subsequently. However, Harford (2005) did not find major differences in merger performance within and outside waves which might suggest no difference in the likelihood of divestitures during wave periods and non-wave periods. Instead of comparing wave and non-wave acquisitions, it might be more interesting to investigate early versus late movers in waves and how they fare during and after the merger and acquisition process. Considering that the majority of merger and acquisitions within waves are unsuccessful (see McNamara et al. 2008, who find that only the first 20–25% of acquisitions generate positive returns), it is likely that more divestitures will be conducted by late movers. Similarly, it could be argued that later movers will be more impatient after conducting an acquisition and will divest faster than early movers. However, will those divestitures happen while the wave is still going or will firms take a "wait-and-see" approach and divest after the wave has finished? Another interesting question that begs an answer is comparing how early versus late movers within waves integrate the acquired target. Since early movers are thought to be driven by synergies (Carow et al. 2004), while later movers have been considered more likely imitators (McNamara et al. 2008), early movers might be better able to transfer knowledge between acquirer and target. In addition, it might be that early movers are more likely to retain target management and thus leverage core capabilities.

Fourth, the performance implications for other stakeholders of the firm have yet to be fully explored. Traditional acquisitions research has shown that acquisitions have beneficial effects for CEO compensation (see Kroll et al. 1997; Wright et al. 2002). Future extensions of this work could explore whether CEO compensation of early movers rises at the same rate as that of later movers—particularly since it has been established that later movers do not perform as well as early movers (McNamara et al. 2008). Mergers and acquisitions within waves could also have implications for board members. Since early movers are seen as having greater foresight and perform better, do board members of early movers benefit from this either in their direct compensation or in career prospects outside the focal firm? In contrast, are the board members of later movers punished for simply following the bandwagon? More broadly, research could also examine the effect of merger and acquisition waves on employees, suppliers, and customers.

Fifth, although we know that early movers fare better than later movers in merger waves, we don't know why. The underlying processes between acquirers and targets during waves have not yet been explored. It may be that early movers experience better knowledge transfer between bidders and targets, as early movers are often driven by synergies (Carow et al. 2004), while later movers are more likely to imitate rather than acquire for synergies (McNamara et al. 2008). Hence, it may be that retaining target firm executives leads to increased knowledge sharing between target and acquirer, which facilitates synergies between firms, particularly early within waves. Evidence shows that target firm top management turnover generally increases following acquisitions; however, retaining target firm management has positive performance implications (Matsusaka 1993). We recommend assessing whether target executive retention is more prevalent for early acquirers, and whether it results in greater knowledge transfer, which may help explain the superior performance of early movers.

Sixth, research could also focus on the societal implications of merger and acquisition waves. More specifically, we see great potential in investigating how waves could affect industry consolidation and lead to the elimination of local small and medium businesses. These consequences appear to be particularly strong during the current period of intense globalization. As entire industries are being transferred to different geographic locations due to lower costs of production and capital, the social and economic cost of this activity to higher cost of production nations should be explored.

Finally, our literature review offers practical implications for managers. Regarding the timing of merger and acquisitions within waves, proactive and alert managers may be able to move early and generate benefits from merger and acquisitions. To do so, they would likely need to build environmental scanning and forecasting skills to identify acquisition opportunities and strike before other potential acquirers. Managers who are not able to develop such skills and instead tend to mimic other firms and are prey to bandwagon pressures are advised to restrain from acquiring, particularly during the later stages of the merger and acquisition wave (McNamara et al. 2008). Moreover, managers should consider the industry conditions surrounding acquisition waves and more carefully assess acquisitions in uncertain and dynamic industries. The latter industries create additional complexities and risks regarding the identification of relevant targets and the appropriate timing of merger execution. Furthermore, while managers have to act quickly to move early in waves—they might be tempted to limit their due-diligence efforts. We would advise managers to quickly yet carefully focus on a detailed evaluation of potential targets to increase the likelihood of a successful early wave acquisition. Of course, managers should also pay careful attention to the preparation and implementation phases of mergers to increase the likelihood of merger success—as these factors should increase acquisition success both within and outside waves. In addition, we advise board members to link more tightly managerial compensation and acquisition performance. Such a decision could limit the execution of bandwagon-driven acquisitions and encourage managers to engage in synergistic and value-enhancing mergers and acquisitions.

CONCLUSION

Our objective was to describe prior merger and acquisitions waves and their characteristics, explore their underlying antecedents, and consider the consequences associated with such waves. In addition, we attempted to identify unexplored topics that deserve scholarly attention, and offered several potential directions in which future research on merger and acquisition waves could go. In terms of antecedents, industry-level (e.g. environmental shocks, such as changes in economic and demand conditions, technology innovations, deregulation), firm-level (e.g. firm misvaluations), and managerial-level (e.g. bandwagon and imitation pressures, and self-interested motives, such as "empire building") factors appear to be the key drivers of industry merger and acquisition waves. As for consequences, early moving acquirers (and all target firms) benefit the most from mergers and acquisitions within waves.

We hope that our review will spur additional interest among researchers from various disciplines that have paid less attention to merger and acquisition waves (e.g. psychology, sociology, anthropology) and lead to more theoretical and empirical findings on the topic of industry merger and acquisition waves.

ENDNOTES

1. Sales shock is defined as a difference in absolute terms between an industry's sales growth and average industry sales growth of 18.12% for the full sample of 51 industries. Employment shock is measured as the difference in absolute terms between an industry employment growth and average industry employment growth of 10.4% for the full sample of 51 industries.
2. The time frame for the CARs measures range from several days to a month.

REFERENCES

Abrahamson, E., & Rosenkopf, L. (1993). "Institutional and Competitive Bandwagons: Using Mathematical Modeling as a Tool to Explore Innovation Diffusion." *Academy of Management Review*, 18: 487–517.

Amihud, Y., & Lev, B. (1981). "Risk reduction as a Managerial Motive for Conglomerate Mergers." *Bell Journal of Economics*, 12: 605–17.

Andrade, G., Mitchell, M., & Stafford, E. (2001). "New Evidence and Perspectives on Mergers." *Journal of Economic Perspectives*, 15: 103–20.

Barmash, I. (1971). *Welcome to our Conglomerate—You're Fired.* New York: Grosset & Dunlap.

Bhagat, S., Shleifer, A., & Vishny, R. (1990). "Hostile Takeovers in the 1980s: The Return to Corporate Specialization." *Brookings Papers on Economic Activity: Microeconomics*, 1–72.

Banerjee, A., & Eckard, E. W. (1998). "Are Mega-Mergers Anticompetitive? Evidence from the First Great Merger Wave." *Journal of Economics*, 29/4: 803–27.

Becketti, S. (1986). "Corporate Mergers and the Business Cycle." Federal Reserve Bank of Kansas City. *Economic Review*, May: 13–26.

Bradley, M. (1980). "Interfirm Tender Offers and the Market for Corporate Control." *Journal of Business*, 53/4: 345–76.

—— & Jarrell, G. A. (1980). "The Economic Effects of Federal and State Regulations of Cash Tender Offers." *Journal of Law and Economics*, 23/2: 371–407.

Carow, K., Heron, R., & Saxton, T. (2004). "Do Early Birds Get the Returns? An Empirical Investigation of Early Mover Advantages in Acquisitions." *Strategic Management Journal*, 25: 563–85.

Chen, M. J. (1996). "Competitor Analysis And Interfirm Rivalry: Toward a Theoretical Integration." *Academy of Management Review*, 21/1: 100–34.

De Bondt, W. F. M., & Thompson, H. E. (1992). "Is Economic Efficiency the Driving Force behind Mergers?" *Managerial and Decision Economics*, 13/1: 31–44.

DiMaggio, P., & Powell, W. (1983). "The Iron Cage Revisited: Institutional Isomorphism and Collective Rationality in Organizational Fields." *American Sociological Review*, 48: 147–60.

Eis, C. (1969). "The 1919–1930 Merger Movement in American Industry." *Journal of Law and Economics*, 12/2: 267–96.

Fiol, C. M., & O'Connor, E. J. 2003. Waking up! Mindfulness in the face of bandwagons. *Academy of Management Review*, 28: 54–70.

Franks, J., Harris, R., & Titman, S. (1991.) "The Postmerger Share-Price Performance of Acquiring firms." *Journal of Financial Economics*, 29: 81–96.

Ghauri, P. N., & Buckley, P. J. (2003). "International Mergers and Acquisitions: Past, Present and Future." *Advances in Mergers and Acquisitions*, 2: 207–9.

Goel, A. M., & Thakor, A. V. (2009). "Do Envious Ceos Cause Merger Waves?" *The Review of Financial Studies*, 23/2: 487–517.

Goergen, M., & Renneboog, L. (2004). "Shareholder Wealth Effects of European Domestic and Cross-Border Takeover Bids." *European Financial Management*, 10/1: 9–45.

Gort, M. (1969). "An Economic Disturbance Theory of Mergers." *Quarterly Journal of Economics*, 83: 623–42.

Gorton, G., Kahl, M., & Rosen, R. J. (2009). "Eat or be Eaten: A Theory of Mergers and Firm Size." *Journal of Finance*, 64/3: 1291–344.

Haleblian, J., & Finkelstein, S. (1999). "The Influence of Organizational Acquisition Experience." *Administrative Science Quarterly*, 44: 29–56.

Harford, J. (2005). "What Drives Merger Waves?" *Journal of Financial Economics*, 77/3: 529–60.

Healy, P. M., Palepu, K. G., & Ruback, R. S. (1992). "Does Corporate Performance Improve after Mergers?" *Journal of Financial Economics*, 31: 135–75.

Hubbard, R. G., & Palia, D. (1999). "A Reexamination of the Conglomerate Merger Wave in the 1960s: An Internal Capital Markets View." *Journal of Finance*, 54/3: 1131–52.

Jensen, M. (1986). "Agency Costs of Free Cash Flow, Corporate Finance, and Takeovers." *American Economic Review*, 76/2: 323–9.

Jensen, M. C., & Meckling, W. H. (1976). "Theory of the Firm: Managerial Behavior, Agency Costs and Ownership Structure." *Journal of Financial Economics*, 3/4: 305–60.

Jovanovic, B., & Rousseau, P. (2002). "The Q-theory of Mergers." *American Economic Review*, 92: 198–204.

—— —— (2008). "Mergers as Reallocation." *Review of Economics and Statistics*, 90/4: 765–76.

Kaplan, S. (1989). "The Effects of Management Buyouts on Operations and Value." *Journal of Financial Economics*, 24: 217–54.

Kroll, M., Wright, P., Toombs, L., & Leavell, H. (1997). "Form of Control: A Critical Determinant of Acquisition Performance and CEO Rewards." *Strategic Management Journal*, 18: 85–96.

Lambrecht, B. (2004). "The Timing and Terms of Mergers Motivated by Economies of Scale." *Journal of Financial Economics*, 72: 41–62.

Leblebici, H., Salancik, G. R., Copay, A., & King, T. (1991). "Institutional Change and the Transformation of Interorganizational Fields: An Organizational History of the U.S. Radio Broadcasting Industry." *Administrative Science Quarterly*, 36: 333–63.

Leeth, J. D., & Borg, J. R. (2002). "The Impact of Takeovers on Shareholder Wealth during the 1920s Merger Wave." *Journal of Financial and Quantitative Analysis*, 35/2: 217–38.

Lieberman, M. B., & Montgomery, D. B. (1988). "First-Mover Disadvantages: Retrospective and Link with Resource-Based View." *Strategic Management Journal*, 19: 1111–25.

Linn, S. C., & Zhu, Z. (1997). "Aggregate Merger Activity: New Evidence on the Wave Hypothesis." *Southern Economic Journal*, 64/1: 130–46.

Martynova, M., & Renneboog, L. (2008). "A Century of Corporate Takeovers: What have we Learned and Where do we Stand?" *Journal of Banking and Finance*, 32: 2148–77.

Matsusaka, J. G. (1993). "Takeover Motives during the Conglomerate Merger Wave." *Journal of Economics*, 24/3: 357–79.

McNamara, G. M., Haleblian, J., & Dykes, B. (2008). "The Performance Implications of Participating in an Acquisition Wave: Early Mover Advantages, Bandwagon Effects, and the Moderating Influence of Industry Characteristics and Acquirer Tactics." *Academy of Management Journal*, 51/3: 113–30.

Mitchell, M., & Mulherin, J. H. (1996). "The Impact of Industry Shocks on Takeover and Restructuring Activity." *Journal of Financial Economics*, 41: 193–229.

Morck, R., Shleifer, A., & Vishny, R. (1990). "Do Managerial Objectives Drive Bad Acquisitions?" *Journal of Finance*, 45/1: 31–48.

Navin, T. R. & Sears, M. V. (1955). "The Rise of a Market for Industrial Securities, 1877–1902." *Business History Review*, 29: 105–38.

Polonchek, J. A., & Sushka, M. E. (1987). "The Impact of Financial and Economic Conditions on Aggregate Merger Activity." *Managerial and Decision Economics*, 8/2: 113–19.

Porter, M. E. (1987). "From Competitive Advantage to Corporate Strategy." *Harvard Business Review*, 65: 43–59.

Qiu, L. D., & Zhou, W. (2007). "Merger Waves: A Model of Endogenous Mergers." *Journal of Economics*, 38(1): 214–26.

Ravenscraft, D. (1987). "The 1980s Merger Wave: An Industrial Organization Perspective," in L. Browne and E. Rosengren (eds.), *The Merger Boom*. Boston: Federal Reserve Bank, 17–37.

—— & Scherer, F. M. (1987). *Mergers, Sell-Offs & Economic Efficiency*. Washington, DC: The Brookings Institution.

Reid, S. R. (1968). *Mergers, Managers, and the Economy*. New York: McGraw-Hill Book Company.

Rhodes-Kropf, M., & Viswanathan, S. (2004). "Market Valuation and Merger Waves." *Journal of Finance*, 59/6: 2685–718.

—— —— (2005). "Valuation Waves and Merger Activity: The Empirical Evidence." *Journal of Financial Economics*, 77: 561–603.

Scott, W. R. (2001). *Institutions and Organizations* (2nd ed). Thousand Oaks, CA: Sage.

Servaes, H. (1991). "Tobin's Q and the Gains from Takeovers." *Journal of Finance*, 46/1: 409–19.

—— (1996). "The Value of Diversification during the Conglomerate Merger Wave." *Journal of Finance*, 51/4: 1201–25.

Shleifer, A., & Vishny, R. W. (1989). "Management Entrenchment: The Case of Manager-Specific Investments." *Journal of Financial Economics*, 25: 123–40.

—— —— (1991). "Takeovers in the '60s and the '80s: Evidence and Implications." *Strategic Management Journal*, 12: 51–9.

—— —— (1992). "Liquidation Values and Debt Capacity." *Journal of Finance*, 32: 337–47.

—— —— (2003). "Stock Market Driven Acquisitions." *Journal of Financial Economics*, 70: 295–311.

Shughart, W. F., & Tollison, R. D. (1984). "The Random Character of Merger Activity." *Journal of Economics*, 15/4: 500–9.

Smith K. G., Ferrier, W. J., & Ndofor, H. (2001). "Competitive Dynamics Research: Critique and Future Directions," in M. A. Hitt, J. R. Harrison, and E. Freeman (eds.), *Handbook of Strategic Management*. Oxford: Blackwell.

Stearns, L. B., & Allan, K. D. (1996). "Economic Behavior in Institutional Environments: The Corporate Merger Wave of the 1980's." *American Sociological Review*, 61: 699–718.

Stigler, G. (1950). "Monopoly and Oligopoly Power by Merger." *American Economic Review*, 40: 23–34.

Suchman, M. C. (1995). "Managing Legitimacy: Strategic and Institutional Approaches." *Academy of Management Review*, 20: 571–610.

Tosi, H. L., Werner, S., Katz, J. P., & Gomez-Mejia, L. R. (2000). "How Much does Performance Matter? A Meta-analysis of CEO Pay Studies." *Journal of Management*, 26/2: 301–39.

Town, R. J. (1992). "Merger Waves and the Structure of Merger and Acquisition Time-Series." *Journal of Applied Econometrics*, 7: 83–100.

Wright, P., Kroll, M., & Elenkov, D. (2002). "Acquisition Returns, Increase in Firm Size, and Chief Executive Officer Compensation: The Moderating Role of Monitoring." *Academy of Management Journal*, 45(3): 599–608.

CHAPTER 3

MERGER AND ACQUISITION TYPOLOGIES: A REVIEW

DUNCAN ANGWIN

INTRODUCTION

The Mergers and Acquisitions (M&A) literature is replete with typologies, many of which have become common currency for practitioners and academics alike. To date, however, there appears to have been little discussion about the value of typologies to these different audiences. Why are they needed—what value can they add to our understanding of M&A? What forms do M&A typologies take and what do they focus upon? What are the risks of relying upon typologies in M&A? What can typologies offer in the future for the mapping of M&A? The purpose of this chapter is to provide an extensive review, comparison, and critique of many prominent typologies in the M&A literature in order to identify the status of these frameworks and to highlight where further refinement and testing is necessary. This is the first critical treatment of typologies in the M&A field and aims to assess their role in making sense of a complex area.

WHAT ARE TYPOLOGIES?

First of all what is meant by "typology"? Literally the study of types, typologies are the investigation of classes with common characteristics. Observed populations are subdivided into groups, subgroups, or sequences according to consideration of their qualitative, quantitative, formal, morphological, technological, functional attributes. This type of exercise has a long and distinguished history stemming from Aristotle's (384–22 BC) instructions to his students to list champions at the Pythian Games, classify the constitutions of various Greek city-states, and his own detailed analysis of animal body parts to rank animals in terms of their physical complexity. It is perhaps not surprising then that the biological sciences seized the idea of classifying types and developed the concept further, with important contributions from Carolus Linnaeus (1707–78), an 18th-century Swedish botanist who devised the system of binomial nomenclature used for naming species, and the English naturalist Charles Darwin (1809–82), who devised a system of evolutionary classification. Strictly speaking, these researchers were engaged in a subset of classification, taxonomy, which involves the study of classification or the methods of classification. The word *taxonomy* can be traced back to Greek origins: *taxis,* or "arrangement," and *nomos,* or "method or law." The search for taxonomies has spread far beyond the biological sciences, with taxonomies in archaeology, enterprise, folk, linguistics, military, personality, politics, theology, urban planning studies. The reason why such effort has been devoted to searching for classificatory systems is humankind's need to make sense, or order, out of the complexities which surround us.

What advantages do typologies offer? The main benefit of establishing a typology is being able to differentiate amongst a population. A typology enables different groups to be identified and named. It creates a framework for embodying knowledge which can then be accessed efficiently. In a way, empirical typologies can be thought of as a form of scientific shorthand as they can replace an entire system of interrelationships and variables. Through organizing into groups, further study can be performed to deepen understanding. A typology also enables subsequent discoveries to be evaluated and classified, or determined as something new. One reason for the popularity of typologies is that they seem to provide parsimonious explanation for describing complex phenomena and their outcomes. The test of a good typology is whether its users, researchers, and practitioners find it helps make sense of diversity amongst a general class of phenomena.

There is some debate over the theoretical status of typologies, with some taking the position that at worst, a typology is a sloppy categorical system, and many are just atheoretical devices used as a means for ordering and comparing organizations and clustering them into categorical types (Rich 1992: 758). However, Doty and Glick (1994: 231) argue that, far from being just a mode of description, at its best, typologies are complex theoretical statements which can and should be subjected to quantitative modeling and rigorous empirical testing. Their more restrictive view of typologies is that they are conceptually derived interrelated sets of ideal types. These multiple ideal types represent a unique combination of organizational attributes that are believed to determine a relevant outcome. For Doty and Glick (1994), typologies can meet the criteria for theory, as they may have constructs, predict relationships among constructs, and these predictions are falsifiable. Typographical theories may be more complex than traditional theories as they include assertions based on both grand theory and middle-range theory.

In the management literature, the terms *classification scheme, taxonomy*, and *typology* have tended to be used interchangeably (Hall 1991; Hambrick 1983). Indeed, there is a proliferation of labels for typologies, including extreme, polar, pure, empirical, classificatory, constructed, heuristic. However, distinctions can be drawn in terms of their underlying purpose, key characteristics, and theoretical statements embedded within them. *Typologies* describe ideal types, each one presenting a unique combination of organizational attributes (Doty and Glick 1994; Narasimhan et al. 2008) and might be termed "explanatory typologies." It is possible no existing organization will perfectly match a proposed ideal type, although closer alignment with an ideal type should result in increased organizational effectiveness (Venkatraman 1989). Good typologies should

(i) provide a generalizable theory; (ii) specify the "unidimensional constructs that are the building blocks of traditional theoretical statements" (Miller 1996)—the importance and appropriate values of these dimensions should be established (Bozarth and McDermott 1998); and (iii) the underlying hypotheses should be empirically testable. These typologies are generally derived conceptually and/or theoretically a priori, after which empirical validation follows. Early examples in the management literature include Max Weber's (1947) classification of social domination into ideal types of patrimonial, feudal, and bureaucratic organization, where each could be characterized by a number of mutually complementary attributes and Talcott Parson's (1956) typology of organizations based upon their chief function for society—those with economic goals, political goals, integrative organizations, and pattern-maintenance organizations. These studies show coherence amongst the attributes of each type, but no empirical data was gathered to support the typologies (Miller and Friesen 1984). Later typologies, such as Miles and Snow's (1978) well-known Strategic Typology of Defenders, Prospectors, Analyzers, Reactors, define types in advance and then use empirical data to study the ways in which the types differ in their processes, structural and decision-making styles for example.

Other typologies, perhaps more accurately labeled as *taxonomies*, do not define "ideal groups" and tend be generated a posteriori. They attempt to classify organizations into mutually exclusive and exhaustive groups (Doty and Glick 1994) through careful choice of variables. Groups are delimited and classified by multivariate analyses of empirical data which uncover predictive regularities in organizational data. They are based on dimensions which can be empirically measured and tested. A well-known early taxonomy in management studies is Pugh et al.'s (1969) taxonomy of structures of work organizations derived from factor analysis of 64 structural variables. Good taxonomies are relatively unaffected by the techniques or sample data used to create them—indeed the sample in the Pugh et al. (1969) study was criticized for not being representative of organizations in general. The descriptive power of a taxonomy, rather than the methods used, is what is important (Miller 1996). One problem for taxonomists in general is that they often do not try to establish the stability and generalizability of their taxonomies, often having used up all their data in the generation of types and having none left for testing (Miller and Friesen 1984). The main differences between typology and taxonomy are summarized in Figure 3.1.

In this chapter, the aim is to provide an overview of typologies in the M&A literature and, for many, this includes a wide range of frameworks from classifications to typographical theories.

WHY ARE TYPOLOGIES NEEDED IN M&A STUDIES?

As a phenomenon, M&A is a massive set of events spanning at least 100 years (US records show M&A taking place as far back as 1897) and probably occurring much further back in business history. In terms of volume of activity, trillions of dollars of deals have taken place worldwide, with a record being set in 2007 with 4.7 trillion dollars of

	Typologies	Taxonomies
Definition	Ideal types	Classifications of real organizations in representative and mutually exclusive groups
Objective	To match one of the ideal types theoretically proposed to obtain better results	To obtain stable groups by using several techniques and data samples
Approach basis	A priori	A posteriori
Key features	Provide generic theories for all types and theories for each type. Specify factors that make up theoretical basis. Can be empirically tested	Right choice of classification variables. Not influenced by techniques or data samples. Capacity to generate knowledge
Result of procedure	Types formed before allocating organizations to each class. Companies are classified according to previous theory rather than on basis of empirical studies	Taxonomies emerge from empirical procedures used to describe groups of companies on the basis of degree of similarity between variables or their characteristics

FIG. 3.1 Differences between the concepts of taxonomy and typology

Source: Martin-Pena and Diaz-Garrido (2008).

transactions.[1] These represent hundreds of thousands of individual deals affecting economies, regions, industries, markets, communities, individuals, and many other stakeholder interests. As a nexus of social and economic ties, the acquisition of a business has the potential to disrupt every aspect of internal and external organization. The volume and variety of transactions, impacting upon a wide range of stakeholders, indicates a large and heterogeneous phenomenon in which a wide range of practitioners and academics have varied interests. The complexity of M&A raises the question of tractability in research terms and this may explain the very substantial literature which has grown up around the phenomenon.

The M&A literature is very large and spans at least half a century (cf. Ansoff et al. 1959). However, it is noticeable that, despite this substantial endeavor, M&A research still struggles to provide answers to some of the most basic questions. For instance, should companies grow through acquisition or organically; acquirers buy related or unrelated companies; acquisition integration be carried out at a fast or slow pace; acquired top executives be retained or released? Indeed, we are still not clear of the extent to which acquisitions really fail or succeed. In all cases, the answers seem to be "it all depends." This underlines a major difficulty in so much M&A research, that the vast majority of empirical endeavors' attempts to find strong significant evidence of simple dyadic relationships to explain aspects of M&A often lead to inconclusive results. That so little strong support for causalities has been found after so much inquiry suggests many confounding variables at work. It suggests substantial variation amongst M&A and this heterogeneity needs to be addressed in other ways. For this reason, typologies can offer valuable insight into M&A. The fact that many typologies have been developed and proven remarkably durable suggests researchers and practitioners alike find them helpful in trying to make sense of M&A. In particular, they appear to offer a parsimonious framework for describing complex organizational forms and for explaining outcomes.

Contingency Theory of Organizational Adaptation

Underlying typological approaches to M&A is the contingency theory of organizational adaption. The theory argues that individual companies must adapt to their environment, which poses requirements for innovation and efficiency in order to survive and prosper. The company's management therefore adopts a strategy which reflects these pressures, but which also meets organizational objectives based upon the strategic advantage of the firm (Christensen et al. 1978). Differences amongst organizations involved in M&A therefore matter. Specifically, (1) required strategic competencies vary across organizations and over time; (2) industry structures vary; (3) managers differ in experience, education, personality, social connectedness, and the competencies they bring to a business; (4) organizations vary by geography, and by sociocultural, political, and economic context. The assumption in many of the typologies described below is that the selection of a particular strategy driving M&A will enable the acquiring firm to improve its fit with the environment in general or in a specific contingency and through this choice, organizational performance will be improved. And there is some empirical support for contingency theory in works such as Donaldson's (1995) review of organizational structure change and fit.

M&A Typologies[2]

The vast majority of typologies in the M&A literature focus upon either pre-acquisition strategies or post-acquisition integration. However, this section follows the M&A process with an opening section on pre-acquisition strategies, followed by a negotiation typology, post-acquisition integration typologies, and an overarching integrative framework. Within the pre-acquisition strategy section, directional policy, strategic fit, extended acquisition strategy, and strategy motivation and performance typologies are reviewed. In the negotiation section, a friendliness–hostility framework is summarized. In the post-acquisition integration section, cultural integration and psychological matrices are reviewed to begin with, followed by human resource typologies, strategic and organizational fit matrices, and speed of integration frameworks. The section ends with a typology which aims to classify M&A types by integrating pre-acquisition strategic considerations with deal-making characteristics and post-acquisition integration styles.

Pre-acquisition Strategy Typologies

Directional Policy Frameworks

Early typologies relevant to M&A occurred in the strategic management literature and concerned corporate strategy issues of when to grow or dispose of businesses and which direction expansion should take. One of the earliest frameworks, Ansoff's (1965) Growth Vector Components Matrix, might be termed a typology in that it conceptualized two dimensions along which firms might expand. Although the matrix did not specify M&A as a method by which growth might be achieved, it certainly underlies the option for diversification. Similarly, the Boston Consulting Group (BCG) Growth Share Matrix (Henderson 1979) developed during the 1970s is another corporate strategy technique allowing firms to evaluate various businesses in terms of which should receive funds and which should be divested. The two underlying concepts are the product life cycle and the experience curve. These concepts determine the cash-flow characteristics of the four types created by this matrix. The BCG typology also lends itself as a way of assessing industries in order to determine their suitability for entry through acquisition (through the distribution of incumbent companies) and as a technique for identifying the best targets amongst them (Ebeling and Doorley 1983) (see Fig. 3.2).

This type of policy matrix approach to strategy was extended significantly in the GE Matrix—the market attractiveness-business strength model developed by General Electric and McKinsey. This matrix believed earlier approaches based upon only two factors, market growth and relative market share, were too simplistic and so used

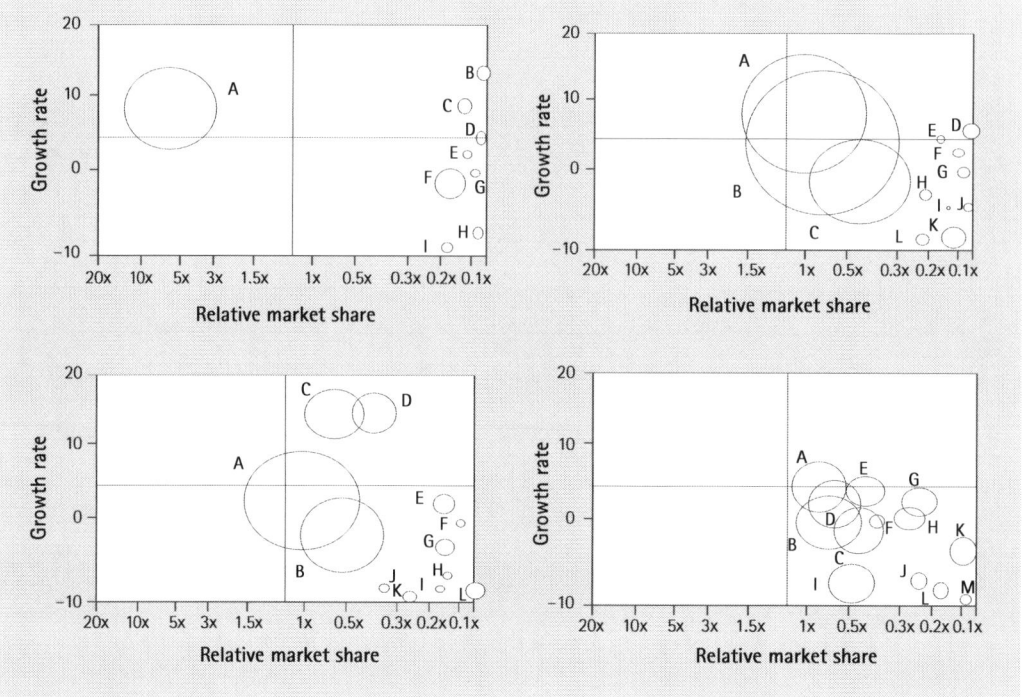

FIG. 3.2 Industry sector graph approach

Source: Braxton Associates.

multiple variables to assess business position and market attractiveness. This assessment allowed conclusions to be drawn about the attractiveness of markets and business position relative to other competitors' positions and so was an effective framework for assessing acquisition opportunities. Many other variations on policy matrices followed, such as the Directional Policy Matrix (Shell) and the Industry Maturity-Competitive Matrix (Arthur D. Little).

Strategic Fit Typologies

The policy matrices originally focused upon potential growth strategies for the firm for which M&A might be a suitable method for expansion. Later typologies focused upon strategic fit in terms of how an acquisition target would complement the acquiring firm in terms of products and markets. Salter and Weinhold (1979) conceptualized distinctions between the relatedness of businesses in terms of product markets and functional resources. These conceptual categories were adopted in subsequent typologies such as that of Shelton (1988), showing different types of strategic fit from a systematic classification of acquirer/target characteristics based upon market and product characteristics (see Fig. 3.3)

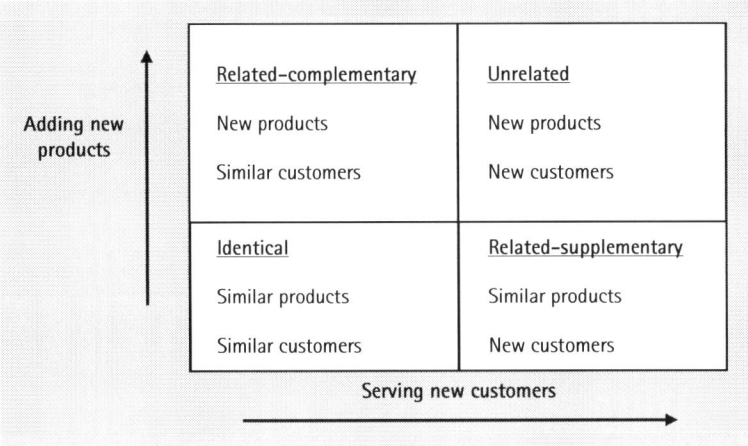

FIG. 3.3 Strategic fits between a target and a bidder business

Source: Shelton (1988).

Probably the most established of these sorts of typologies is the one used by the Federal Trade Commission (FTC) (1975) to indicate the way in which horizontal, and so potentially anti-competitive, M&A might occur. In this typology, M&A are classified as (i) horizontal—combining firms with the same products and markets, i.e. direct competitors; (ii) vertical—combining firms with possible buyer-seller relationships (backward integration would be purchasing a supplier, forward integration would be buying a customer); (iii) product extension—combining firms with non-competing products but functionally related in production and distribution; (iv) market extension—combining firms with the same products but in different geographical markets; and (v) conglomerate—combining unrelated firms with no product market relationships as well as no buyer-seller relationships. Larsson (1990) suggests a way of representing this FTC typology diagrammatically (see Fig. 3.4)

These earlier matrices have focused upon the positioning of businesses in terms of "fit" with their external contexts, i.e. whether they have an attractive or unattractive competitive position. Later typologies have focused upon "fit" between the capabilities of the parent company and the acquisition target to avoid the potential problem of identifying a target which is attractive in terms of market position and business strength, but which may not allow synergies to be achieved once within the acquiring group. One such matrix is the Parenting Matrix (Goold et al. 1994), which focuses upon fit not just between the target company and its external context but also between the parent's capabilities and (i) the potential internal synergies with the target and (ii) what the target needs to do to achieve external advantage (see Fig. 3.5.)

This conceptually derived typology identifies zones which may be deemed attractive for acquisition and those which are not (see Fig 3.6.).

For instance, heartland businesses are those where the target business offers internal opportunities for synergies which fit with parent competencies and also where those parental contributions will not damage the way in which the target company competes

		Market	Relation
		Same	Different
Production	Same	Horizontal M&A	Market extension M&A (concentric technology)
Production	Long-linked	Vertical backward M&A	Vertical forward M&A
Relation	Unrelated	Product extension M&A (concentric marketing)	Conglomerate M&A (unrelated)

FIG. 3.4 A systematic framework for the FTC typology of M&A

Source: Larsson (1990).

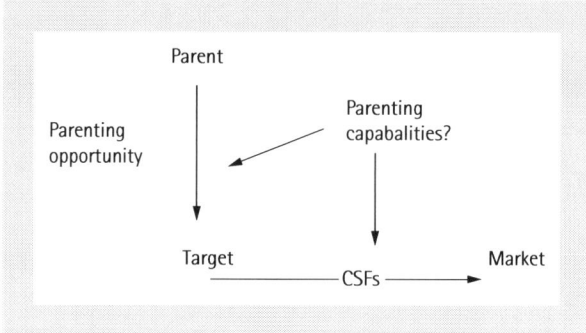

FIG. 3.5 Fit between parenting capabilities and key synergy relationships

in its markets. For the other areas of the matrix, either of these links is challenged, suggesting less optimal acquisitions. Underlying the matrix is the assumption, as with earlier portfolio strategy matrices, that related businesses make better acquisitions. However, as suggested earlier, the empirical evidence on this is not clear. The Parenting Fit Matrix does, however, focus attention upon how the parent may benefit from acquisition and enables its users to quickly assess potential acquisitions in these terms. It also has the benefit of being testable in research terms.

Extended Acquisition Strategy Typologies

Whilst two-by-two typologies have the virtue of visual clarity, more recent research suggests that there are more than just four possible acquisition strategies. Joseph Bower (2001), writing in the *Harvard Business Review*, conceptualized five distinctive M&A

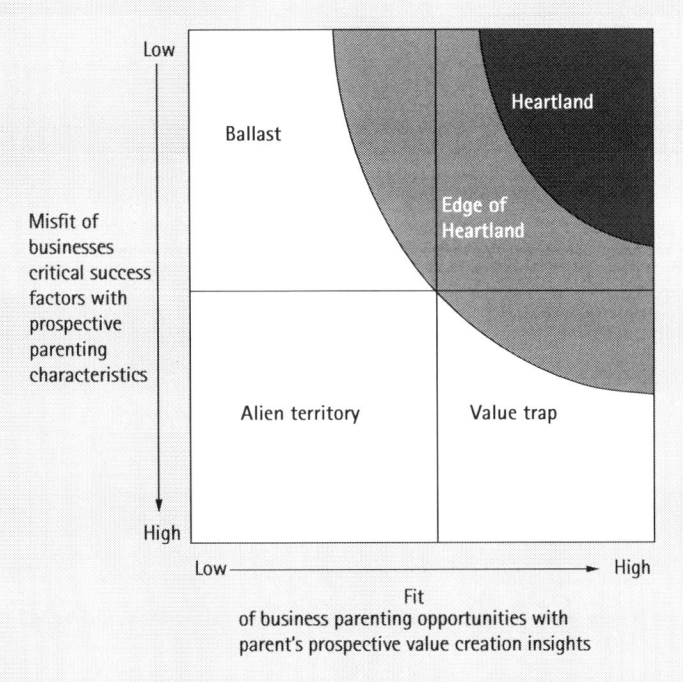

FIG. 3.6 Parenting fit matrix

Source: Goold, M., Campbell, A., and Alexander, M. (1994), *Corporate-Level Strategy: Creating Value in the Multibusiness Company*, Wiley. Reprinted with permission of John Wiley & Sons, Inc.

strategies. Whilst several of these strategies are similar to those in earlier typologies, such as product/market expansion, Bower recognizes the acquisition of innovation, the dynamic aspects of M&A, such as acquiring at different stages in the life cycle, and M&A in anticipation of industry convergence, as additional types. Interestingly, Bower (2001) also mentions the existence of pure financial investments, although he suggests that this type of motivation generally results in underperformance and so is not included explicitly in the classification. It is also evident that there is an underlying performance outcome intended with the five M&A Strategies. Figure 3.7 illustrates Bower's five distinctive strategies and also includes purely financial investment as an additional sixth type of M&A strategy.

Strategy Typologies and M&A Performance

Until recently, all of the typologies focusing upon the motivations behind companies making acquisitions have inferred top management rationality. Many empirical enquiries have attempted to correlate these acquisition motives with post-acquisition performance, with rather disappointing results. This may have been because researchers

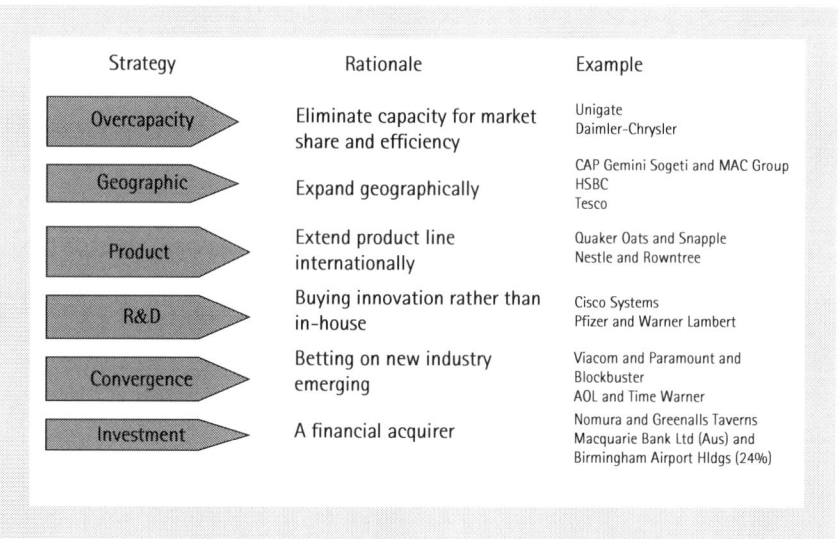

FIG. 3.7 Six rational distinctive M&A strategies

Source: Adapted from Bower (2001).

have over-ascribed M&A to a narrow set of top management prescriptions, such as Walter's (1987) typology of motives for M&A of increasing competitive strength, maximizing earnings, related diversification, limiting risk, and have ignored the role of many other forces which could result in M&A taking place. These forces, such as environmental disturbance (Gort 1969), could lead management to engage in sub-optimal M&A activity. This may help explain why links with performance outcomes are not clear. In order to convey the differing forces at work, Angwin (2007a) proposes a conceptual typology based upon three complex dimensions of (i) acquiring firm competitive strategy motives (ranging from classic value-maximizing motives aimed at improving shareholder value through enhanced competitiveness in the short term to creating opportunities through exploration, stasis, or survival measures); (ii) contextual pressure to engage in M&A (consonant or dissonant with acquiring firm's competitiveness); (iii) top management agendas (ranging from acting selflessly on behalf of the firm and investors to being more interested in their own benefits—the classic agency problem). Each dimension is envisaged as a continuum, where a mixture of motives and pressures is more the norm than the extremes. From the three axes, he conceptualizes the existence of eight distinct M&A of which some are congruent with internal and external forces and others are not (see Fig. 3.8).

Type 1: Classical M&A is the one assumed in the performance literature where the firm is conducting M&A on the basis of rational value-maximizing strategies, such as cost reduction, to enhance shareholder value. The top management are acting as good agents and the contextual drivers are encouraging. This type of M&A can reasonably be expected to succeed in conventional terms.

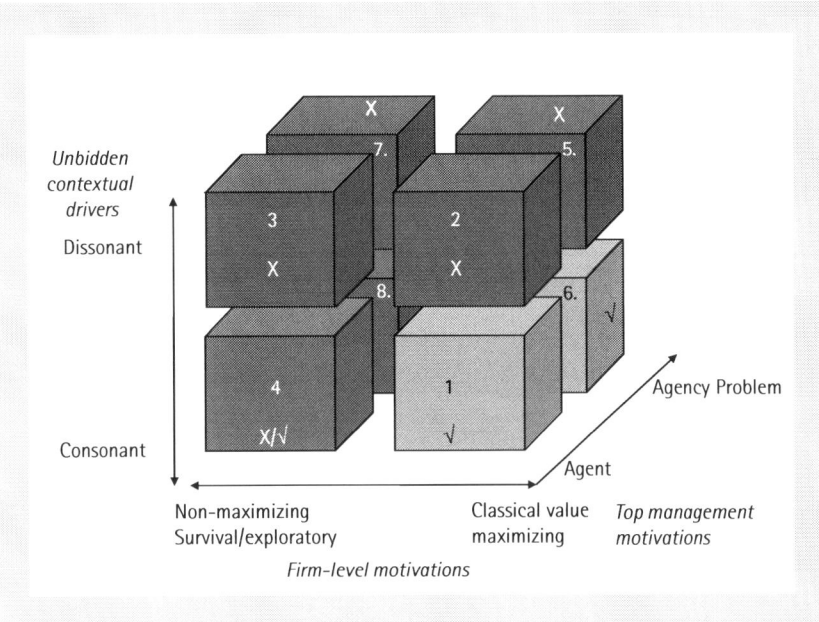

FIG. 3.8 Motivational archetypes in M&A

Source: Angwin (2006).

Type 2: Contextual pressures in this type may be at odds with the firm's wishes to maximize shareholder value. In this type, there may be conflict between firm and top manager rational value-maximizing motivations and those of the context. Although the acquisition will be conducted in classical terms, it may well be very difficult for the acquiring firm to do well out of the deal. For instance, there are a number of examples of M&A taking place more for the good of governments than for acquiring firms.

Type 3: Contextual factors may be at odds with classic firm motivations, but may be accommodated if the firm is motivated by non-maximizing motives. There could be tension with a top management focused upon shareholder value in the short term. It is unlikely that the acquisition will succeed in conventional terms, but it may be beneficial in the long term.

Type 4: Contextual factors set conditions for classic M&A and top management are aligned with this pressure. However, the returns may be in the future, requiring exploratory M&A. For instance, business may be anticipating the convergence of industries/technologies which suggest profitable opportunities in the future. M&A in this situation may not realize short-term returns, and may be risky, but might also result in significant long-term benefits.

Type 5: Contextual pressures may pressure the acquirer into deals which do not fit with classical firm motives and there is also an agency problem. The latter may result in a deal which suits top management and addresses the context, but is unlikely to benefit the firm in conventional terms.

Type 6: Contextual pressures may be propitious for M&A in terms of maximizing firm value. An agency problem may mean that top management seek to benefit personally from the deal, although this does not exclude the possibility of the deal being successful.

Type 7: Contextual pressures may be counter to the firm's classical motives, but could fit with exploratory motives. An agency problem does give top management scope to benefit personally and so it is unlikely that such a deal would bring benefits to the firm.

Type 8: Contextual pressures may be favorable for M&A by the firm, although the firm may be motivated by non-maximizing outcomes. This may enable the firm to engage in speculative acquisitions with low commercial rationale. They may be encouraged by top management where there is an agency problem.

Based upon this set of archetypes, different sorts of outcomes are apparent. Importantly, it is clear that only a few archetypes can be described as classically oriented toward improving shareholder value. Most of the archetypes are likely to result in underperformance in conventional terms. Studies which therefore treat all M&A as homogeneous include those which are not designed primarily to achieve these gains, and so performance outcomes are likely to be biased downwards. A more refined approach to M&A motivations could potentially result in quite different results. Many testable hypotheses are possible from this typology for instance:

Hypothesis 1: Acquirers acquiring in a propitious context with top managers acting as agents, archetype 1, will exhibit higher levels of performance than other archetypes in conventional terms.

Hypothesis 2: Acquirers acquiring in propitious conditions with top managers acting as agents but using exploratory types of M&A (archetype 4), are likely to underperform short term, but may achieve substantial long-term gains.

Hypothesis 3: Acquirers acquiring in dissonant conditions, with top management exhibiting an agency problem, and acquiring in an exploratory way (archetype 7), are likely to be less successful than other archetypes.

NEGOTIATION-STYLE TYPOLOGY

Negotiating style is rarely acknowledged in typologies as a discriminator of M&A. However, its importance was recognized by Pritchett (1985), who classified deals along a cooperative-adversarial dimension. His four M&A categories are (i) organizational rescues, (ii) collaborations, (iii) contested situations, (iv) raids. Based upon these negotiation styles, post-acquisition integration implications are predicted. In organizational rescues, acquirers are coming to the aid of another firm either as a "financial salvage" operation or as a "friendly alternative" (White Knight) to an unwanted hostile takeover. The acquirer in these situations is looked upon favorably by the target company during negotiations as a savior. However, post-deal, this feeling of relief may be short-lived as substantial restructuring may follow. In collaborations, the negotiations are about creating a fair deal for both parties and the firms approach the table with a sense of goodwill and diplomacy. The negotiation atmosphere is one of mutual respect and understanding. However, post-deal, there can be human resource difficulties as employees may not fully understand the importance of the agreement and may find adjusting difficult. Even in the friendliest of atmospheres, there can be collaboration backlash if not managed effectively. In contested combinations, increasing amounts of resistance are shown by the target firm and aggressive negotiations between multiple firms lead to significant tensions and anxiety. The target firm is often well run, but the bidding contest tends to precipitate a loss of productivity and measurable amounts of adversity. The result can be a "reluctant bride," unable to defend itself against being acquired. In raids, a hostile bid and the most adversarial of forms, the greatest amounts of uncertainty and resistance are generated in target firms. The raider approaches the target shareholders directly, bypassing the target management team in order to strong-arm them into capitulation. The efforts made by target management to defend their company can result in the acquisition of an emotional, battle-scarred victim which is almost impossible to manage. Based upon this typology of negotiation approaches, Pritchett (1985) suggests that the degree of friendliness or hostility is a key determinant of how employees and managers will react to the combination. This typology was not tested further but has influenced later work by Buono and Bowditch (1989).

Post-acquisition Integration Typologies

Cultural Integration Typologies

Early research on M&A focused upon strategic and financial fit between acquirer and target companies and tended to assume that good fit in these terms would lead to successful post-acquisition performance. Disappointing outcomes, however, led researchers to consider the importance of the integration process itself as an important determinant of outcome (Jemison and Sitkin 1986). Shrivastava (1986) noted that socio-cultural integration had not been fully examined even though earlier work had suggested that fit between culture and strategy is essential for organizational effectiveness (Schwartz and Davis 1981). Nahavandi and Malekzadeh (1988) address the gap between the strategic classifications of M&A (described earlier in the chapter) and the role culture plays in implementation. Their typology is derived from earlier work by Berry (1983, 1984) on how groups adapt to conflict. Nahavandi and Malekzadeh (1988) argue that the two merging organizations may not have the same preferences regarding mode of acculturation, "the degree of agreement (congruence) regarding each one's preference for a mode of acculturation will be a central factor in the successful implementation of the acquisition " (p. 84). Their a priori typology dimensions for acquired companies are (i) the perceptions of the attractiveness of the acquirer and (ii) how much the members of the acquired company value their own culture. For the acquirer, the two dimensions are (i) the level of multiculturalism existing in the acquiring firm and (ii) the diversification strategy. The four modes of acculturation which result are deemed to determine the preferred mode of acculturation for the acquiring company (see Fig. 3.9). It is the congruence between these two firms' preferences which determine the level of acculturative stress and the smoothness of integration. The proponents of the framework argue that many of the problems of post-acquisition integration can be avoided or managed if the mode of acculturation can be agreed. This typology presents a series of possible integration situations which can be tested empirically.

Nahavandi and Malekzadeh's (1988) typology has subsequently been extended by Elsass and Veiga (1994), who suggest that acculturation is not an outcome but a process. They present an adjusted version of the Nahavandi and Malekzadeh (1988) typology to show how time and the effect of subsequent organizational performance during integration may affect management decisions. This allows them to theorize that, in the face of poor post-acquisition performance, increasing forces of organizational integration may be antithetical to positive organizational performance despite management's natural inclination to take control of the situation with increasing force (Elsass and Veiga 1994).

Following Nahavandi and Malekzadeh's (1988) typology, Siehl and Smith (1990) also consider interpersonal relationships between acquiring and acquired firms and draw upon a marital analogy to convey the emotional effect upon acquired company employees. Based upon a series of interviews with managers to gather dominant post-acquisition integration change characteristics, they conceptualize four discrete integration styles of (i) pillage and plunder; (ii) one night stand; (iii) courtship/just

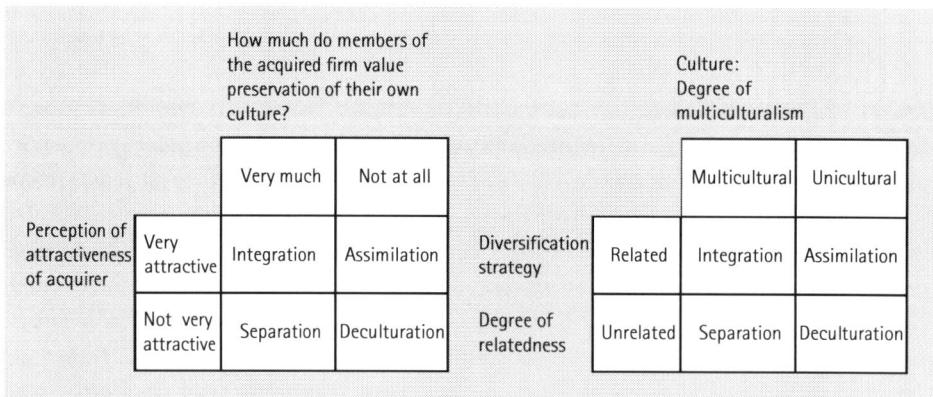

FIG. 3.9 Modes of acculturation

Source: Nahavandi and Malekzadeh (1988).

friends; (iv) love and marriage. (1) "Pillage and plunder," or "asset stripping," is portrayed as the breakup of the acquired firm, with valuable assets retained and the remainder disposed of. They suggest these are underperforming target companies which may require turning around. (2) "One night stand" is characterized as an intense financial but otherwise superficial relationship. There is minimal integration and the retention or disposal of the acquisition is whether the firm continues to meet financial expectations. (3) "Courtship/just friends" focuses upon achieving a stable working relationship whilst maintaining operational and cultural differences between the firms. The acquired firm remains independent. (4) "Love and marriage" represents complete organizational integration of the two firms. It is difficult to determine the dominant party in the relationship and over time the distinctiveness of each party may be lost as a new stronger entity emerges. This typology suggests that M&A can be classified into these categories, but performance outcome is inferred in emotional and moral terms rather than tested empirically.

Mirvis and Marks (1992) argue that taking cultural upheaval together with degree of integration determines the magnitude of post-acquisition change. They position the degree of change in the acquired company against degree of change in the acquiring company to create five different ideal post-acquisition integration styles. They suggest (i) preservation; (ii) absorption; (iii) transformation; (iv) reverse takeover; (v) best of both (see Fig 3.10). (1) "Preservation" is one of cultural autonomy. There are few changes in either company as integration between organizations is low. (2) "Absorption" is about cultural assimilation. The acquired company is absorbed into the acquiring firm. (3) "Transformation" is where both firms undergo fundamental changes in culture and operation. This is a reinvention rather than just a reorganization of businesses. (4) "Reverse takeover" is about cultural assimilation and is viewed as a rare case. Here the acquired company leads the post-acquisition integration efforts, causing the acquiring company to experience considerable change in being absorbed into the acquired firm. (5) "Best of both" is conceived as an acquisition of equals with full cultural integration and partial or full organizational consolidation.

Building upon Nahavandi and Malekzadeh (1988) and Napier (1989—reviewed later), Cartwright and Cooper (1993) focus upon the cultural mechanism of change underlying these typologies by showing the constraints that different cultural types place on merging individuals. They identify a cultural continuum ranging from high to low individual constraint, along which different cultural types are located; power, role, task/achievement, person/support. By plotting the two merging firms on the continuum, the similarity and dissimilarity between them indicates the degree of change that partners may need to adopt. The direction of movement for the firms indicates the potential difficulty in achieving this end. Through their characterization of different cultural types of merging firms, for a "traditional" marriage, Cartwright and Cooper (1992) are able to conceptualize the suitability of culture matches. This allows the creation of a typology that suggests which merging firms are likely to be able to change culturally more successfully than others (see Fig. 3.11).

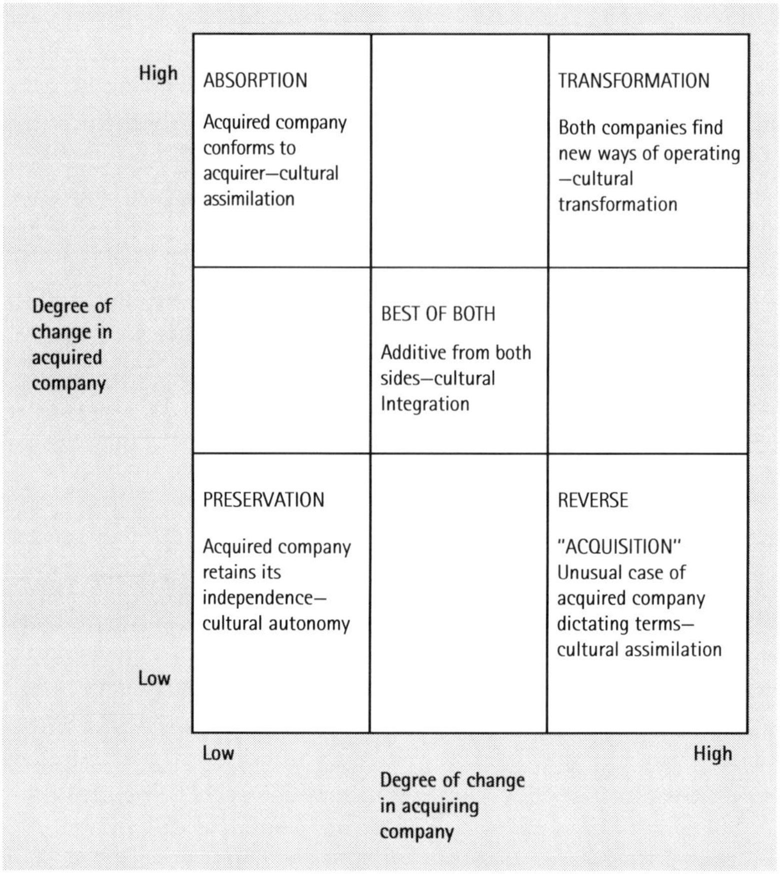

FIG. 3.10 Magnitude of post-acquisition change

Source: Marks, Mitchell Lee and Mirvis, Philip H. (2010: 15), *Joining Forces: Making One Plus One Equal Three in Mergers, Acquisitions, and Alliances* (second edition), San Francisco: Jossey–Bass Publishers.

Human Resource Integration

Recognizing that there could be different approaches to post-acquisition integration due to variations in motives for acquisition and in firm characteristics, Napier (1989) proposed a typology in order to identify the implications for human resources practices and outcomes. Napier (1989) identified extension, collaborative, and redesign mergers and illustrates these types with case examples. Extension mergers are where the acquiring firm leaves the acquired firm alone. Collaborative mergers occur in two forms: "synergy," where both firms join together to blend operations, assets, culture, or "exchange," where there is a transfer of knowledge, technology, or other talent from one firm to the other. In redesign mergers, the acquired firm adopts the policies and practices of the acquirer. The human resource implications of this typology are inferred to be a "hands-off" approach in the case of extension mergers, where there would be little change in

Culture of the acquirer/dominant merger partner	Potentially "good" marriage partners	Potentially "problematic" marriage partners	Potentially "disastrous" marriage partners
Power	—	Power	Role Task Person /Support
Role	Power Role	Task	Person/Support
Task	Power Role Task	Person/Support	—
Person/Support	All culture types	—	—

FIG. 3.11 The suitability of the culture match typology

Source: Cartwright and Cooper (1992: 85).

human resource policy or firm structure. Top management in the acquired company are likely to stay, since their organization remains largely independent of the acquirer. In collaborative mergers, the "synergy" approach is likely to force changes in personnel practices as there are advantages in harmonizing to achieve economies of scale. In order to achieve these ends it is likely that there would be widespread use of teams and also staff reduction. It is likely that top management in the acquired company will also leave, since they perceive a loss of control. There is also likely to be change in human resource performance appraisal and compensation programs as both firms harmonize. It is also probable that new human resource practices will developed out of existing ones. The exchange approach will see specific skills transferred from one firm to the other and this is likely to result in the human resource practices of one firm adapting to the policies of the other firm. In redesign mergers, the policies and practices of the acquired firm are changed far more dramatically than in the other merger integration styles. The intention is to mould to the shape of the buyer or reshape policies or procedures. Often there will be wide-ranging replacements of staff and top management and changes in compensation and benefits policies in the acquired company.

Strategic and Organizational Fit Typologies

Perhaps the best-known post-acquisition contingency typology is by Haspeslagh and Jemison (1991), which directs attention to a resource-based perspective on the transfer of capabilities between two companies in order to create value and the need to protect the acquired company from organizational integration into the parent firm. In their terms, the typology rests upon two dimensions of "strategic interdependence" between companies and level of "organizational autonomy" allowed the acquired firm. These dimensions were derived from primary data capture and iterative analysis. Three distinct ideal types of post-acquisition integration approaches resulted: (i) preservation; (ii) absorption; (iii) symbiotic (see Fig. 3.12).

Preservation acquisitions require high levels of autonomy and have limited strategic interdependence. It is important to maintain the acquired company's sources of benefits and so these acquisitions are managed at arm's length from the parent. Absorption acquisitions have low levels of autonomy and high levels of strategic interdependence. The boundaries between the firms are dissolved and operations, organization, and culture are fully consolidated into the parent firm. Symbiotic acquisitions involve both high strategic interdependence and high organizational autonomy. From a position of coexistence, both firms become increasingly susceptible to a broad range of interactions as interfirm boundaries dissolve. A fourth type of post-acquisition style, "Holding," is conceptualized, where there would be no intention of integrating the acquired firm. Holding acquisitions would have little autonomy and experience little strategic interdependence. They did not encounter any examples of this type of acquisition as their focus was upon strategic acquirers (Haspeslagh and Jemison, 1991: 147).

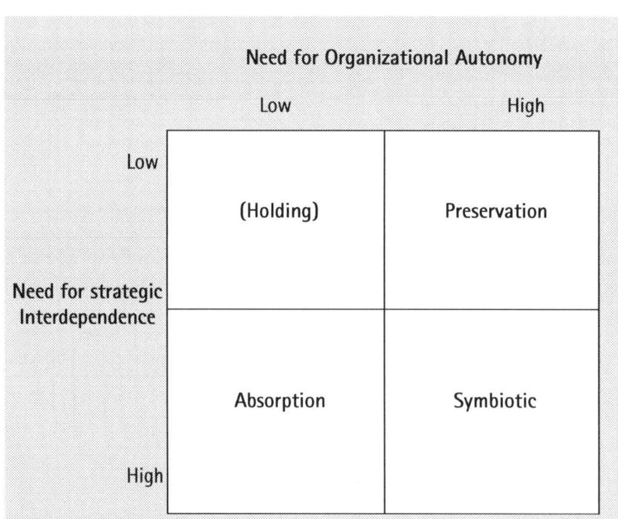

	Need for Organizational Autonomy	
	Low	High
Low	(Holding)	Preservation
High	Absorption	Symbiotic

Need for strategic Interdependence

FIG. 3.12 Types of acquisition integration approaches

Source: Haspeslagh and Jemison (1991: 145).

A later typology also focuses upon synergy creation and draws upon Porter's (1985) value chain in order to provide a parsimonious representation of a complex process. Schweiger et al. (1994: 28) argue that synergistic value can only occur when the value chains of two merging firms are reconfigured in ways which improve the competitive advantage of the combined firm. In order to achieve restructuring for advantage, firms need to reconfigure in technical, sociocultural, and political terms. For Schweiger et al. (1994), there are four configuration options: (i) absorption, (ii) linkage or interrelatedness, (iii) elimination, and (iv) independence. Absorption acquisitions require the greatest amount of change and are likely to trigger severe political and cultural reactions. Absorption requires adaptation of business units either through complete restructuring or adaptation of technical systems, processes, cultural and political configurations. These can be difficult to achieve since individuals and units do not freely or easily change. There is a spectrum of increasing difficulty of change from Novation (the most difficult), to Assimilation, to Integration (least difficult) (Schweiger et al. 1994), so that absorption through integration will result in least resistance, mostly involving changes to technical configurations rather than political and cultural configurations, whereas absorption through Novation, which may be thought of as a "tabula rasa," involves units being rebuilt in order to innovate. This latter style is likely to cause significant clashes in technical systems, cultures, and political battles. "Linked/interrelated" M&A demand few changes within each unit, but require new relationships with other units to be established. This may require some political and cultural changes to manage the new interface. When units are "eliminated," there will be internal changes as people or responsibilities move into or out of various units. In units remaining "independent," the impact of political and cultural factors is likely to be minimal. Having identified the organizational and political implications of each integration approach, Schweiger et al. (1994) suggest five ways in which these strategic objectives may be achieved.

Neither set of authors of the previous two typologies has tested their framework. However, Haspeslagh and Jemison's (1991) typology has been used subsequently to classify acquisition populations and to evaluate whether the ideal types remain distinctive for other post-acquisition variables. Angwin (1999, 2000), using a cross-sectional survey of acquisitions in the UK, classifies them in terms of ideal types similar to those of Haspeslagh and Jemison (1991) and finds significant statistical differences between each type in terms of volume and timing of post-acquisition changes made to the acquired company (see Fig. 3.13).

Similarly, the typology has been used to determine whether different post-acquisition integration strategies affect the deployment of top management in the acquired firm (Angwin 2004a; Angwin and Meadows 2009). In terms of "Maintain" acquisitions, insiders (top managers drawn from the acquired company) dominate, as the maintenance of distinctive capabilities is critical for performance. In "Subjugation" acquisitions, outsiders (top managers brought in from outside the acquired company) dominate, as acquired company synergy benefits are to be found from full organizational integration with the acquirer. In these acquisitions, the distinctiveness of the acquired firm is less valuable than the commonalities between firms. It is more important for profound

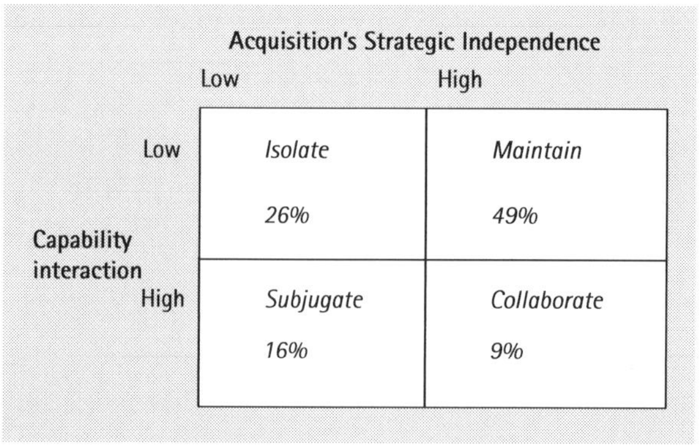

FIG. 3.13 Distribution of post-acquisition integration styles in the UK, 1991–1994

Source: Angwin (1999).

adjustment of the acquired firm than maintaining its uniqueness and so insiders, who are more likely to hinder integration through trying to preserve the acquired firm's integrity, are less valuable. Outsiders are more willing to impose radical changes to achieve the necessary alignment of the acquired company with the new parent. In "Isolation" acquisitions, insiders dominate and this may be explained by the need for rapid improvement in acquired firm performance. Insiders are best placed to deliver rapid and substantial change. Collaboration acquisitions show a more dynamic quality in the deployment of insiders and outsiders, as acquisitions in this context start with the former and later appoint the latter. The insider seems critical in the early stages of integration to preserve the integrity of the acquired firm's capabilities, whereas later in the process, greater benefit can be gained through a gradual convergence with the acquiring firm through inter-organizational change. The existence of differential timings in the types of top executive deployment in Collaboration acquisitions suggests a more dynamic quality in choice than is commonly recognized (Angwin and Meadows 2009).

A typology by Birkinshaw et al. (2000) focuses upon the dynamics of integration as merging companies seek to create value through integration. Drawing upon the strategic management literature, they identify task integration as critical for value creation, a concept which resonates strongly with the strategic interdependence of Haspeslagh and Jemison's (1991) framework—the transfer of capabilities and resources. The other critical sub-process they identify is human integration, which is drawn from the organizational behavior school and which resonates with the earlier frameworks such as those by Nahavandi and Malekzadeh (1988), Siehl and Smith (1990), Mirvis and Marks (1992). This sub-process focuses upon human satisfaction post-acquisition and the building of shared identity. Based upon these two dimensions, Birkinshaw et al. (2000) conceptualize a typology to show how integrating research and development (R&D) departments in Swedish

		Level of completion of task integration	
		Low	High
Level of completion of human integration	High	Mixed success: satisfied employees but operational synergies not achieved	Successful acquisition
	Low	Failed integration	Mixed success: Operational synergies achieved at the expense of employees

FIG. 3.14 Impact of task and human integration processes on acquisition outcome

Source: Birkinshaw, Bresman, and Hakanson (2000).

companies may integrate effectively to achieve the original objectives of the acquisition. Through case-based research, they suggest that there are different trajectories which firms may travel in order to achieve a successful outcome. This process typology aims to understand how the potentials offered by strategic and organizational fit may be realized through effective management of process in symbiotic style acquisitions (see Fig. 3.14).

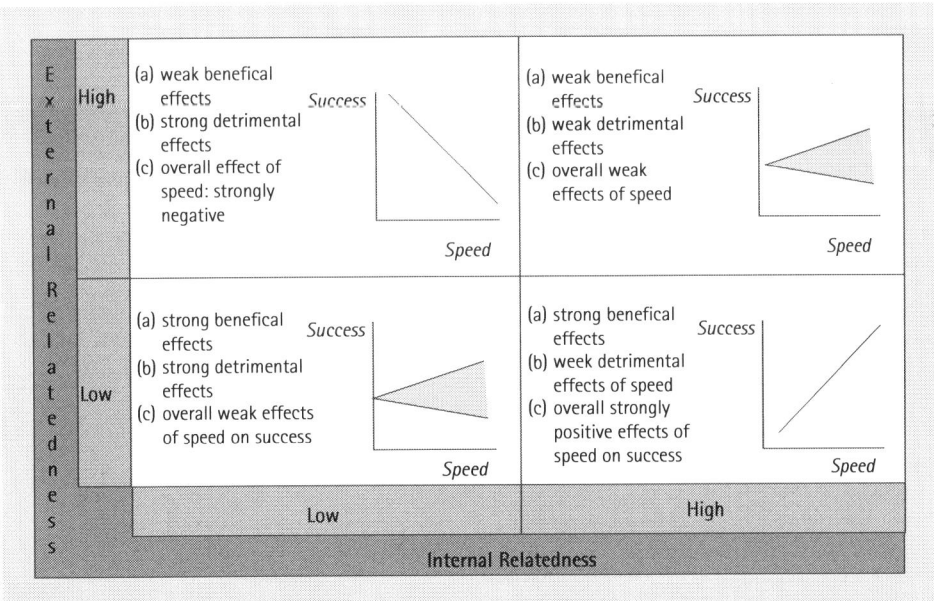

FIG. 3.15 Effects of internal and external alignment on speed of change and performance

Source: Homburg and Bucerius (2006).

Speed of Integration Typologies

Within the process approach to acquisition integration, the timing and speed of change has recently become recognized as a critical factor in post-acquisition integration (Angwin 2004b). In order to examine specifically the effects of speed upon performance in the area of marketing integration, Homburg and Bucerius (2006) created a contingency framework showing the performance implications of speed of change against different contingencies of external and internal organizational fit (see Fig. 3.15). The framework illustrates the complex relationship between speed and performance as conceptualized by Angwin (2004b), showing that contingencies matter.

INTEGRATED M&A TYPOLOGIES

The vast majority of typologies have focused upon one or other of the main acquisition phases, either pre-acquisition strategies or post-acquisition integration. These typologies have tended either to ignore the other phase or to make assumptions which are not clearly articulated. They also tend to ignore an important part of the process which is the

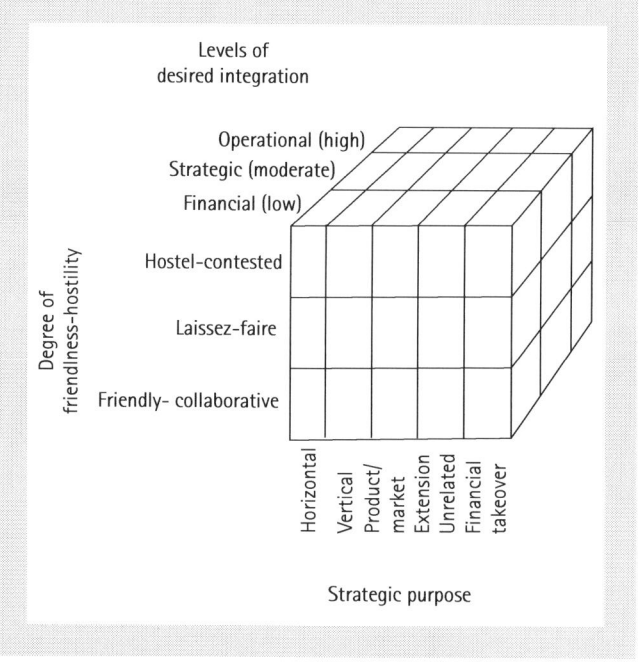

FIG. 3.16 An integrated typology of mergers and acquisitions

Source: Buono, A. F. and Bowditch, J. L. (1989: 75), *The Human Side of Mergers and Acquisitions: Managing Collisions between People and Organisations*. San Francisco: Jossey–Bass. Reprinted with permission of John Wiley & Sons, Inc.

spirit in which the deal is transacted—the negotiation phase. One typology which attempts to integrate the phases of the M&A process is by Buono and Bowditch (1989). They take (i) the classical pre-acquisition strategy types based on the FTC's merger typology (1975) of horizontal, vertical, product/market extension, unrelated and financial takeovers, (ii) the degree of friendliness/hostility in the negotiation phase used by Pritchett (1985), and (iii) choose three aspects of post-acquisition integration intensity, based on the work of Jenster (1987), running from low to high. This generates 45 potential types of M&A (see Fig 3.16), although the authors are quick to acknowledge that certain combinations are far more likely than others. They do not go on to characterize these M&A types, but conjecture that they may exist.

Since Buono and Bowditch's (1989) typology was created, researchers have worked at refining typologies for pre- and post-acquisition phases (see earlier sections), but have not extended this overall integration framework.

SYNTHESIS OF TYPOLOGIES IN M&A

The M&A literature is rich in typologies, although their form, nature, and status vary considerably. Table 3.1 organizes the typologies described in this chapter in terms of whether they are typologies (a priori rigorous conceptualizations/theorizations),

Table 3.1 Typologies, taxonomies and classifications in M&A

	Tested	Untested
Typologies	Ansoff (1965)	Nahavandi and Malekzedah (1988)
	Henderson (1979)	Buono and Bowditch (1989)
	Salter and Weinhold (1979)	Napier (1989)
	Shelton (1988)	Cartwright and Cooper (1992)
	Larsson (1990)	Mirvis and Marks (1992)
	Angwin and Meadows (2009)	Elsass and Veiga (1994)
		Goold, Campbell, and Alexander (1994)
		Schweiger, Csiszar, and Napier (1994)
		Birkinshaw, J., Bresman, H., and Hakanson, L. (2000)
		Angwin (2006)
Taxonomies	Homburg and Bucerius (2006)	Haspeslagh and Jemison (1991)
Classifications		Pritchett (1985)
		Walter (1987)
		Siehl and Smith (1990)
		Bower (2001)
		Angwin (2007a)

taxonomies (a posteriori empirical deductions based upon rigorous multivariate statistical techniques), classifications (less rigorous descriptive categorizations). One observation from the table is that the older strategy frameworks have generally been tested substantially for their links to performance outcomes as well as the robustness of their categories. Many later typologies have tended not to have been subject to rigorous testing, perhaps because (i) the paradigm in which they are located is less amenable to quantitative analysis; (ii) there has been less time to evaluate them; (iii) the perceived value in replication studies is low. However, for the study of M&A to progress, it is valuable to establish stronger foundations which rigorous testing would bring. This presents opportunity for further testing to take place, but also a challenge of how to integrate the dimensions of the typologies in order that more holistic robust frameworks can be created.

Many of the M&A typologies described in this chapter have been influenced by the strategic management field, which itself has been subject to multiple influences, such as industrial economics on the studying of positioning in industries and of the economics and sociology of organization on the study of firm resources and capabilities. They have also been influenced variously by methods which focus on content and process. The earliest typologies mentioned here, Ansoff (1965), Henderson (1979), and other business policy matrixes such as the GE policy matrix, can be located in the Positioning School of strategy, where researchers explored the relationships between various strategies and performance outcomes such as market share or financial results. These strategic fit typologies were later refined to consider capabilities and resources in terms of how firms could generate rents from significant decisions involving changes in firm scope. Difficulties in finding clear relationships between pre-acquisition typologies and post-acquisition outcomes led to M&A scholars recognizing the potentially distorting effects of the acquisition process itself (Jemison and Sitkin 1986). Subsequent typologies located in the Process School of strategy focused upon the post-acquisition phase in order to more closely understand organizational fit. These typologies, such as Haspeslagh and Jemison (1991), resonated with pre-existing M&A frameworks deriving from the Organizational Behavior School which had focused upon the human resource impact of acquisitions and issues of cultural compatibility. Whilst early typologies of this type struggle to capture the dynamic qualities of process—indeed a more general criticism of typologies is that they are static in nature—later typologies focus squarely on change and performance over time (cf. Birkinshaw et al. 2000; Homburg and Bucerius 2006). So far, however, these typologies have been quite narrow in their scope and further research is needed to broaden and test them. Whilst some of these typologies purport to be strategic in terms of linking pre- and post-acquisition phases, most only really capture aspects of the post-acquisition phase. M&A researchers are well aware that the whole M&A process is complex and consists of multiple phases, although there is debate about the nature and extent of its many phases (which can include deal conception, planning, negotiations, transaction, integration, outcomes (cf. Howell 1970; Jemison and Sitkin 1986; Buono and Bowdich 1989; Haspeslagh and Jemison 1991; Angwin and Connell 2008)). These temporal typologies have not been subject to rigorous examination, and an important current challenge is for typologies to successfully capture the dynamics along the whole acquisition process. Recent developments in strategic management, the emergence of a strategy-as-practice school, offer additional opportunities for the development of typologies. The practice approach seeks to open up different levels and dimensions for analysis which are currently black boxed by earlier typologies (Angwin 2007b). In particular, this approach seeks to focus upon individual strategic actors—the people who actually do the work of M&A—and explicitly aims to relate their activities to the macro level. Typologies are well suited to this contingency thinking.

The Limitations of Typologies

A well-constructed typology can bring order out of chaos, but this is not to deny that there can be practical problems with creating and deploying them. All typologies initially identify a finite set of ideal types, but a problem can occur in handling hybrid situations, where strategies, for instance, appear to be a mix of different ideal types. On the one hand, these strategies may simply be deemed confused and far from ideal types or they may represent a different "type" which could be ignored by focusing too much on those conceptualized. If the hybrid situation is highlighted as a new "ideal" type, then this risks undermining the original set of types.

Some typologies have been too narrowly focused to be a basis for reliable prediction or prescription. This narrowness also hinders integrating different typologies, as there is little overlap among them. Unless there are more attempts to integrate M&A typologies through focusing upon a broader array of variables, they will only continue to reveal isolated and irreconcilable slices of reality.

One of the strengths of typologies, particularly in a two-by-two form, is that they are memorable and easy to convey. However, this also presents a risk of reification, that they can come to narrow our view of reality. Typologies may also be perceived to be an end in themselves rather than a means to an end. They have also been criticized for not being sufficiently parsimonious, being based on arbitrary criteria, are essentially static, rely too heavily on dichotomized variables rather than continuous ones and are more descriptive than explanatory or predictive. Many of these criticisms, however, also apply to much social research and are not specific to typologies where a skilful researcher can avoid most of these difficulties.

A further limitation is institutional in nature in management studies—the difficulty of getting replication studies published. This knowledge discourages researchers from rigorous testing of existing typologies, so we are never sure about the robustness and value of those already in existence. This has a deleterious effect upon the study of M&A as we continuously strive for the new and yet are never sure of what has been achieved. Until more unglamorous rigorous testing is recognized as a valuable and legitimate activity, M&A research will always be unsure of its foundations.

Conclusions

> Typologies can transform the complexities of apparently eclectic congeries of diverse cases into well ordered sets of a few rather homogenous types, clearly situated in a property space of a few important dimensions. A sound typology forms a solid foundation for theorizing and empirical research.
>
> Bailey (1994: 33)

Typologies have a lot to offer those concerned with M&A and their enduring nature is evidence of their popularity. They are valuable in enabling audiences to understand the diversity that exists in M&A and appear to provide parsimonious frameworks for describing complexity and outcomes. From a configurational perspective, M&A is best viewed as a holistic synthesis of multiple interdependent characteristics. In order to determine dominant patterns or relationships which are poorly understood or too complex to be modeled using conventional approaches, configurations are useful (Miller 1996). The combination of parsimony and equifinality makes typologies well suited for empirical testing, although this is not carried out as often as it might be in the M&A literature.

The M&A literature exhibits a wide range of typologies from purely classificatory schemes to taxonomies and theoretically derived ideal types. These distinctions are rarely made clear and there is significant variation in the rigor with which they have been created and the extent to which they have been empirically verified. This presents a challenge to the construction of a coherent body of M&A knowledge, but also offers an opportunity for subsequent testing and development.

Looking ahead, these are exciting times for the study of M&A. Its dynamic nature suggests there are many opportunities for examining how organizations move across existing typologies, rather than locating them in a static position. For instance, Haspeslagh and Farquhar (1994) hint at the possibilities of movement between preservation strategy to symbiotic strategy, but there are other possibilities which have not been examined. This moves the typology focus from purely content orientation to a process view of how and why acquirers manage in the way they do. The advantages of typologies for these sorts of questions are that they identify the many elements which must vary as firms change state. For instance, what elements need to change in order for one integration strategy to change to another? In terms of contextual alignment, one might also ask what changes in external conditions may affect integration approach in a recently acquired company.

Many of the typologies reviewed in this chapter can be seen to emerge alongside intellectual developments in the field of strategic management. In the new strategy-as-practice perspective, typologies have been identified as being potentially very useful for pinning down the different types of phenomena or practices that are involved in strategy practice and showing how they work relative to the context in which they are located

(Johnson et al. 2007). This focus upon linking micro activities to strategic outcome resonates strongly with central concerns in the study of M&A (Angwin 2007b) and here typologies can constitute valuable building blocks for developing that knowledge.

In terms of future directions for typological approaches to M&A, meaningful frameworks have been generated to cover many complex aspects of M&A, although many require more empirical testing and refinement. The extremely diverse and heterogeneous nature of M&A still presents significant challenges for the development of an overarching typology—"we can still see the seams" in the literature and in our understanding of the M&A process. There remain many sub-areas where typologies would help to make sense of complex interrelationships in this phenomenon and would allow the generation of testable hypotheses. The recent call for pluralistic approaches to studying M&A (Angwin 2007b; Angwin and Vaara 2005) plays clearly into the hands of a typological approach to M&A, offering up many more legitimate variables for inclusion in analysis. Finally, many M&A typologies have not lived up to the high standards of theory building which are possible, but, as a methodological approach, they continue to offer considerable promise for researchers seeking to understand the complex phenomenon of M&A in a holistic way.

Endnotes

1. Estimates vary for transaction totals for each year, but independent sources agree on the magnitude of the aggregate deal value.
2. The terms Merger and Acquisition are often used interchangeably in the M&A literature. In this chapter, the terms are used as the typology authors intended them to be used.

References

Angwin, D. N. (1999). "Post-Acquisition Management of Corporate Take-Overs in the United Kingdom." Unpublished PhD thesis, Warwick University.

——(2000). *Post-acquisition Management*. London: Financial Times/Prentice Hall, Senior Executive Briefing, Management Series, December.

——(2004a). "Top Management in Acquisitions and Acquisitions." *Advances in Mergers and Acquisitions*. Oxford: JAI Press, 3: 57–82.

——(2004b). "Speed in M&A Integration: The First 100 days." *European Management Journal*, 22/4: 418–30.

——(2007a). "Motive Archetypes in Mergers and Acquisitions: The Implications of a Configurational Approach to Performance." *Advances in Mergers and Acquisitions*, 6: 77–104.

——(2007b). *Mergers and Acquisitions*. Oxford: Blackwell Publishing.

——& R. Connell (2008). "Interrupts in the M&A Decision Making Process." *Journal of Management Studies* Special Conference, St Anne's College, Oxford.

——& Meadows, M. (2009). "The Choice of Insider or Outsider Top Executives in Acquired Companies." *Long Range Planning*, 37: 239–57.

——& Vaara, E. (2005). "Connectivity in Merging Organizations." Special Issue, *Organization Studies*, 26/10: 1447–1635.

Ansoff, H. I., Anderson, T. A., Norton, F. & Weston, J. F. (1959). "Planning for Diversification through Acquisition." *California Management Review*, 1/4: 24–35.

Ansoff, H. I. (1965). *The Concept of Corporate Strategy*. Homewood, IL: Dow-Jones Irwin.

Bailey, K. D. (1994). *Typologies and Taxonomies: An Introduction to Classification Techniques*. Thousand Oaks, CA and London: SAGE publications.

Berry, J. W. (1983). "Acculturation: A Comparative Analysis of Alternative Forms," in R. J. Samuda & S. L. Woods (eds.), *Perspectives in Immigrant and Minority Education*. Lanham, MD: University Press of America, 66–77.

——(1984). "Cultural Relations in Plural Societies: Alternatives to Segregation and their Sociopsychological Implications," in N. Miller & M. B. Brewer (eds.), *Groups in contact*. Orlando, FL: Academic Press, 11–27.

Birkinshaw, J., Bresman, H., & Hakanson, L. (2000). "Managing the Post Acquisition Process: How the Human Integration and Task Integration Processes Interact to Foster Value Creation." *Journal of Management Studies*, 37/3: 395–425.

Bower, J. L. (2001). "Not all M&As are Alike—and that Matters." *Harvard Business Review*, 79/3, March: 92–101.

Bozarth, C., & McDermott, C. (1998). "Configurations in Manufacturing Strategy: A Review and Directions for Future Research." *Journal of Operations Management*, 16: 427–39.

Buono, A. F., & Bowditch, J. L. (1989). *The Human Side of Mergers and Acquisitions: Managing Collisions between People and Organisations*. San Francisco: Jossey–Bass.

Cartwright, S., and Cooper, C. (1992). *Mergers and Acquisitions: The Human Factor*. Oxford: Butterworth Heinemann.

———(1993). "The Role of Culture Compatibility in Successful Organizational Marriage." *Academy of Management Executive*, 7/2: 57–70.

Christensen, C. R., Andrews, K., & Bower, J. L. (1978). *Business Policy: Text and Cases* (4th ed.). Homewood, IL: Richard D. Irwin.

Donaldson, L. (1995). "American Anti-management Theories of Organization: A Critique of Paradigm Proliferation." *Cambridge Studies in Management*, 25. Cambridge: Cambridge University Press, 41.

Doty, D. H., & Glick, W. H. (1994). "Typologies as a Unique Form of Theory Building: Toward Improved Understanding And and Modelling." *Academy of Management Review*, 19, /2: 230–51.

Ebeling, H.W., Jr., & Doorley 111, T. L. (1983). "A Strategic Approach to Acquisitions." *The Journal of Business Strategy*, Winter, 3/3: 45–54.

Elsass, P. M., & Veiga, J. F. (1994). "Acculturation in Acquired Organizations: A Force-Field Perspective." *Human Relations*, 47/4: 431–53.

Goold, M., Campbell, A., & Alexander, M. (1994). *Corporate-Level Strategy: Creating Value in the Multibusiness Company*. New York: Wiley.

Gort, M. (1969). "An Economic Disturbance Theory of Mergers." *Quarterly Journal of Economics*, 83/4: 624–42.

Hall, R. H. (1991). *Organizations, Structures, Processes and Outcomes* (5th ed.). Englewood Cliffs, NJ: Prentice Hall.

Hambrick, D. C. (1983). "An Empirical Typology of Mature Industrial-Product Environments." *Academy of Management Journal*, 26: 213–30.

Haspeslagh, P. C., and Farquhar, A. B. (1994). "The Acquisition Integration Process: A Contingent Framework," in G. von Krogh, A. Sinatra, and H. Singh (eds.), *The Management of Corporate Acquisitions*. London, UK: Macmillan Press Ltd.

——& Jemison, D. B. (1991). *Managing Acquisitions: Creating Value through Corporate Renewal*. New York: Free Press, Macmillan Inc.

Henderson, B. (1979). *Henderson on Strategy*. Boston, MA: ABT Books.

Homburg, C., & Bucerius, M. (2006). "Is Speed of Integration Really a Success Factor of Mergers and Acquisitions? An Analysis of the Role of Internal and External Relatedness." *Strategic Management Journal*, 27/4: 347–67.

Howell, R. A. (1970). "Plan to Integrate Your Acquisitions." *Harvard Business Review*, 48/6, November–December: 66–76.

Jemison, D. B., & Sitkin, S. B. (1986). "Corporate Acquisitions: A Process Perspective." *Academy of Management Review*, 11/1: 145–63.

Jenster, P. V. (1987). "Using Critical Success Factors in Planning." *Long Range Planning*, 20/4: 102–49.

Johnson, G., Langley, A., Melin, L., & Whittington, R. (2007). *Strategy as Practice: Research Directions and Resources*. Cambridge: Cambridge University Press.

Larsson, R. (1990). "Coordination of Action in Mergers and Acquisitions: Interpretive and Systems Approaches towards Synergy." *Lund Studies in Economics and Management*, 10. The Institute of Economic Research. Sweden: Lund University Press.

Martin-Pena, M. L., & Diaz-Garrido, E. (2008). "Typologies and Taxonomies of Operations Strategy: A Literature Review." *Management Research News*, 31/3: 200–18.

Miles, R. E., & Snow, C. C. (1978). *Organizational Strategy, Structure, and Process*. New York: McGraw-Hill.

Miller, D. (1996). "Configurations Revisited." *Strategic Management Journal*, 17: 505–12.

——& Friesen, P. H. (1984). *Organizations: A Quantum View*. Englewood Cliffs, NJ: Prentice Hall.

Mirvis, P. H., & Marks, M. L. (1992). *Managing the Merger: Making it Work*. Englewood Cliffs, NJ: Prentice Hall.

Nahavandi, A., & Malekzadeh, A. R. (1988). "Acculturation in Mergers and Acquisitions." *Academy of Management Review*, 13/1: 79–90.

Napier, N. K. (1989). "Mergers and Acquisitions, Human Resource Issues and Outcomes: A Review and Suggested Typology." *Journal of Management Studies*, 26/3: 271–89.

Narasimhan, R., Kim, S. W., & Tan, K. C. (2008). "An Empirical Investigation of Supply Chain Strategy Typologies and Relationships to Performance." *International Journal of Production Research*, 46/18: 5231–59.

Porter, M. E. (1985). *Competitive Advantage: Creating and Sustaining Superior Performance*. (With a new introduction; 1st Free Press ed.). New York: Free Press.

Pritchett, P. (1985). *After the Merger: Managing the Shock Waves*. New York: Dow Jones–Irwin.

Pugh, D. S., Hickson, D. J., & Hinings, C. R. (1969). "An Empirical Taxonomy of Structures of Work Organizations." *Administrative Science Quarterly*, 14: 115–26.

Rich, P. (1992). "The Organizational Taxonomy: Definition and Design." *Academy of Management Review*, 17: 758–81.

Salter, M. S., & Weinhold, W. A. (1979). *Diversification through Acquisition*. New York: The Free Press.

Schwartz, H., & Davis, S. M. (1981). "Matching Corporate Culture And and Business Strategy,." *Organizational Dynamics*, 10, /1: 30–48.

Schweiger, D. M., Csiszar, E. N., and Napier, N. (1994). "A Strategic Approach to Implementing Mergers and Acquisitions," in G. von Krogh, A. Sinatra, & H. Singh (eds.), *The Management of Corporate Acquisitions*. London, UK: Macmillan.

Shelton, L. M. (1988). "Strategic Business Fits and Corporate Acquisition: Empirical Evidence." *Strategic Management Journal*, 9: 279–87.

Shrivastava, P. (1986). "Postacquisition Integration." *Journal of Business Strategy*, 7/1: 65–76.

Siehl, C., and Smith, D. (1990). "Avoiding the Loss of a Gain: Retaining Managing Executives in an Acquisition." *Human Capabilities Management*, 29/2: 167–85.

Parson, T. (1956). "Suggestions for a Sociological Approach to the Theory of Organizations." *Administrative Science Quarterly*, 1: 68–85.

Venkatraman, N. (1989). "The Concept of Fit in Strategy Research: Toward Verbal and Statistical Correspondence." *Academy of Management Review*, 14/3: 423–44.

Walter, G. A. (1987). "Key Acquisition Integration Processes for Four Strategic Orientations." Western Academy of Management meeting, Hollywood, CA.

Weber, M. (1947). *The Theory of Social and Economic Organization*. New York: Free Press.

CHAPTER 4

....

CREATING VALUE
THROUGH MERGERS
AND ACQUISITIONS

Challenges and Opportunities

....

MICHAEL A. HITT, DAVID KING, HEMA KRISHNAN,
MARIANNA MAKRI, MARIO SCHIJVEN,
KATSUHIKO SHIMIZU, AND HONG ZHU

INTRODUCTION

....

Although a popular strategy, only a minority of firms have achieved significant success using mergers and acquisitions (M&A). In fact, many acquisitions are unsuccessful, some spectacularly so. Several studies have shown that, on average, the value created by M&As varies closely around zero (Hitt et al. 2001a; King et al. 2004). There has been a significant amount of research on M&As, but more is needed to help us understand this important strategy and to provide recommendations that will help strategists enhance their success with this strategy (Hitt et al. 2009). In recent years, a few firms have had more success with M&As, evidently building needed capabilities and completing the acquisition process, including integration, effectively. Yet, the number having success is small.

Our purpose herein is to understand some of the primary reasons for failure and opportunities for achieving success with M&As. Although the goal of all M&As is to create value, many actually create negative value because they produce problems that managers are unable to resolve. Acquisitions are incredibly complex strategies that are highly challenging to complete and implement. For example, several have explained the challenges of completing an effective integration of two businesses involved in a merger (e.g. Haspeslagh and Jemison 1991a). In fact, many believe that ineffective integration is the primary reason for the inability of M&As to create value. Although we agree that integration problems are a major reason for unsuccessful acquisitions, the research suggests that the causes of failure are more complex. Thus, we examine several additional and important reasons why M&As do not create value (e.g. paying an unwarranted premium and executives' delay in divesting poorly performing units that were acquired earlier). We also explore research on learning from M&As and building capabilities which contribute to the success of M&As (e.g. building capabilities necessary to produce innovation). Finally, we discuss cross-border M&A research because of M&As' growing prominence in the global competitive landscape and the challenges they present for creating value. We begin our exploration by reviewing M&A research more generally to identify prominent independent variables used in the research and a concise explanation of what we have learned about them.

Extant Research on Mergers and Acquisitions

We conducted a review of the extant empirical research on M&A performance over the last 25 years (1983–2008). The intent of the review was to identify the most common independent variables used in M&A research and to summarize the key research findings and opportunities for future research. Articles for the review were identified by a combination of computer-aided, keyword searches and manual searches of leading management journals (e.g. *Academy of Management Journal, Administrative Science Quarterly, Journal of Management*, and *Strategic Management Journal*). We also followed the "ancestry" approach of article identification (Cooper 1998). This search process resulted in a list of 89 studies predominantly in economics, finance, and management, as shown in Appendices 4.1 and 4.2. The resulting "top five" most common M&A independent variables used in the research are:

1. The extent that an acquisition increased the diversification of the acquiring firm, or the relatedness of an acquisition (58% of the studies);

2. Firm size or the relative size of the acquired to the acquiring firm (52% of the studies);

3. The acquisition experience of the acquiring firm (28% of the studies);

4. Method of payment for an acquisition (18% of the studies); and

5. Firm performance prior to an acquisition (18% of the studies).

There were some other interesting and potentially important issues identified in our review of the research. First, the review left the definition of M&As to each study. Second, the vast majority of existing M&A research uses samples of firms from the US. However, as explained later in this chapter, research on cross-border M&As is gaining increased attention. Third, research increasingly uses multiple measures of performance (e.g.

event window, long-term stock, and/or accounting-based measures). This positive development is likely the result of recent research recommending the use of multiple measures of M&A performance (Cording et al. 2008; King et al. 2008; Schoenberg 2006; Zollo and Meier 2008). Below, we explain the research involving each of the five most common independent variables in M&A research.

Diversification or Relatedness of Acquisition

The effect of firms diversifying into related or unrelated businesses on subsequent performance has received the most attention in M&A research. While there are logical arguments and some evidence to suggest that target firms with greater relatedness to an acquiring firm should produce higher performance (Bruton et al. 1994; Finkelstein and Haleblian 2002; Shelton 1988), extant research provides mixed evidence. For example, research has found no relationship between relatedness and acquisition performance (Fowler and Schmidt 1989; Lubatkin 1987; Singh and Montgomery 1987), both related and unrelated acquisitions leading to higher performance (Seth 1990a, 1990b), and unrelated acquisitions leading to lower performance (Hoskisson et al. 1993; Megginson et al. 2004). Research by Palich, Cardinal, and Miller (2000) suggests a curvilinear relationship between relatedness and performance. Additionally, a firm's decision to diversify may relate to its core industry being less attractive (Park 2003). The mixed results can be explained by a few studies showing nonlinear relationships or controlling for other contextual factors. Further exploration of and defining nonlinear relationships of diversifying acquisitions represents a future research opportunity.

Firm Size

The next most common research variable involves firm size, and it provides more consistent results. The impact of firm size on acquisition performance likely results from the effectiveness of the integration process. For example, "mergers of equals" involving two large firms which are consistently poor performers (Fanto 2001; Weber and Camerer 2003).While it is usually easier for a firm to integrate a smaller firm than a firm of similar size, a target firm also needs to be large enough to have an impact on an acquiring firm's performance (King et al. 2008). This suggests firm size has a complex relationship with M&A performance in that the relative size of the acquirer and target versus independent considerations of firm size may be of most relevance.

Acquisition Experience

Some research has found that prior acquisition experience predicts success in later acquisitions (Bruton et al. 1994; Fowler and Schmidt 1989; Haleblian and Kim, 2006), while other studies have found no effect (Lahey and Conn 1990) or a decline in acquisition performance as acquisition activity increases (Kusewitt 1985; Haleblian and Finkelstein 1999). The more critical issue is likely the amount learned from making an acquisition. Obviously, a firm with some experience should be able to learn from additional acquisitions, but having more experience does not ensure that greater learning occurs. Early experiences can produce more learning than later experiences, but without adequate absorptive capacity, early lessons may be generalized to subsequent acquisitions where they are not applicable. Thus, the impact of acquisition experience is likely to be curvilinear (Haleblian and Finkelstein 1999), or it may become significant through the interaction with other important factors. Additional research is needed to examine how acquisition experience influences firm performance, especially in future acquisitions and to develop better measures of learning in acquisitions.

Method of Payment

Firms can pay for an acquisition with cash, stock shares (equity), or a combination of both. Research generally suggests that managers will finance an acquisition with equity if their firm's stock is overvalued, and cash if it is not. Therefore, the use of cash may signal manager expectations that performance will be higher after the acquisition. While a meta-analysis of prior research indicated there was no effect for method of payment on acquisition performance (King et al. 2004), subsequent research supports the conclusion that better performance is achieved in acquisitions made with cash (Abhyankar et al. 2005). The influence of the method of payment on M&A performance may be contextual, or influenced by the premium paid with higher premiums for stock payment. The impact of payment method may also depend on the timing of an acquisition in a merger wave or stock market cycle, with acquisitions underperforming in later stages of a cycle, because they are paid for with overvalued stock. Again, research is needed to explore in more detail the complex relationships involving method of payment, especially potential contingency variables such as the amount of premiums paid.

Prior Performance

The general assumption is that acquiring firm performance displays inertia, or firms that performed well before an acquisition will continue to display high performance. Alternatively, the effects of prior performance on the target firms are more nuanced. While some acquirers select acquisition targets independent of their prior performance (Anand and Singh 1997), research generally suggests that firms seek to acquire more profitable targets (e.g. Mahoney and Pandian 1992; Vermeulen and Barkema 2001). Still other research suggests that acquirers are attracted to distressed firms (Bruton et al. 1994). Another consideration is that selecting an acquisition target based on its performance may depend on a firm's industry environment, as profitable firms are more frequently targeted in growing industries (Heeley et al. 2006). In general, M&A research is more focused on acquirers and examining the characteristics of targets represents a largely unexplored area. Thus, future research on the target firms in acquisition offers the potential to advance our understanding of M&As.

Supplementary Review

Our review of M&A research revealed the diversity of foci, so we divided our review into two time segments to identify trends. Period 1 includes 56 studies (see Appendix 4.1), published after Jensen and Ruback's (1983) review and before the meta-analysis by King and others (2004). Meanwhile, Period 2 includes 33 studies published between 2004 and 2008; they are listed in Appendix 4.2. The five most common independent variables for both time periods are shown in Table 4.1.

A comparison of columns in Table 4.1 reveals some consistency in variables considered in M&A research over time, with measures of diversification or relatedness, and firm size or relative size ranking number 1 or 2 for both Period 1 and Period 2. Other variables exhibit differences, with an increased focus on method of payment and prior performance appearing more in M&A research published since 2004. One change that can be readily explained is that contemporary studies do not control for the method of accounting for an acquisition, as purchase accounting has been used for all US acquisitions completed after July 1, 2001 (Weil 2001). While prior research and its conclusions are useful, increased utilization of a common set of independent variables in M&A research could minimize model under-specification and facilitate achieving greater consensus on the drivers of M&A performance. There are two positive trends in the

Table 4.1 Top five acquisition research variables

Rank	1983–2003 56 Studies (no./%)	2004–2008 33 Studies (no./%)
1	Diversification/relatedness 34 (61%)	Firm size/relative size 19 (58%)
2	Firm size/relative size 27 (48%)	Diversification/relatedness 18 (55%)
3	Acquisition experience 11 (20%)	Method of payment 16 (48%)
4	Industry controls 9 (16%)	Prior performance 16 (48%)
5	Accounting method 7 (13%)	Acquisition experience 14 (42%)

M&A research. First, the amount of M&A research conducted is growing, with roughly three articles a year published in Period 1 and approximately six articles a year in Period 2. Second, there is increased emphasis placed on the most common research variables. Still, there is much more to learn about the requirements for creating value through acquisitions. We conclude from this review that an important need in M&A research is to consider more complex relationships among the critical variables (King et al. 2004). In the following sections, we examine additional factors that affect a firm's ability to create value through acquisitions, beginning with acquisition premiums.

Paying Acquisition Premiums and Organizational Performance

The acquisition premium has important effects on M&A outcomes (Krishnan et al. 2007; Sirower 1997). Firms are often willing to pay a substantial price, well exceeding the market value, to acquire the shares of the target firm in the hope of realizing the synergies that may exist in the merged organization. An *acquisition premium* is the price paid for a target that exceeds its pre-acquisition market value. Over the past 20 years, the average premium paid has ranged between 40 and 50% (Laamanen 2007).

While creation of synergy is the stated motive for paying large premiums (Hitt et al. 2001b), there are additional reasons why acquiring firms pay substantial premiums for the target firms. These reasons include agency factors, managerial hubris, the presence of other competing bidders, board interlocks and investment advisors, consolidation trends in the industry, and desire to acquire technology firms.

In theory, firms hope to create synergy by capitalizing on the complementary assets in the acquiring and acquired firms to produce valuable and unique products or services (Ravenscraft and Scherer 1987), to generate economies of scale and scope through asset consolidation, to eliminate inefficiencies and redundancies in the value chains of the firms by combining sales forces and manufacturing facilities, sharing trademarks, brand names, or distribution channels (Capron 1999; Haspeslagh and Jemison 1991b), to redeploy assets to more profitable uses, and to achieve market power via increased bargaining leverage with key constituencies. The synergy motive is vested in the resource-based theory of the firm, where the complementary resource profiles of the two firms, such as physical resources, intangible resources, financial resources, and human resources, are integrated in ways that uniquely position the firm against its competitors (Capron 1999). In order to capture this synergy, the payment of a premium for the shares of the target firm may be justified. However, the premium paid should not exceed the benefits to be achieved through the potential synergy if the acquisition is to produce positive returns (Sirower 1997).

A second reason that acquiring firms often pay large premiums stems from agency factors, when top executives engage in opportunistic behavior that provides them with personal gains (Trautwein 1990). Because acquisitions increase the size of a firm, they often have a positive effect on a top executive's compensation and enhance his/her power. Further, the top executive's employment risk is likely to be reduced if the acquisition diversifies the firm. Slusky and Caves (1991) argue that the alignment of the objectives of the managers with shareholders' interests can influence the amount of premium paid. Managers who gain from a merger can overpay for it or they can undertake mergers which have a value-creating potential that is less than the target's reservation price for yielding control. Alternately, managers who hold a large proportion of their company's shares are more likely to offer a lower price for the target firm (Morck et al. 1988).

A third reason for high premiums is executive hubris (Roll 1986). Managerial or CEOs' hubris is overconfidence by managers in their capabilities to extract synergy from the combined firm. Hubris often results in firms overpaying for their targets (Hayward and Hambrick 1997). This problem surfaces during the acquisition search or the due-diligence process, when fragmented decision making, escalating momentum, and ambiguous expectations cloud the judgment of CEOs and other top managers (Haspeslagh and Jemison 1991a; Jemison and Sitkin 1986). Hubris sometimes causes the CEO to do an inadequate job of due diligence and to ignore negative information provided by this process (Hitt et al. 2001a).

Sirower (1997), however, disputes the notion that self-interest or hubris is at the core of high premiums. Rather, he suggests three alternate reasons for overpayment: (1) unfamiliarity with the fundamentals of the acquisition strategy, (2) lack of adequate knowledge of the target and market conditions, and (3) unexpected problems that may occur during the integration process. Overpayment may also result from decision biases; for example, Baker, Pan, and Wurgler (2009) found that the majority of acquisition announcements use a target firm's 52-week trading high to determine acquisition premiums. However, while lack of capabilities or experience on the part of the executives can result in the acquisition failing to meet expectations, the belief that they can make it work (hubris) likely plays a role in premium payments.

Another reason for premium payments is competitive factors in the environment, such as multiple bidders for the target firm (Varaiya 1988; Slusky and Caves 1991). In this case, the price is usually driven higher when multiple bids are made for the target (Varaiya 1988). When a target firm operates in product markets that are valuable to competing firms or if it operates in a product market that complements the product line of competing firms, multiple firms may place bids for the target. These cases have been termed the "winner's curse," in that the acquiring firm with the winning bid often overestimates a target firm's value (Coff 2002).

Interorganizational relationships that have developed through board interlocks and professional firms including investment advisors and bankers can also influence the amount of premium paid by acquiring firms. Haunschild (1993) found that premiums paid are related to those paid by the interlock partners of the acquiring firm and to those paid by other firms using the same professional firms. In a recent study, Porrini (2006) found that investment bankers (used by 88% of acquiring firms) complete acquisition transactions for their clients that involve the payment of large premiums. Agency factors are likely at play because the fees collected by the bankers from their clients are calculated as a percentage of the final purchase price of the target firm, providing an incentive for investment firms to recommend a high price. Recently, a few researchers have examined some lesser known motives for high premium payments. These motives include the consolidation trends in the industry in which the acquiring and target firms function, and higher growth opportunities in some younger industries. The findings on the relationship between consolidation trends in the industry and premiums are not conclusive. Consolidation in the hospital industry in the 1990s resulted in acquisitions with minimal or no premium payments, whereas the reverse was the case in the pharmaceutical industry. It is likely that, in the pharmaceutical industry, the opportunity to acquire valuable R&D and to realize significantly higher profits increased the price of the target firms, whereas, in the highly regulated low-profit hospital industry, an acquisition was made for survival (Chadwick et al. 2004; Scott et al. 2000). In the high growth technology firms, Kohers and Kohers (2001) and Laamanen (2007) argue that high premiums are paid because the market cannot easily value the resources of the target. There is uncertainty regarding the future cash flows from the accumulated R&D investments in firms operating in younger industries (Chan et al. 2001). An acquirer conducting the required due diligence may value the accumulated R&D investments higher than the stock market and therefore offers a premium.

Overall, a majority of the studies reveal a negative relationship between acquisition premiums and organizational performance. While the announcement of a high-priced acquisition usually benefits the shareholders of the target firm (Hitt et al. 2001b), the shareholders of the acquiring firm typically lose value from the acquisition (Datta et al. 1992; Hayward and Hambrick 1997; Varaiya and Ferris 1987). This loss is often sustained in the long term as evidenced from stock returns (Sirower 1997) and based on accounting performance measures such as the post-acquisition return on sales (ROS) or return on equity (ROE) (Beckman and Haunschild 2002; Krishnan et al. 2007). The negative effect of premium on performance exists even after controlling for the relative size difference between the acquiring and acquired firms, the debt of the acquiring firm, the method of payment, prior performance of both firms, multiple bidders, acquisition climate and time period, composition of the board, and the relatedness of the acquired firm (Haunschild 1994; Krishnan et al. 2007; Slusky and Caves 1991).

One main reason for this negative relationship can be directly attributed to the size of the premium which places a huge burden on the management of the acquiring firm to not only recoup the acquisition costs, but also to extract the synergies from the merged organization. The parent firm is expected to not only meet the performance that the market expects, but also to generate the cash flows imposed by the premium payment. About 70% of the firms fail to deliver the required results. Achieving synergies is challenged when acquiring firms incur huge debt (Jensen 1991) to finance the acquisition, imposing a serious burden on the firm to generate high cash flows. The reaction of the stock market to most acquisition announcements and deal finalization is usually negative; there is great pressure on executives to appease the shareholders. As a result, two types of actions are likely to be taken; the first involves a restructuring process where the assets are consolidated, some of the assets of the acquired firm are sold, and redundancies such as duplicate workforces are eliminated along the value chains of the two firms (Bowman and Singh 1993; Cascio et al. 1997; Ravenscraft and Scherer 1987). This action generates operational synergies from economies of scale and may have motivated the high premium payment (Capron 1999; O'Shaughnessy and Flanagan 1998; Porter 1987). However, operational synergy is rarely sufficient for the firm to recoup the high costs of the acquisition. Therefore, firms under pressure from shareholders often sell off assets of the acquired firm at lower than true market value and resort to large-scale workforce reduction in the merged entity (Johnson et al. 1993; Nixon et al. 2004; Useem 1993; Zuckerman 2000). These drastic actions can seriously erode the human capital and the knowledge and learning that is essential to capitalize on the complementarity between the two firms (Cording et al. 2008; Vermeulen and Barkema 2001). Thus, the transfer of skills vested in the employees, and which represents the heart of synergy realization, is not materialized. Thus, paying excessive premiums increases the probability that an acquisition will be unsuccessful; even potentially creating a need for divestitures.

Summary of the Research on Acquisition Premiums

Acquisition premiums have been studied by strategy and finance researchers for their influence on various organizational outcomes, including post-acquisition performance. While there are reasons for paying a premium to acquire the shares of a target firm, synergy has been identified as the dominant motive. Synergy is created when the merged firm capitalizes on the complementary resource profiles, and from the elimination of redundant activities of the value chains of the two partners. Agency factors, executive hubris, and competitive factors in the environment, such as multiple bidders, consolidation trends in the industry, and growth opportunities for high technology firms, also result in the payment of high acquisition premiums. A majority of studies reveals a negative relationship between acquisition premium and organizational performance. This is because the size of the premium often places a huge burden on the executives of the acquiring firm to extract the synergies and to recoup the acquisition costs in the merged organization. The negative reaction of the stock market to many acquisition announcements places great pressure on the executives to resort to restructuring. Restructuring following a high-priced acquisition involves large-scale workforce reduction, which results in the loss of valuable human capital. It also leads to divestitures of assets in the merged organization. Therefore, most acquisitions in which high premiums are paid do not create positive value.

DIVESTING ACQUIRED BUSINESSES

Because M&As are not always successful (Hitt et al. 2001b), a large proportion of acquired businesses is later divested (Bergh 1997; Kaplan and Weisbach 1992; Porter 1987; Ravenscraft and Scherer 1991). However, research on divestitures of acquired businesses is limited (Brauer 2006; Moschieri and Mair 2008). It is understandable because "[c]ompanies tend to announce acquisitions and other forms of new entry with a flourish but divestments and shutdowns with a whimper, if at all" (Porter 1987: 47). However, given the high percentage of failure, it is important to develop a better understanding of divesture activities. Divested businesses are purchased by other companies, and thus divestitures are, in part, mirror images of M&As (Brauer 2006; Buchholtz et al. 1999). M&As are important and visible strategic decisions; therefore reversing the decision is influenced by various psychological, organizational, and social factors (Shimizu and Hitt 2004). Thus, understanding divestitures of acquired businesses contributes to the M&A literature and also provides broader insights into research on strategic decision making, organizational change, and escalation of commitment (e.g. Duhaime and Grant 1984; Hayward and Shimizu 2006; Shimizu 2007).

Although divestiture is generally regarded as a sign of a failed acquisition (Kaplan and Weisbach 1992), not all divestitures of acquired businesses indicate failure. For example, some funds buy distressed firms, improve their performance, and sell them at a premium. Divestiture may also be a result of appropriating valuable resources from the target and eliminating the remainder of the assets and/or redundant assets (Capron et al. 2001). Our focus is on divestiture of acquired businesses because of poor performance. Divestitures have been examined under the broad umbrella of restructuring research in relation to proliferation of unrelated diversification and resulting performance problems (Brauer 2006; Hoskisson and Hitt 1994; Johnson 1996). Due to such problems as overpayment, illusionary synergy, and cultural clashes, many acquired businesses are not successful and some are eventually divested (Duhaime and Schwenk 1985; Haspeslagh and Jemison 1991b). For example, Porter (1987) found that firms divested more formerly acquired businesses than they kept. Kaplan and Weisbach (1992) also found that 44% of the acquisitions they studied were divested. Although acquisitions became more strategic in the 1990s and 2000s, we still observe several failures.

A major determinant of divestiture is poor unit performance (Johnson 1996; Ravenscraft and Scherer 1991). Other reasons for divestitures include poor performance of the parent firm (Denis and Kruse 2000; Duhaime and Grant 1984), the desire to change the parent's diversification strategy (Bergh 1997; Hoskisson et al. 1994), and change in the top management team of the parent firm (e.g. a new CEO) and/or its governance structure (Weisbach 1995). Acquisition failures typically result from poor decision making, which can be attributed to agency problems within top management as noted earlier (Hoskisson and Hitt 1994). Therefore, most of the early research on divestitures adopts economic and agency theory perspectives, suggesting that the divestiture decision is to "correct" an earlier mistake based on economic performance and governance actions (Hoskisson et al. 1994). In general, the consequences of divestitures are often positive for both sellers and acquirers of the unit based on the stock market response (Jain 1985; Mulherin and Boone 2000).

However seemingly rational, such a "correction" is often influenced by various non-rational factors. Because divestiture of acquired businesses reverses an earlier strategic decision, managerial attachment and organizational inertia also influence divestiture of acquired businesses (Duhaime and Grant 1984; Shimizu and Hitt 2005). Managers may unconsciously delay response to a poorly performing unit because of the managers' assumption regarding the success of their acquisition strategy (Buchholtz et al. 1999; Duhaime and Schwenk 1985). Delays in response to an underperforming unit can also be a result of an acquired unit becoming institutionalized within the larger organization (Shimizu and Hitt 2005). As a result, poorly performing acquired businesses are more likely to be divested when organizational inertia to maintain the acquisition is low, the business unit is small, parent firms are young and small, parent firms have divestiture experience, and unit performance declines precipitately (Duhaime and Baird 1987; Shimizu and Hitt 2005). The effects of CEO turnover and change of directors can also break cognitive and organizational inertia (e.g. Shimizu and Hitt 2005).

More recent studies extend our knowledge of the effects of non-economic factors on divestiture. For example, Hayward and Shimizu (2006) found that high organizational slack and better parent firm performance strengthen the relationship between poor acquired unit performance and divestiture, contradicting a view that divestitures are intended to obtain cash at a time of low slack or low performance by the parent firms (Hamilton and Chow 1993). Their findings are consistent with a behavioral view suggesting that managers are less committed to poor performing acquisitions when strong firm performance and higher slack absorb or mask the acquisition failure (i.e. divestiture) (cf. Boot 1992; Cyert and March 1963). Shimizu (2007) also applied prospect theory (Kahneman and Tversky 1979), behavioral theory (Cyert and March 1963), and the threat-rigidity thesis (Staw et al. 1981) to the divestiture of acquired businesses and discussed how managers deal with uncertainties in reversing their acquisition decisions. He argued and found that the three different forces implied by the unique theories result in an inverse-U shaped relationship between unit business performance and divestiture and that the relationship is moderated by ambiguity (derived from prospect theory), failure to improve performance and resource availability (derived from prospect theory), and divestiture experience and unit size (derived from the threat-rigidity thesis). Divestitures of formerly acquired businesses provide a rich setting to explore various organizational issues, including uncertainty, commitment, and inertia (Shimizu 2007).

There are at least four potentially valuable future research foci. Although divestitures are typically equated with sell-offs (Ravenscraft and Scherer 1991), divestitures are broader. Brauer (2006) argues that divestitures were often regarded as a simple mirror image of M&As and different types of divestitures, such as spin-offs and split-ups (no external buyers) and equity carve-outs (the sale of the unit to the public via an IPO), are rarely considered. Each of these types of divestitures has different and unique characteristics and thus, factors influencing them can be different. By considering different types of divestitures, we can develop a much richer understanding of the divestiture behaviors. M&A researchers have described acquisition processes (e.g. Haunschild et al. 1994), but research on the divestiture process is rare (Brauer 2006). Moschieri and Mair (2008: 417) recommend that researchers examine "a more comprehensive picture of these complex operations." Examining the divestiture processes will provide important insights. For example, divestiture of an acquired business can involve a political process (Hayward and Shimizu 2006). A rich description of the interactions among top managers and stakeholders can help to open the black box on the upper echelon of organizations. Additionally, most M&A research focuses on acquirers with little attention to sellers. Buchholtz et al. (1999: 633) point out that "we know a lot more about the art of 'buying' than we do about the art of 'selling.'" Recently, Graebner (2009) provided an insightful study on trust in the process of acquisition by showing the asymmetries between buyers and sellers. More research is needed to clarify divestiture and selling processes. Given the inherent difficulties involved in M&As, learning from the failures and utilizing the learning for future deals are important. However, research on these topics is surprisingly limited. Moreover, there is little research on the aftermath of divesting a formerly acquired business. Divestitures of units typically indicate an acquisition error. It is reported that Charles Schwab has been hesitant about acquiring weaker rivals and expanding, because Schwab was traumatized by its early unsuccessful acquisition of SpundView Technology Group (Farzad and Palmeri 2009). Because a small but increasing number of studies are examining learning from mistakes and failures, research on this topic can contribute to our knowledge of divestitures and organizational learning. While there are studies that examine the effects of acquisition on the target unit in terms of executive retention (Cannella and Hambrick 1993), the unit of analysis of most of the research is the employee, not the target unit (e.g. Gopinath and Becker 2000). Little research exists on the target unit in the aftermath of the divestiture (Graebner and Eisenhardt 2004). The poorly performing acquired unit often receives little new investment and may be isolated from other units internally grown. As a result, the resources and capabilities may be deteriorated when it is divested. For example, it is reported that Chrysler lacks key engineering functions because they were outsourced under Daimler (Welch 2007). Thus, the price may correctly reflect the weak capabilities of the divested unit. The inherent difficulties involved in M&As increase the probability of divestiture. There is much to learn from divestitures, particularly divestitures of formerly acquired businesses. Of course, the potentially weakened state of many divested units heightens the importance of learning from and building capabilities with acquisitions.

Summary of Research on Divesting Acquired Businesses

As M&As become more popular, both domestically and internationally, the inherent difficulties involved in M&As increase the number of divestitures. Given that such divestitures are strongly influenced by the earlier acquisition decisions, understanding divestitures of acquired businesses contributes to the M&A literature and also provides broader insights into research on strategic decision making, organizational change, and escalation of commitment. Recent studies found that non-rational, behavioral factors had important influences on the divestiture decisions. More studies are needed and specific areas abundant in future research potential include examining different types of divestitures, careful exploration of divestiture processes, understanding the aftermath of divestitures (selling firms), and understanding the outcomes for acquired firms that were later divested.

BUILDING CAPABILITIES WITH ACQUISITIONS

The preceding sections attest to the breadth and depth of our current understanding of the key success factors in M&A. However, despite this sizable body of theoretical insights, many firms seem unable to implement them effectively in practice. After all, evidence suggests that the fate of the average acquirer has improved little over time (see King et al. 2004). It is difficult because the required knowledge and skills are largely tacit. Therefore, learning from prior experience may be crucial to enhance the performance of acquisitions (Barkema and Schijven 2008a).

To be sure, this learning from prior experience by the acquiring firm is different from learning from the focal deal. The next section deals with how the acquirer can learn from the resources and capabilities of its focal acquisition (target-specific learning). In the present section, we focus on how lessons learned from previous acquisitions can help the acquirer make additional acquisitions effectively.

At first sight, the remarkable success of a handful of experienced acquirers such as Cisco Systems (Paulson 2001) and General Electric (Ashkenas et al. 1998)—suggests that acquisition performance might follow a conventional learning curve (Arrow 1962). However, the phenomenon is considerably more complex; unlike the evidence of learning curves in operating settings (see Yelle 1979), research on learning in *strategic* settings has produced inconsistent results. With respect to acquisitions, some scholars have found a positive relationship between experience and performance (Barkema et al. 1996; Barkema and Schijven 2008b; Bruton et al. 1994; Fowler and Schmidt 1989; Power 1982), whereas others have found insignificant (Baum and Ginsberg 1997; Bruton et al. 1994; Hayward 2002; Kroll et al. 1997; Lubatkin 1982; Newbould et al. 1976; Wright et al. 2002; Zollo and Leshchinskii 2004; Zollo and Singh 2004) or U-shaped relationships (Haleblian and Finkelstein 1999; Porrini 2004; Zollo and Reuer 2010).

These inconsistencies in the performance implications of prior acquisition experience suggest that important contingencies are at play, primarily because of the dissimilarities between acquisitions (see Finkelstein and Haleblian 2002; Haleblian and Finkelstein 1999). The acquisition process consists of numerous interdependent sub-activities—such as due diligence, valuation, negotiation, financing, and integration—each of which often must be customized to the specific deal (Haspeslagh and Jemison 1991b; Hitt et al. 2001b). As a result of this multidimensional heterogeneity across acquisitions (Zollo and Singh 2004), acquirers face high causal ambiguity (Lippman and Rumelt 1982), encountering difficulty disentangling "causal relationships between the decisions or actions taken and the performance outcomes obtained" (Zollo and Winter 2002: 348). This lack of insight into underlying causal patterns impedes effective learning because routines developed on the basis of prior experience are not readily generalizable across acquisitions.

Scholarly inquiry into organizational learning in the context of acquisitions can be traced back to the late 1970s (see Newbould et al. 1976). However, whereas early work was largely atheoretical, empirically driven, and almost metaphorical, based on the traditional learning curve perspective (see Arrow 1962; Yelle 1979), three distinct and valuable research streams have developed since the mid-1990s. Collectively, these three streams of work are at the forefront of a more mature theory of organizational learning in strategic settings. Below, we briefly discuss the most important developments in each of these research areas.

Negative Experience Transfer

One implicit assumption of early work on organizational learning was that experience is inherently positive. Haleblian and Finkelstein (1999) made a seminal contribution by breaking with this simplistic assumption. Drawing on experience transfer theory from cognitive psychology (Cormier and Hagman 1987; Ellis 1965), they argued that transferring acquisition routines from one industry to another results in transferring old lessons to new settings where they do not apply. The authors hypothesized and found that a firm's second acquisition will, therefore, typically underperform its first. Although this negative trend persists following the second acquisition, the firm ultimately develops the expertise needed to identify underlying dissimilarities across acquisitions, thus enabling it to generalize prior experience only when it is applicable (see Finkelstein and Haleblian 2002).

Recent research built on this insight, suggesting that the performance of an acquisition is affected by the heterogeneity of the firm's accumulated acquisition experience. Hayward (2002) found that, although heterogeneous experience can complicate learning, experiences that are too homogeneous limit exploration and, thus, may lead to a competency trap for the acquirer. This result suggests that the performance of the focal acquisition tends to benefit from acquisition experience that is neither too heterogeneous nor too homogeneous. Alternatively, Bingham and Eisenhardt (2007) find that learning is more about developing expertise than refining routines, suggesting that experience heterogeneity is beneficial to learning.

Another research stream focuses on experience spillovers across, rather than within, distinct corporate development activities. For example, Porrini (2004) finds a U-shaped relationship between alliance experience and acquisition performance, similar to Haleblian and Finkelstein's (1999) findings on acquisition experience. Similarly, in the international business literature, Nadolska and Barkema (2007) uncover a U-shaped relationship between international joint venture experience and the longevity of international acquisitions. Finally, building on experience transfer theory to offer a more nuanced view, Zollo and Reuer (2010) argue and find that alliance experience is beneficial only if the focal acquisition requires little integration because alliances teach acquirers little about integration.

Overall, this stream of research shows that acquisition experience is not a panacea, but can actually hurt the acquirer's performance as well. As such, it has substantially deepened our insight into the mechanisms underlying the organizational learning process.

Deliberate Learning Mechanisms

Another rapidly growing research stream pursues a better understanding of organizational learning by relaxing a second implicit assumption of the traditional learning curve that experience automatically implies learning. Some of the prior research shows that high levels of heterogeneity in acquisition experience may be overwhelming for boundedly rational actors due to its causal ambiguity. As such, there is an emerging body of research on deliberate learning mechanisms, to explain how firms can learn from heterogeneous experience. The rationale is that firms need to move beyond "semi-automatic" experience accumulation to deliberate learning mechanisms.

Haleblian, Kim, and Rajagopalan (2006) move beyond the traditional notion of routine-based, semi-automatic learning by showing that learning can be enhanced through active evaluation of performance feedback about recent acquisitions. Hence, strong performance reinforces the positive effect of acquisition experience and poor performance reduces it. Strong performance strengthens the firm's belief that it has effective routines, while poor performance leads to reappraisal. As such, performance represents a key mechanism through which routines are refined or discarded.

Hébert, Very, and Beamish (2005) argue that experience is insufficient for acquisition capability development, because the lessons learned may not be available to organization members who need them. They propose that expatriates play a central role in transferring the experience from the acquiring firm to the acquired unit. Examining cross-border acquisitions, they find that general acquisition experience, industry experience, host-country experience, industry acquisition experience, or local acquisition experience do not have independent effects on acquisition longevity. Significant benefits are only found for some of these experience types with expatriates in the focal unit. Apparently, experience only results in learning if there are mechanisms in place to transfer it to appropriate places in the firm.

Zollo and Winter (2002) argue that infrequently performed tasks with high levels of heterogeneity and causal ambiguity require learning mechanisms that are "aimed at uncovering the linkages between actions and performance outcomes" (Zollo and Winter 2002: 342), such as experience articulation and codification. Zollo and Singh (2004) apply this argument and demonstrate an insignificant effect of acquisition experience on performance, but a significant positive effect of knowledge codification tools, such as manuals and checklists, for due diligence and integration. This positive effect increases with the level of acquisition integration, suggesting that the benefits of deliberate learning mechanisms increase with the complexity of the task and the level of causal ambiguity.

Thus, research strongly suggests that experience accumulation is a necessary, but insufficient, condition for successful acquisition capability development. Deliberate organizational learning mechanisms are crucial in dealing with the high levels of complexity and causal ambiguity that firms encounter in acquisitions.

Learning from Others

Some researchers have questioned a third assumption with the traditional learning curve, namely that firms only learn from their own experience. They posit that firms may also learn from other firms, based on sociological theory of imitation (DiMaggio and Powell 1983) and psychological theory of vicarious learning (Bandura 1977). Vicarious learning allows a firm to explore a variety of ways of performing tasks without incurring the costs and risks that such experimentation entails (Miner and Haunschild 1995). In other words, it enables a firm to engage in "exploratory learning" (March 1991), even though each of the firms from which it learns may only be "exploiting" their experiences within their own domains.

A substantial body of evidence suggests that imitation is a common practice in the context of acquisitions. Haunschild (1993) finds that firms imitate the acquisition behavior of other firms to which they are tied through board interlocks, at least for horizontal acquisitions. She and her co-authors also find (1) that firms rely on their interlock partners for information on how much to pay for targets, especially when it is difficult to determine their value (Haunschild 1994), (2) that they rely more on interlock partners which are similar to them and less so if there are alternative information sources (Haunschild and Beckman 1998), and (3) that they decide which investment bank to hire based on how often others have used that bank (frequency-based imitation), how many large and successful firms have used it (trait-based imitation), and size of the average premium that firms using that bank have paid (outcome-based imitation) (Haunschild and Miner 1997). Interestingly, Westphal, Seidel, and Stewart (2001) observe that, apart from imitating their interlock partners' acquisition behavior, firms also imitate the imitative behavior of interlock partners, which they label "second-order imitation."

Focusing on the imitation of competitors' acquisition behavior rather than that of interlock partners, Baum, Li, and Usher (2000) show that firms tend to acquire targets near those of competitors' recent acquisitions. Furthermore, Yang and Hyland (2006) find that firms in the financial services industry are more likely to engage in unrelated, rather than related, acquisitions if their competitors undertake more unrelated acquisitions.

In contrast to the aforementioned studies, several researchers have focused more on actual vicarious learning rather than imitation. For instance, Beckman and Haunschild (2002) show that firms can learn to acquire more successfully by tapping into the experience of their interlock partners. Specifically, they find that this beneficial learning is strongest if the experience of the focal firm's partners is highly heterogeneous. Furthermore, Shaver, Mitchell, and Yeung (1997), focusing on foreign direct investment (including acquisitions), find that the longevity of such investments undertaken by foreign firms, with experience in the US but no target industry experience, benefits from the experiences of prior foreign entrants, suggesting that vicarious learning occurs.

Summary of Research on Building Capabilities through Acquisitions

Given the high failure rate of acquisitions, it seems crucial for acquirers to learn from their prior experience with acquisitions in order to increase the likelihood of success in future acquisitions that they make. However, early work on the performance effects of prior acquisition experience produced highly inconsistent findings. In reaction to this mixed evidence, three research streams have developed since the mid-1990s that, collectively, are at the forefront of a more mature theory of organizational learning in the context of acquisitions and other strategic moves. These streams of work focus on negative experience transfer, deliberate learning mechanisms, and learning from others. Learning new knowledge helps the firm to build capabilities to make acquisitions and manage them in ways that create value. In sum, there is evidence that firms imitate the acquisition behavior of others and that they commonly rely on vicarious learning to enhance the performance of their own acquisitions. Although such learning can be beneficial, direct learning for acquired firms can be used to build capabilities, which is discussed next.

TECHNOLOGICAL LEARNING IN ACQUISITIONS

Rapid technological change and increasing knowledge intensity have made firm innovation an important source of value creation in many industries. The increasing scope of knowledge needed to remain competitive has made M&As a prominent strategy for acquiring new knowledge and capabilities (Makri et al. 2010; Uhlenbruck et al. 2006). Acquisitions of small technology firms, in particular, are an important source of innovation for established firms in high technology industries (McEvily et al. 2004). However, while acquisitions can be a source of external innovation, research has shown that acquisitions can also have a negative effect on both R&D expenditures and patent productivity (Hitt et al. 1991, 1996). Some suggest that firms making acquisitions introduce fewer new products into the marketplace (Hitt et al. 1990) and also that their key inventors either leave the acquired firm after the acquisition or significantly reduce their patenting performance (Ernst and Vitt 2000).

One possible explanation is that the acquisition process often absorbs significant amounts of managerial time and energy, thereby diverting managerial attention from other important activities such as innovation (Haspeslagh and Jemison 1991a; Hitt et al. 1996). Especially if the acquired firm's knowledge base is large in comparison to the acquiring firm's knowledge base, "fairly major changes would have to be made in the acquiring firm leading to a significant disruption of existing processes" to absorb and use this knowledge (Ahuja and Katila 2001: 201). The change processes involved in integrating the target firm with the acquirer may also disturb the routine functioning of the target firm, thus endangering the chances of bringing its products speedily to market. Further, firms following an active acquisition strategy often need substantial resources to complete their acquisitions and thus resort to the use of debt. Doing so creates debt costs that must be traded off against the use of these resources for other purposes such as funding new R&D projects (Hitt et al. 1996). Acquisitions can cause a culture shock or lead to dissatisfaction by key inventors due to modifications in the work environment. Talented engineers are often attracted to smaller organizations because of their ability to offer strong incentives. Such engineers are likely to leave before their firm has been fully integrated into the acquirer, which would critically undermine the target firm's product development capacity (Zenger 1994). As a result, key R&D personnel may decide to leave the firm, causing severe and costly technological gaps (Ernst and Vitt 2000).

The question then becomes how acquiring firms can reap the intended benefits of their acquisitions and successfully complement their internal innovation efforts. The answer to this has two components, one relating to the pre-acquisition target-selection phase and the other relating to the post-acquisition integration phase. The focus of this section is the former, examining how the characteristics of the target and acquirer firms affect the types of innovation outcomes. Specifically, we explore how the acquirer's and target's degree of knowledge relatedness affect innovation outcomes post-M&A.

Knowledge Relatedness and Innovation Outcomes in M&As

For firms that rely on continuous innovations as a source of competitive advantage, knowledge synergies have become increasingly critical. Research on high technology M&As has identified the relatedness of the buyer's and the target's technological knowledge as an important predictor of post-merger innovation performance (Cloodt et al. 2006; Cassiman et al. 2005; Hagedoorn and Duysters 2002). The positive effect on innovation is, in part, based on absorptive capacity; the more similar the two firms' technological knowledge, the more quickly the acquired firm's knowledge can be assimilated and commercially exploited (Cohen and Levinthal 1990; Lane and Lubatkin 1998). However, too much similarity reduces the acquirer's opportunities for learning (Hitt et al. 1996). For example, Ahuja and Katila (2001) examined the impact of technological acquisitions on the subsequent innovation performance in the chemicals industry and found that the relatedness of the acquiring and target firm knowledge bases has a curvi-linear effect on innovation output. Similarly, Cloodt et al. (2006), found an inverted U-shaped relationship between technological relatedness and post-merger innovation performance in a study of several high technology industries. Innovation performance (innovation quantity) was lowest for M&As when the firms were in highly similar or largely unrelated technology areas and highest when there was a moderate degree of overlap. Further, Cassiman et al.'s (2005) in-depth study of 31 high technology M&As found that firms are more likely to reduce R&D effort, shorten the time horizon of projects, and emphasize development over research when they acquire targets in similar technology areas than when they acquire targets in complementary areas. In short, not only do M&As integrating highly similar technologies narrow the range of potential learning, they also reduce the incentives to explore the divergent research opportunities available. The M&As that most improve innovation performance are those in which the technological knowledge is similar enough to facilitate learning, but different enough to provide both new opportunities and the incentives to explore them.

Makri et al. (2010) disentangle knowledge relatedness into science and technology and consider knowledge complementarities as well as similarities. They suggest that knowledge heterogeneity in terms of type (science, technology) and in terms of combination potential (complementarity) affects the exploration and exploitation processes and consequently the innovation outcomes achieved. The authors argue that similarities and complementarities in science and technology can affect firms' innovative outcomes in two ways. First, they can influence the maximum potential novelty of innovations by affecting either core design concepts or linkages between components. Second, they can influence the ease and speed of innovation. First, we examine the role of science and technology in innovation.

The Role of Science and Technology in Innovation

Despite the tendency to treat technology and science interchangeably, "technology is not science—engineers are not scientists" (Allen 1984: p.307). Technology is theoretical and practical knowledge, skills, and artifacts that can be used to develop products and services. A firm's *technology domain* is the set of applied technological problems that the firm has experience in solving. It is about exploitation, adapting, and combining what is known to respond to pressures from markets for products and services (Clark 1987; Rip 1992; Balmer and Sharp 1993). Alternatively, science is knowledge about the general characteristics, antecedents, and relationships of natural, social, and technological phenomena that are openly shared. A firm's *science domain* is the set of scientific research topics of which it has demonstrated some understanding, typically via employee publications (Kuhn 1970; Latour 1987; Tushman and Rosenkopf 1992). These differences between science and technology suggest that technological knowledge facilitates an incremental recombination of components (Fleming and Sorenson 2004), leading to incremental or architectural innovations (Henderson and Clark 1990). Scientific knowledge, on the other hand, can play an *enabling* role by stimulating a better understanding of the problem at hand, which suggests that science-based innovations could overturn core design concepts underlying existing technology and lead to radical innovations (Henderson and Clark 1990). Simply put, technology facilitates an *exploitative* recombination process most likely leading to incremental innovations, and science enables an *exploratory* process most likely leading to radical innovations.

Science and Technology Relatedness and Innovation Outcomes in M&As

When two firms have very similar science and technology domains, the most novel innovations possible are incremental because the lack of new scientific knowledge encourages incrementally moving to adjacent points on the technological landscape (Cyert and March 1963). Knowledge similarities (technology similarity in particular) facilitate the exchange and combination of existing knowledge (Nonaka et al. 1996) and encourage exploitation of what is known. Thus, knowledge similarity facilitates innovation productivity because firms need less time and effort to integrate their R&D activities. However, while knowledge similarity encourages exploitation of what is known, it is less likely to result in novel recombinations. In fact, the path dependency created by strong similarity reduces the probability of developing radical innovations because there is a limit to the number of new recombinations that can be created using the same set of knowledge elements. Additionally, science similarity suggests that the two firms' scientists have similar understandings of how technologies work and thereby search for new solutions in the "neighborhood" of old or existing solutions. Such knowledge redundancy diminishes the opportunities for creating radically new knowledge and leading to novel innovation.

Alternatively, when two firms have high complementarity in both their science and technology domains, new technologies may be discovered, leading to more radical innovations (Henderson and Clark 1990). In other words, while knowledge similarities (technology similarities in particular) facilitate a process of exploitation by refining and extending existing competencies and technologies, knowledge complementarities (science complementarities in particular) facilitate a process of exploration by experimenting with new competencies and technologies (March 1991). Research in organizational learning suggests that the potential for new innovations increases when different knowledge bases are combined (Tushman and Rosenkopf 1992), hence the potential for new configurations increases when knowledge bases are complementary. Exploring diverse realms of knowledge can increase the probability that a radically different approach to problem solving emerges (Fiol and Lyles 1985; Levinthal and March 1993) and exposure to a new set of routines, new modes of reasoning, and challenges to existing cause-effect understandings help firms discover novel solutions to its problems. In Ahuja and Lampert's words, "… the irritant of new, imperfectly understood streams of knowledge can foster the pearls of insight" (2001: 527). If the acquirer has to assimilate and integrate a complementary science knowledge base in addition to a complementary technology knowledge base, such a combination can have an increasingly positive effect on invention novelty (Hall et al. 2001; DeCarolis and Deeds 1999; Deng et al. 2001; Rosenkopf and Nerkar 2001). However, integrating complementary technology and complementary science is more time consuming and difficult than integrating similar knowledge domains because combining complementary knowledge requires integrating related but dissimilar sets of technological problems and scientific patterns. Assimilating and integrating a complementary science knowledge base and a complementary technology knowledge base could have a negative effect on innovation productivity because they require significant managerial attention (Haspeslagh and Jemison 1991a).

Implications for Management Practice

A major challenge for managers and boards of directors is managing the breadth and depth of the firm's own scientific and technological knowledge to support its short- and long-term strategic needs (Norling et al. 2000). Few firms can survive long term if they focus exclusively on incremental innovation. However, in most companies, there are strong institutional and individual biases towards incremental innovations (Hoskisson et al. 2002). At the other extreme, firms that focus exclusively on seeking radical innovations face great uncertainty, and must often wait years to learn whether their efforts will pay off. Corporate R&D executives seeking to use acquisitions to strengthen their firm's innovation pipeline must be clear as to the type of innovations they desire. If the firm needs to quickly reinforce its existing product market positions, targets with relatively similar science and technology are likely to be the most useful. If the firm needs to improve or redefine its existing products and services, targets with similar technology and complementary science can help them accomplish that over the near to medium term. If the firm is seeking to reinvent itself, reinvent its industry, or enter a new industry as a disruptive innovator, it should select targets with complementary science and technology, but must be willing to invest the time and effort needed to make such collaborations successful.

The differences in the amount of time needed to realize innovations from different combinations of similarity and complementarity in science and technology suggest that the evaluation criteria for M&As, and the incentives for R&D managers, should vary according to the similarity or complementarity of the science and technology involved. Acquisitions involving highly complementary knowledge should be evaluated based on longer time frames and more subjective criteria, because those types of interactions take longer to come to fruition. The R&D managers involved in those M&As should have long-term incentives, perhaps tied to the innovations or patents produced, or changes in the firm's market value. Shorter time frames and more objective financial criteria reinforce the short-term, incremental innovation bias and make it difficult to realize the potential benefits of complementary science and technology of other firms.

Summary of Research on Technological Learning from Acquisitions

Recent studies on high technology M&As suggest that the knowledge relatedness of the buyer and target firms is an important antecedent to post-merger innovation performance. The M&As that most improve innovation performance are those where scientific and technological knowledge is similar enough to facilitate learning but different enough to provide both businesses with new learning opportunities. More specifically, if the acquirer has to assimilate and integrate complementary science knowledge in addition to complementary technology knowledge, such a combination is likely to have a positive effect on invention novelty, but a negative effect on innovation productivity. When firms are able to enhance their innovation (amount and novelty) through an acquisition, it increases the probability that the acquisition will create positive value for the firm.

Gaining complementary knowledge in M&As is not limited to domestic acquisitions. Cross-border M&As have become increasingly common not only for the purpose of taking advantage of economies of scale and scope, but also for gaining access to complementary technological and science knowledge.

MAKING CROSS-BORDER MERGERS
AND ACQUISITIONS

Cross-border M&As are an increasingly common strategy adopted by firms to create value in the fiercely competitive global market. In the most recent M&A wave, M&As occur predominantly across borders (Shimizu et al. 2004). Firms increasingly acquire targets in foreign countries to increase market power, overcome market entry barriers, enter new markets, reduce competition, change the competitive landscape, increase efficiency, access new and diversified technologies and knowledge, and create new knowledge, products, and services (Brakman et al. 2008; Hitt et al. 2001b). Cross-border M&A has received much scholarly attention in recent years (e.g. Hitt et al., 2001a, 2001b). Prior research has primarily examined cross-border M&As as a foreign market entry mode and cross-border M&A performance from several theoretical perspectives: transaction cost economics (TCE), ownership-location-internationalization (OLI) framework, resource-based view (resource management), institutional theory, learning theory, and the synergy perspective (Barney 1991; Dunning 1993; Hitt et al. 2000; North 1990; Scott 2001; Sirmon et al. 2007; Vermeulen and Barkema 2001; Williamson 1975).

Cross-Border M&A as an Entry Mode

Most prior research investigated factors influencing firms' choice of cross-border M&As to enter foreign markets rather than an international joint venture (IJV), international alliance, Greenfield venture, or exporting (Hitt et al. 2000, 2004, 2006; Isobe et al. 2000; Zahra et al. 2000). According to TCE, cross-border M&A allows foreign acquirers to internalize specific assets (e.g. patents, advanced technologies) and thus, helps protect acquirers' intellectual property rights (Barkema and Vermeulen 1998; Brouthers and Brouthers 2000; Hitt et al. 2004; Williamson 1975). Cross-border M&As can decrease transaction costs associated with knowledge expropriation by local firms (Williamson 1975). Cross-border M&A also affords more control to acquirers than IJVs and international alliances.

Researchers have suggested that acquirers generally lack knowledge about host-country culture, regulations, and business norms, which poses unique challenges for them when integrating targets and creating value from cross-border M&As (Eden and Miller 2004). Acquirers encounter a liability of foreignness (LOF) (Eden and Miller 2004). Using a learning theory perspective, Nadolska and Barkema (2007) found that firms experienced in cross-border M&As are more likely to engage in cross-border M&As, suggesting that learning from previous cross-border M&As could help decrease LOF.

Prior research has found that cultural distance affects firms' entry mode choice, though findings are mixed (Brouthers and Brouthers 2000; Hennart and Reddy 1997; Tihanyi et al. 2005). Recently scholars have used institutional theory to investigate how country institutions (e.g. host-country institutions, institutional distance between home and host countries) affect firms' choice of foreign market entry mode (Brouthers 2002; Eden and Miller 2004; Habib and Zurawicki 2002; Uhlenbruck et al. 2006; Xu and Shenkar 2002). Researchers found that the level of corruption in the host country influences firms to choose cross-border M&As as their entry mode (Habib and Zurawicki 2002; Uhlenbruck et al. 2006). Institutional scholars also suggested that regulatory, normative, and cognitive institutional distance affects firms' choice of foreign market entry mode (Eden and Miller 2004; Xu and Shenkar 2002).

Building on the resource-based view and resource management, cross-border M&As facilitate firms' entry into foreign countries to obtain target firms' resources, including physical facilities, technology, human capital, and established relationships with suppliers, distributors, and government officials (Barney 1991; Shimizu et al. 2004; Sirmon et al. 2007). Cross-border M&As could further act as "an admission ticket" for acquirers to navigate in host countries, exploiting local business opportunities and discovering potential yet unknown resources and services that could add new value to acquirers (Barney 1991; Sirmon et al. 2007; Smit 2001).

Cross-Border M&A Performance

Researchers have primarily examined cross-border acquirers' short-term abnormal returns as a performance measure (Amihud et al. 2001; Berger et al. 2000; Bruner 2004; Correa 2008; Cybo-Ottone and Murgia 2000; Goergen and Renneboog 2004; Harris and Ravenscraft 1991; Moeller and Schlingemann 2005; Seth et al. 2002; Shimizu et al. 2004). Some finance researchers have recently focused on acquirers' long-term abnormal return (e.g. 36 months) after the date of a cross-border M&A announcement (Chakrabarti et al. 2009; Mitchell and Stafford 2000). Yet, the results provide no definitive conclusions. For example, Seth et al. (2002) found that acquirers are more likely to create value by obtaining resources from foreign targets, and yet, less likely to create value due to managers' actions to reduce their job risk (i.e. managerialism). Further, King et al.'s (2004) meta-analysis showed that the commonly examined variables, such as acquirers' M&A experience, and resource complementarities between the acquirer and the target, have little effect on M&A value creation.

Cross-border M&As represent a strong commitment and high expectation to create value from acquiring foreign targets in the long term. Value creation is more based on firms' resources and capabilities to compete successfully in the dynamic global market. As discussed earlier, cross-border M&As expand acquirers' knowledge base, including new technology, and various ways of managing resources. Vermeulen and Barkema (2001) found a positive relationship between the number of the firm's preceding international acquisitions in related domains and the survival rate of subsidiaries, suggesting that cross-border M&As broaden a firm's knowledge base, decrease inertia, and enhance the viability of its later ventures. So, cross-border M&A could be an important strategy for firms to continuously create value and compete in the fiercely competitive global market (Hitt et al. 2001a; Vermeulen and Barkema 2001).

A few exceptions that examined cross-border M&As' long-term performance include Uhlenbruck and DeCastro (2000) and Zhu et al. (2010). Uhlenbruck and DeCastro (2000) found that acquirers are likely to create value by acquiring targets in countries with lower risks. Building on institutional theory, Zhu et al. (2010) extended the synergy perspective prevailing in M&A research to the country level, suggesting that acquirers need to identify the right host country in which an appropriate target with potential synergy hopefully exists. Zhu et al. (2010) demonstrated that host-country institutional environments, including regulatory, economic, physical, and political institutions, affect cross-border M&A performance (Holmes et al. 2010).

Other Cross-Border M&A Research

Researchers have investigated other important topics related to cross-border M&As, such as the premiums that acquirers pay for foreign targets (Krishnan et al. 2007; Weitzel and Berns 2006), and the transfer of organizational practices between acquirers and foreign targets (Berger et al. 2004). Krishnan et al. (2007) suggested that acquirers are likely to pay too high premiums for foreign targets than domestic ones because acquirers are constrained by large information asymmetries and thus, face the risk of adverse selection in identifying the right foreign target. Weitzel and Berns (2006) examined 4979 cross-border and domestic takeovers to test the relationship between host-country corruption and premiums paid for targets. Interestingly, they found that host-country corruption is negatively related to target premiums, after controlling for other governance-related factors such as political stability, legal systems, and financial disclosure standards.

Building upon institutional theory, researchers have suggested that acquirers transfer their organizational practices to foreign targets to facilitate the integration between acquirers and their foreign targets (Kostova and Zaheer 1999). Berger et al. (2004) found that acquirers from highly developed economies are more likely to export financial institution management to foreign targets.

Researchers have also investigated diverse cross-border M&A strategies (e.g. Klaus and Tran 2006; Reuer 2001). For example, Klaus and Tran (2006) identified three cross-border M&A strategies, including staged, multiple, and indirect cross-border M&As. A staged cross-border M&A refers to partial acquisitions in which the foreign acquirers have the option to acquire full control later; multiple cross-border M&As suggest that each acquisition is only a small building block in foreign countries; and an indirect cross-border M&A represents a post-acquisition investment that exceeds the investment in the original one (Klaus and Tran 2006). Reuer (2001) found that firms' abnormal returns from IJV partner buyouts are positively related to the firms' R&D intensity. Additionally, Krug and Nigh (2001) suggested that executives have different perspectives on cross-border M&As from domestic ones regarding (1) organizational cultural differences between acquirer and the target; (2) system changes in the target; (3) acquisition negotiations; and (4) executives staying or leaving after the acquisition.

Future Research

While prior research has advanced our understanding of cross-border M&A as an important entry mode, more fruitful future research is needed on their performance outcomes.

Emerging economy firms from Asia, Latin America, Eastern Europe, and the Middle East have become active in acquiring foreign firms in recent years (*The World Investment Report* 2006). For example, the China Merger & Acquisition Annual Report (2007) showed that the transaction value of 63 cross-border M&As was about US$18.67 billion—an increase of 105.4% from 2006. The number of deals in 2007 increased 117.6%. Prior cross-border M&A research has focused on acquirers from developed countries, as they dominated cross-border M&A transactions in the last century. Future research is needed to examine cross-border M&As by acquirers from less developed countries. Major research questions include: (1) Are previous theoretical models and findings applicable to emerging economy acquirers? (2) If not, what causes these differences? What new theoretical models could provide insights about emerging economy firms' acquiring foreign targets?

Second, integration between acquirers and targets is vital to synergy creation and thus, cross-border M&A value creation (Hitt et al. 2001a, 2001b). Yet, it is a challenging process (Cording et al. 2008), involving merging of operations, technology, resources, decision making, organizational culture, national culture, and norms, often requiring a long period of time (Barkema and Schijven 2008a). Prior research has demonstrated the effects of cultural distance on the integration between acquirers and foreign targets (Chakrabarti et al. 2009; Stahl and Voigt 2008; Teerikangas and Véry 2006). More research is needed on how integration can be effectively achieved in cross-border M&As. Third, prior research established that firm and country-level factors influence cross-border M&A performance (King et al. 2004; Seth et al. 2002; Zhu et al. 2010). Based on institutional theory, country-level factors (institutions) affect their embedded firms' behavior (North 1990; Scott 2001). Certainly host (home) country institutions affect targets' (acquirers') behavior, which affects cross-border M&A performance. Further, home and host-country institutions influence the integration between the acquirer and the target, such as transferring resources from the acquirer/target to the target/acquirer, and the percentage of the target's top managers in the combined firms' top management team (Stahl et al. 2010). Yet, we lack understanding of the mechanisms through which country-level factors (institutions) affect firm behavior and the integration between acquirers and foreign targets. Future research should examine acquirers' due diligence, the role of investment banks, and selection of financing in cross-border M&As (Hitt et al. 2001a).

Summary of Research on Cross-Border Acquisitions

Cross-border M&As have become an increasingly important strategy employed by firms to enhance their ability to compete in globally competitive markets and to create value. In fact, acquisitions used to enter international markets have been on the increase in recent years. In so doing, the foreign firm gains an immediate foothold in the market entered and acquires the knowledge of how to operate there effectively. Yet, creating value with cross-border acquisitions is highly challenging. The research suggests that firms often gain benefits from a cross-border acquisition, but also experience more serious problems that are difficult to resolve. Therefore, creating value in these cases is difficult. The research suggests that acquiring firms are more likely to create value when they enter countries with more favorable institutional environments and thereby, experience lower risks. Additionally, because of larger information asymmetries, firms are more likely to pay too high a premium in making cross-border acquisitions, which lowers the probability of creating value as discussed earlier, herein. More research is needed, especially in understanding the effects of institutional distance on value creation in cross-border acquisitions and on such acquisitions made by emerging market firms.

Thus, research has advanced our understanding of cross-border M&A from multiple theoretical perspectives. More research is needed to provide insights on cross-border M&As to advance our understanding, and improve their value creation, particularly in this changing global landscape.

CONCLUSIONS

M&As have become a strategy used by many companies across the globe. And, while they can be successful, many of them create little or no value. Prior research suggests that firms that use acquisitions to diversify, especially into unrelated businesses and those distant from their core business, are unlikely to create value. But, the mixed results of research may also suggest that the relationship is more complex (i.e. nonlinear). Research also suggests that the difference in size between the acquiring and target firms influences value creation. When the target firm is much smaller than the acquiring firm, it is unlikely to affect value creation. However, as the difference narrows, the potential influence on value creation grows, although, when the two firms are of similar size, integration often is a problem leading to value loss rather than creation. M&A experience can lead to capabilities to make effective M&As if the acquiring firm's managers learn from their acquisitions. Care must be taken, however, because they can attribute the positive and negative outcomes from prior M&As to the wrong factors, thereby increasing the likelihood of value disintegration instead of value creation.

The research suggests that when acquiring firms pay cash, they are more likely to create value from the acquisition than if they use stock. They are more likely to use stock to pay for acquisition when their own firm is undervalued. However, the firm may have a low value because of poor management, suggesting that they may be unable to manage the merged firm to create value. High performance by the acquiring firm in prior years has been shown as a positive predictor of value creation in acquisitions. Prior high performance likely suggests good management, thus predicting that managers are more likely to make and implement (i.e. integrate the two businesses) acquisitions that create value.

The specific research examined herein suggests that firms paying high premiums have a low probability of creating value in the acquisition because they are unlikely to create enough synergy to recoup the premium paid. These problems are often exacerbated by actions taken by executives when they realize that inadequate returns are likely to be created. In these cases, they sometimes engage in excessive downsizing and thereby, lose valuable human capital. Although this action creates short-term cost savings, it also weakens the firm's capabilities, harming its potential to achieve longer-term returns. And, when these actions fail, executives often delay divesting the poorly performing business and may even escalate their commitment to it. There are several reasons for this, including escalation of commitment to the failed decision. Firms can learn from acquisitions if they select their targets carefully and use processes that enhance knowledge creation from the merged firm. In particular, they are most likely to enhance their innovation if they acquire firms with complementary science and technological knowledge.

Finally, the global competitive landscape that has developed over the last two decades has motivated and facilitated an increasing number of cross-border acquisitions. It is exceedingly complex and challenging to create the value desired from such acquisitions. Differences in culture and in formal institutional environments only enhance the difficulties. Yet, they also pose significant opportunities because of access to new markets and valuable resources. They must be very careful in selecting targets, especially because of higher information asymmetry and they have to integrate the newly acquired firm quickly and effectively in order to enjoy the potential advantages the acquired firm affords.

All of the research reviewed herein suggests that value creation in M&As is possible, but does not occur often. The most critical element here is highly knowledgeable managers who are intent on creating value. They must avoid the common problems (e.g. hubris and paying too high premiums) and overcome the significant challenges that M&As present. Therefore, M&As are likely to create value only when they are made by highly capable managers who avoid psychological biases and who have developed acquisition capabilities through learning from previous M&As. They carefully select targets to ensure complementary resources and capabilities and integrate the two businesses in ways that enhance the synergy between them.

We conclude that, since M&As have become increasingly common because of their importance in the global competitive landscape, more research is needed. More M&A-based research on premiums, divestitures, learning, capability development, innovation, and cross-border strategies could inform theory, empirical work, and practice. Thus, scholars interested in M&As have significant opportunities to make important contributions to our knowledge in these areas.

APPENDIX 4.1: EMPIRICAL RESEARCH ON M&A PERFORMANCE, 1983–2003

Agrawal, A., Jaffe, J. F., & Mandelker, G. N. (1992). "The Post-merger Performance of Acquiring Firms: A Re-Examination of an Anomaly." *Journal of Finance*, 47: 1605–21.

Ahuja, G., & Katila, R. (2001). "Technological Acquisitions and the Innovation Performance of Acquiring Firms: A Longitudinal Study." *Strategic Management Journal*, 22: 197–220.

Anand, J., & Delios, A. (2002). "Absolute and Relative Resources as Determinants of International Acquisitions." *Strategic Management Journal*, 23: 119–34.

—— & Singh, H. (1997). "Asset Redeployment, Acquisitions and Corporate Strategy in Declining Industries." *Strategic Management Journal*, 18: 99–118.

Bergh, D. D. (1998). "Product-Market Uncertainty, Portfolio Restructuring, and Performance: An Information-Processing And Resource-Based View." *Journal of Management*, 24: 135–55.

Bresman, H., Birkinshaw, J., & Nobel, R. (1999). "Knowledge Transfer in International Acquisitions." *Journal of International Business Studies*, 30: 439–62.

Brush, T. H. (1996). "Predicted Change in Operational Synergy and Post-acquisition Performance of Acquired Businesses." *Strategic Management Journal*, 17: 1–24.

Bruton, G. D., Oviatt, B. M., & White, M. A. (1994). "Performance of Acquisitions of Distressed Firms." *Academy of Management Journal*, 37: 972–89.

Buckholtz, A. K., Ribbens, B. A., & Houle, I. T. (2003). "The Role of Human Capital in Post-acquisition CEO Departure." *Academy of Management Journal*, 46: 506–514.

Cannella, A. A., & Hambrick, D.C. (1993). "Effects of Executive Departures on the Performance of Acquired Firms." *Strategic Management Journal*, 14: 137–52.

Capron, L. (1999). "The Long-Term Performance of Horizontal Acquisitions." *Strategic Management Journal*, 20: 987–1018.

—— & Hulland, J. (1999). "Redeployment of Brands, Sales Forces, and General Marketing Management Expertise Following Horizontal Acquisitions: A Resource-Based View." *Journal of Marketing*, 63: 41–54.

—— & Pistre, N. (2002). "When do Acquirers Earn Abnormal Returns?" *Strategic Management Journal*, 23: 781–94.

Carper, W. B. (1990). "Corporate Acquisitions and Shareholder Wealth: A Review and Exploratory Analysis." *Journal of Management*, 16: 807–23.

Chatterjee, S. (1986). "Types of Synergy and Economic Value: The Impact of Acquisitions on Merging and Rival Firms." *Strategic Management Journal*, 7: 119–39.

—— & Lubatkin, M. (1990). "Corporate Mergers, Stockholder Diversification, and Changes in Systematic Risk." *Strategic Management Journal*, 11: 255–68.

Datta, D. K., Pinches, G. P., & Narayanan, V. K. (1992). "Factors Influencing Wealth Creation from Mergers and Acquisitions: A Meta-analysis." *Strategic Management Journal*, 13: 67–84.

Dickerson, A., Gibson, H., & Tsakalotos, E. (2003). "Is Attack the Best Form of Defence? A Competing Risk Analysis of Acquisition Activity in the UK." *Cambridge Journal of Economics*, 27: 337–58.

Finkelstein, S., & Haleblian, J. (2002). "Understanding Acquisition Performance: The Role of Transfer Effects." *Organization Science*, 13: 36–47.

Fowler, K. L., & Schmidt, D.R. (1988). "Tender Offers, Acquisitions, and Subsequent Performance in Manufacturing Firms." *Academy of Management Journal*, 31: 962–74.

—— —— (1989). "Determinants of Tender Offer Post-acquisition Financial Performance." *Strategic Management Journal*, 10: 339–50.

Gerpott, T. J. (1995). "Successful Integration of R&D Functions after Acquisitions: An Exploratory Study." *R&D Management*, 25/2: 161–78.

Haleblian, J., & Finkelstein, S. (1999). "The Influence of Organizational Acquisition Experience on Acquisition Performance: A Behavioral Learning Perspective." *Administrative Science Quarterly*, 44: 29–56.

Harrison, J. S., Hitt, M. A., Hoskisson, R. E., & Ireland, R. D. (1991). "Synergies and Post-acquisition Performance: Differences versus Similarities in Resource Allocations." *Journal of Management*, 17: 173–90.

Hayward, M. L. A. (2002). "When do Firms Learn from their Acquisition Experience? Evidence from 1990–1995." *Strategic Management Journal*, 23: 21–39.

—— & Hambrick, D. C. (1997). "Explaining the Premiums Paid for Large Acquisitions: Evidence of CEO Hubris." *Administrative Science Quarterly*, 42: 103–27.

Healy, P. M., Palepu, K. G., & Ruback, R. S. (1992). "Does Corporate Performance Improve after Mergers?" *Journal of Financial Economics*, 31: 135–75.

Hitt, M. A., Harrison, J. S., Ireland, R. D., & Best, A. (1998). "Attributes of Successful and Unsuccessful Acquisition of U.S. Firms." *British Journal of Management*, 9: 91–114.

—— Hoskisson, R. E, Ireland, R. D., & Harrison, J. S. (1991). "Effects of Acquisitions on R&D Inputs and Outputs." *Academy of Management Journal*, 34/3: 693–706.

—— —— Johnson, R. A., & Moesel, D. D. (1996). "The Market for Corporate Control and Firm Innovation." *Academy of Management Journal*, 39: 1084–119.

Hopkins, H. D. (1987). "Long-Term Acquisition Strategies in the U.S. Economy." *Journal of Management*, 13: 557–72.

Hoskisson, R. E., Hitt, M. A., Johnson, R. A., & Moesel, D. D. (1993). "Construct Validity of an Objective (Entropy) Categorical Measure of Diversification Strategy." *Strategic Management Journal*, 14: 215–35.

Jensen, M. C., & Ruback, R. (1983). "The Market for Corporate Control: The Scientific Evidence." *Journal of Financial Economics*, 11: 5–50.

Jones, G. K., Lanctot, A., & Teegen, H. J. (2000). "Determinants and Performance Impacts of External Technology Acquisition." *Journal of Business Venturing*, 16: 255–83.

Krishnan, H. A., Miller, A., & Judge, W. Q. (1997). "Diversification and Top Management Team Complementarity: Is Performance Improved by Merging Similar or Dissimilar Teams?" *Strategic Management Journal*, 18: 361–74.

Kusewitt, J. B. (1985). "An Exploratory Study of Strategic Acquisition Factors Relating to Performance." *Strategic Management Journal*, 6: 151–69.

Lahey, K. E., & Conn, R. L. (1990). "Sensitivity of Acquiring Firms' Returns to Alternative Model Specification and Disaggregation." *Journal of Business and Accounting*, 17: 421–39.

Larsson, R., & Finkelstein, S. (1999). "Integrating Strategic, Organizational, and Human Resource Perspectives on Mergers and Acquisitions: A Case Survey of Synergy Realization." *Organization Science*, 10: 1–26.

Lubatkin, M. (1987). "Merger Strategies and Stockholder Value." *Strategic Management Journal*, 8: 39–53.

—— Srinivasan, N., & Merchant, H. (1997). "Merger Strategies and Shareholder Value during Times of Relaxed Antitrust Enforcement: The Case of Large Mergers during the 1980s." *Journal of Management*, 23: 59–81.

—— Schulze, W. S., Mainkar, A. & Cotterill, R. W. (2001). "Ecological Investigation of Firm Effects in Horizontal Mergers." *Strategic Management Journal*, 22: 335–7.

Palich, L. E., Cardinal, L. B., & Miller, C. C. (2000). "Curvilinearity in the Diversification-Performance Linkage: An Examination of over Three Decades of Research." *Strategic Management Journal*, 21: 155–74.

Park, C. (2003). Prior Performance Characteristics of Related and Unrelated Acquirers, *Strategic Management Journal*, 24: 471–480.

Ramaswamy, K. (1997). "The Performance Impact of Strategic Similarity in Horizontal Mergers: Evidence from the U.S. Banking Industry." *Academy of Management Journal*, 40: 697–716.

Rau, P. R., & Vermaelen, T. (1998). "Glamour, Value and the Post-Acquisition Performance of Acquiring Firms." *Journal of Financial Economics*, 49: 223–53.

Ravenscraft, D. J., & Scherer, F. M. (1987). *Mergers, Sell-Offs, and Economic Efficiency*. Washington, DC: The Brookings Institution.

—— —— (1989). "The Profitability of Mergers." *International Journal of Industrial Organization*, 7: 101–16.

Schmidt, D. R., & Fowler, K. L. (1990). "Post-acquisition Financial Performance and Executive Compensation." *Strategic Management Journal*, 11: 559–69.

Seth, A. (1990a). "Value Creation in Acquisitions: A Re-examination of Performance Issues." *Strategic Management Journal*, 11: 99–115.

—— (1990b). "Sources of Value Creation in Acquisitions: An Empirical Investigation." *Strategic Management Journal*, 11: 431–46.

—— Song, K. P., & Pettit, R. (2000). "Synergy, Managerialism, or Hubris? An Empirical Examination of Motives for Foreign Acquisitions of U.S. Firms." *Journal of International Business Studies*, 31: 387–405.

Shelton, L. M. (1988). "Strategic Business Fits and Corporate Acquisition: Empirical Evidence." *Strategic Management Journal*, 9: 279–87.

Singh, H., & Montgomery, C. A. (1987). "Corporate Acquisition Strategies and Economic Performance." *Strategic Management Journal*, 8: 377–86.

Sirower, M.L. (1997). *The Synergy Trap: How Companies Lose the Acquisition Game*. New York: The Free Press.

Vermeulen, F., & Barkema, H. (2001). "Learning through Acquisitions." *Academy of Management Journal*, 44/3: 457–76.

Wright, P., Kroll, M., & Elenkov, D. (2002). "Acquisition Returns, Increase in Firm Size, and Chief Executive Officer Compensation: The Moderating Role of Monitoring." *Academy of Management Journal*, 45: 599–608.

APPENDIX 4.2: EMPIRICAL RESEARCH ON M&A PERFORMANCE, 2004–2008

Abhyankar, A., Ho, K., & Zhao, H. (2005). "Long-Run Post-Merger Stock Performance of UK Acquiring Firms: A Stochastic Dominance Perspective." *Applied Financial Economics*, 15: 679–90.

Alexandridis, G., Antoniou, A., & Petmezas, D. (2007). "Divergence of Opinion and Post-acquisition Performance." *Journal of Business Finance and Accounting*, 34: 439–60.

Andre, P., Kooli, M., & L'Her, J. (2004). "The Long-Run Performance of Mergers and Acquisitions: Evidence from the Canadian Stock Market." *Financial Management*, 33/4: 27–43.

Barkema, H., & Schijven, M. (2008). "Toward Unlocking the Full Potential of Acquisitions: The Role of Organizational Restructuring." *Academy of Management Journal*, 51: 696–722.

Capron, L., & Shen, J. (2007). "Acquisitions of Private vs. Public Firms: Private Information, Target Selection and Acquirer Returns." *Strategic Management Journal*, 28: 891–911.

Carow, K., Heron, R., & Saxton, T. (2004). "Do Early Birds Get the Returns? An Empirical Investigation of Early-Mover Advantages in Acquisitions." *Strategic Management Journal*, 25: 563–85.

Casciaro, T., & Piskorski, M. (2005). "Power Imbalance, Mutual Dependence, and Constraint Absorption: A Closer Look at Resource Dependence Theory." *Administrative Science Quarterly*, 50: 167–90.

Christensen, K. (2006). "Losing Innovativeness: The Challenge of Being Acquired." *Management Decision*, 44/9: 1161–82.

Cloodt, M., Hagedoorn, J., & Kranenburg, H. (2006). "Mergers and Acquisitions: Their Effect on the Innovative Performance of Companies in High-Tech Industries." *Research Policy*, 35: 642–54.

Cording, M., Christmann, P., & King, D. (2008). "Reducing Causal Ambiguity in Acquisition Integration: Intermediate Goals as Mediators of Integration Decisions and Acquisition Performance." *Academy of Management Journal*, 51: 744–67.

Deutsch, Y., Keil, T., & Laamanen, T. (2007). "Decision Making in Acquisitions: The Effect of Outside Directors' Compensation on Acquisition Patterns." *Journal of Management*, 33: 30–56.

Dong, M., Hirshleifer, D., Richardson, S., & Teoh, S. (2006). "Does Investor Misevaluation Drive the Takeover Market?" *Journal of Finance*, 61: 725–62.

Fan, J., & Goyal, V. (2006). "On the Patterns and Wealth Effects of Vertical Mergers." *Journal of Business*, 79: 877–902.

Haleblian, J., & Kim, J. (2006). "The Influence of Acquisition Experience and Performance on Acquisition Behavior: Evidence from the U.S. Commercial Banking Industry." *Academy of Management Journal*, 49: 357–70.

Heeley, M., King, D., & Covin, J. (2006). "Effects of Firm R&D Investment and Environment on Acquisition Likelihood." *Journal of Management Studies*, 43: 1513–35.

Homburg, C., & Bucerius, M. (2005). "A Marketing Perspective on Mergers and Acquisitions: How Marketing Integration Affects Postmerger Performance." *Journal of Marketing*, 69: 95–113.

Iyer, D., & Miller, K. (2008). "Performance Feedback, Slack, and the Timing of Acquisitions." *Academy of Management Journal*, 51: 808–22.

Kapoor, R., & Lim, K. (2005). "The Impact of Acquisitions on the Productivity of Inventors at Semiconductor Firms: A Synthesis of Knowledge-Based and Incentive-Based Perspectives." *Academy of Management Journal*, 50: 1133–55.

Kavanagh, M., & Ashkanasy, N. (2006). "The Impact of Leadership and Change Management Strategy on Organizational Culture and Individual Acceptance of Change during a Merger." *British Journal of Management*, 17: S81–S103.

King, D., Dalton, D., Daily, C., & Covin, J. (2004). "Meta-Analyses of Post-acquisition Performance: Indications of Unidentified Moderators." *Strategic Management Journal*, 25: 187–200.

King, D, Slotegraaf, R., & Kesner, I. (2008). "Performance Implications of Firm Resource Interactions in the Acquisition of R&D-Intensive Firms." *Organization Science*, 19: 327–40.

Krishnan, H., Hitt, M., & Park, D. (2007). "Acquisition Premiums, Subsequent Workforce Reductions and Post-Acquisition Performance." *Journal of Management Studies*, 44: 709–32.

McNamara, G., Haleblian, J., & Dykes, B. (2008). "The Performance Implications of Participating in an Acquisition Wave: Early Mover Advantages, Bandwagon Effects, and the Moderating Influence of Industry Characteristics and Acquirer Tactics." *Academy of Management Journal*, 51: 113–20.

Megginson, W., Morgan, A., & Nail, L. (2004). "The Determinants of Positive Long-Term Performance in Strategic Mergers: Corporate Focus and Cash." *Journal of Banking and Finance*, 28: 523–52.

Moeller, S., Schlingemann, F., & Stulz, R. (2004). "Firm Size and the Gains from Acquisitions." *Journal of Financial Economics*, 73: 201–28.

Porrini, P. (2004). "Can a Previous Alliance between an Acquirer and a Target Affect Acquisition Performance?" *Journal of Management*, 30: 545–62.

Puranam, P., Singh, H., & Zollo, M. (2006). "Organizing for Innovation: Managing the Coordination-Autonomy Dilemma in Technology Acquisitions." *Academy Management Journal*, 49: 263–80.

Rosen, R. (2006). "Merger Momentum and Investor Sentiment: The Stock Market Reaction to Merger Announcements." *Journal of Business*, 79: 987–1017.

Saxton, T., & Dollinger, M. (2004). "Target Reputation and Appropriability: Picking and Deploying Resources in Acquisitions." *Journal of Management*, 30: 123–47.

Sorescu, A., Chandy, R., & Prabhu, J. (2007). "Why Some Acquisitions Do Better than Others: Product Capital as a Driver of Long-Term Stock Returns." *Journal of Marketing Research*, 44: 57–72.

Sudarsanam, S., & Mahate, A. (2006). "Are Friendly Acquisitions Too Bad for Shareholders and Managers? Long-Term Value Creation and Top Management Turnover in Hostile and Friendly Acquirers." *British Journal of Management*, 17: S7–S30.

Uhlenbruck, K., Hitt, M., & Semadeni, M. (2006). "Market Value Effects of Acquisitions Involving Internet Firms: A Resource-Based Analysis." *Strategic Management Journal*, 27: 899–913.

Zollo, M., & Singh, H. (2004). "Deliberate Learning in Corporate Acquisitions: Post-Acquisition Strategies and Integration Capability in U.S. Bank Mergers." *Strategic Management Journal*, 25: 1233–56.

REFERENCES

Abhyankar, A., Ho, K., & Zhao, H. (2005). "Long-Run Post-Merger Stock Performance of UK Acquiring Firms: A Stochastic Dominance Perspective." *Applied Financial Economics*, 15: 679–90.

Ahuja, G., & Katila, R. (2001). "Technological Acquisitions and the Innovation Performance of Acquiring Firms: A Longitudinal Study." *Strategic Management Journal*, 22: 197–220.

—— & Lampert, C. M. (2001). "Entrepreneurship in the Large Corporation: A Longitudinal Study of How Established Firms Create Breakthrough Inventions." *Strategic Management Journal*, 22: 221–38.

Allen, T. J. (1984). *Managing the Flow of Technology*. Cambridge, MA: MIT Press.

Amihud, Y., DeLong, G. L., & Saunders, A. (2001). "The Geographic Location of Risk and Cross-Border Bank Mergers." Working Paper at New York University.

Anand, J., & Singh, H. (1997). "Asset Redeployment, Acquisitions and Corporate Strategy in Declining Industries." *Strategic Management Journal*, 18: 99–118.

Arrow, K. J. (1962). "The Economic Implications of Learning by Doing." *Review of Economic Studies*, 29: 166–70.

Ashkenas, R. N., DeMonaco, L. J., & Francis, S. C. (1998). "Making the Deal Real: How GE Capital Integrates Acquisitions." *Harvard Business Review*, 76: 165–78.

Baker, M., Pan, X., & Wurgler, J. (2009). "The Psychology of Pricing in Mergers and Acquisitions." Working Paper. Available at <http://papers.ssrn.com/sol3/papers.cfm?abstract_id=1364152>.

Balmer, B., & Sharp, M. (1993). "The Battle For Biotechnology: Scientific and Technological Paradigms and the Management of Biotechnology in Britain in the 1980s." *Research Policy*, 22: 463–78.

Bandura, A. (1977). *Social Learning Theory*. Englewood Cliffs, NJ: Prentice Hall.

Barkema, H. G., Bell, J. H. J., & Pennings, J. M. (1996). "Foreign Entry, Cultural Barriers, and Learning." *Strategic Management Journal*, 17: 151–66.

—— & Schijven, M. (2008a). "How do Firms Learn to Make Acquisitions? A Review of Past Research and an Agenda for the Future." *Journal of Management*, 34: 594–634.

—— —— (2008b). "Toward Unlocking the Full Potential of Acquisitions: The Role of Organizational Restructuring." *Academy of Management Journal*, 51: 696–722.

—— & Vermeulen, F. (1998). "International Expansion through Start-Up Or Acquisition: A Learning Perspective." *Academy of Management Journal*, 41: 7–26.

Barney, J. B. (1991). "Firm Resources and Sustained Competitive Advantage." *Journal of Management*, 17: 99–120.

Baum, J. A. C., & Ginsberg, A. (1997). "Acquisition Experience and Profitability: Exploring the Value of Learning by Doing." Working Paper, New York University.

—— Li, S. X., & Usher, J. M. (2000). "Making the Next Move: How Experiential and Vicarious Learning Shape the Locations of Chains' Acquisitions." *Administrative Science Quarterly*, 45: 766–801.

Beckman, C. M., & Haunschild, P. R. (2002). "Network Learning: The Effects of Partners' Heterogeneity of Experience on Corporate Acquisitions." *Administrative Science Quarterly*, 47: 92–124.

Berger, A. N., Buch, C. M., DeLong, G., & DeYoung, R. (2004). "Exporting Financial Institutions Management via Foreign Direct Investment Mergers and Acquisitions." *Journal of International Money and Finance*, 24: 831–59.

Berger, A. N., DeYoung, R., Genay, H., & Udell, G. (2000). "Globalization of Financial Institutions: Evidence from Cross-Border Banking Performance." *Brookings-Wharton Papers on Financial Services*, 3: 23–158.

Bergh, D. D. (1997). "Predicting Divestiture of Unrelated Acquisitions: An Integrative Model of Ex Ante Conditions." *Strategic Management Journal*, 18: 715–31.

Bingham, C. B., & Eisenhardt, K. M. (2007). "Opening the Black Box of What Firms Learn from their Process Experience." Working Paper, University of Maryland.

Boot, A. W. (1992). "Why Hang on to Losers? Divestitures and Takeovers." *Journal of Finance*, 47: 1401–23.

Bowman, E. H., & Singh, H. (1993). "Corporate Restructuring: Reconfiguring the Firm." *Strategic Management Journal*, 14: 5–14.

Brakman, S., Garita, G., Garretsen, H., & Marrewijk, C. V. (2008). "Unlocking the Value of Cross-Border Mergers and Acquisitions." CESIFO Working Paper No. 2294.

Brauer, M. (2006). "What Have We Acquired and What Should We Acquire in Divestiture Research? A Review and Research Agenda." *Journal of Management*, 32: 751–85.

Brouthers, K. D. (2002). "Institutional, Cultural and Transaction Cost Influences on Entry Mode Choice and Performance." *Journal of International Business Studies*, 33: 203–21.

—— & Brouthers, L. E. (2000). "Acquisitions or Greenfield Start-Up? Institutional, Cultural and Transaction Cost Influences." *Strategic Management Journal*, 21: 89–97.

Bruner, R. F. (2004). *Applied Mergers & Acquisitions,* University Edition. New Jersey: John Wiley & Sons.

Bruton, G. D., Oviatt, B. M., & White, M. A. (1994). "Performance of Acquisitions of Distressed Firms." *Academy of Management Journal*, 37: 972–89.

Buchholtz, A. K., Lubatkin, M., & O'Neill, H. M. (1999). "Seller Responsiveness to the Need to Divest." *Journal of Management*, 25: 633–52.

Cannella, A. A. Jr., & Hambrick, D. C. (1993). "Effects of Executive Departures on the Performance of Acquired Firms." *Strategic Management Journal*, 14 (Special Issue): 137–52.

Capron, L. (1999). "The Long-Term Performance of Horizontal Acquisitions." *Strategic Management Journal*, 20: 987–1018.

Capron, L., Mitchell, W., & Swaminathan, A. (2001). "Asset Divestiture Following Horizontal Acquisitions: A Dynamic View." *Strategic Management Journal*, 22: 817–44.

Cascio, W. F., Young, C. E., & Morris, J. R. (1997). "Financial Consequences of Employment-Change Decisions in Major U.S. Corporations." *Academy of Management Journal*, 40: 1175–89.

Cassiman, B., Colombo, M., Garrone, P., & Veugelers, R. (2005). "The Impact of M&A on the R&D Process: An Empirical Analysis of the Role of Technological- and Market-Relatedness." *Research Policy*, 34: 195–220.

Chadwick, C., Hunter, L. W., & Walston, S. L. (2004). "Effects of Downsizing Practices on the Performance of Hospitals." *Strategic Management Journal*, 25: 405–27.

Chakrabarti R., Jayaramam, N., & Mukhaerjee, S. (2009). "Mars-Venus Marriages: Culture and Gross-Border M&A." *Journal of Independence Studies*, 40: 216–37.

Chan, L. K. C., Lakonishok, J., & Sougiannis, T. (2001). "The Stock Market Valuation of Research and Development Expenditures." *Journal of Finance*, 56: 2431–56.

Clark, N. (1987). "Similarities and Differences between Scientific and Technological Paradigms." *Futures*, 19/1 (February): 26–42.

Cloodt, M., Hagedoorn, J., & Van Kranenburg, H. (2006). "Mergers and Acquisitions: Their Effect on the Innovative Performance of Companies in High-Tech Industries." *Research Policy*, 35: 642–68.

Coff, R. (2002). "Human Capital, Shared Expertise, and the Likelihood of Impasses in Corporate Acquisitions." *Journal of Management*, 28: 107–28.

Cohen, W. M., & Levinthal, D. A. (1990). "Absorptive Capacity: A New Perspective on Learning and Innovation." *Administrative Science Quarterly*, 35: 128–52.

Cooper, H. (1998). *Synthesizing Research: A Guide for Literature Reviews*. Thousand Oaks, CA: Sage Publications.

Cording, M., Christmann, P., & King, D. R. (2008). "Reducing Causal Ambiguity in Acquisition Integration: Intermediate Goals as Mediators of Integration Decisions and Acquisition Performance." *Academy of Management Journal*, 51: 744–67.

Cormier, S. M. & Hagman, J. D. (1987). *Transfer of Learning: Contemporary Research and Applications*. New York: Academic Press.

Correa, R. (2008). "Board of Governors of the Federal Reserve System." International Finance Discussion Papers no. 922.

Cybo-Ottone, A., & Murgia, M. (2000). "Mergers and Shareholder Wealth in European Banking." *Journal of Banking & Finance*, 24: 831–59.

Cyert, R. M., & March, J. G. (1963). *A Behavioral Theory of the Firm*. Englewood Cliffs, NJ: Prentice Hall.

Datta, D. K., Narayanan, V. K., & Pinches, G. E. (1992). "Factors Influencing Wealth Creation from Mergers and Acquisitions: A Meta Analysis." *Strategic Management Journal*, 13: 67–84.

DeCarolis, D. M., & Deeds, D. (1999). "The Impact of Stocks and Flows of Organizational Knowledge on Firm Performance: An Empirical Investigation of the Biotechnology Industry." *Strategic Management Journal*, 20: 953–68.

Deng, Z., Lev, B., & Narin, F. (2001). "Science and Technology as Predictors of Stock Performance." *Financial Analysts Journal*, 20: 953–68.

Denis, D. J., & Kruse, T. A. (2000). "Managerial Discipline and Corporate Restructuring Following Performance Declines." *Journal of Financial Economics*, 55: 391–424.

DiMaggio, P. J., & Powell, W. W. (1983). "The Iron Cage Revisited: Institutional Isomorphism and Collective Rationality in Organizational Fields." *American Sociological Review*, 48: 147–60.

Duhaime, I. M., & Baird, I. S. (1987). "Divestment Decision-Making: The Role of Business Unit Size." *Journal of Management*, 13: 483–98.

—— & Grant, J. H. (1984). "Factors Influencing Divestment Decision-Making: Evidence from a Field Study." *Strategic Management Journal*, 5: 301–18.

—— & Schwenk, C. R. (1985). "Conjectures on Cognitive Simplification in Acquisition and Divestment Decision Making." *Academy of Management Review*, 10: 287–95.

Dunning, J. (1993). *Multinational Enterprises and the Global Economy*. Reading, MA: Addison-Wesley Publishing.

Eden, L., & Miller, S. (2004). "Distance Matters: Liability of Foreignness, Institutional Distance and Ownership Strategy," in M. A. Hitt & J. Cheng (eds.), *Advances in International Management*, vol. 16. New York: Elsevier, 187–221.

Ellis, H. (1965). *The Transfer of Learning*. New York: Macmillan.

Ernst, H., & Vitt, J. (2000). "The Influence of Corporate Acquisitions on the Behavior of Key Inventors." *R&D Management*, 30/2: 105–20.

Fanto, J. (2001). "Quasi-Rationality in Action: A Study of Psychological Factors in Merger Decision-Making." *Ohio State Law Journal*, 62: 1333–408.

Farzad, R., & Palmeri, C. (2009). "Can Schwab Seize the Day?" *Business Week*, July 27: 36–9.

Finkelstein, S., & Haleblian, J. (2002). "Understanding Acquisition Performance: The Role of Transfer Effects." *Organization Science*, 13: 36–47.

Fiol, C. M., & Lyles, M. (1985). "Organizational Learning." *Academy of Management Review*, 10: 803–13.

Fleming, L., & Sorenson, O. (2004). "Science as Map in Technological Search." *Strategic Management Journal*, 25: 909–28.

Fowler, K. L., & Schmidt, D. R. (1989). "Determinants of Tender Offer Post-Acquisition Financial Performance." *Strategic Management Journal*, 10: 339–50.

Goergen, M., & Renneboog, L. (2004). "Shareholder Wealth Effects of European Domestic and Cross-Border Takeover Bids." *European Financial Management*, 10: 9–45.

Gopinath, C., & Becker, T. M. (2000). "Communication, Procedural Justice, and Employee Attitudes: Relationships under Conditions of Divestiture." *Journal of Management*, 26: 63–83.

Graebner, M. E. (2009). "Caveat Venditor: Trust Asymmetries in Acquisitions of Entrepreneurial Firms." *Academy of Management Journal*, 52: 435–72.

—— & Eisenhardt, K. M. (2004). "The Seller's Side of the Story: Acquisition as Courtship and Governance as Syndicate in Entrepreneurial Firms." *Administrative Science Quarterly*, 49: 366–403.

Habib, M., & Zurawicki, L. (2002). "Corruption and Foreign Direct Investment." *Journal of International Business Studies*, 33: 291–307.

Hagedoorn, J., & Duysters, G. (2002). "The Effect of Mergers and Acquisitions on the Technological Performance of Companies in a High-Tech Environment." *Technology Analysis & Strategic Management*, 14: 67–89.

Haleblian, J., & Finkelstein, S. (1999). "The Influence of Organizational Acquisition Experience on Acquisition Performance: A Behavioral Learning Perspective." *Administrative Science Quarterly*, 44: 29–56.

—— & Kim, J. (2006). "The Influence of Acquisition Experience and Performance on Acquisition Behavior: Evidence from the U.S. Commercial Banking Industry." *Academy of Management Journal*, 49/2: 357–70.

—— —— & Rajagopalan, N. (2006). "The Influence of Acquisition Experience and Performance on Acquisition Behavior: Evidence from the U.S. commercial banking industry." *Academy of Management Journal*, 49: 357–70.

Hall, B., Jaffe, A., & Trajtenberg, M. (2001). "The NBER Patent Citations Data File: Lessons, Insights and Methodological Tools." NBER Working Paper no. 8498, National Bureau of Economic Research.

Hamilton, R. T., & Chow, Y. K. (1993). "Why Managers Divest: Evidence from New Zealand's Largest Companies." *Strategic Management Journal*, 14: 479–84.

Harris, R. S., & Ravenscraft, D. (1991). "The Role of Acquisitions in Foreign Direct Investment: Evidence from the U.S. Stock Market." *Journal of Finance*, 46/3: 825–44.

Haspeslagh, P. C., & Jemison, D. B. (1991a). *Managing Acquisitions: Creating Value through Corporate Renewal*. New York: The Free Press.

—— —— (1991b). "The Challenge of Renewal through Acquisitions." *Planning Review*, 19/2: 27–32.

Haunschild, P. R. (1993). "Interorganizational Imitation: The Impact of Interlocks on Corporate Acquisition Activity." *Administrative Science Quarterly*, 38: 564–92.

—— (1994). "How Much is that Company Worth? Interorganizational Relationships, Uncertainty, and Acquisition Premiums." *Administrative Science Quarterly*, 39: 391–411.

—— & Beckman, C. M. (1998). "When do Interlocks Matter?: Alternate Sources of Information and Interlock Influence." *Administrative Science Quarterly*, 43: 815–44.

—— Davis-Blake, A., & Fichman, M. (1994). "Managerial Overcommitment in Corporate Acquisition Processes." *Organization Science*, 5: 528–40.

—— & Miner, A. S. (1997). "Modes of Interorganizational Imitation: The Effects of Outcome Salience and Uncertainty." *Administrative Science Quarterly*, 42: 472–500.

Hayward, M. L. A. (2002). "When do Firms Learn from their Acquisition Experience? Evidence from 1990–1995." *Strategic Management Journal*, 23: 21–39.

—— & Hambrick, D. C. (1997). "Explaining the Premiums Paid for Large Acquisitions: Evidence of CEO Hubris." *Administrative Science Quarterly*, 42: 103–27.

—— & Shimizu, K. (2006). "De-commitment to Losing Strategic Action: Evidence from the Divestiture of Poorly Performing Acquisitions." *Strategic Management Journal*, 27: 541–57.

Hébert, L., Very, P., & Beamish, P. W. (2005). "Expatriation as a Bridge over Troubled Water: A Knowledge-Based Perspective Applied to Cross-Border Acquisitions." *Organization Studies*, 26: 1455–76.

Heeley, M. B., King, D. R., & Covin, J. G. (2006). "R&D Investment Level and Environment as Predictors of Firm Acquisition." *Journal of Management Studies*, 43: 1513–36.

Henderson, R. M., & Clark, K. B. (1990). "Architectural Innovation: The Reconfiguration of Existing Product Technologies and the Failure of Established Firms." *Administrative Science Quarterly*, 35: 9–30.

Hennart, J. F., & Reddy, S. (1997). "The Choice between Mergers/Acquisitions and Joint Ventures: The Case of Japanese Investors in the United States." *Strategic Management Journal*, 18: 1–12.

Hitt, M. A., Ahlstrom, D., Dacin, M. T., Levitas, E., & Svobodina, L. (2004). "The Institutional Effects on Strategic Alliance Partner Selection in Transition Economies: China versus Russia." *Organization Science*, 15: 173–85.

—— Dacin, M. T., Levitas, E., Arregle, J., & Borza, A. (2000). "Partner Selection in Emerging and Developed Market Contexts: Resource-Based and Organizational Learning Perspectives." *Academy of Management Journal*, 43: 449–67.

—— Franklin, V., & Zhu, H. (2006). "Culture, Institutions, and International Strategy." *Journal of International Management*, 12: 222–34.

—— Harrison, J. S. & Ireland, R. D. (2001a). *Mergers and Acquisitions: A Guide to Creating Value for Stakeholders*. New York: Oxford University Press.

—— Hoskisson, R. E., & Ireland, R. D. (1990). "Mergers and Acquisitions and Managerial Commitment to Innovation in M-Form Firms." *Strategic Management Journal*, 11: 29–47.

—— —— Ireland, D. R, Harrison, S. J. (1991). "Effects of Acquisitions on R&D Inputs and Outputs." *Academy of Management Journal*, 34: 693–711.

—— —— Johnson, R. A. & Moesel, D. D. (1996). "The Market for Corporate Control and Firm Innovation." *Academy of Management Journal*, 39: 1084–119.

—— Ireland, R. D., & Harrison, J. S. (2001b). "Mergers and Acquisitions: A Value Creating or Value Destroying Strategy?" in M. A. Hitt, R. E. Freeman, & J. S. Harrison (eds.), *The Blackwell Handbook of Strategic Management*. Oxford: Blackwell Publishers Ltd., 384–408).

—— King, D., Krishnan, H., Makri, M., Schijven, M, Shimizu, K., & Zhu, H. (2009). "Mergers and Acquisitions: Overcoming Pitfalls, Building Synergy, and Creating Value." *Business Horizons*, 52/6: 523–29.

Holmes, R. M., Miller, T., Hitt, M. A., and Salmador, M. P. (2010). "The Origins and Implications of Formal Institutions: Informal Institutions and FDI." Working Paper, Texas A&M University.

Hoskisson, R. E., & Hitt, M. A. (1994). *Downscoping: How to Tame the Diversified Firm*. New York: Oxford University Press.

—— —— Johnson, R. A., & Grossman, W. (2002). "Conflicting Voices: The Effects of Institutional Ownership Heterogeneity and Internal Governance on Corporate Innovation Strategies." *Academy of Management Journal*, 45: 697–736.

Hoskisson, R. E., Hitt, M. A., Johnson, R. A. & Moesel, D. D. (1993). "Construct Validity of an Objective (Entropy) Categorical Measure of Diversification Strategy." *Strategic Management Journal*, 14: 215–35.

—— Johnson, R. A., & Moesel, D. D. (1994). "Corporate Divestiture Intensity in Restructuring Firms: Effects of Governance, Strategy, and Performance." *Academy of Management Journal*, 37: 1207–51.

Isobe, T., Makino, S., & Montgomery, D. B. (2000). "Resource Commitment, Entry Timing, and Market Performance of Foreign Direct Investments in Emerging Economies: The Case of Japanese International Joint Ventures in China." *Academy of Management Journal*, 43: 468–84.

Jain, P. (1985). "The Effect of Voluntary Sell-Off Announcements on Shareholder Wealth." *Journal of Finance*, 40: 209–24.

Jemison, D. B., & Sitkin, S. B. (1986). "Corporate Acquisitions: A Process Perspective." *Academy of Management Review*, 11: 145–63.

Jensen, M. (1991). "Corporate Control and the Politics of Finance." *Journal of Applied Corporate Finance*, 4: 13–33.

—— & Ruback, R. (1983). "The Market for Corporate Control: The Scientific Evidence." *Journal of Financial Economics*, 11: 5–50.

Johnson, R. A. (1996). "Antecedents and Outcomes of Corporate Refocusing." *Journal of Management*, 22: 439–83.

—— Hoskisson, R. E., & Hitt, M. A. (1993). "Board of Directors' Involvement in Restructuring: The Effects of Board versus Managerial Controls and Characteristics." *Strategic Management Journal*, 14: 33–50.

Kahneman, D., & Tversky, A. (1979). "Prospect Theory: An Analysis of Decision under Risk." *Econometrica*, 47: 263–91.

Kaplan, S. N., & Weisbach, M. S. (1992). "The Success of Acquisitions: Evidence from Divestitures." *Journal of Finance*, 47: 107–38.

King, D. R., Dalton, D. R., Daily, C. M., & Covin, J. G. (2004). "Meta-analyses of Post-acquisition Performance: Indications of Unidentified Moderators." *Strategic Management Journal*, 25: 187–200.

—— Slotegraaf, R., & Kesner, I. (2008). "Performance Implications of Firm Resource Interactions in the Acquisition of R&D-Intensive Firms." *Organization Science*, 19: 327–40.

Klaus, M. E., & Tran, Y. T. T. (2006). "Market Penetration and Acquisition Strategies for Emerging Economies." *Long Range Planning*, 39: 177–97.

Kohers, N., & Kohers, T. (2001). "Takeovers of Technology Firms: Expectations vs. Reality." *Financial Management*, 30: 35–54.

Kostova, T., & Zaheer, S. (1999). "Organizational Legitimacy under Conditions of Complexity: The Case of the Multinational Enterprise." *Academy of Management Review*, 24: 64–81.

Krishnan, H. A., Hitt, M. A., & Park, D. (2007). "Acquisition Premiums, Subsequent Workforce Reductions and Post-acquisition Performance." *Journal of Management Studies*, 44: 709–32.

Kroll, M., Wright, P., Toombs, L., & Leavell, H. (1997). "Form of Control: A Critical Determinant of Acquisition Performance and CEO Rewards." *Strategic Management Journal*, 18: 85–96.

Krug, J. A., & Nigh, D. (2001). "Executive Perceptions in Foreign and Domestic Acquisitions: An Analysis of Foreign Ownership and its Effect on Executive Fate." *Journal of World Business*, 36: 85–105.

Kuhn, T. S. (1970). *The Structure of Scientific Revolutions*. Chicago: University of Chicago Press.

Kusewitt, J. B. (1985). "An Exploratory Study of Strategic Acquisition Factors Relating to Performance." *Strategic Management Journal*, 6: 151–69.

Laamanen, T. (2007). "On the Role of Acquisition Premium in Acquisition Research." *Strategic Management Journal*, 28: 1359–69.

Lahey, K. E., & Conn, R. L. (1990). "Sensitivity of Acquiring Firms' Returns to Alternative Model Specification and Disaggregation." *Journal of Business and Accounting*, 17: 421–39.

Lane, P. J., & Lubatkin, M. (1998). "Relative Absorptive Capacity and Interorganizational Learning." *Strategic Management Journal*, 19: 461–77.

Latour, L. (1987). *Science in Action.* Cambridge, MA: Harvard University Press.

Levinthal, D., & March, J. (1993). "The Myopia of Learning." *Strategic Management Journal*, 14: 95–112.

Lippman, S. & Rumelt, R. (1982). "Uncertain Imitability: An Analysis of Interfirm Differences in Efficiency under Competition." *Bell Journal of Economics*, 13: 418–38.

Lubatkin, M. H. (1982). "A Market Model Analysis of Diversification Strategies and Administrative Experience on the Performance of Merging Firms." Unpublished doctoral dissertation, University of Tennessee.

—— (1987). "Merger Strategies and Stockholder Value." *Strategic Management Journal*, 8: 39–53.

Mahoney, J., & Pandian, J. (1992). "The Resource-Based View within the Conversation of Strategic Management." *Strategic Management Journal*, 13: 363–80.

Makri, M., Hitt, M. A., & Lane, P. J. (2010). "Complementary Technologies, Knowledge Relatedness, and Invention Outcomes in High Technology M&As." *Strategic Management Journal*, 31: 602–28.

March, J. G. (1991). "Exploration and Exploitation in Organizational Learning." *Organization Science*, 2: 71–87.

McEvily, S. K., Eisenhardt, K. M., & Prescott, J. E. (2004). "The Global Acquisition, Leverage, and Protection of Technological Competencies." *Strategic Management Journal*, 25: 713–23.

Megginson, W., Morgan, A., & Nail, L. (2004). "The Determinants of Positive Long-Term Performance in Strategic Mergers: Corporate Focus and Cash." *Journal of Banking and Finance*, 28: 523–52.

Miner, A. S., & Haunschild, P. R. (1995). "Population Level Learning." *Research in Organizational Behavior*, 17: 115–66.

Mitchell, M. L., & Stafford, E. (2000). "Managerial Decisions and Long-Term Stock Price Performance." *Journal of Business*, 73: 287–329.

Moeller, S. B., & Schlingemann, F. P. (2005). "Global Diversification and Bidder Gains: A Comparison between Cross-Border and Domestic Acquisitions." *Journal of Banking and Finance*, 29: 533–64.

Morck, R., Schleifer, A., & Vishny, R. (1988). "Management Ownership and Market Valuation: An Empirical Analysis." *Journal of Financial Economics*, 20: 293–315.

Moschieri, C., & Mair, J. (2008). "Research on Corporate Divestitures: A Synthesis." *Journal of Management & Organization*, 14: 399–422.

Mulherin, J. H., & Boone, A. L. (2000). "Comparing Acquisitions and Divestitures." *Journal of Corporate Finance*, 6: 117–39.

Nadolska, A., & Barkema, H. G. (2007). "Learning to Internationalise: The Pace and Success of Foreign Acquisitions." *Journal of International Business Studies*, 38: 1170–86.

Newbould, G. D., Stray, S. J., & Wilson, K. W. (1976). "Shareholders' Interests And Acquisition Activity." *Accounting and Business Research*, 23: 201–13.

Nixon, R. D., Hitt, M. A., Lee, H., & Jeong, E. (2004). "Market Reactions to Announcements of Corporate Downsizing Actions and Implementation Strategies." *Strategic Management Journal*, 25: 1121–9.

Nonaka, I., Takeuchi, H., & Umemoto, K. (1996). "A Theory of Organizational Knowledge Creation." *International Journal of Technology Management*, 11: 833–46.

Norling, P., Herring, J., Rosenkrans, W., Stellpflug, M., & Kaufman, S. (2000). "Putting Competitive Technology Intelligence to Work." *Research-Technology Management*, 43/5: 23–8.

North, D. C. (1990). *Institutions, Institutional Change, and Economic Performance*. Cambridge and New York: Cambridge University Press.

O'Shaughnessy, K. C., & Flanagan, D. J. (1998). "Determinants of Layoff Announcements Following M&As: An Empirical Investigation." *Strategic Management Journal*, 19: 989–99.

Palich, L. E., Cardinal, L. B., & Miller, C. C. (2000). "Curvilinearity in the Diversification-Performance Linkage: An Examination of over Three Decades of Research." *Strategic Management Journal*, 21: 155–74.

Park, C. (2003). "Prior Performance Characteristics of Related and Unrelated Acquirers." *Strategic Management Journal*, 24: 471–80.

Paulson, E. (2001). *Inside Cisco*. New York: John Wiley & Sons.

Porrini, P. (2004). "Alliance Experience and Value Creation in High-Tech and Low-Tech Acquisitions." *Journal of High Technology Management Research*, 15: 267–92.

——(2006). "Are Investment Bankers Good for Acquisition Premiums?" *Journal of Business Research*, 59: 90–9.

Porter, M. E. (1987). "From Competitive Advantage to Corporate Strategy." *Harvard Business Review*, 5/3: 43–59.

Power, D. J. (1982). "Acquiring Small And Medium Size Companies: A Study of Corporate Decision Behavior." Unpublished doctoral dissertation, University of Wisconsin, Madison.

Ravenscraft, D. J., & Scherer, F. M. (1987). *Mergers, Sell-Offs, and Economic Efficiency*. Washington, DC: Brookings Institution.

————(1991). "Divisional Sell-Off: A Hazard Function Analysis." *Managerial and Decision Economics*, 14: 429–38.

Reuer, J. J. (2001). "From Hybrids to Hierarchies: Shareholder Wealth Effects of Joint Venture Partner Buyouts." *Strategic Management Journal*, 22: 27–44.

Rip, A. (1992). "Science and Technology as Dancing Partners," in P. Kroes & M. Bakker (eds.), *Technological Development and Science in the Industrial Age*. Netherlands: Kluwer, 231–70.

Roll, R. (1986). "The Hubris Hypothesis of Corporate Takeovers." *Journal of Business*, 59: 197–216.

Rosenkopf, L., & Nerkar, A. (2001). "Beyond Local Search: Boundary-Spanning, Exploration, and Impact in the Optical Disk Industry." *Strategic Management Journal*, 22: 287–304.

Schoenberg, R. (2006). "Measuring the Performance of Corporate Acquisitions: An Empirical Comparison of Alternative Metrics." *British Journal of Management*, 17: 361–70.

Scott, R. (2001). *Institutions and Organizations* (2nd ed.). Thousand Oaks, CA: Sage.

Scott, W., Ruef, M., Mendel, P., & Caronna, C. (2000). *Institutional Change and Healthcare Organizations: From Professional Dominance to Managed Care*. Chicago, IL: University of Chicago Press.

Seth, A. (1990a). "Value Creation in Acquisitions: A Re-examination of Performance Issues." *Strategic Management Journal*, 11: 99–115.

——(1990b). "Sources of Value Creation in Acquisitions: An Empirical Investigation." *Strategic Management Journal*, 11: 431–46.

—— Song, K., & Pettit, R. (2002). "Value Creation and Destruction in Cross-Border Acquisitions: An Empirical Analysis of Foreign Acquisitions of U.S. Firms." *Strategic Management Journal*, 23: 921–40.

Shaver, J. M., Mitchell, W., & Yeung, B. (1997). "The Effect of Own-Firm and Other-Firm Experience on Foreign Direct Investment Survival in the United States, 1987–1992." *Strategic Management Journal*, 18: 811–24.

Shelton, L. M. (1988). "Strategic Business Fits and Corporate Acquisition: Empirical Evidence." *Strategic Management Journal*, 9: 279–87.

Shimizu, K. (2007). "Prospect Theory, Behavioral Theory, and Threat-Rigidity Thesis: Combinative Effects on Organizational Divestiture Decisions of a Formerly Acquired Unit." *Academy of Management Journal*, 50: 1495–514.

—— & Hitt, M. A. (2004). "Strategic Flexibility: Organizational Preparedness to Reverse Ineffective Strategic Decisions." *Academy of Management Executive*, 18/4: 44–59.

—— —— (2005). "What Constrains or Facilitates Divestitures of Formerly Acquired Firms? The Effects of Organizational Inertia." *Journal of Management*, 31: 50–72.

—— —— Vaidyanath, D., & Pisano, V. (2004). "Theoretical Foundations of Cross-Border Mergers and Acquisitions: A Review of Current Research and Recommendations for the Future." *Journal of International Management*, 10: 307–53.

Singh, H., & Montgomery, C. A. (1987). "Corporate Acquisition Strategies and Economic Performance." *Strategic Management Journal*, 8: 377–86.

Sirmon, D. G., Hitt, M.A., & Ireland, R.D. (2007). "Managing Firm Resources in Dynamic Environments to Create Value: Looking inside the Black Box." *Academy of Management Review*, 32: 273–93.

Sirower, M. L. (1997). *The Synergy Trap: How Companies Lose the Acquisition Game*. New York: The Free Press.

Slusky, A. R., & Caves, R. E. (1991). "Synergy, Agency and the Determinants of Premia Paid in Mergers." *Journal of Industrial Economics*, 39: 277–96.

Smit, H. T. J. (2001). "Acquisition Strategies as Option Games." *Journal of Applied Corporate Finance*, 14: 79–89.

Stahl, G. K., Maznevski, M. L., Voigt, A., & Jonsen, K. (2010). "Unraveling the Effects of Cultural Diversity in Teams: A Meta-Analysis of Research on Multicultural Work Groups." *Journal of International Business Studies*, 41: 690–709.

—— & Voigt, A. (2008). "Do Cultural Differences Matter in Mergers and Acquisitions? A Tentative Model and Examination." *Organization Science*, 19: 160–76.

Staw, B. M., Sandelands, L. E., & Dutton, J. E. (1981). "Threat-Rigidity Effects in Organizational Behavior: A Multilevel Analysis." *Administrative Science Quarterly*, 26: 501–24.

Teerikangas, S. & Véry, P. (2006). "The Culture-Performance Relationship in M&A: From Yes/No to How." *British Journal of Management*, 17: S1–48.

Tihanyi, L., Griffith, D. A., & Russell, C. J. (2005). "The Effect of Cultural Distance on Entry Mode Choice, International Diversification, and MNE Performance: A Meta-analysis." *Journal of International Business Studies*, 36: 270–83.

Trautwein, F. (1990). "Merger Motives and Merger Prescriptions." *Strategic Management Journal*, 11: 283–96.

Tushman, M. L., & Rosenkopf, L. (1992). "Organizational Determinants of Technological Change: Toward a Sociology of Technological Evolution." *Research of Organizational Behavior*, 14: 311–47.

Uhlenbruck, K., & DeCastro, J. O. (2000). "Foreign Acquisitions in Central and Eastern Europe: Outcomes of Privatization in Transitional Economies." *Academy of Management Journal*, 43: 381–402.

—— Hitt, M. A., & Semadeni, M. (2006a). "Market Value Effects of Acquisitions Involving Internet Firms: A Resource-Based Analysis." *Strategic Management Journal*, 27: 4–26.

—— Rodriguez, P., Doh, J., & Eden, L. (2006b). "The Impact of Corruption on Entry Strategy: Evidence from Telecommunication Projects in Emerging Economies." *Organization Science*, 17: 402–14.

Useem, M. (1993). *Executive Defense: Shareholder Power and Corporate Reorganization*. Cambridge, MA: Harvard University Press.

Varaiya, N. P. (1988). "The Winner's Curse Hypothesis and Corporate Takeovers." *Managerial and Decision Economics*, 9: 209–20.

—— Ferris, K. R. (1987). "Overpaying in Corporate Takeovers: The Winner's Curse." *Financial Analysts' Journal*, 43/3, May–June: 64–70.

Vermeulen, F., & Barkema, H. (2001). "Learning through Acquisitions." *Academy of Management Journal*, 44: 457–76.

Weber, R., & Camerer, C. (2003). "Cultural Conflict and Merger Failure: An Experimental Approach." *Management Science*, 49: 400–15.

Weil, J. (2001). "Goodwill Hunting: Accounting Change May Lift Profits, But Stock Prices May Not Follow Suit." *Wall Street Journal*, 25 January, p. C1.

Weisbach, M. S. (1995). "CEO Turnover and the Firm's Investment Decisions." *Journal of Financial Economics*, 37: 159–88.

Weitzel, U., & Berns, S. (2006). "Cross-Border Takeovers, Corruption, and Related Aspects of Governance." *Journal of International Business Studies*, 37: 786–806.

Welch, D. (2007). "Buyer Beware at Chrysler." *Business Week*, April 23: 34.

Westphal, J. D., Seidel, M. D. L., & Stewart, K. J. (2001). "Second-Order Imitation: Uncovering Latent Effects of Board Network Ties." *Administrative Science Quarterly*, 46: 717–47.

Williamson, O. E. (1975). *Markets and Hierarchies*. New York, NY: Free Press.

World Investment Report (2006). *FDI from Developing and Transition Economies: Implications for Development*. New York and Geneva: United Nations.

Wright, P., Kroll, M., Lado, A., & Van Ness, B. (2002). "The Structure of Ownership and Corporate Acquisition Strategies." *Strategic Management Journal*, 23: 41–53.

Xu, D., & Shenkar, O. (2002). "Institutional Distance and the Multinational Enterprises." *Academy of Management Review*, 27: 608–18.

Yang, M., & Hyland, M. A. (2006). "Who do Firms Imitate? A Multilevel Approach to Examining Sources of Imitation in the Choice of Mergers and Acquisitions." *Journal of Management*, 32: 381–99.

Yelle, L. E. (1979). "The Learning Curve: Historical Review and Comprehensive Survey." *Decision Sciences*, 10: 302–28.

Zahra, S. A., Ireland, R. D., & Hitt, M. A. (2000). "International Expansion by New Venture Firms: International Diversity, Mode of Market Entry, Technological Learning, and Performance." *Academy of Management Journal*, 43: 925–50.

Zenger, T. R. (1994). "Explaining Organizational Diseconomies of Scale in R&D: Agency Problems and the Allocation of Engineering Talent, Ideas, and Effort by Firm Size." *Management Science*. 40: 708–30.

Zhu, H., Hitt, M. A., Eden, L., & Tihanyi, L. (2010). "Host Country Institutions and the Performance of Cross-Border M&As." Working Paper, Chinese University of Hong Kong.

Zollo, M., & Leshchinskii, D. (2004). "Can Firms Learn to Acquire? Do Markets Notice?" Working Paper 99-82-SM, INSEAD.

—— & Meier, D. (2008). "What is M&A Performance?" *Academy of Management Perspectives*, 22/3: 55–77.

—— & Reuer, J. (2010). "Experience Spillovers across Corporate Development Activities." *Organization Science*, 21/6: 1195–212.

—— & Singh, H. (2004). "Deliberate Learning in Corporate Acquisitions: Post-acquisition Strategies and Integration Capability in U.S. Bank Mergers." *Strategic Management Journal*, 25: 1233–56.

—— & Winter, S. G. (2002). "Deliberate Learning and the Evolution of Dynamic Capabilities." *Organization Science*, 13: 339–51.

Zuckerman, E. W. (2000). "Focusing the Corporate Product: Securities Analysts and De-diversification." *Administrative Science Quarterly*, 45: 591–619.

CHAPTER 5

UNBUNDLING ACQUISITION PERFORMANCE: HOW DO THEY PERFORM AND HOW CAN THIS BE MEASURED?

IOANNIS C. THANOS AND VASSILIS M. PAPADAKIS

INTRODUCTION

During the previous century, five major M&A waves occurred (see Chapter 2 by Kolev, Haleblian, and McNamara in this *Handbook* for a comprehensive presentation). The last wave ended in 2001. Recently, we have again witnessed a boom in the volume and value of M&As. In 2007 the value of M&As globally reached the astonishing amount of US$4.367 trillion (Moschieri and Campa 2009). In today's turbulent environment, M&As are seen by firms as a fast way to enter new markets, improve their competitive position, introduce new brands, spread the financial risk, and achieve economies of scale. Yet, their success is by no means guaranteed as recent empirical research indicates (Papadakis 2005; King et al. 2004).

The aim of this chapter is to take stock of what we know as regards the performance of M&As and to set the stage as to where future research on the topic should be directed. By conducting a comprehensive review of 13 top US and European management journals, we aim to provide answers to the following crucial questions: How do M&As perform? How is M&A performance measured in the literature? What are the advantages and disadvantages of each performance measure utilized by previous researchers? What validity tactics and robustness tests have been adopted by previous researchers in their efforts to improve their measures of M&A performance?

The rest of the chapter is organized as follows. In the next section we outline the method used for identifying papers dealing with M&A performance issues. The following section is about reviewing the literature. Finally, we provide a list of substantive future research priorities.

METHOD

In our efforts to better understand the alternative measures of M&A performance used in the literature, we adopted a six-step process following recent reviews (Haleblian et al. 2009). First, we focused on empirical (quantitative and qualitative) M&A research in the management area. Second, we focused only on top academic journals as these are likely to have a considerable impact on the field (Hutzschenreuter and Kleindienst 2006). We deliberately excluded from our study list well known practitioner outlets such as *Harvard Business Review, California Management Review, Academy of Management Perspectives, Long Range Planning, European Management Journal*, etc. Also, we did not include in our review journals publishing theoretical papers without empirical data (i.e. *Academy of Management Review*). Following reviews from other management areas such as decision making (Papadakis et al. 2010), strategy processes (Hutzschenreuter and Kleindienst 2006), and strategic alliances (Walter 2011), we selected 13 academic journals. Nine of them are published in North America (*Academy of Management Journal, Administrative Science Quarterly, Decision Sciences, Journal of Business Research, Journal of International Business Studies, Journal of Management, Organization Science, Strategic Management Journal*, and *Strategic Organization*) and four in Europe (*British Journal of Management, Human Relations, Journal of Management Studies, Organization Studies*). Our review of empirical evidence covers three decades of research (1980–2010).

In step three, we conducted an online search of titles and abstracts of the 13 target journals using three general keywords: merger(s), acquisition(s) and mergers and acquisitions/M&As. This procedure resulted in an initial set of 1345 results. The fourth step included an initial screening of the titles and abstracts of these 1345 results. Here, we eliminated a significant number of articles referring to other themes, such as acquisition of tacit knowledge, information acquisition, etc. In step 5, we reviewed each of the remaining papers and selected these papers which used an M&A performance measure as a dependent variable. After this extensive review, we created a core list of 137 empirical papers. Table 5.1 describes the results from steps 3, 4, and 5.

Finally, in step 6, we classified the papers according to the approach taken to measuring M&A performance. Results from this analysis indicate that management scholars have used seven broad approaches to measure the performance of M&As. These include

Table 5.1 Number of hits using keywords such as: merger, acquisition, mergers and acquisitions, in abstracts of articles in 13 management journals, using the Business Source Premier Publications

Journal	Merger(s)	Acquisition(s)	Mergers & Acquisitions	Papers selected*
Academy of Management Journal (AMJ)	53	43	30	18
Administrative Science Quarterly (ASQ)	22	30	14	2
British Journal of Management (BJM)	19	17	10	7
Decision Sciences (DS)	4	29	1	0
Human Relations (HR)	12	29	7	4
Journal of Business Research (JBR)	31	61	18	6
Journal of International Business Studies (JIBS)	42	75	36	9
Journal of Management Studies (JMS)	48	47	28	5
Journal of Management (JOM)	33	32	23	15
Organization Science (OS)	29	37	22	8
Organization Studies (OStudies)	13	13	8	7
Strategic Management Journal (SMJ)	150	144	105	53
Strategic Organization (SO)	9	13	8	3
Total	465	570	310	137

Note:* Papers included in the review are those which used an M&A performance metric as a dependent variable.

short-term financial performance, accounting performance, long-term financial performance, key informants' retrospective assessments of performance, divestiture, integration process performance, and innovation performance. Table 5.A1 in the Appendix provides an analytical categorization of the studies and Figure 5.1 depicts these alternative approaches.

To get an idea of how the literature on M&A performance has evolved in the management literature, we plotted the studies by performance measure (Figure 5.2). Figure 5.2

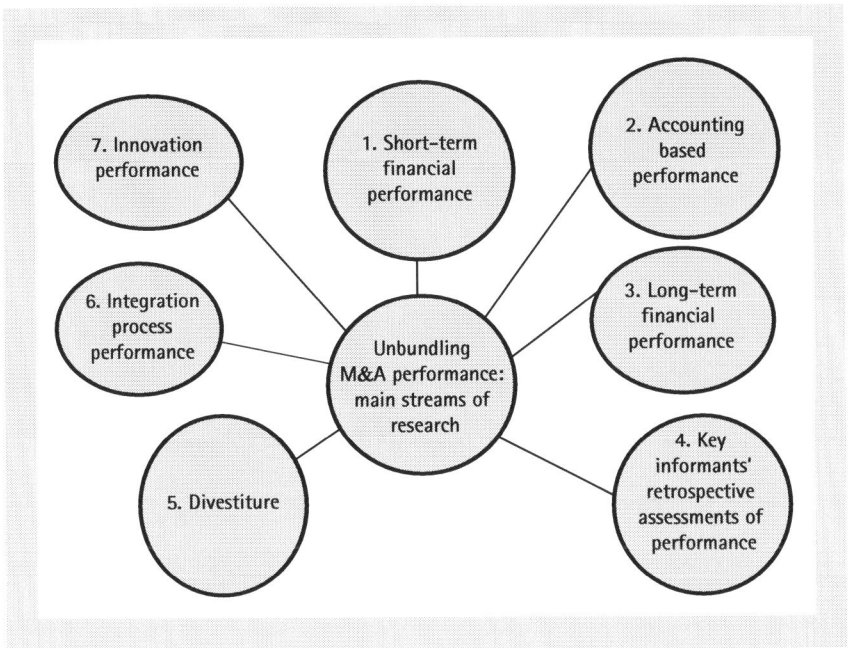

FIG. 5.1 Main streams of research in the study of M&A performance

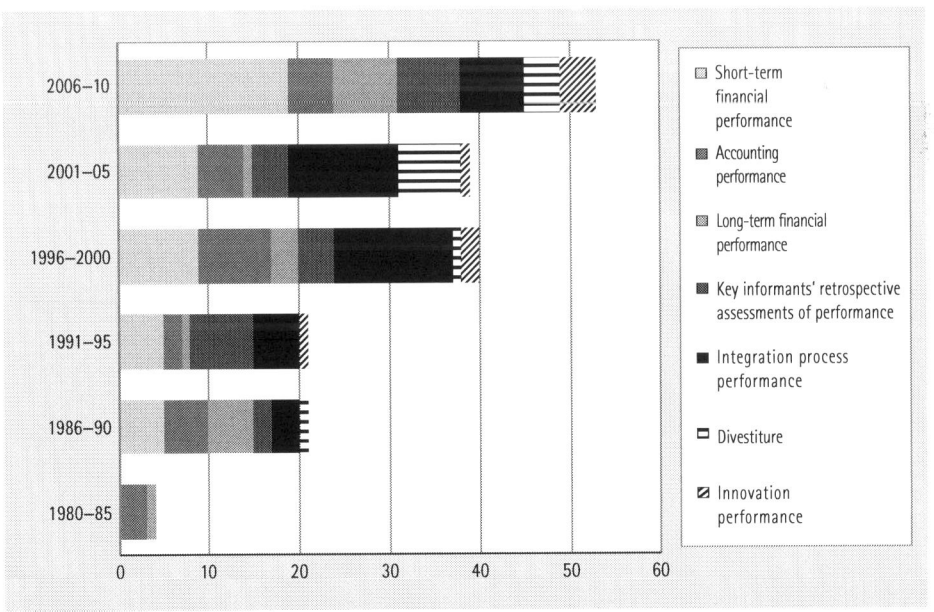

FIG. 5.2 The trends in M&A performance: number of articles by performance metric

suggests that the number of studies utilizing M&A performance as a dependent variable is constantly increasing in the management area. There were just four studies during the 1980–5 period, rising to the record number of 53 studies during the past five years. Another interesting conclusion is that the first paper measuring M&A performance from our select list of 13 journals appeared in 1982. This shows that interest in M&A performance is relatively young in the management area, as opposed to the finance area, where scholars have published influential papers on M&A performance since the early 1950s. This may explain why during the period 1980–5 we see only finance and accounting measures of M&A performance.

In the next section, we review the literature, focusing on the seven adopted streams of research. It should be stressed that apart from the 137 papers identified from the previous six steps, our literature review takes into account a select number of highly cited papers from practitioner outlets. In addition, we incorporate the results of recent reviews of M&As from related areas such as finance, accounting, and strategy (e.g. Cording et al. 2010; Haleblian et al. 2009; Barkema and Schijven 2008a; Zollo and Meier 2008; Tuch and O'Sullivan 2007). Finally, useful insights were obtained by looking at recent meta-analyses of post-acquisition performance (e.g. Stahl and Voigt 2008; King et al. 2004). All these diverse sources of information were taken into account in an effort to capture the existing knowledge base on the topic of M&A performance.

LITERATURE REVIEW

Short-Term Financial Performance

Short-term measures of M&A performance have been used in 47 of the 137 papers reviewed (34.31%) and represent the largest group of studies. We can speculate that management scholars have relied heavily on short-term measures first because they are the only direct measure of stockholder value and second because these kinds of data are relatively easily accessible for all publicly traded firms (Cannella and Hambrick 1993; Lubatkin and Shrieves 1986). The majority of these papers have adopted the event study methodology which assumes market efficiency. Researchers usually compare the results for shareholders of acquiring firms or target firms, during a period surrounding the acquisition announcement (window) with "normal returns" from a period unaffected by the event (benchmark period) (Sudarsanam 2003). There is no consensus among researchers on what should be the proper length of the event window (McWilliams et al. 1999). In the management literature, previous studies have adopted multiple windows, with examples including two-day (e.g. Anand and Delios 2002; Markides and Ittner 1994), 11-day (e.g. Gubbi et al. 2010; Walters et al. 2007; Haleblian and Finkelstein 1999) and 21-day (e.g. Aybar and Ficici 2009; McNamara et al. 2008; Capron and Pistre 2002; Seth et al. 2002) windows.

Results from this stream of research suggest that on average target firms' shareholders gain significant positive returns due to the large premiums often paid for acquisitions (Sudarsanam and Mahate 2006; Markides and Oyon 1998). For example, Arnold and Parker (2007) studied 50 mergers in the UK from 1989 to 2002 and concluded that target firms' shareholders obtain more gains than acquiring firms' shareholders over a three-day period surrounding the announcement.

Regarding shareholders of the acquiring firm, a recent review of finance and accounting journals concluded that results are somewhat mixed, with studies showing negative significant returns or positive insignificant returns around the bid announcement (Tuch and O'Sullivan 2007). Our review from the management area provides support for the former (Papadakis and Thanos 2010; Schoenberg 2006; King et al. 2004). For example, Schoenberg (2006) studied 61 cross-border acquisitions made by British acquisitions of continental European firms over the period 1988–90 and concluded that the acquisition announcement created positive negative abnormal returns for the acquirers in 50% of cases. Papadakis and Thanos (2010), in a study of 50 domestic horizontal acquisitions made in Greece, echoed this finding by reporting negative and significant returns for acquiring firms in 52% of their cases.

To conclude, the use of short-term window event methodology has received a great deal of criticism from several researchers for four main reasons. The first is that they are ex-ante and not ex-post measures of performance. They do not measure actual performance, but investors' expectations (Montgomery and Wilson 1986). Second, they measure only financial performance, ignoring other important influences on M&A success such as organizational integration and employee reactions (Larsson and Finkelstein 1999: 3). Third, short-term measures of performance can be used only for public listed firms and not for privately held firms. A final limitation is that the results of the short-term measures might be influenced by the length of the event window, the length of the estimation period, and the method used (e.g. market and risk adjusted model, market adjusted model, etc.). In an effort to overcome the latter limitation, researchers have recently employed a number of robustness tests. For example, Haleblian and Finkelstein (1999) used both the market adjusted and the market and risk adjusted models, which yielded similar results. Other robustness tests refer to the computation of abnormal returns with multiple time windows. Again, results from these analyses report no variation in the findings (Kroll et al. 2008; Carow et al., 2004). More recently, researchers have validated their cumulative abnormal returns (CAR) results with accounting data for a subset of their samples (Kim and Finkelstein 2009; Desai et al. 2005).

Accounting-Based Performance

Accounting-based measures have been used in 28 of the 137 studies reviewed (20.44% of the total). Scholars adopting these types of measures usually compare the average post-M&A returns of the acquiring or the combined firm with the weighted pre-M&A average returns of the target and acquiring firm. To obtain further robust results, they also adjust for industry returns by subtracting from the above calculation the mean average industry profitability and exclude from the analyses the year the M&A took place (Ramaswamy 1997). The use of accounting-based measures as a proxy for M&A performance has two main advantages. First, they measure actual performance as reported in the annual financial statements and not investors' expectations for the future as short-term measures of M&A performance do (Grant et al. 1988). Second, the relevant literature holds that potential synergies from an M&A are best depicted in long-term accounting-based ratios such as ROA (return on assets), ROE (return on equity), etc. (Hitt et al. 1998). Following this line of argumentation, it would seem that the best way to evaluate potential synergies is to use accounting-based measures of M&A performance.

A series of accounting ratios has been employed by M&A researchers, the most popular of which is undoubtedly the ROA (used by e.g. Barkema and Schijven 2008b; Desai et al. 2005; Zollo and Singh 2004; Hitt et al. 1998; Ramaswamy 1997; Krishnan et al. 1997; Weber 1996; Harrison et al. 1991; Kusewitt 1985). Other accounting measures include ROE (used by e.g. Kroll et al. 1990; Fowler and Schmidt 1989, 1988) and Growth in Sales (used by e.g. Stahl and Voigt 2008; Morosini et al. 1998).

In the management literature, our review of the 28 studies indicated that accounting-based measures have been mainly used as dependent variables in models explaining the antecedents of M&A performance. Thus, when using accounting-based measures, we cannot be certain as to the average failure rate of M&As. However, a paper by Papadakis and Thanos (2010) seems to have overcome this limitation. By using a weighted ROA adjusted for both size and industry effects, they have found that 50% of the firms saw their financial condition deteriorating two years after the M&A as opposed to two years before the M&A.

To further enrich our discussion, we drew on the findings of a recent review on accounting-based measures from finance and accounting journals (Tuch and O'Sullivan 2007). According to these authors, there exist some studies providing evidence of negative returns (Dickerson et al. 1997; Meeks 1977) and some studies showing that on average M&As lead to higher operating cash flow returns over a five-year period for acquiring firms (e.g. Healy et al. 1992). The authors, however, conclude that on average accounting measures suggest no evidence of improved post-acquisition performance.

Despite the profound advantages of accounting-based measures, they have been criticized for a number of shortcomings. Prevalent among them is that they reflect past performance (Chenhall and Langfield-Smith 2007; Montgomery and Wilson 1986); and that they are narrow in their orientation as they measure only the economic performance of the firm (Papadakis 2005; Lubatkin and Shrieves 1986). Additional limitations are that they are offered at the firm level, thus they do not capture the effects of isolated events such as acquisitions (Larsson and Finkelstein 1999; Capron 1999; Bruton et al. 1994; Datta 1991) and that they cannot be used in cross-national, interfirm or intra industry comparison of studies of M&A performance due to the different accounting standards and rules followed by firms (Tuch and O'Sullivan 2007; Hitt et al. 1998; Montgomery and Thomas 1988). A final limitation is that results might be influenced by the different accounting ratios used (King et al. 2008). Cording et al. (2010) in their study used three different accounting measures to evaluate the performance of M&As. They used adjusted three-year ROA,

ROE, and ROS (return on sales). Their empirical analyses showed that changes in ROA capture a different construct than changes in ROE and ROS. Hence, they supported the view that results might differ based on the selection of the accounting measures employed.

Long-Term Financial Performance

Apart from short-term performance and accounting-based measures, researchers have evaluated the success of acquisitions by measuring the long-term financial performance of the acquiring firm after the acquisition announcement. Our review indicates that such measures have been used in 18 of the 137 papers reviewed (13.14% of the total). The use of long-term measures answers the need for longitudinal data (Puranam et al. 2006) in M&A research. Unlike short-term measures, they are considered to be of vital importance since they measure "realized" and not "expected" performance (King et al. 2008).

In long-term studies, management scholars usually employ the event study methodology and extend the length of the event window from some days to several months or years. Examples of windows adopted in the literature include 12 months (e.g. Hayward and Hambrick 1997), 24 months (e.g. Carper 1990), 36 months (e.g. Zollo 2009; Laamanen and Keil 2008; King et al. 2008), and nine years (e.g. Fowler and Schmidt 1988).

Empirical results from UK and US studies are consistent in pointing out that on average acquisitions generate negative abnormal returns for the acquiring firm in the long term (Tuch and O'Sullivan 2007). For example, Sudarsanam and Mahate (2006) find significantly negative abnormal returns for half of the acquisitions they studied. Furthermore, Laamanen and Keil (2008) find in a study of 611 US acquirers that acquisitions did not create long-term value. However, when they split their sample into frequent and not frequent acquirers, they concluded that the former outperformed the latter in the long run.

To conclude, studies measuring long-term financial performance have some limitations. As in the case of short-run studies, they cannot assess the impact of an acquisition on the private target firm. Also, the results from the studies utilizing the event window methodology may be influenced by the period of the event window and the benchmark chosen. Furthermore, the models available to estimate abnormal returns over a long period have been criticized for having limited power in statistical significance (see Sudarsanam and Mahate 2006: S15).

Key Informants' Retrospective Assessments of Overall M&A Performance

In contrast to the aforementioned objective criteria, researchers have also utilized subjective performance measures in their effort to assess the performance of M&As (24 articles, or 17.51% of the total). In this stream of research, "key informants" are asked to rate the extent to which a series of goals set before the acquisition have been effectively met after the M&A. These goals usually refer to either financial (e.g. ROA, sales growth, growth in profits, earnings per share, cash flows, market share, etc.) or non-financial aspects (e.g. new product development, competitive position, developing new customer relationships, etc.) or both. Typical "key informants" include managers of the acquiring firm (e.g. Ellis et al. 2009; Homburg and Bucerius 2006; Angwin 2004; Capron 1999; Datta 1991; Datta and Grant 1990), consultants (Zollo and Meier 2008), security analysts (Hayward 2002; Cannella and Hambrick 1993), and academics (Bruton et al. 1994). The use of subjective measures has been justified in cases where objective measures of performance are not available (Dess and Robinson 1984). Among the main advantages of this approach is that it allows for a composite evaluation of performance and that it takes into account the multiple motives for M&As (Larsson and Finkelstein 1999; Brouthers et al. 1998).

Results from this stream of research suggest that on average 45–60% of M&As tend to fail. For example, Hunt (1990) and Rostand (1994) found that 45% of the managers participating in their research believed that the expectations that existed before the deal were not met. Schoenberg (2006), in a UK study, found that 44% of both managers and experts perceived the acquisitions as unsuccessful. More recently, Papadakis and Thanos (2010) calculated the failure rate for Greek domestic acquisitions to be approximately 60%. In addition, studies by consultants (e.g. Adolph et al. 2001) and academics publishing in practitioner journals (e.g. Kitching 1974) have reported similar failure rates.

It should be stressed that, as with any other performance metric, subjective assessments of performance have some limitations. Prevalent among them is that the views expressed by a single "key informant" might be subject to respondent bias (Bowman and Ambrosini 1997), to his/her accurate recollection of past events (Miller et al. 1997; Kumar et al. 1993), to ex-post rationalization symptoms (Golden 1992), and to his/her actual familiarity with the particular M&A (Datta 1991). In an effort to overcome these limitations, researchers have followed a number of validity and robustness tests. First, to overcome individual bias, they have employed responses from multiple managers (e.g. Ambrosini et al. 2011) and have sought responses from different categories of "key informants." For instance, Cannella and Hambrick (1993) averaged the perceptions of six executives from the acquiring firm and six security analysts, for each M&A included in their sample. Furthermore, to overcome the potential existence of retrospective bias, some studies have proceeded to an ex-post analysis of archival data (e.g. Datta 1991). Others, in addition to managerial perceptions, calculated cumulative abnormal returns for a sub-sample of acquisitions in their sample and computed correlations between these two measures to establish convergent validity (e.g. Reus and Lamont 2009). Ellis et al. (2009) validated managerial perceptions by calculating correlations with a series of objective accounting data (e.g. sales growth, return on assets).

Divestiture

Divestiture (sometimes called acquisition survival) has been utilized in 13 studies of our sample (9.49% of the total). According to Schoenberg (2006: 3) "this measure identifies whether an acquired firm has subsequently been divested, with divestment deemed to show manage-ments' dissatisfaction with the acquisition's performance." The time period for assessing divestiture in the literature varies greatly. Examples include five years (e.g. Bergh 2001, 1997), seven years (e.g. Kaplan and Weisbach 1992), ten years (e.g. Hebert, Very, and Beamish 2005) and 13 years after the acquisition (e.g. Porter 1987; Montgomery and Wilson 1986).

Divestiture rates reported in the literature range from a low 20% to a high 74% depend-ing on whether acquisitions are related or not, and whether they are in new fields/indus-tries for acquiring firms. The time frame used to monitor divestitures seems to play a major role. For example, Porter (1987) reported a divestiture rate of 60% for firms enter-ing new fields and a divestiture rate of 74% for unrelated acquisitions. Kaplan and Wiesbach (1992) reported a divestiture rate of 44% seven years after the acquisition, higher than the 33% reported by Ravenscraft and Scherer (1987). Schoenberg (2006) reported an 11% divestiture rate within six years, rising to 30% after nine years, and 56% after 13 years. Finally, Hayward and Shimizu (2006) and Shimizu (2007) report a low divestiture of 20% for recent US acquisitions.

As with perceived performance, the use of divestment data has been encouraged in cases where objective data for post-M&A performance of target firms are not available (Bergh 1997). However, it has been characterized as a "coarse-grained measure" (Cannella and Hambrick 1993). Critics stress its fundamental limitation, i.e. that divest-ment might take place not because of poor performance of the target firm, but because the acquiring firm has decided to change its corporate strategy or received a high pre-mium to sell it (Kaplan and Weisbach 1992). In addition, divestment as a measure of performance is frequently used in the academic literature. It should be stressed that this is not the case in the practitioner area where we found hardly any studies utilizing it as a performance measure. Overall, this suggests that practitioners see this metric with some skepticism.

Integration Process Performance

Apart from financial, accounting, perceptions and divestiture, management scholars have also evaluated the effects of a series of variables on the post-acquisition integration processes, based on the premise that "all value creation takes place after the acquisition" (Haspeslagh and Jemison 1991). Following Birkinshaw, Bresman, and Hakanson (2000) and Stahl and Voigt (2008), we distinguish between task integration and human/socio-cultural integration in our discussion. It should be made clear to the reader that these two aspects of integration are not independent of one another but exert interactive effects on influencing the overall effectiveness on the integration process which in turn influences firm's overall performance.

Task Integration (or Operational Integration)

This type of integration refers to components that need to be integrated between the acquiring and target firm (Zollo and Meier 2008). Such components might include alignment of the operations and systems between the two organizations, transfer of capabilities, resource sharing and learning (Stahl and Voigt 2008). Our review indicates that aspects of task integration have been studied in 20 of the 137 papers reviewed (14.60%). Examples of tasks examined in the management literature include integrating mechanisms between acquiring and target firms (Birkinshaw et al. 2000), the level of alignment of production, R&D, and marketing (Datta 1991), the transfer of technological know-how (Puranam and Srikanth 2007; Bresman et al. 1999), and the creation of knowledge structures leading to learning (Vermeulen and Barkema 2001; Barkema and Vermeulen, 1998). All these studies suggest that these tasks are important in influencing the success of integration, which in turns influences the success of an acquisition.

Human Integration or Sociocultural Integration

Our review concluded that 20 studies (14.60%) have dealt with aspects of human integration and performance. These refer to such outcomes as employee turnover, cultural convergence, employee commitment, stress, job satisfaction, and security (Stahl and Voigt 2008; Birkinshaw et al. 2000). In the following, we review aspects of human integration and link them to performance.

With respect to employee turnover, M&A studies have examined what drives target firms' CEO departures (e.g. Buchholtz et al. 2003), target firms' top management turnover (Krug and Hegarty 2001; Lubatkin et al. 1999; Krug and Hegarty 1997; Hambrick and Cannella 1993; Walsh 1989, 1988) and workforce reductions (Krishnan et al. 2007). Another focal point of this research stream is whether these departures influence target firms' performance. Krug and Aguilera (2004) reviewed previous literature on the topic and reported that the average top management turnover rate over a five-year period following the acquisition is 68% in acquired companies and 34.5% in non-acquired firms.

Also, top management turnover has been linked to lower ROA (Krishnan et al. 1997), lower perceived overall performance (Cannella and Hambrick 1993), and an increased possibility of divestiture (Bergh 2001).

Regarding cultural convergence or acculturation, studies explore their antecedents (Larsson and Lubatkin 2001) and their effects on M&A performance (Weber 1996). Results indicate that corporate cultural differences influence negatively the effectiveness of integration outcomes and post-M&A performance (Weber 1996).

Finally, research has shown that an acquisition can influence several employee outcomes. In one notable study, Schweiger and Denisi (1991) found that the announcement of a merger increases employee uncertainty, stress, and absenteeism. All these employee outcomes lead to poor synergy realization.

This stream of research has its own limitations. These are mainly related to their subjective versus objective measurement. Subjective measures based on survey data (e.g. top management turnover, employee turnover, employee outcomes, stress, motivation) have the same limitations as the method of using survey data to measure key informants' retrospective assessments. Also, objective data (e.g. R&D spending) are susceptible to the reliability of the secondary source of data.

Innovation Performance

The final stream of research to gauge M&A performance explores the extent to which an acquisition influences the innovation performance of the acquiring and/or the target firm. Innovation outcomes have been utilized in 6% of the studies reviewed (eight papers out of 137). Researchers in this area utilize such variables as number of patents (Kapoor and Kwanghui 2007; Ahuja and Katila 2001), R&D intensity (Hitt et al. 1998), both patents and R&D intensity (Hitt et al. 1991), and product innovativeness (Puranam et al. 2006). Recently, Makri, Hitt, and Lane (2010: 610) used multiple criteria to assess a firm's innovativeness. Their study operationalized innovation performance as a complex construct consisting of invention quantity (patent counts), invention quality (extent to which a firm's patents are cited in subsequent patents), and invention novelty (extent to which a firm's patent portfolio extends to a range of technology classes).

Studies utilizing innovation outcomes as a dependent variable assert that multiple acquisitions over time reduce an acquirer's innovative outputs (e.g. ability to create new products). This is attributed to the fact that acquisitions emphasize financial controls which ultimately discourage innovation (Hitt et al. 2005).

Innovation outputs, although useful in measuring the performance of technological acquisitions, have some drawbacks. For instance, the use of patents as a proxy for innovative output assumes that all inventions can be patented, which is not always the case (Ahuja and Katila 2001). Other drawbacks relate to the way innovation performance is measured (survey vs. secondary data). The use of survey data for measuring innovation might suffer from informant bias as explained in the perceived performance measure and the reliability of secondary data is sometimes questionable.

Research on M&A Performance: Where do we Go from Here? A List of Substantive Priorities

So far we have critically reviewed the literature from 13 top management journals and have found that past researchers have used seven broad approaches in their attempt to capture the multifaceted construct of M&A performance. All the studies reviewed have greatly added to our level of knowledge, yet there are still some controversies and inconsistencies. In the following sections, we propose a list of substantive priorities which need to be addressed by researchers in coming years.

The Inherent Limitations of Cumulative Abnormal Returns (CARs) and the Need for Carefully Aligning M&A Performance with the Research Question Explored

Previously in the review, we reported that almost one-third of papers in the management area have used short-term event windows (CARs) to assess the performance of acquisitions. The major advantage of this method is that changes in stock prices can be attributed to a particular acquisition. We argue that despite this primary advantage, the use of CARs for assessing post-M&A performance should be treated with due caution. CARs do not measure realized (actual) performance but investors' expectations about future performance, based on the efficient market hypothesis.

However, in the accounting and finance area, it has been argued that CARs efficiently predict post-financial long-term performance. For instance, Healy, Palepu, and Ruback (1992) showed that short-term event study results were positively associated with subsequent long-term cash flows. In the same vein, Harrison and Godfrey (1997) showed that they are correlated with industry-adjusted ROA.

A contrary view has been suggested in the management literature. Recently, scholars have provided empirical evidence that in complex events (e.g. horizontal acquisitions), the initial market response may provide biased or misleading results (Oler et al. 2008), meaning that the market hypothesis may not hold. For example, Schoenberg (2006) found in the UK that short-term CARs are related neither to long-term divestment data, nor to the assessments of managers and experts. Oler, Harrison, and Allen (2008: 151) found that the positive initial market response to an acquisition announcement is contradicted by negative long-run post-acquisition returns in a sample of 2500 US acquisitions.

In summary, in a study including cross-border and domestic acquisitions made by European firms, Zollo and Meier (2008) found that CARs are not linked to a series of other post-acquisition performance measures such as accounting returns, long-term financial performance, experts' assessments, customer and employee retention, and integration process performance.

More recently, Papadakis and Thanos (2010) further echoed these results by reporting no statistically significant correlations between CARs and ROA and managers' perceptions in a Greek sample. The aforementioned studies lend credence to the argument that short-term measures fail to predict post-M&A performance. It seems that they do not measure post-acquisition realized performance. In the words of Zollo and Meier (2008: 71), "CARs gauge the collective cognitive heuristic, the overall market sentiment about how a given typology of acquisitions should perform."

Of course we do not argue that CARs should be abandoned by future researchers and that results from CAR studies are not useful. We only suggest that researchers should bear in mind that they do not measure actual performance, but investors' short-term expectations. Thus, we encourage future researchers to continue adopting this method, but at the same time to avoid using general terms such as "acquisition performance" when adopting the CAR methodology and also to complement their analyses with longer-term performance measures. Maybe a term such as "short-term expectations for the merger" or "market expectations about firm performance" or "short-term market response to acquisition announcements" would be more appropriate, as recent reviews suggest (Haleblian et al. 2009; Zollo and Meier 2008).

The same holds for the other six broad performance criteria identified in our review. Zollo and Meier (2008) showed that M&A performance is a multidimensional construct, with the available measures tapping only parts of it. Similarly, Cording et al. (2010) performed a series of confirmatory factor analyses and showed that acquisition performance is a multilevel construct with no available measure capturing its entirety. Given Cording et al.'s (2010) and Zollo and Meier's (2008) results, we are of the opinion that future researchers should avoid using general terms such as M&A performance and be more specific as to what they measure. For example, when employing managers' personal opinions in survey data, they could label them as managers' perceived performance (Papadakis and Thanos 2010) or managers' retrospective assessments of acquisition performance (Haleblian et al. 2009). Similarly, when employing accounting ratios such as ROA, ROE, growth in sales, they could be described as post-accounting returns to the acquiring firm and not post-M&A performance.

A related issue has to do with the necessity of carefully aligning the measure of M&A performance with the research question of the study (Haleblian et al. 2009; Zollo and Meier 2008). We hold the view that researchers should clearly defend why they decided to use this particular measure instead of another one. Lately we have seen such notable examples in the management literature clearly aligning their selection of their dependent variable with their research question (McNamara et al. 2008; Haleblian et al. 2006; Zollo and Singh 2004). For example, McNamara et al. (2008) examined the effects of participating in an acquisition wave and whether the point in time that a firm participates (early or late) has any effects on the success of individual M&As. They adopted CARs as a measure of M&A performance, since these measures capture the performance of individual acquisitions as opposed to accounting-based measures which measure overall firm performance.

The Need for Multiple Performance Criteria

Apart from paying attention to the inherent limitations of CARs and aligning the performance construct with the research question explored in the study, we believe that a second future challenge concerns the adoption of multiple measures for evaluating performance within a single study. Previously, we cited papers demonstrating that acquisition performance is a multidimensional construct, with existing measures capturing only parts of it. Also, we cited recent empirical papers (e.g. Zollo and Meier 2008; Schoenberg 2006) utilizing multiple measures of performance which demonstrated that there is a lack of comparability among the various measures of performance. This suggests that an acquisition measured with one performance criterion (e.g. CARs) might be considered as successful and at the same time as unsuccessful if we use another criterion (e.g. divestiture).

Along with previous research, we argue that to overcome these limitations of previous studies, future researchers should evaluate M&A performance with multiple criteria. This will shed further light on the contradictory results published with respect to the impact of some variables (e.g. past experience, cultural differences, premiums, etc.) on M&A performance. For instance, we have seen studies publishing all possible types of relationships (e.g. positive, negative, no relationship) between previous past experience in making acquisitions and M&A performance (Papadakis 2005; Haleblian and Finkelstein 1999). Cording et al. (2010: 27) employed multiple performance criteria in their effort to provide a basis for explaining these contradictory results. They found that the relationship between acquisition experience and acquisition performance is (1) positive when acquisition performance is measured with accounting-based measures, (2) negative when it is measured with long-term stock measures, and (3) insignificant when it is measured with short-term stock measures. Hence, we encourage future researchers to consider utilizing multiple performance criteria.

The Need to Develop New Measures of M&A performance Taking into Account Multiple Stakeholders (e.g. Customers, Employees, Suppliers)

Apart from studying M&A performance with multiple performance criteria, we believe that there is a need for new measures of M&A performance that take account of multiple stakeholders (Haleblian et al. 2009). Traditional research has studied the effects of an acquisition on stakeholders and has ignored shareholders such as customers, suppliers, borrowers, rivals etc. (Haleblian et al. 2009). For instance, losing important customers might lead to poor post-acquisition returns. However, our review indicates that no study from the 137 reviewed has considered this criterion as a measure of M&A performance. Zollo and Meier's (2008) review of 89 articles from top management and finance journals and Haleblian et al.'s (2009) review of 164 articles further support this argument. Similarly, we found no study in the management area measuring the impact of acquisitions on suppliers, borrowers, rivals, or other aspects such as corporate brands. As an acquisition is likely to impact various shareholders in different ways (Schoenberg 2006), we believe that developing new measures that take account of these shareholders represents a promising avenue for future research. Recently, in the marketing area, Öberg, Henneberg, and Mouzas (2007) examined whether an M&A has an impact on the business network and existing customers. We see this as a positive trend and encourage future researchers to consider the retention of customers as a measure of M&A success.

From the Examination of Acquisitions as Isolated Events to the Examination of Acquisition Programs

Our review recognized that management scholars have focused on the characteristics and performance implications of individual acquisitions. But individual acquisitions are usually part of a sequence of acquisitions (acquisition program) aimed at implementing a broader strategy and this might have an impact on the performance of an isolated acquisition (Kusewitt 1985). Barkema and Schijven (2008b) established the validity of this point. Their empirical data demonstrated that the success of an individual acquisition is contingent upon its position within the acquirer's acquisition sequence. Laamanen and Keil (2008) have argued for examining the performance implications of serial acquirers rather than the examination of acquisitions per se. We believe that both papers represent novel approaches and we strongly support the view that by examining acquisition patterns of serial acquirers, the field can progress toward understanding the true antecedents of M&A performance (for more on this topic, please see Chapter 6 by Keil, Laamanen, and Mäkisalo in this *Handbook*).

The Potential Impact of New Regulatory Changes (e.g. Sarbanes–Oxley) on the Performance of M&As

Corporate scandals from the USA (e.g. Enron, Arthur Andersen) led investors to lose their trust in the financial system and view the annual financial statements with some skepticism. To prevent similar scandals in the future, the US government introduced an act of law named the Sarbanes–Oxley (SOX) in 2002. The enactment of SOX created a new business environment with important consequences for companies. Business analysts suggest that SOX has created a new M&A environment in which firms proceed with more caution in carrying out acquisitions, pay lower premiums, and overall conduct more successful acquisitions (Karan and Sharifi 2006; Mamdani and Noah 2004). However, with two recent exceptions (Devers et al. 2008; Papadakis and Thanos 2008), there is no study that directly examines empirically whether the allegations of business analysts hold in reality. Devers et al. (2008) concluded that firm strategy has become more conservative after SOX, as firms tend to avoid taking unjustified risks. In their study, Papadakis and Thanos (2008) contrasted M&A processes and outcomes between the merger boom period of 1997–2000 (pre-SOX) and the merger bust period of 2000–2004 (post-SOX). Their results suggested that there exists no difference in the performance of M&As between these two periods and this can be attributed to the fact that acquiring firms did not significantly change the processes followed both before and after the deal closure. These results contradict the aforementioned conclusions from non-academic sources. However, Papadakis and Thanos (2008) utilized data from domestic deals made by Greek firms. As a matter of fact, we do not know for sure whether their findings can be replicated in the US context. Thus, we advise future researchers to examine how (and if) SOX and other regulatory changes impacted acquisition performance.

Our belief in the importance of this issue is echoed by a recent review on M&As whose authors have argued along similar lines (Haleblian et al. 2009: 485). Also, the reader is advised to read Chapter 23 by Gary Dymski in the current *Handbook* for more on regulatory changes and frameworks.

The Need to Overcome the "Geographical Bias" of M&A studies

As with any other management topic, research on M&A performance comes mainly from the US or the UK (Cartwright and Schoenberg 2006). This reflects the so-called "geographical bias" problem of previous management work (Pettigrew et al. 2002). We argue that to overcome this trend, there is a need for cross-national studies from both developed and emerging economies in order to understand whether the country of origin of the studies has any impact on the conclusions we are drawing. Such studies will shed further light on the impact of national culture on M&A processes and outcomes (Teerikangas and Véry 2006). Please also see Chapter 16 in this *Handbook* by Satu Teerikangas and Philippe Véry.

Domestic vs. Cross-Border Acquisitions: Implications for performance

Our review identified studies with domestic (e.g. Shimizu 2007), cross-border (e.g. Nadolska and Barkema 2007; Markides and Ittner 1994), and mixed samples (e.g. Zollo and Meier 2008). What is still missing in the literature is a study examining whether acquiring firms follow different M&A strategies in domestic and international environments and whether these strategies have effects on the performance of domestic and international acquisitions respectively. Of course, particular caution should be paid to definitional issues of domestic and international acquisitions.

CONCLUSIONS

The aim of this chapter was to review the literature on M&A performance. To do so we conducted a review of the topic in 13 top management journals and also drew on the results of recent reviews. Results suggest that significant progress has been made on the topic during the past 30 years. Nonetheless, challenges such as aligning measures of M&A performance with the research question, using multiple performance criteria for evaluating M&A performance, implementing cross-national studies, examining acquisition programs instead of individual acquisitions, and considering the impact of recent regulatory changes on performance, remain unresolved.

Table 5.A1 Studies reviewed categorized by performance measure*

Study	Short-term financial performance	Accounting performance	Long-term financial performance	Key informants' retrospective assessments	Divestiture	Integration process performance	Innovation performance	Journal
Ahuja and Katila (2001)							******	SMJ
Anand and Singh (1997)	******							BJM
Ambrosini et al. (2011)				******				SMJ
Arikan and Capron (2010)	******							BJM
Arnold and Parker (2007)	******							JIBS
Aybar and Ficici (2009)	******							SMJ
Balakrishnan (1988)	******							SMJ
Barkema and Schijven (2008b)		******						AMJ
Bergh (1997)					******			SMJ
Bergh (2001)					******			JOM
Bettis and Hall (1982)		******						AMJ
Birkinshaw et al. (2000)						******		JMS
Bresman et al. (1999)						task		JIBS
Brush (1996)		******				task		SMJ
Bruton et al. (1994)				******		******		AMJ
Buchholtz et al. (2003)						human		JOM
Calori et al. (1994)				******				Ostudies
Cannella and Hambrick (1993)				******		******		SMJ
Capron (1999)				******		task		SMJ

(Continued)

Table 5.A1 Continued

Study	Short-term financial performance	Accounting performance	Long-term financial performance	Key informants' retrospective assessments	Divestiture	Integration process performance	Innovation performance	Journal
Capron et al. (2001)	***				***			SMJ
Capron and Pistre (2002)	***							SMJ
Capron and Shen (2007)	***							SMJ
Carow et al. (2004)			***					SMJ
Carper (1990)			***					JOM
Castrogiovanni and Bruton (1994)				***				JBR
Chakrabarti et al. (2009)			***					JIBS
Chang (1996)		***						SMJ
Chatterjee (1991)	***							AMJ
Chatterjee (1992)			***					SMJ
Chatterjee et al. (1992)	***							SMJ
Clougherty and Duso (2009)	***							JMS
Cording et al. 2008			***					AMJ
Cording et al. 2010	***	***	***					SO
Datta and Grant (1990)				***				JOM
Datta (1991)		***		***				SMJ
Datta et al. (1992)	***	***						SMJ
Desai et al. (2005)	***			***				JBR
Ellis et al. (2009)				task		***		SMJ
Empson (2001)						***		HR
Finkelstein and Haleblian (2002)	***					task		OS
Flanagan (1996)								JOM
Fowler and Schmidt (1988)		***	***					AMJ
Fowler and Schmidt (1989)	***	***	***	***				SMJ

Study	C1	C2	C3	C4	C5	C6	C7	C8	Journal
Graebner (2004)				both		******		******	SMJ
Gubbi et al. (2010)	******								JIBS
Haleblian and Finkelstein (1999)	******								ASQ
Hambrick and Cannella (1993)	******								AMJ
Harris and Shimizu (2004)	******								JMS
Harrison et al. (1991)				******		human	******	******	AMJ
Hayward (2002)	******								SMJ
Hayward (2003)	******								SMJ
Hayward and Hambrick (1997)	******				******	******			ASQ
Hayward and Shimizu (2006)									SMJ
Hebert et al. (2005)		******			******				JOM
Hitt et al. (1991)									Ostudies
Hitt et al.(1996)		******					******		JOM
Hitt et al. (1998)							******		BJM
Holl and Kyriazis (1997)	******	******							SMJ
Homburg and Bucerius (2006)	******			******					SMJ
Hopkins (1987)		******							JOM
Hunt (1990)				******		task		******	SMJ
Kapoor and Lim (2007)						task	******		AMJ
Kim and Finkelstein (2009)	******								SMJ
King et al. (2004)	******	******							SMJ
King et al. (2008)			******						OS
Kobeissi et al. (2010)	******								JBR
Krishnan et al. (1997)	******	******							SMJ
Kroll et al. (1990)		******							JBR
Kroll et al. (1997)	******								SMJ
Kroll et al. (2008)	******							******	SMJ

(Continued)

Table 5.A1 Continued

Study	Short-term financial performance	Accounting performance	Long-term financial performance	Key informants' retrospective assessments	Divestiture	Integration process performance	Innovation performance	Journal
Krishnan et al. (2007)		*****				human		JMS
Krishnan and Krishnan (2003)		*****						JBR
Krug and Hegarty (1997)						*****		SMJ
Krug and Hegarty (2001)						human		SMJ
Kusewitt (1985)		*****	*****			*****		SMJ
Laamanen and Keil (2008)			*****					SMJ
Lamont and Anderson (1985)		*****						AMJ
Larsson and Finkelstein (1999)				*****		both *****		OS
Larsson and Lubatkin (2001)						human		HR
Lubatkin (1987)	*****		*****					SMJ
Lubatkin et al. (1997)	*****		*****			*****		JOM
Lubatkin et al. (1998)						both *****		OS
Lubatkin et al. (1999)	*****					human		JOM
Makri et al. (2010)							*****	SMJ
Markides and Ittner (1994)	*****							JIBS
McDonald et al. (2008)	*****							SMJ
McNamara et al. (2008)	*****					*****		JOM
Meyer and Altenborg (2007)					*****	task		BJM
Montgomery and Wilson (1986)								SMJ

Study	(1)	(2)	(3)	(4)	(5)	Journal
Morosini et al. (1998)	*****					JIBS
Mtar (2010)				both		Ostudies
Nadolska and Barkema (2007)			*****			JIBS
Oler et al. (2008)				*****		SO
Olie (1994)				human		Ostudies
Pangarkar and Lie (2004)	*****	*****				SMJ
Papadakis and Thanos (2010)	*****					BJM
Paruchuri et al. (2006)					*****	OS
Phan and Hill (1995)	*****					JOM
Porrini (2004)	*****					JOM
Puranam et al. (2006)					*****	AMJ
Puranam and Srikanth (2007)	*****			task		SMJ
Ramaswamy (1997)				*****		AMJ
Ranft and Lord (2002)				task		OS
Reus and Lamont (2009)			*****			JIBS
Sanders (2001)		*****				AMJ
Saxton and Dollinger (2004)		*****				JOM
Schweiger and Denisi (1991)		*****		human		AMJ
Schmidt and Fowler (1990)		*****	*****			SMJ
Schoenberg (2006)	*****					BJM
Schweiger and Goulet (2005)		*****	*****	*****		Ostudies
Schweizer (2005)			*****	task		AMJ
Seth (1990)	*****					SMJ
Seth et al. (2000)	*****					JIBS
Seth et al. (2002)	*****					SMJ
Shanley and Correa (1992)		*****				SMJ

(Continued)

Table 5.A1 Continued

Study	Short-term financial performance	Accounting performance	Long-term financial performance	Key informants' retrospective assessments	Divestiture	Integration process performance	Innovation performance	Journal
Shelton (1988)	*****							SMJ
Shimizu and Hitt (2005)					*****	*****		JOM
Shimizu (2007)					*****	*****		AMJ
Singh and Montgomery (1987)	*****							SMJ
Stahl and Voigt (2008)	*****					both		OS
Sudarsanam and Mahate (2006)		*****	*****					BJM
Uhlenbruck et al. (2006)	*****							SMJ
Uhlenbruck and Castro (2000)				*****				AMJ
Vaara (2003)						*****		JMS
Vermeulen and Barkema (2001)					*****	both		AMJ
Véry et al. (1997)				*****				SMJ
Villinger (1996)						task *****		O studies
Walsh (1988)						human *****		SMJ
Walsh (1989)						human *****		SMJ
Walsh and Ellwood (1991)						human		SMJ

Study	Task	Human	Both	Journal
Walters et al. (2007)	*****			JBR
Walters et al. (2008)	*****			SO
Wan and Yiu (2009)	*****			SMJ
Weber (1996)	*****	human		HR
				HR
Yu et al. (2005)	******	human		Ostudies
Zollo (2009)	******			OS
Zollo and Singh (2004)	******		******	SMJ

* *Note*: In integration process performance, we distinguish between task, human and both types of integration.

REFERENCES

Adolph, G., Buchanan, I., Hornery, J., Jackson, B., Jones, J., Kihlstedt, T., Neilson, G., & Quarls, H. (2001). *Merger Integration: Delivering on the Promise*. Fairfax, VA: Booz-Allen & Hamilton.

Ahuja, G., & Katila, R. (2001). "Technological Acquisitions and the Innovation Performance of Acquiring Firms: A Longitudinal Study." *Strategic Management Journal*, 22, 197–220.

Ambrosini, V., Bowman, C., & Schoenberg, R. (2011). "Should Acquiring Firms Pursue More Than One Value Creation Strategy? An Empirical Test of Acquisition Performance." *British Journal of Management*, 22: 173–85.

Anand, J., & Delios, A. (2002). "Absolute and Relative Resources as Determinants of International Acquisitions." *Strategic Management Journal*, 23: 119–34.

—— & Singh, H. (1997). "Asset Redeployment, Acquisitions and Corporate Strategy in Declining Industries." *Strategic Management Journal*, 18/S1: 99–118.

Angwin, D. (2004). "Speed in M&A Integration: The First 100 Days." *European Management Journal*, 22: 418–30.

Arikan, A. M., & Capron, L. (2010). "Do Newly Public Acquirers Benefit or Suffer from their Pre-IPO Affiliations with Underwriters and VCs?" *Strategic Management Journal*, 31/12: 1257–89.

Arnold, M., & Parker, D. (2007). "UK Competition Policy and Shareholder Value: The Impact of Merger Inquiries." *British Journal of Management*, 18: 27–43.

Aybar, B., & Ficici, A. (2009). "Cross-Border Acquisitions and Firm Value: An Analysis of Emerging-Market Multinationals." *Journal of International Business Studies* 40: 1317–38.

Balakrishnan, S. (1988). "The Prognostics of Diversifying Acquisitions." *Strategic Management Journal*, 9/2: 185–96.

Barkema, H. G., & Schijven, M. (2008a). "How do Firms Learn to Make Acquisitions? A Review of Past Research and an Agenda for the Future." *Journal of Management*, 34: 594–634.

—— —— (2008b). "Toward Unlocking the Full Potential of Acquisitions: The Role of Organizational Restructuring." *Academy of Management Journal*, 51: 696–722.

—— & Vermeulen, F. (1998). "International Expansion through Start-Up or Acquisition: A Learning Perspective." *Academy of Management Journal*, 41: 7–26.

Bergh, D. (1997). "Predicting Divestiture of Unrelated Acquisitions: An Integrative Model of Ex Ante Conditions." *Strategic Management Journal*, 18: 715–31.

—— (2001). "Executive Retention and Acquisition Outcomes: A Test of Opposing Views on the Influence of Organization Tenure." *Journal of Management*, 27: 603–22.

Bettis, R. A., & Hall, W. K. (1982). "Diversification Strategy, Accounting Determined Risk, and Accounting Determined Return." *Academy of Management Journal*, 25/2: 254–64.

Birkinshaw, J., Bresman, H., & Hakanson, L. (2000). "Managing the Post-acquisition Integration Process: How the Human Integration Processes Interact to Foster Value Creation." *Journal of Management Studies*, 37: 395–425.

Bowman, C., & Ambrosini, V. (1997). "Using Single Respondents in Strategy Research." *British Journal of Management*, 8: 119–31.

Bresman, H., Birkinshaw, J., & Nobel, R. (1999). "Knowledge Transfer In International Acquisitions." *Journal of International Business Studies*, 30: 439–62.

Brouthers, K. D., van Hastenburg, P., & van den Ven, J. (1998), "If Most Mergers Fail Why Are They So Popular?" *Long Range Planning*, 31: 347–53.

Brush, T. H. (1996). "Predict Change in Operational Synergy and Post-acquisition Performance of Acquired Businesses." *Strategic Management Journal*, 17/1: 1–24.

Bruton, G. D., Oviatt, B. M., & White, M. A. (1994). "Performance of Acquisitions of Distressed Firms." *Academy of Management Journal*, 37: 972–89.

Buchholtz, A. K., Ribbens, B. A., & Houle, I. T. (2003). "The Role of Human Capital in Postacquisition CEO Departure." *Academy of Management Journal*, 46: 506–14.

Calori, R., Lubatkin, M., & Véry, P. (1994). "Control Mechanisms in Cross-Border Acquisitions: An International Comparison." *Organization Studies*, 15/3: 361–79.

Cannella, A. A. J., & Hambrick, D. C. (1993). "Effects of Executive Departures on the Performance of Acquired Firms." *Strategic Management Journal*, 14: 137–52.

Capron, L. (1999). "The Long-Term Performance of Horizontal Acquisitions." *Strategic Management Journal*, 20: 987–1018.

—— Mitchell, W., & Swaminathan, A. (2001). "Asset Divestiture following Horizontal Acquisitions: A Dynamic View." *Strategic Management Journal*, 22/9: 817–44.

—— & Pistre, N. (2002). "When do Acquirers Earn Abnormal Returns?" *Strategic Management Journal*, 23: 781–94.

—— & Shen, J.-C. (2007). "Acquisitions of Private vs. Public Firms: Private Information, Target Selection, and Acquirer Returns." *Strategic Management Journal*, 28/9: 891–911.

Carow, K., Heron, R., & Saxton, T. (2004). "Do Early Bids Get the Returns? An Empirical Investigation of Early-Mover Advantages in Acquisitions." *Strategic Management Journal*, 25: 563–85.

Carper, W. B. (1990). "Corporate Acquisitions and Shareholder Wealth: A Review and Exploratory Analysis." *Journal of Management*, 16: 807–23.

Cartwright, S., & Schoenberg, R. (2006). "Thirty Years of Mergers and Acquisitions Research: Recent Advances and Future Opportunities." *British Journal of Management*, 17: S1–5.

Castrogiovanni, G. J., & Bruton, G. D. (1994). "Business Turnaround Processes following Acquisitions: Reconsidering the Role of Retrenchment." *Journal of Business Research*, 48/1: 25–34.

Chakrabarti, R., Gupta-Mukherjee, S., & Jayaraman, N. (2009). "Mars-Venus Marriages: Culture and Cross-Border M&A." *Journal of International Business Studies*, 40/2: 216–36.

Chang, S. J. (1996). "An Evolutionary Perspective on Diversification and Corporate Restructuring: Entry, Exit, and Economic Performance during 1981–89." *Strategic Management Journal*, 17/8: 587-611.

Chatterjee, S. (1991). "Gains in Vertical Acquisitions and Market Power: Theory and Evidence." *Academy of Management Journal*, 34/2: 436–48.

—— (1992). "Sources of Value in Takeovers: Synergy or Restructuring—Implications for Target and Bidder Firms." *Strategic Management Journal*, 13/4: 267–86.

—— Lubatkin, M. H., Schweiger, D. M., & Weber, Y. (1992). "Cultural Differences and Shareholder Value in Related Mergers: Linking Equity and Human Capital." *Strategic Management Journal*, 13/5: 319–34.

Chenhall, R. H., & Langfield-Smith, K. (2007). "Multiple Perspectives of Performance Measures." *European Management Journal*, 25: 266–82.

Clougherty, J. A., & Duso, T. (2009). "The Impact of Horizontal Mergers on Rivals: Gains to Being Left Outside a Merger." *Journal of Management Studies*, 46/8: 1365–95.

Cording, M., Christmann, P., & King, D. R. (2008). "Reducing Causal Ambiguity in Acquisition Integration: Intermediate Goals as Mediators of Integration Decisions and Acquisition Performance." *Academy of Management Journal*, 51/4: 744–67.

Cording, M., Christmann, P. & Weigelt, C. (2010). "Measuring Theoretically Complex Constructs: The Case of Acquisition Performance." *Strategic Organization*, 8: 11–41.

Datta, D. K. (1991). "Organizational Fit and Acquisition Performance: Effects of Post-acquisition Integration." *Strategic Management Journal*, 12: 281–97.

—— & Grant, J. H. (1990). "Relationship between Type of Acquisition, the Autonomy Given to the Acquired Firm, and Acquisition Success: An Empirical Analysis." *Journal of Management*, 16: 29–44.

—— Pinches, G. E., & Narayanan, V. K. (1992). "Factors Influencing Wealth Creation from Mergers and Acquisitions: A Meta-Analysis." *Strategic Management Journal*, 13/1: 67–84.

Desai, A., Kroll, M., & Wright, P. (2005). "Outside Board Monitoring and the Economic Outcomes of Acquisitions: A Test of the Substitution Hypothesis." *Journal of Business Research*, 58: 926–34.

Dess, G. G., & Robinson, R. B., Jr. (1984). "Measuring Organizational Performance in the Absence of Objective Measures: The Case of the Privately-Held Firm and Conglomerate Business Unit." *Strategic Management Journal*, 5: 265–73.

Devers, C. E., McNamara, G., Wiseman, R. M., & Arrefelt, M. (2008). "Moving Closer to the Action: Examining Compensation Design Effects on Firm Risk." *Organization Science*, 19: 548–66.

Dickerson, A., Gibson, H., & Tsakalotos, E. (1997). "The Impact of Acquisitions on Company Performance: Evidence from a Large Panel of UK Firms." *Oxford Economics Papers*, 49: 344–61.

Ellis, K. M., Reus, T. H., & Lamont, B. T. (2009). "The Effects of Procedural and Informational Justice in the Integration of Related Acquisitions." *Strategic Management Journal*, 30: 137–61.

Empson, L. (2001). "Fear of Exploitation and Fear of Contamination: Impediments to Knowledge Transfer in Mergers between Professional Service Firms." *Human Relations*, 54/7: 839–62.

Finkelstein, S., & Haleblian, J. (2002). "Understanding Acquisition Performance: The Role of Transfer Effects." *Organization Science*, 13/1: 36–47.

Flanagan, D. J. (1996). "Announcements of Purely Related and Purely Unrelated Mergers and Shareholder Returns: Reconciling the Relatedness Paradox." *Journal of Management*, 22/6: 823–35.

Fowler, K. L., and Schmidt, D. R. (1988). "Tender Offers, Acquisition, and Subsequent Performance in Manufacturing Firms." *Academy of Management Journal*, 31: 962–74.

—— & Schmidt, D. R. (1989). "Determinants of Tender Offer Post-acquisition Financial Performance." *Strategic Management Journal*, 10: 339–50.

Golden, B. R. (1992). "The Past is the Past—or Is It? The Use of Retrospective Accounts as Indicators of Past Strategy." *Academy of Management Journal*, 35: 848–60.

Graebner, M. E. (2004). "Momentum and Serendipity: How Acquired Leaders Create Value in the Integration of Technology Firms." *Strategic Management Journal*, 25/8–9: 751–77.

Grant, R. M., Jammine, A. P., & Thomas, H. (1988). "Diversity, Diversification, and Profitability among British Manufacturing Companies 1972–1984." *Academy of Management Journal*, 31: 771–801.

Gubbi, S. R., Aulakh, P. S., Ray, S., Sarkar, M. B., & Chittoor, R. (2010). "Do International Acquisitions by Emerging-Economy Firms Create Shareholder Value? The Case of Indian Firms." *Journal of International Business Studies*, 41: 397–418.

Haleblian, J., Devers, C. E., McNamara, G., Carpenter, M. A., & Davison, R. B. (2009). "Taking Stock of What We Know About Mergers and Acquisitions: A Review and Research Agenda." *Journal of Management*, 35: 469–502.

—— & Finkelstein, S. (1999). "The Influence of Organizational Acquisition Experience on Acquisition Performance: A Behavioral Learning Perspective." *Administrative Science Quarterly*, 44: 29–56.

—— Kim, J.-Y., & Rajagoplan, N. (2006). "The Influence of Acquisition Experience and Performance on Acquisition Behavior: Evidence From The U.S. Commercial Banking Industry." *Academy of Management Journal*, 49: 357–70.

Hambrick, D. C., & Cannella, A. A. J. (1993). "Relative Standing: A Framework for Understanding Departures of Acquired Executives." *Academy of Management Journal*, 36: 733–62.

Harris, I. C., & Shimizu, K. (2004). "Too Busy to Serve? An Examination of the Influence of Overboarded Directors." *Journal of Management Studies*, 41/5: 775–98.

Harrison, J., & Godfrey, P. (1997). "Do Event Studies Predict Acquisition Success? An Empirical Test." Annual Academy of Management Conference, Boston, MA.

—— Hitt, M. A., Hoskisson, R. E., & Ireland, R. D. (1991). "Synergies and Post-acquisition Performance: Differences versus Similarities in Resource Allocations." *Journal of Management*, 17: 173–90.

Haspeslagh, D., & Jemison, D. B. (1991). *Managing Acquisitions: Creating Value through Corporate Renewal*. New York: Free Press.

Hayward, M. L. A. (2002). "When do Firms Learn from their Acquisition Experience? Evidence from 1990 to 1995." *Strategic Management Journal*, 23: 21–39.

—— (2003). "Professional Influence: The Effects of Investment Banks on Clients' Acquisition Financing and Performance." *Strategic Management Journal*, 24/9: 783–801.

—— & Hambrick, D. C. (1997). "Explaining the Premiums Paid for Large Acquisitions: Evidence of CEO Hubris." *Administrative Science Quarterly*, 42: 103–29.

—— & Shimizu, K. (2006). "De-commitment to Losing Strategic Action: Evidence from the Divestiture of Poorly Performing Acquisitions." *Strategic Management Journal*, 27: 541–57.

Healy, P., Palepu, K., & Ruback, R. (1992). "Does Corporate Performance Improve after Mergers?" *Journal of Financial Economics*, 23: 135–75.

Hebert, L., Véry, P., & Beamish, P. W. (2005). "Expatriation as a Bridge Over Troubled Water: A Knowledge-Based Perspective Applied to Cross-Border Acquisitions." *Organization Studies*, 26: 1455–76.

Hitt, M., Harrison, J., Ireland, R. D., & Best, A. (1998). "Attributes of Successful and Unsuccessful Acquisitions of US Firms." *British Journal of Management*, 9: 91–114.

—— Hoskisson, R. E., Johnson, R. A., & Moesel, D. D. (1996). "The Market for Corporate Control and Firm Innovation." *Academy of Management Journal*, 39/5: 1084–119.

—— Ireland, D., & Harrison, J. (2005). "Mergers and Acquisitions: A Value Creating or Value Destroying Strategy," in M. Hitt, E. Freeman, & J. Harrison (eds.), *The Blackwell Handbook of Strategic Management*. Malden, MA & Oxford: Blackwell Publishing.

—— —— —— & Hoskisson, R. E. (1991). "Effects of Acquisitions on R&D Inputs and Outputs." *Academy of Management Journal*, 34: 693–706.

Holl, P., & Kyriazis, D. (1997). "Wealth Creation and Bid Resistance in U.K. Takeover Bids." *Strategic Management Journal*, 18/6: 483–98.

Homburg, C., and Bucerius, M. (2006). "Is Speed of Integration Really a Success Factor of Mergers and Acquisitions? An Analysis of the Role of Internal and External Relatedness." *Strategic Management Journal*, 27: 347–67.

Hopkins, H. D. (1987). "Long-Term Acquisition Strategies in the U.S. Economy." *Journal of Management*, 13/3: 557–72

Hunt, J. W. (1990). "Changing Pattern of Acquisition Behaviour in Takeovers and the Consequences for Acquisition Processes." *Strategic Management Journal*, 11: 69–77.

Hutzschenreuter, T., & Kleindienst, I. (2006). "Strategy-Process Research: What have we Learned and What is Still to be Explored." *Journal of Management*, 32: 673–720.

Kaplan, S. N., and Weisbach, M. S. (1992). "The Success of Acquisitions: Evidence from Divestitures." *Journal of Finance*, 47: 107–38.

Kapoor, R., & Kwanghui, L. I. M. (2007). "The Impact of Acquisitions on the Productivity of Inventors at Semiconductor Firms: A Synthesis of Knowledge-Based and Incentive-Based Perspectives." *Academy of Management Journal*, 50: 1133–55.

Karan, V., & Sharifi, M. (2006). "Will SOX Kill the Deal?" *The Journal of Corporate Accounting & Finance*, 17: 37–44.

Kim, J.-Y., & Finkelstein, S. (2009). "The Effects of Strategic and Market Complementarity on Acquisition Performance: Evidence from the U.S. Commercial Banking Industry, 1989–2001." *Strategic Management Journal*, 30: 617–46.

King, D., Dalton, D. R., Daily, C. M., & Covin, J. G. (2004). "Meta-analyses of Post-acquisition Performance: Indications of Unidentified Moderators." *Strategic Management Journal*, 25: 187–200.

——Slotegraaf, R. J., & Kesner, I. (2008). "Performance Implications of Firm Resource Interactions in the Acquisition of R&D-Intensive Firms." *Organization Science*, 19, 327–40.

Kitching, J. (1974). "Winning and Losing with European Acquisitions." *Harvard Business Review*, 52: 124–36.

Kobeissi, N., Sun, X., & Wang, H. (2010). "Managerial Labor-Market Discipline and the Characteristics of Merger and Acquisition Transactions." *Journal of Business Research*, 63/7: 721–8.

Krishnan, H. A., Hitt, M. A., & Park, D. (2007). "Acquisition Premiums, Subsequent Workforce Reductions and Post-acquisition Performance." *Journal of Management Studies*, 44: 709–32.

——Miller, A., & Judge, W. Q. (1997). "Diversification and Top Management Team Complementarity: Is Performance Improved by Merging Similar or Dissimilar Teams?" *Strategic Management Journal*, 18: 361–74.

Krishnan, R. A., & Krishnan, H. (2003). "Effects of Hospital Mergers and Acquisitions on Prices." *Journal of Business Research*, 56/8: 647–56.

Kroll, M., Simmons, S. A., & Wright, P. (1990). "Determinants of Chief Executive Officer Compensation Following Major Acquisitions." *Journal of Business Research*, 20: 349–66.

——Walters, B. A., & Wright, P. (2008). "Board Vigilance, Director Experience, and Corporate Outcomes." *Strategic Management Journal*, 29: 363–82.

——Wright, P., Toombs, L., & Leavell, H. (1997). "Form of Control: A Critical Determinant of Acquisition Performance and CEO Rewards." *Strategic Management Journal*, 18/2: 85–96.

Krug, J. A., & Aguilera, R. V. (2004). "Top Management Team Turnover in Mergers & Acquisitions." *Advances in Mergers and Acquisitions*, 4: 121–49.

—— & Hegarty, W. H. (1997). "Postacquisition Turnover among U.S. Top Management Teams: An Analysis of the Effects of Foreign vs. Domestic Acquisitions of U.S. Targets." *Strategic Management Journal*, 18: 667–75.

—— —— (2001). "Predicting Who Stays and Leaves after an Acquisition: A Study of Top Managers in Multinational Firms." *Strategic Management Journal*, 22: 185–96.

Kumar, N., Stern, L. W., & Anderson, J. C. (1993). "Conducting Interorganizational Research Using Key Informants." *Academy of Management Journal*, 36: 1633–51.

Kusewitt, J. B., Jr. (1985). "An Exploratory Study of Strategic Acquisition Factors Relating to Performance." *Strategic Management Journal*, 6: 151–69.

Laamanen, T., & Keil, T. (2008). "Performance of Serial Acquirers: Toward an Acquisition Program Perspective." *Strategic Management Journal*, 29: 663–72.

Lamont, B. T., & Anderson, C. R. (1985). "Mode of Corporate Diversification and Economic Performance." *Academy of Management Journal*, 28/4: 926–34.

Larsson, R., & Finkelstein, S. (1999). "Integrating Strategic, Organizational, and Human Resource Perspectives on Mergers and Acquisitions: A Case Survey of Synergy Realization." *Organization Science*, 10: 1–26.

—— & Lubatkin, M. (2001). "Achieving Acculturation in Mergers and Acquisitions: An International Case Survey." *Human Relations*, 54: 1573–607.

Lubatkin, M. (1987). "Merger Strategies and Stockholder Value." *Strategic Management Journal*, 8/1: 39–53.

—— Calori, R., Véry, P., & Veiga, J. F. (1998). "Managing Mergers across Borders: A Two-Nation Exploration of a Nationally Bound Administrative Heritage." *Organization Science*, 9/6: 670–84.

—— Schweiger, D., & Weber, Y. (1999). "Top Management Turnover in Related M&As: An Additional Test of the Theory of Relative Standing." *Journal of Management*, 25: 55–73.

—— & Shrieves, R. E. (1986). "Towards Reconciliation of Market Performance Measures to Strategic Management Research." *Academy of Management Review*, 11: 497–512.

—— Srinivasan, N., & Merchant, H. (1997). "Merger Strategies and Shareholder Value during Times of Relaxed Antitrust Enforcement: The Case of Large Mergers during the 1980s." *Journal of Management*, 23/1: 59–81.

Makri, M., Hitt, M. A., & Lane, P. J. (2010). "Complementary Technologies, Knowledge Relatedness, and Invention Outcomes in High Technology Mergers and Acquisitions." *Strategic Management Journal*, 31: 602–28.

Mamdani, M., & Noah, D. (2004). "Pathways to Success in M&As." *Journal of Applied Corporate Finance*, 16: 77–81.

Markides, C. C., & Ittner, C. D. (1994). "Shareholder Benefits from Corporate International Diversification: Evidence from U.S. International Acquisitions." *Journal of International Business Studies*, 25: 343–66.

—— and Oyon, D. (1998). "International Acquisitions: Do they Create Value for Shareholders?" *European Management Journal*, 16: 125–35.

McDonald, M. L., Westphal, J. D., & Graebner, M. E. (2008). "What Do They Know? The Effects of Outside Director Acquisition Experience on Firm Acquisition Performance." *Strategic Management Journal*, 29/11: 1155–77.

McNamara, G. M., Haleblian, J., & Dykes, B. J. (2008). "The Performance Implications of Participating in an Acquisition Wave: Early Mover Advantages, Bandwagon Effects, and the Moderating Influence of Industry Characteristics and Acquirer Tactics." *Academy of Management Journal*, 51: 113–30.

McWilliams, A., Siegel, D., & Teoh, S. H. (1999). "Issues in the Use of the Event Study Methodology: A Critical Analysis of Corporate Social Responsibility Studies." *Organizational Research Methods*, 2: 340–65.

Meeks, G. (1977). *Disappointing Marriage: A Study of the Gains from Mergers*. Cambridge: Cambridge University Press.

Meyer, C. B., & Altenborg, E. (2007). "The Disintegrating Effects of Equality: A Study of a Failed International Merger." *British Journal of Management*, 18/3: 257–71.

Miller, C. C., Cardinal, L. B., & Glick, W. H. (1997). "Retrospective Reports in Organizational Research: A Reexamination of Recent Evidence." *Academy of Management Journal*, 40: 189–204.

Montgomery, C. A., & Thomas, A. R. (1988). "Divestment: Motives and Gains." *Strategic Management Journal*, 9: 93–7.

—— & Wilson, V. A. (1986). "Mergers that Last: A Predictable Pattern?" *Strategic Management Journal*, 7: 91–6.

Morosini, P., Shane, S., & Singh, H. (1998). "National Cultural Distance and Cross-Border Acquisition Performance." *Journal of International Business Studies*, 29: 137–58.

Moschieri, C., & Campa, J. M. (2009). "The European M&A Industry: A Market in the Process of Construction." *Academy of Management Perspectives*, 23: 71–87.

Mtar, M. (2010). "Institutional, Industry and Power Effects on Integration in Cross-Border Acquisitions." *Organization Studies*, 31/8: 1099–127.

Nadolska, A., & Barkema, H. G. (2007). "Learning to Internationalise: The Pace and Success of Foreign Acquisitions." *Journal of International Business Studies*, 38: 1170–86.

Öberg, C., Henneberg, S & Mouzas, S. (2007). "Changing Network Pictures: Evidence from Mergers and Acquisitions." *Industrial Marketing Management*, 36: 926–40.

Oler, D. K., Harrison, J. S., & Allen, M. R. (2008). "The Danger of Misinterpreting Short-Window Event Study Findings in Strategic Management Research: An Empirical Illustration Using Horizontal Acquisitions." *Strategic Organization*, 6: 151–84.

Olie, R. (1994). "Shades of Culture and Institutions in International Mergers." *Organization Studies*, 15/3: 381–405.

Pangarkar, N., & Lie, J. R. (2004). "The Impact of Market Cycle on the Performance of Singapore Acquirers." *Strategic Management Journal*, 25/12: 1209–16.

Papadakis, V. M. (2005). "The Role of Broader Context and the Communication Program in Merger and Acquisition Implementation Success." *Management Decision*, 43: 236–55.

—— & Thanos, I. (2008). "Contrasting M&As in Boom and Bust Periods: An Empirical Investigation of Processes and Outcomes." Paper presented at the Academy of Management, Anaheim, California, USA.

—— —— (2010) Measuring the Performance of Acquisitions: An Empirical Investigation Using Multiple Criteria. *British Journal of Management* 21, 859–73.

—— —— & Barwise, P. (2010). "Research on Strategic Decisions: Taking Stock and Looking Ahead," in P. Nutt & D. Wilson (eds.), *Handbook of Decision Making*. Chichester: Wiley & Sons Ltd.

Paruchuri, S., Nerkar, A., & Hambrick, D. C. (2006). "Acquisition Integration and Productivity Losses in the Technical Core: Disruption of Inventors in Acquired Companies." *Organization Science*, 17/5: 545–62.

Pettigrew, A., Thomas, H., & Pettigrew, R. (2002). "Strategic Management: The Strengths and Limitations of a Field," in A. Pettigrew, H. Thomas, & R. Pettigrew (eds.), *Handbook of Strategy and Management*. London: Sage Publications Ltd.

Phan, P. H., & Hill, C. W. L. (1995). "Organizational Restructuring and Economic Performance in Leveraged Buyout: An Ex Post Study." *Academy of Management Journal*, 38/3: 704–39.

Porrini, P. (2004). "Can a Previous Alliance between an Acquirer and a Target Affect Acquisition Performance?" *Journal of Management*, 30/4: 545–62.

Porter, M. E. (1987). "From Competitive Advantage to Corporate Strategy." *Harvard Business Review*, 65: 43–59.

Puranam, P., Singh, H., & Zollo, M. (2006). "Organizing for Innovation: Managing the Coordination-Autonomy Dilemma in Technology Acquisitions." *Academy of Management Journal*, 49: 263–80.

—— & Srikanth, K. (2007). "What they Know vs. What they Do: How Acquirers Leverage Technology Acquisitions." *Strategic Management Journal*, 28: 805–25.

Ramaswamy, K. (1997). "The Performance Impact of Strategic Similarity in Horizontal Mergers: Evidence from the U.S." *Academy of Management Journal*, 40: 697–715.

Ranft, A. L., & Lord, M. D. (2002). "Acquiring New Technologies and Capabilities: A Grounded Model of Acquisition Implementation." *Organization Science*, 13/4: 420–41.

Ravenscraft, D., & Scherer, F. M. (1987). *Mergers, Sell-Offs, and Economic Efficiency*. Washington, DC: Brookings Institution.

Reus, T. H., & Lamont, B. T. (2009) The double-edged sword of cultural distance in international acquisitions. *Journal of International Business Studies*, 40: 1298–316.

Rostand, A. (1994). "Optimizing Managerial Decisions during the Acquisition Integration Process." Paper presented to 14th Annual Strategic Management Society Conference, Paris, France.

Sanders, W. G. (2001). "Behavioral Responses of CEOs to Stock Ownership and Stock Option Pay." *Academy of Management Journal*, 44/3: 477–92.

Saxton, T., & Dollinger, M. (2004). "Target Reputation and Appropriability: Picking and Deploying Resources in Acquisitions." *Journal of Management*, 30/1: 123–47.

Schmidt, D. R., & Fowler, K. L. (1990). "Post-acquisition Financial Performance and Executive Compensation." *Strategic Management Journal*, 11/7: 559–69.

Schoenberg, R. (2006). "Measuring the Performance of Corporate Acquisitions: An Empirical Comparison of Alternative Metrics." *British Journal of Management*, 17: 361–70.

Schweiger, D. M., & Denisi, A. S. (1991). "Communication with Employees Following a Merger: A Longitudinal Field Experiment." *Academy of Management Journal*, 34: 110–35.

—— & Goulet, P. K. (2005). "Facilitating Acquisition Integration through Deep-Level Cultural Learning Interventions: A Longitudinal Field Experiment." *Organization Studies*, 26/10: 1477–99.

Schweizer, L. (2005). "Organizational Integration of Acquired Biotechnology Companies into Pharmaceutical Companies: The Need for a Hybrid Approach." *Academy of Management Journal*, 48/6: 1051–74.

Seth, A. (1990). "Sources of Value Creation in Acquisitions: An Empirical Investigation." *Strategic Management Journal*, 11/6: 431–46.

—— Song, K. P., & Pettit, R. (2000). "Synergy, Managerialism or Hubris? An Empirical Examination of Motives for Foreign Acquisitions of U.S. Firms." *Journal of International Business Studies*, 31/3: 387–405.

—— —— —— (2002). "Value Creation and Destruction in Cross-Border Acquisitions: An Empirical Analysis of Foreign Acquisitions of U.S. Firms." *Strategic Management Journal*, 23: 921–40.

Shanley, M. T., & Correa, M. E. (1992). "Agreement between Top Management Teams and Expectations for Post Acquisition Performance." *Strategic Management Journal*, 13/4: 245–66.

Shelton, L. M. (1988). "Strategic Business Fits and Corporate Acquisition: Empirical Evidence." *Strategic Management Journal*, 9/3: 279–87.

Shimizu, K. (2007). "Prospect Theory, Behavioral Theory, and the Threat-Rigidity Thesis: Combinative Effects on Organizational Decisions to Divest Formerly Acquired Units." *Academy of Management Journal*, 50: 1495–514.

Shimizu, K., & Hitt, M. A. (2005). "What Constrains or Facilitates Divestitures of Formerly Acquired Firms? The Effects of Organizational Inertia." *Journal of Management*, 31/1: 50–72.

Singh, H., & Montgomery, C. A. (1987). "Corporate Acquisition Strategies and Economic Performance." *Strategic Management Journal*, 8/4: 377–86.

Stahl, G. K., & Voigt, A. (2008). "Do Cultural Differences Matter in Mergers and Acquisitions? A Tentative Model and Examination." *Organization Science*, 19: 160–76.

Sudarsanam, S. (2003). *Creating Value from Mergers and Acquisitions: The Challenges*. Harlow, UK: Financial Times–Prentice Hall.

——& Mahate, A. A. (2006). "Are Friendly Acquisitions Too Bad for Shareholders and Managers? Long-Term Value Creation and Top Management Turnover in Hostile and Friendly Acquirers." *British Journal of Management*, 17: S7–30.

Teerikangas, S., & Véry, P. (2006). "The Culture-Performance Relationship in M&As: From Yes/No to How." *British Journal of Management*, 17: S31–48.

Tuch, C., & O'Sullivan, N. (2007). "The Impact of Acquisitions on Firm Performance: A Review of the Evidence." *International Journal of Management Reviews*, 9: 141–70.

Uhlenbruck, K., & De Castro, J. O. (2000). "Foreign Acquisitions in Central and Eastern Europe: Outcomes of Privatization in Transitional Economies." *Academy of Management Journal*, 43/3: 381–402.

——Hitt, M. A., & Semadeni, M. (2006). "Market Value Effects of Acquisitions Involving Internet Firms: A Resource-Based Analysis." *Strategic Management Journal*, 27/10: 899–913.

Vaara, E. (2003). "Post-acquisition Integration as Sensemaking: Glimpses of Ambiguity, Confusion, Hypocrisy, and Politicization." *Journal of Management Studies*, 40/4: 859–94.

Vermeulen, F., & Barkema, H. (2001). "Learning through Acquisitions." *Academy of Management Journal*, 44: 457–76.

Véry, P., Lubatkin, M., Calori, R., & Veiga, J. (1997). "Relative Standing and the Performance of Recently Acquired European Firms." *Strategic Management Journal*, 18/8: 593–614.

Villinger, R. (1996). "Post-acquisition Managerial Learning in Central East Europe." *Organization Studies*, 17: 181–206.

Walsh, J. P. (1988). "Top Management Turnover Following Mergers and Acquisitions." *Strategic Management Journal*, 9: 173–83.

——(1989). "Doing a Deal: Merger and Acquisition Negotiations and their Impact upon Target Company Top Management Turnover." *Strategic Management Journal*, 10: 307–22.

——& Ellwood, J. W. (1991). "Mergers, Acquisitions, and the Pruning of Managerial Deadwood." *Strategic Management Journal*, 12/3: 202–17.

Walter, J. (2011). "Strategic Decision Processes in the Realm of Strategic Alliances," in P. Mazolla & F. Kellermans (eds.), *Handbook of Strategy Process Research*. Cheltenham, UK: Edward Elgar Publishing.

Walters, B. A., Kroll, M. J., & Wright, P. (2007). "CEO Tenure, Boards of Directors, and Acquisition Performance." *Journal of Business Research*, 60: 331–8.

————— (2008). "CEO Ownership and Effective Boards: Impacts on Firm Outcomes." *Strategic Organization*, 6/3: 259–83.

Wan, W. P., & Yiu, D. W. (2009). "From Crisis to Opportunity: Environmental Jolt, Corporate Acquisitions, and Firm Performance." *Strategic Management Journal*, 30/7: 791–801.

Weber, Y. (1996). "Corporate Cultural Fit and Performance in Mergers and Acquisitions." *Human Relations*, 49: 1181–203.

Yu, J., Engleman, R. M., & Van de Ven, A. H. (2005). "The Integration Journey: An Attention-Based View of the Merger and Acquisition Integration Process." *Organization Studies*, 26/10: 1501–28.

Zollo, M. (2009). "Superstitious Learning with Rare Strategic Decisions: Theory and Evidence from Corporate Acquisitions." *Organization Science*, 20: 894–908.

—— & Meier, D. (2008). "What Is M&A Performance?" *Academy of Management Perspectives*, 22: 55–77.

—— & Singh, H. (2004). "Deliberate Learning in Corporate Acquisitions: Post-acquisition Strategies and Integration Capability in U.S. Bank Mergers." *Strategic Management Journal*, 25: 1233–56.

CHAPTER 6

....

ACQUISITIONS, ACQUISITION PROGRAMS, AND ACQUISITION CAPABILITIES

....

THOMAS KEIL, TOMI LAAMANEN,
AND AINO MÄKISALO[1]

INTRODUCTION

....

Performance of acquisitions has been among the most actively studied topics in research on mergers and acquisitions (see Chapters 4 and 5 in this volume for detailed reviews). Yet, despite decades of research and literally thousands of published articles, findings continue to be mixed on the overall performance impact of acquisitions. What has clearly become established, however, is that acquisitions are characterized by a high degree of performance variance. As a result, research has over time increasingly moved from trying to explain the performance of acquisitions to identifying antecedents that would explain the variance in performance.

One argument that has received particular attention is that firms differ in their abilities to perform acquisitions. Whereas early studies suggested that these differences are mainly due to differences in acquisition experience, paralleling similar arguments in the alliance literature (e.g. Heimeriks and Duysters 2007; Kale et al. 2002; Kale and Singh 2007; Zollo et al. 2002) a more refined view on how acquisition capabilities contribute to acquisition performance has emerged during recent years (e.g. Barkema and Schijven 2008; Zollo 2009).

In this chapter, we provide a review of research on acquisition experience and the emergence of acquisition capabilities. We build on the organizational learning literature and provide a systematic analysis of how firms build acquisition capabilities and how these capabilities contribute to acquisition performance. While prior research has studied acquisitions capabilities predominantly at the level of the individual transaction, our chapter emphasizes the importance of acquisition programs and program-level acquisition capabilities as a novel level of analysis.

The acquisition program perspective has recently moved to the forefront of acquisition research, triggered by the observation that there are a number of firms that engage in series of acquisitions (Laamanen and Keil 2008). These acquisitions often aim at a common goal. Acquisition programs can therefore be defined as sequences of acquisitions initiated by an acquiring firm, with the intention of achieving a specific business goal or market position. We contribute to an improved understanding of this acquisition program perspective by discussing the main elements of acquisition program capabilities and how they differ from the ordinary acquisition capabilities that are observed at the level of individual acquisitions.

Our chapter starts with a brief overview of the literature on the role of acquisition experience on acquisition performance. Next we distinguish between the concepts of acquisition capability and acquisition program capability, and provide an in-depth discussion of their sub-components. We examine the path-dependent processes of interpretation and codification of how firms develop these acquisition capabilities and conclude our review with an agenda for future research. Figure 6.1 helps illustrate the structure and flow of this chapter.

ACQUISITION EXPERIENCE AND ACQUISITION PERFORMANCE

The first wave of research on the effects of acquisition experience appeared in the early 1980s. Studies within this stream started from the basic learning curve arguments suggesting that acquisition experience should improve the performance of a focal acquisition (Lubatkin 1983). However, the initial empirical results were mixed. In one of the

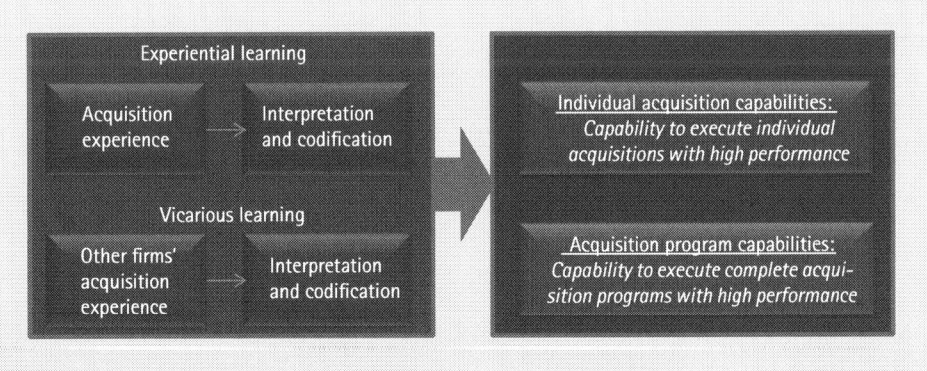

FIG. 6.1 Structure of the chapter

first systematic studies, Kusewitt (1985) found a negative relationship between the acquisition rate and acquisition performance, a result that he and others (Fowler and Schmidt 1989) interpreted as the result of indigestion, that is, the difficulty faced by an acquiring firm of integrating acquired firms into its operations.

During the 1990s, several studies revisited the acquisition experience construct, investigating its effect in a more fine-grained manner. One of the first findings from this stream of research was that the effect of acquisition experience is contingent upon a number of factors. For example, Li (1995) found that acquisition experience would seem to matter more in some industries, for example the computer industry, and less in other industries, such as pharmaceuticals. Similarly, research on international acquisitions found that experience with home country acquisitions would not always seem to translate into improved performance in international acquisitions (Lee and Caves 1998; Markides and Ittner 1994).

Starting from the mid-1990s, a second wave of literature on experience effects appeared. These studies questioned the implicit original argumentation that all acquisition experience, irrespective of its type, has positive performance effects for a focal acquisition. In their seminal papers on this topic, Haleblian and Finkelstein (Finkelstein and Haleblian 2002; Haleblian and Finkelstein 1999) showed that overgeneralization and negative transfer effects would indeed seem to occur when a firm transfers experiences from initial acquisitions to subsequent acquisitions that have fundamentally different characteristics. As a result, studies drawing on Haleblian and Finkelstein have tended to focus on the effects of different types of acquisition experience on acquisition performance (e.g. Hayward 2002).

In addition to literature questioning the positive performance effects of acquisition experience, a second stream of literature emerged in the mid-1990s that pointed to the effects of learning from the experience of others. Such vicarious learning might take place by observing the acquisition moves of others or transferring the knowledge of others through board interlocks or personnel transfers (Baum et al. 2000; Haunschild 1993). While most of the other literature on acquisition experience has tended to focus on organizational learning theories, research on imitation and learning from others also tends to incorporate arguments from institutional theory (Dimaggio and Powell 1983; Yang and Hyland 2006). One of the main challenges of this line of research is that it is empirically very hard to distinguish between vicarious learning from other firms' experiences and imitation that can happen without any learning taking place.

The most recent research has concluded that irrespective of the type of acquisition experience, the effects of acquisition experience are not automatic. They require explicit investments in deliberate learning and capability building (Haleblian et al. 2006; Hébert et al. 2005; Zollo and Singh 2004) in order to be able to make the correct causal inferences and develop acquisition capabilities. These studies point to the importance of gradually evolving acquisition capabilities as one of the key factors affecting the performance of acquisitions. We build on this in more detail in the next section.

From Acquisition Experience to Acquisition Capabilities

Before we detail the building blocks of acquisition capabilities, a brief discussion of the nature of organizational capabilities is in order. Organizational capabilities have their roots in the resource-based view of strategic management (RBV). The RBV distinguishes between resources, that is, tangible assets that are tied at least semi-permanently to the firm (Barney 1991; Wernerfelt 1984), and organizational capabilities, that is, a firm's ability to deploy these resources to productive ends (Amit and Schoemaker 1993; Collis 1994; Henderson and Cockburn 1994). Organizational capabilities consist of individual skills and expertise, but also of organizational routines, rules, and procedures that the firm can draw upon in its activities. Against this backdrop, acquisition capability refers to the ability of a firm to execute acquisitions. There is, however, an important difference between developing the capability to perform individual acquisitions and the capability to perform acquisition programs. Next, we will elaborate this distinction, which we have adopted from Laamanen and Keil (2008), in more detail.

Capabilities to Manage Individual Acquisitions

In their pioneering book, Haspeslagh and Jemison (1991) identified capabilities related to three specific tasks in mergers and acquisitions. These include the capabilities (1) to identify acquisition targets, (2) to negotiate the agreement to purchase or to merge, and (3) to decide how to manage the post-acquisition integration and implement it. Capabilities to identify promising targets often rest on the ability to assess how strategic, organizational, and cultural characteristics of potential targets fit with those of the acquiring firm (Jemison and Sitkin 1986; Larsson and Finkelstein 1999; Seth 1990). Among those characteristics, the strategic fit of a potential acquisition determines the potential value the acquisition can create, whereas cultural and organizational fit affect the realization of value (Jemison and Sitkin 1986).

Capabilities to negotiate the agreement affect how the potential value of an acquisition is distributed among the owners of the acquiring firm and the target. Research on these capabilities has focused, for example, on the ability of a firm to carry out effective due diligence (Zollo and Reuer 2010), structured negotiation (Ashkenas et al. 1998), and the importance of avoiding paying a premium over the stock price of the target (Laamanen 2007).

Capabilities to engage in acquisition integration reflect the ability to decide what functions of the target to integrate and at what pace. Drawing on a rich literature on the role of post-merger integration, Zollo and Singh (2004) find that a firm's ability to manage this stage of the acquisition process is an important element of a firm's overall ability to successfully acquire or merge. This argument is further underlined by Schweiger and

DeNisi (1991) who argue that firms experienced in mergers and acquisitions tend to perform more appropriate interventions in the acquired firm. Also, Uhlenbruck argues that acquisition capabilities allow multinational enterprises to configure the acquisition target's resources so as to gain local competitive advantage when entering new markets (Uhlenbruck 2004).

The original division into three groups of acquisition capabilities has since been refined and extended by several other scholars. For example, Capron and Anand (2007) distinguish between the ability to identify when acquisitions are the appropriate strategic tool and the ability to identify acquisition targets. In addition, they add the ability to reconfigure resources for acquisition integration. They define acquisition selection capability as the capability to recognize when acquisition would be the most appropriate method of obtaining new resources. The company should always be able to compare acquisitions to other alternatives, such as alliances, greenfield investments, commercial agreements, or organic growth.

Capron and Anand (2007) define acquisition identification capability as the company's ability to detect and negotiate with appropriate targets. Acquisition identification capability requires the company to carry out effective due diligence regarding all potential targets in order to determine the target value and to negotiate appropriate terms with the target's owner. The company should additionally acknowledge when to withdraw from the negotiations. Finally, Capron and Anand (2007) also discuss the acquisition reconfiguration capabilities. An acquirer should be able to reshape the target's resources and combine them with its own asset base in order to create entirely new resources. Reconfiguration capability requires an acquirer to selectively divest unneeded resources from the target and dispense with its own resources that have become obsolete.

Capabilities to Manage Acquisition Programs

Capabilities to engage in individual acquisitions assume every acquisition is an independent transaction with relatively little connection to other activities of the firm. However, a substantial number of firms engage in multiple acquisitions to execute their strategy (Schipper and Thompson 1983). For instance, firms such as Cisco, Dow Chemicals, General Electric, Microsoft, Philips, and Oracle, have engaged in acquisition programs that have involved the acquisition of hundreds of companies. For such serial acquirers, it is not enough to focus on executing the individual deals well. Also, coordination across acquisitions within an acquisition program is critical for the success of the overall program. It is surprising that although series of acquisitions are widely used by firms to advance their strategies, very little prior research exists on the acquisition program-level capabilities (Fuller et al. 2002; Kusewitt 1985). There is an extensive amount of anecdotal evidence on, for example, how Cisco was able to make acquisitions a systematic practice for enhancing a firm's strategy. Also, many other firms, such as Philips in its medical electronics business or Dow Chemicals in the chemicals industry

(Heimeriks and Gates 2010), have used acquisitions in a systematic manner to strengthen their positions in their existing businesses or in entering new business areas. The way Philips describes its use of acquisitions to enhance its position in the medical electronics business is quite illustrative in this respect (see Figure 6.2).

We define an acquisition program as "a sequence of acquisitions that is initiated by an acquiring firm with the intent to reach a specific business goal or market position." As is common also more generally with intended and emergent strategies, an acquisition program may not always become realized as intended. The stream of acquisitions may be discontinued prematurely or receive a new meaning in the acquiring firm. An acquisition program itself can also be emergent. As a firm enters a new business area, it may find it useful to perform so-called learning acquisitions to learn how to operate in the new business area or in a new kind of business environment. The initial acquisitions may result in positive experiences and gradually build up a momentum for subsequent acquisitions that then become a systematic practice for strengthening one's position and expanding in the business area.

We can identify multiple different kinds of acquisition programs based on the motivation of the acquiring firms. For example, when entering the Russian beer market, the Baltic Beverages Holding (BBH) adopted a systematic geographic roll-up acquisition program, where it mapped the Russian territory according to logistics distances and drew up a visionary picture that defined the cities in which it should buy breweries in the future in order to cover the whole former Soviet Union beer market. During the next decade, the management team then acquired, one-by-one, on average one-to-two breweries per year, when suitable breweries gradually came up for sale that matched the "acquisition map." In addition to the overall program-level vision, the acquisition program involved systematic practices for involving the sellers in the further development of the acquired brewery's business, renewal of the brewery's brewing technology, and investments in revitalizing the brand in the local market. The acquisition program turned out to be phenomenally successful as it led to a more than 50% share of the Russian beer industry and an estimated business valuation of over 10 billion euro when the Baltic Beverages Holding was acquired by Carlsberg as part of Scottish and Newcastle.

We call this kind of geographic expansion strategies a geographic roll-up acquisition program, consistent with the terminology used by Bower (2001) to distinguish between archetypical acquisition motivations. Similarly, we can identify systematic industry consolidation acquisition programs, product or market extension acquisition programs, industry convergence acquisition programs, and R&D-motivated acquisition programs. Some programs may also share characteristics of multiple archetypical acquisition programs. For example, the expansion of health care organizations by acquiring small health care clinics could be regarded as both a geographic roll-up acquisition program as well as an industry consolidation-motivated acquisition program. Similarly, acquisition programs aimed at product extension tend to share similar characteristics with acquisition programs motivated by R&D.

While different types of acquisition programs are likely to require different capabilities, there are also likely to be more generic capabilities that are associated with the

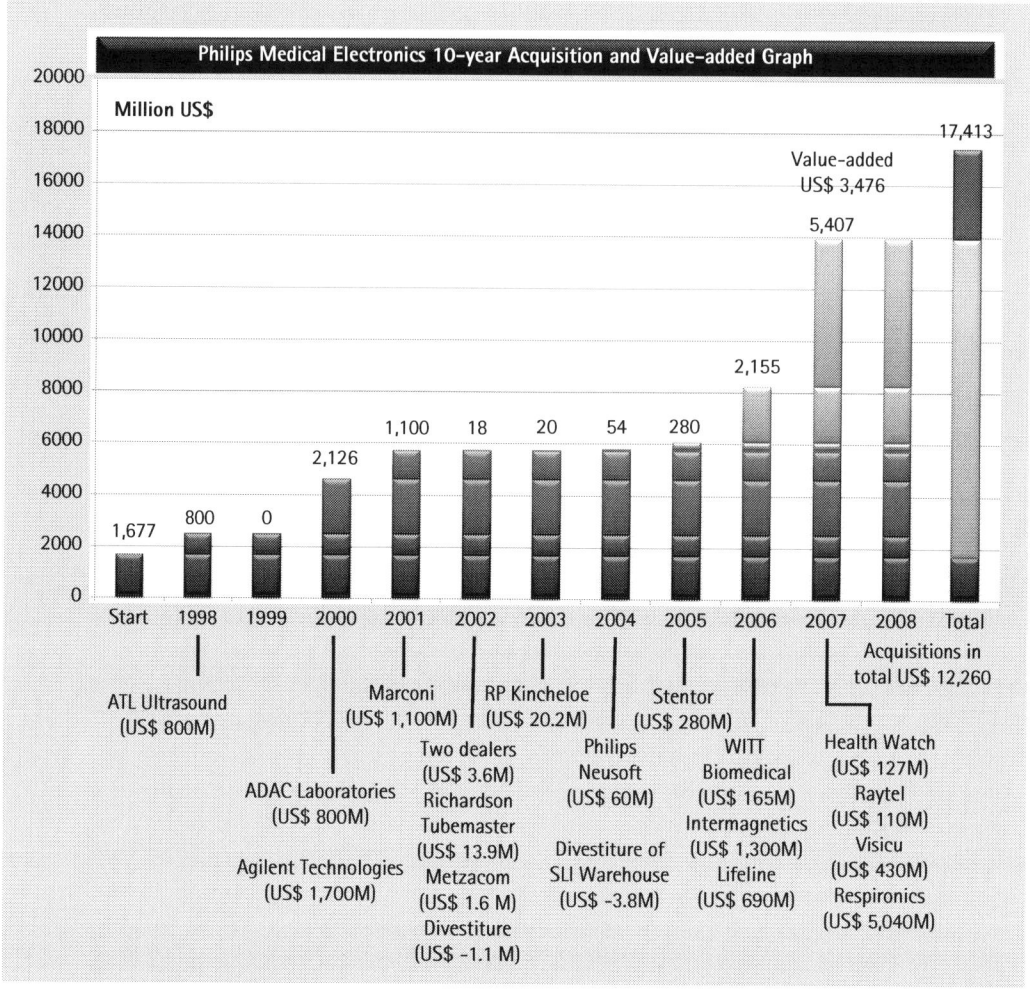

FIG. 6.2 Philips Medical Electronics ten-year acquisition and added value analysis
Source: Developed on the basis of data provided in Philips Corporation's 2008 Annual Report Presentation.

ability to carry out acquisition programs in general. For example, Laamanen and Keil (2008) argue that capabilities to manage acquisition programs include the ability to decide on the optimal number of firms to acquire, the timing of individual acquisitions and types of firms to acquire, the optimal scope of an acquisition program, etc. They examined over 5500 acquisitions performed in the United States during the ten years between 1990 and 2000. They studied whether different acquisition frequency patterns affect the acquirer's performance and whether company-level influences moderate the relationship between the frequency patterns and performance. They present the capability to manage acquisition programs as a higher-level capability than the capability to perform an individual acquisition or the capability to learn from previous acquisitions. Performing well in acquisition programs requires a more holistic understanding of the structure of the industry in order to be able to lay out a plan of which kind of sequence of acquisitive activities would lead to the most optimal outcome from the perspective of the firm. This is quite different from being able to evaluate the consequences of an individual acquisition or to be able to perform an acquisition operatively.

Acquisition program-level capabilities tend to reside either in the top management, strategic planning organization, or a firm's acquisition team. This is consistent with the research that has tended to emphasize the importance of a well-planned M&A strategy and a professional M&A function. Accordingly, transparent and professional M&A methodology should steer acquisition processes and develop templates for target screening (Hitt et al. 1998). Routinizing target selection, evaluation, and integration reduces the cognitive effort and time spent on individual acquisitions (Levitt and March 1988; Nelson and Winter 1982) and is therefore an important element of an acquisition strategy.

We will next discuss in more detail four different capability areas that we have found particularly relevant when examining the acquisition program-level capabilities of firms that have engaged in acquisition programs. These include (1) the capability to pace the acquisition program, (2) the capability to optimize the program scope, (3) the capability to acquire optimally sized and strategically, organizationally, and culturally fit targets, and (4) the capability to manage multiple simultaneous integration processes.

Capability to Pace the Acquisition Program

The acquisition rate is traditionally taken to be the number of acquisitions a company undertakes during a certain time period. Acquisition rhythm refers to the variability of the acquisition rate and is measured as the standard deviation of the annual number of acquisitions across the same time period. Laamanen and Keil (2008) found that a high acquisition frequency and a high variability have a negative impact on an acquirer's performance. However, the sizes of the acquirer, the scope of the acquisition program, and acquisition experience were seen to alleviate these negative effects.

In general, acquiring at a very fast speed does not appear to generate superior returns. Hayward (2002) found that, on average, companies benefit from acquisition intervals of six to twelve months, but in case of the prior acquisition being larger, the optimal interval was longer. This can be explained by the smaller acquisitions having less demanding integration requirements. Rather, the relationship between the time elapsed between two acquisitions and acquisition performance has been found to be inversely U-shaped (Hayward 2002). More specifically, Hayward (2002) found that the point of inflection was approximately 220 days before the announcement of the acquisition. As the time period grew further, acquisition performance started to decline slowly.

Thus, acquisitions should not be temporally too close or too distant from the prior one and they should be carried out steadily during both economic bust and boom times (Hayward 2002; Rovit and Lemire 2003). Multiple acquirers seem to outperform occasional acquirers or companies refraining from acquisitions, although a high acquisition rate has been found to have a negative impact on short-term performance.

Capability to Optimize the Acquisition Program Scope

The degree of business relatedness—both between the acquiring firm and the target firms and across target firms themselves—determines the acquisition program scope. Therefore, the capability to optimize the acquisition program scope requires optimizing acquirer-to-target and target-to-target relatedness. Voss (2007) determined acquisition type as the other significant factor contributing to acquisition capability development in addition to acquisition frequency. Pehrsson (2006) found that managers tend to view acquirer-to-target relatedness from five different aspects: product technology, general management skills, end customers, brand recognition, and types of supply channels.

Target-to-target relatedness is seen to be determined by the industry the target operates in, its relative market share, organizational structure, and its size relative to the acquirer. Acquiring highly dissimilar targets in an acquisition program creates additional strain for the individual acquisition-level capabilities. Significant business logic diversity among the firms acquired may force a firm to master multiple businesses to such an extent that the added complexity may put too much strain on a firm's capabilities to manage its acquisition program.

Capability to Acquire Optimally Sized, and Strategically, Organizationally, and Culturally Fit Targets

In addition to business area diversity, international acquisitions tend to introduce cultural diversity into the acquisition program (Barkema et al. 1996; Birkinshaw et al. 2000; Vaara 2003). Similarly, small and large firms can be argued to differ from each other quite dramatically in terms of the optimal approach toward integration. The "optimal size" of a target is a subjective, firm-specific measure. It mainly depends on the characteristics of the acquirer and the objectives of the acquisition program. The scale of acquisitions should be in the right proportion to the acquirer's business activity. It has been argued that larger companies should avoid acquisitions that are too small, since they only take up resources without providing sufficient shareholder value (Fuller et al. 2002). Smaller acquirers, on the other hand, tend to avoid acquiring companies that are too large, since they have a higher likelihood of wealth losses for the target's shareholders. In addition, the larger the target, the more it has negotiation power and ability to extract value from the transaction.

Larsson and Finkelstein (1999) found in a study of 60 acquisitions that strategic fit contributed positively to synergistic benefits. Applying this in the context of acquisition programs, we can argue that successful implementation of an acquisition program requires the company to know when to discard acquisition opportunities that fall outside the scope of its strategy and when to embrace them as a new potential thrust. The capability to acquire optimally sized targets that are also strategically, culturally, and organizationally a good match, requires an acquirer to emphasize the target screening phase, supported by a well-planned acquisition strategy. In this respect, for example, Cisco Systems gained negative experiences when it acquired a larger firm that had already developed its own distribution network, with the result that Cisco decided to focus the scope of its acquisition program predominantly on entrepreneurial technology-driven firms that had not yet built distribution networks.

Capability to Manage Multiple Simultaneous Integration Processes

Successful acquisition program integration requires a clear allocation of responsibilities among the acquiring and acquired organizations. One determinant of successful integration is to involve the acquirer's and target's employees in the process. Zollo and Leshchinskii (2001) found that a higher degree of knowledge codification leads to better performance. Information should be distributed also to the parts of the organization that have not been closely involved in the acquisition process.

The entire personnel of the acquiring and acquired company should be involved in the integration process to the extent that it ensures the motivation to work for common goals. An acquired company's existing management team should not be substituted, or removed, without a careful assessment, since it is likely to destroy shareholder value and increase the complexity of the integration process (Zollo and Leshchinskii 2001). In acquisition programs, the ability to manage multiple simultaneous integration processes is particularly critical, because due to the larger number of firms acquired, there tend to be multiple integration processes ongoing in parallel in the acquiring organization. Multiple simultaneous integration processes put a heavy strain on the corporate-level acquisition team to support the different business units in their processes and inability to do so may result in a rapid escalation of complexity.

Performance Effects of Acquisition Capabilities

The link between acquisition capabilities and acquisition performance has received only limited attention. One of the reasons for this may be that most research on acquisition performance has emphasized easily observable characteristics of acquisitions, thereby obscuring the link between decision making and an acquirer's performance (Zollo and Winter 2002). The research that has aimed at investigating acquisition capabilities and the performance relationship has usually drawn on various experience measures to proxy for acquisition capabilities and few studies have utilized direct measures of different acquisition capability aspects.

The performance effects of acquisition capabilities in acquisition programs have been studied even less. Kusewitt (1985) studied the effects of different factors on long-term performance by focusing on serial acquirers. Schipper and Thompson (1983) indicated the difficulties in identifying market reaction to an individual acquisition when the acquisition is carried out as part of an announced acquisition program. Kusewitt (1985) used accounting returns on assets and market returns as the performance measures. He explored the effect of a number of factors on the post-transaction performance of 140 active acquirers from 1967 to 1976. Based on his analysis, Kusewitt (1985) came up with the following guidelines for achieving success through an acquisition program:

- The acquisition rate should be sufficiently high to develop and maintain expertise but not so high that it detracts attention from the proper assimilation and integration of the acquisition.
- Acquisitions should be performed when the market cycle is low.
- Stock rather than cash should be preferred as the method of payment, as the analysis indicates a significant and negative relationship between the percentages of acquisitions accomplished by cash. Cash acquisitions are believed to be associated with poorer performance, owing to the risk to liquidity and a balanced capital structure.
- The targets should have higher profitability and growth potential than companies on average have. Unfriendly takeovers should also be avoided, since they often lead to management attrition. In order to promote early and effective integration between the companies, compatibility of management styles should be ensured.
- In order to achieve synergies, acquisitions should preferably be performed in related businesses.
- Acquisitions that are remarkably large or excessively small in relative terms should be avoided. A significant negative relationship was found between relative size and performance. It appears that acquiring relatively large firms increases the risk to performance, whereas acquiring very small firms on the other hand may constitute more trouble than they are actually worth. Kusewitt (1985) suggests that the target's assets should be on average less than 5% of the acquirer's assets at the end of the year prior to the acquisition.
- Value is gained through synergies. Overpayment and bidding competitions should be avoided since they decrease the profitability of the acquisition.

Many of the conclusions of Kusewitt are valid even today. Guest et al. (2004) examined whether acquisitions by multiple acquirers have a more favorable impact on performance than individual acquisitions. They examined 1476 UK public firms that made more than 4000 acquisitions during 1984–1998. They found that the short-term and long-term performance of multiple acquirers decline significantly with each subsequent acquisition. Furthermore, they found that this decline only takes place when the first acquisition is successful. For acquirers whose first bid is unsuccessful, the result is contrary: they experience an improvement in performance, signaling that they learn from their mistakes. However, they do not appear to be able to catch up with their more successful counterparts when overall performance is measured.

Fuller et al. (2002) also found that cumulative abnormal returns (CARs) are significantly lower for the fifth and higher-order bids than for the first one and reasoned that after making many acquisitions rapidly, the bidders become less efficient in negotiating with targets and end up creating less synergy due to overconfidence and hubris. They also found differences in how the gains and synergies are divided between takeovers involving public and private targets and subsidiaries: the CARs were significantly negative only for public targets, whereas they were significantly positive for private targets and subsidiaries. There are also other empirical studies that have recently appeared in finance journals. These studies in finance have further investigated the performance effects of acquisition sequences, yet findings continue to be mixed (e.g. Ahern 2010; Aktas et al. 2007, 2009).

To summarize, it would seem that there is a gradual shift taking place from a predominant focus on acquisition experience to acquisition capabilities and from a focus on acquisitions as stand-alone events to acquisition sequences and programs. We do not yet know much about acquisition programs, program-level acquisition capabilities, and their performance consequences. This is captured quite well in Laamanen and Keil's (2008) paper, where the authors show that the short-term performance effects of an intensive acquisition activity tend to be negative, as shown also by several other studies. At the same time, however, they find that the programmatic systematic acquirers that pace their acquisition activity evenly over a longer time period (a 13-year time period in their study), tend to earn the highest long-term shareholder returns and have a lower likelihood of bankruptcy than firms with more opportunistic acquisition profiles. At the outset, the positive findings of Laamanen and Keil regarding the higher longer-term value creation of serial acquirers would seem to contradict the findings of Guest et al. (2004). This is, however, not the case, because the time period used by Guest et al. to study longer-term performance was shorter than that used by Laamanen and Keil, and Guest et al. did not distinguish between different kinds of serial acquirers in terms of how they paced their acquisition programs.

How Firms Develop Acquisition Capabilities

When considering how acquisition capabilities emerge, Salvato and colleagues (Salvato et al. 2006) suggest a three-stage model in which firms first actively create acquisition knowledge, then store this knowledge in individuals, documents, tools, routines, and practices, and in the third phase activate the knowledge by creating structures and practices that put this knowledge into use in new acquisitions.

As we argued above, firms can also develop acquisition capabilities by learning from others. They might observe the acquisition strategies of their competitors and imitate them (Barkema and Schijven 2008; Baum et al. 2000). Some research suggests that an inexperienced acquirer is likely to learn more from others before it is able to gain remarkable experience itself. At later stages, the ability to learn from others reduces somewhat due to increasing organizational inertia. Learning from others might be particularly pronounced in times of uncertainty or change (Karim and Mitchell 2000). While imitation of others might be based on observation of successful strategies only, some studies suggest that the likelihood of imitation increases when a focal firm is connected to the source through board interlocks (Haunschild 1993). Vicarious learning from competitors' successful actions and strategies is often seen as a method to overcome the bounds of experience (Levinthal and March 1993) and as a complement to experiential learning. In particular, given that highly heterogeneous experience has been found to attenuate experiential learning, vicarious learning may be more effective in initially developing learning of very different experience (Barkema and Schijven 2008).

When examining and interpreting the capabilities to learn from others, there is one essential point to reflect on: in spite of several studies implying that companies learn by imitating their competitors in order to improve their own performance, this research still provides very little insight into developing acquisition capabilities. Most of the studies tend to infer acquisition capabilities without measuring them. Only a small number of studies have moved to capture how firms build these capabilities in detail. These studies suggest that firms have to engage in deliberate learning efforts for successful learning. Such deliberate learning processes can be influenced by a number of factors. For instance, the work by Zollo and Singh (2004) suggests that knowledge codification plays a key role in capturing knowledge from acquisition experience. This knowledge-based capability development may emerge through explicit manuals,

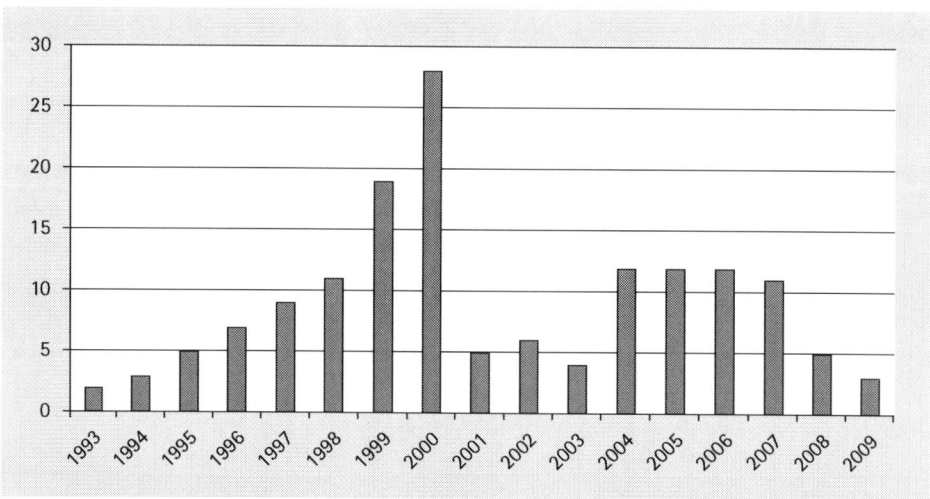

FIG. 6.3 Development of Cisco Systems' acquisition volumes over time

forms, and information systems, as well as in the intangible form of human capacity. The ideal outcome is that the intangible form of prior know-how could be transferred also to the tangible form. The unavoidable downside to explicit codification of knowledge can be that it reduces the firm's ability to protect its expertise and know-how from replication and imitation. However, the advantages are likely to offset the disadvantages (Zollo and Singh 2004).

Others have pointed to the importance of sophisticated cognitive strategies as a prerequisite for successful capability building (Bingham et al. 2007; Hayward 2002). Effective knowledge management and knowledge transfer routines are essential in order to learn from experience (Keil 2004). Simply transferring acquisition routines from one industry to another is similar to trying to apply old lessons to new settings where they do not work (Barkema and Schijven 2008). Given that acquisitions exhibit a great degree of diversity, being able to apply the right kind of experience and know-how in the right situations and being able to discard unusable knowledge, i.e. unlearning (Hedberg 1981), is a key skill for successful acquirers. Unlearning and learning require explicit learning mechanisms (Zollo and Winter 2002). Learning needs to be deliberate and it requires the company to create expertise instead of only refining already familiar routines. "Semi-automatic" experience accumulation does not enhance learning, quite the contrary (Barkema and Schijven 2008). Zollo and Leshchinskii (2001) found that developing acquisition-specific tools such as manuals and decision-support systems has a positive effect on performance, although this positive effect diminishes in the long run. Documenting, for example, due diligence-check-lists, system conversion manuals, branch staffing and product mapping software, and human resource manuals therefore tends to result in better performance.

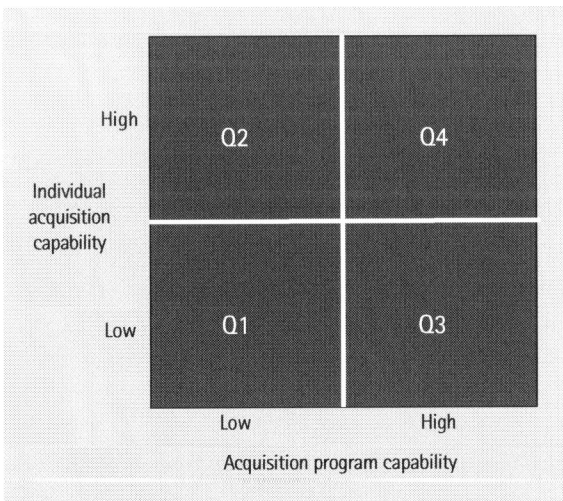

FIG. 6.4 Individual acquisition capability versus acquisition program capability

TOWARD A RESEARCH AGENDA ON ACQUISITION CAPABILITIES

To summarize, we propose that one should go even further in distinguishing between capabilities to perform individual acquisitions and the capability to perform an acquisition program. Acquisition program capability is a higher-level capability to envision, create, and execute acquisition programs in some selected market segments or geographic regions. A firm may be able to reach high operative proficiency in both pre- and post-acquisition processes and excel at individual acquisitions, but it may still not be able to use acquisitions systematically to advance its strategy.

On the contrary, becoming increasingly good at individual acquisitions may cause a firm to build its capability to perform individual acquisitions too much and the management may end up becoming too careless at the level of the acquisition program. Cisco Systems provides a good example in this respect. Figure 6.3 shows the number of acquisitions that Cisco Systems performed in different years. It shows how the development of individual acquisition-level capabilities led Cisco over time to rely increasingly on acquisitions to realize its strategy. Codification of important key heuristics into the "Cisco acquisition blueprint" boosted Cisco Systems' performance in its acquisitions, but did not yet lead into acquisition program-level capabilities. Even though Cisco's first acquisition program that focused on acquiring certain key technology assets was highly successful, its second acquisition program focused on optical networking turned out to be a failure. After the failure of the second acquisition program, which coincided with the internet bubble burst, Cisco established its third acquisition program focused on the creation of selected new business areas. This third program turned out to be successful again, with systematic pacing of acquisitions at the acquisition program level.

We distinguish between four types of acquisition capability combinations as illustrated by a matrix shown in Figure 6.4. While traditional research on the development of acquisition capabilities has tended to focus on quadrants Q1 and Q2, we find that the performance of Cisco Systems and many other acquirers is also significantly affected by how their acquisition program capabilities in quadrants Q3 and Q4 develop over time. As demonstrated by the Cisco Systems example, reaching Q2 too fast may be dangerous without simultaneous development of the capability to envision, develop, and execute acquisition programs. Similarly, there are also examples of firms that have engaged in carefully crafted systematic acquisition programs, without yet having individual acquisition capabilities in place. ABB is a good example of a firm that was created through a large number of carefully planned acquisitions, with a vision of a global firm that integrates previously national organizations into a single firm. While the acquisition program itself was a success, the breakdown of due diligence in connection with an asbestos liability of an acquired firm, led the firm to the brink of bankruptcy at a later point.

We call for more research on interactions between the capability development processes leading to the development of capabilities for executing individual acquisitions and the capability development processes leading to capabilities for executing full-scale acquisition programs. Recognizing that these capability development processes interact with each other and that they differ across different types of acquisition programs, provides a rich basis for future research on acquisition capability development. Finally, building on the dynamic capabilities literature, we note that if dynamic capabilities are regarded as capabilities to develop capabilities, there are different kinds of (dynamic) capabilities needed for developing individual acquisition capabilities and acquisition program capabilities. Since individual acquisition capabilities tend to be associated with singular acquisition transactions, they tend to have a more restricted scope and be more operative than acquisition program-level capabilities. Thus, also dynamic capabilities are likely to be more operative, related to a firm's ability develop heuristics, systematize its processes, and codify its lessons learned from previous acquisitions. Since this is largely driven by routinization and systematization of behaviors, behavioral learning theory could be expected to work well in explaining the emergence of individual acquisition capabilities.

On the other hand, the development of acquisition program-level capabilities cannot be explained using experiential learning theory only, since there is too little repetition to develop experiential inferences. Development of program-level capabilities or the lack of it can better be explained by cognitive learning theories, such as learning from others, learning from analogies, and being able to make causal inferences from a more fragmented set of clues. Even though engaging in a study of the development of acquisition program-level capabilities is likely to be more demanding than a study on the development of individual acquisition capabilities, recent developments in research on the cognitive aspects of dynamic capabilities can prove helpful in this respect. We have in this respect tried to provide several pointers to relevant articles on dynamic capabilities, that can help researchers extend their toolkits for analyzing how management's cognition is tied to the development of capabilities and how, in particular, acquisition program-level capabilities emerge.

CONCLUSION

In this chapter we have reviewed and synthesized literature on acquisition capabilities, with a special focus on acquisition capabilities for acquisition programs. Our review shows that significant progress has been made toward understanding the nature of acquisition capabilities in connection with individual acquisitions, but that significant gaps exist, in particular in our understanding of acquisition programs and the capabilities needed to successfully manage them.

Acquisition programs and the need for acquisition program capabilities have important implications for practitioners. For example, acquisitions are frequently managed through a team where senior management is the decision maker, frontline executives manage the integration process, and a corporate M&A function supports the process. In an acquisition program, this division of labor becomes more challenging as the need emerges to coordinate across acquisitions and manage the program at large. As the necessary acquisition program capabilities naturally reside in corporate development or a corporate mergers and acquisitions function, executing acquisition programs suggests a stronger and longer-lasting role for this function in the overall acquisition process.

In our view, acquisition programs and the related capabilities to design and manage them, are an important meso-level between the study of individual acquisitions and firm-level performance outcomes, such as financial performance or innovation performance. An improved understanding of this meso-level analysis might hold the key to reconciling many of the contradictory findings that prior acquisition research has produced. We therefore believe that future research addressing this level of analysis and the gaps in our current understanding, has the potential to strengthen not only our understanding of the acquisition phenomenon, but is also likely to allow us to better integrate it with theorizing issues related to corporate strategy more generally.

ENDNOTE

1. Authors in alphabetical order.

REFERENCES

Ahern, K. R. (2010). "Q-Theory and Acquisition Returns." AFA 2008 Meetings, New Orleans. Available at: http://ssrn.com/abstract=970345.

Aktas, N., de Bodt, E., & Roll, R. (2007). "Learning, Hubris, and Corporate Serial Acquisitions." Working Paper in Finance. Los Angeles: Anderson Graduate School of Management, UCLA.

—— —— —— (2009). "Learning, Hubris and Corporate Serial Acquisitions." *Journal of Corporate Finance*, 15/5: 543–61.

Amit, R. & Schoemaker, P. (1993). "Strategic Assets and Organizational Rent." *Strategic Management Journal*, 14/1: 33–46.

Ashkenas, R. N., DeMonaco, L. J., & Francis, S. C. (1998). "Making the Deal Real: How GE Capital Integrates Acquisitions." *Harvard Business Review*, 76/1: 165–78.

Barkema, H. G., Bell, J. H. J., & Pennings, J. M. (1996). "Foreign Entry, Cultural Barriers, and Learning." *Strategic Management Journal*, 17/2: 151–66.

—— & Schijven, M. (2008). "How do Firms Learn to Make Acquisitions? A Review of Past Research and an Agenda for the Future." *Journal of Management*, 34/3: 594–634.

Barney, J. B. (1991). "Firm Resources and Sustained Competitive Advantage." *Journal of Management*, 17/1: 99–120.

Baum, J. A. C., Li, S. X., & Usher, J. M. (2000). "Making the Next Move: How Experiential and Vicarious Learning Shape the Locations of Chains' Acquisitions." *Administrative Science Quarterly*, 45/4: 766–801.

Bingham, C. B., Eisenhardt, K. M., & Furr, N. R. (2007). "What Makes a Process a Capability? Heuristics, Strategy, and Effective Capture of Opportunities." *Strategic Entrepreneurship Journal*, 1/1–2: 27–48.

Birkinshaw, J., Bresman, H., & Hakanson, L. (2000). "Managing the Post-Acquisition Integration Process: How the Human Integration and Task Integration Processes Interact to Foster Value Creation." *Journal of Management Studies*, 37/3: 395–425.

Bower, J. L. (2001). "Not all M&As are Alike—and That Matters." *Harvard Business Review*, 79/3: 92–101.

Capron, L. & Anand, J. (2007). "Acquisition-Based Dynamic Capabilities," in C. E. Helfat, S. Finkelstein, W. Mitchell, Margaret Peteraf, H. Singh, D. Teece, & S. Winter (eds.), *Dynamic Capabilities: Understanding Strategic Change in Organizations*. Malden, MA: Blackwell Publishing, 80–99.

Collis, D. J. (1994). "Research Note: How Valuable are Organizational Capabilities?" *Strategic Management Journal*, 15 (Winter Special Issue): 143–52.

Dimaggio, P. J. & Powell, W. W. (1983). "The Iron Cage Revisited: Institutional Isomorphism and Collective Rationality in Organizational Fields." *American Sociological Review*, 48/2: 147–60.

Finkelstein, S. & Haleblian, J. (2002). "Understanding Acquisition Performance: The Role of Transfer Effects." *Organization Science*, 13/1: 36–47.

Fowler, K. L. & Schmidt, D. R. (1989). "Determinants of Tender Offer Post-Acquisition Financial Performance." *Strategic Management Journal*, 10/4: 339–50.

Fuller, K., Netter, J., & Stegemoller, M. (2002). "What do Returns to Acquiring Firms Tell Us? Evidence from Firms that Make Many Acquisitions." *Journal of Finance*, 57/4: 1763–93.

Guest, P. M., Cosh, A., Hughes, A., & Conn, R. L. (2004). "Why Must All Good Things Come to An End? The Performance of Multiple Acquirers," in Academy of Management (ed.), *Creating Actionable Knowledge: Academy of Management Best Paper Proceedings (64th), 6–11 August 2004*, New Orleans, LA. Published on CD-ROM, pp. BPS: S1–S6.

Haleblian, J. & Finkelstein, S. (1999). "The Influence of Organizational Acquisition Experience on Acquisition Performance: A Behavioral Learning Perspective." *Administrative Science Quarterly*, 44/1: 29–56.

—— Kim, J. Y. J., & Rajagopalan, N. (2006). "The Influence of Acquisition Experience and Performance on Acquisition Behavior: Evidence from the US Commercial Banking Industry." *Academy of Management Journal*, 49/2: 357–70.

Haspeslagh, P. C. & Jemison, D. B. (1991). *Managing Acquisitions: Creating Value through Corporate Renewal*. New York: The Free Press.

Haunschild, P. R. (1993). "Interorganizational Imitation: The Impact of Interlocks on Corporate Acquisition Activity." *Administrative Science Quarterly*, 38/4: 564–92.

Hayward, M. L. A. (2002). "When Do Firms Learn from their Acquisition Experience? Evidence from 1990–1995." *Strategic Management Journal*, 23/1: 21–39.

Hébert, L., Véry, P., & Beamish, P. W. (2005). "Expatriation as a Bridge Over Troubled Water: A Knowledge-Based Perspective Applied to Cross-Border Acquisitions." *Organization Studies*, 26(10): 1455–76.

Hedberg, B. (1981). "How Organizations Learn and Unlearn," in P. C. Nystrom & W. H. Starbuck (eds.), *Handbook of Organizational Design: Adapting Organizations to their Environments*, Vol. 1. Oxford, UK: Oxford University Press, 3–27.

Heimeriks, K. H. & Duysters, G. (2007). "Alliance Capability as a Mediator between Experience and Alliance Performance: An Empirical Investigation into the Alliance Capability Development Process." *Journal of Management Studies*, 44/1: 25–49.

—— and Gates, S. (2010). *Dow's Acquisition Program*. Case study. London, ON: Ivey Publishing.

Henderson, R. & Cockburn, I. (1994). "Measuring Competence? Exploring Firm Effects in Pharmaceutical Research." *Strategic Management Journal*, 15: 62–84.

Hitt, M., Harrison, J., Ireland, R. D., & Best, A. (1998). "Attributes of Successful and Unsuccessful Acquisitions of US Firms." *British Journal of Management*, 9/2: 91–114.

Jemison, D. B. & Sitkin, S. B. (1986). "Corporate Acquisitions: A Process Perspective." *Academy of Management Review*, 11/1: 145–63.

Kale, P., Dyer, J. H., & Singh, H. (2002). "Alliance Capability, Stock Market Response, and Long-Term Alliance Success: The Role of the Alliance Function." *Strategic Management Journal*, 23/8: 747–67.

—— & Singh, H. (2007). "Building Firm Capabilities through Learning: The Role of the Alliance Learning Process in Alliance Capability and Firm-Level Alliance Success." *Strategic Management Journal*, 28/10: 981–1000.

Karim, S. & Mitchell, W. (2000). "Path-Dependent and Path-Breaking Change: Reconfiguring Business Resources Following Acquisitions in the U.S. Medical Sector, 1978–1995." *Strategic Management Journal*, 21/10–11: 1061–81.

Keil, T. (2004). "Building External Corporate Venturing Capability." *Journal of Management Studies*, 41/5: 799–825.

Kusewitt, J. B. (1985). "An Exploratory Study of Strategic Acquisition Factors Relating to Performance." *Strategic Management Journal*, 6/2: 151–69.

Laamanen, T. (2007). "On the Role of Acquisition Premium in Acquisition Research." *Strategic Management Journal*, 28/13: 1359–69.

—— & Keil, T. (2008). "Performance of Serial Acquirers: Toward an Acquisition Program Perspective." *Strategic Management Journal*, 29/6: 663–72.

Larsson, R. & Finkelstein, S. (1999). "Integrating Strategic, Organizational, and Human Resource Perspectives on Mergers and Acquisitions: A Case Survey of Synergy Realization." *Organization Science*, 10/1: 1–26.

Lee, T. J. & Caves, R. E. (1998). "Uncertain Outcomes of Foreign Investment: Determinants of the Dispersion of Profits after Large Acquisitions." *Journal of International Business Studies*, 29/3: 563–81.

Levinthal, D. A. & March, J. G. (1993). "The Myopia of Learning." *Strategic Management Journal*, 14: 95–112.

Levitt, B. & March, J. G. (1988). "Organisational Learning." *Annual Review of Sociology*, 14: 319–40.

Li, J. T. (1995). "Foreign Entry and Survival: Effects of Strategic Choices on Performance in International Markets." *Strategic Management Journal*, 16/5: 333–51.

Lubatkin, M. (1983). "Mergers and the Performance of the Acquiring Firm." *Academy of Management Review*, 8/2: 218–25.

Markides, C. C. & Ittner, C. D. (1994). "Shareholder Benefits from Corporate International Diversification: Evidence from United States International Acquisitions." *Journal of International Business Studies*, 25/2: 343–66.

Nelson, R. R. & Winter, S. G. (1982). *An Evolutionary Theory of Economic Change*. Cambridge, MA: The Belknap Press of Harvard University Press.

Pehrsson, A. (2006). "Business Relatedness and Performance: A Study of Managerial Perceptions." *Strategic Management Journal*, 27/3: 265–82.

Rovit, S. & Lemire, C. (2003). "Your Best M&A Strategy." *Harvard Business Review*, 81/3: 16–17.

Salvato, C., Lassini, U., & Wiklund, J. (2006). "Dynamics of External Growth in SMEs: A Process Model of Acquisition Capabilities Emergence," in J. Wiklund & D. Dimov & J. A.

Katz & D. A. Shepherd (eds.), *Advances in Entrepreneurship, Firm Emergence and Growth*, vol. 9. Amsterdam: Elsevier.

Schipper, K. & Thompson, R. (1983). "Evidence on the Capitalized Value of Merger Activity for Acquiring Firms." *Journal of Financial and Economics*, 11/1–4: 85–119.

Schweiger, D. M. & DeNisi, A. S. (1991). "Communication with Employees Following a Merger: A Longitudinal Experiment." *Academy of Management Journal*, 34/1: 110–35.

Seth, A. (1990). "Value Creation in Acquisitions: A Reexamination of Performance Issues." *Strategic Management Journal*, 11: 99–115.

Uhlenbruck, K. (2004). "Developing Acquired Foreign Subsidiaries: The Experience of MNEs in Transition Economies." *Journal of International Business Studies*, 35/2: 109–23.

Vaara, E. (2003). "Post-acquisition Integration as Sensemaking: Glimpses of Ambiguity, Confusion, Hypocrisy, and Politicization." *Journal of Management Studies*, 40/4: 859–94.

Voss, I. (2007). *M&A Capability Evolution: The Art of Balancing Standardization and Flexibility*. Göttingen: Cuvillier Verlag.

Wernerfelt, B. (1984). "A Resource-Based View of the Firm." *Strategic Management Journal*, 5: 171–80.

Yang, M. & Hyland, M. (2006). "Who do Firms Imitate? A Multilevel Approach to Examining Sources of Imitation in the Choice of Mergers and Acquisitions." *Journal of Management*, 32/3: 381–99.

Zollo, M. (2009). "Superstitious Learning with Rare Strategic Decisions: Theory and Evidence from Corporate Acquisitions." *Organization Science*, 20/5: 894–908.

—— & Leshchinskii, D. (2001). "Can Firms Learn to Acquire." Working Paper 99-82-SM. Fontainebleau, France: INSEAD.

—— & Reuer, J. J. (2010). "Experience Spillovers across Corporate Development Activities." *Organization Science*, 21(6): 1195–212.

—— Reuer, J. J., & Singh, H. (2002). "Interorganizational Routines and Performance in Strategic Alliances." *Organization Science*, 13/6: 701–13.

—— & Winter, S. G. (2002). "Deliberate Learning and the Evolution of Dynamic Capabilities." *Organization Science*, 13/3: 339–51.

—— & Singh, H. (2004). "Deliberate Learning in Corporate Acquisitions: Post-acquisition Strategies and Integration Capability in US Bank Mergers." *Strategic Management Journal*, 25/13: 1233–56.

PART II

A FINANCIAL LENS FOR M&A

CHAPTER 7

PRE-DEAL MANAGEMENT

BRENDAN MCSWEENEY
AND ELINA HAPPONEN

INTRODUCTION

The acquisition process is often represented as a step-by-step logical chain of events. Typically, these steps are said to flow from acquisition strategy and objectives, passing through the phases of systematic search and screening, strategic evaluation, financial evaluation, negotiations, purchase, and ultimately integration. This characterization is useful in highlighting different challenges and stages through time. But it has two limitations.

Depicting the acquisition process as a chain of sequential and discrete steps neglects the extensive interrelationships between the different stages (Ashkenas et al. 1998). Furthermore, acquisitions are usually undertaken within contexts characterized by considerable uncertainty. Discrete stage descriptions of acquisitions overstate the predictability of outcomes, including strategic fit, organization fit, and economic value. These are judged, supposed, anticipated as much as they are objectively found. This chapter considers the management of the interrelated acquisition activities undertaken prior to a merger or acquisition (hereafter, acquisition) deal.

PLACING THE PRE-DEAL PHASE INTO AN ACQUISITION PROCESS

This chapter situates the pre-deal phase within the context of an acquisition process. In addition, it also presents a pre-deal process framework providing an overview of the multiple pre-deal (i.e. candidate search, evaluation, and purchase) considerations and issues.

Discrete Stages View vs. a Process View

The discrete stages view sees the acquisition process as a sequential segmented process (Figure 7.1) in which the pre-acquisition analysis of strategic fit and financial valuation are the most important factors (Haspeslagh and Jemison 1991).

In contrast to a discrete stages view, a process perspective shifts the focus from acquisition results to the drivers that generate these results (Figure 7.2). It recognizes that the acquisition process itself is an important determinant of acquisition activities and outcomes. Yet, it retains important roles for strategic and organizational fit that have historically been emphasized by scholars and practitioners employing a rational choice perspective (Jemison and Sitkin 1986).

Acquisition Process Stages

Haspeslagh and Jemison (1991: 5, 12–14) divide the acquisition process into two main phases, suggesting that the pre-deal decision-making phase and the post-deal integration process are integrative determinants of the acquisition's success, and thus, should be considered together. Their process perspective widens the view from looking only at the pre-deal process to considering the post-acquisition issues during, not after, the acquisition's decision-making and justification phase.

While Haspeslagh and Jemison (1991) divide the process into only two main, pre- and post-deal, phases, Voss (2007) has identified three interdependent, yet distinct phases:

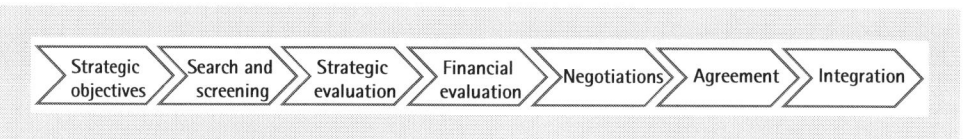

FIG. 7.1 Conventional view of acquisitions

Source: Haspeslagh and Jemison (1991: 13).

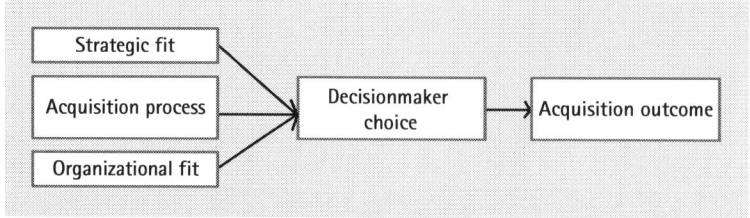

FIG. 7.2 A process perspective on corporate acquisitions

Source: Jemison and Sitkin (1986).

preparation; transaction; and integration. The preparation phase can be further divided into five stages: strategy; screening; selection; justification; and investment decision. Ashkenas et al. (1998) provide an even more detailed division of the pre-deal stages of the acquisition process: selecting possible acquisitions; narrowing the field; agreeing on a first-choice candidate; assessing compliance with regulations; convening preliminary discussions; formulating the letter of intent; conducting due diligence; completing financial negotiations; making the announcement; signing the agreement; and closing the deal. Also Ashkenas et al. (1998) note that integration is not a stage which should be addressed only following the deal.

DePamphilis (2005) highlights that good planning expedites sound decision making and his view of a structured acquisition process contains ten phases: business plan; acquisition plan; search; screen; first contact; negotiations; integration plan; closing; integration; and post-integration evaluation. The negotiations stage consists of four largely concurrent and interrelated activities (due diligence, refined valuation, deal structuring, and financing plan) and is a crucial phase in an acquisition process.

Pre-acquisition Process Framework

As the pre-deal phase has an evident link to overall acquisition success, it is important to understand the process elements and considerations in each process stage (Figure 7.3). However, understanding the process is not enough. In order to manage the pre-deal process adequately, it is also essential to acknowledge that the pre-deal phase can be shaped and affected by several factors (Figure 7.3). Some affect the work flow and analysis, some relate to framing ideas and conceptions, and some are potential acquisition decision-making problems. Moreover, acquirers should consider how the pre- and post-deal phases could be better linked (e.g. Kitching 1967; Marks 1982), and start the integration planning and relationship building during the pre-deal phase (Howell 1970; Hunt 1990).

THE ACQUISITION TEAM

Acquisitions are complex processes which require a wide range of specialized capabilities. When considering the possibility of an acquisition, the potential buyer should establish a dedicated acquisition team that includes people with different areas of expertise depending on the size, importance, and nature of the possible deal. The acquisition team should contain expertise on aspects such as the process and negotiations, pricing, deal-structuring options, business issues, security aspects related to post-deal risks, human resource issues, and integration planning and implementation. This chapter describes the key roles in an acquisition team.

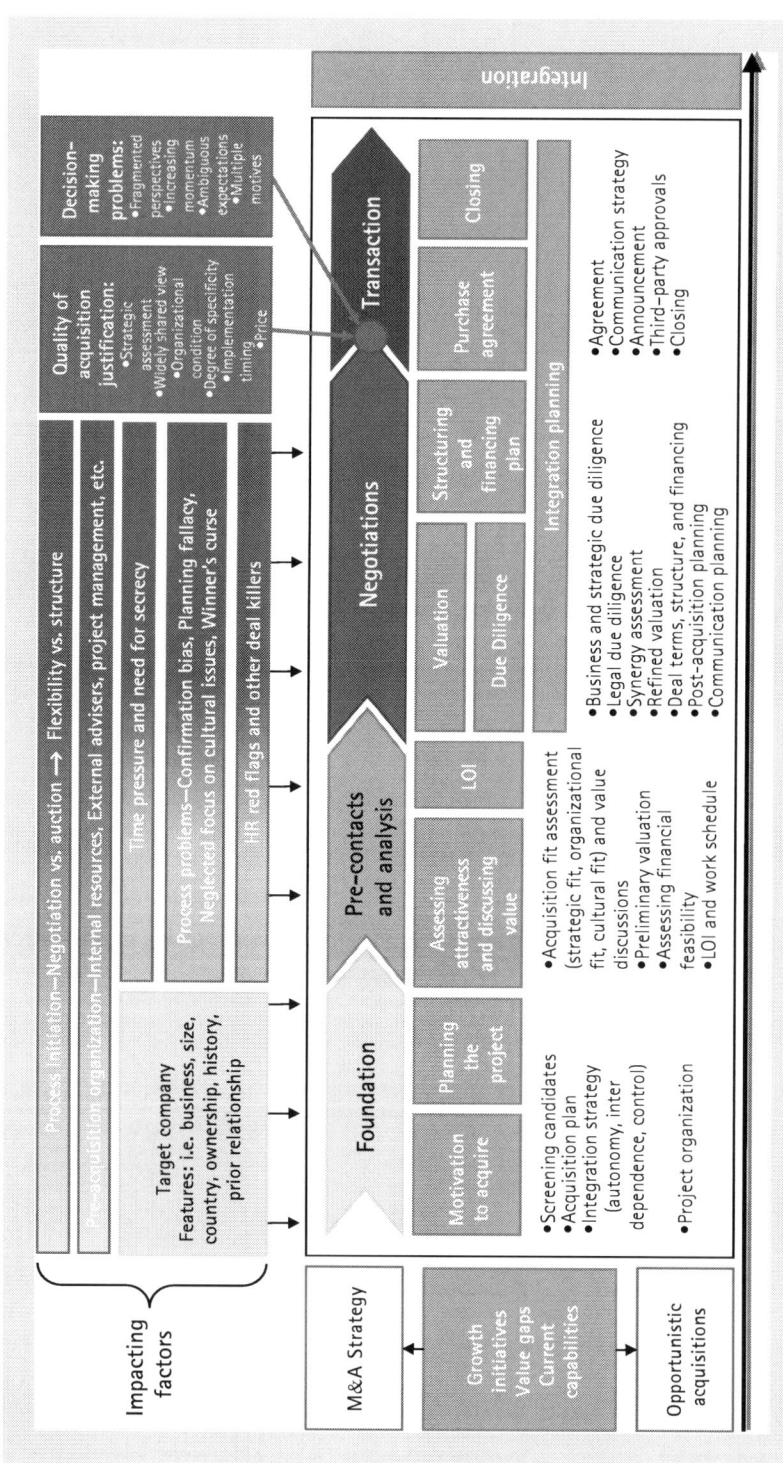

FIG. 7.3 Pre-deal acquisition process

Source: Happonen (2009).

Process Leader

The technical complexity of acquisition process activities and the functional back-grounds of the process participants may lead to grooved (segmented and silo) thinking (Jemison and Sitkin 1986). Thus, it is important that efforts are made to undertake the analytical challenge holistically and that intra-team information flows are soundly coordinated. There is evidence that the appointment of one person in the team as the ultimate deal-maker is beneficial. The chosen person should champion the successful completion of an acquisition, understand why the acquisition is being made, have com-mitment to it, and know how to make the best use of the talents and knowledge of the other members of the team (Dionne 1988).

Integration Manager

The involvement of an integration manager in the pre-acquisition phase is likely to guarantee more efficiency in the management of the integration phase (Véry 2004). As the integration and its successful implementation are an essential part of the entire acquisition process, it is highly desirable that the person who would be responsible for the integration, and ideally, if different, the person responsible for eventually managing the new business, are included in the acquisition team from the start (Haspeslagh and Jemison 1991). They serve as a bridge between the pre- and post-deal stages, and thus ensure that views and information about post-acquisition inte-gration is gathered and fed into the screening and valuation processes as well as being used after a deal.

Human Resource (HR) Function

The role of human resources (HR) representatives as part of the acquisition team has been increasingly been recognized as important (e.g. Mirvis and Marks 1992; Schweiger and Lippert 2005). HR knowledge about the human side of the acquisitions, for exam-ple, employees' motivation, can be essential to planning and managing the post-merger integration. However, the "soft" people issues and the management of the human side of acquisition activity are often neglected (e.g. Schuler and Jackson 2001; Schweiger et al. 1989). This has its dangers, as many acquisition motives are human resource related, as in for example the acquisition of key talent, competencies, and capabilities. In some cases, the post-acquisition retention of talent may be a major concern. Furthermore, the HR function has an important role in searching and selecting potential targets (Schuler and Jackson 2001), including the evaluation of the organizational and cultural fit between the two companies (Harding and Rouse 2007). Thus, it is advisable to have an HR expert on the team from the outset.

External Resources

In addition to internal expertise and resources, using experienced external advisors, such as investment bankers, valuation experts, and insurance or employee benefits experts (Sherman and Hart 2006), may be appropriate at different stages of the acquisition process (e.g. Jemison and Sitkin 1986; Saorím-Iborra 2008; Sherman and Hart 2006). The more complex the acquisition, the more different groups of outside advisers are usually involved in the analysis (e.g. Jemison and Sitkin 1986). Regardless of the level of complexity, legal advice is always required.

External advisers can save time and money as well as provide information that would otherwise be unavailable to the buyer. Areas requiring specific expertise might at times be best acquired. Companies new to acquisitions should consider recruiting some acquisition-experienced staff. However, the involvement of internal staff is also vital as they have unique company-specific knowledge, crucial in determining the degree of fit between the firms.

The Acquisition Plan

The acquisition process starts by developing an acquisition plan. A well-prepared acquisition plan can be a valuable negotiation tool in dealing with a seller's concern on the value and continued growth of buyer's stock. Furthermore, the plan also provides a road map and serves as a screen to filter out deals that do not meet acquisition criteria or long-term objectives (Sherman and Hart 2006).

Acquisition plans usually include a list or statement of objectives. In effect, the statement helps the team address the following questions about a proposed acquisition: (1) Why are we considering an acquisition? (2) Are we convinced that it is the right choice compared to other forms of growth strategies? (3) Would an acquisition improve our competitive position? (4) Would it enhance shareholder value? (5) What impacts would it have on other stakeholders? and (6) Have we identified and evaluated the key value drivers of the proposed acquisition (Sherman and Hart 2006)? In addition, the plan will usually include specific financial objectives such as a minimum rate of return and operating profit, revenue, and cash-flow targets to be achieved within a specific time period (DePamphilis 2005).

When the deal objectives are clear, the acquisition plan can be created. Table 7.1 (below) distinguishes between a "general acquisition plan" and a "candidate specific plan." The former defines the specific objectives that management hopes to achieve by completing an acquisition. The core of this plan sets boundaries and lists the criteria for evaluating candidates within target industries and provides guidance for those responsible for finding and valuing the target. In addition, the plan provides a schedule of milestones to keep the process on track and also defines the authority and responsibility of the individuals charged with managing the acquisition process. The latter is developed when a potentially suitable acquisition candidate, or candidates, has been identified. This plan additionally includes the initial offer price, guidelines for precise negotiations, and implications of the proposed acquisition.

Table 7.1 Contents of an acquisition plan

General acquisition plan

- Plan objectives: Identify the specific purpose for the acquisition and precise goals to be achieved
  - The desired financial returns and/or operating synergies to be achieved as an acquisition result
- Search plan: Develop screening criteria for identifying potential target firms. Explain plans for conducting the search—why the target was selected, and how the initial contact is made
  - The minimum and maximum ranges and rates of acceptable revenue, growth, earnings, and net worth of the seller
  - The desired geographic location of the company
  - The desired demographics and buying habits of the seller's customers
  - The method for finding candidates (e.g. internal research vs. intermediaries)
- Timetable: Establish a timetable for completing the acquisition including integration
- Resource and capability evaluation: Evaluate the acquirer's financial and managerial capability to complete an acquisition. Identify affordability limit (maximum price) and explain its determination
  - The members of the acquisition team including external advisers and each of their roles
  - The targeted size of the acquisition candidates (maximum purchase price etc.)
  - The source of acquisition financing and amount available
- Management preferences: Indicate preferences for a "friendly" acquisition, controlling interest, method of payment, etc.
  - Openness to full versus partial ownership of the seller's entity, or willingness to consider a spin-off sale, such as purchase of the assets of an operating division or the stock of subsidiary
  - Interest or willingness to launch an unfriendly takeover
  - Willingness to consider turnaround or roundtable companies
  - Tax and financial preferences for asset vs. stock transaction
  - The nature and type of risks the buyer is willing to assume (vs. those that are unacceptable)

Candidate specific plan

- Initial offer price: Determine the value for the company with and without expected synergies
  - Develop preliminary minimum and maximum purchase prices for the target
  - Considerations on closing the gap between seller's and offered prices
- Negotiation strategy and financing plan: Identify key buyer/seller issues. Comment on the characteristics of the deal structure
  - The acquisition vehicle (i.e. the legal structure used in acquiring the target firm)
  - The post-closing organization (i.e. the post-closing legal structure to manage the combined firm)
  - The form of payment (i.e. cash, stock, or combination)
  - The form of acquisition (i.e. whether the asset or stock is being acquired)
  - The tax structure (i.e. taxable or non-taxable acquisition)
  - The likely competing bidders for qualified candidates
- Implications: Consider how the deal affects some primary stakeholders
  - The obvious integration challenges
  - The impact of the acquisition on existing shareholders of your company
  - The plans to retain or replace the management team of the target company—this policy may vary by candidate

Source: Modified from Sherman and Hart (2006); DePamphilis (2005).

CANDIDATE SEARCH AND SCREENING

When the acquisition objectives are clear, the acquisition team and responsibilities are set, and an acquisition plan has been developed, the search for acquisition candidates can begin, or be extended, and the screening of these candidates can commence. In some instances, the process has been initiated by the identification of a candidate company, for example, through a "cold-call" by an investment bank. In these circumstances, the prospective buyer may already be in a "state of readiness," in the sense that they have already defined their strategic acquisition vision, or further still, have developed a general acquisition plan. Alternatively, the acquisition possibility might be the initiating trigger. Regardless of when or how a candidate company is identified, the process described above (the establishment of an acquisition team, and so forth) is desirable.

The range and quality of analysis of a target company will influence not only the valuation of a candidate company, but also a host of other views and decisions. Issues which require early analysis include: proceed or abandon? make a direct or indirect approach? is the response likely to be friendly or hostile? if the latter, what defensive tactics could the target company employ and what effective counter-actions are possible? who are the influential owners (institutional shareholders, family trust, or whoever)? who are the key managers and directors? what are its core competences? and which parts of the company underperform and which parts excel? It is therefore vital that the characteristics of the candidate company should be considered very early in the process. Relevant data to be collected about candidate companies includes: financial performance; market value (if available), asset age and structure; brand strengths and values; tax planning; size; market share and position within industry; locations; ownership composition; corporate governance; prior relationships (if any) with the buyer; contingent liabilities; court actions; and attractiveness to other potential buyers.

The acquisition team should be alert to its own biases. There is extensive evidence that people tend to seek out information to validate their initial hypothesis and ideas (Lovallo et al. 2007; Nisbett and Ross 1980). This "confirmation bias" may be intensified by the speed and secrecy of an acquisition process. Managers and other analysts need to be sensitive to potential biases generated by this cognitive preconception when estimating an acquisition candidate's potential and value.

Other cognitive problems in the acquisition process are the "planning fallacy," the "winner's curse," and "herd behavior." The planning fallacy means that acquirers tend to underestimate the time, money, and other resources required to complete major projects (Lovallo et al. 2007). The winner's curse refers to situations where the acquirer overestimates the benefits of the deal due to its strong desire to win the bid. Herd behavior—a tendency to follow and imitate others—has been observed not only in stock markets but also in the field of acquisitions (Ghemawat and Ghadar 2000).

Estimating Value and Future Growth Potential

As the acquisition candidate or candidates have been found, the acquirer starts estimating their value and future growth potential. Corporate valuation is always challenging, but estimating the value of an acquisition is even more problematic as central to it is an additional and key uncertainty: the extent and consequences of the fit between two previously separate entities, the acquirer and the acquired. Simplistic formulae, such as multiples of one or other financial indicator; earnings per share, for example, do not work. Almost always they turn out to be precisely wrong (Fernández 2007). A vaguely right valuation requires a synthesis of knowledge of the inner and outer contexts of both companies and some luck in anticipating future uncertainties.

Acquisition Value

A number of frameworks which may help in structuring the valuation analysis by an acquisition team are available. Kruger and Müller-Stewans (1994: 68), for instance, provide a typology of *acquisition fit*, in which higher fit leads to higher acquisition value for the target (Figure 7.4).

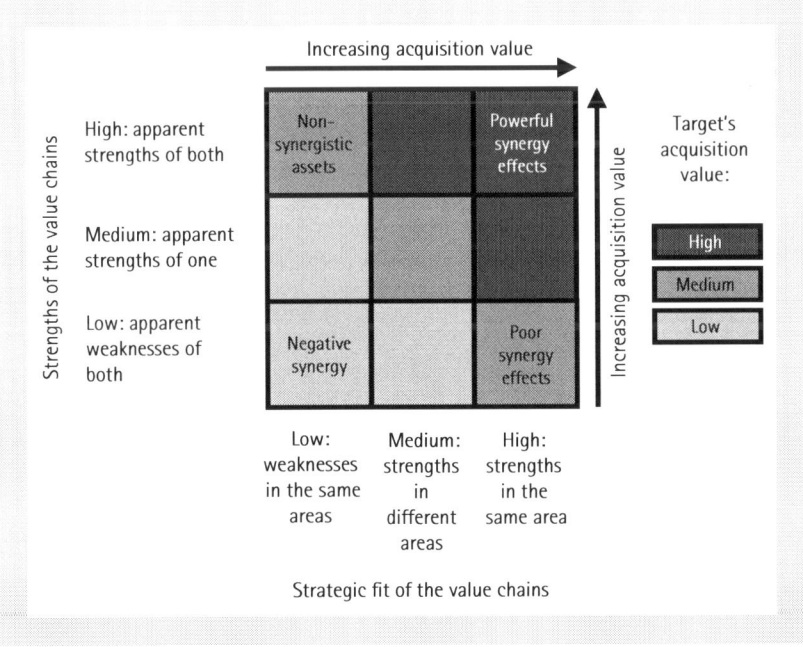

FIG. 7.4 Acquisition-fit matrix: combining acquirer with candidate

Source: Krüger and Müller-Stewens (1994: 68).

Table 7.2 Nine tests of corporate growth

External tests	Internal tests	Strategic tests
1. *Competitive analysis:* (a) capabilities and competencies of competitors; (b) competitors' intentions and future directions; and (c) broader dynamics of the market	1. *Core competencies and operational efficiency:* e.g. procurement, communications, logistics, distribution, outsourcing, and workflow process	1. *Strategic planning:* investigations into the direction that the company is heading, the process utilized to arrive at this direction, and the company's perceived value of strategic planning as an ongoing process
2. *Customer awareness:* (a) customer needs, behaviors, and interests; (b) perceptions of suppliers; and (c) the current state of relationships	2. *Human capital assessment:* e.g. recruitment, selection, training, leadership development, culture, system's performance management, and feedback loops	2. *Wild card analyses:* gaining awareness of the potential for disruptive, disintermediating, playing-field-altering opportunities and threats
3. *Market knowledge:* (1) attractiveness of the market (growth, profit potential, customer needs, industry trends, etc.); and (2) target's position in the market	3. *Growth capital analysis:* financial performance analysis, and investigation of whether the company has the resources it needs to achieve its goals, objectives, strategies, and tactics	3. *Value proposition and brand strategy:* identify the company's unique selling point, determine whether that point might be valued by target customers, and consider the extent to which awareness of the company's unique value offering is being communicated to current and target customers via branding and other mechanisms

Source: Adapted from Lisle (2008: 133–6).

Lisle (2008: 133–6) proposes that companies can benefit from using a systematic test of nine predictors of target growth (Table 7.2): three tests of external strategic opportunities; three tests of internal capabilities to execute these opportunities; and three strategic or balancing tests which include strategic planning, wild cards, and value proposition. Every one of the nine tests has the potential to "kill" a deal.

Sources of Synergies

Synergies (operational and financial) are a common acquisition objective as they can be a major source of value enhancement. But estimating synergies is difficult (Christofferson et al. 2004). Many companies overestimate the value of acquisition synergies and underestimate the difficulty of achieving them (Cools et al. 2006; Cullinan et al. 2004; McKinsey & Company, Inc. et al. 2005; Lovallo et al. 2007). Lovallo et al. (2007) argue that using a reference class of comparable prior deals to estimate synergies can reduce bias towards overestimation.

Cullinan et al. (2004) state that a good approach to hinder synergy overestimations is to use due-diligence processes to carefully distinguish between different kinds of synergies, estimate their potential value and probability of being realized, assess the speed with which the synergies can be realized, and define the required investments. They argue that it is useful to think of potential synergies as a series of concentric circles, as a map of synergies (Figure 7.5), since categorizing synergies provides a useful framework for valuing them. Analysts can assign a potential value for each circle, assess the probability of achieving the synergies concerned, and provide a timetable for implementation. The timetable can then be used to model the synergies' effect on the combined cash flows. Synergies that lie close to the center tend to be cost-saving and can be realized quickly and are likely to succeed. Those on the outside circles are revenue-generating synergies, which require greater time and management and are less likely to succeed.

According to McKinsey & Company, Inc. et al. (2005), even the most experienced acquirers sometimes forget to estimate the implementation costs which are required to capture the synergies. Some synergies may be negative, arising, for example, from potential conflicts between aspects of the merged businesses. Furthermore, acquirers often make overly optimistic assumptions about how long it will take to capture synergies (Christofferson et al. 2004; Cullinan et al. 2004).

When estimating and quantifying synergies, it is useful to divide them into two groups: cost and revenue synergies. Cost synergies can be divided into six groups based on their source: R&D; procurement; manufacturing; sales and marketing; distribution; and administration. Revenue synergies, on the other hand, often involve acquiring a specific technology or product, and they come from one or more of four sources: increasing each product's peak sales level; reaching the increased peak sales faster; extending each product's life; and adding new products or features that could not have been developed if the two companies had remained independent. Moreover, revenue synergies can also come from higher prices through reduced competition (McKinsey & Company, Inc. et al. 2005).

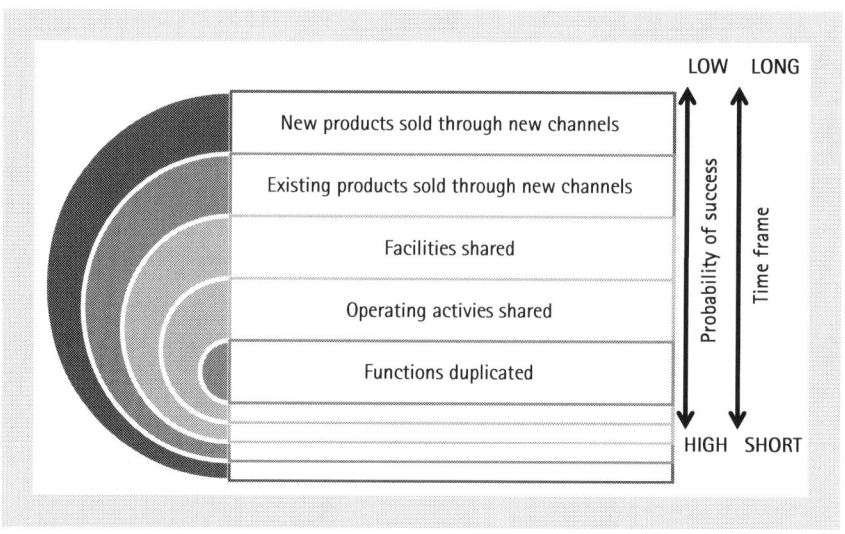

FIG. 7.5 A map of synergies

Source: Based on Cullinan et al. (2004).

MANAGING THE NEGOTIATION PROCESS

The negotiation phase is an intensely interactive and iterative process where many activities are conducted simultaneously by various acquisition team members. Acquisition negotiations consist of four concurrent activities: (1) conducting due diligence; (2) refining valuation; (3) structuring the deal; and (4) developing a financing plan. The new information that emerges from the due-diligence investigation of the company is used to refine the valuation and determine the actual purchase price for the acquisition. This purchase price may differ significantly from the initial offer (DePamphilis 2005).

A number of characteristics of acquisitions tend to make the process even more complicated and risky than a normal resource allocation process or internal investment. These characteristics include, for example, the irregular and opportunistic nature of acquisitions, acquisitions' dissimilarity from managers' regular experiences, unusually high levels of uncertainty, and the required speed in decision making (Haspeslagh and Jemison 1991).

Auctions vs. Direct Negotiations

There are two different ways of making a deal: direct negotiations and controlled auctions. The former is the main method used for selling and buying a company. In a direct deal, contacts and information exchange happen directly between the seller and buyer.

Direct deals are the most prevalent for unlisted companies or for companies for whom the target presents only a small part of their total business. While direct negotiations usually are exclusive, auctions typically include multiple potential buyers. As the process affects the outcome, understanding the auction as a pre-acquisition process driver is important. Auctions proceed through several stages, during which one or more buyer candidates are excluded. Competition among bidders can help in realizing higher prices for sellers in auctions than in direct deals (Bulow and Klemperer 2009).

Negotiations have few rules and deadlines, and there is some uncertainty as to whether the target will be sold at all. Auctions, on the other hand, are more structured and create pressure for interested buyers due to competitive bids. Negotiations give flexibility in the transaction design and deal makers may be able to accommodate multiple objectives more easily than in auctions. In addition, when compared to auctions, negotiations proceed more slowly.

Time Pressure and Increasing Momentum

The pre-bid process is characterized by time pressure (e.g. Reuer 2005; Saorím-Iborra 2008; Bruner 2004). As the pressure, pace, and involvement levels rise, the acquisition team may feel unable to stop the process or slow its tempo. Prime drivers for this increasing momentum are increased personnel commitment, secrecy and intense concentration, and the pressure from outside advisers, such as investment bankers. It results in escalating desires to complete the process quickly and "close the deal". If this issue is left unchecked, it can lead to overvaluation and inadequate considerations of integration issues (Haspeslagh and Jemison 1991).

Fragmented Perspectives and Unresolved Expectations

Independent goals of the specialists and analysts involved as well as their particular experience may result in multiple fragmented views of the agreement. If specialists work without coordination in isolation from one another, the outcome may emphasize quantification of financial estimates rather than strategic and organizational considerations, and thus limits the firm's ability to develop a rich acquisition justification. In addition, unresolved expectations on the key aspects of the acquisition between the negotiating parties can create substantial post-deal problems (Haspeslagh and Jemison 1991).

Information Asymmetries and the Risk of Adverse Selection

Acquisition negotiations are often characterized by information asymmetries. As an acquisition is a terminal sale, the buyer bears the primary risk of overpayment. To cope with this problem, Reuer (2005) suggests that when the acquirer has an inadequate understanding of the resources to be acquired, and when that information deficit is irredeemable, a joint venture or other form of alliance may be a more attractive option. In addition, instead of implementing hybrid organizational forms (such as joint ventures), decision makers can devise bespoke contracts to manage the risk of adverse selection, while still obtaining complete control of the target (Ghemawat and Ghadar 2000).

Acquisition Justification Challenge

The acquisition justification process is too often focused on financial valuation rather than strategic issues. Yet, unless the justification is based on the combination of a solid strategic assessment, a shared purpose, a specific examination of benefits and problems, a regard for organizational conditions, and attention to timing, the mechanically sophisticated financial case is simply a storyline. The quality of the acquisition justification is closely related to acquisition performance and can be judged by the dimensions identified above (Haspeslagh and Jemison 1991).

Deal Killer Management

"Deal killers" can come in all shapes, sizes, and varieties with different reasons, justifications, and rationalizations. They can originate from the buyer, the seller, or any of the third parties, such as lenders, investors, and key customers or suppliers (Sherman and Hart 2006). Table 7.3 provides a list of potential deal killers.

Deal killers are legitimate for deals that deserve to die, but in many cases deal killers can and should be resolved with creative restructuring or careful document redrafting. In managing the acquisition process, it is important to distinguish between different types of deal killers as they require different approaches. This means that the leader of the acquisition team should have enough transactional business experience, business intelligence, and communication skills to diagnose the source and nature of the problem. Strong leadership and extensive communication between the parties and key people are needed.

Due Diligence

Due diligence includes legal, financial, and strategic reviews of all of the seller's documents, contractual relationships, operating history, and organizational structure. The heart of "due diligence" is research (Table 7.4). Within the acquisition process, its purpose is to support the valuation, guide negotiators, test the exactness of representa-

Table 7.3 Deal killers

Trust and relationship	Unexpected changes in performance or business
• Egos clashing • Inexperienced players • Internal and external politics (board-level, executives, venture investors, etc.) • Loss of trust/integrity during the transaction process • Nepotism • Breakdowns in leadership and coordination/too little or too many points of communication • Too little or too much "principal to principal" communication	• Changes in seller performance during the transactional process (upside surprises vs. unexpected downside surprises) • Unexpected changes in the buyer's strategy or operations during the transactional process (including a change in management or strategic direction) • Loss of a key customer or strategic relationship during the transaction process • Employee and customer issues
Due diligence red flags/surprises	**Deal structuring difficulties**
• Accounting/financial statement irregularities • Incompatibility of culture and/or business systems (e.g. IT infrastructure, costs and budgeting policies, compensation and reward programs, accounting policies)	• Valuation problems (tax/source of financing/in general) • Pricing and structural challenges (price vs. terms) • Seller's/buyer's source of capital remorse
Negotiations and closing	**Post-closing considerations**
• Crowded auctions • Force-feeding deals that do not meet acquisition objectives (square peg/round hole; bad deal avoidance/good deal capture, systems and filters) • Misalignment of objectives • Different perceptions: merger vs. acquisition • Impatience to get to closing versus loss of momentum (flow and timing issues) • Shareholder approvals	• Overdependence on the founder/key employee/key customer or relationship • Failure to develop a mutually agreeable post-closing integration plan • Failure to agree on post-closing obligations, roles, and responsibilities • Environmental problems (buyers less willing to rely on indemnification and insurance protections)

Source: (adopted from Sherman and Hart 2006)

tions and warranties, fulfill disclosure requirements to investors, and inform integration planners (Bruner 2004). Due diligence is not only a process, but also serves as a reality check—as a test that determines whether the factors driving and making the deal are valid or illusory. This chapter presents important due-diligence features and principles, and discusses the contents of business, legal, HR, and cultural due-diligence efforts.

Due-Diligence Principles

Due diligence acts as a counterweight to the excitement and "deal fever" that builds when managers begin to pursue a target. It can be tedious, frustrating, time consuming, and expensive, yet it is a necessary prerequisite of a well-planned acquisition (Sherman and Hart 2006). When conducting the process, the buyer confronts a trade-off between "surprise me now" versus "surprise me later", as the research approach can be either narrow (brief, limited, and focused), or broad (detailed and time consuming). Both approaches are equally costly but they differ on the timing of cash flows and how they bear risk (Bruner 2004).

Not infrequently, due diligence narrowly focuses on the mere verification of financial statements rather than conducting a reasonable analysis of the deal's strategic logic and the acquirer's ability to realize value from it. Cullinan, Le Roux, and Weddigen (2004) have found that successful acquirers view due diligence as much more than an exercise in verifying data. While going through the numbers thoroughly, due diligence also puts the broader strategic rationale for their acquisition under the "microscope." An effective due-diligence process challenges superficial impressions that are often drawn from the target's public profile or its reputation. It looks beyond the surface and builds a bottom-up view of the target and its industry, suppliers, and competitors.

Business and Legal Due Diligence

The level and extent of the general financial and strategic business due diligence vary depending on the experience of the industry and familiarity with the target company. Some key questions focus on the target company's capabilities and performance in all of its functional areas, including operations, marketing, human resources, and financial management. Added to this analysis, it is important to investigate its customer and supplier relationship activities, as well as to form a view of the target's cultures, leadership style, and motivation and commitment to the acquisition (Cullinan et al. 2004).

When analyzing the target from a business perspective, the due diligence undertaken by the acquisition team is likely to identify some financial problems and risks. In such circumstances, typical findings are undervalued inventory, overdue tax liabilities, inadequate management information systems, related-party transactions, an unhealthy reliance on a few key customers or suppliers, aging accounts receivable, unrecorded liabilities, or an urgent need for significant expenditure resulting from obsolete equipment, inventory, or computer systems (Sherman and Hart 2006). The buyer should also be aware of the wide range of accounting tricks that companies can use to buff their numbers (Cullinan et al. 2004).

In legal due diligence, the buyer's team reviews and analyzes legal documents and records concerning corporate matters, financial matters, management and employee matters, tangible and intangible assets of the seller, material contracts and obligations of the seller, actual and contingent litigation and claims, and other miscellaneous issues, such as press releases, management team résumés and speeches, schedules of all outside advisors and consultants, financial analyst reports, and surveys (Sherman and Hart 2006).

HR Due Diligence

When compared to strategic business development, finance, operations, and sales functions, the priority assigned to HR and communications functions in due diligence is usually relatively low (Cartwright and Cooper 1992). The human relations due diligence effort, that is, gathering and analyzing detailed information about the composition and characteristics of the target company's employees at all levels, can have considerable impact on the long-term success of an acquisition. HR due diligence should evaluate the adequacy of the target company's human talent and leadership and identify any unusual workforce competences or weaknesses, inefficiencies in compensation and benefit schemes, contingent liabilities, past and pending employee discrimination claims, and the compatibility of organizational and HR policies with the buyer's. Burrows (2000) has identified some HR due-diligence "red flags," such as the difficulty of gaining access to one-to-one meetings with employees, employee fears of talking openly, lack of employee affiliation or affection for the company, absence of trust between the management and employees, absence of an HR function within the company, and high employee turnover.

Cultural Due Diligence

The research findings that cultural/practice differences between the firms are a major source of conflict in acquisitions, especially post-deal (Buono et al. 1985; Schweiger 2002; Teerikangas and Véry 2006), underline the importance of assessing cultural fit as part of due-diligence research. The acquirer should assess the cultures or practices of both the target and itself in order to determine whether the target's cultures/practices are important to the deal, whether differences are so severe that the deal should be killed, or whether some interventions can be employed to ensure that differences become a source of value rather than a weakness (Schweiger and Lippert 2005). According to Marks (1999), the goal is not to exclude firms that have somewhat different cultures/practices from consideration as targets, but to understand the differences and to begin developing plans to bridge them.

Reliable information on a target's cultures/practices is often difficult to obtain. Mission statements and statements of core values should not be taken at face value. In addition to their construction for public relations purposes, such statements wrongly ignore the diversity of values in companies. However, they may give some indication of the values the company aspires to. Some insights can be gleaned from interaction between the negotiating teams, organizational folklore, court actions (if any), and secondhand reports from individuals with previous or current contacts within the organization (Cartwright and McCarthy 2005).

Table 7.4 Attained knowledge from due diligence

Legal	Finance
• Corporate organization and ownership • Litigation risk: existing and potential • Compliance with laws and regulations	• Adequacy of cash management system • Exposure to covenants and guarantees (e.g. in debt contacts, other acquisitions, etc.) • Compatibility of financial policies with strategy of buyer

Market presence and sales issues	Accounting
• General image of the firm, and the strength of brand, franchise, or goodwill with customers • Strength of marketing and sales organization, and the effectiveness of sales and marketing efforts (coverage, cost, profitability etc.) • Perception of product or service quality and variety in the market place • Competitive advantages/disadvantages vs. peers • Potential for improvement and synergies • Exposure to product or service warranties • Sales and marketing policy compatibility • Outlook for future performance: customer base, units sold, revenues, and collections	• Adequacy of accounting procedures, and compliance with generally accepted accounting principles, and acceptability of financial statements • Identification of good and bad trends in reported financial results, comparisons with industry peers • Identification of financial management issues in the areas of cash balances, backlogs, inventory management, obsolescence, bad debts, costs, obligations to suppliers, contingent liabilities such as unfounded pension obligations and guaranties, forecasts etc. • Effectiveness of internal auditing procedures • Exposure to fraud

Operations	Organization, HR, and ethics
• Strength of manufacturing or service operations • Opportunities for improvement, and potential synergies • Innovativeness • Exposure to unions or other workforce-related risks • Exposure to technological change risks • Congruence of operational policies with buyer, and with customer demand or competitive positioning • Outlook for future performance: operating cost trends, efficiency trends, inventory management, etc.	• Adequacy of talent and leadership, compensation, and benefits • Exposure to workforce problems • Exposure to benefits claims • Compatibility of organization and HR policies with buyer • Compliance with existing policies and laws related to ethics, and exposure to liabilities arising from ethics issues • Compatibility of ethics policies with buyer

IT	Tax
• Adequacy of MIS systems • Evaluation of effectiveness of target's IT Department • Compatibility between target and buyer	• Compliance with tax laws and regulations • Tax policy inefficiencies, and exposure of unpaid taxes • Indemnification • Exposure to fraud

Culture	Risk management
• Congruence of target culture with beliefs and vision, and with its strategic threats and opportunities • Congruence of target and buyer cultures	• Adequacy of insurance • Compatibility with buyer

Real and personal property

- Condition of the properties being acquired
- Implications for integration with the buyer, and opportunities to create value
- Ownership of assets
- Exposure to encumbrances by other existing or potential claimants
- Compatibility of property policies with buyer

Intellectual and intangible assets

- Ownership or rights to use
- Exposure to infringement
- Compatibility of protection policies with strategy of buyer

Environmental

- Compliance with laws and regulations
- Exposure to environmental liabilities, and estimate of costs to remediate
- Compatibility with buyer's environmental strategy
- Inefficiencies in recycling and/or sale of scrap and waste

Cross–border

- Exposure to foreign currencies, foreign laws, and foreign regulations
- Adequacy of management and monitoring of foreign operations

Source: Adapted from Bruner (2004).

Structuring the Consideration

The final step or end of due diligence is to determine a walk-away price, which is a top price that the buyer is willing to pay for the target. Cullinan, Le Roux, and Weddigen (2004) suggest that the acquiring company assembles a body, separate from the acquisition team, to determine the walk-away price, since such a team are less likely to have an emotional commitment to the deal.

In deciding what form the payment for the acquisition should be, four questions need to be addressed: (1) will the buyer acquire stock or assets of the target? (2) in what form will the consideration from the buyer to the seller be made (e.g. cash, notes, securities)? (3) will the purchase price be fixed, contingent, or payable over time on an installment basis? and, (4) what will the consequences of the proposed structure of the payment be for the acquisition? In addition, a variety of corporate, tax, and securities law issues affect the final decision of how to structure any transaction (Sherman and Hart 2006).

Acquisitions always include a variety of financial, cultural, and legal risks which should be considered when structuring the deal. The buyer has available a wide spectrum of risk management tools and devices, including: toehold stake; termination fees; exit clauses; lock-up options; warranties; escrow accounts; post-transaction price adjustments; other contingent payments; claw-back provisions; making staged investments; choosing the form of payment and financing terms carefully; and the initiative in drafting documents and designing the deal (Bruner 2004).

INTEGRATION PLANNING

The post-acquisition integration has been commonly cited as an important consideration in the acquisition process (e.g. Ashkenas et al. 1998; Askhenas and Francis 2000; Cartwright and Cooper 1993; Epstein 2004; Shrivastava 1986). The importance integration planning stage has been referred to by existing research as a critical factor and a facilitator in ensuring successful integration (e.g. Schuler and Jackson 2001; Schweiger 2002; Cullinan et al. 2004; McKinsey & Company, Inc. et al. 2005; Schweiger et al. 1994; Krüger and Müller-Stewens 1994; Marks 1999). A well-prepared and detailed integration plan, accompanied by strict responsibilities, clear objectives, and timetables, creates the basis for successful post-acquisition integration (e.g. Dionne 1988; McKinsey & Company, Inc. et al. 2005).

The integration planning and design phase should begin well before the acquisition is signed and sealed (e.g. Cullinan et al. 2004; Dionne 1988; Epstein 2004; Schweiger 2002; Shrivastava 1986) and should include a blueprint for organizational changes, for example structures, processes, systems, and people (Schweiger et al. 1994). Lovallo et al. (2007) have found that, at this stage, acquirers often face planning fallacy: a tendency to underestimate the time, money, and other resources needed to complete an acquisition. Table 7.5 presents an example of contents found in an integration plan.

Table 7.5 Post–deal plan contents

Business plan	Integration plan
• Strategic logic of the acquisition, and integration objectives and scope: ○ *The desired financial returns* and/or *operating synergies* to be achieved as an acquisition result (note: defined and measurable objectives) ○ *Integration approach* in terms of interdependence, organizational autonomy, and control mechanism • Management model of the acquired company • Employee exchange/reduction • Corporate identity and the name of the company	• Timetable and schedule for staged integration: milestones, deadlines, check points, work plans, etc. • Integration budget: synergy benefits, negative synergies, communication costs, stage-setting costs, travelling costs, etc. • Day one plan: communication, events, etc. • 100-day plan: customer operations, management planning meeting, objective, budget, and risk analysis, integration team, cultural integration, and values • Cultural integration plan: corporate values

Integration management

• Resources and responsibilities:
  ○ Full-day *integration manager*, and the *integration team* members
  ○ External *advisers and specialists*
• Performance measures (KPIs, i.e. key performance indicators) and progress milestones (requires specified objectives and goals that can be measured)

Sources: See e.g. Haspeslagh and Jemison (1991: 328–31); Lajoux (1998).

The Closing Phase

The closing phase consists of obtaining all necessary shareholder, regulatory, and third-party consents, as well as signing the definitive agreement of the purchase. Following the issue of a Letter of Intent, the negotiations, and a thorough due-diligence process, buyers and sellers look to their legal counsel for guidance on a variety of strategic, regulatory, and financial tasks. It is important that the lawyers have an understanding of the key issues and challenges to the closing of the transaction, the key transaction motivations, and the special issues and risks that need to be dealt with in the documents. The final closing takes place as soon as all approvals have been met and all relevant documents have been filed with the appropriate authorities.

Conclusions and Future Research Directions

As a number of contributions to this *Handbook* have discussed, measuring the consequences of acquisitions is challenging. Impact identification requires contestable choices about time horizon (over what time period should and can consequences be considered?); about ambit (consequences from whom—the shareholders of the acquiring company, the acquired company, and/or wider stakeholders?); about geographical boundaries (should the consequences be considered only for those within the country of the acquired company or more globally?); about weighing trade-offs (how should intra- and inter-stakeholder benefits and losses be compared?); and other factors. Nonetheless, whilst the exact scale of acquisition consequences is contested, there is a consensus that whilst there have been spectacular successes, there have also been many spectacular failures. Overall results have been disappointing. This largely, but not wholly, negative record contrasts sharply with the optimistic predictions acquirers invariably make about proposed acquisitions. The frequent gap between (pre-bid) expectations and the often dull, and in some instances, disastrous outcome demonstrates the importance of sober and effective pre-deal management. A bid made in haste usually leads to inescapable remorse.

The performance of an acquisition or a merger is unavoidably characterized by uncertainty. There is no perfect analytical framework—there is no answering machine. But the vision and exuberance that often motivates a proposed acquisition needs to be steered and fashioned by relevant knowledge and experience. Some advice on shaping and controlling pre-deal management is provided in the chapter. Three aspects were especially considered—the roles of leadership; the roles of holistic analysis, that is, the avoidance of disconnected functional thinking; and the vital importance of undertaking early analysis of the implementation challenges. As the number of cross-border acquisitions continues to increase, so too does uncertainty about business contexts. Much pre-deal management literature has been overly normative—sometimes promoting a favored framework of analysis. Hopefully, a greater portion of future pre-deal management research will focus on action, on how pre-deal management is actually undertaken, rather than how the researchers think it ought to be done. And out of that more positive approach should emerge especially useful advice.

REFERENCES

Ashkenas, R., DeMonaco, L., & Francis, S. (1998). "Making the Deal Real: How GE Capital Integrates Acquisitions." *Harvard Business Review*, 76/1: 165–78.

—— & Francis, S. (2000). "Integration Managers: Special Leaders for Special Times." *Harvard Business Review*, 78/6: 108–16.

Bruner, R. (2004). *Applied Mergers and Acquisitions*. New Jersey: John Wiley & Sons, Inc.

Bulow, J., & Klemperer, P. (2009). "Why do Sellers (Usually) Prefer Auctions?" *American Economic Review*, 99/4: 1544–75.

Buono, A., Bowditch, J., & Lewis, J. (1985). "When Cultures Collide: The Anatomy of a Merger." *Human Relations*, 38/5: 477–500.

Burrows, D. (2000). "How People Problems can Sap Value from a Deal." *Mergers and Acquisitions*, 35/9: 36–9.

Cartwright, S., & Cooper, C. L. (1992). *Managing Mergers, Acquisitions and Strategic Alliances: Integrating People and Cultures*. Oxford: Butterworth-Heinemann.

—— —— (1993). "The Role of Cultural Compatibility in Successful Organizational Marriage." *Academy of Management Executive*, 7/2: 57–70.

Cartwright, S., & McCarthy, S. (2005). "Developing a Framework for Cultural Due Diligence in Merger and Acquisitions," in G. Stahl & M. Mendenhall, *Mergers and Acquisitions: Managing Culture and Human Resources*. Stanford, CA: Stanford University Press, 253–67.

Christofferson, S., McNish, R., & Sias, D. (2004). "Where do Mergers Go Wrong." *McKinsey Quarterly*, (2): 92–9.

Cools, K., Gell, J., and Roos, A. (2006). *Successful M&A: The Method in Madness*. Chicago: Boston Consulting Group.

Cullinan, G., Le Roux, J., & Weddigen, R. (2004). "When to Walk Away from the Deal." *Harvard Business Review*, 82/4: 96–104.

DePamphilis, D. (2005). *Mergers, Acquisitions, and Other Restructuring Activities: An Integrated Approach to Process, Tools, Cases, and Solutions* (3rd ed.). San Diego, CA: Elsevier/Academic Press.

Dionne, J. (1988). "The Art of Acquisitions." *The Journal of Business Strategy*, 9/6: 13–17.

Epstein, M. (2004). "The Drivers of Success in Post-merger Integration." *Organizational Dynamics*, 33/2: 174–89.

Fernández, P. (2007). "Company Valuation Methods: The Most Common Errors in Valuation." IESE Working Paper no. 499.

Ghemawat, P., & Ghadar, F. (2000). "The Dubious Logic of Global Megamergers." *Harvard Business Review*, 78: 65–74.

Happonen, E. (2009). "The Role of Pre-deal Management in Ensuring Correct M&A Decisions." Thesis. Department of Industrial Engineering and Management (Institute of Strategy), Helsinki University of Technology.

Harding, D., & Rouse, T. (2007). "Human Due Diligence." *Harvard Business Review*, 85/4: 124–31.

Haspeslagh, P., & Jemison, D. (1991). *Managing Acquisitions: Creating Value through Corporate Renewal*. New York: The Free Press.

Howell, R. A. (1970). "Plan to Integrate your Acquisitions." *Harvard Business Review*, 48/6, November–December: 66–76.

Hunt, J. W. (1990). "Changing Patterns of Acquisition Behaviour in Takeovers and the Consequences for Acquisition Processes." *Strategic Management Journal*, 11: 69–77.

Jemison, D., & Sitkin, S. (1986). "Corporate Acquisitions: A Process Perspective." *Academy of Management Review*, 11/1: 145–63.

Kitching, J. (1967). "Why Do Mergers Miscarry?" *Harvard Business Review*, 45/6, November–December: 84–100.

Krüger, W., & Müller-Stewens, G. (1994). "Matching Acquisition Policy and Integration Style," in G. von Krogh, A. Sinatra, & H. Singh, *The Management of Corporate Acquisitions: International Perspectives*. New York: Palgrave, 50–87.

Lajoux, A. (1998). *The Art of M&A Integration: A Guide to Merging Resources, Processes, and Responsibilities*. New York: McGraw-Hill.

Lisle, C. (2008). "Commercial Due Diligence and the Nine Levers of Corporate Growth." In *International Mergers and Acquisitions*. Birmingham: Financier Worldwide, 133–6.

Lovallo, D., Viguerie, P., Uhlaner, R., & Horn, J. (2007). "Deals without Delusions." *Harvard Business Review*, 85/12: 92–9.

McKinsey & Company, Inc., Koller, T., Goedhart, M., & Wessels, D. (2005). *Valuation: Measuring and Managing the Value of Companies* (4th ed.). New Jersey: John Wiley & Sons, Inc.

Marks, M. L. (1982). "Merging Human Resources: A Review of the Literature." *Mergers and Acquisitions*, 17/2, Summer: 38–44.

—— (1999). "Adding Cultural Fit to your Due Diligence Check List." *Mergers and Acquisitions*, 34/3: 14–20.

Mirvis, P., & Marks, M. (1992). "The Human Side of Merger Planning: Assessing and Analyzing." *Human Resource Planning*, 15: 69–93.

Nisbett, R. I. & Ross, L. (1980) *Human Inference: Strategies and Shortcomings of Social Judgment*, Englewood Cliffs, NJ: Prentice Hall.

Reuer, J. (2005). "Avoiding Lemons in M&A Deals." *MIT Sloan Management Review*, 46/3: 15–17.

Saorím-Iborra, M. (2008). "Time Pressure in Acquisition Negotiations: Its Determinants and Effects on Parties' Negotiation Behavior Choice." *International Business Review*, 17/3: 285–309.

Schuler, R., & Jackson, S. (2001). "HR Issues and Activities in Mergers and Acquisitions." *European Management Journal*, 19/3: 239–53.

Schweiger, D. (2002). "Merge Right." *Business and Economic Review*, 48/3: 3–11.

—— Csiszar, E., & Napier, N. (1994). "A Strategic Approach to Implementing Mergers and Acquisitions," in G. von Krogh, A. Sinatra, & H. Singh, *The Management of Corporate Acquisitions: International Perspectives*. New York: Palgrave, 23–49.

—— & Lippert, R. (2005). "Integration: The Critical Link in M&A Value Creation," in G. Stahl & M. Mendenhall, *Mergers and Acquisitions: Managing Culture and Human Resources*. Stanford, CA: Stanford University Press, 18–45.

—— Weber, Y., and Power, F. (1989). "Strategies for Managing Human Resources during Mergers and Acquisitions: An Empirical Investigation." *Human Resource Planning*, 12/2: 69–87.

Sherman, A., & Hart, M. (2006). *Mergers and Acquisitions from A to Z* (2nd ed.). New York: American Management Association, AMACOM.

Shrivastava, P. (1986). "Post-merger Integration." *Journal of Business Strategy*, 7/1: 65–76.

Teerikangas, S., & Véry, P. (2006). "The Culture–Performance Relationship in M&A: From Yes/No to How." *British Journal of Management*, 17: 31–48.

Véry, P. (2004). *The Management of Mergers and Acquisitions.* Chichester: Wiley.

Voss, I. (2007). *M&A Capability Evolution.* Göttingen: Cuvillier Verlag.

CHAPTER 8

VALUE CREATION AND VALUE APPROPRIATION IN M&A DEALS

SUDI SUDARSANAM

INTRODUCTION

Valuation of the target in an acquisition is an important part of the process of determining the consideration to be offered to the target shareholders. The value that the bidder places on the target sets the maximum or "walk-away" price that the bidder can afford to offer the target shareholders. This price is only one point in a range that the bidder should derive to guide negotiation. The value of the target from the bidder's point of view is the sum of the pre-bid stand-alone value of the target and the incremental value the bidder expects to add to the target's assets. The latter may arise from improved operation of the target or synergy between the two companies. Added value may also come from profitable target asset disposals, as in a bust-up takeover.

Valuation of the target requires valuation of the totality of the incremental cash flows and earnings. The expected incremental value may be reflected in the earnings and cash flows of both the target and the bidder in the post-acquisition period. The incremental earnings and cash flows may include those arising from reduced corporation tax liability. They also include the effects of combining and leveraging the target's and the acquirer's resources and capabilities.

Valuation of a target is based on expectations of both the magnitude and the timing of realization of the anticipated benefits. Where these benefits are difficult to forecast, the valuation of the target is not precise. This exposes the bidder to valuation risk. The degree of this risk depends on the quality of information available to the bidder, which, in turn, depends upon whether the target is a private or a public company, whether the bid is hostile or friendly, the time spent in preparing the bid, and the pre-acquisition due diligence and audit of the target.

There are a number of models employed by firms to evaluate targets. These may be broadly divided into those based on (1) earnings and assets multiples and (2) discounting of accounting earnings or cash flows. The earnings and assets multiples are less information intensive than the discounting models, and less rigorous, although they can be shown as attempting to capture the underlying earnings or cash flow discounting process. In this chapter, we describe how these models can be applied in target valuation. In recent years, new models have been developed to take into account the sequential nature of many corporate investments, with the initial investment being an option on subsequent investments. Such options allow managers to determine if and when subsequent investments will be made and, if the investment has already been made, if and when it may be abandoned. This managerial flexibility adds value to corporate investments such as acquisitions and divestitures. These options are called real or strategic options and valuation models developed for valuing financial assets have been extended to valuing real options. This chapter provides an introduction to how real options may be valued. Real option valuation is fraught with great imprecision and therefore increases valuation risk.

Value from acquisitions is derived from cost or efficiency savings, revenue enhancement while maintaining costs, and real options. While the first two may be valued using traditional valuation tools, these tools fail to capture the essence of real options. We need new tools for valuing real options. Value creation from an acquisition is a necessary condition for the shareholders of acquirers to benefit from the acquisition. It is not a sufficient condition, which is that the created value is appropriated by the acquirer. Value appropriation depends on the relative bargaining strengths of the acquirer and the target firm, bid strategies and tactics leading up to the acquisition, deal characteristics such as deal structure, timing, nature of the target, etc. It also depends on other process characteristics such as the top managers' cognitive and behavioral biases, their monetary and psychological incentives, and the robustness of corporate governance in acquirers. We review the impact of these aspects of the acquisition process on the valuation of the acquisition from the acquirer shareholders' point of view.

In this chapter, we first identify the sources of value in M&A and the factors that may influence how the value created is appropriated by the acquirers. We then present a range of valuation models and discuss their limitations and suggest the contexts in which each model is appropriate. This is followed by a discussion of the impact of deal and firm characteristics and the negotiation process upon value appropriation. Top managers' behavioral and cognitive biases and their potential impact on value creation and value appropriation are highlighted. We then discuss the role of corporate governance in influencing choice of value-creating acquisitions and in ensuring optimal appropriation of value for shareholders.

Sources of Value in Acquisitions

Value in acquisitions may be broadly derived from various cost efficiencies (scale, scope, and learning economies), revenue enhancement (through leveraging each merging company's current resources such as brands or distribution channels), and future growth opportunities (through leveraging each other's resources to create future competitive advantages). These sources are depicted in Figure 8.1, which relates strategy drivers to sources of value in acquisitions. The competitive strategy underlying the acquisition determines the relative importance of the three different sources of value. In a single acquisition, there may be primary and secondary sources of value.[1]

Value Creation versus Value Appropriation

Value creation needs to be distinguished from value appropriation by the acquirer. Value creation depends on the robustness of the corporate strategy that drives the acquisition and the validity of the specific acquisition strategy chosen to implement

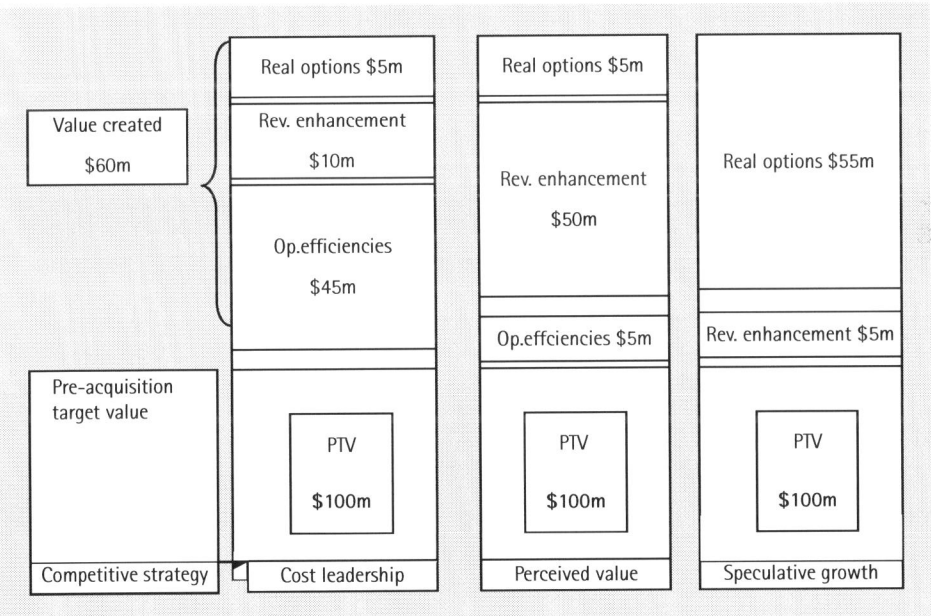

FIG. 8.1 Value creation in acquisitions with different strategy drivers

Notes: Op. efficiency = operational efficiency; PTV=Pre-acquisition target value; Rev. enhancement = revenue enhancement; boxes not drawn to scale.

that business strategy. An acquirer having undertaken such an acquisition may never-theless find that it is not able to appropriate an adequate share of that added value to yield the required rate of return. Of course, where there is no value creation, there is little to appropriate and the deadweight transaction costs will inevitably lead to value destruc-tion for the acquirer. Thus value creation is a necessary, but not a sufficient, condition. The sufficient condition is that both value creation and value appropriation take place.

The ability to appropriate value depends on a host of factors:

1. whether the synergies are unique to the bidder and target;
2. whether there are several targets for each bidder;
3. whether there are several bidders for each target;
4. whether the offer price is subject to any regulatory determination; and
5. the relative bargaining strengths of the bidder and target.

Case 1 means the appropriation is subject to bilateral negotiation between the bidder and target. Under case 2, the targets will compete down the takeover price. Under case 3, targets can play off one bidder against another; the competition among targets and bidders under these circumstances may be actual or potential. The last factor, while reflecting the impact of factors 1 to 3, may also reflect the behavioral imperatives of each party to negotiate a deal even if there is little appropriation, e.g. when managers seek to make a deal to satisfy their ego, overconfidence, or due to the bandwagon or the "herd" effect. This factor depends not only on the relative contribution of the target and bidder to synergies but also on an understanding that each has about its own contribu-tion as well as that of the other firm. Such an understanding, while difficult to accom-plish given that information asymmetry between bidder and target normally characterizes M&A valuation and negotiation, can nevertheless lead to realistic deal negotiation strategies.

Connecting Strategic Drivers and Financial Drivers

Mergers and acquisitions are aimed at strengthening the competitive advantage of the acquirer or the target or both merging firms. But such enhanced competitive advantage needs to be reflected in incremental value creation. Further, the value sources are rooted in the business model leading to such advantage and driving the merger. Figure 8.2 depicts the relation between strategic drivers and financial drivers. Valuation models rely on financial drivers and where there is a disconnect between strategic drivers and financial drivers, val-uation can lead to an under- or overestimate of incremental value. In general, since strategic drivers are often articulated in vague and unquantified terms, value drivers such as revenue growth, profit margin, incremental investment, etc. are also measured with imprecision. This results in misevaluation of merger benefits and mispricing of the deal.

Disconnect between strategic and value drivers is due to poor specification of the business model underpinning the merger and poor articulation of its implications for

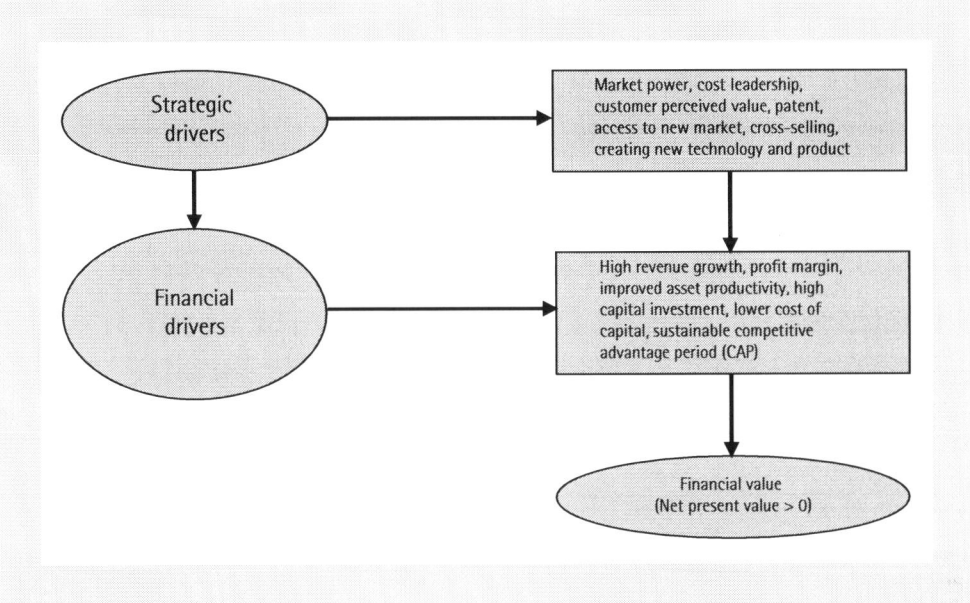

FIG. 8.2 Connecting strategic and value drivers

revenue, costs, investments, risk, and cost of capital. Strategies may often be expressed in grandiloquent terms based on excessive optimism about the world, the economy, the industry, and the firm's own prospects. An important reality check on such exuberance is to convert the strategic drivers into financial drivers and financial value and see whether the financial numbers, e.g. the growth rate, competitive advantage period (CAP), profit margin, etc., are way too optimistic (Eccles 1999). Another caveat is that financial drivers do not always reflect the full range of strategic drivers. For example, valuation of a merger inherently driven by revenue enhancement through common branding or cross-selling may fail to reflect the resulting synergies and may place undue emphasis on cost efficiencies. Similarly, a merger resting on speculative real options may be justified on the basis of cost efficiency and revenue growth. While most mergers may combine all these different sources of synergies, establishing a clear and transparent link between strategic and financial drivers is an important step in the valuation process. It is generally recognized that realizing revenue enhancement opportunities is much more difficult than cost efficiency realization. In a study of bank mergers in the US, Houston et al. (2001) report that value gains from revenue growth are of a much smaller magnitude than from cost savings and have an insignificant impact on the value gains to bidders and targets.[2] In the next section, we present a range of valuation models that allow the estimation of synergies and the value of the acquisition to acquirers. Such valuation determines the offer price and the bid premium to the target shareholders.

VALUATION MODELS

We first present the traditional valuation models that are appropriate for valuing the first two components. We then discuss real option valuation models. We indicate the data and other limitations of these models and how the choice of these models is dictated by the nature of the deal and the sources of value in a deal.

Traditional Valuation Models

With these models, the earnings or assets of the target are estimated after taking into account any changes the acquirer plans to make to the operations and asset structure of the target in the post-acquisition period. The estimated earnings or assets are capitalized into target value using an appropriate benchmark earnings or assets multiplier. The choice of this benchmark multiplier is very important and can present problems when the target is a private company or a multi-business firm. These multiples are single-number valuation tools but are derived from the economic fundamentals of the firm. We start with the residual income models that lead to the earnings and asset multiples.

Residual Income Models[3]

Starting from the fundamental premise that the equity value of a firm is the present value of its future dividends discounted at the appropriate risk-adjusted discount rate, we can derive the simple Gordon growth valuation model:

$$Equity \text{ value at time } t = \frac{\text{dividend at time } t + 1}{K^e - g} \qquad (8.1)$$

where K^e is the cost of equity capital and g is the expected constant dividend growth rate. For example, if company X is expected to pay a dividend of \$1 next year, this dividend is expected to grow indefinitely at the rate of 6%, and the cost of equity is 16%, the firm's equity value now is \$10. The ratio of the expected (or forecast) dividend to current share price is the dividend yield, i.e. 10%.

We can express the Gordon model in terms of earnings and return on equity at $t = 0$:

$$Equity \text{ value} = BE_0 + \frac{NI_1 - K^e.BE_0}{(1+K^e)} + \frac{NI_2 - K^e.BE_1}{(1+K^e)^2} + \frac{NI_3 - K^e.BE_2}{(1+K^e)^3} + \ldots \qquad (8.2)$$

where NI_t = net income for equity holders for year t and BE_{t-1} = book value of equity at $t-1$. The firm or asset value is expressed similarly (BE at the end of $t-1$ is the same as at the beginning of t). Since asset value is the sum of the capital from equity and debt, the following formula uses the after-tax profit for both these capital providers rather than just net income for equity:

$$Asset\ value = BA_0 + \frac{NOP_1 - K^e.BA_0}{(1+K^w)} + \frac{NOP_2 - K^w.BA_1}{(1+K^w)^2} + \frac{NOP_3 - K^w.BA_2}{(1+K^w)^3} + \dots \ (8.3)$$

where NOP_t = net operating profit after tax (NOPAT) for year t and K^w = weighted average cost of equity and debt (see below on weighted average cost of capital), BA_{t-1} = book value of assets represented by sum of equity and debt at $t-1$.

Equation (8.2) is based on the clean surplus relation (CSR) among book value of equity, net income, and dividend.[4] The interpretation of the above formulae is simple. Asset value equals the book value of assets in place plus the value due to future growth, at a rate of return in excess of the dollar cost of capital. A similar relation holds for the equity-funded portion of the firm assets. The growth component specifies the conditions under which growth creates value. In the case of equity, the net income, NI_t, must exceed the opportunity cost of using the assets for equity, $K^e.BE_{t-1}$. The excess is known as residual income (RI). Similarly, profit made by the company from all assets, NOPt, should exceed the opportunity cost of using them, $K^w.BA_{t-1}$. If the assets do not generate returns in excess of the relevant cost of capital, there is no value addition.

The important question, therefore, is "under what competitive conditions can the acquirer generate returns in excess of the cost of capital?" Another aspect of the above equations is that the growth component can extend over several years. Each growth term on the right-hand side represents the value addition from maintaining the competitive edge in that year. Competitive equilibrium is reached when profit equals the dollar cost of capital. Value destruction happens when the profit fails to match the latter. It is now clear why RI models are also called economic profit or abnormal returns models. Economic profit arises from economic rents that a firm enjoys and economic rent depends on its superior competitive position. In competitive equilibrium, firms can earn only the minimum return, i.e. the risk-adjusted cost of capital. Return in excess of that is "abnormal" and can arise only from superior competitive positioning.

Equity Value to Book Value of Equity (EVBV)

The above value equations can be transformed into asset multiples as follows:

$$\frac{Equity\ value}{Book\ value} = 1 + \frac{ROE_1 - K^e}{(1+K^e)} + \frac{(ROE_2 - K^e)(1+g_1)}{(1+K^e)^2} + \frac{(ROE_3 - K^e)(1+g_1)(1+g_2)}{(1+K^e)^3} + \dots \tag{8.4}$$

where ROE_t is return on equity = NI_t/BE_{t-1} and g_t is percentage growth in book value (GBV) of equity BE from $t-1$ to t, i.e. $\left(\dfrac{BE_t - BE_{t-1}}{BE_{t-1}}\right)$. The equation tells us that a firm has equity to book value of 1 when the return on equity equals the cost of capital in every period.[5] An acquirer may be able to improve the target's performance and its ROE and deliver shareholder value. The difference (ROE - K^e) is the abnormal return and represents the value spread. This spread will be high when a firm enjoys any competitive advantage, but will be competed away if it fails to maintain that advantage.

Market or Price to Book Ratio

The ratio, equity value/book value when expressed on a per share basis is known as the price to book (PTBV) ratio. This is done by dividing both the numerator and denominator by the number of shares at issue at the time of calculation of the ratio. It is also known as market to book ratio (MTBV) since equity value is the share price times the number of shares at issue of the firm. PTBV or MTBV exceeds 1 when RI is positive at least in some periods in the future and the sum of the present values of the spreads in Equation (8.4) is positive. Since MTBV depends on the competitive conditions in a sector, there is wide variation in sector MTBVs.

We can derive a similar formula for equity plus debt to book value of total assets. In the latter case, the return on assets (ROA) should exceed the weighted average cost of capital in every period in the future. With competition eroding profit margins, ROE (ROA) as well as the growth rate g will decline over time. This is competitive attrition of profitability.

Price to Earnings Ratio

Price/earnings ratio (PER), also known as the earnings multiple, expresses the relation between a firm's earnings for equity NI and its equity market capitalization. This can be derived from the equity value model above.[6] It can be shown that

$$P_0/NI_0 = \{(1+K^e)/K^e\}\ \{1+(\Sigma\Delta RI_t/(1+K^e)^t NI_0)\}-(Dividend_0/NI_0) \qquad (8.5)$$

where Σ is over $t = 1$ to ∞ and ΔRI_t is the change in RI from $t-1$ to t. This shows that PER

- increases with growth in RI ($\Delta RI_t > 0$) and, therefore, in NI, and
- declines with an increase in the cost of capital, K^e, and, therefore, risk.

It is also a positive function of the length of time over which residual income increases.

In practice, the equity value is proxied by the market value of the company's equity:

$$Price\ /\ earnings\ ratio = \frac{Market\ value\ of\ equity}{Earnings\ for\ equity}$$
$$= \frac{Share\ price}{Earnings\ per\ share\ (EPS)}$$

We can relate the MTBV and PER ratios:

$$MTBV = P_0\ /\ BE_0 = (NI_0\ /\ BE_0) \times (P_0\ /\ NI_0) = ROE_0 \times PER_0$$

Thus, the higher the PER, the higher is the MTBV, for a given ROE. If PER is 20 and ROE is 10%, MTBV will be 2. For the period 1974–2004 in the US, Lundholm and Sloan report PER ranging from 5 to 20. This suggests a range of 10% in 1974 to about 9% in 2004 for ROE.[7] During takeover bids, the PER is often argued by both offerors and targets to indicate whether the price being offered is generous or inadequate.

Investment analysts employ alternative definitions of the PER: the historic and the prospective. The historic PER relates the current market value of equity to the earnings of the most recent accounting year. Prospective PER relates the current market value of equity to the earnings expected to be reported at the end of the current accounting year. Prospective PER requires a forecast of prospective earnings.[8]

Interpretation of the PER

The PER is a function of three factors: K^e, ROE, and the length of time the firm can earn returns on its investments in excess of the investor-required return, i.e. the speed to establishment of competitive equilibrium. Valuable growth comes from the firm's ability to invest in acquisitions, yielding higher returns than the investors' required return, i.e. with a positive RI. This ability depends upon the competitive advantages the firm realizes through acquisition: for example, a low-cost production process, product differentiation through branding, exclusive access to a distribution network, or privileged access to raw materials. The profitable growth phase does not last for ever and is terminated by the emergence of competitors. However, the longer the competitive advantage can be maintained, the greater the value of the firm to its shareholders. The competitive advantage period (CAP) is therefore a critical variable for acquirers to estimate.

The time to competitive equilibrium when the acquirer's competitive advantage is eroded, i.e. CAP, depends on factors such as replicability, imitability, cost of developing countervailing competitive advantage by its rivals, and the payoffs to being a second or third mover. If the competitive opportunities are shared and not unique to the acquirer and the rivals can replicate the resources and capabilities that gave the acquirer the first mover advantage, the competitive equilibrium may be quickly established. In the light of the incidence of merger waves at industry level and at the economy level (see Sudarsanam, 2010, and Ch. 2, for a review of merger waves), triggered, *inter alia*, by the rapid proliferation of "me-too" acquisition strategies by rivals, any presumption of unassailable competitive positioning through acquisitions may be unwarranted.

Empirical evidence suggests that such positioning may last four to five years before reversion to the mean. Palepu et al. (2007) show that many value drivers such as sales growth rate, return on equity, and profit margin are mean-reverting.[9] This evidence suggests that maintaining relatively high-growth sales rates and high profitability is also a great challenge. The rapid emergence of competitive equilibrium must therefore be factored into the assumptions behind valuation models.

CAP can be eroded by any of Porter's five forces or by the erosion of complementors: buyer power may increase, substitutes may appear, current competitors may unleash a ferocious counter-attack, new competitors may enter, or complementors may suffer a similar fate and its loss of competitive advantage then contaminates the merged entity's competitive advantage. Any or all of these forces may be causing the mean reversion in revenue growth or profitability. Where these potential threats take a long time to materialize, the merged entity can enjoy a long and fruitful CAP. CAP is lengthened by robust *isolating mechanisms* that protect against challenges by the five forces.

In Equations (8.4) and (8.5), CAP may be defined as the length of time, T, over which $RI_t > 0$, for $t = 1$, T. In equilibrium, $RI_t = 0$ for all t. Where RI increases over time ($\Delta RI_t > 0$), the firm is operating with increasing returns to scale, e.g. a firm with network externality.

Residual Income Model with Earnings Attrition

A level or constant growth assumption for the RI may be unrealistic when RI is eroded by competition. If RI regresses towards the mean as a result, then future long-term RI will be less than the near-term RI. Equity value P_0 is then

$$P_0 = BE_0 + \sum_{t=1}^{T-1} \frac{(NI_1 - rBE_{t-1})}{(1+K_e)^t} + \frac{NI_T - rBE_{T-1}}{(1+K_e - \omega)(1+K_e)^{T-1}} \tag{8.7}$$

where the RI persistence parameter is ω ($0 \leq \omega \leq 1$). Here profit attrition sets in after T periods. The higher the profit persistence, the higher is the value of the firm.

Estimating Target Value using the PER Model

Application of the PER model proceeds in the following steps: (1) Examine the most recent profit performance of the target firm and the expected future performance under the current target management; (2) Identify those elements of revenue and costs that will be raised or lowered under the acquirer management; (3) Re-estimate the target's future, post-acquisition earnings for equity shareholders on a sustainable basis; (4) Select a benchmark PER; and (5) Multiply the sustainable earnings by the benchmark PER to arrive at a value for equity. Re-estimation of sustainable earnings reflects the improvements in the target operation that the acquirer plans to make after the acquisition. For example, the combined operation of the two firms may be expected to lead to higher prices or lower cost of sales, thus improving the gross profit margin. Reduction of sales and administration costs resulting from the acquisition may lead to improved net profit margins. The acquirer's post-acquisition management plans for the target, based on the acquisition logic, determine the extent of cost saving or revenue enhancement. The assumptions behind the plans, such as higher output prices, lower input costs, or reduced selling and administration costs, must be carefully vetted and must reflect the genuine capabilities of the two firms and not just wishful thinking. The costs of achieving the planned operational efficiencies must be allowed for in estimating the purchase price. For example, rationalization of production or sales force may lead to redundancy costs or relocation costs.[10] In estimating the future earnings for equity shareholders, the capital structure—that is, the proportion of debt and equity in financing the acquired firm—is an important consideration due to the tax deductibility of interest on debt (see below on leverage and cost of capital).

Since equity earnings are estimated post-tax, the impact of accumulated trading losses must be taken into account in estimating the corporation tax on profits. In many countries, e.g. the UK and US, there are strict rules for offsetting past losses against future profits, and these rules dictate the extent of benefits from tax losses. Provided the conditions are satisfied, past losses reduce the effective rate of corporation tax. Some of the adjustments that the acquirer has to make to the target earnings, such as profits from asset disposals, redundancy costs, and tax savings due to accumulated tax losses, are of a transitory nature. Since the PER model requires an estimate of sustainable earnings, one solution to the estimation problem is to identify and value the transitory components separately. Their value can then be incorporated in the purchase price.

Selecting the Benchmark PER

A number of PER benchmarks are available: the target's prospective PER at the time of the bid; the PER of firms comparable to the target; the target's sector average PER; the PER reflected in the M&A transactions in the same sector in recent years; or the PER reflected in the M&A transactions of similar size in recent years.[11] In choosing the benchmark, we must ensure its comparability in terms of risk and growth to the target. It is the risk–growth configuration of the target post-acquisition and not its historic profile that forms the basis of comparison. The benchmark is normally adjusted to reflect this expected configuration. Such an adjustment is often a matter of subjective judgment, since the relation between PER and risk and growth is, in practice, only imperfectly understood. Sustainable earnings are then capitalized at the adjusted benchmark PER to give a target value.

Determining the Purchase Price

Estimation of the sustainable post-acquisition earnings of the target involves a concomitant appraisal of the investment needed to sustain those earnings. This appraisal helps the acquirer identify those target assets that are not needed and can be disposed of, as well as the new investment to be made, such as new plant and equipment. The proceeds of such disposals reduce the purchase price. Acquirers are often faced with the obligation to top up employee post-retirement benefits or pension schemes and this can add substantially to the acquisition cost. Trustees of such pension schemes negotiate hard with potential acquirers. Several bids have in recent years failed because of bidders' failure to meet the trustees' demands.[12] Where rationalization is contemplated by the acquirer, the associated costs must be added to the purchase price if they have been excluded from the computation of sustainable earnings. It must be remembered that profits on asset disposals and refund of pension fund surpluses are generally subject to corporation tax, and rationalization costs are tax deductible. The cost of new investments must be added to the purchase price.

Limitations of the PER Model

The PER model estimates the post-acquisition earnings for the target for a single period, and assumes that this level will be maintained. There is no explicit recognition of the time pattern of earnings growth. The acquirer needs to make realistic estimates of future revenues, costs, investments, etc. Moreover, the model does not directly consider the investor-perceived risk of the target firm's earnings. Problems also arise in the selection of the benchmark PER, as indicated above. Despite these limitations, the PER model provides a valuation based on the capital market consensus view of the value of earnings. It is widely used by the investment community and makes for ease of communication during a bid.

ENTERPRISE VALUE MULTIPLE

In recent years, analysts have used an alternative measure of valuation. The ratio, enterprise value/earnings before interest and tax (EV/EBIT) or its "cash flow" variant, enterprise value/earnings before interest, tax, depreciation, and amortization (EV/EBITDA) has been employed. It is called enterprise value multiple (EVM). EBIT represents the pre-tax return to both shareholders and debt holders. Since most firms are overwhelmingly funded by equity and debt, the sum of equity and debt values represents the value of the firm or enterprise. Depreciation (D) and amortization (A) are non-cash expenses deducted in deriving EBIT. Adding them back, we get EBITDA, which is widely regarded as a measure of operating cash flow. As in the case of PER, the EVM requires an appropriate benchmark.

Sum of Parts Valuation

Where a target firm has several distinct businesses differing in their competitive environment and performance, it makes little sense to value the firm as a whole using a single multiple PER or EVM. More fine-grained valuation can be obtained by valuing each individual business and then summing up the individual values. Targets with multi-business portfolios often feel that the overall firm valuation does not truly value the underlying businesses correctly, i.e. the firm is valued at a "conglomerate discount" (on conglomerate discount, see e.g. Graham et al. 2002; Lamont and Polk 2002; Vilalonga 2004). They are therefore keen to establish that "sum of parts" (SOP) valuation gives a more realistic firm value. Acquirers which may buy the target and then unbundle it to divest some of the acquired businesses may also find SOP valuation more insightful of the true value of their purchase and what unbundled business would likely fetch if they were divested. Another reason for SOP valuation is that valid benchmark multiples such as EV/EBITDA and EV/sales may be easier to obtain at the business level than at the firm level for a multi-business firm.[13]

ASSET-BASED VALUATION

The best known of the asset-based models is Tobin's q, which is the ratio of the market value of a firm to the replacement cost of its assets. The replacement cost of an asset is the cost of acquiring an asset of identical characteristics, such as the production capacity of a plant:

$$Tobin's = \frac{Market\ value\ of\ a\ firm}{Replacement\ cost\ of\ its\ assets}$$

For example, if the market value of a firm is $500m and the replacement cost of its assets is $250m, its q is 2. The excess value may also be regarded as the value of the option to exploit these opportunities. The value of a firm is thus made up of two components:

Firm value = Replacement cost of assets + Value of growth options

This relationship is similar to the one between firm value, book value of assets, and the value of residual income we discussed above.[14]

Tobin's q can also be used as a valuation tool in the same way as the PER. Selection of a benchmark q is, however, much more difficult than in the case of the PER. The asset structures of firms could differ considerably, even if they are in the same business. Moreover, evaluation of the underlying growth options is not easy. Growth options available to different firms in the future are not always identical. For example, two oil exploration and production companies operating in different parts of the world may have different growth opportunities. In some other sectors such as property, although valuation of the firm's individual assets can be done more easily, there is nevertheless the problem of valuing the growth options. There are other limitations in the use of Tobin's q for valuation purposes.

As regards the numerator of the q ratio, the market value of the firm is the sum of the market values of all the financial claims on the firm, such as equity and debt. Since corporate debt in many countries is generally not traded, market value of debt is difficult to ascertain. Often analysts use the sum of the market value of equity and the book value of debt, but this is only an approximation of the firm market value. A widely used approximation of the q in practice is the market to book value of equity (MTBV) derived earlier. This ratio is also known as the valuation ratio. MTBV is interpreted broadly in the same way as the q ratio.

Valuation Using other Multiples

In addition to earnings and asset multiples, analysts use other multiples such as price to sales revenue or price to cash flow. In each case, the variables are measured per share.

Cash flow is in theory the free cash flow (see the discounted cash flow model below), but in practice it is proxied by EBITDA. Price to sales is used for valuing young businesses where earnings or cash flow data are not available, i.e. when the firm makes losses in the initial years of its life. Price to sales revenue was used to value start-up companies such as Amazon.com, a company that did not make any profit for its shareholders for several years. This provides a cautionary tale, since no matter how big the revenue, what fattens shareholder wallets is not revenue but cash flows and dividends (Damodaran 2001). Thus multiples based on variables far removed from cash flows to investors must be carefully used.

DISCOUNTED CASH FLOW MODEL

The earnings-based models described above can be transformed into a cash flow-based valuation model. The numerator of the equity value model is expressed in terms of free cash flow to equity holders (FCFE) in each period. This cash flow model is known as the equity residual model since the FCFE is the residual cash flow after meeting the claims of debt holders, e.g. interest. The numerator of the asset value model above is expressed in terms of the free cash flow to the firm (FCFF), i.e. to both equity and debt holders.[15]

The discounted cash flow (DCF) model is applied in the following steps to derive the value of the target's equity to the bidder: (1) Estimate the future cash flows of the target based on the assumptions for its post-acquisition management by the bidder over the forecast horizon; (2) Estimate the terminal value of the target at the forecast horizon; (3) Estimate the cost of capital appropriate for the target, given its projected post-acquisition risk and capital structure; (4) Discount the estimated cash flows to give a value of the target; (5) Add other cash inflows from sources such as asset disposals or business divestments; (6) Subtract debt and other expenses, such as tax on gains from disposals and divestments, and acquisition costs, to give a value for the equity of the target; (7) Compare the estimated equity value for the target with its pre-acquisition stand-alone value to determine the added value from the acquisition; and (8) Decide how much of this added value should be given away to target shareholders as control premium. The cash flow forecast is based on assumptions about the changes to the operation of the target to be introduced by the bidder. In particular, these assumptions relate to the value drivers.

Value drivers are those key revenue, cost, or investment variables that determine the level of a firm's cash flows, and hence its value to the shareholders. We can identify six key value drivers: forecast sales growth in volume and revenue terms; operating profit margin; new fixed capital investment; new working capital investment; the competitive advantage period (CAP); and the cost of capital (see Rappaport, 1986 on these value drivers except CAP).

The bidder's post-acquisition management plan normally aims at altering the above value drivers, so that additional value can be created from the acquisition. Alteration of the value driver levels depends upon the value creation logic underlying the acquisition. Changes in the driver levels are often interdependent. For example, higher sales growth may be achieved only by increasing expenditure on marketing, advertising, or product development, or by additional investment in fixed assets and current assets. These changes in the value drivers are then translated into a forecast of cash outflows and inflows.

Operating cash inflows, arising from the operations of the firm, are after-(corporation) tax cash flows but before payment of interest on borrowing that has been used to finance the target. Any changes in the effective tax rates as a result of reduction in potential corporate tax liabilities should be added to the cash inflows. Examples of such incremental tax benefits include writing off the accumulated tax losses of the acquired company against its future, post-acquisition profits, or any saving from stepped-up depreciation under certain tax regimes. Cash outflows are due to additional fixed capital and working capital investments.

Target cash flows are generally forecast for the next five to ten years. In general, the longer the forecast horizon, the less accurate is the forecast. Where CAP is short, it can form the forecast horizon. The terminal value (TV) of the target at the end of that period based on free cash flows (FCFs) thereafter also needs to be forecast. Often this terminal value is based on the assumption of perpetual free cash flows at the same level of operations as in the last year of the forecast period. The level of perpetual cash flows are then capitalized at, i.e. divided by, the cost of capital to yield the terminal value. The forecast FCFs, when discounted, provide the acquirer with the present value of the target as a whole. From this firm value, debt is subtracted to give the equity value. TV can also be based on assumptions about the rate of sustainable growth. For most industries and firms, the sustainable growth rate may be just the economy's growth rate of 3 to 5%. Overconfident/overoptimistic managers may project much higher rates, but such projections need to be exposed to very rigorous and skeptical scrutiny. A healthy dose of skepticism is warranted by the mean reversion phenomenon (see above on evidence of such mean reversion), although high performers seem able to sustain their *relative* (not *absolute*) high performance over several years.

Cost of Capital

The cost of capital is the weighted average cost of capital (WACC), estimated from the target's pre-acquisition costs of equity and debt. If, after the acquisition, the risk profile of the target changes, perhaps due to product or market diversification of the target, the cost of equity and of debt will change. The pre-acquisition cost of capital has, therefore, to be adjusted to reflect this change in risk. Further, if the post-acquisition capital structure for the target differs from its pre-acquisition structure, the WACC has to be adjusted for the difference. Thus,

$$\text{WACC} = K^e\, E/V + (1-T^c)K^d D/V + K^p\, P/VP \qquad (8.8)$$

where

K^e = cost of equity;

K^d = cost of debt;

K^p = cost of preference shares (relevant if capital structure includes preference shares);

E = market value of equity;

D = market value of debt;

P = market value of preference shares;

T^t = corporation tax rate;

$V = E + D + P$, the value of the firm.

In general, P is a negligible source of capital and in the following discussion of WACC, we focus on cost of equity and cost of debt.

Estimating the Weighted Average Cost of Capital

This requires estimation of the costs of the various components of long-term capital, including equity, preference shares, and debt. As regards equity, earning yield (earnings/share price) and dividend yield (dividend/share price) do not fully reflect the opportunity cost of equity to the shareholder. The capital asset pricing model (CAPM) may be used to estimate the historic cost of equity for the target. The CAPM estimates the investor-required return as the sum of a risk-free rate and a risk premium based on the overall market risk premium and the risk of the stock in relation to the market. The systematic risk, beta, is measured by the coefficient β.

Equity cost of capital, $K^e = R_F + \beta (R_M - R_F)$
= Risk-free rate+Equity risk premium×Beta of equity stock   (8.9)

Equity risk premium = Expected return on market, R_M − Risk-free rate, R_F
Equity Beta = Sensitivity of stock return to market return
$$= \frac{\text{Covariance of stock with market returns}}{\text{Variance of the market return}}$$

Beta is estimated by time series regression models using historical share price data. For public companies, betas are also readily available from investment advisory services in different countries, such as Value Line in the US and the Risk Measurement Service of the London Business School in the UK. For a private company, the beta of a similar public company may be used. The risk-free rate is in practice often the return on a short-dated, say 90-day, government Treasury bill or the return on a government Treasury bond. The market is generally proxied by a broad-based stock market index such as Standard & Poor's (S&P) in the US and the Financial Times All-Share Index in the UK.

The pre-acquisition expected return on equity for the target needs to be adjusted for a possible change in the target beta after the acquisition. This adjustment, necessitated by changes in the underlying operating characteristics of the target due to the acquisition, is somewhat subjective, since the relation between the operating characteristics of a firm and its betas is not definitively understood.

Having estimated the individual components of cost of capital, we then weight them by the proportion of each type of capital in the capital structure of the target. The relevant capital structure is the post-acquisition capital structure contemplated by the bidder.

Estimating the Cost of Equity

Although the empirical validity of the CAPM has been questioned by numerous studies and alternative asset pricing models have been proposed and tested (see Sudarsanam 2010, ch. 4 on CAPM and the other models), CAPM still remains the workhorse of the valuation industry and is discussed at length in textbooks on corporate finance. One of the important issues in employing the CAPM is the equity risk premium (ERP), which is the difference between the expected return on the market portfolio and the risk-free rate. Estimates of the ERP have been made by numerous researchers, some using time series data stretching back to the beginning of the 20th century! One estimate based on data from 1900 to 2005 of the ERP, with the long-term bond rate as the proxy for the risk-free rate for the US (UK and the world) is 5.5% (4.4% and 4.7% respectively). This estimate is sensitive to the choice of the risk-free rate proxy. With the government Treasury bill rate as the proxy the ERP, for the US (UK and the world) is 4.5% (4.1% and 4% respectively) (Dimson et al. 2008).[16]

Apart from these historic estimates, many researchers have also made "forward looking" estimates based on some measure of expectation of stock market earnings/dividends growth rates. In this regard, the dividend growth model and the residual income model have been put to service. These efforts yield the implied expected cost of equity for the market as a whole from which the ERP can be calculated by subtracting the risk-free rate. ERP is model sensitive.[17] It is better to work with a reasonable range of ERP and test the sensitivity of value estimates to the choice of ERP and therefore the cost of equity. ERP, as well as the risk-free rate, vary from one country to another.

Cost of Debt

Cost of debt is generally different from the coupon rate when the face value of debt is different from its market value. It also varies with the maturity of debt, in general, increasing with increasing maturity. The rate at which a firm can borrow is influenced by the firm's default risk. Debt rating agencies like Standard & Poor's, Moody's, and Fitch rate corporate debt and the debt issuing companies and the rating category is a reflection of the expected default risk. The ratings go down from AAA (highest quality debt with little default risk) through AA down to BBB and further down to B, C, D etc. The lower the rating, the greater is the likelihood of default and the higher is the coupon to attract debt investors. Such ratings reflect both the likelihood of default and any financial loss suffered in the event of default and the spread depends on the rating category. The spread increases non-linearly as the rating is lowered. The default risk also increases similarly.

The cost of debt is measured as a base rate plus a spread. The base rate is the London Interbank Offered Rate (LIBOR) or a similar base rate. BBB is an important threshold as it represents the minimum investment grade bond. Categories below BBB are variously referred to as "junk," "sub-investment," "speculative," or "high yield".[18] Sub-investment grade bonds have to pay considerably higher spreads to compensate investors for higher default risk. Spreads widen very substantially for grades below BBB. The calculations above provide only the coupon, i.e. the nominal interest rate on the bond. The cost of debt itself may be higher or lower than the coupon, depending on the level of interest rates in the economy as reflected in the LIBOR. For example, the bond yield to maturity will be less if the interest rates have risen and more if they have fallen. In WACC calculations, we need the cost of debt represented by the expected yield to maturity and the coupon may or may not be a good proxy for that.[19] Some estimates for debt beta range from 0 at low levels of leverage debt to about 0.20 or 0.30 at high leverage levels. It also follows that low credit rating will be associated with high debt beta.[20]

Determining the Purchase Price

The value of target-free cash flows to the bidder is:

$$TGTVAL_a = \sum_{t=1}^{T} \frac{FCF_t}{(1+WACC)^t} + \frac{TV_T}{(1+WACC)^T} \tag{8.10}$$

where

$TGTVALa$ = target value after the acquisition;
$FCFt$ = free cash flow of target in period t;
TVT = terminal value of target at $t = T$; and
T = terminal period for forecast, and $t = 1 ..., T$.

The total value of the target to the bidder may also include the proceeds of the sale of assets and divestments, reorganization costs, or pension fund deficits discussed earlier. These sale proceeds and pension fund deficits must be calculated on an after-tax basis. From the target value, the debt of the target must be subtracted to yield the target equity value to the bidder. The actual consideration paid to target shareholders must fall short of this value if the bidder shareholders are to receive any gains from the acquisition.

Terminal Value, TVT

The DCF model back end-loads corporate value with the present value of TV_T, accounting often for 80% of target value. TV_T can vary widely (and wildly) depending on whether the growth assumption is optimistic, realistic, or pessimistic. The terminal value assumption is quite critical and must be chosen with a thorough understanding of the current and, even more importantly, the future competitive dynamics of the market in which the bidder will be selling its goods and services.

Where the target can grow initially at a high rate and then settle at the long-run equilibrium for a mature economy, say 3%, its competitive advantage, though temporary, is not completely eroded. The target may achieve high growth, but severity of competition may flatten its growth rate after five years down to 0%. Finally, competitors may retaliate so fiercely as to quickly erode its competitive advantage. The appropriateness of each assumption depends on the anticipated competitive rivalry, as well as the competitive reactions of buyers and sellers. A scenario analysis, by raising questions about the post-acquisition competitive advantage and its durability, can aid realistic acquisition pricing.

Sensitivity Analysis of the DCF Valuation

Given the uncertainty surrounding the forecast process, it is sensible that the acquirer examines how sensitive the target value is to any variation in the assumptions. This kind of analysis highlights those critical value drivers that the acquirer needs to focus on. In particular, the assumptions behind the critical drivers need to be robustly justified. Forecasting their post-acquisition levels also demands greater accuracy. The impact of changing some of the value driver forecasts while maintaining others has to be assessed so that critical value drivers and the risk of not achieving them can be assessed. Such a sensitivity analysis allows for a range of realistic target values, with their associated risks of non-realization to be estimated, and may prevent overpayment for the target.

One can reverse-engineer the DCF model to figure out the rate of growth of FCF after the forecast horizon, which can justify a given acquisition premium.

Adjusted Present Value (APV) Model

In the above DCF model, we forecast cash flows to the firm and discounted them at the WACC to arrive at the firm value, but inclusive of the benefit of leverage reflected in WACC. An alternative to the DCF model in Equation (8.10) is the APV:

Value of firm = Value of firm if it were fully equity financed
+ the value of tax benefits of debt

Thus firm value is estimated in two steps. To calculate the value of a 100% equity-funded firm we need the cost of equity of such a firm. This cost of equity is also called unlevered cost of equity to distinguish it from the levered cost of equity.

$$TGTVAL_a = \sum_{t=1}^{T} \frac{FCF_t}{(1+K_{ue})^t} + \frac{TV_T}{(1+K_{ue})^T} + \sum_{t=1}^{T} \frac{Taxbenefit_t}{(1+K_d)^t} + \frac{TV \text{ of } Taxbenefit_T}{(1+K_d)^T} \quad (8.11)$$

In Equation (8.11), K_{ue} = Cost of unlevered equity; $Taxbenefit_t$ = coupon on debt times the corporation tax rate at t; and K_d is the cost of debt, which may be different from the coupon (see above for discussion of cost of debt).

From Equation (8.11) we can see that the operating cash flows to the firms are discounted at the unlevered cost of equity. This is also known as the cost of capital for the firm's assets and is independent of the way the firm finances its assets, i.e. of its leverage. The tax benefits are separately valued. Since the APV model estimates firm value and the benefit of debt separately, it is particularly useful when leverage changes over time. In the case of leveraged buyouts (LBOs), private equity firms raise leverage substantially after buyout. The pre-buyout equity beta is therefore an inappropriate measure of the cost of equity, which consequently increases after buyout. WACC falls with increased leverage since lower-cost debt is substituted for high-cost equity (see Equation (8.8) above).

Equation (8.9) above estimates the levered cost of equity from the observed stock returns of the company as a function of levered equity beta. We calculate the firm's asset beta from the levered equity beta by de-levering it. We then substitute the estimate of the asset beta in the CAPM equation to calculate the cost of unlevered equity, K_{ue}. The following formulae are used for this purpose:

$$\beta Asset = \beta Equity \ (E/D + E) + \beta Debt \ (D/D+E) \tag{8.12}$$

$$\beta Levered \ Equity = \beta Asset + (D/E) \ (\beta Asset - \beta Debt) \tag{8.13}$$

βAsset is invariant to leverage and it measures the pure business risk. βLevered Equity increases with business risk and leverage but decreases with βDebt. This effect may be somewhat offset by increasing βDebt as leverage increases. Using Equation (8.12), we can estimate the asset beta, given the current leverage. To re-calculate the levered equity beta if leverage increases, we can use Equation (8.13). This procedure is known as re-levering beta.

Valuation for Private Equity Buyouts

Private equity firms expect to exit their investments within defined periods in order to return the capital to equity investors. They forecast possible exit dates, e.g. three or five years from the date of investment in a portfolio company. They then work out the return to equity investors conditional on that exit. For this purpose they normally estimate the internal rate of return (IRR) to their investment in the LBO target during the investment holding period. IRR is the rate of return that equates the future cash flows from an investment, when discounted at that rate, to the cost of that investment. To calculate the IRR, they forecast a possible exit value of equity. For this purpose one can use the DCF model described earlier. In this case, the terminal value becomes the exit value. Instead of using the DCF to estimate the exit value, PE firms often use an exit multiple, e.g. the FCF at the end of the assumed exit horizon of say five years is converted into exit value by using an appropriate FCF multiple. This is then used in the IRR calculation. Intermediate cash flows that the PE firm receives from the portfolio company are also factored into the IRR model. PE investors normally aim for an IRR of 25–30% per year.

Cost of Capital for Different Synergy Sources

It may be argued that cost efficiencies, revenue enhancement, and real options give rise to risks of varying magnitudes and therefore merit different costs of capital (see Figure 8.1). In general, cost savings do not fundamentally alter the business profile. Similarly, when the merged firms' revenue grows but they remain in the same lines of business, the business/asset risk does not change. If the merged entity diversifies into related or unrelated businesses to achieve revenue enhancement, there is likely to be a change in asset risk. This needs to be modeled and the revised asset beta can be used to calculate the equity beta assuming the expected leverage level. Where the value source is a real option that the acquisition carries, the systematic risk of the merged entity depends on the nature of the option. In general, an option to expand into new products or services may increase the systematic risk, whereas the options to divest (abandon) the acquisition at a later date will reduce that risk. The option component needs to be valued separately and incorporated into the overall valuation of the acquisition.

Valuation of Private Companies

While the principles of valuation of private companies are the same as for public companies, an important difference is that for private company targets we do not have the benchmark valuation provided by the stock market. Use of the PER model or the discounted cash flow model requires that we locate a stock market proxy for the private company. This proxy must be as similar as possible to the target. Often the proxy is matched by industry or sector and size to the target. The proxy's PER or its cost of capital may then be used to value the target. Even where the proxy is well matched to the target in terms of industry and size, the proxy PER needs to be discounted for the potential non-marketability of target shares before it can be applied to the target. Similarly, the cost of capital has to be raised to compensate for this additional risk. Compared to a public company that is often widely researched by investment analysts, information about the private target may be sparse. Forecasting the future cash flows is thus a more difficult exercise. Offsetting this disadvantage is the fact that private company bids are almost always friendly, with easier access to the target's management information, thereby facilitating a more thorough due diligence.

Impact of Tax on Target Valuation

In the past, some of the acquisitions were driven by tax factors. For example, a target with accumulated trading losses (called tax losses) which could be offset against the acquirer's profits would be an attractive target. The acquirer could reduce the tax liability for the group after acquisition. Use of tax losses is subject to strict conditions in various countries. For example, in the UK, the trading losses can be carried forward only for offset against future profits of the same business. That is, there is no immediate transfer of losses and profits between the target and the acquirer after the acquisition. Further, there should be no major change in the target's trade in the period three years before and three years after the change of ownership. The practical implication of this rule is that the acquirer has to run the same business of the target as before, turn around that company, and then use the tax losses to reduce future tax liability. Tax law provisions in the UK also restrict the carry back by the target of losses incurred after a change of ownership to the pre-change periods (Scott 1996).

Accumulated capital losses of a target cannot be set against a chargeable capital gain (i.e. a gain liable to capital gains tax, CGT) made by another member of the group. It is also difficult to buy a target with accumulated capital losses, and transfer to it from the acquirer assets pregnant with capital gain, thus offsetting the gain against the losses. In pricing a target, the buyer therefore has to examine very carefully whether the potential tax benefits can be reliably factored into the valuation. Tax rules differ widely across countries and so merit careful consideration of each country's rules.

REAL OPTIONS FRAMEWORK FOR
VALUING TARGETS

The abnormal earnings models, the multiples, and the DCF all suffer from an important shortcoming. Corporate investments are often multi-stage investments, with the later stage investments being contingent upon the outcome of the prior stage investments. For example, investment in a patent will necessarily be followed up with investment in product development, production, and marketing. However, often the subsequent investments rely on the outcome of early stage investments. For example, production decisions will be made on the basis of results from clinical trials of a patented drug. The subsequent stages may even not be undertaken if information from the early stage investment is adverse. That is, management gains an option from the first-stage investment on the follow-on investments. Further, managers have the flexibility to time their investments and to adapt to emerging new information such as an alternative drug from a competitor.

Examples of such contingent investments are research and development, advertising, pilot marketing, license for oil exploration, geological testing for mineral reserves, etc.

In some cases, managers may make an initial investment, knowing that they can exit or abandon that investment. Acquisitions generally include a range of such options. These options available to corporate managers may be modeled using decision trees in conjunction with the DCF.

We can use the decision tree model (DTM) to derive the NPV of the initial investment. For this we calculate the NPV of each decision branch, starting with the final stage. We weight each branch's NPV by the probability of its occurrence. We then trace these NPVs backwards to the prior decision nodes and finally to the first decision. For example, suppose we have a two-stage investment decision problem. The first stage is a small pilot investment and the second stage is investment to scale up. There are two outcomes from the second stage (see Fig 8.3). The favorable outcome has an NPV of £100 in a strong economy with a probability of 60%. The unfavorable outcome has a negative NPV of £20 in a weak economy with a probability of 40%. If the firm is committed no matter what the outcome, the NPV is £52, the probability-weighted average of the NPVs of the two outcomes. When this overall second-stage NPV is discounted to the time of the initial decision, the NPV is say £40 (assuming a discount rate of 30%). If the initial investment is £46, then at the first stage the NPV becomes −£6. So the project is not worthwhile.

If, however, the firm makes the second-stage investment on the basis of the information available after the first stage, e.g. about the unfavorable outcome of the first stage, it will not make the investment. Thus the second-stage negative NPV investment will be avoided. The overall second-stage NPV is then £60 and, by discounting back, we find that the initial investment is a break-even decision.

While a decision tree is useful as a way of mapping out alternative decision choices contingent on outcomes of prior decisions, it is restricted to dichotomous outcomes at each stage rather than a continuous range of outcomes. Moreover, the discount rate

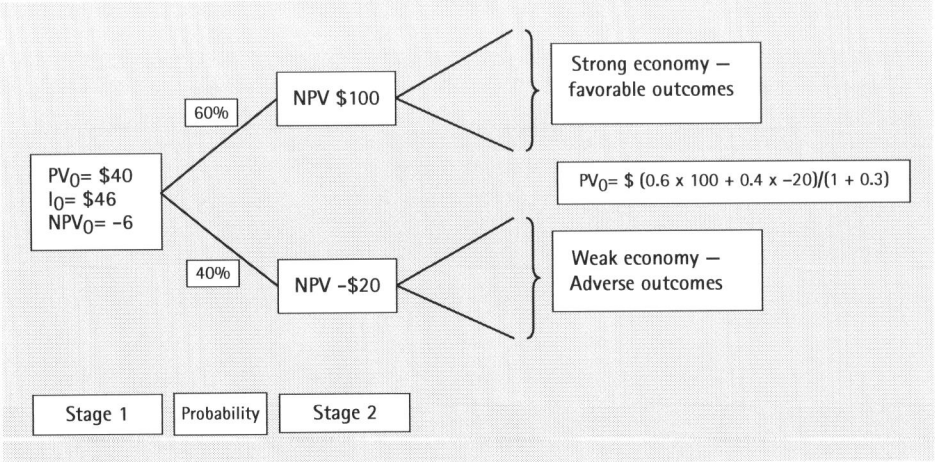

FIG. 8.3 Real options in a multi-stage investment

assumed is constant for all outcomes and over different time periods. These shortcomings are avoided in the real options models derived from the Black–Scholes (BS) option-pricing model first developed for application to financial options, i.e. options written on financial assets such as stocks, bonds, and currencies. To understand the real options valuation we need an understanding of the model.

Call and Put Options on Financial Assets

A call option gives the buyer of that option the right, but not the obligation, to buy the asset on which it is written at an agreed price (the exercise price) at maturity of the option contract (in the case of a European option) or at any time before maturity (in the case of a US option). The price of the option is called the option premium. A put option gives the buyer the right, but not the obligation, to sell the asset at the agreed price at or before maturity. An investor buys a call option when he or she expects the asset to increase in value beyond the exercise price. An investor buys a put when he expects the asset to decline in value below the exercise price.

Black–Scholes Option Pricing Model (BSOPM)

The BS model is one of the best-known models in financial economics. Myron Scholes, and Robert Merton who developed a similar model independently, received the Nobel Prize in Economics for the model. The BSOPM, based on stochastic calculus, is as shown below: C, the value of a European call option is

$$C = S\,N(d_1) - E\,e^{-rt}\,N(d_2)$$

Where $d_1 = [\text{In}(S/E) + (r + 1/2\sigma^2)t]/\sqrt{\sigma^2 t}$

$d_2 = d_1\sqrt{\sigma^2 t}$
S = current stock price;
E = exercise price;
r = annual risk-free continuously compounded rate;
σ^2 = annualized variance of the continuous return on the stock;
t = time to expiry of the option

The exponential term, e^{-rt}, discounts the exercise price to the present value.

$$\text{Call value} = S\,N(d_1) - \text{Present value of } E \times N(d_2)$$

$N(d_1)$ and $N(d_2)$ represent the probability distributions. Values of $N(d_1)$ and $N(d_2)$ are obtained from normal probability distribution tables available from books on valuation or finance. They give us the probability that S or E will be below d_1 and d_2. In the BS model, they measure the risk associated with the volatility of the value of S. Software is available to calculate the BS option prices for various parameter values.

Interpretation of the BS Model

- The underlying asset value (S)—high S increases call value and reduces put value.
- The exercise price (X)—high X reduces call value but increases put value.
- The volatility of the value of S (s)—high s increases both call and put values.
- The time to maturity (t)—high t increases both call and put values.
- Any dividend payment—high dividend reduces call value and increases put value.
- The risk-free rate (r_f)—high r_f increases call value and reduces put value.

One of the most intriguing relationships is that high volatility enhances the option value. Since an option restricts the downside loss to the option premium but does not restrict the upside potential, high volatility benefits the option. This perspective has particular relevance to real options as we discuss below.

Financial Options and Real Options

A real option is an option to buy or sell an investment in physical or intangible assets rather than in financial assets. Thus any corporate investment in plant, equipment, land, patent, brand name, etc. can be the assets on which real options are "written." Purchase of a brand is an option on the related product or service. A license to explore for oil is an option on oil. Many investment projects have call and put option features. Investment in R&D is a call option since it may lead to "buying," i.e. investing in, a second-stage production facility. Any exploratory investment in a growth opportunity such as the internet or biotechnology is a call option. An investment that can be sold if it does not meet the investor's expectations may be regarded as a put option, e.g. a mine that is abandoned when the price of gold falls and is unlikely to recover.

In addition to the examples of real options cited above, we can identify many other types of real options. These are listed in Figure 8.4. A compound option combines two or more of these options. For example, in a bust-up takeover, the acquirer plans to break up the target and sell some of the businesses while retaining others. The potential sale represents a put option to the acquirer. Serial acquisitions represent compound options as the value of the first acquisition depends on the value of the options on subsequent acquisitions (see below for further discussion of serial acquisitions). Many of these options drive acquisition strategies (Smith and Triantis 1995).[21]

Valuation of Real Options

The BSOPM may be used to value real options (Luehrman 1998a). We first show such a valuation application and then discuss the limitations and caveats in valuing real options using the BSOPM. The variables in the BS model when applied to real options are as follows:

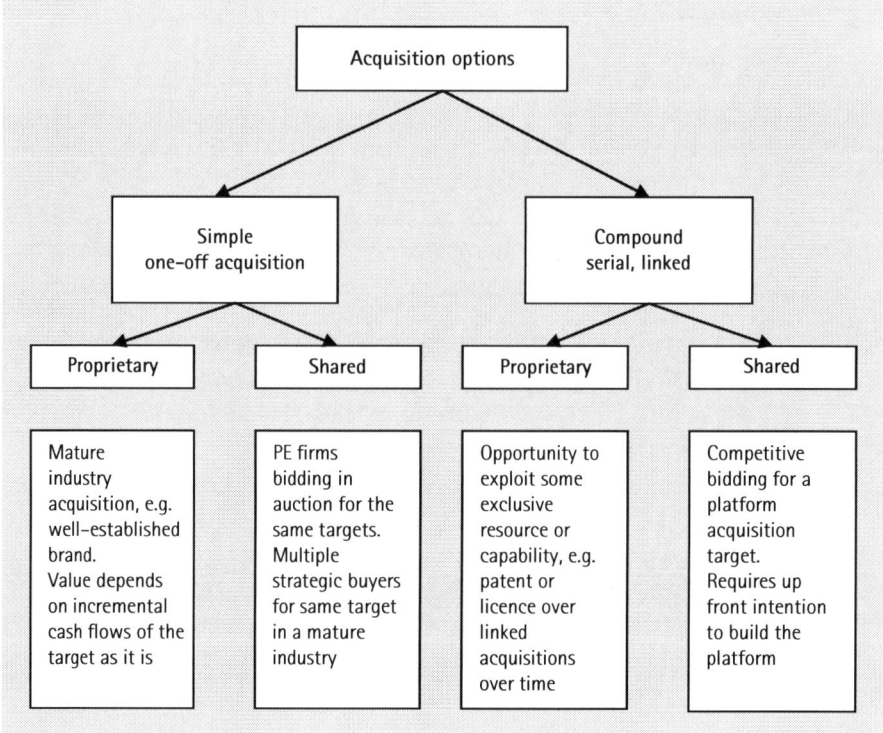

FIG. 8.4 Types of real options in acquisitions

Source: Smit and Trigeorgis (2004).

- C = the first-stage investment;
- S = present value of the second-stage investment;
- t = the time to making the second-stage investment, i.e. how long that opportunity will be open or how long the second-stage investment can be deferred;
- X = present value of the cost of the second-stage investment;
- Dividend = intermediate costs to keep the second-stage investment opportunity open, e.g. maintenance costs, rents;
- σ = the volatility of the value of the second-stage investment.

The risk-free rate has the same connotation as in the financial asset case. While waiting to make the second-stage investment, the company is gathering information that flows from the first-stage investment, e.g. about feasibility of technology, and from the outside world, e.g. the size of the potential market or the price of the output, say, gold or a drug or a regulatory change. This learning covers learning what the company's resources and capabilities are and how they can be adapted to the environmental changes (a process of self-discovery) as well as learning about the environment (intelligence gathering) (Bernardo and Chowdhry 2002; Kogut and Kulatilaka 2001).

Real Options and Game Theory

What is the value of an option that a firm has acquired when there is competition? How soon will the competitors catch up and acquire similar options? Real options may give rise to unique non-imitable claims on the underlying second-stage investment opportunity or they can be replicated by competitors, in which case the opportunity is shared. This is a fundamental issue in competitive strategy and not peculiar to the real options framework (Luehrman, 1998b; Bowman and Moskowitz 2001; and Smit 2001). However, the real options framework may be used to shed light on value implications of shared options.

Whether competitors enter and spoil the game for the first mover depends on whether the claims on the growth opportunities are shared and also on entry barriers and what the first option holder does to forestall such entry. The game theory framework can be used to figure out how the game will be played with shared opportunities and the entry and pre-emptive (also called "commitment") strategies of different players. One way we can model the threat of entry is to incorporate an estimate of competitive erosion (proxied by "dividend" payment in the BSOPM). Where there is more than one competitor, this attrition can be increased to reflect the effect of such competition on the option value.[22]

Another way to model competitor reactions and value strategic flexibility is to use the DTM described earlier. Suppose a serial acquirer (SA) has a program of acquisitions to build its competitive strength and the value of each acquisition is path-dependent and influenced by the reaction of the SA's competitors. The decision tree to map a serial acquisition program of three acquisitions is shown in Figure 8.5. Having made the first acquisition, the firm awaits the response from its rival(s). If the rival responds with a matching acquisition, the payoff to the firm is likely to be less than if the rival makes no such acquisition. The payoff to each acquisition in the program can be estimated conditional upon the rival making a matching acquisition and the payoff without such a rival acquisition may also be estimated (we assume a single rival for simplicity). In Figure 8.5, these payoffs to SA are shown as P1, P2, and P3. By estimating the probability of a rival acquisition at each acquisition stage and discounting the expected payoffs, we can estimate the present value of these payoffs for these contingencies and identify the optimal serial acquisition strategy. The DTM can be extended to more acquisitions in a serial acquisition program. The upward branch represents acquisitions that are not matched by the rival (NRA, no rival acquisition) and the downward branch represents acquisitions that are matched (RA, rival acquires). The bold pathway represents a possible optimal serial acquisition strategy for SA. The DTM can also help SA decide at what stage in the acquisition program it should cease further acquisitions since it is no longer optimal.[23]

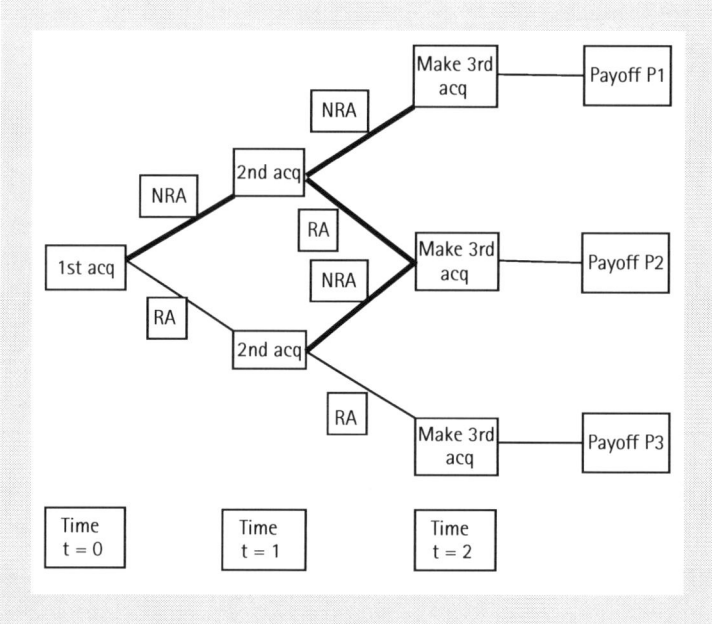

FIG. 8.5 Decision tree model of three serial acquisitions

Notes: acq = acquisition; NRA = no rival makes acquisition; RA = rival acquires.

Limitations of Real Option Valuation Models

Extrapolation of the BSOPM model to real options and strategic options is fraught with problems. Many of the assumptions that underlie financial options do not hold in the real options context. Data such as volatility are difficult to estimate since the underlying investment opportunities are not traded. By their very nature, many of these are of an exploratory nature and historical data about them will not be available. Many other differences between financial and real options make valuation of real options using BSOPM less reliable.

Summary of Valuation Models

We have presented a range of valuation models that differ in terms of their assumptions, forecast horizon, conceptual foundation, simplicity, and data limitations. The multiples-based models are widely used, but they rely on simple assumptions about the future. The DCF models allow for more finely grained assumptions about the pattern of future cash flows and the equilibrium determination of discount rates. The real option models are useful in those acquisitions where future growth options rather than cash flows from the current assets in place are important as a source of value. It is generally the case that no single model is adequate to capture the complexity of the valuation process. In the next section, we turn to how the estimated value from the proposed acquisition is shared between the acquirers and target firms. The impediments to value appropriation by acquirers are highlighted.

VALUE APPROPRIATION IN M&A DEALS

What we have described so far are the tools of valuation that may be used to value the benefits flowing from an acquisition. These benefits represent the overall value creation from an acquisition. As highlighted in our discussion of scenario analysis above, valuation itself is subject to errors arising from the forward-looking nature of cash flow and earnings forecasts and the errors that surround the estimation of cost of capital. Such valuation errors may be compounded by the behavioral biases of acquirer managers and the various deal and firm-specific characteristics. Among the latter are the payment currency employed in the acquisition, how cash offers are financed, whether an acquisition is a one-off acquisition or is part of a series of acquisitions informed by a business model such as buy-and-build (also known as platform strategy), the target characteristics, bidder characteristics, and the timing of acquisition. These influence, not the value creation, but the value appropriation in an acquisition.

Value appropriation is a matter of negotiation between the bidder and its target. The negotiation process is not necessarily a rational process in which managers seek to maximize shareholder value. Managers are often motivated to undertake acquisitions for personal interests that may conflict with the interests of shareholders. Behavioral finance literature provides evidence that corporate managers are often driven by cognitive biases such as overoptimism, overconfidence, or hubris. When these biases influence acquisition decisions and the negotiation process, it is likely that acquirers fail to appropriate the value expected to be created from an acquisition. This failure will be reflected in shareholder value losses to acquirers. Target shareholders may gain inordinately at the expense of acquirer shareholders. In the following sections, we examine the impact of these factors and review the related empirical evidence.

VALUE APPROPRIATION AND DEAL CHARACTERISTICS

Value Impact of Payment Currency for Acquisitions

An acquirer can pay for its acquisition in a variety of ways: cash, its own shares in exchange for the shares in the target, its own loan stock, or a mixture of these. A cash offer may be financed with accumulated free cash flows or the cash can be raised ahead of the acquisition by issue of new shares or bonds or by raising bank loans. Each of these methods carries associated risks to the acquirer. In a cash offer, however financed, the acquirer assumes all the risk of overvaluation of the target and overpayment for the acquisition, thereby falling victim to adverse selection. Cash acquisitions financed with bond issues or bank loans increase the financial leverage of the acquirer and hence its financial risk. The bidder can alleviate its own adverse selection problem by offering a share exchange rather than cash. In Hansen's model, common stock due to its contingent pricing effect reduces the target valuation risk for the bidder by forcing the target shareholders to share the risk.[24] The bidder can also mitigate the target's adverse selection problem with a generous share exchange ratio (ER). This may take the form of higher ER if the bidder's stock price falls below an agreed threshold.[25]

Cash as a payment currency can provide a bidder with tactical advantages in deterring potential rival bidders. Fishman (1989) argues that cash acquirers signal their high valuation of the target, thereby deterring rival low-value bidders. This suggests that cash acquirers are likely to experience value gains from their acquisition.

Franks, Harris, and Mayer (1988), in their extensive study of payment methods and their impact on shareholder returns for the UK and the US for the period 1955–85, reported a negligible use of convertibles in the UK, but a significant use in the US. They found that shareholders of target companies earned a risk-adjusted abnormal return of 30% in all-cash offers and 15% in all share offers in the month of bid announcement.[26] For the bidder shareholders, the returns were 0.7 and 21.1% respectively. The returns for "cash or equity" for the same month were close to all-cash offers, and for "cash and equity" offers the returns were higher than in pure equity offers. The relative superiority of cash offers in the returns to shareholders is also observed in other countries like France (Eckbo and Langohr 1989).

This pattern of superior returns to cash acquirers is replicated in more recent studies in the US as well as Europe. Table 8.1 shows the abnormal returns (%) around announcement dates. One interesting point is that in the case of private targets, in contrast to public targets, stock acquisitions outperform cash acquisitions, in both the US and Europe. In general, acquirers earn higher returns from private than from public company acquisitions (see below for review of evidence). This is explained as an illiquidity discount to the private targets. Since private target shareholders should gain greater liquidity in cash offers than in stock offers, the expected order of performance of the acquirer will be cash and stock offers. What we observe is the opposite. Thus increased liquidity to private targets may not explain the latter pattern. An alternative explanation is that acquirers do better in private target acquisition because such targets have concentrated ownership and this, when converted into acquirer's equity, creates a large block of shareholders that can better monitor the acquirer in the post-acquisition period. This corporate governance benefit cannot materialize in cash acquisitions but only in stock acquisitions. The superior returns to acquirers in stock acquisitions of private targets are consistent with this rationale (Chang 1998).

Many other US and UK studies have reported broadly similar results for cash and equity offers (Huang and Walkling 1987; Travlos 1987; Draper and Paudyal 1999; and Peterson and Peterson 1991).[27] In terms of post-acquisition operating performance,

Table 8.1 Abnormal returns (%) to acquirers by payment method*

Study and sample period	All cash	Mixed	All stock
Moeller et al. (2004) (US), 1980–2001	1.38	1.45	0.15
Bouwman et al. (2003) (US), 1979–98	0.88	2.33	−0.79
Bradley and Sundaram, 2004 (US), 1990–2000	0.83		−1.29
	0.71		1.39
Faccio et al. (2006) (Europe), 1996–2001	0.30	−0.66	−1.81
	1.17	2.14	3.90
Martynova and Renneboog (2006) (Europe), 1993–2001	1.03	1.03	0.66

* *Note*: The first row in Bradley and Sundaram and in Faccio et al. reports returns to public targets and the second row to private targets. In other studies, the returns are mixed. Blank means study does not report any result.

however, Heron and Lie (2002) do not find any significant difference between cash and stock exchange acquirers for a sample of US acquisitions during 1985–97. If, as documented by the several studies cited above, cash offers generate significantly more value than stock exchange offers, why do acquirers choose the latter? One answer is that acquirer managers are motivated by considerations other than shareholder value enhancement. However, these managers may have information on the basis of which they rationally prefer one method over another. In an interesting empirical study of the returns to cash acquirers and stock acquirers, Emery and Switzer (1999) estimated the returns to the optimal payment method predicted from an expectations model comprising the various motivational factors. This model also allowed them to compare the actual announcement period abnormal returns to the expected returns from the optimal choice and the expected returns from the wrong choice. The results, based on a US sample of completed acquisitions during 1967–87, show that managers correctly chose the method with the higher expected abnormal return. Further, bidders making cash acquisitions earned higher returns than if they had made a stock offer. Emery and Switzer also reported that managers' choices were motivated by the target shareholders' personal tax liability and the need to minimize valuation risk.

Valuation of Cash Offers and Source of Financing

While the bidder may choose one (or more) of several payment methods, a separate issue is how such methods will be financed. In the case of a pure, i.e. 100% stock exchange offer, the bidder will issue its own stock.[28] In the case of a debt offer, it can issue its own loan stock or bonds. Thus the two coincide. For a pure cash offer, however, a range of financing options is available. Here the source of cash becomes an important consideration. Some of the financing methods are seemingly equivalent, e.g. a loan stock offer is similar to selling the stock in the market and using the proceeds to make a cash offer and a stock exchange offer is similar to making a seasoned equity issue and using the proceeds to make a cash offer. Nevertheless, each source has its own implications for the leverage of the merged entity, cost of capital, the monitoring it brings to bear upon the acquisition itself, regulatory burden, the success of the bid etc., and hence for the value gains to bidders. Separating payment method from its financing allows the bidder greater flexibility in terms of timing and exploiting any arbitrage opportunities between capital markets, currency markets, etc.

Bidders may choose to use debt financing in order to gain an advantage over potential competitive bidders. A low leverage allows the bidder the financial slack to raise the necessary financing for its bid quickly, whereas a high leverage constrains the bidder. Thus a bidder can time its takeover bid when it enjoys this slack. A low leverage bidder also signals a stronger commitment to a takeover bid than a highly levered competitor. Such a commitment may persuade the target managers (or target shareholders in a tender offer) to accept its bid more readily than a bid from a rival, more highly levered, bidder. Following the success of the bid, the acquirer may lever up.[29] Bharadwaja and Shivdasani (2003) test whether the source of cash for a cash offer signals the quality of the acquisition. They find, for a sample of cash tender offers in the US, that bank financing has a favorable impact on the value gains to bidders. This is attributed to the monitoring of the acquisition decision by the lending banks. Under this monitoring, the higher the bank debt, the higher are the returns to bidders on announcement.[30] Martynova and Renneboog provide similar evidence on the impact of the source of cash for a cash offer.

Value Impact of Deferred Consideration

As discussed earlier, both bidders and target shareholders face valuation risk in negotiating a price and the payment currency in a takeover. One way of mitigating this risk is to make the consideration payable to the vendors contingent upon the future performance of the target under their own management. This method, called "earnout," is used to finance acquisitions of private companies operating in the service or high technology sectors, e.g. advertising agencies, or software development businesses. In such companies, the value of the company often depends on the intangible asset of human creativity and the flair of one or two individuals. Retaining the target management after acquisition to ensure that the target performs as expected by the acquirer may be a key consideration.[31] Valuing such companies, however, is immensely difficult. Earnout provides a solution when price negotiation between buyer and seller stalls (Sherman and Janatka 1992).

In an earnout, consideration to the vendor is made up of the following:

- an immediate payment in cash or shares of the acquirer;
- a deferred payment contingent upon the target-turned-subsidiary achieving certain predetermined performance levels.

The performance level may be expressed in terms of sales revenue or pre-tax profits.[32, 33]

Value Impact of Earnouts and Collars in Stock Exchange Acquisitions

Kohers and Ang (2000) compare the abnormal returns to earnout acquirers with those of cash and stock acquirers. Earnout acquirers outperform the latter in terms of two-day abnormal returns when acquiring private targets (corporate subsidiaries): 2.2% (2.1%) for earnout acquirers compared to 1.8% (1.5%) for cash acquirers and 1.13% (2.0%) for stock acquirers.

Such outperformance is even greater when the targets are associated with greater information uncertainty about their value, e.g. high-tech or service sector targets, consistent with the rationale that earnout reduces risk to the acquirer due to information asymmetry. Barbopoulos and Sudarsanam (forthcoming), analyzing a large UK sample of acquirers using different payment methods including earnouts, find similar results: 1% for non-earnout acquirers and 1.5% for earnout acquirers, the difference being statistically significant. They also find that acquirers who choose earnout as payment currency when it is optimal, conditional on the transactional and bidder and target characteristics, earn superior returns.

Officer et al. (2008) find that straight stock acquirers earn a three-day median abnormal return of −2.0%, whereas stock acquirers with collar protection perform better—with fixed exchange rate collar −0.9% and with fixed price collar −0.8%. Targets in these deals receive similar returns, between 13.8% and 14.3%. Thus offering protection reduces the information risk to the targets and the bidder avoids having to excessively compensate them for this risk. This may explain the collar offers' superior value creation.

Value Impact of Serial Acquisitions

Serial acquisitions are part of a pre-meditated consolidation strategy. Serial acquisitions also provide the acquirer with the opportunity to learn from the preceding acquisitions about the problems of making and integrating acquisitions and these lessons, if internalized by the acquirer's organization, can enhance its capacity to make successful acquisitions. Thus successful acquisition-making becomes the firm's core competence. Of course no two acquisitions are alike and the learning process must intelligently differentiate between similar and dissimilar acquisitions and judiciously apply the lessons and not apply them indiscriminately.

Serial acquisitions may be announced by a firm as its sustained competitive strategy. This may have the advantage of a firm commitment that deters its rivals from imitative acquisitions, thereby maintaining its competitive advantage. However, this depends on how the rivals react. The serial acquirer may therefore wish to preserve its flexibility by waiting for its rivals' reactions before embarking upon further acquisitions in the series. If the rivals' reactions are robust, then the firm may follow a less aggressive and more accommodating strategy that will avoid a "no-holds-barred" war, and cease its acquisition program. We illustrated above how the real options framework can be used to model the choice between strategic commitment and flexibility and how valuable such flexibility is.

When a firm engages in serial acquisitions as part of its long-term strategic positioning, it is reasonable to surmise that, at the outset of the series, its investment opportunities are quite profitable. As it makes successive acquisitions to carry out its strategy, these opportunities get exhausted and the marginal returns from follow-on acquisitions fall off. When the returns turn negative, it is an indication that such opportunities exist no more. If this scenario plays out, we shall observe that high returns to acquirers from initial acquisitions in the series are followed by lower returns to later acquisitions.

Klasa and Stegemoller (2007) find that 25% of acquisitions during 1982–99 in the US are in the form of serial acquisitions defined as those made by the same acquirer over a period separated by 24 months of no acquisitions before and after the series. 1285 acquisitions were made in 487 sequences compared to 3796 acquisitions out of sequence. They estimate the buy-and-hold abnormal returns (%) for the first, middle, and last acquisition in a sequence as follows:

	Year −1	Year+1	Year+2	Year +3	Year+4
1st acquisition	17	25	21	−10	15
Mid acquisition	32	3	−21	−27	−28
Last acquisition	−3	−14	−24	−20	−19

Klasa and Stegemoller find that investment opportunities do diminish from before the first acquisition to after the last one.

Sudarsanam and Huang (2008) examine the performance of serial acquirers which make at least five acquisitions from the first acquisition over a five-year period. They find, in a sample of 2527 US acquisitions from 1993 to 2004, 149 serial acquirers making 1223 acquisitions. They observe that the three-day abnormal returns at bid announcements are positive at the first acquisition and no different from those of non-serial (occasional) acquirers, but as the series progresses these returns fall and turn negative. The abnormal returns to the fifth and later acquisitions in a series are also significantly lower than those of non-serial acquirers. This pattern is consistent with diminishing marginal returns to later acquisitions. It is also consistent with later acquisitions, stirring up the five competitive forces we discussed earlier. It is also consistent with more acquisitions adding to complexity and making the integration effort more demanding (Barkema and Schijven 2008). Sudarsanam and Huang also estimate the three-year abnormal return to a portfolio of serial acquirers and compare it to the abnormal return to a control portfolio of non-acquirers and the return to the US stock market. Figure 8.6 shows that serial acquirers seem to outperform occasional acquirers and the stock market.[34, 35] Thus, while later acquisitions add less, and diminishing, value, serial acquisitions as a whole may add value.

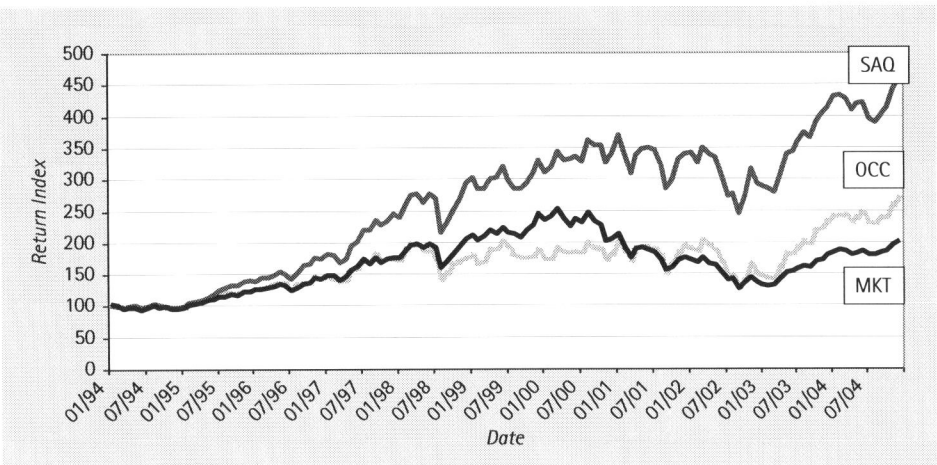

FIG. 8.6 Cumulative returns to serial acquirers

Notes: The cumulative returns are excess returns over the one-month US Treasury bill rate
and the portfolios are value weighted. SAQ = portfolio of serial acquirers;
OCC = portfolio of occasional acquirers; MKT = Market portfolio.

Source: Sudarsanam (2010: 404).

Value Impact of Target Characteristics

Many prior studies have evidenced that several characteristics of a takeover deal and of
the bidder and target influence the value gains to bidders and targets. Several empirical
studies have found that acquirers of private companies make significantly higher value
gains at announcement as well as in the post-acquisition period than those of publicly
listed companies. From a very comprehensive sample of 4429 acquisitions by Western
European firms during 1996–2001, Faccio, McConnell, and Stolin (2006) find that[36] the
cumulative abnormal return around announcement to acquirers is −0.4% for public
targets and 1.5% for private company or subsidiary business acquisition (subsidiary businesses being generally unlisted and hence "private"). This listing effect prevails in all
sample years and most sample countries. Officer et al. (2008) also find superior returns
to private company acquisitions with US data. For a sample of 735 private and 1944 public company targets during 1995–2004, the acquirer's three-day abnormal returns are
respectively 3.8% and −1.3%. For a sample of 6224 UK acquisitions during 1986–2008,
Barbopoulos and Sudarsanam (forthcoming) find that five-day announcement period
abnormal returns are: 1.4% (private targets); 1.5% (subsidiary targets); and −0.8% (public
targets), all significant at 1%.[37, 38]

Moeller, Schlingemann, and Stulz (2004) report that over a three-year post-acquisition period, large (small) acquirers of private firms generate 0.3% (−0.3%) monthly
abnormal return, the difference being significant. In the three-day announcement
period, the small (large) acquirers generate 2.14% (0.7%). Thus while large acquirers

generate significant positive gains in both periods, small acquirers experience gains in the short term, but losses in the long term. Moreover, both in the short and long term, all stock acquirers experience larger gains than all-cash acquirers with private targets, whereas the opposite is true of public company returns. This is consistent with the monitoring benefit of the target owners becoming block shareholders of the acquirer. In the UK, non-cash acquirers of private targets perform worse than cash acquirers over three years, indicating no evidence of such monitoring benefit. There is also no value gain from reduction in valuation risk through stock exchange offers (see also Antoniou et al. 2007).

Smaller targets are easier to integrate after acquisition. The cost to the acquirer of misvaluation is less when the target is smaller. On the other hand, the expected synergies are also smaller with smaller targets. Several empirical studies show that the smaller the target relative to the acquirer, the larger are the announcement period returns to acquirers. This result is, however, not uniform across studies.[39] The size effect is also not similar across public and private company targets. Acquirers generate significant positive abnormal returns when they buy large private targets and significant negative returns with large public targets.[40]

A takeover bid may be made on an opportunistic impulse because a seemingly attractive target company is being offered as a takeover candidate. Often companies with a poor performance record, limited growth opportunities, or management succession problems when the founder manager retires look for potential acquirers or become available for acquisition. Sometimes a company may be bounced into a bid because of an acquisition move made by a rival. Unplanned takeover bids may turn out, serendipitously, to be winners. However, there is an element of risk in such acquisitions in that the underlying value creation logic is glossed over, or the target is overvalued and a high bid premium paid, or the post-acquisition integration problems are not foreseen. It is, therefore, important to undertake acquisitions only after much deliberation and as part of the firm's strategic planning. In July 2007, the board of Royal Bank of Scotland (RBS) faced a critical decision. For the previous two months, an RBS-led consortium had been pursuing a break-up bid for ABN Amro (ABN), the Dutch bank. But a Dutch court had just ruled that ABN Amro was allowed to complete a controversial deal to sell its US subsidiary—a business that RBS coveted. After a brief deliberation, the RBS board—led by Sir Tom McKillop, chairman, and Sir Fred Goodwin, chief executive—chose to press ahead with the ABN Amro bid for €72bn.The true cost of that decision became clear in April 2008 when the bank launched the largest rights issue in European history for £12bn to repair its battered balance sheet. RBS executives attempted to blame the rights issue— and losses of £5.9bn on complex debt securities held on the bank's balance sheet—on the recent turmoil in the capital markets. Sir Tom said the market's slide in March had forced RBS to recognize additional losses and raise fresh capital. But in retrospect, the precarious state of RBS's balance sheet, and a substantial proportion of its writedowns, can be traced back to the decision to push on with the ABN Amro deal. RBS's total losses on debt securities amounting to £8.8bn, about a third of which come from ABN, were written off. Sir Tom acknowledged *the timing of the deal was wrong*, but suggested the board could not have foreseen the impact the turmoil in the markets would have on the business.[41]

Value Impact of Timing

If buying at the top of a stock market cycle is that bad, is it a good idea to buy after a market crash or at the bottom of a cycle? There are several advantages to this timing strategy:

- The acquirer is in a buyers' market rather than in a sellers' market with the collapse of the M&A market; this enhances the bidder's bargaining power;
- The acquirer is not making the acquisition under peer pressure to "keep up with the Jones's" and therefore can consider what it is buying and why;
- With increased bargaining leverage, the bidder can secure a more thorough due diligence and avoid any nasty post-acquisition surprises; this reduces acquisition risk and potentially its cost of capital;
- Assuming the bidder has not already exhausted its war chest in reckless acquisitions during the boom, its liquidity is likely to be large enough to finance an attractive acquisition;
- As is witnessed during 2008–09, the credit crunch that normally accompanies a recession might have hit financial buyers that rely on high levels of debt more harshly than strategic buyers;
- The acquisition premium is much lower than at the top of an M&A boom.[42, 43]

The foregoing discussion is concerned with the impact of deal structure and deal timing on shareholder value. It is also about the impact of the characteristics of bidder and target firms. In the next section, we discuss how the negotiation process impacts on value appropriation. This discussion encompasses organizational processes and the behavior of top managers in the context of acquisitions. It highlights the critical importance of corporate governance in determining the acquirer's value gains.

VALUE IMPACT OF THE NEGOTIATION PROCESS

Neglecting the Discipline of the "Walk-Away" Price

Negotiation is not an unambiguously rational process and requires both understanding of the perspectives of the other party to the negotiation and an appreciation of the emotions driving the negotiators. The end objectives of negotiation are often a mixture of pecuniary gains and non-pecuniary or psychological gains. The negotiators may often appeal to the greed, fear, and ego of the leaders of the merging firms. Fear arises from the threats faced by the firm in the absence of a deal. The SWOT (strengths, weaknesses, opportunities, and threats) analysis is a useful tool in understanding the weaknesses of the other party and the threats it faces. This can be linked to the familiar concept in negotiation literature known as the best alternative to no agreement (BATNA). For example, the BATNA for a target firm may be an unwanted and unloved existence as an independent firm or being taken over by a predator. For a bidder, BATNA may be the loss of competitive advantage and shareholder value decline, possibly causing the bankruptcy of the firm. Loss of competitive advantage may come from the failure to realize the unique re-configuration of its resources and capabilities that the failed acquisition might have facilitated or from a rival acquiring the target and gaining competitive advantage.

Given that negotiations may often happen at both the rational and emotional levels, BATNA must be assessed at both the firm level, i.e. what is best for the firm, and the negotiators' level, i.e. what is the best for the negotiators. The interactions between financial and non-financial parameters of the two negotiating teams are shown in Panel A of Figure 8.7. Panel B of that figure shows how wide apart the two teams are and what the feasible negotiation range is as regards the price. The "walk-away" price equals the value of BATNA for each team. Deals result from the trade-off between financial and non-financial parameters during the negotiation stage. Deals may collapse because of insufficient appreciation of the other party's non-financial motivation for doing a deal. However, often a bidder may reach a trade-off from which the target or its managers gain at the expense of the bidder shareholders.

An important characteristic of a win-win deal is that it is perceived by each party to be so even though the reality may be different. For example, one type of merger deal is the so-called merger of equals. In practice, however, in such deals there is a barely concealed dominant partner who in effect takes over the weaker partner. The $40bn merger of Daimler-Benz (DB) and Chrysler in 1998 was touted as a merger of equals but the dominant partner was Daimler-Benz. The deal was dressed up as a merger of equals so that it could win acceptance by a number of important stakeholders, e.g. top managers and large minority shareholders of Chrysler. This illustrates how presentational, face-saving considerations, essentially, psychological props, facilitate conclusion of a deal. A merger of equals may often hide, behind its warm and sentimental semantics, a skewed power structure with clearly a discernible acquirer and the acquired. Thus, in substance the deal is a takeover and not a merger of equals. In the post-acquisition period, the veneer is stripped away and the fiction of a merger of equals gives way to the situation where one firm dominates the other. In October 2000, Jürgen Schrempp, DB's CEO, admitted that it had always been his intention that the deal would be an acquisition by Daimler. This led to a large shareholder in Chrysler, Kirk Kerkorian, launching an $8bn claim against Daimler-Chrysler (DC) for fraud (Burt et al. 2000). Empirical evidence from the US suggests that target CEOs in mergers of equals may be trading power for premium, by negotiating shared control in the merged firm in exchange for lower shareholder premium (Wulf 2004). For the acquirer this is good news, provided it does not create post-merger problems similar to the ones that DC faced.

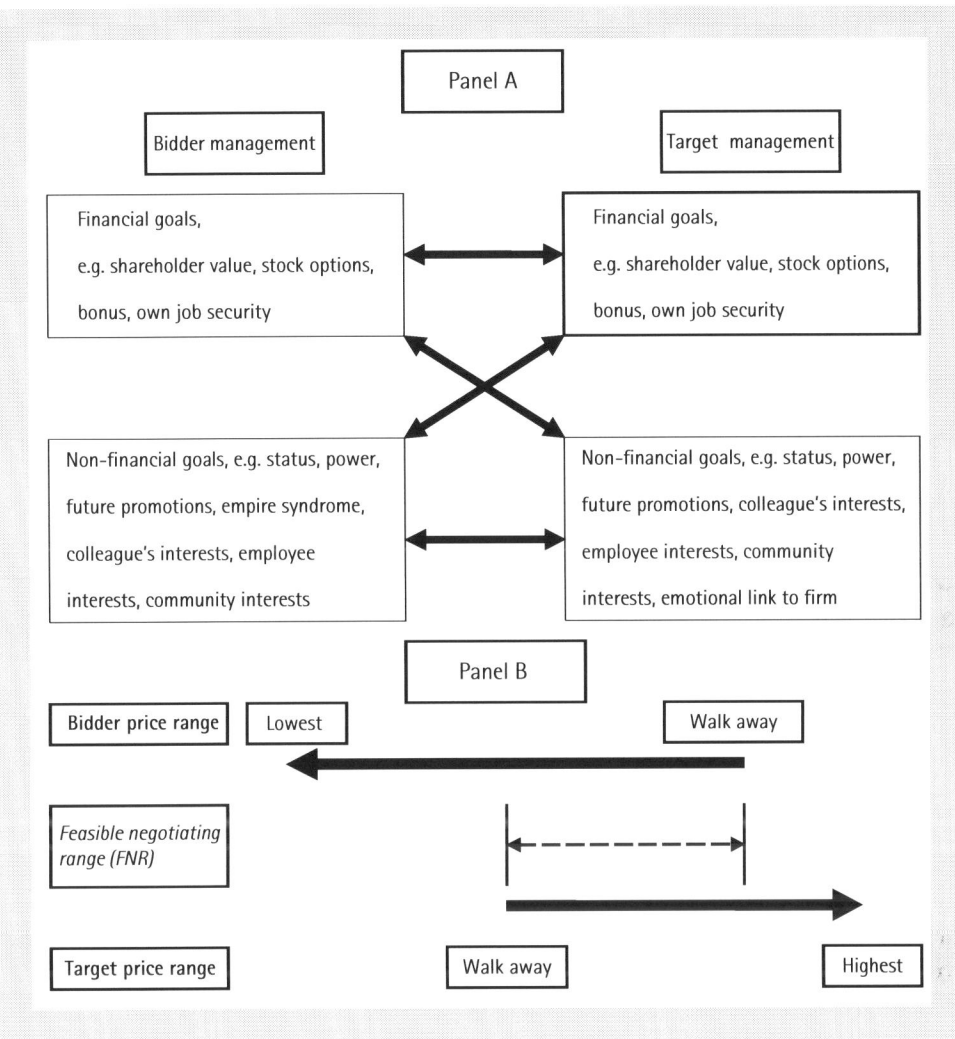

FIG. 8.7 Negotiation parameters and limits

Source: Sudarsanam (2010: 638).

Pricing the target and determining the takeover premium are a matter of negotiation between the bidder and target. In general, each side will have done its own valuation of the target as a stand-alone entity and as part of the acquirer contributing to synergy and value creation. The estimate of synergy depends on a lot of assumptions and these may not be the same between the two sides. The negotiation price range would coincide perfectly if both made identical assumptions for all future conditions. However, such coincidence may be just that! It is part of the negotiation exercise to get these assumptions out into the open so that valuation models can be harmonized. Then the arguments move from the set of assumptions to the validity of those assumptions. Here each side may be biased, with the target being more optimistic and the bidder more pessimistic. Of course the bidder should not overdo the pessimism since that begs the question "why merge at all if there is not much value to be created?"

Negotiators normally benchmark their valuations and takeover premia against those applied in recent mergers of similar size, status, e.g. "best of breed" companies but in different sectors, or the same industry/sector. Arguments about the appropriate benchmark will then ensue! Acquisition prices are often benchmarked against the earnings, cash flow, or asset multiples—EV/EBITDA, PER, or market to book value of assets multiples—in recent "comparable deals" in the same sector. Such benchmarks can, however, give rise to a self-reinforcing escalating spiral of bid premium and need to be guarded against by testing facile assumptions of comparability and the true value creation potential that may be peculiar to a deal.

Value Impact of High Bid Premium

In US takeovers during 1980–2001, the average (median) premium paid for public targets was 68% (61%) by large acquirers and 62% (52%) by small acquirers. A high premium is generally treated as evidence of overpayment, sometimes due to bidder managers' hubris or overconfidence. Large acquirers pay higher bid premiums but also experience significant value destruction over a three-year post-acquisition period compared to value creation by small acquirers (Moeller et al. 2004). Antoniou, Arbour, and Zhao (2008) find that, for a large UK sample, acquirers that pay a high four-week premium do not underperform those paying relatively low premiums in the three-year post-acquisition period. Although they do not analyze the impact of acquirer size on bid premium and post-acquisition abnormal returns, they report that there is little difference in these returns between relatively large and relatively small acquirers, i.e. relative to targets. Thus evidence on the link between high premium and post-acquisition shareholder value performance is inconclusive.[44]

VALUE IMPACT OF MANAGERS'
BEHAVIORAL BIASES

Another perspective that may shed light on the factors that allow firms to undertake value-destroying mergers and acquisitions is rooted in individual psychological attributes and behavior of the CEO and in the collective social dynamics of the board of directors. The behavioral corporate finance literature has identified several psychological traits of CEOs, including:

- hubris;
- overconfidence; and
- overoptimism.

When managers consider taking over another firm, hubris causes managers to underestimate the risks inherent in acquisitions, leading to overvaluation of the target and an excessive takeover premium (Roll 1986). March and Shapira (1987) find managers are *overconfident* and consider themselves able to distinguish between gambling, i.e. where the chances of win or loss are uncontrollable, and risk taking, i.e. where uncertainty can be reduced by skill or information. *Overoptimistic* individuals also underestimate the likelihood of hazards affecting them. Heaton (2002) and Malmendier and Tate (2005) find that overoptimistic managers often show an upward bias in their cash flow forecasts for investment projects. The impact of these behavioral biases is that CEOs may underestimate the risk of the acquisitions they make and overpay for them.

Rovenpor (1993) examines the role that four CEO personal characteristics, including preference for organizational growth, belief in synergy, need for power, and self-confidence, play in encouraging companies to engage in mergers and acquisitions. Rovenpor finds that these four CEO characteristics are highly and positively related to the level of mergers and acquisitions activities. There is a thin line between confidence and overconfidence. Jack Welch, the former CEO of GE, notes the thin line between self-confidence and hubris. After describing GE's disastrous acquisition of Kidder Peabody, Welch (2001: 229) says: "There is only a razor's edge between self-confidence and hubris. This time hubris won and taught me a lesson we'd never forget." This suggests that behavioral biases can provide the tipping point between optimal and excessive risk taking by top managers.

Overconfident managers may be particularly attracted to high-tech acquisitions being opportunities to demonstrate their capability in "creating miracles." Available empirical evidence points to the negative value impact of different behavioral biases. Acquisitions driven by managerial hubris destroy acquirer shareholder value. Managerial overconfidence induced by glamour stock rating leads to a risky acquisition strategy, excessive acquisition premium, and value destruction for acquirer shareholders. Overconfident managers are more likely to conduct mergers, in particular, value-destroying mergers, than are rational CEOs.

Malmendier and Tate (2008) test the proposition that overconfident CEOs overestimate their ability to generate value from acquisitions and overpay for target companies, resulting in value-destroying mergers. These predictions are tested using two proxies for overconfidence: CEOs' personal overinvestment in their company and their press portrayal. They find that the odds of making an acquisition are 65% higher if the CEO is classified as overconfident. The effect is largest if the merger is diversifying and does not require external financing. The market reaction at merger announcement (0.9%) is significantly more negative than for non-overconfident CEOs (−0.12%) (see Kohers and Kohers 2001 and Sudarsanam and Gao 2004 on overconfidence being correlated with more risky, high-tech acquisitions; Hayward and Hambrick 1997 on hubris being associated with value-destroying acquisitions).

Leaders often exhibit overoptimism either because of intense desire to succeed or to inspire the "troops" to fight hard and win. Such optimism may again engender unrealistic overstatement of the benefits of an acquisition and an understatement of the problems in achieving those benefits. Such overoptimism, combined with overconfidence in their own ability to manage risks, may induce managers to venture ahead of other firms, i.e. be first movers, even though technological and market uncertainties are unlikely to be resolved soon. Overoptimism may often be manifested in grandiose visions of the future and the firm's positioning in that future. The disastrous merger of AOL and Time Warner (TW) was crafted on the basis of exuberant optimism about internet broadband as a transformative technology and visionary faith in its potential.[45]

Overoptimism may also be engendered by the social process at work within organizations. Lovallo and Kahneman (2003) note the "organizational pressures" to conform and to be optimistic: "Organizations also actively discourage pessimism, which is often interpreted as disloyalty. The bearers of bad news tend to become pariahs, shunned and ignored by other employees. When pessimistic opinions are suppressed, while optimistic ones are rewarded, an organization's ability to think critically is undermined. The optimistic biases of individual employees become mutually reinforcing, and unrealistic views of the future are validated by the group." This process may explain why non-CEO directors on the board may often fall in line with the CEO's overoptimism and thus fail to rein in the CEO.

Psychologists who have studied individual and group decision making have identified several other behavioral biases that may dilute the quality of decisions made by CEOs. Tversky and Kahneman (1974), in their path-breaking studies of decision behavior under uncertainty, identify a number of such biases, many of which afflict acquisition decisions e.g. *representativeness*—the decision maker draws upon another situation in which a successful decision was made to validate the decision in the present context, even though the former may have only superficial similarity to the latter, e.g. a past successful acquisition is used to justify the case for another, seemingly similar acquisition. Other biases are: *availability, anchoring, prospect-driven* (see Shefrin 2007 for a discussion of these in the context of corporate finance).

CEOs often launch the bid for a target because they want to acquire it. Given this initial commitment, they are predisposed to see what they want to see. They will selectively use information that reinforces the validity of their decision to acquire, by relying on representativeness and availability heuristics. Moreover, any discordant facts or revelations, e.g. from due diligence that might call for questioning or abandoning the acquisition, may be dismissed as non-representative. This behavior is characteristic of self-delusion (Pfeffer 2007).

Commitment to a deal often turns into overcommitment from which it is difficult to *walk away* even when there is a cause and an opportunity to do so, e.g. during the pre-negotiation due-diligence stage. Haunschild, Davis-Blake, and Fichman (1994), in their experimental study of commitment in the acquisition process, find evidence that personal responsibility for proposing the acquisition, competition for the target, and a publicly announced acquisition bid all lead to escalating commitment even in the face of emerging signals that the acquisition is likely to destroy value. The decision maker is thus in denial and has low tolerance of cognitive dissonance. All three conditions for escalation are associated with loss of face or power or authority that may follow a decision to walk away. The commitment escalates even during the due-diligence stage, which normally should allow the bidder to walk away without loss of face since the purpose of due diligence is to allow re-assessment of risk in making the acquisition, offering a perfect opportunity to walk away. Negative signals thrown up by due diligence may be dismissed as non-representative. Commenting on such cognitive biases, Langevoort (1997) observes: "The management literature strongly suggests that once executives have committed to a course of action, their subsequent survey of information is strongly biased to bolster their choice.... Bolstering evidence is actively sought, while disconfirming information is subconsciously resisted." Thus self-delusion trumps rational risk assessment.

In a survey of 250 senior managers involved in M&A deals, Bain & Company found the following (Elton and Eddigen 2006):

- 50% (of respondents) said that their due diligence had overlooked significant problems;
- 50% found the targets had been dressed up to look good;
- Two-thirds said their approach routinely overestimated synergies from the acquisition;
- Only 30% were satisfied with their due diligence process; and
- A third acknowledged that they had not walked away from deals despite nagging doubts.

Often the pressures on firms to merge arise from both internal and external factors. As noted above, competition for a target increases the commitment to make an acquisition. Another form of competition also gets the CEOs' adrenalin pumping overtime. In an atmosphere in which the firms' rivals are making an acquisition, not to make matching acquisitions will project the executives as corporate wimps. Jeffrey Pfeffer (2007), a foremost scholar of organizational behavior, identifies three forces that drive firms to merge even though the vast majority of mergers and acquisitions create little value or destroy value:

- Executive ego leading to hubris and overconfidence—mergers get attention from analysts and sometimes from the media and the ego-driven CEO likes that attention;
- Executives find mergers exciting, i.e. they enjoy the thrill of the chase; mergers often seem like a faster and less risky solution to problems than solving those problems internally. "Mergers have sex appeal";
- In a world in which everyone else is doing a deal, who wants to be left out! This may explain imitative acquisitions and herd-like behavior causing takeover waves (on various theories of merger waves including the imitative theory, see Sudarsanam 2010, chs. 2 and 12).

Narcissistic CEOs and Acquisitions

Behavioral biases such as overconfidence and overoptimism may themselves be rooted in the personalities of the CEOs or other top executives. Clinical psychologists have identified a personality disorder called narcissism. Narcissus is a Greek mythological character who fell hopelessly in love with his own image and pined away to death. The lesson is that excessive self-love is self-destructive. Manfred Kets de Vries (2006), a trained clinical psychologist and management professor who has specialized in leadership development in organizations, differentiates between different forms of narcissism, from "healthy self-esteem to self-destructive egotism." He argues that "a moderate measure of self-esteem contributes to positive behaviors such as assertiveness, confidence, and creativity, all desirable qualities for an individual in any walk of life, but particularly so for business leaders. At the other end of the spectrum, however, extreme narcissism is characterized by egotism, self-centredness, grandiosity, lack of empathy, exploitation, exaggerated self-love and failure to acknowledge boundaries..." and within an organization "the combination of a leader's overly narcissistic disposition and his or her position of power can have devastating consequences."

CEO narcissism may find manifestation in frequent and high profile acquisitions based on grand visions. Chatterjee and Hambrick (2007) argue that "corporate chieftains with supersized egos favour grandiose and high risk strategies... acquisitions, large scale product launches and aggressive international expansion.... they can hit big but they can also miss big." The authors provide empirical evidence that their proxies for CEO narcissism increase the chances of value-destroying acquisitions. In recent years, there have been many examples of such narcissistic behavior by chairmen and CEOs, leading to massive value destruction and great misery for thousands of employees and investors of the corporations they led.[46, 47] Sudarsanam and Huang (2007) find a close correlation between the number of overconfident CEOs and the number of M&A deals in the US during the same period, as shown in Figure 8.8.[48]

Psychological traits such as overconfidence cannot be directly observed but only inferred. However, several empirical studies have used variables that may be considered reasonable proxies for overconfidence to examine its impact on shareholder value following acquisitions. Media profile can give rise to celebrity status and overconfidence, as argued above. Serial acquirers are likely to be overconfident because they have done many deals before and can ride on their success. Longholder is a definition of an overconfident CEO, based on a CEO not exercising deep-in-the-money stock options. Low book-to-market ratio (the reciprocal of high market value of equity to its book value) is generally used as a measure of the glamour status of the firm's stock. Self-importance is measured by the CEO's compensation relative to other executives' compensation. Media profile is the profile of a CEO in media accounts of that CEO. Thus both CEO-level indicators, e.g. CEO self-importance and non-exercise of stock options, and firm-level indicators of performance, e.g. book-to-market ratio, are used to infer CEO overconfidence.

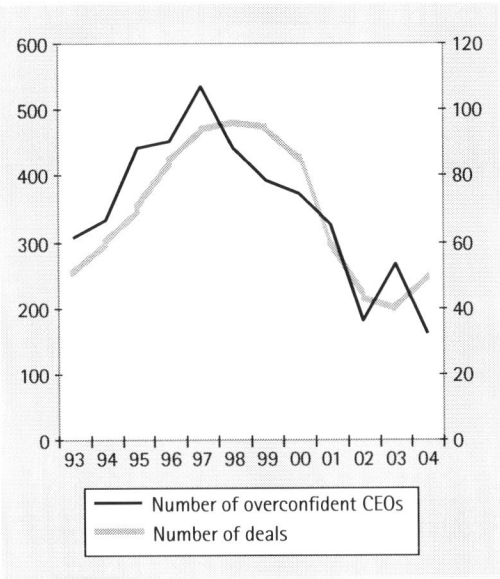

FIG. 8.8 Number of acquisitions and number of overconfident CEOs

Note: Data based on S&P 500 companies.

Table 8.2 lists the results from various studies that examine the impact of overconfidence on acquirer share price performance around acquisition announcement or over the longer term following it. From this table we find that overconfidence is in general associated with value-destroying acquisitions either in the short or in the long term.

The Imperial Overstretch

Moeller, Schlingemann, and Stulz (2004) find that large acquirers make more value-destroying acquisitions than small acquirers. They attribute this to the hubris of large acquirers. Large acquirers pay higher bid premia to acquire their targets, although bid premium does not significantly influence bid success. Large acquirers also experience synergy losses, i.e. the abnormal returns to the portfolio of bidders and targets. Moeller et al. (2004) estimate that the three-day abnormal dollar returns to the bidder-target combined are −$56mn when the bidder is large and are $5mn when the bidder is small, both statistically significant. Large acquirers thus "*hit big and miss big*," as noted by Chatterjee and Hambrick (2007).

While our discussion has so far focused on the organizational decision processes and top managements' behavioral biases leading to poor acquisition decisions and suboptimal value appropriation, the next section discusses another factor leading to similar

Table 8.2   Impact of overconfidence on shareholder gains to acquirers

Study (year of publication)	Country (sample period)	Acquirer's share performance (%)	Proxy for overconfidence
Hayward and Hambrick (1997)	US (1989–92)	– 4 [11 days]	• Past performance
			• Media appraisal
		– 11 [1 year]	• CEO self-importance
Rau and Vermaelen (1998)	US (1980–91)	– 4.04 [3 years]	• Book-to-market ratio
Kohers and Kohers (2001)	US (1984–95)	0.92ᵃ [2 day]	• Book-to-market ratio
		– 18.68ᵃ [3 years]	
Sudarsanam and Mahate (2003)	UK (1983–95)	– 1.39ᵃ [2 days]	• Book-to-market ratio
		– 8.71 [3 years]	
Doukas and Petmezas (2006)	UK (1980–2004)	1ᵃ [5 days]	• Serial acquisition
Malmendier and Tate (2005)	US (1980–94)	– 0.5 [3 days]	• Longholder
			• Media appraisal

Notes: 1. Except for Sudarsanam and Mahate, who employ buy-and-hold abnormal returns (BHARs), all studies use cumulative abnormal returns to measure shareholder value gains (see Sudarsanam, 2010, chapter 4 for definitions of these return metrics).
2. The period in brackets is the period over which performance is measured.
3. indicates significance at 1%, 5%, and 10% levels, respectively.

outcomes—the agency conflict between managers and shareholders. It also highlights the role of robust corporate governance in minimizing such conflict, improving acquisition decision making and mitigating behavioral biases.

VALUE IMPACT OF AGENCY CONFLICT IN ACQUIRERS

Conflicts of interests between shareholders and managers in the agency model of the firm may be managed in a number of different ways—internally through efficient board monitoring and control or through large shareholder monitoring, and externally through the threat and actual incidence of hostile takeovers. Among the tools available for internal control are appropriately designed compensation contracts for the CEO and other executives. Such contracts include various forms of compensation—cash salary, cash bonus, long-term incentive plans (LTIPS) that grant the firm's stock and stock option grants. Both stock and stock option grants are subject to performance benchmarks and vesting periods. They become exercisable after vesting periods of say three to five years. These different compensation components bring about different degrees of alignment to shareholder interests.

Cash salary has little relation to shareholder value. Similarly, cash bonus based on annual accounting performance benchmarks, i.e. revenue or profits, is not directly related to share price to the extent that share price does not reflect accounting performance. Values of stock and stock option grants are obviously determined by the share price. The components also offer different risk incentives to the executives in terms of reward and retribution for risk taking. Salary and bonus encourage risk avoidance since managers endanger these by taking too much risk with the firm's future financial performance. Since stock grant value goes up and down with the share price, if a risky decision drags the share price down, the value of the grant also goes down. This suggests that stock grants may discourage risk taking. Finally, stock option has value only if the share price rises about the exercise (which at the time of the grant is often the current share price). Above the exercise price, the stock option value increases exponentially. Stock option value is more volatile than that of the firm's stock, but an option holder gains far more from the upswing of the share price than he or she loses from the downswing. A stock option is often described as a punt on volatility. Thus, far more than any other compensation element, stock option is designed to encourage risk taking.

In this section, we discuss the relation between executive compensation and acquisitions from opposite angles:

- how acquisitions affect compensation; and
- how compensation affects acquisition behavior.

We also review the empirical evidence from some recent studies for the impact of stock options on acquisition risk.

Does Executive Compensation Increase with Acquisition?

Acquisition can affect current or future compensation of the top management in several ways. In recent years, CEOs and other top managers have been paid bonuses for acquisition completion, thus providing incentives for managers to complete deals even if in the long run they destroy value. Acquisitions also increase firm size and it is well documented that firm compensation increases with firm size. Managers may also increase firm risk by undertaking high risk acquisitions and gain from the stock options they have awarded themselves. Thus while compensation affects the nature of acquisitions, it is also, in turn, influenced by acquisitions. Table 8.3 summarizes a number of empirical studies of the impact of acquisitions on executive compensation. The studies reveal a positive link between good acquisitions (those that add value) and executive compensation. But bad acquisition do not impact at all or, perversely, they increase compensation. This is consistent with the self-attribution bias discussed earlier—managers claim reward for good performance but probably disclaim responsibility for bad performance. Where compensation is sensitive to firm size, this incentivizes managers to go for larger acquisitions.

Table 8.3 Impact of corporate acquisitions on executive compensation

Study, country, and sample period	Major results
Lambert and Larcker (1987), US (1976–1980)	• Increases in executive compensation and wealth observed only if acquisition increases shareholder wealth
Firth (1991), UK (1974–1980)	• Acquisition leads to increase in managerial remuneration due to increased firm size
Khorana and Zenner (1998), US (1982–1986)	• *Ex ante* compensation-to-size sensitivity makes large acquisition more likely • *Ex post*, large acquisitions have a small positive effect on total compensation • Good acquisitions increase compensation, whereas bad acquisitions do not reduce compensation
Bliss and Rosen (2001), US (1986–1995)	• Mergers increase compensation, mainly due to firm size effect • Compensation increases even if mergers cause acquiring bank's stock price to decline • CEOs make fewer wealth-reducing mergers when they own more stock
Grinstein and Hribar (2004), US (1993–1999)	• More powerful CEOs gain more in acquisition-related bonus • Bonuses larger with larger deals • Deal announcement performance in stock returns unrelated to variation in compensation
Harford and Li (2007), US (1993–1999)	• CEOs' total pay and overall wealth increase substantially following an acquisition • In poorly governed acquirers, CEOs' pay following merger insensitive to performance • CEO's wealth increases even if he makes a poor acquisition
Coakley and Iliopoulou (2006), UK (1998–2001)	• Less independent and larger boards award CEOs significantly higher bonuses and salary following M&A completion, consistent with CEO power

SUMMARY AND CONCLUSIONS

In this chapter, we have approached valuation from the acquirer's point of view as a process that consists of valuing the expected benefits from acquisitions and of appropriating the created value for the benefit of the acquirer's shareholders. Valuation being about converting forecast benefits and costs into current value to guide the acquirer in pricing the acquisition is inherently an imprecise exercise subject to numerous valuation errors. Creating value from an acquisition is a necessary but not a sufficient condition for the acquirer shareholders to benefit from it. Value appropriation is critical to assuring such benefit. Value appropriation is influenced by the structuring of the acquisition deal and the negotiation between the acquirer and the target firm. It is influenced by a host of deal characteristics and the characteristics of the bidder and the target firms. The negotiation process is not a clinically rational process in which acquirer managers seek to deliver the maximum value to its shareholders. This process is influenced by the cognitive and behavioral biases of managers and the incentives that resolve the agency conflicts between them and their shareholders.

This chapter has introduced a range of valuation models used in the M&A context and discussed their limitations. It has reviewed the extant empirical literature and discussed the evidence for the way the deal structure, deal characteristics, and firm characteristics influence value creation and value appropriation in M&A. It also highlights the empirical evidence for the way managerial biases and skewed managerial incentives can lead acquirer managers to fail to appropriate value from the acquisitions they make. Managers who craft value-creating acquisitions may nevertheless fail in their value-appropriation strategies.

END NOTES

1. In acquisitions driven by cost leadership, the lower post-acquisition cost may increase sales and market share and contribute to revenue enhancement, depending on the price elasticity of demand for the firms' products. Similarly, where revenue enhancement through product differentiation is the primary driver, there may be cost efficiencies resulting from the increased operating scale. Thus the sources of value may not be mutually exclusive.

2. "Revenue synergies tend to be particularly suspect and hard to deliver...investors tend to respond positively to acquisitions that involve cost reductions...But revenue synergies are viewed as being in the realm of speculation" (Pozen 2008). Academic views support this skepticism about revenue enhancement as a source of value. Houston et al. (2001), in their study of value gains in bank mergers cited above, find evidence that bidder managements typically overvalue merger-related gains and "this is particularly true for revenue estimates." They also find that analysts are more skeptical of high revenue growth forecasts than cost savings forecasts made by merging firms. Palepu et al. (2007, ch. 6) provide empirical evidence that high fliers, having achieved high revenue growth, are unable to maintain it after two to three years.

3. This section draws on Palepu et al. (2007, ch. 7). See also Lundholm and Sloan (2007, ch. 10).

4. CSR means that closing equity book value = opening equity book value + net income during year – dividends. This assumes that the increase (surplus) in the book value of equity at the end of the fiscal year is due to retained profits alone. In practice, there are a number of accounting adjustments that may distort CSR, e.g. reserves created on the balance sheet without affecting the income statement. In such cases, the surplus is said to be "dirty." See Lundholm and Sloan (2007). These authors demonstrate that the RI valuation model is robust to such accounting distortions since any bias in the book value of equity creates an opposite bias in the residual income estimate, e.g. higher book value increases the cost of capital and reduces the residual income over several periods. Equation 8.3 assumes CSR at the assets' level

5. Where the firm maintains the policy of 100% payout of its net income as dividends, $g_t = 0$ for all t. Even then the firm can add value if residual income is positive. MTBV will

increase if ROEt > K^e. Where the firm retains some of its net income, then it will add to firm value in a multiplicative way. On the other hand, if $ROE_t = K^e$, even 100% retention of net income will not add value and the equity to book value will be just 1.

6. See Lundholm and Sloan, ibid: 234.

7. See Lundholm and Sloan, ibid, section 11.5.

8. Analysts' forecasts are available for publicly listed companies of many countries in databases such as IBES on Thomson Financial.

9. See Palepu et al. (2007, ch. 6 and appendix). For US data from 1979 to 1998, firms with high sales growth of the order of above 50% per annum experienced a similarly rapid decline to the average growth rate of just below 10% within the third year. ROE fell from nearly 30% to nearer 15% over six or seven years for the top quintile firms in their sample. While top performers maintained their lead over several years, it was gradually eroded. These numbers are the author's interpretations of these graphs.

10. Houston et al. (2001) note several sources of overoptimism bias in the bidder management forecasts of cost savings and revenue growth in mergers: underestimate of lost revenue due to consolidation, a loss often ignored by analysts as well, and consequent overestimate of efficiency savings; underestimate of the costs of integrating the merged businesses; and a tendency to include cost savings that would have been realized even without the merger.

11. Bidders or their financial advisers often benchmark their chosen PER against PERs observed in recent takeovers of comparable firms, e.g. targets from the same sector. For examples, see Bruner (2004).

12. See, for example, Davoudi and Burgess (2007).

13. For an example of sum-of-parts valuation using a range of multiples, see Applegate's (2002) case study of AOL Time Warner.

14. Tobin's q has been used in the acquisition context to spot undervalued companies. In the early 1980s, many firms were selling at q values below 1: that is, at a discount on their assets at replacement cost. This discount was seized upon by many predators who bid for those undervalued companies. *Business Week* captioned one of its articles "The Q-Ratio: Fuel for the Merger Mania" (24 August 1981), reflecting the wild spirit of the times.

15. In principle, merger synergies should lead to revaluation of both bidder and target. In practice, for simplicity, the target is attributed all the synergistic benefits reflected in the forecast cash flows and the estimated cost of capital. So only the target value is determined.

16. The numbers are geometric averages. Arithmetic averages are generally higher than geometric averages, which smooth out the fluctuations in year-on-year returns. In general, historic arithmetic average overestimates future ERP and geometric average underestimates it. Some analysts consider that the arithmetic average is a better predictor of forward-looking, especially short-term, ERP than the geometric average.

17. For the UK this ranges from 2 to 5.4 (arithmetic) and from 1.7 to 4.1 (geometric). See the Report of the Inquiry into the Price Regulation of Stansted Airport, October 2008. For publication details of the cited studies, see that report at <http://www.competition-commission.org.uk>.

18. Under the law in the US, certain prudential financial institutions are not allowed to invest in corporate bonds with a lower rating than BBB. Hence the name "sub-investment" grade.

19. In the extreme, if a firm finances all its assets with debt, the debt beta will equal the asset beta and if it finances only with equity, the equity beta will equal the asset beta. Thus, debt

risk must have a systematic risk component. One way to calculate the cost of debt is to use the CAPM to estimate the systematic risk of corporate debt. The statistical procedure is the same as for estimating equity beta. However, because corporate debt is either untraded or traded infrequently, such estimation may result in debt beta estimates subject to a lot of error and therefore unreliable. An alternative method is to break down the excess of the coupon over the risk-free rate into its various components: systematic risk which may include economy-wide default risk; firm-specific risk which may include firm-level default risk; liquidity risk, i.e. the secondary market in debt is not deep and investors cannot disinvest without selling at a high discount. Attempts to estimate by disaggregating the coupon have not so far yielded universally agreed conceptual and procedural models. Nevertheless, it is intuitively plausible that high levels of leverage will increase the systematic risk of debt, i.e. debt beta.

20. On the use of debt betas in calculating the WACC in merger situations, see Gilson (2004). This case illustrates how asset beta can be calculated from observed equity and assumed debt betas and also how asset beta can be re-levered to arrive at equity beta appropriate for any level of gearing.

21. For further discussion of various types of real options in acquisitions see Smit and Trigeorgis (2004: 353–6).

22. Based on Damodaran (2000) (which extends the BS model to dividend-paying (competitive attrition) real options. Damodaran (2001) provides easily accessible software to calculate option values. To allow for dividend payment, d_1 in the BSOPM is modified:

$$d_1 = \left[In\,(S\,/\,E) + \left(r - y + \frac{1}{2}\sigma 2 \right) t \right]$$

where y is annual dividend yield or the annual rate of reduction in the value of S. We attribute this attrition to competitive rivalry in the real option context. The call option value is now:

$$C = S\,e^{-yt}\,N(d_1) - E\,e^{-rt}\,N(d_2)$$

23. For an extended and numerical illustration of DTM involving five serial acquisitions, see Sudarsanam (2010, ch. 14).

24. See Hansen (1987). Within the same adverse selection framework, Eckbo et al. (1990) derive the result that high-value bidders, i.e. bidders whose post-acquisition value will be high offer cash, and low-value bidders offer equity as a way of risk sharing. Officer et al. (2008) find evidence supportive of the Hansen model in their analysis of methods of payment by US acquirers. Where the targets are young companies at development stage (or are relatively intensive of intangible assets) and hence subject to high valuation risk, the announcement period abnormal return to acquirers is 6% (10%) compared to returns with non-development stage (less intangible intensive) targets of -6% (5%). The differences are statistically significant. Thus acquiring high risk targets with stock generates more value than acquiring them with non-stock consideration. See their Table IV.

25. With stock exchange offers, the bidder can protect target shareholders against adverse movements in relative share prices of bidder and target shares by offering derivative contracts in the form of caps, floors, and collars. This protection converts a fixed ER offer to a fixed exchange value offer within agreed bounds of relative share price movements (see Sudarsanam 2010, ch. 16 on the structure of such derivative contracts).

26. Abnormal returns are returns in stock returns in excess of a "normal" or benchmark return. In the empirical finance literature, there is a wide range of benchmarks and abnormal returns can vary depending on the "normal" asset pricing model used. Traditionally, the most frequently employed model is the Capital Asset Pricing Model (CAPM) (see Sudarsanam 2010, ch. 4 for further discussion of the abnormal returns methodology).

27. Peterson and Peterson (1991) attribute higher gains to targets in cash offers to the need to compensate for capital gains tax.

28. A bidder, instead of issuing new equity, may choose to buy back its shares ahead of a bid and re-issue it to target shareholders. To buy back the shares, it needs cash. This method is therefore effectively a cash offer. However, the rationale for this exercise is that it avoids the earnings and control dilution that accompanies a new share issue. Further the buy-back often raises the share price, thereby making the stock exchange more attractive. There may also be tax advantages to this two-stage process if target shareholders demand a higher price to compensate them for any CGT in a straight cash offer. See Wilber (2007).

29. See Morellec and Zhdanov (2008) for further development of this model. They also cite evidence that, post-takeover, the leverage of the merged entity increases and argue that this is supportive of their model.

30. It could be argued that banks' and bidder shareholder interests are not always aligned and that banks may influence bidder managers to make acquisitions that serve their interests, e.g. risk reducing diversifying acquisitions. The evidence is, however, more consistent with robust monitoring by banks to the benefit of shareholders.

31. In some cases preventing the defection of key managers to rivals or to set up their own shop, rather than retention, may motivate an earnout. See Marino (2008).

32. See *Mergers and Acquisitions, Almanac,* February 2002. Kohers and Ang provide evidence that earnouts are rarely used in public company takeovers in the US. In their sample of 938 acquisitions with earnout during 1984 to 1996, 96% are non-public targets, i.e. private companies or divested subsidiaries. The earnout component as a proportion of the deal value is 45% (average value $10.4m) for private companies and 33% ($27.2m) for divested subsidiaries. Earn-outs are generally used in small or medium-sized deals. They are difficult to use in public company acquisitions because the target managers generally own only a fraction of the firm equity. In the US, during 1997–2001, the total number, value of M&A deals, and the earnout component of the value are respectively 737, $94bn, and 22bn. The earnout value represents 24% of the deal value. See also Officer et al. (2008) who report that the proportion of earnouts in their sample is about 9%.

33. In a European sample of 4342 acquisitions during 1997–2000, Faccio and Masulis (2005) report 478 with earnouts.

34. *SAQ* is the value-weighted returns of the serial acquirers' portfolio minus the one-month Treasury bill. *OCC* is the value-weighted returns of occasional acquirers' portfolio minus the one-month Treasury bill. *MKT* is the excess return on the market portfolio, which is the value-weighted return on all NYSE, AMEX, and NASDAQ stocks (from CRSP) minus the one-month Treasury bill rate. In order to facilitate our comparison, we set the full index levels of these three portfolios to 100 on January 1, 1994. For SAQ and OCC, the acquirer stock is placed in the portfolio at announcement and then held in the portfolio for three years when it leaves the portfolio. For further details, see Sudarsanam and Huang (2007).

35. This evidence is consistent with results reported by Harding and Rovit (2004). In a sample of 110 US acquirers making at least 20 deals during the sample period 1986–2001, constant

acquirers outperformed those making acquisitions only during recessions, growth phase, or the period in between in an economic cycle. Continuous acquirers in Europe (sample of 52) outperformed early acquirers in an economic cycle and both outperformed late acquirers. The sample sizes are small and the study does not provide tests of significance of the intra-group differences (see Figures A-2 and A-3, p. 183).

36. They conclude that this listing effect is still strong after controlling for other relevant factors. For the US, see Ang and Kohers (2001) who report 1 to 2% significant two-day CARs for all private targets, whereas for public companies the CAR is either negative or insignificant. See also Masulis et al. (2007); Chang (1998); and Fuller et al. (2002). For UK studies reporting similar results, see Antoniou et al. (2007), and Draper and Paudyal (2006).

37. Among the reasons for this superior performance of private company acquirers are: (1) No free-ride and hold up: private companies have concentrated ownership often held by the founder and his family. In a public company with dispersed ownership, individual shareholders can hold up tendering their shares and thereby reduce the chances of a successful bid unless the premium offered to target shareholders is high. In a private company, such free-riding is not possible, thereby reducing the bid premium. (2) Liquidity discount: for owners a takeover is a way of encashing their equity invested in the target firm. The offer price from the bidder reflects this liquidity discount and is therefore lower than for a public target whose shares are traded on a stock market. This effect should be larger for relatively large targets. Available empirical evidence suggests that the median liquidity discount may be as high as 17%. (3) Post-acquisition monitoring: since the owners of the target, in a stock for stock deal, become block shareholders in the acquirer, they can monitor the latter's performance. The stock market reaction on announcement reflects this positively. If this were true, we would expect to see higher acquirer returns on stock offers than on pure cash offers. Since stock exchange acquisitions of private companies are a small fraction of cash acquisitions, this cannot be a very strong reason for the higher-value gains.

38. This superior performance of acquirers of private companies is, however, not sustained in long-term returns. Over a three-year post-acquisition period, their abnormal returns are either zero or negative. For the UK and the same period, acquirers of both public and private targets experience significant value losses, but these are larger in the former case (−0.6% vs. −0.4% respectively) (see Antoniou et al. 2007) Note that this sample consists only of multiple, i.e. repeat acquirers.

39. Relative size of target to acquirer is normally one of several "control" variables used in multiple regressions of returns to acquirers on explanatory variable. These are too numerous to list here. For example, see Faccio et al. (2006) or Masulis et al. (2007).

40. See Officer et al. (2008, Tables VI and VII), where target size is measured relative to the acquirer's size. This result may be due to large public targets having greater negotiating power against bidders and the free-rider problem is much more severe in large public targets than in large private targets where large block shareholdings are more likely.

41. In contrast to RBS, which had to be rescued by the UK government in a bail-out, Barclays, which had been outbid by RBS for ABN, did not seek or accept any government bail-out offer. Barclays had a fortunate escape. RBS bought ABN not only at the top of the stock market but also in an auction against Barclays. A double dose of winner's curse indeed!

42. See Baghai et al. (2008), who note that companies often "freeze" in a downturn, more so than in an upturn—60% compared to 40%—and forego many value-creating acquisition opportunities.

43. For evidence that buyers in a recession earn better returns for their shareholders than acquirers during a growth phase or between recession and growth, see Harding and Rovit (2004). In a sample of 110 US acquirers making at least 20 deals during the sample period 1986–2001, constant acquirers outperformed those making acquisitions only during recession, the growth phase, or the period in between in an economic cycle.

44. Moeller et al. (2004). Their measure of bid premium is 50-day target value difference to announcement day. For the UK, see Antoniou et al. (2008). Interestingly, they report that the combined announcement period abnormal returns to bidders and targets are positive and significant, suggesting market expectation of synergies. According to the authors, since these synergies are already capitalized at announcement, the acquirers experience zero post-acquisition abnormal returns. A high premium, when driven by expected synergies, may lead to deeper restructuring of the merged firms, e.g. larger job losses, than a low premium, since the high premium acquirer has to work harder to justify the high price paid for the target. For a test of this proposition, see Krishnan et al. (2007). Laamanen (2007) argues that a high premium may reflect target valuation difficulties and not overpayment. For a sample of 458 acquisitions they find that, although high premia are paid for R&D-related assets, these acquirers do not suffer negative abnormal returns.

45. A respected portfolio manager, Gordon Crawford, reflecting on the AOL–TW merger said of Jerry Levin, the CEO of TW and one of the prime movers behind the deal: "This was a breathtaking deal. Everyone was surprised by it. But it turned out to be the wrong company at the wrong time and at the wrong price. *The crux of the issue here is Levin's ego.... Levin got caught up in his self-image as a leading thinker about transformative technology*" (Bruner 2005: 278; emphasis added). Crawford does not fault Levin's vision about the internet, but the timing of the deal, the choice of the merger partner, and the price paid to realize the vision.

46. The rogues' gallery of such leaders includes: Gary Winnick, Chairman of Global Crossing, made $735m from his stock holding in the company in the four years of his leadership while the company collapsed into bankruptcy; Kenneth Lay, chairman of Enron, Jeffrey Skilling, the CEO and Andrew Fastow, the CFO, were all convicted of fraud and other felonies; Dennis Kozlowski, the CEO of Tyco, was convicted of fraud, conspiracy, and grand larceny for looting his own company of $600m; and Bernie Ebbers, the CEO of Worldcom, was found guilty of accounting fraud amounting to $11bn. He was sentenced to a 25-year prison term. All these leaders "ignored the rules of civilized organizational behavior" since "narcissists often develop a sense of entitlement, believing that they deserve special treatment and that rules and regulations only apply to others" (Kets de Vries 2006: 28 and 39).

47. The behavior of Jean-Marie Messier, the CEO of the French conglomerate Vivendi Universal, who through a series of grandiose and expensive acquisitions led his company to the largest loss in French corporate history and to the brink of bankruptcy, reeks of narcissism. Jean-Marie Messier was granted the title of the "perfect Frenchman" by the French media. However, after the telecom bubble burst in 2000, Vivendi fell into substantial financial difficulties. Jean-Marie Messier was sacked and convicted of fraud. "Without his [Messier's] vision and personality—a strange blend of French technocratic arrogance, wannabe Hollywood showmanship and investment banker charm—Vivendi Universal would never have come into existence. Without Jean-Marie Messier's weakness—a love of deal-making, self-promotion, obfuscation and risk—the dream of a French champion might have survived" (Johnson and Orange 2003: 3).

48. Sudarsanam and Huang (2007) define a CEO as overconfident if he fails to exercise his stock option that is at least 67% in the money during the year prior to acquisition announcement. A risk-averse CEO may be expected to exercise such options when they are so deep in the money. The delay in exercise is treated as a measure of the CEO's high confidence that the future performance and, hence, its share price will be even higher and the value of the stock options will be even greater.

REFERENCES

Ang, J., & Kohers, N. (2001). "The Takeover Market for Privately Held Companies: The US Experience." *Cambridge Journal of Economics*, 25: 723–48.

Antoniou, A., Arbour, P., & Zhao, H. (2008). "How Much is Too Much: Are Merger Premiums Too High?" *European Financial Management*, 14/2: 268–87.

—— Petmetzas, D., & Zhao, H. (2007). "Bidder Gains and Losses of Firms Involved in Many Acquisitions." *Journal of Business Finance and Accounting*, 34/7–8:/ 1221–44.

Applegate, L. (2002). AOL Time Warner, Harvard Business School case 9-802-098.

Baghai, M., Smit, S. & Viguerie, P. (2008). "M & A Strategies in a Downmarket." *McKinsey Quarterly*, September.

Barkema, H., & Schijven, M. (2008). "Towards the Full Potential of Acquisitions: The Role of Organizational Restructuring." *Academy of Management Journal*, 51/4: 696–722.

Barbopoulos, L., & Sudarsanam, S. (forthcoming). "Determinants of Earnout as Acquisition Payment Currency and Bidder's Value Gains." *Journal of Banking and Finance*.

Bernardo, A., & Chowdhry, B. (2002). "Resources, Real Options and Corporate Strategy." *Journal of Financial Economics*, 63: 211–34.

Bharadwaja, A., & Shivdasani, A. (2003). "Valuation Effects of Bank Financing in Acquisitions." *Journal of Financial Economics*, 67: 113–48.

Bliss, R., & Rosen, R. (2001). "CEO Compensation and Bank Mergers." *Journal of Financial Economics*, 61/1: 107.

Bouwman, C., Fuller, K. P., & Nain, A. (2003). "Stock Market Valuation and Mergers." *Sloan Management Review*, 45/1: 9–11.

Bowman, E., & Moskowitz, G. T. (2001). "Real Options Analysis and Strategic Decision Making." *Organization Science*, 12/6: 772–7.

Bradley, M., & Sundaram, A. (2004). "Do Acquisitions Drive Performance or Does Performance Drive Acquisitions?" SSRN Working Paper.

Bruner, R. (2004). "The Merger of Hewlett-Packard and Compaq (B): Deal Design." Darden Business School case (UVA-F-1451).

—— (2005). *Deals from Hell, M & A Lessons that Rise Above the Ashes*. New Jersey: Wiley.

Burt, T., Mason, J., & Harnischfeger, U. (2000). "Tracinda Gains More Support for Lawsuit." *Financial Times*, 29 November

Chang. S (1998). "Takeovers of Privately Held Targets, Methods of Payment and Bidder Returns." *Journal of Finance*, 53: 773–84

Chatterjee, A., & Hambrick, D. (2007). "It's All About Me: Narcissistic CEOs and their Effects on Company Strategy and Performance." *Administrative Science Quarterly*, 52: 351–86.

Coakley, J., & Iliopoulou, S. (2006). "CEO Compensation for Bidders in UK M & As," *European Financial Management*, 12/4: 609–31.

Damodaran, A (2000). "The Promise of Real Options." *Journal of Applied Corporate Finance*, 13/20 (Summer): 29–44.

—— —— (2001). *The Dark Side of Valuation*. New York: *Financial Times*–Prentice Hall.

Davoudi, S., & Burgess, K. (2007). *Financial Times*, 17 June.

Dimson, E., Marsh, P., & Staunton, M. (2008). "The Worldwide Equity Premium: A Smaller Puzzle." Available at <http://ssrn.com/abstract=891620>.

Doukas, J., & Petmezas, D. (2006). "Acquisitions, Overconfident Managers and Self-Attribution Bias." Working Paper, Old Dominion University.

Draper, P., & Paudyal, K. (1999). "Corporate Takeovers: Mode of Payment, Returns and Trading Activity." *Journal of Business Finance & Accounting*, 26/5–6: 521–58.

—— —— (2006). "Acquisitions: Private vs Public." *European Financial Management*, 12: 57–80.

Eccles, R. (1999). "Are You Paying Too Much for that Acquisition?" *Harvard Business Review*, July–August: 136–46.

Eckbo, E., Giammarino, R., & Henkel, R. (1990). "Asymmetric Information and the Medium of Exchange in Takeovers." *Review of Financial Studies*, 3: 651–75.

—— & Langohr, H. (1989). "Information Disclosure, Method of Payment and Takeover Premiums." *Journal of Financial Economics*, 24: 363–403.

Elton, G., & Eddigen, R. (2006). "Top Tips to Make the Best Acquisition or Not." *Financial Times* (FTfm), 27 May.

Emery, G., & Switzer, J. A. (1999). "Expected Market Reaction and the Choice of Method of Payment for Acquisitions." *Financial Management*, 28/4: 73–86.

Faccio, M., & Masulis, R. W. (2005). "The Choice of Payment Method in European Mergers & Acquisitions." *Journal of Finance*, 60/3: 1345–88.

—— McConnell, J., & Stolin, D. (2006). "Returns to Acquirers of Listed and Unlisted Targets." *Journal of Financial and Quantitative Analysis*, 41/1: 197–220.

Firth, M. (1991). "Corporate Takeovers, Stockholder Returns and Executive Rewards." *Managerial and Decision Economics*, 12: 421–8.

Fishman, M. (1989). "Preemptive Bidding and the Role of the Medium of Exchange in Acquisitions," *Journal of Finance*, 44/1: 41–57.

Franks, J., Harris, R., & Mayer, C. (1988). "Means of Payment in Takeovers: Results for the UK and the United States," in A. J. Auerbach (ed.), *Corporate Takeovers: Causes and Consequences*. Chicago, IL: University of Chicago Press.

Fuller, K., Netter, J., & Stegemoller, M. (2002). "What do Returns to Acquiring Firms Tell Us? Evidence from Firms that Make Many Acquisitions." *Journal of Finance*, 57: 1763–93.

Gilson, S. (2004). "Seagate Technology Buyout." Harvard Business School case 9-201-063.

Graham, J., Lemmon, M. L., & Wulf, J. G. (2002). "Does Corporate Diversification Destroy Value?" *Journal of Finance*, 52, April: 695–720.

Grinstein, Y., & Hribar, P. (2004). "CEO Compensation and Incentives: Evidence from M & A Bonuses." *Journal of Financial Economics*, 73/1: 119–43.

Hansen, R. (1987). "A Theory for the Choice of Exchange Medium in Mergers and Acquisitions." *Journal of Business*, 60: 75–95.

Harding, D., & Rovit, S. (2004). *Mastering the Merger*. Boston, MA: Harvard Business School Press.

Harford, J. & Li, K. (2007). "Decoupling CEO Wealth from Firm Performance: The Case of Acquiring CEOs." *Journal of Finance*, 62: 917–49.

Haunschild, P., Davis-Blake, A., & Fichman, M. (1994). "Managerial Overcommitment in Corporate Acquisition Processes." *Organization Science*, 5/4, November: 528–40.

Hayward, M. L. A. & Hambrick, D. C. (1997). "Explaining the Premiums Paid for Large Acquisitions: Evidence of CEO Hubris." *Administrative Science Quarterly*, 42: 103–27.

Heaton, J. (2002). "Managerial Optimism and Corporate Finance." *Financial Management*, 31: 33–45.

Heron, R., & Lie, E. (2002). "Operating Performance and the Method of Payment in Takeovers." *Journal of Financial and Quantitative Analysis*, 37/1: 137–55.

Houston, J. F., James, C., & Ryngaert, M. D. (2001). "Where do Merger Gains Come From? Bank Mergers from the Perspective of Insiders and Outsiders." *Journal of Financial Economics*, 60: 285–331.

Huang, Y., & Walkling, R. A. (1987). "Target Abnormal Returns Associated with Acquisition Announcements, Payment Method, Acquisition Form and Managerial Resistance." *Journal of Financial Economics*, 19: 329–49.

Kets de Vries, M. (2006). *The Leader on the Couch: A Clinical Approach to Changing People and Organizations*. San Francisco, USA: Josey-Bass, 24–5.

Khorana, A., & Zenner, M. (1998). "Executive Compensation of Large Acquirers in the 1980s." *Journal of Corporate Finance*, 4: 209–40.

Klasa, S., & Stegemoller, M. (2007). "Takeover Activity as a Response to Time-Varying Changes in Investment Opportunity Sets: Evidence from Takeover Sequences." *Financial Management*, 36/2, Summer:19–43, Table XII.

Kogut, B., & Kulatilaka, N. (2001). "Capabilities as Real Options." *Organization Science*, 12/6: 744–58.

Kohers, N., & Ang, J. (2000). "Earnouts in Mergers and Acquisitions: Agreeing to Disagree and Agreeing to Stay." *Journal of Business*, 73: 445–76.

—— & Kohers, T. (2001). "Takeovers of Technology Firms: Expectations vs Reality." *Financial Management*, 30: 35–54.

Krishnan, H., Hitt, M. A., & Park, D. (2007). "Acquisition Premiums, Subsequent Workforce Reductions and Post-Acquisition Performance." *Journal of Management Studies*, 44/5: 709–32.

Johnson, J., & Orange, M. (2003). *The Man Who Tried to Buy the World: Jean-Marie Messier and Vivendi Universal*. London: Penguin Books Ltd.

Laamanen, T (2007). "On the Role of Acquisition Premium in Acquisition Research." *Strategic Management Journal*, 28: 1359–69.

Lambert, R. A., & Larcker, D. F. (1987). "Executive Compensation Effects of Large Corporate Acquisitions." *Journal of Accounting and Public Policy*, 6: 231–43.

Lamont, O., & C. Polk (2002). "Does Diversification Destroy Value? Evidence from Industry Shocks." *Journal of Financial Economics*, 63: 51–77.

Langevoort, D. (1997). "Organized Illusions: A Behavioral Theory of Why Corporations Mislead Stock Market Investors (and Cause Other Social Harms)." *University of Pennsylvania Law Review*, 101: 142–3.

Lovallo, D., & Kahneman, D. (2003). "Delusions of Success: How Optimism Undermines Executives' Decisions." *Harvard Business Review*, 56, July: 57–8.

Luehrman, T. (1998a). "Investment Opportunities as Real Options: Getting Started on the Numbers." *Harvard Business Review*, July/August: 51–67.

—— (1998b). "Strategy as a Portfolio of Real Options." *Harvard Business Review*, September/October: 89–99.

Lundholm, R., & Sloan, R. (2007). *Equity Valuation and Analysis*. New York: McGraw-Hill–Irwin.

Malmendier, U., & Tate, G. (2005). "CEO Overconfidence and Corporate Investment." *Journal of Finance*, 60: 2662–700.

——— (2008). "Who Makes Acquisitions? CEO Overconfidence and the Market's Reaction." *Journal of Financial Economics*, 89: 20–43.

March, J., & Shapira, Z. (1987). "Managerial Perspective on Risk and Risk-Taking." *Management Science*, 33: 1404–18.

Marino, J. (2008). "Resisting Defection." *Mergers and Acquisitions*, 43/10, October: 60–1.

Martynova, M., & Renneboog, L. (2006). "Mergers and Acquisitions in Europe," in L. Renneboog (ed.), *Advances in Corporate Finance and Asset Pricing*. Amsterdam: Elsevier.

Masulis, R., Wong, C., & Xie, F. (2007). "Corporate Governance and Acquirer Returns." *Journal of Finance*, 62/4: 1851–89.

Moeller, S., Schlingemann, F. P., & Stulz, R. (2004). "Firm Size and the Gains from Acquisitions." *Journal of Financial Economics*, 73: 201–28.

Morellec, E., & Zhdanov, A. (2008). "Financing and Takeovers." *Journal of Financial Economics*, 87: 556–81.

Officer, M., Poulsen, A., & Stegemoller, M. (2008). "Target-Firm Information Asymmetry and Acquirer Returns." *Review of Finance*, 1: 1–27

Palepu, K., Healy, P. M., Bernard, V. L., & Peek, E. (2007). *Business Analysis and Valuation*. London: Thomson Learning.

Peterson, D., & Peterson, P. P. (1991). "The Medium of Exchange in Mergers and Acquisitions." *Journal of Banking and Finance*, 15: 383–405.

Pfeffer, J. (2007). *What Were They Thinking? Unconventional Wisdom about Management*. Boston, MA: Harvard Business School Press.

Pozen, R. (2008). "Corporate Portfolio Management Roundtable." *Journal of Applied Corporate Finance*, 20/2: 12–14.

Rappaport, A. (1986). *Creating Shareholder Value*. New York: Free Press.

Rau, R., & Vermaelen, T. (1998). "Glamour and the Post-acquisition Performance of Acquiring Firms." *Journal of Financial Economics*, 49: 223–53.

Roll, R. (1986). "The Hubris Hypothesis of Corporate Takeovers." *Journal of Business*, 12/1986: 371–86.

Rovenpor, J. (1993). "The Relationship between Four Personal Characteristics of Chief Executive Officers and Company Merger and Acquisition Activity." *Journal of Business and Psychology*, 8/1: 27–55.

Scott, T. (1996). "Tax Planning," in *Company Acquisitions Handbook*. Croydon: Tolley Publishing Co. Ltd.

Shefrin, H. (2007). *Behavioral Corporate Finance*. New York: McGraw-Hill.

Sherman, S., & Janatka, D. A. (1992). "Engineering Earn-Outs to Get Deals Done and Prevent Discord." *Mergers and Acquisitions*, September/October: 26–31.

Smit, H. (2001). "Acquisition Strategies as Option Games." *Journal of Applied Corporate Finance*, 14/2: 79–89.

——— & Trigeorgis, L. (2004). *Strategic Investment, Real Options and Games*. Princeton, NJ: Princeton University Press.

Smith, K., & Triantis, A. J. (1995). "The Value of Options in Strategic Acquisitions," in L. Trigeorgis (ed.), *Real Options in Capital Investment: Models, Strategies and Applications*. Westport, CT: Praeger.

Sudarsanam, S. (2010). *Creating Value from Mergers and Acquisitions: The Challenges* (2nd ed.). Harlow: *Financial Times*–Pearson.

—— & Gao, L. (2004). "Value Creation in UK High Technology Acquisitions." Financial Management Association (USA) Annual Meeting, New Orleans, October.

—— & Huang, J. (2007). "Executive Compensation and Managerial Overconfidence: Impact on Risk Taking and Shareholder Value in Corporate Acquisitions," in G. N. Gregoriou & L. Renneboog (eds.), *International Mergers and Acquisitions Activity since 1990: Recent Research and Quantitative Analysis*. Amsterdam: Elesevier.

—— —— (2008). "Are CEOs Bidding for Higher Pay? Evidence from Firms that Make Serial Acquisitions." Cranfield School of Management Working Paper, March.

—— & Mahate, A. (2003). "Glamour Acquirers, Method of Payment and Post-acquisition Performance: The UK Evidence." *Journal of Business Finance & Accounting*, 30: 299–341.

Travlos, N. (1987). "Corporate Takeover Bids, Methods of Payment and Bidding Firms' Stock Returns." *Journal of Finance*, 42/4: 943–63.

Tversky, A., & Kahneman, D. (1974). "Judgement under Uncertainty: Heuristics and Biases." *Science*, 185: 1124–31.

Vilalonga, B. (2004). "Diversification Discount or Premium? New Evidence from the Business Information Tracking Series." *Journal of Finance*, 59/2: 479–506.

Welch, J. (2001). *What I've Learned Leading a Great Company and Great People*. London: Headline.

Wilber, R. (2007). "Why do Firms Repurchase Stock to Acquire Another Firm?" *Review of Quantitative and Financial Analysis*, 29: 155–72.

Wulf, J. (2004). "Do CEOs in Mergers Trade Power for Premium? Evidence from 'Mergers of Equals,'" *The Journal of Law, Economics and Organization*, 20: 60–101.

CHAPTER 9

....

STRUCTURING THE TRANSACTION

....

RICHARD J. JOSEPH AND BILL RYAN

INTRODUCTION

....

Despite doubts that mergers create significant economic value, merger and acquisition (M&A) activity sharply increased in the New Millennium. While the reasons for this phenomenon are many and varied (see Part I of this *Handbook*), this chapter will focus on an important phase in the merger process: deal structuring. In doing so, it will draw primarily on the US experience, while placing deal structuring in a broader market context.

To date, researchers have devoted considerable attention to the pre-acquisition phase. Sherman and Hart (2006) identify 14 steps in this phase, including defining acquisition objectives, assembling an acquisition team, conducting due diligence, structuring the transaction, arranging for acquisition financing, and pursuing negotiations. Under a similar approach, DePamphilis (2005) breaks down the pre-acquisition phase into several distinct steps that include developing an acquisition plan, searching for acquisition candidates, screening for finalists, valuing a potential target company, and developing an integration plan.

Likewise Erkkilä (2001) identifies four main stages in the acquisition process, namely, devising an acquisition strategy, identifying and screening potential acquisition candidates, buying or acquiring, and integrating. Voss (2007) characterizes the pre-acquisition, or "preparation," phase as proceeding in five steps: formulating strategy, screening candidates, selecting a target company, justifying the acquisition, and reaching an investment decision. Finally, Ashkenas, DeMonaco, and Francis (1998) divide this phase into several distinct categories, including complying with applicable regulations, drafting a letter of intent, announcing the transaction, concluding an agreement, and closing the deal. (For a more detailed discussion of the pre-acquisition phase, see Chapter 7 of this *Handbook*.)

While the current literature supplies useful categories for delineating the pre-acquisition process (Happonen 2009), relatively little has been written about the technical aspects of deal structuring, including key factors that influence how the deal is structured. As a general guideline, "deal structuring" refers to the specific process of defining the terms of the transaction, identifying the parties to the merger, and selecting appropriate consideration, all within a given contractual, regulatory, statutory, and constitutional framework, with the ultimate aim of achieving a reasonably foreseeable institutional outcome. By elaborating on this process, this chapter will attempt to bridge the research gap and thus foster a better understanding of a critical component of the merger process.

The chapter proceeds as follows: first, it presents an overview of the context of deal structuring, with particular emphasis on trends in the United States and Europe. It then explains the "continuity of interest" principle, a judicial doctrine that has influenced deal structuring in the United States since the 1930s. Next, it discusses a variety of strategic, institutional, operational, and regulatory factors that influence how the deal is structured. (A more elaborate listing of these factors is presented as an appendix to this chapter.) The chapter then critiques conventional accounting methods by which transactional outcome has been analyzed, and presents a new accounting paradigm that could provide greater insights into how the deal is structured. It offers examples of European merger deals that bear on the "value added" by transactional form. Finally, it proposes ways in which non-workable deals can be "unstructured" to accommodate key stakeholder interests.

Although the sections relating to "continuity of interest," corporation and securities law, and tax accounting are US-specific, because US policies relating to M&A have inspired the formulation of M&A policies in other parts of the world, they are relevant to a discussion of transactional structuring in general. The exposé of recent market trends is intended to place the more technical aspects of deal structuring in broader market perspective.

The Context of Deal Structuring

As most companies that are non-serial acquirers (see Chapter 6 for a discussion on serial acquirers) engage in merger activity infrequently, M&A deals are generally regarded as extraordinary transactions to be concluded expeditiously so that managers can get on with the "normal" course of business (Ashkenas et al. 1998). Just as company M&A activity remains infrequent, so too there is a sense of cyclicality in the overall environs of M&A, particularly in Europe (Golbe and White 1993). By far the most active period was in the 1990s, i.e. the fifth merger wave (see Chapter 2), when European M&A activity reached a level comparable to that attained in the United States. Increasing globalization, the expanded use of the euro, government deregulation and privatization, and the explosive growth of financial markets, all served as catalysts for an acceleration of European M&A activity.

As an example of this trend, in 2010, the number and value of M&A deals in Europe stood at slightly less than 3,800 and $268 billion, respectively, relative to 2,955 and $187

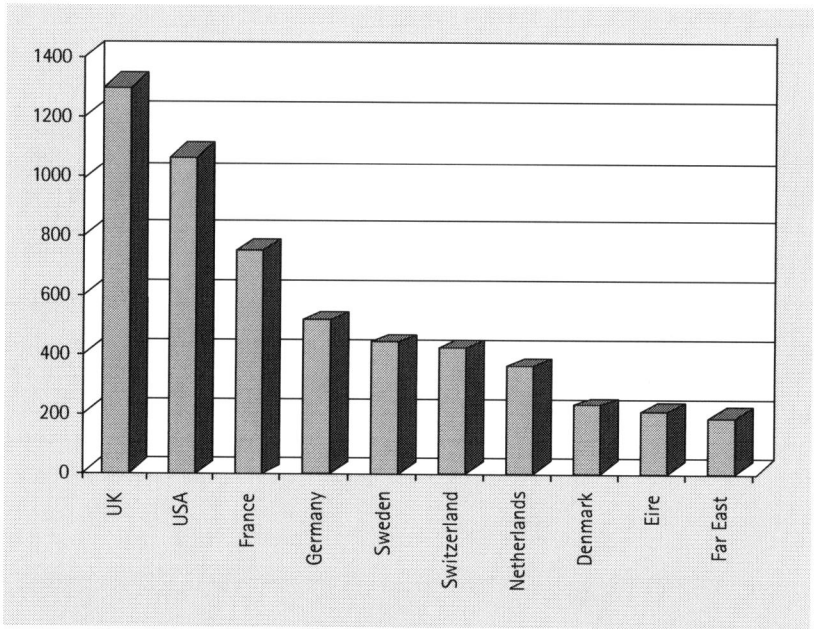

FIG. 9.1 Number of deals of European cross-border activity by country, 1985–1995

Source: Angwin and Savill (1997).

billion for deals in the United States in roughly the same period (Factset, Mergerstat, August 2010). Compared with the 1980s, European merger activity in the 1990s displayed phenomenal growth, with UK companies leading the way.

Underlying this broad market trend were fundamental technical principles relating to deal structuring. In the United States, where the M&A legal and institutional infrastructure is perhaps more established and integrated than that in Europe, one such principle is "continuity of interest."

STRUCTURING THE DEAL: THE "CONTINUITY OF INTEREST"

In the US market, the universe of merger transactions falls into two broad categories: taxable and non-taxable. A key factor that differentiates the two is "continuity of interest," a judicial doctrine articulated by US courts (*Cortland Specialty Co. v. Commissioner*, 1932, and US Treasury Regulation Sec. 1.368-1). In general, non-taxable transactions effectively "continue" a shareholder's interest in the enterprise, whilst taxable transactions "discontinue" this interest. What is the rationale for this doctrine and what are its implications for structuring the deal?

Continuity of interest embodies two key propositions to stakeholders. The first proposition implies liquidating the stakeholder's investment in return for specific benefits. The second implies exchanging this investment for equivalent rights in a reorganized business. The ensuing effect of the first proposition is *taxability* (Internal Revenue Code (IRC) Sec. 1001 and US Treasury Regulation Sec. 1.368-1). The corresponding effect of the second is *tax deferral* (IRC Secs. 354, 361, and 1032). These effects seem disparate and inconsistent. They raise a fundamental question: Why is continuity of interest preferred, and why does it result in more favorable tax treatment?

From a policy perspective, continuity of interest promotes capital retention in a reorganized business. It ensures that parties to a merger have sufficient resources to perpetuate a going concern without resorting to additional financing. But why not institute a tax regime that facilitates, and even promotes, the liquidation of unproductive stakeholder investments? Why not encourage stakeholders to channel their capital to efficient ventures that promise the highest return?

A tax regime that makes "discontinuity of interest" (i.e. liquidating a stakeholder investment) a taxable event effectively penalizes the diversion of capital to other, more productive, more efficient, and potentially more profitable ventures—or, at least makes the endeavor more costly. In the context of an increasingly globalized economy, such a regime risks subverting tax neutrality (Simons 1938) on an increasingly globalized scale. In light of this effect, should not "continuity of interest" be re-defined to encompass reinvesting capital in *any* productive enterprise? Should not the doctrine be reformed so as to penalize liquidating a stakeholder investment and diverting the proceeds to pure consumption?

Undoubtedly, taxing "discontinuity" can be justified on policy grounds. The State has a paramount interest in promoting the reorganization of productive resources so as to minimize economic disruption, promote social stability, increase organizational efficiency, and maximize wealth generation. However, defining "continuity of interest" in such a way as to exclude reinvestment in other, more productive ventures could ultimately disserve these ends. A tax policy based on so narrow a definition could in fact encourage the retention of capital in grossly inefficient, relatively unproductive, and marginally profitable businesses.

Under existing US policy, the tax benefits associated with continuity of interest do not accrue equally to every class of stakeholder. Rather, they accrue primarily to debt and equity investors whose interests are represented in the permanent capital structure of the enterprise. This policy appears to be premised on the "primacy of financial capital" in production and wealth generation. It neglects, for example, the contribution of labor to productivity, growth, and value creation. Accordingly, under the existing US tax regime, to compensate an employee with stock for services rendered would not be regarded as "continuity of interest," and thus would be taxable as "compensation." By contrast, in a reorganization, to compensate a lender with stock for credit extended would be regarded as "continuity of interest," and thus would be non-taxable as an equivalent stake.

Though biased toward investors, this essential principle underlies *the whole of US merger transactions*. The US taxability of these transactions depends, in the first instance, on whether the underlying interests are capital in character, and in the second instance, on whether these interests are continued through the exchange of "equivalent interests" (e.g. stock) or discontinued through the payment of substantially different "consideration" (e.g. cash). What constitutes an "equivalent interest" and substantially different "consideration" is statutorily defined (IRC Sec. 361(c)(2)(B)).

Accordingly, in most US merger transactions, if payment consists primarily of voting stock, and this stock is exchanged for voting stock in another party to the merger, the transaction generally is non-taxable. On the other hand, if payment consists primarily of cash or other assets, and such property is exchanged for voting stock in another party to the merger, the transaction generally is taxable. This basic tenet is key to understanding how the deal is structured.

Factors that Influence Transactional Form

While continuity of interest underlies the "economic substance" of a US merger transaction, a multiplicity of strategic, operational, and institutional factors influence "transactional form," that is, whether the merger should be conducted as an asset purchase or a stock purchase, and whether it should be structured as a simple merger, direct acquisition, triangular merger, or consolidation. Among these factors are high target company asset values, the concentration of target shareholdings, the complexity of applicable statutory procedures, the magnitude of target liabilities, the lack of cultural or operational synergies, distinct brands, peculiar business risks, and local regulations.

As a practical matter, the deal should be structured as a negotiated stock purchase or tender offer where target asset values exceed target share values, target shareholdings are concentrated in the hands of a single parent or relatively few investors, target management opposes a takeover, the acquiring company wants to utilize target tax attributes, or obtaining formal shareholder approval for a merger is impractical or difficult. On the other hand, the deal should be structured as an asset purchase where target fixed or contingent liabilities are substantial, target holds relatively few assets valued by the acquirer, or target plans to restructure or discontinue a line of business. Preserving target as a subsidiary of the acquirer makes sense where target and acquirer brands are distinct, their cultural or operational synergies are weak, or their business risks are substantially different. Structuring the deal as a triangular merger is advisable where, in addition to the foregoing factors, jurisdictional or regulatory issues weigh in favor of the cross-border merging of a subsidiary. Finally, a consolidation works well where both the acquirer and target find value in the creation of a new corporate entity to supplant pre-existing ones. (For a more detailed discussion of these factors, see Appendix 9.1.)

Acquiring with Cash or Stock

Another major factor that impacts transactional form is the liquidity of the acquiring firm. Indeed, the cash position of the acquirer and its access to acquisition financing bears heavily on the decision as to the type of consideration to be used. In general, low liquidity companies with poor access to bank financing are likely to use stock as consideration. High liquidity companies, and companies with easy access to bank financing, are likely to use cash. Hovakimian, Opler, and Titman (2001) draw a positive correlation between tangible asset values and debt capacity. They observe that companies with high tangible asset values generally have a greater capacity to issue debt and borrow from banks. This finding suggests that acquiring companies with high tangible asset values, and by implication substantial borrowing capacity, should structure the deal as a leveraged buyout, so as to take advantage of post-merger interest deductions.

Often, the type of offer made by the acquiring firm sends subtle signals to the market. In general, a cash offer signals that the acquirer intends to liquidate the interests of shareholders so as to exclude them from future investment risks and rewards. By contrast, a stock offer signals that the acquirer wants target shareholders to share these risks and rewards. If the acquiring firm believes that underlying target asset values are greater than the market value of target as a going concern, then logically it should structure the deal as a stock purchase, using either cash or acquirer stock as consideration. On the other hand, if the acquiring company believes that underlying target asset values are less than the market value of target as a going concern, then in principle, it should structure the deal as an asset purchase, using either cash or acquirer stock as consideration. A major factor in this decision is the expected market reaction to the type of consideration used. For example, if the acquirer uses cash, the market might view the cash-for-stock offer as a sign of target company undervaluation, triggering a positive correction to target company share price. On the other hand, if the acquirer uses stock, the market might view the stock-for-stock offer as ultimately diluting target company earnings per share, triggering a negative correction to target share price.

Regulations and Statutes

In many jurisdictions, two institutional factors weigh heavily against the use of stock as consideration: first, the disclosure requirements of that jurisdiction's securities law, and second, the procedural requirements of its corporation law.

Securities Law

If the acquirer's stock is publicly traded on a national securities exchange, the issuance of additional acquirer shares to purchase target stock or assets will be subject to national or local securities regulation (for example, US Securities Act of 1933 and the regulations thereunder), as well as the listing requirements of that exchange. These regulations and requirements mandate the full disclosure of material information relating to the acquirer, its officers, directors, and shareholders. Releasing such information could be sensitive to acquirer's principal stakeholders, especially if stock in acquirer is closely held.

Corporation Law

Moreover, the acquirer's capacity to issue additional shares could be limited by its articles of incorporation, or corporate charter. This instrument sets forth the number of shares that the acquirer is authorized to issue. If the number of additional shares required to purchase target stock or assets exceeds this limitation, the acquirer must amend its charter to increase the number of shares that it is authorized to issue. So doing would necessitate strict adherence to the procedural requirements of the jurisdiction's corporation law, including giving adequate notice to shareholders, and obtaining shareholder approval by a majority vote (see, for example, Delaware Corporation Law Sec. 242).

By implication, significant factors in the decision to use stock as consideration include the need to register additional shares with the appropriate regulatory authorities, list these shares on major securities exchanges, and register these shares in more than one jurisdiction; the time and cost required to register or list, the sensitivity of the information that must be disclosed; the feasibility of convening a shareholder's meeting to amend the corporation's charter; and the time required to convene such a meeting, in light of the notice and due process requirements of corporation law. By contrast, significant factors in the decision to use cash as consideration include the shareholders' interest in retaining voting control of the board of directors, and in maintaining a high level of earnings per share.

To summarize, the structure of the deal is influenced by a multiplicity of strategic, financial, operational, institutional, and legal factors, including the liquidity of the acquirer, its access to capital markets, legal restrictions, and securities exchange requirements. In a sense, these factors provide transactional form to economic substance based on continuity of interest.

TOWARD A NEW CONCEPTUAL PARADIGM

Typically, M&A deals in the US and Europe (and worldwide, bearing in mind the growing number of emerging market M&A deals) are structured on the basis of conventional accounting concepts and principles. On the one hand, these concepts and principles establish a uniform paradigm for planning and assessing transactional outcome. On the other hand, they are grossly deficient in representing social and economic realities, as well as underlying investment values. For example, they reveal little about disparities in market and book value that frequently inspire a takeover, social and economic interests that prevail in the outcome, and relationships among key stakeholders that are reinforced, discontinued, or modified as a result of a corporate reorganization. Moreover, they fail to account for key intangibles, such as human talent and organizational efficiency that add value to the enterprise as a whole.

These concepts have been derived from traditional accounting and corporation law, major tenets of which were formulated in the early stages of industrialization. They portray the corporation as an amorphous being, devoid of organization, skills, and know-how, the value of whose assets remains constant in the context of a fluctuating economic environment.

Richer concepts can be drawn from modern commercial practice, which assigns value to talent, technology, and organization, and from contemporary US and European bankruptcy law, which recognizes a hierarchy of stakeholders with divergent, often conflicting interests. These latter concepts capture the social and economic essence of a merger, as well as key considerations that often motivate M&A transactions. They portray the corporation as an association of stakeholders, each with differing objectives, bound by contract, organized in a productive venture, and united in the pursuit of wealth. Giving order to this collectivity is a system of governance defined by law and sanctioned by the State. Associated with it are peculiar fiscal obligations, legal entitlements, tax attributes, and stakeholder claims. These claims are fundamentally different, unequal, often competing, and at times irreconcilable.

Seen in this light, asset purchases tend to strengthen the hand of acquirer and target managers, who negotiate transactional value on behalf of their shareholders. By contrast, tender offers tend to undermine the position of target managers, who are neither privy to the deal nor a party to the merger. Consolidations ultimately reinforce the position of target shareholders, who exchange target rights for equity in an enlarged enterprise. Triangular mergers benefit acquirer shareholders, who insulate themselves from target liability, acquire non-transferable rights, and preserve acquirer brand and customer loyalty.

In a similar vein, mechanisms for assuming liabilities generally reinforce the position of target creditors in the reorganized business order. Such mechanisms include assumption of liabilities "by mutual assent," and assumption of liabilities "by operation of the law." Both mechanisms facilitate the substitution of a generally stronger debtor (i.e. the acquirer) for a generally weaker one (i.e. the target). In addition, they preserve the creditor's superior standing in the legal hierarchy of claims and preferences. Notwithstanding this order, the financial stake of acquirer and target creditors is likely to be jeopardized to the extent that the acquirer leverages off incremental debt. The risk of default can be minimized where pre-deal creditors subordinate this debt to their own financial claims.

In general, from a US stakeholder perspective, "continuity of interest" mergers based on stock-for-stock exchanges tend to weaken the position of both target and acquirer shareholders in the short run. For the issuance of additional acquirer shares both dilutes earnings per share and erodes shareholder voting control. On the other hand, by continuing the shareholder's capital interest, such mergers extend the shareholder's claim to the earnings and assets of a consolidated enterprise. Through the achievement of increased efficiency and improved productivity, corporate reorganization could ultimately lead to higher earnings per share and enhanced share value.

To some extent, the ultimate "losers" in the post-acquisition order are stakeholders whose essential interests are protected neither by contract nor by statute. Such stakeholders include at-will employees, short-term suppliers, temporary service providers, and non-contract labor. The claims of these stakeholders may be summarily dismissed or discontinued by management, subject to the due process requirements of the jurisdiction's labor law. On the other hand, if protected by contract, such interests must be respected by management, and "continued" until the contract is lawfully terminated. In principle, post-acquisition managers may not abridge the contract rights of stakeholders, absent a judicial proceeding.

Conceptually, this stakeholder view is consistent with that articulated by Freeman (1984), who has highlighted the distinct interests of a firm's principal constituents, such as suppliers, customers, employees, and "society-at-large." Along the same lines, Hillman and Keim (2001) have argued that adopting a stakeholder approach to business could ultimately benefit an enterprise by enabling it to develop long-term relationships with primary stakeholders, such as employees, suppliers, and customers; expand its value-creating networks; and as a result, improve its competitive advantage. Kay (1993) has pointed out that relational contracting in building a firm's "architecture" could be a major factor in the company's long-term success, for business relationships cannot be easily replicated or eroded by competitors. Mallin (2004) suggests that shareholders can play a critical social role, because they have a vested interest in ensuring that a company's resources be used efficiently for the benefit of society as a whole.

To return to the central argument, the existing conceptual paradigm for understanding transactional outcome is deficient in that it "dehumanizes" the process of deal structuring and understates the value of key intangibles. It portrays the corporation as an amorphous being, devoid of organization, skills, and know-how, the value of whose assets remains constant in a fluctuating economic environment. In so doing, it reveals little about disparities in value that frequently inspire a takeover, social and economic interests that prevail in the outcome, and stakeholder relationships that are impacted as a result of corporate reorganization. A new paradigm is needed to emphasize the primary role of stakeholders in the deal-structuring process. This paradigm should recognize the value of key intangibles such as human talent, efficient organization, and productive technology in the inexorable drive to merge. It should also shed light on the identity of stakeholders whose interests ultimately prevail in the transactional outcome.

ACCOUNTING FOR VALUE

For similar reasons, the current methodology for accounting for intangibles, and for reconciling intangible values with going-concern values warrants review and reform. From a merger perspective, equity markets assign value to the enterprise as a whole, while factor input markets (i.e. markets for raw materials, capital, and labor) assign value to its component parts. These parts include not only conventional assets, such as land, buildings, and equipment, but also unconventional assets, such as human talent, operational processes, distribution networks, and business organization. When equity values significantly diverge from factor values, arbitrage opportunities arise. Exploiting these opportunities to realize wealth is a recurring theme in successive merger waves.

Seen in this light, takeovers frequently are driven by a perceived disparity in equity and factor values, present and future, real and potential. They are consummated through a meticulous effort to realize these values through an extensive process of consolidation and reorganization. They are structured with a multiplicity of strategic, operational, marketing, and institutional objectives in mind. Their ultimate effect is to advance the interests of some, though not all, stakeholders, often to the detriment of other stakeholders.

Conventional US tax accounting offers little insight into the arbitrage effect of a merger. Rather, it provides a mixed bag of quantitative results that are inconsistent, anomalous, and confusing. These results hinge largely on whether the transaction preserves continuity of interest, and whether equity values exceed asset values. For example, where target interests are liquidated, and equity values exceed asset values, conventional tax accounting adjusts asset values to market, and records the excess of equity over asset values as amortizable "Goodwill" (US Treasury Regulation Sec. 1.338-6). Where target interests are liquidated, and asset values exceed equity values, conventional tax accounting adjusts asset values to market by order of liquidity, and records no amortizable Goodwill (ibid.). Where target interests are continued—regardless of any difference in equity and asset values—conventional tax accounting makes no adjustment to asset values and records no amortizable Goodwill. In the latter case, assets simply take a carry-over basis, and newly issued acquirer stock takes a substituted basis (IRC Sec. 362).

These results reveal little about disparities in value that could have motivated the merger, intangible factors that the merging parties might have valued highly, or to what material, human, and technological resources residual value, if any, should be assigned. Rather, they give the impression that the most liquid assets are the most essential, that asset values depend on "continuity of interest," and that the amorphous category "Goodwill" provides adequate insight into the factors that add value to the sum total of a corporation's component parts.

Basically, the problem is several-fold. Conventional tax accounting fails to adequately account for intrinsic factors that often represent the "crown jewels" of a merger. Such factors include managerial talent, employee skills, productive organization, efficient processes, distributional networks, and company brand. As a consequence, it assigns little or no value to these factors, which frequently play a key role in merger decisions. What residual value it does assign to these factors is relegated to the amorphous category "Goodwill." Moreover, as an inherent deficiency, conventional accounting records the value of non-liquid assets at historical cost. This approach often understates the value of key assets, such as real estate, that are highly coveted in an acquisition. In addition, conventional tax accounting adjusts asset and enterprise values to market only after the fact. Thus, Goodwill is created only after consummation of the merger, and the value of major tangibles, such as real estate, is adjusted to market only after acquirer has paid consideration. Finally, conventional accounting prescribes "expensing" in situations where "capitalization" would more adequately reflect pre-merger values. For example, the cost of product advertising that enhances company brand is typically expensed, instead of capitalized. Likewise, the cost of professional training that sharpens employee skills and improves productivity is usually expensed, instead of capitalized.

An alternative approach involves deconstruction, capitalization, periodic adjustment, and separate statement. Under this approach, the generic category "Goodwill" first would be deconstructed into special accounts designed to record intrinsic value. Such accounts might include "Human Resources," "Organization," "Distribution Channels," "Supplier Networks," and "Company Brand."

Second, costs assigned to these accounts would be capitalized, instead of expensed. Thus, for example, executive search fees and professional development outlays would be capitalized and allocated to "Human Resources." Likewise, the cost of a corporate restructuring would be capitalized and recorded in the "Organization" sub-account.

Third, periodically, and at least on an annual basis, the value of all assets and liabilities would be adjusted to market. These asset adjustments would be based on average market value per quarter, current costs, or projected costs discounted to present value. This approach is built on the assumption that if liquidated, such assets would command value in the marketplace. The liability adjustments would be based on benchmark short-, medium-, and long-term corporate bond rates, on the assumption that if extinguished through borrowed funds, such values would reflect the borrower's cost of capital.

Finally, the adjusted asset and liability values would be set forth in a separate valuation statement. Decoupled from the income statement, and devoid of retained earnings, this statement would supplement, not supplant, the traditional balance sheet.

A valuation statement would more adequately reflect asset, liability, and enterprise values. Its primary purpose would be to inform shareholders of the market value of their equity investment, creditors of the risks associated with the extension of credit, and managers/investors of net asset values, enterprise worth, and company solvency. Furthermore, by assigning value to intrinsic factors, capitalizing costs that contribute to enterprise value, and adjusting historical costs to market, valuation accounting would bring about a greater convergence in equity and factor values. It would bridge the "arbitrage gap" between market and book values and thus provide greater insight into the factors that contribute to enterprise wealth.

To summarize, under the current US tax regime, the methodology for accounting for intangibles and for reconciling intangible asset values with going-concern values is deficient in that it understates intrinsic asset values, offers little insight into the arbitrage effect of a merger, and generates quantitative results that are inconsistent, anomalous, and confusing. An alternative and more insightful approach would involve deconstruction, capitalization, periodic adjustment, and preparation of a separate valuation statement. Such a statement would supplement conventional financial statements, more adequately reflect asset, liability, and enterprise values, and thus contribute to a better understanding of factors that likely influenced the structure of the deal.

Intangibles from a European Perspective

In recent times, the notion of intangibles has taken on a new meaning in a European business environment characterized by "mentofacture," as opposed to manufacturing. This new knowledge-based environment poses methodological challenges for the European accounting profession, which for decades has debated appropriate standards for valuing internally developed "knowledge resources." A prime example is the case of UK soccer club Manchester United, which employed star player David Beckham early in his career. As Beckham's skill and talent increased over the years, so did his "value added." Under conventional accounting standards, Manchester United could not appropriately recognize and accrue this "value added" as an intangible asset. Yet clearly, from a market perspective, this value added was realizable: in 2007, when Beckham joined the Los Angeles Galaxy, the US soccer club valued his skill and talent (and by implication, his previous employer's unrecorded intangible) at more than $250 million.

The failure of European accounting to recognize and accrue human intangibles, such as employee skill and talent, has resulted in a gross understatement of the market value of certain company employers. Not surprisingly, professional, service, and sports firms, whose principal "knowledge resource" consists of human talent, generally command a premium in the market well above their stated book values. As a result of a perceived disparity between their "internal" and "external" worth, they typically become prime targets for acquirers, bent on realizing the market potential inherent in their unrecorded intangibles. To return to the Manchester United case, in the aftermath of Los Angeles Galaxy's bid for Beckham's skill and talent, debt-free UK soccer clubs became a magnet for investors. Ironically, Manchester United was acquired by a US investor, which valued the UK club's roster of human talent considerably more than the club's net worth.

Post-merger Divestitures

Mergers create not only synergies, but also incompatibilities. If these incompatibilities cannot be reconciled through marriage and integration, they generally must be addressed through divorce and separation. In a sense, mergers and divestitures go hand-in-hand, for that which cannot be effectively integrated, reconciled, or incorporated into the merged enterprise should be divested from the business. In the long run, divestitures frequently result in improved synergies, greater efficiencies, higher productivity, and increased profitability. US tax law provides a mechanism for the merged entity to divest itself of unwanted assets, business segments, or profit centers in a manner that benefits key stakeholders (IRC Sec. 355).

To avoid liability for US tax, the divesting firm (transferor) must transfer assets to one or more controlled corporations (controlled) in exchange for controlled stock. The transferor must then distribute the stock to its shareholders. The ensuing transactional result will depend on the number of controlled corporations to which assets are transferred, whether some or all of the assets are transferred, and the manner in which controlled stock is distributed to transferor shareholders; i.e. proportionately, disproportionately, or in exchange for transferor stock. The principal scenarios are three:

- First, if only some of transferor's assets are transferred to controlled, and controlled stock is distributed pro rata to all shareholders, the result is a "spin-off." In a spin-off, the shareholder group that owns transferor eventually acquires an equity stake in controlled.
- Second, if all of transferor's assets are transferred to more than one controlled, and the controlled stock is distributed pro rata to all shareholders in exchange for their transferor stock, the result is a "split-up." In a split-up, transferor eventually goes out of existence, and its former shareholders acquire an equity interest in more than one controlled.
- Third, if only some of transferor's assets are transferred to controlled, and controlled stock is distributed to some, though not all shareholders, in exchange for their transferor stock, the result is a "split-off." A split-off effectively divides the shareholder group into two or more groups, each group acquiring an equity stake in a separate controlled.

Each type of divestiture can be tailored to suit the business, strategic, and institutional needs of a merged enterprise and its shareholders. For example, if the merged entity wants to divest itself of a high-risk business segment, it might spin the segment off into a wholly-owned subsidiary. If it wants to divest itself of a non-synergistic subdivision, it might split off the subdivision into a separate sister company. If it wants to settle an intractable dispute between majority and minority shareholders, it might split up its business segments into two or more independent companies. Each type of transaction is not subject to US taxation so long as transferor shareholder interests are continued. Such interests are continued where controlled voting stock is distributed to transferor shareholders.

CONCLUSION

While much of the pre-deal literature focuses on the various phases of the M&A process, this chapter has elaborated on essential principles and factors underlying a key phase—deal structuring—with particular emphasis on US deals, and the broader global context of M&A transactions in general. In so doing, it has attempted to "bridge the gap" in the pre-deal literature relating to an essential M&A activity. It has also opened the door for future research in the areas of transactional accounting, reporting, and analysis; essential principles that shape deal structures in other parts of the world; the creation of a new conceptual paradigm for understanding the role of stakeholders in deal structuring, disparities in intangible value that often catalyze a transaction, and the identity of economic interests that ultimately prevail in the outcome.

As discussed in the chapter, a key principle underlying the whole of US merger transactions is "continuity of interest." This principle determines whether an M&A transaction is taxable to principal stakeholders, and by implication, how the deal should be structured to avoid or minimize taxability. In general, merger transactions that continue the stakeholders' interests are non-taxable, while merger transactions that discontinue these interests are taxable. Linked to the notion of "continuity" is the type of consideration used. In general, if the acquiring company uses voting stock to acquire the target company or its assets, stakeholder interests are "continued." By contrast, if the acquiring company uses cash to acquire the target company or its assets, stakeholder interests are "discontinued" (i.e. liquidated). While in a sense, continuity of interest underlies economic substance, a variety of strategic, operational, and institutional factors influence transactional form.

Finally, emanating from the essential "micro-activity" of deal structuring are broader M&A "macro-trends," including a recent surge in the number of cross-border deals and a steady increase in transactional value. Whether these numbers and value will translate into greater economic efficiency, productivity, and growth across borders is yet to be seen.

APPENDIX 9.1

TRANSACTIONAL STRUCTURE

Asset Purchase

In addition to those mentioned in this chapter, key factors that weigh in favor of structuring the deal as an asset purchase include the following:

The Value and Quality of Target Assets

In some situations, the acquirer will attach greater value to individual target assets than to target as a going concern. In such situations, the acquirer should structure the deal as an asset purchase. Typically, in an asset purchase, the acquirer contracts with target management to purchase specific assets. The target transfers title to, and conveys the assets in a bulk transfer. The acquirer pays consideration directly to the target. Such consideration may take the form of voting stock, which continues target shareholders' interest, or non-voting stock, which discontinues it. If substantially all the assets are conveyed, the target usually distributes the consideration to its shareholders and then liquidates.

The Nature and Extent of Target Liabilities

Likewise, if the acquirer wants to avoid responsibility for target debts, it should structure the deal as an asset purchase. In this type of transaction, the acquirer contractually agrees to assume some, all, or none of target liabilities. Thus, it may "cherry pick" the type and amount of liabilities it explicitly assumes. Those target liabilities not explicitly assumed by the acquirer generally become the responsibility of target directors.

However, in some jurisdictions, if the acquirer purchases substantially all of target assets, it is deemed to assume most, if not all, of target liabilities by operation of the law.

The Feasibility of Obtaining Shareholder Approval

In some jurisdictions, because the sale of substantially all of target assets is an "extraordinary event," the transaction requires shareholder approval by a significant margin. The feasibility of obtaining such approval will largely depend on the degree to which shareholdings are dispersed, the type and value of the consideration offered, and shareholder willingness to sell. The approval process is simplified where the target is "controlled" by a single parent corporation or by a few institutional investors. In the latter case, the majority holders of target shares typically negotiate the sale of target assets to the acquirer.

Stock Purchase

Factors that weigh in favor of structuring the deal as a stock purchase include the following:

Management Opposition

Where target management resistance to a takeover is strong, the acquirer should consider a stock purchase. Typically, in this type of transaction, the acquirer purchases target stock directly from target shareholders, who tender their shares to the acquirer. Where the majority of target shares are held by a few investors or by a parent corporation, a negotiated stock purchase is feasible. By contrast, where the majority of target shares are dispersed among numerous investors, a tender offer provides the best acquisition route.

Relatively High Asset Values

The deal also should be structured as a stock purchase where aggregate target asset values exceed total target share values. The value differential is usually reflected in the share price premium. It is realized if and when the acquirer subsequently sells target assets.

Corporate Integration or Separation

Following the acquisition, acquirer may merge the target into the acquirer, or preserve the target as a separate subsidiary. Merging the target into the acquirer is advisable where operational synergies, cultural compatibilities, and economies of scale so warrant. Preserving the target as a subsidiary is advisable in the following circumstances:

Target Licenses, Franchises, and Contracts are Exclusive or Non-transferable

Where merging the target into the acquirer would work a forfeiture of target contractual and proprietary rights, maintaining the target as a separate subsidiary should be considered. A parent-subsidiary relationship gives the acquirer effective control of the target, while preserving target non-transferable rights and licenses. For example, so as not to work a forfeiture of a non-transferable broadcast license, an acquirer of a broadcast company might maintain the licensee company as a separate subsidiary.

The Acquirer and Target have Peculiar Brands and Strong Customer Loyalties

Preserving the target as a subsidiary also makes sense where acquirer and target brands are unique, and customer loyalty to each is strong. In such situations, merging the target into the acquirer could significantly weaken their respective brands and erode their respective customer bases. By contrast, maintaining the target and acquirer as separate companies could significantly enhance the value of these intangibles through cross-branding and co-marketing.

The Risks Associated with Acquirer and Target Businesses are Substantially Different

Where target and acquirer business risks are dissimilar, maintaining the target as a separate subsidiary could serve to segregate and isolate these risks. In addition, because both parent and subsidiary enjoy limited liability, it could effectively insulate acquirer from target creditor claims. For example, following its acquisition of a consumer finance company, an automobile manufacturer might maintain the company as a separate subsidiary to insulate itself from the risks associated with a consumer credit business.

Acquirer and Target Synergies are Weak

Corporate cultures, operational processes, and business approaches that are difficult to integrate weigh in favor of preserving the target as a separate subsidiary. Because the cost of successfully integrating these cultures, processes, and approaches could be prohibitively high, segregating them could effectively avoid dysfunctionalities, improve efficiencies, and ensure acquirer control.

Tax Attributes

An additional consideration relating to how the deal should be structured concerns target tax attributes. Subject to limitations, these attributes may be used by the acquirer to reduce its overall tax liability.

In many jurisdictions, the tax attributes with which corporations are endowed include net operating and capital loss carry-overs, accounting methods, and tax credits. In general, mergers that continue stakeholder interests preserve these attributes. Mergers that liquidate these interests extinguish them. By implication, in non-taxable transactions where the acquirer uses voting stock to acquire target stock or assets, the successor entity may, subject to limitations, use target net operating losses to shelter income. By contrast, in taxable transactions where the acquirer uses cash to acquire target stock or assets, the successor entity derives no comparable tax benefit.

Selected Bibliography

Angwin, D. & Savill, B. (1997). "Strategic Perspectives on European Cross-Border Acquisitions: A View from Top European Executives." *European Management Journal*, 15: 423–35.

Ashkenas, R., DeMonaco, L., & Francis, S. (1998). "Making the Deal Real: How GE Capital Integrates Acquisitions." *Harvard Business Review*, 76/1: 165–78.

—— & Francis, S. (2000). "Integration Managers: Special Leaders for Special Times." *Harvard Business Review*, 78/6: 108–16.

Bower, J. (2001). "Not All M&As are Alike—And That Matters." *Harvard Business Review*, 79/3: 92–101.

Brockhaus, W. (1975). "Model for Success in Mergers and Acquisitions." *Sam Advanced Management Journal*, 40: 40–9.

Bruner, R. (2004). *Applied Mergers and Acquisitions*. New Jersey: John Wiley & Sons, Inc.

Burch, T. (2001). "Locking out Rival Bidders: The Use of Lock-Up Options in Corporate Mergers." *Journal of Financial Economics*, 60/1: 103–41.

Cartwright, S., & McCarthy, S. (2005). "Developing a Framework for Cultural Due Diligence in Merger and Acquisitions," in G. Stahl & M. Mendenhall, *Mergers and Acquisitions: Managing Culture and Human Resources*. Stanford, CA: Stanford University Press, 253–67.

Cools, K., Gell, J., and Roos, A. (2006). *Successful M&A: The Method in Madness*. Chicago: Boston Consulting Group.

Cullinan, G., Le Roux, J., & Weddigen, R. (2004). "When to Walk away from the Deal." *Harvard Business Review*, 82/4: 96–104.

Delaware Corporation Law Secs. 251–67.

DePamphilis, D. (2005). *Mergers, Acquisitions, and Other Restructuring Activities: An Integrated Apporoach to Process, Tools, Cases, And Solutions* (3rd ed.). San Diego, CA: Elsevier/Academic Press.

Dionne, J. (1988). "The Art of Acquisitions." *The Journal of Business Strategy*, 9/6: 13–17.

Erkkilä, K. (2001). *Haltuunoton ja yhdistämisen haasteet—integraatio yrityskaupassa*. Porvoo: WSOY.

Freeman, R. E. (1984). *Strategic Management: A Stakeholder Approach*. Boston, MA: Pitman publishing.

Golbe, D., & White, L. (1993). "Catch a Wave: The Time Series Behavior of Mergers." *Review of Economics and Statistics*, 75/3: 493–9.

Grundy, T. (1996). "Strategy, Acquisition, and Value." *European Management Journal*, 14/2: 181–8.

Happonen, E. (2009). "The Role of Pre-deal Management in Ensuring Correct M&A Decisions." Master's thesis, Helsinki University of Technology.

Harding, D., & Rouse, T. (2007). "Human Due Diligence." *Harvard Business Review*, 85/4: 124–31.

Haspeslagh, P., & Jemison, D. (1991). *Managing Acquisitions: Creating Value through Corporate Renewal*. New York: The Free Press.

Henderson, R., & Clark, K. (1990). "Architectural Innovation: Reconfiguring of Existing Product Technologies and the Failure of Established Firms." *Administrative Science Quarterly*, 35/1: 9–30.

Hillman, A. J., & Keim, G. D. (2001). "Shareholder Value, Stakeholder Management, and Social Issues: What's the Bottom Line?" *Strategic Management Journal*, 22/2: 125–39.

Hovakimian, A., Opler, T., & Titman, S. (2001). "The Debt Equity Choice." *Journal of Financial and Quantitative Analysis*, 36/1: 1–24.

Internal Revenue Code of 1986, as amended, and US Treasury Regulations thereunder.

Jemison, D., & Sitkin, S. (1986a). "Corporate Acquisitions: A Process Perspective." *Academy of Management Review*, 11/1: 145–63.

——— (1986b). "Acquisitions: The Process Can be a Problem." *Harvard Business Review*, 64/2: 107–10.

Kay, J. (1993). *Foundations of Corporate Success: How Business Strategies Add Value*. New York: Oxford University Press.

Lisle, C. (2008). "Commercial Due Diligence and the Nine Levers of Corporate Growth," in *International Mergers and Acquisitions*. Birmingham: Financier Worldwide, 133–6.

MacDougal, G., & Malk, F. (1970). "Master Plan for Merger Negotiations." *Harvard Business Review*, 48/1: 71–82.

Mallin, C. A. (2004). *Corporate Governance*. Oxford: Oxford University Press.

Marks, M. (1999). "Adding Cultural Fit to your Due Diligence Check List." *Mergers and Acquisitions*, 34/3: 14–20.

Mirvis, P., & Marks, M. (1992). "The Human Side of Merger Planning: Assessing and Analyzing." *Human Resource Planning*, 15: 69–93.

Nolop, N. (2007). "Rules to Acquire By." *Harvard Business Review*, 85/9: September: 129–39.

Officer, M. (2003). "Termination Fees in Mergers and Acquisitions." *Journal of Financial Economics*, 69/3: 431–67.

Ravid, A., & Spiegel, M. (1999). "Toehold Strategies, Takeover Laws and Rival Bidders." *Journal of Banking and Finance*, 23/8: 1219–42.

Reuer, J. (2005). "Avoiding Lemons in M&A Deals." *MIT Sloan Management Review*, 46/3: 15–17.

Salter, M., & Weinhold, W. (1981). "Choosing Compatible Acquisitions." *Harvard Business Review*, 59/1: January–February: 117–27.

Simons, Henry (1938). *Personal Income Taxation*. Chicago: University of Chicago Press.

Saorím-Iborra, M. (2008). "Time Pressure in Acquisition Negotiations: Its Determinants and Effects on Parties' Negotiation Behavior Choice." *International Business Review*, 17/3: 285–309.

Schweiger, D. (2002). "Merge Right." *Business and Economic Review*, 48/3: 3–11.

——— Csiszar, E., & Napier, N. (1994). "A Strategic Approach to Implementing Mergers and Acquisitions," in G. von Krogh, A. Sinatra, & H. Singh, *The Management of Corporate Acquisitions: International Perspectives*. New York: Palgrave, 23–49.

Selden, L., & Colvin, G. (2003). "M& A Needn't be a Loser's Game." *Harvard Business Review*, 81/6: 70–9.

Sherman, A., & Hart, M. (2006). *Mergers and Acquisitions from A to Z* (2nd ed.). New York: American Management Association, AMACOM.

Shleifer, A., & Vishney, R.W. (2003). "Stock Market Driven Acquisitions." *Journal of Financial Economics*, 70/3: 295–311.

Trautwein, F. (1990). "Merger Motives and Merger Prescriptions." *Strategic Management Journal*, 11: 283–95.

Voss, I. (2007). *M&A Capability Evolution*. Göttingen: Cuvillier Verlag.

CHAPTER 10

....

ACQUIRING DISTRESSED
AND BANKRUPT CONCERNS

....

SCOTT MOELLER AND MARIA CARAPETO

INTRODUCTION

....

The recent financial crisis which arguably started in April 2007 with the Chapter 11 bankruptcy of New Century Financial, the largest subprime lender in the US, has revived the debate on ways of resolving financial distress and their effectiveness. Jensen (1991), a keen supporter of the takeover approach whereby distressed targets are acquired either inside or outside bankruptcy, argues that mergers and acquisitions (M&A) are an effective means for resolving financial distress. This view is also shared more recently with others, including Betton et al. (2008). This chapter reports further on this important topic by bringing together updated research on issues related to the structure and success of the acquisition of distressed and bankrupt companies.

The acquisition of distressed targets is one of three routes to the reorganization of firms in financial distress, which together with corporate restructuring in the strict sense (asset, operational, financial, and managerial) and liquidation (piecewise sale), constitute the full portfolio of turnaround measures. Each of these three routes has variations, especially by country as will be noted later with their differing legal regimes and even differing cultural acceptances of some of these alternatives (that is, in some countries it is culturally more acceptable for management to allow their company to be placed into bankruptcy, for example). This chapter focuses on acquisitions of distressed and bankrupt concerns, and as such highlights the reasons why these deals take place, the importance of economic cycles and their effect on distressed and bankrupt sales levels, the differences between reorganization and liquidation as end-game alternatives, and the comparisons between the different processes used, such as auctions, "fire sale" discounts, and divestitures (including asset stripping). The chapter ends with a brief discussion of the financial services as an example of an industry that has recently been in distress and therefore presents timely examples of these activities.

Distinction between Deals involving
Distressed and Bankrupt Companies

It is useful first to look at how observers and researchers have identified some of the differences between distressed and bankrupt deals and what distinguishes them from deals involving "healthy" companies. Bankruptcy is easiest to define, because it is a legal term, albeit with differing definitions by country (and different terminology as well: for example, in the United Kingdom, the term "insolvency" is typically used). The definition of distress is less clear, but has been addressed by a number of studies.

It is not surprising to see that these target firms are typically highly leveraged and in economic distress, as noted by Hotchkiss and Mooradian (1998). Bergström et al. (2005) support Hotchkiss and Mooradian's findings, using data from Sweden, in so far as targets in mergers (those not involving a bankrupt firm) are more likely to have lower leveraging power compared to the bankrupt targets. However, Faccio and Sengupta (2006) argue that there should be more distressed mergers when targets are already highly leveraged, which is supported by the findings of Carapeto et al. (2009), who also provide some clarification on the type of distress that targets may be facing. Using global data, they show that, compared to acquisitions of healthy targets, distressed acquisitions involve acquirers and targets that are both generally smaller and more distressed. However, while distressed targets, as well as their respective industries, seem to suffer from both financial and economical distress, bankrupt targets are insolvent. Following Wruck's (1990) definitions of insolvency, distressed targets display flow-based insolvency and bankrupt targets show evidence of stock-based insolvency. In contrast, Buehler et al. (2006), using data from Switzerland, show that large firms are less likely to fail but more likely to merge, while Clark and Ofek (1994) argue that acquirers of distressed targets show similar performance to their industry peers.

The deals that include distressed and bankrupt targets occur in waves, as with overall M&A activity. It is well established that there have been six merger waves so far (see e.g. Martynova and Renneboog 2006 and Sudarsanam 2010), although the early waves were principally concentrated in the US and therefore not global in nature. The first five waves correspond to the early 1900s, 1920s, 1960s, 1980s, and the 1990s, while the sixth wave started in 2001/2 and peaked in 2006/7 before the beginning of the credit crunch crisis. Many authors have highlighted the high correlation between merger and acquisition activity and the performance of worldwide stock markets (see e.g. Lambrecht 2004). Figure 10.1 provides evidence of the procyclical characteristics of M&A using the MSCI World stock market index as a proxy for economic cycles, monthly from 1984 to 2008, enabling identification of the latest two waves. More importantly, close inspection validates the continuing correlation during periods of distress, i.e. there are fewer deals during recessions compared to market peaks, as expected. The nature of such deals is extremely illuminating as Figure 10.2 shows that the acquisition of distressed and bankrupt firms is somewhat counter-cyclical, with bankrupt deals even more numerous than

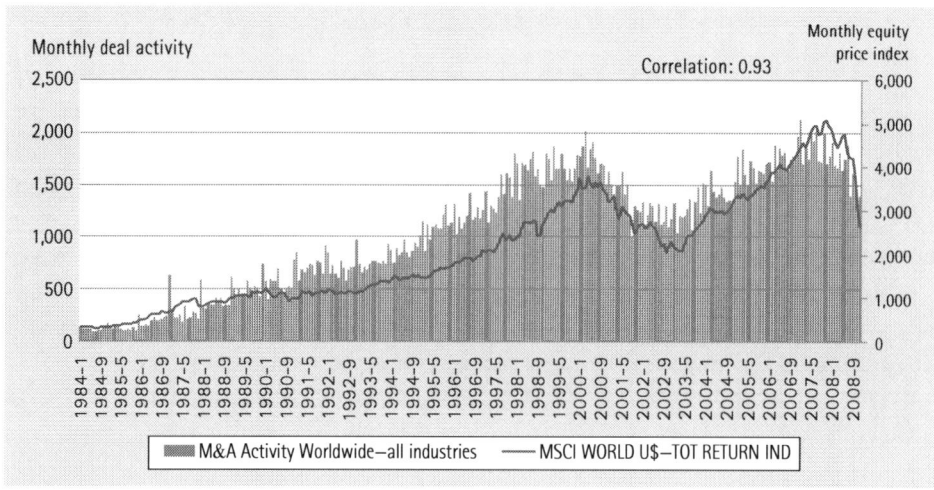

FIG. 10.1 Merger activity worldwide

Source: Carapeto et al. (2009).

those involving distressed targets. Bergström et al. (2005) and Buehler et al. (2006) examine the determinants of mergers and bankruptcies in Sweden and Switzerland, respectively, and find evidence of more merger activity during prosperous periods than recessions. It is interesting to note that following major crises, acquisitions of distressed and bankrupt companies increase and remain higher than average for three to four years, even if markets start showing signs of recovery, as argued by Carapeto et al. (2009).

Jovanovic and Rousseau (2001) show that there is a strong association between periods of high merger activity and high market valuations. Rhodes-Kropf and Viswanathan (2004) and Bouwman et al. (2009) find that acquisitions in booming stock markets are of poorer quality than those in depressed markets, evidence of firms buying late in the merger wave. Bouwman et al. (2009) argue that the long-term underperformance of high market acquirers is most likely a result of managerial herding.

Having defined deals involving distressed and bankrupt firms and establishing from the research that these deals tend to cluster, as expected, it is useful then to look at the existing research related to the frequency of such acquisitions.

ACQUISITIONS AS A MEANS
OF CORPORATE RESTRUCTURING

Research from the late 1990s and the first decade of the new millennium observes that sales of bankrupt firms have become more frequent over time. Kaiser (1996) finds that nearly 50% of UK firms are sold as going concerns in administrative receivership, while

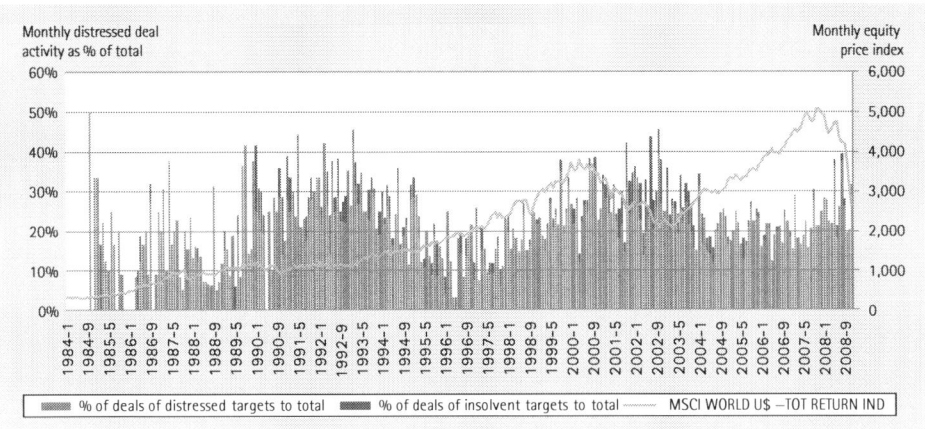

FIG. 10.2 Monthly distressed merger activity

Source: Carapeto et al. (2009).

Baird and Rasmussen (2003) report 56% of sales under Section 363 of the US Bankruptcy Code or following a plan of reorganization. More recently, Carapeto et al. (2009) show that in 12,339 deals between 1984 and 2008, almost one-quarter involved a distressed or bankrupt target (although only 2% of this total sample were bankruptcies). This evidence thus emphasizes the importance of studying the distressed acquisition market as a topic within the overall field of M&A.

Despite the increased recognition in academia and the press of topics relating to M&A on one hand and distress/bankruptcy on the other, research on distressed acquisitions is still scarce and has so far focused on acquisitions of distressed companies outside bankruptcy (Clark and Ofek 1994); the comparison of acquisitions of companies in bankruptcy and those of healthy companies outside bankruptcy (Hotchkiss and Mooradian 1998); the comparison of acquisitions and bankruptcies as exit strategies (Bergström et al. 2005 and Buehler et al. 2006); and recently, the comparison of acquisitions of companies in bankruptcy and those of healthy and distressed companies outside bankruptcy (Carapeto et al. 2009[1]).

Clark and Ofek (1994) investigate mergers of distressed firms in the US and state that both acquirer and target are frequently in the same industry. Hotchkiss and Mooradian (1998) extend Clark and Ofek's (1994) findings to Chapter 11 acquisitions, as in their study the acquirer is often found to be in the same industry as the target or to have had some prior relationship, e.g. a previous asset purchase with the target. Carapeto et al. (2009) study a large global sample over a 25-year span and show that, compared to acquisitions of healthy targets, in distressed acquisitions acquirer and target typically belong to the same industry. All three papers thus support the argument of Gertner and Picker (1992) that asymmetric information may deter bidding by potentially less well-informed firms.

In what concerns the duration of the deal process, Carapeto et al. (2009) support the generally accepted argument that bankruptcy acquisitions are typically very fast procedures compared to the other cases, particularly in downturns, in light of the timing issues inherent to the whole process (the median number of days to deal completion is 34 when markets are falling compared to 52 for rising markets).

Having looked at when these deals occur and their general characteristics, it is necessary to delve deeper to identify the alternatives within this overall category of deals. Rarely is acquisition the only option for a bankrupt or distressed firm.

SHOULD THE BANKRUPT CONCERN
BE REORGANIZED OR LIQUIDATED?

Reorganization is one of two routes that a bankrupt company may take; liquidation is the other alternative. Then, within reorganization, assuming the agreement of the major creditors, there is the choice to grow out of bankruptcy (which is rare) or be acquired.

Reorganization may enable claimants to capture a larger value than liquidation, in particular when a going concern is more valuable than a piecemeal sale of the firm. However, while reorganization may save economically efficient firms from liquidation, it is possible that it may also facilitate the continuation as a going concern of some economically inefficient firms (see e.g. Bulow and Shoven 1978). The reverse may also hold true. An efficient bankrupt code is thus one whereby firms that should be reorganized are done so effectively and those that should be liquidated are indeed liquidated. The key concept is not so much financial distress, i.e. companies with profitable operations but the wrong capital structures, but economic distress, i.e. companies with unprofitable operations, hence typically in financial distress as well.

White (1989) identifies inefficient outcomes as Type-I and Type-II errors, whereby economically inefficient firms are allowed to reorganize and economically efficient firms are liquidated, respectively. However, assessing economic efficiency may not be possible and, as a result of asymmetric information problems, even if managers are aware of economic inefficiency, investors will not necessarily know the true type of the firm. Furthermore, even if some know, the presence of multiple classes of creditors renders decisions more difficult, which may result in inefficient outcomes, as observed by Bulow and Shoven (1978) and Gertner and Scharfstein (1991). Specifically, senior claimants have the incentive to promote inefficient liquidation while junior claimants may favor inefficient continuation.

In order to assess the efficacy of the decision to reorganize or liquidate the bankrupt concern, the literature has so far concentrated on studying the performance of the two firms involved in the merger and subsequently the merged entity, both short term (event studies) and long term (accounting ratios).

Using event study methodology and comparing acquisitions in bankruptcy with those outside bankruptcy, Hotchkiss and Mooradian (1998) find positive abnormal returns for both acquirer and bankrupt target in the former, i.e. evidence of value creation, but only for the target in non-bankrupt acquisitions. For a sample of distressed acquisitions, Clark and Ofek (1994) show however that, in general, abnormal returns for both acquirers and distressed targets are similar to those for the general population of acquirers and targets. Carapeto et al. (2009) examine a large global sample of healthy, distressed, and bankrupt acquisitions, and argue that acquirers of distressed and bankrupt targets on one hand, and healthy and distressed targets on the other, typically enjoy positive announcement abnormal returns. Hence, there is evidence that acquirers tend to perform well in acquisitions of distressed and bankrupt targets, while bankrupt targets seem to lose out, a reflection of more limited bargaining power.

Using cash-flow performance, and in line with the short-term analysis, Hotchkiss and Mooradian (1998) compute value creation for the merged entity when the target is bankrupt but not when the target is acquired outside bankruptcy. Identified sources of gains include reductions in operating expenses and employment. Clark and Ofek (1994) find, however, evidence of poor post-merger performance for the combined firm when the target is distressed; worse for deals with lower announcement abnormal returns, larger premiums, and larger subsequent combined leverage, though better for relatively smaller and more financially (as opposed to economically) distressed targets. Carapeto et al. (2009) extend the results of Hotchkiss and Mooradian (1998) and Clark and Ofek (1994) to confirm that when the target is either distressed or bankrupt, the newly combined firm generally benefits from an overall improvement in performance over the long term compared to its combined pre-bid performance, which emphasizes the realization of synergies. Eckbo and Thorburn (2003) show that the performance of merged companies following mandatory auctions in Sweden is similar to that of their industry peers.

Carapeto et al. (2009) find, however, that the performance of the combined entity is worse than that of the acquirer pre-bid, with clear deterioration over time. A word of caution is warranted at this stage. Even if some research may indicate that acquirer firms tend to lose out in the process, Clark and Ofek (1994) argue that it is not fair to state that mergers are an inefficient outcome for distressed targets since it is impossible to ascertain the effects on total welfare of other restructuring means and, as such, unsuccessful restructurings may be actually the best alternative. Hotchkiss and Mooradian (1998) add that there should be fewer "bad acquirers" of bankrupt firms compared to healthy deals since the acquisition of bankrupt firms is very complex and involves sophisticated bargaining because it requires negotiation with each class of claimant over both the bid and the subsequent distribution of payments. The process of a bankruptcy is also most often very public, in contrast to most M&A deals, which are negotiated in private between two parties, with a final deal being announced only when both parties have negotiated the details of the deal confidentially.

Thus, although the research would appear to be inconclusive regarding the success of merged entities where the target has been in distress or bankrupt, the short-term results are usually found to be positive (and certainly for the acquired firm). Overall, the effect of synergies does contribute to longer-term efficiency, but may not offset the other costs of acquiring a distressed or bankrupt company.

EFFECTS OF AUCTIONS AND "FIRE SALE" DISCOUNTS

Zender (1991) argues that the decision to liquidate or continue bankrupt firms should lie with the residual claimant, i.e. the claimant who might not be fully paid (typically the unsecured creditors). As Hotchkiss et al. (2008) point out, one alternative could be to sell the firm in an auction, with the winner (potentially the marginal claimant) deciding the best way forward. Hart (1995) classifies bankruptcy procedures in two main categories: cash auctions and structured bargaining, ruled by the auction and reorganization codes, respectively.[2] Auctions mandate a public sale of a company, supervised by an appointed trustee, thus using the market approach, with the price being compared to the estimate of piecemeal liquidation. The proceeds are then distributed among the claimants according to absolute priority rules (secured debt, priority claims, unsecured debt, subordinated debt, and equity, in this order). Pre-pack auctions occur when a sale is negotiated immediately prior to filing for bankruptcy. Bankruptcy reorganization is built upon the idea of structured bargaining. In this way, all claimants are encouraged to negotiate over the future of the company, especially whether it should be liquidated or kept operating, and how to divide its value based on absolute priority rules.

Published research on auctions of bankrupt firms has been conducted mainly in Sweden. Thorburn (2000) documents that about 75% of auctions end up as going-concern sales, in contrast with prevailing views that auctions promote excessive piecewise liquidation. Povel and Singh (2007), however, point out that insiders are better informed and, as such, auctions should be biased against them to mitigate the winner's curse that typically plagues outsiders.

Shleifer and Vishny (1992) show that mandatory auctions of bankrupt companies may promote offer discounts when the whole industry is also in distress. Specifically, Shleifer and Vishny (1992) and Aghion et al. (1992) argue that competitors of distressed companies might be financially constrained themselves if the whole industry is financially distressed and, as such, offers will suffer from large discounts, so-called "fire sales," potentially producing sub-optimal allocation of assets. Acharya et al. (2007) say that in periods of industry distress most bankrupt firms tend to emerge as restructured entities, instead of being acquired or liquidated, probably as a way to avoid costly "fire sales." Buehler et al. (2006) find lower merger rates in industries and regions with high bankruptcy rates. Bergström et al. (2005) argue however that, when the economy is not doing well, firms in industries with high bankruptcy rates are less likely to initiate bankruptcy proceedings (see also Faccio and Sengupta 2006). Carapeto et al. (2009) also show more acquisitions of distressed targets and fewer acquisitions of healthy/bankrupt targets when the target industry is in financial distress, with evidence of more distressed acquisitions and fewer healthy acquisitions in distressed industries in stressed times.

Moreover, there seems to be an unwritten "first-in, first-out" rule at industry level, in so far as industries that fall early in a crisis tend to emerge from the trough much earlier.

Pulvino (1998, 1999) shows evidence of "fire sales" for financially constrained airlines when the airline industry is depressed, with offers for used aircraft even lower in bankruptcy. Specifically, sales of aircraft suffer from 14% discounts compared to their market value, and this discount is 30% in market downturns/recessions, probably because acquirers are more likely to be outsiders, e.g. financial institutions. The laws of supply and demand operate here as well. Thus, as the market for a distressed firm's assets is likely to be rather illiquid, the winning bidder may potentially operate in another industry and bid below the fundamental value of the assets. In fact, Bergström et al. (2005) and Buehler et al. (2006) find that in depressed times distressed sellers are more likely to sell to industry outsiders, and Clayton and Ravid (2002) argue that industry debt overhang may potentially prevent rivals from bidding for bankrupt concerns. Other studies compute liquidity discounts in distressed sales with similar magnitudes to those observed by Pulvino (1998). Kim (1998) investigates the contract drilling industry, Ramey and Shapiro (2001) focus on the aerospace industry, while Officer's (2007) sample is not industry-specific. However, Maksimovic and Phillips (1998) find no difference in the productivity of assets whether in the hands of bidders or targets, regardless of the degree of distress of the target's industry (see also Andrade and Kaplan 1998).

Both Clark and Ofek (1994) and Hotchkiss and Mooradian (1998) provide evidence of few hostile acquisitions of distressed and bankrupt targets, respectively. As such, offers are typically small compared to non-distressed/bankrupt deals, despite one-third of transactions involving multiple acquirers in the bankrupt cases. Hotchkiss and Mooradian (1998) report mean discounts in the region of 40%, similar to those documented by Faccio and Sengupta (2006) during the Asian financial crisis, with higher offers for targets in better profitability shape. This result contrasts with Eckbo and Thorburn (2008), who find no evidence of fire sale discounts in acquisitions of bankrupt concerns. Carapeto et al. (2009) show that compared to distressed/bankrupt targets, healthy targets benefit from higher premiums, especially in falling markets.

One cause for concern with the widespread use of auctions is the issue of the illiquidity of the markets for the assets of distressed firms which may produce "fire sales," in particular when the target's industry as a whole also suffers from distress. One solution to overcoming this problem involves Strömberg's (2000) suggestion of sale-backs to incumbent management financed by the current creditors, e.g. banks. Eckbo and Thorburn (2009) also point out that targets' banks improve liquidity by providing the necessary funding for the bidding. Interestingly, Baird and Rasmussen (2003) highlight the reduction in asset specificity[3] over time, which consequently promotes increased liquidity in the market for assets of distressed firms and the eventual mitigation of "fire sales." Eckbo and Thorburn (2008) indeed find no evidence of "fire sales" in going-concern auctions (though there are large discounts in piecemeal liquidations), regardless of the degree of relatedness of acquirer/target or industry distress level. Many bids are structured as LBOs to overcome liquidity constraints, thus widening the participation of bidders, an issue initially raised by Aghion et al. (1992).

Post-Acquisition Bust-Up
and Asset-Stripping

Porter (1987), Ravenscraft and Scherer (1987), and Kaplan and Weisbach (1992) all show that, in general, divestitures of recently acquired assets are fairly frequent. Kaplan and Weisbach (1992) emphasize that divestitures of unrelated business lines are more common than those of related businesses, which must be a continuing trend since the end of the conglomerate merger wave of the late 1960s and the subsequent decline in the market attractiveness of conglomerate firms.

Carapeto et al. (2010a) find evidence of newly hired managers favoring divestitures over acquisitions during their first year in office when the firms had been underperforming prior to their appointment. Lang et al. (1995) also argue that divestitures tend to follow periods of stock price underperformance, with positive short-term abnormal returns, though Brown et al. (1994) find no significant stock price reactions for divestitures of financially distressed firms.

Asquith et al. (1994) suggest that divestitures are used to generate much needed liquidity and thus avoid bankruptcy. Alternatively, divestitures may be used to generate liquidity while in bankruptcy, as Hotchkiss (1995) finds substantial asset sales for bankrupt companies. However, and using a global sample from the financial services industry, Carapeto et al. (2010b) argue that distressed banks that have divested assets increase significantly in size three years after the deals, which implies subsequent growth either internally or through acquisition.

Financial Services Industry

As a case study, it is helpful to look at one industry, financial services. This industry is chosen in light of its importance, impact, and influence on the economy as a whole and on other companies, and its relevance as a driver (if not the catalyst itself) in the most recent global downturn. The industry also includes a number of high profile large institutions requiring distressed company sales both with and without government assistance. These, therefore, allow an examination of the resolution of company distress using the acquisition method.

Interestingly, the research so far is sparse and most covers distressed and bankrupt deals prior to the most recent wave of such deals. One such study compared acquisitions and bankruptcies as exit strategies (Wheelock and Wilson 2000), another the acquisitions of distressed banks outside bankruptcy (Elsas 2007), and a third the comparison between distressed banks involved in an M&A deal and banks not involved in M&A (Koetter et al. 2007). More recently, and incorporating the events of the company sales during the recession that began in 2007, there is a comparison of acquisitions and government intervention in distressed banks (Carapeto et al. 2010b).

The findings of these four pieces of research are enlightening and consistent with the non-industry-specific findings presented earlier in this chapter. Wheelock and Wilson (2000) demonstrate that small banks with low leverage and high asset quality, profitability, liquidity, and efficiency are more prone to being acquired than liquidated. This is especially interesting in light of Koetter et al. (2007), who argue that, compared to banks not involved in M&A deals, distressed participants in M&A deals exhibit poor financial profiles, i.e. lower capital reserve ratios, lower exposure to the securities business, higher net loan loss provisions, and below average efficiency. Elsas (2007) nevertheless finds a positive relationship between distress and the likelihood of acquisition, with the combined entity enjoying increased asset quality, albeit with a temporary decrease in profitability, with no significant change in default risk or cost efficiency. There is also evidence of diversification gains for the combined entity compared to non-distressed acquisitions.

In the most recent study, Carapeto et al. (2010b) argue that the distressed banks which have government intervention are in better financial shape than those acquired by other banks in an M&A transaction, apart from liquidity, which is evidence of critical short-term flow issues. While foreign acquirers seem to "cherry pick" the least distressed targets, the post-acquisition performance of targets reveals no significant differences between those acquired by domestic and foreign banks. Thus, although it would appear that governments and foreign acquirers have an ability to succeed or at least to perform better than domestic acquirers, this talent may not lead to better performance overall.

Conclusion

The academic literature on bankrupt and distressed acquisitions mirrors the market itself. These acquisitions are cyclical, and in the past two decades have shown three periods of higher activity (the early 1990s, early 2000s, and post-2007). The academic analysis of these bankrupt and distressed acquisitions also intensified for a brief period following these peaks of market activity. Yet this chapter has shown a remarkable consistency in the analytical results over the past 20 years, irrespective of the period analyzed.

For the management and owners of distressed or bankrupt firms, acquisition by another company is an important alternative to liquidation or corporate restructuring. For such distressed firms, the acquisition alternative has increased in use since the late 1980s. Research has also shown that these acquisitions take place faster, on average, than acquisitions of companies that are not in distress, which means that this process may be useful in saving what is salvageable in a company that is struggling. Yet despite the possibility of acting quickly, the process is not simple and for managers, the decision to reorganize, liquidate, or be acquired is not a simple one with easy answers, as shown by the research covered in this chapter. The decision process includes the need to choose between the type of sale, such as the use of an auction process or not, and whether to keep the company whole or break it up whilst trying to save it.

In conclusion, one of the most recent studies (Carapeto, et al. 2009) shows that the performance of acquirers does tend to deteriorate over time after having purchased a distressed firm, despite short-term gains around the time of the announcement of the deal. But it must be remembered that practitioners in the M&A industry have a tendency to emphasize that "every deal is unique." This observation may be especially true when looking at distressed and bankrupt targets, especially because, as shown above, the evidence is not fully consistent. Therefore, although it might be an alternative that appears attractive to the distressed company itself, from the buyer's perspective the decision to purchase a distressed or bankrupt firm must be entered into carefully: "*caveat emptor.*" No practitioner, in executing a distressed or bankrupt acquisition, would be likely to disagree with that advice.

Endnotes

1. According to Carapeto et al. (2009), a target is distressed when two criteria are met: (1) Interest Coverage Ratio (ICR) less than unity in the year prior to the acquisition; (2) ICR in the first quartile of the industry ICR in the same year.
2. For example, Sweden follows the auction code while the US follows the reorganization code, though evidence from Baird and Rasmussen (2003) suggests that the majority of Chapter 11 large cases uses the auction approach.
3. Machinery and equipment that can be used for few specific purposes only, i.e. not easily redeployable.

References

Acharya, V. V., Bharath, S. T., & Srinivasan, A. (2007). "Does Industry-Wide Distress Affect Defaulted Firms? Evidence from Creditor Recoveries." *Journal of Financial Economics*, 85: 787–821.

Aghion, P., Hart, O., & Moore, J. (1992). "The Economics of Bankruptcy Reform." *Journal of Law, Economics and Organization*, 8: 523–46.

Andrade, G., & Kaplan, S. N. (1998). "How Costly is Financial (Not Economic) Distress? Evidence from Highly Leveraged Transactions that Became Distressed." *Journal of Finance*, 53/5: 1443–93.

Asquith, P., Gertner, R., & Scharfstein, D. (1994). "Anatomy of Financial Distress: An Examination of Junk Bond Issuers." *Quarterly Journal of Economics*, 109: 625–58.

Baird, D. G., & Rasmussen, R. K. (2003). "Chapter 11 at Twilight." *Stanford Law Review*, 56: 673–99.

Bergström, C., Eisenberg, T., Sundgren, S., & Wells, M. T. (2005). "The Fate of Firms: Explaining Mergers and Bankruptcies." *Journal of Empirical Legal Studies*, 2/1: 49–85.

Betton, S., Eckbo, B. E., & Thorburn, K. S. (2008). "Corporate Takeovers," in B. E. Eckbo (ed.), *Handbook of Corporate Finance: Empirical Corporate Finance*, vol. 2. Handbooks in Finance Series. North Holland: Elsevier, ch. 15, 291–430.

Bouwman, C. H. S., Fuller, K., & Nain, A. S. (2009). "Market Valuation and Acquisition Quality: Empirical Evidence." *Review of Financial Studies*, 22: 633–79.

Brown, D. T., James, C. M., & Mooradian, R. M. (1994). "Asset Sales by Financially Distressed Firms." *Journal of Corporate Finance*, 1: 233–57.

Buehler, S., Kaiser, C., & Jaeger, F. (2006). "Merge or Fail? The Determinants of Mergers and Bankruptcies in Switzerland, 1995–2000" *Economics Letters*, 90: 88–95.

Bulow, J. I., & Shoven, J. B. (1978). "The Bankruptcy Decision." *Bell Journal of Economics*, 9: 437–56.

Carapeto, M., Moeller, S., & Faelten, A. (2009). "The Good, the Bad, and the Ugly: A Survival Guide to M&A in Distressed Times." Unpublished manuscript.

—— —— —— (2010a). "What should I do next? CEO succession, M&A deals, and company performance." Unpublished manuscript.

—— —— —— Vitkova, V., & Bortolotto, L. (2010b). "Distress Resolution Strategies in the Banking Sector: Implications for Global Financial Crises," in S. J. Kim & M. D. McKenzie (eds.), *International Finance Review 11—International Banking in the New Era: Post-Crisis Challenges and Opportunities*, Bingley: Emerald, 337–62. By invitation.

Clark, K., & Ofek, E. (1994). "Mergers as a Means of Restructuring Distressed Firms: An Empirical Investigation." *Journal of Financial and Quantitative Analysis*, 29: 541–65.

Clayton, M. J., & Ravid, S. A. (2002). "The Effect Of Leverage on Bidding Behavior: Theory and Evidence from the FCC Auctions." *Review of Financial Studies*, 15: 723–50.

Eckbo, B. E., & Thorburn, K. S. (2003). "Control Benefits and CEO Discipline in Automatic Bankruptcy Auctions." *Journal of Financial Economics*, 69: 227–58.

—— —— (2008). "Automatic Bankruptcy Auctions and Fire-Sales." *Journal of Financial Economics*, 89: 404–22.

—— —— (2009). "Creditor Financing and Overbidding in Bankruptcy Auctions: Theory and Tests." *Journal of Corporate Finance*, 15: 10–29.

Elsas, R. (2007). "Preemptive Distress Resolution through Bank Mergers." Unpublished manuscript.

Faccio, M., & Sengupta, R. (2006). "Corporate Response to Distress: Evidence from the Asian Financial Crisis." Unpublished manuscript.

Gertner, R., & Picker, R. (1992). "Bankruptcy and the Allocation of Control." Unpublished manuscript.

—— & Scharfstein, D. (1991). "A Theory of Workouts and the Effects of Reorganization Law." *Journal of Finance*, 46: 1189–222.

Hart, O. (1995). *Firms, Contracts, and Financial Structure*. Oxford: Clarendon Press.

Hotchkiss, E. S. (1995). "Postbankruptcy Performance and Management Turnover." *Journal of Finance*, 50: 3–21.

—— John, K., Mooradian, R. M., & Thorburn, K. S. (2008). "Bankruptcy and the Resolution of Financial Distress," in B. E. Eckbo (ed.), *Handbook of Corporate Finance: Empirical Corporate Finance*, vol. 2, Handbooks in Finance Series. North Holland: Elsevier, ch. 14, 235–90.

—— & Mooradian, R. M. (1998). "Acquisitions as a Means of Restructuring Firms in Chapter 11." *Journal of Financial Intermediation*, 7/3: 240–62.

Jensen, M. C. (1991). "Corporate Control and the Politics of Finance." *Journal of Applied Corporate Finance*, 4/2: 13–33.

Jovanovic, B., & Rousseau, P. (2001). "Mergers and Technological Change: 1885–1998." Unpublished manuscript.

Kaiser, K. M. J. (1996). "European Bankruptcy Laws: Implications for Corporations Facing Financial Distress." *Financial Management*, 25: 67–85.

Kaplan, S., & Weisbach, M. (1992). "The Success of Acquisitions: Evidence from Divestitures." *Journal of Finance*, 41: 107–38.

Kim, C. E. (1998). "The Effects of Asset Liquidity: Evidence from the Contract Drill Industry." *Journal of Financial Intermediation*, 7: 151–76.

Koetter, M., Bos, B., Heid, F., Kool, C., Kolari, J., & Porath, D. (2007). "Accounting for Distress in Bank Mergers." *Journal of Banking and Finance*, 31/10: 3200–17.

Lambrecht, B. M. (2004). "The Timing and Terms of Mergers Motivated by Economies of Scale." *Journal of Financial Economics*, 72: 41–62.

Lang, L., Poulsen, A., & Stulz, R. (1995). "Asset Sales, Firm Performance, and the Agency Costs Of Managerial Discretion." *Journal of Financial Economics*, 37: 3–37.

Maksimovic, V., & Phillips, G. M. (1998). "Asset Efficiency and the Reallocation Decisions of Bankrupt Firms." *Journal of Finance*, 53: 1495–532.

Martynova, M., & Renneboog, L. (2006). "Mergers and Acquisitions in Europe," in L. Renneboog (ed.), *Advances in Corporate Finance and Asset Pricing*. Amsterdam: Elsevier.

Officer, M. S. (2007). "The Price of Corporate Liquidity: Acquisition Discounts for Unlisted Targets." *Journal of Financial Economics*, 83: 571–98.

Porter, M. (1987). "From Competitive Advantage to Corporate Strategy." *Harvard Business Review*, 65/3: 43–59.

Povel, P., & Singh, R. (2007). "Sale-Backs in Bankruptcy." *Journal of Law, Economics, and Organization*, 23/3: 710–30.

Pulvino, T. C. (1998) "Do Asset Fire Sales Exist? An Empirical Investigation of Commercial Aircraft Transactions." *Journal of Finance*, 53: 939–78.

——(1999). "Effects of Bankruptcy Court Protection on Asset Sales." *Journal of Financial Economics*, 52: 151–86.

Ramey, V. A., & Shapiro, M. D. (2001). "Displaced capital: A study of aerospace plant closings." *Journal of Political Economy*, 109: 958–92.

Ravenscraft, D., & Scherer, F. (1987). *Mergers, Selloffs, and Economic Efficiency*. Washington, DC: Brookings Institution.

Rhodes-Kropf, M., & Viswanathan, S. (2004). "Market Valuation and Merger Waves." *Journal of Finance*, 59: 2685–718.

Shleifer A., & Vishny, R. W. (1992). "Liquidation Values and Debt Capacity: A Market Equilibrium Approach." *Journal of Finance*, 47: 1343–66.

Strömberg, P. (2000). "Conflicts of Interest and Market Illiquidity in Bankruptcy Auctions: Theory and Tests." *Journal of Finance*, 55: 2641–92.

Sudarsanam, S. (2010). *Creating Value from Mergers and Acquisitions: The Challenges*. Harlow: Pearson Education.

Thorburn, K. S. (2000). "Bankruptcy Auctions: Costs, Debt Recovery, and Firm Survival." *Journal of Financial Economics*, 58: 337–68.

Wheelock, D., & Wilson, P. (2000). "Why Do Banks Disappear? The Determinants of U.S. Bank Failures and Acquisitions." *Review of Economics and Statistics*, 82/1: 127–38.

White, M. (1989). "The Corporate Bankruptcy Decision." *Journal of Economic Perspectives*, 3: 129–51.

Wruck, K. H. (1990). "Financial Distress, Reorganization, and Organizational Efficiency." *Journal of Financial Economics*, 27: 419–44.

Zender, J. F. (1991). "Optimal Financial Instruments." *Journal of Finance*, 46: 1645–63.

....

CHAPTER 11

TAKEOVER STRATEGIES, COMPETITIVE BIDDING, AND DEFENSIVE TACTICS

....

BRENDAN MCSWEENEY

INTRODUCTION

....

The financial benefits and costs of takeovers for shareholders (and other stakeholders) of acquiring and acquired companies and for economies and societies more generally are varied and contested. They are discussed elsewhere in the *Handbook*. This chapter is agnostic about this debate and instead considers the main mechanisms employed in takeover situations (negotiated and hostile) to enable or frustrate completion of a takeover. The distinction between "negotiated" (or friendly) and "hostile" is not always clear-cut as negotiated takeovers of quoted companies may occur under a more or less explicit threat that a friendly acquirer would, if initially thwarted, launch a hostile bid.

Takeover tactics do not have inherent power. Both their choice and effects are influenced by larger dynamics. Before considering specific tactics, three key contexts (corporate governance; takeover strategies; and peaks-troughs) which shape, albeit do not determine, the choice and efficacy of tactics are discussed.

TAKEOVER STRATEGIES

....

Reasons for attempting a takeover include: reduction of industry overcapacity; expansion in domestic or foreign markets; acquisition of brands or technical knowledge; diversification; consolidation; buying a "honey-pot"; reducing competition; opportunistically using an acquirer's overvalued shares; empire building; following fashion; the thrill of the chase; grabbing a bargain (Bower 2001; Shleifer and Vishny 2003). In some instances, multiple motives may drive the action. The most common reasons for take-overs are discussed below to illustrate why the motivation for a particular takeover strategy may influence the choice of tactics of the initiating and/or the target companies.

Capacity Reduction A high proportion of takeover activity occurs in industries which have overcapacity. Most mega-takeovers aim at capacity reduction. Industries with over-capacity are large and mature and the main companies in these industries are usually quoted, that is, their shares are publicly traded and their ownership is dispersed. Apart from capacity reduction caused by corporate failure, such change rarely takes place except as a result of a takeover.

As the motive is capacity reduction and as historically there has been a bias towards retaining more of the acquiring companies' operations, management, and procedures, the directors and management of the targeted company(ies) will feel vulnerable and thus have incentives to reject a takeover attempt and to employ counter-bid (defensive) tactics. "Hostile bids," that is, an unsolicited bid which is unwelcomed (at least initially) by the directors/management of a target company, are therefore common when the takeover aim is capacity reduction. Successful hostile bids lead not only to ownership change but also usually to very substantial control changes.

Michael Jensen argues that takeovers are a major component of the managerial labor market. They are, he states, "the arena in which alternative management teams compete for the right to manage corporate resources" (1988: 4). This is an accurate, if oversimplified, description of takeovers seeking to consolidate mature industries. It is also a good reductive description of hostile takeovers, regardless of what is the takeover strategy. But as discussed below, competition between alternative management does not necessarily characterize all takeover strategies.

Defragmentation In contrast with capacity reduction, which typically occurs in mature industries, defragmentation takes place in industries which, though often containing firms of long standing, are at an earlier stage in their life cycle. Such strategies, often called "roll-ups" (Bower 2001), are associated with growth not contraction. Typically, larger companies acquire smaller companies. For the latter the acquisition provides greater access to capital, and greater marketing and technological resources. For founders of firms it provides a way of selling out which is an alternative to an expensive initial public offer. For the acquirer, the deal provides growth, access to new markets, opportunities to reduce costs through economies of scale; and the immediate involvement of tested local management. For both parties it reduces the threat from rivals. As the context is generally one of growth, this strategy results in far fewer hostile takeovers than when capacity reduction is the aim.

Scope or Scale Extension The motivation for this strategy varies and includes empire building; a desire to benefit from economies of scale; and expansion into new activities or territories. Rather than developing or getting them through slow organic growth, an acquirer can rapidly obtain someone else's product line, someone's distribution system, someone's customers, someone's talent. Whether this is ultimately a more effective way is an open question. If a company's firm-specific advantages are, or are perceived to be, home location-bound, then foreign takeovers are one way to get host country-pertinent capabilities (Verbeke 2009). Local success requires local knowledge and expertise. Other methods of going local include minority shareholding or partnership or distribution agreements. Each has different comparative advantages and disadvantages.

In 2007, for the first time in recent history, the value of cross-border takeovers equalled the value of intra-border takeovers (OECD 2007). Go-it-alone expansions into foreign markets have produced some spectacular failures. As for all takeovers, foreign acquisitions are shaped by local, including legal and other institutional, circumstances. Foreign takeovers may be constrained by cost, by national prohibitions, the extent to which stakeholders additional to shareholders have formal influence; political opposition; or competition laws. Capabilities may be home location-bound and thus not transferable to another country. Both vertical and horizontal takeovers occur under this strategy. National sensitivities encourage negotiated rather than hostile cross-border takeovers. The successful hostile takeover by the UK-headquartered Vodaphone of the German-based Mannesmann might seem to be a spectacular counter-example, but arguably this was not in ownership terms a cross-border acquisition as more than two-thirds of the shares in Mannesmann were held by foreigners, mainly institutional investors based in the UK and the US (Keida 2001). Furthermore, Mannesmann had failed to implant any pre-bid defensive devices (Höpner and Jackson 2004).

Acquisition or Localization of Technical Capability Shortening product life cycles, increasing specialization of technical knowledge, and the growth in customer diversity make the need for effective innovation all the more necessary. But developing sustainable within-company research and development (R&D) is costly and R&D in large long-established companies tends to become sluggish. A company may be targeted for a takeover to provide a substitute for, or an addition to, the takeover initiator's technical knowledge and innovative capability. Alternatively, a takeover might seek to prevent a competitor from getting access to that knowledge. International acquisitions may also be undertaken to localize (R&D)—to make it more responsive to the specifics on individual markets.

The key asset of companies with strong R&D capabilities (whether small or large) is the R&D people. Hostile bids or aggressive offers are rare in takeovers of such companies. The main asset of those companies walks out the door at the end of every day. But pre- and post-takeover management exodus is commonplace. It is vital to retain these people; a hostile bid would be counter-productive. In the UK, for instance, approximately 90% of top management and board members of the acquired companies resigned after the consummation of a hostile takeover compared with only 50% in negotiated takeovers (Franks and Mayer 1996).

It is in the interests of the acquiring company to offer incentives to key R&D personnel to remain post-acquisition. The required incentives are likely to include the non-monetary, specifically some credible assurances that the conditions which enabled technical creativity will not be damaged. If, however, the aim of a takeover is to acquire already established knowledge, say that protected by patents, rather than to buy research capability and potential, then retention of R&D and other personnel in the acquired company is less significant and thus opposition from management, or factions within management, but not necessarily from shareholders, of the target company is more likely. Having acquired the "crown jewel," the other assets are likely to be disposed of. A similar logic operates when the main asset sought by means of a takeover is a brand, or brands, and not the target's operating capabilities.

As with every takeover type, there is a danger of overvaluation (in the sense of paying more than will be achieved after gaining control) and incompatibility between the acquiring and the acquired. The speed of technical change and strong information asymmetry (as well sometimes as acquirer hubris) has resulted in a host of companies buying second-rate R&D intense companies for inflated prices. The degree of information asymmetry varies between industries. It is low, for example, in brewing but high in biotechnology.

Financialized Gains Although financial gain may be the primary or exclusive aim of the participants in the varieties of takeovers described above, the common means of achieving that end is largely through attempted improvement in operational performance. However, since around the 1980s, takeover activity, and business life more generally, in Anglophone countries and elsewhere have become more financialized in the sense that the productive parts of the economies have become more subordinated to capital markets. An indication of this is the rise to centrality of the notion "shareholder value"—a theoretically ambiguous notion which to an even greater extent than hitherto marshals and intensifies pressures on quoted companies to focus on short-term financial returns. The short-termism of the shareholder-value model, its emphasis on distribution of profits rather than their retention, and even more speculative activity in capital markets discourages patient investment (O'Sullivan 2000).

In more shareholder value-focused countries at least, the power of capital markets (and the financial institutions within them) over business and economic life has grown enormously as has the scale of its capture of governments (McSweeney 2009). In a greater proportion of takeovers than hitherto, the primary aim is financial gain, speculative short-term trading gains on share price changes or saddling the acquired company with the debt used to acquire it. Financial extraction with consequent debilitation and not positive transformation has been the dominant consequence of this focus on maximizing shareholder value (Porter 1992; Froud et al. 2006).

Financialized strategies featured much more in the major takeover waves of the 1980s and late 1990s than they did in the major wave at the turn of the 20th century and that in the 1920s. That is not, of course, to suggest that speculative activity, what John Maynard Keynes called the economically "functionless activity" of the "rentier" (1936: 376) is new, there have always been speculative "bubbles on a steady stream of enterprise" (1936: 159), but the scale and frequency of such speculative activities have grown, facilitated by a variety of changes in political economies. Whether leveraged buyouts have any social or national economic value is contested, but large numbers undoubtedly debilitate the acquired companies. As Ben Franklin states: "It is hard for an empty sack to stand upright" (in Cunningham 2002: 172). That is not to dismiss the desirability or acceptability of financial gain, but the notion that making it the sole objective always benefits everyone, that such exclusiveness is "a virtuous circle" (Bughin and Copeland 1997), that it makes winners of us all, relies on an unreal notion of markets. Ironically, as John Kay points out, making maximization of shareholder value a corporation's primary goal is in the longer term likely to be the least effective way of achieving that goal (2010).

In financialized takeovers, there are no obvious synergies between the bidder and the target and the bidders often sell off core assets and/or run down the remaining assets to repay debt incurred in the takeover. Not surprisingly, financialized takeovers are sometimes called "bust-up" takeovers (Kahan and Rock 2002). Given the likely consequences of financialized takeovers, a high proportion of hostile bids might seem likely, but in fact the great majority are negotiated takeovers despite frequent opposition from a range of interested parties (employees and so forth). The reason is that in these cases the key decision makers—whether top management/boards or the shareholder body in general—have incentives to accept bids which may outweigh concerns for the longer-term welfare of the firm (Bolton, Scheinkman and Xiong 2006). As a practice, stock option schemes for top management which began in the US now dominate remuneration at that level in other Anglophone countries (Barron and Waddell, 2003) and have spread elsewhere, albeit not always as extensively. Legislative changes in 1998 in Germany, for instance, significantly facilitated the implementation of stock option plans (Langmann 2007). Financialized takeover bids are often characterized by large premiums, so that negotiated takeovers are arguably in effect coercive, as the target's stock optioned board/top management and shareholders in general are made offers which encourage them to "cut and run" with their gains regardless of the wider or longer-term consequences for the target. Oliver Williamson bizarrely states that shareholders, unlike other stakeholders, "invest for the life of the firm" (1984: 1210). In reality, employees of and the suppliers to firms have more at stake in the continuity of a firm than do shareholders whose risks are usually widely dispersed and whose relationship may be very brief.

CORPORATE GOVERNANCE

Regardless of the disparate views on who the beneficiaries of takeovers are, there is consensus that takeovers are economically and socially significant. Because of this importance, the activity is regulated and thus certain strategies and tactics are prohibited, restricted, or encouraged. The location—regional, national, or specific federal state—of the target company will influence the permissibility of tactics and may determine the comparative emphasis put on them and the timing of their use.

At one extreme are societies with few restrictions on takeovers and limited, if any, influence over the ultimate decision to accept or reject the bid, of any stakeholders, other than shareholders. In such societies, such as the UK, it is the shareholders of the target company whom both the potential purchaser and the incumbent management must exclusively persuade to accept or reject the bid. The fundamental foundations of that position are: a commitment to shareholder primacy; a view that shareholders of the same class should be afforded equivalent treatment by an offeror; and a suspicion of management—a belief that, unless controlled, management will give priority to their own interests to the detriment of shareholders. Illustrative of this view is the City (of London) Code's position on takeover defenses:

> During the course of an offer, or even before the date of the offer if the board of the offeree company has reason to believe that a bona fide offer might be imminent; the board must not, without the approval of the shareholders in general meeting…take any action which may result in any offer or bona fide possible offer being frustrated or its shareholders being denied the opportunity to decide on its merits. (The Panel on Takeovers and Mergers 2010: 21.1)

In contrast, in most US states, the "business judgement rule" dominates. Courts are reluctant to second-guess company directors. The highly influential Supreme Court of Delaware (a state in which the great majority of publicly quoted US companies are registered) has demonstrated in a number of cases that there are few decisions not involving outright self-dealing that shareholders could prevent boards of directors from making (Marens and Wicks 1999). In the UK, the requirement in the 1985 Companies Act that company directors must have regard to employees' interests was effectively removed from the 2006 Companies Act. Over time a number of European Union (EU) countries have moved their takeover laws and regulations towards the UK's shareholder primacy model rather than the US-type "business judgement" rule model. On competition and industrial policy, the European Commission has demonstrated an increasing enthusiasm for neo-liberalism—notwithstanding "the wishful thinking of trade unions and the 'social dimensions' rhetoric of politicians" (Streeck 2007: 540). The EU's *Thirteenth Directive on Takeover Regulations* (2004) is broadly modelled on the UK's "City Code" (The Panel on Takeovers and Mergers 2010), but it leaves margins of freedom to Member States (Ventoruzzo 2005). A range of defense tactics employable in the US are either prohibited within many EU countries or are only exercisable with prior shareholder approval. The majority of US academic commentators (from law, economics, and management) seem to favor restricting boards of directors' ability to veto takeovers and favor leaving the matter to shareholders (Arlen 2002), but ironically it is European public policy which is shaped by that view not policy in the US.

PEAKS AND TROUGHS

Takeover activity flows in peaks and troughs—both quantitatively and qualitatively. Whilst takeovers are an ongoing feature of the business world, the quantity of takeovers has long peaks and troughs. The conventional description of these peaks is "merger waves." This is both an inaccurate and an accurate label. Inaccurate in that very few of the new relationships are mergers in the sense of a future relationship of equals—overwhelmingly acquirers dominate and frequently discriminate against the acquired's management. Instead the acquisitions are takeovers—the acquirer gets control of the acquired. But the description is accurate in the sense that historically takeover activity has come in waves—activity is clustered rather than constant. Peaks of intense activity are followed by troughs of relatively few transactions.

Within each wave (and indeed each trough) takeovers are driven by diverse strategies (of the types discussed above). However, each major wave is also characterized by a predominance of one type of takeover strategy. For example, the takeover wave of the 1890s and early 1900s—this in Europe and especially the US created many huge dominant companies. This wave of horizontal, within industry, takeovers created industrial giants in steel, oil, and mining (McNamara et al. 2008). The focus in the second major wave which occurred in the 1920s was on vertical takeovers (that is, between firms with prior buyer-seller relationships). The majority of the takeovers in the 1960s were of firms in unrelated businesses. Conglomerates were then fashionable. A reaction to this diversification was the long "refocusing wave" of the 1980s. The wave in the late 1990s was dominated by overseas takeovers to expand scope or scale. Predictions are risky, but it is possible that the next takeover wave will be an intensification of overseas scope and scale expansion, but unlike the 1990s wave in which share exchanges dominated, the new wave will be cash focused and the acquirers will predominantly come from the East not the West.

BUY-SIDE TACTICS

The two primary aims of buy-side takeover tactics are to achieve control of an appropriate acquisition and at the lowest possible price. As Warren Buffet puts it: "the aim is to buy good businesses at fair prices rather than fair businesses at good prices" (in Cunningham 2002: 159). A third desirable—but often neglected key objective—is the enhancement of, or at least minimizing difficulties for, post-takeover integration and operation of the acquired company. That is assuming the aim of the takeover is not asset stripping. Tactics will be influenced by whether the target is publicly quoted or not and whether the prospect of a takeover is likely to be welcomed or opposed by the incumbent management. In effect, hostile bids are made only for publicly quoted companies—those with comparatively dispersed share ownership. Hostile bids—bids which are unwelcomed (at least initially) by the directors of a target company—are the type of takeover activity best known to the public in general. Often these types of bids are for large and sometimes iconic companies. The ongoing and changing drama of attack and defense (below) results in great amounts of media coverage.

The key buy-side tactics are described below. A number, such as "Saturday night specials" are prohibited in some jurisdictions.

Premium Price   If a bid is to be successful, the consideration offered must be sufficient to attract a sufficient portion of the target company's shareholders. It has to be high enough to deliver a "knock-out" (Sudarasanam 1995: 224). The challenge for the bidder is to neither under- nor over-offer. But as bidders (and indeed incumbent management) will have incomplete knowledge of shareholder wishes and in any event shareholders are a heterogeneous, not a homogeneous, group with diverse risk preferences, liquidity desires/requirements, time horizons, extent of risk spread, tax status, and so forth, determining the knock-out price is a judgment based on considerable uncertainty. As auctions generally generate higher prices for sellers, buyers will in the main try to achieve a negotiated sale. A substantial bid premium is one tactic to try to conclude matters through negotiations rather than subsequently getting involved in what is likely to be an even more costly auction. In a survey of private equity firms, 90% said that they preferred to avoid auctions when acting as buyers, but 80% of the same firms said they would prefer to use auctions when acting as sellers (Bulow and Klemperer 2009).

Composition of the Consideration   An offer to the target's shareholders can be wholly in the form of cash; of shares; or a mix of both. The shares offered are usually ordinary shares, but may include in part, or in whole, preference shares.

A share-exchange offer avoids the problem of obtaining the substantial amounts of cash required for a cash bid—a particularly problematic task in the current lending context. However, there are potential downsides. Organizing a share offer may be slower, with the attendant dangers allowing more time for a rival bidder and, in a hostile bid situation, giving incumbent management more time to prepare its defenses. Furthermore, in a share-exchange bid, target shareholders may view the offered shares as overvalued. The extent to which they do so is determined both by the reputation and anticipated prospects of the bidder and the wider market mood. Share exchanges are more acceptable in bull market periods. The evidence and views on target valuation in share-exchange bids is mixed. It may reduce the downside for the bidder of overvaluing the target because of information asymmetry and uncertainty (Sudarsanam 1995), but on the other hand for the target company's shareholders (and other stakeholders if pertinent) the same conditions (namely, information asymmetry and uncertainty) put an upward pressure on the desired price. Warren Buffet strongly prefers cash bids and reports that "When I've issued stock, I've cost you [the shareholders of 'his' company—Berkshire Hathaway] money" (in Cunningham 2002: 168).

The valuation of the shares offered is often the object of disagreement between bidder and targets—especially so in hostile takeover contexts. Unlike shares whose value is dependent on expectations, the value of cash itself is immediate and evident. But that is no guarantee that the size of a cash offer will be seen as adequate. A cash bid, a share-exchange bid, a mixed consideration bid can all be criticized by incumbent management, and commentators, as undervaluing the target.

Toehold   A "toehold" is a bidder's share ownership in the target, acquired prior to making a takeover bid. Such holdings reduce the portion of the target's share which a bidder must newly acquire to gain control. A toehold also reduces the cost of an acquisition as these shares will have been acquired without the additional cost of the bid premium. Despite these advantages, Betton, Eckbo, and Thorburn (2009) report that bidders rarely have a toehold in the target despite (as a consequence) paying substantial control premiums. In the period 1973–2002, they report that only 13% of 10,000 initial bidders seeking control of publicly traded US targets had toeholds. However, that data obscures the differences between negotiated and hostile takeovers. They observe that in the latter type of takeover, toehold bidding is the norm (50%). A likely explanation for the very small number of toeholds by bidders in negotiated takeovers is that approaching a target with a toehold already acquired might impede or sour negotiations. When toeholds are acquired, they tend to be large (Betton et al. 2009).

Dawn-Raid This is a means of rapidly acquiring a toehold (above). A substantial number of shares in a target company are bought when the market or markets in which its shares are traded open for the day, that is, in the morning. Hence the description of the "raid" as *dawn*-raid. Because the bidding company builds a substantial stake in its target at the prevailing stock market price, a price which does not incorporate anticipation of a takeover bid, the takeover costs are likely to be significantly lower than they would be had the acquiring company first made a formal takeover bid.

Blind Bid Bids may be based only on publicly available information or they may also be grounded on confidential information. The former are described as blind bids. The management of a target company will, because of their position as insiders, have information not in the public domain. A blind bid is almost always made without the prior knowledge of the incumbent management and the financial markets. Because of this information asymmetry, a blind bid is a risky strategy which is subject to the well-known "lemons problem" (Akerlof 1970). The "lemons" problem can lead to companies being sold cheaply. Buyer ignorance drives the price of good companies down. But conversely, that "blindness" or asymmetrical information drives up the prices of weak companies, thus increasing the risk of the buyer paying too much or even getting a dud. Cooper, Orlin, and Raghavendra (2001), for instance, found in a study of the period June 1998 to July 1999—a time of exuberance for shares in Internet companies—that the inclusion of a ".com" suffix in a firm's name resulted in a 53% increase in price. Even firms with very limited links to the Internet who added a ".com" suffix got a 23% increase in price. As Warren Buffett humorously but critically says:

> I've observed that many acquisition hungry managers are apparently mesmerized by their childhood reading of the story about the frog-kissing princess. Remembering her success, they pay dearly for the right to kiss corporate toads, expecting wondrous transformations. (in Cunningham 2002: 159)

A blind bid may be made after early attempts at a negotiated takeover have broken down. But more usually it is made without an approach to incumbent management or after an approach has been rebuffed.

Jump Bids These bids are made in the context of a bid auction. A new bid is made substantially above a previous bid by a competitor. Akin to bluffing on poker, a jump bid discourages other bidders by signaling that the jump bidder values the target more than anyone else and that anyone who competes with that bidder risks overpaying. The intention is to end the auction (Avery 1998). But whilst jump bids create incentives for rival bidders to cease bidding—as such bids signal the determination of the jump bidder to succeed—there is a contrary incentive for the rivals to continue bidding, since financial markets may perceive a lost competition as a missed opportunity to acquire a valuable addition and therefore downgrade the losers (Bradley et al. 1983).

Seeking to Avoid a Hostile Takeover In some cases, a hostile bid may be the only means of acquiring a target company but everything else being equal, hostile takeovers generate two additional types of cost. First, the price paid (the consideration) will be higher. Secondly, there will be post-takeover costs—higher costs of integration. Assuming the acquirer wishes the acquired company to continue as a going concern, the commitment of retained staff at the acquired company and their willingness to share tacit knowledge is likely to be lower. "Romancing" top management of a target company is widely recommended prior to even discussing a possible price if a negotiated takeover is deemed to be possible.

Reputational Protection Promises made as inducements to stakeholders are often not fulfilled after a hostile takeover. And, as already described above, the departure (voluntary or required) of management of acquired companies is much higher after hostile takeovers than after negotiated takeovers. For an acquiring company—which anticipates that it will undertake significant takeovers in the future—a hostile bid has the associated danger of reputational costs as future targets may be less willing to initiate negotiations with a bidder who has reneged on promises made previously.

In addition, a number of tactics, often described as "coercive," may be employed. The main criticism of these tactics is that they prevent all or some shareholders receiving a "fair price" for their shares. As a result, some regimes impose prohibitions or restrictions on these tactics.

Saturday Night Specials This is an offer which is open only for a short period of time, thereby forcing shareholders to decide quickly whether or not to tender and limiting the ability of the incumbent management to effectively present arguments against takeover. Most regimes now prohibit such coercion.

Two-tier-Tender Offers This is an offer to purchase a sufficient number of shares so as to gain effective control of a firm at a certain price per share, followed by a lower offer at a later date for the remaining shares. Two-tier tender offers rely on the ignorance of a shareholder whether or not other shareholders will tender their shares and thus whether the bid will be successful or not. Even shareholders believing that the "front-end" price is too low will rationally tender, fearing that they might be forced to take the lower "back-end" price. The greater the difference between the "front-end" and the back-end' price, the greater the coercive pressure on shareholders to tender (Mucciarelli 2006). Two-tier bids are not allowed in the EU—the bid price must be uniform—but are permissible in most US states.

Bid Defenses

The discussion above of takeover strategy illustrated how the motivation for a proposed takeover may influence the decision of incumbent management to support or oppose a takeover bid. From an exclusively shareholder returns perspective, the employment of defenses against the initiation or completion of a takeover has been both supported as a means to increase those returns or alternatively criticized for protecting incumbent management to the financial detriment of the target company's shareholders (Hartzell et al. 2004).

A host of defensive tactics have been fashioned to discourage bids and to defeat hostile ones. The major tactics are discussed below. Two key influences on the choice of tactics are the institutional context (the extent to which particular defenses are permitted and if so on whose authority—management or shareholders) and timing (whether the defenses are put in place pre-bid or post-bid).

Although the tactics employed by a target company are widely labeled as "defensive," their aim is not always necessarily to prevent a takeover but instead may, in effect, be a way of giving the directors/management of the target company more time to search for an alternative bidder, or to enable them to put more pressure on the bidder to raise the bid. The main defensive tactics are now discussed.

Enhancing Share Price Arguably, a major pre-bid defense is a sustained and strong share price performance in order to ensure high valuation and satisfied shareholders. Sound operational performance should provide the basis for a strong shareholder valuation of a company, but given market irrationalities it is not a guarantee of such an evaluation (Shleifer 2000). Some mechanisms employed to sustain or enhance share performance may ironically make companies more vulnerable to being taken over. Excessive cash payouts either as dividends or in buying-back shares may deplete the company of financial resources, weakening (not strengthening) the company. Prior to the 2007/8 financial crisis, demands for share price growth, and relatedly large dividend payments (and/or share buybacks to boost share prices), encouraged corporations to increasingly rely on external funds, rather than retained profits, so their debt ratios grew. Corporations were urged not to "turn their backs on opportunities for shareholder value offered by the easier availability of debt" (Bhide 1988: 98). Now, in a period of more constrained lending, the prior pressure to disgorge cash has left many companies vulnerable to takeover by cash-rich companies.

Good Investor Relations A parallel practice to operational actions to enhance a company's share price is a program to strengthen relations with shareholders, especially institutional shareholders, and with investment analysts, in ways which seek to create longer-term loyalty and awareness of the future benefits of activities requiring costly upfront investments. A balance has to be struck between extensive briefings of such parties and the danger of being seen to reveal price-sensitive information to selective shareholders only. Building good investor relations is a long-term task. To be effective the groundwork has to have been undertaken well before any takeover bid.

Repellents This is an umbrella term for a variety of procedures with the common aim of deterring or repelling takeovers. Broadly, they are of four types: procedural restrictions; "poison pills;" "golden parachutes;" and divestments. A colloquial description of repellents is "shark repellents," but this supposes that the motive of potential acquirers is always predatory, which it may be but is not always so.

Procedural restrictions include removing the mandatory retirement age for directors; changing corporation byelaws to make takeovers more difficult (for instance, increasing the proportion of shares needed to call a meeting of shareholders required to approve a takeover) or increasing the proportion of shareholders required to approve a takeover. As the term "poison pills" suggests, these are warnings to would-be acquirers that should they "swallow" the target company, they are likely to be "poisoned" (Kesner and Dalton 1985). The aim is to make a hostile takeover prohibitively expensive. Examples include: a requirement that anyone buying a specified significant portion of a company's shares (typically between 10–20%) would be obliged to also redeem the company preferred shares for cash and at a premium; allowing existing shareholders (except the acquirer) to buy more shares at a discount; and/or requiring an acquirer to sell its shares to the acquired company's shareholders at a discounted price.

The employability and power of a "pill," as with most other tactics, varies because of differences in national or sub-national (state) corporate law. In some countries they can be implemented by the directors without prior approval by shareholders. Since the Delaware Supreme Court's 1989 decision in *Paramount Communications, Inc. v. Time-Warner, Inc.*, no Delaware court has ever ordered a board of directors to redeem its poison pill (Gordon 2002). The court gave approval to a board to employ any defensive measures it chose, provided the measures were not "preclusive or coercive" (Arlen 2002: 918). However, in some other regimes, for instance the UK, the use of poison pills must be expressly authorized by the shareholders (The Panel on Takeovers and Mergers 2010). If a bidder gains control of the target's board, it would be able to remove the "pill" and proceed with an offer for the majority of the shares. But mechanisms to prevent such control include a staggered board, forcing the bidder to wait through at least two annual elections of directors before it could get a majority of seats on the target's board. Another mechanism for preventing the redemption of a pill, where permitted by corporate law, is a "dead hand" or "slow hand" pill. Dead hand provisions determine that the pill can only be redeemed by the continuing directors, that is, the directors who were in office when the pill was adopted, or their approved successors. A slow hand (or "delayed redemption") provision prevents any redemption of the pill for a defined limited period after a change in board composition.

"Golden parachutes" are provisions which guarantee a company's top management immense cash payments if the company is taken over. Often the provisions cover lengthy periods such that the payments would be required even some years after a takeover. However, "golden parachutes" may also have the opposite effect. Whilst making takeover targets more expensive and thus less attractive, they provide an incentive for potential beneficiaries (the chief executive officer and whoever else) to support a takeover. The latter effect is made all the more powerful if the potential beneficiaries have stock options from which they acquire substantial benefits when the company is acquired in premium bid.

Divestments are of two types. One way is the sale of parts of the target especially coveted by bidder—the "crown jewels." This makes the target less attractive to a bidder and encourages abandonment of the bid. A different form of divestment is sale not of the "crown jewels" but of underperforming parts of the target. Paradoxically, this action might increase the attractiveness of the target, but ideally the tactic is employed when the bidder plans—may even have announced—that they would sell off those parts posttakeover. Pre-emptive action by incumbent management undermines the rationale for the takeover and may boost its image amongst shareholders.

Paying Greenmail The term "greenmail" is a neologism derived from blackmail and greenbacks (i.e. dollar bills). As the notion of blackmail suggests, this tactic is a response to a threat (explicit or implicit). In these cases, a predator acquires a substantial block of company's shares. It then threatens, or is anticipated to threaten, a tender offer for the company as a whole. Incumbent management, afraid of losing control, or other reasons, for instance, fearing asset stripping, buys out the potential acquirer at a premium. The amount paid is sometimes colloquially called a "goodbye kiss" or a "bon voyage bonus." The tactic, whilst effective in warding off the immediate takeover threat, may increase a company's susceptibility to takeovers or takeover threats as it cues other potential raiders that the company is vulnerable to takeover or to be milked of cash.

Usually share prices of target firms fall after the payment of greenmail. Some writers have used this evidence as support for the "management entrenchment" hypothesis that bidder elimination tactics are used primarily to perpetuate the reign of self-serving managers. But whatever the motivation of incumbent management for such tactics, succumbing to greenmail may not ensure continuing control as firms paying greenmail have above-average management turnover in the following year. The "management entrenchment" hypothesis has also been challenged on the grounds that paying greenmail can be a way of encouraging a bidding war for the company, thus increasing the takeover premium. Greenmail has been very controversial and is debarred, discouraged, or prohibited in some jurisdictions or where permitted, its payment may require prior shareholder approval.

Once a hostile bid is made, or is imminent, a range of additional defense tactics may be employed.

Standstill Agreements Management of listed companies which provides inside information to a potential purchaser during friendly discussions or further down the line at the negotiation stage face the risk that the potential buyer—having acquired the information—makes an offer directly to the shareholders on terms unacceptable to the incumbent management. The prior information disclosures would have revealed weaknesses as well as strengths in the target company. The former then provide grounds to criticize incumbent management and legitimate a lower price. A defense against this tactic is a standstill agreement under which the potential acquirer agrees not to make a hostile bid, not to increase his stake in the target without the approval of the target's board, for a specified period. In exchange, the potential acquirer is allowed to conduct diligence with full access to the target's inside information (documents, records, reports, and so forth) (Subramanian 2003).

White Knights The management of the target company may approach another company to place a rival bid. For whatever reason, the rival is seen by the incumbent management as desirable, or at least less undesirable, than the company which has made the hostile bid. The desire to attract a rival (and friendly) bidder will be shaped by the takeover context. So, for instance, if the takeover strategy is capacity reduction, the incumbent management may see their position as less threatened than by the hostile party. If the takeover strategy is market expansion, the friendly bidder may be seen as having greater compatibility with the target company. In addition, the motive may be to increase the takeover premium by encouraging a bidding contest. An alternative to a takeover by a rival, but one which prevents the hostile takeover, is a partial bid for the shares of the company, thus providing protection for the target company *but* without acquiring control of it. Another company (or companies) may enter the fray without the approval—implicit or explicit—of the incumbent management.

The term "white knight" may not be an appropriate description of all such new bidders. If a rival second bidder (encouraged or not by the incumbent management) is successful, it will control the acquired company and thus incumbent management may be no more secure than if the hostile bid had succeeded. The new bidder, or bidders, are simply rivals to the original bidder, but for a range of reasons incumbent management may prefer the rival bid(s) to the original hostile bid. A grey knight, rather than a white knight, is perhaps a better description of the rival bidder(s). An acquirer of a portion of the target company's shares with the intention of preventing a takeover but not controlling the target is sometimes described as a "white squire" in that it protects but does not control. Whilst partial bids are legal in many countries, they are not allowed in some others.

Other Post-Bid Tactics These include issue of additional shares which can disperse ownership more widely or effectively place shares in friendly hands; issue of shares to employees as they are likely to oppose a takeover; share buybacks which increase share price and increase company debt; defensive divestments (particularly of a subsidiary or subsidiaries which the predator especially wants); acquisitions (making the target company more expensive); management buyout; regulatory appeal (usually on the grounds that the takeover would be anti-competitive); lawsuits (for example, on the grounds that the bidder misrepresented material facts in their bid or breaches of confidentiality or conflicts of interest—even when the grounds for such complaint are thin, they have the effect of delaying a takeover and creating more space for the arrival of a "white knight"); intensified communications to shareholders critical of the takeover bid (this may also be underpinned by increased dividend payouts; asset revaluations; and/or improved profit announcements); changing the country of incorporation or in federal countries, changing the state of incorporation where hostile takeovers are more difficult; voting right restrictions and/or dual voting rights (prohibited in many countries); and turning the tables by launching a counter-attack on the bidding company (the so-called "Pac-Man defense" named after a video game character).

Encouraging Opposition by Employee Organizations In countries where trade unions or other employee representative organizations have formal influence on corporate governance—including board of director membership in some countries—opposition to a takeover by an employee organization can be very influential. Where such influence does not exist—such as in Anglo-American countries—this form of opposition has no direct value. However, even in those countries, the tactic may have benefits for incumbent management. If the aim of the bidder is operational synergy with the target (post-takeover), employee opposition might suggest implementation difficulties because of resentment and departures. This reduces the attractiveness of the target. However, if the object is only to acquire assets other than employees (such as brands, patents, or distribution channels), the tactic is likely to be ineffectual.

Discussion

Takeover activity is a contextually shaped activity between parties with asymmetrical information and in conditions of uncertainty. Because of the economic and social importance of takeovers, the activity is regulated. Whilst cross-national border takeovers have increased considerably and notwithstanding greater liberalization and globalization, legal, institutional, and other rules vary across borders. These differences influence and shape the frequency, the scale, and type of takeovers within and between countries, the variety and effectiveness of different tactics employed by those seeking to obtain control of a corporation, and the response (welcoming or hostile) of the management of the latter.

Hyper efficient notions of stock market efficiency widely employed in the takeover literature suppose that shareholders are a homogeneous group (with for instance a common time horizon); that perfect information is available, that management is always rational, and that what is good for shareholders is necessarily good for all stakeholders. Each assumption is problematic. In contrast with the idealized situation of perfect information (and thus the absence of uncertainty) and the equal distribution of power, the reality of takeover events is far messier. Necessarily, there is knowledge which insiders have and outsiders do not. Subsequent activities, especially due-diligence processes, reduce, but do not eliminate, that opaqueness.

The employment of formal analytical processes, for example discounted cash flow, to value a company may beneficially increase the rigor of takeover analysis, but they cannot eliminate uncertainty about the future (Arzac 2008). As Gigerenzer et al. (1989) observe, "no amount of mathematical legerdemain can transform uncertainty into certainty." To make a game analogy, takeovers are much more like poker than Sudoku. Success in the latter depends wholly on technical skill. But in the former, whilst calculation is significant, asymmetrical information, uncertainty, emotion, bluffing, and sheer luck are all unavoidable ingredients.

Should there be a "free market" in takeover tactics (buy and sell-side) or is there an essential role for regulation? If legal intervention is deemed to be essential—which it currently is in every major country—which offensive and defensive tactics should be permitted or curtailed and to what extent? And whose interests should the regulation of tactics protect? Should shareholder choice be the default rule? As we have seen, different national corporate governance regimes give different answers depending on the underlying view of the role of takeovers. Identifying the consequences of takeovers is complicated by choice of time frame, measures, range of recognized stakeholders, and comparators. A post-takeover decline in "value" (however measured) and/or a reduction in the workforce (managerial or other) is not, of itself, an indication of failure. The appropriate comparison is not with the past but with what would have happened without the takeover. But "value" for whom? Much of the literature which evaluates takeovers focuses only on the consequences for shareholders (of the acquired and acquiring companies) and implicitly or explicitly supposes that what is good for shareholders is always good for everyone else. Objective and comprehensive evaluations need to review the longer-term consequences for all, including the wider community and nation—not narrowly focus just on the consequences for shareholders. A departing "boat" does not necessarily take everyone on it.

References

Akerlof, G. A. (1970). "The Market for 'Lemons': Quality Uncertainty and the Market Mechanism." *Quarterly Journal of Economics*, 84/3: 488–500.

Arlen, J. (2002). "Designing Mechanisms to Govern Takeover Defenses: Private Contracting, Legal Intervention, and Unforeseen Contingencies." *The University of Chicago Law Review*, 69/3: 917–32.

Arzac, E. R. (2008). *Valuation for Mergers, Buyouts and Restructuring* (2nd ed.). New York: John Wiley & Sons.

Avery, C. (1998). "Jump Bidding in English Auctions." *The Review of Economic Studies*, 65/2: 185–210.

Barron, J. M., & Waddell, G. R. (2003). "Executive Rank, Pay and Project Selection." *Journal of Financial Economics*, 67/2: 305–49.

Betton, S., Eckbo, B. E., & Thorburn, K. S. (2009). "Merger Negotiations and the Toehold Puzzle." *Journal of Financial Economics*, 91: 158–78.

Bhide, A. (1988). "Why Not Leverage Your Company to the Hilt?" *Harvard Business Review*, 66/3: 92–8.

Bolton, P., Scheinkman, J., and Xiong, W. (2006). "Executive Compensation and Short-Termist Behaviour in Speculative Markets." *Review of Economic Studies*, 73: 577–610.

Bower, J. L. (2001). "Not All M&As are Alike—and that Matters." *Harvard Business Review*, 79, March: 93–101.

Bradley, M., Desai, A., and Kim E. H. (1983). "The Rationale behind Interfirm Tender Offers: Information or Synergy?" *Journal of Financial Economics*, 11: 183–206.

Bughin, J., and Copeland, T. E. (1997). "The Virtuous Cycle of Shareholder Value Creation." *The McKinsey Quarterly*, 2: 156–67.

Bulow, J., and Klemperer, P. (2009). "Why Do Sellers (Usually) Prefer Auctions?" *American Economic Review*, 99/4: 1544–75.

Cooper, M., Orlin, D., and Raghavendra, R. (2001). "A Rose.com By Any Other Name." *Journal of Finance*, 56/6: 2371–88.

Cunningham, L. A. (2002). *The Essays of Warren Buffett: Lessons for Investors and Managers.* Singapore: John Wiley & Sons.

Franks, J., and Mayer, C. (1996). "Hostile Takeovers and the Correction of Managerial Failure." *Journal of Financial Economics*, 40/1: 163–81.

Froud, J., Johal, S., Leaver, A., and Williams, K. (2006). *Financialization and Strategy: Narrative and Numbers.* London: Routledge.

Gigerenzer, G., Swijtink, Z., Daston, L., Beatty, J., and Krüger. L. (1989). *The Empire of Chance.* Cambridge: Cambridge University Press.

Gordon, M. (2002). "Takeover Defences: Is That Such a Bad Thing?" *Stanford Law Review*, 55/3: 819–37.

Hartzell, J. C., Ofek, E., and Yermack, D. (2004). "What's in It for Me? CEOs Whose Firms Are Acquired." *The Review of Financial Studies*, 17/1: 37–61.

Höpner, M., and Jackson, G. (2004). "An Emerging Market for Corporate Control? The Mannesmann Takeover and German Corporate Governance." Working Paper 01/04 Max-Planck-Institut für Gesellschaftsforschung. Available at: <http://papers.ssrn.com/sol3/papers.cfm?abstract_id=285232>.

Jensen, M. C. (1988). "Takeovers: Their Causes and Consequences." *Journal of Economic Perspectives*, 2/1: 21–48.

Kahan, M., and Rock, E. B. (2002). "How I Learned to Stop Worrying and Love the Pill: Adaptive Responses to Takeover Law." *The University of Chicago Law Review*, 69/3: 871–915.

Kay, J. (2010). "*Obliquity: Why Our Goals Are Best Achieved Indirectly.*" London: Profile Books.

Keida, S. (2001). "Vodaphone Air Touch's Bid for Mannesmann." Harvard Business School Case Study No. 9-201-096.

Kesner, I. F., and Dalton, D. R. (1985). "Antitakeover Tactics: Management 42, Stockholders 0." *Business Horizons*, 5, September–October: 17–25.

Langmann, C. (2007). "Stock Market Reaction and Stock Options Plans: Evidence from Germany." *Schmalenbach Business Review*, 59: 85–106.

Marens, R., and Wicks, A. (1999). "Getting Real: Stakeholder Theory, Managerial Practice and the General Irrelevance of Fiduciary Duties to Shareholders." *Business Ethics Quarterly*, 9/2: 272–93.

McNamara, G. M., Haleblian, J., and Dykes, B. J. (2008). "The Performance Implications of Participating in an Acquisition Wave: Early Mover Advantages, Bandwagon Effects, and the

Moderating Influence of Industry Characteristics and Acquirer Tactics." *Academy of Management Journal*, 51/1: 113–30.

McSweeney, B. (2009). "The Roles of Financial Asset Market Failure Denial and the Economic Crisis: Reflections on Accounting and Financial Theories and Practices." *Accounting, Organizations & Society*, 43: 835–48.

Mucciarelli, F. M. (2006). "White Knights and Black Knights: Does the Search for Competitive Bids Always Benefit the Shareholders of 'Target' Companies?" Working Paper. Available at: <http://amsacta.cib.unibo.it/2129/1/White_knights_and_black_knights.pdf>.

Organization for Economic Cooperation and Development (2007). *International Investment Perspectives: Freedom of Investment in a Changing World*. Paris: OECD.

O'Sullivan, M. A. (2000). *Contests for Corporate Control*. Oxford: Oxford University Press.

Porter, M. (1992). "Capital Disadvantage: America's Failing Investment System." *Harvard Business Review*, 70, September–October: 65–82.

Shleifer, A. (2000). *Inefficient Markets: An Introduction to Behavioural Finance*. Cambridge: Cambridge University Press.

Shleifer, A., & Vishny, R. W. (2003). "Stock Market Driven Acquisitions." *Journal of Financial Economics*, 70, December: 295–311.

Streeck, J. (2007). "Endgame? The Fiscal Crisis of the German State." Cologne: Max-Planck-Institut für Gesellschaftsforschung, Discussion Paper 07/7. Available at: <http://federation. ens.fr/ydepot/semin/texte0809/STR2009END.pdf>.

Subramanian, G. (2003). "Bargaining in the Shadow of Takeover Defences." *Yale Law Journal*, 113/3: 621–86.

Sudarasanam, P. S. (1995). "The Role of Defensive Strategies and Ownership Structure of Target Firms: Evidence from UK Hostile Takeover Bids." *European Financial Management*, 1/3: 223–40.

The Panel on Takeovers and Mergers (2010). *The City Code on Mergers and Takeovers*. Available at: <http://www.thetakeoverpanel.org.uk/wp-content/uploads/2008/11/code.pdf>.

Ventoruzzo, M. (2005). "The Thirteenth Directive and the Contrasts between European and U.S. Takeover Regulation: Different (Regulatory) Means, Not so Different (Political and Economic) Ends?" Bocconi Legal Studies Research Paper No. 06-07. Available at SSRN: <http://ssrn.com/abstract=819764>.

Verbeke, A. (2009). *International Business Strategy*. Cambridge: Cambridge University Press.

Williamson, O. (1984). "Corporate Governance." *The Yale Law Journal*, 93/7: 1197–230.

CHAPTER 12

LEVERAGED BUYOUTS

VIKTORIA DALKO

INTRODUCTION

The current chapter aims to provide an introduction for the reader to the world of one of the most exciting developments of the M&A market, those acquisitions (and divestitures) made by a specialized financial buyer, from relatively minor equity and large borrowed funds, to be returned in 10–12 years. These investments are usually not liquid, and allow almost negligible influence for the equity investors—yet, equity committed to such funds (LBO funds) have grown exponentially since the mid-1980s, and especially since 2001. We review the key characteristics of these M&A transactions, from acquisition to divestiture.

THE ROLE OF PRIVATE EQUITY IN LEVERAGED BUYOUTS

What is a leveraged buyout (LBO) and what is private equity (PE)? A leveraged buyout is a transaction whereby the majority or the entire business of a public or private corporation, or a business unit, is acquired by a firm that specializes in such transactions. Much of the purchase price is paid from debt (Kaplan and Strömberg 2009). The firm that is subject to an LBO will be referred to in the chapter as the LBO target firm, or portfolio firm, or individual investment by the PE fund. Three main types of buyers can be involved in an LBO transaction: private equity buyout firms; hedge funds, with or without the cooperation of the incumbent management; and the incumbent management, without the sponsorship of PE or hedge fund (the latter called non-sponsored management buyout (MBO)).

Private equity is risk capital, and as an industry, it includes private equity buyout firms (that are engaged in leveraged buyouts, mainly as equity owners), and also venture capital firms (VCs) that invest in early stage business, are less leveraged, and do not aim for majority control. In the literature, some use the terminology private equity firm and leveraged buyout investment firm interchangeably (Kaplan and Strömberg 2009). We will follow this tradition in the current chapter, and we call PE firms the leveraged buyout investment firms (not VCs.) Most PE firms are diversified, operating numerous types of funds, including real estate, infrastructure, natural resource, turnaround, distressed debt, mezzanine, and secondaries, besides buyout and venture funds (Bain & Company 2010). Some also have their own hedge funds.

In the US, PE funds usually are set up as private limited liability partnerships with 10–12-year terms. The PE firm is the general partner and outside investors are passive limited partners (Metrick and Yasuda 2010). The main reason for the choice of limited partnership is its favorable pass-through tax treatment. In addition, limited partnerships provide contractual flexibility and a certain default setting for fiduciary responsibilities (Birdthistlet and Henderson 2009). However, this legal form brings certain problems with it. General partners have clear discretion ahead of limited partners. Limited partners have very few legal avenues to challenge the decisions made by general partners, even though there is an obvious difference in interest (Harris 2010). PE funds raise equity primarily from institutional investors (Cumming 2010, chapter 2), and more recently, and to a much smaller degree, from the investing public. In 2006, in the US, 57% of capital committed was from pension funds. This proportion is much higher than for European contributors from pension funds.

The second type of buyers in an LBO transaction are hedge funds, which increasingly have been participating in LBOs over the last decade, finding the returns to be attractive to complement their traditional investment activities. Recently, hedge funds and private equity buyout firms have clearly converged (Blassberg 2006). The third type of buyers are the incumbent management without PE sponsorship—that is, non-sponsored MBO. Although this is a potentially different type of LBO, there is very little information available for research. When a buyout is originated by the incumbent management, it is always referred to as a management buyout (MBO), whether it is PE sponsored or not. It is usually contrasted with management buy-ins (MBI), which are PE-led LBOs, if the PE fund does not retain the original management but brings in its own.

Who are the investors in PE firms? One of the relatively few distinguishing characteristics remaining between hedge funds and private equity is the significance of institutional investors in PE, as opposed to hedge funds, 80% of whose investors are wealthy individuals (Edwards 1999). In particular, considering the worldwide distribution of assets under management in 2008, we find that pension funds have the greatest share, at over $22 billion, followed by mutual funds and insurance companies. Sovereign wealth funds, which are both a source of equity investment for private equity and sometimes direct competitors for the deal, had about $3 trillion in assets under management—still double that of hedge funds and private equity (Fotak et al. 2008).

Value, Location and Type of LBO Deals

In the US, LBO had three cycles; each lasted a decade and each ended with a collapse: the 1980s, the 1990s, and 2000–2010. The LBO boom was driven in the 1980s by the inefficiency of conglomerates and the flourishing junk bond market, in the 1990s by GDP growth, and in the 2000s by the liquidity surge and the credit bubble (Bain & Company 2010).

Globally, the picture is somewhat different. The number of leveraged buyouts and the value of the firms that were undertaken in LBO have grown exponentially globally between 2001 and 2007 (see Figure 12.1).

Industry sources provide a much smaller LBO deal value than Kaplan and Strömberg (2009). According to Bain & Company (2010), rising from $28 bn in 1995, the peak global buyout deal value in 2007 was only $503 bn. After the peak, between 2007–9 deal activity sank in all regions, declining by a compound annual rate of 66% in North America and in Europe, 32% in Asia, and 58% in the rest of the world (Bain & Company 2010). The difference between Bain's and Kaplan and Strömberg's numbers are due to two reasons: Kaplan and Strömberg (2009) estimate enterprise value and not equity value, even though Thomson Reuter's data used in the Bain study include deals made not only by the PE funds but also by the portfolio firms.

In Rubenstein's (2009) opinion, this phenomenal rise in transaction value was due to the increased demand by institutional investors for higher returns from PE funds, and it was enabled by the increasingly more accommodating debt markets, and less extreme stock market valuations prior to the second half of 2007. In addition, it is very likely that

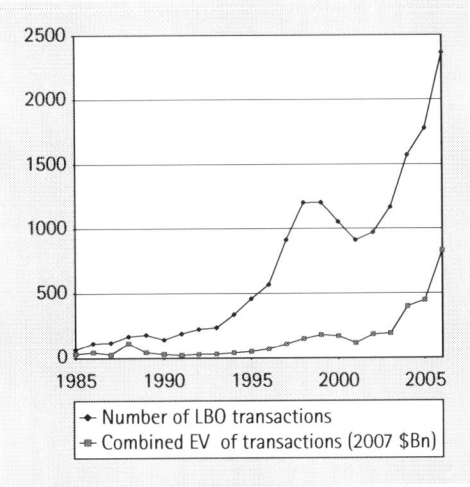

FIG. 12.1 Number of LBO transactions and combined enterprise value of transactions (measured in 2007 $bn)

Source: Kaplan and Strömberg (2009).

the geographical shift contributed to the size of the boom. A very significant change in geographical distribution of global LBO deals happened recently. Since 1985, the United States has fallen in significance, and by 2007 was below 50% of the combined enterprise value of global LBO deals. Western Europe (outside of the UK) was the main target location fueling the spectacular rise, from 3% to 30% of global deal value. Meanwhile, Asia and Australia have doubled their share of a fast-growing total (Axelson et al. 2010).

In a previous version of their paper, Axelson et al. (2008) report not only the geography but also the dominant type of LBO transactions over time. During the first five years of the PE industry, from 1985 to 1989, 49% of the combined enterprise value was public to private. In the following decade, between 1990 and 2000, independent private transactions were dominant, with 54–44% of enterprise value. Immediately following the dot-com bubble burst, between 2000 and 2004, divisional buyouts dominated, with 41% of deal value. In the two years leading up to the 2007 financial crisis, public-to-private transactions became dominant again, accounting for 34% of enterprise value.

Over the entire 37 years between 1970 and 2007, divisional buyout had the largest share globally, 30% of overall enterprise value (Axelson et al. 2010). This was due mainly to the remarkable post-dot-com boom divisional buyout activities, when other forms of financing, besides what PE could provide, became relatively scarce, while many firms suddenly had limited access to capital and faced possible financial distress in the future. However, it is interesting to note that distressed LBOs never exceeded 2% of the deals; therefore, the common vision of PE funds rescuing failing corporations is not supported by the available statistics.

The only type of activity that has increased steadily over time is secondary LBO— when one PE fund sells a portfolio firm to another PE fund. This segment grew from 2% of enterprise value to 26% between 1985–9 and 2005–7. Was this shift a result of the choice of PE funds or were they responding to new constraints? When funds close, general partners are required to distribute capital back to the limited partners; there is a pressing need to sell the portfolio companies. Is it possible that portfolio firms that could not be sold to the public or to a strategic buyer had to be sold to other PE funds? Cumming, Siegel, and Wright (2007) argue that secondary, tertiary, and fourth-time-around buyouts are due to the mounting difficulties of traditional exit strategies, and are unlikely to result in further efficiency gains for the company. This increasingly frequent phenomenon deserves further investigation. In particular, it would be interesting to know if the buyer and seller PE funds have common general partners, or are related in other ways or not.

In summary, we have reviewed the value, the type of LBO deals, and the geographic location of the target. All these characteristics exhibit rapid and major changes over time, as opportunities and constraints evolve. In particular, there is an interesting fact: the rise in significance of secondary LBOs, becoming the second most frequent type of LBO during the last peak of 2005–7, signals maturity, saturation, and possible future problems for the industry.

In the next section we review the critical and distinguishing features of LBO deal structuring relative to other M&A deals.

How Acquisitions Have been and Should be Structured?

Optimally, LBOs should be structured to harmonize the interests of every related party, based on their existing and diverse priorities. There are numerous areas of acquisition structuring that influence one another, and usually are subject to negotiation. The first of the three main categories of acquisitions structuring questions involve the legal issues, including the type of acquisition vehicle, and the post-closing organization. In a leveraged buyout, the PE fund usually creates a new entity, Newco, which is the entity that acquires the target company. The Newco borrows from the lead banker, which in turn deals with the rest of the debt providers. Often, several Newcos are established, to match the needs of the different funding sources (Gilligan and Wright 2010). The second issue of acquisition structuring is that of accounting and tax, which is treated in a separate chapter of the *Handbook*. The third type of structuring question is the amount of payment, the form and timing of payment, and what is acquired (asset or stock) (DePamphilis 2010). We focus on these third types of questions in the following section.

Most often in LBOs, the past debt of the target firm is paid off as part of the transaction. Regarding the amount of payment, or the valuation issues of the LBO, it has been shown by numerous studies that the price PE pays for the target company is strongly correlated to the amount of debt it is able to take on (Axelson et al. 2010). That is to say, the lower the interest rate on leveraged loans—bank loans intentionally structured as high risk—the higher the leverage and higher the price paid for the LBO target firm. More liquid and "forgiving" debt markets contribute to higher pricing for LBO transactions. Therefore, we discuss LBO valuation issues in the following section, as part of the decision on the degree of leverage. Regarding the form of payment for LBO, it is so critical to the business that, in practice, there is widespread agreement on viewing private equity as a special way of financing deals. We will consider this issue in two steps: the division between debt and equity and the choice among the variety of debt instruments.

Degree of Leverage

As of the spring of 2010, it was estimated that the leveraged buyout community had accumulated $3 trillion bank debt (Griffiths and Mathiason 2010). How did this happen? First, we review the data that are available regarding the degree of leverage of LBOs, on average and its change over time.

For the 873 LBO samples of Axelson et al. (2010), the median proportion of non-contingent debt to enterprise value overall was 70%. This ratio was highest for public-to-private transactions, and lowest for independent private buyouts. One measure frequently used by the industry, total debt ratio to EBITDA (earnings before interest, tax, depreciation, and amortization—an incomplete but often used substitute for free cash flows), had a median of 5.2. These averages, however, changed significantly over time. For example, according to a CNBC interview with David Rubenstein (2009) before the financial crisis, debt commonly reached 10–11 times EBITDA.

According to Thomas (2010), the equity portion of PE transactions fluctuated between 12.7% in 1987–90 and 32.8% for 2005–7. The 2007–9 increase in equity participation in PE deals was due to the need to partially replace the disappeared debt financing with equity (Bain & Company 2010).

Leverage on the Portfolio Company Level

Traditional finance theory has recommended an optimal capital structure that maximizes the value of the firm (Damodaran 1997, 2002). There is a striking difference between the capital structure of current US firms and those that underwent LBO. In general, US public firms are on average 75% equity financed and 25% debt financed, while target companies undergoing a leveraged buyout are 25% equity and 75% debt financed (Axelson et al. 2010). Is the level of debt raised at the time of the LBO transaction optimal?

In theory, the capital structure of the LBO is primarily determined by the balance between the increased firm value due to the tax shield of the debt and the increased probability of bankruptcy (Olsen et al. 2003). Therefore, the critical test of whether the debt is optimal for the portfolio company level is to check whether the PE firm estimates the probability of bankruptcy and the cost of bankruptcy well enough, so that value of the portfolio company increases—that the gain from the tax shield is not offset by the expected increase in the cost of bankruptcy caused by the added leverage. Real options have been recommended by financial experts as a viable method of valuation of LBO (Damodaran 2002). The key idea is that a PE firm does not have any commitment to keep its portfolio company alive. If at any time in the future, the return on equity is higher when allowing the portfolio company to go bankrupt relative to paying its debt, the PE firm will select bankruptcy.

The sources of the value added from leverage for equity holders is the expectation that the effective after-tax interest expense will be low enough so that it is below the operating return on assets; therefore, the spread increases the return on equity (Palepu and Healy 2008). The standard way to incorporate the value of the tax shield in the enterprise value is through applying the discounted cash flow (DCF) technique, valuing the firm with all equity financing, and adding the value of the interest tax shield separately. This technique is the adjusted present value (Ross et al. 2002). The variable risk method (DePamphilis 2010) proposes to adjust the discount rate each year, while the capital structure changes according to the DCF method. Equity cash flow methodology is a more practical alternative valuation method for valuing highly leveraged transactions (Luehrman 2009; Baldwin 2001). Using comparable firm and comparable transaction ratios is common in the industry, but has a limited theoretical base (Palepu and Healey 2008).

This way of considering the benefit of leverage partly explains the interesting phenomenon of why, in the Middle East and North Africa region (MENA), PE funds often do not employ leverage for investment—since tax is in general very modest, the tax shield gives little increase in value, and the corporate debt market is underdeveloped or non-existent (Abillama et al. 2010). One way to evaluate if the level of debt is optimal for the portfolio firm is to weight the two sides of the equation: return on assets and the risk of default. Cumming, Siegel, and Wright (2007) provide a detailed analysis of the existing literature on the firm-level returns of buyouts and private equity, including shareholder return, investor return, and accounting return. In addition, Phalippou and Gottschalg (2009) provide critical assessment of data and correct for many shortcomings of the commonly used databases. We will review their results and compare it with the evidence regarding the increased risk of default later in the chapter.

There is another way to decide if the leverage is optimal at the fund level—by econometric analysis. That is, after controlling for other known factors, increased leverage should result in higher fund return. However, with a large global matched database, Axelson et al. (2010) find the opposite: funds with more leveraged deals have lower returns. That means that increasing target firm leverage is not optimal from the PE fund limited partners' point of view. In fact, according to Axelson et al. (2010), factors that influence leverage for public firms have no impact on leverage for LBO targets. Indeed, they find that the most important factor defining leverage for buyout targets is the interest rate and availability of debt. Lower interest rates for buyout that is readily available result in more leverage and higher prices. Therefore, they find strong evidence of an agency problem behind the size of leverage, and not the principle of maximization of equity investors' return. This is especially so when we take into account that general partners benefit from larger fund size directly, but limited partners do not. Metrick and Yasuda (2010) found that 80% of general partners' remuneration depends on the fund size. Only 20% depends on the return on investment. Therefore, larger and older funds are providing a higher revenue stream for general partners, while more leverage results in a lower return to limited partners.

In summary, after reviewing the degree of leverage historically taken for LBO deals, we ask what finance theory can tell us about the optimal capital structure. We consider two approaches, the trade-off between increased risk of bankruptcy and increased value of the firm and a new econometric study that directly addresses the question of whether higher leverage increases the return to PE fund investors. The risk/return trade-off is discussed later in the chapter. The direct econometric analysis by Axelson et al. (2010) points to the suboptimality of existing leverage: decisions are based on the availability and the interest rate of the debt, and not on the characteristics of the firm that is being bought out with the debt. In practice, higher leverage increases the purchase price of the LBO target firm, and reduces the return to limited partners, just the opposite to what one would expect based on neoclassical financial theory. This is evidence of a conflict of interest between limited and general partners.

Sources and Terms of Debt Financing

According to Blassberg (2006), the main development of the past ten years is that the financing options for PE have expanded greatly, including the growth of the EU

Table 12.1 Typical LBO transaction structure

Offering	Percent of Transaction	Cost of Capital	Lending Parameters	Likely Sources
Senior debt	50–60%	7–10%	5–7 years payback 2.0x–3.0x EBITDA 2.0x interest coverage	Commercial banks Credit companies Insurance companies
Mezzanine Financing	20–30%	10–20%	7–10 years payback 1.0–2.0x EBITDA	Public Market Insurance companies LBO/Mezzanine Funds
Equity	20–30%	25–40%	4–6 year exit strategy	Management LBO funds Subordinated debt holders Investment banks

Source: Olsen et al. (2003).

high-yield bond market, the second lien debt market, and the use of asset-backed securities (ABS). The complex financial structure of LBO by PE has not received appropriate attention from academic circles. There are only two good examples; one is Cotter and Peck (2001), who describe the debt structure of 64 US public-to-private buyout transactions in the 1980s, and Axelson et al. (2010), who provide a detailed study of 1,157 global buyouts.

The two main types of non-equity financing for LBO are bank debt, of different seniority, and bonds, also of different seniority. Assumed debt, off balance sheet financing, and vendor loans are minority additions to these two main types of debt financing. Note that the large majority of non-equity funding coming from bank debt is frequently securitized and sold to non-bank investors (or the shadow-banking system). In this way, bank lending was not subject to bank lending regulations, including capital adequacy ratio requirements. Olsen et al. (2003) propose the following capital structure to be typical (see Table 12.1).

As the table shows in principle, debt for buyout can be provided by commercial banks, investment banks, mezzanine debt providers, hedge funds, and other lending institutions. Some of the lending is syndicated, and kept within the banks. Some lending is structured and sold on the capital markets through collaterized debt obligations (CDO) or collaterized loan obligations (CLO). Mezzanine or subordinated debt is usually offered by insurance firms, hedge funds, and other specialty finance companies. It often includes interest and detachable warrants. Another way of categorizing lending is by its basis: asset-based or cash flow-based.

The following section, including the categorization of the types of debt, relies on the DePamphilis (2010) summary. Accordingly, most of the debt for LBO is asset-based.

The type of asset used as collateral influences the type of borrowing it can be used for. Those assets, relatively easy to liquidate, like inventories or accounts receivable, would be acceptable for a loan for a short term (one year). Term loans (two to ten years) use capital equipment or land as collaterals. Term loans are negotiated privately with the bank; therefore, they are expected to be less costly than public floating. Those who lend on a cash-flow basis have no collateral. These loans often are called mezzanine financing. The name suggests that its seniority is below senior debt, but above equity in case of borrower's default. The types of mezzanine financing include senior subordinated debt, subordinated debt, bridge financing, and high-yield bonds.

A different terminology, besides the above classification, that appears to have multiple meaning is leveraged loan. A leveraged loan, a bank loan intentionally structured as high risk, is a segment of the syndicated loan market. It is higher yielding and higher risk than senior secured loan. It has greatly and systematically exceeded the amount of junk bonds issued globally since 1995. Bain & Company (2010) reveals that the LBO boom, especially after 2003, was enabled by the exponential growth in leveraged loan issuance. At the same time, the 2008–9 collapse of the LBO market also was due to the disappearance of liquidity from the leveraged loan market. High-yield debt issue was stable and certainly was not the driving force behind the last boom and bust of the LBO market.

In summary, we can conclude that the sources of debt and terms of debt financing have a very significant impact on boom and bust in the global LBO market. The first, 1980s, boom was based on high-yield bond market growth, and the most recent boom is related to the exponential growth of leveraged loans and its securitization. By the same mechanism, once securitized debt lost its liquidity and much of its value during the 2007–9 financial crisis, the LBO market subsequently collapsed.

Post-buyout Capital Structure: Financial and Legal Strategies to Minimize Risk of Bankruptcy

How much is the debt service for the LBO firm initially? How many years does it take to reduce debt service to the level public firms have? Do PE firms manage the risk of default of their portfolio firms well? Is the rate of default comparable or higher than for public companies? These are the questions we set out to answer. According to Axelson et al. (2010), in their large global sample of LBOs, 22.8% of the principal is paid back during the first five years. Since during the observation period of the study, the typical spread of senior bank debt is between 271–306 basis points, and for subordinated debt it is 519–543 basis points, the interest coverage ratio as EBITDA/cash interest payment is about 2. As the numbers are measured as a percentage of previous years' EBITDA, over the first five years, an average of about 60% EBITDA is spent on net working capital and debt service, and the rest is used for tax, depreciation, or amortization, and investment in long-term assets.

The second consequence of the payment schedule is that after five years, about 22.8% of principal is paid off—leaving the firm with about 50% debt and 50% equity capital structure. Cao and Lerner (2009) support the previous findings on change in leverage: PE portfolio firms sold back to the public—known as reverse LBO (RLBO)—have a median total debt/assets ratio of 29.52%, compared with a 9.36% industry-adjusted total debt/asset ratio for mature firms; and interest expense/operating income of 25.99%, compared with 14.92% for mature firms in the same industry. This implies that during the average 3.46 years spent in private ownership, firms' capital structures change dramatically, but they are still significantly more highly leveraged relative to public firms at the time of RLBO.

Can portfolio companies avoid default if the macroeconomic environment, the industry, or the business itself is changing? With severe constraints on the use of cash, can portfolio companies avoid default on their borrowing, once they have such a difficult-to-service capital structure? In order to answer this question, we next consider observed failure and default rates.

Bankruptcy

Studying an early sample, Kaplan and Stein (1993) document that more than 30% of management buyouts (MBOs) completed after 1985 later defaulted. Kaplan and Andrade (1998) calculated a 23% default rate of larger public-to-private firms, at least for transactions in the 1980s. On a longer time horizon, with comparisons, a number of studies have been completed so far (see Table 12.2).

Table 12. 2 Estimates of portfolio company default rates

Study	Period	Default Rate
Kaplan and Stein 1993	1980–4	0.41%
Kaplan and Stromberg 2009	1970–2	1.20%
BIS 2008	1982–6	2.13%
BIS 2008	1992–6	2.63%
Chapman and Klein 2009	1984–6	2.66%
Private Equity Council	2008–09	2.84%
Guo, Hotchkiss, and Son 2010	1990–6	3.14%
BIS 2008	1987–1	3.14%
BIS 2008	1997–1	3.84%
Kaplan and Stein 1993	1985–89	5.17%
Non–PE		
S&P Overall Default Rate		4.19%
Moody's Default Rate (Speculative)		4.32%

Source: Thomas (2010)

In a study for the Private Equity Council, Thomas (2010) argues that PE-backed companies exhibit a low default rate, even at the time of the "Great Recession" of 2008–9. There are several reasons why PE portfolio firms may have lower bankruptcy rates than would be expected based on their extreme leverage. First of all, we documented above the importance of bank lending and the unimportance of bonds in the deals. Bank lending can more easily facilitate renegotiation of terms outside of bankruptcy procedure, and such ability reduces the possible cost of bankruptcy (Gertner and Scharfstein 1991). In addition, payment-in-kind or RESET bonds often are used for this purpose, avoiding default on bonds when the firm cannot pay its interest (Opler 1993). Second, PE firms often have equity at hand that has been committed by limited partners but has not been invested. This equity often is known as "dry powder." PE firms can therefore apply an equity injection should a portfolio company be in temporary need. This "dry powder" was estimated to be of the magnitude of $1.07 trillion at the beginning of 2010 (Bain & Co. 2010).

Third, PE firms can launch a so-called "loan to re-own" campaign, buying up debt from other investors that was issued for their LBO transaction, before their portfolio firm becomes distressed. All three methods can reduce the likelihood of the portfolio firm's bankruptcy. However, the size of the PE firms could make a difference. The reason is because the borrowing conditions are different for PE firms with the highest reputation than for the others (Ivashina and Kovner 2008; Demiroglu 2008). In fact, there is an expectation that portfolio companies, at least those of the larger PE firms, exhibit a lower rate of default than comparable publicly held firms, during financial distress (Thomas 2010). That would result in a higher leverage than for publicly held corporations being optimal for LBO portfolio firms.

In addition, whether PE-sponsored firms can go bankrupt or not is in part a legal expertise question and not so much a question of finance or management. PE portfolio firms default less frequently on their debt partly because of the specific structure of the debt. Jensen (1989) pointed out that portfolio firms avoid the bankruptcy court, and carry out a private resolution of claims out of court, once the portfolio firm becomes insolvent. In addition, Jensen (1989) also provides an explanation for LBO firms' very high rate of restructuring and M&A activity—which is about double the rate of public corporations. PE portfolio firms may restructure and get involved in other M&A activity as a strategy to avoid bankruptcy.

Therefore, when we evaluate the risk to PE portfolio firms, due to their capital structure, it is not enough to consider the rate of bankruptcy and compare it with public companies. We also need to take into account the very high rate of restructuring and M&A activities, covenant lightness, and out-of-court negotiation as a bankruptcy defense strategy often applied by PE.

Default

According to Asquith, Mullins, and Wolff (1989), junk bonds issued in the first wave of LBO in the 1970s reached a cumulative default rate of 34%. According to Moody's

Investors Service study, when a company gets acquired by a private equity fund, the probability of default increases materially (Emery and Cantor 2007). In 2008, more than half of PE portfolio firm loans carried single B ratings from Standard & Poor's (S&P)—that is, they faced a more than 13% risk of default in three years. In March 2007, according to S&P, more than 90 US firms were facing bankruptcy, having a credit rating of B– or below, and more than half of them were involved in LBO during the last few years (Basar, May 13, 2008). Taking high recovery rates from bankruptcy into account, Altman and Kishore (1996) calculated that the realized spread between junk bonds and ten-year US Treasury bonds, between 1978 and 1994, was 2%—as opposed to the 4% spread offered at the time of issue. The difference is due to bond default and limited recovery after default.

In summary, on one hand, since PE firms themselves do not borrow, and they usually are set up as limited liability companies (LLCs), PE firms cannot go bankrupt, even if all of their portfolio companies go bankrupt. At most, general partners of failed funds might have problems raising money for a new fund (Gilligan and Wright 2010). On the other hand, the post-buyout capital structure exposes the portfolio company to a serious risk of bankruptcy. Bank loan renegotiation, bonds default, covenant-light borrowing, loan to re-own, out-of-court negotiations, and in particular, the very vivid restructuring, acquisition, and divestiture activities of the portfolio companies are among the financial and legal strategies employed to prevent the bankruptcy of their portfolio firms.

Transitioning the Target from Private to Public Ownership

The life of a private equity fund is usually ten years. At the end, the fund is dissolved and investors' equity is returned. There are several exit routes, i.e. ways for the PE fund to liquidate its equity holdings. One exit strategy is reverse LBO (RLBO). In an RLBO, the PE fund sells its equity in the portfolio firm to the investing public through an initial public offering on the stock market. This transaction often is called "from private to public." According to Kaplan and Strömberg (2009), the most common exit strategy of a PE fund is the sale of its equity interest in a portfolio firm to a strategic buyer, which happens 38% of the time. The second most popular choice is the secondary LBO, that is, a sale of equity holdings in a portfolio firm to another PE fund, in 24% of cases. RLBO accounts for 14% of exits, and this is the type of exit strategy that has declined the most in significance, giving rise to more secondary LBOs over time. Therefore, when we consider the private-to-public transition, it actually is only 14% of the exits for the PE firm.

DeGeorge and Zeckhauser (1993) analyzed 62 RLBO cases between 1983 and 1987, and studied both operating performance and stock price behavior. They found that RLBOs are timed to be at the peak of their operating performance, and they outperform those portfolio firms that remain private. After the initial public offering (IPO), the firm's operating performance drops in the first year, but improves the second year. The model that is consistent with their finding is a pure selection model combined with asymmetric information. Mian and Rosenfeld (1993), like DeGeorge and Zeckhauser (1993), found that over three years after the RLBO, the former portfolio companies outperform their industrial peers, matched by their size, although the first year is less impressive. Holthausen and Larcker (1996), focusing on the five-year window between 1983 and 1988, found no evidence of accounting or stock underperformance of RLBOs. However, they also found that pre-RLBO, the accounting performance of the firm is significantly better than the average for the sectors. After RLBO, accounting performance declines, but it still remains above the industry average during the first four years. The change in performance is driven by the change of insider ownership—and not by change in leverage.

Chou, Gombola, and Liu (2006) find, from a sample of 247 cases, that there is no long-run underperformance of RLBO after equity offering, in contrast to other IPOs and secondary equity offerings (SEOs). This is most unexpected, as they find evidence of earnings manipulation prior to RLBO, similar to other IPOs. Observing the stock market performance of 526 reverse LBOs between 1981 (the first documented RLBO) and 2003, Cao and Lerner (2009) found that both the three-year and five-year RLBO performance is comparable with the broader market and other IPOs, and that it outperforms its peers in cross-sectional analysis. However, superior performance deteriorates over time. There is one particularly striking result: higher leverage did not result in worse stock performance for RLBO. This result is unexpected since higher leverage is supposed to increase the company's beta, and therefore the volatility of its stock price.

In summary, the portfolio firm subject to RLBO—returning to public shareholding after a partial exit through a PE sponsor—has a temporary ability to outperform the stock market or its own industry. There are signs of earnings manipulation prior to RLBO, which normally, in the case of public companies, would lead to underperformance for several years to come, after a short period of high stock return. Therefore, there must be some reasons why RLBOs do not follow the common trend of IPOs.

Von Drathen and Faleiro (2008) show that the higher the percentage equity that the PE fund retains after the RLBO, the more the stock outperforms other non-LBO-backed IPOs and the stock market index. Usually, the RLBO involves the flotation of only about 15% of outstanding shares, therefore allowing the PE firm to benefit from further appreciation of the stock on the public market. This finding deserves further study; in particular, if we want to understand the behavior of PE funds as investors in publicly traded corporations, and the methods they apply to achieve superior stock returns.

Summary

In this chapter, we have considered the primary distinguishing factor of leveraged buyout by PE firms, namely the financing and capital structure of their deals, the sources of debt financing, the change in capital structure over time, and some of the exit strategies available to PE firms. We aimed to present data, as much as possible, from peer-reviewed journals and from industry publications. However, a key characteristic of PE is secrecy, and the data voluntarily provided are fragmented and biased. The quality and representativeness of data and their availability is therefore problematic. A rare example of systematic improvement and completion of the commonly used database, in Phalippou and Gottshalg (2009) and Phalippou (2010), led to surprising results: the average return on equity from PE investment by limited partners is underperforming the S&P 500 by 3% annually (without even adjusting for risk).

PE became a very significant player in the M&A market, through LBO transactions, and it became a global player in the early years of the twenty-first century. Its expansion was based on regulatory changes in the US and followed by the UK, the temporary ease and low cost of borrowing, and the innovative legal and financial strategies PE funds apply to reduce the probability of bankruptcy of their highly levered portfolio firms. However, defaults and bankruptcies still occur. In addition, an increasing share of portfolio firms is not sold to the public or to strategic investors at the time of the PE fund closing, but to another PE fund—an alarming trend, signaling possible problems with the viability of portfolio firms.

We have identified numerous gaps in the current knowledge of LBO—which should provide us with directions for future research. How significant is the gap between the perceived and real success of PE-backed LBOs? What is the link between business media reporting and the public perception of the superior performance of PE-sponsored LBOs? In addition, non-PE-sponsored LBOs have so far been rather neglected, but without them, we can only have a partial picture. Which characteristics do non-PE-sponsored LBOs share with PE-sponsored LBOs? We have no way to decide as of today. It is not clear if hedge funds participate in the LBO market in a way that is different from PE. The question of how often and why PE funds succeed or fail should also be addressed in more rigorous ways. It would be very helpful to study systematically what other kinds of business relationships exist between the LBO firm and some of its limited partners (such as banks and investment banks)—in order to calculate the comprehensive return to certain groups of investors, and to distinguish it from the return to "pure" equity investors in PE (like pension funds or individual investors). Also, the phenomenon that secondary LBOs grew significantly over time would warrant a more concentrated effort to understand the returns, accounting performance, and possible partnerships or other linkages between PE funds. Last but not least, future research should find a way of putting previous studies on the success of LBO—some based on a small number or limited selection of cases—within the framework generated by recent and more comprehensive empirical studies, such as Axelson et al. (2010), Phalippou and Gottshalg (2009), and Phalippou (2010).

At the time of the infancy of the industry, PE firms were heralded as the solution to the fundamental problem of conflict of interest between shareholders and management. Instead, current research is confronted with a much less optimistic reality. The regulation of PE firms, hedge funds, and other alternative investment vehicles is under review by the EU as well as by the US government. Regulation will likely affect the strategies and techniques of PE firms in the future, therefore continuing interest in the study of this very significant industry and asset class is certainly warranted.

REFERENCES

Abillama, Jean, Bolurfrushan, Arya, & Mammadov, Zaur (2010). "The Anatomy of Private Equity Investments in the MENA Region." Harvard Business School MBA, Class of 2010, supervised by Prof. Josh Lerner.

Altman, Edward I., & Kishore, Vellore M. (1996). "Almost Everything You Wanted to Know about Recoveries on Defaulted Bonds." *Financial Analysts Journal*, 52/6: 57–64.

Asquith, Paul, Mullins, Jr., David W., & Wolff, Eric D. (1989). "Original Issue High Yield Bonds: Aging Analysis of Defaults, Exchanges and Calls." *The Journal of Finance*, 44/4: 923–52.

Axelson, Ulf, Jenkinson, Tim, Strömberg, Per, & Weisbach, Michael (2008). "Leverage and Pricing in Buyouts: An Empirical Analysis." Working Paper, Swedish Institute for Financial Research.

—— —— —— —— (2010). "Borrow Cheap, Buy High? The Determinants of Leverage and Pricing in Buyouts." NBER Working Paper No. 15952.

Bain & Company. (2010). "Global Private Equity Report 2010." Boston, MA. Available at: <http://www.bain.com/publications/articles/global-private-equity-report-2010.aspx>.

Baldwin, Carliss (2001). "Technical Note on LBO Valuation (A): LBO Structure and the Target IRR Method of Valuation." Harvard Business School No. 9-902-004.

Bank for International Settlements (2008). "Private Equity and Leveraged Finance Markets." *Committee on the Global Financial System, Publication No. 30*. Available at: <http://www.bis.org/publ/cgfs30.htm>. Accessed July 8, 2010.

Basar, Shanny (2008). "Apollo Acts to Protect its Stake in Linens Holding." *eFinancialNews*, May 13. Available at: <http://www.efinancialnews.eom/archive/keyword/linensholding/l/content/2350610801>. Accessed June 21, 2010.

Birdthistlet, William A., & Henderson, M. Todd (2009). "One Hat Too Many? Investment Desegregation in Private Equity." *University of Chicago Law Review*, 76/1: 45–82.

Blassberg, Franci J. (ed.) (2006). *The Private Equity Primer: The Best of Debevoise & Plimpton Private Equity Report*. New York: Debevoise & Plimpton LLP.

Cao, Jerry, & Lerner, Josh (2009). "The Performance of Reverse Leveraged Buyouts." *Journal of Financial Economics*, 91/2: 139–57.

Chou, De-Wai, Gombola, Michael, & Liu, Feng-Ying (2006). "Earnings Management and Stock Performance of Reverse Leveraged Buyouts." *Journal of Financial and Quantitative Analysis*, 41/2: 407–38.

Cotter, J. F., & Peck, S. W. (2001). "The Structure of Debt and Active Equity Investors: The Case of the Buyout Specialist." *Journal of Financial Economics*, 59/1: 101–47.

Cumming, Douglas (ed.) (2010). *Private Equity, Fund Types, Risks and Returns, and Regulation*. Hoboken, NJ: John Wiley & Sons.

—— Siegel, Donald S., & Wright, Mike (2007). "Private Equity, Leveraged Buyouts and Governance." *Journal of Corporate Finance*, 13/4: 439–60.

Damodaran, Aswath (1997). *Corporate Finance: Theory and Practice*. New York: John Wiley & Sons, 502–37.

—— (2002). *Investment Valuation: Tools and Techniques for Determining the Value of Any Asset*. New York: John Wiley & Sons.

DeGeorge, Francois, & Zeckhauser, Richard (1993). "The Reverse LBO Decision and Firm Performance: Theory and Evidence." *The Journal of Finance*, 48/4: 1323–48.

Demiroglu, Cem (2008). "Lender Control and the Role of Private Equity Group Reputation in Buyout Financing." PhD thesis, University of Florida.

DePamphilis, Donald M. (2010). *Mergers, Acquisitions, and Other Restructuring Activities: An Integrated Approach to Process, Tools, Cases, and Solutions* (5th ed.). Burlington, MA: Academic Press.

Edwards, Franklin R. (1999). "Hedge Funds and the Collapse of Long-Term Capital Management." *The Journal of Economic Perspectives*, 13/2: 189–210.

Emery, Kenneth, & Cantor, Richard (2007). "Default and Migration Rates for Private Equity-Sponsored Issuers." *The Journal of Private Equity*, 10/2: 38–48.

Fotak, Veljko, Bortolotti, Bernardo, & Megginson, William (2008). "The Financial Impact of Sovereign Wealth Fund Investments in Listed Companies." Working Paper. Available at: <http://www.ssrn.com/abstract=1108585>. Accessed June 3, 2010.

Gertner, R., & Scharfstein, D. (1991). "A Theory of Workouts and the Effects of Reorganization Law." *The Journal of Finance*, 46/4: 1189–222.

Gilligan, John, & Wright, Mike (2010). *Private Equity Demystified: An Explanatory Guide* (2nd ed.). London, UK: ICAEW Corporate Finance Faculty.

Griffiths, Ian, & Mathiason, Nick (2010). "Debt Crisis: AA Becomes Latest Private Equity Flotation to Fall by the Wayside: The Leveraged Buyout Boom is Over—And Now Thousands of Jobs are at Risk in the UK." *Guardian* (London), February 22, p. 29.

Harris, Lee (2010). "A Critical Theory of Private Equity." *Delaware Journal of Corporate Law*, 35: 259–93.

Holthausen, Robert W., & Larcker, David K. (1996). "The Financial Performance of Reverse Leveraged Buyouts." *Journal of Financial Economics*, 42/3: 293–332.

Ivashina, Victoria, & Kovner, Anna (2008). "The Private Equity Advantage: Leveraged Buyout Firms and Relationship Banking." EFA 2008 Athens Meetings Paper.

Jensen, Michael C. (1989). "The Eclipse of the Publicly Held Corporations." *Harvard Business Review*, 67: 61–74.

Kaplan, Steven N., & Andrade, Gregor (1998). "How Costly is Financial (Not Economic) Distress? Evidenced from Highly Leveraged Transactions that Became Distressed." *Journal of Finance*, 53: 1443–94.

—— & Stein, Jeremy (1993). "The Evolution of Buyout Pricing and Financial Structure in the 1980s." *Quarterly Journal of Economics*, 108/2: 313–57.

—— & Strömberg, Per (2009). "Leveraged Buyouts and Private Equity." *Journal of Economic Perspectives*, 23/1: 121–46.

Luehrman, Timothy (2009). "Note on Valuing Equity Cash Flows." Harvard Business School Note 9-295-085.

Metrick, Andrew, & Yasuda, Ayako (2010). "The Economics of Private Equity Funds." *The Review of Financial Studies*, 23/6: 2303–41.

Mian, Shehzad, & Rosenfeld, James (1993). "Takeover Activity and the Long-Run Performance of Reverse Leveraged Buyouts." *Financial Management*, 22/4: 46–57.

Opler, Tim C. (1993). "Controlling Financial Distress Costs in Leveraged Buyouts with Financial Innovations." *Financial Management*, 22/3: 79–90.

Olsen, Jon, Gagliano, Salvatore, & Wainwright, Fred (2003). "Note on Leveraged Buyouts." Case no. 5-0004, Center for Private Equity and Entrepreneurship, Tuck School of Business, Dartmouth College.

Palepu, Krisna, & Healy, Paul (2008). *Business Analysis & Valuation: Using Financial Statements, Text and Cases* (4th ed.). Mason, OH: Thomson/South-Western.

Phalippou, Ludovic (2010). "Risk and Return of Private Equity: An Overview of Data, Methods, and Results," in Douglas Cumming (ed.), *Private Equity, Fund Types, Risks and Returns, and Regulation*. Hoboken, NJ: John Wiley & Sons.

—— & Gottschalg, Oliver (2009). "The Performance of Private Equity Funds." *Review of Financial Studies*, 22/4: 1747–76.

Ross, Stephen A., Westerfield, Randolph W., & Jaffe, Jeffrey (2002). *Corporate Finance* (6th ed.). New York: McGraw-Hill.

Rubenstein, David M. (2009). "The Future of Private Equity." Interview by CNBC on October 22, 7.55 a.m.

Thomas, Jason M. (2010). "The Credit Performance of Private Equity-Backed Companies in the 'Great Recession' of 2008–2009." The Private Equity Council, March.

Von Drathen, C., & Faleiro, F. (2008). "The Performance of Leveraged Buyout-Backed IPOs in the UK." Available at: <http://ssrn.com/abstract=1117185>. Accessed August 13, 2010.

CHAPTER 13

....

SHAREHOLDER VALUE

A Driver of Merger and Acquisition Activity

....

BILL RYAN

INTRODUCTION

....

Much of the mergers and acquisitions (M&A) literature explores reasons for and aspects of success rates (Sudarsanam and Mahate 2006; Jensen and Meckling 1976), often quoting rates typically as low as 30%. There are, inevitably, winners and losers in such activity, with the recent deal between Kraft and Cadbury illustrating the difficulties of gaining both effectiveness and popularity for such ventures. In the case of Cadbury Kraft, it is arguably one of the most unpopular deals in recent times and one where there was concern as to who was going to benefit. Kraft had looked sickly in recent quarters prior to the takeover. Their need for continued growth was driven by shareholder demands. The financial firm Sandford Bernstein noted in a brief to its clients that "Kraft would benefit from all of Cadbury's strengths." The British firm boasts "dominant positions," strong market presence, and potential for massive margin improvements (<http://www.time.com>). However, there are many who believe that Kraft paid too much (£12 billion) and that the cost of the takeover is weighing heavily on the debt burden of the company. Looking at Kraft's share price over the past three years, it peaked around the time of the takeover but has more recently (December 2010) dropped to about $30.75. The question remains whether the debt-ridden Kraft did a good deal in the takeover. To pay down the debt creates massive pressure on management to deliver shareholder value. As an example of a deal that was supposed to be a "win-win" for both parties, the Kraft Cadbury takeover is also arguably an example of the drive for shareholder value operating at the extremes.

Eccles et al. (1999) discuss the question of whether a firm pays too much for an acquisition and why. They argue that despite 30 years of evidence that M&A does not create value for shareholders, firms continue to take this route to growth. They quote the famous Snapple acquisition by Quaker Oats and argue that the $1.7 billion purchase price was about $1 billion too much. In both cases, company stock prices declined and less than three years later Quaker sold off Snapple to Triarc for less than 20% of what it had cost them originally. The search for shareholder value growth is not a guaranteed option for growth and it is one that needs discussion.

This chapter will review developments within the area of shareholder value, a major driver of M&A activity. It will include discussion on the movements within shareholder value and the capital markets, along with influences on the firm for continued growth as, for example, via M&A activity. The framework for this chapter will draw on the notion of boundaries (Llewellyn 1994), especially as it relates to movements in the boundary of activities undertaken by the firm as it tries to mediate a relationship for itself within the business context, including, importantly, the shareholding community.

PROMISES AND MEASURES

Shareholder value became the business cliché of the 1990s. However, it started as a consultancy product of the 1980s. Stern Stewart and LEK/Alcar were leading proponents of the ideology, arguing that there was "one best way" to share value creation. Other firms, such as Price Waterhouse, adopted a more flexible approach, using different techniques to increase shareholder value (Froud et al. 2000). At this time, the emphasis was less on M&A growth and more on consultancy offers of implementation packages to increase shareholder value by means of various firm activities. However, much of this was nothing more than business common sense, such as making assets work harder and investing in activities with a positive economic value added (EVA). The speed of this new value-based management approach resulted in massive growth for consulting firms such as Stern Stewart, with the value-based consultancy idea going global with offices around the world, such as in London, Bangkok, and Paris etc. However, by the late 1990s, the *Sunday Times* performance list showed that only 87 out of 200 companies were creating EVA (*Sunday Times*, September 17, 1998). Despite publicity to the contrary in terms of acquiring firms' null returns, firms continue to be driven to M&A activity in the search for growth. This pressure increasingly comes from the investment community and restricted domestic markets that offer fewer opportunities for such growth (Angwin 2001; Campa and Hernando 2004).

FROM PRODUCT MARKET TO SHAREHOLDER VALUE

Since the 1960s the conventional business strategy recommended by researchers such as Drucker (1955), Porter (1980), Chandler (1962), and Prahalad and Hamel (1990) has focused on the ability of firms to develop a product-market advantage in order to generate profits. Such strategies were orientated round the positioning of the company relative to its business relationships, structure, and core competencies, and in many respects encompassed a holistic view of the organization as serving a balanced set of stakeholders. Indeed, the ability of firms to satisfy customers, create employment, and gain product-market share was often considered the pinnacle of corporate management, nurturing as it did sustainability and economic performance for the organization. This in turn required firms to retain and reinvest profits (Lazonick and O'Sullivan 2000), which reflected the faith, loyalty, and trust placed by owners in the organization's ability to generate sufficient returns and adequately account for performance. However, the boundary of relationships started to change with the increased importance and influence of the shareholders.

ORGANIZATION BOUNDARY DISCOURSE

The relationship between the organization and wider society is one that is constantly under review and subject to change. Llewellyn (1994) identifies the duality of boundary essence, describing it as both the limits of the organization as it meets its environment as well as a boundary maintaining the organization as a unified entity. In this way, the organization and its boundary is in constant negotiation as to its simultaneous pursuit of stability and reconfiguration. For example, the traditional model of business interaction (see Figure 13.1) sees the firm as primarily interacting with the product market, with direct links between the resource conversion process of the firm and its product market. This was regarded as constituting the main boundary or threshold of the firm. More recently, this boundary of activity has been extended to include not only the product market but also the capital markets, with the firm having, for example, this duality of interrelationships (Figure 13.1). How the discourse of these relationships has evolved and how it has been affected by and influential on organizational growth and activity is an essential aspect of this chapter.

Llewellyn (1994) considers boundaries as "thresholds" and as "binding" structures. She discusses the notion of the universal natural ordered organization and examines the notion that boundary maintenance was bypassed due to the assumption of the universal natural ordered organization. Organizations appeared to be fixed relative to their relationship with the outside business environment. For example, organizations managed their relationship with their shareholders mainly via dividends, which were indicators of the well-being of the firm. Organizational theory since Weber has stressed the enduring nature of the organization in a changing world. This modernist view was prevalent until the 1970s.

The development of this way of thinking has led to the development of a post-modern approach to organizational theory that focuses on what is termed "an assault on unity," a changing of the boundary relationships. This provides a challenge to the position of the organization as being the single generator of growth and value for the firm (Clegg 1990).

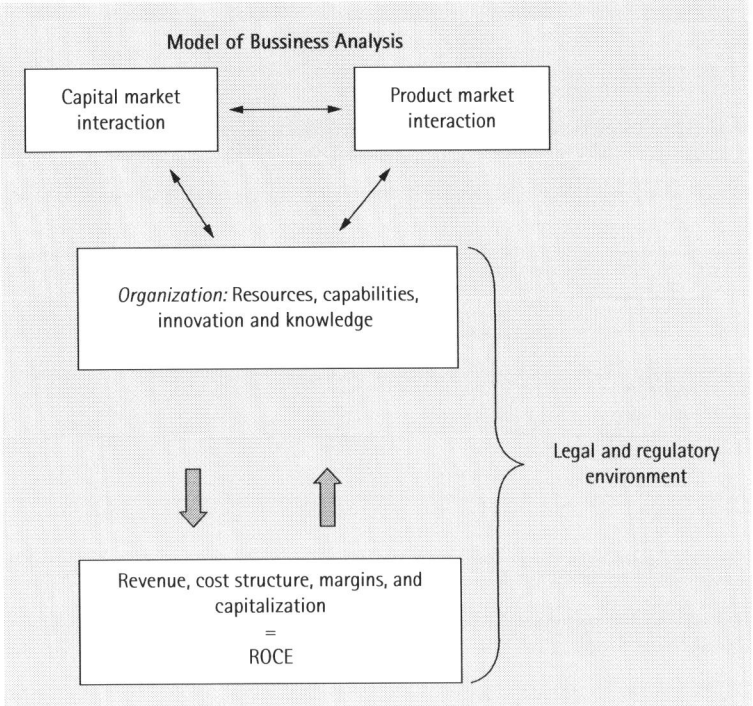

FIG. 13.1 Model of business analysis

Source: The chart is adapted from MSN Money Investor.

The post-modern organization is flatter, less bureaucratic, more fragmented and decentralized than its predecessor. The basis of boundary maintenance is the acceptance of the notion that the organization is no longer a given fixed entity but one where the processes make it possible for it to exist (Turner 1990). Thus, boundary management constitutes the achieved relations of relative autonomy and relative dependence that exist between organizations and their business environment (Clegg 1990). This increasingly includes the influential shareholder group.

An aspect of boundary discourse that is important is that of organization goals. Organization goals can include the generation of wealth in the context of sustaining and growing the organization. Traditionally this was achieved by the firm's interaction with the product market. However, sustaining and growing the organization had become problematic due to the changing nature of the organization and the dynamic boundary of relationships with outside stakeholders, particularly the investment community (Haslam et al. 2000; Goldenberg 2000). Developments in mainstream economics following agency theory (Jensen and Meckling 1976) argued that the separation of ownership and control left corporate management focusing on their own objectives as opposed to the interest of the "real" owners (i.e. shareholders), resulting in a "value-gap".[1] From this perspective, corporate governance was constructed as an agency problem.[2] That proposition, among others, increased awareness that corporate management might not be maximizing profits, which, according to economists including Friedman (1970), was the major purpose of the organization. "There is one and only one social responsibility of business... to increase its profits... without deception and fraud" (Friedman 1970: 125).

Through social and business discourse, the notion of profit maximization and "shareholder value"[3] became embedded in the business arena and coincided with the emergence of the "new economy." Rapid advances in technology, increasing international trade, and the growing nature of mature product markets made sectors within the Anglo-Saxon economies competitively "aggressive." One of the biggest threats came from Japanese corporations who had been able to "integrate the capability of people into a broader array of functional specialist and processes of organisational learning" (Lazonick and O'Sullivan, 2000: 15). This increased level of competition placed intense pressure on corporations to sustain profitability and yield adequate returns on capital employed (ROCE).[4] For example, in the US, Stern Stewart (2003) observed that out of 2,717 companies listed on the Russell 3000 index, well over half were earning negative economic profit—meaning they were unable to cover the cost of capital and generate value for shareholders.

Shareholders: Financialization and the Search for Corporate Credibility

In the current business context, shareholders are the dominant interest group exercising influence on management, and the major goal pursued by companies is the maximization of shareholder value, that is, of the financial value of the firm. The USA and UK are leading examples of shareholder systems.

The expectations of shareholders impact in a number of ways and one issue to be considered is that of corporate credibility. The business world has been going through a period of time compression where everything is demanded more quickly and in the case of products and services, more economically and at a consistently high quality. This is a part of what has been described as a movement in the 19th century from an agrarian to an industrial society and in the 20th century to a knowledge-based post-industrial society (Drucker 1999; Quintas 2002). While this is a broad area of change, the general business environment has, for some time now, been characterized by levels of extreme competitiveness, where technologies and processes have become increasingly transferable and more easily copied (Teece 2000). However, in recent years, shortening product life cycles and increased competition has meant that this advantageous situation has been difficult to maintain, resulting in shortfalls in actual as opposed to predicted results. The demand for organizational credibility in the attainment of results has been led by shareholders, who no longer show longer-term loyalty to organizations (Handy 1995; Haslam et al. 2000; Rappaport 1986; Drucker 1999).

Shareholder loyalty has undergone major change, led by a movement from individual ownership to larger fund management groups (Handy 1995). The growth in fund management has institutionalized share dealing and ownership (Haslam et al. 2000). The traditional holding of shares has increasingly been delegated to the fund management community who along with the investment analysts (for example, the Wall Street analysts), exercise major steering power and influence over organizations and their strategies. The separation of ownership and management has long meant the delegation of operational responsibility from the owners to management. However, this separation has become even more remote with the growth in importance and power of the fund management community (Drucker 1999; Handy 2002). They have had an increasing policy of engaging in what has been described as the active management of funds rather than the previously more common practice of long-term share ownership. Rappaport (1986) notes that portfolio managers compete for best returns by moving in and out of individual stocks and the implication is that this is not necessarily based on a company's long-term future goals but on short-term return expectations. Traditionally, individual investor loyalty was strong, with shareholders often maintaining their shares in a company over the period of a lifetime. Haslam, Neale, and Johal (2000) discuss the changing turnover rates of shareholding for UK shares. This has changed from an average of roughly five years in the mid-1960s to three years in the 1980s, to about 18 months and less towards the end of the 1990s. The point here is that the changing emphasis of share ownership/management has led to a more active investment discourse and influential share-dealing environment, changing the boundary of those relationships. Institutional investors are able to intervene and can influence the manner in which managers carry out their duties. They can influence for example expectations as to what constitutes a fair return on funds invested and the time frame in which it is expected. Historically, share ownership was more dispersed and that dispersion meant more limits to the boundary of impact that individual owners could make (Berle and Means 1932; Haslam et al. 2000).

This changing shareholder loyalty, along with the intensity of competition and lowering profit margins, has led to immense pressure on organizations. This is exemplified by the power of the Wall Street analyst community, who exercise a major influence on corporate strategy through their buy-or-sell recommendations to fund managers. Riley (2000) compares traditional stocks to technology growth stocks and notes that apart from cyclical interruptions, there has been a weakening in profit margins for about 25 years. Businesses have been facing pressures on profit margins from both price-conscious consumers and the increasing intensity of competitive forces. However, while natural competitive discourse shapes and influences financial returns, there is no lessening in the expectations of shareholders who have become accustomed to a certain level of returns. The quest for profit and the retention of shareholders' funds has forced the organization to adopt a different view of value generation and one that will be shown to rely heavily on the application of a more systemized approach to the search for organizational credibility in terms of their results.

For reasons such as those described above, the boundary of relationships shifted, with firms exposed to the changing, more increased demands of the financial community. This movement developed into a challenge for corporate management to raise funds efficiently and effectively from capital markets to compete on a global scale.

INCREASING SHAREHOLDER INFLUENCE

In the light of these developments, many of the traditional organic strategies for long-term growth have arrived at a crossroads. This change was supported by an influx in "value-based investors" that represented an unequivocal shift to the boundary and pattern of financialization, with a major shift in the concentration of share ownership from direct to large institutions as in pension and insurance funds (Froud et al. 2006: 40; see Table 13.1).

With the movement to major shareholding influence, the drive was on for significant returns, along with growth trajectories and expectations of increasing shareholder value. But more importantly, due to the sheer size of their investment position, they had become powerful agents of corporate control, able to influence corporate strategy and the way in which organizations account for performance[5] (Useem 1999; Pozen 1994; Andersson et al. 2006).

The increase in international trade and especially the growth of international capital markets, it is claimed, is leading to a borderless control of economic activity. In general, such claims herald the development of a move to more global coordination and a lessening of different kinds of national economic organization (Hirst and Thompson 1996). This globalization of approach also creates a uniformity of measurement.

One performance metric commonly used by firms (e.g. Coca-Cola[6]) to "manage for value" is economic value added (EVA),[7] despite the fact that it pays no explicit attention to strategy (Otley 2001: 245). The underlying dynamics of this metric essentially places a cost on the utilization of company resources, which suggests that, in the short term, shareholders can only be privileged at the expense of the other stakeholders.

Table 13.1 Share ownership in Britain, distribution by sector (quoted share) (%)

Sector	1963	1975	1990	2000	2004
Individuals	54.0	37.5	20.3	16.0	14.1
Pension funds	6.4	16.8	31.7	17.7	15.7
Insurance companies	10.0	15.9	20.4	21.0	17.2
Rest of the world	7.0	5.6	11.8	32.4	32.6
Others (banks, public sector, unit trusts, investment banks)	22.6	24.2	15.8	12.9	20.4

Source: Based on Office for National Statistics, Share Ownership Report 2004. Available at: <http://www.statistics.gov.uk>.

Nevertheless, in this system of "investor capitalism" the underlying dynamics of share ownership and loyalty has radically changed. Investors and money managers are now quick to liquidate their investment position in the face of corporate adversity, and the inability of firms to meet analyst expectations and earnings forecasts. Their power to do so has led to an increasing shortening of corporate horizons, under which profit maximization has been perceived to be the optimal measure of organizational legitimacy (Ramanathan 1976). This change has been highlighted by Handy (2002), who makes a theoretical distinction between owners and investors, arguing that investors "have none of the pride or responsibility of ownership ... and are only there for the money" (Handy 2002: 51). However, despite increasing stakeholder debates, the name of the game continues to be about shareholder value. The fact of the matter remains—restrained by the jurisdictions of institutional investors and analysts, firms continue to embark on various approaches to influence profits and share price. This includes a number of routes to growth, including the all-important M&A activity.

While internal development and organic growth provide great scope for sustainable profitability in the long term, a more contemporary view has been to focus on the short-term liquidity of the organization as a "sure-fire" way to increase profits. Most notably, firms have actively engaged in restructuring their organization by disposing of diversified product lines (Zuckerman 2000), share buy-back schemes, downsizing or rightsizing their workforce (Murphy et al. 1995 and Cappelli 2000), and strategically engaging in M&A activity—all of which can include labor force reduction in the search for shareholder value. As highlighted by Lazonick and O'Sullivan (2000), while the profit distribution rates of US companies have substantially risen, there has been a decline in corporate workforces, which they argue is due to the propensity of firms to employ a strategy of "downsize and distribute" rather than the previously held view of retain and reinvest.

In Europe, British Airways (BA) has used restructuring as a strategic approach to reducing the company's cost base by means of labor adjustments. The company's workforce has been reduced from 65,000 to 47,000 in six years, with plans to cut costs by £450m over the next two years—warning staff to expect more job cuts (Tran 2006). In many respects, this is a reflection of BA's strategy to increase earnings and achieve shareholder expectations in recovering from its poor share price and lower levels of shareholder return in recent years (see Figure 13.2).

Although such measures can increase efficiency, extracting value through structural changes is essentially limited, because it is a redistribution of cost from the organization to other stakeholders. Froud et al. (2000: 776) notes, "Many of the benefits for shareholders appear to be coming not from reallocation gains, as managers shuffle their asset portfolios, but from redistribution as managers squeeze other stakeholders, especially labour."

While it is important for management to meet the expectations of its investors, it would also appear that the combination of contracting product markets, excessive demands of the capital markets, and the vested economic interest of management, has encouraged dysfunctional and opportunistic management behavior through earnings management. When considering the imperfections found in auditing, and the resulting avalanche of accounting scandals such as Enron, WorldCom,[8] and more recently iSOFT,

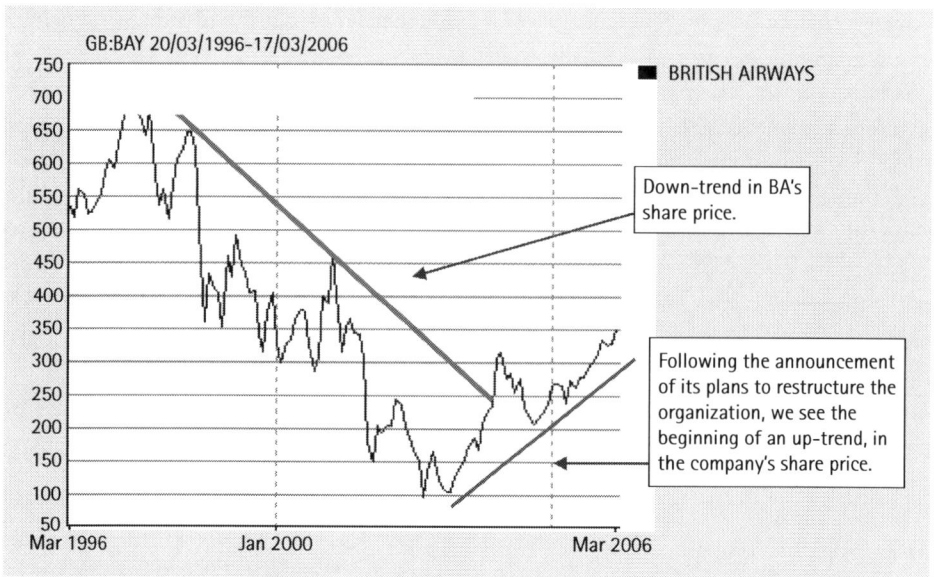

FIG. 13.2 British Airways share price

one may challenge the orthodoxy of the shareholder ideology as the principal govern-ance mechanism, and subsequently raise the question as to whether the obsession of profit maximization has gone too far. These developments have certainly heightened social and environmental expectations in recent years, where the ethics and morals of extreme individualism often found in liberal societies are beginning to change.

However, at the same time, it is also worth noting that many companies have success-fully used the pursuit of value as a guiding governance principle, arguing that it provides a clear focus for management. For example, between 1982–2001 Lloyds TSB was able to increase its market capitalization from "1 billion to 40 billion." According to Pitman (2003), the company was able to do so by institutionalizing the notion of shareholder value within the internal boundaries of the organization:

> We always maintained a clear focus...generating greater value for sharehold-ers...we found this objective created value for everyone...customer satisfaction rose and our employees were better remunerated. (Pitman 2003: 42)

New Approaches to Value

Nonetheless, with the growing concerns of social and environmental issues, it is eco-nomically beneficial for firms to effectively communicate with the wider stakeholder community through democratic engagements. Indeed, the notion of stakeholder dialogue has of late become the foundation of many theoretical developments in economic, social, ethical, and environmental control (see e.g. O'Dwyer 2005; Unerman and Bennett 2004; Owen et al. 2000).

The current knowledge-based economy is an example of this wider stakeholder perspective. Here, the ability of firms to innovate, enhance quality, increase productivity, and build "distinctive"[9] relationships with customers and employees (Kay 1993) has pragmatically become a crucial dimension to survive and remain competitive. Crucially, this requires a greater integration of organization stakeholders rather than a single focus on shareholders.

It could then be argued that the basis and boundary of wealth creation is shaped by the ability of firms to manage their intellectual capital, of which knowledge, intellectual property, and competence are the most important (Teece 2000, 2005).

Yet despite the growing importance and acknowledgement of human capital, market practitioners and analysts continue to ignore these aspects when assessing a company's performance and future earnings. So even though stakeholders such as customers, employees, and society are crucial to business practices, the "bottom line" still remains the most important measure of performance for many organizations. This in turn makes it difficult for management to reconcile the changing boundary of responsibility to various stakeholders. (Mintzberg et al. 2002: 70).

From this point of view, traditional financial performance measures[10] appear to be somewhat oblivious to the wider boundaries of the organization, as they are unable to engage, and account for, the skills required by firms to strategically compete in the future and generate consistent results. Thus, focusing solely on the financial aspects of business practices can often be misleading, a view supported by Hamel and Prahalad (1994: 124) who argue that "Financially driven managers are asleep behind the wheel."

Consistent with this perspective, we have seen major advances stemming from stakeholder theory.[11] For example, Kaplan and Norton's (1992) "Balance Scorecard" offers a multidimensional framework that integrates the financial and non-financial aspects of the enterprise into the taxonomy of social and organizational control.[12] This can assist management to consolidate short- and long-term objectives in corporate strategy. Similarly, Hart and Milstein's (2003) "Sustainable Value Framework" illustrates the prolific relationship between social and environmental issues and shareholder value:

> The global challenges associated with sustainability...can help identify strategies that contribute to a more sustainable world and simultaneously drive shareholder value (Hart and Milstein 2003: 57)

While such frameworks can often be difficult to implement at the operational level, they certainly accentuate the budding nature of profitability and shareholder value in the current business environment, where the current challenge for management is to "ethically" re-engineer strategy to administer the product-market relationship while simultaneously mediating the intrusion of financial markets into the normative business model. These areas are, however, by no means mutually exclusive but rather can be naturally reinforcing. A prime example of this is Marks and Spencer, who in the year 2001 recorded a pre-tax fall in profits of £74m due to declining sales, inviting the wrath of the corporate

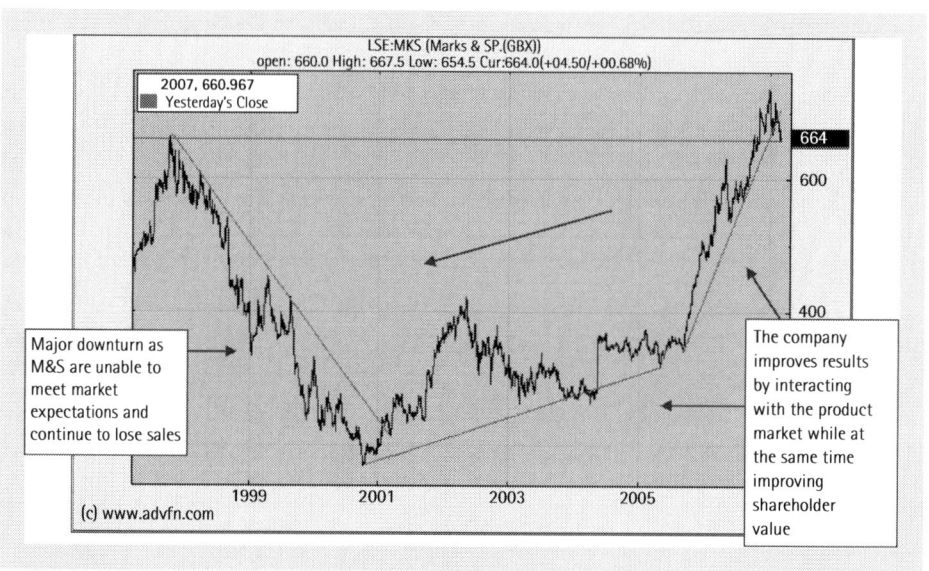

FIG. 13.3 Marks and Spencer share price, 1997–2007

Source: Advfn Stock Charts. Available at: <http://www.advfn.com>.

financial world and opening up supposed opportunities for corporate raiders. However, having fought off takeover bids, the company has revived its sales figures and profits by engaging with the product market and introducing new product lines, as well as refining its internal operations. This in turn has rejuvenated analysts' expectations and the company's share price in recent years (Figure 13.3), which reflects the fact that generating value requires "performance on multiple dimensions" (Hart and Milstein 2003: 58).

As noted earlier, M&A activity is often perceived to be a feasible mechanism to gain synergistic benefits and growth, yet evidence shows that 70–80% of acquisitions are unable to create wealth for the shareholders of the acquiring company (Selden and Colvin 2003; Sudarsanam and Mahate 2006, 2001; Jensen and Meckling 1976). These observations suggest that a company's value proposition rests on its long-term capacity to generate cash, which can be used to finance value-creating activities. Therefore, at some point in time, firms must once more excel at the core of their operations and grow organically as the ultimate source of value, ongoing success, and global sustainability. This will require a longer-term outlook and a move away from myopic business practices and expectations.

Conclusion

The literature has intermittently questioned the value of "growth for the sake of growth." Many managers have a view of their company's future that is remarkably similar to the child's view of himself. When asked what they want their companies to become over the next few years, the reply is "bigger." Associating creation of shareholder value with growth in earnings, sales, or other metrics is commonplace in the investment industry, and the use of such metrics has greatly influenced managerial compensation schemes and thus provided the impetus for mergers and acquisitions as well as internal growth. In traditional incentive schemes, compensation is often tied to the manager's ability to beat budgeted increases in earnings or sales, but a formal mechanism for determining whether growth activities enhance shareholder returns is lacking. Kay (1993) discussed the undesirable consequences of linking executive pay and managerial compensation to measures of corporate growth. The investment industry demands that managers maximize sales and earnings growth over time. This prescription is based on the presumption that growth is synonymous with shareholder value creation. Empirical results indicate that maximizing growth does not maximize corporate profitability or shareholder value. On the contrary, companies with moderate growth in sales or earnings show the highest rates of return and value creation for their owners. The results support the general warning regarding the dangers of conforming to market pressures for growth. The financial press is full of examples of once rapidly growing companies that have "gone south." Recent crises have shown that growth without profitability cannot be sustained. The empirical results of the "crisis" show that corporate managers need to abandon the habit of blindly increasing company size and investors need to carefully consider the drawbacks of diseconomies of scale, while managers also need to make a fundamental shift in their strategic orientation from "growth now, profitability later" to "profitable growth now." Unfortunately, all too often management succumbs to pressures from Wall Street, which is always in search of higher growth rates. Stated plans and budgets may fall short of Wall Street's expectations. Fearing the results of missing the Street's expectations, managers sometimes start the budgeting process with consensus expectations and mandate that internal budgets are set to meet them. This sets the company up for failure if external expectations are impossible to meet. Ending the expectations game requires the CEO to reclaim the initiative in terms of setting growth forecasts. Growth should not be the input to strategic planning but the outcome of a sound investment strategy that is geared to accepting value-creating activities, perhaps with a return to a focusing on what the organization is good at and a renewed interaction with its product market.

It is evident that within the sphere of an institutional framework, firms are building strategy based on the demands of capital markets, where the importance of the investor and the drive for shareholder value echoes a short-term strategy affecting long-term investment. However, many companies are oblivious to the fact that long-term investment can often be the source of continuous short results and sustainability.

There certainly appears to be a common misconception that the organization should only exist to maximize profits. Although profits are undoubtedly an important aspect, firms must begin to look deeper into the capabilities and competencies of their business practices as a key driver of success, whereby increased attention needs to be paid to the way in which progress is made.

The recent financial crisis shows evidence of this phenomenon, with the ever hungry pursuit of shareholder value outweighing all logic and our ability to control the organization from within. The movement from a "retain and reinvest" to a "downsize and distribute" approach (Lazonick and O'Sullivan 2000) provides a major shift in the boundary of managerial strategic orientation and one which, post-crisis, may come back to a more solidly based approach to performance and its management. The realities of the market place appear to suggest that the current overemphasis on shareholder value is not sustainable and that companies exploring growth opportunities over the long term will generate more value for all stakeholders. In the opinion of Rappaport (2006), "the shareholder value principle has not failed management; rather it is management that betrayed the principle." This implies a return to the reasons for the firm's existence, which historically was the production of goods and services over the longer term rather than the provision of shareholder value. In doing so, we still have a connection to shareholder value, but importantly remain within the historical boundary of performance and its control.

Endnotes

1. The "value gap" refers to the discrepancy between the current market value of the firm and the potential market value of the firm. The firm was managed to maximize returns on capital and organizational resources (Rappaport 1998: 2).

2. Agency problem refers to the issue of aligning the interests of owners (principals) and those who control the organization (agents), the solution to which many corporate financial specialists believe is to actively incentivize executives through various remuneration packages (e.g. share option schemes) that are tied directly to financial performance and share price.

3. From a shareholder perspective, the term "value" is essentially a summation of the share price increase and increasing returns, commonly known as total shareholder return (TSR) (Johnson and Scholes 1993).

4. For instance, in recent years a post-tax ROCE of 10–12% has been considered a proxy or benchmark for expectations, with a view to increasing shareholder value (see e.g. Froud et al. 2000 and Rappaport 1998).

5. For example, Useem (1999), an organizational theorist, interviews a range of financial actors such as fund managers and corporate directors to illustrate how large institutions influence corporate strategy and structure. He concludes that there are close network relationships between financial agents where institutions increasingly shape business practices and drive national economic performance.

6. Robert Goizueta, CEO of Coca-Cola, clarifies: "We raise capital to make concentrate, and sell it at an operating profit, then we pay the cost of capital and shareholders pocket the difference" (Tully 1994: 143).

7. The economic value added was formulated by Stern Stewart and Company and is essentially "a company-level residual income measure of earnings after subtracting a charge for capital" (Haslam et al. 2000: 779).

8. See e.g. Unerman (2004).

9. e.g. from a resource-based theory of the firm, Kay (1993) argues that the ability to add value requires "distinctive capabilities" which include innovation, architecture, and corporate reputation. This is seen as the basis of wealth creation and competitive advantage.

10. Traditional financial measures include ROCE, return on investment (ROI), and earnings per share (EPS) for example.

11. Stakeholder theory conceptualizes the corporation as part of a broad social system whereby the firm influences and is influenced by various groups within society (see e.g. Freeman 1984).

12. The balance scorecard consists of four key areas: financial perspective, customer perspective, innovation and learning, and internal business perspective (Kaplan and Norton 1992).

References

Andersson, T., Haslam, C., & Lee, E. (2006). "Financialized Accounts: Restructuring and Return on Capital Employed in the S&P 500." *Accounting Forum*, 30/1: 21–41.

Angwin, D. (2001). "Mergers and Acquisitions across European Borders: National Perspectives on Preacquisition Due Diligence and the Use of Professional Advisers." *Journal of World Business*, 36/1: 32–57.

Berle, A., & Means, G. (1932). *The Modern Corporation and Private Property*. London: Macmillan.

Campa, J. M., & Hernando, I. (2004). "Shareholder Value Creation in European M&As." *European Financial Management*, 10/1, March: 47–81.

Cappelli, P. (2000). *Examining the Incidence of Downsizing and its Effect on Establishment Performance*. New York: Sage Foundation.

Chandler, A. (1962). *Strategy and Structure*. Cambridge, MA: MIT Press.

Clegg, S. (1990). *Modern Organizations: Organization Studies in the Postmodern World*. London: Sage.

Drucker, P. (1955). *The Practice of Management*. Oxford: Elsevier publications.

——— (1999). "Knowledge-Worker Productivity: The Biggest Challenge." *California Management Review*, 41: 79–94.

Eccles, R. C., Lanes, K. L., & Wilson, T. C. (1999). "Are You Paying Too Much for that Acquisition?" *Harvard Business Review*, 77, July–August: 136–46.

Freeman, E. R. (1984). *Strategic Management: A Stakeholder Approach*. Boston, MA: Pitman.

Friedman, M. (1970). "The Social Responsibility of Business is to Increase its Profits." *The New York Times Magazine*, September: 32–3.

Froud, J., Haslam, C., Johal, S., & Williams, K. (2000). "Restructuring for Shareholder Value and its Implications for Labour." *Cambridge Journal of Economics*, 24: 771–92.

——— Johal, S., Leaver, A., & Williams, K. (2006). *Financialization Strategy: Narrative and Number*. London: Routledge.

Goldenberg, D. (2000). "Shareholder Value Debunked." *Strategy and Leadership*, 28/1: 30–6.

Hamel, G., & Prahalad, C. K. (1994). *Competing for the Future*. Boston, MA: Harvard Business School.

Handy, C. (1995). "Balancing Corporate Power: A New Federalist Paper," in *Beyond Certainty*. London: Hutchinson, 33–56.

——— (2002). "What's a Business For?" *Harvard Business Review*, 80/12: 49–56.

Hart, S., & Milstein, M. B. (2003). "Creating Sustainable Value." *Academy of Management Executive*, 17/2: 56–67.

Haslam, C., Neale, A., & Johal, S. (2000). *Economics in a Business Context* (3rd ed.). London: Thomson Learning.

Hirst, P., & Thompson, G. (1996). "Multinational Corporations and the Globalization Thesis," in P. Hirst & G. Thompson, *Globalization in Question*. London: Polity, 76–98.

Jensen, M., & Meckling, W. (1976). "Theory of the Firm: Managerial Behaviour, Agency Costs and Ownership Structure." *Journal of Financial Economics*, 3: 305–60.

Johnson, G., & Scholes, K. (1993). *Exploring Corporate Strategy: Text and Cases* (3rd ed.). Hemel Hempstead, Hertfordshire: Prentice Hall.

Kaplan, R., & Norton, D. (1992). "The Balanced Scorecard: Measures that Drive Performance." *Harvard Business Review*, January–February: 71–9.

Kay, J. (1993). *Foundations of Corporate Success*. Oxford: Oxford University Press.

Lazonick, W., & O'Sullivan, M. (2000). "Maximising Shareholder Value: A New Ideology for Corporate Governance." *Economy and Society*, 29: 13–35.

Llewellyn, S. (1994). "Managing the Boundary: How Accounting is Implicated in Maintaining the Organisation."*Accounting, Auditing and Accountability Journal*, 7: 4–23.

Mintzberg, H., Simons, R., & Basu, K. (2002). "Beyond Selfishness." *MIT Sloan Management Review*, 44: 67–74.

Murphy, K., & Jay, D. (1995). "Incentives Downsizing and Value Creation: General Dynamics." *Journal of Financial Economics*, 37: 261–314.

Otley, D. (2001). "Extending the Boundaries of Management Accounting Research: Developing Systems for Performance Management." *British Accounting Research*, 44: 243–61.

O'Dwyer, B. (2005). "Stakeholder Democracy: Challenges and Contributions from Social Accounting." *Business Ethics: A European Review*, 14/1: 24–41.

Owen, D., Swift, T., Humphrey, C., & Bowerman, M. (2000). "The New Social Audits: Accountability, Managerial Capture or the Agenda of Social Champions?" *European Accounting Review,* 9/1: 81.

Pitman, B. (2003). "Leading for Value." *Harvard Business Review*, 81/4, April: 41–6.

Porter, M. (1980). *Competitive Strategy*. New York: Free Press.

Pozen, R. C. (1994). "Institutional Investors: The Reluctant Activists." *Harvard Business Review,* 1: 140–9.

Prahalad, C. K., & Hamel, G. (1990). "The Core Competence of the Corporation." *Harvard Business Review*, May–June: 79–91.

Quintas, P. (2002). "Managing Knowledge and Innovation across Boundaries," in S. Little, P. Quintas, & T. Ray (eds.), *Managing Knowledge*. London: The Open University and Sage Publications.

Ramanathan, K. V. (1976). "Towards a Theory of Corporate Social Accounting." *The Accounting Review*, 21: 516–28.

Rappaport, A. (1986). *Creating Shareholder Value*. New York: Free Press.

—— (1998). *Creating Shareholder Value: A Guide for Managers and Investors*. New York: Free Press.

—— (2006). "Ten Ways to Create Shareholder Value." *Harvard Business Review*, September: 66–77.

Riley, R. (2000). "Stock Price Discussion." *Financial Times*.

Selden, L., & Colvin, G. (2003). "M&A Needn't Be All Game." *Harvard Business Review*, 81(6): 70–9.

Stern Stewart & Co. (2003). Russell 3000 Annual Ranking Data.

Sudarsanam, S., & Mahate, A. A. (2006). "Are Friendly Acquisitions Too Bad for Shareholders and Managers? Long Term Value Creation and Top Management Turnover in Hostile and Friendly Acquirers." *British Journal of Management*, 17/1: s7–s30.

Teece, D. J. (2000). *Managing Intellectual Capital.* Oxford: Oxford University Press.

Tran, M. (2006). "British Airways Abandons the High Street." *Guardian*, Wednesday, March 15: 12.

Tully, S. (1994). "The Real Key to Creating Wealth." *Fortune*, November 28: 143.

Turner, B. (1990). "The Rise of Organizational Symbolism," in J. Hassard & D. Pym (eds.), *The Theory and Philosophy of Organizations.* London: Routledge.

Unerman, J. (2004). "Enron, WorldCom, Andersen et al: A Challenge to Modernity." *Critical Perspectives on Accounting*, 15/6–7: 971.

—— & Bennett, M. (2004). "Increased Stakeholder Dialogue and the Internet: Towards Greater Corporate Accountability or Reinforcing Capitalist Hegemony?" *Accounting, Organizations and Society*, 29/7: 685–707.

Useem, M. (1999). *Investor Capitalism: How Money Managers are Changing the Face of Corporate America.* New York: Basic Books.

Zuckerman, E. W. (2000). "Focusing the Corporate Product: Securities Analysts and De-diversification." *Administrative Science Quarterly*, 45: 591–619.

PART III

A SOCIOCULTURAL LENS FOR M&A

CHAPTER 14

POST-DEAL INTEGRATION

An Overview

SATU TEERIKANGAS AND
RICHARD J. JOSEPH

INTRODUCTION

Interest in mergers and acquisitions (M&A) as strategic moves for corporations has rocketed throughout the 20th century and continues to do so at the dawn of the 21st century. Faced with an increasingly rapidly changing, competitive marketplace with global reach, M&A transactions have established themselves as a means of strategic growth, expansion, diversification, and reorganization. All the while, they have also been associated with managerial hubris and overconfidence (see Chapter 8), as well as a systemic effect—how can one avoid getting involved in M&A when it is by definition one of the sought-after ways of growth for the modern, globalizing firm (see Chapter 13)? Under the conventional wisdom, M&A has become "a" or "the" way of promoting corporate growth, without much criticism, or critical review (see Chapter 13). Today, many a multinational firm consists of a number of companies acquired over the firm's corporate history—as a result, these firms host a plethora of cultures, structures, ways of working, and cultures (Teerikangas 2006; Barkema and Schijven 2008).

Despite a noticeable increase in the number of M&A transactions over the last century, and a significant surge since the early 1990s, individual accounts of practitioners point to the daily challenge in making M&A work. Indeed, once the deal has been signed off, a new phase in the participating organizations' corporate life begins. This post-deal phase has been referred to in a number of ways: the post-acquisition integration phase, the post-merger integration phase, or the post-acquisition implementation phase. Regardless of the terminology used, it is at this juncture that M&A integration activity starts in earnest. It is from here onward that the desired objectives, synergies, and cost efficiencies should be achieved (Haspeslagh and Jemison 1991).

The practicing managers' accounts and consulting reports' findings have been echoed by academic research evidence (Hunt 1990; Haspeslagh and Jemison 1991; Larsson and Finkelstein 1999) pointing to the central, yet challenging task posed by post-deal integration management in making mergers or acquisitions work. Interest in the study of the post-M&A integration phase relates to the fact that this phase has repeatedly been cited as the most challenging in ensuring the success of M&A (Olie 1994; Datta 1991; Cartwright and Cooper; 1993; Child et al. 2001, Ranft and Lord 2002).

Among the earliest academic works on M&A, basing their findings on 275 interviews, Mace and Montgomery (1962) posit the critical significance of post-acquisition integration: "Many potentially valuable acquired corporate assets have been lost by neglect and poor handling during the integration process" (1962: 230). In another seminal work, Haspeslagh and Jemison (1991: 105) note: "The integration process is key to making acquisitions work." Further, in their study, the authors found that whilst the interviewed managers acknowledged the importance of integration, this part of the acquisition process is the one that managers feel least comfortable with: "They find it difficult, time consuming, uncertain, and fraught with risks and setbacks" (ibid. 105).

What is intriguing is that the view of (1) integration being the most challenging aspect of making acquisitions work, (2) managers paying insufficient attention to this phase, and (3) a lack of systematic academic study of integration resonates across much of the M&A integration literature. Indeed, we find this argument in the earliest works from the 1960s and 1970s (Mace and Montgomery 1962; Howell 1970), as well as from subsequent work since the 1980s, when post-acquisition integration established itself as a stream of research. Whilst the 1960s and the 1970s were characterized by individual academic studies on M&A, it was the advent of the 1980s that marked the beginning of more widespread academic interest in studying integration (as in e.g. Lindgren 1982; Duhaime and Schwenk 1985; Jemison and Sitkin 1986; Shrivastava 1986). At the time, researchers lamented the lack of "solid scientific" evidence on M&A integration, despite the availability of a myriad of anecdotal or case-study reports (see e.g. Jemison and Sitkin 1986; Haspeslagh and Jemison 1991).

This chapter proceeds as follows. We begin with a historical overview of the field; we discuss the "process" view of M&A management that has prevailed since the mid-1980s as the preferred lens through which integration has been examined. We then move on to explore later approaches to M&A integration, highlighting the need to take a long-term perspective to integration. Third, we present and synthesize the key success factors of M&A integration, based on existing case-based evidence. Having defined the broad context in which M&A integration occurs, the following sections expound on critical facets of integration management: integration strategy, organizational fit, change processes, integration management best practices, the roles involved, and performance effects. To illustrate the practical difficulties of merging, at the end of the chapter we present a case study of a merger involving two prominent educational institutions, focusing on the integration challenges therein. A final section concludes and provides pointers for future research.

Toward a Process Perspective to M&As

Whilst pointers to the significance of post-acquisition integration can be found in early publications (e.g. Mace and Montgomery 1962; Kitching 1967; Howell 1970), it was the work of Jemison and Sitkin (1986) and Haspeslagh and Jemison (1991) that formally posited the "process" view of M&A. Prior to these publications, whilst the term "process" had been attached to M&A integration and its importance had been highlighted, most M&A scholars and practitioners continued to treat M&A as unfolding sequentially over various phases. In this respect, Howell (1970) identified the sequential acquisition phases as (1) strategy formation, (2) investigation and selection, (3) negotiating the contract, and (4) integrating the operations. Hunt (1990) defined the phases of an acquisition process as: (1) targeting the seller, (2) negotiations following the bid, (3) implementation, (4) converting the seller's staff to the new configuration. Meanwhile, De Noble et al. (1988) described the acquisition process as proceeding from pre-merger planning, through negotiations, to integration, and acculturation.

In contrast, the work of Jemison and Sitkin (1986) linked the formerly disconnected fields of strategic management and organizational behavior by arguing that the progress of M&A should not be regarded as a sum of sequential parts, but rather as a process, the management of which determines the potential for value creation from the deal (Haspeslagh and Jemison 1991; see also Chapter 8). At the time of publication, Jemison and Sitkin (1986) observed that acquisitions were approached by practitioners and academics alike from a strategic and financial "choice" perspective, i.e. the rational executive decision-maker's viewpoint. Given the number of stakeholders involved in the various phases of an acquisition, the reality was not only a discontinuous approach to acquisitions, but also a fragmented, multiple stakeholders' view. It was in response to this seemingly disparate conception that Jemison and Sitkin (1986) introduced the "process" perspective to acquisitions. The authors argued that ultimately, the successful outcome of an acquisition depends on how the entire acquisition process, from pre- to post-deal phases, is orchestrated. Acquisitions are not only about "choice" (choosing the right target), but also about the "process" (the way in which the entire process is managed). The authors identified several factors that impede pre-acquisition decision-making and subsequent integration:

1. The segmentation of activities by multiple stakeholders, leading to an overemphasis on strategic fit at the expense of organizational fit;
2. Escalating momentum to close the deal, leading to premature conclusions, inattention to integration issues, and consequently, a lower probability of the acquisition succeeding;
3. Ambiguity regarding expectations of the acquisition, resulting in cycles of escalating conflict following the deal, and, at worst, in polarized mutual attitudes;
4. Lack of confidence on both sides or overconfidence on the buyer's side, leading to mutual defensiveness or parent firm chauvinism.

Whilst the focus of the 1986 work was on the pre-deal phase, the 1991 book extended the argument to the integration phase. On the basis of a series of in-depth case studies of international acquisitions, Haspeslagh and Jemison (1991) articulated the tenet that what distinguishes successful acquisitions is an understanding of the processes through which acquisition decisions are made and through which acquisition integration is managed.

Prior to this perspective, the authors claimed that acquisitions were viewed as individual deals, with a primary focus on price. Moreover, the decision-making process leading to acquisitions tended to be considered a sequential, linear process, involving setting strategic objectives, search and screening, strategic evaluation, financial evaluation, negotiation, agreement, and integration. In contrast, the process view advocated by Haspeslagh and Jemison (1991) portrays acquisitions not as independent, once-off deals, but rather as belonging to a firm's long-term renewal strategy. What is more, they contend, whilst concluding a deal is significant, value is realized only if the target is integrated in the right way—hence, "integration management" matters. Their key argument is that, whilst (pre-acquisition) decision-making and (post-acquisition) management do present distinct challenges, instead of viewing them as separate activities and phases, as often happens in M&A practice, M&A scholars and practicing managers should treat them as interdependent.

In summary, the acquisition process consists of two interrelated phases: the phase preceding the deal (the pre-acquisition phase) and the phase following the deal (the post-acquisition phase). The aim of the pre-acquisition evaluation process is to decide whether to engage in an acquisition or not. The acquiring company has a strategic rationale for the purchase, including potential value creation, against which it assesses the attractiveness of the deal. The integration process can be defined as a guided process to implementing organizational change, affecting mainly the acquired unit(s) (possibly the acquiring organization too, depending on the integration strategy), and ultimately the parties involved, with the aim of aligning the new unit(s) with the desired strategic direction. According to the process view, the aim of the integration phase is to create an "atmosphere supportive of capability transfer" (Haspeslagh and Jemison 1991). The progress of acquisitions further depends upon the kinds and quality of interactions between the two parties (Haspeslagh and Jemison 1991).

Despite the fact that both Jemison and Sitkin's (1986) and Haspeslagh and Jemison's (1991) models integrated the pre- and post-acquisition phases, subsequent research has largely focused on each of these phases as independent occurrences. The significance of linking the pre- and post-deal phases has been emphasized (Marks 1982; Hunt 1990; Haspeslagh and Farquhar 1994; Krüger and Müller-Stevans 1994), together with the complex nature of this interrelationship (Kitching 1967; Marks 1982; Shanley 1994). For example, Hunt (1990) finds that the implementation phase is the outcome of the two earlier pre-deal phases: pre-acquisition behaviors during targeting affect the progress of negotiations. As a result, the quality of the interpersonal relationships created will affect the extent to which target stakeholders will be motivated to join and work for the buying firm. Nevertheless, it seems that the dynamics of this relationship, i.e. how the pre-deal phase impacts on the integration phase, still requires more systematic research (Greenwood et al. 1994; Schweiger and Goulet 2000; Teerikangas 2010).

TIME-SPAN PERSPECTIVE TO INTEGRATION

Proceeding from Haspeslagh and Jemison's (1991) findings, subsequent phase- or process-based studies on M&A have highlighted the need to adopt a long-term perspective on integration.

Birkinshaw et al. (2000) conceptualize integration from the dual perspective of task integration and human integration. They define "task integration" as the integration strategy adopted and the degree of communication and socialization between units. They define "human integration" as leadership, communication during integration, retention of staff, cultural convergence, and respect. Birkinshaw et al. (2000) find that during the first five to seven years following the conclusion of the deal, the connections between task and human integration are limited. The authors also point to the slow and difficult task of human integration. They advise that as human integration can facilitate task integration, it should ideally precede the latter.

Angwin (2004) finds that the perceptions of the success of an acquisition tend to diminish over time. Yet, perceptions of the success of integration tend to improve three to four years following the deal. Consequently, Angwin (2004) argues, the issue of time in integration should be addressed in greater detail.

More recently, Quah and Young (2005) reported the results of their study of an American automobile multinational's acquisitions in Europe. They found that these acquisitions could be delineated conceptually as follows:

1. The pre-acquisition phase: what happens in the six months prior to the deal;
2. The first year following the acquisition;
3. The second to fifth year following the acquisition;
4. Beyond the first five years following the acquisition.

Quah and Young (2005) found that the automobile manufacturer they studied adopted a gradual approach to integration, with few changes implemented in the first post-deal year. They further noted that it took on average five years for the acquired units to become absorbed. Yet, performance-wise, the planned synergies were not captured until approximately eight years following the deal. This study highlights the long-term nature of acquisitions integration-wise as well as performance-wise.

Further, it would seem that acquisitions should be set in the buying firm's wider corporate context. In a study of 25 Dutch multinationals' acquisition patterns 1966–2005, Barkema and Schijven (2008) find that whilst post-acquisition integration is the single most important determinant of synergy realization, this factor should not be treated as unique, but rather, should be incorporated into the acquiring firm's long-term acquisition strategy. The authors claim that by focusing on single acquisitions, current research efforts have failed to account for the systemic variables that nevertheless impact integra-tion progress and ultimate acquisition performance. The authors reconfirm an earlier estimate by Biggadike (1979) that full post-acquisition performance might be achieved as late as 12 years following a deal. A sequence of acquisitions increases the need for internal restructuring, in turn affecting the management of a single acquisition. Placing acquisitions in the acquiring firm's sequence of takeovers, Barkema and Schijven (2008) find that a particular acquisition's position in the acquirer's overall acquisition sequence dictates performance; specifically, the performance of an acquisition tends to be weaker if it occurs late in a sequence of acquisitions.

In summary, recent research findings point to the need to take a long-term post-acquisition perspective. Conceptually, post-acquisition integration can be delineated into phases. The length of the integration process is estimated at as much as five to twelve years post-deal. Instead of focusing on single acquisitions, the challenge of integration should be placed in the context of the acquiring firm's acquisition strategy and stream of acquisitions.

Success Factors in Integration

In order to understand the challenge of succeeding in post-acquisition integration, we will next proceed to an overview of studies that posit key success factors in M&A inte-gration. Our focus has been on studies that draw from direct industry, or case-study evidence.

Based on a study of McGraw-Hill, Dionne (1988) finds that acquisition success rests on (1) knowing why the acquisition is needed, (2) appointing an integration champion to head the pre-acquisition team, (3) assigning the right people to the team, i.e. includ-ing responsible business managers, (4) managing expectations, (5) keeping the court-ship phase short and smooth, (6) planning integration, (7) melding the teams, (8) maintaining surveillance and support.

Through their review of existing literature and an in-depth case study of two capital equipment leasing companies, De Noble et al. (1988) identify the following success fac-tors in mergers: (1) focusing on sources, not symptoms; (2) ensuring line management involvement from the pre-deal phase onward; (3) cross-fertilizing management teams; (4) remembering that people count; (5) identifying the hidden costs; (6) recognizing that corporate cultures exist, and might need to be changed; (7) linking strategy and structure; and (8) getting started early enough rather than too late. They argue that post-merger integration issues should be addressed from the pre-deal phase onward: whilst potentially helpful in the negotiations phase, ambiguities turn into difficulties at the start of integration planning. In the latter phase, clarifying and defining mutual expectations, roles, and responsibilities, is important. In terms of roles, De Noble et al. (1988) highlight the risk of having some individuals plan the acquisition, and others implement it.

Schweiger et al. (1993) present implementation tips for international M&A from a human resource management perspective. The authors highlight the importance of managing the depth, location, and nature of changes, whilst considering the speed of the change process. They advise that at the start of integration, the stability of the workforce should be ensured through clear communications and retention contracts. Also, the change process during integration should be effectively managed. Key questions should be addressed. What is the decision-making process? How will differences between the firms be managed? How will employee dislocation be managed?

In another work on international mergers, Olie (1990) found that integration of a cross-border merger is a long-term process facilitated through a sense of parity and common management programs, tasks, and goals. The author proposes leadership, symbolic reconstruction of a new identity, the implementation of super-ordinate goals, and introducing new multi-group membership as means of easing integration (Olie 1994). Evolutionary change promotes learning, as it enables the merging parties to get acquainted with each other's practices (Napier et al. 1993).

Ranft and Lord (2002) find that post-acquisition implementation consists in the speed or pace of change, the amount of mutual communications, the degree of autonomy granted to the target firm, as well as the extent to which target firm employees are retained. Epstein (2004) identifies the key drivers of successful post-merger integration as follows: (1) a coherent integration strategy, (2) a strong integration team, i.e. a project management approach to integration, involving both firms, and with dedicated integration managers in charge, (3) internal and external communications, (4) rapid speed, and (5) clear measurements of success. Epstein further notes that these drivers will manifest themselves differently depending on deal type, i.e. whether the deal is an acquisition, a merger, or a conglomerate. Epstein (2004) finds that in the JPMorgan Chase merger, success factors related to (1) the design of the integration process, (2) early critical decisions, (3) optimal tools and methods, (4) managing people and change, and (5) disciplined integration management.

Based on Pitney Bowes' experience with acquisitions, Nolop (2007) draws up the following checklist of success factors: (1) buying related firms, (2) taking a portfolio approach, i.e. acquiring multiple small firms, (3) finding a business sponsor to drive and execute the deal, (4) formulating different criteria for assessing the progress and success of different deal types, (5) avoiding acquiring for the sake of acquiring.

In synthesis, based on extant research, key success factors in making M&A integration work relate to acquisition strategies, integration management, and performance expectations. Key characteristics of successful integration revolve around planning, using effective change/integration teams, starting early, managing employee expectations, communicating, and allowing for a degree of autonomy relative to complete absorption, depending on the deal type. Given the plethora of possible M&A types and contexts, the authors caution against using absolute metrics to measure integration progress; rather, they recommend developing deal-specific progress and performance measures. In the discussion that follows, to further our understanding of M&A integration, we will delve into the most discussed facets of integration.

THE DEGREE OF INTEGRATION DICTATES
THE LEVEL OF CHALLENGE IN AN M&A

A key question regarding post-deal integration concerns the optimal degree of integration. In mergers, the question becomes to which degree the two organizations should be merged. In acquisitions, this issue relates to the extent to which the target firm should be integrated into the acquiring firm's organization. Often, the acquiring firm has an interest in learning from the target firm and adopting some of its best practices. Thus, integration need not be one-way, for the transfer of post-deal knowledge and capabilities can be mutual.

Extant research has confirmed that the integration strategy (alternatively termed "integration approach," or "degree of structural integration") adopted by the buying firm in the post-deal integration phase defines the location, nature, extent, and direction of change in that phase. What is more, the degree of integration has been found to impact post-deal performance (King et al. 2004), and mediate the effect of differences in national cultures on the latter (Slangen 2006). Pablo (1994) found that the degree of integration opted for in the post-acquisition phase depends on the involved managers' experience with acquisitions, as well as the industry in which they operate. Moreover, she found decisions on integration strategies to be primarily based on strategic task demands, rather than cultural and political ones. This finding suggests a strategic bias in decision-making on acquisition integration.

Available typologies

Integration strategies reflect the different degrees to which the acquired firm can be integrated into the buying firm. Several typologies of M&A integration strategies have been proposed. The seminal work of Haspeslagh and Jemison (1991) has come to be much used. Typologies have also been proposed by, for example, Kitching (1967), Howell (1970), Buono and Bowditch (1989), Napier (1989), Cartwright and Cooper (1990, 1992), and Bower (2001).

One approach to typologies is to distinguish from a management perspective on the basis of friendly and hostile acquisitions of healthy vs. unhealthy targets. In a replication of the seminal study by Kitching (1967), Hunt focused on 40 cases of British acquisitions. He finds that acquisitions should be placed in context (i.e. buyer strategy, ownership, compatibility of industry or size, health of seller, buyer or seller experience of acquisitions, and access to audit information) in order to understand the keys to their success. Hunt (1990) identifies three contextual scenarios for acquisitions, and proposes that each requires a different managerial approach in order to succeed, be it in the pre- or post-acquisition phase. The three acquisition contexts are: (1) the friendly acquisition of a healthy firm, (2) the friendly acquisition of a fairly healthy firm, and (3) the hostile bid for an unhealthy seller. Hunt (1990) emphasizes that the behavioral processes throughout an acquisition are critical to its success.

A much quoted approach is the typology proposed by Haspeslagh and Jemison (1991), identifying four possible integration strategies for the post-deal era: absorption, symbiosis, preservation, and holding. These integration strategies differ with respect to the desired degree of (1) acquiring firm–target firm strategic interdependence, and (2) target firm autonomy.

In "holding" acquisitions, the acquiring firm does not seek to integrate the target nor to create value from the deal; rather, it might seek financial integration or managerial cooperation. This strategy is appropriate for the acquisition of unrelated entities, or acquisitions that are not inherently strategic in nature. In the "preservation" mode, the target firm retains autonomy, usually as a separate subsidiary or division of the acquiring firm. It is likely that little integration takes place, and as a result, the target is not likely to incur much change in the post-deal era. By contrast, in "absorption" acquisitions, where the aim is explicitly to "absorb" the acquired firm into the acquiring firm's organization, a strong integration of the acquired into the acquiring firm is expected. Integration is likely to be one-way only, in that the acquiring firm's best practices and operational processes are "imposed" on the target, with little interest in mutual learning or knowledge transfer. In "symbiotic" acquisitions, the aim is to ensure a balance between target firm autonomy on the one hand, and integration into the acquiring firm on the other hand. Central to the implementation of the symbiotic approach is the reciprocal exchange of knowledge, skills, and capabilities between the two firms. Given that the process is inherently bi-directional, the management of symbiotic acquisitions is deemed the most challenging of all integration types (Haspeslagh and Jemison 1991).

In synthesis, what the four-quadrant typology of integration strategies suggests is that not all acquisitions are alike in terms of their integration process, management challenges, and requirements. Using the Haspeslagh and Jemison typology, integration management seems to be most critical and demanding in "absorption" or "symbiotic" acquisitions. The limitation of any categorical scheme is that the integration strategies adopted by acquiring firms rarely fit neatly into existing typologies. In practice, acquiring firms tend to adopt integration strategies that combine various features of different integration approaches (Haspeslagh and Jemison 1991). Another limitation is that the typological schemes assume that acquiring firms explicitly decide on post-acquisition integration strategies. This decision might not always be explicit, nor might it involve the entire firm. In practice, there are likely to be a myriad of different post-deal strategies implemented throughout the organizations. Ultimately, the number of different post-acquisition strategic regimes is reflected in the number of parallel integration processes at work (Ranft and Lord 2002; Teerikangas 2006).

Adopting a third approach by bridging the work of Kitching (1967) and Haspeslagh and Jemison (1991), Salk (1994) proposes that the appropriate integration strategy depends on merger type (see Appendix 1 for an introduction to M&A types): a "preservation" approach would befit conglomerate mergers, a "symbiosis" approach would suit both vertical and concentric mergers, whilst "absorption" would befit concentric and horizontal mergers. Salk (1994) further argues that each merger and integration regime parallels a governance mode. Salk likens preservation to pluralism, symbiosis to federation, and absorption to unification. She concludes that integration challenges differ from one merger type to another, and through this typology, are made more predictable.

Integrate or Not?

A key issue in the debate on integration strategies has centered on autonomy vs. integration, i.e. whether buying firms should provide the acquired firm with autonomy or vigorously seek to integrate the latter into their operations (Graebner 2004; Puranam et al. 2006, 2009).

Some scholars argue that autonomy ensures better performance than centralization (for a review, see Schweiger and Goulet 2000), although this argument might be more relevant for mergers in the knowledge and service-intensive sectors rather than to those in the manufacturing sector (Weber 1996). Thus, in high-technology firm acquisitions, autonomy granted to the target firm correlates with high employee retention (Ranft and Lord 2000).

By contrast, in their case-survey, Larsson and Finkelstein (1999) emphasize the significance of interaction and coordination to the degree of synergy realization in the post-deal era. All the while, Ranft and Lord (2002) argue that different units of the target firm might be integrated to different degrees, thus suggesting that integration strategies based on autonomy vs. absorption can coexist (Graebner 2004). Moreover, the degree of integration can change over time (Ranft and Lord 2002). In the case of acquisitions of small high-technology firms, where potential synergies are high, Puranam et al. (2009) find that despite potential integration costs and disruption, these consequences are outweighed by the opportunities gained. Puranam et al. (2006) find that the decision to integrate the high-technology target also depends on the position of the latter on its innovation trajectory. The disruptive consequences of lost target autonomy were found to be particularly salient for targets positioned in an exploration (vs. exploitation) phase of their innovation trajectory. A high integration level was found to have the strongest adverse effects on the innovation sequences of target firms that have not launched any products prior to the acquisition, and on the first post-acquisition innovation project. In line with these findings, some scholars have emphasized the need to be more sensitive to the type of M&A studied, and to managerial requirements per M&A type (Napier 1989; Greenwood et al. 1994).

In addition to varying with sector, integration strategies have been found to be culturally and institutionally dependent. Acquirers from different countries adopt different due-diligence (Angwin 2000) and integration approaches (Child et al. 2001). In a study of acquisitions conducted by multinational firms in emerging countries, Kale et al. found that these firms did not follow the traditional integration approach, as advocated in the literature on M&A (see Chapter 22). Instead of "integrating" the target firm into the acquiring firm, these firms adopted a "partnering" approach, which gives the target autonomy in the post-acquisition phase, whilst seeking to partner and find synergies in selected vs. all areas.

In synthesis, we find that the degree of "integration depth" is perhaps one of the most central issues in integration management. Essentially, the question is to what extent the target should be left autonomous or absorbed into the acquiring firm, and further, how much mutual coordination sought. The answer might not be straightforward; it might emerge and change over time, and it might differ across the acquisition's units and businesses. To complicate matters further, the appropriate answer will be context-dependent, i.e. it will depend on the sector in which the deal is made, and the country of the acquiring firm.

ORGANIZATIONAL FIT

Like integration strategy, organizational fit is considered a significant variable likely to impact the ease vs. challenge of post-deal integration (Datta 1991; Chatterjee et al. 1992; Weber 1996; Weber et al. 1996; Larsson and Finkelstein 1999). The better known the target firm, the better the managerial resource deployment decisions in the target firm, and the better the acquisition's performance (Colombo et al. 2007). Yet, historically, the research and practice of M&A have been plagued with the assumption that concerns for strategic fit override concerns for organizational fit in the pre-acquisition courtship phase (Jemison and Sitkin 1986). Calls have been made to evaluate the organizational and cultural aspects of the target firm during due diligence; there is a tendency to over-estimate financial and technical aspects related to the deal in this phase (Jemison and Sitkin 1986; Datta 1991; Chatterjee et al. 1992). Prior research has shown that acquiring firms realize the impact of organizational fit (or a lack thereof) only over time, as the firms begin working together after conclusion of the deal (Greenwood et al. 1994).

However, until now there have been few attempts to provide a means of assessing such aspects of inter-firm differences (Cartwright and Cooper 1993; Gertsen et al. 1998). This is noticeable in the debate on organizational fit. The notion of organizational fit has been raised as a factor impacting the level of difficulty of M&A integration (David and Singh 1994). Examining prior research on "organizational fit," the earliest works (Marks 1982; Sales and Mirvis 1984) were based on single-case-study anecdotal evidence regarding the need to account for organizational differences between the merging firms. This shortcoming led Jemison and Sitkin (1986) to call for a broader perspective on organizational fit, relative to the prevailing fragmented ones. Ultimately, they defined organizational fit as "the match between administrative practices, cultural practices, and personnel characteristics" (ibid. 147).

Subsequent studies have addressed organizational fit at the level of organizational cultures in domestic deals (Datta 1991; Chatterjee et al. 1992; Cartwright and Cooper 1992; Weber 1996), including national (Morosini and Singh 1994; Olie 1994; Weber et al. 1996), and functional cultures (David and Singh 1994) in the study of cross-border deals. A review of these studies shows, however, that there are inconsistencies within the research stream as to the way the concept of organizational fit is defined and operationalized.

What is more, the 1986 definition of organizational fit combined elements of organizational culture and structure, albeit at the level of practices only. Since then, with few exceptions, most studies have defined organizational fit exclusively as "cultural fit," ignoring its structural dimensions (as in e.g. Buono and Bowditch 1989; Olie 1990; Datta 1991). One exception is Franck (1990), who cautioned that implicit differences in information systems, human resource management policies, decision-making processes, values, and ethics can cause major difficulties in the implementation of M&A. Also Datta (1991) defined organizational fit as the differences in management styles, and reward and evaluation systems. Greenwood et al. (1994) highlight the difficulty of separating cultures, structures, and processes from one another, given that they are mutually related (Ranson et al. 1980). Yet, they acknowledge that cultural, rather than structural, differences have a negative impact on acquisition performance (Greenwood et al. 1994).

However, subsequent studies have not recognized the importance of the structural dimensions of organizational fit. Rather, these studies have merely continued the cultural discourse. Hence, the prevailing view on organizational fit remains dominated by the cultural dimension, with the result that a more inclusive definition of organizational fit that accounts for both its cultural and structural dimensions is lacking. This deficiency explains why, for example, Gertsen et al. (1998: 18) argue that despite the acknowledgement of the importance of pre-deal evaluation, researchers have little to say about *how* to carry out such an analysis.

NATURE OF POST-DEAL CHANGE

Focusing on the changes occurring in the post-acquisition phase, different, but related functional integration processes have been identified, to correspond with the array of possible post-deal changes.

Among the earliest studies, Howell (1970) identified post-acquisition integration as applicable to (1) the corporate organization, (2) functional areas, and (3) planning and control systems. In his view, the challenge of integration in these three domains depends on the type and strategy of the acquisition. Lindgren (1982) defined integration in terms of the administrative, organizational (organizational structures, reward and communication systems, financial systems), social (i.e. cultural systems), and operational (i.e. production, marketing, R&D) systems involved. Shrivastava (1986) referred to these systems as procedural (i.e. legal and accounting integration), physical (i.e. product line and technology integration), and managerial and sociocultural integration processes (i.e. changes in organization structure, development of an organizational culture, and selection of managers). Haspeslagh and Jemison (1991) contend that the transfer of strategic capabilities is at the heart of integration. This transfer can relate to (1) operational resource sharing, (2) the transfer of functional skills, (3) the transfer of general management skills, and (4) other combination benefits. In his work on the integration of R&D

units, Håkanson (1995) alluded to procedural (i.e. budget and reporting, work routines), technical (i.e. infrastructure and joint projects), and managerial and sociocultural integration processes.

In synthesis, both structural (i.e. technical and procedural changes) and cultural integration-related changes would appear to occur in the post-deal era. Yet these changes tend to be treated as occurring in parallel with one another, as though they bear no mutual relationships. Most studies do not address the relationship between these "cultural" and "structural" changes, and assume that they take place in parallel. In contrast, a study of three cross-border R&D units' acquisitions (Teerikangas and Laamanen 2006) found the cultural and structural integration processes to be not only intertwined, but also sequentially ordered. This finding emphasizes the need for additional research on the ways in which post-acquisition change unfolds.

INTEGRATION MANAGEMENT

In this section, we explore "integration management." We start with an overview of the "best practices" in integration management, followed by a discussion of the "attitudes" that prompt or hamper the progress of post-acquisition integration.

An Overview of Integration Best Practices

Planning

Planning has been referred to in extant research as a critical factor in ensuring the success of M&A integration. As early as 1970, Howell's study of over 40 acquiring companies found many companies to be poorly prepared for acquisitions owing to a lack of planning. In their survey of 751 cross-border acquisitions in Italy and by Italian firms, Colombo et al. (2007) confirm that planning, through its positive impact on the post-acquisition climate and managerial appointments in the target firm, significantly impacts acquisition performance.

Speed and Timing

Timing is critical to the success of acquisitions. Haspeslagh and Jemison (1991) note that, at worst, companies prepare for integration in the pre-acquisition phase by viewing integration from the perspective of a "static end point," instead of considering how to achieve the desired outcome. The authors posit that having a clear view of how to start, with what speed to proceed, and how to reach desired objectives is critical if acquisitions are to succeed.

There is an ongoing debate as to the significance of the speed of integration actions. There are diverging views as to whether a quick or slow start to integration activities is best (Schweiger et al. 1993; Schweiger and Goulet 2000; Ranft and Lord 2002).

Calls have been made for more conceptual research on the way in which speed of post-deal action influences the progress of post-acquisition integration (Ranft and Lord 2002). Whilst practitioner cases point to the need for "swift" action (De Noble et al. 1988; Epstein 2004), academic findings have maintained a more nuanced stance.

Among proponents of swift post-deal action, the immediate post-deal period has been referred to as the "window of opportunity" (Ranft and Lord 2002). In the weeks and months following the acquisition, the target organization expects and awaits change to take place. Implementing change has thus been found to be easier in this period, as change is expected. A link to performance has also been identified. In their large-scale survey of acquisitions related to Italian firms, Colombo et al. (2007) find a negative correlation between a temporal lag (i.e. time between deal closure and start of integration), performance, and climate.

It is in this respect that the concept and arguably the importance of the "first 100 days" (e.g. Angwin 2004) is well-known in M&A practice. In a study of GE Capital's acquisitions, Ashkenas et al. (1998) report that the first 100 days are typically spent creating an integration plan. It is argued that the first 100 days constitute the time frame during which all critical actions should be launched. Yet, in a study of whether and how the first 100 days impact the performance of acquisitions, Angwin (2004) finds little evidence of such an impact, thus suggesting that this time frame might be "more of convenience than substance" (2004: 428). On the other hand, Angwin (2004) finds a correlation between the volume of changes implemented in the first 100 days and perceptions of success three to four years post-deal.

By contrast, in the context of cross-border acquisitions, recent research evidence suggests that changes should *not* be made immediately after a deal. Rather, post-deal changes should be made over time, as the acquiring firm will be better able to target the changes required, once its knowledge of the acquired organization increases (Quah and Young 2005).

Possibly, both slow and rapid integration speeds are required, at different intervals. Teerikangas (2006) finds that rapid action is needed early in the integration phase, with regard to communications and changes that require implementation soon after the deal, and to ensure that staff of the acquired firm know what is taking place. Thereafter, a gradual integration pace creates space for making longer-term decisions on more significant, larger-scale changes required in the acquired firm. These findings suggest that both kinds of integration actions are needed and that the choice between quick vs. slow pace is not "either/or."

Homburg and Bucerius (2006) conducted the first empirical study of the impact of speed in acquisitions. In their survey of 232 horizontal M&As, they find no simple answer. The optimal speed of post-acquisition integration is found to depend on the extent to which the merging firms are related. Where the internal relatedness of the firms is high (i.e. similar management styles, strategic orientation, and performance), but their external relatedness is low (i.e. the firms' geographical markets and customers are not similar), speed of integration has a positive effect on acquisition success. By contrast, where internal relatedness is low, but external relatedness is high, speed has an adverse, negative effect.

In synthesis, we find that timing and speed are critical, yet they depend on the deal type, context, relatedness of firms, as well as the acquisition/integration strategy. This strategy should be embodied in an integration plan that is not only implemented expeditiously, but also communicated clearly to key internal and external stakeholders.

Socialization and Interactions

M&A are, at heart, organizational encounters; i.e. encounters of people. In this respect, it is not surprising that socialization and interactions have been established as critical to successful post-deal integration.

To this end, Calori et al. (1994) studied "informal control mechanisms" (Ouchi 1981; Bartlett and Ghoshal 1989) in M&A integration. Larsson and Lubatkin (2001) emphasized the importance of "social controls" in fostering acculturation following M&A. The role of mutual interaction in the success of M&A integration has been addressed by, among others, Buono and Bowditch (1989), Olie (1990), Cartwright and Cooper (1992), and Larsson and Finkelstein (1999). These studies call for recognizing the importance of exchange and interaction in promoting learning, sharing knowledge, and ensuring successful post-deal integration (Schweiger and Goulet 2000; Larsson and Lubatkin 2001). Given the significance of knowledge transfer in the context of R&D acquisitions, work on the integration of acquired R&D units (Håkanson 1995) also mentions the importance of informal means of communication. Larsson and Finkelstein (1999) regard the degree of organizational integration and the ensuing degree of inter-firm interaction as critical for the success of M&A.

Communications

The centrality of integration-related communications has come to be amply emphasized by M&A scholars (Bastien 1987; Ivancevich et al. 1987; Schweiger and Denisi 1991). Haspeslagh and Jemison (1991) posit that inter-firm interactions are "at the heart of integration" (1991: 117). Nonetheless, a distinction should be made between different kinds of post-acquisition communications.

Extant research on post-deal communications has focused on corporate-level post-deal communications and the role of the transition team (Bastien 1987; Burke 1987; Ivancevich et al. 1987; Cartwright and Cooper 1992; Schweiger et al. 1993). Also counseling for employees in the post-deal phase has been advised (Cabrera 1982).

Haspeslagh and Jemison (1991) identify three types of interactions: "substantive interactions," which refer to ensuring that the objectives of the acquisition are met; "administrative interactions," which relate to setting the reporting and control relationships in place; finally, "symbolic interactions," which relate to establishing the long-term vision for the firms as well as the "rules of behavior."

In their study of technology acquisitions, Ranft and Lord (2002) found the construct of post-acquisition communications to be multidimensional in terms of content and frequency. They argued that frequent and open communications facilitate post-deal integration. In particular, they found the richness of exchanges to be determinative of the effectiveness of communication, i.e. face-to-face contact has more effect than virtual contact. They concluded that rich communications in turn support knowledge transfer and the establishment of a climate favorable to change.

Ellis et al. (2009) found that the degree of open communications (i.e. informational justice) is positively related to value creation during and after integration. Involving target firm managers in decision-making (i.e. procedural justice) was found to have positive performance effects only if previously supported by open communications. In other words, according to this study, openness in communications seems to be a first priority, which then can support the extent to which acquired firm managers become involved. Intriguingly, communications and involvement impact acquisition performance in different ways: whilst open communications have a positive effect on financial returns, involvement has a positive effect on gains in market position. This would mean that managers involved in acquisitions should revert to different managerial approaches, depending on the desired objectives in the deal.

In synthesis, communications lie at the heart of successful post-acquisition integration. Communication should occur at several levels, from top management to the teams managing change. Also, various kinds of communications are required, depending on the context. The significance of open and "rich" face-to-face communications should be emphasized, given the breadth and significance of the organizational upheaval in an M&A.

Attitudes

Attitudes have both value-enhancing and value-destructive effects on the progress and outcomes of M&As.

In their seminal work, Haspeslagh and Jemison (1991) place the "right" atmosphere for capability transfer at the heart of integration. Based on their research, the authors view the optimal atmosphere as embodying several factors. First, both firms should appreciate their respective organizational backgrounds and differences, thus creating a context for capability transfer. Further, there should be a willingness to work together. Third, there needs to be sufficient capacity to transfer and receive the desired capabilities. Given the resources that integration absorbs, it is critical that slack resources are made available in both firms, thus creating a capability-supportive atmosphere in both firms. Finally, managers should communicate the purposes and objectives of the acquisition to the organizations at large. This "cause-effect understanding" then supports employees in working toward mutual goals.

M&A literature has reflected on the importance of the buying firm's attitudes in enhancing mutual cooperation in the post-deal phase (Olie 1994; Deiser 1994), the need to create an atmosphere supportive of capability transfer (Haspeslagh and Jemison 1991), the need for "assertive tolerance" in managing the post-deal integration phase (Napier et al. 1993), and the importance of fairness during post-acquisition integration (Hambrick and Cannella 1993). The importance of "respect" in the way acquired firm management and employees are treated was noted by Krug and Nigh (2001) in their study of acquired firm executive departures.

More recent findings support this view. A study of European and American firms' acquisitions in East Germany (Thomson and McNamara 2001) cites the potential role of "corporate entrepreneurship" in enabling integration, thereby affecting acquisition success.[1] In her study of acquisitions by worldwide industry leaders, Kanter (2009) finds that successful buyers are firms that have been able to integrate and motivate new staff members. Such "winners" can be distinguished from other firms on the basis of their attitudes: they do not act like conquerors. Rather, they act as "welcoming hosts," "eager learners," "fixers vs. destroyers." Within their respective organizations, managerial leaders are effective communicators, who can read the emotional and cultural cues given by their co-workers. Processes are transparent, and investments in the future are made without hesitation.

Whilst fairness and equality are often raised as cornerstones of successful mergers, cases of failed mergers point to the potential ambiguities therein. In a study of the failed Telia and Telenor merger, Meyer and Altenborg (2007) contend that the notion of equality is in practice not an objective concept, but subject to a myriad of local interpretations. Moreover, they point out that in the context of a merger, the principles of equality in roles and responsibilities might lead to "structural paralysis" because decisions cannot be taken, and national interests cannot be bridged.

Scholars have also cautioned against the presence of potentially negative attitudes in the aftermath of M&A. Deiser (1994) alludes to the impact of the buying firm's attitudes in the post-acquisition process and advises against the buying firm blindly imposing its ideas upon the acquired firm. The presence of a "not-invented-here" syndrome has been referred to by Blake and Mouton (1984) and Buono and Bowditch (1990). They note that interpersonal relations can be tense in times of M&A, even moving toward hostility, owing to group dynamics. They caution that employees are likely to resent ideas that do not come from their group. Third, inter-organizational problems in times of M&A typically relate to "competing claims," "secrecy vs. deception" (Buono and Bowditch 1990), "us vs. them," "superior vs. inferior," "attack and defend," and "win vs. lose" behaviors (Marks 1991). These findings touch on the debate on inter-group relations in social psychology, where it is argued that social conditions should be positive for inter-group encounters to succeed. Otherwise, the groups will revert to dysfunctional behavior, through which each will favor their in-group members at the expense of the out-group members (Sherif 1962; Tajfel 1978a, 1978b).

Among potentially destructive attitudes, Haspeslagh and Jemison (1991) identify "determinism" as a problem in acquisitions. By determinism, they refer to situations where managers cling to their initial goals for the deal, regardless of mounting evidence of the need to change these objectives. The source of determinism can be traced to how and when the acquisition decision was justified in the pre-deal phase. Indeed, in retrospect, the initial justification for the acquisition might be flawed, based on limited information, or might have been purposefully communicated in simplistic terms in order to be understood. Also, unexpected events such as industry or contextual changes might have prompted changes to the initial strategy.

Vaara (2003) takes a more critical perspective of events occurring in the post-acquisition era. Through the study of a Finnish furniture manufacturer's three Swedish acquisitions, he finds that cultural and social identity differences result in ambiguity and cultural confusion, thus potentially resulting in a perceived hypocrisy in decision-making and politicization of integration issues. As a result of such ambiguity and confusion, there is a lack of action to implement integration activities.

To summarize, attitudes can bear positively or negatively on M&A. Whilst attitudes of fairness, experimentation, learning, ambition, and humility underlie experiences of successful integration, one must beware of the potential for destructive reactions in the post-acquisition encounter of two organizations. Such negative outcries might relate to hostility, secrecy, overdeterminism, or superiority claims.

Who is in Charge of Integration?

Extant research has found that the following roles bear significantly on M&A success: top management teams, change agents, acquired firm managers, and key target firm talent. These roles will be reviewed in this section.

Top Management Attention

In addition to demanding the attention of business or integration managers, acquisitions require the attention of senior managers (Haspeslagh and Jemison 1991). Without such attention, a "leadership vacuum" might emerge in the post-acquisition phase. At worst, top managers forget the acquisition soon after the deal. Yet this omission masks the parallel employee need for top management attention and direction in the integration phase. At worst, such inattention can result in the failure to make, implement, or effectively communicate the right decisions. The role of top management is to set the right atmosphere or tone for integration, so that both sides are interested in sharing ideas and are willing to collaborate in a mutually respectful manner. Haspeslagh and Jemison (1991) term this "institutional leadership."

Integration Teams and Boundary-Spanning Change Roles

Who is responsible for integration? In their study of General Electric's (GE) acquisition process across a number of deals, Ashkenas et al. (1998) identify the integration manager as key to the success of the company's acquisitions. The authors note that it was after significant acquisition experience that GE realized that the appointment of a manager in charge of the integration process is critical to acquisition success. Regarding GE Capital's acquisitions, Ashkenas et al. (1998) identified the integration manager's role as (1) facilitating and managing integration activities, (2) helping the acquired business to understand GE Capital, (3) helping GE Capital to understand the target business, and

(4) building a connective tissue between the organizations. In a follow-up study of companies across industries, Ashkenas and Francis (2000) clarified the role of the integration manager. In this study, they observed that so-called "enlightened" companies typically appoint an executive, "guide," or "shepherd" to coordinate post-acquisition phase activities.

In a similar vein, Haspeslagh and Farquhar (1994) found interface management or "gatekeeping" between the buying and acquired firms to be a critical variable that impacts the progress of post-acquisition integration. Effectively this task is incidental to the role of the "integration manager." In acquisitions where exchange and integration between the combined firms is to be expected, "interface management" becomes important, to the extent that "the quality of interface management becomes a key to unlocking acquisition value" (Haspeslagh and Jemison 1991: 156). The role of interface management is to control the pace, nature, and timing of inter-firm interactions. Depending on the integration approach, interface management serves a gatekeeping function either to (1) provide transitional management in a full integration "absorption" acquisition, (2) support mutual knowledge transfer in a "symbiotic acquisition," or (3) protect target firm boundaries in a "preservation" acquisition where granting target firm autonomy is a high priority.

What capabilities are required of such individuals? In a study of individuals engaged in boundary-spanning activities in times of organizational change including mergers, Balogun et al. (2005) find that these individuals typically engage in aligning agendas and selling the initiative, manipulating situations to ensure that the message is effectively delivered, gathering intelligence, and lobbying for help from senior managers. All these activities relate to influencing others involved in the transition. The extent to which change agents are successful depends on the strength and breadth of their network. A key factor characterizing these individuals is that they work within social networks and strongly rely on their networks to achieve results. By implication, the work of these individuals is highly network-dependent.

Use Insiders of Outsiders in Management?

In the academic literature, a major discussion centers on the destiny of top managers in the post-deal regime: in a merger or acquisition, should top managers stay or go? Angwin and Meadows (2009) suggest that the choice of whether to use target or outsider managers depends on the integration strategy. Where there is low interdependency between the firms or the target is given considerable autonomy following the deal (i.e. "preservation" acquisitions), the tendency to use insiders, i.e. target firm managers, is predominant. Insiders also appear to be favored when the target is granted little autonomy and is in financial difficulty: an insider is best positioned to deal with the dire situation. In contrast, where there is high interdependency between the firms (i.e. "absorption" acquisitions), and change and new perspectives are required, the tendency to opt for outsiders in top managerial positions prevails. In "symbiotic" acquisitions, firms typically start with an insider manager, only to replace him or her later by an outsider. In "holding" acquisitions, although insiders are predominant, outsiders, when used, tend to achieve better results. In sum, integration strategy as well as acquisition context jointly dictate the choice of management. As Chapter 22 indicates, this choice might relate to the national background of the acquiring firm.

The Selling Side and Involving Acquired Firm Management

M&A scholars have advised involving the acquired organization (Haspeslagh and Farquhar 1994; Angwin 2004; Graebner 2004) as a means of fostering integration and mutual learning. Véry and Schweiger (2001) stressed the importance of such involvement, especially where the acquisition occurred in a country in which the acquiring firm had no prior experience. Graebner's (2004) study of technology acquisitions suggested that target firm managers have a distinct and crucial role in ensuring the successful integration of their entity into the new parent firm. These managers usually enable the realization of expected and serendipitous value creation in acquisitions. In order to realize expected value, acquired firm managers typically engage in "mobilizing actions" that help maintain the momentum of change, be it by setting goals and clear tasks for target firm employees or coordinating with acquiring firm management for support. Moreover, in successful acquisitions, acquired firm leaders also engage in "mitigating actions" that address personnel issues and uncertainties in times of the change. Graebner (2004) further found that serendipitous value was created when acquired firm engineers and managers were provided with cross-organizational responsibilities.

The work of Graebner and Eisenhardt (2004) takes the seller's view of an acquisition. In contrast, the majority of M&A research has focused on the buying firm. The authors find that sellers are triggered to be positive toward their firm being acquired, if they are facing strategic hurdles or have a personal motivation to sell the firm, be it owing to a fear of failure, stress, financial gain, or dilution risk. Moreover, target company leaders were found to be ready to sell their firm, when they identified combination potential between the acquiring and target firms, or when organizational rapport—e.g. cultural fit, personal fit, trust, and respect—between the two firms coexisted. The authors see that these findings provide not only a seller-focused, but also a relationship-focused perspective on acquisitions, in contrast to a buyer-focus and an agency-theory focus in the existing literature. In light of this result, Graebner and Eisenhardt (2004) posit the acquisition process not as a takeover, but rather as at best a courtship.

Key Talent

In terms of ensuring future performance, retaining key employees is critical. This applies especially to sectors that are highly reliant on human capital.

In biotechnology acquisitions (see Chapter 26), retaining engineers is perhaps more critical than retaining senior managers, owing primarily to the unique technical expertise of the former. In their study of targets acquired by pharmaceutical companies, Paruchuri et al. (2006) find that negative effects of acquisitions are not homogeneous across employee types: acquisitions affect the productivity of some employees more than others, depending on their particular skill-set. The authors find that acquisition integration has an overall negative effect on the productivity of inventors following acquisitions. Yet, inventors whose work is far from the acquiring firm's core tend to suffer more than other engineers. Moreover, engineers who boasted a strong pre-acquisition network are likely to suffer most in the aftermath of a takeover, because the acquisition and resulting integration tend to redefine the structure of social networks. Whilst these changes are constructive from an integration perspective, they are destructive from an innovation perspective, because inventors tend to rely strongly on social networks to collaborate. It generally takes time after the acquisition for these networks to become functional again.

Synthesis

The task of achieving M&A integration rests on a number of shoulders. It falls on the acquiring firm's top management, who should be fully committed to integration, and should visibly express this commitment to the target. Second, successful integration rests on the work of transition teams and integration managers, appointed for an interim period to coordinate change efforts. At best, such teams should involve members of both organizations. In particular, the involvement of acquired firm managers has been found to have beneficial effects. The question of whether acquired firm managers should stay or go depends on the acquisition and integration type. Finally, it should be remembered that the effects of M&A are different, depending on employee class and profession; thus some professions and employees might be more valuable in terms of future value creation. This applies especially to acquisitions in human capital-intensive and dependent sectors.

VALUE CREATION AND MEASUREMENT
DURING INTEGRATION

Integration has been found to matter in terms of operational performance. For example, in their survey of M&A case studies, Larsson and Finkelstein (1999) find that synergy is realized across different functional areas when (1) the firms to be combined are complementary, (2) the degree of organizational integration is high, and (3) the degree of employee resistance is low. Achieving these results requires an effective integration effort. More recently, Ranft and Lord (2002) find that implementation, together with the nature of the knowledge to be transferred, affect the extent to which capabilities are transferred post-acquisition in technology acquisitions.

This brings us to the central question of how, in practice, value is created through integration, and how integration progress can be measured. Whilst M&A performance has been the subject of ample research (see Chapters 4 and 5), more work is warranted on the micro dynamics that link actions in the integration phase with long-term acquisition performance (King et al. 2004; Haleblian et al. 2009). In the following section, we have handpicked studies conducted in this promising research arena.

One study viewed M&A as a dual process of (1) value creation, and (2) value leakage or destruction (Gates and Véry 2003). Value is created when, through the deal, it is possible to exploit sources of revenue enhancement and cost reduction, and when it is possible to preserve each firm's intrinsic value (Gates and Véry 2003). Value is destroyed when the firms are unable to deliver synergies, or they decrease one firm's intrinsic value; also, where the cost of managing post-merger integration exceeds potential benefits. Furthermore, value leakage can be economic or psychological. Acquisitions that adversely impact employees and managers through stress, strain, and uncertainty at worst destroy value (Haspeslagh and Jemison 1991). Economic value destruction relates to potential economic losses resulting from diminished job security, pay, and benefits, whilst psychic value destruction refers to the potential intangible costs resulting from a myriad of emotional and psychological grievances.

Continuing the theme of value leakage, through in-depth case studies on several North-European M&A transactions, Meyer (2008) identifies several means through which sought value is eroded. First, whether in mergers or in acquisitions, managers tend to seek governance structures that allow for independence rather than integration—as a result, synergies take longer to realize. Meyer terms this "rent-seeking managerial behavior." Second, employees engage in "rent-seeking behavior," either by arguing for increased compensation or by resisting efforts to change. Third, M&A transactions often result in "reduced effort," owing to employee demotivation and stress, loss of identity, perceptions of unfairness, or the sheer loss of talent. Finally, the change brought about by a merger or an acquisition also leads to a "reallocation of effort" through an extensive focus on organization-internal matters during integration; alternatively, wastes of effort occur as personnel and managers spend excessive time negotiating their personal gains in the deal. By comparing different deal types and their eroding effects, Meyer (2008) finds that value leakage can be expected to be the greatest in horizontal mergers involving multiple parties, and lesser in single, expansion-type acquisitions.

Whilst M&A performance has been studied extensively, less attention has been paid to measuring integration progress. Gates and Véry (2003) argue that there is no best way to measure M&A integration performance, because each process within the integration phase is geared to specific contingencies. Consequently, the tips given by the authors toward measuring integration progress relate to the parties' identifying as early as possible: (1) the objectives, strategy, potential synergies, and plan for the deal, (2) the main sources of value creation and value leakage, (3) measures of following up both of the latter, (4) milestones and targets per measure, and (5) how the measures are used to efficiently control and monitor the entire process.

In synthesis, whilst value creation is the oft sought goal in acquisitive arrangements, there are a myriad ways in which value can leak, resulting in lower than expected performance. Value leakage is likely to be higher, the more parties are involved, and the greater the desired degree of integration. Value leakage can result from strategic decisions. It is often associated with intangible dysfunctionalities: do managers and employees seek the benefit of the deal or their own benefit? How much time is spent grieving and worrying? How much effective time does integration consume? These micro-dimensions of M&A performance warrant additional research. Moreover, the issue of how to measure integration progress merits greater attention. It seems that M&A performance research has largely remained at a macro-organizational level.

Case Study of M&A Integration: Enterprise Acquisition of Fidelity

The following case study illustrates the challenges associated with post-merger integration, as well as the need to adequately plan for them in the pre-merger phase. The authors have selected a "real-world" example from the educational sector to highlight many of the cultural, organizational, and "intangible" aspects of integrating two distinct institutions within the same industry.

In October 2007, a Chicago-based business school (referred to under the fictitious name "Enterprise"), which offered a highly ranked MBA program, acquired a London-based college (referred to under the fictitious name "Fidelity"), which conferred four US-accredited degrees: the MBA, Bachelor of Science, Master of Finance, and Master of Marketing. Before the acquisition, Fidelity's financial position had deteriorated as a result of a steady decline in undergraduate enrollments. By contrast, Enterprise's financial position had been bolstered by a dramatic surge in MBA enrollments, propelled by an effective global recruiting effort.

Inspiring Enterprise's takeover of Fidelity were three key strategic objectives. First, Enterprise wanted to acquire a European-based institution that offered programs similar to those offered by Enterprise, but in different markets. Enterprise's MBA program catered primarily to South American, Western European, Indian, and East Asian markets, whilst Fidelity's MBA programs catered primarily to North American, Eastern European, and Middle Eastern markets. Second, Enterprise wanted to obtain a "portfolio" of degree programs that could both complement its MBA program and "leverage off" its marketing, administrative, and instructional resources. Enterprise's key intangible asset was its highly ranked MBA program. In Enterprise's eyes, Fidelity's Bachelor of Science, Master of Finance, and Master of Marketing programs could complement the Enterprise MBA and benefit from Enterprise's marketing, administrative, and instructional expertise. Third, Enterprise wanted to acquire valuable real estate in a unique urban setting; i.e. Central London. It realized that acquiring such real estate in a separate asset transaction could be costly and difficult from a zoning and regulatory perspective.

Apart from these strategic objectives, Enterprise also believed that by injecting funds into Fidelity, capitalizing on Enterprise's extensive administrative and market expertise, and tapping its enormous recruiting capability, it could ultimately augment Fidelity's enrollments, restore Fidelity to economic viability, upgrade its facilities, improve its academic quality, and replicate Fidelity's accredited degree programs in other parts of the world. Thus, it executed its strategy with speed and agility.

Five years later, Enterprise's strategy largely succeeded, thanks to an effective management team, the financial backing of its key investors, and support from Fidelity's accreditors, who abhorred the prospect of a final teach-out if Fidelity became insolvent. However, Enterprise's implementing this strategy proved difficult from a financial, operational, and integration perspective. In the aftermath of the takeover, Enterprise faced the formidable task of eliminating redundancies in administrative and academic personnel (a key human resource integration issue). Undertaking this task required strict compliance with UK and EU labor law, faithful adherence to US accreditation guidelines, the hiring of numerous HR consultants and legal counselors, and the expenditure of additional funds to pay severance to employees deemed redundant and to give raises to faculty and staff deemed indispensable.

Enterprise was also compelled to reconcile incongruous organizational structures, governance systems, operational processes, and employee roles (essential for operational integration). It had to standardize degree requirements, academic policies, courses, curricula, admissions guidelines, grading criteria, and academic calendars. In the process, it encountered stiff resistance on the part of former Fidelity administrators, instructors, and staff, who felt deceived by what they believed to be "false promises" and betrayed by those in whom they had placed their utmost trust, thus posing a major communications problem for Enterprise management.

Finally, Enterprise faced the monumental task of reconciling seemingly disharmonious institutional milieus, thus highlighting the challenge of cultural integration. The work environment it fostered before the acquisition was entrepreneurial, market-oriented, and culturally diverse. Its approach to education was more practical than theoretical, with a heavy emphasis on teaching. For course delivery, it relied primarily on the deployment of highly paid part-time "specialists." It had no tenure system, no academic departments, and no gradations in faculty rank. Fidelity, by contrast, was bureaucratic, internally focused, and culturally homogeneous. Its approach to education was more theoretical than practical, with a heavy emphasis on research. For course delivery, it relied primarily on the deployment of moderately paid full-time "generalists." It had a traditional tenure system, five academic departments, and five gradations in faculty rank.

In the end, Enterprise made great strides in overcoming most of these difficulties, primarily because its administrators were willing to spend the time, effort, and resources necessary to rectify operational and organizational dysfunctionalities; its key stakeholders were willing to invest the funds necessary to upgrade facilities, integrate operations, and raise salaries; its staff and faculty were deeply committed to the paramount mission of providing a quality education for deserving students; and both Fidelity's and Enterprise's accreditors staunchly supported the takeover. However, financial and strategic success was not without a corresponding human cost. Nor was it accompanied by success in fully eliminating cultural incompatibilities. Were these results "value destructive"? Or do they represent incidental, or even "ordinary" costs associated with post-merger integration? The jury is still out.

The lessons to be learned from the Enterprise-Fidelity case are primarily four. First, mergers that make perfect sense from a strategic and financial perspective may not make sense from an operational and cultural perspective, given the "human element" involved. Second, just as mergers can fail because of the "human element," so too can they succeed because of this element: specifically, competent managers who are aware of operational and cultural pitfalls, adequately plan and provide for them in the pre-deal phase, and are willing to devote ample time and resources to "manage" them in the post-deal phase. Third, the real costs of a merger go well beyond share price and market value, paramount considerations in the pre-deal planning phase. To be sure, they encompass the unpredictable financial, operational, and human costs of merging distinct entities, cultures, and systems of organizational behavior. (Query: if such costs are indeed unpredictable, how can they be provided for, or even estimated with reasonable certainty, in this phase?) Finally, notwithstanding the limited success of some managers at "reconciling" distinct organizational cultures, there remains the thorny issue of post-merger identity. In the context of rapid institutional change, rare are the instances of unscathed personal identity, for individual self-certainty is integrally bound up with the stability of the institutional order. The Enterprise-Fidelity case offers no exception to the rule.

Conclusions and Future Research Directions

The aim of this chapter has been to provide a state-of-the-art review of our knowledge of M&A integration to date. To this end, we embarked on a review of the published academic literature on M&A integration in key management journals since the 1960s. Whilst not aiming at exhaustive coverage, our goal was to focus on the key dynamics and characteristics underlying successful M&A integration. Our findings highlight how since the 1960s, M&A integration has been acknowledged as *the* difficult phase in making M&A work. In this respect, we can critically ask what has been achieved since the early works (e.g. Mace and Montgomery 1962). Whilst many of the fundamentals of M&A integration management have remained the same across the five decades covered by this review chapter, we have witnessed an increasingly nuanced and fine-grained understanding of the dynamics inherent in M&A integration.

When reviewing work on M&A integration, one needs to bear in mind the practical difficulty of separating integration from the overall acquisition process and the related human (see Chapter 15) and cultural (see Chapter 16) challenges that further complicate the integration phase. Chronologically speaking, whilst research on M&A integration has existed since the 1960s, we note that reviews of this stream of research remain rarer than those, for example, of the human or cultural stream on M&A (as in e.g. Napier 1989; Cartwright and Cooper 1990; Teerikangas and Véry 2006). It would almost seem that research on the post-deal integration phase has become an "amalgam" of inquiries that moves in many directions without becoming confined to the space of a review chapter, as here. This means that notwithstanding the expanded scope of this chapter, not all relevant literature has been covered. We highlight the difficulty of a thorough review of the literature on M&A integration—a topic that is at once multifaceted, multidimensional, and multilevel.

Our review of M&A integration-related studies indicates that the topic has been studied primarily in the contexts of high-technology acquisitions (Ranft and Lord 2002), biotechnology acquisitions (Schweizer 2005), professional service firms (Greenwood et al. 1994; Empson 2004), research and development units (Håkansson 1995), banking (Epstein 2004), the automobile industry (Quah and Young 2005), industrial firms (Teerikangas 2010), and multinational firms' units (Haspeslagh and Jemison 1991; Birkinshaw et al. 2000). In terms of countries studied, considerable work relates to a US or North American context (Greenwood et al. 1994; Ranft and Lord 2002; Graebner 2004), American acquisitions in Europe (Quah and Young 2005), or European acquisitions in Europe (Håkansson 1995). The relative absence and only recent disclosure of evidence from emerging markets or other continents is worth highlighting (see Chapter 22).

In synthesis, the field has moved from a paradigm of M&A management based on a sequential phase-based view to one of appreciating M&A as a process that unfolds from strategic decision-making, through pre-deal decision-making, to integration management (Haspeslagh and Jemison 1991). In this transformation, a view of integration as a long-term venture spanning as many as seven (Birkinshaw et al. 2000) or twelve years post-deal (Biggadike 1979; Barkema and Schijven 2008) has emerged. Moreover, an appreciation of the "key success factors" in making M&A work has, by and large, taken hold. Having said this, the more subtle micro-dynamics at work during M&A integration warrant more study. Whilst the assessment of organizational fit has been established as key to acquisition decision-making, rare are the analytical tools for evaluating whether or not a fit exists. Moreover, the present understanding has defined organizational fit purely through a cultural lens, thereby omitting its other, e.g. structural, operational, dimensions. With respect to post-acquisition change, since the scholarly advances of the 1980s, little effort has been devoted to this topic. Post-acquisition change still is regarded as consisting of a set of parallel, functional, processes. This largely static view of post-acquisition change could be replaced by a more dynamic one, incorporating the interrelationships between post-acquisition processes, as well as their potential dynamic or emergent nature. In this respect, we note that the current literature posits post-acquisition change as a linear, predetermined process, a view that runs counter to more recent advances in strategy and organization theory (Burnes 2009).

Regarding the role of key people involved in making integration work, we note a paucity of research on this topic. A few articles tend to focus on managers in the buying firm, as opposed to those in the acquired firm (Graebner 2004) or on the selling side (Graebner and Eisenhardt 2004). Moreover, extant research suggests that M&A integration is merely a "managerial enterprise"—the sole responsibility of top management (Haspeslagh and Jemison 1991), integration managers (Ashkenas and Francis 2000), or acquired firm managers (Graebner 2004). There is a surprising gap in the literature regarding the role of the ordinary employee in M&A integration (see Chapter 21). Yet, for the last few decades, empowerment and employee engagement have been at the core of change management and organization development efforts (Burnes 2009). Finally, whilst M&A performance has been the focus of extensive research for years, we found little evidence of scholarly interest in exploring how the progress of integration comes to affect M&A performance (Haleblian et al. 2009). Indeed, M&A scholars seem to have neglected the impact of actions in the integration phase upon M&A performance.

What this synthesis implies is that M&A integration research is conducted primarily through a macro-organizational, static, linear, deterministic, and prescriptive lens. This view omits the micro-organizational (i.e. individual actors, behaviors, attitudes, etc.), the dynamic, the emergent, the practice-based aspects of M&A. Current research seems to be dominated by a process perspective that assumes neatness and linearity; yet, this approach begs the question, "Where is ambiguity, where is uncertainty?" All the while, it is this view that has come to dominate academic discourses in organization theory, change management, and strategy over the last decades (Lynch 2006; Burnes 2009). Critically speaking, we ask—is it time for a fresh look at M&A integration, from a dynamic, evolving, non-linear, 21st-century perspective? This proposition is supported by the observation that much of M&A integration scholarship occurs within the boundaries set by the M&A literature itself (Teerikangas and Geraldi 2011). Yet, M&A integration embodies dynamic concepts such as emergence, change, uncertainty—all relevant to the study of organizations in general. Critically speaking, one might consider that, as a research topic, "integration management" has been around for so long that it must have been thoroughly addressed. Is it now time for M&A integration researchers to go beyond their own discipline to develop new concepts and lenses from which to view integration? Is it now time for researchers to renew, refresh, and re-enliven the study of M&A integration?

Regardless of research advances, important questions remain unresolved. A fundamental question concerns the differences between mergers and acquisitions. The extant literature tends to treat the two as synonymous, despite important differences in their management. Also, research findings are biased toward integration in domestic, rather than international, settings. In this respect, there is a need for qualitative, longitudinal studies on integration dynamics in small-scale acquisitions vs. large-scale mega mergers. What dynamics are at play in cross-border vs. domestic acquisitions? From an integration perspective, in which ways do these acquisition types differ? And what about integration management in the context of a multi-site global merger, spanning several countries? Most research on integration is conducted by North American or European scholars. What about M&A in other continents? Furthermore, how are the pre- and post-acquisition phases interrelated? How are parallel change processes during integration interrelated? Finally, what are the cultural and structural dynamics of M&A integration?

Another area for exploration is how to link the study of M&A performance to the study of M&A integration. Hitherto, these two areas of inquiry have led almost disparate lives. Yet, if we are to respond to calls to elucidate the micro-dynamics behind M&A performance (King et al. 2004; Haleblian et al. 2009), such an inquiry becomes necessary. Questions such as—When is integration complete? How long does integration take? What is integration success? Through what means is value created vs. destroyed in the course of integration?—would need to be answered. Finally, the challenge of post-deal integration research is to shed light on the firm's overall acquisition strategy, instead of focusing on a single acquisition (Barkema and Schijven 2008).

In summary, by presenting an overview of the M&A integration literature over the past five decades, this chapter has highlighted the potential inherent in this stream for repositioning. Undoubtedly, additional research in this critical field is needed.

End Notes

1. Corporate entrepreneurship refers to post-acquisition behaviors characterized by a learning capability, a team orientation, a culture of experimentation, and ambition in terms of high aspirations.

References

Angwin, D. (2000). "Mergers and Acquisitions across European Borders: National Perspectives on Pre-acquisition Due Diligence and the Use of Professional Advisers." *Journal of World Business*, 36/1: 32–57.

—— (2004). "Speed in M&A Integration: The First 100 Days." *European Management Journal*, 22/4: 418–30.

—— & Meadows, M. (2009). "The Choice of Insider or Outsider Top Executives in Acquired Companies." *Long Range Planning*, 42: 359–89.

Ashkenas, R. N., DeMonaco, L. J., & Francis, S. C. (1998). "Making the Deal Real: How GE Capital Integrates Acquisitions." *Harvard Business Review*, 76/1: 165–78.

—— & Francis, S. C. (2000). "Integration Managers: Special Leaders for Special Times." *Harvard Business Review*, 78/6: 108–16.

Balogun, J., Gleadle, P., Hope Hailey, V., & Willmott, H. (2005). "Managing Change across Boundaries: Boundary-Shaking Practices." *British Journal of Management*, 16: 261–78.

Barkema, H. G., & Schijven, M. (2008). "Toward Unlocking the Full Potential of Acquisitions: The Role of Organizational Restructuring." *Academy of Management Journal*, 51/4: 696–722.

Bartlett, C. A., & Ghoshal, S. (1989). *Managing across Borders: The Transnational Solution*. London: Random House Business Books.

Bastien, D. T. (1987). "Common Patterns of Behaviour and Communication in Corporate Mergers and Acquisitions." *Human Resource Management*, 26: 17–33.

Biggadike, R. (1979). "The Risky Business of Diversification." *Harvard Business Review*, 57/3: 103–11.

Birkinshaw, J., Bresman, H., & Håkansson, L. (2000). "Managing the Post-acquisition Integration Process: How the Human Integration and Task Integration Processes Interact to Foster Value Creation." *Journal of Management Studies*, 37/3: 395–425.

Blake, R. B., & Mouton, J. S. (1984). "How to Achieve Integration on the Human Side of the Merger," in R. B. Black & J. S. Mouton (eds.), *Solving Costly Organisational Conflicts: Achieving Intergroup Trust, Cooperation and Teamwork*. San Francisco: Jossey-Bass, 41–56.

Bower, J. L. (2001). "Not All M&As are Alike—And That Matters." *Harvard Business Review*, 79/3: 93–101.

Buono, A. F., & Bowditch, J. L. (1989). *The Human Side of Mergers and Acquisitions: Managing Collisions between People, Cultures and Organizations*. London: Jossey-Bass.

—— —— (1990). "Ethical Considerations in Merger and Acquisition Management: A Human Resource Perspective." *SAM Advanced Management Journal*, Autumn: 18–33.

Burke, R. J. (1987). "Managing the Human Side of Mergers and Acquisitions." *Business Quarterly*, 5/2–3: 18–23.

Burnes, B. (2009). *Managing Change* (4th ed.). Harlow: Pearson.

Cabrera, J. C. (1982). "Takeovers: The Risks of the Game and How to Get Around Them." *Management Review*, 71/11: 17–21.

Calori, R., Lubatkin, M., & Véry, P. (1994). "Control Mechanisms in Cross-Border Acquisitions: An International Comparison." *Organization Studies*, 15/3: 361–79.

Cartwright, S., & Cooper, C. L. (1990). "The Impact of Mergers and Acquisitions on People at Work: Existing Research and Issues." *British Journal of Management*, 1: 65–76.

—— —— (1992). *Managing Mergers, Acquisitions and Strategic Alliances: Integrating People and Cultures*. Oxford: Butterworth-Heinemann.

Cartwright, S., & Cooper, C. L. (1993). "The Role of Culture Compatibility in Successful Organizational Marriage." *Academy of Management Executive*, 7/2: 57–70.

Chatterjee, S., Lubatkin, M. H., Schweiger, D. M., & Weber, Y. (1992). "Cultural Differences and Shareholder Value in Related Mergers: Linking Equity and Human Capital." *Strategic Management Journal*, 13: 319–34.

Child, J., Faulkner, D., & Pitkethly, R. (2001). *The Management of International Acquisitions.* Oxford: Oxford University Press.

Colombo, G., Conca, V., Buongiorno, M., & Ghan, L. (2007). "Integrating Cross-Border Acquisitions: A Process-Oriented Approach." *Long-Range Planning,* 40: 202–22.

Datta, D. K. (1991). "Organizational Fit and Acquisition Performance: Effects of Post-Acquisition Integration." *Strategic Management Journal,* 12: 281–97.

David, K., & Singh, H. (1994). "Sources of Acquisition Cultural Risk," in G. Von Krogh, A. Siknatra, & H. Singh (eds.), *The Management of Corporate Acquisitions.* London: Macmillan, 251–92.

Deiser, R. (1994). "Post-acquisition Management: A Process of Strategic and Organisational Learning," in G. Von Krogh, A. Siknatra, & H. Singh (eds.), *The Management of Corporate Acquisitions.* London: The Macmillan Press, 359–90.

De Noble, A. F., Gustafson, L. T., & Hergert, M. (1988). "Planning for Post-merger Integration: Eight Lessons for Merger Success." *Long-Range Planning,* 21/4: 82–5.

Dionne, J. L. (1988). "The Art of Acquisitions." *The Journal of Business Strategy,* 9/6: 13–17.

Duhaime, I. M., & Schwenk, C. R. (1985). "Conjectures on Cognitive Simplification in Acquisition and Divestment Decision-Making." *Academy of Management Review,* 10: 287–95.

Ellis, K. M., Reus, T. H., & Lamont, B. T. (2009). "The Effects of Procedural and Informational Justice in the Integration of Related Firms." *Strategic Management Journal,* 30: 137–61.

Empson, L. (2004). "Organisational Identity Change: Managerial Regulation and Member Identification in an Accounting Firm Acquisition." *Accounting, Organisations and Society,* 29/8: 759–81.

Epstein, M. J. (2004). "The Drivers of Success in Post-merger Integration." *Organisational Dynamics,* 33/2: 174–89.

Franck, G. (1990). "Mergers and Acquisitions: Competitive Advantage and Cultural Fit." *European Management Journal,* 8/1: 40–3.

Gates, S., & Véry, P. (2003). "Measuring Performance during M&A Integration." *Long Range Planning,* 36/2: 167–85.

Gertsen, M. C., Soderberg, A.-M., & Torp, J. E. (1998). *Cultural Dimensions of International Mergers and Acquisitions.* Berlin: De Gruyter.

Graebner, M. E. (2004). "Momentum and Serendipidity: How Acquired Firm Leaders Create Value in the Integration of Technology Firms." *Strategic Management Journal,* 25/8–9: 751–77.

—— & Eisenhardt, K. M. (2004). "The Seller's Side of the Story: Acquisition as Courtship and Governance as Syndicate in Entrepreneurial Firms." *Administrative Science Quarterly,* 49: 366–403.

Greenwood, R., Hinings, C. R., & Brown, J. (1994). "Merging Professional Service Firms." *Organization Science,* 5/2: 239–57.

Håkanson, L. (1995). "Learning through Acquisitions, Management and Integration of Foreign R&D Laboratories." *International Studies of Management and Organization,* 25/1–2: 121–57.

Haleblian, J., Devers, C. E., McNamara, G., Carpenter, M. A., & Davison, R. B. (2009). "Taking Stock of What We Know About Mergers and Acquisitions: A Review and Research Agenda." *Journal of Management,* 35: 469–502.

Hambrick, D. C., & Cannella, A. A. (1993). "Relative Standing: A Framework for Understanding Departures of Acquired Executives." *Academy of Management Journal,* 36/4: 733–62.

Haspeslagh, P. C., & Jemison, D. B. (1991). *Managing Acquisitions: Creating Value through Corporate Renewal*. New York: The Free Press.

—— & Farquhar, A. B. (1994). "The Acquisition Integration Process: A Contingent Framework," in G. von Krogh, A. Siknatra, & H. Singh (eds.), *The Management of Corporate Acquisitions*. London: The Macmillan Press, 414–47.

Homburg, C., & Bucerius, M. (2006). "Is Speed of Integration Really a Success Factor in Mergers and Acquisitions? An Analysis of the Role of Internal and External Relatedness." *Strategic Management Journal*, 27: 347–67.

Howell, R. A. (1970). "Plan to Integrate your Acquisitions." *Harvard Business Review*, 48/6, November–December: 66–76.

Hunt, J. W. (1990). "Changing Patterns of Acquisition Behaviour in Takeovers and the Consequences for Acquisition Processes." *Strategic Management Journal*, 11: 69–77.

Ivancevich, J. M., Schweiger, D. M, & Power, F. R. (1987). "Strategies for Managing Human Resources during Mergers and Acquisitions." *Human Resource Planning*, 10/1: 19–35.

Jemison, D. B., & Sitkin, S. B. (1986). "Corporate Acquisitions: A Process Perspective." *Academy of Management Review*, 11/1: 145–63.

Kanter, R. M. (2009). "Mergers that Stick." *Harvard Business Review*, 84/10, October: 121–5.

King, D. R., Dalton, D. R., Daily, C. M., & Covin, J. G. (2004). "Meta-Analyses of Post-acquisition Performance: Indications of Unidentified Moderators." *Strategic Management Journal*, 25/2: 187–200.

Kitching, J. (1967). "Why Do Mergers Miscarry?" *Harvard Business Review*, 45, November–December: 84–100.

Krug, J. A., & Nigh, D. (2001). "Executive Perceptions in Foreign and Domestic Acquisitions: An Analysis of Foreign Ownership and its Effect on Executive Fate." *Journal of World Business*, 36/1: 85–98.

Krüger, W., & Müller-Stevans, G. (1994). "Matching Acquisition Policy and Integration Style," in G. von Krogh, A. Siknatra, & H. Singh (eds.), *The Management of Corporate Acquisitions*. London: Macmillan, 50–87.

Larsson, R., & Finkelstein, S. (1999). "Integrating Strategic, Organizational, and Human Resource Perspectives on Mergers and Acquisitions: A Case Survey of Synergy Realization." *Organization Science*, 10/1: 1–26.

—— & Lubatkin, M. (2001). "Achieving Acculturation in Mergers and Acquisitions: An International Case Study." *Human Relations*, 54/12: 1573–607.

Lindgren, U. (1982). "Strategic Aspects of Postacquisition Management in Multinational Corporations." *International Studies of Management and Organisation*, 12/1: 83–123.

Lynch, R. (2006). *Corporate Strategy* (4th ed.). Harlow: Prentice-Hall.

Mace, M. L., & Montgomery, G. (1962). *Management Problems of Corporate Acquisitions*. Cambridge, MA: Harvard University Press.

Marks, M. L. (1982). "Merging Human Resources: A Review of the Literature." *Mergers and Acquisitions*, 16, Summer: 38–44.

—— (1991). "Combating Merger Shock before the Deal is Closed." *Mergers and Acquisitions*, 25/4: 42–8.

Meyer, C. N. (2008). "Value Leakages in Mergers and Acquisitions: Why they Occur and How they can be Addressed." *Long Range Planning*, 41: 197–224.

Meyer, C. B., & Altenborg, E. (2007). "The Disintegrating Effects of Equality: A Study of a Failed International Merger." *British Journal of Management*, 18: 257–71.

Morosini, P., & Singh, H. (1994). "Post-Cross-Border Acquisitions: Implementing National Culture-Compatible Strategies to Improve Performance." *European Management Journal*, 12/4: 390–400.

Napier, N. K. (1989). "Mergers and Acquisitions, Human Resource Issues and Outcomes: A Review and Suggested Typology." *Journal of Management Studies*, 26/3: 271–89.

——, Schweiger, D. M., & Kosglow, J. J. (1993). "Managing Organisational Diversity: Observations from Cross-Border Acquisitions." *Human Resource Management*, 32/4: 505–23.

Nolop, B. (2007). "Rules to Acquire by." *Harvard Business Review*, 85/9: 129–39.

Ouchi, W. G. (1981). *Theory Z: How American Business can Meet the Japanese Challenge.* Reading, MA: Addison-Wesley.

Olie, R. (1990). "Culture and Integration Problems in International Mergers and Acquisitions." *European Management Journal*, 8/2: 206–15.

——(1994). "Shades of Culture and Institutions in International Mergers." *Organization Studies*, 15/3: 381–405.

Pablo, Amy L. (1994). "Determinants of Acquisition Integration Level: A Decision-Making Perspective." *Academy of Management Journal*, 37/4: 803–36.

Paruchuri, S., Nerkar, A., & Hambrick, D. C. (2006). "Acquisition Integration and Productivity Losses in the Technical Core: Disruption of Inventors in Acquired Companies." *Organization Science*, 17/5: 545–62.

Puranam, P., Singh, H., & Chaudhuri, S. M. (2009). "Integrating Acquired Capabilities: When Structural Integration is (Un)necessary." *Organization Science*, 20/2: 313–28.

—— —— & Zollo, M. (2006). "Organizing for Innovation: Managing the Coordination-Autonomy Dilemma in Technology Acquisitions." *Academy of Management Journal*, 49/2: 263–80.

Quah, P., & Young, S. (2005). "Post-Acquisition Management: A Phases Approach for Cross-Border M&A." *European Management Journal*, 23/1: 65–75.

Ranft, A. L., & Lord, M. D. (2000). "Acquiring New Knowledge: The Role of Retaining Human Capital in Acquisitions of High-Tech Firms." *The Journal of High-Tech Management Research*, 11/2: 295–319.

—— ——(2002). "Acquiring New Technologies and Capabilities: A Grounded Model of Acquisition Implementation." *Organization Science,* 13/4: 420–41.

Ranson, S., Hinings, C. R., & Greenwood, R. (1980). "The Structuring of Organizational Structures." *Administrative Science Quarterly*, 25: 1–17.

Sales, A. L., & Mirvis, P. H. (1984). "When Cultures Collide: Issues in Acquisitions," in J. Kimberley & R. E. Quinn (eds.), *New Futures: The Challenges of Managing Corporate Transitions.* Homewood, IL: Dow Jones-Irvin, 107–33.

Salk, J. (1994). "Generic and Type Specific Challenges in the Strategic Implementation and Legitimation of Mergers and Acquisitions." *International Business Review*, 3/4: 497–512.

Schweiger, D. M., Csiszar, E. N., & Napier, N. K. (1993). "Implementing International Mergers and Acquisitions." *Human Resource Planning*, 16/1: 53–70.

—— & Denisi, A. S. (1991). "Communication with Employees Following a Merger: A Longitudinal Field Experiment." *Academy of Management Journal*, 34/1: 110–35.

—— & Goulet, P. K. (2000). "Integrating Mergers and Acquisitions: An International Research Review," in C. Cooper & A. Gregory (eds.), *Advances in Mergers and Acquisitions*, vol. 1. Amsterdam: JAI Press, 61–91.

Schweizer, L. (2005). "Organizational Integration of Acquired Biotechnology Companies into Pharmaceutical Companies: The Need for a Hybrid Approach." *Academy of Management Journal*, 48: 1051–74.

Shanley M. T. (1994). "Determinants and Consequences of Post-Acquisition Change," in G. Von Krogh, A. Sinatra, & H. Singh (eds.), *Managing Corporate Acquisitions: A Comparative Analysis*. London: Macmillan, 391–413.

Sherif, M. (1962). *Intergroup Relations and Leadership*. New York: Wiley.

Shrivastava, P. (1986). "Postmerger Integration." *Journal of Business Strategy*, 7/1: 65–76.

Slangen, A. (2006). "National Cultural Distance and Initial Foreign Acquisition Performance: The Moderating Effect of Integration." *Journal of World Business*, 41: 161–70.

Tajfel, H. (1978a). *Differentiation between Social Groups: Studies in the Social Psychology of Intergroup Relations. European Monographs in Social Psychology*, 14. London: Academic Press.

——(1978b). "Interindividual Behaviour and Intergroup Behaviour," in H. Tajfel (ed.), *Differentiation between Social Groups: Studies in the Social Psychology of Intergroup Relations. European Monographs in Social Psychology*, 14. London: Academic Press.

Teerikangas, S. (2006). *Silent Forces in Cross-Border Acquisitions: An Integrative Perspective on Post-acquisition Integration*. Helsinki: Helsinki University of Technology, Institute of Strategy and International Business, Doctoral Dissertation Series, 1/2006.

——(2010). "Dynamics of Acquired Firm Pre-acquisition Employee Reactions." *Journal of Management*. Published online, October 19. DOI: 10.1177/0149206310383908.

——& Geraldi, J. (2011). "Bridging Trouble Waters: A Comparative Analysis of the M&A and Project Literatures." Paper presented at 11th Annual Conference of the European Academy of Management, Tallinn, June 1–4.

——& Laamanen, T. (2006). "Cultural and Structural Dynamics of Post-Acquisition Integration." Paper presented in the IM Division of the Academy of Management Annual Conference, Atlanta, USA, August 11–16.

——& Véry, P. (2006). "The Culture-Performance Relationship in M&A: From Yes/No to How." *British Journal of Management*, 17: S31–S48.

Thomson, N., & McNamara, P. (2001). "Achieving Post-acquisition Success: The Role of Corporate Entrepreneurship." *Long Range Planning*, 34: 669–97.

Vaara, E. (2003). "Post-acquisition Integration as Sense-making: Glimpses of Ambiguity, Confusion, Hypocrisy, and Politicization." *Journal of Management Studies,* 40/4: 859–94.

Véry, P., & Schweiger, D. (2001). "The Acquisition Process as a Learning Process: Evidence from a Study of Critical Problems and Solutions in Domestic and Cross-Border Deals." *Journal of World Business*, 36/1: 11–31.

Weber, Y. (1996). "Corporate Cultural Fit and Performance in Mergers and Acquisitions." *Human Relations*, 49/9: 1181–202.

——Shenkar, O., & Raveh, A. (1996). "National and Corporate Cultural Fit in Mergers/Acquisitions: An Exploratory Study." *Management Science,* 42/8: 1215–27.

CHAPTER 15

....

INDIVIDUAL RESPONSE TO MERGERS AND ACQUISITIONS

....

SUSAN CARTWRIGHT

INTRODUCTION

....

One of the consequences of global recession and tough economic times is an increase in merger and acquisition (M&A) activity. M&As provide an opportunity to create value through economies of scale, consolidating or extending markets, or by acquiring new products, technologies, or knowledge.

Importantly, they minimize the costly time lag in the development of products, markets, and the supporting structures associated with organic growth (Brock 2005). In recessionary times, as share values fall, prices become more competitive and markets shrink, many businesses face growing debt problems, limited access to credit, and so suffer from lack of investment. Hence such companies become attractive targets for acquisition by more financially robust and cash-rich competitors that are more able to weather the storm of recession.

Whilst often justified on rational economic and strategic grounds, M&As can also be motivated by psychological factors such as executive greed, fear of obsolescence, and the need to exercise power and leadership to prove individual worth. As it is widely recognized that executive pay and benefits are closely related to organizational size (Fitzroy et al. 1998), M&As provide a means of not only enhancing prestige but also of achieving personal financial gain. Displaced CEOs in acquired or merged firms are often well compensated in the receipt of so-called "golden parachutes." It is therefore not surprising that Hunt (1988) found that the initial identification of a potential acquisition target was made either by the chairman or the CEO.

Napier (1989) draws a distinction between financial or value-maximizing motives and managerial or non-value-maximizing motives. Mergers are considered to be initiated by financial or value-maximizing motives when the main objective is to increase shareholder wealth and financial synergy through economies of scale, transfer of knowledge, and increased control. Non-value-maximizing motives relate to mergers which occur primarily for other strategic reasons, for example, to increase market share, management prestige, or to reduce uncertainty and restore market confidence.

As discussed in an earlier chapter, M&A activity tends to occur in waves. Ghauri and Buckley (2003) identify the first wave as having occurred in the USA in 1898–1902, resulting in over 3,000 deals. Up until the end of 2000 there were four further waves (Grotenhuis 2009). Activity then declined as a result of recession only to reappear in the biggest wave so far in 2004–7. In 2004 alone, there were 30,000 acquisitions globally, equivalent to one transaction every 18 minutes, with a total transactional value of $1,900 billion (Cartwright and Schoenberg 2006). Activity may have dipped slightly in 2008, but reports suggest that 2009 has sparked a further round of mergers and acquisitions (Reuters Press Release, October 7, 2009).

Despite the popularity and strategic importance of M&A activity to businesses and wider society, many transactions fail to create shareholder value, increase profitability, or achieve the anticipated strategic and financial goals (Ashkenas and Francis 2000; Schweiger and Lippert 2005). Indeed, estimates of domestic M&A failure have remained fairly consistent over time as being between 46–50% (Kitching 1974; Rostand 1994; Sirower 1998). As international activity has increased, evidence suggests that cross-border mergers and acquisitions may carry an even greater risk, with failure rates estimated to be in the region of 50–80% (Grotenhuis 2009).

Extensive reviews (Sudarsanam 2003) have shown that short-term beneficiaries of M&A activity are the target firm shareholders who experience positive and statistically significant wealth gains at the time of the bid announcement due to share inflation values. The other significant beneficiaries of M&A activity are the "marriage brokers" or intermediaries, i.e. the bankers, accountants, and lawyers who arrange, advise, or execute the deals for fees typically reflecting 10–15% of the bid price (McManus and Hergert 1988). In contrast, overall evidence regarding the performance of merged companies tends to show small positive and negative abnormal returns over a two-to-five-year period post-merger. Although it is hostile takeovers which attract the most public attention, these account for only about 10% of all acquisitions. However, poor success seems to occur irrespective of whether the takeover is regarded as friendly or hostile and is unrelated to previous acquisition experience (Sudarsanam and Mahate 2006).

Traditionally, M&A underperformance has been the focus of considerable scrutiny by scholars of finance and strategy (e.g. Agrawal et al. 1992; Burt and Limmack 2001, 2003). Variables such as poor strategic fit, changes in market and economic conditions, and overinflated purchase price, as well as financial mismanagement in achieving economies of scale have been blamed for M&A underperformance. It is also often the case that acquiring management are overoptimistic in their expectations of the short- to medium-term gains that a newly merged firm can realistically achieve in their desire to convince new investors and existing shareholders of the attractiveness of a proposed deal. At the same time, it should be recognized that some M&As are not instigated for value-maximizing motives but rather to increase status and prestige. According to Seth, Song, and Pettit (2000), non-value-maximizing motives account for about a quarter of all M&A activity. However, it is further argued that scholars of finance and strategy may be simply continuing to look for explanations in the wrong place. As recent findings from a meta-analytical study conducted by King et al. (2004) concluded, despite decades of research, the most frequently studied variables in the finance and strategic literature offered no significant explanation of M&A outcomes.

From the 1980s onwards, the literature on M&As has expanded to reflect a growing increase of interest in the human and psychological aspects of the phenomenon, regarded as representing the "hidden costs" in M&A accounting, as a means of understanding why identified and anticipated synergies are not realized in the post-merger period. In emphasizing the disruptive nature of major organizational change and restructuring, this stream of literature has highlighted the way in which individuals respond both behaviorally and emotionally to the merger event and the way in which the process of integration is managed (Appelbaum et al. 2000). In particular, the literature has placed great emphasis on the difficulties of integrating previously separate and distinct employee groups and their cultures (Weber 1996; Shrivastava 1986).

Consequently, we do know considerably more about the human aspects of M&A than we did 30 years ago. However, there is still much that we do not know, particularly in terms of the exact impact that cultural differences make in determining M&A outcomes. This chapter seeks to review what we currently know about M&As in terms of how individuals respond to M&As and how this may impact on M&A outcomes. There are personality differences in the way that individuals respond to change more generally. Those who are excited by, easily embrace, and cope well with change tend to display personality traits associated with extraversion, openness to experience, sensation seeking, and tolerance of ambiguity (Oreg 2003), whereas those who find change difficult tend towards neuroticism, dogmatism, and are averse to risk. However, evidence suggests (Cartwright and Cooper 1996) that the complex dynamics of mergers and acquisition tend to have a fairly universal impact on the individual which is little moderated by personality factors.

The Dynamics of Mergers and Acquisitions

A merger is defined as a combination of the assets of two (or more) previously separate companies into a new legal entity, whereas an acquisition or takeover is said to occur when the control of assets is transferred from one company to another (Ghauri and Buckley 2003). According to the *Oxford English Dictionary*, an acquisition is described as "an outright gain of something (especially useful)" and a merger, less rapaciously, as "the joining and blending of two previously discrete entities." Mergers, publicly at least, are presented as a co-operative agreement, usually between organizations more closely matched in terms of size. Pritchett (1985) suggests there are four types of merger, described as rescue, collaborative, contested, and raid, which influence the degree of co-operativeness. Whilst the terms merger and acquisition are used almost interchangeably in much of the literature, most transactions fall into the category of acquisitions rather than mergers. Evidence suggests that less than 3% of all cross-border deals are "real" mergers (UNCTAD 2000), although many acquisitions are publicly presented to the press and employees as mergers, implying that the announcement signifies a co-opera-tive union between partners of equal standing. Irrespective of whether a combination is described as a merger or an acquisition, in the eyes of involved employees there is always an employee group who feel that they have been "sold out" by the deal.

According to Schweiger and Lippert (2005), synergistic value can be created in M&A by achieving cost reductions, revenue enhancements, increased market power, and intangibles. Intangibles are difficult to quantify but are generally considered to be fac-tors such as brand name and knowledge management and transfer. The successful reali-zation of these synergies is dependent to a greater or lesser extent on the degree of integration required between the combining organizations in order to achieve these outcomes. For example, when organizations use acquisitions as means of extending their operations into a very different business area, as in vertical M&As, then the necessary level of integration is likely to be low since the newly acquired company will often con-tinue to function as a separate entity—at least in the short term.

However, the later waves of M&A activity from the 1980s onwards have mainly involved related combinations, i.e. organizations within the same sector and so require a greater degree of integration of people and resources than in conglomeration or vertical integration, i.e. companies in a buyer-seller, client-supplier, and value-chain linkages. Ghauri and Buckley (2003) describe contemporary mergers and acquisitions as "the most dramatic demonstration of vision and strategy" in that in a single move the course of a company, and the careers of its managers and employees, are dramatically changed.

As mergers are rarely a marriage of equals, in terms of power or size (Bower 2001), it is the dominant partner who has the upper hand in the restructuring and change process post-merger. Therefore, fears surrounding a merger and its impact on the working lives of the acquired employee groups induce cohesion and potential for conflict (Alderfer 1977; Matteson and Ivancevitch 1990). According to Hambrick and Cannella (1993), typ-ically acquired employees view the acquisition as a defeat and the resultant loss of status and autonomy leads to feelings of inferiority and low self-esteem. In contrast, the mem-bers of an acquiring organization perceive themselves to be victorious and superior—a state best described as cultural imperialism.

EMOTIONAL AND BEHAVIORAL PERSPECTIVES ON M&A

While Crouch and Wirth (1991) consider that the individual impact of M&A is often exaggerated, there is a substantial body of research that has linked M&A experiences with lowered morale (Sinetar 1981), job dissatisfaction, increased stress, unproductive behavior, acts of sabotage, petty theft (Cartwright 2005; Cartwright and Cooper 1996), loss of identity (Kroon et al. 2009; Van Knippenberg and Hogg 2003), increased labor turnover and absenteeism (Marks and Mirvis 2001; Birkenshaw et al. 2000; Schweiger and DeNisi 1991). Importantly, it has been increasingly recognized that an inherent tension exists between implementing radical change to match the strategy and culture of the acquirer or dominant partner, whilst, at the same time, promoting and maintaining what is valuable within the acquired organization (Meyer and Lieb-Doczy 2003).

From an emotional-behavioral perspective, the main research themes can usefully be grouped as follows:

(i) M&As as loss experiences (the coping/adjustment perspective) A number of researchers have likened the intensity of emotional feelings experienced by acquired employees to the loss of a close family member (McManus and Hergert 1988; Mirvis 1985; Schweiger et al. 1987) and so set the experience apart from other forms of organizational change. The sudden and unexpected nature of M&A, like bereavement, requires adjustment over time and produces feelings of anger, denial, and depression, as well as a shared sense of misery and grief, before acquired employees can start to adjust to the reality of the situation and move on. Both Hunsaker and Coombs (1988) and Mirvis (1985) have developed stage models to describe the way in which individuals adjust to the loss experience associated with M&A. Employees that have difficulty in coping and adjusting to both the sense of loss and the resultant merger-related changes are unlikely to perform optimally. Central to the concept of change is the notion of letting go and leaving someone or something behind. Those who have difficulty in leaving behind their old loyalties to the legacy company and its identity and practices are likely to be labeled by acquiring management as resistant to change. However, there is some evidence to suggest that as M&As become more commonplace, individuals become more resilient to the adverse psychological consequences of M&A (Cartwright and Hudson 2000) and are less inclined to engage in "wishful thinking" and collective remembering.

(ii) M&As as disruption promoting uncertainty, negative emotions, and stress (the emotions/well-being perspective) Change, more generally, has been shown to result in increased stress, confusion, and reduced productivity (Gibbons 1998; Nelson et al. 1995). Such findings have been replicated in specific studies conducted in M&A settings (McHugh 1995; Cartwright et al. 2007; Siu et al. 1997). The stressors associated with M&As are many and various and include job insecurity, loss of self-esteem and identity, increased workload, and changes in work practices. Interestingly, these studies have highlighted that the most stressful period in the merger process is during the pre-integration process, i.e. the period of "limbo" following the announcement but prior to any physical or socio-cultural integration.

The findings of Kavanagh and Ashkansay (2006) suggest that about half of the merged workforce report that M&A-related change has had significant personal consequences for them. In terms of physical and psychological health outcomes, studies have shown that the greater adverse impact is experienced by employees of the less powerful and smaller partner (Cartwright and Cooper 1993; Siu et al. 1997) even when there are seemingly few cultural differences between the firms.

Evidence (Pritchett 1985) suggests that employees' attitudes towards M&A are linked to their individual appraisal as to the impact the event is likely to have on their own career and job future, irrespective of any potential organizational benefits. Matteson and Ivancevitch (1990) found that acquired employees at the mid-career stage are most likely to have negative attitudes because they feel their chances of progression to be limited in the new merged company. Also, those at the mid-stage of their working life may feel frustrated because they consider they are too young to benefit from any offer of early retirement packages and too old to start a career elsewhere (Bucholtz et al. 2003).

Although the overwhelming balance of evidence (Marks and Mirvis 1992; Morrison and Robinson 1997) has emphasized that M&As generally result in negative attitudes amongst employees of the acquired or smaller merger partner, in some circumstances, acquired employees experience positive emotions if they feel that there may be positive outcomes for them, such as increased career opportunities or association with a higher status organization (Buono et al. 1985).

(iii) M&As a process of acculturation (the cultural perspective) Without doubt, the dominant paradigm adopted by scholars of organizational behavior in the study of M&A integration has been from a cultural perspective (Angwin and Vaara 2009; Stahl and Mendenhall 2005). Culture is generally accepted to concern the shared symbols, values, assumptions, beliefs, and behavior of a group, an organization, or a nation, which serve to guide their cognitions and actions and reflect a shared sense of reality and agreement on a certain set of appropriate ways of behaving toward others.

Culture is perceived to be learnt through socialization processes that help to "programme the mind" (Hofstede 1980) to see the world in a particular way and obstruct the understanding or acceptance of alternative views. Importantly, cultural assumptions are often unconscious in nature and hence difficult to modify or change (Gagliardi 1986).

The argument presented by many academics that merging employee groups are unwilling to co-operate with each other and lack commitment to the newly merged company because they come from different organizational or national cultures, and so do not think or feel in the same way, has had a great deal of resonance with practitioners. As a result, in some ways "culture" has become something of a linguistic scapegoat—in that anything and everything that goes wrong in the post-merger period is put down to irreconcilable cultural differences. According to Lane et al. (2004), M&As fail because acquiring management underestimate the difficulties associated with integrating acquired employees and the potential for culture clash. Numerous surveys of managers involved in M&As have cited failure to integrate cultures as a major reason for M&A failure (British Institute of Management 1986; Coopers & Lybrand 1999; Cartwright and Price 2003). A survey by A.T. Kearney (1999) found that cultural differences were regarded as the primary factor in the failure of 35% of US banking mergers. A subsequent survey of chief executives of Fortune 500 companies (Schweiger and Goulet 2000) found that the ability to manage human integration was rated as more important than financial or strategic factors.

Cultural differences are believed to result in tension and a lack of co-operation between employee groups which frustrate the efforts of acquiring management to effectively integrate the merging firms. These differences can occur in domestic M&As when different organizational cultures clash or in international deals when there are differences in national cultures. Although the balance of evidence tends to support the notion that differences in organizational cultures are problematic to M&A success (Chatterjee et al. 1992; Buono and Bowditch 1989), the role of national culture in international M&As is less clear cut. Compared to domestic mergers, managers perceive cross-border M&As to be more risky (Angwin and Savill 1997). However, whereas some studies (Datta and Puia 1995; Slangen 2006) found that differences in national culture negatively impacted on performance, others have shown a positive (Morosini et al. 1998) or negligible impact (Schoenberg and Norburn 1998). A very recent study (Chakrabarti et al. 2009) based on over 1,150 large cross-border acquisitions between 1991 and 2004 and using Hofstede's framework, demonstrated that acquisitions perform better in the long term (i.e. three years post-acquisition) if the acquirer and target firm are from countries that are culturally different. The widespread attention that the culture variable has received in the M&A literature in relation to human integration problems has been successful and useful in raising awareness that mergers are about people and not just property and assets. However, even after 30 decades of research on cultural issues in M&As, the specific role of culture in determining merger outcomes still remains rather imprecise and muddled and so remains a continuing source of debate (Cartwright and Schoenberg 2006).

(iv) M&As as a threat to identity (the social identity perspective)   Researchers (Hogg and Terry 2000; Kramer 1991; Van Knippenberg and Hogg 2003) who have focused on the impact of M&A at the work group/departmental level have drawn upon social identity theory (Tajfel and Turner 1979) to explain why invariably a "them vs. us" mentality develops between employee groups following M&A. Weber (2000) asserts that tension and conflict between members of the top management teams is often the result of a protective need of the two groups to assert their pre-existing identities and belief systems in the decision-making process.

Kleppesto (1998) suggests that culture becomes a convenient metaphor through which to assert and convey group distinctiveness. According to Riad (2005), despite its many critics, the notion of "organizational culture" has provided a useful platform for discourse whereby employees can voice their concerns about the human side of merger.

(v) M&As as violations of the psychological contract (the organizational justice perspective)   Many years ago, Schein (1985) defined the psychological contract as "an unwritten set of expectations operating at all times between every member of an organization and the various managers and others in that organization." Robinson and Rousseau (1994) highlighted that the psychological contract was about promissory and reciprocal obligations as well as expectations on the part of both employer and employees. Expectations might include the right to be consulted about changes in working practices or fair treatment with regard to career progression and role or work allocation. According to Rousseau (1995), broken expectations lead to feelings of disappointment

and possibly anger. In approaching M&A from an organizational justice perspective (Meyer 2001), scholars have argued that employees respond negatively to M&A because they perceive an injustice in the way in which roles are allocated and/or lack of fairness and equity in the operation of HRM policies and practices.

(vi) M&As as forming new highly emotional and significant relationships In applying a metaphorical lens, researchers have likened M&As to marriage or the acquisition of a step family and hinted at the need for independent agencies to help a merged organization to build new relationships. However, whereas most individuals are able to choose their marriage partner, there is no option of choice for employees in organizational marriages.

HRM Perspectives

This stream of literature has emphasized that M&A is a process of task and human integration which requires effective management. As such, management of the process is affected by a wide range of potential variables, including language and communication, trust, autonomy, leadership, and HR policies and practices, and better M&A outcomes could be achieved by better and more sensitive management of the process (Cartwright and Cooper 1996; Mangham 1973). According to DeNisi and Shin (2005), senior merger management tends to adopt a crisis management approach because of the uncertainty of the situation and so tends to centralize and minimize the amount of communication provided to employees, which fuels anxiety. In a well-designed longitudinal study of a domestic merger, Schweiger and DeNisi (1991) demonstrated that effort invested in delivering an extensive realistic merger communication program had a more significant impact on reducing uncertainty, maintaining job satisfaction, and promoting trust and confidence in the new management team than minimal communication effort and leads to a greater acceptance of change (Appelbaum et al. 2000).

Communication can also be effective in promoting shared values and breaking down the negative stereotypes that one employee group may have of another. Stahl and Sitkin (2005) found that mode of takeover, extent of imposed control, and interaction history were all factors which impacted on trust following M&A. However, the most significant factor was the attractiveness of the acquiring company's HR policies and practices.

Post-Merger Integration, Culture, and Performance

Researchers who have emphasized the importance of culture fit to M&A outcomes differentiate between the goodness of the strategic fit in terms of the recognized potential synergies which exist between the combining organizations and the goodness of the culture fit as the trigger which enables the release and realization of these synergies. As examples of widely reported mergers such as Daimler–Chrysler have demonstrated, even when there is an excellent strategic fit between the companies this is insufficient of itself if there are resultant conflicts around cultural issues between senior managerial groups.

Culture fit is generally taken to mean the extent to which the management style, rewards and sanctions, values etc. are similar between the merging organizations. Hence it is argued that the greater the similarity, the better the fit, and therefore the smoother the integration process (Jemison and Sitkin 1986; Bijlsma-Frankema 2001). This would suggest that better M&A outcomes could be achieved if deal makers paid more attention to cultural issues before committing to an organizational marriage and included these factors in the due-diligence procedure. Indeed evidence shows that mergers which occur following a period of working together as part of a strategic alliance agreement, and so are founded on a pre-existing trust and mutual respect, are more likely to be successful (Donnelly et al. 2005). Daly et al. (2004) conducted a retrospective study of 59 mergers and acquisitions in which they compared the values between the partners as expressed in the annual company reports prior to the merger. They found that similarities in pre-existing values had a significant positive influence on financial performance post-merger and explained 11% of the variance. Earlier studies (Chatterjee et al. 1992; Datta 1991) on domestic M&As have also demonstrated links between poor financial performance and cultural differences and increased managerial turnover (Weber and Menipaz 2003).

However, in the main, research has tended to highlight the influence of cultural differences in producing negative attitudes, diminished co-operation and commitment, and increased stress amongst employees rather than showing any direct link with financial performance (Buono et al. 1985; Dackert et al. 2003; Irrmann 2002).

In a study of a financially successful domestic merger in the financial services sector, Cartwright and Cooper (1996) found that objective measures indicated a high degree of cultural similarity between partners. However, the merger also resulted in high levels of managerial stress amongst members of the smaller merger partner. Larsson and Finkelstein (1999) suggest that M&As between culturally similar partners have the potential to achieve "economies of sameness." Indeed, there is evidence that given a choice, decision makers do prefer to select acquisition targets which are perceived to be culturally similar (Van Oudenhoven and de Boer 1995; Larsson and Risberg 1998; Cartwright and Price 2003) and hence easier to absorb and assimilate into their existing structure and culture.

Cartwright and McCarthy (2005) argue that culture fit is not simply a matter of cultural similarity but depends more upon the intended integration strategy of the dominant partner or acquirer and the nature of the synergies that they wish to realize. Veiga et al. (2000) found that high-performing mergers occurred more often in situations where a new "best of both worlds" culture emerged. Therefore, whilst cultural differences can be a source of disturbance and anxiety to employees, they can also enhance learning and effectiveness in providing opportunities for synergetic complementarities that improve the competitive position of the resultant merged company (Larsson and Finkelstein 1999). This view has received some support from the findings of a recent meta-analysis (Stahl and Voight 2003) which found that whilst cultural distance had a negative impact on socio-cultural integration, it had no direct effect on financial performance unless account was taken of the mode of integration and how this was managed.

In a recent review of the literature, Cartwright (2005) highlighted that in the past a great deal of attention had addressed the criticality of the early stages of M&A, particularly the first three months post-acquisition (Barrett 1973; Mangham 1973; Mirvis 1985). As a result, it focused more on the role of pre-acquisition factors such as context, type, and size as affecting interpersonal relationships at the group, usually senior managerial, level. Shrivastava (1986) conceptualizes post-merger/acquisition integration as occurring at three levels; the physical, procedural, and the socio-cultural level. According to Shrivastava (1986), integration at the physical and procedural level is likely to be achieved on a shorter time scale than managerial and wider socio-cultural integration. Socio-cultural integration or acculturation (Berry 1980) is considered to occur within three to five years (Cartwright 2005) or even longer (Schein 1985), yet few research studies have examined the evolving cultural dynamics and the process of acculturation within the same M&A over time.

Nahavandi and Malekzadeh (1988) propose that the unfolding cultural dynamics of a merger or acquisition are a reflection or outcome of the process of adaptation and acculturation. Acculturation is an anthropological term, generally defined as "changes introduced in (two cultural systems) as a result of the diffusion of cultural elements in both directions." Although this suggests a balanced two-way flow, in reality this is not usually the case as members of one culture frequently attempt to dominate members of the other culture. There are four proposed modes through which acculturation takes place which result in different cultural dynamics and outcomes dependent upon the willingness of acquired members to abandon their old culture and their perceptions of the attractiveness of the culture of the acquiring. In conditions of high willingness/high attractiveness, the resultant mode of acculturation will be assimilation/absorption.

In contrast, conditions of low willingness/low attractiveness will result in cultural separation. In conditions of low willingness/high attraction, there is potential for successful integration to create a new "best of both worlds" culture, but also a "culture clash." Finally, in circumstances where there is low willingness/low attractiveness, there is deculturation, whereby members of the acquired culture become marginalized and experience feelings of confusion and alienation as they become dismembered from both the old and the new cultures. Deculturaton, unsanctioned separation, and unsatisfactory integration are likely to have an adverse impact on both organizational and individual M&A outcomes. At an individual level, employees may choose to avoid the acculturation process by leaving the organization. At the organizational level, the acquirer may avoid or escalate the process by replacing a substantial number of employees who disagree or are out of line with the proposed mode of acculturation, given that cultural transitions are likely to be more problematic for individuals who have not self-selected themselves for change.

Haspeslagh and Jemison (1991) suggest that the degree of integration depends upon the need for strategic interdependence and the need for organizational autonomy. According to their typology, an acquiring organization can choose (i) preservation—maintaining separate operations and cultures, (ii) absorption—acting to assimilate the target into its own culture, (iii) symbiosis—gradually integrating operations and cultures, or (iv) transformation—re-inventing and radically changing the operations and cultures of both companies. Lubatkin et al. (1998) have shown that managers from different countries have different management styles. Research has shown also that the choice of integration strategy is often linked to national culture. American and British acquirers have been shown to overwhelmingly favor an absorption strategy (Child et al. 2001) and since traditionally, these nations have dominated M&A activity from its very beginning, this is the dominant intervention strategy adopted in M&A integration management. In contrast, Japanese acquirers, having only engaged in M&A activity in recent years, prefer a preservation strategy. As the majority of evidence on the role of culture in domestic mergers and acquisitions has emanated from the USA and the UK, it is perhaps not unexpected that cultural differences, as a potential obstacle to effective assimilation, have emerged as a key factor in determining M&A outcomes.

However, as participation in M&A activity internationally has widened, it is perhaps also not surprising that the relationship between culture and performance has become more intriguing. The influence of national culture on attitudes and behavior from childhood onwards is considered to be more deep rooted and less easy to modify than organizational culture, which is only experienced as an adult.

Studies which have addressed the role of culture in international M&As have drawn heavily upon the work of Hofstede (1980) on cultural dimensions. Based on a study of the attitudes and values of managers and employees of IBM across 53 countries, Hofstede (1980) originally proposed four cultural dimensions—individualism/collectivism, uncertainty avoidance, power distance, and masculinity/femininity. Using this typology to produce a composite measure of cultural distance, Krug and Nigh (1998, 2001) found that US executives in firms acquired by foreign nationals were more likely to quit when there was a high cultural distance between the acquirer and the acquired. Yet, Morosini et al. (1998) found that the performance of cross-border acquisitions was enhanced by cultural differences, possibly because less integration is necessary or because foreign acquirers are more sensitive in their approach to integration management (Evans et al. 2002; Larsson and Risberg 1998). However, Morosini et al. only studied cross-border M&As in Italy. In a study of over 100 domestic and cross-border M&As across Europe, Véry et al. (1997) found that cultural differences can generate employee stress in both domestic and international M&As, but that this stress was more acute in circumstances where members of the acquired organization felt their status or "relative standing" had diminished or where they had experienced an erosion in autonomy.

The issue of social status has been echoed in other studies (Panchal and Cartwright 2001; Empson 2001). In a study of sales employees in a merged organization, Panchal and Cartwright (2001) found that members of the acquired company were more likely to accept post-acquisition change if they considered that the merger was likely to enhance their social status. Empson (2001) similarly found that acquired employees were less likely to be co-operative if they felt that they were being exploited for their knowledge or were being taken over by a "downmarket" company.

Cartwright and Cooper (1996) suggest that mergers are most problematic when the culture of the acquirer or dominant partner is more constraining and less autonomous than that of the acquired. In a study of 103 related acquisitions in Australia and New Zealand, Brock (2005) found that parent or acquiring companies from a culture which, in Hofstede's terms (1980), is high on power distance and so favors centralization, a lack of consultation, and autocratic leadership encountered significantly more difficulty in resource sharing and achieved fewer synergies than combinations more closely matched on this dimension. However, the findings suggested that cultural differences on the individualism/collectivism dimension were even more salient. Combinations between acquirers from a culture low on individualism with an acquired organization with a culture high on individualism resulted in significant difficulties in both integration and resource sharing and the realization of fewer synergies. Whilst not testing the impact of cultural combinations between high individualism-acquirers and low individualism-acquired companies, Brock (2005) considers that such combinations are equally likely to be very problematic because they expose major areas of difference and potential conflict surrounding autonomy, challenge, and accountability. However, one of the limitations of this study is that data was collected retrospectively and both New Zealand and Australia are regarded as being predominantly individualist, masculine, low power distance, and low uncertainty-avoiding cultures.

EXECUTIVE TURNOVER

Individuals have been shown to cope with change more positively if they have chosen to make the change rather than if change is imposed upon them and therefore they have no control over the event. Many individuals at all levels in a merged organization decide to leave the company as a means of regaining control over their job future, hence merged organizations tend to experience above average rates of voluntary as well as involuntary staff turnover, especially among executives (Bucholtz et al. 2003; Krug and Hegarty 1997; Walsh 1988). Walsh (1988) found that 60% of senior executives in the USA left acquired companies within the first five years post-acquisition. Other studies (e.g. Cannella and Hambrick 1993; Krug and Hegarty 2001) suggest that about one in three executives in acquired firms have their contracts terminated involuntarily and a further third leave voluntarily within two years of the acquisition. Turnover of CEOs follows a similar pattern, based on UK data (Angwin 1996), which shows that only around 40% are still in post two years after an acquisition. Krug (2002) has shown that merged organizations are also less able to retain new hires than non-acquired organizations.

This discontinuity in senior leadership is likely to adversely impact on employee trust and confidence and impede the likelihood of a smooth and swift transition by a merged company to a more stable state.

LEADERSHIP AND MERGER MANAGEMENT

Evidence from the 1997 merger of Ciba Geigy and Sandos to form Novartis indicates that success is dependent upon an agreement between management groups as to the proposed integration strategy and mode of acculturation. In the case of Novartis, the selection of a new company name, derived from the Latin words meaning "new skills," was intended to communicate that the merger was a new start for both companies and this was reinforced by the message from the new CEO, Daniel Vasella, that all employees would be treated fairly and with parity. Whilst Hatch and Schultz (2000) emphasizes that culture change is shaped by both leaders and followers, in uncertain and anxious times, groups are more likely to be receptive to strong and unambiguous leaders. Importantly, competent leaders have the potential to frame strategies in a way that ensures that followers cognitively accept the resultant changes. Rather than typically distancing themselves from the presentation of bad news, studies have shown that leaders who actively explain difficult decisions to employees reduce the intensity of negative reactions and behaviors to unfavorable events. In the case of Novartis, employees were provided with a 40-page-long document describing the economic and financial background to the merger in detail. Furthermore, a charter on the integration process was produced which set out a list of guiding principles as to how managers should approach and behave. This document emphasized the importance of being candid, simple, and clear, repeatedly informing and explaining decisions and presenting fact-based arguments to justify actions.

In a longitudinal study of three Australian public sector organizations over a seven-year period, Kavanagh and Ashkanasy (2006) emphasized that successful merger integration was very much about the quality of the change management skills exercised by organizational leadership. They concluded that a gradual and incremental approach to change produced more satisfactory results than an immediate or indifferent approach, since it met with less employee resistance and a more positive view of leaders. However, their findings also highlight that the direction of cultural change is important in that shifts in culture which impose greater constraints on the individual than was present in their pre-existing culture are met with greater resistance than shifts in the opposite direction.

Disagreements about the pace and scheduling of change have been voiced in the change literature more generally. Incremental change is by its nature a slow process which may prolong employee uncertainty and stress, whereas radical and immediate change may be more painful and disruptive in the short term but then normalize and so achieve swifter results. Whereas leaders may be able to exercise an incremental approach to change in public sector organizations, the shareholder pressures on private sector leaders to turn a company around often means that this approach is not an option.

Conclusions and Future Directions

Whilst there is consensus amongst scholars and managers that culture matters in mergers and acquisitions, as Stahl and Mendenhall (2005) conclude, the extent to which it matters, and when, how, and under what conditions still remain uncertain.

Otte (2005) suggests that what matters is whether the culture of an organization is functional or dysfunctional as measured against its own mission and goals and whether it is consistent. Hence, he argues for the necessity of treating every acquisition or merger as a single case rather than searching for a single theoretical framework to explain the dynamics of all mergers and acquisitions. Although this view is not widely shared (e.g. Weber et al. 2009), it is the case that the interdependencies of the various aspects of culture typically assessed, e.g. decision-making style, communication, etc. are complex and do not necessarily demonstrate any clear relationship with performance, particularly when there is no account taken of the merger context, in relation to the degree of integration required and the integration strategy itself.

Perhaps the key to successful M&A outcomes is more a matter of leadership and change management skills. M&A managers who are aware of the cultural strengths and weaknesses, who are able to articulate them well, and are honest, fair, and sensitive in their dealings with others are more likely to be able to effectively deal with conflict and reduce tension. Some degree of labor turnover following M&A may not only be inevitable but also desirable as employees are likely to be well able to make their own decisions as to whether they will fit into the new merged organization provided they are given sufficient information. As Jones (1983) observed many years ago: "When people believe that they will be treated fairly and that if they are honest, they will have time to learn a new paradigm, they seem quite willing to experiment with new ideas" (p. 465).

References

Agrawal, A., Jaffe, J. F., & Mandelker, G. N. (1992). "The Post Merger Performance of Acquiring Firms: A Re-examination of an Anomaly." *The Journal of Finance*, 67: 1605–21.

Alderfer, C. P. (1977). "Organization Development." *Annual Review of Psychology*, 28: 197–223.

Angwin, D. (1996). "After the Fall." *Management Today*, April: 56–8.

——& Savill, B. (1997). "Strategic Perspectives on European Cross Border Acquisitions: A View from the Top." *European Management Journal*, 15/4: 423–35.

——& Vaara, E. (2009). "Introduction to the Special Issue: Connectivity in Merging Organizations: Beyond Traditional Cultural Perspectives." *Organization Studies*, 26/10: 1445–53.

Appelbaum, S. H., Gandell, J., Yortis, A., Proper, S., & Jobin, F. (2000). "Anatomy of a Merger: Behaviour of Organizational Factors and Processes throughout the Pre- During- Post Stages." *Management Decision*, 38/9: 649–61.

Ashkenas, R. N., & Francis, S. C. (2000). "Integration Managers: Special Leaders for Special Times." *Harvard Business Review*, 78/6: 108–16.

A.T. Kearney (1999). "Corporate Marriage: Blight or Bliss? A Monograph on Post Merger Integration." April. A.T. Kearney.

Barrett, P. F. (1973). *The Human Implications of Mergers and Takeovers*. London: Institute of Personnel Management.

Berry, J. W. (1980). "Social and Cultural Change," in H. C. Triandis & R. W. Brislin (eds.), *Handbook of Cross Cultural Psychology*, vol. 5. Boston, MA: Allyn & Bacon, 211–79.

Bijlsma-Frankema, K. (2001). "On Managing Cultural Integration and Cultural Change Processes in Mergers and Acquisitions." *Journal of European Industrial Training*, 25: 192–207.

Birkenshaw, J., Bresman, H., & Håkanson, L. (2000) "Managing the Post-acquisition Process: How the Human Integration and Task Integration Processes Interact to Foster Value Creation." *Journal of Management Studies*, 37/3: 395–425.

Bower, J. L. (2001). "Not all M&As are Alike—And That Matters." *Harvard Business Review*, 79/3: 92–101.

British Institute of Management (1986). "The Management of Acquisitions and Mergers." Discussion Paper No. 8. London: Economics Department, September.

Brock, D. M. (2005). "Multinational Acquisition Integration: The Role of National Culture in Creating Synergies." *International Business Review*, 14: 269–88.

Bucholtz, A. K., Ribbens, B. A., & Houle, I. T. (2003). "The Role of Human Capital in Post Acquisition CEO Departure." *Academy of Management Journal*, 46/4: 506–14.

Buono, A., & Bowditch, J. L. (1989). *The Human Side of Mergers and Acquisitions*. San Francisco: Jossey Bass.

————— & Lewis, J. W. (1985). "When Cultures Collide: The Anatomy of a Merger." *Human Relations*, 38: 477–500.

Burt, S., & Limmack, R. J. (2001). "Takeover and Shareholder Returns in the Retail Industry." *International Review of Retail, Distribution and Consumer Research*, 11: 1–21.

————— (2003). "The Operating Performance of Companies Involved in Acquisitions," in C. Cooper & A. Gregory (eds.), *Advances in Mergers and Acquisitions*, vol. 2. London: JAI Press, 147–76.

Cannella, A. A., & Hambrick, D. C. (1993). "Effects of Executive Departure on the Performance of Acquired Firms." *Strategic Management Journal*, 14, Summer Special Issue: 137–52.

Cartwright, S. (2005). "Mergers and Acquisitions: An Update and Appraisal," in G. P. Hodgkinson & J. K. Ford (eds.), *International Review of Industrial and Organizational Psychology*, 20: 1–38.

——— & Cooper, C. L. (1993). "The Psychological Impact of Mergers and Acquisitions on the Individual : A Study of Building Society Managers." *Human Relations*, 46: 327–47.

——— & Cooper, C. L. (1996). *Managing Mergers, Acquisitions and Strategic Alliances: Integrating People and Cultures*. Oxford: Butterworth Heinemann.

——— & Hudson, S. L. (2000). "Coping with Mergers and Acquisitions," in R. Burke & C. L. Cooper (eds.), *The Organization in Crisis: Downsizing, Restructuring and Renewal*. Oxford: Blackwell.

——— & McCarthy, S. (2005). "Developing a Framework for Cultural Due Diligence in Mergers and Acquisitions," in G. Stahl & M. E. Mendenhall (eds.), *Mergers and Acquisitions: Managing Culture and Human Resources*, Stamford: Stamford University Press, 253–67.

——— & Price, F. (2003). "Managerial Preferences in International Merger and Acquisition Partners Re-visited: How are they Influenced?" in C. L. Cooper & A. Gregory (eds.), *Advances in Mergers and Acquisitions*, vol. 2. London: JAI Press, 81–95.

—— Robertson, S., & Tytherleigh, M. (2007). "Are Mergers Always Stressful ? Some Evidence from the Higher Education Sector." *European Journal of Work and Organizational Psychology*, 16/4: 456–78.

—— & Schoenberg, R. (2006). "Thirty Years of Mergers and Acquisitions Research: Recent Advances and Future Opportunities." *British Journal of Management*, 17 (Special Issue): S1–S6.

Chakrabarti, R., Gupta-Mukherjee, S., & Jayaraman, N. (2009). "Mars–Venus Marriages: Culture and Cross Border M&A." *Journal of International Business Studies*, 40: 216–36.

Chatterjee, S., Lubatkin, M., Schweiger, D., & Weber, Y (1992). "Cultural Differences and Shareholder Value in Related Mergers: Linking Equity and Human Capital." *Strategic Management Journal*, 13: 319–34. `

Child, J., Faulkner, D., & Pitkethly, R. (2001). *The Management of International Acquisitions*. Oxford: Oxford University Press.

Coopers & Lybrand (1999). *Making a Success of an Acquisition*. London: Coopers & Lybrand.

Crouch, A., & Wirth, A. (1991). "Managerial Responses to Mergers and Other Job Changes." *Journal of Managerial Psychology*, 6/2: 3–8.

Dackert, L., Jackson, P. R., Brenner, S.-O., & Johansion, C. R. (2003). "Eliciting and Analysing Employees' Expectations of a Merger." *Human Relations*, 56/6: 705–25.

Daly, J. P., Pounder, R. W., & Kabanoff, B. (2004). "The Effect of Firms' Espoused Values on their Post Merger Performance." *Journal of Applied Behavioral Science*, 6: 323–43.

Datta, D. K. (1991). "Organization Fit and Post Acquisition Performance: Effects of Post Acquisition Integration." *Strategic Management Journal*, 12: 281–98.

—— & Puia, G. (1995). "Cross Border Acquisitions: An Examination of the Influence on Relatedness and Cultural Fit on Shareholder Value Creation in US Acquiring Firms." *Management International Review*, 35: 337–59.

DeNisi, A. S., & Shin, S. J. (2005). "Psychological Communication Interventions," in G. K. Stahl & M. E. Mendenhall (eds.), *Mergers and Acquisitions: Managing Culture and Human Resources*, Stanford, CA: Stanford University Press, 228–49.

Donnelly, T., Morris, D., & Donnelly, T. (2005). "Renault-Nissan: A Marriage of Necessity?" *European Business Review*, 17/5: 428–40.

Empson, L. (2001). "Fear of Exploitation and Fear of Contamination: Impediments to Knowledge Transfer in Mergers between Professional Services Firms." *Human Relations*, 54/7 (Special Issue): 839–62.

Evans, P., Pucik, V., & Barsoux, J. L. (2002). *The Global Challenge: Frameworks for International Human Resource Management*. Boston, MA: McGraw-Hill.

FitzRoy, J., Acs, Z. J., & Gelwoski, D. A. (1998). *Management and Economics of Organization*. Europe: Prentice Hall.

Gagliardi, P. (1986). "The Creation and Change of Organizational Cultures: A Conceptual Framework." *Organization Studies*, 7/2: 117–34.

Ghauri, P. N., & Buckley, P. J. (2003). "International Mergers and Acquisitions: Past, Present and Future", in C. Cooper & A. Gregory (eds.), *Advances in Mergers and Acquisitions*, vol. 2. London: JAI Press, 207–29.

Gibbons, R. (1998). "Incentives in Organizations." *Journal of Economic Perspectives*, 12/4: 115–32.

Grotenhuis, F. J. (2009). "Mergers and Acquisitions in Japan: Lessons from a Dutch-Japanese Case Study." *Journal of Global Business and Organizational Excellence*, March/April: 45–54.

Hambrick, D. C., & Cannella, A. A. (1993). "Relative Standing: A Framework for Understanding Departures of Acquired Executives." *Academy of Management Journal*, 36/4: 733–62.

Haspeslagh, P. C., & Jemison, D. B. (1991). *Managing Acquisitions: Creating Value through Corporate Renewal*. New York: Free Press.

Hatch, M., & Schultz, M. (2000). "Scaling the Tower of Babel: Relational Differences between Identity, Image and Culture in Organizations," in M. Schultz, M. J. Hatch, & M. H. Lawson (eds.), *The Expressive Organization*. Oxford: Oxford University Press, 11–35.

Hofstede, G. (1980). *Culture's Consequences: International Differences in Work Related Values*, Beverly Hills, CA: Sage Publications.

Hogg, M. A., & Terry, D. J. (2000). "Social Identity and Self Categorization Processes in Organizational Contexts." *Academy of Management Review*, 25/1: 121–40.

Hunsaker, P. L., & Coombs, M. W. (1988). "Mergers and Acquisitions: Managing the Emotional Issues." *Personnel Journal*, 65: 56–63.

Hunt, J. (1988). "Managing the Successful Acquisition: A People Question." *London Business School Journal*, Summer: 2–15.

Irrmann, O. (2002). "Organizational Culture and Identity Strategies in International Management: An Interdisciplinary Review." European International Business Academy Conference, Stockholm, Sweden, July 10–13.

Jemison, D., & Sitkin, S. (1986). "Corporate Acquisitions: A Process Perspective." *Academy of Management Review*, 11: 145–63.

Jones, G. R. (1983). "Transaction Costs, Property Rights and Organizational Culture: An Exchange Perspective." *Administrative Science Quarterly*, 28: 454–67.

Kavanagh, M., & Ashkansay, N. (2006). "The Impact of Leadership and Change Management Strategy on Organizational Culture and Individual Acceptance of Change during Merger." *British Journal of Management*, 17: S83–S105.

King, D., Dalton, D., Daily C., & Covin, J. (2004). "Meta-analyses of Post Acquisition Performance: Indications of Unidentified Moderators." *Strategic Management Journal*, 25: 187–200.

Kitching, J. (1974). "Winning and Losing with European Acquisitions." *Harvard Business Review*, 52: 124–36.

Kleppesto, S. (1998). "A Quest for Social Identity: The Pragmatics of Communication in Mergers and Acquisitions," in M. Gertsen, S. Soderberg, & J.-E. Torp (eds.), *Cultural Dimensions of International Mergers and Acquisitions*. Berlin: de Gruyter.

Kramer, R. M. (1991). "Intergroup Relations and Organizational Dilemmas: The Role of Categorization Processes," in L. L. Cummings & B. M. Straw (eds.), *Research in Organizational Behavior*, vol. 13. Greenwich, CT: JAI Press, 199–227.

Kroon, D., Noordehaven, N., & Leufkens, A. (2009). "Organizational Identification and Cultural Differences: Explaining Employee Attitudes and Behavioural Intentions during Post-merger Integration," in C. L. Cooper & S. Finkelstein (eds.), *Advances in Mergers and Acquisitions*, vol. 8. London: JAI Press, 19–42.

Krug, J. A. (2002). "Executive Turnover in Acquired Firms: A Longitudinal Analysis of Long Term Integration Effects." Paper presented at the Academy of Management Meeting, Seattle, August.

—— & Hegarty, W. H. (1997). "Post Acquisition Turnover among US Top Management Teams: An Analysis of the Effects of Foreign vs Domestic Acquisitions of US Targets—Research Notes and Communications." *Strategic Management Journal*, 18: 667–75.

—— —— (2001). "Predicting Who Stays and Leaves after Acquisition: A Study of Top Managers in Multinational Firms." *Strategic Management Journal*, 22: 185–96.

—— & Nigh, D. (1998). "Top Management Departures in Cross Border Acquisitions: Governance Issues in an International Context." *Journal of International Management*, 4/4: 267–87.

—— —— (2001). "Executive Perceptions in Foreign and Domestic Acquisitions: An Analysis of Foreign Ownership and its Effect on Executive Fate." *Journal of World Business*, 36/1: 85–105.

Lane, H. W., Greenberg, D., & Berdrow, I. (2004). "Barriers and Bonds to Knowledge Transfer in Global Alliances and Mergers," in H. W. Lane, M. Maznevski, & M. Mendenhall (eds.), *Blackwell Handbook of Global Management: A Guide to Managing Complexity*. Oxford: Blackwell, 342–61.

Larsson, R., & Finkelstein, S. (1999). "Integrating Strategic Organizational and Human Resource Perspectives on Mergers and Acquisitions: A Case Study of Synergy Realization." *Organization Science*, 10/1: 1–26.

—— & Risberg, A. (1998). "Cultural Awareness and National versus Corporate Barriers to Acculturation," in M. Gertsen, S. Soderberg, & J.-E. Torp (eds.), *Cultural Dimensions of International Mergers and Acquisitions*. Berlin: de Gruyter

Lubatkin, M., Calori, R., Véry, P., & Veiga, J. F. (1998). "Management Mergers across Borders; A Two Nation Exploration of a Nationally Bound Administrative Heritage." *Organization Science*, 9: 670–84.

Matteson, M. T., & Ivancevitch, J. M. (1990). "Merger and Acquisition Stress: Fear and Uncertainty at Mid Career Prevention." *Human Sciences Journal*, 8/1: 139–58.

McHugh, M. L. (1995). "Organizational Merger: A Stressful Challenge." *Review of Employment Topics*, 3/1. Belfast: Labour Relations Agency.

McManus, M. L., & Hergert, M. L. (1988). *Surviving Merger and Acquisition*. Glenview, IL: Scott Foresman & Co.

Mangham, I. (1973). "Facilitating Intra Organizational Dialogue in a Merger Situation." *Journal of Interpersonal Development*, 4: 133–47.

Marks, M. L., and Mirvis, P. H. (1992). "Rebuilding after the Merger: Dealing with Survivor Sickness." *Organizational Dynamic*, 21/2: 18–35.

—— —— (2001). "Making Mergers and Acquisitions Work: Strategic and Psychological Preparation." *Academy of Management Executive*, 15/2: 80–94.

Meyer, C. B. (2001). "Allocation Processes in Mergers and Acquisitions: An Organizational Justice Perspective." *British Journal of Management*, 12/1: 47–67.

Meyer, K. E., & Lieb-Doczy, E. (2003). "Post Acquisition Restructuring as Evolutionary Process." *Journal of Management Studies*, 40/2: 459–82.

Mirvis, P. H. (1985). "Negotiations after the Sale: The Roots and Ramifications of Conflict in an Acquisition." *Journal of Organizational Behavior*, 6/1: 72–84.

Morosini, P., Shane, S., & Singh, H. (1998). "National Cultural Distance and Cross Border Acquisition Performance." *Journal of International Business Studies*, 29/1: 137–58.

Morrison, E. W., & Robinson, S. L. (1997). "When Employees Feel Betrayed: A Model of How Psychological Contract Violation Develops." *Academy of Management Review*, 22/1: 226–56.

Nahavandi, A., & Malekzadeh, A. R. (1988). "Acculturation in Mergers and Acquisitions." *Academy of Management Review*, 13/1: 79–90.

Napier, N. K. (1989). "Mergers and Acquisitions: Human Resource Issues and Outcomes: A Review and Suggested Typology." *Journal of Management Studies*, 25: 3–13.

Nelson, A., Cooper, C. L., & Jackson, P. (1995). "Uncertainty amidst Change: The Impact of Privatisation on Employee Job Satisfaction and Well Being." *Journal of Occupational and Organizational Psychology*, 68: 57–71.

Oreg, S. (2003). "Resistance to Change: Developing an Individual Measure." *Journal of Applied Psychology*, 88/4: 680–93.

Otte, M. (2005). "Executive Commentary," in G. K. Stahl & M. E. Mendenhall (eds.), *Mergers and Acquisitions: Managing Culture and Human Resources*. Stanford, CA: Stanford University Press, 268–76.

Panchal, S., & Cartwright, S. (2001). "Group Differences in Post Merger Stress." *Journal of Managerial Psychology*, 16/6: 424–34.

Pritchett, P. (1985). *After the Merger: Managing the Shock Waves*. New York: Dow Jones & Irwin.

Riad, S. (2005). "The Power of 'Organizational Culture' as a Discursive Formation in Merger Integration." *Organization Studies*, 26/10: 1529–54.

Robinson, E. W., & Rousseau, D. M. (1994). "When Employees Feel Betrayed: A Model of How Psychological Contract Violation Develops." *Academy of Management Review*, 22/1: 226–56.

Rostand, A. (1994). "Optimising Managerial Decision Making during the Acquisition Integration Process." Paper presented at the 14th Annual Strategic Management Society International Conference, Paris.

Rousseau, D. (1995). *Psychological Contracts in Organizations*. Los Angeles: Sage.

Schein, E. (1985). *Organizational Culture and Leadership*. San Francisco: Jossey Bass.

Schoenberg, R., & Norburn, D. (1998). "Leadership Compatibility within Cross Border Acquisition Outcome." Paper presented to the 18th Annual Strategic Management Society International Conference, Orlando.

Schweiger, D. M., & DeNisi, A. (1991). "Communication with Employees Following A Merger: A Longitudinal Field Experiment." *Academy of Management Journal*, 34: 110–35.

—— & Goulet, P. K. (2000). "Integrating Mergers and Acquisitions: An International Review," in C. L. Cooper & A. Gregory (eds.), *Advances in Mergers and Acquisitions*, vol. 1. New York: JAI Press, 61–93.

—— Ivancevich, J., & Power, F. (1987). "Executive Action in Managing Human Resources Before and After Being Acquired." *Academy of Management Executive*, 1: 127–38.

—— & Lippert, R. L. (2005). "Integration—The Critical Link in M&A Value Creation," in G. Stahl & M. E. Mendenhall (eds.), *Mergers and Acquisitions: Managing Culture and Human Resources*. Stanford, CA: Stanford University Press, 17–43.

Seth, A., Song, K. P., & Pettit, R. R. (2000). "Synergy, Managerialism or Hubris? An Empirical Examination of Motives for Foreign Acquisitions of US Firms." *Journal of International Business Studies*, 13: 387–405.

Shrivastava, P. (1986). "Post-merger Integration." *Journal of Business Strategy*, 7: 65–76.

Sinetar, M. (1981). "Mergers, Morale and Productivity." *Personnel Journal*, 6: 863–67.

Sirower, M. L. (1998). *The Synergy Trap: How Companies Lose the Acquisition Game*. New York: The Free Press.

Siu, O., Cooper, C. L., & Donald, I. (1997). "Occupational Stress, Job Satisfaction and Mental Health amongst Employees of an Acquired TV Company in Hong Kong." *Stress Medicine*, 13/2: 99–107.

Slangen, A. H. L. (2006). "National Cultural Distance and Initial Foreign Acquisition Performance: The Moderating Effect of Integration." *Journal of World Business*, 41/2: 161–70.

Stahl, G., & Mendenhall, M. (2005). *Mergers and Acquisitions: Managing Culture and Human Resources*. Stanford, CA: Stanford University Press.

—— & Sitkin, S. B. (2005). "Trust in Mergers and Acquisitions," in G. K. Stahl & M. E. Mendenhal (eds.), *Mergers and Acquisitions: Managing Culture and Human Resources*. Stanford, CA: Stanford University Press, 82–102.

—— & Voight, A. (2003). "Meta-analyses of the Performance Implications of Cultural Differences in Mergers and Acquisitions: Integrating Strategic, Financial and Organizational Perspectives." INSEAD Working Paper Series Working Paper 2003/99/ABA.

Sudarsanam, P. S. (2003). *Creating Value from Mergers and Acquisitions: The Challenges, An Integrated and International Perspective*. Harlow: FT Prentice Hall.

—— & Mahate, A. A. (2006). "Are Friendly Acquisitions Too Bad for Shareholders and Managers? Long Term Value Creation and Top Management Turnover in Hostile and Friendly Acquirers." *British Journal of Management*, 17: S7–S30.

Tajfel, H., & Turner, J. C. (1979). "An Integrative Theory of Inter Group Conflict," in W. G. Austin & S. Worchel (eds.), *Psychology of Intergroup Relations*. Monterey, CA: Brooks-Cole.

UNCTAD (2000). *Cross-Border Mergers and Acquisitions*. World Investment Report. New York: United Nations.

Van Knippenberg, D., & Hogg, M. A. (2003). "A Social Identity Model of Leadership Effectiveness." *Organizational Behaviour*, 25: 243–96.

Van Oudenhoven, J. P., & de Boer, T. (1995). "Complementarity and Similarity of Partners in International Mergers." *Basic and Applied Social Psychology*, 17/3: 343–56.

Veiga, J., Lubatkin, M., Calori, R., & Véry, P. (2000). "Measuring Organizational Culture Clashes; A Two Nation Post Hoc Analysis of a Cultural Compatibility Index." *Human Relations*, 53/4: 539–57.

Véry, P., Lubatkin, M. & Veiga, J. (1997). "Relative Standing and the Performance of Recently Acquired European Mergers." *Strategic Management Journal*, 18: 593–614.

Walsh, J. P. (1988). "Top Management Turnover following Mergers and Acquisitions." *Strategic Management Journal*, 9/2: 173–83.

Weber, Y. (1996). "Corporate Cultural Fit and Performance in Mergers and Acquisitions." *Human Relations*, 49/9: 1181–202.

—— (2000). "Measuring Cultural Fit in Mergers and Acquisitions," in N. M. Ashkanasy, C. P. M. Wilderom, & M. F. Peterson (eds.), *Handbook of Organizational Culture and Climate*. Thousand Oaks, CA: Sage.

—— & Menipaz, D. (2003). "Measuring Culture Fit in Mergers and Acquisitions." *International Journal of Business Performance Management*, 5/1: 54–72.

—— Tarba, S.Y., & Reichel, A. (2009). "International Mergers and Acquisitions Revisited: The Role of Cultural Distance and Post Acquisition Integration Approach," in C. L. Cooper & S. Finkelstein (eds.), *Advances in Mergers and Acquisition*, vol. 8. Bingley: Emerald Group, 1–18.

CHAPTER 16

CULTURE IN MERGERS AND ACQUISITIONS

A Critical Synthesis and Steps Forward

SATU TEERIKANGAS AND PHILIPPE VÉRY

INTRODUCTION

The practice and research on mergers and acquisitions (M&A) converge on the fact that it is the post-deal implementation or integration phase that explains the difficulty of making M&A work, and ultimately perform according to or beyond expectations (Ashkenas et al. 1998; Larsson and Finkelstein 1999). Taking a closer look at the implementation challenge in M&A, three significant themes arise, all three having been raised by both managers and consultants involved in the practice of M&A, as well as researchers involved in understanding their underlying dynamics. These three themes are: (1) the management of the post-acquisition integration phase (Haspeslagh and Jemison 1991; Birkinshaw et al. 2000), (2) ensuring employee motivation and retention (Napier 1989; Cartwright and Cooper 1990), and (3) dealing with the cultural challenge inherent in the combination of formerly distinct organizations (Buono and Bowditch 1989; Schweiger and Goulet 2000). Whilst other chapters in this *Handbook* deal with the first two of the challenges identified above (see Chapters 14, 15, 21), in this chapter, our focus is on reviewing how extant academic literature has studied the cultural issue at stake in M&A.

One could ask: why is there a need to separately study the cultural encounter taking place in M&A? Should that not form part of the generic study of the management of M&A and their integration?

As is often the case with research on social sciences, ranging from psychology to management, research on M&A has tended toward a "culture-general" approach, i.e. assuming the findings to hold universally. In this respect, the "cultural discourse" on M&A has emerged as a means of ensuring that sufficient interest is paid to this dimension of M&A activity. Moreover, the cultural challenge in cross-border M&A has been pointed to by prominent organizational scholars as a prime example of the importance of the cultural complexities at stake in today's organizations (Schein 1985; Hofstede 2001). This view is supported by corporate evidence: a recent study found that more than 90% of European M&A fall short of forecast objectives, owing to difficulties in combining corporate cultures and governance structures (Hay Group 2007).

The cultural view of M&A is not without its problems, however. In a critical analysis of the field, Riad (2005) finds that the "culture" discourse has become so prevalent and natural to the discipline that it has become "naturalized" as part of the M&A discourse. The term itself has become normative, quasi-institutionalized in the discourse on M&A. Subsequently, any critical voices regarding culture in M&A are likely to feel ignored. Riad (2005) calls for scholars to become more aware of their own role in forming and producing this discourse.

Despite ongoing M&A activity and research, reviews of the field point to its advances on the one hand, as well as its continuing inability to tap into the core of the issue—what happens, actually, when two formerly distinct organizations meet, be it in a merger, or an acquisition (for reviews of the field, please see Schweiger and Walsh 1990; Vaara 1999; Schweiger and Goulet 2000; Schoenberg 2000; Stahl and Voigt 2008; Teerikangas and Véry 2006; Teerikangas 2007). In the present review, our aim is to re-address the field from the following perspectives: (1) how has culture been conceptualized, (2) what is known about the culture-performance relationship in M&A, (3) what is the nature of the cultural encounter in M&A, and how to manage cultural change in M&A, (4) in what ways do national cultures impact international M&A? Conclusions and pointers toward future research end the chapter.

What Culture is Present in M&A?

A Brief Historical Tour

Taking a brief historical look at this stream of research, we notice it has undergone a gradual internationalization and globalization in terms of the foci of research as well as the academics undertaking research in this area (see Cartwright 1998). The study of culture began in the social sciences, where anthropologists, sociologists, social psychologists, and cross-cultural psychologists have been studying culture throughout the 20th century.

Research on the cultural challenge at stake in M&A emerged in the early 1980s with a focus on domestic deals in the US context; thus the emphasis was on the clash of organizational cultures (Marks 1982; Buono et al. 1985; Buono and Bowditch 1989). These advances parallel the emergence of the "cultural" paradigm in the broader management sciences in the early 1980s that led to an interest in the role of organizational culture as a driver of corporate success (for reviews, see e.g. Vaara 1999; Burnes 2009).

A decade later, from the early 1990s onward, the rise of European cross-border M&A activity led to the proliferation of the study of cross-border M&A; here, the relevant cultural encounter includes both organizational and national cultures (Cartwright 1998; Gertsen et al. 1998). Since the early 21st century, interest in the cross-border dimensions of M&A activity has expanded to the study of M&A in the Asian context, looking at acquisitions of Japanese companies (Olcott 2008), acquisitions of Chinese state-owned companies (Cooke 2006), acquisitions undertaken by emerging market multinationals (Chapter 22), and more specifically by Indian (Gubbi et al. 2010) and Chinese firms (Deng 2009).

What Type of Cultural Diversity is at Play?

A historical tour of research on culture in M&A points to the term at the core of the work, namely "culture," as having been given differing connotations over time.

From an early focus on organizational culture in domestic deals (e.g. Buono and Bowditch 1989), the field started studying national cultures in cross-border deals (e.g. Morosini 1998), and the simultaneous effects of organizational and national cultures (e.g. Véry et al. 1996; Weber et al. 1996). In other words, the "cultural challenge" at stake in M&A can range from a clash of organizational cultures in domestic deals, to a clash of both organizational and national cultures in cross-border transactions.

To complicate matters still further, David and Singh (1994) identify the need to account for the presence of professional cultures in addition to organizational and national ones. Chatterjee et al. (1992) note the diversity of subcultures in the workplace. The latter findings remind us that all M&A represent cultural diversity at the subcultural, functional, and organizational levels of analysis, in addition to national cultures in the case of cross-border deals.

Moving beyond the organizational boundaries, Pioch's study on retail sector acquisitions points to the impact of the underlying industry culture that impacts all players in the retail sector, and their acquisition approaches (Pioch 2007). Teerikangas (2006) finds that within-country regional cultures matter in parallel with national cultures: some cross-border acquisitions might seem easy owing to the similarity between the firms' regional cultures, or between one firm's national and the other's regional culture (see also McSweeney 2009). For example, the Alsace region in France is culturally close to Germany; hence, an acquirer is likely to meet cultural challenges similar to those in Germany when buying a company from the Alsace region. In synthesis, this leads us to conclude that cultural diversity in all M&A exists at the subcultural, functional, organizational, and industrial levels of analysis, in addition to regional and national cultures in the case of cross-border transactions.

Such an emerging multi-level view of the cultural challenge at stake in M&A is supported by recent findings in social sciences that claim that a focus on multiple levels of analysis and the acknowledgement of the simultaneous presence of multiple cultures in organizations reflects the complex cultural reality in today's organizations. Traditionally, the disciplines most concerned with the study of culture, namely anthropology, cross-cultural psychology, organization theory, and cross-cultural management have each focused on a specific level of analysis. This has been either the culture of a tribe or nation, the culture of an organization, or the culture of a society or country. For example, management scholars have traditionally argued for the existence of one unified corporate culture (Deal and Kennedy 1982; Schein 1985; Handy 1999) and specific national cultures (Hofstede 1980; House et al. 2004).

There have been, over the years, a growing number of voices arguing that the trend is away from a unitary view of corporate culture toward a view of organizations as consisting of multiple cultures (Martin 1992). In this regard, professional and occupational subcultures (Van Maanen and Barley 1984; Trice 1993; Trice and Beyer 1993; Raelin 1986; Sackmann 1997), site cultures (Sackmann 1997), departmental cultures (Sackmann 1997), functional cultures (Tannenbaum 1973), and industrial cultures (Turner 1971; Reynolds 1986; Chatman and Jehn 1994; Philips 1994) have been discussed. The parallel presence of cultures at multiple levels of analysis has also become acknowledged. Fombrun (1983) made a distinction between societal (i.e. national), industrial, and corporate cultures. Sackmann (1997) distinguished between national, corporate, and subculture levels in an organization. In his work on societal culture, Hofstede (2001) discusses the parallel existence of industrial, corporate, functional, and social class cultures. Still, Alvesson (2002) argues that extant research on corporate culture continues to largely omit the issue of levels of analysis. Based on a review of extant research in the social sciences, he identifies cultures at the level of societies, regions, industries, organizations, functions, professions, and social groups.

These views are rooted in research in the more traditional social sciences. In sociology, Merton (1968) argued for the use of multiple levels of analysis in addition to the societal one, e.g. organizational, institutional and group levels. In contrast to anthropologists looking at culture at the societal level, sociologists have long been interested in the study of subcultures within a society (Ritzer 2000). Today, the issue of ethnic relations and multicultural societies remains central to the sociologists' agenda (Bauman and May 2001). This line of thinking is mirrored in the sociological view of organizations as one in which multiple subcultures interact (Cuche 2001). In social psychology, Social Identity Theory (Tajfel and Turner 1986) explains the impact that the membership in many cultures has on a person's identity.

Whilst the trend in sociological and organizational research has been toward a multi-level view of culture, extant research in M&A has continued to retain a more traditional outlook, focusing on one or a maximum of two levels of culture simultaneously. What is more, the notion of a "unitary" corporate culture has prevailed as the dominant paradigm, overlooking the possibility that organizations might consist of fragmented cultures (Vaara 1999). Moreover, these studies have tended to approach culture as "something an organization has," rather than "something an organization is" (Vaara 1999). This realistic and positivist approach to culture could be complemented by interpretive and critical approaches (Vaara 2000). Looking forward, it would seem that the field could gain from more fragmented and multi-level perspectives to the study of culture.

DOES CULTURAL DIVERSITY IMPACT THE PERFORMANCE OF M&A?

One of the main questions in the work on culture in M&A relates to answering the question—"is there a relationship between cultural diversity and M&A performance?" This question parallels the work of finance and strategy scholars on M&A, where the question of "what drives the performance of M&A?" has been a concern since the 1970s (Jensen and Ruback 1983). In the cultural stream, the assumption is that "the greater the cultural discrepancy between the organizations involved, the worse the performance of the deal" (Teerikangas and Véry 2006).

This question has been studied in the context of organizational cultures clashing in domestic deals (Datta 1991; Chatterjee et al. 1992), national cultures conflicting in cross-border M&A either independently (Morosini et al. 1998) or together with the effect of organizational cultures (Weber et al. 1996; Véry et al. 1996, 1997). Despite the appeal of the argument, research reviews find little conclusive evidence of the impact of cultural differences on M&A performance (Schweiger and Walsh 1990; Schoenberg 2000; Schweiger and Goulet 2000; Teerikangas and Véry 2006; Stahl and Voigt 2008). It has thus been argued that an in-depth understanding of the progress of the post-deal integration process and the nature of the cultural challenge therein would be needed (Teerikangas and Véry 2006; Stahl and Voigt 2008).

We proceed next to reviewing findings from this interesting area of research thematically, depending on whether the focus of these studies has been on the level of (1) organizational culture, (2) national culture, or (3) the mix of organizational and national cultures. The reader is advised to refer to Table 16.1 for a thorough synthesis.

Our review highlights how the focus of these studies has shifted not only culture-wise, but also as regards the way in which M&A performance has been defined. From the study of corporate performance using accounting, stock market, or perceptual measures, researchers have become interested in the impact of cultural differences on integration and resource sharing (Brock 2005), attitudinal and behavioral variables (Weber et al. 1996), post-acquisition conflict (Sarala 2010), knowledge transfer (Sarala and Vaara 2010), and capability transfer (Björkman et al. 2007). Also, the conjoint impact of cultural distance on perceived performance and acculturation (Véry et al. 1996), relative standing (Véry et al. 1997), as well as attitudinal and behavioral variables (Weber 1996; Reus and Lamont 2009) has been emphasized. This points to the concept of M&A performance as amenable to a multiplicity of definitions, and to the complexity of the causal mechanisms by which the impact of culture on M&A performance has come to be operationalized.

Organizational Culture and the Performance of M&A

Work on the impact of organizational culture on post-acquisition performance has looked at the significance of organizational fit to performance (Datta 1991), cultural fit to performance (Chatterjee et al. 1992), the impact of cultural differences on autonomy removal and commitment (Weber, 1996), and top management team complementarity and performance (Krishnan et al. 1997). Performance has been measured using either accounting measures three years post-deal (Krishnan et al. 1997), stock measures (Chatterjee et al. 1992), perceptions of performance (Datta 1991), or a mix of behavioral and accounting measures (Weber 1996). What have these studies taught us?

In his study of the impact of organizational fit on the performance of US domestic acquisitions, Datta (1991) found differences in top management styles to have a negative performance impact, using both accounting and stock market measures. In contrast, differences in reward and evaluation systems were not found to impact acquisition performance. The findings prevailed regardless of the level of integration.

Chatterjee et al.'s (1992) study was among the first systematic attempts to bridge hitherto separate fields of study on M&A performance on the one hand, and their cultural consequences on the other hand. They consolidated two streams of research on the impact of "fit" on merger performance, namely research on strategic fit and cultural fit. Consistently with their hypotheses, the market expectation of the performance of the studied mergers was associated with the target firm managers' perceptions of cultural fit. Cultural differences in this study were operationalized as the perceived differences between the two firms' top management teams (as perceived by the target firm managers). Chatterjee et al. (1992) find that strategic fit and cultural fit both contribute to merger performance.

Later, Weber (1996)'s study was the first systematic large-scale study to link corporate cultural fit, autonomy removal, and commitment of managers to the progress of integration and the financial performance of a transaction. Financial performance was measured in terms of return on assets in the four years following the deal. He sampled US deals in both the banking and manufacturing sectors. Weber (1996) found evidence of the negative effect of differences in corporate culture on the progress of integration. This effect was visible for both the full sample and the banking sample, but not the manufacturing sample. However, corporate culture differences were not found to affect the financial performance of the transactions studied. Commitment was in turn found to be negatively associated with cultural differences, especially in the bank sample.

Second, Weber (1996) found that cultural differences are more likely to surface when the degree of integration, i.e. the degree of autonomy removal, is high. In such instances, encounters between the two parties are likely to be manifold, potentially leading to cultural conflict. This is prevalent, for example, in service sector mergers including banks, but less prevalent in manufacturing mergers. Differences in organizational culture tend to become more prevalent, the more there is contact between the firms involved, as in the professional services sector, e.g. banking.

Krishnan et al. (1997) studied the impact of complementarity of acquired and acquiring firms' top management teams on acquisition performance. Financial performance was measured in terms of return on assets in the three years following the transaction. They found differences in functional backgrounds to have a positive impact on the performance of related and unrelated mergers. Complementarity was seen as a means of enhancing organizational learning, as top management team members with different backgrounds bring specific skills to the team. Further, they found that in acquisitions where management teams were complementary, turnover rates were lower. This finding would suggest that differences can provide opportunities, and thus bear value.

Recently, experimental laboratory studies of the cultural encounter in mergers have been undertaken. Weber and Camerer (2003) conducted an experiment to study the clashing of cultures in mergers. They find that both firms' performance decreases following the merger. The two experimental groups involved in the study both blamed the other party for the decrease in performance, instead of recognizing that the latter can also be caused by the sheer situational complexity of a merger. In a similar vein, Van den Steen (2010) develops an economic theory of the costs and benefits of corporate culture in the context of mergers. Within-firm organizational cultures, if assumed to be homogeneous, are argued to be resource-efficient owing to, for example, faster coordination and communication, since organizational members share similar beliefs. At the time of a merger, this cultural homogeneity is lost, as two formerly disparate firms merge into one. The costs of the merger will show immediately after the deal, whereas benefits from merging dissimilar firms will take time to materialize. Both studies provide more detailed pointers as to *why* the merging of firms might have performance effects.

To synthesize, what do we learn from these studies? As regards the impact of corporate cultural differences on firm performance, the results are contradictory. Whilst Datta (1991), Chatterjee et al. (1992), and Weber and Camerer (2003) find that cultural differences have a negative impact on performance, Krishnan et al. (1997) find that differences in top management team functional backgrounds have a positive impact on the financial performance of the firm. However, Weber (1996) did not find a direct relationship between cultural differences and M&A financial performance. He does, however, find that corporate culture differences have a negative impact on both integration progress as well as commitment. The relationships are likely to be stronger for service than for manufacturing firms (Weber 1996). The impact of cultural differences is also likely to be stronger, when high degrees of integration and autonomy removal are sought (Weber 1996). All the while, Datta's (1991) findings were robust regardless of the degree of integration. Thus, even the question of "depth of integration" needs to be treated with caution.

In other words, a lack of cultural fit would seem to impact investor expectations of the future success potential of a merger (Datta 1991; Chatterjee et al. 1992). However, the impact on the two- to four-year accounting performance of a firm remains contested, with negative (Datta 1991), neutral (Weber 1996), and positive (Krishnan et al. 1997) findings reported. A direct impact of cultural differences on integration and commitment is found, however (Weber 1996). The results might partly be explained by the fact that Chatterjee et al. (1992) and Weber (1996) focus on mergers, the latter tending toward greater cultural issues, whilst Krishnan et al. (1997) focus on acquisitions.

A comparison of these studies (see Appendix 16.1, Table 16.A1) further points to the fact that all of these studies have been conducted in the US domestic M&A context, studying deals made in the period of 1980–8. Sample sizes vary between 30 to 173 M&A. Studies focus either on all industries (Chatterjee et al. 1992; Krishnan et al. 1997), manufacturing (Datta 1991; Weber 1996), or banking (Weber 1996) sectors. Acquired firm (Chatterjee et al. 1992; Weber 1996), buying firm respondents (Datta 1991), or both are used (Krishnan et al. 1997). Performance-wise, the focus is on accounting measures or stock measures (Chatterjee et al. 1992), both (Datta 1991), or attitudinal and behavioral measures (Weber 1996). Studies using accounting measures analyze M&A performance in the three- to four-year window following a deal (Weber 1996; Krishnan et al. 1997). It is noteworthy that all of the above studies (Chatterjee et al. 1992; Weber 1996; Krishnan et al. 1997) use management teams' cultural dis/similarity as a proxy for organizational culture. To be specific, what the above studies measure is not organizational culture differences per se, but differences between the involved firms' top management team cultures. This points to the difficulty of capturing organizational culture differences in the study of M&A. Ultimately, this begs the questions—has organizational culture been addressed in these studies; and what are they actually measuring?

National Culture and the Performance of M&A

Studies on the effects of national cultures on M&A performance have continued the tradition of "whether culture affects M&A performance." In this stream of research, two arguments can be found: whilst some studies paint the impact of national cultures on M&A performance in a positive light, more recently this image has come to be more nuanced. Performance has been assessed in terms of financial performance, using either accounting measures two to five years post-deal (Morosini et al. 1998), stock measures (Chakrabarti et al. 2009; Gubbi et al. 2010), perceptions of performance (Slangen 2006), or a mix of the latter (Reus and Lamont 2009). Also non-financial metrics have been used (Brock 2005).

We begin with an overview of the studies that find a positive impact of national culture differences on M&A performance. The earliest study was conducted by Morosini et al. (1998), looking at differences in national cultures as sources of competitive advantage for globally operating firms. Morosini et al. (1998) found that cross-border acquisitions conducted in the US and Europe performed better as the distance between the national cultures involved increased. Performance was measured in terms of return on sales in the two years following the deal. Drawing from the resource-based view of the firm, it was argued that global companies need a diverse set of organizational routines to maintain their competitive advantage.

More recently, this finding has received confirmation. Based on an extensive sample of 800 cross-border acquisitions undertaken across four continents over the period of

1991–2004, Chakrabarti et al. (2009) find that in the long term, cross-border acquisitions perform better the more culturally distant the partners. Performance is measured in terms of stock market returns up to three years post-deal. These positive performance effects are, however, not visible in the immediate post-deal era when measured with announcement period returns. The findings further point to overall cultural distance as being of significance in contrast to per dimension analyses of cultural differences. Furthermore, synergy effects would seem to occur when the buying firm comes from an economically more developed country than the target.

Recently, studies have begun to look not only at acquisitions undertaken by American and European firms, but also at those by emerging market firms. A study of 425 acquisitions by Indian firms (Gubbi et al. 2010) finds that acquisitions undertaken by Indian firms overseas create value for shareholders. Performance is measured as regards the market reaction in an 11-day window. The findings point to positive performance when the target is from a more developed economic and institutional host country environment than the acquirer. The authors argue that positive gains from acquisitions occur, when acquirers undertake acquisitions where capability transfer occurs. In the case of Indian acquirers acquiring in developed economies, the latter contexts offer a myriad of opportunities for the acquirers to learn from.

In parallel, another stream of studies points to more nuances in the ways that national culture differences come to impact the performance of M&A. To this end, Slangen (2006) finds that the effect of cultural differences depends on the degree of integration (Haspeslagh and Jemison 1991). Through a study of 103 cross-border acquisitions undertaken by Dutch acquiring firms, Slangen finds support for his argument that the impact of cultural distance increases when acquiring firms integrate the acquired firm into their operations. The more the members of the formerly distinct organizations interact post-acquisition, the more opportunities there are for misunderstandings to occur, and hence the greater the likelihood that there is an impact on subsequent performance. The managerial implication is that cultural differences can be beneficial, if the acquired firm is left with autonomy and not forcefully integrated into the acquiring firm.

Other authors have identified an indirect culture-performance relationship. In a survey of 103 international, related, acquisitions, Brock (2005) argues that the relationship between national culture and the creation of synergies following an acquisition does not follow a direct, but rather, an indirect process. Brock (2005) identifies a causal chain linking cultural differences (as regards Hofstede's dimensions of (1) power distance, and (2) individualism vs. collectivism) to the degree of resource sharing and post-acquisition integration. The latter, in turn, have an effect on the extent to which synergies are created in the acquisition. Brock notes that specific dimensions of cultural differences have differing performance implications. Whilst individualism is likely to affect integration, power distance affects the degree of resource sharing. Thus, when a buying firm from a collectivistic tradition buys a firm from an individualistic culture, integration-related problems are likely to occur; and when a buying firm from a high power distance country buys a firm with a tradition for lower power distance, resource-sharing problems are likely to occur.

Continuing on the indirect argument, based on a sample of 118 international acquisitions undertaken by US firms, Reus and Lamont (2009) posit cultural distance as being a double-edged sword in international acquisitions. Cultural distance is argued to withhold both positive and negative performance effects. Whilst previous literature has argued as to whether cultural distance brings positive or negative consequences, work by Reus and Lamont (2009) effectively points out that both tend to occur simultaneously, hence the challenge of the cultural debate in international acquisitions. In the study, cultural distance is found to impede integration capabilities by having a negative effect on understandability between the parties, communication, and key employee retention. Through this effect on integration, cultural differences come to have an indirect effect on acquisition performance. All the while, cultural distance is found to moderate the extent to which integration capabilities result in performance outcomes: in parallel to their negative effect, cultural differences are found to exert a simultaneous positive effect on communication and understandability through learning opportunities. In sum, the study posits that international acquisition performance largely depends on the adopted integration parameters, here conceptualized as understandability, communication, and key employee retention.

In summary, researchers focused on national cultures in M&A posit two types of findings. On the one hand, the positive effects of differences in national cultures have been identified, using both accounting and stock measures, and across continents (Morosini et al. 1998; Chakrabarti et al. 2009; Gubbi et al. 2010). On the other hand, researchers argue for a more nuanced picture of the impact of national culture on post-deal performance. Extending Weber's findings on organizational culture (1996), Slangen (2006) finds that the effect of national culture depends on the degree of integration, i.e. it is not static from one deal to another. Brock (2005) and Reus and Lamont (2009) argue that national cultures have an indirect effect on acquisition performance, through their effect on "interim" metrics, such as resource sharing and integration (Brock 2005), communication, retention, and understanding (Reus and Lamont 2009). Also, differing dimensions of cultures bring differing performance effects (Brock 2005). Buyers from economically more developed countries would seem to score better (Chakrabarti et al. 2009; Gubbi et al. 2010). The performance effect would become all the more positive the greater the distance between the participating firms' home countries (Morosini et al. 1998; Chakrabarti et al. 2009). Finally, Reus and Lamont (2009) note a simultaneous negative and positive impact of national cultures.

A comparison of these studies (see Table 16.A1) further points to the fact that this stream of research follows time-wise the previous stream that focused on corporate culture and M&A performance, in that the deals studied by the present stream were conducted between the late 1980s and 2007. In contrast with only US acquirers, in this stream acquirers from across the world have been studied, with an early focus on European and US acquirers (Morosini et al. 1998), to a more recent focus on acquirers from emerging markets (Gubbi et al. 2010), or a global representation of acquirers (as in Chakrabarti et al. 2009). Samples range from 52 (Morosini et al. 1998) to 118 acquisitions (Reus and Lamont 2009) in survey-based studies, to between 425 (Gubbi et al. 2010) and

800 (Chakrabarti et al. 2009) in database studies. Performance is measured two to five years post-deal for both accounting and stock measures of performance, with only one study using a shorter, 11-day window (Gubbi et al. 2010).

National culture is operationalized either using Hofstede's (1980) dimensions, the more recent findings from the Globe project (House et al. 2004), at times conjointly with the cultural distance index (Kogut and Singh 1988). Other measures include language, religion, legal origin, and economic and institutional distance (as in Chakrabarti et al. 2009; Gubbi et al. 2010). In other words, this stream has not aimed at furthering our understanding of what types of dimensions of national cultures are at stake in international M&A; rather, existing operationalizations of national culture have been taken as a given.

Organizational and National Cultures and the Performance of M&A

Work that has combined national and organizational cultures in the study of post-acquisition performance has measured "performance" as perceptions of performance combined with the effect of behavioral variables (Véry et al. 1996; 1997). Most studies in this stream have used non-financial performance metrics, however, measuring the impact of culture on attitudinal and behavioral variables (Weber et al. 1996), knowledge transfer (Sarala and Vaara 2010), post-acquisition conflict (Sarala 2010), and capability transfer (Björkman et al. 2007). We highlight the relative paucity of financial performance measures in this research stream.

Two studies have attempted to measure perceptions of financial performance combined with the behavioral variables of acculturative stress and relative standing. The earliest study by Véry et al. (1996) found that the prevalence of acculturative stress in international M&A is not straightforward. Depending on the dimensions of acculturative stress and the home countries of the participating companies, acculturative stress can be attractive or repulsive. Moreover, acculturative stress was found to influence post-acquisition performance; yet different dimensions of acculturative stress are salient depending on the country. In some cases, cultural issues are more significant in domestic than in cross-border settings. Managers should thus not forget about the cultural problematique when acquiring domestically.

Relative standing has been another focus of study. Relative standing sees that the status individuals ascribe themselves in a social setting is based on how they compare their status to others in a proximate social setting (Frank 1985). In M&A, this means that the more autonomy is removed from managers in a merger situation, the more likely they are to react against the acquiring culture. In the earliest work on relative standing in cross-border M&A, Véry et al. (1997) looked at relative standing and its impact on the post-merger performance of European firms. Performance was analyzed as the self-reported impact that the deal had on the firm's earnings, sales, and market share in the one to three years following the deal. Overall, the performance effect of the studied mergers was neutral. Performance was better for related mergers, the longer the time had elapsed since the merger, the more compatible the cultures, and the less autonomy was removed. It was noted that buying firms from some countries tended to perform better, e.g. British acquirers' performance was better than that of French acquirers. Moreover, no evidence of "cultural clash" was to be found, as the studied firms' cultures were reported as being somewhat compatible. Finally, no performance difference between domestic and cross-border mergers was evidenced.

Moving on to the use of non-financial performance metrics, Weber et al. (1996) studied the role of national and organizational culture fit in determining effective integration in domestic and cross-border mergers. They looked at the impact of cultural distance on top management teams. In domestic mergers, differences in corporate cultures were found to negatively impact all studied attitudinal and behavioral variables (autonomy removal, stress, attitudes, commitment, and cooperation). In contrast, in cross-border mergers, corporate cultures had a positive effect on the same variables, whilst national cultures had a negative effect. The study is significant in that it highlighted the simultaneous, yet differing effects that national and corporate cultures exert on post-merger integration. Both need to be taken into account in cross-border transactions.

Björkman et al. (2007) propose a conceptual model linking cultural differences to post-acquisition performance, defined as the degree of post-acquisition capability transfer between the firms. Capability transfer is argued to depend on the degree of social integration achieved, potential absorptive capacity, and capability complementarity, each of these in turn affected by the cultural distance between the merging parties. In other words, the greater the differences between the merging parties, the less likely it is that capability transfer takes place. The use of social integration mechanisms and the degree of operational integration are claimed to reduce the negative effects of cultural differences on social integration and potential absorptive capacity respectively.

Another recent example is work by Sarala and Vaara (2010) that studies the effect of cultural distance on knowledge transfer. Differences in national cultures are found to provide opportunities for knowledge transfer in international acquisitions. Whilst static organizational culture differences per se were not found to influence knowledge transfer, the dynamic changes in post-acquisition organizational cultures, i.e. through cultural integration, were found to have a positive effect, moderating the impact of national cultures on knowledge transfer.

Cultural differences have also been studied conjointly with acculturative modes. In a recent study, Sarala (2010) studies how cultural differences and acculturation factors come to jointly impact the degree of post-acquisition conflict. National cultural differences were not found to have an effect on the degree of post-acquisition conflict. Organizational culture differences, as well as acquiring firm's organizational culture preservation, tend to increase conflict, whereas partner attractiveness reduces conflict.

A recent meta-analysis of publications on the culture-performance relationship (Stahl and Voigt 2008) finds that cultural differences impact the degree and progress of sociocultural integration in times of M&A, as well as synergy realization, and share-holder value. The impact can be different, depending on the study. Further, the impact of cultural differences will depend on the degree of relatedness of the firms involved as well as the level of culture studied. Stahl and Voigt point to the difficulty of assessing this rela-tionship owing to the number of variables involved. They posit the significance of cul-tural differences on post-acquisition integration.

In synthesis, research on the dual impact of organizational and national culture on M&A performance points to an increasingly nuanced, yet mixed picture. Whilst organi-zational culture is found to positively affect attitudes, stress, and behaviors (Weber et al. 1996), it is in parallel found to increase post-acquisition conflict (Sarala 2010), but not to affect knowledge transfer (Sarala and Vaara 2010). National culture is found to nega-tively impact attitudes, stress, and behaviors (Weber et al. 1996), impact acculturative stress positively or negatively depending on the dimensions of acculturative stress and the countries involved (Véry et al. 1996), have no impact on post-acquisition conflict (Sarala 2010), and yet provide opportunities for knowledge transfer (Sarala and Vaara 2010). Further, buyers from some countries tend to outperform others (Véry et al. 1997). In general, related deals perform better, the longer the time frame of measurement (Véry et al. 1997). What is at stake?

First, in this stream of research, "performance" tends not to be measured finance-wise. Only Véry et al.'s work (1996, 1997) uses accounting measures of performance, whilst Stahl and Voigt's (2008) meta-analysis of existing studies uses synergy realization as a proxy. In contrast, most studies in this stream are interested in the nuanced ways in which national and organizational cultures, separately or conjointly, come to impact acquisition-related outcome variables such as autonomy removal, stress, attitudes, com-mitment, acculturation, relative standing, employee resistance, knowledge transfer, capability transfer, and sociocultural integration. At times, the joint impact of cultural differences and acculturative modes or cultural integration is under review (Sarala 2010; Sarala and Vaara 2010). In sum, a more complete, yet results-wise mixed, view of the influence mechanisms of cultural diversity on M&A outcomes emerges.

Taking a closer comparative look at these studies, samples range from 52 (Weber et al. 1996) to 133 deals (Sarala and Vaara 2010), including conceptual work (Björkman et al. 2007), a case-survey (Larsson and Risberg 1998), and a meta-analysis (Stahl and Voigt 2008). A majority of the studies focus on American or European acquirers, with a not-able absence of acquirers from other continents. In terms of respondents, studies aim for multiple respondents per acquisition, with a focus on either the acquired firm (Weber et al. 1996; Véry et al. 1996, 1997) or both firms' managers (Sarala 2010; Sarala and Vaara 2010). Organizational culture is again largely operationalized as regards differences in management team styles, with the exception of more recent work, which has included other types of organizational culture differences (Sarala 2010; Sarala and Vaara 2010). As regards national culture, either Hofstede (1980), or more recently Globe (House et al. 2004) and Kogut and Singh's (1988) cultural distance index have been used. These oper-ationalizations point to the difficulty of studying the impact of culture, however defined, on international operations such as M&A. In their work, Sarala (2010) and Sarala and

Vaara (2010) discuss the difficulty of moving beyond the much used management team proxy for culture, given that no other measures exist.

Synthesis

In synthesis, debate on the issue of whether and how cultural differences impact merger and acquisition performance continues to rage. The field has moved from an initial focus on US deals, to a focus on European, Asian, and worldwide transactions as well. Whilst a focus on organizational culture initially dominated, there was a rapid shift to studies on national culture, and studies combining the effects of national and organizational cultures on performance. It is worth noting that studies rely on existing models of national cultural differences, especially Hofstede's or more recently House et al.'s (2004) dimensions, without seeking to find out what types of differences in national culture exist in "the reality" of M&A. Likewise, organizational culture is largely proxied as regards differences at the level of management teams. As Figure 16.1 illustrates, in terms of performance measurement, the study of organizational or national cultures on M&A performance has largely relied on financial metrics, whilst the study of national and organizational cultures has operationalized performance using non-financial measures.

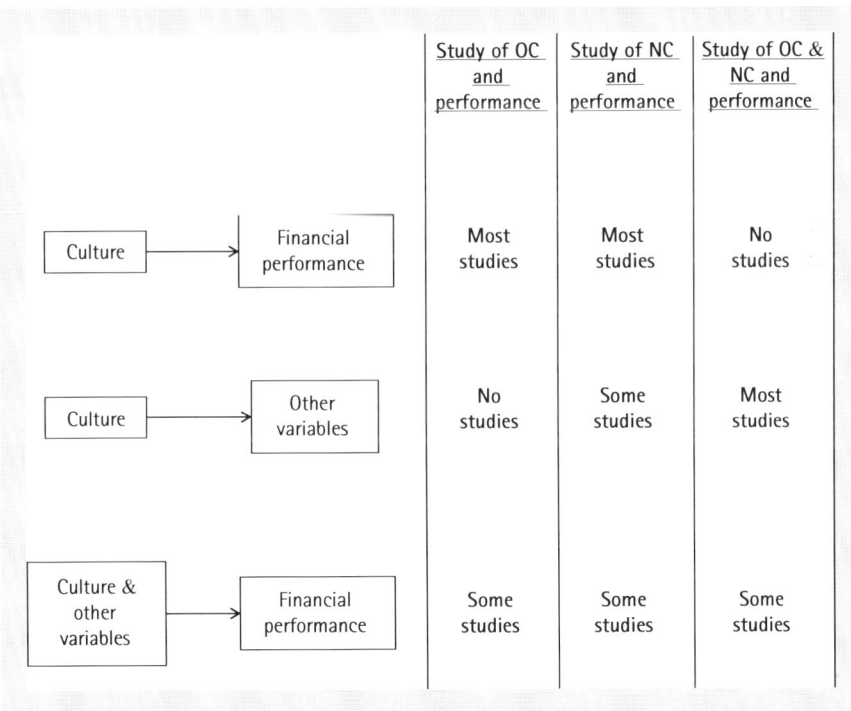

	Study of OC and performance	Study of NC and performance	Study of OC & NC and performance
Culture → Financial performance	Most studies	Most studies	No studies
Culture → Other variables	No studies	Some studies	Most studies
Culture & other variables → Financial performance	Some studies	Some studies	Some studies

FIG. 16.1 Relationships assessed in the study of a culture-performance link in M&A

Notes: OC refers to organizational culture; NC refers to national culture.

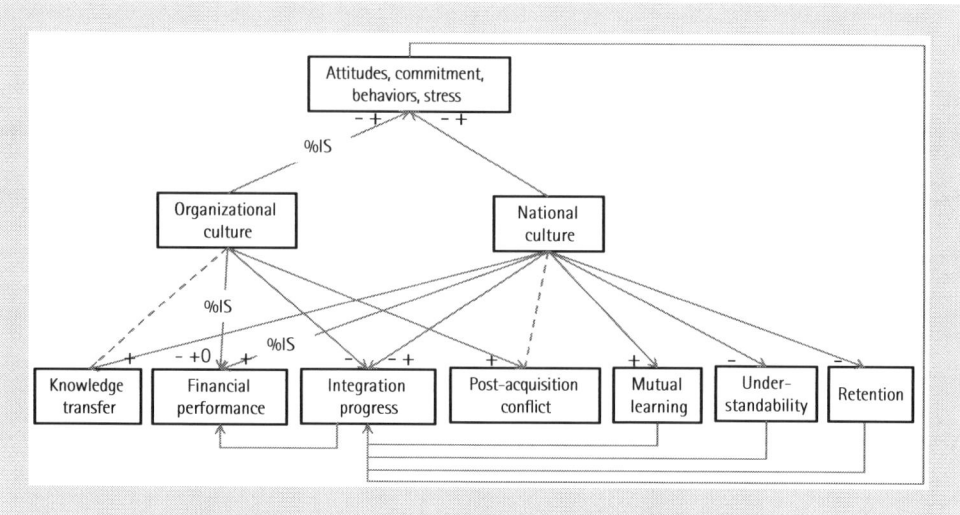

FIG. 16.2 Impact of cultural differences on M&A performance—a synthesis

Notes: IS stands for integration strategy, + refers to a positive relationship,
− to a negative relationship, and a dotted line to a neutral relationship.

Figure 16.2 represents an effort to synthesize the current understanding of the impact of cultural distance on M&A performance. The conventional wisdom claims that cultural differences have a negative impact on the outcome of a merger. Such wisdom has been proven for organizational cultures in some of the studies (Datta 1991; Chatterjee et al. 1992; Weber and Camerer 2003; Sarala 2010) as regards integration progress and conflict; all the while, the relationship to financial performance, attitudes, stress, and behaviors lends conflicting evidence. As regards national cultures, the impact analysis provides a more positive outlook: national cultures have been found to bear positively on financial performance, knowledge transfer, and mutual learning. They impact understandability and retention negatively, and have mixed effects on attitudes, stress and behaviors. Cultural distance should thus not only be viewed from a negative lens. As Figure 16.2 illustrates, the picture is more complicated. Cultural differences, at organizational and national levels, have both positive and negative effects, but these effects depend upon the outcome measure. One can further question the extent to which the two cultures—organizational and national—can be conceptually separated in this analysis.

It is further intriguing that the field has moved from an initial focus on a direct culture-financial performance link to a focus on studying the more intricate ways in which various cultures might impact on non-financial performance outcomes, including knowledge transfer, capability transfer, synergy realization, integration, acculturation, behaviors, or stress. The argument being that it is through their effect on these aspects of M&A that cultural differences come to impact financial performance. Recent findings point to the fact that this indirect link between cultural diversity and M&A performance is mediated by the actions of the managers concerned: the degree of integration (Slangen

2006), the degree of social interaction (Bjorkman et al. 2007), and the evolving process of cultural integration (Sarala and Vaara 2010). Put together, these findings point to the fact that cultural distance, per se, is both an asset and a liability, depending on the actions taken during integration.

CULTURAL DYNAMICS AT PLAY IN TIMES OF M&A

Parallel to the performance debate, another central question that the researchers interested in the study of culture in M&A continue to look at is: what are the nature and the dynamics of the cultural encounter taking place at the time of M&A and how can this encounter be enabled, facilitated, and possibly managed? This stream of research can be seen as an extension of the literature looking at the culture-performance link in M&A, taking a step further and entering the organizations to understand what is happening in this encounter. Also this stream of research began with the study of the cultural encounter in domestic M&A, moving since the 1990s to studying this encounter in cross-border settings. In parallel, cultural change and its management has been studied, but surprisingly, largely in domestic deals only.

Cultural Dynamics in Domestic M&A

Among the early studies was that of Marks (1982), who found that cultural clashes occur in the merging of domestic firms. Buono et al. (1985) introduced the concept of "culture shock," occurring when two organizational cultures merge. They defined culture shock as the shock when two corporate cultures merge, "affecting the acquired firm members by contributing to changing feelings and discomfort." As culture provides a frame of life for its members, cultural changes are among the most difficult for people to cope with. Buono et al. found that culture shock follows an organizational merger and affects the members by contributing to changing feelings and discomfort. Despite the employees' rational understanding of the need to merge, culture shock impacts their willingness to view the deal in a positive light. These findings were among the first in the study of M&A to point to the fact that the cultural side of mergers warrants attention (Buono et al. 1985; Buono and Bowditch 1989).

The introduction of the concept of acculturation by Nahavandi and Malekzhadeh (1988) was the next notable, conceptual, milestone in this direction. The concept of acculturation, borrowed from cross-cultural psychology (Berry 1983), represents the cultural adaptation process and alternative scenarios in the merging of two organizational cultures. The choice of the acculturative mode depends on both the acquirer and the acquired company. When an acculturative mode accepted by both companies is chosen, less acculturative stress is expected to occur. The acculturative mode will affect the cultures of both companies. Nahavandi and Malekzhadeh's article is significant in that it recognizes different approaches to, and choices in, cultural integration. Cultural integration is thus not a static matter, but can be influenced upon upfront. Further, the concept of acculturative stress is useful for highlighting the emotional distress incurred by the acquired company's members. It is also noted that different sub-units within a company can experience different levels of acculturative stress. Finally, Nahavandi and Malekzhadeh note that even unrelated acquisitions can be made to succeed if the correct acculturative mode is chosen. Just a year later, Buono et al. (1985) defined four modes of integrating cultures in M&A: cultural pluralism, cultural blending, cultural takeover, and cultural resistance. These modes mirror the acculturative modes presented by Nahavandi and Malekzadeh.

These early initiatives, based on either US domestic mergers or conceptual work, have thereafter maintained an almost "unrivalled" position in the literature on M&A, given that few works have since sought to understand the cultural dynamics at stake in domestic deals. A notable step in this direction was the introduction of the stepfamily metaphor (Allred et al. 2005) as a means of understanding the challenge of managing M&A. The two phenomena are argued to share similar characteristics (e.g. culture shock, high levels of stress, role ambiguity), tasks (e.g. establishing new relationships), and issues (e.g. high failure rates, power issues). Based on the stepfamily literature, the authors posit that challenges experienced in times of M&A could be extrapolated from those experienced by stepfamilies. Drawing a parallel, this would mean that M&A would suffer from biological discrimination (i.e. buying firm discrimination), incomplete institutionalization (i.e. leading to misunderstandings), and deficit-comparison (i.e. acquired firms ending up in a disadvantageous position as compared with the buying firm and competitors). In order to sustain high success rates in M&A, the authors suggest that firms (a) acquire similar targets, (b) properly evaluate the target prior to the deal, and (c) ensure the buying firm's full commitment to the venture.

Cultural Dynamics in Cross-Border M&A

If interest in the domestic dimensions of the culture clash following M&A has been relatively scant since the 1980s, this seeming disinterest has been replaced by an emerging interest in the cultural dynamics at stake in cross-border M&A. Authors point to the fact that in cross-border deals, both organizational and national cultures need to be considered.

The first papers to address the cultural encounter in cross-border mergers were by Olie (1990, 1994), who focused on cross-border merger integration, highlighting that both organizational and national cultures meet in cross-border mergers, the latter influencing the former. Olie (1990) found that obstacles in international M&A were related to the way people react as culture-bearers. First, there is resistance to changing working methods and opposition to any alienation from the national character of the environment. Second, there is a perceived threat to one's own position in the company. A third issue concerns nationalism in the countries concerned owing to their historical backgrounds. He argues that the integration success of cross-border mergers will depend on the degree of interaction between the two firms, the degree of integration, and the extent to which the firms value their original cultures. In a later study, Olie (1994) looked at the nation and firm-specific factors influencing cross-border mergers. He found that the degree of compatibility of administrative practices, management styles, organizational structures and cultures, the kind and degree of post-merger consolidation, the extent to which parties value and want to retain their organizational integrity, and the nature of the relationship between the two organizations together contribute to explaining the difficulties encountered in the post-merger integration process in a cross-border merger setting.

Building on the work of Nahavandi and Malekzadeh (1988) in a cross-border setting, Larsson (1993) points out that national cultures create additional barriers to the development of joint corporate cultures in the post-acquisition era. In a similar vein, Malekzadeh and Nahavandi (1998) discuss acculturation in the context of cross-border M&A, where double-layered acculturation (Barkema and Bell 1996), i.e. changes in both national and corporate cultures, occurs. They conclude, however, that the area is in its infancy and requires more research. The work of Quah and Young (2005) on a phased approach to M&A points to the parallel impact of organizational and national cultures in cross-border M&A. Despite these advances, we note a relative scarcity of research on the dual impact of national and organizational cultures on cross-border M&A, notwithstanding the paucity of research considering other levels of culture.

Critical Perspectives

Some authors have adopted critical views on the way that culture is conceptualized and studied in the literature on M&A.

In a conceptual paper, Risberg (1997) argues for an "ambiguity" perspective to cross-cultural acquisitions. She sees that most approaches at present take an "integration" perspective to culture in the post-acquisition era, seeking to merge the acquired firm's culture with the acquiring firm, in so doing, erasing cultural differences altogether. Alternatively, a "differentiation" perspective is adopted, in which case both firms' cultures are allowed to coexist in parallel. Risberg (1997) calls for an "ambiguity" perspective in which both sides' differences and the ambiguities arising therefrom are acknowledged. The acquired firm is not forced culturally into the buying firm's regime, and potential areas of difference and ambiguity are negotiated. Two-way communication emerges as of critical importance.

Vaara (1999) takes a theoretical position and argues that most studies on culture in M&A adopt a realist approach to culture, treating culture as a given that "can be managed." Following the constructionist tradition, according to which culture is seen as the continuous interpretations of its members, Vaara (2000) uncovers the sense-making processes in cross-border mergers. In addition to the traditional cultural sense-making process, he also identifies new processes as regards manipulation of cultural conceptions and suppressed emotional identification with one of the merger sides. This finding suggests that the culture shock experienced by members participating in M&A is possibly more complex than traditional studies have led us to believe. Perhaps a shift toward more interpretative approaches would enable more nuanced perspectives to be highlighted. Since the end of the 1990s, a stream of research has adopted a constructionist approach to cross-border M&A (Gertsen et al. 1998), looking at how cultural differences are constructed through interpretations and sense-making processes of the actors concerned (Vaara 1999, 2000; Söderberg and Vaara 2003), the process of social identity construction (Kleppesto 1993, 1998), and the role of metaphors therein (Vaara et al. 2003).

Based on ethnographic research, Riad (2007) criticizes existing research on culture in M&A for forcing what she terms a "binary opposition" between coherence of cultures on the one hand, and pluralism of cultures on the other hand. Riad finds that this is not an either/or issue; instead, employees can be simultaneously united and divided in their cultural allegiance. Further, a cohesive culture might not exist, but might result from having been socially constructed in the merger process. Riad cautions against the tradition in the M&A literature to categorize cultures into certain types, or focusing on "differences" between cultures. She asks whether cultures and their potential differences could not simply be embraced as such at times of M&A, as they are in multicultural societies.

In synthesis, there would seem to be a need for a more complex view of the cultural encounter taking place in M&A, one that accounts for the ambiguities in the encounter, for the way that culture-carriers make sense and construct cultures, for the possibility that employees maintain plurality in their cultural allegiances, and for cultures also to have positive effects on M&A.

The Dynamics of Cultural Change

A fourth stream has focused on cultural change following M&A. The management of cultural change during post-acquisition integration has been addressed mainly in domestic M&A (Sales and Mirvis 1984; Buono et al. 1985; Buono and Bowditch 1989; Cartwright and Cooper 1992, 1993). Here, work has focused on (1) cultural change strategies, (2) phases of cultural change and tips for managing cultural change, and (3) other matters.

To begin with, different types of cultural integration strategies have been identified, depending on the buying firm's aim with regard to cultural integration and the type of merger or acquisition in question (Buono and Bowditch 1989; Olie 1990; Cartwright and Cooper 1992, 1993; Schweiger et al. 1993; David and Singh 1994; Forstmann 1998). The direction of cultural change has been found to dictate the ease of change, especially if the change is paralleled by increased levels of openness in the practiced organizational culture (Cartwright and Cooper 1992, 1993). Where beliefs are widely shared and strongly held, cultural change is likely to be challenging (Buono and Bowditch 1989).

Cartwright and Cooper (1992) identify approaches to culture change: aggressive, conciliative, corrosive, and indoctrinative. They find that a combinative use of these approaches is fruitful. They provide recommendations for a program for culture change. Such a program would begin with an understanding of both participating cultures. Next, it would proceed to unfreezing these cultures. Further, it would present a positive and realistic view of the future to both organizations. It would ensure the wide-scale involvement of organizational members and adopt a realistic timescale for the integration process. Finally, it would monitor the change process and take corrective action where necessary.

Sales and Mirvis (1984) argue that there are three phases of cultures coming into contact. Managing a culture in transition requires understanding not only the factors influencing acculturation, but also the processes underlying them. First, the existing cultures perceive a threat to their cultures. This phase can best be managed by preparing strategically and emotionally for the change, rehearsing the possible implications, and developing ground rules for cross-cultural contact. Second, there is cross-cultural contact between the two firms. The management of this phase entails managing the processes of polarization, evaluation, and ethnocentrism, as well as the conflicts resulting from cultural differences. Third, acculturation begins. This phase should be accompanied by a conscious scanning of culture and its re-examination.

Buono et al. (1985) unfold the process of culture change and identify the following factors as meaningful ways of influencing integration in M&A: changing the behavior of organizational members, justifying this change, using cultural communication to facilitate the change, hiring and socializing new recruits to speed up the change, and removing deviants. The extent to which cultural change can be achieved has also been questioned (Buono and Bowditch 1989). The importance of attitudes (Napier et al. 1993; Deiser 1994; Morosini 1998) when implementing cultural change has been emphasized. In a review of existing literature, Schraeder and Self (2003) find that training, support, and socialization are means of fostering acculturation in the post-acquisition era.

In her study of organizational culture change following M&A, Bijlsma-Frankema (2001) identifies factors that promote the progress of cultural integration following M&A. The factors identified include the degree of mutual trust between the parties, which is furthered by shared norms, itself enabled by dialogue, even in instances of deviance or conflict resolution. Trust can also be enabled by shared goals. Monitoring the progress of agreed tasks is a means of tracking progress. In this respect, people might be rewarded for right behaviors, for example. In order to decrease employee fears, managers need to explain the need for changes, i.e. change needs to be legitimized in the minds of the employees. In a similar vein, clarity of goals helps reduce employee uncertainties. A culture that promotes psychological safety will allow members on both sides to raise their concerns and propose ideas. Finally, providing feedback on the progress and early successes is critical. Whilst Bijlsma-Frankema notes that many of the aforementioned factors have already been identified in the literature, the same factors were present in all of the successful M&A cases in her study, and likewise absent in the unsuccessful cases.

More recent findings focus on the human reactions to cultural change as well as the practice of cultural change. In this respect, Styhre et al. (2006) point to "cultural anxieties" that are raised in employees' minds in times of cross-border mergers. In other words, cultural changes following cross-border mergers represent an emotionally painful process for organizational members who have to gradually let go of their previous culture, whilst developing an allegiance toward the new one.

In a study of cultural change following a cross-border acquisition in the retail sector in the UK, Pioch (2007) finds that whilst top management sees post-acquisition cultural change from a company-wide integration perspective, the majority of employees experience a daily differentiation of cultures on the shop floor. The former have internalized the new organizational culture at Schein's (1985) level of assumptions, whereas for the majority of employees only surface-level cultural changes are experienced. Moreover, Pioch points to the presence and impact of industrial cultures and notes that in industries that increasingly share global practices, such as the retail sector, an acquisition does not necessarily entail as much change as one might suppose, given that industry-wide, the sector has been globally moving in a similar direction for years.

In conclusion, existing research has highlighted that there are various alternative approaches to cultural change. Cultural change occurs and can be approached in phases. Best practices with regard to enabling cultural change revolve around attitudes conveying trust and safety, communications, dialogue, clarity of goals, and employee rotation.

Synthesis

The stream of research looking at the cultural encounter occurring in M&A has established that culture clashes occur during domestic and cross-border transactions alike. The level of the resulting acculturative stress depends on the acculturative mode chosen and whether this mode is accepted by both organizations. Cultural change can be influenced by participating firms and by the decisions made in the M&A process. Different managerial means can be used to this end. These findings are supported by the more recent constructionist and critical approaches that argue for more fine-tuning, ambiguity, and complexity in the encounter than is presently acknowledged. These findings would seem to suggest that the merger of cultures in M&A is a complex phenomenon, warranting more systematic research. Interestingly, little emphasis has been placed on national culture encounters as of yet, as most of the aforementioned research focuses on the integration of corporate cultures. Figure 16.3 synthesizes this understanding, pointing to the types of cultural encounters taking place in times of M&A. Making a link back to the culture-performance debate, it is possibly owing to this type of complexity that findings on the impact of culture on M&A performance continue to provide mixed results.

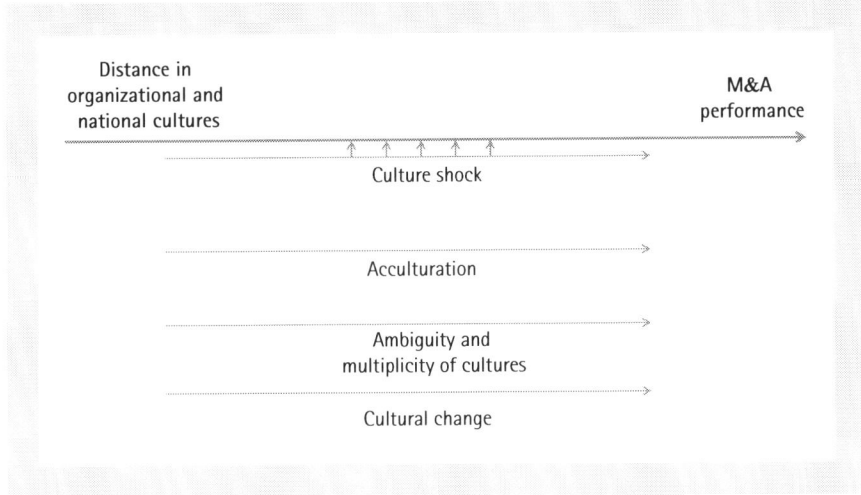

Distance in
organizational and
national cultures

M&A
performance

Culture shock

Acculturation

Ambiguity and
multiplicity of cultures

Cultural change

FIG. 16.3 Overview of the cultural encounters in M&A

National Culture in M&A: Impact and Management

So what is it known about national culture in M&A? Research has looked at how acquired and buying firm behaviors are conditioned by national cultures on the one hand, and how national cultures should be accounted for in times of international M&A on the other hand. We will review findings from both streams next.

National Culture and the Behavior of Buying and Target Firms

Some studies have explicitly focused on the impact of national culture on M&A. These findings confirm that acquirers from different countries tend to adopt different kinds of due diligence (Angwin, 2000) and integration approaches (Dunning 1958; Jaeger 1983; Calori et al. 1994; Lubatkin et al. 1998; Child et al. 2000, 2001; Larsson and Lubatkin 2001; Faulkner et al. 2003; Pitkethly et al. 2003), reflecting their national culture origin. All the while, some constants across acquirers have been found, just as some acquiring nations would not seem to conform to their cultural stereotype when acquiring (see Chapter 17). In this respect, based on a recent study of international firms' acquisitions in Japan, Olcott (2008) points to there being no single approach that characterizes international firms' integration styles in Japan.

In parallel, target firms from different countries have been found to prefer different kinds of integration approaches, in line with their home countries' national cultures (Morosini 1998; Cartwright and Price 2003). Particular emphasis has been placed on the dimensions of uncertainty avoidance (Morosini 1998; Schoenberg 2000), risk orientation (Schoenberg 2000), and individualism vs. collectivism (Morosini 1998). Despite these preferences, it seems that acquisitions in which the target firm has been involved in the integration through informal activities meet greater success than others (Calori et al. 1994; Child et al. 2001; Larsson and Lubatkin 2001). This would seem to suggest that the involvement of acquired firms is a critical success factor in M&A.

Surprisingly little effort has been devoted to studying the reality of national cultures interacting in times of M&A. In this respect, the findings of Barmeyer and Mayrhofer (2008) on the European Aeronautic Defence and Space Company (EADS) tri-party merger bear consideration. They found that intercultural team-working was negatively affected by the French, German, and Spanish participants' differing perceptions and interpretations of what teamwork and cooperation meant. This resulted in misunderstanding as regards how one ought to behave in a team. What is more, Barmeyer and Mayrhofer (2008) identified differences as regards perceptions and interpretations of leadership, especially around the notion of "authority" and what it means across country contexts. The authors conclude that these differences are likely to complicate the process of integration, as members involved in the merger adopt different behavioral strategies to reach their goals. Whilst the strategies are aligned with their respective national cultural backgrounds, their everyday presence makes intercultural work prone to misunderstandings.

Working across National Cultures in M&A

Some studies have taken a step further to understanding how national cultures should be accounted for throughout the international M&A process. It is argued that cultural differences should be managed throughout the process.

Pre-acquisition Target Evaluation

In a study on the impact of organizational fit on post-acquisition performance, Datta (1991) found that organizational fit should be evaluated together with financial evaluation of the deal. Datta defined organizational fit as the differing management styles, reward, and evaluation systems of the acquired and acquiring firms. He found that management styles were especially prone to cause difficulties in all types of acquisitions. Cartwright and Cooper (1993) noted that effective evaluation of the partners' cultural differences and similarities prior to entering the deal and starting integration is an early means of assessing the success potential for the merger.

Integration Strategy

In a study on the human resource implications of M&A, Schweiger et al. (1993) highlight that strategy is critical in guiding the change. Morosini and Singh (1994) studied the management of cultural differences during post-acquisition integration and suggested acquirers adopt a culture-related post-acquisition strategy, coherent with the target country's national culture. They termed this a "national culture compatible strategy." This was deemed especially relevant in cross-border acquisitions, as characteristics influenced by national culture are especially difficult to change. This kind of strategy was seen as a way of ensuring that the aspects of national culture most likely to cause problems would be adequately managed.

Interactive Ties between the Organizations

In their study of the creation of EADS, a tri-party merger between the French Aerospatiale Matra, the German DASA, and the Spanish CASA, Barmeyer and Mayrhofer (2008) describe how shared organization structures, the development of an organizational culture geared toward an "EADS spirit," as well as specific human resource management practices geared toward enhancing team-working and cooperation between members of the formerly separate organizations, along with leadership and career development, were used to further the ties between the formerly disparate organizations.

Integration Attitudes

Tolerance has been found to be key in intercultural management. Napier et al. (1993) looked at how organizational diversity is managed in cross-border mergers from a human resource management perspective. They found that assertive tolerance is a powerful integration tool. Chatterjee et al. (1992) found that a tolerant attitude is a positive factor in ensuring acquisition success; an over-controlled approach should thus be avoided.

Training

Intercultural training has been established as a means of enhancing awareness of cultural differences (Thomas and Inkson 2005). The assumption is that cultural differences can be learnt about, and in so doing, managed or even manipulated (David and Singh 1993). Schweiger and Goulet (2005) tested the effect of deep vs. surface-level cultural learning interventions on acquired firm employees' experiences of being acquired. They argue that the positive experience of an acquisition is not a matter of merging similar cultures, but rather a matter of cultural learning. Consistent with their hypotheses, they find that deep-level cultural learning interventions resulted in enhanced intercultural awareness, understanding, and communication, as well as gearing attitudes toward cooperation and integration, in contrast to units that received no learning interventions, where, as a result, cultural misunderstandings flourished. Despite these positive findings, surface-level cultural interventions did not result in the partner being better accepted. Interestingly, surface-level learning interventions were found to have a limited effect, possibly even reinforcing existing stereotypes.

In a recent study of the European merger that formed the EADS, Barmeyer and Mayrhofer (2008) identified distinct intercultural training practices geared to improving organizational members' intercultural skills. This was particularly salient in the context of this merger, which was formed on the basis of a simultaneous merger of three formerly separate European national organizations (French, German, and Spanish respectively) in the aerospace industry. The intercultural training sessions were part of EADS's management's goal of creating the "Corporate Business Academy" that trained the organization's managers in leadership, change management, business excellence skills, in addition to intercultural management.

Pragmatic Cross-Cultural Skills

Morosini (1998) looked at how cultural differences can be managed in cross-border M&A. He argues that pragmatic cross-cultural skills are required to successfully manage in the international arena. National cultural differences also provide a competitive advantage to the firm, as each national culture introduces new organizational routines into the organization.

Synthesis

In synthesis, we find the following (see Figure 16.4). First, the behaviors of both the buying and acquired parties are dependent on their national culture heritage. Second, differences in the merging partners' national cultures should be included in the management of the acquisition process, starting with evaluation, through strategy, and skills in integration. These insights can be regarded as one answer to the earlier debate

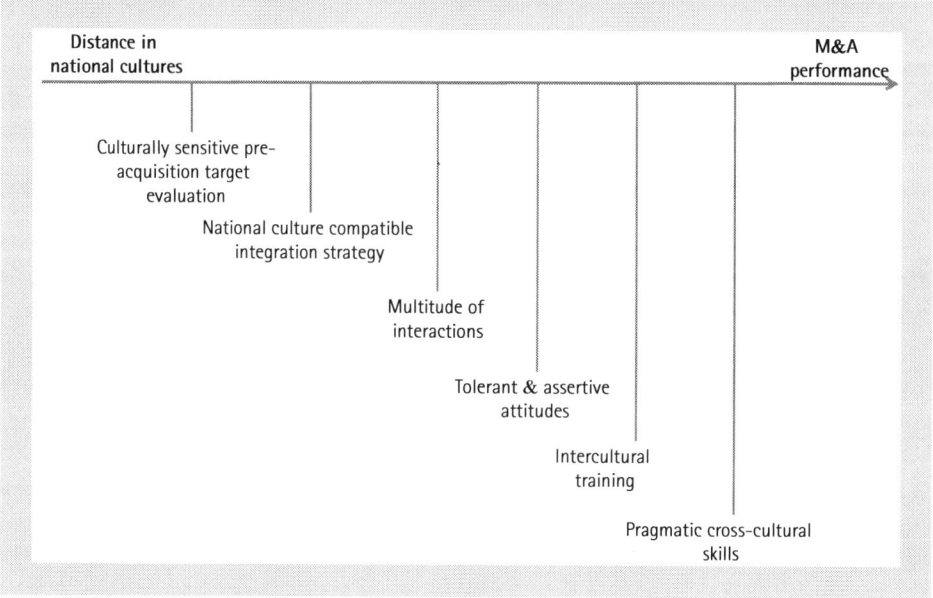

FIG. 16.4 Working across national cultures in M&A

on the culture-performance relationship in that the impact of national cultural distance is likely to be all the more positive if these measures are undertaken.

Conclusions and Future Research Directions

The aim of this chapter has been to provide a review of how the academic literature on M&A has treated the topic of "culture." In the following, we start by providing a critical analysis of the key findings of this stream of research, continuing thereafter with an overview of future gaps to be addressed in order to take work in this promising area further.

First, research on culture in M&A has identified cultural diversity as existing at the subcultural, functional, organizational, and industrial levels of analysis, in addition to regional and national cultures in the case of cross-border deals. As Table 16.1 shows, we find that the concepts of organizational and national culture are predominantly used to conceptualize the cultural challenge at stake in times of domestic and cross-border M&A. Whilst other cultures are mentioned, including professional, regional and industrial cultures, the field has not yet explicitly delved into the complexity of the cultural encounters taking place in M&A. This brings us to a first future research direction: unearthing the real complexity of cultural encounters in times of M&A. What are their performance effects? Which level of culture is salient to manage, in which context, in order to ensure the success of an acquisition? Such questions remain unexplored as yet.

Second, as Table 16.1 points out, we find that a large portion of research on the cultural issue at stake in M&A is ontologically geared toward realism and an objective

Table 16.1 Synthesis of the levels of analysis in the study of the cultural challenge in M&A

Theme studied	The culture-performance relationship in M&A	Cultural dynamics in times of M&A	Cultural change in M&A	Impact and management of national cultures
Level of analysis	Organizational culture	Organizational culture	Organizational culture	
	National culture			National culture
	Organizational and national culture	Organizational and national culture		
Research paradigm	Realist	Realist & Interpretive	Realist	Realist

epistemology. Interpretive studies have emerged, but remain rare. Also, critical voices are rare. This state of affairs is noticeable in that M&A literature tends to treat "culture" unquestioningly as a monolith that an organization "has," instead of seeing culture as something the organization "is," "lives," "breathes," and is continually creating. In this respect, there is a role for more fine-grained, interpretive, and critical studies on culture in M&A.

Third, research into the culture-performance relationship paints an increasingly nuanced, yet continuously mixed, picture of the ways in which cultural differences, be they at organizational and/or at national levels, impact the performance of M&A. Several questions remain unanswered. For one, how should M&A performance be measured against culture? Should performance be measured in terms of financial or non-financial metrics; over which time frame following the deal? For another, who are the respondents, and how does the choice of buying or target firm respondents affect the results? Are there industry effects, or possibly country effects?

Moreover, the impact of cultural differences would not seem to occur in isolation, but rather in conjunction with other factors, including acculturation mode, degree of integration, and behavioral reactions following the deal (stress, commitment, conflict, learning, etc.). The assumption that culture can be isolated and treated separately appears simplistic. All the while, national culture differences would seem to impact the progress of integration itself, whilst integration and socialization can help reduce distance in national cultures. What emerges is a view of national cultural differences as deeply embedded in the integration "fabrique" at times of M&A. Therefore, it might be interesting to introduce new concepts, such as the coevolution of culture and integration, to get a better understanding of this "fabrique." What occurs in the interactions between the two sides during M&A, and how is culture present vs. absent from these interactions?

Fourth, looking at the way in which dimensions of differences in organizational and national cultural distance are conceptualized, we find rather simplistic views. As regards national culture, the field's weakness, as with other cross-border studies in the international management and strategy literatures, is its overreliance on existing frameworks of national culture, such as Hofstede's (1980) or House et al.'s (2004). The field takes the existence of national cultures and the particular dimensions of Hofstede or House et al. for granted (for a critique, see McSweeney 2002). The same holds for the way that organizational culture is conceptualized: as differences in management team culture. We argue that research *on* the national and organizational culture dimensions at work in times of domestic and cross-border M&A is needed.

Fifth, in contrast to the large amount of work on the culture-performance relationship, we find some work, though it is relatively meager, on understanding the cultural dynamics that unfold following M&A. Intriguingly, much of this work was done in the 1980s and early 1990s by Buono and colleagues, as well as Cartwright and Cooper. Thereafter, work on the cultural encounter in domestic M&A has been less vocal. This begs the question: has everything been found? Where are the bold ethnographers studying mergers of the 21st century? Likewise, whereas some studies on cross-border cultural encounters in times of cross-border M&A exist, this stream remains meager. There are opportunities to further our understanding of M&A through more in-depth, qualitative, ethnographic studies, large-scale interview studies, action research, or longitudinal, mixed methods studies. Alarmingly, research on cultural change following acquisitions exists largely for domestic, less for cross-border, deals. As a result, our understanding of the fine-tuned ways in which organizational and national cultures, intertwined, come to affect M&A, remains scarce. Further, work on cultural integration has tended to view the latter in isolation from other changes that occur following M&A, be it as regards e.g. integration or identification.

Our literature review also encourages us to highlight three neglected questions, or gaps, in our current understanding of the cultural issues at stake in times of M&A.

Intriguingly, we find that whilst some research focuses explicitly on mergers or on acquisitions, the field of cultural encounters in M&A tends to treat these two phenomena as equivalent, as though findings from one could be transferred to the other. Culturally speaking, the merger of two organizations does present a different challenge from that of acquiring another organization. What are the differences in the cultural encounter between these phenomena? Would it be time to unveil their "cultural" differences instead of assuming similarity?

Another gap apparent in M&A research relates to the fact that researchers generally consider the cultural encounter as a "uniform" issue for organizations. It is often assumed that the cultural reactions of employees, as well as integration processes, are uniform across business units, departments, services, countries, etc. We do not know much about this uniformity, but there is a chance it is not true. We concluded earlier that research has identified the embeddedness of cultural differences within the integration "fabrique." Consequently, cultural issues and their management are likely to vary according to the degree of integration in each unit. More exploration in this direction is worthwhile; for example, at a sub-organizational level, what are the linkages between culture and performance?

Finally, as with other domains in the study of M&A, we find that work on the cultural challenge at stake is largely restricted to a within-stream debate. Whereas practitioners involved in making M&A work need to deal simultaneously with financial, strategic, cultural, managerial issues, academics have the luxury of choice: we can decide to focus on a particular lens. In so doing, however, we risk losing overall focus. As regards future research, it would seem of significance that work on the cultural side of M&A be linked to findings from other disciplines and other M&A research streams, e.g. integration, strategy, identity, or performance in M&A. Only then will we have moved toward a more holistic view of M&A, and the role of culture therein.

Table 16.A1 Comparative overview of research on the culture–performance relationship in M&A*

Article details	Number of acquisitions	Bf country	Af country	Sector	Time period	Respondent	Operationalization of organizational culture	Operationalization of national culture	Non-financial performance measures	Time frame of performance	Accounting measure	Stock measure
Organizational culture and M&A performance												
Datta (1991)	173 acquisitions	US	US	Manufacturing	1980–1984	One senior Bf executive	• Perceived differences in top management • Perceived differences in management styles • Perceived differences in reward and evaluation systems	--	• Post-acquisition integration	Min. two years after deal	Perceptions of: • ROI • EPS • Cash flow • Sales growth	Perceptions of: • Stock price
Chatterjee et al. (1992)	30 related mergers	US	US	Across industries	1985–1987	One to five senior Af executives	• Perceived differences in top management team management styles	--	• Tolerance of multicultural-ism	7 and 16 day pre/post-deal windows	--	• Stock price
Weber (1996)	73 related mergers	US	US	Manufacturing & banking	1985–1987	One to five senior Af executives	• Perceived differences in top management team management styles	--	• Autonomy removal • Commitment • Effectiveness of integration	Four years after deal	ROA	--
Krishnan et al. (1997)	147 acquisitions	US	US	Across industries	1986–1988	Bf and Af top management team responses.		--	--	Three years after deal	ROA	--

National culture and M&A performance

Study	Sample	Acquirer	Target	Industry	Years	Respondent		Cultural measure	Integration variables	Time frame	Performance measure	
Morosini et al. (1998)	52 cross-border acquisitions in Italy	Europe & US	Italy	Across industries	1987–1992	Bf or Af respondent based in Italy	--	• Hofstede (1980) cultural dimensions • Kogut & Singh (1988) cultural distance index	--	Two years after deal	Sales growth	--
Brock (2005)	103 international related acquisitions	North America, Europe, Asia	New Zealand, Australia	Across industries	NA	Af respondent	--	• Hofstede (1980) cultural dimensions: individualism, power distance	• Resource sharing • Integration • Synergy (expectations met)	--	--	--
Slangen (2006)	102 international acquisitions	Dutch	Across continents (30 countries)	Across industries	1995–2001	Af respondent	--	Kogut & Singh (1988) cultural distance index based on Hofstede's (1980) dimensions	• Integration (autonomy removal)	Two years after deal	Perceptions of: sales level, market share, profit level, overall performance	--
Reus & Lamont (2009)	118 international acquisitions	US	North America, Europe, Asia, Africa, Central & South America	Across industries	1998–2000	Bf managers	--	Kogut & Singh (1988) cultural distance index GLOBE project's dimensions	• Understandability • Communication • Employee retention	• Three to five years following the deal • 240–40 day window for stock measure	Perceptions of: profitability, market share, sales volume, new product development	Cumulative abnormal returns (for subsample)

(Continued)

Table 16.A1 Continued

Article details	Number of acquisitions	Bf country	Af country	Sector	Time period	Respondent	Operationalization of organizational culture	Operationalization of national culture	Non-financial performance measures	Time frame of performance	Accounting measure	Stock measure
Chakrabarti et al. (2009)	800	North America, Europe, Asia, South Africa	North America, Europe, Asia	Across industries	1991–1994	--	--	• Hofstede (1980) cultural dimensions • Language • Religion • Legal origin		30–36 months after deal	--	Excess return over market
Gubbi et al. (2010)	425 acquisitions	India	North America, Europe, Asia, South Africa, Middle-East	Across industries	2000–2007	--	--	• Developed market acquisition • Economic distance • Institutional distance	• 11 day window • Past three years' net profit margins	--		Cumulative abnormal returns

Organizational and national culture and M&A performance

Article details	Number of acquisitions	Bf country	Af country	Sector	Time period	Respondent	Operationalization of organizational culture	Operationalization of national culture	Non-financial performance measures	Time frame of performance	Accounting measure	Stock measure
Weber et al. (1996)	52 mergers	North America, Europe	US	Across industries	1985–1987	On average seven Af managers	Degree of similarity between management teams	Hofstede (1980) cultural dimensions	• Autonomy removal • Stress • Attitudes toward cooperation & new organization • Commitment • Cooperation	--	--	--
Véry et al. (1996)	106 domestic and international mergers	France, UK, US	France, UK	Across industries	1987–1989	One to several Af managers	Perceived cultural compatibility using Denison (1990), Chatterjee et al. (1992)	Perceived cultural compatibility using Hofstede (1980) cultural dimensions, Bond (1987)	• Acculturative stress	One to three years after the deal	Perceptions of: Earnings, sales, market share	--

Study	Sample	Countries	Industries	Period	Respondents	Perceived cultural compatibility using Denison (1990), Chatterjee et al. (1992)	Perceived cultural compatibility using Hofstede (1980) cultural dimensions, Bond (1987)	Moderators	Timing	Outcomes
Very et al. (1997)	106 domestic and international mergers	France, UK, US	France, UK	1987–1989	One to several Af managers	NA	NA	• Relative standing • Removal of autonomy	One to three years after the deal	Perceptions of: Earnings, sales, market share
Larsson and Risberg (1998)	45 domestic M&A 17 international M&A	Domestic deals in US, Sweden, UK and Finland International deals by Swedish, North-American and European firms	Variety of countries, not specified	Across industries	1960–1989	NA	NA	• Level of acculturation • Employee resistance		synergy realization
Björkman et al. 2007	Conceptual							• Social integration • Potential absorptive capacity • Capability complementarity • Use of social integration mechanisms • Degree of operational integration		Post-acquisition capability transfer

(Continued)

Table 16.A1 Continued

Article details	Number of acquisitions	Bf country	Af country	Sector	Time period	Respondent	Operationalization of organizational culture	Operationalization of national culture	Non-financial performance measures	Time frame of performance	Accounting measure	Stock measure
Sarala (2010)	118 acquisitions	Finland	North America, Europe, South America, Asia	Across industries	2001–2004	One to multiple responses from Af & Bf managers	Perceptions of: • cultural differences across key organizational functions • cultural differences in key decision makers' values	National culture distance using Kogut and Singh (1988), GLOBE project scores (House et al., 2004)	• Partner attractiveness in Af & Bf • Bf & Af multiculturism • Bf & Af organizational culture preservation	One to three years after the deal	Post-acquisition conflict	--
Stahl and Voigt (2008)	10,710 acquisitions	Worldwide	Worldwide	Across industries	Meta-analysis of existing studies		Top management team compatibility	• Kogut & Singh (1988) cultural distance index • Hofstede (1980) cultural dimensions	• Sociocultural integration outcomes	• One to 30 day event windows for short-term effect • Over 120 day event windows for long-term effect	Synergy realization: sales growth, ROA	Stock market reactions: cumulative abnormal returns (CAR)
Sarala and Vaara (2010)	133 acquisitions	Finland	North America, Europe, South America, Asia	Across industries	1993–1996 1997–2000 2001–2004	1–5 responses from Af & Bf managers	Perceptions of: • cultural differences across key organizational functions • differences in company values • differences in values of key decision makers Cultural change in: • organizational functions • company values • values of key decision makers A shared new culture, identity, and practices created post-deal	GLOBE project scores (House et al., 2004)		• One to three years after the deal	Knowledge transfer	

Notes: Af refers to the acquired or target firm; Bf refers to the buying or acquiring firm.

References

Allred, B. B., Boal, K. B., & Holstein, W. K. (2005). "Corporations as Stepfamilies: A New Metaphor for Explaining the Fate of Merged and Acquired Companies." *Academy of Management Executive*, 19/3: 23–37.

Alvesson, M. (2002). *Understanding Organisational Culture*. London: Sage.

Angwin, D. (2000). "Mergers and Acquisitions across European Borders: National Perspectives on Pre-acquisition Due Diligence and the Use of Professional Advisers." *Journal of World Business*, 36/1: 32–57.

Ashkenas, R. N., DeMonaco, L. J., & Francis, S. C. (1998). "Making the Deal Real: How GE Capital Integrates Acquisitions." *Harvard Business Review*, 76/1: 165–78.

Barkema, H. G., & Bell, H. J. (1996). "Foreign Entry, Cultural Barriers, and Learning." *Strategic Management Journal*, 17: 151–66.

Barmeyer, C., & Mayrhofer, U. (2008). "The Contribution of Intercultural Management to the Success of International Mergers and Acquisitions: An Analysis of the EADS Group." *International Business Review*, 17/1: 28–38.

Bauman, Z., & May, T. (2001). *Thinking Sociologically* (2nd ed.). Oxford: Blackwell.

Berry, J. W. (1983). "Acculturation: A Comparative Analysis of Alternative Forms," in R. Samuda & S. Woods (eds.), *Perspectives in Immigrant and Minority Education*. New York: University Press of America, 65–78.

Bijlsma-Frankema, K. (2001). "On Managing Cultural Integration and Cultural Change Processes in Mergers and Acquisitions." *Journal of European Industrial Training*, 25: 192–207.

Birkinshaw, J., Bresman, H., & Håkansson, L. (2000). "Managing the Post-acquisition Integration Process: How the Human Integration and Task Integration Processes Interact to Foster Value Creation." *Journal of Management Studies*, 37/3: 395–425.

Björkman, I., Stahl, G. K., & Vaara, E. (2007). "Cultural Differences and Capability Transfer in Cross-Border Acquisitions: The Mediating Roles of Capability Complementarity, Absorptive Capacity, and Social Integration." *Journal of International Business Studies*, 38: 658–72.

Bond, M. (1987). "Chinese Values and the Search for Culture-Free Dimensions of Culture." *Journal of Cross-Cultural Psychology*, 18/2: 143–64.

Brock, D. (2005). "Multinational Acquisition Integration: The Role of National Culture in Creating Synergies." *International Business Review*, 14/3: 269–88.

Buono, A. F., & Bowditch, J. L. (1989). *The Human Side of Mergers and Acquisitions: Managing Collisions between People, Cultures and Organizations*. London: Jossey-Bass Inc.

—— —— & Lewis, J. W. (1985). "When Cultures Collide: The Anatomy of a Merger." *Human Relations*, 38/5: 477–500.

Burnes, B. (2009). *Managing Change*. Harlow, UK: Prentice Hall.

Calori, R., Lubatkin, M., & Véry, P. (1994). "Control Mechanisms in Cross-Border Acquisitions: An International Comparison." *Organization Studies*, 15/3: 361–79.

Cartwright, S. (1998). "International Mergers and Acquisitions: The Issues and Challenges," in M. Gertsen, A.-M. Söderberg, & J. E. Torp (eds.), *Cultural Dimensions of International Mergers and Acquisitions*. Berlin: De Gruyter, 5–16.

—— & Cooper, C. L. (1990). "The Impact of Mergers and Acquisitions on People at Work: Existing Research and Issues." *British Journal of Management*, 1: 65–76.

—— —— (1992). *Managing Mergers, Acquisitions and Strategic Alliances: Integrating People and Cultures*. Oxford: Butterworth-Heinemann.

Cartwright, S. & Cooper, C. L. (1993). "The Role of Culture Compatibility in Successful Organizational Marriage." *Academy of Management Executive*, 7: 2: 57–70.

——— & Price, F. (2003). "Managerial Preferences in International Merger and Acquisition Partners Revisited: How Much are They Influenced?," in C. Cooper & A. Gregory (eds.), *Advances in Mergers and Acquisitions*, vol. 1. Amsterdam: JAI Press, 81–95.

Chakrabarti, R., Gupta-Mukherjee, S., & Jayaraman, N. (2009). "Mars-Venus Marriages: Culture and Cross-Border M&A." *Journal of International Business Studies*, 40: 216–36.

Chatman, A. J., & Jehn, A. K. (1994). "Assessing the Relationship between Industry Characteristics and Organisational Culture: How Different Can You Be?" *Academy of Management Journal*, 37/3: 522–53.

Chatterjee, S., Lubatkin, M. H., Schweiger, D. M., & Weber, Y. (1992). "Cultural Differences and Shareholder Value in Related Mergers: Linking Equity and Human Capital." *Strategic Management Journal*, 13: 319–34.

Child, J., Faulkner, D., & Pitkethly, R. (2000). "Foreign Direct Investment in the UK 1985–1994: The Impact on Domestic Management Practice." *Journal of Management Studies*, 37/1: 141–67.

——— ——— ——— (2001). *The Management of International Acquisitions*. Oxford: Oxford University Press.

Cooke, F. L. (2006). "Acquisitions of Chinese State-Owned Enterprises by Multinational Corporations: Driving Forces, Barriers and Implications for HRM." *British Journal of Management*, 17: S105–S121.

Cuche, D. (2001). *La Notion de Culture dans les Sciences Sociales*. Paris: La Découverte.

Datta, D. K. (1991). "Organizational Fit and Acquisition Performance: Effects of Post-acquisition Integration." *Strategic Management Journal*, 12: 281–97.

David, K., & Singh, H. (1993). "Acquisition Regimes: Managing Cultural Risk and Relative Deprivation in Corporate Acquisitions," in D. E. Hussey (ed.), *International Review of Strategic Management*, 4. New York: Wiley, 227–76.

——— ——— (1994). "Sources of Acquisition Cultural Risk," in G. Von Krogh, A. Siknatra, & H. Singh (eds.), *The Management of Corporate Acquisitions*. Basingstoke: Macmillan, 251–92.

Deal, T. E., & Kennedy, A. A. (1982). *The Rites and Rituals of Corporate Life*. Reading, MA: Addison-Wesley.

Deiser, R. (1994). "Post-acquisition Management: A Process of Strategic and Organisational Learning," in G. Von Krogh, A. Siknatra, & H. Singh (eds.), *The Management of Corporate Acquisitions*. London: The Macmillan Press, 359–90.

Deng, P. (2009). "Why do Chinese Firms Tend to Acquire Strategic Assets in International Expansion?" *Journal of World Business*, 44: 74–84.

Denison, D. (1990). *Corporate Culture and Organizational Effectiveness*. New York: Free Press.

Dunning, J. H. (1958). *American Investment in British Manufacturing Industry*. London: Allen & Unwin.

Faulkner, D., Child, J., & Pitkethly, R. (2003). "Organisational Change Processes in International Acquisitions," in C. Cooper & A. Gregory (eds.), *Advances in Mergers and Acquisitions*, vol. 1. Amsterdam: JAI Press, 59–80.

Fombrun, C. (1983). "Corporate Culture, Environment and Strategy." *Human Resource Management*, 22/1; 139–52.

Forstmann, S. (1998). "Managing Cultural Differences in Cross-Cultural Mergers and Acquisitions," in M. Gertsen, A-M. Söderberg, & J. E. Torp (eds.), *Cultural Dimensions of International Mergers and Acquisitions*. Berlin: De Gruyter, 57–84.

Franck, G. (1990). "Mergers and Acquisitions: Competitive Advantage and Cultural Fit." *European Management Journal*, 8/1: 40–3.

Frank, R. H. (1985). *Choosing the Right Pond: Human Behaviour and the Quest for Status*. New York: Oxford University Press.

Gertsen, M. C., Soderberg, A.-M., & Torp, J. E. (1998). *Cultural Dimensions of International Mergers and Acquisitions*. Berlin: De Gruyter.

Gubbi, S. R., Aulakh, P. S., Ray, S., Sarkar M. B., & Chittoor, R. (2010). "Do International Acquisitions by Emerging-Economy Firms Create Shareholder Value? The Case of Indian Firms." *Journal of International Business Studies*, 41: 397–418.

Handy, C. (1999). *Understanding Organizations* (4th ed.). London: Penguin.

Haspeslagh, P. C., & Jemison, D. B. (1991). *Managing Acquisitions: Creating Value through Corporate Renewal*. New York: The Free Press.

Hay Group (2007). "Dangerous Liaisons: Hay Group Finds Most European Mergers Fail to Deliver." *Business Wire*, March 26.

Hofstede, G. (1980). *Culture's Consequences: International Differences in Work-Related Values*. Beverly Hills, CA: Sage Publications.

—— (2001). *Culture's Consequences: Comparing Values, Behaviors, Institutions and Organizations across Nations*. Thousand Oaks, CA: Sage Publications.

House, R. J., Hanges, P. J., Javidan, M., Dorfman, P. W., & Gupta, V. (2004). *Culture, Leadership, and Organizations: The GLOBE Study of 62 Societies*. Thousand Oaks, CA: Sage Publications.

Jaeger, A. M. (1983). "The Transfer of Organizational Culture Overseas: An Approach to Control in the Multinational Corporation." *Journal of International Business Studies*, 14/2: 91–114.

Jensen, M. C., & Ruback, R. S. (1983). "The Market for Corporate Control." *Journal of Financial Economics*, 11/1–4: 5–50.

Kleppesto, S. (1993). *Social Identitet vid Uppköp och Fusioner*. Lund: Lund University.

—— (1998). "A Quest for Social Identity: The Pragmatics of Communication in Mergers and Acquisitions," in M. Gertsen, A.-M. Söderberg & J. E. Torp (eds.), *Cultural Dimensions of International Mergers and Acquisitions*. Berlin: De Gruyter, 147–66.

Kogut, B., & Singh, H. (1988). "The Effect of Culture on the Choice of Entry Mode." *Journal of International Business Studies*, 19/3: 411–32.

Krishnan, H. A., Miller, A., & Judge, W. Q. (1997). "Diversification and Top Management Team Complementarity: Is Performance Improved by Merging Similar or Dissimilar Teams?" *Strategic Management Journal*, 18/5: 361–74.

Larsson, R. (1993). "Barriers to Acculturation in Mergers and Acquisitions: Strategic Human Resource Implications." *Journal of European Business Education*, 2/2: 1–18.

—— & Finkelstein, S. (1999). "Integrating Strategic, Organizational, and Human Resource Perspectives on Mergers and Acquisitions: A Case Survey of Synergy Realization." *Organization Science*, 10/1: 1–26.

—— & Lubatkin, M. (2001). "Achieving Acculturation in Mergers and Acquisitions: An International Case Study." *Human Relations*, 54/12: 1573–607.

—— & Risberg, A. (1998). "Cultural Awareness and National versus Corporate Barriers to Acculturation," in M. Gertsen, A.-M. Söderberg & J. E. Torp (eds.), *Cultural Dimensions of International Mergers and Acquisitions*. Berlin: De Gruyter, 39–56.

Lubatkin, M., Calori, R., Véry, P., & Veiga, J. (1998). "Managing Mergers across Borders: A Two-Nation Exploration of a Nationally Bound Administrative Heritage." *Organization Science*, 9/6: 670–84.

Malekzadeh, A. R., & Nahavandi, A. (1998). "Leadership and Culture in Transnational Strategic Alliances," in M. C. Gertsen, A.-M. Söderberg & J. E. Torp (eds.), *Cultural Dimensions of International Mergers and Acquisitions*. Berlin: De Gruyter, 111–28.

Marks, M. L. (1982). "Merging Human Resources: A Review of the Literature." *Mergers and Acquisitions*, 16, Summer: 38–44.

Martin, J. (1992). *Cultures in Organizations: Three Perspectives*. New York: Oxford University Press.

McSweeney, B. (2002). "Hofstede's Model of National Cultural Differences and their Consequences: A Triumph of Faith—A Failure of Analysis." *Human Relations*, 55/1: 89–118.

——(2009). "Dynamic Diversity: Variety and Variation Within Countries." *Organization Studies*, 30/09: 933–57.

Merton, R. K. (1968). *Social Theory and Social Structure*. New York: Free Press.

Morosini, P. (1998). *Managing Cultural Differences: Effective Strategy and Execution Across Cultures in Global Corporate Alliances*. Oxford: Pergamon.

——Shane, S., & Singh, H. (1998). "National Cultural Distance and Cross-Border Acquisition Performance." *Journal of International Business Studies*, 19/1: 137–58.

——& Singh, H. (1994). "Post-Cross-Border Acquisitions: Implementing National Culture-Compatible Strategies to Improve Performance." *European Management Journal*, 4: 390–400.

Nahavandi, A, & Malekzadeh, A. R. (1988). "Acculturation in Mergers and Acquisitions." *Academy of Management Review*, 13/1: 79–90.

Napier, N. K. (1989). "Mergers and Acquisitions, Human Resource Issues and Outcomes: A Review and Suggested Typology." *Journal of Management Studies*, 26/3: 271–89.

——Schweiger, D. M., & Kosglow, J. J. (1993). "Managing Organizational Diversity: Observations from Cross-Border Acquisitions." *Human Resource Management*, 32/4: 505–23.

Olcott, G. (2008). "The Politics of Institutionalization: The Impact of Foreign Ownership and Control on Japanese Organizations." *International Journal of Human Resource Management*, 19/9: 1569–87.

Olie, R. (1990). "Culture and Integration Problems in International Mergers and Acquisitions." *European Management Journal*, 8/2: 206–15.

——(1994). "Shades of Culture and Institutions in International Mergers." *Organization Studies*, 15/3: 381–405.

Phillips, E. M. (1994). "Industry Mindsets: Exploring the Cultures of Two Macro-organizational Settings." *Organization Science*, 5/3: 384–403.

Pioch, E. (2007). "'Business as Usual?' Retail Employee Perceptions of Organizational Life Following Cross-Border Acquisition." *International Journal of Human Resource Management*, 18/2: 209–31.

Pitkethly, R., Faulkner, D., & Child, J. (2003). "Integrating Acquisitions," in C. Cooper & A. Gregory (eds.), *Advances in Mergers and Acquisitions*, vol. 1. Amsterdam: JAI Press, 27–58.

Quah, P., & Young, S. (2005). "Post-acquisition Management: A Phases Approach for Cross-Border M&A." *European Management Journal*, 23/1: 65–75.

Raelin, J. A. (1986). *The Clash of Cultures*. Boston, MA: Harvard Business School Press.

Reus, T. H., & Lamont, B. T. (2009). "The Double-Edged Sword of Cultural Distance in International Acquisitions." *Journal of International Business Studies*, 40: 1298–316.

Reynolds, P. D. (1986). "Organisational Culture as Related to Industry, Position and Performance: A Preliminary Report." *Journal of Management Studies*, 23/3: 334–558.

Riad, S. (2005). "The Power of 'Organizational Culture' as a Discursive Formation in Merger Integration." *Organization Studies*, 26/10: 1529–54.

——(2007). "Of Mergers and Cultures: 'What Happened to Shared Values and Joint Assumptions?" *Journal of Organizational Change Management*, 20/1: 26–43.

Risberg, A. (1997). "Ambiguity and Communication in Cross-Cultural Acquisitions: Towards A Conceptual Framework." *Leadership and Organization Development Journal*, 18/5: 257–66.

Ritzer, G. (2000). *Sociological Theory* (5th ed). Singapore: McGraw-Hill.

Sackmann, S. A. (1997). *Cultural Complexity in Organizations: Inherent Contrasts and Contradictions*. London: Sage.

Sales, A. L., & Mirvis, P. H. (1984). "When Cultures Collide: Issues in Acquisitions," in J. Kimberley & R. E. Quinn (eds.), *New Futures: The Challenges of Managing Corporate Transitions*. Homewood, IL: Dow Jones-Irvin, 107–33.

Sarala, R. (2010). "The Impact of Cultural Differences and Acculturation Factors on Post-acquisition Conflict." *Scandinavian Journal of Management*, 26/1: 38–56.

——& Vaara, E. (2010). "Cultural Differences, Convergence, and Crossvergence as Explanations of Knowledge Transfer in International Acquisitions." *Journal of International Business Studies*, 41: 1365–90.

Schein, E. (1985). *Organizational Culture and Leadership: A Dynamic View*. London: Jossey-Bass.

Schoenberg, R. (2000). "The Influence of Cultural Compatibility within Cross-Border Acquisitions," in C. Cooper & A. Gregory (eds.), *Advances in Mergers and Acquisitions*, vol. 1. Amsterdam: JAI Press, 43–60.

Schraeder, M., & Self, R. D. (2003). "Enhancing the Success of Mergers and Acquisitions: An Organizational Culture Perspective." *Management Decision*, 41/5: 511–22.

Schweiger, D. M., Csiszar, E. N., & Napier, N. K. (1993). "Implementing International Mergers and Acquisitions." *Human Resource Planning*, 16/1: 53–70.

——& Goulet, P. K. (2000). "Integrating Mergers and Acquisitions: An International Research Review," in C. Cooper & A. Gregory (eds.), *Advances in Mergers and Acquisitions*, vol. 1. Amsterdam: JAI Press, 61–91.

————(2005). "Facilitating Acquisition Integration through Deep-Level Cultural Learning Interventions: A Longitudinal Field Experiment." *Organization Studies*, 26/10: 1477–99.

——& Walsh, J. P. (1990). "Mergers and Acquisitions: An Interdisciplinary View," in B. B. Shaw & J. E. Beck (eds.), *Research in Personnel and Human Resources Management*, vol. 8. Greenwich, CT: JAI Press, 41–107.

Slangen, A. (2006). "National Cultural Distance and Initial Foreign Acquisition Performance: The Moderating Effect of Integration." *Journal of World Business*, 41: 161–70.

Söderberg, A-M., & Vaara, E. (2003). *Merging across Borders*. Copenhagen: Copenhagen Business School Press.

Stahl, G. K., & Voigt, A. (2008). "Do Cultural Differences Matter in Mergers and Acquisitions? A Tentative Model and Examination." *Organization Science*, 19/1: 160–76.

Styhre, A., Börjesson, S., & Wickenberg, J. (2006). "Managed by the Other: Cultural Anxieties in two Anglo-Americanized Swedish Firms." *International Journal of Human Resource Management*, 17/7: 1293–306.

Tajfel, H., & Turner, J. (1986). "The Social Identity Theory of Intergroup Behavior," in S. Worchel & W. G. Austin (eds.), *Psychology of Intergroup Relations* (2nd ed.). Chicago: Nelson, 7–24.

Tannenbaum, A. S. (1973). *Social Psychology of the Work Organisation*. London: Tavistock.

Teerikangas, S. (2006). "Silent Forces in Cross-Border Acquisitions: An Integrative Perspective on Post-acquisition Integration." Espoo: Helsinki University of Technology, Department of Industrial Engineering and Management, Institute of Strategy, Doctoral Dissertation Series, 1/2006. Available online.

—— & Véry, P. (2006). "The Culture-Performance Relationship in M&A: from Yes/No to How." *British Journal of Management*, 17/S1: 31–48.

Teerikangas, S. (2007). "A Comparative Overview of the Impact of Cultural Diversity on Inter-organizational Encounters," in C. Cooper & S. Finkelstein. (eds.), *Advances in Mergers and Acquisitions*, vol. 6. Amsterdam: JAI Press, 37–76.

Thomas, D. C., & Inkson, K. (2005). "Cultivating your Cultural Intelligence." *Security Management*, 48/8: 30–2.

Trice, H. M. (1993). *Occupational Subcultures in the Workplace*. Ithaca, NY: ILR Press.

—— & Beyer, J. M. (1993). *The Cultures of Work Organizations*. New York: Prentice Hall.

Turner, B. (1971). *Exploring the Industrial Subculture*. Basingstoke: Macmillan.

Vaara, E. (1999). "Cultural Differences and Post-Merger Problems: Misconceptions and Cognitive Simplifications." *Organisasjonsstudier*, 1/2: 59–88.

—— (2000). "Constructions of Cultural Differences in Post-merger Change Processes: A Sense-Making Perspective on Finnish-Swedish cases." *Management*, 3/3: 81–110.

—— Tienari, J., & Säntti, R. (2003). "The International Match: Metaphors as Vehicles of Social Identity Building in Cross-Border Mergers." *Human Relations*, 56/4: 419–51.

Van den Steen, E. (2010). "Culture Clash: The Costs and Benefits of Homogeneity." *Management Science*, 56/10: 1718–38.

Van Maanen, J., & Barley, S. (1984). "Occupational Communities: Culture and Control in Organizations," in B. M. Staw & L. L. Cummings, *Research in Organizational Behavior*, vol. 6. Greenwich, CT: JAI Press.

Véry, P., Lubatkin, M., & Calori, R. (1996). "A Cross-National Assessment of Acculturative Stress in Recent European Mergers." *International Studies of Management and Organization*, 26/1: 59–86.

—— —— —— & Veiga, J. (1997). "Relative Standing and the Performance of Recently Acquired European Firms." *Strategic Management Journal*, 18/8: 593–614.

Weber, R. A., & Camerer, C. F. (2003). "Cultural Conflict and Merger Failure: An Experimental Approach." *Management Science*, 49/4: 400–15.

Weber, Y. (1996). "Corporate Cultural Fit and Performance in Mergers and Acquisitions." *Human Relations*, 49/9: 1181–202.

—— Shenkar, O., & Raveh, A. (1996). "National and Corporate Cultural Fit in Mergers/Acquisitions: An Exploratory Study." *Management Science*, 42/8: 1215–27.

CHAPTER 17

COUNTRY CULTURAL DIFFERENCES IN ACQUISITION MANAGEMENT[1]

DAVID FAULKNER, ROBERT PITKETHLY,
AND JOHN CHILD

INTRODUCTION

There has been growing foreign direct investment (FDI) into the UK in recent years, particularly from the United States, Japan, Germany, and France, a dominant proportion of it through merger and acquisition (M&A). In fact, the UK has been the most popular European country for foreign investors and acquirers (KPMG 1997). M&A activity of course raises the potential problems associated with corporate cultural interaction. For long, national cultures were thought to be of little relevance in determining "best practice" in management (Hickson et al. 1974), or merely one contingency to which adjustment had to be made (Child 1981). More recent academic literature suggests that companies from each of the major investing countries tend to use different approaches to management (Hampden-Turner and Trompenaars 1993; Whitley 1992). Thus acquisitions of UK companies offer a good opportunity to examine whether nationally distinct approaches to management are introduced within the same country location. This is a particularly lively area of debate. Some researchers hold that the growth of transnational corporations will lead to convergence of management practices (Bartlett and Ghoshal 1989), whilst others hold that multinational companies (MNCs) tend to use the organization models most popularly espoused in the country where their corporate headquarters are located (Ruigrok and van Tulder 1995). Indeed, some suggest (Ferner and Quintanilla 1998) that many MNCs from non-UK/US countries go through a process of "Anglo-Saxonization" as their international activities expand. "Nonetheless," they claim "there is clear evidence of a nationality effect."

A study of UK acquisitions by US, Japanese, German, French, and UK companies was carried out to examine the main post-acquisition changes and national differences in management practice that were introduced, and the perceived influence of the acquiring companies on the changes, in order to gain insights into the convergence or otherwise of management methods from acquiring companies from different countries.

Scale and Nature of FDI into the UK

Table 17.1 summarizes the amount of direct investment into the UK over the period 1986 to 1995, as estimated by the DTI's Invest in Britain Bureau.

Information technology, mechanical and instrument engineering, the financial services industry, business services, and the chemical and pharmaceutical industries have been the most popular industries for FDI in the UK (Child et al. 2000). However, a very wide range of sectors have been touched by FDI. The trend over the last decade is on the whole similar for the four countries surveyed. It grew during the late 1980s, then fell as world recession hit.

Potential Impact of M&A FDI on UK Management Practice

Corporate and national culture have come to be seen by many researchers as critically important in selecting management methods, strategies, and structures (cf. Hofstede 1991; Hampden-Turner and Trompenaars 1993). Kogut and Singh (1988) claim that:

> No matter how superior the current MNC may be in replacing the skills of traders by the international extension of organizational boundaries, the management of these firms are likely to be influenced by the dominant country culture.

For example, Calori, Lubatkin, and Véry (1994) in their research conclude that the French exercise higher formal control of strategy and operations, and lower informal control through teamwork in UK acquisitions, than do the Americans. They also conclude that the Americans exercise higher procedurally based control than do the British in French acquisitions:

Table 17.1 Direct investment into the UK, 1986–1995

Countries of Origin: Years to March (£m)

	1986/7	1988/9	1990/1	1992/3	1994/5
USA	594.2	1502.4	1002.3	1213.1	2876.9
Japan	443.9	293.9	1085.0	109.1	1156.7
Germany	58.3	174.9	544.4	402.3	1535.4
France	80.9	215.5	198.8	59.2	1188.2
TOTAL	1537.7	2891.2	3876.9	2520.2	8351.3
% of Total	76.6	75.6	73.0	70.8	80.9

Source: Invest in Britain Bureau.

being conscious of the influence of national administrative heritage should help reduce anticipated cultural problems in the integration process following international acquisitions...Firms are prone to carry their home practice with them as they move into foreign markets. (Calori et al. 1994)

Perlmutter (1969) had long ago warned of the risk of ethnocentricity, where the buyer does not make any adaptation to local practice, and carries on as though in its domestic market. Gates and Engelhoff (1986) concentrate on the importance of the country of origin of MNCs in their choice of control mechanisms over new acquisitions. Whitley (1992) addresses the issue from the viewpoint of the local company, and stresses the importance of local institutional and infrastructural circumstances in influencing effective consolidation of acquisitions across borders.

Hunt (1988) claims that almost all acquirers adopt a "hands-on" attitude towards structure, people, budgets, plans, and systems in the first year after an acquisition, although our research shows that this is by no means a universal form of behavior. Bartlett and Ghoshal (1989) in their description of the transnational corporation (TNC) pay little attention to differing national managerial styles. Similarly Olie (1994) highlights leadership, appropriate organization structures, and compatibility of merger motives as the best predictors of merger success, rather than sensitivity to national practice.

However, a growing body of research on national management systems and relevant national cultural differences has led to the expectation that companies of different nationalities will introduce distinctive management practices. At the same time, markets and corporations have been globalizing rapidly, and many more companies now face two distinct cultures; their own, and that of a foreign partner or parent. Work on acquisitions and their performance (Haspeslagh and Jemison 1991; Norburn and Schoenberg 1994), as well as on the effects of differing national management cultures on the performance of acquisitions (Véry et al. 1996; Morosini and Singh 1994), has also led to interest in the wider implications of national and managerial culture for acquisitions.

There is considerable interest in the literature on post-acquisition performance, the integration of the new subsidiary, and cross-border modes of market entry. Nahavandi and Malekzadeh (1988) find that the success of implementation and of effective acculturation is highly dependent upon the attitudes to the mode of acculturation held by both the acquirer and the acquired company. They see the four possible modes as integration, assimilation, separation, and deculturation. Sales and Mirvis (1984) see conflict, and hence probable failure of the acquisition, as most likely when firms with radically different corporate cultures come together. Kogut and Singh (1988) find that the greater the cultural distance between the two countries involved, and the higher the level of uncertainty avoidance in the potential market-entering firm, the less likely it is to adopt acquisition as a method of market entry, preferring greenfield development or joint venture.

The impact of the acquirer's national management practice on the post-acquisition behavior and performance of the acquired company is also an issue of concern. The implication of the globalization of markets and the multiple management cultures faced by UK management is that inward FDI, through the control and influence it gives to foreign management, will stimulate the adoption of management practices which contrast with past practices of the acquired UK firm. As Shrivastava (1986) points out, there are several areas in which management practice influence might come about; for example, in accounting and budgeting systems, in physical assets, product lines, production systems and technologies, and, most importantly, at a managerial and socio-cultural level. Integration, or at least influence, is not always needed or in fact achieved at all these levels. It might be suggested that the managerial and socio-cultural level is the most important one, since Buono and Bowdich (1985) find in their research that where cultures collide and cause a merger to fail, the predominant observed factor is that of discontent seen in the non-dominant partner based on subjective, i.e. cultural, rather than objective facts.

The importance of the national origin of the acquiring company in cross-border acquisitions is thus by now a well-established and much studied phenomenon. However, past study of the balance between direct application of foreign management practice and its adaptation to local conditions leaves open the question of how far and in what manner FDI induces domestic changes in the management practices of acquired companies.

As Eltis (1996) puts it:

> United Kingdom producers have learnt work habits from inward investors which have proved extremely favourable…British producers used to utilise their resources less efficiently, but as a result of inward investment, they are now performing closer to their technical potential. (Eltis 1996)

Japanese practices, especially operational methods centered around lean production and continuous improvement, have received the most attention from British and American industry (UNCTAD 1995). However, other factors may also be relevant. First, there may be *"background changes"* which would have occurred anyway even in the absence of an acquisition. These changes may result from general conditions affecting UK industry during the period of study.

Second, there may be some *"acquisition effects."* Amongst these are changes which would have occurred anyway eventually, but which proceed faster because of the acquisition. For example, new investment may be made in plant and information technology, providing opportunities for new practices to be introduced. Acquisitions are normally justified to achieve synergies, which in itself gives an impetus for change in management practice within the subsidiary. A "new broom sweeps clean" effect is also to be seen in most acquisition situations.

Third, there is change which is specific to the nationality of the new owner, and may be called the *"transfer of foreign practice effect."* These considerations pose the questions of "what is being transferred" from foreign investing companies, and "what are we comparing?" (Morris and Wilkinson 1996: 727). The first question concerns the differences one might expect to find between companies coming from each of the "big four" foreign investing countries into the UK. The second question concerns itself with comparing the differences in management practice that emerge when UK companies buy other UK companies. The study does not address the question of what changes might have happened anyway, independently of the impact of acquisition.

SAMPLE AND METHOD

This chapter discusses research involving a questionnaire survey of 201 UK acquisitions by US, Japanese, German, French, and UK companies (split: Japanese 29, US 69, French 32, German 21, UK 50).

The questionnaires aimed to address a wide range of nationality-specific topics, as well as areas where change might be expected following any acquisition. In addition, respondents were also asked some more open-ended questions to identify the greatest changes they perceived to have taken place and that had the most impact on the company. Questions were also asked about the size and growth of sales and turnover of the company. A key feature of the questions was the distinction between the direction and strength of change and the degree of influence of the new parent company in bringing about that change.

Following the completion of the questionnaire survey, 40 senior managers of acquired companies in the sample were selected, ten from each of the US, Japanese, German, and French acquirers. They were then interviewed, using a semi-structured interview format, to study how acquiring companies approached the issue of change management in relation to their new UK acquisitions.

Not only were the industries covered in the questionnaire extremely wide and varied, but this was also the case for the companies interviewed, as shown in Table 17.2 below.

In the sample, Japanese and German companies acquired more traditional manufacturing companies and US and French companies more service companies, but all three categories were adequately covered by the interviewing to minimize the risk of skew in the results. The companies interviewed are therefore reasonably representative of the sample surveyed using questionnaires, save for the exclusion of UK companies acquired by UK companies from the interviews. These were excluded since the aim of the interviews was to explore any cross-cultural interactions occurring in the transfer process, which would obviously not be present in UK/UK cases.

Table 17.2 Spread of interviewed acquisitions between sectors of industry

	USA	Japanese	French	German
High-tech	3	3	2	2
Services	4	1	3	1
Manufacturing	3	6	5	7

The prior international experience of the acquirers varied from high to negligible, the size of the acquirers varied from medium-sized domestic companies to major MNCs, and the condition of the acquirees varied from strongly loss-making to very profitable. Furthermore, the risk that MNCs would import practices from experience gained in other countries, and thus distort the attempt to identify specifically national practices amongst the acquirers, as suggested by Buckley and Ghauri (1999), was minimized by ensuring that MNCs were not overly dominant in the interviewed sample, as shown in Table 17.3 below.

A further possible distorting factor might be the variety of different motives for making the acquisitions. Dunning (1993: 56–61) suggests four principal motives for foreign acquisitions: (1) resource seeking; (2) market access; (3) efficiency; (4) strategic asset or new capability seeking. This was also investigated in the interview sample, and it was judged that the strongest motive for the acquisitions concerned was the desire for greater market access, no doubt as part of a globalization strategy (cf. Table 17.4 below). However, another important motive was the acquisition of strategic assets and new capabilities, and some motives could only be categorized as "other", e.g. the purchase of an upmarket UK perfume company by a US grocery company for the purely personal reasons of the US chief executive.

Checks were made for potential sources of bias contained within the sampling of companies and respondents. Respondents divided fairly evenly between those who had joined the subsidiary before acquisition (52%) and those who joined after (48%). As

Table 17.3   Spread of acquirers between MNCs and nationals

	USA	Japanese	French	German
MNCs	4	5	7	4
National companies	6	5	3	6

Table 17.4   *Motives for acquisitions amongst companies interviewed

	USA	Japanese	French	German
Resource seeking	0	1	2	1
New market access	5	8	7	6
Efficiency	0	0	1	2
Gain strategic assets or new capabilities	4	1	5	5
Other	2	1	0	0

Note: * The total adds up to more than 40 since some acquisitions were judged to have more than one motive.

expected, there was a tendency for those appointed after acquisition to perceive that more change had taken place and that the parent company had exerted greater influence. They also tended to take a more positive view of post-acquisition profitability, though not of sales. This bias was, however, only significant in 28% of items for the strength of change, 18% of items for the direction of change, and 12% of items for acquirer influence. It accounted on average for a difference of 0.18 within the 7.0 range of possible scores on the scale of post-acquisition profitability. There was also some skew in the distribution of pre- and post-acquisition appointees by acquirer nationality, with Japanese, French, and UK acquirers having larger numbers of post-acquisition appointees responding than the norm. This means that the assessments of change, acquirer influence, and profitability may be somewhat inflated for these nationalities.

The interview schedule covered a wide range of management practices. Background information on the story behind the acquisition was also gathered. Respondents were asked some open-ended questions about which changes they felt had been the greatest and had made the most impact on the company. Of the 40 companies interviewed, the interviewees were the managing director or chief executive of the subsidiary in 35 cases. Only three had been appointed from the parent, and only two were non-British. It is accepted therefore that the results may show something of a constructivist bias as the perceptions are generally seen through British eyes. Had it been possible to interview more widely within the companies, it is conceded that some impressions might have varied from those received. However, resources did not permit more extensive interviewing, and therefore the results in the chapter must be regarded as somewhat exploratory.

KEY FINDINGS

The differences in the reported levels of influence which acquiring companies from different national groups had on the changes were quite marked. French and US acquirers exercised more influence than Japanese and German acquirers. In certain areas, there were significant differences between parent company influence. In *human resource management and marketing*, US acquirers tended to exercise the greatest influence, closely followed by French acquirers. In *organization, supply, and strategy* areas, French acquirers seem to have exercised the greatest influence, closely followed by US parent companies. In each of these areas, Japanese and German acquirers exercised less influence. National differences in influence for *company philosophy, communications, and operations* were smaller.

The *acquisition effect* supposes that acquisition has a significant impact on changes in management practice through the influence exercised by the acquiring company. Managers in the subsidiaries generally reported that the fact of acquisition has itself been a lever for change. Table 17.5 lists the correlations between an aggregation of post-acquisition changes reported by respondents and their perceptions of the parent

Table 17.5 Correlations between the overall level of change and reported change due to acquirer*

Category	N	Correlation	p
Total sample	124	0.52	0.000
US acquisitions	43	0.58	0.000
French acquisitions	19	0.66	0.001
German acquisitions	9	0.58	0.05
Japanese acquisitions	17	0.42	0.047
UK acquisitions	36	0.45	0.003

*Overall level of change + sum of the moduli of change on all items except for job rotation, type of planning, R&D/development of products and services, and operations.

Influence of acquiring company = sum of influence scores for the same items.

company's influence on each change. The indicators of both change and influence relate to all the areas of management covered by the survey, except for development of new products and services, and operations.

Across the sample as a whole, approximately one-quarter of the variation in the degree of post-acquisition change was ascribed to the influence of the foreign parent. However, this figure varied considerably according to the acquiring company's nationality. As Table 17.5 indicates, the correlations between perceived parent company influence and the degree of change in the acquired firm were noticeably higher in the case of US, French, and German companies, than they were among companies with Japanese and UK parents.

Investigation of the reported acquisition and transfer of practice effects together requires a closer look at the data with reference to three specific questions. First, there were some areas of management practice in which little change was reported, suggesting that these may be relatively immune from either effect, or possibly that the major motive was the acquisition of a strategic asset or new capability. Second, there were some areas in which changes were reported that were similar across acquirer nationalities. This would suggest that acquisition acted as a vehicle for promoting general trends in management fashion. Third, there were areas of practice in which acquisition appears to have had an impact, but where the practices being transferred clearly differed, i.e. there were clear national differences.

Little or No Change

Whilst, as Haspeslagh & Jemison (1991) found in their research, there were few acquisitions which were clear examples of a total lack of integration, there were several examples where the management of the new subsidiary involved little or no change as shown in Table 17.6.

There were three main reasons suggested for this. One was that acquiring companies assumed that the new subsidiary understood its business better than the parent and so

Table 17.6 Areas of management practice: little reported post-acquisition change

1. Job rotation of managers between different functions
2. Scientific or technically qualified staff as a percentage of total employment
3. Emphasis on formal qualifications for selection and advancement
4. Employment philosophy—recruitment and termination: short term vs. long term
5. Approach to promotion: slow vs. rapid
6. Methods of distribution: subcontracted vs. internal
7. Customer involvement in marketing decisions
8. Emphasis on managing the total supply chain
9. Degree of outsourcing
10. Range of suppliers (single source/multi-source)

Notes: In these areas of management practice, the average modulus of change was less than 1 on a scale from 0 to 3, but the probability of any differences between national categories of acquirer arising from chance was greater than 5%.

left it alone. The second was where the company was acquired for reasons unrelated to the acquiring company, for example companies acquired as a by-product of the acquisition of the company's former parent group. The third reason was where the acquiring company recognized that it could learn from the new subsidiary in specific areas and was therefore concerned to preserve the relevant skills in the subsidiary, i.e. the acquisition of new capabilities or strategic assets.

For example, a major German safety equipment manufacturer acquired a small entrepreneurial firm in the same line of business. Unusually, the entrepreneur remained with the company, the MD of the German parent saying: "We don't want you to change. Stay the way you are, because you have the ability to move in a market place more than we can." Where little change occurred it was, it seems, often due to the subsidiary's management gaining trust and acceptance in the eyes of the new parent's management.

Another factor in the little or no change category may reflect a reluctance of the new parent to act. In one acquisition of a UK pharmaceutical company by a Japanese company, the UK MD said that: "The slight negative is...that perhaps we could have made faster improvement in our business, or development of our business, with more interchange of ideas and operations between the two companies." There is of course the risk that leaving a new subsidiary alone in the hope of preserving its good side may neglect the possibility of achieving useful synergies in other areas.

Similar Changes

Changes which are similar across all acquisitions, as shown in Table 17.7, may be categorized into three main areas: underlying change which would have occurred anyway, catalyzed change which would have occurred anyway but perhaps somewhat more slowly, and finally, acquisition change due to the acquisition but without distinction of parent nationality.

Where change would have occurred anyway, new management trends within the UK are generally the main factors involved. As one manager of a UK firm acquired by a German company said, "We have adopted a lot of new production and process techniques, but not as a result of the link-up with our new parent." A USA company acquired a small UK toiletries manufacturer, but took little interest in it. Despite this, in the last few years the subsidiary has adopted more formal planning systems, become more professional at marketing, learnt to communicate with employees in a more open way, adopted several forms of automation, increased its outsourcing, adopted a longer time horizon, improved its cost control, and increased formal training. But it claims that " . . . there has been no effective influence on us by the US company at all."

The interviews also confirmed the existence of several areas where the survey found significant change but no significant differences between nationalities, for example in the adoption of new IT systems.

Acquiring companies of whatever nationality generally pay attention to image projection. This was often marked by something more than just a change of name of the subsidiary. It varied from a complete re-branding to the addition of a minor logo on the bottom of the letterhead. A UK insurance-related company was acquired by a far larger US group with a global reputation in the new but specialist field it was operating in. This association, and what amounted to a seal of approval from the larger company, greatly assisted the subsidiary in breaking into some highly conservative markets. With smaller

Table 17.7. Changed management practice: no discrimination by nationality

Area of Change	Direction of Change
* Strategy: competing on price; offering unique products/services; development of new products/services	More emphasis
* Amount of training	More
*Reward systems: performance-oriented vs. annual increments	Performance-oriented
*Level of image projection	Higher
*Communication philosophy: open vs. need-to-know	More open
* R&D/product development: team-based vs. sequential	Team-based
*Use of automation and IT	More
*Cost control	More
Operations: employee responsibility for quality; continuous improvement; group working/work teams	More

Notes: *Scored on binary scales. More than half the sample had introduced these features post-acquisition, and there were no significant differences between acquirer nationalities (significant probability of differences occurring by chance was 0.05% or less).

acquiring companies, a wish to build a global reputation often fueled efforts to re-brand newly acquired subsidiaries.

The other universal forms of change were in operations, cost controls, technology, and management methods. Acquisition also has a drastic effect on the confidence felt in a company by its customers, suppliers, bankers, and other associates. In order to keep the company trading successfully, substantially more in the way of financial support than is at first apparent may be necessary. Also in the 16 acquirers included in the top 100 global companies no doubt new management methods adopted were less likely to show ethnocentric qualities than in the more nationally based acquirers.

NATIONAL DIFFERENCES

Table 17.8 provides a general summary of those areas of post-acquisition change in management practice in which clear differences were apparent between the national acquirer categories.

We now examine post-acquisition changes where the *degree of difference from the rest of the sample* is significant. This is a more stringent test of national differences in acquisition effects than that presented in Table 17.8, because it requires that the change is greater than the differences in *all* the remaining companies sampled, not just one or two of the other national groups. For example, whereas Table 17.8 indicates that German and Japanese acquirers contrasted with US and UK acquirers, this contrast may not remain evident unless, say, a particular management practice introduced by Japanese parent companies was sufficiently different from all the others.

US Acquirers

Companies acquired by US parents, *compared with the rest of the sample*, reported moves toward a shorter planning time horizon and employment philosophy. Table 17.9 lists the types of US acquisitions interviewed.

They tended to retain a larger managerial superstructure and to have more frequent managerial job rotation between functional areas. US acquired companies had more senior managerial posts in the UK subsidiaries held by people from the parent company. On the other hand, and perhaps as a result, the subsidiaries tended to have more autonomy over capital expenditure and changes in strategy. There was evidence of greater formalization being introduced than in other national groups, notably in the methods of securing market intelligence, the use of financial control systems, and communications. US acquired companies also tended to have more systematic training through courses, rather than being trained on-the-job. All the distinctive features of US management practice identified in the literature were thus evident in the comparison of US acquisitions with others. The introduction of performance-related reward systems, however,

Table 17.8 National differences by functional area

Area of Practice	Nature of difference
Formal meetings	German acquirers: fewer
	Other acquirers: more
CEO appointed by acquiring company	UK acquirers: 78% of cases
	US acquirers: 53% of cases
	Other acquirers: under 50% of cases
Sales & marketing director appointed by acquiring company	US acquirers: more likely than others
Managers without mainline functional portfolio appointed by acquiring company	Japanese acquirers: more likely than others
Capital expenditure requires final approval by parent company	US acquirers: 75% of cases
	Other acquirers: 89% or more of cases
Use of financial control systems	French, US, & UK acquirers: considerably more use than German & Japanese acquirers
Communication mechanisms	German acquirers: less formal
	Other acquirers (esp. US): more formal
Primary orientation of the subsidiary	Japanese & German acquirers more strategic: UK & US more financial

Table 17.9 US acquisitions interviewed

Acquirer	Acquiree	Industry	Condition
US1 Major MNC (H) *	Small family co.	Medical implants	Just profitable
US2 Large nat'l retailer (L)	Perfumier	Cosmetics	Losses
US3 Major transport co. (H)	4 local transp't cos.	Courier	Losses
US4 Major MNC (H)	Specialist manuf'r	Automobiles	Losses
US5 Major int'l consult'y (H)	Nat'l IT consult'y	IT consult'y	Profitable
US6 Large nat'l high-tech co. (L)	High-tech defense co.	Electronics	Profitable
US7 Major MNC (H)	National FM co.	Facilities mgt	Profitable
US8 Major MNC (H)	Small mfg Co.	Synthetic fibres	Just profitable
US9 Large nat'l Co (H)	Specialist start-up	Insurance	Profitable
US10 Large int'l Co (H)	Small national co.	Engineering	Just profitable

Notes: *International experience: H = High, M = Medium, L = Low; information gleaned from interviews.

was common to all the national acquirer groups. The strength with which the apparently typical American pattern of management practice is reproduced in their UK acquisitions is undoubtedly enhanced by the greater influence that US acquirers exercised.

The American mode of post-acquisition management appears to be hands-on, forceful, and distinctive. In the case of a diversified US manufacturer's subsidiary, the new US manager said: "By linking in to the parent worldwide all the necessary skills and facilities became available to the new acquisition. In this case the company was very much 'absorbed'. The US parent's mission statement hangs in every office, the structure was integrated into the parent's European structure, course training has increased, open communication is compulsory, a sophisticated planning system has been introduced, team working, high turnover of personnel, informality, and market driven rather than R&D driven attitudes now prevail."

An emphasis on financial control and shorter financial time horizons is typical of the US subsidiaries interviewed. The MD of a small UK company US6Co. acquired by a much larger US company said, "They put in financial reporting systems much quicker and ones which were compatible with their own systems, and what they have done has improved the business. It needed a financial controller rather than a part time accountant."

The need for continuous financial returns by US companies facing quarterly reporting constraints is well-nigh universal. According to the UK MD of another US parent this has given rise to a style of management depending very much on trust, but with a heavy emphasis on performance: "The US CEO...left us to get on with it but he made himself familiar with the operation and went around the branches and at the end of the day he asked 'is this British Management delivering that which we require?' If it was he didn't interfere." Very often along with the financial controls came a requirement for consistency with the corporate profile, sometimes tempered by a realization that in some cases there had to be a balance between instilling big company values and preserving the small company's entrepreneurial spirit and flexibility. That was not to say that US parents were very formal, but as one MD of a US multinational manufacturing company's subsidiary US8Co. said: "I was at the site when the takeover took place and the CEO of US8Co. came over and said, 'Call me Hank.'...So, on the one hand there's a high degree of informality but also a very high degree of toughness and an insistence on conformity. You've got to conform—or you're dead."

Companies, acquired by US parents, reported moves towards a shorter planning time horizon and employment philosophy and the toughness mentioned above also extended to employee relations, as the MD of US8Co. also said, "I find American business culture pretty difficult. UK1Co. never talked about caring and valuing people but its actions showed that it did. US8Co. talks a huge amount about caring and valuing people, but when the going gets tough...it doesn't care at all."

At the same time, the disparate size of some US parent companies relative to their UK subsidiaries meant that very significant investments are still made in the subsidiaries. The MD of a small UK technology-based company, US9Co., said that the main benefit of the acquisition of his company was that "Our company was going down the tubes fast.

US9Co. has been very successful in turning around the business, and putting in huge sums of money."

However, in parallel with the financial demands of US ownership, the subsidiaries of US companies have tended to have more autonomy over capital expenditure and changes in strategy. One MD of a US company's subsidiary, US10Co., said that if one is fairly dynamic in one's approach, it may be possible to adopt strategies which the parent company might not think of. In the case of the UK company, this was mainly apparent through marketing initiatives which it, not its US parent, had initiated.

Virtually all the distinctive features of US management practice identified in the literature were thus evident in the comparison of US acquisitions with others. The strength with which the American stereotype emerges is undoubtedly enhanced by the greater influence that US acquirers were reported to exercise. As the MD of US7Co., which had been German owned and was bought by a US company, put it: "They expect instant returns—the day after. There's no 'we'll wait for three years and make sure there's synergies there and then we look for a return'—they want it *now*."

Japanese Acquirers

Japanese acquirers tended to introduce a stronger strategic orientation, with a longer-term financial time horizon and less emphasis on the use of financial control systems than other nationalities. Their employment philosophy was also longer term. They favored a bottom-up approach and collective managerial decision making. They also introduced less managerial job rotation between functions. Market intelligence tended to be gained mostly through use of personal contacts. Although regarded as having lower influence in bringing about post-acquisition change, Japanese companies introduced significantly more "advisers" than the other national groups. They generally permitted rather more decision-making autonomy to their new subsidiaries. "I've been surprised how hands-off they have been, contrary to the popular perception about wearing boiler-suits and so forth. We've had none of that" said the MD of a UK consumer products company (J1Co.). Table 17.10 indicates the nature of the Japanese acquisitions that were the subject of interviews.

The Japanese long-term, strategic collective orientation was clearly apparent, and consistent with traditional characterizations. However, Japanese human resource management (c) changes are generally adjusted to local conditions (Abo 1994; Botti 1995) and most companies, across the national groups, had introduced some or all of the operational practices associated with the Japanese approach as Oliver and Wilkinson (1992) concluded. They were very detailed in their planning techniques and expected the plans to be achieved.

The MD of a UK pharmaceutical company J3Co., acquired along with its US parent by the Japanese licenser of the US parent, said: "I think we have benefited from the takeover from being able to address issues which prior to the takeover would have been difficult to address, through lack of funding or lack of strategic direction..." Another UK

Table 17.10 Japanese acquisitions interviewed

Acquirer	Acquiree	Industry	Condition
J1 Major national co. (L)	Small family co.	Engineering	Losses
J2 Major national co. (L)	Ex-sub'y of MNC	Engineering	Losses
J3 Major national co. (L)	Old branded co.	Household goods	Losses
J4 Major MNC (M)	Nat'l branded co.	Computers	Losses
J5 Large domestic bank (L)	City merchant bank	Banking	Losses
J6 MNC (H)	Medium eng. co.	Engineering	Just profitable
J7 MNC (H)	National branded co.	Men's clothing	Just profitable
J8 Major int'l co. (M)	Ex Danish sub'y co.	Polymers	Losses
J9 Major MNC (H)	Old mfg co.	Engineering	Just profitable
J10 Large nat'l family co. (L)	Old ex-sub'y of US	Pharmaceuticals	Just profitable

company, J4Co., which manufactured a specialist consumer product and was bought by a major Japanese firm, said that: "The main benefit has to be the investment that was made. Our subsequent success has stemmed from the fact that it gave us the breathing space to move forward in the market."

Some Japanese parent companies were perceived to have slowed down progress in their subsidiary due to their slow decision-making process. One UK manufacturer, J4Co., having received design help from its Japanese parent and produced both a Japanese line and a UK line of goods, said that: "In a couple of instances we actually brought products to the market place based on their tooling and their designs before they got into the market place." One MD of a UK retailing company, J5Co., said that one problem with their Japanese parent was "Getting a clear answer, a clear 'yes go ahead'. We keep battling away and sometimes they'll never say no. If they said no, go away, we'd know where we stand, but their culture doesn't permit them to say no."

On the other hand, where trust over a particular issue or over a general range of management issues had been established, considerable independence was granted. But the trust and respect had to be earned. Japanese "advisers" were often managers being sent abroad for two to four years in order to gain international exposure prior to promotion to senior management posts. In the case of one subsidiary, this was described thus: "There are no formal links, there have been some placements of Japanese personnel, but they've been in new posts in staff roles, not direct involvement in the day-to-day business. It's more for training." However, in some cases these advisers had substantial expertise in some specialist area. J7Co.'s MD said that: "I think that the most beneficial thing that happened is that we had a Japanese gentleman on this site who was dealing with general matters but who had a production background. Once I noticed that he was very strong on production-related matters, I changed his responsibilities to production and he has really done some nice things in production. Because he was an expert... he really took it on board and did some really good work..."

Japanese acquirers seem to be much like their accepted stereotypes. As one MD of a pharmaceutical company's subsidiary J9Co. said, "There is a feeling that we should know what we need to do and that we don't need to go to [our parent] for counsel. But they do know what is going on, and they have been very supportive." In all acquisitions there is a balance between independence and intervention along the spectrum of integration. In the case of Japanese acquisitions, the balance is often one where supportive independence outweighs any suggestion of stifling intervention.

German Acquirers

German subsidiaries made much less use of formal meetings, had less formal planning, made less use of financial control systems, had a less planned approach to career development, used formal communication mechanisms less, and placed less emphasis on a cost control strategy. Table 17.11 shows the nature of the German acquisitions interviewed.

German acquisitions were less likely to have parent company managers as CEOs, or as marketing and R&D directors. This is a quite distinctive profile and to some degree reflects the perception of subsidiary managers that their German parent companies exercised comparatively less influence over their acquisitions.

The remarkable aspect of these findings is that they directly contradict one of the assumptions about German management practice found in the literature. Generally, commentators tend to stress a high level of formality, rule-orientation, orderliness, and formal provisions for participation as defining characteristics of German management. These features did *not* distinguish the changes brought about by German investors in the UK; in fact, it was quite the contrary. This may reflect, to some extent, the observation made by Stewart et al. (1994) that German "order" is demonstrated in

Table 17.11 German acquisitions interviewed

Acquirer	Acquiree	Industry	Condition
G1 Major MNC (H)	Family co.	Pharmaceutical	Profitable
G2 Large national co. (L)	Small regional co.	Engineering	Losses
G3 Major landesbank (H)	City bank	Banking	Just profitable
G4 Major MNC (H)	Specialist Mfr	High-tech medical	Just profitable
G5 Major MNC (M)	Truck agency	Automobiles	Losses
G6 MNC (H)	Small family co.	Fire security	Just profitable
G7 Medium national co. (L)	Small local co.	Furniture	Losses
G8 Medium national co. (L)	Med. national	Trailers	Profitable
G9 Major MNC (H)	Small family co.	Chemicals	Profitable
G10 Domestic co. (L)	Small national co.	Construction	Profitable

organizational structure rather than in process. Nevertheless, our findings question the accepted German characterization at least as regards acquisitions.

Various explanations were offered for this apparent contradiction. One MD held that it was a generational issue. "The Germans are quasi-formal, and the first management team was very traditional and formal. The new management however is much younger and much less formal. We have 'casual days', 'funny tie days' and 'sandals days' and this sort of thing!" Other managers saw increased informality as a reaction to the problems of the recession in the early 1990s, in that a more hands-off informal approach would preserve some of the small company characteristics that a large German company might learn from in the recession. This approach was contrasted with an earlier approach which involved management quite literally "by the book," with the rigid use of set procedures. There was some support for Ferner and Quintanilla's (1998) views that...

> In German MNCs there is a tension between the cross-national isomorphism exerted by the institutional features of the German national business system; and on the other hand the global inter-corporate isomorphism that we have described as Anglo-Saxonization, that is the pressure to adopt corporate governance and management control systems that approximate more to those of the UK/US multinationals.

Thus German acquisitions illustrate the effect of management methods in the home country influencing but also adapting to practices abroad. German managers were perceived to be closer to UK culture than many other nationalities. As the manager of a financial services company G4Co. observed: "The culture is not that different. A bit more formal, but they are in my opinion far closer to us than any other European lot. You wouldn't have any trouble having dinner with them ..." As one MD put it: "We found that consensual board decision making (as in Germany), might seem like a very cosy way to run a company, but at the end of the day you need a focus for someone to say 'let's do this chaps'. Even if you disagree with him about it; then you can have an argument about it." Another MD in a very similar position with another company acquired by a German company said that, having completed the acquisition, the German parent company actually fired the MD of the UK company, not for any failing on his part, but because he was not seen to have any functional responsibility. This was despite the insistence of the other managers that an MD was a necessity. The interviewee speculated that German companies which until 1991 had experienced very little recession in the post-war period, had not until recently needed the unifying and directing influence of an MD. Notably, with the coming of the recession in the early 1990s, both the German company and the UK subsidiary acquired MDs.

The German acquirers also took a long-term view of investment decisions, and provided financial support. However, the MD of a UK manufacturing company G6Co. said: "I think our financial director ... would almost have welcomed being pressed more to be self-sufficient. It was almost a failing of the Germans to be as supportive as they were." It seems that for such support to lead to success, the subsidiary must have some idea about the long-term direction of the company—whether that direction is self-generated or dictated by the parent. Support or direction by themselves are insufficient. This was reflected by the above MD's sense that the UK company under its German owners suffered from a lack of strategic direction: "it failed to have a long-term strategic objective. The business objectives were not known by the board, so how on earth could they be transmitted to the rest of the troops?"

German management seems to be influenced by the less demanding nature of the home financial markets, compared to the US. The manager of a German subsidiary said something that would be very difficult for anyone in a US company to say: "They are long-termist. They do not have making a profit itself as a prime matter. They are not profit driven. They want to know about quarterly results but they are not dominated by them."

French Acquirers

French acquirers tended to simplify subsidiaries' management structures, with fewer hierarchical levels, and a smaller managerial component. French parent companies also introduced a stronger emphasis on formal qualifications as criteria for selection and advancement, and planned career development within the subsidiaries. The nature of French acquisitions interviewed is shown in Table 17.12.

Companies acquired by French parents rarely had parent company appointees as CEOs, or as directors, especially in the R&D and HRM areas. However, key decision powers tended to be reserved for the parent more than in the other companies sampled.

French parent company influence was also greater than in Japanese, German, and UK acquisitions. At the strategic level, the only issue which distinguished French acquisitions was that they emphasized the development of new products more strongly. The

Table 17.12 French acquisitions interviewed

Acquirer	Acquiree	Industry	Condition
F1 Major MNC (M)	2 small private cos.	Defense	Losses
F2 Large MN bank (H)	City firm	Banking	Losses
F3 Small Parisian bank (L)	City firm	Banking	Just profitable
F4 Major domestic co. (L)	Domestic co.	Engineering	Profitable
F5 Major MNC (H)	Small domestic co.	Marketing	Just profitable
F6 MNC (H)	IT consultancy co.	IT consultancy	Profitable
F7 MNC (H)	Brand name co.	Adhesives	Losses
F8 Major MNC (H)	Regional co.	Water	Profitable
F 9 family co. (L)	Ex-sub'y of UK plc	Pharmaceuticals	Profitable
F 10 major MNC (H)	2 regional cos.	Water	Profitable

distinctly French changes were not those that support the picture of French management in the literature. There was no compelling evidence that French companies adopt a strategic rather than a financial orientation, are more specialized, use more written media or prefer individual decision making. The expectation that French companies tolerate tall hierarchies is in fact directly challenged by what has happened in the French take-overs in our sample. The only major feature attributed to French management practice which has survived present scrutiny is the tendency for subsidiary autonomy to be relatively restricted.

Certainly the criteria for promotion at the top levels of French companies is fairly stereotypical. According to one manager: "What happens in Paris as regards appointments is all French and depends on which year you were at the Polytechnique." Such comments may spring from denied opportunities, since one UK manager observed that: "Brits can make it only to a glass ceiling level."

French parent company influence was also high compared with all except the Americans. This may be linked to the fact noted by some interviewees that it was fairly common for French managers to be installed, and hand over to a UK manager. As one MD commented, "The form is to put a Frenchman in to run a new company, then after a few years replace him with a local."

Where interviewees did refer to a French parent company taking a strategic view, it was usually by force of circumstances in the context of persevering in the face of financial losses. A manager in a major French electronics company's subsidiary said: "A strategic rather than a financial orientation exists; it has to, since the company loses money. However, it is thought to be important to stay in the market." Certainly, on the financial/strategic axis, the MD of a UK financial services provider acquired by a Parisian Bank said "To us relationship management is important, but to them if something doesn't show profits in six months, they lose interest. They are very short-term. This is unsettling as you can't motivate people on this basis." As regards individual decision making, one MD observed that: "They veer towards collective decision making. The main problem has been the bureaucratic nature of the French decision-making process, and the style of management." Another interviewee said: "Decision making is collective, but the French are very autocratic, but on big strategic issues only." This shows that the issue may depend on the size of the decision being made.

A French financial services company, for example, was said to reserve larger decisions for itself, but to allow its British subsidiary a lot of local autonomy over operational matters. One personnel director related an incident shortly after being acquired: "A (UK) director said, 'What do you want us to do?', and there was a pregnant silence and the visiting French director paused, looked straight down the table, and said 'Monsieur if we have to tell you what to do we have the wrong people'. So I thought this is good news because nobody is going to tell us what has to be done." This apparently surprised the UK manager concerned, who said he had always regarded the French as bureaucratic and centralist. This also illustrates the point that to a certain extent, it is up to a subsidiary to manage its owners as much as be managed by them.

The possibility of being fairly autonomous in some respects though can have disadvantages as pointed out earlier. The MD of a high-tech manufacturing firm acquired by a French company said: "The way in which the business is being approached is interesting, 'the center and several self-sufficient satellites', but in my opinion it was never going to be a workable philosophy because it weakens the whole thing rather than strengthens it...It's wonderful to manage a subsidiary where one is totally empowered, but on the other hand how is one going to grow the business without the help of the group?"

The expectation that French companies tolerate tall hierarchies was not confirmed in the survey. One UK MD commented, "The levels of hierarchy are much fewer. UKCo. had eight grades. Now there are far fewer." More generally, this is part of the view that French companies have tried to absorb their acquired companies to fit in with their existing French management structure.

The overall view of French acquisitions provided by the interviews and survey results thus tends to belie the conventional views of what constitutes "French" management style, with hierarchical structures and centralized decision making.

Conclusions

It is clear from our survey and interviews that the very fact of the acquisition led to major changes in the way the companies were run. Some changes were common across all nationalities, no doubt reflecting changes that were fashionable or ones carried out by transnational companies who learn "best practices" where they find them. Such changes may well have been prompted by the acquisition, but were not necessarily individually caused by it. Some common changes may have been due to the acquisition, but were common to the acquisitions, irrespective of the nationality of the acquirer. All the national acquirer groups reported a move toward performance-related payment systems (which has been associated with the American approach), and the adoption of team-based work organization and continuous improvement systems (which has been associated with the Japanese approach). Such management practices are therefore no longer limited national practices, but now general "best practice" across nations.

Many other changes, however, did vary by nationality of acquirer, but did not all fit the received accepted characteristics of the nation in question as described in the literature. The ways in which the types of management practice were transferred from the foreign acquirers of UK companies varied according to their nationality and were quite distinct for the US and the Japanese. For example, Japanese acquirers were much more likely to adopt a long-term view than their equivalents from the USA. Indeed, it became clear that many companies owed their survival through the recession of the early 1990s to the willingness of their new Japanese owners to afford them financial support without an expectation of any short-run return. The US acquirers, on the other hand, seem to be much more likely than other nationalities to absorb their acquisitions into their group in a very integrationist way. These and some other contrasts between

American and Japanese acquirers tally with the characteristics generally reported in the literature of their respective approaches to management.

Very little support was found, however, for the characteristics which have previously been associated with French and German management. Even though French and German acquirers were found to introduce some management practices of a kind which contrasted with the rest of the sample, these did not on the whole conform to the national characteristics generally reported. There was a pronounced tendency for German companies to make long-term financial investments in a similar way to Japanese parent companies, but to be rather uncertain in their strategic approach to their acquisitions. It is important here perhaps to remember Ferner and Quintanilla's (1998) comments that there are tensions in the transition from traditional German companies to German-based MNCs. That can lead to a conflict of objectives in the German acquiring company. In addition, two of the distinctive post-acquisition changes French and German companies tended to introduce fly in the face of the conclusions to be drawn from existing assumptions about French and German management. These are, respectively, the relatively strong tendency of French acquirers in the sample to reduce hierarchical levels and simplify management structures, and the marked tendency among German acquirers to reduce formalization among their new UK subsidiaries. This suggests that our present views of French and German management practice may be in need of revision. French and German management practice has, in fact, received much less attention than is the case for Japanese and US approaches—at least in the English-language literature—and further research might well refine our existing conceptions of their typical management practices. In any event, from this research they appear less easy to caricature than their US or Japanese counterparts, although the French approach was described in the interviews as somewhat "colonial," in that there was a tendency for French acquirers to leave day-to-day management to the native Brits but to take all strategic decisions in France.

ENDNOTES

1. This chapter is based on a Judge Institute of Management Studies Working Paper (2002).

REFERENCES

Abo, T. (ed.) (1994). *The Hybrid Factory: The Japanese Production System in the United States.* New York: Oxford University Press.

Bartlett, Christopher, & Ghoshal, Sumantra (1989). *Managing across Borders.* London: Hutchinsons.

Botti, H. F. (1995). "Going Local: The Hybridization Process as Organizational Learning." Paper presented to the Workshop on the Production, Diffusion and Consumption of Management Knowledge in Europe, IESE, Barcelona, January.

Buckley, P. J., and Ghauri, P. N. (1999). *The Internationalisation of the Firm: A Reader* (2nd ed.). London: International Thomson Business Press.

Buono, Anthony F., & Bowditch, James (1985). "When Cultures Collide: The Anatomy of a Merger." *Human Relations*, 38/5: 477–501.

Calori, Roland, Lubatkin, Michael, & Véry, Philippe (1994). "Cross-Border Acquisitions: An International Comparison." *Organization Studies*, 15/3: 361–99.

Child, John (1981). "Culture, Contingency and Capitalism in the Cross-National Study of Organizations." *Research in Organizational Behavior*, 3: 303–56.

—— Faulkner, David, and Pitkethly, Robert (2000). "Foreign Direct Investment in the UK 1985–1994: The Impact on Domestic Management Practice." *Journal of Management Studies*, 37/1: 141–66.

Dunning, J. H. (1993). *Multinational Enterprises and the Global Economy*. Wokingham, UK: Addison-Wesley.

Eltis, Walter (1996). *The Political Economy of United Kingdom Foreign Direct Investment*. London: Foundation for Manufacturing and Industry.

Ferner, A., & Quintanilla, J. (1998). "Multinationals, National Business Systems and HRM ." *International Journal of Human Rights Management*, 9/4: 710–31.

Gates, Stephen R., & Engelhoff, William G. (1986). "Centralization in Headquarters-Subsidiary Relationships." *Journal of International Business Studies*, 17/2: 71–92.

Hampden-Turner, Charles, & Trompenaars, Fons (1993). *The Seven Cultures of Capitalism*. London & New York: Doubleday.

Haspeslagh, Philippe D., & Jemison, David B. (1991). *Managing Acquisitions*. New York: Free Press.

Hickson, David J., Hinings, Christopher R., McMillan, Charles J., & Schwitter, J. P. (1974). "The Culture-Free Context of Organization Structure: A Tri-National Comparison." *Sociology*, 8: 59–80.

Hofstede, Geert (1991). *Cultures and Organizations: Software of the Mind*, Maidenhead, UK: McGraw-Hill.

Hunt, John (1988). "Managing the Successful Acquisition: A People Question." Stockton lecture, London Business School.

Kogut, Bruce, & Singh, Harbir (1988). "The Effect of National Culture on the Choice of Entry Mode." *Journal of International Business Studies*, 19/3: 411–33.

KPMG (1997). *Corporate Finance Survey*. London: KPMG.

Morosini, Piero, & Singh, Harbir (1994). "Post Cross-Border Acquisitions: Implementing National Culture Compatible Strategies to Improve Performance." *European Management Journal*, 12: 390–400.

Morris, J., & Wilkinson, Barry (1996). "The Transfer of Japanese Management to Alien Institutional Environments." *Journal of Management Studies*, 32: 719–30.

Nahavandi, Afsaneh, & Malekzadeh, Ali R. (1988). "Acculturation in Mergers and Acquisitions." *Academy of Management Review*, 13/1: 79–90.

Norburn, David, and Schoenberg, Ralph (1994). "European Cross-Border Acquisition: How Was it For You?" *Long Range Planning*, 27/4: 25–34.

Olie, Rene (1994). "Shades of Culture and Institutions in International Managers." *Organisation Studies*, 15/3: 381–405.

Oliver, Nick, & Wilkinson, Barry (1992). *The Japanization of British Industry: New Developments in the 1990s* (2nd ed.). Oxford: Blackwell.

Perlmutter, H. (1969). "The Tortuous Evolution of the Multinational Corporation." *Columbia Journal of World Business*, (4): 9–18.

Ruigrok, W., & van Tulder, R. (1995). *The Logic of International Restructuring*. London: Routledge.

Sales, Amy, & Mirvis, Philip (1984). "When Cultures Collide: Issues of Acquisition," in J. R. Kimberly and R. E. Quinn (eds.), *Managing Organizational Transition*. Homewood, IL: Irwin, 103–33.

Shrivastava, Paul (1986). "Postmerger Integration." *Journal of Business Strategy*, 7/1: 65–76.

Stewart, R., Barsoux, J.-L., Kieser, A., Ganter, H.-D., & Walgenbach, P. (1994). *Managing in Britain and Germany*. Basingstoke: Macmillan.

United Nations Conference on Trade and Development (UNCTAD) (1995). *World Investment Report 1995*. New York: United Nations.

Véry, Philippe, Lubatkin, Michael, and Calori, Roland (1996). "A Cross-National Assessment of Acculturative Stress in Recent European Mergers." *International Studies of Management and Organisations*, 26/1: 59–86.

Whitley, Richard (ed.) (1992). *European Business Systems: Firms and Markets in their National Contexts*. London: Sage.

CHAPTER 18

....

KNOWLEDGE MANAGEMENT IN MERGERS AND ACQUISITIONS

....

SAJJAD M. JASIMUDDIN

INTRODUCTION

....

Over the last thirty years, mergers and acquisitions (in short M&As) activity has been seen as one of the popular methods of organizational survival and growth (Lynch and Lind 2002; Schoenberg 2003; Huyghebaert and Laypaert 2010). Arguably, global M&A activity has become an important mode of foreign entry into a host country (Chua and Goh 2009; Liu and Zou 2008). Parallel to this, Segal-Horn and Faulkner (2010) state that rapid globalization has influenced cross-border M&A activity to a high degree.

The M&A literature (e.g. Huber 1991; Madhok 1997; Story and Helft 2007; Chua and Goh 2009; Bresman et al. 1999; Rumyntseva et al. 2002) discusses the opportunity to access the knowledge of other companies via M&As. Casal and Fontela (2007), for example, contend that organizational knowledge is constantly treated as crucial to materialize the potential of M&As.

As a result, knowledge management seems to help the exploration and exploitation of knowledge available in two units of an amalgamated firm. It is found in the relevant literature that knowledge management is loosely used as knowledge transfer. Some define it as organizational learning, others as knowledge creation, still others as knowledge storage (Barlett and Ghosal 1989; Westney 1993; Hedlund 1994; Nonaka and Takeuchi 1995). Since knowledge transfer is a critical factor for successful merger or acquisition, we use knowledge transfer and knowledge management interchangeably for the purpose of this study.

In the knowledge management literature, considerable attention has focused on knowledge management under different modes of governance, e.g. joint ventures, strategic alliances, and foreign subsidiaries. More specifically, the relevant literature has focused much on knowledge management within an organization (Szulanski 1996; Tsai 2001), knowledge management in alliances and joint ventures (Doz 1996; Morwery et al. 1996; Kogut 1988; Simonin 1999; Hamel 1991; Inkpen 1992; Inkpen and Crossan 1992; Tsang 2002), and knowledge transfer activities between independent companies (Carrillo and Anumba 2002; Bresman et al. 1999).

However, knowledge management is still in its infancy in the M&A context. It is important to understand the relationship between knowledge management within M&A activity. Unfortunately, the knowledge management literature has not exclusively discussed the potential of knowledge management for the success of M&As. To the author's knowledge, no study has explicitly attempted to discuss the relationship between knowledge management and M&As.

Against this backdrop, the purpose of the chapter is to address the phenomenon of knowledge management in the case of M&As so as to develop a better understanding of knowledge management with M&A. The objective of the chapter then is twofold: first, to understand the role of knowledge management in the M&A context; and second, to identify the factors that facilitate its implementation in M&As. The chapter is structured as follows. The next section will focus on the issues associated with M&As. The following section justifies M&A as a means of gaining access to organizational knowledge. The notion of knowledge management is then elaborated. Next, the relevance of knowledge management in M&As is discussed. Subsequently, the challenges of M&A activity from a knowledge management perspective are explored. After that, an effort will be made to provide guidelines for companies considering the introduction of a knowledge management initiative in order to explore and exploit knowledge within a structural change. The final section provides concluding remarks.

MERGERS AND ACQUISITIONS

In a real sense, mergers and acquisitions are two different strategies of organizational growth for a firm. M&As provide a popular means of achieving rapid growth and market entry (Schoenberg 2003). Reflecting this view, Kumar and Bansal (2008) assert that M&A has increasingly become the most widely used strategy of a firm which seeks to establish a competitive advantage over its rivals. Cross-border M&As constitute a large share of global FDI flows, reaching 80% in the years of merger waves (UNCTAD 2007, as cited in Stiebale and Reize 2011). In 2007 alone, 35,982 M&A deals were announced worldwide, with an aggregate deal value of $4.4 trillion; and the volume of deals was 21% higher than in 2006 (Huyghebaert and Laypaert 2010; Dealogic 2008; Rumyntseva et al. 2002). Almost every renowned multinational corporation (MNC) has been engaged in some form of M&A activity in recent years. For instance, the largest global conglomerates Siemens and General Electric acquired as many as 166 and 110 firms respectively during the period from 1984 to 2000 (Desylla and Hughes 2008).

Many definitions of merger and acquisition have been produced in the M&A litera-ture. A few scholars (e.g. Stewart et al. 1963; Segal-Horn and Faulkner 2010) constantly discuss the notion of "mergers" and "acquisitions" synonymously. Others (e.g. Bresman et al. 1999; Schraeder and Self 2003; Desylla and Hughes 2008) use the two words "merg-ers" and "acquisitions" separately, treating them as two distinct strategies. This will be dealt in the following paragraphs.

Researchers loosely define "merger" as the consolidation of two previously separate companies into a single firm. According to Schraeder and Self (2003), a merger is when two or more entities combine to form one new entity. Merger is viewed as the amalgamation of two separate organizations into a single enterprise, which allows their available assets, liabilities, and cultural values to be combined on a compara-tively equal basis across different businesses and industries (Horwitz et al. 2002, as cited in Kongpichayanond 2009). Likewise, Segal-Horn and Faulkner (2010) define a merger as a collaborative agreement by two companies to combine their interests, ownership, and company structures into one company. It should be mentioned that the largest merger deal to date is the $73 billion amalgamation of Travelers and Citicorp (Teternbaum 1999).

On the other hand, several scholars have loosely defined "acquisition" as the purchase of one company by another. In their seminal work, Bresman, Birkinshaw, and Nobel (1999) argue that an acquisition represents the bringing together of two "social commu-nities" into a single social community over a period of years. According to Schraeder and Self (2003), acquisition refers to when one firm buys or takes over the operations of another. Parallel to this, Segal-Horn and Faulkner (2010) makes a similar comment, say-ing that:

> An acquisition is an outright purchase of one company by another. It occurs when one company acquires enough of another company's shares to gain control or ownership. (p. 222)

Put differently, acquisitions occur when one organization acquires sufficient shares to increase the level of control, gain ownership of another firm, and maintain their identity (Horwitz et al. 2002, as cited in Kongpichayanond 2009). Desylla and Hughes (2008) view acquisitions as deals where the acquiring firm owns less than 50% of the target's voting shares before the takeover and increases its ownership to at least or above 50% as a result of the takeover. It is worth noting that the largest acquisition deal to date is the $86 billion announced acquisition of Mobil by Exxon so as to unite two giant oil compa-nies (Teternbaum 1999).

However, in some of the M&As literature, a few authors (e.g. Gerpott 1995; Carrillo and Anumba 2002; Rumyntseva et al. 2002) set out to define the words "merger" and "acquisition" side by side so as to explain that the terminologies are not synonymous, but rather distinct. Carrillo and Anumba (2002), for example, contend that "the termi-nology 'merger' is used when the two companies have a similar size in terms of number of employees and annual turnover while 'acquisition' is used when one partner is much larger than the other." Rumyntseva et al. (2002) argue that in an acquisition, the acquiring company gains control over the acquired company which loses its economic and legal autonomy, but in a merger, two or more companies create a new entity. While merger can occur through a mutual agreement between two organizations in a friendly environment, an acquisition emerges in either a hostile (popularly termed a hostile takeover) or a friendly environment that prevails between the two companies.

As evidenced in the extant management literature, the terms "mergers" and "acquisitions" are also interchangeably used. For the purposes of this chapter, the terminology "mergers" and "acquisitions" will be used to mean a mode of governance, be it merger or acquisition, and jointly to indicate a change in company ownership. One important aspect of understanding M&As is to examine the motives that drive such activity. The motives behind undertaking M&As will be elaborated next.

MERGERS AND ACQUISITIONS—A MEANS OF GAINING ACCESS TO KNOWLEDGE

As evidenced in the M&As literature (e.g. Cooper and Gregory 2003; Pablo and Javidan 2004; Daniel and Metcalf 2001; Schmidt 2002; Stahl et al. 2005; Hitt and Pisano 2004; Kongpichayanond 2009; Brouthers et al. 1998), a firm engaging in M&As can improve its performance and thereby strengthen its competitive advantage. The fact is that the primary objectives for both "mergers" and "acquisitions" seem to be similar. In this regard, several researchers (e.g. Haspeslagh and Jemison 1991; Segal-Horn and Faulkner 2010; Greenwood et al. 1994; Rumyntseva et al. 2002) provide a list of the common objectives of "mergers" and "acquisitions," which include an increase in shareholder value, a quick response to change in industrial structure, exploitation of economies of scale and scope, and the realization of synergy benefits.

Most specifically, the literature emphasizes that a combined firm in M&As can strengthen market positioning, achieve a reduction of operational costs, obtain needed competencies, improve the image of the amalgamated firm, and ensure better services for potential customers. Huyghebaert and Laypaert (2010), for example, report that a combined firm in M&As gains synergy benefits, that is, a combined firm has the potential to be more profitable than the individual units that are combining. Furthermore, Hopkins (1999) identifies four distinct but related motives in understanding M&As: strategic, market, economic, and personal. Consistent with this, Brouthers et al. (1998) rightly observe that the motives for M&As range from increasing profitability to increasing managerial prestige.

Interestingly, another strategic motive of M&As activity is the acquisition and transfer of knowledge to create value for a combined firm. Several writers (e.g. Story and Helft 2007; Chua and Goh 2009; Bresman et al. 1999; Larsson and Finkelstein 1999; Gupta and Roos 2001; Yildiz and Fey 2010) contend that one of the most cited reasons for M&As activity is to expand a firm's knowledge base in a shorter time. While organic growth seems to be excessively time-consuming, M&A allows a firm to quickly exploit in an acquired firm available knowledge resources that could be developed internally (Karim and Mitchell 2000), but might take more time to develop.

Parallel to this, Empson (2001) rightly explains that the creation of knowledge from scratch is costly in terms of time and resources. Moreover, there is no guarantee of its success. By contrast, M&As activity can provide an organization with the opportunity to gain access to a knowledge base from the acquired firm. If the requisite knowledge is already available in the acquired firm, and if it is not used by the acquiring firm, reinventing the wheel is a serious waste of time and resources for the restructured organization. The M&As activity is treated as an attractive means to quickly develop new products and services because two firms can bring and utilize their core competences within an amalgamated firm. For example, IBM's hostile takeover of Lotus allowed it to become a software-driven company, transforming it from its mainframe image. Similarly, Story and Helft (2007, as cited in Chua and Goh 2009) mention that by acquiring DoubleClick, Google is able to move quickly in its transformation from search engine to online advertising powerhouse.

The M&As literature (e.g. Haspeslagh and Jemison 1991; Madhok 1997; Rumyntseva et al. 2002; Bresman et al. 1999; Pablo and Javidan 2004; Carrillo and Anumba 2002) has stressed the importance of gaining access to a competitive firm's knowledge base via M&A. Madhok (1997), for example, suggests that one of the main objectives of M&As is to gain access to and utilize an acquired company's existing knowledge and R&D activity. Resonating with this, Bresman, Birkinshaw, and Nobel (1999) point out that a key reason for M&As has often been to capture knowledge available in an acquired firm, which is then disseminated across the combined organization. Likewise, Pablo and Javidan (2004) argue that M&As create integrating knowledge. It is essential to understand the notion of knowledge management in order to comprehend how knowledge can be managed in an M&A context. The notion of knowledge management will be discussed next.

THE NOTION OF KNOWLEDGE MANAGEMENT

Being a relatively new discipline of the 1990s, scholars from many different backgrounds have contributed to popularizing the emerging interdisciplinary discourse of knowledge management by organizing conferences, and publishing articles in academic and professional journals. Knowledge management focuses on the discovery and deployment of knowledge that helps an organization to gain an edge in the market place. The meanings and features of knowledge management reflect researchers' disciplinary backgrounds. Most specifically, academics and practitioners from information systems, human resources management, strategic management, innovation management, organizational learning, and organization theory have shown an interest in this field (Jasimuddin 2006a).

Knowledge management can be defined as managing knowledge in a way that helps enhance the sustainable competitive advantage of an organization. Many attempts have been made to define knowledge management. According to Wiig (1997), knowledge management is the systematic creation and use of knowledge to maximize the knowledge-related effectiveness of an organization. Snowden (1999) views the subject as the identification, optimization, and active management of intellectual assets, either in the form of explicit knowledge held in artifacts or as tacit knowledge possessed by employees. However, the definition used in this chapter refers to the effective and efficient discovery and deployment of knowledge available in a combined organization in M&As so as to enhance sustainable competitive advantage.

The majority of the knowledge management research focuses on topics such as knowledge typology, knowledge transfer, knowledge creation, and knowledge storage and retrieval (Jasimuddin 2006b). A common theme seems to be that managing knowledge is linked to the capacity for action. Various processes of knowledge management have emerged and been discussed by researchers. But no consensus has been reached, even on a core knowledge management process. The knowledge management process consists of various stages, which are frequently repetitive and sometimes not sequential. The generic processes of knowledge management are given below.

- *Knowledge transfer*—Knowledge transfer involves both the transmission of knowledge to a recipient and absorption from one person to another person (Davenport and Prusak 1998). Knowledge transfer is widely regarded as a strategic element in knowledge management. Most researchers (e.g. Albino et al. 1999) in knowledge management tend either to view knowledge transfer as "an act of transmission and reception" (the information system), or to think in terms of "a process of reconstruction" (the interpretative system). The process of knowledge transfer is increasingly seen as crucial to organizational success.
- *Knowledge creation*—Knowledge creation is another key task of knowledge management. Knowledge creation is defined as a spiralling process of interactions between tacit knowledge and explicit knowledge (Nonaka and Takeuchi 1995). Nonaka (1994) points out that knowledge creation embraces a continual dialogue between explicit and tacit knowledge, which boosts the creation of new ideas.
- *Knowledge storage*—Viewing knowledge as a crucial resource, organizations recognize the value of knowledge storage for present and future use. Organizational storage is an important strategic element of knowledge management, by which knowledge is stored and retrieved for present and future (re)use in problem solving or decision making, thereby resulting in the enhancement of the firm's competitive advantage. The preservation of knowledge seems to be a major building block in re-using and creating knowledge.

It has been recognized that managing knowledge is important for organizational survival and growth (e.g. Sutton 2001; Jasimuddin, 2005; Neef 1999; Beckman 1999). Accordingly, effective knowledge management seems to enhance the success of M&A activity as well. The following section will elaborate the generic role of knowledge management, along with its relevance in the M&A context.

THE ROLE OF KNOWLEDGE MANAGEMENT IN M&AS

As noted earlier, successful M&As seem to result in increasing market share and gaining access to an organization's core knowledge (Hitt et al. 2001; McIntyre 2004). However, empirical studies provide mixed results about the undertaking of M&A activities (Covin et al. 1996; Carlton and Lineberry 2004; Schraeder and Self 2003; Bertoncelj and Kovac 2007; Schweiger and Lippert 2005; Cartwright and Schoenberg 2006; Weber and Tarba 2010). Hassan et al. (2007) suggest that more than half of M&As were failures. On the other hand, Cartwright and Schoenberg (2006) report that only 56% of M&As are successful. In this connection, Schweiger and Lippert (2005, as cited in Weber and Tarba 2010) argue that "the sharp increase in M&A activity stands in contrast to their high rate of failure."

There are scholars who attempt to identify the causes of M&As failure. Parallel to this, others (e.g. Grotenhuis and Weggeman 2002; McIntyre 2004; Carrillo and Anumba 2002; Mitleton-Kelly 2006) state that such failure occurs when the combined organization overlooks the importance of the knowledge that resides in the two firms. Carrillo and Anumba (2002), for example, argue that inadequate knowledge exchange does not create the synergy anticipated and may lead to duplication of effort and even repetition errors within the restructured organization. In order to understand the role of managing knowledge in M&A success, the following paragraphs will take a closer look at this.

The role played by knowledge management in an organization has been receiving growing recognition in the management literature (e.g. Brown & Duguid 1998; Nonaka and Takeuchi 1995; Choo 1996; Binney 2001; Jasimuddin et al. 2005; Kogut and Zander 1992). The benefits derived from knowledge management initiatives are many. Knowledge management seeks to improve the performance of an organization by leveraging the existing knowledge assets. In this connection, Sutton (2001) considers it critical to improve the exploitation of the knowledge resources of an enterprise. Petrash (1996) supports this, arguing that knowledge management ensures the availability of "right knowledge to the right people at the right time" so that the best decisions are made.

Reflecting this view, KPMG (1999) provides a list of benefits derived from applying knowledge management, including the generation of new ideas and the exploitation of the organization's thinking power, supporting innovation, capturing insight and experience to make them available when, where, and by whom required, and fostering collaboration and knowledge sharing.

Scholars in M&As (e.g. Boeh and Beamish 2007; Daniel and Metcalf 2001; Schmidt 2002; Kongpichayanond 2009) have suggested that knowledge of the combined organization should be considered vital, since this strongly influences the success of M&A activity. In the M&A context, there is the possibility of loss of an organization's knowledge resources. Resonating with this, Collins and Wickham (2002) contend that M&As seem also to involve the loss of tacit knowledge built up by experience with the organization.

Against this backdrop, the acquired company's knowledge has to be managed within changing organizational structures and cultures (Carrillo and Anumba 2002).

The extant literature reveals that there is some research that has paid limited attention to knowledge management in M&As (Bresman et al. 1999; Grotenhuis and Weggeman 2002; Carrillo and Anumba 2002; Greenwood et al. 1994; Hakanson 1995; Haspeslagh and Jemison 1991; Yoo et al. 2007). For example, Carrillo and Anumba (2002) state that organizational knowledge that resides in the two firms in the pre-M&A situation plays a central role in the success or failure of M&A activity. Alberto Almansa, Chief Knowledge Officer of Cap Gemini Ernst & Young, rightly quotes: "When Cap Gemini purchased Ernst & Young, knowledge management was strategic. Not only for the business but also for the merger's success" (as cited in Segal-Horn and Faulkner 2010).

Kongpichayanond (2009) contends that organizational knowledge and knowledge management are soft sides of M&As that play a vital role in creating the synergy which is a common goal of M&A. Resonating with this, Segal-Horn and Faulkner (2010) emphasize that one of the ways to achieve the synergy benefit goal of M&A activity is through the exchange of knowledge. In this regard, Grotenhuis and Weggeman (2002) explore the need for knowledge management in M&As. In their widely cited article, Bresman, Birkinshaw, and Nobel (1999) support this, remarking that due to the failure to transfer knowledge properly, a combined firm can fail to realize the expected synergy. Instead the firm may make the same errors or waste resources in solving its problems. Hence, knowledge management is critical for a successful M&A.

Despite the importance of knowledge management in M&As, there appear to be challenges for M&As in implementing knowledge management. The following section addresses the challenges of M&As in terms of knowledge management implementation.

CHALLENGES OF M&AS FROM A KNOWLEDGE MANAGEMENT PERSPECTIVE

Child, Faulkner, and Pitkethly (2006) describe M&As as "among the most important strategic decisions companies ever make." Such a decision has long-term implications for the combined firm that may sometimes pose a threat to its survival. As mentioned earlier, M&As allow the gaining of expertise, technology, and products in an amalgamated firm (e.g. Chua and Goh 2009; Barney 1996; Haspeslagh and Jemison 1991; Empson 2001). The exploration and exploitation of knowledge assets that are available in the units of a combined company is regarded as a critical factor in the success of M&A. The following paragraphs highlight the challenges faced by a combined firm in effectively implementing a knowledge management initiative in M&A.

It is argued that there is the possibility of losing an organization's knowledge resources while undertaking M&A. Resonating with this, Collins and Wickham (2002) consider that mergers may also lead to the loss of knowledge, particularly tacit knowledge.

Likewise, Carrillo and Anumba (2002) state that organizations find it difficult to manage their own knowledge when they go for an organizational change. Furthermore, Carrillo and Anumba (2002) argue that knowledge management becomes more complicated in M&A. Table 18.1 demonstrates three different scenarios of M&A, based on whether knowledge management (KM) is common practice in the two companies' pre-M&A activity.

The challenge of M&As is to properly manage the knowledge assets available in both the units of combined organizations, because it becomes increasingly difficult to determine "what the organization knows" and "who knows what" in a scenario where two firms have amalgamated (Carrillo and Anumba 2002). Similarly, other researchers (e.g. Kamara et al. 2001; Kongpichayanond 2009) contend that the challenge for managers of M&As is to ensure that knowledge management practices fit the respective structural configurations and communication patterns.

Moreover, it is strongly believed that M&As activity may create a climate of fear and loss of trust among the employees of the two units of an amalgamated firm, which may make knowledge transfer difficult. Consistent with this, Empson (2001) identifies fear of exploitation and fear of contamination as hurdles to knowledge transfer in M&As between professional services firms (PSFs), arguing that

> Developing knowledge "organically" is costly, both in terms of time and resources, and success cannot be guaranteed. By contrast, mergers provide firms with the opportunity to gain access to a pre-existing knowledge base of proven value. The challenge for managers of merging PSFs is to convert the opportunity for knowledge transfer into a reality. (p. 843)

As evidenced by the literature, knowledge management has been implemented in different modes of governance, including joint ventures. Contrarily, Kamara, Anumba, and Carrillo (2001, as cited in Kongpichayanond 2009) argue that knowledge management becomes more difficult to implement when organizations are transformed through M&A. In this regard, Chua and Goh (2009) elaborate the flipside of M&As with regard

Table 18.1 Different scenarios of M&As with respect to knowledge management

Scenario	Knowledge management practice in pre-M&A		Combined firm after M&A activity
	Company A	Company B	
I	Yes	Yes	Matter of integration—but not difficult
II	Yes	No	Difficult to integrate
III	No	No	Daunting task—introduce KM initiative from scratch for the first time

to knowledge, such as the departure of experts from the acquired firm, destruction of the acquired organization's knowledge ecology, and mixed perceptions of the acquired firm's knowledge.

While proposing a process model of post-merger knowledge exchange, Yoo, Lyytinen, and Heo (2007) identify several problems associated with knowledge. These problems include:

- a lack of shared context,
- the incompatibility of existing knowledge systems, and
- the handling of tacit dimension of knowledge.

Since effective implementation of knowledge management is a prerequisite for the successful integration of the two units in a combined firm, the next section will address the critical factors that may help in the successful implementation of knowledge management in a restructured firm post-M&A.

CRITICAL DETERMINANTS OF M&AS SUCCESS FROM A KNOWLEDGE MANAGEMENT PERSPECTIVE

Despite overwhelming evidence of mixed results on the success of M&As activities, many researchers argue that the effective utilization of knowledge management may lead to the success of M&As. In this regard, Chua and Goh (2009) point out that within the current literature the success and failure of M&As are rarely framed as a knowledge management issue. As mentioned earlier, one distinct motive for a firm to undergo M&A is to grab a competitive firm's knowledge base via M&A. It is interesting to observe that companies in every sector still continue to use M&As as a strategy for growth. For example, automobile manufacturing giant Daimler-Benz acquired Chrysler, another giant in the automobile industry, for $40 billion (Teternbaum 1999).

It is believed that an underemphasis on knowledge management may have led to M&As' failure. Grotenhuis and Weggeman (2002) suggest that the knowledge base needs to be managed carefully in M&As in order to maintain resources and to be able to achieve the intended synergies. There is a need to understand how knowledge management can be launched and implemented in the M&A context in order to exploit its potential.

The relevant literature reveals that it is difficult to manage knowledge when two firms undergo M&A activity. Recently, Chua and Goh (2009) explain why an acquiring company is unable to leverage the knowledge of an acquired firm even though both organizations were highly successful in their own right prior to the amalgamation. However, Kongpichayanond (2009) seeks to propose a system-based framework, suggesting the relationship between knowledge management and M&As. Haspeslagh and Jemison

(1991) suggest that effective implementation of knowledge management is contingent on the successful integration of the acquired firm. M&As actually need to create the conditions for efficient knowledge management practice between the units of a combined firm. Parallel to this, in their classic work, Bresman, Birkinshaw, and Nobel (1999) rightly comment that the transfer and utilization of knowledge through M&As can be a daunting task. The following paragraphs will set out the key factors that seem to help implement knowledge management successfully in M&As in order to realize knowledge-based synergies.

The Nature of the Knowledge

Organizational knowledge of the companies affected by M&A activity has both tacit and explicit components. The primary factor that influences the choice of knowledge transfer mechanism in a combined firm is the tacitness of knowledge. Several researchers, most notably Ranft (1997) and Bresman et al. (1999), contend that for knowledge management in M&As to be successful, it is necessary to take into account the nature of the knowledge to be transferred. To put it differently, the nature of the underlying knowledge will have an important impact on the knowledge management process.

It is worth mentioning that tacit knowledge resides in the human brain, and may be ambiguous. Since tacit knowledge that is not well defined requires more interpretation, Gupta and Govindaranjan (2000) suggest that the ability to disseminate such knowledge requires rich transmission channels, such as face-to-face (F-2-F) communication and the movement of experts. Again, tacit knowledge does not always remain tacit. A large portion of such knowledge is articulated in some way, and subsequently stored for future use so that it becomes easier to transfer. Knowledge available in a repository is thought to be a more formal way of transferring knowledge which is actually explicit in nature.

Several researchers (e.g. Connell et al. 2003; Gupta and Govindaranjan 2000; Lam 1997; Storey and Barnett 2001) suggest active direct communication between individuals as a means of tacit knowledge transfer and F-2-F interaction is recommended as the most suitable way of facilitating the transfer of tacit knowledge. On the other hand, explicit knowledge can be transferred via a codification approach (Hansen et al. 1999; Jasimuddin et al. 2005; Earl 2000). The restructured company should be aware of the nature of knowledge and accordingly follow a strategy that suits it best.

A Unified Strategy to Explore and Exploit Knowledge

While undertaking a M&A, two organizations come along with different strategies and priorities at different levels. Even though they are amalgamated, they may intend to continue their corporate strategy. This may lead them to differ slightly from one another as far as knowledge exploitation is concerned. In the post-M&A situation, their strategy and focus may remain different, which will definitely have an influence on knowledge management implementation in the combined firm. When it comes to launching a knowledge management initiative, there should be a unified strategy to explore and exploit knowledge from both the units of M&A.

It could be argued that in order to achieve the best possible outcome of M&A, the two companies should integrate their strategy within the combined firm in order to get better results out of knowledge management use. It should be noted that E&Y has explicitly recognized knowledge management as an outstanding part of its strategy (Segal-Horn and Faulkner 2010). Similarly, Cap Gemini has its knowledge management strategy. Together, Cap Gemini E&Y has one unified knowledge management strategy. Hence it could be suggested that knowledge management in M&As requires specific management processes, since the combination of firms involves the joining of two corporate strategies into a single knowledge management strategy.

The Combination of Different Cultures at Different Levels

While undertaking a M&A, two organizations seem to have different cultures. There is overwhelming evidence (e.g. Teternbaum 1999; Hasegawa 2000; McCann III 1996) to suggest that one important issue in the effective implementation of knowledge management, as well as for the success of M&A, is culture. For example, Hasegawa (2000) argues that corporate culture is the biggest of the initial changes to occur with M&A. Parallel to this, McCann III (1996) suggests that managing cultural differences requires a long-term perspective on an M&A deal. Integration of different issues relating to culture is a much more immediate concern after such a deal has been completed. The notion of cultural clash is taken seriously, as it is frequently identified as a factor explaining why M&A has failed to produce results. Resonating with this, Ardichvili, Page, and Wentling (2003) contend that cultural differences loom large in knowledge transfer during M&As.

Shrivastava (1986) claims that in order to achieve the best possible outcome of M&A, the two companies should be integrated to make them as similar as possible by attaining a mutual corporate culture. Napier, Simmons, and Stratton (1989) produce evidence that, in reality, acquired companies often adapt to the acquiring company's culture and routines. That is why Yoo, Lyytinen, and Heo (2007) encourage a combined firm to develop a shared culture in M&A. During the selection of a firm (to be acquired or merged), companies need to consider the compatibility of cultural values and management practice. In this regard, several authors, most notably Lafiax (2002), Schmidt (2002), and Kongpichayanond (2009), suggest that if a firm selects the wrong organization to merge with or acquire, the result will be the incompatibility of cultural values, clashes in management practice, and loss of key experts, which may eventually lead to the collapse of the restructured firm. Hence, among others, Grotenhuis and Weggeman (2002) also suggest the two cultures need to be combined in M&As.

The Compatibility of Existing Knowledge Systems

While amalgamating through M&A, the two organizations seem to have different ways of treating knowledge assets. Chua and Goh (2009) point to differences in technology infrastructure and knowledge management processes between the two organizations. Yoo, Lyytinen, and Heo (2007) view the incompatibility of existing knowledge systems as a problem in the post-merger environment. For example, both Cap Gemini and E&Y had followed their own knowledge management systems in the past (Segal-Horn and Faulkner 2010).

However, efforts need to be made to design a holistic approach to knowledge management systems that seems to ensure compatibility. In line with this, Grotenhuis and Weggeman (2002) suggest two systems of knowledge integration in M&A situations so as to be able to achieve the intended synergies. It is worth mentioning that the merger of Cap Gemini and E&Y early in 2000 made clear the requirement for an integrated system.

Trust

A knowledge-hoarding tendency hampers the flow of knowledge between the personnel of two companies. The free and frequent flow of knowledge is necessary to make a success of M&As. In this connection, Rumyntseva, Gurgul, and Enkel (2002) argue that knowledge transfer between the merging organizations depends on the development of a cooperative relationship. Reflecting this view, Kongpichayanond (2009) suggests two important elements relating to knowledge management that create a congenial atmosphere for M&As: the willingness of employees in each firm to transfer knowledge, and to receive the knowledge necessary for value creation.

In this regard, Norman (2001) points out that trust is one of the most important characteristics that influence knowledge exchange, an essential aspect of knowledge management. Similarly, Bresman, Birkinshaw, and Nobel (1999) postulate that knowledge transfer between the merging organizations depends on the development of a cooperative relationship. The fact is that trust between individuals has been shown to be a prerequisite for the successful transfer of knowledge.

Early empirical research efforts have begun to shed some light on trust and the knowledge transfer process (e.g. Keong and Al-Hawamdeh 2002; Bouty 2000). When a partner is more highly trusted, fewer or less stringent mechanisms are needed to control potential opportunism. Bresman, Birkinshaw, and Nobel (1999) remark that knowledge transfer can be facilitated by communication, visits, and meetings, while Keong and Al-Hawamdeh (2002) contend that an environment of trust is conducive to knowledge sharing. Likewise, Bouty (2000) makes a similar comment, saying that "trust is crucial in the sense that the provider needs to trust the receiver not to exploit the shared knowledge for purposes other than those agreed upon, implicitly as well as explicitly."

Davenport and Prusak (1998) assert that greater levels of trust tend to promote higher levels of knowledge transfer. Drawing on scholars' work, it could be said that building trust among the members of the two amalgamating units is thought to be a necessary condition for the success of a restructured organization.

CONCLUSIONS

The terminology "mergers and acquisitions" refers to a mode of governance which indicates a change in company ownership. A combined firm through M&A facilitates several benefits, including strengthening market position, reducing operational costs, enhancing competencies, improving the image of the combined firm, ensuring better services to potential customers, and realizing synergy. Most specifically, cross-border M&A is constantly used as a strategy for market entry. Moreover, M&A provides a firm with an opportunity to gain access to the knowledge and technology of the other company being acquired or merged with.

However, empirical studies provide mixed results about the undertaking of M&A activities. Failure of M&A activity seems to occur when the amalgamated organization overlooks the importance of the knowledge that resides in the two firms. Organizational knowledge is increasingly treated as crucial to realize the potential of M&As. In other words, knowledge that resides in the two firms in the pre-M&A situation plays a central role in the success of M&A activity. Knowledge management is regarded as a strategic tool in an M&A's success. However, the topic associated with the connection between knowledge management and M&As represents a relatively limited strand in the extant literature. This chapter provides insights into understanding the relationship between knowledge management and M&As.

One of the objectives of this chapter is to understand the role of knowledge management in the M&A context. Knowledge management has the potential to bring about the success of M&As. Scholars have stressed that knowledge is a critical component in successful M&As, and knowledge management is important in managing the knowledge available in the two units of the combined firm to create value. In order to exploit the existing knowledge available in the two units, the combined organization should make full use of knowledge management that influences the success of M&A activity.

The implementation of knowledge management in the M&A context is not an easy task. Another objective of this chapter has been to identify the factors that facilitate the implementation of knowledge management initiative in M&As. In reality, a combined firm faces challenges when implementing a knowledge management initiative successfully in M&A. The chapter identifies those factors in the effective implementation of knowledge management that seem to enhance the success of an M&A activity. For example, in M&A situations, two knowledge bases need to be combined in the expectation of synergies to be derived from the joint forces. Similarly, the two different cultures of the two units need to be combined in M&As.

Mergers and acquisitions (M&As) activity is a popular strategy of organizational survival and growth for a firm, which eventually enhances its competitive advantage over its rivals. This chapter provides some insights into the relationship between knowledge management and M&As, in that M&As can be used to gain access to other firms' knowledge, and knowledge management can be utilized to discover and deploy organizational knowledge leading to the M&A success. Since the chapter is based on the extant relevant literature, further research is required to collect data in order to empirically explore the factors that help in the effective implementation of knowledge management in M&As, and to examine the implications of knowledge management in M&As' success.

References

Albino, V., Claudio, G. A., & Schiuma, G. (1999). "Knowledge Transfer and Inter-firm Relationships in Industrial Districts: The Role of the Leader Firm." *Technovation*, 19: 53–63.

Ardichvili, A., Page, P., & Wentling, T. (2003). "Motivation and Barriers in Participation in Virtual Knowledge Sharing Communities of Practice." *Journal of Knowledge Management*, 7/1: 64–77.

Barney, J. B. (1996). *Gaining and Sustaining Competitive Advantage*. Reading, MA: Addison-Wesley.

Bartlett, C. A., & Ghosal, S. (1989). *Managing across Borders: The Transnational Solution*. Boston, MA: Harvard Business School Press.

Beckman, T. J. (1999). "The Current State of Knowledge Management," in J. Liebowitz (ed.), *Knowledge Management Handbook*. Florida: CRC Press LLC, 1–22.

Bertoncelj, A., & Kovac, D. (2007). "An Integrated Approach for a Higher Success Rate in Mergers and Acquisitions." *Journal of Economics and Business, Proceedings of Rijeka Faculty of Economics*, 25/1: 167–88.

Binney, D. (2001). "The Knowledge Management Spectrum: Understanding the KM Spectrum." *Journal of Knowledge Management*, 5/1: 33–42.

Boeh, G. W., & Beamish, P. W. (2007). *Mergers & Acquisitions: Text and Cases*. Thousand Oaks, CA: Sage.

Bouty, I. (2000). "Interpersonal and Interaction Influences on Informal Resources Exchanges between R&D Researchers across Organizational Boundaries." *Academy of Management Journal*, 43/1: 50–65.

Bresman, H., Birkinshaw, J., & Nobel, R. (1999). "Knowledge Transfer in International Acquisitions." *Journal of International Business Studies*, 30/3: 439–62.

Brouthers, K. D., van Hustenburg, P., & van den Ven, J. (1998). "If most Mergers Fail Why are They so Popular?" *Long Range Planning*, 31/3: 347–53.

Brown, J., & Duguid, P. (1998). "Organizing Knowledge." *California Management Review*, 40/3: 90–111.

Carlton, J. P., & Lineberry, C. S. (2004). *Achieving Post-merger Success*. San Francisco: John Wiley & Sons.

Carrillo, P., & Anumba, C. (2002). "Knowledge Management in the AEC A Sector: An Exploration of the Mergers and Acquisitions Context." *Knowledge and Process Management*, 9/3: 149–61.

Cartwright, S., & Schoenberg, R. (2006). "Thirty Years of Mergers and Acquisitions Research: Recent Advances and Future Opportunities." *British Journal of Management*, Special Edition, 17:1–5.

Casal, C. C., & Fontela, E. N. (2007). "Transfer of Socially Complex Knowledge in Mergers and Acquisitions." *Journal of Knowledge Management*, 11/4: 58–71.

Child, J., Faulkner, D., & Pitkethly, R. (2006). *The Management of International Acquisitions.* Oxford: Oxford University Press.

Choo, C. W. (1996). "The Knowing Organization: How Organizations Use Information to Construct Meaning, Create Knowledge and Make Decisions." *International Journal of Information Management*, 16/5: 329–40.

Chua, A. Y. K., & Goh, D. H. (2009). "Why the Whole is less than the Sum of its Parts: Examining Knowledge Management in Acquisitions." *International Journal of Information Management*, 29: 78–86.

Collins, G., & Wickham, J. (2002). "Experiencing Mergers: A Woman's Eye View." *Women's Studies International Forum*, 25/5: 573–83.

Connell, N. A. D., Klein, J. H., & Powell, P. L. (2003). "It's Tacit Knowledge but Not as we Know it: Redirecting the Search for Knowledge." *Journal of Operational Research Society*, 54: 140–52.

Cooper, C., & Gregory, A. (2003). *Advances in Merger and Acquisitions.* New York: Elsevier Science.

Covin, T. J., Sightler, K. W., Kolenko, T. A., & Tudor, K. R. (1996). "An Investigation of Post-Acquisition Satisfaction with the Merger." *The Journal of Applied Behavioral Science*, 32/2:125–37.

Daniel, T. A., & Metcalf, G. S. (2001). *The Management of Merger and Acquisitions.* Westport, CT: Quorum.

Davenport, T. H., & Prusak, L. (1998). *Working Knowledge: How Organizations Manage What They Know.* Boston, MA: Harvard Business School Press.

Dealogic (2008). "Mergers & Acquisitions, M&A Analytics." Available at: <http://www.dealogic.com>.

Desylla, P., & Hughes, A. (2008). "Sourcing Technical Knowledge through Corporate Acquisition: Evidence from an International Sample of High Technology Firms." *The Journal of High Technology Management Research*, 18: 157–72.

Doz, Y. L. (1996). "The Evaluation of Cooperation in Strategic Alliances: Initial Conditions or Learning Processes?" *Strategic Management Journal*, 17: 55–84.

Earl, M. (2000). "Knowledge Management Strategies: Toward a Taxonomy." *Journal of Management Information Systems*, 18/1: 215–33.

Empson, L. (2001). "Fear of Exploitation and Fear of Contamination: Impediments to Knowledge Transfer in Mergers between Professional Service Firms." *Human Relations*, 54: 839–62.

Gerpott, T. J. (1995). "Successful Integration of R&D Functions after Acquisition: An Exploratory Empirical Study." *R&D Management*, 25: 161–78.

Greenwood, R., Hinings, C. R., & Brown, J. (1994). "Merging Professional Service Firms." *Organizational Science*, 5/2: 239–57.

Grotenhuis, F. D. J., & Weggeman, M. P. (2002). "Knowledge Management in International Mergers." *Knowledge and Process Management*, 9/2: 83–9.

Gupta, A. K., & Govindaranjan, V. (2000). "Knowledge Management's Social Dimension: Lessons from Nucor Steel." *Sloan Management Review*, 42/1, Fall: 71-80.

Gupta, O., & Roos, G. (2001). "Mergers and Acquisitions through an Intellectual Capital Perspective." *Journal of Intellectual Capital*, 2/3: 297–309.

Hakanson, L. (1995). "Learning through Acquisitions: Management and Integration of Foreign R&D Laboratories." *International Studies of Management and Organization*, 25/1–2: 121–58.

Hamel, G. (1991). "Competition for Competence and Inter-partner Learning within International Strategic Alliances." *Strategic Management Journal*, 12: 83–104.

Hansen, M. T., Nohria, N., & Tierney T. (1999). "What's Your Strategy for Managing Knowledge?" *Harvard Business Review*, 77/2: 106–16.

Hasegawa, H. (2000). "Global Acquisition and Knowledge Transfer: A Case Study of Company D." *International Business Review*, 9: 587–98.

Haspeslagh, P., & Jemison, D. (1991). *"Managing Acquisitions: Creating Value through Corporate Renewal."* Oxford: The Free Press.

Hassan, M., Patro, D. K., Tuckman, H. & Wang, X. (2007). "Do Mergers and Acquisitions Create Shareholder Wealth in the Pharmaceutical Industry?" *International Journal of Pharmaceutical and Healthcare Marketing*, 1/1: 58–78.

Hedlund, G. (1994). "A Model of Knowledge Management and the N-form Corporation." *Strategic Management Journal*, 15: 3–91.

Hitt, M. A., Ireland, R. D., & Harrison, J. S. (2001). "Mergers and Acquisitions: A Value Creating or Value Destroying Strategy?" in M. A. Hitt, R. D. Ireland, & J. S. Harrison (eds.), *Handbook of Strategic Management*. Oxford: Blackwell, 384–432.

—— & Pisano, V. (2004). "Cross-Border Mergers and Acquisitions: Challenges and Opportunities?" in A. L. Pablo & M. Javidan (eds.), *Mergers and Acquisitions: Creating Integrated Knowledge*. Malden, MA: Blackwell, 45–59.

Hopkins, H. D. (1999). "Cross-Border Mergers and Acquisitions: Global and Regional Perspectives." *Journal of International Management*, 5: 207–39.

Horwitz, M. F., Anderson, K., Bezuidenhout, A., Cohen, S., Kirsten, F., & Moseunyne, K. (2002). "Due Diligence Neglected: Managing Human Resources and Organisational Culture in Mergers and Acquisitions." *South African Journal of Business Management*, 33/1: 1–10.

Huber, G. P. (1991). "Organizational Learning: The Contributing Process and the Literatures." *Organization Science*, 2/1: 88–115.

Huyghebaert, N., & Laypaert, M. (2010). "Antecedents of Growth through Mergers and Acquisitions: Empirical Results from Belgium." *Journal of Business Research*, 63: 392–403.

Inkpen, A. (1992). "Learning and Collaboration: An Examination of North American-Japanese Joint Ventures." Unpublished doctoral dissertation, University of Western Ontario.

—— & Crossan, M. (1992). "Believing is Seeing: Joint Ventures and Organisational Learning." *Journal of Management Studies*, 22/5: 595–618.

Jasimuddin, S. M. (2005). "Knowledge of External Sources' Knowledge: New Frontier to Actionable Knowledge," in M. A. Rahim, & K. D. Mackenzie (eds.), *Current Topics in Management*, vol. 10. New Brunswick, NJ: Transaction Publishers, 39–50.

—— (2006a). "Disciplinary Roots of Knowledge Management: A Theoretical Review." *International Journal of Organizational Analysis*, 14/2: 171–80.

—— (2006b). "Knowledge Transfer: A Review to Explore Conceptual Foundations and Research Agenda," in L. Moutinho, G. Hutcheson, & P. Rita (eds.), *Advances in Doctoral Research in Management*, vol. 1. Singapore: World Scientific, 3–20.

—— Klein, J. H., & Connell, C. (2005). "The Paradox of Using Tacit and Explicit Knowledge: Strategies to Face Dilemmas." *Management Decision*, 43/1: 102–12.

Kamara, M., Anumba, C. J., & Carrillo, P. M. (2001). "Knowledge Management in a Multi-Project Environment in Construction," in A. Singh (ed.), *Proceedings of the First International Structural and Construction Conference (ISEC-01)*. Hawaii and Rotterdam: A. A. Balkema, 321–26.

Karim, S., & Mitchell, W. (2000). "Path-Dependent and Path-Breaking Change: Reconfiguring Business Resources Following Acquisitions in the US Medical Sector, 1978–1995." *Strategic Management Journal*, 21/10/11: 1061–81.

Keong, L. C., & Al-Hawamdeh, S. (2002). "Factors Impacting Knowledge Sharing." *Journal of Information & Knowledge Management*, 1/1: 49–56.

Kogut, B. (1988). "Joint Ventures: Theoretical and Empirical Perspectives." *Strategic Management Journal*, 9: 319–22.

—— & Zander, U. (1992). "Knowledge of the Firm, Combinative Capabilities, and the Replication of Technology." *Organization Science*, 3/3: 383–97.

Kongpichayanond, P. (2009). "Knowledge Management for Sustained Competitive Advantage in Mergers and Acquisitions." *Advances in Developing Human Resources*, 11: 375–87.

KPMG (1999). *The Power of Knowledge: A Business Guide to Knowledge Management*. London: The KPMG Management Consulting.

Kumar, S., & Bansal, L. K. (2008). "The Impact of Mergers and Acquisitions on Corporate Performance in India." *Management Decision*, 46/10: 1531–43.

Lafaix, F. (2002). "The Pre-deal Stage," in J. A. Schmidt (ed.), *Making Mergers Work: The Strategic Importance of People*. Alexandria, VA: Tower Perrin/SHRM, 49–76.

Larsson, R., & Finkelstein, S. (1999). "Integrating Strategic, Organisational and Human Resource Perspectives on Mergers and Acquisitions: A Case Study of Synergy Realisation." *Organisation Science*, 10/1:1–26.

Liu, X., & Zou, H. (2008). "The Impact of Greenfield FDI and Mergers and Acquisitions on Innovation in Chinese High-Tech Industries." *Journal of World Business*, 43: 352–64.

Lynch, J. G., & Lind, B. (2002). "Escaping Merger and Acquisition Madness." *Strategy & Leadership*, 30/2: 5–12.

Madhok, A. (1997). "Cost, Value and Foreign Market Entry Mode: The Transaction and the Firm." *Strategic Management Journal*, 18/1: 39–53.

McCann III, J. E. (1996). "The Growth of Acquisitions in Services." *Long Range Planning*, 29/6: 835–41.

McIntyre, T. L. (2004). "A Model of Levels of Involvement and Strategic Roles of Human Resource Development (HRD) Professionals as Facilitators of Due Diligence and the Integration Process." *Human Resource Development Review*, 3/2:173–82.

Mitleton-Kelly, E. (2006). "Co-evolutionary Integration: The Co-creation of a New Organisational Form Following M&A." *Emergence: Complexity & Organisation*, 8/2: 36–47.

Morwery, D. C., Oxley, J. E., & Silverman, B. S. (1996). "Strategic Alliances and Interfirm Knowledge Transfer." *Strategic Management Journal*, 17: 77–92.

Napier, N. K., Simmons, G., & Stratton, K. (1989). "Communications during a Merger: The Experience of Two Banks." *Human Resource Planning*, 12/2: 105–22.

Neef, D. (1999). "Making the Case for Knowledge Management: The Bigger Picture." *Management Decision*, 37/1: 72–8.

Nonaka, I. (1994). "A Dynamic Theory of Organizational Knowledge Creation." *Organization Science*, 5/1: 14–37.

—— & Takeuchi, H. (1995). *The Knowledge Creating Company*. Oxford: Oxford University Press.

Norman, P. C. (2001). "Are Your Secrets Safe? Knowledge Protection in Strategic Alliances." *Business Horizons*, 44/6: 51–60.

Pablo, L. A., & Javidan, M. (2004). *Mergers and Acquisitions: Creating Integrating Knowledge*. Boston, MA: Blackwell.

Petrash, G. (1996). "Dow's Journey to a Knowledge Value Management Culture." *European Management Journal*, 14/4: 365–73.

Ranft, A. L.(1997). "Preserving and Transferring Knowledge-Based Resources during Post-Acquisitions Implementation." PhD dissertation. University of North Caroline, Chapel Hill, NC.

Rumyntseva, M., Gurgul, G., & Enkel, E. (2002). "Knowledge Integration after Mergers & Acquisitions." Discussion Paper No. 42.

Schmidt, A. J. (2002). *Making Mergers Work: The Strategic Importance of People*. Alexandria, VA: Tower Perin/SHRM.

Schoenberg, R. (2003). "Mergers and Acquisitions: Motives, Value Creation, and Implementation," in D. Faulkner & A. Campbell (eds.), *The Oxford Handbook of Strategy*. Oxford: Oxford University Press, 587–609.

Schraeder, M., & Self, D. R. (2003). "Enhancing the Success of Mergers and Acquisitions." *Management Decision*, 41/5: 511–22.

Schweiger, D. M., & Lippert, R. L. (2005). "Integration: The Critical Link in M&As Value Creation," in G. K. Stahl & M. E. Mendenhall (eds.), *Mergers and Acquisitions: Managing Culture and Human Resources*. Stanford, CA: Stanford University Press.

Segal-Horn, S. & Faulkner, D. (2010). *Understanding Global Strategy*. Oxford: Oxford University Press,

Shrivastava, P. (1986). "Postmerger Integration." *Journal of Business Strategy*, 7/1: 65–76.

Simonin, B. L. (1999). "Ambiguity and the Process of Knowledge in Strategic Alliances." *Strategic Management Journal,* 20: 595–623.

Snowden, D. (1999). "A Framework for Creating a Sustainable Knowledge Management Program," in J. W. Cortada and J. A. Woods (eds.), *The Knowledge Management Yearbook 1999-2000*. Boston, MA: Butterworth-Heinemann, 52–64.

Stahl, G. K., Mendenhall, M. E., Pablo, A. L., & Javidan, M. (2005). "Social-cultural Integration in Mergers and Acquisitions," in G. K. Stahl & M. E. Mendenhall (eds.), *Mergers and Acquisitions: Managing Culture and Human Resources*. Stanford, CA: Stanford University Press.

Stewart, R., Wingate, P., & Smith, R. (1963). *The Impact of Mergers*. London: The Action Society Trust.

Stiebale, J., & Reize, F. (2011). "The Impact of FDI through Mergers and Acquisitions on Innovation in Target Firms." *International Journal of Industrial Organisation*, 29/2: 155–67.

Storey, J., & Barnett, E. (2001). "Knowledge Management Initiatives: Learning from Failure." *Journal of Knowledge Management,* 4/2: 145–56.

Story, L., & Helft, M. (2007). "Google Buys an Online Ad Firm for $3.1 Billion." *New York Times*, p. 1. Accessed at <http://www.nytimes.com/2007/04/14/technology/14DoubleClick.html>.

Sutton, D. C. (2001). "What is Knowledge and Can it be Managed?" *European Journal of Information Systems*, 10/2: 80–8.

Szulanski, G. (1996). "Exploring Internal Stickiness: Impediment to the Transfer of Best Practice with the Term." *Strategic Management Journal*, 17: 27–43.

Teternbaum, T. J. (1999). "Beating the Odds of Merger & Acquisitions Failure: Seven Key Practices that Improve the Chance for Expected Integration and Synergies." *Organisational Dynamics*, 28/2: 22–36.

Tsai, W. (2001). "Knowledge Transfer in Intraorganisational Networks: Effects of Network Position and Absorptive Capacity on Business Unit Innovation and Performance." *Academy of Management Journal*, 44/5: 996–1004.

Tsang, E. M. K. (2002). "Acquiring Knowledge by Foreign Partners from International Joint Ventures in a Transition Economy: Learning-by-Doing and Learning Myopia." *Strategic Management Journal*, 23/9: 835–54.

UNCTAD (2007). *World Investment Report 2007: Transnational Corporations, Extractive Industries and Development*. New York: United Nations.

Weber, Y., & Tarba, S. Y. (2010). "Human Resources Practices and Performance of Mergers and Acquisitions in Israel." *Human Resource Management Review*, 20: 203–11.

Westney, D. E. (1993). "Institutionalisation Theory and the MNC," in S. Ghosal & D. E. Westney (eds.) *Organization Theory and the Multinational Corporation*. New York: St Martin's Press.

Wiig, K. M. (1997). "Knowledge Management: Where did it Come From and Where will it Go?" *Expert Systems with Applications*, 13–14(Fall): 1–14.

Yildiz, H. E., & Fey, C. F. (2010). "Compatibility and Unlearning in Knowledge Transfer in Merger and Acquisitions." *Scandinavian Journal of Management*, 26: 448–56.

Yoo, Y., Lyytinen, K., & Heo, D. (2007). "Closing the Gap: Towards a Process Model of Post-merger Knowledge Sharing." *Information System Journal*, 17: 321–47.

CHAPTER 19

....

A SOCIAL IDENTITY
ANALYSIS OF MERGERS
AND ACQUISITIONS

....

STEFFEN R. GIESSNER, JOHANNES ULLRICH,
AND ROLF VAN DICK

UNDERSTANDING employees' relationship with the organization is crucial for successful mergers and acquisitions (M&As). Nearly 80 years ago, James O. McKinsey identified the "development of a proper *esprit de corps* among the employees of the new organization" (McKinsey 1929: 334; emphasis in original) as a major challenge for merging companies. He argued that employees' loyalty to the former organization would hinder post-merger success. Furthermore, it takes time and "the exerting of a considerable amount of diplomacy on the part of the management" (p. 334) to increase employees' loyalty to the post-merger organization. The financial failure of 50–80% of M&A activities is at least partly explained by this human side of the merger (Cartwright and Cooper 1996).

Employees' psychological reactions during the merger process have, therefore, received substantial attention from theorists and researchers alike (Cartwright 2005; Hogan and Overmyer-Day 1994) and the group psychology of reactions to M&As has been described using terms like *esprit de corps* (McKinsey 1929), commitment (Schweiger and DeNisi 1991), merger support (Giessner et al. 2006), culture collisions (Cartwright and Cooper 1993; Stahl and Voigt 2008), morale (Levinson 1970), family atmosphere and camaraderie (Buono, Bowditch, and Lewis 1985), trust (Jemison and Sitkin 1986; Stahl and Sitkin 2005), employee resistance (Larsson and Finkelstein 1999; cf. van Dijk and van Dick 2009), acculturation (Larsson and Lubatkin 2001; Marks and Mirvis 2001; Nahavandi and Malekzadeh 1988), ingroup bias (Terry 2001), or post-merger identification (van Knippenberg and van Leeuwen 2001; Ullrich and van Dick 2007).

Although each of these labels carries a unique meaning and theoretical depth, they share a focus on employees' relationship to the organizations involved in a merger: pre-merger organization and post-merger organization. One influential approach to study-ing the effects of group membership on perceptions, evaluations, and behavior is the social identity approach (SIA) which is grounded in social identity theory (Hogg and Abrams 1988; Tajfel and Turner 1986) and self-categorization theory (Turner et al. 1987), as well as the optimal distinctiveness theory (Brewer 1991). Not surprisingly then, research on the group psychology of M&As has greatly benefitted from applying such a social identity analysis (Giessner 2009; Terry 2001; Ullrich and van Dick 2007; van Knippenberg and van Leeuwen 2001). An identity-based analysis of M&As is fruitful because M&As can affect various employee identities. The most important identities affected by an organizational merger are the pre-merger identity of the organizations prior to the merger and the post-merger identity of the merged organizations. However, there are also subgroups affected by an M&A such as smaller groups within the merger partners (Lupina-Wegener et al. 2011) or the identities of individuals as employees (who often resist the change) or as agents of change (who have to cope with resistance) (van Dijk and van Dick 2009).

In this chapter, we review M&A research that is based on a social identity approach (see Haslam 2004; van Dick 2004). We will not differentiate between acquisitions and mergers, but we will be using these terms interchangeably. Although their distinction is obviously necessary and useful from a legal perspective, a social identity analysis finds more value in examining status and power relations between the two organizations in question. And perceptions of power or status can often be independent of who acquires and who is acquired. In this way, the old adage that there is never a merger of equals holds true. In the following, we will first introduce the central theoretical assumptions of the SIA, which provides a coherent framework for understanding and managing psy-chological reactions to M&As. Next, we review important insights from empirical research applying such a perspective. Finally, we discuss open questions and promising areas for future research.

The Social Identity Approach (SIA)

The SIA represents a general theory of group processes and intergroup relations. The important assumption of this approach is that individuals perceive the social world in terms of social categories. The perceived membership of social categories contributes to the self-definition of the individuals. In other words, people define themselves not only on the basis of their individual characteristics and the interpersonal relations that dis-tinguish them from other individuals (i.e. *personal identity*), but also in terms of the characteristics of the social groups to which they belong (i.e. *social identity*). This group membership renders an individual similar to (or, in fact, interchangeable with) other (in)group members and different from members of distinct (out)groups. These two dif-ferent aspects of the self mark the ends of a theoretical continuum from *interpersonal* to *intergroup behavior*. One of the great insights of Tajfel and Turner (1986) was that the situational *salience* of different aspects of the self (i.e. personal vs. social) can fundamentally alter the kind of comparisons people make, so that the resulting motivation to act can vary considerably. As an example, a banker whose personal identity is salient may try to maximize his salary by selling more products to customers and working longer office hours. But when his social identity as a member of his workgroup is salient, he may reduce effort in personal sales to avoid outperforming his teammates and he might, thus, perform in accord with the group's norms.

Organizational theorists and researchers have applied these insights from the SIA and argue that organizational identification plays an important part in predicting and understanding employees' motivations, perceptions, and performance. Organizational identification can be defined as a "relatively enduring state that reflects an individual's willingness to define him- or herself as a member of a particular organization" (Haslam 2004: 281; see also Ashforth and Mael 1989; Hogg and Terry 2000). Meta-analyses have shown that organizational identification is positively associated with job satisfaction and extra-role behaviors, and negatively with turnover intentions (Riketta 2005; Riketta and van Dick 2005). Findings such as these have led scholars to conclude that "[i]nsofar as the firm can profitably motivate its employees through such attachments, these investments should be considered a part of the capital of the organization, its *motivational capital*" (Akerlof and Kranton 2005: 29; emphasis in original).

Different motives may underlie individuals' tendency to identify with a social group (i.e. to "take on" the social identity). First, individuals have a desire for a positive self-concept (Tajfel and Turner 1986). As with all evaluative judgments, self-evaluations are made with reference to a comparative standard. In other words, most people feel good about themselves when they compare favorably to others. Self-categorizing as a group member can serve this motive if their ingroup compares favorably to a relevant outgroup. A second motive stimulating group (i.e. social) identification is uncertainty reduction (Hogg 2000, 2007). Individuals dislike feelings of uncertainty (i.e. who one is and how one should behave). As a result, they strive for meaningful and stable group affiliations as their group memberships can give clarity about these uncertainties. Two additional motives are outlined by optimal distinctiveness theory (Brewer 1991), which seems particularly relevant to the analysis of M&As. According to this theory, when people identify with social groups, they seek to strike a balance between two fundamental human motives. On the one hand, people have a need to belong and to validate their worldviews (Baumeister and Leary 1995). On the other hand, they also have a need to be special and unique (Snyder and Fromkin 1980). Combining these two needs, optimal distinctiveness theory predicts that identification will be strongest for social categories that are neither too large nor too small or satisfy the conflicting needs in other ways (Hornsey and Jetten 2004). In line with this prediction, a recent meta-analysis has shown that people tend to identify more strongly with their workgroup than with the larger organization (Riketta and van Dick 2005).

It is this nuanced view on the antecedent motives of social identification and resulting changes in individual's behavior and motivations that has sparked considerable interest in applying the SIA in the context of M&As. Simply put, and to foreshadow our review, the promise of the SIA is to provide insights into when and how employees involved in an organizational merger (e.g. Air-France-KLM) do identify themselves as members of the merged organization (e.g. "I am an employee of Air-France-KLM"), identify them-selves as members of the pre-merger organization (e.g. "I am an employee of KLM"), or plainly perceive themselves as individuals (e.g. "I am Mrs Smith") who care much less about any of the organizations than what is in the merger for themselves. Many M&A theorists (see also our opening quotes from James O. McKinsey) would agree that only the first of these alternatives would provide a basis for a successful organizational merger. The SIA helps us to clarify the underlying conditions and implications in detail.

After having introduced the essentials of the SIA, we will now review the literature using an identity-based analysis to better understand the human side of M&As. We first review literature indicating the importance of post-merger identification for the merger and the potential detrimental effects of pre-merger identification. Next, we will discuss contextual factors that influence how employees of the merger partners will respond to the new situation post-merger. Finally, we review the literature on two factors—continuity and fairness—that may help in achieving positive merger integration.

The SIA of Pre-merger and Post-merger Identification

Organizational mergers are characterized by a certain structural condition—two (or more) companies merge to become one company. A merger often increases employees' awareness of the identities of the pre-merger organizations and the post-merger organi-zation (Giessner and Mummendey 2008; Haunschild et al. 1994). The SIA suggests that when employees adopt (i.e. identify with) the post-merger company identity as a viable self-definition, this would give rise to group behavior aimed at furthering the interests of the collective defined by the merger. However, M&As often create an "us-versus-them" dynamic which refers to a heightened salience of the distinct pre-merger group memberships (Blake and Mouton 1985; Buono and Bowditch 1989; Gleibs et al. 2008). In other words, employees often identify with their pre-merger organization and perceive the other organization as a potential "enemy." Hence, identification with the pre-merger organization hinders the merger integration process and creates the potential for con-flict, competition, and even discrimination (Buono et al. 1985; Giessner 2009; Gleibs et al. 2010; Haunschild et al. 1994).

As the main challenge of merger integration is to have employees cooperate effec-tively across the boundaries of pre-merger organizational memberships, it is highly desirable to encourage a common post-merger identification, which is the foundation of cooperative intergroup behavior (Richter et al. 2006; van Knippenberg 2003). Without identifying with the post-merger organization comprising the two former organizations as subgroups (e.g. Gaertner et al. 1994; Giessner and Mummendey 2008), employees will have little incentive to cooperate with colleagues from the other merger partner beyond what is absolutely necessary. Empirical research demonstrates that post-merger identification is related to core organizational behavior variables like job satisfaction, organizational citizenship behavior, and emotional well-being, stronger team performance, and reduced turnover intentions (Jetten et al. 2002b; Lipponen et al. 2004; Terry 2001; van Dick et al. 2006; van Dick et al. 2004). In addition, strong post-merger identification relates to less friction between the employees of the merging organizations (Amiot et al. 2007a; Haunschild et al. 1994; Terry 2001) even if the merger does not meet its overall goals (Giessner and Mummendey 2008). Consequently, post-merger identification is a "valid indicator of the extent to which an employee is psychologically engaged with (i.e. has 'signed onto') the change" (Millward and Kyriakidou 2004: 17).

STATUS RELATIONSHIPS AND INTERGROUP TENSIONS BETWEEN MERGER PARTNERS

Unfortunately, post-merger identification often does not develop as fast as management would wish (cf. Gleibs et al. 2008). A social identity analysis helps to understand why this is the case. A simple explanation can be given by applying an optimal distinctiveness perspective (Brewer 1991). By definition, an organization will grow through an M&A so that the social category associated with the pre-merger organization will become larger because of the merger. However, people do prefer memberships in smaller groups to maintain their sense of uniqueness and individuality. This implies that the new organization will become less attractive as a target for identification. On the basis of the general finding that employees feel less strongly attached to their organization as a whole compared with smaller subunits (Riketta and van Dick 2005; van Knippenberg and van Schie 2000), one would expect post-merger identification to be lower compared to pre-merger identification. Indeed, this is what a number of studies find (Amiot et al. 2007a; Boen et al. 2005a; Gleibs et al. 2008; Newman and Krzystofiak 1993; van Dick et al. 2004; van Knippenberg et al. 2002).

Another explanation relates to the heightened salience of pre-merger organizational identities during the merger process, which implies that employees compare themselves with the "other" organization and their employees. Such comparisons will result in status evaluations (i.e. which is the "better" organization?). As already stated at the beginning of this chapter, although some M&As pretend to be between organizations of equal status, most organizational mergers are not mergers of equals (Cartwright and Cooper 1996; van Oudenhoven and de Boer 1995). Following the SIA, membership in low-status groups fails to provide members with a positive social identity (i.e. motive of self-enhancement). Therefore, employees of the low-status organization feel more threatened (Terry and O'Brien 2001) and may seek to enhance their status position (Ellemers, Wilke, and van Knippenberg 1993). In contrast, members of the high-status organization have a positive social identity and try to maintain their status position (Ellemers et al. 1992), because a low-status organization might drag down the status of the whole organization (cf. Hornsey et al. 2003). To be clear, status is not always determined by which is the acquirer and which is the acquired. Status can also relate to reputation, size, or power relationships during the merger integration and instances of reverse takeovers have shown that status relationships can also change during the different stages of integration.

According to the SIA, there are a number of strategies that employees of the low-status organization can use to improve or enhance their social identity (Tajfel and Turner 1986; Ellemers 1993). Employees could engage in individual mobility by seeking membership in the higher-status organization. They would consider such a strategy only, however, if they believe that the boundaries with other higher-status organizations are permeable. For instance, highly qualified employees of the relatively low-status organization may either decide to leave the organization in favor of another high-status organization or see the merger as an opportunity for career progress in the newly merged firm. In contrast to this individualistic response, employees of the low-status organization may engage in collective strategies based on their pre-merger organizational identity. Social competition is one such response. It involves direct actions to change the negative standing of the organization. This can be accomplished via collective protest, a decrease in performance, or even sabotage. The SIA suggests that this strategy will be applied if employees perceive group boundaries to be impermeable and the status differential as illegitimate (which is often the case during a merger), and if cognitive alternatives to the present situation are available. Another collective response is social creativity: making or changing comparisons that change the outcome of the comparison process to a positively evaluated social identity. The employees could select a new organization to compare with (e.g. organization X was more unlucky with the merger partner), use new dimensions of comparison (e.g. we have a better working climate), or modify the values assigned to comparison dimensions (e.g. working is not about performance and money, but about working climate).

Empirical work suggests that, the last two social creativity strategies are especially prevalent during organizational mergers. A study by Terry and Callan (1998) with more than 1,000 employees examined an intended merger of two hospitals—a high-status metropolitan teaching hospital and a relatively low-status local area hospital. Employees of the low-status hospital showed stronger ingroup bias, especially on dimensions that were not related to the status difference (e.g. good communication by management, relaxed work environment). In contrast, employees of both hospitals agreed upon the superiority of the high-status organization on the status-relevant dimensions (e.g. high prestige in the community, high variety in patient type). Furthermore, employees of the low (vs. high) status hospital experienced higher levels of threat during the merger—indicating that self-enhancement seemed to be particularly impaired for employees of the low-status hospital. These results have been replicated in another field study with fleet staff involved in an airline merger (Terry et al. 2001; see also Terry and O'Brien 2001). In addition, this study indicates that permeable group boundaries have a positive impact on the adjustment of the employees of the low-status airline. This, in turn, increased post-merger identification of low-status employees. However, permeable group boundaries yielded the opposite effects on employees of the high-status airlines. These employees felt there was a threat to maintaining their status and tended to react with lowered post-merger identification.

Potentially more harmful than such social creativity strategies are strategies of social competition. Given that most mergers are characterized by high uncertainty and unstable situations (cf. Schweiger and DeNisi 1991), as well as perceptions of low permeability (Terry 2001), employees might apply such strategies. A case study of a bank merger nicely supports this assumption. Buono and colleagues (1985) conducted this longitudinal case study with employees and managers. Although the merger started with enthusiasm and positive attitudes among employees from both merger partners, differences in the identity of the organization became salient during the merger. Increased pre-merger identification and an unstable situation resulted first in collective behaviors like gossiping. Subsequently, cross-organizational cooperation decreased, prejudice about the other bank concerned and its employees increased, and employees from different pre-merger banks grew more competitive about management positions. All of these behaviors decreased trust and impaired the performance of the merged company.

Experimental research has also shown that such collective strategies are very much rooted in identification processes with the pre-merger organization, especially in the absence of a common post-merger identification. For instance, Weber and Camerer (2003) conducted a laboratory experiment in which participants had to take on the roles of managers and employees and communicate to each other which of several photographed work environments they preferred. Over the course of the experiment, participants developed their own norms of accomplishing the task, which became evident in decreased task completion times. After the dyads were merged with another group, however, they lost their efficiency and developed hostile attitudes toward each other. For instance, one "employee" was quoted as angrily saying: "Stop telling me what they're wearing and just tell me how many people are in the picture!" (p. 412). Furthermore, decreased performance was attributed to the other group.

Giessner and Mummendey (2008) found similar effects for interacting groups. In a first phase of their study, participants were randomly placed in groups and interacted on a task. Furthermore, a group identity was developed by means of, for instance, creating a common group name, wearing similar dress, or working cooperatively on a task. In a second phase, two groups were merged. The type of merger was, however, manipulated. Either the groups developed a new common identity or they were merged without developing this new shared post-merger identity. Finally the merged groups received either success or failure feedback about their performance on the common task. The results indicated that negative feedback about task accomplishment was attributed to the other pre-merger group only if no common post-merger identity was developed. Furthermore, when no post-merger identity was developed, group members indicated that they would not like to cooperate with group members of the other team in future tasks. Thus, these experiments show how merely combining people from previously distinct groups can result in frustration and hostility even in the absence of other risk factors typically surrounding M&As, such as job insecurity and fear of downsizing (see van Dick et al. 2006, for an elaboration of this point).

In sum, heightened pre-merger identification during the merger integration process presents a potential threat to the M&A integration and the post-merger performance. The SIA explains how and under what conditions employees might show biased perceptions (e.g. ingroup bias) or even collective behaviors against the other merger partner and its employees (e.g. gossiping, competition, exclusion). After having clarified the importance of post-merger identification, the question arises as to how post-merger identification can be established. There is certainly no single magic bullet. However, theory and research on M&As applying the SIA provide fruitful insights.

Sense of Continuity and Post-merger Identification

As decreased post-merger identification is partly caused by an increase in inclusiveness of the post-merger identity and the resulting threat to pre-merger identity, one simple strategy might be to make the post-merger organization appear distinctive at the level of the larger post-merger identity—by pointing out dimensions of superiority to competitors etc. For instance, a large and potentially over-inclusive club such as Mensa (i.e. an organization of the gifted) provides its members with distinctiveness by setting them apart from people with less exceptional intelligence (cf. Hornsey and Jetten 2004). A similar strategy in M&As might amount to pointing out that, due to the merger, the company is now industry leader or uniquely capable of creating a new product or service. Unfortunately, however, distinctiveness concerns are not the only threat to organizational identification. At the most fundamental level, organizational identification is threatened by changes in content of organizational identity rather than by changes in the size of the organization (Ullrich and van Dick 2007).

Social identity researchers have paid substantial attention to this issue. They have studied how organizational identification is affected by the perceived continuity of pre-merger identity and the nature of the representation of the pre-merger organization within the post-merger organization. It is important to realize that organizational change per se is not the most important factor influencing organizational identification (Rousseau 1998). Indeed, employees know that organizations have to change from time to time. However, despite all change, employees generally want to feel that they are continuing to work for essentially the same organization (Ellemers 2003; Jetten et al. 2002b; van Knippenberg et al. 2002). Rousseau (1998) termed this feeling a "sense of continuity" and argued that this sense of continuity is essential if employees are to maintain their identification with the organization in the wake of major organizational changes.

Daan van Knippenberg and colleagues argued and have demonstrated that the relationship between organizational identification before and after a merger depends on a sense of continuity of one's pre-merger identification (van Knippenberg et al. 2002; van Knippenberg and van Leeuwen 2001; van Leeuwen and van Knippenberg 2003; van Leeuwen et al. 2003; see also Boen et al. 2005b; Boen et al. 2007; Jetten et al. 2002b). They demonstrated in laboratory as well as field studies that the stronger an employee's sense of continuity, the more that employee tends to identify with the post-merger organization. In other words, employees who feel that the merged organization is still *their* organization tend to transfer their pre-merger identification to the post-merger organization (see also Ellemers 2003; Jetten et al. 2002b). Further, because one of the merging organizations is bound to be more dominant in shaping the merger entity, its employees are likely to perceive the new identity as a continuation of their pre-merger organization's identity to a greater extent than members of the dominated organization(s).

In line with van Knippenberg's model of continuity of identity, recent research has found that members of high-status organizations (which are expected to dominate the merger process) prefer different ways of merging than members of low-status organizations (Giessner et al. 2006). Giessner and colleagues varied the type of representation of the two merger partners. In a series of three studies, they found that members of high-status organizations prefer assimilation (i.e. low-status organization is assimilated to the high-status organization) and an integration pattern that follows a proportional rule by representing more of the high (vs. low) status organization's features in the new post-merger identity. In contrast, members of low-status organizations prefer a merger pattern where their group is equally well represented in the merger as the high-status group (i.e. as represented by an integration-equality pattern and a transformation pattern). This study also corroborates the assumption that establishing a sense of continuity is more of a problem for the low-status or less dominant merger partner, because the low-status organization was more sensitive regarding the type of merger pattern than the high-status organization.

One may argue, however, that the fact that the members of the low-status organization most often experience a sense of discontinuity of their identity does not solve the problem of how to increase post-merger identification for all employees of the merged organization. What can be done to salvage post-merger identity among employees who experience a discontinuity of their organizational identity? Employees who experience a discontinuity (vs. continuity) of their organizational identity tend to experience higher levels of uncertainty, which hinders identification with the unknown post-merger organization (cf. Ullrich et al. 2005). Given that organizational mergers generally imply dramatic changes for at least one of the merging partners, it is important to know which factors might positively influence the degree of post-merger identification among the employees most affected by the merger. Two interesting lines of SIA research help address this issue.

Ullrich and colleagues (2005) explored the possible antecedents of post-merger identification in a qualitative field study of a large industrial merger. Their research revealed that middle management considered not only the subjective experience of the transition from the past to the present as an important factor in their degree of post-merger identification, but also the expected transition from the present to the merged organization's future. More specifically, they presented evidence that the asymmetry of continuity may be confined to what the authors called observable continuity, i.e. the past-to-present changes in identity and job contents (i.e. reflecting the continuity of identity discussed above). Equally important to employees, however, is the clarity about the merged organization's future and the employees' role in it. In contrast to observable continuity, projected continuity refers to the "subjective belief that the relationship between path and goal is clear and controllable" (Ullrich et al. 2005: 1562) and can equally be established for all parties involved in a merger—thus, for employees of the low- and high-status organizations. A recent field study by Giessner (2011) confirmed and extended this inductive finding. Giessner operationalized projected continuity as the perceived necessity to merge (i.e. the subjective understanding of the goals of the merger), which can be seen as part of projected continuity (see also Boen et al. 2005b). This research indicates that especially those employees who perceive a low observable continuity of identity show an increase in post-merger identification when the perceived necessity of the merger increases. Thus, there is qualitative and quantitative evidence that observable and projected continuity together can increase post-merger identification.

To our knowledge, there is no conclusive evidence on the differential success of cross-border versus domestic mergers. Related to continuity, however, one can assume that cross-border mergers are less likely to result in high post-merger identification and are ultimately more likely to fail. Van Knippenberg and van Leeuwen (2001) suggested that larger differences between the merger partners would result in lower perceptions of continuity. They referred to differences in general, but also noted that differences in organizational culture would be particularly damaging to continuity. In a related vein, Cartwright and Cooper (2000) argue that cross-border mergers might be problematic because employees use stereotypes and guesswork regarding the merger partner's culture and that if the merger happens across cultures, national stereotypes about differences might accentuate the problems of perceived differences. Stahl and Voigt's (2008) meta-analytic results seem to confirm these suggestions; they found a negative correlation between cultural differences (operationalized as both organizational and national differences) and sociocultural integration.

Another stream of SIA research focuses on the role of leadership in M&As. Leading change is considered a defining aspect of leadership (Yukl 2001) and as such it should play a key role in M&As (Jetten et al. 2002a; van Knippenberg et al. 2008). Leaders play a central role in fostering collective change and even mobilizing employees to contribute actively to the change process (Bass 1985; Shamir et al. 1993). From our analysis it follows that effective leadership in terms of accomplishing high post-merger identification within the workforce implies the creation of a strong sense of continuity of identity for all the employees concerned. Taking such a perspective, van Knippenberg and colleagues (2008) argue that effective leadership does not only require the leader to be the agent of change, but also the agent of continuity (cf. Reicher and Hopkins 2003; van Knippenberg and Hogg 2003).

The starting point for the SIA view of leadership is the notion that leadership processes are enacted in the context of a shared group membership. Consequently, a leader's characteristics as a group member impact the leader's effectiveness in influencing and mobilizing followers. Importantly, two leader characteristics are central in this analysis: leader group prototypicality (i.e. leaders' representativeness or embodiment of the shared social identity; Hogg 2001), and leader group-orientedness (the extent to which the leader is seen to be committed to the group's best interest; van Knippenberg and van Knippenberg 2005). In other words, it is important to what degree the leader embodies the norms and characteristics of the organization (i.e. group prototypicality) and behaves in a way that shows the leader's endorsement of the organization (i.e. group-orientedness). Further, perceptions of leader group-orientedness are influenced by perceptions of leader group prototypicality, because a prototypical leader is more likely to be trusted to have the collective interest at heart (Giessner and van Knippenberg 2008; Giessner et al. 2009; van Knippenberg and van Knippenberg 2005). Therefore, leader group-orientedness and leader group prototypicality interact in predicting leadership influence. Because prototypical (vs. non-prototypical) leaders are more likely to be trusted to be group-oriented, their influence on followers is less contingent on acts of group-oriented behavior (van Knippenberg and Hogg 2003). In other words, prototypical leaders are trusted by their followers and have, therefore, more leeway in their behaviors (Giessner and van Knippenberg 2008; Ullrich et al. 2009).

Applying these principles to the context of M&As and, more specifically, to the issue of the continuity of the post-merger identity, the SIA would predict that group prototypical leaders are positioned particularly well to promote organizational change. Given that these leaders are trusted by their employees to have the collective interest at heart, their envisioned organizational changes should be perceived by the employees as more identity consistent compared with the envisioned changes of a non-prototypical leader. Thus, in line with Rousseau's (1998) observation that it is not organizational change per se but the employees' perception of change related to their identity that is the most important factor influencing organizational identification, the SIA suggests that prototypical leaders might be able to influence employees' perceptions of change.

Recent research by Bobbio and colleagues (Bobbio et al. 2005) provides the first evidence in support of this assumption. They conducted two scenario studies, describing a potential merger scenario to their participants. In all scenarios, participants had to put themselves in the role of an employee involved in a merger. The merger was described as a potential threat to the organization's identity. In the first study, the leader announcing the merger was described either as prototypical (i.e. very representative of the pre-merger organization identity) or non-prototypical. Afterwards, participants had to indicate their willingness to contribute to the change and rate their perceptions of the leader as ensuring the identity of the pre-merger organization in the post-merger identity. As predicted by the SIA, participants indicated more willingness to change when the leader was prototypical (vs. non-prototypical). This effect was explained by the perception of the leader as ensuring the identity of the organization. In a follow-up study, Bobbio and colleagues added another twist: half of the participants were informed that the threat to the organizational identity due to the merger was rather small; the other half that the threat to the organizational identity was large. Following the SIA logic, one would assume that the effects of leader prototypicality should be more pronounced when the threat is large (vs. small). This was exactly what the researchers found. Thus, the more effectively a leader represents the pre-merger identity of the organization, the more willing are employees to support the merger, and this effect is even stronger the greater the discontinuity. One obvious problem is, however, that it will be hard for a leader to represent all merger partners simultaneously. The leader can only be representative of one pre-merger organization, but not of all merger partners at the same time. At least, this is true for leaders at the start of any merger integration and might be different at later stages where the two partners develop a truly new identity shaped by the "best of both" former organizations' identities.

However, even at the beginning of a merger, a leader who is not perceived as prototypical by employees of one organization might show behaviors that favor these employees (Jetten et al. 2002a) and in this way express his or her group-orientedness toward these employees as well. Although this stream of research holds great potential for applications in merger integration, there is sparse empirical evidence so far. Hence, the SIA of M&As has great potential to explore the role of leadership in greater depth.

In sum, the SIA suggests that continuity of identity is an important predictor of post-merger identification. However, the observable continuity of identity is not the only predictor of post-merger identification. Projected continuity can also increase post-merger identification by clarifying paths and goals, and this is especially true for members experiencing identity discontinuity. In addition, leaders have the potential to act as agents of continuity when organizational identities change. Thus, leaders clarifying observable and projected continuity to all employees and revealing behaviors that indicate group-orientedness are needed in M&As. Although there is plenty of research on the potential benefits of identity continuity, a recent study by Gleibs and colleagues (2008) indicates some potential drawbacks. Gleibs conducted a longitudinal study over three points of measurement with students experiencing a university merger. Data were collected four months, ten months, and 22 months after the merger. The studies confirmed previous cross-sectional research by indicating that post-merger identification only increased slowly over time, whereas pre-merger identification was consistently stronger than post-merger identification. The study also provided evidence that pre-merger identification translates into post-merger identification for members of the high-status organization. However, this effect dissipated over time. In other words, observable continuity of identity may have less impact during the course of the merger.

FAIRNESS AND POST-MERGER IDENTIFICATION

Research applying the SIA has pointed to various other factors influencing post-merger identification. For instance, communication (Bartels et al. 2006; van Dick et al. 2006), perceived external prestige (Bartels et al. 2009), and merger success (Boen et al. 2005b) have been identified as predictors of post-merger identification. Gleibs and colleagues (2008) showed that over the course of the merger issues of fairness seem to become more important in predicting post-merger identification. Perceptions of fairness are employees' beliefs about the distribution of resources and outcomes during the merger (i.e. distributive justice) and employees' perceptions of how new procedures and rules are implemented, as well as how employees feel they are treated within the merged organization (i.e. procedural justice). Because both types of justice have been found to have consequences for employees' adjustment during the merger (Citera and Rentsch 1993; Citera and Stuhlmacher 2001; Greenberg and Folger 1983), researchers have explored the influence of justice concerns on employees' post-merger identification (Amiot et al. 2007a; Giessner et al. 2006; Gleibs et al. 2008; Lipponen et al. 2004; Tyler and de Cremer 2005). Based on the group engagement model (Tyler and Blader 2003), the perceived fairness of the procedures and treatment was predicted and found to be especially important for group identification, because it conveys identity-relevant information about the quality of the relationship between oneself and the authorities (or other group members). Thus, procedural justice creates particular feelings of pride and respect which, in turn, increases identification. Lipponen and colleagues (2004) provided evidence of this relationship in a cross-sectional field study of a merger between two Finnish service organizations (see also Amiot et al. 2007a; Gleibs et al. 2008, 2010 for longitudinal evidence).

Although procedural justice seems to be especially important during M&As, some researchers argue that procedural and distributive forms of justice are not completely independent in the context of a merger (Meyer 2001; cf. Brockner and Wiesenfeld 1996). Furthermore, the influence of procedural and distributive justice on post-merger identification may depend on the degree of pre-merger identification. A recent series of studies by van Knippenberg, Martin, and Tyler (2006) revealed how these different types of justice might be related to organizational identification during change. Applying the SIA, the researchers argue that employees with low organizational identification are generally less interested in change-related procedural information (e.g. procedures, voice, and participation options, etc.) than highly identified employees. This corroborates the general finding that the people identifying more with the organization are more likely to take the organization's interest to heart (van Knippenberg and Hogg 2003). Further, Barbara van Knippenberg and colleagues (2006) predicted that low identification would result in more interest in distributive (vs. procedural) justice aspects (e.g. salary, expenses, etc.), because these tangible outcomes relate to the personal (vs. collective) interest of the employees. Results of both a scenario experiment and a survey study yielded support for this assumption. Although this research has not been conducted in contexts specific to M&As and, therefore, did not tap into the issue of pre-merger and post-merger identification, the results seem important to better understand the relationship between employees' justice concerns and their post-merger identification. More specifically, the results suggest that employees high in pre-merger identification might be especially concerned about issues of procedural justice. Thus, these employees might identify with the post-merger organization only if they can participate in the merger process, receive information about the merger, and can voice their concerns during the integration (cf. Schweiger and DeNisi 1991). In contrast, employees low in pre-merger identification are more concerned about distributive justice. Thus, these employees may seek clarifications about salary, career, or bonuses involved in the merger process. Unfortunately, no research has yet tapped into this issue and it remains a task for future research in the SIA tradition.

Conclusion

The considerations discussed above provide some reason for being optimistic about the potential to diminish negative group-based reactions to M&As and to improve their track record. To be sure, established strategies for optimal communication, the management of job insecurity or stress (see Cartwright and Cooper 2000), or management training involving the management of both merger partners (e.g. the interface conflict-solving model, Blake and Mouton 1985; combination preparation workshop, Marks and Mirvis 2001) are still valid and useful. The contribution of a social identity analysis to mainstream management knowledge consists of a coherent and robust theoretical framework to better understand the human side of the merger. Processes of social identification and self-categorization impact almost every stage of the merger integration. Understanding how, when, and why these processes influence employee motivation and company performance is the key to M&A success. Figure 19.1 summarizes the main variables studied using a SIA. This list is certainly not exhaustive, but represents the processes summarized in this chapter.

Although a lot of empirical research over the past ten years has clarified identity dynamics during M&As, it should be noted that there are still many important questions to answer. To give but one example, identity dynamics do not only matter to employees involved in an organizational merger, but also emerge among leaders and change agents developing their own identities as promoters of change. Van Dijk and van Dick (2009) recently demonstrated that this may cause a vicious cycle. Employees feel threatened by the expected impact of the change on their identities; therefore, they show resistance. Change agents, in turn, perceive this resistance as a threat to their *identity as leaders of the change* and therefore do not respond adequately, which causes more resistance by employees and so on.

Another issue to consider is the fact that most of the research cited in this chapter is in some ways "European" based. Social identity theory has been developed in the United Kingdom and has been applied to a variety of phenomena in the UK and other European countries for the last 40 years. Most empirical work on mergers from this tradition has been conducted in Belgium, the Netherlands, and Germany—Australia seems to be the exception, but one has to consider that John Turner, one of the founding fathers of the SIA, is Australia-based and has influenced many colleagues on this continent. Why might it be important to think about the researchers' origin or the place where this

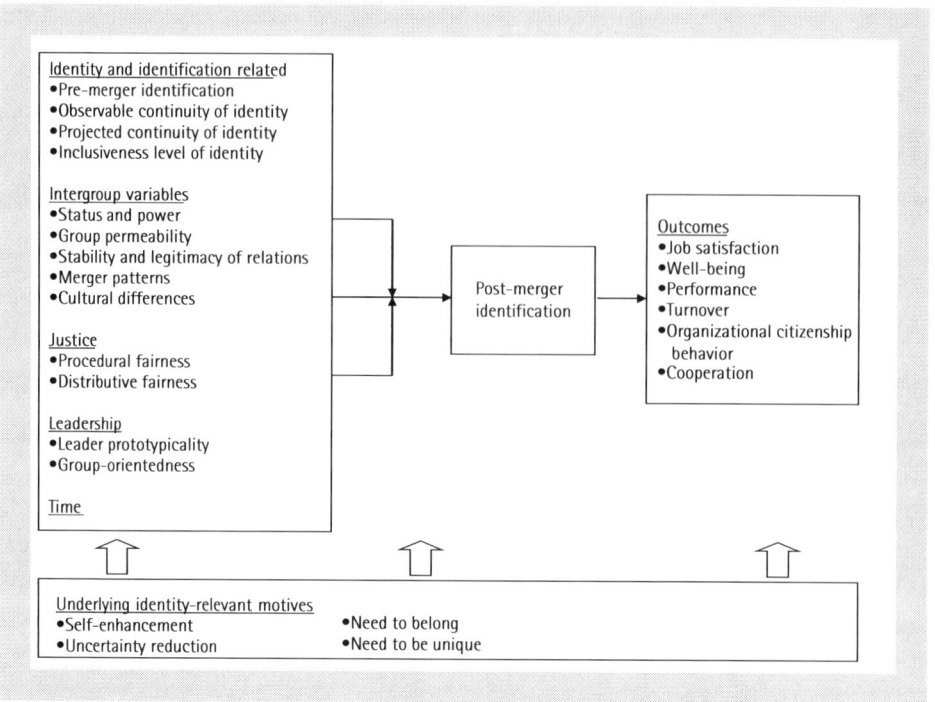

FIG. 19.1 Overview of antecedents and effects of post-merger identification

research is conducted? Social identity theory in some way emphasizes the importance of our lives as social beings and stresses group membership for individuals' thoughts, feelings, and actions (Haslam 2004). In this respect, US-American researchers, with a focus on individualism and individuality, have been a little hesitant to fully utilize the SIA. It was not before 1989, with Ashforth and Mael's influential overview article on social identity theory in the *Academy of Management Review*, that the theory became more and more prominent in the US. Applications of the theory in the field of M&As are still rare though and it would be interesting to see whether some of the theoretical predictions would find differential support in Asian or US contexts. Related to the geographic heritage, social identity analyses as presented throughout this chapter are clearly utilizing empirical and experimental methods based in (social) psychology. Most of the existing studies are based on either laboratory experiments or field surveys and in both approaches the individual's attitudes are the focus. Although this provides a rich understanding of the "human side" of M&As, it would be helpful to combine such analyses with research approaches from other fields such as accounting and finance, to name but two.

Third, with few exceptions (e.g. Gleibs et al. 2008, 2010), most of the existing research presented in this chapter has adopted laboratory or cross-sectional field designs. What is largely absent is research that looks at the pattern of identity issues as they evolve during a merger—from its announcement, execution, and through the various stages of the integration process. Future research should aim to collect longitudinal field data to answer open questions of identity development (cf. Amiot et al. 2007b).

Fourth, and related to the above, most studies have used self-reported data on important but subjective variables such as job satisfaction or turnover intentions. It is highly desirable to combine such research in the future with hard evidence on merger performance in terms of real employee turnover or accountancy-based figures of financial performance.

Finally, it is striking that no social identity-based research has yet considered the specific case of cross-border M&As. This is surprising because differences between cultural and/or ethnic groups have been the focus of attention of decades of social psychological research in general and social identity work in particular. As we have mentioned above, because national-cultural differences might play a role in cross-border M&As—above and beyond the usual organization-based cultural differences—future research that helps understand the impact of such differences would be interesting.

We hope that future research puts the issues raised above to the empirical test which will further deepen our knowledge of how to "merge right." However, even at this stage, the practicing manager who is at the helm of an M&A integration process can already start learning from our analysis. This analysis has focused on two key issues that now seem well supported by the existing evidence. First, creating a vision for the future and a sense of continuity will help maintain employees' old identities and translate them into stronger identification with the new, post-merger organization. And second, fairness and transparency are important. The call for managers to act fair might seem almost trivial. But if we look at organizational reality, this call is frequently violated. Particularly when a merger is announced, the statement that there would be no lay-offs seems to be almost a managerial reflex-phrase which is followed by lay-offs a few months down the line. We believe that this is damaging not only to those who have lost their jobs, but also to those who stay on and who suffer from so-called survivor syndrome (see e.g. Worrall et al. 2004). We believe that a large part of this syndrome is due to threats to people's identities. Therefore, change leaders and change agents should learn from our analyses and carefully consider their actions' impact on employees' identities—or employees' perceptions thereof.

References

Akerlof, G. A., & Kranton, R. E. (2005). "Identity and the Economics of the Organization." *Journal of Economic Perspectives*, 19: 9–32.

Amiot, C. E., Terry, D. J., & Callan, V. J. (2007a). "Status, Equity and Social Identification during an Intergroup Merger: A Longitudinal Study." *British Journal of Social Psychology*, 46: 557–77.

Amiot, C. E., de la Sablonnière, R., Terry, D. J., & Smith, J. R. (2007b). "Integration of Social Identities in the Self: Toward a Cognitive-Developmental Model." *Personality and Social Psychology Review*, 11: 364–88.

Ashforth, B. E., & Mael, F. A. (1989). "Social Identity Theory and the Organization." *Academy of Management Review*, 14: 20–39.

Bartels, J., Douwes, R., de Jong, M., & Pruyn, A. (2006). "Organizational Identification during a Merger: Determinants of Employees' Expected Identification with the New Organization." *British Journal of Management*, 17: 49–67.

—— Pruyn, A., & de Jong, M. (2009). "Employee Identification Before and After an Internal Merger: A Longitudinal Analysis." *Journal of Occupational and Organizational Psychology*, 82: 113–28.

Bass, B. M. (1985). *Leadership and Performance beyond Expectations*. New York: Free Press.

Baumeister, R. F., & Leary, M. R. (1995). "The Need to Belong: Desire for Interpersonal Attachments as a Fundamental Human Motive." *Psychological Bulletin*, 117: 497–529.

Blake, R. R., & Mouton, J. S. (1985). "How to Achieve Integration on the Human Side of the Merger." *Organizational Dynamics*, 13: 20–39.

Bobbio, A., van Knippenberg, D., & van Knippenberg, B. (2005). "Leading Change: Two Empirical Studies from a Social Identity Theory of Leadership Perspective." Paper presented at the EAESP Medium Sized Meeting, Academy Colloquium on Social Identity in Organizations, June. Amsterdam, The Netherlands.

Boen, F., Vanbeselaere, N., Brebels, L., Huybens, W., & Millet, K. (2007). "Post-merger Identification as a Function of Pre-merger Identification, Relative Representation and Pre-merger Status." *European Journal of Social Psychology*, 37: 380–9.

—— —— Hollants, K., & Feys, J. (2005a). "Predictors of pupils' and teachers' identification with a merged school." *Journal of Applied Social Psychology*, 35: 2577–605.

—— —— & Swinnen, H. (2005b). "Predicting Fans' Support for a Merged Soccer Team: A Social-Psychological Perspective." *International Journal of Sport Psychology*, 36: 65–85.

Brewer, M. B. (1991). "The Social Self: On Being the Same and Different at the Same Time." *Personality and Social Psychology Bulletin*, 17: 475–82.

Brockner, J., & Wiesenfeld, B. M. (1996). "An Integrative Framework for Explaining Reactions to a Decision: The Interactive Effects of Outcomes and Procedures." *Psychological Bulletin*, 120: 189–208.

Buono, A. F., & Bowditch, J. L. (1989). *The Human Side of Mergers and Acquisitions: Managing Collisions between People, Cultures, and Organizations*. San Francisco, CA: Jossey-Bass.

—— —— & Lewis, I. J. W. (1985). "When Cultures Collide: The Anatomy of a Merger." *Human Relations*, 5: 477–500.

Cartwright, S. (2005). "Mergers and Acquisitions: An Update and Appraisal," in G. P. Hodgkinson & J. K. Ford (eds.), *International Review of Industrial and Organizational Psychology*, vol. 20. Chichester, UK: Wiley, 1–38.

—— & Cooper, C. L. (1993). "The Role of Culture Compatibility in Successful Organizational Marriage." *Academy of Management Executive*, 7: 57–70.

—— —— (1996). *Managing Mergers, Acquisitions and Strategic Alliances: Integrating People and Cultures*. Oxford: Butterworth-Heinemann.

—— —— (2000). *HR Know-How in Mergers and Acquisitions*. London: CIPD.

Citera, M., & Rentsch, J. R. (1993). "Is there Justice in Organizational Acquisitions? The Role of Distributive and Procedural Fairness in Corporate Acquisitions," in R. Cropanzano (ed.), *Justice in the Workplace: Approaching Fairness in Human Resource Management*. Hillsdale, NJ: Lawrence Erlbaum, 211–30.

—— & Stuhlmacher, A. F. (2001). "A Policy Modeling Approach to Examining Judgments in Organizational Acquisitions." *Journal of Behavioral Decision Making*, 14: 309–27.

Ellemers, N. (1993). "The Influence of Socio-Structural Variables on Identity Enhancement Strategies." *European Review of Social Psychology*, 4: 27–57.

Ellemers, N. (2003). "Identity, culture, and change in organizations: A social identity analysis and three illustrative cases," in S. A. Haslam, D. van Knippenberg, M. J. Platow, & N. Ellemers (eds.), *Social Identity at Work: Developing Theory for Organizational Practice*. Philadelphia, PA: Psychology Press, 191–203.

—— Doosje, B. J., van Knippenberg, A., & Wilke, H. (1992). "Status Protection in High-Status Minority Groups." *European Journal of Social Psychology*, 22: 123–40.

—— Wilke, H., & van Knippenberg, A. (1993). "Effects of Legitimacy of Low Group or Individual Status on Individual and Collective Status Enhancement Strategies." *Journal of Personality and Social Psychology*, 64: 766–78.

Gaertner, S. L., Rust, M. C., Dovidio, J. F., Bachman, B. A., & Anastasio, P. A. (1994). "The Contact Hypothesis: The Role of a Common Ingroup Identity on Reducing Intergroup Bias." *Small Group Research*, 25: 224–9.

Giessner, S. R. (2009). "Diskriminierung und Toleranz bei Unternehmensfusionen," in A. Beelman & K. Jonas (eds.), *Diskriminierung und Toleranz: Psychologische Grundlagen und Anwendungsperspektiven*. Wiesbaden: VS Verlag, 399–418.

—— (2011). "Is the Change Necessary? The Interactive Effect of Perceived Necessity and Continuity of Identity on Post-Merger Identification." *Human Relations*, 64: 1079–98.

—— & Mummendey, A. (2008). "United We Win, Divided We Fail? Effects of Cognitive Representations and Performance Feedbacks on Merging Groups." *European Journal of Social Psychology*, 32: 412–35.

—— & van Knippenberg, D. (2008). "'License to Fail': Goal Definition, Leader Group Prototypicality, and Perceptions of Leadership Effectiveness after Leader Failure." *Organizational Behavior and Human Decision Processes*, 105: 14–35.

—— —— & Sleebos, E. (2009). "License to Fail? How Leader Group Prototypicality Moderates the Effects of Leader Performance on Perceptions of Leadership Effectiveness." *The Leadership Quarterly*, 45: 434–51.

—— Viki, G. T., Otten, S., Terry, D. J., & Täuber, S. (2006). "The Challenge of Merging: Merger Patterns, Premerger Status, and Merger Support." *Personality and Social Psychology Bulletin*, 32: 339–52.

Gleibs, I., Mummendey, A., & Noack, P. (2008). "Predictors of Change in Post-merger Identification throughout a Merger Process: A Longitudinal Study." *Journal of Personality and Social Psychology*, 95: 1095–112.

—— Noack, P., & Mummendey, A. (2010). "We are Still Better than Them: A Longitudinal Field Study of Ingroup Favouritism during a Merger." *European Journal of Social Psychology*, 40: 819–36.

Greenberg, J., & Folger, R. (1983). "Procedural Justice, Participation, and the Fair Process Effect in Groups and Organizations," in P. B. Paulus (ed.), *Basic Group Processes*. New York: Springer Verlag, 235–56.

Haslam, S. A. (2004). *Psychology in Organizations: The Social Identity Approach* (2nd ed.). London: Sage.

Haunschild, P. R., Moreland, R. L., & Murell, A. J. (1994). "Sources of Resistance to Mergers between Groups." *Journal of Applied Social Psychology*, 24: 1150–78.

Hogan, E. A., & Overmyer-Day, L. (1994). "The Psychology of Mergers and Acquisitions," in C. L. Cooper & L. T. Robertson (eds.), *International Review of Industrial and Organizational Psychology*, vol. 9. Chichester, UK: Wiley, 247–81.

Hogg, M. A. (2000). "Subjective Uncertainty Reduction through Self-Categorization: A Motivational Theory of Social Identity Processes." *European Review of Social Psychology*, 11: 223–55.

—— (2001). "A Social Identity Theory of Leadership." *Personality and Social Psychology Review*, 5: 184–200.

—— (2007). "Uncertainty-Identity Theory," in M. P. Zanna (ed.), *Advances in Experimental Social Psychology*, vol. 39. San Diego, CA: Academic Press, 69–126.

—— & Abrams, D. (1988). *Social Identifications: A Social Psychology of Intergroup Relations and Group Processes*. London: Routledge.

—— & Terry, D. J. (2000). "Social Identity and Self-Categorization Processes in Organizational Contexts." *Academy of Management Review*, 25: 121–40.

Hornsey, M. J., & Jetten, J. (2004). "The Individual within the Group: Balancing the Need to Belong with the Need to be Different." *Personality and Social Psychology Review*, 8: 248–64.

—— van Leeuwen, E., & van Santen, W. (2003). "Dragging Down and Dragging Up: How Relative Group Status Affects Responses to Common Fate." *Group Dynamics: Theory, Research, and Practice*, 7: 275–88.

Jemison, D. B., & Sitkin, S. B. (1986). "Corporate Acquisitions: A Process Perspective." *Academy of Management Review*, 11: 145–63.

Jetten, J., Duck, J., Terry, D., & O'Brien, A. (2002a). "Being Attuned to Intergroup Differences in Mergers: The Role of Aligned Leaders for Low Status Groups." *Personality and Social Psychology Bulletin*, 28: 1194–201.

—— O'Brien, A., & Trindall, N. (2002b). "Changing Identity: Predicting Adjustment to Organizational Restructure as a Function of Subgroup and Superordinate Identification." *British Journal of Social Psychology*, 41: 281–97.

Larsson, R., & Finkelstein, S. (1999). "Integrating Strategic, Organizational, and Human Resource Perspectives on Mergers and Acquisitions: A Case Survey of Synergy Realization." *Organization Science*, 10: 1–26.

—— & Lubatkin, M. (2001). "Achieving Acculturation in Mergers and Acquisitions: An International Case Survey." *Human Relations*, 54: 1573–607.

Levinson, H. (1970). "A Psychologist Diagnoses Merger Failures." *Harvard Business Review*, 48: 139–47.

Lipponen, J., Olkkonen, M.-E., & Moilanen, M. (2004). "Perceived Procedural Justice and Employee Responses to an Organizational Merger." *European Journal of Work and Organizational Psychology*, 13: 391–413.

Lupina-Wegener, A., Schneider, S. C., & Van Dick, R. (2011). "Different Experiences of Socio-Cultural Integration: A European Merger in Mexico." *Journal of Organizational Change Management*, 24: 65–89

Marks, M. L., & Mirvis, P. H. (2001). "Making Mergers and Acquisitions work: Strategic and Psychological Preparation." *The Academy of Management Executive*, 15: 80–94.

McKinsey, J. O. (1929). "Effect of Mergers on Marketing, Production, and Administrative Problems." *The Journal of Business of the University of Chicago*, 2: 326–37.

Meyer, C. B. (2001). "Allocation Processes in Mergers and Acquisitions: An Organizational Justice Perspective." *British Journal of Management*, 12: 47–66.

Millward, L., & Kyriakidou, O. (2004). "Linking Pre- and Post-Merger Identities through the Concept of Career." *Career Development International*, 9: 12–27.

Nahavandi, A., & Malekzadeh, A. R. (1988). "Acculturation in Mergers and Acquisitions." *Academy of Management Review*, 13: 79–90.

Newman, J. M., & Krzystofiak, F. J. (1993). "Changes in Employee Attitudes after an Acquisition." *Group & Organization Management*, 18: 390–410.

Reicher, S., & Hopkins, N. (2003). "On the Science of the Art of Leadership," in D. van Knippenberg & M. A. Hogg (eds.), *Leadership and Power: Identity Processes in Groups and Organizations*. London: Sage, 197–209.

Richter, A., West, M. A., van Dick, R., & Dawson, J. F. (2006). "Boundary Spanners' Identification, Intergroup Contact and Effective Intergroup Relations." *Academy of Management Journal*, 49: 1252–69.

Riketta, M. (2005). "Organizational Identification: A Meta-analysis." *Journal of Vocational Behavior*, 66: 358–84.

—— & van Dick, R. (2005). "Foci of Attachment in Organizations: A Meta-analytic Comparison of the Strength and Correlates of Workgroup Versus Organizational Identification and Commitment." *Journal of Vocational Behavior*, 67: 490–510.

Rousseau, D. M. (1998). "Why Workers Still Identify with Organizations." *Journal of Organizational Behavior*, 19: 217–33.

Schweiger, D. M., & DeNisi, A. S. (1991). "Communication with Employees Following a Merger: A Longitudinal Field Experiment." *Academy of Management Journal*, 34: 110–35.

Shamir, B., House, R., & Arthur, M. B. (1993). "The Motivational Effects of Charismatic Leadership: A Self-Concept Based Theory." *Organization Science*, 4: 577–94.

Snyder, C. R., & Fromkin, H. L. (1980). *Uniqueness: The Human Pursuit of Difference*. New York: Plenum.

Stahl, G. K., & Sitkin, S. B. (2005). "Trust in Mergers and Acquisitions," in G. K. Stahl & M. E. Mendenhall (eds.), *Mergers and Acquisitions: Managing Culture and Human Resources*. Stanford, CA: Stanford University Press, 82–102.

—— & Voigt, A. (2008). "Do Cultural Differences Matter in Mergers and Acquisitions? A Tentative Model and Examination." *Organization Science*, 19: 160–76.

Tajfel, H., & Turner, J. C. (1986). "The Social Identity Theory of Intergroup Behavior," in S. Worchel & W. G. Austin (eds.), *Psychology of Intergroup Relations*. Chicago: Nelson-Hall, 7–24.

Terry, D. J. (2001). "Intergroup Relations and Organizational Mergers," in M. A. Hogg & D. J. Terry (eds.), *Social Identity Processes in Organizational Contexts*. Brighton: Psychology Press, 229–47.

—— & Callan, V. J. (1998). "In-group Bias in Response to an Organizational Merger." *Group Dynamics: Theory, Research, Practice*, 2: 67–81.

—— Carey, C. J., & Callan, V. J. (2001). "Employee Adjustment to an Organizational Merger: An Intergroup Perspective." *Personality and Social Psychology Bulletin*, 27: 267–80.

—— & O'Brien, A. (2001). "Status, Legitimacy, and Ingroup Bias in the Context of an Organizational Merger." *Group Processes & Intergroup Relations*, 4: 271–89.

Turner, J. C., Hogg, M. A., Oakes, P. J., Reicher, S. D., & Wetherell, M. S. (1987). *Rediscovering the Social Group: A Self-Categorization Theory*. Oxford, UK: Basil Blackwell.

Tyler, T. R., & Blader, S. (2003). "Procedural Justice, Social Identity, and Cooperative Behavior." *Personality and Social Psychology Review*, 7: 349–61.

—— & De Cremer, D. (2005). "Process Based Leadership: Fair Procedures, Identification, and the Acceptance of Change." *Leadership Quarterly*, 16: 529–45.

Ullrich, J., Christ, O., & van Dick, R. (2009). "Substitutes for Procedural Fairness: Prototypical Leaders are Endorsed Whether they are Fair or Not." *Journal of Applied Psychology*, 94: 235–44.

—— & van Dick, R. (2007). "The Group Psychology of Mergers & Acquisitions: Lessons from the Social Identity Approach," in C. L. Cooper & S. Finkelstein (eds.), *Advances in Mergers and Acquisitions*, vol. 6. Greenwich, CT: JAI Press, 1–15.

Ullrich, J., Christ, O., & van Dick, R. Wieseke, J., & Van Dick, R. (2005). "Continuity and Change in Mergers and Acquisitions: A Social Identity Case Study of a German Industrial Merger." *Journal of Management Studies*, 42: 1549–69.

van Dick, R. (2004). "My Job is My Castle: Identification in Organizational Contexts," in C. L. Cooper & I. T. Robertson (eds.), *International Review of Industrial and Organizational Psychology*, vol. 19. Chichester, UK: Wiley, 171–204.

—— Ullrich, J., & Tissington, P. A. (2006). "Working under a Black Cloud: How to Sustain Organizational Identification after a Merger." *British Journal of Management*, 17: 69–79.

—— Wagner, U., & Lemmer, G. (2004). "The Winds of Change. Multiple Identifications in the Case of Organizational Mergers." *European Journal of Work and Organizational Psychology*, 13: 121–38.

—— & Van Dick, R. (2009). "Navigating Organizational Change: Change Leaders, Employee Resistance and Work-Based Identities." *Journal of Change Management*, 9: 143–63.

van Knippenberg, B., Martin, L. & Tyler, T. R. (2006). "Process Orientation versus Outcome Orientation during Organizational Change: The Role of Organizational Identification." *Journal of Organizational Behavior*, 62: 307–26.

—— & van Knippenberg, D. (2005). "Leader Self-Sacrifice and Leadership Effectiveness: The Moderating Role of Leader Prototypicality." *Journal of Applied Psychology*, 90: 25–37.

van Knippenberg, D. (2003). "Intergroup Relations in Organizations," in M. A. West, D. Tjosvold, & K. G. Smith (eds.), *International Handbook Of Organizational Teamwork and Cooperative Working*. Chichester, UK: Wiley, 381–400.

—— & Hogg, M. A. (2003). "A Social Identity Model of Leadership Effectiveness in Organizations," in B. Staw & R. M. Kramer (eds.), *Research in Organizational Behavior*, vol. 25. Greenwich, CT: JAI Press, 245–97.

—— van Knippenberg, B., & Bobbio, A. (2008). "Leaders as Agents of Continuity: Self Continuity and Resistance to Collective Change," in F. Sani (ed.), *Self-Continuity: Individual and Collective Perspectives*. New York: Psychology Press, 175–86.

—— —— Monden, L., & de Lima, F. (2002). "Organizational Identification after a Merger: A Social Identity Perspective." *British Journal of Social Psychology*, 41: 233–52.

—— & van Leeuwen, E. (2001). "Organizational Identity after a Merger: Sense of Continuity as the Key to Postmerger Identification," in M. A. Hogg & D. J. Terry (eds.), *Social Identity Processes in Organizational Contexts*. Sussex: Psychology Press, 249–64.

—— & van Schie, E. C. M. (2000). "Foci and Correlates of Organizational Identification." *Journal of Occupational and Organizational Psychology*, 73: 137–47.

van Leeuwen, E., & van Knippenberg, D. (2003). "Organizational Identification Following a Merger: The Importance of Agreeing to Differ," in S. A. Haslam, D. van Knippenberg, M. Platow, & N. Ellemers (eds.), *Social Identity at Work: Developing Theory for Organizational Practice*. New York: Psychology Press, 205–21.

—— —— & Ellemers, N. (2003). "Continuing and Changing Group Identities: The Effects of Merging on Social Identification and Ingroup Bias." *Personality and Social Psychology Bulletin*, 29: 679–90.

van Oudenhoven, J. P., & de Boer, T. (1995). "Complementarity and Similarity of Partners in International Mergers." *Basic and Applied Social Psychology*, 17: 343–56.

Weber, R. A., & Camerer, C. F. (2003). "Cultural Conflict and Merger Failure: An Experimental Approach." *Management Science*, 49: 400–15.

Worrall, L., Parkes, C. L., & Cooper, C. (2004). "The Impact of Organizational Change on the Perceptions of UK Managers." *European Journal of Work & Organizational Psychology*, 13: 139–63.

Yukl, G. (2001). *Leadership in Organizations* (5th ed.). New York: Prentice Hall.

CHAPTER 20

POWER AND POLITICS IN MERGERS AND ACQUISITIONS

JANNE TIENARI AND EERO VAARA

INTRODUCTION

Mergers and acquisitions (M&A) are complex social phenomena that bring together different people in conditions of uncertainty and ambiguity. M&A give rise to competing versions of strategy, disputes over resource allocation, and confrontation between groups with varying vested interests. Although their own future is typically insecure, employees are expected to work together and take part in integration efforts. Hence, it is not surprising that issues related to power are crucial for M&A. Power relations are often intertwined with organizational politics and politicking.

In this chapter, we attempt to shed light on power-related issues that arise when previously separate organizations merge or when one organization acquires another. As a basis for this endeavor, we provide a brief overview of the ways in which power as a concept has been treated in management and organization studies. This overview is followed by an analysis of the ways in which power (and politics) has been conceptualized in different strands of M&A literature. We revisit seminal studies in the field where the treatment of power is often implicit. We reread some of the classics in terms of how they (seem to) conceptualize power, and also provide examples of more explicit takes on power and politics in the M&A context. We highlight important contributions, but also point out some of the limitations of extant theorizing.

It is reasonable to assume that power and politics are salient to M&A performance. At the core of social interaction in M&A are power relations and politicking, which concern choosing between alternative and competing directions for the future. It is virtually impossible—and indeed unfruitful—to search for direct and unambiguous connections between power and performance. However, the high failure rate of M&A, which is frequently cited by researchers and practitioners alike, suggests that connections probably do exist. For example, one might expect that power relations and politics contributed to the apparent failure of the merger between Daimler (Germany) and Chrysler (US) or that the conflicts labeled cultural in the Travelers and Citibank merger in the US had to do with power struggles and politicking.

How exactly power- and politics-related processes unfold in M&A over time is a matter that needs to be studied further, although problems of access are likely to continue to hamper researchers' attempts to do so. Moreover, power is not only a tricky subject for empirical study, but also a theoretically challenging concept. As our review below demonstrates, power and politics are notoriously vague and malleable conceptual tools for researchers. They can be defined and used in a number of ways. Also, power is likely to attain different meanings in mergers as opposed to acquisitions and in domestic maneuvers as opposed to cross-border ones. Based on our tentative analysis of M&A literature in the light of power, we argue that advancements in our understandings of this complex phenomenon will require more in-depth and context-sensitive inquiries.

This chapter is structured as follows. We first provide a brief introduction to power and politics in management and organization studies and beyond. We then move on to outline different perspectives on power and politics in M&A research. Finally, we offer some suggestions for key points and sketch avenues for future research.

POWER: A MALLEABLE CONCEPT

Power is pervasive, and power relationships are of crucial importance for social analyses. Power has, however, been understood in a variety of ways in literatures relevant to M&A (Clegg et al. 2006). A crude distinction can be made between those who theorize power as a resource, as something held and used, and those who advocate a relational view of power in social interaction. These two perspectives are outlined next. We then move on to a brief introduction to a multidimensional definition of power, and conclude this section with a reflection on politics and an outline of literatures that are still not typically drawn upon by M&A scholars, but which may prove helpful in taking us beyond the obvious.

In the 1960s and 1970s, political and sociological analyses advanced the conceptualization of *power as a resource* (Clegg et al. 2006). Management theorists drew on these analyses and distinguished between legitimate (or official) decision-making power deriving from the hierarchical positions of those who exercise power over their subordinates on the one hand and illegitimate (or unofficial) power embedded in social networks and relationships on the other (Pettigrew 1973; Pfeffer 1992; Thompson 1956). In fact, it has been argued that these informal relationships are particularly relevant power mechanisms in organizations (Mintzberg 1983). In general, most management and organization analyses of decision-making power have more or less shared the resource-based view, where power is considered a property of particular actors or groups of actors (Miller et al. 1996).

When power is viewed as something held and used, questions of resistance acquire a particular meaning. In managerialist accounts, resistance has been presented as a hindrance to organizational development; something to be overcome by means of management. This is reflected in the plethora of popular books on (and for) managers pursuing change in organizations (Kotter 1996). Sometimes the advice may be to "share" power to achieve particular goals, but the overarching message is clear.

In contrast, research on labor processes has concentrated primarily on the collective, conscious, and organized responses to managerial power of male blue-collar workers in factory settings (Thomas and Davies 2005). Power and resistance have been presented as antithetical, that is, related to management and employees and their (often tense) relationships in organizations. While in the 1970s and 1980s this focus was the exclusive domain of a marginalized group of Marxist intellectuals, by the mid-1990s theorizations on resistance had made a dramatic reappearance in new forms (Fleming and Spicer 2008).

Critical management studies (CMS) provided an intellectual counterpoint to mainstream management research (Alvesson and Willmott 1996). Critical analyses of management typically address how cultural traditions and the acts of powerful agents contribute to "freezing" social reality for the benefit of certain sectional interests at the expense of others (Alvesson and Deetz 2000). Management is understood as a concept and category, as a social construction that is filled with history and political motives. Studying management critically means addressing asymmetrical relations of power in depth. However, central to this work is also an appreciation of the difficult position of managers: "Caught between contradictory demands and pressures, managers encounter ethical problems; they run the risk of dismissal; they are 'victims' as well as perpetrators of discourses and practices that (un-)necessarily constrain ways of thinking and acting (Jackall, 1988)" (Alvesson and Willmott 2003: 14).

Power and resistance have come to be viewed as a complex issue that cannot be reduced to relationships between managers and employees. Industrial sociologists, too, began to open up the notion of resistance in the 1990s to see "more quotidian variants like cynicism, foot dragging, dis-identification, and alternative articulations of selfhood" (Fleming and Spicer 2008: 302). In brief, while the more mainstream literature on management continued to embrace power as a resource, more critical work slid toward processual and relational understandings.

A post-structuralist conception of *power as relations* in organization and management studies grew out of Michel Foucault's (1977, 1984) work in particular. Foucault conceptualized social actors as controlled and disciplined by social practices and discourses, rather than vice versa. Practices and discourses, Foucault suggested, construct subject positions and identities for actors. In the Foucauldian view, power relationships are understood to be multifaceted in the sense that those conventionally seen as powerless also exercise power over those conventionally seen as the dominators. Acts of resistance—conventionally seen as a counterforce to power—are in the Foucauldian view an inherent part of the (re)construction of power relations. Resistance is not considered to be separate from power; rather, it is inherent in its exercising (Knights and Vurdubakis 1994). Resistance can even be conceptualized to constitute a form of power (Collinson 1994).

The Foucauldian view can be used not only to point out limits in mainstream takes on power, but also to scrutinize more critical understandings in management studies. In her distinction between mainstream, critical, and Foucauldian perspectives, Foldy (2002) suggests that the critical perspective typically treats power as something negative. A Foucauldian perspective, she argues, is apt for exploring the terrain of identity as a key site for the reproduction of power relations, thus also offering opportunities for resistance and change. Central to Michel Foucault's conceptualization of power is that it is both productive and transformative as well as exacting and limiting (Foucault 1980). Power is viewed as action on action. It is fundamentally relational; modifying, directing, and guiding rather than dominating. In the Foucauldian scheme, domination is the result of the application of force rather than the effect of power.

In management and organization theory, many scholars have been inspired by post-structuralist ideas. They have paid attention to discourses and discursive mechanisms that (re)produce power relationships. Such studies have often examined the (re)produc-tion of inequalities in organizations. Foucauldian perspectives have been found useful in, for example, studies of disciplinary practices (Townley 1993), subjugation and sub-jectification (McKinlay and Starkey 1998), and normalization (Ahonen and Tienari 2009). Studies have also found Foucault's work useful in making sense of discursive struggles in and around organizations (Hardy and Phillips 1999). Struggle refers here, first, to the interplay of different discourses that shape organizational reality and, sec-ond, to a struggle over meanings. To put it crudely, the key question (to study) is how and why a particular version of social reality, carrying specific meanings, becomes accepted and normalized as "truth" at a given time and place, and what opportunities for alternatives it opens up. In brief, the relational view on power draws attention to histor-icity and discursivity and understands resistance as an integral part of power relations.

Power remains a contested terrain in management and organization research. Both views—power as resources and power as relations—have been criticized. On the one hand, to understand power as a resource to be acted on and used by individual decision-makers and dominant groups is to run the risk of simplification. At the extreme, power may be reduced to qualities and possessions of individuals and groups and the positions they hold. On the other, post-structuralist conceptions of power relations have been criticized for an overly deterministic view where the role given to individual subjects and selves remains limited. At the extreme, individuals are seen as puppets moved around by invisible and faceless discourses. It has also been pointed out that by ques-tioning the very existence of "stable" structures, post-structuralists run the risk of offer-ing a relativist scenario where the possibility of a critique of apparent structural inequalities and subordination remains limited.

More *multidimensional views on power* have also been advocated.[1] Steven Lukes (1974) presented a model of three dimensions that advanced power analyses so that in addition to concrete decision-making and non-decision-making the institutionalized power that is exercised to construct social reality also became highlighted. This directed research attention to the ways in which meaning is controlled by some to render others power-less, while the others do not necessarily even become aware of this exercise of power.

Contributions by Lukes and others paved the way for understanding power not solely as something that is possessed by specific actors, but something that is embedded in social structures, traditions, and conventions. A similarly influential view was advocated by Anthony Giddens (1984), who considered power the (causal) ability of agents working within a framework of specific structures to mobilize particular rules and resources.

Stewart Clegg's (1989) circuits of power framework is an example of multidimensional conceptualizations in management and organization theory. Clegg brings together (1) episodic power relationships manifested in concrete situations where different social actors interact, (2) rules of practice that fix relations of meaning and membership (that both define identities and subjectivities for the actors interacting in specific episodes and are affected by these interactions), and (3) structures of domination constituted by social practices and techniques empowering or disempowering actors. The term "circuit" refers to the coexistence and connections between all three levels of analysis.

If power is a vague and malleable concept, so is *politics*. Mainstream management and organization research has found it difficult to grasp the dynamics of politicking in organizations. In contrast, critical studies have embraced such inquiry. For example, in *Moral Mazes*, Robert Jackall (1988) provides an intriguing study of the controversial aspects of managerial work. Jackall suggests that to climb up the organizational ladder, managers need to engage in power play and politicking, and they need to learn to live with ethical dilemmas. For example, by virtue of their position, managers are frequently asked to take part in questionable practices that they may personally find uncomfortable. Yet, at the same time, sensitivity to the necessity of organizational politics—making the right choices in paradoxical conditions—determines their success in making a career, and persuades them to turn a blind eye and take part in, and contribute to, questionable practices.

A Foucauldian view offers an alternative vocabulary to study micro-politics in organizations. For example, increasing attention has been paid to "resistance strategies" as an essential part of organizational power relationships, bringing to the fore the idea that resistance can be seen as a continuous process of adaptation and reinscription of the dominant discourses, as well as inventive in terms of creating new types of practice and discourse-level responses to challenging social situations (Thomas and Davies 2005). Hence, power, resistance, and politics often overlap, both in organizational practice and in research.

Finally, apart from management and organization studies, power is also central to fields that have only recently received attention from M&A theorists. Feminist and postcolonial studies are examples thereof. Different traditions notwithstanding, making unequal gendered power relationships in society and in organizations visible lies at the heart of feminist theory. Marta Calás and Linda Smircich (2009) postulate that feminism implies more than a focus on gender relations; in its various strands and forms, feminism is always political. It is guided by feminist theory, ongoing criticism of nonfeminist scholarship, and an aim to create social change. As an example, in the book edited by Robyn Thomas, Albert J. Mills, and Jean Helms-Mills (2004), different scholars theorize on gender and resistance to offer nuanced understandings of identity politics, and to highlight different ways in which individuals and groups struggle to appropriate and transform gendered norms in organizations.

Post-colonialist researchers, in turn, have examined the relationship between colonizing and colonized cultures and people from a specific power/domination perspective. The seminal work of Edward Saïd (1979) has been influential in illustrating how the cultural and socio-political hegemony of the West continues to subordinate people in the non-West. More broadly, post-colonialist analyses have provided keys for understanding how relationships between specific peoples, ethnic groups, and nations are overshadowed by (problematic) historical heritages. For example, the post-colonial lens has inspired scholars to attempt to understand the social forces behind marginalization and exclusion in contemporary multinational organizations (Prasad 2003; Frenkel 2008).

In sum, power and politics have been defined and put to use in a variety of ways by management, organization, and other scholars. However, this abundance has only of late become visible in M&A research, where the resource-based understanding of power has been notably dominant.

PERSPECTIVES ON POWER IN M&A

The chapters of this edited volume show that research on M&A reflects a range of traditions, foci, and interests. Our analysis suggests that different ways of looking at M&A also tend to incorporate particular understandings of power (as well as resistance and politics). They draw from particular fields of inquiry, prefer specific methodologies, and frame the researched phenomena differently. It is interesting to note, however, that in practice power often remains implicit in the research reports; M&A theorists talk about power-related issues without referring to them as such, or only do so in passing. In the following, we outline seven perspectives on M&A in relation to power (see Table 20.1).

Motives and Performance

Since the 1960s, mergers and acquisitions have been studied from a strategic viewpoint (Kitching 1967) with close links to economics and later finance theory. Such studies have concentrated on the firm-level strategic motives and performance effects of M&A, often with a particular focus on various aspects of decision-making. This kind of research has been based on attempts to understand management as a rational agent solving problems related to market conditions and organization resources in different stages of M&A processes.

Friedrich Trautwein (1990) reviewed theories of merger motives and considered these theories in the light of their prescriptions for merger strategies. According to Trautwein, theories of merger motives—or researchers' explanations for why mergers are carried

Table 20.1 Perspectives on M&A

Perspective	Key concerns	Focus on power and politics
Motives and performance	Different strategic motives for M&A, and their connections to performance and value creation	Attaining market power
		Empire-building
		Strategy as political process
Employee concerns	Employees' change-related uncertainty and sense of loss in relation to compliance and resistance in M&A processes	Employee perceptions of domination and subordination
Cultures and cultural politics	Cultural differences, collisions, and resolution through integration in M&A processes	Employee perceptions of dominant and dominated cultures
	M&A as culturally politicized spaces	Political actions in cultural encounters
Identities and identification	(Lack of) employees' organizational identification following M&A decisions	Identifications of the dominant as opposed to the dominated
Institutions	M&A as elements of particular societal configurations of institutions and markets	Structural power in the form of "rules of the game" in and across societies
Legitimation and discursive struggles	Particular representations of M&A, drawing on wider discourses in society	Struggles for meanings
		Legitimation strategies
	M&A stories and narratives-in-the-making	(Re)constructions of success and failure as well as winners and losers
Marginalization and exclusion	Cross-border M&A as constituted in historical relations between peoples and cultures.	Reification of post- and neo-colonial structures of domination
	M&A as gendered spaces	(Re)production of gender-based segregation

out—fall into distinct categories.[2] Efficiency theories view mergers as planned maneuvers that are executed to achieve synergies, be they financial, operational, or managerial. Monopoly theory, in turn, views mergers as planned and executed to achieve market power. Horizontal, vertical, and conglomerate mergers provide different opportunities for firms to embark upon cross-subsidization of products, limiting competition in different markets, and deterring potential entrants. Valuation theory is interested in the effects of managers' information about the target's value. In brief, efficiency, monopoly, and valuation theories present particular understandings of why mergers take place, and on this basis attempt to explain their relative success and failure.

Trautwein (1990) also outlined empire-building, process, raider, and disturbance theories of merger motives. According to Trautwein, empire-building theories view mergers to be planned and executed by managers who attempt to maximize their own utility instead of value for shareholders. Process theory, in turn, is said to produce models that describe strategic decisions not as comprehensively rational choices, but as outcomes of processes governed by individuals' limited information-processing capabilities, organizational routines, and political power. Raider theory focuses on wealth transfers from stockholders to bidders. Finally, rather than focusing on individual mergers, disturbance theory looks at waves of mergers in time vis-à-vis economic disturbances, which increase uncertainty and cause change in the expectations of owners and non-owners.

In recent years, strategy scholars have expanded their focus on M&A motives and effects.[3] For example, attention has been paid to the combination of assets (Haspeslagh and Jemison 1991), capability development, and innovation performance (Ahuja and Katila 2001) and acquirers' development of capabilities to carry out acquisitions (Haleblian and Finkelstein 1999). Tomi Laamanen, and Thomas Keil (2008: 670) put forth a "third layer of acquisition capabilities: the capability to manage acquisition programs," that is, series of acquisitions in time. They considered the impact of an acquirer's size, the scope of its program, and acquisition experience vis-à-vis the performance effects of acquisitions.

From the point of view of power, different theories of strategic merger motives seem to have different foci (Trautwein 1990). For example, a focus on empire-building hinges on theorizing power relations between managers and shareholders. In process theories, organizational political power is a core category in, for example, the seminal studies by Allinson (1971) and Pettigrew (1977). Trautwein interpreted these studies to frame strategic decisions as the outcome of political games played between actors. In this view, tactical considerations and mutual adjustments dominate the decision process. In more recent strategic takes on M&A such as Haleblian and Finkelstein (1999), Ahuja and Katila (2001), and Laamanen and Keil (2008), power is not explicitly discussed in any way.

In sum, in the strategic perspective on M&A, power—whether or not explicitly addressed—is typically considered a resource. This is often implicit as power as a concept remains unarticulated. The notion of market power, however, seems to be particularly pertinent to the more economics-oriented studies. On the one hand, it directs attention to the environmental conditions of M&A activity, leading to various firm-level strategic responses to attaining a powerful position in the market. On the other, it downplays power relations within and between the merging organizations. Processual understandings of strategic motives in M&A, with an often explicit focus on politics, provide an exception in the strategic literature.

Employee Concerns

M&A typically unfold in conditions of ambiguity, uncertainty, and insecurity, and this presents particular challenges for employees and managers alike (Risberg 1999). Studies focusing on employees and other human actors in the M&A context have for some time provided a contrast to more strategically oriented analyses (Marks and Mirvis 1986; Napier 1989; Schweiger et al. 1987; Shrivastava 1986). These studies have often sympathized with employees in the emergent, merger-related change processes, and closely examined employee reactions leading to compliance or resistance to change. Schweiger et al. (1987) identified five major employee concerns in M&A: loss of identity, lack of information, obsession with self-survival, loss of talent, and family repercussions. Fubini, Price, and Zollo (2007) used the metaphor of "corporate health" to make sense of how mergers need to be managed in order to mitigate such concerns.

The point of departure in Susan Cartwright and Cary L. Cooper's (1990) seminal treatise on the human side of M&A was the high-risk nature and failure rate of these maneuvers. Cartwright and Cooper reviewed classifications of M&A, and concluded that human and social issues were ignored in most analyses. Drawing from the field of psychology, Cartwright and Cooper (1990) focused on employees' sense of loss and stress. A sense of loss, particularly prevalent in acquisitions, was compared to bereavement for a close friend or relative. It was suggested that feelings of loss may be accentuated in conditions of uncertainty associated with major organizational change such as M&A. This is likely to be stressful for human beings, and to lead to a variety of reactions.

The relative power of the merging organizations seems to be a recurring theme in studies focusing on the human side of M&A. Employees' perceptions of domination and subordination often lie at the heart of the research. Cartwright and Cooper's (1990: 69) treatise on the human aspects of M&A addressed issues of power as follows: "Mergers and acquisitions are about power, differing perceptions, cultures and definitions of the situation, and so are potentially conflictual; the social and cultural ramifications extend beyond the boardroom." The difference between mergers and acquisitions was pointed out as crucial in terms of power: "In an acquisition, there are clear winners and losers; power is not negotiable but is immediately surrendered to the new parent on completion of the deal (Mangham 1973). Merger is rarely a marriage between equals (Humpal 1971), but the parties are likely to be more evenly matched in terms of size, and the distribution of power is more likely to evolve over time" (Cartwright and Cooper 1990: 70).

Cartwright and Cooper (1990: 70–1) concluded that "there will be greater initial conflict and resistance to change within bitterly fought takeovers, particularly if the issue has mobilized the entire workforce (Turner 1987) than in voluntary mergers or acquisitions, in that feelings of defeat and powerlessness are likely to be heightened (Mirvis 1985)." In mergers, however, "the distribution of power is important in the longer term, as the culture of the dominant party will invariably be expected to become the culture of the new or revamped organization. However, in considering theories which have addressed employee responses to merger, it is useful to draw the distinction between reactions to (i) the announcement itself, and (ii) the changes which subsequently result." Connections between employees' perceptions of power and powerlessness,[4] with feelings of loss, uncertainty, and stress, are of specific importance in this kind of an approach to M&A.

In sum, literature on the human side of M&A builds on perceptions of the relative power of the merging organizations. It is typically implied that this affects a variety of employee reactions, including compliance and more often than not questioning and resistance. In practice, studies of M&A as human activity often overlap with cultural analyses of M&A processes.

Cultures And Cultural Politics

In the early 1980s, with the rise of a more general interest in the study of culture in social sciences, researchers started to explore M&A from a cultural perspective (Buono et al. 1985; Nahavandi and Malekzadeh 1988). Also, a stream of research emerged with a focus on cultural differences and contradictions in international M&A (Olie 1994; Calori et al. 1994; Lubatkin et al. 1998). Cultural differences, whether between organizations or national collectives, have received a lot of attention in the literature. The need to integrate the merger partners began to be framed as a cultural issue, and the impact of cultural differences on merger performance raised interest among M&A scholars (Stahl and Voigt 2005; Teerikangas and Very 2006).

In their seminal work, Anthony F. Buono, James L. Bowditch, and John W. Lewis III (1985) directed attention to the notion of culture in understanding domestic M&A and their outcomes. Buono et al. aimed to complement what in the 1980s was a literature dominated by a strategic perspective. Their study of a merger between two mutual savings banks in the US brought to the fore a novel view of the merger process as an attempt to combine different organizational cultures. Buono et al. examined the cultures of the merging organizations, the attitudes and perceptions of organizational members before and after the merger, the emerging culture of the newly formed organization, and the cultural implications of the merger and its effects on organizational members. With this agenda, Buono et al. paved the way for what became a stream of cultural studies on M&A in the 1980s and 1990s. Cartwright and Cooper's (1990) contribution discussed above is an example, as they explicitly connect their ideas to the language of organizational culture, discussing cultural (in)compatibility, rivalry, and combination in relation to employee perceptions of loss, uncertainty, and stress.

The question of cultures in M&A was soon taken to the international level. René Olie (1994) provides an example in his study of difficulties emanating from "firm-specific" and "nation-specific" differences in cross-border mergers. To reconcile these potentially problematic consequences of differences, and to achieve an adequate level and form of integration,[5] Olie suggested that questions of leadership, symbolic reconstruction of a new identity, superordinate goals, and multi-group memberships would be crucial.

Buono et al. (1985) focused specifically on cultural collisions and their resolution. They discussed at length perceptions of the "organizational locus of power" in the merging firms. This discussion centered on perceptions of individual top managers and their behavior. While in one of the merging firms studied the locus of power was presented as egalitarian and bureaucratically dispersed, in the other firm it was portrayed as being consolidated in the hands of the president. Although not explicitly articulated, the conception of power in Buono et al.'s study is clearly resource based. This is illustrated by their descriptions of the post-merger setting: "Soon after the merger actually took place, each parent organization was seen by the employees of the other bank as an 'invading enemy,' rather than as a co-equal partner (despite the relatively equal size of the banks)" (ibid. 492). Buono et al. identified stages in the unfolding of the merger, for example, with labels such as "negative stereotyping" and "arm wrestling." In the merger studied, "it was becoming increasingly clear that although this was to be a 'merger of equals,' the culture of the new institution, in terms of its subjective interpretations and its objective artifacts and symbols, more closely resembled Bank B than Bank A" (ibid. 495).

Power is not always explicitly addressed, but it is implicitly assumed in cultural studies of international M&A. It typically becomes framed as a question of national (cultural) balance of power. In describing his merger cases, for example, Olie (1994) contended that "every indication that one of the two parties was dominating the new venture was studiously avoided. A [national] balance was applied to the overall distribution of management positions, the composition of the management and supervisory boards, presidency, new investments and location of the new head office" (ibid. 399). Olie went on to suggest that "despite...attempts to symbolize the binational character and the co-equal status of the two partner firms, it was often perceived differently by national groups" (ibid. 400).

In brief, cultural studies of M&A typically frame power as the dominance of one merger party over the other, and the cultural dynamics involved receive particular attention. Buono et al.'s (1985) study exemplifies this. Olie's (1994) study, in turn, is typical of the significant body of literature on international M&A in the sense that it seeks to understand the dominance of one national culture over another, as well as the effects of integrating the two different cultures. It also attempts to prescribe suitable managerial activities for achieving success in the cross-border M&A context.

Some studies have taken a more processual perspective on cultural differences and their implications for power. Eero Vaara (2003) viewed post-acquisition integration as a culturally politicized space and focused on the ways in which managers made sense of key issues in post-acquisition integration. His analysis illustrated the ways in which the ambiguity surrounding integration issues and cultural confusion may lead to the politicization of post-acquisition integration.

Finally, cultural studies of mergers and acquisitions have been shown to lack critical reflection. Sally Riad (2005) offered a critical reading of the use of organizational culture in both researchers' and practitioners' attempts to make sense of M&A. She applied a Foucauldian perspective in arguing that knowledge on "organizational culture" (a contested term, hence the quotation marks) has acquired authority and constitutes a "truth" (ditto) in mergers. Riad viewed organizational culture as a discursive formation implicated in a regime of truth. She confronted issues of power explicitly, and argued that when used in making sense of mergers, the "truth" of the organizational culture construct has both enabling and constraining power effects.

Identities and Identification

With the rise of cultural studies on M&A, employees' identities and identification emerged as a related topic that raised interest among scholars. Drawing from the field of social psychology, Daan van Knippenberg, and colleagues (2002) analyzed social identity processes in mergers. They argued that organizational identification following a merger is contingent on a sense of continuity of identity, and suggested that this sense of continuity is contingent on the extent to which the individual's own pre-merger organization dominates or is dominated by the merger partner. Van Knippenberg et al. went on to argue that pre- and post-merger identification are more positively related for members of dominant as opposed to dominated organizations, and that perceived differences between the merger partners are more negatively related to post-merger identification for members of the dominated organization.

Steve Maguire and Nelson Phillips (2008) followed the same line of reasoning, paying particular attention to the notion of institutional trust. They focused on how issues of organizational identity and identification processes contributed to the loss of institutional trust—the trust that members have in their organization—among a group of employees from one merger party following the merger decision. Maguire and Phillips suggested that this includes two mechanisms. First, the ambiguity surrounding the identity of the newly merged organization can undermine trust. Second, in time, as ambiguity is reduced, those employees who are highly identified with their legacy organization may continue to experience low institutional trust because they do not identify with the new organization.

With regard to identities and identification in the M&A context, domination (and subordination) is—again—a crucial issue. This is explicit in van Knippenberg et al.'s (2002) study. Maguire and Phillips (2008: 395), in turn, remain relatively silent about power, but maintain that the "efficiency-driven decisions to make headcount reductions and to increase the hours in a work week [in the new organization] were interpreted as signs that [merger partner 1] was emerging as the more dominant partner and that [the new organization] would resemble that legacy organization rather than [merger partner 2]."

Institutions

It is evident that different strands of institutional theory have influenced research on M&A, although not to the same extent as the strategic, human, and cultural views outlined above. The specific contribution of institutionalist research is to consider M&A in the "big picture" and to view them as elements of particular societal configurations of institutions and markets. A form of institutional view was already inherent in seminal historical studies that highlight long-term waves of M&A activity in society (Chandler 1990), as well as in studies of M&A as social movements and fashions (Davis and Stout 1992; Thornton 1995). To put it crudely, these studies considered M&A as constituent parts of their operating environments and, more specifically, of particular industries and their evolution.

The crux in institutionalist theory is that particular societal configurations of institutions and markets determine the rules of the game for economic and social activity. In this vein, Glenn Morgan (2007) set out to explain, first, why M&A take place and, second, how they play out in practice. He pointed out that this entails a focus on "how institutions of society (the underlying patterns of political power, authority, trust, ownership, labor relations and skill formation) pre-structure the game that individual firms and actors play." Hence, Morgan took distance from the human and cultural understandings of power in M&A literature: "my interest is not so much in what may be termed the microdynamics of power (i.e. how individuals assert their will over others; how one side of an M&A deal overcomes another), it concerns what authors (such as Lukes (1974) and Clegg (1989)) have referred to as 'structural power'" (Morgan 2007: 116).

Morgan's (2007) work on "structural power" was in the tradition of comparative capitalisms and national business systems literature, which can be considered particular strands of institutionalist theory (cf. Hall and Soskice 2001; Whitley 1992). Morgan's fundamental argument was that power (in M&A and in other economic activities) is already distributed by the rules themselves, which reflect a process of social negotiation arising from social conflict between actors with differential power. Morgan maintained that the rules of the game reflect and reproduce power differences. This, he claimed, has significant consequences for the ways in which M&A play out in practice. On the one hand, different rules of the game in different societies create different conditions for M&A. On the other, M&A become a crucial mechanism of power in the restructuring of firms and societies.

However, for scholars such as Morgan the increasing influence of transnational governance bodies and organizations has become crucial for understanding the shift in the rules of the game for M&A activity. The "big picture" has become global. On the one hand, transnational governance bodies such as the OECD, IMF, WTO, and the World Bank and on the other, multinational corporations (MNCs), work to promote a global playing field with universal rules of the game. However, at the same time nation-states continue to pursue their own agendas in coordinating economic activity. M&A need to be viewed in context, and today this includes both societal (national) and global forces and their intertwining.

Legitimation and Discursive Struggles

The discursive and narrative aspects of M&A have lately received increasing research attention. Influential early studies were carried out by Hirsch and Andrews (1983) and Hirsch (1986), who examined the metaphors and vocabularies of hostile takeovers, and Schneider and Dunbar (1992), who presented a psychoanalytic reading of texts in relation to such events. Vaara (2002) examined the discursive construction of success and failure in decision-makers' accounts of mergers and acquisitions, and Vaara and Tienari (2002) studied types of discourse through which the changes involved in M&A are justified and legitimized, and how they come to be viewed as "natural" in the media. Cummings and Riad (2007) noted that M&A are frequently described with expressions drawn from war and battle, and showed how this has implications for the ways in which M&A are made sense of by focal actors and the public at large.

Andrew D. Brown and Michael Humphreys (2003) provide an intriguing study of a merger of two colleges into an institution of further education in the United Kingdom. In their narrative analysis of organizational members' sense making of the merger, Brown and Humphreys reported a contradiction: while the merger strategists (the senior management team) told a distinctly heroic narrative of epic change, the subordinate groups in the merging colleges authored recognizably tragic narratives. Brown and Humphreys argued that these different narrations and narratives were influenced both by psychological processes and by broadly available cultural resources. Categorization, self-enhancement, and uncertainty reduction were the key psychological processes that influenced how people made sense of the mergers. Cultural resources such as literary genres, in turn, provided means for articulating stories of the merger and its outcomes.

Brown and Humphreys (2003) illustrated the precarious and sometimes contested nature of success and failure in mergers. The senior management team in Brown and Humphreys' study understood the merger to have been largely successful and attributed this success to their own efforts. They expressed optimism regarding the future of the new merged institution. In stark contrast, while subordinate groups in the two merging colleges had different understandings of the merger and each other, they agreed that the merger had been ill planned and poorly executed by an incompetent, uncaring, and careerist senior management team. Brown and Humphreys' findings resonate with Vaara's (2002) study on the discursive construction of success and failure in narratives of post-merger integration. Vaara concluded that the success stories of senior managers were likely to lead to overly optimistic views of the management's ability to control change processes in the merger context. Stories of failure, in turn, led to overly pessimistic views. Questions of power and of dominance and submission came to be understood as more ambiguous and multifaceted than in the more established strategic, human, and cultural perspectives on M&A.

As institutional theory posits in its idiosyncratic ways, discursive and narrative studies also point out that M&A do not exist in a vacuum. Stakeholders often considered to be outside the merging organization may in fact emerge as key actors in the ways in which merger and acquisition processes take shape and are understood. The media is an example of this. How journalists choose to cover M&A may affect the ways in which shareholders, customers, and employees make sense of these complex and ambiguous phenomena (Vaara et al. 2006). Merger strategists, for example, attempt to justify and legitimize their views in the media, while other actors may promote competing understandings (Vaara and Tienari 2008). For example, Vaara and Monin (2010) showed how legitimation is an inherent part of post-merger integration and how successful or failed legitimation effects have a fundamental impact on organizational action.

Discursive and narrative analyses have recently been complemented by novel approaches. Eero Vaara and Janne Tienari (2011) offer an antenarrative lens to international M&A. While classical narrative analyses make sense of organizations through fully formed stories, antenarrative analysis focuses on narratives and storytelling *in action* as they are crafted in organizations undergoing change (Boje 2001; Bakhtin 1981). Antenarratives are fragments of organizational discourse that construct identities and interests in time and space. Vaara and Tienari suggest that antenarratives are particularly useful for understanding international M&A, where different stories-in-the-making coexist and jockey for position. In their model, antenarratives exist in a dialogical relationship and provide alternative ways of giving sense to, or making sense of, the merger and its implications. Vaara and Tienari also illustrate the crucial role that stories-in-the-making play in both the legitimation and the resistance of change in post-merger integration.

Marginalization and Exclusion

Finally, although M&A may have fundamental implications for economies, societies, communities, and various groups of people, explicitly critical analyses of M&A have been scarce. The study of Vaara et al. (2005), focusing on the choice of corporate language as a question of power and politics in an international merger, is a rare example. Vaara et al. used Clegg's (1989) circuits of power framework and pointed to the multifaceted implications of corporate language policies. Language skills became empowering or disempowering resources in organizational communication that were associated with professional competence and led to the creation of new social networks. Language also became an essential element in the construction of international confrontation, led to a construction of superiority and inferiority, and reproduced post-colonial identities in the merging organization. Vaara et al.'s analysis also illustrated how language policies lead to the reification of post- and neo-colonial structures of domination in multinational corporations.

Drawing on feminist organization theory, in turn, Tienari (2000) studied a domestic merger from a gender perspective. He illustrated how women became marginalized in the merger process and typically ended up in less attractive managerial positions than men. He also showed how the status of feminized positions declined in time. His study brought to the fore how the merger process contributed to the (re)production of gender-based segregation in the new organization. Tienari, Søderberg et al. (2005) elaborated on this with a focus on the making of a multinational firm through cross-border mergers. They explored how male executives explained away the exclusion of women from the top echelons in processes of internationalization. Among other things, their study brought to the fore how understandings of women's family responsibilities serve as an excuse for excluding them from top management (Calás and Smircich 1993). Tienari, Vaara, and Meriläinen (2010) provided another reading of men and masculinity in cross-border M&A. They showed how becoming international induces a particular masculine identity for the top managers involved, but also demonstrated how the managers' national identification persists. Masculine identity construction re-enforces the position of men, while, again, excluding women from positions of authority.

Summary

Different approaches and perspectives form a varied and fragmented field of M&A research, not only in terms of conceptualizing power, but also more generally. Prominent scholars continue to call for more coherence and paradigmatic unity in the field, typically around positivist principles and more "rigorous" research (Larsson and Finkelstein 1999; King et al. 2004). The issue can, however, be turned around. It has been suggested that it is precisely the hegemonic position of positivist methods of inquiry that prevent a rich, multiform, and comprehensive understanding of M&A dynamics from developing (Meglio and Risberg 2010). Conceptualizations of power are arguably a case in point.

Categorizations always remain analytical exercises that merely attempt to organize messy social reality—in this case, academic. Our review above is not intended to be exhaustive. Individual pieces of M&A research may also combine ideas from different perspectives. Our distinction between the seven perspectives and the labels we have given to them can be contested. It is merely offered as a tool for M&A researchers to make sense of the variety in the field, and to develop it further with respect to enhanced understandings of power and politics.

CONCLUSIONS

In this chapter, we have shed light on power-related issues in mergers and acquisitions. We have provided an outline of how power has been addressed in management and organization theory. We have revisited seminal studies in the field of M&A and reread them from the point of view of power, and also provided examples of more explicit takes on power and politics in M&A research. Based on our review and analysis of extant literature, we have offered seven perspectives to make sense of power and politics in M&A. These include motives and performance; employee concerns; cultures and cultural politics; identities and identification; institutions; legitimation and discursive struggles; and marginalization and exclusion.

Power and politics are extremely challenging theoretical concepts. We have highlighted important contributions in the M&A literature, but also pointed out some of the limitations of extant theorizing. While power and politics have been understood in a variety of ways by management, organization, and other scholars, they remain ambiguous concepts that are defined and put to use in a variety of ways. This abundance has only recently become visible in M&A research, where scholars have for some time been bound by resource-based understandings of power, focusing on questions such as the perceived (im)balance of power between the merging organizations and their representatives, the various consequences of this (im)balance (strategic, human, cultural, or identity related), and the managerial efforts to coordinate the integration of the merging organizations. The focus has been on distinguishing between the dominant (powerful) and dominated (powerless), and on dealing with the (often) negative consequences of this "power asymmetry."

However, it is important to add to these conventional views on power. Studies that have focused on cultural politics, those taking a narrative or discursive approach to M&A, and those exploring marginalization and exclusion have made a clear leap from a resource-based view on power to a more relations-based view. Yet, alternative framings of power and politics remain scarce in M&A literature. In particular, we lack openly critical studies that would elaborate on topics such as marginalization and exclusion. In international settings, post- or neo-colonial lenses would be particularly helpful in providing M&A scholars with ideas and concepts for understanding the complex ways in which historically constituted relations between peoples and cultures impact upon the dynamics of power relations in cross-border mergers and acquisitions. There are also many other interesting and useful perspectives that M&A scholars could draw upon (Clegg et al. 2006). By so doing, M&A scholars could also aim to contribute to analyses of power in organizations more generally.

At the same time, it is our conviction that making sense of power and politics calls for in-depth understandings of particular mergers and acquisitions. One must zoom in and address the specific dynamics at hand as they unfold in M&A planning, negotiation, and implementation. In short, there is a need for context-sensitivity and a deep understanding of the various dynamics of human and social interaction, whether they are framed in terms of strategy, human resources, culture, identity, or discourse. Sensitivity to context and contextualization of research endeavors have been recognized in fields ranging from anthropology (Dilley 2002) and communication studies (Sillince 2007) to management (Bamberger 2008), strategic management (McKiernan 2006), and international business (Michailova 2011; Welch et al. 2011). In-depth, context-sensitive studies are also likely to advance the development of theory on power in M&A. This would also be practically relevant, as corporate managers have little use for abstract variables and bogus quantification (Kay 2010).

ENDNOTES

1. For a genealogy of (research on) power and organizations, we advise M&A scholars to consult the comprehensive treatise on the subject by Stewart Clegg, David Courpasson, and Nelson Phillips (2006).
2. Trautwein's (1990) research report contains a typical flaw in M&A research: the distinction between mergers and acquisitions remains blurry and unarticulated. Although mergers and acquisitions are legally different transactions (Hovers 1973) and their points of departure differ significantly in terms of social interaction (Cartwright and Cooper 1990), they are often presented as synonymous.
3. In the international business (IB) literature, motives and outcomes of cross-border M&A have been discussed through several thematic perspectives, for example, as a question of strategic choice of entry mode, value-creating strategy, and learning process (Shimizu et al. 2004).
4. Scholars have also focused on issues such as organizational justice in the M&A context. Perceptions of procedural justice, for example, have been found useful in understanding employee reactions to M&A (Lipponen et al. 2004; Meyer 2001; Véry et al. 1998).
5. Olie (1994: 386) conceptualizes integration as the "combination of firms into a single unity or group, generating joint efforts to fulfill the goals of the new organization."

REFERENCES

Ahonen, P., & Tienari, J. (2009). "United in Diversity? Disciplinary Normalization in an EU Project." *Organization*, 16/5: 655–79.

Ahuja, G., & Katila, R. (2001). "Technological Acquisitions and the Innovation Performance of Acquiring Firms: A Longitudinal Study." *Strategic Management Journal*, 22: 197–220.

Allinson, G. T. (1971). *The Essence of Decision: Explaining the Cuban Missile Crisis*. Boston, MA: Little Brown.

Alvesson, M., & Deetz, S. (2000). *Doing Critical Management Research*. London: Sage.

—— & Willmott, H. (1996). *Making Sense of Management: A Critical Introduction*. London: Sage.

——— (2003). "Introduction," in M. Alvesson & H. Willmott (eds.), *Studying Management Critically*. London: Sage, 1–22.

Bakhtin, M. M. (1981). *The Dialogic Imagination*, ed. M. Holquist. Austin, TX: University of Texas Press.

Bamberger, P. (2008). "Beyond Contextualization: Using Context Theories to Narrow the Micro-Macro gap in Management Research." *Academy of Management Journal*, 51/5: 839–46.

Boje, D. M. (2001). *Narrative Methods for Organization and Communication Research*. New York: Sage.

Brown, A. D., & Humphreys, M. (2003). "Epic and Tragic Tales. Making Sense of Change." *Journal of Applied Behavioral Science*, 39/2: 121–44.

Buono, A. F., Bowditch, J. L., & Lewis, J. W., III (1985). "When Cultures Collide: The Anatomy of a Merger." *Human Relations*, 38/5: 477–500.

Calás, M. B. & Smircich, L. (1993). "Dangerous Liaisons: The 'Feminine in Management' Meets 'Globalization.'" *Business Horizons*, 36: 73–83.

——— (2009). "Feminist Perspectives on Gender in Organizational Research: What Is and is Yet to Be," in D. Buchanan & A. Bryman (eds.), *The SAGE Handbook of Organizational Research Methods*. London: Sage, 246–69.

Calori, R., Lubatkin, M., & Véry, P. (1994). "Control Mechanisms in Cross-Border Acquisitions: An International Comparison." *Organization Studies*, 15/3: 361–79.

Cartwright, S., & Cooper, C. L. (1990). "The Impact of Mergers and Acquisitions on People at Work: Existing Research and Issues." *British Journal of Management*, 1/1: 65–76.

Chandler, A. D. (1990). *Scale and Scope: The Dynamics of Industrial Capitalism*. Cambridge, MA: Belknap Press.

Clegg, S. R. (1989). *Frameworks of Power*. London: Sage.

—— Courpasson, D., & Phillips, N. (2006). *Power and Organizations*. London: Sage.

Collinson, D. (1994). "Strategies of Resistance," in J. Jermier, D. Knights, & W.E. Nord (eds.), *Resistance and Power in Organizations*. London: Routledge, 25–68.

Cummings, S., & Riad, S. (2007). "M&A as Warfare: Warspeak in Mergers and Acquisitions," in D. Angwin (ed.), *Mergers and Acquisitions*. Oxford: Blackwell Publishing, 87–115.

Davis, G. F., & Stout, S. K. (1992). "Organization Theory and the Market for Corporate Control: A Dynamic Analysis of the Characteristics of Large Takeover Targets, 1980–1990." *Administrative Science Quarterly*, 37/4: 605–33.

Dilley, R. M. (2002). "The Problem of Context in Social and Cultural Anthropology." *Language and Communication*, 22/4: 437–56.

Fleming, P., & Spicer, A. (2008) "Beyond Power and Resistance: New Approaches to Organizational Politics." *Management Communication Quarterly*, 21/3: 301–9.

Foldy, E. G. (2002). "'Managing' Diversity: Identity and Power in Organizations," in I. Aaltio & A. J. Mills (eds.), *Gender, Identity and the Culture of Organizations*. London: Routledge, 92–112.

Foucault, M. (1977). *Discipline and Punish: The Birth of the Prison*. Harmondsworth: Penguin.

—— (1980). *Power/Knowledge: Selected Interviews and Other Writings 1972–1974*. ed. C. Gordon. Brighton: Harvester Press.

—— (1984). *The History of Sexuality: An Introduction*. Harmondsworth: Penguin.

Frenkel, M. (2008). "The Multinational Corporation as a Third Space: Rethinking International Management Discourse on Knowledge Transfer through Homi Bhabha." *Academy of Management Review*, 33/4: 924–42.

Fubini, D., Price, C., & Zollo, M. (2007). *Mergers: Leadership, Performance and Corporate Health*. Basingstoke: Palgrave Macmillan.

Giddens, A. (1984). *The Constitution of Society*. Cambridge: Polity Press.

Haleblian, J., & Finkelstein, S. (1999). "The Influence of Organization Acquisition Experience on Acquisition Performance." *Administrative Science Quarterly*, 44/1: 29–56.

Hall, P. A., & Soskice, D. (2001). *Varieties of Capitalism: The Institutional Foundations of Comparative Advantage*. New York: Oxford University Press.

Hardy, C., & Phillips, N. (1999). "No Joking Matter: Discursive Struggle in the Canadian Refugee System." *Organization Studies*, 20/1: 1–24.

Haspeslagh, P., & Jemison, D. B. (1991). *Managing Acquisitions: Creating Value through Corporate Renewal*. New York: Free Press.

Hirsch, P. M. (1986). "From Ambushes to Golden Parachutes: Corporate Takeovers as an Instance of Cultural Framing and Institutional Integration." *American Journal of Sociology*, 91/4: 800–37.

—— & Andrews, J. A. (1983). "Ambushes, Shootouts, and Knights of the Roundtable: The Language of Corporate Takeovers," in L. Pondy, P. Frost, G. Morgan, & T. Dandridge (eds.), *Organizational Symbolism*. Greenwich, CT: JAI Press.

Hovers, J. (1973). *Expansion through Acquisition*. London: Business Books.

Humpal, J. J. (1971). "Organizational Marriage Counselling: A First Step." *Journal of Applied Behavioral Science*, 7: 103–9.

Jackall, R. (1988). *Moral Mazes: The World of Corporate Managers*. New York: Oxford University Press.

Kay, J. (2010). *Obliquity: Why Our Goals Are Best Achieved Indirectly*. London: Profile Books.

King, D. R., Dalton, D. R., Daily, C. M., & Covin, J. (2004). "Meta-analysis of Post-acquisition Performance: Indicators of Unidentified Moderators." *Strategic Management Journal*, 25/2: 187–200.

Kitching, J. (1967). "Why do Mergers Miscarry?" *Harvard Business Review*, 45 (November–December): 84–101.

Knights, D., & Vurdubakis, T. (1994). "Foucault, Power, Resistance and All That," in J. Jermier, D. Knights, & W. E. Nord (eds.), *Resistance and Power in Organizations*. London: Routledge, 167–98.

Kotter, J. (1996). *Leading Change*. Boston, MA: Harvard Business School Press.

Laamanen, T., & Keil, T. (2008). "Performance of Serial Acquirers: Toward an Acquisition Program Perspective." *Strategic Management Journal*, 29, 663–72.

Larsson, R., & Finkelstein, S. (1999). "Integrating Strategic, Organizational, and Human Resource Perspectives on Mergers and Acquisitions: A Case Survey of Synergies Realization." *Organization Science*, 10/1: 1–26.

Lipponen, J., Olkkonen, M., & Moilanen, M. (2004). "Perceived Procedural Justice and Employee Responses to an Organizational Merger." *European Journal of Work and Organizational Psychology*, 13: 391–413.

Lubatkin, M., Calori, R., Véry, P., & Veiga, J. (1998). "Managing Mergers across Borders: A Two Nation Test of Nationally Bound Administrative Heritage." *Organization Science*, 9/6: 670–84.

Lukes, S. (1974). *Power: A Radical View*. London: Macmillan.

Maguire, S., & Phillips, N. (2008). "'Citibankers' at Citigroup: A Study of the Loss of Institutional Trust after a Merger." *Journal of Management Studies*, 45/2: 372–401.

Mangham, I. (1973). "Facilitating Intraorganizational Dialogue in a Merger Situation." *Journal of Interpersonal Development*, 4: 133–47.

Marks, M. L., & Mirvis, P. H. (1986). "The Merger Syndrome." *Psychology Today*, 20/10: 36–42.

McKiernan, P. (2006). "Understanding Environmental Context in Strategic Management—Preface to a Special Issue." *International Studies of Management and Organization*, 36/3: 3–6.

McKinlay, A., & Starkey, K. (eds.) (1998). *Foucault, Management and Organization Theory*. London: Sage.

Meglio, O., & Risberg, A. (2010). "Mergers and Acquisitions: Time for a Methodological Rejuvenation of the Field?" *Scandinavian Journal of Management*, 26/1: 87–95.

Meyer, C. B. (2001). "Allocation Processes in Mergers and Acquisitions: An Organizational Justice Perspective." *British Journal of Management*, 12/1: 47–66.

Michailova, S. (2011). "Contextualizing in International Business Research: Why do We Need More of It and How Can We Be Better At It?" *Scandinavian Journal of Management*, 27/1: 129–39.

Miller, S. J., Hickson, D. J., & Wilson, D. C. (1996). "Decision-Making in Organizations," in S. R. Clegg, C. Hardy, & W. R. Nord (eds.), *Handbook of Organization Studies*. London: Sage.

Mintzberg, H. (1983). *Power In and Around Organizations*. Englewood Cliffs, NJ: Prentice Hall.

Mirvis, P. H. (1985). "Negotiations after the Sale: The Roots and Ramifications of Conflict in an Acquisition." *Journal of Occupational Behaviour*, 6: 65–84.

Morgan, G. (2007). "M&A as Power," in D. Angwin (ed.), *Mergers and Acquisitions*. Oxford: Blackwell Publishing, 116–52.

Nahavandi, A. and Malekzadeh, A. R. (1988). "Acculturation in Mergers and Acquisitions." *Academy of Management Review*, 13/1: 79–90.

Napier, N. K. (1989). "Mergers and Acquisitions, Human Resource Issues and Outcomes: A Review and Suggested Typology." *Journal of Management Studies*, 26/3: 271–89.

Olie, R. (1994). "Shades of Culture and Institutions in International Mergers." *Organization Studies*, 15/3: 381–405.

Pettigrew, A. M. (1973). *The Politics of Organizational Decision-Making*. London: Tavistock.

—— (1977). "Strategy Formulation as a Political Process." *Journal of International Management Studies*, 7: 78–87.

Pfeffer, J. (1992). *Power in Organizations*. Boston, MA: Pitman.

Prasad, A. (2003). *Postcolonial Theory and Organisational Analysis: A Critical Engagement*. Basingstoke: Palgrave Macmillan.

Riad, S. (2005). "The Power of 'Organizational Culture' as a Discursive Formation in Merger Integration." *Organization Studies*, 26/10: 1529–54.

Risberg, A. (1999). *Ambiguities Thereafter: An Interpretive Approach to Acquisitions*. Malmö, Sweden: Lund University Press.

Saïd, E. W. (1979). *Orientalism*. New York: Vintage.

Schneider, S. C., & Dunbar, R. L. M. (1992). "A Psychoanalytic Reading of Hostile Takeover Events." *Academy of Management Review*, 17/3: 337–567.

Schweiger, D. M., Ivancevich, J. M., & Power, F. R. (1987). "Executive Action for Managing Human Resources Before and After the Acquisition." *Academy of Management Executive*, 1/2: 127–38.

Shimizu, K., Hitt, M. A., Vaidyanath, D., & Pisano, V. (2004). "Theoretical Foundations of Cross-Border Mergers and Acquisitions: A Review of Current Research and Recommendations for the Future." *Journal of International Management*, 10: 307–53.

Shrivastava, P. (1986). "Post-merger Integration." *Journal of Business Strategy*, 7/1: 65–71.

Sillince, J. A. A. (2007). "Organizational Context and the Discursive Construction of Organizing." *Management Communication Quarterly*, 20/4: 363–94.

Stahl, G., & Voigt, A. (2005). "Impact of Cultural Differences on Merger and Acquisition Performance: A Critical Research Review and an Integrative Model." *Advances in Mergers and Acquisitions*, 4: 51–82.

Teerikangas, S., & Véry, P. (2006). "The Culture-Performance Relationship in M&A: From Yes/No to How." *British Journal of Management*, 17(S1): 31–48.

Thomas, R., & Davies, A. (2005). "Theorizing the Micro-Politics of Resistance: New Public Management and Managerial Identities in the UK Public Services." *Organization Studies*, 26/5: 683–706.

Thomas, R., Mills, A. J. & Helms-Mills, J. (eds.) (2004). *Identity Politics at Work: Resisting Gender, Gendering Resistance*. London: Routledge.

Thompson, J. D. (1956). "Authority and Power in Identical Organizations." *American Journal of Sociology*, 62: 290–301.

Thornton, P. (1995). "Accounting for Acquisition Waves: Evidence from the U.S. College Publishing Industry," in W.R. Scott & S. Christensen (eds.), *The Institutional Construction of Organizations: International and Longitudinal Studies*. Thousand Oaks, CA: Sage.

Tienari, J. (2000), "Gender Segregation in the Making of a Merger." *Scandinavian Journal of Management*, 16/2: 111–44.

Tienari, J. Søderberg, A.-M., Holgersson, C., & Vaara, E. (2005). "Gender and National Identity Constructions in the Cross-Border Merger Context." *Gender, Work and Organization*, 12/3: 217–41.

—— Vaara, E., & Meriläinen, S. (2010). "Becoming an International Man: Top Manager Masculinities in the Making of a Multinational Corporation." *Equality, Diversity and Inclusion: An International Journal*, 29/1: 38–52.

Townley, B. (1993). "Foucault, Power/Knowledge and its Relevance for Human Resource Management." *Academy of Management Review*, 18: 518–45.

Trautwein, F. (1990). "Merger Motives and Merger Prescriptions." *Strategic Management Journal*, 11: 283–95.

Turner, J. (1987). "The Pilkington Experience." *Personnel Management*, July.

Vaara, E. (2002). "On the Discursive Construction of Success/Failure in Narratives of Post-merger Integration." *Organization Studies*, 23/2: 211–48.

—— (2003). "Post-acquisition Integration as Sensemaking: Glimpses of Ambiguity, Confusion, Hypocrisy, and Politicization." *Journal of Management Studies*, 40/4: 859–94.

—— & Monin, P. (2010). "A Recursive Perspective on Discursive Legitimation and Organizational Action in Mergers and Acquisitions." *Organization Science*, 21/1: 3–22.

—— & Tienari, J. (2002). "Justification, Legitimization and Naturalization of Acquisitions: A Critical Discourse Analysis of Media Texts." *Organization*, 9/2: 275–304.

—— —— (2008). "A Discursive Perspective on Legitimation Strategies in MNCs." *Academy of Management Review*, 33/4: 985–93.

—— —— (2011). "On the Narrative Construction of MNCs: An Antenarrative Analysis of Legitimation and Resistance in a Cross-Border Merger." *Organization Science*, 22/2: 370–90

—— —— & Laurila, J. (2006). "Pulp and Paper Fiction: On the Discursive Legitimation of Global Industrial Restructuring." *Organization Studies*, 27/6: 789–810.

—— —— Piekkari, R. & Säntti, R. (2005). "Language and the Circuits of Power in a Merging Multinational Corporation." *Journal of Management Studies*, 42/3: 595–623.

van Knippenberg, D., van Knippenberg, B., Monden, L., & De Lima, F. (2002). "Organizational Identification after a Merger: A Social Identity Perspective." *British Journal of Social Psychology*, 41: 233–52.

Véry, P., Lubatkin, M. H., & Calori, R. (1998). "A Cross-National Assessment of Acculturative Stress in Recent European Mergers," in M. C. Gertsen, A.-M. Söderberg & Torp, J. E. (eds.), *Cultural Dimensions of International Mergers and Acquisitions*. Berlin: De Gruyter.

Welch, C., Piekkari, R., Plakoyiannaki, E., & Paavilainen-Mäntymäki, E. (2011). "Theorising from Case Studies: Towards a Pluralistic Future for International Business Research." *Journal of International Business Studies*, 42/5: 740–62.

Whitley, R. (1992). *European Business Systems: Firms and Markets in their National Contexts*. London: Sage.

··

CHAPTER 21

SILENT FORCES SHAPING THE PERFORMANCE OF CROSS-BORDER ACQUISITIONS

··

SATU TEERIKANGAS

Introducing M&A—A Fragmented Field?

··

Why is it that M&A, despite years of experience and evidence, would seem to continue to underperform (King et al. 2004)? Whilst the difficulty in making M&A succeed has been traced back to an inadequate strategic rationale and a lack of pre-deal evaluation, researchers seem to agree that it is the post-deal implementation phase that presents the greatest challenge in making M&A work (Jemison and Sitkin 1986; Datta 1991; Haspeslagh and Jemison 1991).

However, the study of the challenges inherent in the post-deal implementation phase has evolved in parallel research streams, with little cross-fertilization between them (Haspeslagh and Jemison 1991; Larsson and Finkelstein 1999; Shimizu et al. 2004; Haleblian et al. 2009). The challenges of post-acquisition integration have thus been studied separately from the perspectives of (1) managing the integration process (Mace and Montgomery 1962; Kitching 1967; Haspeslagh and Jemison 1991; Birkinshaw et al. 2000; Ranft and Lord 2002); (2) dealing with the human challenge (Marks 1982; Napier 1989; Cartwright and Cooper 1990); as well as (3) understanding and dealing with the impact of differences in organizational and/or national cultures (Sales and Mirvis 1984; Nahavandi and Malekzadeh 1988; Buono and Bowditch 1989; Weber et al. 1996). More strikingly, these research streams have surprisingly few connections with research on M&A performance (Lubatkin 1983; Chatterjee 1986; Datta et al. 1992; King et al. 2004). In contrast to the prevailing departmentalization of M&A research, in their case-survey covering qualitative studies on M&A, Larsson and Finkelstein (1999) pointed out the significance of adopting an integrative perspective on M&A. In the study, key variables, namely employee motivation, firm complementarity, and organizational integration, were all strongly correlated with M&A performance and the realization of potential synergies in the deal.

Given the apparent departmentalization of M&A research, it has further been suggested that there is a general lack of "theory" on M&A. Trautwein (1990) argues that research on M&A should "move away from efficiency theories toward more process-related theories." Sinatra and Dubini (1994) claim that, owing to the methodological weakness of existing studies, a "theory of M&A" is still lacking. Greenwood et al. (1994) agree, claiming that, at present, M&A research is focused on specific "themes" rather than on theory development. Schweiger and Goulet (2000) have argued the need for "a comprehensive theory" on M&A. In a recent review, Haleblian et al. (2009) note the scarcity of comprehensive reviews and models of the M&A literature.

The lack of theory on M&A is paralleled by concern as to the lack of understanding on the drivers of M&A performance (Hoskisson and Hitt 1993; Hitt et al. 1998; King et al. 2004). In their extensive meta-analytical study of research on M&A performance, King et al. (2004) identified no significant M&A performance antecedents, concluding that "additional, unknown variables may impact M&A performance," and subsequently calling for more theory-building research on M&A, using novel methods. A lack of understanding of the dynamics of the post-acquisition integration process has also been raised. Von Krogh et al. (1994) call for "a better understanding of the post-acquisition integration process." Based on their extensive review of extant research, Schweiger and Goulet (2000) argue that there is a need for an improved understanding of "managing the post-acquisition integration process." In particular, they regret the lack of "empirical research on the relationships between the pre- and post-acquisition phases to the successful outcome of M&A." In their comprehensive review of the M&A literature, Haleblian et al. (2009) emphasize the need for qualitative studies on M&A integration dynamics.

These concerns would seem to be particularly salient in the context of cross-border M&A that present the challenge of differing country contexts in addition to the traditional burden of post-acquisition organizational integration. Surprisingly, cross-border M&A have received scantier research attention than domestic ones (Olie 1994; Shimizu et al. 2004; Quah and Young 2005). More specifically, while cross-border mergers have been studied (see work by e.g. Olie 1994; Zaheer et al. 2003), cross-border acquisitions remain an under-studied phenomenon (Shimizu et al. 2004; Quah and Young 2005). This is all the more important given that most so-called "M&A" are in practice acquisitions, not mergers (UNCTAD 2000, quoted by Buckley and Ghauri 2002; Zaheer et al. 2003).

As a result, the discussion on the impact of cultural differences in times of M&A, traceable to organizational or national cultures, seems to be raging without conclusive evidence either way (Teerikangas and Véry 2006; Stahl and Voigt 2008). Thus, based on current research evidence, it is difficult to say whether domestic or cross-border M&A are more difficult to undertake: do differences in national cultures make cross-border M&A more challenging than domestic M&A, and if so, what is the nature of this challenge? Calls have been made for research to unearth the complex nature of the cultural challenge in cross-border M&A, and the ways in which this challenge is related to the dynamics of post-acquisition integration (Teerikangas and Véry 2006).

To summarize, the review of extant research on M&A suggests that the field needs an enhanced theoretical understanding of M&A as an organizational phenomenon. Thus, an appreciation of (1) the antecedents of M&A performance, (2) the dynamics of post-acquisition integration, and (3) the cultural and integration dynamics inherent in cross-border M&A would seem to be lacking. These gaps in current knowledge could explain why M&A remain such managerially challenging undertakings. This chapter aims to contribute to research on M&A by addressing these gaps in the context of cross-border acquisitions.

RESEARCH SETTING AND OBJECTIVES

Based on the study of one domestic and eight cross-border acquisitions, in this chapter, a grounded, integrative perspective on the post-acquisition integration dynamics of cross-border acquisitions, is presented, using the grounded theory method (Glaser and Strauss 1967; Glaser 1978). The grounded model points to the need to simultaneously attend to (1) "visible" strategic, structural, and financial factors, and (2) "less visible," more intangible, behavioral, human, and cultural factors in order to appreciate the dynamics and causal links predicting the progress and ultimate outcome of cross-border acquisitions.

The findings are based on extensive qualitative material relating to a total of 166 interviews with 141 interviewees in nine acquisitions in France, Denmark, Germany, the US, the UK, and Finland. This study ranks among the most extensive qualitative interview-based studies on M&A (see Teerikangas 2010). The acquisitions took place during the period of 1990–2000 and were made by four Finnish multinationals operating in a variety of industrial sectors (ranging from dynamic high-technology sectors to process-based industries). Interviewees' experiences with eight other former parent firms of European and American origin were also used to inform the findings. For a detailed overview of the research setting and method, please see Teerikangas (2006).

The research project focused on cross-border acquisitions wherein the buying firms followed a symbiotic integration strategy (Haspeslagh and Jemison 1991), i.e. aiming to integrate the acquired firm into their operations, whilst simultaneously seeking to learn from the latter. The unit of analysis was either the acquisition of one company, or one site in a multi-site firm's acquisition.

Consistent with the aim of grounded theory research, the research process focused on understanding what takes place in the basic social process under study (Glaser and Strauss 1967), i.e. post-acquisition integration, as seen from the perspectives of the actors involved. A grounded theory culminates in identifying a "core category" (Glaser 1978) that explains most variation in the studied phenomenon. To this end, the concept of "silent forces" emerged in the research process as the core category explaining variation in the studied phenomenon—the social process of "post-acquisition integration." "Silent forces" represent factors that tend to go unnoticed and unrecognized by managers involved in acquisitions. In the present-day corporate context, they typically relate to the behavioral, human, and cultural dimensions of organizational life. In other words, buying firms typically emphasize the strategic, structural, and financial dimensions of M&A to the detriment of the "silent forces" therein. All the while, unattended factors have the potential to turn into "silent forces." Non-attention to the presence of silent forces throughout the acquisition process has consequences for the outcome and subsequent performance of the transaction. Ultimately, the "hidden" dimension in the silent forces at work in M&A relates to the type of cognitive attention span of the managers involved. Indeed, silent forces are "silent" only for those actors whose cognitive attention span does not attend to such dimensions of organizational behavior.

SILENT FORCES AND THE PERFORMANCE OF CROSS-BORDER ACQUISITIONS

In this section, we proceed to an overview of the types of "silent forces" at play throughout the cross-border acquisition process. In so doing, we also identify their impact on the progress and performance of cross-border acquisitions. We show that it is the interplay of the more easily "visible" strategic, structural, and financial dimensions, and the less "visible" behavioral, human, and cultural dimensions that explains the difficulty of making cross-border acquisitions succeed. This interplay takes place throughout the acquisition process, beginning with the pre-deal evaluation phase, moving on to the integration phase, and ultimately affecting the outcome of the acquisition and the long-term outlook for both firms. The challenge of post-acquisition integration lies in the involved managers' needing to simultaneously account for this wide array of factors. Hence there is a need for an "integrative perspective" in the management of cross-border acquisitions (Figure 21.1). In support of this reading, Table 21.1 summarizes the findings in the acquisitions studied.

Silent Forces in the Pre-acquisition Phase

The findings pointed to the significance of the pre-deal phase as determining the level of the managerial challenge to be expected at the start of the post-deal era. In other words, the integration period does not begin in a void, but is influenced by the pre-deal era. Extant M&A research has largely focused on the management of the post-deal period (see Teerikangas 2010, for an overview). The role of the pre-deal period in the success of the post-deal integration phase has surprisingly not been the subject of

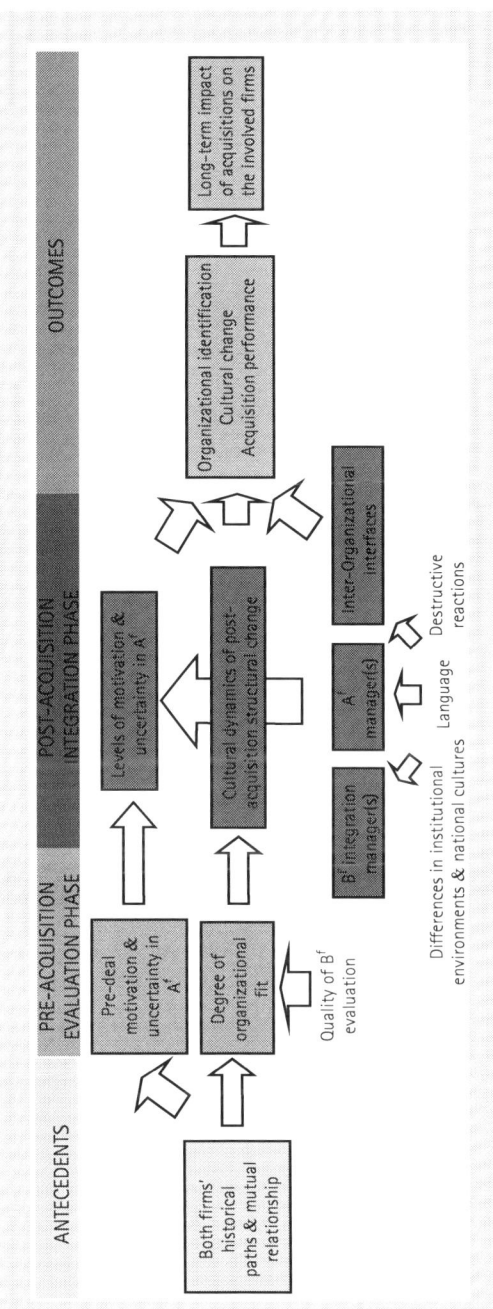

FIG. 21.1 An integrative perspective on cross-border acquisitions

NOTE: A^f refers to the acquired firm, and B^f refers to the buying firm.

Table 21.1 The management of the cross-border acquisition process and the outcome of the studied acquisitions*

	Danish R&D unit no. 1	German R&D unit no. 2	UK firm no. 3	German firm no. 4	US firm no. 4	Unit of French multi-site firm no. 5	Finnish firm no. 6	French site no. 7	Unit of US multi-site firm no. 8
PRE-DEAL ANTECEDENTS TO ACQUISITION OUTCOME									
Pre-deal motivation	Very positive	Very positive	Negative	Positive	Positive	Positive	Very positive	Very positive	Negative
Degree of organizational fit	High	Medium	Low	Low	Low	Low	Low	Low	Low
Surprises emerging from due diligence	Negative surprises	Negative surprises	Negative surprises	Negative surprises	Negative surprises	Negative & positive surprises	Negative surprises	Negative surprises	Negative surprises
POST-DEAL ANTECEDENTS TO ACQUISITION OUTCOME									
Post-deal motivation	Very positive	Positive	Negative	Very positive	Positive	Negative	Positive	Positive	Negative
Quality of integration management	Very well-managed integration	Well-managed integration	Poorly managed integration	Well-managed integration	Little integration management	Well-managed integration	Well-managed integration	Well-managed integration	Well-managed integration
B[f] negative emotions	Some	Some	Some	None	None	Some	Some	Some	Disturbing
A[f] negative emotions	None	None	None	Disturbing	Disturbing	Disturbing	None	None	None
Cultural side of change considered	Somewhat	Poorly	Poorly	Somewhat	Little change implemented	Poorly	Poorly	Somewhat	Somewhat

Country institutional & cultural differences	Small impact	Negative impact	Very negative impact	Negative impact	Negative impact	Negative impact	Negative impact	Negative impact	Negative impact
Language barriers	Harmful	Harmful	Harmful	Harmful	Harmful	Harmful	Harmful	Harmful	Harmful

ASSESSING THE OUTCOME OF THE STUDIED ACQUISITIONS

Speed of cultural change	Rapid	Rapid	Slow	Rapid	Slow	Medium	Medium	Rapid	Medium
Speed of identification	Rapid	Rapid	Slow	Rapid	Slow	Medium	Medium	Rapid	Medium
Progress of integration & change	On target	On target	Lagging significantly	On target	Lagging significantly	On target	Some delay	Some delay	Some delay
Business targets met	On target	On target	Negative for years	Depends on department	Depends on department	Depends on department	Depends on department	On target some years after deal	Initial targets are not met
A^f financial performance	Positive	Positive	Negative	Positive	Positive	Negative	Positive	Positive	Positive
B^f financial performance	Positive	Positive	Negative	Positive & negative	Positive & negative	Positive & negative	Positive & negative	Positive & negative	Positive & negative

* Note: A^f refers to the acquired firm, and B^f refers to the buying firm.

extensive research (Hunt 1990; Haspeslagh and Farquhar 1994; Schweiger and Goulet 2000). Calls have been made for more research into its effect on the acquisition process (Greenwood et al. 1994; Schweiger and Goulet 2000).

The present findings extend those of Jemison and Sitkin (1986) and Haspeslagh and Jemison (1991) on a process perspective on M&A by showing that the pre-acquisition phase impacts upon the challenge of post-deal integration through (1) the degree of pre-deal level motivation vs. uncertainty that acquired firm employees enter the new parent firm with, and (2) the degree of organizational and strategic fit between the firms. These findings point to the need for an integrative perspective on cross-border acquisitions, starting from the pre-deal phase.

Target firm employee motivation   Prior to the deal, employee reactions have been found to relate to preoccupation, imagining the worst, and stress reactions (Marks 1991). Ivancevich et al. (1987) and Buono and Bowditch (1989) have shown how employee reactions change in the course of the M&A process. The studied acquisitions point to factors explaining fluctuations in pre-deal levels of motivation in the acquired firm as stemming from the way the acquired firm employees react to (a) the news of being acquired, (b) the identity of the buying firm, (c) the buying firm managers' pre-deal behaviors and actions, and (d) the local acquired firm managers' within-firm communications on the forthcoming era (Teerikangas 2010). The news of a cross-border vs. domestic acquisition visibly increases the amount of staff worries regarding their future; this was particularly noticeable for targets with scant international exposure.

Given the multitude of organizational histories within a larger multi-site firm, motivation levels were found to vary from one acquired firm's unit to another. Hence, the pre-acquisition era tends to be characterized by a plethora of reactions and differing motivation levels across the acquired firm's units, and possibly also across departments within each unit. Whilst prior research tends to emphasize the negative employee reactions to M&A (Buono and Bowditch 1989; Cartwright and Cooper 1992; Risberg 2001), the present study showed pre-deal examples of acquired firms wherein high to low degrees of motivation existed (Teerikangas 2010). Thus, the reality would not seem to be as glum as often depicted by research.

The studied acquisitions pointed to target firm employee reactions not being attended to by acquiring firm managers in the pre-acquisition phase. This results in target firm employee reactions turning into a "silent force," with the potential to impact the subsequent integration phase and the long-term performance of the acquisition. The studied acquisitions showed how instances of low levels of pre-deal motivation can result in the departure of key staff, knowledge leaks, and the strengthening or formation of new competitors, and hence can have long-term consequences on the financial performance of the acquiring firm. They can also result in pre-acquisition action against the buying firm, be it in the form of negative press coverage resulting in a damaged public image, or even in delaying the deal through lobbying of local administrators. Pre-deal levels of motivation were further found to impact the extent to which acquired firm managers were willing to engage in post-acquisition integration efforts. As a result, the pre-deal motivation levels in the acquired firm will be reflected in the short- to long-term performance of the acquisition.

Quality of pre-deal evaluation In addition to ongoing negotiations in the pre-deal phase (O'Connor 1985), the buying firm representatives are busy being involved in due diligence. Strategic, legal, financial, and technical analyses have repeatedly been found to override human and organizational analyses in this phase (Madura et al. 1991; Kissin and Herrera 1990; Greenwood et al. 1994; Cartwright 1998; Marks 1999), and the difficulty of assessing cultural differences has been recognized (Napier 1989; Greenwood et al. 1994). These findings received confirmation in the present study. Indeed, buying firms were more at ease with the evaluation of the technical and financial sides of the acquired firm, at the expense of an in-depth understanding of the acquired firm's cultural make-up. The short time frame in which the pre-deal evaluation has to be made and the difficulty of gaining access to reliable information about the acquired firm further complicate the evaluation task. All the while, any omission in the pre-acquisition phase does not go unnoticed in the post-acquisition phase. Any omission was found to turn into a "silent force" hampering the success of the post-acquisition phase.

The involved managers' limited attention span is exemplified in the way that pre-acquisition organizational fit is assessed. The present findings point to the fact that the analysis of organizational fit needs to be made in terms of structural and cultural dimensions of interfirm differences at departmental, unit, corporate, and national levels of analysis. "Cultural fit" here refers to the analysis of departmental, unit, organizational and national cultures, whereas "structural fit" refers to the analysis of operational, technical, systems, administrative, and organization structural differences. Moreover, many parallel analyses of organizational fit need to be made when acquiring a firm consisting of many sites, possibly spread across countries. This analysis is critical given that it provides clues as to both the attractiveness of the transaction and to the foreseeable areas of difficulty in the post-deal era. Omissions were found to induce slower progress in post-acquisition change. However, managers involved in pre-acquisition evaluation tend to focus on the technical and structural facets of organizational fit, whilst partly ignoring its cultural dimensions. The latter would thus often turn into "silent forces" hampering the progress of the post-acquisition phase.

In synthesis, based on the study of nine acquisitions, this section has identified target firm employee reactions to the forthcoming acquisition as well as the quality of pre-deal evaluation as critical in that they impact the progress of the post-deal integration phase, as well as the outcome and performance of the acquisition. As a result, it is argued that managers involved in the pre-acquisition phase need to adopt an integrative perspective in the management of the acquisition process, starting with the pre-deal phase and also a broader perspective traceable to the participating firms' historical paths, as these shape both firms' respective organizational cultures, identification patterns, and provide cues as to the reactions with which acquired firm employees greet the new era. In other words, post-acquisition integration does not start on "day one" after the deal, and the two firms do not enter the acquisition in a "void," stripped of their prior histories, affiliations, cultures, and motivations. The deal should rather be regarded as the point at which the firms' relationship becomes official, the success of which depends on the extent to which pre-deal dynamics have been appreciated.

However, more often than not, buying firms tend to omit the less visible factors related to M&A success. For this reason, the acquired firm's motivation levels, the cultural dimensions of organizational fit, and the buying and acquired firm's managers' behaviors during the pre-deal phase are here termed "silent forces." Unless the managers concerned adopt an "integrative" perspective in the pre-deal phase and attend to both the visible strategic, technical, and financial dimensions as well as the less visible dimensions identified here, these "silent forces" will be left free to hamper and deter the progress and outcome of post-acquisition integration efforts, and thus come to hinder the performance potential inherent in the transaction.

Silent Forces in the Post-acquisition Phase

The studied acquisitions pointed to the smooth progress of the post-acquisition integration phase as depending on the extent to which (a) integration management, (b) emotional reactions, (c) country differences, (d) the progress of post-acquisition change, and (e) acquired firm employees' motivation levels were accounted for (Figure 21.1).

Integration management The organization of post-acquisition integration, i.e. integration management, plays a central role in capturing the value sought from M&A (Haspeslagh and Jemison 1991; Larsson and Finkelstein 1999). The present findings have shown that the management of the post-acquisition era needs the attention of *both* the integration managers directly responsible for its success as well as that of *all* buying firm representatives.

"Integration management" is defined here as the activities that the integration manager(s)/team(s) coordinate(s). First, strategic decisions regarding the post-acquisition phase have to be made, as regards business and integration strategies. Moreover, well-known "fundamentals" of integration management, including the provision of a clear vision (Haspeslagh and Jemison 1991), integration planning (Howell 1970), sufficient communications (Schweiger et al. 1993), timing of actions (Ranft and Lord 2002), fostering interaction (Larsson and Finkelstein 1999), need to be catered for. These efforts prove to be of little use, however, unless the integration teams' attitudes are aligned and supportive of integration. These include attitudes enhancing mutual cooperation between the firms (Hambrick and Cannella 1993; Olie 1994; Deiser 1994; Krug and Nigh, 2001), attitudes to spur the desired post-acquisition change (Napier et al. 1993), and attitudes to enhance mutual exchange of know-how (Haspeslagh and Jemison 1991). The studied acquisitions pointed to the fact that whilst the "fundamentals of integration management" tend to be catered for, poorly performing acquisitions often suffer from a lack of the right mix of attitudes. Attitudes would seem to reflect an easily forgotten dimension in post-acquisition management, thus turning into a "silent force" hampering the acquisition's progress. In cases of poorly managed acquisitions, the "fundamentals of integration management" were also not accounted for.

Paralleling the central role of integration managers and teams (Haspeslagh and Jemison 1991; Ashkenas and Francis 2000), the progress of post-acquisition integration depends on the proactivity of buying firm expatriates present in acquired overseas sites (Harzing 2001; Hebert et al. 2005), the support of the buying firm's subsidiaries in the country where the acquisition takes place, the support of the buying firm's top management, as well as the extent to which proactive acquired firm managers are involved in the integration efforts (Graebner 2004).

Effectiveness of interfirm interfaces   In addition to the importance of the different managerial roles, the findings pointed to the influence of the firms' mutual organizational interface on the progress and outcome of post-acquisition integration (Haspeslagh and Jemison 1991). The successful management of post-acquisition change was not found to depend only on the actions of the responsible managers. Instead, anyone from the parent firm's side who is in touch with the acquired firm's employees at any point in the post-acquisition era plays a role as a daily micro-level "change agent." Unless the significance of this micro-level change agent role is recognized, buying firm employee behaviors unwittingly become "silent forces" potentially destroying value. Indeed, while managers responsible for integration are able to support the acquired firm employees with strategic-level direction, the daily support and guidance for how to operate in the parent firm falls upon the buying firm employees. Unless their role in ensuring the success of the acquisition is clearly communicated and rewarded, employees might not realize the systemic impact that their behaviors, e.g. in terms of a lack of support and attentiveness to the needs of their new colleagues, has on the outcome of the transaction.

Destructive reactions   The effectiveness of integration management and especially of the interfirm organizational interface tends to be reduced by destructive reactions and emotional tensions arising in times of M&A. On the one hand, one can witness the buying firm's not-invented-here syndrome (Blake and Mouton 1984; Buono and Bowditch 1990; Szulanski 1996) and protective reactions against the acquired firm, these often referred to as "competing claims," "secrecy vs. deception" (Buono and Bowditch 1990), "us vs. them," "superior vs. inferior," "attack and defend," and "win vs. lose" behaviors (Marks 1991).

On the other hand, destructive reactions can also arise from within the acquired firm, resulting in the acquired firm units' distrust and competitive and biased behaviors toward one another. These destructive reactions, whether originating in the buying or the acquired firm, were found to slow the progress of post-acquisition integration, and also to have an impact on the financial performance of the transaction. As these reactions tended to go unrecognized, they were allowed to turn into "silent forces" hampering the value-creation potential inherent in the transaction.

Country differences   The effectiveness of interactions and integration progress in cross-border contexts was further found to depend on whether the presence and impact of country differences as regards (a) institutional differences, (b) national cultures, and (c) language was recognized. These findings provide an emerging answer to recent calls for more research on the impact of national cultures in M&A (e.g. Stahl and Voigt 2008).

For one thing, an inattention to institutional country characteristics (Davis and North 1970; DiMaggio and Powell 1991), e.g. as regards competitive and customer dynamics, and legislation, was found to lead to a lack of appreciation of foreign market and organization dynamics. This resulted in lower international sales and a lack of appreciation of how to run global organizations in foreign countries. This had direct performance consequences for the transaction concerned.

For another, inattention to the behavioral, managerial, and communication-related dimensions of national cultures (Hall 1967; Hofstede 1980) was found to lead to different expectations with regard to appropriate organizational behavior, and to result in misunderstandings that reduced the potential effectiveness of cross-border interactions. Moreover, the national cultural roots of both parties' behaviors helped to explain the challenge that acquired firm managers experienced in adapting to a new parent firm's managerial environment (Morosini 1998; Teerikangas 2006). Indeed, the prevailing management style in the buying firm is influenced by its respective home country's national culture (Calori et al. 1994; Lubatkin et al. 1998; Child et al. 2001). Unless this influence is recognized, however, "mistakes" made by acquired firm managers tend to be termed as "deviant" or "wrong" behavior. In other words, for successful intercultural cooperation to occur, both parties need to recognize the influence of their respective cultural heritage on their interactions. Until this occurs, both sides will continue to complain about the other's seemingly "deviant" or "wrong" behavior.

In the context of the present study, buying firms tended to ignore the cultural roots of their behavior, and hence underestimated the challenge that acquired firms face in making the required post-acquisition cultural shift toward the new parent firm. In such situations, national cultures have become "silent forces" that slow the progress of post-acquisition integration. Overall, the findings pointed to the fact that the breadth of the cultural challenge in acquiring across borders remains today largely underestimated and misunderstood. In essence, the need for pragmatic cross-cultural skills (Morosini 1998) and for national culture-compatible integration strategies following M&A (Morosini and Singh 1994; Forstmann 1998; Morosini 1998) seems still to be lacking in the practice of M&A.

In cross-border contexts, the effectiveness of interorganizational interfaces is further impacted by language (Marschan et al. 1997; Feely and Harzing 2003). The lack of a joint native language was experienced as slowing down the progress of cooperation, causing misunderstandings, and ultimately making it more difficult and time-consuming to develop a relationship based on trust. Moreover, acquired firm managers complained that in the long term, the lack of a joint language has consequences for their potential to climb the parent firm's corporate career ladder (Teerikangas 2006).

Post-acquisition change   The pre-deal degree of organizational fit, when combined with the post-acquisition integration strategy (Haspeslagh and Jemison 1991), was found to translate into the experienced "integrative challenge" in the acquired firm, i.e. the likely degree of difficulty in implementing the desired post-deal changes in the acquired firm (Teerikangas 2006). We saw in the pre-deal phase the need to analyse both the structural and cultural dimensions of organizational fit. In the post-acquisition phase, the successful implementation of structural changes was found to have cultural roots traceable to national cultures, corporate-wide cultures, local organizational cultures, and possibly also departmental cultures. These findings mirror the debate in sociology with regard to integrative theories (see e.g. Bate 1994; Parker 2000) that argue for the interdependent nature of the culture-structure relationship. In the present study, a failure to acknowledge the cultural dimensions of a firm's structural choices resulted in the latter being treated from a purely "structural" perspective, ultimately leading to slower post-acquisition change, as the behavioral and cultural changes required to enable and parallel the desired structural changes were not occurring. As a result, the cultural dimensions of structural change were allowed to become "silent forces" impeding the implementation of post-deal change.

Given the interrelatedness of the cultural and structural dimensions of post-acquisition change, any post-acquisition "structural" change was found to be paralleled by cultural change in the acquired firm. In other words, all post-deal structural change was found to be a form of cultural change. However, as buying firms tended to regard post-acquisition change from a purely structural perspective, the resulting cultural change went largely unnoticed and unsupported. In sum, the lack of attention to the cultural dimensions of post-acquisition structural change resulted in its slower progress, reflected in escalating integration costs, and also in slower progress of post-acquisition cultural alignment and change in the acquired firm.

Employee motivation Negative employee stamina preceding and following acquisitions has been the subject of considerable research interest (Sinetar 1981; Buono and Bowditch 1989; Cartwright and Cooper 1993; Risberg 2001). The present findings point to there being varying degrees of uncertainty vs. motivation in the post-acquisition phase depending on how this phase is experienced by acquired firm employees.

The degree of pre-deal motivation that acquired firm employees enter the post-deal phase with was found to act as a lever pointing toward the relative ease vs. challenge of the integration phase. Indeed, pre-deal levels of motivation across the acquired firm tended to predict the likely degrees of motivation across the acquired firm in the post-acquisition months. In the post-acquisition phase, the degree of acquired firm employee motivation further depended on the way in which the integration phase was managed, the direction of post-deal structural and cultural change, the amount of country differences, and contextual factors such as economic downturns and reorganizations. In other words, if the post-deal phase is well managed, well organized, and the types of interventions and post-deal changes taking place in the acquired firm were perceived as bringing positive news for its staff, the latter are more likely to remain motivated to work for the new parent firm. In contrast, a badly managed and organized integration phase and/or negative post-deal news for the acquired firm tends to decrease its employees' willingness to be integrated into the new parent firm and is likely to be paralleled by high levels of uncertainty.

Ensuring the motivation of acquired firm staff is critical, because it affects the willing-ness with which they take part in the integration efforts, and reduces the likely forma-tion of nests of resistance. High levels of uncertainty are likely, in turn, to translate into a more cumbersome integration period. More effort will have to be focused on assuaging employee worries than on building a joint future together. The key question is: Are tar-get firm employees motivated to work for a shared vision, or are they turned off? In the long term, uncertainty and motivation levels were found to impact the willingness of the acquired firm's staff to identify themselves with the new parent firm and their eagerness to accept cultural change. In sum, a lack of attention to uncertainty and motivation lev-els across the acquired firm in the post-acquisition era results in such factors becoming "silent forces" that impact the progress and outcome of integration.

In summary, the post-acquisition integration phase was found to be an arena in which the swift progress of post-acquisition change and the motivation of acquired firm employees tend to get hampered by a lack of attention to attitudes supportive of integra-tion, poorly functioning interfirm interfaces, destructive reactions, and country differ-ences. Though a wealth of literature exists on post-acquisition integration management (see Chapter 14), the present findings point to the strategic and operational/structural facets of post-acquisition integration being more easily catered for. All the while, the less visible behavioral, human, and cultural factors tend to get omitted. As the latter factors nevertheless exist, though they are not necessarily accounted for to a sufficient degree, they become "silent forces" that start to hamper the progress and deter the successful outcome of cross-border acquisitions.

Silent Forces and Acquisition Performance

The analysis of the studied acquisitions led to conceptualizing the successful outcome of cross-border acquisitions in terms of (1) the degree of post-acquisition cultural change and (2) the degree of organizational identification in the acquired firm, as well as (3) the strategic and financial performance of the acquisition. These are termed "outcomes" of successfully managed cross-border acquisitions, given that they were the result of what had taken place throughout the acquisition process, i.e. the motivation of employees toward the acquisition, the progress of post-deal change, the management of post-acquisition integration, and effectively functioning interfirm organizational interfaces. Conceptualized in this way, successful post-acquisition integration is not only reflected in the strategic and financial performance of the acquisition, but also in longer-term sustainable integration results: the degrees of cultural change and organ-izational identification induced in the acquired firm in the years following the transaction.

Cultural change Cultural change (Buono and Bowditch 1989; Cartwright and Cooper 1992) was found to result from the ongoing post-acquisition structural changes induced in the acquired firm, the extent of interfirm interactions taking place in the post-acquisition years (Cartwright and Cooper 1992; Larsson and Lubatkin 2001), as well as the buying firm's efforts to align the acquired firm's corporate value base with its own (Cartwright and Cooper 1992; Schweiger et al. 1994). As post-acquisition structural changes and interactions with buying firm members both reflect the buying firm's national and organizational cultural heritage, the resulting cultural change in the acquired firm was found to take place at the levels of both organizational and national cultures.

The findings further pointed to the fact that post-acquisition cultural change takes place regardless of whether the buying firm actively seeks it or not. Indeed, cultural change in the acquired firm was found to result from successful integration efforts. Indeed, cultural change was found to take place gradually through the structural changes implemented, as well as through daily interfirm interactions, regardless of whether a "formal" cultural change program was under way.

More specifically, the more the buying firm's structures and ways of working were aligned with its corporate values, the more post-acquisition cultural change in the acquired firm was found to move in the direction of the buying firm's official value base. In general, buying firms tended to be unaware of the need to embed their advertised corporate values in their organization's structures, behaviors, and management styles. Unless this happened, the buying firm's organizational culture reflected a "practiced" organizational culture rather than the advertised value base. As buying firms tended, in parallel, to openly recognize only their advertised values, the practiced organizational culture was allowed to turn into a "silent force" impacting the behavior of its members. As a result, post-acquisition cultural change in the acquired firm came to reflect the buying firm's practiced organizational culture, rather than that officially advertised. In sum, post-acquisition cultural change in cross-border acquisitions undertaken by multinational firms was found to represent a multifaceted and complex process. Managers involved in acquisitions need a broad attention span to cope with its dynamics.

Organizational identification In parallel with cultural change, organizational identification (Albert and Whetten 1985) with the new parent firm was also found to be an outcome of successful post-acquisition integration. However, acquired firms cannot be expected to "erase" their affiliation toward previous owners, especially the firm's founding owner (see Chapter 19). The findings highlighted that an acquired firm's patterns of organizational identification reflect its acquisitive history. Consequently, a multinational firm's units are likely to portray a plethora of patterns of organizational identification reflecting each unit's respective ownership history. The strength of identification with previous owners was found to depend on the way in which each ownership era had been experienced. Through active post-acquisition change efforts, proactively involved and supportive acquired firm managers, motivated employees, and the parent firm's overall sincere efforts to develop a "One Company" identity, gradually, over time, the acquired firm's staff can be expected to start developing a positive identification toward the new parent firm. In the absence of such efforts, buying firms might mistakenly expect acquired firms to automatically identify themselves with the parent firm over time and be disappointed if this does not occur.

Performance What M&A performance is and how it should be measured is subject to debate (King et al. 2004; Schoenberg 2006; Zollo and Meier 2008; see Chapters 4, 5). The present findings led to defining post-acquisition performance in terms of (1) the progress of integration, (2) the extent to which strategic targets set for the acquisition have been met, (3) the acquired units' and the buying firm's post-acquisition financial performance using accounting measures. Each of these indicators gave a different view of the studied acquisitions' performance (see also Cording et al. 2010).

The performance of the studied acquisitions along these performance indicators was found to materialize only if the post-acquisition efforts led to the increased performance of the sales, product development, and production functions of both firms, in parallel with enhanced organizational effectiveness. Whether this occurred depended on the extent to which the pre- and post-acquisition phases had been successfully managed. Thus, the extent to which the "visible" strategic, structural, and financial, as well as the "less visible" behavioral, human, and cultural, dimensions had been accounted for was found to impact the performance of the studied acquisitions. This finding further explains the need to adopt an integrative perspective on post-acquisition integration and acquisition performance: an acquisition's performance can be traced back to the way that the acquisition process has been managed.

Long-Term Impact of Acquisitions

Based on the above analysis, a long-term perspective on the consequences of acquisitions for both participating firms emerges.

For the acquired firm, an acquisition is reflected in long-term changes to its structural make-up, organizational culture, patterns and location of emotional tensions, patterns of organizational identification, and financial performance, all of which will shape its future. For the buying firm, an acquisition means that its organizational make-up has been made more complex through the addition of another organizational entity that brings an additional layer of structural choices, organizational culture(s), emotional inter-unit tensions, and identification patterns to those which already exist (Teerikangas 2006; Barkema and Schijven 2008).

Given the amount of M&A taking place in today's corporate arena, many medium to large firms that have grown through M&A can thus be regarded as consisting of a myriad of structural, cultural, emotional, and identity-based entities. The extent to which the parent firm has been able to successfully manage the post-acquisition integration of each of these individual acquisitions was found to predict the extent of alignment across its operations and the types of tensions between these formerly separate entities.

In sum, the consequences of M&A for the firms concerned need to be placed in a long-term context. The present findings have shown that acquisitions do not just have three-month or one-year consequences. Rather, their consequences reach out to impact the subsequent structural and cultural make-up, emotional inter-unit tensions, patterns of identification, and the financial performance of both firms. In sum, the short period of post-acquisition integration can be regarded as the "theatrical arena" of the firms' organizational encounter that draws the greatest amount of attention, yet it represents only a short moment in the long-term success of an acquisition. The challenges faced during this period can to a large extent be traced back to the historical development of both firms, whilst they simultaneously extend into both firms' futures. This invests post-acquisition integration management with greater significance in that its role is not only short term, but ultimately impacts the long-term successful structural, cultural, identity-related, and emotional integration of the target into the acquiring firm.

Conclusions and Discussion

Based on extensive qualitative material relating to 166 interviews with a total of 141 interviewees in one domestic and eight cross-border acquisitions in Germany, France, Denmark, Finland, the UK, and the US respectively, this chapter has extended our understanding of the array of dimensions that need to be attended to in the management of cross-border acquisitions. Whilst strategic, structural, and financial factors tend to be part of the regular M&A checklist, the studied acquisitions point to the fact that the difficulty experienced in making acquisitions work often stems from neglecting the behavioral, human, and cultural dimensions therein. In so doing, the chapter makes the following contributions to extant research.

Integrative Perspective to the Management of Cross-Border Acquisitions

The chapter highlights the need for an integrative perspective in the study and management of post-acquisition integration. During the research process, it became clear that the challenges of post-acquisition integration in cross-border acquisitions were not reducible to a single factor, be it behavioral, human, or cultural. Instead, the difficulty experienced by both first-time and experienced buying firms was found to relate to the extent to which they were able to appreciate, understand, and manage the dynamics unfolding throughout the pre-acquisition and post-acquisition integration phases, both impacting the subsequent outcome of the transaction. What emerged was an appreciation of the systemic and multifaceted nature of the cross-border acquisition process, given the way in which its "visible" strategic, structural, financial, and "less visible" behavioral, human, and cultural dimensions were interwoven throughout its progress. The challenges experienced in the integration of cross-border acquisitions stemmed from the *combined presence* and the *relationships* between these factors rather than from any one factor alone. Together, they were found to explain the outcome of the studied acquisitions, conceptualized in terms of the degrees of cultural change and organizational identification induced in the acquired firm, the extent to which targets set for the acquisition had been met, the swift progress of the integration phase, and the financial performance of the combined entity in the post-deal years.

In so doing, the findings provide one answer to prevailing worries in the research community as regards (1) the need for an improved theoretical understanding of M&A (Trautwein 1990; Greenwood et al. 1994; Sinatra and Dubini 1994; Schweiger and Goulet 2000), (2) the lack of understanding of the dynamics within M&A integration (von Krogh et al. 1994; Schweiger and Goulet 2000; Haleblian et al. 2009), and (3) the lack of understanding of the antecedents of M&A performance (Hoskisson and Hitt 1993; Hitt et al. 1998; Sirower 1997). The present findings show how these research gaps are fundamentally related to one another. This argument is mirrored in the work of Larsson and Finkelstein (1999), who through an extensive case-survey of existing qualitative studies on M&A integration were able to show that the success of M&A depends on simultaneously accounting for employee motivation, organizational integration, and firm complementarity, since these factors all relate to M&A performance. Hence, they argued that an integrative perspective is necessary to understand M&A performance.

All the while, the present findings have woven together threads related to the progress and outcome of acquisitions that have to date largely been studied separately and in parallel to one another (Haspeslagh and Jemison 1991; Larsson and Finkelstein 1999; Shimizu et al. 2004; Haleblian et al. 2009). It seems that owing to a departmentalization of scientific research and the resulting lack of cross-fertilization of research findings, current M&A research has lacked integrative perspectives. Whilst prior research on M&A has studied the managerial, human, and cultural aspects related to post-acquisition integration, much of this work has remained specific to just one of these disciplines.

Silent Forces and the Managerial Attention Span

In parallel, this chapter introduces the concept of "silent forces" into the M&A discourse. The underlying argument is that the observed poor performance of M&A and the difficulty of making them work stems from too narrow an attention span on the part of the managers concerned.

"Silent forces" are defined as factors that escape the attention of managers involved in M&A; they refer to the *blind spots* in buying firms' approaches to M&A. The findings presented in this chapter highlight that "silent forces" typically pertain to the behavioral, human, and cultural dimensions of M&A activity. "Silent forces" can be identified by asking the following set of questions:

1. *Behavioral*: Is integration management adequately catered for? Are the attitudes of both parties mindful of mutual interest and integration throughout the acquisition process? Who is involved? Is the role of all employees recognized as impacting the outcome of the transaction?
2. *Human*: How to ensure employee motivation throughout the acquisition process? Are negative emotions allowed to distort long-term performance?

3. *Cultural*: Are the cultural dimensions in the merger/acquisition appreciated? How to cater for the target firm's host country environment? Do language differences hamper cooperation? How to ensure that employees develop a positive identity toward the new firm? How to spur cultural change post-acquisition?

Managers involved in M&A would seem to adequately focus on the strategic, structural, and financial dimensions of M&A activity, whilst at least partly omitting the herein-identified "silent forces." It is argued that this neglect and omission leads to the oft-reported difficulty of reaching the desired performance targets following M&A. Indeed, as long as "silent forces" are ignored, they are allowed to exert a powerful negative impact on the progress and ultimate outcome of post-deal integration. These omissions lead to M&A not reaching their performance expectations. Attaining the strategic and financial benefits sought from M&A was found to depend on the way in which post-acquisition organizational integration is managed and the extent to which the presence of "silent forces" therein is acknowledged. Consequently, these findings argue for the need to adopt an integrative perspective on the management M&A, a perspective that accounts not only for the strategic, structural, and financial dimensions inherent therein, but also for their behavioral, human, and cultural sides.

Unless an integrative perspective on acquisitions is adopted, behavioral, human, and cultural dimensions have the potential to turn into silent forces that impact the progress and outcome of cross-border acquisitions (Figure 21.2). Indeed, the findings show how inattention to the presence, manifestations, and impact mechanisms of these factors results in slower post-acquisition cultural change in the acquired firm, slower organizational identification with the new parent firm, slower progress of post-acquisition integration efforts, a failure to meet the targets set for the acquisition, and poorer acquired and buying firm financial performance in the post-deal years. In such circumstances, instead of only being the result of rational business decisions and managerial actions, *the outcome of acquisitions was found to largely result from a set of silent forces that were free to "roam around," quietly influencing the progress and outcome of the post-acquisition integration process*, without the actors in charge being fully aware of them.

At heart, the "hidden" and "silent" dimension inherent in the silent forces at work during M&A relates to the type of *cognitive attention span* (Simon 1947; March and Simon 1958; Cyert and March 1963; Weick 1979; Stillings et al. 1995; Ocasio 1997) and subsequent behavior of the managers and actors involved in the integration efforts. Indeed, silent forces are "silent" only for those actors whose cognitive attention span does not attend to such dimensions of organizational behavior. By identifying these forces as "silent," the aim is to shed light and place emphasis on their presence so that over time, the prevailing management style can evolve into one that accounts for their presence. In sum, the present findings call for the involved managers to shift their attention span to include not only the strategic, structural, and financial domains of decision-making (i.e. the overt and visible forces), but also to attend to the more subtle, less visible, yet no less important silent forces at work during M&A transactions.

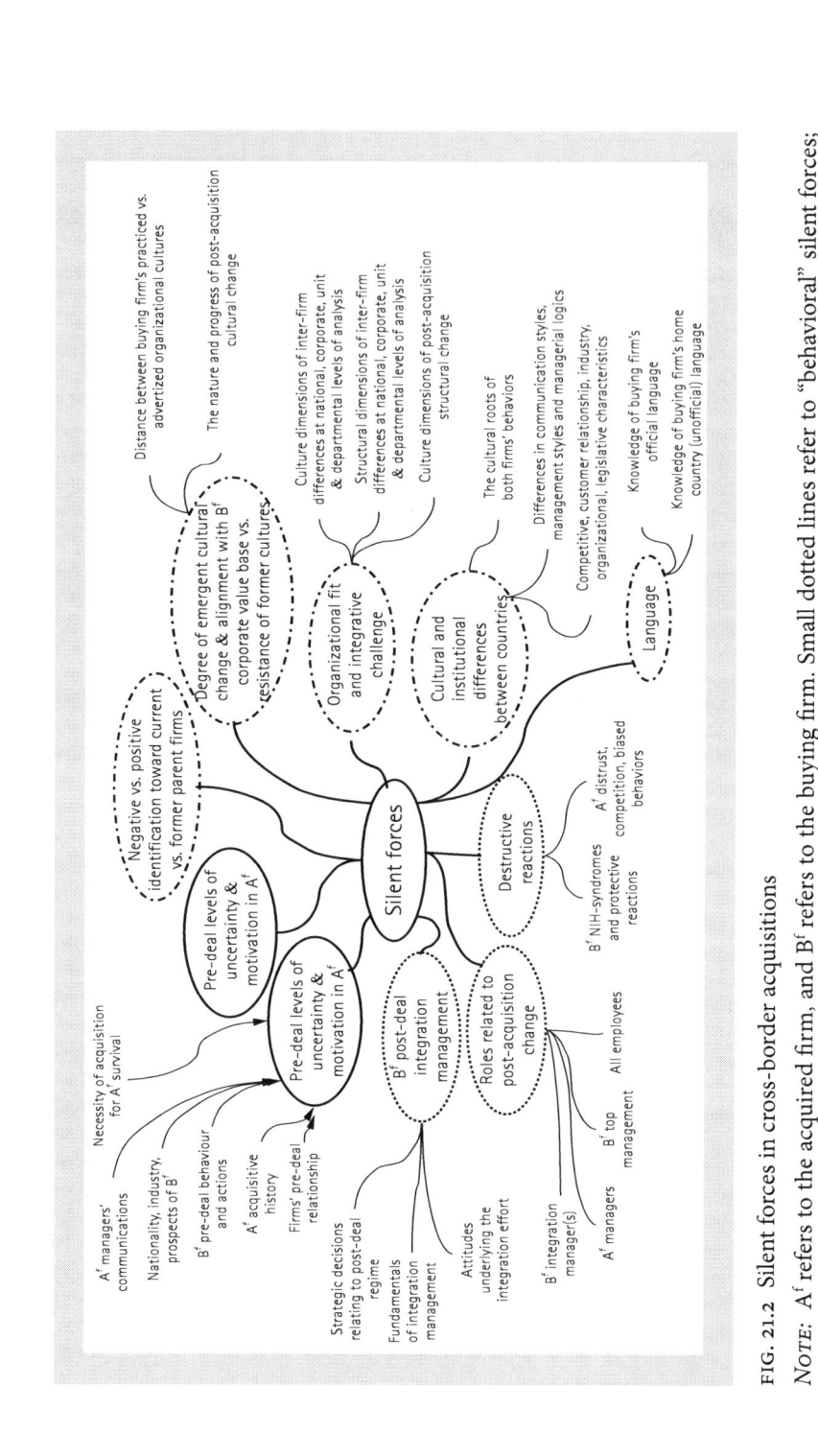

FIG. 21.2 Silent forces in cross-border acquisitions

NOTE: A^f refers to the acquired firm, and B^f refers to the buying firm. Small dotted lines refer to "behavioral" silent forces; semi-dotted lines to "cultural" silent forces, and non-dotted lines to "human" silent forces.

Managerial Contributions, Limitations, Future Research Directions

The findings have important managerial implications. For one, they provide an outline of the post-acquisition integration dynamics in times of cross-border acquisitions: the developed integrative framework allows for a "bird's-eye" perspective on the cross-border acquisition process. By drawing attention to the "silent forces" at work therein, the findings are a call for managers to step back and reflect on the extent to which they engage in cross-border acquisitions with too "shallow" an appreciation of the ensuing challenges. The present findings thus offer managers an opportunity to get acquainted with the myriad of the less advertised, but nonetheless powerful factors impacting the progress and outcome of cross-border acquisitions. The findings encourage managers involved in acquisitions to consider the areas they focus their attention on, and the extent to which the latter attends to the "silent forces" identified here. In the absence of such attention, one can ask if buying firms are fully aware of the challenge they are about to embark upon, and whether they tend to engage in cross-border acquisitions with too limited an estimation of the ensuing difficulties.

As with any research, this study has limitations. The main concern is the fact that the buying firms studied were all from the same country of origin. Consequently, the findings are bound to reflect a "Nordic" twist to M&A. Having said this, this concern can be partly countered by the tenets of the grounded theory method (Glaser and Strauss 1967): the aim being to move beyond description (i.e. of acquisitions made by Finnish multinationals) to a higher-level conceptualization of the findings. Here, the experiences of the acquired firms in their eight prior acquisitions and of parent firms from other European, Asian, and North-American backgrounds proved useful. These experiences were compared with and included in the present findings. This limitation was further countered by the fact that the buying firms represented different industries and that the acquired firms were from a variety of different country backgrounds. In this respect, selecting buying firms from one country was a constructive way of dealing with the otherwise great variety in the cultural backgrounds of the firms studied.

Future studies on M&A are called for. There continues to be a relative lack of qualitative research on post-acquisition integration (see also Haleblian et al. 2009; Cartwright et al. 2010; Meglio and Risberg 2010). Moreover, studies on cross-border acquisitions undertaken with a qualitative design remain equally scarce. Such studies could focus more specifically on the dynamic relationship between organizational and national cultures throughout the (cross-border) M&A process. Also, the relationship between integration management and M&A performance warrants more study. Active future research efforts in the area of M&A are encouraged, given the amount of M&A activity that continues to take place in today's corporate arena. It is important that the scientific community remains interested in a phenomenon of such societal importance and is willing to further develop its theoretical and practical understanding thereof.

To conclude, this chapter extends our understanding of M&A by bringing forth an integrative perspective to the study and management of cross-border acquisitions. Such a perspective highlights the importance of qualitative, systemic studies, and the need to account for a wide array of variables when studying a phenomenon as complex and multifaceted as M&A. The notion of "silent forces" is introduced to denote those integration-related factors that rarely reach the cognitive attention span of managers involved in acquisitions, and yet impact the deal's performance. In the present corporate context, they typically relate—but are not limited—to the behavioral, human, and cultural dimensions of organizational life. In other words, buying firms tend to emphasize the strategic, structural, and financial dimensions of cross-border acquisitions to the detriment of the silent forces therein. Unless these forces are recognized, however, they will continue to exert a detrimental impact on the progress and successful outcome of cross-border acquisitions.

References

Albert, S., & Whetten, D. (1985). "Organizational Identity," in B. M. Staw & L. L. Cummings (eds.), *Research in Organizational Behavior*. Greenwich, CT: JAI Press: 263–95.

Ashkenas, R. N., & Francis, S. C. (2000). "Integration Managers: Special Leaders for Special Times." *Harvard Business Review*, 78/6: 108–16.

Bate, P. (1994). *Strategies for Cultural Change*. Oxford: Butterworth-Heinemann.

Barkema, H. G., & Schijven, M. (2008). "Toward Unlocking the Full Potential of Acquisitions: The Role of Organizational Restructuring." *Academy of Management Journal*, 51/4: 696–722.

Birkinshaw, J., Bresman, H., & Håkansson, L. (2000). "Managing the Post-acquisition Integration Process: How the Human Integration and Task Integration Processes Interact to Foster Value Creation." *Journal of Management Studies*, 37/3: 395–425.

Blake, R. B., & Mouton, J. S. (1984). "How to Achieve Integration on the Human Side of the Merger," in R. B. Black & J. S. Mouton (eds.), *Solving Costly Organizational Conflicts: Achieving Intergroup Trust, Cooperation and Teamwork*. San Francisco: Jossey-Bass, 41–56.

Buckley, P. J., & Ghauri, P. N. (2002). *International Mergers and Acquisitions: A Reader*. London: Thomson.

Buono, A. F., & Bowditch, J. L. (1989). *The Human Side of Mergers and Acquisitions: Managing Collisions between People, Cultures and Organizations*. London: Jossey-Bass.

—— —— (1990). "Ethical Considerations in Merger and Acquisition Management: A Human Resource Perspective." *SAM Advanced Management Journal*, 55/4, Autumn: 18–23.

Calori, R., Lubatkin, M., & Véry, P. (1994). "Control Mechanisms in Cross-Border Acquisitions: An International Comparison." *Organization Studies*, 15/3: 361–79.

Cartwright, S. (1998). "International Mergers and Acquisitions: the Issues and Challenges," in M. Gertsen, A.-M. Söderberg, & J. E. Torp (eds.), *Cultural Dimensions of International Mergers and Acquisitions*. Berlin: De Gruyter, 5–16.

—— & Cooper, C. L. (1990). "The Impact of Mergers and Acquisitions on People at Work: Existing Research and Issues." *British Journal of Management*, 1: 65–76.

—— —— (1992). *Managing Mergers, Acquisitions and Strategic Alliances: Integrating People and Cultures*. Oxford: Butterworth-Heinemann.

—— —— (1993). "The Role of Culture Compatibility in Successful Organizational Marriage." *Academy of Management Executive*, 7/2: 57–70.

—— Teerikangas, S., Rouzies, A., & Wilson-Evered, E. (2010). "The Study of Inter-organizational Encounters: Initiating A Research Methodological Debate." *Scandinavian Journal of Management*, Special issue: Call for papers, September.

Chatterjee, S. (1986). "Types of Synergy and Economic Value: The Impact of Acquisitions on Merging and Rival Firms." *Strategic Management Journal*, 7/2: 119–39.

Child, J., Faulkner, D., & Pitkethly, R. (2001). *The Management of International Acquisitions*. Oxford: Oxford University Press.

Cording, M., Christmann, P., & Weigelt, C. (2010). "Measuring Complex Constructs: The Case of Acquisition Performance." *Strategic Organization*, 8/1: 11–41.

Cyert, R. M., & March, J. G. (1963). *A Behavioral Theory of the Firm*. Englewood Cliffs, NJ: Prentice-Hall.

Datta, D. K. (1991). "Organizational Fit and Acquisition Performance: Effects of Post-acquisition Integration." *Strategic Management Journal*, 12: 281–97.

—— Pinches, G. E., & Narayanan V. K. (1992). "Factors Influencing Wealth Creation from Mergers and Acquisitions: A Meta-analysis." *Strategic Management Journal*, 13/1: 67–84.

Davis, L., & North, D. C. (1970). *Institutional Change and American Economic Growth*. Cambridge: Cambridge University Press.

Deiser, R. (1994). "Post-acquisition Management: A Process of Strategic and Organisational Learning," in G. Von Krogh, A. Siknatra, & H. Singh (eds.), *The Management of Corporate Acquisitions*. London: The Macmillan Press, 359–90.

DiMaggio, P., & Powell, W. (1991). "Introduction," in W. Powell & P. DiMaggio (eds.), *The New Institutionalism in Organizational Analysis*. Chicago: University of Chicago Press.

Feely, A. J., & Harzing, A.-W. (2003). "Language Management in Multinational Companies." *Cross Cultural Management*, 10/2: 37–52.

Forstmann, S. (1998). "Managing Cultural Differences in Cross-Cultural Mergers and Acquisitions," in M. Gertsen, A.-M. Söderberg, & J. E. Torp (eds.), *Cultural Dimensions of International Mergers and Acquisitions*. Berlin: De Gruyter, 57–84.

Glaser, B. J., & Strauss, A. L. (1967). *The Discovery of Grounded Theory*. Chicago, IL: Aldine Publishing Company.

Glaser, B. J. (1978). *Theoretical Sensitivity*. Mill Valley, CA: Sociology Press.

Graebner, M. E. (2004). "Momentum and Serendipidity: How Acquired Firm Leaders Create Value in the Integration of Technology Firms." *Strategic Management Journal*, 25/8–9: 751–77.

Greenwood, R., Hinings, C. R., & Brown, J. (1994). "Merging Professional Service Firms." *Organization Science*, 5/2: 239–57.

Haleblian, J., Devers, C. E., McNamara, G., Carpenter, M. A., & Davison, R. B. (2009). "Taking Stock of What We Know about Mergers and Acquisitions: A Review and Research Agenda." *Journal of Management*, 35: 469–502.

Hall, E. T. (1967). *Beyond Culture*. New York: Doubleday.

Hambrick, D. C., & Cannella, A. A. (1993). "Relative Standing: A Framework for Understanding Departures of Acquired Executives." *Academy of Management Journal*, 36/4: 733–62.

Harzing, A.-W. (2001). "Of Bears, Bumble-bees and Spiders: The Role of Expatriates in Controlling Foreign Subsidiaries." *Journal of World Business*, 36/4: 366–79.

Haspeslagh, P., & Farquhar, A. B. (1994). "The Acquisition Integration Process: A Contingent Framework," in G. von Krogh, A. Siknatra, & H. Singh (eds.), *The Management of Corporate Acquisitions*. London: The Macmillan Press, 414–47.

Haspeslagh, P., & Farquhar, A. B. & Jemison, D. B. (1991). *Managing Acquisitions: Creating Value through Corporate Renewal.* New York: The Free Press.

Hebert, L., Véry, P., & Beamish, P. (2005). "Expatriation as a Bridge over Troubled Water: A Knowledge-Based Perspective Applied to Cross-Border Acquisitions." *Organization Studies,* 26/10: 1455–76.

Hitt, M., Harrison, J., Ireland, R. D., & Best, A. (1998). "Attributes of Successful and Unsuccessful Acquisitions of US firms." *British Journal of Management,* 9: 91–114.

Hofstede, G. (1980). *Culture's Consequences: International Differences in Work-Related Values.* Beverly Hills, CA: Sage Publications.

Hoskisson, R. E., & Hitt, M. A. (1993). "Antecedents and Performance Outcomes of Diversification: A Review and Critique of Theoretical Perspectives." *Journal of Management,* 16: 461–509.

Howell, R. A. (1970). "Plan to Integrate your Acquisitions." *Harvard Business Review,* 48/6: 66–76.

Hunt, J. W. (1990). "Changing Patterns of Acquisition Behaviour in Takeovers and the Consequences for Acquisition Processes." *Strategic Management Journal,* 11: 69–77.

Ivancevich, J. M., Schweiger, D. M., & Power, F. R. (1987). "Strategies for Managing Human Resources during Mergers and Acquisitions." *Human Resource Planning,* 10/1: 19–35.

Jemison, D. B., & Sitkin, S. B. (1986). "Corporate Acquisitions: A Process Perspective." *Academy of Management Review,* 11/1: 145–63.

King, D. R., Dalton, D. R., Daily, C. M., & Covin, J. G. (2004). "Meta-analyses of Post-acquisition Performance: Indications of Unidentified Moderators." *Strategic Management Journal,* 25/2: 187–200.

Kissin, W. D., & Herrera, J. (1990). "International Mergers and Acquisitions." *The Journal of Business Strategy,* 11, July/August: 51–5.

Kitching, J. (1967). "Why Do Mergers Miscarry?" *Harvard Business Review,* 45, November–December: 84–100.

Krogh von, G., Siknatra, A., & Singh, H. (1994). *The Management of Corporate Acquisitions.* London: The Macmillan Press Ltd.

Krug, J. A., & Nigh, D. (2001). "Executive Perceptions in Foreign and Domestic Acquisitions: An Analysis of Foreign Ownership and its Effect on Executive Fate." *Journal of World Business,* 36/1: 85–98.

Larsson, R., & Finkelstein, S. (1999). "Integrating Strategic, Organizational, and Human Resource Perspectives on Mergers and Acquisitions: A Case Survey of Synergy Realization. *Organization Science,* 10/1: 1–26.

—— & Lubatkin, M. (2001). "Achieving Acculturation in Mergers and Acquisitions: An International Case Study." *Human Relations,* 54/12: 1573–607.

Lubatkin, M. (1983). "Mergers and the Performance of the Acquiring Firm." *Academy of Management Review,* 8/2: 218–25.

—— Calori, R., Véry, P., & Veiga, J. (1998). "Managing Mergers across Borders: A Two-Nation Exploration of Nationally Bound Administrative Heritage." *Organization Science,* 9/6: 670–84.

Mace, M. L., & Montgomery, G. (1962). *Management Problems of Corporate Acquisitions.* Cambridge, MA: Harvard University Press.

Madura, J., Vasconcellos, G. M., & Kish, R. J. (1991). "A Valuation Model for International Acquisitions." *Management Decision,* 29/4: 31–8.

March, J. G., & Simon, H. A. (1958). *Organizations.* New York: Wiley.

Marks, M. L. (1982). "Merging Human Resources: A Review of the Literature." *Mergers and Acquisitions*, 16, Summer: 38–44.

—— (1991). "Combating Merger Shock Before the Deal is Closed." *Mergers and Acquisitions*, 25/4, January–February: 42–8.

—— (1999). "Adding Cultural Fit to your Due Diligence Checklist." *Mergers and Acquisitions*, 34/3: 14–20.

Marschan, R., Welch, L., & Welch, D. (1997). "Language—the Forgotten Factor in Multinational Management." *European Management Journal*, 15/5, October: 591–8.

Meglio, O., & Risberg, A. (2010). "Mergers and Acquisitions—Time for a Methodological Rejuvenation of the Field?" *Scandinavian Journal of Management*, 26: 87–97.

Morosini, P. (1998). *Managing Cultural Differences*. Oxford: Pergamon.

—— & Singh, H. (1994). "Post-Cross-Border Acquisitions: Implementing National Culture-Compatible Strategies to Improve Performance." *European Management Journal*, 12/4: 390–400.

Nahavandi, A., & Malekzadeh, A. R. (1988). "Acculturation in Mergers and Acquisitions." *Academy of Management Review*, 13/1: 79–90.

Napier, N. K. (1989). "Mergers and Acquisitions, Human Resource Issues and Outcomes: A Review and Suggested Typology." *Journal of Management Studies*, 26/3: 271 89.

—— Schweiger, D. M., & Kosglow, J. J. (1993). "Managing Organisational Diversity: Observations from Cross-Border Acquisitions." *Human Resource Management*, 32/4: 505–23.

O'Connor, C. W. (1985). "Packaging your Business for Sale." *Harvard Business Review*, 64/2: 52–8.

Ocasio, W. (1997). "Toward an Attention-Based View of the Firm." *Strategic Management Journal*, 18: 187–206.

Olie, R. (1994). "Shades of Culture and Institutions in International Mergers." *Organization Studies*, 15/3: 381–405.

Parker, M. (2000). *Organisational Culture and Identity*. London: Sage Publications.

Quah, P., & Young, S. (2005). "Post-acquisition Management: A Phases Approach for Cross-border M&A." *European Management Journal*, 23/1: 65–75.

Ranft, A. L., & Lord, M. D. (2002). "Acquiring New Technologies and Capabilities: A Grounded Model of Acquisition Implementation." *Organization Science*, 13/4: 420–41.

Risberg, A. (2001). "Employee Experiences of Acquisition Processes." *Journal of World Business*, 36/1: 58–84.

Sales, A. L., & Mirvis, P. H. (1984). "When Cultures Collide: Issues in Acquisitions," in J. Kimberley & R. E. Quinn (eds.), *New Futures: The Challenges of Managing Corporate Transitions*. Homewood, IL: Dow Jones-Irvin, 107–33.

Schoenberg, R. (2006). "Measuring the Performance of Corporate Acquisitions: An Empirical Comparison of Alternative Metrics." *British Journal of Management*, 17/4: 361–70.

Schweiger, D. M., Csiszar, E. N., & Napier, N. K. (1993). "Implementing International Mergers and Acquisitions." *Human Resource Planning*, 16/1: 53–70.

—— —— —— (1994). "A Strategic Approach to Implementing Mergers and Acquisitions," in G. von Krogh, A. Siknatra, & H. Singh (eds.), *The Management of Corporate Acquisitions*. London: Macmillan, 23–49.

Schweiger, D. M., & Goulet, P. K. (2000). "Integrating Mergers and Acquisitions: An International Research Review," in C. Cooper & A. Gregory (eds.), *Advances in Mergers and Acquisitions*, vol. 1. Amsterdam: JAI Press, 61–91.

Shimizu, K., Hitt, M., Vaidyanath, D., & Pisano, V. (2004). "Theoretical Foundations of Cross-Border Mergers and Acquisitions: A Review of Current Research and Recommendations for the Future." *Journal of International Management*, 10: 307–53.

Simon, H. A. (1947). *Administrative Behavior: A Study of Decision-Making Processes in Administrative Organizations*. Chicago, IL: Macmillan.

Sinatra, A., & Dubini, P. (1994). "Predicting Success after the Acquisition: The Creation of a Corporate Profile," in G. von Krogh, A. Siknatra, & H. Singh (eds.), *The Management of Corporate Acquisitions*. London: The Macmillan Press, 480–512.

Sinetar, M. (1981). "Mergers, Morale and Productivity." *Personnel Journal*, 60: 863–7.

Sirower, M. L. (1997). *The Synergy Trap: How Companies Lose the Acquisition Game*. New York: The Free Press.

Stahl, G. K., & Voigt, A. (2008). "Do Cultural Differences Matter in Mergers and Acquisitions? A Tentative Model and Examination." *Organization Science*, 19/1: 160–76.

Stillings, N. A., Weisler, S. W., Chase, C. H., Feinstein, M. H., Garfield, J. L., & Rissland, E. L. (1995). *Cognitive Science* (2nd ed.). Cambridge, MA: MIT Press.

Szulanski, G. (1996). "Exploring Internal Stickiness: Impediments to the Transfer of Best Practice within the Firm." *Strategic Management Journal*, 17: 27–43.

Teerikangas, S. (2006). *Silent Forces in Cross-Border Acquisitions: An Integrative Perspective on Post-Acquisition Integration*. Helsinki: Helsinki University of Technology, Institute of Strategy and International Business, Doctoral Dissertation Series, 1/2006.

——(2010). "Dynamics of Acquired Firm Pre-acquisition Employee Reactions." *Journal of Management*, Published online October 19, 2010: DOI: 10.1177/0149206310383908.

——& Véry, P. (2006). "The Culture-Performance Relationship in M&A—From Yes/No to How." *British Journal of Management*, 17: S31–S48.

Trautwein, F. (1990). "Merger Motives and Merger Prescriptions." *Strategic Management Journal*, 11: 283–95.

UNCTAD (2000). *World Investment Report 2000*. New York and Geneva: UNCTAD.

Weber, Y., Shenkar, O., & Raveh, A. (1996). "National and Corporate Cultural Fit in Mergers/Acquisitions: An Exploratory Study." *Management Science*, 42/8: 1215–27.

Weick, K. M. (1979). *The Social Psychology of Organizing* (2nd ed.). New York: Random House.

Zaheer, S., Schomaker, M., & Genc, M. (2003). "Identity versus Culture in Mergers of Equals." *European Management Journal*, 21/2: 185–91.

Zollo, M., & Meier, D. (2008). "What is M&A Performance?" *The Academy of Management Perspectives*, 22/3: 55–77.

PART IV

A SECTORIAL LENS FOR M&A

CHAPTER 22

CHARACTERISTICS OF EMERGING MARKET MERGERS AND ACQUISITIONS

PRASHANT KALE AND HARBIR SINGH

INTRODUCTION: COLLABORATING YOUR WAY TO INTEGRATING ACQUISITIONS

Since the early 1990s, emerging economies, including China, India, Russia, and countries in Latin America and Central/Eastern Europe have become a more visible and integral part of the global business environment. These economies not only present a huge market opportunity given their large populations, but since the mid-1990s they have also liberalized their hitherto closed and regulated economies. This has made it easier for foreign companies to do business there, as well as enabling companies from these countries to expand outside their home markets. From the early part of this century, this latter trend has accelerated as companies from various emerging economies rapidly expand their global footprint. The term, "emerging market multinational" (Aulakh 2007; *Economist* 2008) has been used to refer to these up-coming global giants (Khanna and Palepu 2006). These companies are expanding their international reach and enhancing their domestic and global advantage by gaining customers in new geographical markets, accessing world-class brands, technological know-how and managerial talent, and building their operational size and scale in order to derive greater efficiencies. Indian companies belonging to multi-business conglomerates such as Mahindra and Mahindra, Aditya Birla Group, and Tata, as well as single business companies like Bharat Forge, Dr. Reddy's, and Suzlon, represent this trend. Companies including Lenovo, Haier, and TCL from China; Cemex and Telemex from Mexico; Vale and AmBev from Brazil; and Ulker from Turkey, also fall within this category.

Aside from organic growth, cross-border mergers and acquisitions (M&A) represent a large part of their international growth strategies. The slice of international M&A activity from emerging economy-based multinational corporations has increased from approximately $30 billion (3% of the world M&A value) in 2001 to over $200 billion (over 10% of the world M&A value) in 2008 (Accenture 2008). Indian companies alone have raised the value of their overseas acquisitions from less than $2 billion in 2002 to well over $30 billion in 2007. Some of the most well-publicized overseas acquisitions include the Tata Group's acquisitions of Tetley, Brunner Mond, Corus, and Jaguar Land-Rover; Aditya Birla Group's acquisition of Novelis in Canada; Lenovo's acquisition of IBM's global PC business; TCL's acquisition of Thomson of France; Vales' acquisition of INCO in Canada, and Coteminas' acquisition of Spring Industries in the US; Cemex's acquisition of Rinker in UK; and Ulker's acquisition of Godiva in the US. Although this trend slowed down a bit during the recessionary years of 2008–9, it is not likely to end.

Acquisitions are usually viewed as completely distinct from alliances or partnerships with respect to control and management. Yet, partnering can actually be a very useful lens through which to view acquisitions, especially when addressing the post-acquisition management phase: a perennial problem in most transactions. While acquisitions have continued to occur frequently over the past decade, a relatively unnoticed new wrinkle has been the rising salience of acquisitions originating from multinationals from emerging economies, and their unique methods of integrating those transactions. In this chapter, we suggest that a "collaborative or partnering approach," a method that is widely seen in the cross-border acquisitions of emerging market multinationals, is a novel way of undertaking post-acquisition management in companies as compared to the approach generally used by established multinationals from developed economies.

A strategic alliance is a phenomenon where "two companies partner with each other to achieve a set of mutually agreeable objectives, while simultaneously retaining their respective independence and identity" (Doz 1996; Kale et al. 2002). On the other hand, in an acquisition, one company purchases another company to acquire controlling rights over the latter's assets and operations; here both companies merge to become one in order to realize the desired benefits of coming together. Generally, most companies view an alliance or partnership as being a different mode of inorganic growth from a merger or acquisition. Consequently, most companies see a distinction in the best practices presumably required in the management of these two types of transactions. However, a partnering approach, which incorporates many alliance management best practices, has merits in managing some of the dynamics of post-acquisition integration too. Briefly speaking, in applying this approach to acquisitions, the acquired company remains structurally separate from the acquirer with its own organization and identity left intact. Expected synergies are instead achieved through the selective coordination of core and supporting activities, as is the case in most alliances (Gulati and Singh 1998). Additionally, the acquirer retains most senior management executives from the acquired company, viewing them as partners and ensuring they retain a fair degree of autonomy in decision-making. Joint purpose is achieved through the alignment of core business values and incentives negotiated between the two. This approach allows an acquirer to leverage the key organizational drivers of competitive advantage in a non-threatening way, reduces many unintended consequences of structural integration that arise in most acquisitions, and provides the opportunity to learn and share the best practices of both organizations. This collaborative mind-set is succinctly reflected in a comment by Mr. Ratan Tata, Chairman of India's $38 billion Tata Group, upon the acquisition of Daewoo Commercial Vehicles of Korea by Tata Motors:

> Tata Motors will operate Daewoo as a Korean company in Korea, managed by Koreans, but it will work as a part of a global alliance with its Indian counterpart.

Mr. R Mukundan, the Managing Director of Tata Chemicals and responsible for several large overseas acquisitions in recent years, said,

> We show a great deal of respect for the acquired company. Hence, we always refer to it as an alliance rather than an acquisition.

The Tata Group is not an isolated case of this phenomenon. In fact, many companies from other emerging economies are following a similar style in their overseas acquisitions. We term this unique approach, wherein an acquisition is managed more like an alliance, as a "collaborative approach" to acquisitions. Of course, there are costs to this approach too: it is counter-intuitive vis-à-vis the rationale for acquisition, and it appears to be more indirect in the achievement of organizational purpose. In the rest of this chapter, we detail the antecedents and main elements of the collaborative approach, explore its implications for the companies involved, and identify the conditions when this approach might be suitable.

KEY ELEMENTS OF A PARTNERING APPROACH

Academic studies and practitioner accounts (Haspeslagh and Jemison 1991; Pablo 1994; Zollo and Singh 2004) suggest that an acquirer has to make decisions about some of the following critical issues in post-acquisition management: the "nature and level of integration" of the acquired company; the extent to which some of the "pre-existing resources of the acquired firm are replaced"; the "autonomy given to the acquired firm"; and the "speed" with which post-acquisition issues are managed by the acquiring firm (see Figure 22.1). A partnering approach differs from the more traditional approach to acquisitions in terms of how these decisions and choices are made.

"Structural Separation" of the Acquired Company

In the post-acquisition phase, acquirers must attend to two separate dimensions of integration: the structural integration of the acquired and acquiring firms and the coordination of activities between them. As the first dimension of integration, *structural integration* involves the grouping of two distinct organizational units within a common organizational or administrative boundary (Puranam and Srikanth 2007). On the one hand, an acquirer can pursue complete structural integration, whereby the acquired firm is fully absorbed into the acquiring firm so the former ceases to exist as a separate,

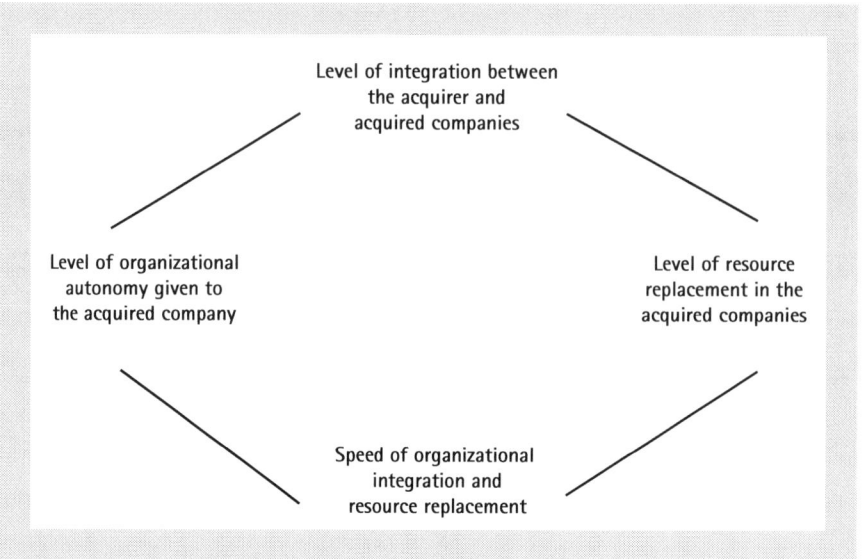

FIG. 22.1 Post-acquisition management: key elements

independent entity with its own distinct identity. If high levels of coordination are anticipated to effectively manage the interdependence between the joining companies in order to achieve the desired synergy benefits, seasoned US acquisition giants such as General Electric will opt instead for complete structural integration of the target firm within the existing structure of acquirer (Ashkenas et al. 1998). Structural integration results in common goals, procedures, and, most importantly, common authority and reporting relationships. Structural integration also facilitates a thorough integration of operations whereby key and often duplicated activities of the two companies are either combined or homogenized, resulting in a reduction of overhead and operational costs. Greater integration of this kind is beneficial, particularly in "related acquisitions" where the acquirer and target companies are in the same line of business (Capron 1999), and there is significant operational interdependence between them. Greater integration enables companies to better realize synergies by eliminating duplication of similar assets and by combining activities, thus leveraging potential economies of size, scale, or scope within key operations. On the other hand, where there is little interdependence, and hence less need for coordination, acquirers are apt to follow a "preservation" strategy, whereby they minimize the structural integration of the two organizations (Haspeslagh and Jemison 1991).

Contrary to the traditional approach (i.e. structural integration for high coordination), in adopting the partnering approach, many emerging multinationals forgo structural integration of their acquired company; instead, the overseas company remains "structurally separate" from the new parent organization even if the two companies are in related business with high expected levels of coordination (see Figure 22.2, based on Haspeslagh and Jemison 1991). In other words, the acquired company continues to operate as a

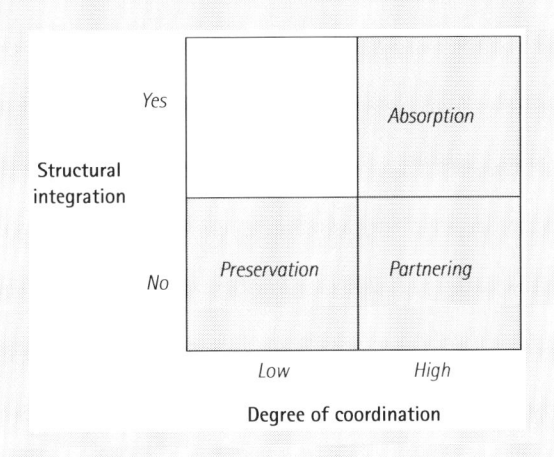

FIG. 22.2 Structural integration and coordination

separate organizational entity with its own structure kept intact. While this might appear contraindicated, it is perhaps not surprising when one considers *why* most emerging market multinationals acquire overseas companies in developed countries—companies are often acquired as a means to enter into or expand within new geographic markets (Deng 2009). Keeping the new firm structurally separate allows the acquiring firm to benefit from their acquisition's unique and distinctive identity in that market place. This is particularly valuable when the acquired firm provides a service or product that is popular among, or valued by, its customers, vendors, or cultural community at large. An executive of VIP Industries, India's largest producer of luggage products, had this to say when his company acquired Carlton Brands, the maker of high-end luggage products in the UK.

> The structure was designed to preserve Carlton's brand integrity by maintaining two separate organizations, distinct from VIP in many ways. The idea was also to keep Carlton's UK heritage.

Tata Steel of India used a similar rationale when they acquired NatSteel in Singapore, as did Ulker of Turkey when they acquired Godiva Chocolatier in the US.

Being structurally separate also implies that activities of the two companies are not combined or integrated, which in turn has some advantages. First, attempts to integrate activities and operations often result in disruptions of resources and operating routines in both firms (Schweizer 2005), the adverse effects of which can outweigh any benefits of operational integration. Second, integration of activities also calls for highly interdependent decision processes that involve different organizational levels, and multiple individuals or sub-units. This makes it harder for companies to execute the planned integration and increases the risk of performance disruption in both organizations. Third, these complexities increase the hidden and often unanticipated costs of integration in terms of the sharp increases in management time required to address them, lower employee satisfaction and morale, and higher turnover (Chaudhuri and Tabrizi 1999).

Finally, emerging multinationals get another benefit by not integrating the acquired company with the parent firm. As explained by the CEO of Blue Star of China when it acquired Adisseo,

> Our purpose was to learn about international business practices through the acquired company and to gain from its experience. We know that we have to learn the rules of today's market economy and that those rules are not defined in China. Learning from the acquired company is also a critical element of acquisition.

Therefore, by maintaining structural separation, emerging multinationals are successfully avoiding some of the negative consequences associated with greater integration.

"Selective Coordination" of Core Activities with the Acquired Company

The question one might ask is: by keeping the acquired company structurally separate, do these companies give up on the synergy benefits linked to the business interdependence between them? The answer: not necessarily so. Acquiring firms attempt to recoup these benefits through "selective high coordination" and "alignment" between the two companies, an approach that has been effectively used in some of the most highly regarded alliances, including the CFM alliance between GE and Snecma, and the Renault-Nissan alliance. In those alliances, despite remaining separate companies, partners have a variety of "linking mechanisms" (Gulati et al. 2005; Thompson 1967), such as the use of joint teams, and boundary-spanning individuals to coordinate those selective core activities that underlie expected synergies. Many emerging multinationals have done the same in their overseas acquisitions. For instance, when Tata Tea acquired Tetley, they formed a team to jointly coordinate their tea purchases from the open market to mutually ensure quality and reduce costs. Additionally, they had three other teams coordinating other operational aspects. The same was true when Tata Steel and Corus established teams to coordinate their zinc and scrap purchases to reduce their input costs through economies of size, and to reduce their joint logistics costs. Tata Steel also created a joint forum to share selective operational know-how, whereby Corus was able to adopt some of Tata Steel's hot metal steel-making technology to reduce its dependence on scrap and lower its energy consumption. Conversely, Tata Steel was able to adopt Corus' technology to reduce the heating time of its coke ovens from 24 to 9 days, thus increasing their production of steel by nearly 2% without increasing fixed costs. Aside from joint teams selectively coordinating activities, senior executives play a boundary-spanning role by sitting on dual Boards—a few executives from Tata Steel joined Corus' Board of Directors and vice versa, to coordinate their strategic actions.

Apart from using various linking mechanisms, emerging multinationals also align key supporting activities to facilitate desired coordination across core activities. For example, companies may choose to align their annual planning or budgeting calendars so they can synchronize the formulation and implementation of their operational coordination plans. Aligning or homogenizing financial reporting formats or IT systems also helps because it creates a common language or platform to enable better communication between partners. Anand Mahindra, the Vice Chairman of India's Mahindra and Mahindra, which has acquired several European companies in the last four years, follows this approach, saying,

> While we value the independence of our overseas companies, some things have to change through benign but impactful points of intervention—one of them is that we strongly encourage all overseas companies to move on to the MAPC (Mahindra Annual Planning Cycle) as fast as possible so that we are in step with each other and speak a common language as we work together.

"Limited Resource Replacement" in the Acquired Company

In the post-acquisition period, acquirers have also to decide the extent to which they will replace or eliminate pre-existing resources in the acquired company with equivalent resources from their own organization. One key resource in question is the top management team of the acquired company. In line with Drucker's old but widely cited rule for successful acquisitions, which states that an acquirer must supply top management to the acquired company, many acquirers tend to replace the top management team of the acquired company with their own. Change in top management is not only a symbolic ratification of the intention to change the acquired company, but also a means to fully align or integrate the strategy, management style, and operating routines of the two companies to achieve desired synergies. This same philosophy is also reflected in the "market for corporate control" thesis which is widely prevalent in Western economies, including the US, wherein an acquirer takes over another company mainly to create value by replacing the top management team of the acquired company with its own, supposedly more skilled, managers (Jensen and Ruback 1983).

Many emerging multinationals, however, take a very different approach in this respect, especially when they acquire companies in developed economies, which is most often the case. In most situations, emerging multinationals opt to retain most senior executives of the acquired company. For example, John Kerrigan, Managing Director of Brunner Mond in the UK; Jim Goldman, CEO of Godiva Chocolatier in the US; Martha Finn Brooks, President of Novelis in Canada; Oo Soon Hee, erstwhile CEO of NatSteel Singapore; Tom O'Conner of Springs Industries USA; and Thomas Koerner, CEO of JECO Holdings in Germany, all stayed on with their companies even after being acquired by emerging multinationals from Asia, Latin America, or Central Europe. This has also been the case in many other overseas acquisitions by emerging multinationals. Mr. Tata, Chairman of the Tata Group said in a recent interview,

> We have sought to keep the management in place after we acquire a company, and we pride ourselves on our ability to motivate their plans. This is contrary to the traditional approach where a team from the acquirer descends on the target company to run it.

Emerging market multinationals seek several advantages in this practice. Retaining the top management team of the acquired company signals their vote of confidence in the overall resource quality of that company. More important, the human and social capital and the industry or context-specific knowledge of that management team is not lost; instead, it can be harnessed for the mutual benefit of both companies (Cannella and Hambrick 1993; Graebner 2004). Debu Bhattacharya of India's Hindalco sees many Novelis executives as "institutions" in their specific areas and says,

> We not only bought assets, but also the talent. Do not disturb the management structure just to prove a point.

This approach has the added benefit of creating a positive climate and reducing uncertainty within the acquired organization. Employees, customers, and the suppliers of that organization are assured of their continued working relationships. The CEO of another emerging multinational that has acquired several European companies says,

> We didn't want to send wrong signals to anyone, so we made sure that we were not high-handed with any of the employees.

The brands of the acquired company are another resource that emerging multinationals often retain in their overseas acquisitions. This is not surprising as brands in acquired European or US companies may enjoy a much better recognition and loyalty in the global market place and emerging multinationals can leverage that to accelerate their own growth. Mr. Adi Godrej, whose company has acquired several overseas companies, says,

> Ownership and retention of strong brands was a key driver of the (Keyline) acquisition. Without this, it is difficult to penetrate markets such as the UK.

Mr. Wang of China's NAC, which has acquired another UK company, concurs,

> The Chinese recognize the need to retain the brand and its British heritage. We are looking for a good balance between heritage and creativity that includes both a Chinese distinctiveness, but also a British one.

"High Organizational Autonomy" to the Acquired Company

Greater integration of the acquired company, and/or replacement of its top management team, sends the message that the acquired organization will have very little autonomy in running its operations after the deal is consummated. In some cases, even if the acquired company is not fully integrated into the acquirer, as in the case of some of Cisco's acquisitions, the acquired company nevertheless has less autonomy in running its operations. However, the situation in acquisitions by many emerging multinationals seems to be somewhat different. A senior executive of one UK-based company we interviewed, said,

> Our new parent hardly interferes in our day-to-day decision-making. While we have to be in general agreement with them about the main products or markets we want to be in or some very large investments we need to make, we pretty much

make our own decisions when it comes to other things—such as staffing, investments in operational improvements, pricing or promotion terms in our markets. They also don't breathe down upon us to accept all their practices or norms.

The CEO of the acquiring company said,

> They know their markets and business better than we do, and I am sure they will make decisions in the interest of both our companies. Also, we don't believe that the push approach works in acquisitions. We don't want to appear like someone who dictates what others should do. Yes, we have some useful practices they can adopt, and I urge my team to constantly think of creative ways in which we can help them appreciate that…but when there is a natural pull from them, and they decide they would like to take from us what we have to offer, it will work much better.

While giving autonomy to the acquired company can cause periodic misalignment between the organizations concerned, or perhaps even slow down the pace of expected change, it has advantages too. First, it minimizes the likelihood of disruption or poor performance should the acquirer make suboptimal decisions based on its insufficient understanding of the acquired company's business context. Second, greater decision-making autonomy for the employees of the acquired company signals the acquirer's respect for and confidence in them. In return, this has a positive effect on their morale and commitment, not only toward their own company, but also toward their new owner. Jim Goldman, the CEO of Godiva whose company enjoys such a privilege, says,

> It results in a huge sense of responsibility. The truth is I feel so committed to try to justify the trust that we've been getting and I have been communicating to our people that you've got to understand we're really lucky that we have a parent who wants to do the right thing, and is willing to invest in the business—but that results in a significant obligation on our part to make sure we deliver.

Third, greater autonomy helps prevent the slow decision-making that typically paralyzes many companies after being acquired, impairing their effectiveness in the market place. Collectively, these benefits create a positive organizational climate for both companies to work effectively with each other.

While many emerging multinationals retain most senior executives in acquired companies and grant them high autonomy, some companies will place one or two of their senior executives to work in the acquired organization. The role of these individuals is not to oversee, second-guess, or curb the management team of the acquired company, but to act as a bridge between their two companies in manner that is mutually beneficial (Ashkenas et al. 1998). Jim Goldman of Godiva, whose Turkish parent Ulker has placed one such executive in his company, says,

> Barack will make sure that the resources there (at Ulker) are positively channeled to us as opposed to getting in our way, and he'll also make sure Mr. Ulker understands where I am coming from. So, that was a brilliant move…I don't feel like I report to Barack. I feel like we're actually partners—he's truly here to make this successful for us and for Yildiz.

Alignment of Values and Incentives

Retaining senior management and giving them decision-making autonomy does not mean that everything continues fully as before. Satish Pradhan, Executive Vice President of Human Resources for the Tata Group, comments,

> We adopt a policy of respectful intrusion. Our approach is inclusive and our tradition supports it. The question is how do you move together with a philosophy and value system that the Tata Group carries?

For the Tata Group, which has recently been recognized as one of the most reputable companies in the world for their business integrity and ethical values by the Reputation Institute of the US, this means that all acquired companies sign up for, live, and practice the values and principles enshrined in the Tata Business Excellence Model and the Tata Code of Conduct. In fact, it is widely believed that the retention of management and decision-making autonomy is viable only when the core values of the two companies are aligned.

Incentive mechanisms are frequently used to achieve joint purpose and to encourage cooperation between two entities that, until recently, were separately owned and managed. To be sure, incentives are also at play in acquisitions with structural integration— the difference here is that incentives are used to achieve joint purpose despite the fact that the two organizations are structurally separate. India's Mahindra and Mahindra, which has acquired several European auto component companies in the last four years, has taken a step in that direction. When it first began acquiring these companies, Mahindra took a majority equity stake in each company, leaving the rest to be held by their earlier owners or managers (through stock options). Subsequently, they launched a new publicly traded company called Mahindra Forging, and shareholders in all the acquired companies (including the managers) received proportionate Mahindra Forging shares in lieu of shares in their respective acquired companies. Consequently, Mahindra has observed higher cooperation between individual companies operating autonomously otherwise. Additionally, they found that despite the fact that senior managers in each company retain their autonomy, they are more likely to make decisions considering the joint interests of all concerned.

Table 22.1 provides an overview of how the partnering approach to managing acquisitions differs from the more traditional approach in terms of the elements we have described.

ANTECEDENTS TO THE PARTNERING APPROACH

Why do several emerging multinationals follow the acquisition approach described above? Unique combinations of some of the reasons discussed next are to likely explain their behavior.

Table 22.1 The traditional versus partnering approach

Decision Elements	The Traditional Integration Approach	The Partnering Approach
Structure	Structural integration (acquired company is structurally absorbed into the acquirer company)	Structural separation (acquired company is structurally separate and retains its independent identity)
Core and supporting activities	Complete integration or homogenization of core and supporting activities	High "coordination of selective" core activities and "alignment" of supporting activities
Acquired company's people and resources	Replacement of managerial and other resources	Retention of managerial and other resources
Decision-making autonomy	Limited autonomy to acquired company	High autonomy for acquired company
Speed of post-acquisition management	Rapid integration and replacement	Gradual coordination and alignment

Nature of the Acquired Company's Resources

Given their relative late-mover status in terms of internationalization (Luo and Tung 2007), emerging multinationals are quite keen to acquire overseas companies not only to increase their geographical reach, but also to enhance their global advantage (Makino et al. 2002). These motives influence the type of companies they acquire in terms of the resources they possess. Many acquired companies have a large presence in developed economies (where the markets are more competitive or advanced), are larger in size than the acquirers (e.g. Corus and Novelis), have globally recognized brands (e.g. Tetley, Godiva) or technology (Jeco Holdings, IBM), and have strong management teams. All of these assets can be leveraged by emerging market multinationals to improve their scope and reputation. In this situation, it would seem advisable to retain their separate identities and operations. By structurally integrating them into the parent organization, combining their activities with those of the acquirer, or replacing their superior practices or resources with equivalent elements from the acquirer, they would effectively run counter to every reason for acquiring them in the first place. Moreover, even if some emerging multinationals would want to acquire and integrate them in the traditional manner, it might be difficult or disruptive to do so. Given their larger size, greater international visibility, or technological superiority, these foreign targets might strongly resist integration or direction from an acquiring company from an emerging economy. In this context, taking a collaborative rather than acquisitive approach to running these organizations minimizes disruption and creates shared value and interest for all concerned.

Second, it is often found in this type of acquisition that the resources of the acquirer (coming from an emerging economy) and the resources of the acquired company (often from a developed country) are "complementary" (i.e. non-overlapping) rather than being similar or redundant in nature (Rui and Yip 2008). The acquired company frequently brings superior technology, brands, and talent to the relationship, whereas the emerging multinational may offer access to less expensive inputs and manufacturing. Also, in return for proprietary access to their superior resources, emerging multinationals provide the acquired company with patient capital to be used for investment/growth, as well as the "inspiration" to grow faster than before. Greater or full integration between companies is usually required only when acquisition value creation is based on cost reductions through the elimination or combination of similar and redundant resources. Nevertheless, in the case of complementary resources, companies are able to create value by combining their complementary assets in the development of new or improved products/services as well as accelerated growth in new markets. For such synergies, selective coordination has proven sufficient to manage the complementary interdependence without the complete loss of their separate identities.

Organizational Bandwidth and Experience

Emerging multinationals have started expanding their international footprint, through acquisitions or otherwise, only recently. Additionally, their domestic markets were neither very competitive until only a few years ago, nor were these companies required to make acquisitions domestically. As a result, it is likely that many of these acquirers simply lack the required organizational or managerial capabilities and bandwidth to manage the complexities of overseas acquisitions. It is likely that they lack not only sufficient experience or capabilities to manage bigger companies in competitive, international markets, but also the skills to manage acquisitions in general (Zollo and Singh 2004). If this is the case, is a "partnering approach to acquisitions" simply a necessity they face in light of their limitations? A comment from an executive in one of Asia's largest companies suggests this might be true,

> Let's face it—we are still novices in running large international companies or brands. In fact, the leadership in the acquired company had a deeper bench-strength than us in running a dispersed global operation, so it seemed like a good idea to retain them and take them into confidence as equal partners.

Lenovo's Liu Wong, which acquired IBM's PC business, echoes a similar sentiment,

> A lot of failure of Asian companies is that they simply did not have the right people to run the business; they were over optimistic about their capabilities.

Thus, a partnering approach that emphasizes retention of local management with the latitude to run their operations might be the way to go.

Conglomerate Operating Style of Emerging Economy Companies

Some practices in the partnering approach may simply be a reflection of the conglomerate or federation-like management style often prevalent in emerging economy companies (Khanna and Palepu 1997). In this approach, the corporate center acts as the primary custodian of core values and business principles by providing common support services, outlining the broad direction and policy for major sectors and companies, facilitating best-practice sharing between companies, and monitoring their performance. As Anand Mahindra, the Vice Chairman of India's Mahindra and Mahindra, said,

> I have to write the music and then stick to my role of conducting the orchestra rather than trying to play the music myself. The players know what's not negotiable: the pace, the tempo, the traditions. But, at some point, I've got to step back and allow the organizations to operate independently...I don't want to micro-manage the process.

This implies that, apart from adhering to a few core principles, individual group companies are quite independent in terms of running their operations and do not need to avail themselves of nor adopt all the practices or services suggested by the Corporate Center. In accordance with this philosophy, the corporate center does not unilaterally thrust its practices upon individual group companies; instead, it works collaboratively, helping them appreciate the benefits of any suggested practice and opt for its implementation. It is plausible that this operating style is replicated when emerging multinationals acquire a new company overseas. A collaborative, rather than unilateral, working style governs the nature of the interaction between the acquirer and target, because the parent is familiar and comfortable with this approach, given its traditional way of doing things at home.

Traditional Organizational Culture

In some cases like Tata in India, the group's traditional organizational culture may influence how they manage overseas acquisitions. Universally regarded as a group that places very high value on the human side of business (Lala 2009), one of the guiding principles of J. R. D. Tata, the longest-serving chairman of the group, and of the Tata Group as a whole is,

> ...good human relationships not only bring great personal rewards, but are essential to the success of any enterprise.

A partnering approach to acquisitions, emphasizing the retention of human capital and preserving the autonomy and respect of its individuals, is perhaps just a reflection of this culture, which avoids disruption to an individual's work and well-being. Mr. Homi

Khusrokhan, a veteran of many successful acquisitions during his tenure with the Tata Group as well as with Western multinationals like GlaxoSmithKline, comments,

> At Tata, we come across as very humane and gentle in our dealings. Jobs are very valued in the Tata culture. Historically, the group has placed a lot of emphasis on employment creation—so replacing people in the acquired companies and cutting back on people is relatively alien to the Tatas.

Unintentional, Evolutionary Trajectory

Finally, a partnering approach to acquisitions as exemplified by emerging multinationals may have simply, based on early events or experiences, become the norm over time. Reportedly, TCL's attempt to have greater integration in 2004 with Thomson of France met several obstacles. In contrast, Tata Motor's acquisition of Daewoo Commercial Vehicles in Korea and the "light-touch" model used to manage it were deemed quite successful. As these initial experiences were reported in the external business press and shared internally with other companies, the partnering approach may have gradually become the "model" or norm for other emerging multinationals to replicate in their own future acquisition endeavors.

Please refer to Figure 22.3 for an overview of antecedent factors to the partnering approach.

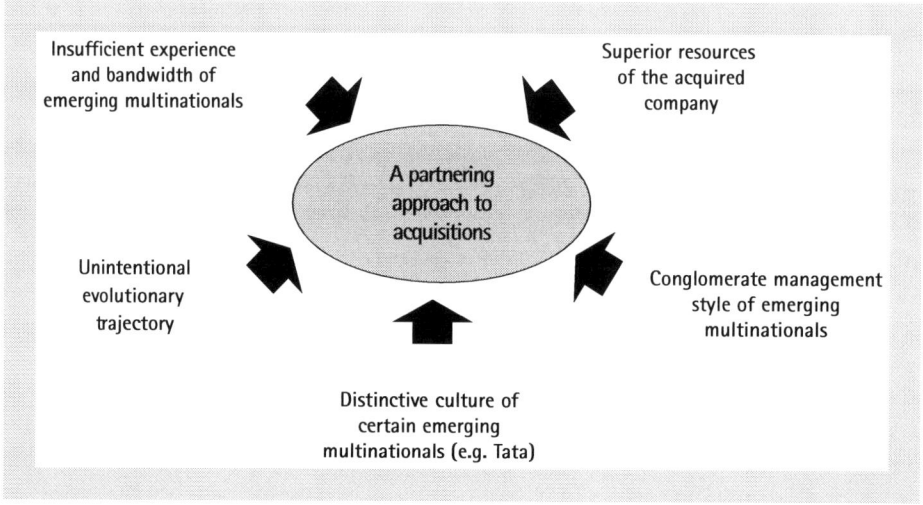

FIG. 22.3 Antecedents of the partnering approach

Performance Implications: Opportunities and Challenges

The partnering approach addresses what may be the most critical and fatal area of the acquisition process: post-acquisition management. In a cross-border setting, it is reasonable to think this element would be even more daunting. In fact, many studies show that over 50% of acquisitions end in failure, destroying shareholder value for the majority of acquirers (King et al. 2004; Shimuzu et al. 2004). Considering the looming likelihood of failure represented by this statistic, one must wonder how emerging multinationals have performed with their overseas acquisitions thus far. We conducted some fieldwork and large-sample analysis to investigate this question. For the purposes of the large-sample analysis, we collected data on overseas acquisitions by Indian firms, since in recent years they have been the most active among all emerging economy firms in doing overseas acquisitions (Ray and Gubbi 2009). We chose the large sample by first identifying all overseas acquisitions by publicly listed Indian firms between the years 2000–7. Of the 536 such transactions during this period, for the results reported in this study we were able to collect performance data for 213 acquisitions. We first measured acquisition performance by calculating the abnormal stock market returns for the acquirer firm, following the announcement of its acquisition. This measure of performance has been widely used by finance and management scholars in the field (Cording et al. 2008). We also measured long-term performance using managerial assessments (Saxton and Dollinger 2004). We sent out a survey instrument to relevant senior executives of the acquired company in all the 213 transactions mentioned above and we received completed responses for 73 of these transactions. The senior executives concerned used a seven-point scale (1 = strongly disagree; 7 = strongly agree) to rate a given transaction on the following two items: (i) "We have achieved most of your expected objectives in doing this acquisition," and (ii) "We are satisfied with the overall outcome and performance of this acquisition." Apart from this large sample analysis, we also conducted in-depth interviews with 31 senior executives across 18 different companies in the large sample. 21 of these interviews were with senior executives in the Indian acquirer firm and the remaining ten interviews were with managers in the companies they had acquired.

Our study reveals some interesting findings. The large-sample analysis of overseas acquisitions done by Indian companies revealed that, on average, Indian acquirers have created positive value for their shareholders. That is, following the announcement/completion of the acquisition, their stock price has shown a significant and positive, abnormal *gain* of +1.76%. The survey of senior executives in 73 of these transactions showed that Indian acquirers felt they had fared quite well. On a seven-point rating scale, senior executives submitted scores averaging 5.69 when presented with the statement, "You have achieved most of your expected objectives in doing this acquisition," and a score of 5.47 regarding the statement, "You are satisfied with the overall outcome and performance of this acquisition." The in-depth interviews with senior executives revealed the same trend. While clarifying that managing the acquisition was by no means an easy task, they were quite satisfied with its progress in terms of meeting desired milestones and creating a positive organizational climate. The ten managers in the acquired overseas company also reported being quite happy with their Indian parent and its approach to post-acquisition management. One senior executive in a large European company said,

> Clearly we had concerns in the beginning. But, to be fair to them, they were very sharp and slick and had done a lot of homework. They have a very people-centric approach, which has been very good.

Another person reported,

> We have a just partnership with them. We have retained our voice; the company has grown and the employees have benefited.

Given their partnering approach to acquisitions and their considered avoidance of large-scale replacements and layoffs within the acquired company, emerging multinationals may also be received favorably by their potential targets in future overseas acquisition attempts. If this happens, they could become an "acquirer of choice" and will enjoy the advantages of that status, including the ability to attract more deals than before, or buy targets at a lower cost. Hemant Luthra, the architect of Mahindra's successful overseas acquisition foray who refers to the partnering approach as a "light-touch model with the right balance between independence and control," says,

> Now our management teams in the acquired companies have become my biggest salesmen. If people in any new company I am trying to acquire have concerns, I simply put them in touch with those managers.

In spite of its benefits, a partnering approach to acquisitions has some limitations as well. Given the model's emphasis on limited structural integration, selective coordination and intervention, people-centricity, and relative independence and autonomy given to the acquired company, this approach may entail a slower realization of the potential benefits associated with the coming together of two companies. This point came up frequently in our discussions with executives, including those who had followed this approach and appreciated its merits. Due to the non-intrusive nature of partnering, the capacity of the acquirer to wring substantial cost reductions, especially those derived from the elimination of human or asset redundancies, is limited. Thus, managers interested in using this practice in their own acquisitions should prepare themselves and their stakeholders for such a possibility. Finally, it would appear that because of the initial success of a few leading emerging multinationals, as they began using this approach to manage their overseas acquisitions, other companies from those regions simply followed their lead and used this approach as a de facto template for their own overseas acquisitions without regard to the size, industry, or type of company being considered for acquisition. However, executives must recognize that this approach may not be well suited to all acquisition types or conditions. The discussion in this chapter provides some clues to considerations that must be taken into account when adopting a partnering approach.

A PARTNERING APPROACH: WHEN IS IT USEFUL AND WHAT DOES IT CALL FOR?

Broadly speaking, the value and relevance of the partnering approach can be determined by answering four essential questions:

- What are the attributes and nature of the company to be acquired?
- What are the primary value-creation drivers underlying the transaction?
- What is the nature of the general business environment(s) in which the transaction will be conducted?
- What are the attributes of the acquiring organization?

(Please see Table 22.2 for an overview.)

First, if the acquired company possesses some unique or superior resources or capabilities such as well-established brands, technology, or management talent, its complete and rapid integration by the acquirer risks the destruction or loss of these resources. In these cases, a partnering approach is worth considering, especially if the acquirer intends

Table 22.2 The partnering approach: when does it work?

Conditions	The Partnering Approach	The Traditional Integration Approach
Nature of the acquired company's resources	Superior and unique resources (e.g. global brands, technology, talent) Complementary and non-overlapping resources	Similar or redundant resources
Primary driver of value creation	Revenue growth by entry or expansion into new markets, development of new products Sharing and learning of best practices	Cost reduction through elimination of duplicate assets or activities, economies of scale in operations
Attributes of the acquirer company	Collaborative and inclusive management style and culture	Hierarchical and "command and control" management style
	Higher tolerance for ambiguity and cultural differences	Lower tolerance for ambiguity and cultural differences
	Patience	Inclination to teach
	Willingness to learn Humility and respect for others	Emphasis on speed
Nature of the external business environment	Benign Supportive of long-term performance improvement Conducive to growth	Competitive and demanding Pressure for short-term performance improvement Recessionary or slow growth

to leverage those resources for its benefit. On the other hand, if the acquired company brings similar or redundant resources to the relationship, value may be better created using a heavy-handed approach of complete integration and replacement. However, if the resources in question are complementary (i.e. non-overlapping) and value is derived through coordination (instead of integration), a partnering approach relying on the use of linking mechanisms could be most beneficial.

The second issue is separate yet associated with the first—what is the primary driver of value creation in the acquisition? If the main goal of the acquisition is to create value by reducing costs as quickly as possible, a partnering approach may not be the best course of action. Substantive and rapid cost reduction is often realized through the elimination of redundant activities or through scale economies, both of which cannot be fully achieved in a partnering approach. On the other hand, the acquirer may see the transaction as a means to generate new revenue or growth opportunities. They may achieve this by entering the new market through their acquisition, collectively creating new or improved products, and sharing best practices and know-how. With these goals in mind, a partnering approach is useful as it allows each player to maintain and focus on what they are each best at doing, while leveraging the complementary resources and capabilities of the other to achieve these goals.

Third, the acquirer needs to take into account the general external business environment surrounding the deal. If the business environment is very competitive and demanding, as was the case in most countries during the 2008–9 recession, companies might be more hard-pressed to achieve cost reduction and efficiencies as rapidly as possible, rather than pursue growth or innovation. In such circumstances, the traditional approach targeting greater integration of the two companies might be preferred. On the other hand, if the business environment is benign and growth oriented, especially in the home or major markets of the acquirer company, a partnering approach may be acceptable because it attempts to realize the benefits of two companies coming together, without risking some of the unintended but adverse consequences of complete and rapid integration between them. Such an environment typically provides the acquirer with more time to achieve benefits in a less desperate or urgent climate.

Finally, the partnering approach is not meant for all companies. Given its key elements, some acquirers may be better suited to adopt this approach than others. Companies with existing collaborative or inclusive cultures and management styles will have an easier time partnering than those with a more traditional, hierarchical or "command-and-control" operating style. Senior executives in acquirer companies, and those working at the interface of the two organizations, must be comfortable achieving their goals through "influence" rather than control. A partnering approach also requires individuals with a higher than average tolerance for ambiguity and cultural differences as both are likely to be higher in such situations. Additionally, humility and respect are critical attributes if the acquirer is to recognize the strengths of the acquired company, and resist the urge to impose its own way of doing things on that company. This approach may also work better for those companies that exhibit patience in their business dealings and have a relatively high willingness to take risks. This is important because, as mentioned before, the gains from managing acquisitions in this manner are not always quickly realized, and frequently, there is an element of uncertainty about their magnitude. Some of these traits may simply be encoded in an acquirer's organizational DNA, but other traits may not—in which case, companies may need to consciously develop them over time. Companies that have greater experience of alliances or other forms of interfirm relationships (i.e. vertical relationships with suppliers, relationships with key customer accounts) can tacitly acquire these skills through their partnering experience. These skills can also be built by taking proactive steps to create a well-developed codified playbook that contains lessons and best practices from their own partnering experience (or from that of other alliance leaders). The tone set by top management and the support they provide are also very critical in this regard.

FUTURE RESEARCH AND CONCLUSIONS

In this chapter, we have discussed how emerging multinationals might adopt a somewhat distinct approach to managing their overseas acquisitions. From an empirical standpoint, we have validated this approach and its implications mainly by collecting large-sample data from overseas acquisitions done by emerging multinationals from India. In future, however, it would be useful to collect similar data from firms in other emerging economies to validate the generalizability of our findings. From a conceptual standpoint, we have proposed several reasons outlining when and why emerging multinationals might adopt the partnering approach to acquisitions. However, it is possible that the use of this approach might change dynamically under certain situations. For example, in some transactions, the acquirer firm may adopt the partnering approach to manage the acquired company only in the initial phase of the post-acquisition period, because doing so would help alleviate some of the adverse effects and anxieties typically felt in the acquired firm. However, at a later stage when the early anxieties have disappeared and/or the acquirer firm better understands where the synergies are and how to manage them, it may pursue a more complete absorption of the acquired firm. As we have mentioned earlier, acquirers are more likely to use this approach when they are relatively inexperienced in doing acquisitions and conducting business overseas. But if an emerging multinational acquires sufficient experience, it is quite plausible that it will adopt a more heavy-handed approach to managing its future acquisitions, right from the outset. In this chapter, we have not collected data to verify some of these possibilities but future research may like to do so.

To conclude, many emerging multinationals are increasingly handling overseas acquisitions and post-acquisition management issues using a unique blend of alliance, or partnering, best practices. Their collaborative approach, entailing the maintenance of the structural separation of the acquired company, "selective coordination" instead of complete integration with the partner, retention of human and social capital in the acquired company, and promotion of cooperation through alignment of core values and incentives, is a more benign but gradual way of realizing the benefits accrued through the transaction. The virtues and opportunities of this approach are many, but there are challenges and limitations too. Thus, executives need to understand the elements of this approach and the contours of the business conditions under which partnering would be most effective.

REFERENCES

Ashkenas, R., DeMonaco, L., & Francis, S. (1998). "Making the Deal Real: How GE Capital Integrates Acquisitions." *Harvard Business Review*, January–February: 45–54.

Aulakh, P. (2007). "Emerging Multinationals from Developing Economies: Motivations, Paths and Performance." *Journal of International Management*, 13: 235–40.

Cannella, A. A., & Hambrick, D. C. (1993). "Effects of Executive Departures on the Performance of Acquired Firms." *Strategic Management Journal*, 14: 137–52.

Capron, L. (1999). "The Long-Term Performance of Horizontal Acquisitions." *Strategic Management Journal*, 20: 987–1018.

Chaudhuri, S., & Tabrizi, B. (1999). "Capturing the Real Value in High-tech Acquisitions." *Harvard Business Review*, 77: 123–31.

Cording, M., Christmann, P., & King, D. (2008). "Reducing Causal Ambiguity in Acquisition Integration: Intermediate Goals as Mediators of Integration Decisions and Acquisition Performance." *Academy of Management Journal*, 51: 744–68.

Deng, P. (2009). "Why do Chinese Firms Tend to Acquire Strategic Assets in International Expansion?" *Journal of World Business*, 44: 74–84.

Doz, Y. (1996). "The Evolution of Cooperation in Strategic Alliances: Initial Conditions or Learning Processes?" *Strategic Management Journal*, 17: 55–83.

Economist (2008). "Emerging Market Multinationals: The Challengers." January 12–19: 62–76.

Graebner, M. E. (2004). "Momentum and Serendipity: How Acquired Leaders Create Value in the Integration of Technology Firms." *Strategic Management Journal*, 25: 751–77.

Gulati, R., Lawrence, P., & Puranam, P. (2005). "Adaptation in Vertical Relationships: Beyond Incentive Conflict." *Strategic Management Journal*, 26: 415–40.

—— & Singh, H. (1998). "The Architecture of Cooperation: Managing Coordination Costs and Appropriation Concerns in Strategic Alliances." *Administrative Science Quarterly*, 43: 781–814.

Haspeslagh, P., & Jemison, D. (1991). *Managing Acquisitions*. New York: Free Press.

Jensen, M. C., & Ruback, R. (1983). "The Market for Corporate Control: The Scientific Evidence." *Journal of Financial Economics*, 11: 5–50.

Kale, P., Dyer, J. H., & Singh, H. (2002). "Alliance Capability, Stock Market Response and Long-Term Alliance Success: The Role of the Alliance Function." *Strategic Management Journal*, 23: 747–67.

Khanna, T., & Palepu, K. (1997). "Why Focused Strategies may be Wrong for Emerging Markets." *Harvard Business Review*, July–August: 41–51.

—— —— (2006). "Emerging Giants: Building World-Class Companies in Developed Economies." *Harvard Business Review*, October: 60–70.

King, D. R., Dalton, D. R., Daily, C. M., & Covin, J. G. (2004). "Meta-analysis of Post-acquisition Performance." *Strategic Management Journal*, 25: 187–200.

Lala, R. M. (2009). *The Creation of Wealth—The Tatas from the 19th to 21st Century*. New Delhi: Penguin.

Luo, Y., & Tung, R. (2007). "International Expansion of Emerging Market Enterprises: A Springboard Perspective." *Journal of International Business Studies*, 38: 481–98.

Makino, S., Lau, C., & Yeh, R. (2002). "Asset Exploitation versus Asset Seeking: Implications for Location Choice of Foreign Direct Investment from Newly Industrialized Economies." *Journal of International Business Studies*, 33: 403–22.

Pablo, A. (1994). "Determinants of Acquisition Integration Level: A Decision-Making Perspective." *Academy of Management Journal*, 37: 803–37.

Puranam, P., & Srikanth, K. (2007). "What They Know Versus What They Do: How Acquirers Leverage Technology Acquisitions." *Strategic Management Journal*, 28: 805–25.

Ray, S., & Gubbi, S. (2009). "International Acquisitions by Indian Firms: Implications for Research on Emerging Multinationals." *Indian Journal of Industrial Relations*, 45: 11–26.

Rui, H., & Yip, G. S. (2008). "Foreign Acquisitions by Chinese Firms: A Strategic Intent Perspective." *Journal of World Business*, 43: 213–26.

Saxton, T., & Dollinger, M. (2004). "Target Reputation and Appropriability: Picking and Deploying Resources in Acquisitions." *Journal of Management*, 30: 123–47.

Schweizer, L. (2005). "Organizational Integration of Acquired Biotechnology Companies into Pharmaceutical Companies: Need for a Hybrid Approach." *Academy of Management Journal*, 48: 1051–74.

Shimuzu, K., Hitt, M., Vaidyanathan, D., & Pisano, V. (2004). "Theoretical Foundations of Cross-Border Mergers and Acquisitions: A Review of Current Research and Recommendations for the Future." *Journal of International Management*, 10/3: 307–53.

Thompson, J. (1967). *Organizations in Action*. New York: McGraw-Hill.

Zollo, M., & Singh, H. (2004). "Deliberate Learning in Corporate Acquisitions." *Strategic Management Journal*, 25: 1233–56.

CHAPTER 23

....

FINANCIAL MERGERS
AND ACQUISITIONS

*From Regulation to Strategic Repositioning
to Geo-economics*

....

GARY A. DYMSKI

INTRODUCTION

....

Mergers and acquisitions (M&As) are often evaluated by comparing the increased operating efficiencies that merging firms can achieve with the losses their customers may experience due to increased monopoly in pricing. Until the 1980s, the literature on financial M&As used these terms of reference. But then things changed. Concerns about monopoly power were set aside due to acceptance of the "contestability" doctrine (Brock 1983), wherein monopoly will not lead to inefficient pricing as long as new competitors can freely enter. Financial deregulations and a merger wave in the 1980s and 1990s appeared to bring about just such a situation.

The 1980s also saw the first instances of large-scale banking crises; these have affected nations throughout the world recurrently until the present day. Arriving as deregulation came into effect (if not hurrying deregulation along), these events have led banks to transform their strategies and many of their core practices. They also expanded the focus of research on bank mergers to include attention to the stability of banking and financial markets. By the early 2000s, many researchers concluded that more concentration leads to more stability. By implication, bank mergers that led to large diversified megabanks were to be encouraged. The engagement of many of the participating banks in ever more opaque and diverse sets of activities, with escalating levels of leverage, did not cause worries. It instead suggested that large banks should manage their risks on their own.

But with the ink barely dry on the first publications that used this expanded approach, many of the largest megabanks melted down in 2008 and 2009. Precipitous action by central banks, involving previously unimaginable levels of intervention, prevented the collapse of the global megabanks. These bailouts achieved market stability only by picking survivors and, in effect, turning "too big to fail" into government policy. Studies of bank M&As have consequently become more skeptical of the benefits of bank concentration.

This evolving story of deregulation and financial crisis provides the backdrop for this chapter. The next section identifies the forces driving bank M&As. The evolution of— and research about—bank M&As in four periods is then analyzed: the post-war period to the end of the 1970s; the deregulation era, the 1980s and 1990s; the post-regulation era beginning in 2000; and finally, the global financial crisis of 2008 and its uncertain aftermath.

A Framework for Understanding Financial M&As

Financial M&As result from the intersection of banking-firm strategies with structural conditions in the market(s) in which the bank operates or hopes to operate. We consider market structures first. These operate at three possible scales—microeconomic, macro-structural, and geo-economic.[1]

Microeconomic factors

Banking firms generally seek to maximize expected profit, and as such will implement M&As when to do so is profit-enhancing. One primary factor in merger decisions is the regulatory regime: the degree of constraint imposed by regulators and law on intra-market and geographic entry. If banks are not free to move into new geographic areas, then mergers may be undertaken intra-market, if the merging bank can either diversify its credit risk or establish a higher degree of monopoly pricing power. The latter has been the traditional concern of US antitrust policy: that firms (including banks) with monopoly power in local markets may extract economic rents by imposing above-equilibrium prices.

When banks are free to enter other geographic markets, we can distinguish between defensive and offensive financial mergers. *Defensive mergers* involve efforts to preserve core bank activities in given market areas in the face of heightened external competition. Costs can be cut by eliminating workforce or closing duplicate offices. Defensive mergers may also permit the surviving entity to offload bad debts, declare capital losses, and even become "too big to eat." Gains from geographic diversification may also result, as noted above. *Offensive mergers* involve efforts to expand the range of bank activities—by entering new product markets, capturing new customers within market areas, or entering new geographic markets.

Macro-structural Factors

"Macrostructural" factors consist of the key elements of national or regional market structure: the size of the firm relative to its national or regional market, and the scale of the national or regional market relative to the world market; the national and regional growth rate; whether the national (or regional) currency has reserve-currency status; the presence or absence of robust capital markets within national or regional borders; and whether the banking firm's national government makes capital available and is willing to offload bad debt.

Taken together, microeconomic and macrostructural factors help delineate what financial mergers are feasible in any one time and place, and whether feasible mergers happen. National regulatory regimes determine which domestic and cross-border acquisitions are possible. Whether possible acquisitions are optimal—whether they enhance expected profits—depends on the size and expected growth rate of domestic and overseas markets, as well as on these markets' degree of competition. And whether optimal mergers are feasible depends on whether they can be financed, which in turn rests on merging banks' retained earnings, on the presence of state funds to underwrite bank mergers, and on banks' proximity to robust equity markets. Overall, then, the scale of the firm and of the national market in which it operates, together with its degree of access to capital markets, determines the scale at which it can make merger/partnership plans.

Geo-economic Factors

Overlaid on any given global structure of banking markets at any point in historic time are two "geo-economic" factors. First, which country or set of countries issues currency that is universally accepted as means of payment, and in which country or set of countries does (do) the central bank(s) operate as a lender-of-last resort in the event of financial crises? The answer to both questions is often the same: those nations whose currency is most readily accepted are most able to undertake whatever liquidity creation is necessary to resolve financial crises. At present, this privileged list of currencies includes the US dollar, the British pound, the Swiss franc, the Euro, and the Japanese yen. Second, are there countries that have—and that can sustain—systematically positive or negative balances on current and capital account?

These two factors are identified as "geo-economic" because there are only a handful of countries across the globe that are able to provide global monies and intervene at will in financial crises, and to sustain continued cross-border imbalances. An extreme example of intervention-at-will is the provision of too-big-to-fail (TBTF) protection to a subset of a country's financial firms. The two factors are linked. A country can run a systematic current-account deficit only if counter-parties in other countries are willing to accumulate assets denominated in its currency. The recent example here is the United States.

These geo-economic factors, when they are active, have important implications for financial intermediation. Banks in countries with sustained current-account surpluses tend to become large (Japan in the 1980s, China in the 2000s). Banks in countries with lender-of-last resort capacities enjoy an extra margin of safety, as they are more likely to be protected in any downturn. In sum, the degree of national "hegemony" implicitly underlies firm strategies, including merger plans.

Strategy

This brings us to the role of strategy in financial acquisitions. Strategies have varied over time in part because of changes in market structures (at the micro-, macro-structural, and geo-economic scales), and in part because of the transformation of banking and finance itself in the past half-century. So rather than identifying fixed strategies, we can identify the factors that underlie the strategy formation that can lead to M&As.

- Two intertwined factors are the means of revenue extraction, and the nature of the bank-customer relationship. The bank can seek to capture customers from whom it hopes to derive business over a period of time; in this case, it must meet basic customer needs, shape customers' preferences and habits, and use cross-subsidies to hold them. Alternatively, the bank can focus on maximizing point-in-time revenues; this involves services—wire-transfers, loan origination and funding, underwriting, and so on—provided without an expectation of customer retention. Mergers can enhance either approach.
- A third strategic element (adapted from ECLAC 2001) is whether an acquisition aims at increasing liabilities—depositors, investors in hedge funds, and customers for wealth-management tools—or focuses on increasing asset production—more loans, more securities, and even more derivatives based on loan and security production. Unbalanced strategies are especially risky for cross-border mergers.
- A fourth element of strategy is whether to defend existing market turf or to attempt to expand it. Mergers or acquisitions may be considered for either purpose. Acquiring former rivals within a given market area, for example, can deter entry by new rivals.
- A fifth element is a bank's approach to risk: whether the bank wants to expand the risky assets on its balance sheet, or to create and offload risky assets via securitization; and the banks' amount of leverage (and hence dependence on short-term borrowing markets).

As noted, in deciding on these strategic elements, banks must consider how they are impacted by the geo-economic structure of power and by macro-structural shifts (for example, in the pace of economic growth and of deregulation or reregulation). Whether banks focus on traditional banking activities or strike out into new areas, and whether banks operate as principals or intermediaries, reflects the influence of all these factors.

BANK M&AS IN THE REGULATED ERA

M&As in finance were relatively rare after World War II until the end of the 1970s. A key reason was that the first half of the 20th century involved repeated experiences of financial meltdown, depression, and war. In the early 20th century, financial panics led to efforts to build up structures of governance and liquidity sharing to protect against systemic meltdowns. These were far from sufficient; and in the Great Depression, banks failed in large numbers. Acquisitions and mergers took second place to efforts to redefine and stabilize the very business of banking. Banks in the US entered the 1940s as closely regulated businesses with well-defined, segmented markets, with little or no ability to set prices in the markets in which they could compete. Elsewhere in the world, banks were also implicated in—and central to—the massive war efforts of World Wars I and II. As such, they were components of the controlled economies of the war years, and then were under clouds of suspicion in the years following.

So coming out of World War II, banking systems were tame institutions whose scope of activity was carefully controlled. These tight controls inhibited banks strategic planning; so mergers were infrequent. In the US, for example, although the banking structure was composed of thousands of individual banks—a legacy of the nation's 19th-century geographic expansion—there were only nine unassisted mergers (and one assisted merger) annually for every 1000 banks, from 1946 to 1976. With time, banking regulations and national controls over the ownership and control of banks loosened. The initial impetus came from money-center banks, pushing against regulations that prevented them from maintaining corporate and large-balance customers who had access to money markets. A second impetus was the growing euro-dollar market.

But the decisive turn of events occurred in the 1970s, when the conditions for stable macroeconomic growth deteriorated. The US unlinked the dollar from a fixed gold price in 1973; thereafter, inflationary pressure built up through the 1970s, spurred by two oil-price spikes. Market interest rates followed price inflation upward, and economic growth stalled. These forces had several impacts. The oil-price spikes changed global financial flows and forced "petro-recycling," that is, the internationalization of banking (Mullineux 2006). Domestically, banks lost customers on both sides of their balance sheets. On the liability side, depositors with larger balances fled to non-bank funds. On the asset side, non-financial firms increasingly obtained the finance they needed directly from money and bond markets.

FINANCIAL MERGERS IN THE
DEREGULATION ERA

As the 1980s opened, a period of stagnant growth and high interest and inflation rates created a sustained period of banking distress. Under pressure, bank owners and managers attempted to adjust; but regulatory structures boxed them in. US laws prohibiting banks from maintaining unified operations across state lines generated higher administrative costs and limited economies of scale; laws restricting lines of commerce for banks, in turn, eliminated many potential economies of scope. Banking in Europe was also constricted by dissimilar rules and legal barriers involved in crossing national borders; added challenges were also posed there because of language differences and even deeper cultural divides than are found in the US.

M&As in the 1980s

During the 1980s and 1990s, national regulators were gradually forced to loosen controls over what instruments banks could emit, and on what terms. The US was the first to move; Congress passed a bank deregulation act in 1980. This act permitted banks to offer new instruments to customers that were abandoning their balance sheets—both depositors leaving for money-market funds, and larger business customers beginning to borrow directly in commercial-paper and corporate-bond markets. Then, in 1982—after a period of sustained high nominal interest rates—much of the US thrift industry collapsed. Its long-term mortgages were locked into fixed interest rates lower than the marginal cost of funds. In that same year, oil prices plunged. Many banks in oil-rich domestic areas of the US—Texas, Oklahoma, Louisiana—experienced non-performing loan problems, and Mexico defaulted on its foreign-loan obligations. The latter action led to the Latin American debt crisis, which especially affected money-center banks. Later in the 1980s, these same banks experienced renewed problems when loans they had made for commercial real-estate and corporate mergers went bad.

Further deregulation was undertaken; and banks began to look for new strategies. In the US, this search focused on the retail market. One key strategy was upscale-retail banking: identifying a preferred customer base to which the bank can deliver traditional banking services—consumer loans, mortgages, deposits—as well as non-traditional services such as mutual funds, insurance, and investment advice. Whereas cross-subsidies were previously extended between customer classes within product lines, cross-subsidies were now implemented between product lines within customer classes. Fees and charges were reduced for desired customers who purchased multiple banking services; fees were increased for customers using only basic banking services.

A second strategy shifted attention from interest-based to fee-based income. This meant using secondary-market sales—and eventually securitization—to reduce maturity-transformation-based liquidity risk. Large banks increasingly provided only transaction services to small businesses; for the larger businesses that met financing needs directly, banks provided risk-management services—such as financial derivatives, foreign exchange hedging, and lines of credit. Initially, these shifts toward desirable upmarket customers and toward fee-based services were mutually reinforcing. Banks began to market more standardized financial services—credit cards, specialized investment accounts, and so on—to the upper tier of the middle market. The larger banks pioneering these changes were led naturally to look for acquisitions that would expand their market areas. Once banks identified the most profitable customers in their market areas and saturated these areas with new products, growth depended on a spatial extension of the customer base.

A new breed of big bank, "super-regional banks" such as NationsBank and BancOne, pioneered these mergers.[2] The crises of the savings-and-loan industry and of commercial banks in "oil-patch" states created opportunities for them to acquire weaker or failing institutions. For example, in the late 1980s, the five largest banks in Texas, all insolvent, were acquired by expansion-oriented banks (NationsBank, BancOne, Wells Fargo, Chemical Bank, and RepublicBank) in "assisted" mergers (underwritten by government guarantees or subsidies).

This period of deregulation, distress mergers, and shifting bank strategies was paralleled by a changed regulatory philosophy. Until this period, regulators had relied on antitrust law and the Bank Holding Company (BHC) Acts of 1956 and 1970 to block the emergence of undue monopoly power or interconnections between banking and non-banking financial activities. However, in the 1980s, the Reagan Administration cut regulatory agencies' staffing levels, and many regulatory economists adopted the Chicago "new learning" approach, which shifts attention from monopoly position to "contestability." The Federal Reserve used regulatory flexibility to force "modernization" in US banking laws—that is, the expansion of banking activities and market areas. And indeed, half the 6,350 bank mergers after 1980 (and a higher proportion after 1985) were aimed at extending banks' geographic markets (Dymski 1999).

The Thatcher Administration in the UK also embraced deregulation and market forces. The defining moment came with the "Big Bang" of October 1986, which deregulated trading on the London Stock Exchange. This led to a huge influx of high-end financing activity in the City of London, and in turn to many M&As involving City firms.

Explaining Financial Mergers and Bank Crisis in the Deregulation Era

The literature on bank mergers in the 1980s and early 1990s focused on laws that segmented banking markets and limited opportunities for the industry to capture operating efficiencies. The empirical literature showed that banking consolidation, by creating larger banks, would permit the realization of economies of scale and scope (Gilbert 1984; Hannan 1991; Berger 1995). At the same time, these economies were exhausted at relatively modest asset levels: there was no evidence that would support the creation of multi-billion dollar banks on efficiency grounds.

The outbreak of the savings-and-loan and Latin American crises stimulated a broadening of research into the key links between restrictions on depository activity and crisis. Research focused on two problems with thrifts. One was their lack of portfolio diversification; in most states, they were required to hold primarily residential mortgages. A number of studies demonstrated the possibility that banks could realize economies of scope and achieve gains from diversification; see, for example, Liang and Rhoades (1988) and Boyd et al. (1993).

Researchers also highlighted the problem of moral hazard in these crises. Moral hazard arises in financial markets primarily when those making risky decisions (such as granting credit to borrowers) face no (or limited) adverse consequences if their decisions go wrong. Market mechanisms with this design flaw will induce excessive riskiness. Vis-à-vis thrifts (and other domestic credit crises), researchers' argument was that deposit insurance removes depositors' incentives to discipline intermediaries whose managers or boards take undue credit-market risks (Kane 1989; Kaufman and Benston 1990). Vis-à-vis the Latin American debt crisis, the argument was that the penalties facing non-paying borrowers were set too low. The prescription for Latin American banking was better regulation and more entry by overseas banks. The prescription for the US domestic market was continued deregulation: the key was to get incentives right so that the financial system could be self-policing. Government intervention would only lead to mismanagement. As George Kaufman put it in a 1995 essay,

> The government first created many of the underlying causes of the problem by forcing Savings and Loan associations (S&Ls) to assume excessive interest rate risk exposure and preventing both S&Ls and banks from minimizing their credit risk exposure through optimal product and geographic diversification and then delayed in applying solutions to the problem by granting forbearance to economically insolvent or near-insolvent institutions. That is, the banking debacle was primarily an example of government failure rather than market failure. (Kaufman 1995: 259)

M&As in the 1990s

As Figure 23.1 shows, the number of OECD-related bank M&As grew steadily through the 1990s, reaching a peak (of 4,663) in 2000. While most of these mergers involved OECD acquirers and acquirees, 34% of OECD-related mergers in the 1990s involved a non-OECD acquirer (22%) or an OECD acquiree (11%). Table 23.1, drawn from Buch and DeLong (2004, 2008), shows an acceleration in the number of mergers in the 1990s, across all continental areas. For Europe and the Americas in the 1994–2001 period, an increasing share of mergers extended across national borders. This was not the case for the other continental areas, though their share of cross-border mergers already stood at very high levels.

In the US, this surge in mergers was facilitated by the 1994 Riegle-Neal Act, which finally ended all prohibitions against interstate banking. A study of the impact of this Act concluded that "the elimination of these constraints through the adoption of intrastate and interstate banking laws has improved the efficiency with which banks operate." Large bank mergers produced more gains than small ones, and profit increases were

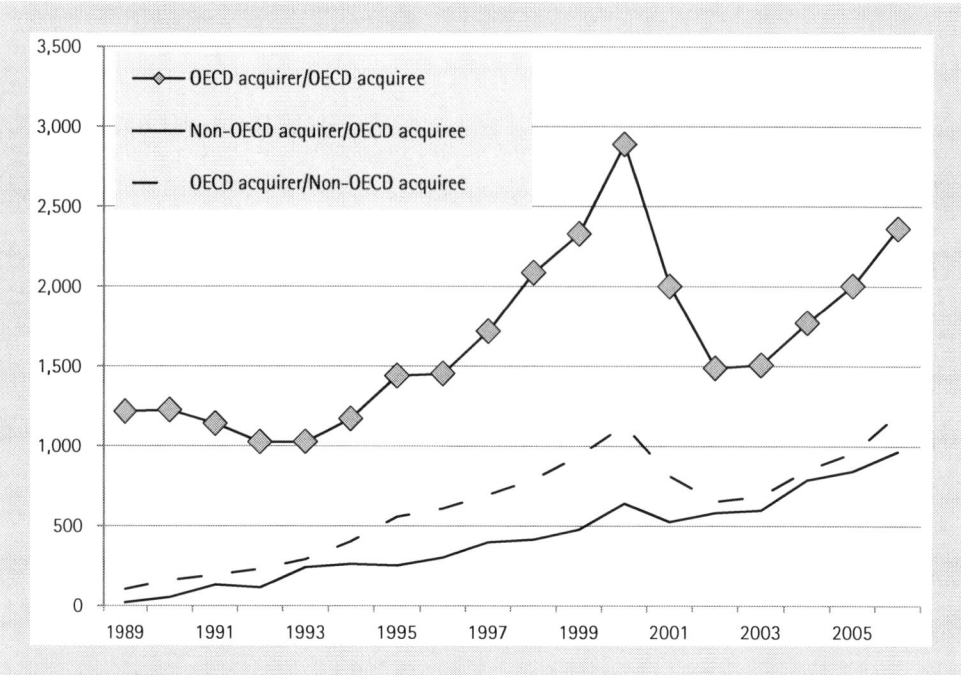

FIG. 23.1 Number of bank mergers and acquisitions—OECD and non-OECD trends, 1989–2006

Source: Hyun and Kim (2010), table 1, p. 293.

Table 23.1 Bank mergers by continental area, 1985–2006*

	Europe	America	Africa/Middle East	Asia	Australia-Asia	Total
Average mergers per year						
1985–1993	234	390	8	29	14	675
1994–2001	479	607	36	100	23	1244
2002–2006	368	391	30	137	21	946
Cross-border mergers as % of all mergers						
1985–1993	32.4	9.1	40.8	57.4	56.5	20.6
1994–2001	40.2	14.2	48.6	35.2	47.3	27.5
2002–2006	49.1	17.3	63.5	52.1	60.2	37.0

* *Source*: Buch-DeLong (2004, 2008). Calculations by author.

greatest "for cost cutting activities, i.e., activity focusing and geographically focusing mergers" (Cornett et al. 2006: 1049).

As Mullineux (2006) observes, one response of large banks to deregulation has been conglomeration, wherein banks combine insurance, retail, and wholesale banking activities. Figure 23.2, which complements Figure 23.1 by showing the value of bank mergers (in billions of US dollars), illustrates the systemic importance of large mergers within the OECD. The gap between the value of intra-OECD and other mergers (Figure 23.2) is far higher than the gap in the number of mergers (Figure 23.1). For intra-OECD mergers, the highest number recorded (2,891 in 2000) is 2.8 times higher than the lowest number (1,026 in 1992); but the highest value recorded ($1.051 trillion in 1999) is 14 times higher than the lowest value ($75 billion in 1993).

The momentum of banking conglomeration slowed in the US in the late 1980s (Rose 1989: 11–12); the money-center banks most inclined to push this envelope were weakened by successive adverse earnings shocks from their recurrent 1980s lending crises. With some money-center banks sidelined, "super-regional" banks pushed across state lines and into new markets in the 1990s, setting up a showdown with money-center banks that came to a head only with the 2008 crisis. Bank consolidation activity outside the US also picked up momentum, for different reasons: in the case of Asia and Latin America, financial crisis; in the case of Europe, market opening (especially for Eastern Europe) and economic consolidation (Western Europe).

Japan: Asset-Bubble Collapse and Consolidation

As the 1990s began, the Japanese banking system and economy was decimated by the collapse of a huge real-estate and stock-market bubble. At the center of the bubble and

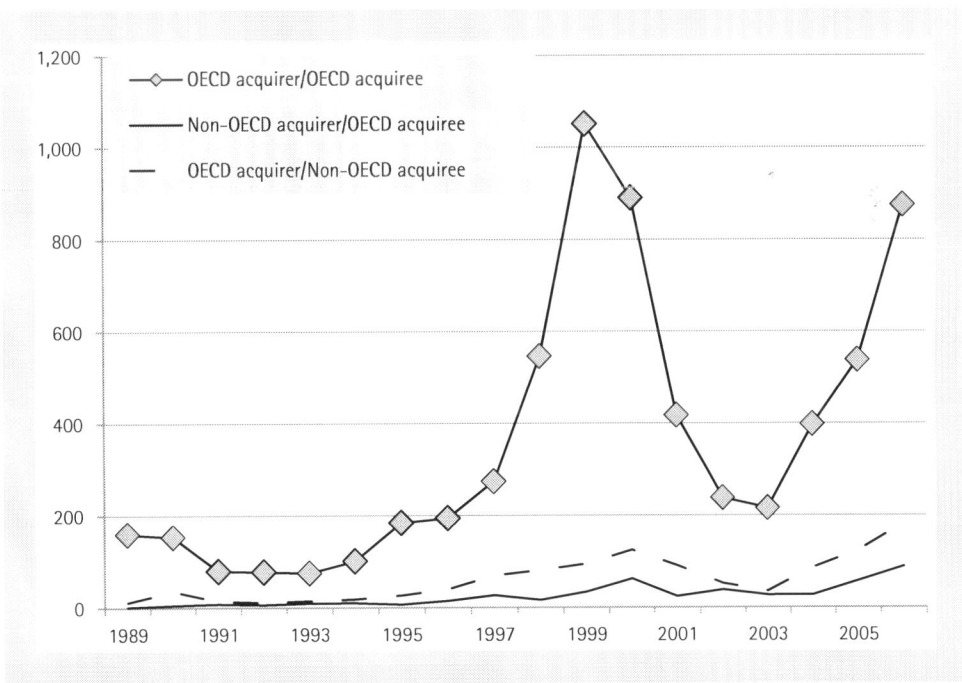

FIG. 23.2 Value of bank mergers and acquisitions—OECD and non-OECD trends, 1989–2006 (US$ billion)

Source: Hyun and Kim (2010), table 1, p. 293.

its aftermath were the Japanese main banks. While these banks had famously spurred Japan's vaunted post-war growth, the growing profit margins of the Japanese non-financial companies with which they had been closely linked led them to seek new investment outlets. They made loans supporting, and invested in, real estate and shares.

The Japanese government responded in a two-fold manner. On one hand, it sponsored financial deregulation, including "Big Bang" changes between 1997 and 1999 which removed barriers between different types of financial activity, the deregulation of brokerage commissions (as in the City of London in 1986), and accounting reforms. Foreign direct investment in finance was also encouraged, though with little success. On the other hand, government regulators guided Japan's large banks through a series of defensive mergers that permitted the offloading of bad debt. In 1990, Mitsui Bank and Taiyo Kobe Bank formed Sakura Bank. In 1991, Kyowa Bank and Saitama Bank created Asahi Bank. A potential merger between Daiwa—damaged by a bond-trading scandal involving its US affiliate—and Sumitomo was undermined when Sumitomo's hard bargaining violated prevailing industry norms. In April 1996, the Bank of Tokyo and Mitsubishi Bank merged into the then largest Bank of Tokyo-Mitsubishi. These "bigger is better" mergers did not resolve the large bank sector's problems: gains in microeconomic efficiency were slight, and these banks' inability to lend compromised economic recovery.

As Japan sank into stagnation, the signing of the Maastricht Treaty in February 1992 led to the establishment of the European Union in November 1993. The EU embraced the "single market" principle, which meant a leveling of the playing field for the provision of goods and services across Europe—and thus a synchronization of financial regulations and supervision (in the direction of deregulation). These events initiated increasingly adventurous struggles among Europe's banks to both defend market turf and to break through into new markets.

EU: Defensive Mergers and the Coming of the Single Market

While Western Europe experienced deregulation and market integration since the mid-1980s, the combination of the creation of the EU and increasing competitive pressure from US-based investment banks spurred action. The explicit goal set by the European Central Bank was "to complete financial integration in Europe by 2005" (Cabral et al. 2002). But throughout the 1990s, even the largest European mergers focused not just on market integration but on defensive positioning. Spain offers an illustrative case. The second largest Spanish bank, Banco Bilbao Vizcaya, was created by a merger of two Basque banks in 1988. Banco Central Hispanomericano (BCH) was created in 1992 by a defensive merger made in light of the emerging single European market. In January 1999, the largest Spanish bank, Banco Santander, consolidated its position by merging with BCH, then third largest.

Throughout Europe, such defensive mergers permitted branch closings, cost cutting, and increases in market capitalization. And sometimes one set of mergers triggered another, as remaining banks sought to insure they had the heft to survive. For example, in March 1999, Italy's two largest banking groups made merger bids—UniCredito Italiano for Banca Commerciale Italiana (BCI), and Sanpaolo IMI for Banca di Roma. Both were aimed at cutting costs and increasing market capitalization. In June 1999, Italy's fourth largest bank, Banca Intesa, merged with the fifth largest, Banca Commerciale Italiana (BCI).

These sometimes featured combinations of different types of intermediaries. And as Altunbas and Marqués report in their survey of EU bank mergers:

> the overall statistical picture is of large, generally more efficient banks merging with relatively smaller and better capitalised institutions with more diversified sources of income. By contrast with the results of most of the US literature, we found that there are improvements in performance after a merger has taken place, particularly in the case of cross-border M&As. (Altunbas and Marqués 2008: 216)

So increased capitalization and larger service menus permitted many institutions to protect their balance sheets and their share prices for Europe-wide competition. Small-business borrowers in Europe were often adversely affected, as has often been found in merger studies (Montoriol-Garriga 2008). Further, in some cases, these mergers generated strong resistance from employees that remained loyal to pre-merger firm cultures. Consider an example from France: the March 1999 bid by Banque Nationale de Paris (BNP) to acquire both Paribas and Société Générale, just after these two institutions had publicly affirmed their interest in a "marriage of equals." Paribas was an investment bank, while the other two were primarily commercial banks, so this merger offered the prospect of both cost-cutting and product-line expansion. However, a huge public controversy erupted over BNP's aggressive offer. In June 1999, BNP succeeded in buying Paribas. This did not work out well; since Paribas had no branch network, few cost economies were available on the commercial-banking side; and a mass exodus of personnel ensued on the investment-banking side.

EU: Seeking Global Reach

In this period, entry by overseas banks was initially resisted in Europe, as it was in the US. For example, the first foreign takeover of a French bank came when HSBC (UK) bought CCF in April 2001. As Buch and DeLong write in their survey of cross-border bank mergers, "If anything, deregulation of entry has lowered rather than increased merger activity within Europe and North America, respectively" (2004: 2099). Pozzolo notes that merger activity in banking, from 1990 onward has lagged behind that in manufacturing. Further, he observes,

> Within EMU, despite a much higher variability, the share is substantially higher, although on average still lower than that calculated considering operations all over the world. Banks from G10 countries, OECD countries and, especially, from the EMU are much more likely to do cross border M&As with banks in less developed

countries than within themselves. Moreover, this share is higher and it is increasing faster for OECD than for G10 countries. (Pozzolo 2008: 11)

Some banks—especially European banks with domestic markets of limited size—thus implemented the opposite strategy. The outstanding examples of this strategy are ABN Amro and ING of the Netherlands, institutions that *The Banker's 2000* listing ranked as the fourth and ninth largest in continental Europe.[3]

ABN Amro descended from a 19th-century trading company, expanded its brokerage and market operations aggressively in the 1990s, and also entered overseas markets. ABN Amro acquired a major interest in Thailand's Bank of Asia in the early 1998, and in mid-1998 became the first international bank in Kazakhstan. In late 1998, ABN Amro became the first Dutch bank permitted into Beijing, and bought Banco Real, the fourth largest bank in Brazil. It operated branch networks in Costa Rica, Guatemala, Hungary, and South Africa. In the US, ABN Amro sold its New England-based European American Bank to Citibank (*The Banker*, March 2001), so as to focus on its US Midwest assets (LaSalle Bank in Illinois and Standard Federal in Michigan). ABN Amro moved aggressively to expand its cross-border consumer-banking operations, especially in Asia and Latin America. Its cross-border expansion emphasized consumer banking, embodying the upscale retail banking approach discussed above. As the *Harvard Business Review* (1999) put it: "Consumer banking is a loosely defined notion. ABN AMRO Bank defines it as providing financial services to the affluent sector in a given market. At the lower end of the socio-economic scale, consumer banking borders on mass retail banking; at the high end, on private banking."

Another ambitious Dutch bank, Internationale Nederlanden Group (ING), has also used mergers to become a large-scale "financial supermarket" that, like Citigroup, combines insurance and commercial banking. ING was created by a 1991 merger; like ABN Amro, the merged bank had a base in Latin America. It bought Barings in 1995, after that bank had been ravaged by Nick Leeson's exchange speculation, and later Equitable of Iowa. In the 1990s, it purchased banks in Poland, Germany, Belgium (Banque Bruxelles Lambert), Romania, and the Czech Republic; and it also bought insurance companies in the US (Equitable of Iowa) and Chile (Cruz Blanca Securos de Vida). In 2000, it purchased two more US insurers (Aetna, Reliastar). ING built up its market capitalization, but was unable to enter the top echelon of European banks. Its attempt to buy Crédit Commercial de France was rebuffed in December 1999, despite an offer 15% over CCF's market value. In effect, these two banks from small national market areas pursued strategies resembling those of HSBC and Citigroup.

Latin American and Asian Lending Crises

It should be emphasized that opportunities for entering markets were not exploited only by these two institutions. To the contrary, the Latin American debt crisis and its aftermath—which included liberalization programs under pressure in several South

American nations (including Brazil and Argentina), NAFTA, and the subsequent "Tequila" crisis of 1994–5—permitted numerous banks to enter Latin American markets. Santander and BBV of Spain, for example, joined Citibank as owners of large banks in Mexico. Foreign-owned banks also dominated the banking market in Mexico and in Argentina.

The East Asian financial crisis of 1997, in turn, generated a new set of opportunities for foreign bank entry. Tightly regulated and credit-focusing domestic banking systems had been key elements of East Asia's envied rapid growth in the 1980s and early 1990s (Stiglitz and Uy 1996). These banking systems had been partially liberalized prior to 1997 (Crotty and Dymski 1998). However, they were opened wide to foreign owners and entrants once the International Monetary Fund entered to manage the currency and economic crises. Significant new entry by overseas banks then occurred. By 2002, the owners of Korean banks included JPMorgan, Bank of America, Commerzbank, Allianz, Goldman Sachs, Bank of New York, and ING (Dymski 2002). However, US private-equity funds also made purchases; and overall, foreign investment in banking was less than hoped. Further, these retooled banks' focus was on upscale consumers. The result, in Korea, was a second crisis of bank insolvency in 2003 (Dymski 2006). Some other East Asian nations' experience was like Korea's; but banks in nations that had avoided insolvency or currency crisis emerged unscathed. Indeed, Singapore's United Overseas Bank (UOB) acquired Thai and Philippine banks; and the Development Bank of Singapore (DBS), South East Asia's largest bank, bought banks in the Philippines, Thailand, and Hong Kong.

M&As in the Post-regulation Era

The new century brought a new phase in financial regulation and in bank mergers. After 2000, the number of mergers slowed. Table 23.1 shows that this slowdown occurred in Europe and the Americas in the 2002–6 period; at the same time, in these two global regions, the trend toward more cross-border mergers continued. Figures 23.1 and 23.2 permit a more detailed analysis of bank mergers involving OECD countries. Figure 23.1 demonstrates that the slowdown in the number of mergers after 2000 was completely due to fewer intra-OECD mergers; mergers involving non-OECD acquirers or acquirees grew at a steady pace. Intra-OECD mergers regained momentum in 2005 and 2006. Figure 23.2 suggests that when the slowdown in the value of completed mergers was reversed in 2005 and 2006, intra-OECD, larger mergers led the way.

This data reflects the trend noted by Mullineux (2006): nearly simultaneous deregulation in many countries led large banks to diversify into activities beyond core banking, usually via acquisitions. In the US, late-1980s balance-sheet distress was wiped away for large banks by several years of record profits in the early 1990s. This reflated their equity prices and positioned them to push for combinations with insurance providers, brokerages, and investment banks. These efforts to create "one-stop shopping" for financial services tested the remaining strength of Glass-Steagall and BHC Act prohibitions on the scope of bank activities.

The Federal Reserve was more than willing to push the issue by playing an activist regulatory hand. Bankers Trust agreed in April 1997 to buy Alex. Brown, a Baltimore investment bank, a move that *The Economist* (April 12, 1997) hailed as the practical end of the Glass-Steagall Act. Both BankAmerica and NationsBank bought San Francisco investment-banking firms later in 1997: BankAmerica, Robertson, Stephens for $540 million; NationsBank, Montgomeries Securities for $1.2 billion. In September 1998, the Federal Reserve tentatively approved a proposed merger that violated the Bank Holding Company Act—the planned combination of Citicorp and Travelers—with the proviso that the law be appropriately modified within 24 months.[4] Two months later, the Gramm-Leach-Bliley Act repealed the Glass-Steagall Act's firewalls between investment and commercial banking, and also eliminated the BHC prohibition of combinations among banks, securities companies, and insurance companies. This cleared the way for a $70 billion deal that created the world's largest financial services firm (*Wall Street Journal*, April 13, 1998).

These moves were greeted skeptically by *The Economist*, which argued, "Many companies have tried, in various ways, to market both insurance policies and savings accounts, or to offer business customers both traditional bank loans and share underwriting. The success stories are few. Cross-selling motor insurance or emerging-market mutual funds to credit-card holders is easy in theory, but turns out to be extremely hard to do. . . . perhaps, not for the first time, the world's leading financiers are mistaking size for profitability" (April 11, 1998).

The Economist's assessment proved to be a step behind large banks' rapidly-evolving practices, as these banks were already opening a second front in their competition to dominate the new financial world. If one front was the "financial supermarket," aimed at repeat consumer business, the second front involved new ways to generate cash-flow through making, securitizing, insuring, and betting on risky loans (and risky financial positions more generally). This new approach was made possible by the maturation of markets for securitized debt, which permitted the widespread use of the "originate-and-distribute" lending model. Originally developed to facilitate the making of high-cost, high-fee (that is, subprime) mortgage loans in formerly redlined neighborhoods (Dymski 2010a), securities based on highly risky paper proved attractive to a then-emerging set of lightly regulated non-bank intermediaries. These entities—hedge funds, private-equity funds, offshore accounts, in particular—were designed to avoid existing regulations, and were captained by managers who commanded high fees and promised above-market returns to their investors.

At the same time, global banks were pioneering new contingent financial instruments—derivatives, interest-rate swaps, and so on—that could be used either to take on insurance against adverse price movements or to take bets on the future direction of prices (or price ratios). Many such contingent contracts were custom designed (sold "over the counter") and thus had no secondary market. The spread of these unregulated and unregistered instruments was contested by the Commodity Futures Trading

Commission (CFTC), which oversaw the Chicago futures markets. This effort did not succeed. The Commodity Futures Modernization Act of 2000 clarified that most over-the-counter derivatives transactions would be overseen under general federal "safety and soundness" guidelines, and would not be subject to either the CFTC or to laws governing financial securities. This pushed the door to the post-regulation era fully open.

Facilitating the rise of securities-based risk-taking was the structural current-account deficit of the US economy; this deficit created a chronic capital-account surplus, which resulted in billions of dollars annually of overseas earnings deposited in US banks and funds and, in turn, invested in US-dollar-denominated securities. Overseas investors did not lead the charge into speculative position-taking, but their dollar inflows maintained liquidity in markets that became increasingly dependent on overnight financing. Ironically, the lion's share of the securitized credit (known as collateralized debt obligations, or CDOs) was financed by credit-default swaps, instruments that originated in the market for insuring against downside subprime risk.[5]

Given the pro-liberalization sentiment of national authorities in the US and Europe, the protocols approved in 1986 to guard against the recurrence of a money-center bank meltdown (as had happened in the Latin American debt crisis) were effectively suspended. These older—Basel I—rules had imposed uniform asset-based capital requirements on large multinational banks. Under the proposed Basel II rules, ratio tests would be replaced by a requirement that all large banks run their own stress tests designed to test whether individual mixtures of derivatives, futures-market commitments, and so on, would survive various worst-case scenarios. In effect, banks' large CDO volumes were not counted against required capital, nor were their contingent obligations based on their derivatives positions subjected to regulatory scrutiny. This amounted to regulatory surrender, a green flag for further bank innovation and combination.

Evaluating Financial Consolidation in the Post-regulation Era

Reflecting changed circumstances in institutional developments, the focus of research on bank mergers shifted in several ways after 2000. For one thing, more studies of cross-border mergers were produced. These studies used traditional approaches—event studies and ratio analysis—and generally concluded that cross-border mergers had positive impacts on bank stockowners and on institutional cost levels. Generally, these studies take as a premise that banking performance improves because more efficient foreign firms enter less efficient domestic markets; see Buch and DeLong (2004, 2008), Pozzolo (2008), and Fraser and Zhang (2009).

In another shift, Europe received more attention. Altunbas and Marqués (2008) found bank mergers in Europe would increase bank efficiency; Cabral, Dierick, and Vesala (2002) argued that mergers would facilitate financial integration; and Méon and Weill (2005) argued that they would help European banks reduce home-lending bias by diversifying their loans.

Countering this optimism that mergers would improve European banking were a set of more skeptical results based primarily on US data. Many studies found that mergers had negative impacts on small businesses' access to credit: higher post-merger interest rates (Montoriol-Garriga 2008); loss of access to credit (Degryse et al. 2004); and increased non-price terms or a deterioration in service provision (Scott and Dunkelberg 2003). An article surveying the post-2000 literature (DeYoung et al. 2009) acknowledges these difficulties, but points to the counter-finding that small firms eventually identify satisfactory substitute sources of credit.

In another new thread, some papers acknowledged the need to explain the lack of compelling evidence for the beneficial effects of bank mergers. DeLong (2003) argues that this "paradox" arises because benefits from mergers are realized only in the long run, not the short run. In another paper, she and a co-author argue that academic studies have not found "value creation in bank mergers…[because] until recently, large bank acquisitions were a new phenomenon, with no best practices history to inform bank managers or market investors" (DeLong and DeYoung 2007: 181). The authors argue bankers and investors can only "learn by observing information that spills over from previous bank mergers" (ibid. 181), because "the banking industry experienced a series of substantial and unpredictable strategic shocks during the 1980s and 1990s" (ibid. 182), including the end of prohibitions against interstate banking.

The increasing level of banking concentration and frequency of financial crises led to new research on the relationships among concentration, competition, and stability. During the Asian crisis, World Bank researchers constructed a database on financial crises drawn from across the globe over the past 50 years. Included were data on financial structure. These data have been used to explore interrelationships between regulation, concentration, and outcomes in banking markets. Demirgüç-Kunt and Levine (2004) conclude—based on 150 countries' experience with financial crisis, financial structure, and development—that maintaining outside investors' legal rights and efficient contract enforcement will insure effective financial-sector development. Barth, Caprio, and Levine (2004) used a 107-country study to show that direct government regulation of banking markets is not effective, and leads often to fragility. Financial development and stability is better fostered by empowering and properly incentivizing private-sector corporate control of banks. Beck, Demirgüç-Kunt, and Levine (2006) use data from 69 countries from 1980 to 1997 to show—after controlling for regulatory and macroeconomic policies, and nation-specific shocks—that systematic banking crises are less likely in countries with more concentrated banking systems.

The summary of banking-structure research by Berger et al. (2004) relies heavily on the results from this new approach. They conclude that markets can be both competitive and concentrated: monopoly or oligopoly power does not in itself imply banks are unfairly taking rents from customers. Further, more concentrated banking markets can be more stable and less crisis prone. Paralleling the Federal Reserve's regulatory approach, this conclusion from research constitutes a green flag for market-driven, lightly regulated bank consolidation.

Banking Strategies and Acquisitions in the Post-regulation Era

As large banks jumped to exploit the possibilities of this new competitive landscape, they found competition on two fronts. On the consumer-services front, resurgent money-center banks faced super-regional banks and well-established regional competitors. On the securitization and derivatives front, they faced US investment banks and foreign competitors. As noted above, banks have had to choose whether to try to walk one of two paths (or whether to try to walk both): to continue to generate income by taking deposits from and making loans to an established customer base, or to generate income from point-in-time transactions in markets for financial services, securitized credit, derivatives, and swaps. Healthy industry profits and equities prices facilitated banks' use of M&As to move in one or the other direction as this post-regulation era dawned.

Consider several examples. Super-regional banks raced to consolidate and add market share. NationsBank was at the front of this line; it followed its 1987 purchase of Texas' RepublicBank with purchases of C&S/Sovran of Georgia (1991), Maryland National (1993), BankSouth (1995), Boatmen's Bancshares of Missouri (1996), Barnett Bank of Florida (1997), Montgomery Securities (1997), and then Bank of America (1998), whose name it took on. Meanwhile, Wachovia merged with First Union in September 2001, and bought the California-based and then the second largest thrift in the US, Golden West Financial, for $25 billion in May 2006. In May 2007, Wachovia purchased AG Edwards, the second largest US retail brokerage. Washington Mutual (WaMu), which had de-mutualized in 1983, expanded its retail banking operations with 1990s purchases of banks in Washington, Utah, and Oregon, with the 1997 and 1998 purchases of California's Great Western and Home Savings, and also the 2002 purchase of Dime Bancorp. These mergers made WaMu the largest thrift in the US. It also moved aggressively to expand its mortgage and credit-card lending via acquisitions: in 2001 and 2002, it acquired PNC Mortgage, Fleet Mortgage, and Homeside Lending (mortgages); then in 2005, it bought Providian Financial Corporation (credit cards).

Among money-center and investment banks, acquisitions and mergers occurred at no less hectic a pace. Apart from the Citigroup-Travelers merger, other notable deals included the February 1997 purchase by Morgan Stanley of Dean Witter, Discover, the third largest US retail broker and a leading credit-card provider. Chase acquired the British investment-banking house Robert Fleming Holdings in April 2000, and then in September 2000 purchased JPMorgan, the fifth largest US commercial bank, for $36 billion. In February 1999, Deutsche Bank took over the stumbling Bankers Trust to build up its trading and investment banking capacity. In July 2000, Switzerland's UBS purchased the brokerage firm PaineWebber for $12 billion. A month later, Credit Suisse First Boston acquired the brokerage firm Donaldson, Lufkin, & Jenrette.

One indication of the frantic pace of mergers in those years is that of the 25 largest US BHCs as of December 1997, only 13 remained in December 2004 (and another nine of those 13 would be bought out or merged by December 2008). The growth of super-regionals and the mergers and failures of money-center banks had eliminated these two categories. For example, in 1999, HSBC, which had entered the US via its purchase of Marine Midland of Buffalo in 1980, bought Republic National Bank, an old-line money-center bank, and moved its headquarters to New York City. By 2007, US retail banking was dominated by three giant BHCs (BankAmerica, JPMorgan Chase, and Citi) who dominated the market, with Wachovia and Wells Fargo close behind. Meanwhile, US investment banking was dominated by four surviving firms—Goldman Sachs, Morgan Stanley, Lehman Brothers, and Bear Stearns.

In Europe, an even more complex scenario played out in the 2000s. A thick competition among large banks was sustained by several factors: the existence of banking-firm champions in several different nations; the competition between Wall Street and the City of London, and the fact that continental Europe had no financial center of equal status; and the widening market possibilities created by the EU and the opening of Eastern Europe. So while there were only two US banks in 2004 that had more than 50% of the assets of the largest US bank, there were 11 banks with more than 50% of the largest European bank's assets. In 2007 and 2010, there were still seven European banks in this category. Further, this competition at the top was unstable, as in the US. Seven of the top 25 European banks (measured by tier-one capital) as of 2000 no longer existed in 2008.[6]

So if 1990s European mergers had focused on bolstering domestic market position, the most significant 2000s mergers in Europe were expansion oriented. Some centered on opening new customer markets: for example, the Italian bank Unicredit bought Germany's HypoVereinsbank in 2005, while Santander bought Abbey National of the UK in 2004. Halifax Bank merged with the Bank of Scotland in 2001 to form HBOS, which specialized in mortgage lending. Other banks—among them UBS, Credit Suisse, and Deutschebank—made moves and undertook acquisitions with the aim of competing more effectively for top-niche global status. The most dramatic cases involved the Royal Bank of Scotland (RBS). RBS bought National Westminster in 2000, a move that helped it become the second largest bank in the world. It then engaged in an extended battle with several other large European banks to buy the Dutch bank ABN Amro. After a multi-year struggle, a coalition of RBS, Santander, and Fortis (another Dutch bank) succeeded in 2009. The merger was completed just as the global financial crisis hit home. Fortis failed and was taken over by the Dutch government. RBS was taken over by the UK government.

The Financial Crisis and Geo-Economic Bank Mergers

A detailed account of the 2008 meltdown of the subprime, asset-backed commercial paper and interbank markets is beyond our scope. Instead, we focus here on one aspect of this crisis: the reformulation of financial structure that it triggered. For the 2008 crisis triggered a new phase in bank M&As—that is, governmental guidance for, and underwriting and subsidies of, combinations and changes in status for large banks and financial firms. The only governments that engaged in this behavior were those with geo-economic power. In effect, this most recent phase of banking-industry consolidation has been defined by the exercise of geo-economic power. How many of these actions were necessary to save the financial system from collapse is unknowable and is not considered here.[7] What is undeniable is that the government-led restructuring in 2008–09 has been so extensive and so forceful as to transform thenceforward the fundamental categories of US and European financial structure.

The crisis was inaugurated in September 2007 with a run by depositors on Northern Rock PLC, one of the five largest mortgage lenders in the UK. This precipitous event, the culmination of months of mounting problems with subprime mortgages and of failures by small US subprime lenders, forced the Bank of England to make loans and guarantees available; in January 2008, Northern Rock was nationalized. In September 2007, the Northern Rock run and accumulated worries about securitized subprime paper led to a collapse in the asset-backed commercial paper market. This in turn forced the Federal Reserve and the Bank of England to purchase securities so as to maintain market liquidity; this forceful balance-sheet intervention ("quantitative easing") deepened in 2008 and has persisted into 2012.

The next major steps occurred in the US: in May 2008, Bear Stearns, one of the "big four" US investment banks, was sold for a bargain price to JPMorgan Chase in a government-orchestrated deal. The money markets wobbled further and liquidity continued to dry up. On September 14, BankAmerica announced its intentions to purchase Merrill Lynch, whose fortunes were declining precipitously due to its large subprime-debt exposure.[8] The next day, the investment bank Lehman Brothers failed. For the next month, a drama of global proportions ensued (Sorkin 2009). On September 15, a ten-day bank run began on WaMu, the largest S&L in the US.[9] On September 20, a New York bankruptcy court approved Barclays' offer to buy the investment banking and trading divisions of Lehman Brothers. The next day, Goldman Sachs and Morgan Stanley, the two surviving US investment banks, were converted into bank holding companies, bringing these two firms under the protective umbrella of the Federal Reserve without public hearings due to the "emergency conditions" (Board of Governors of the Federal Reserve System 2008) affecting the financial markets. On September 25, WaMu was seized by federal regulators, in the largest banking failure in US history; the next day, WaMu branches opened under the ownership of JPMorgan Chase. On the next day, Wachovia share prices fell 27%. On the morning of September 29th, the sale of Wachovia to Citigroup was announced; however, on October 3, Wells Fargo announced an agreement to purchase Wachovia. That same day, President Bush signed a bill creating the Troubled Asset Relief Program (TARP), whereby the US government allocated $700 billion to save the US financial system. About half of this allocation was used to provide equity support for a significant number of banks and non-bank financial firms.

European governments were equally involved in reacting to the crisis. The British government proposed ring-fencing the toxic assets on UK banks' balance sheets. However, market reactions and the complexities of EU policies precipitated other events.

On September 17, HBOS' share prices neared collapse, and it was revealed that Lloyds TSB was engaged in takeover talks which included partial nationalization. A week later, this arrangement was ruled out by EU officials (Parker et al. 2009). Subsequently, in October 2008, the British government infused £37 billion into RBS, Lloyds TSB, and HBOS. On October 5, the Belgian government announced its purchase of Fortis, and its subsequent sale of a portion of Fortis' assets to BNP Paribas of France. In December 2008, Lloyds TSB's takeover of HBOS was approved.

Over the next several months, the US Treasury Department and the Federal Reserve made decisions about which banking firms should receive TARP money and which additional companies should be given BHC status, respectively.[10] The Federal Reserve issued orders approving further BHC applications as follows: for example, American Express, November 10, CIT Group, December 22, and GMAC, December 24. Further acquisitions were also approved: for example, PNC of Pittsburgh acquired National City of Cleveland in December 2008.

The intense crisis period in the US, UK, and EU created pressures for legal and regulatory reform. Nonetheless, policy reforms were limited and partial. EU leaders made an effort to regulate hedge and private-equity funds for the first time in early 2009, but UK and Continental officials disagreed on the balance between freedom of action and control. Later in 2009, these same authorities disagreed over the imposition of restrictions on bankers' pay. Lorenzo Bini Smaghi, a board member of the European Central Bank, stated the core problem facing Europe financial reform succinctly in the *Financial Times*: the three aims of "financial integration, financial stability and national supervisory autonomy...cannot be achieved simultaneously" (Smaghi 2009). In the US, a financial reform effort started belatedly in 2010; the resulting legislation made only marginal changes in the degree of control over megabanks' freedom of action (Braithwaite et al. 2010). In late 2010, the G-20 nations made an effort to harmonize financial regulations globally via a new set of balance-sheet safety standards (Basel III); however, this effort has neither calmed fears nor been greeted as a fair and impartial new set of rules of the road (Braithwaite and Guerrera 2010).

CONCLUSION: RISING SKEPTICISM, UNRESOLVED QUESTIONS

The challenges posed by bank mergers linked to geo-economic considerations have received increasing attention in the academic literature on bank mergers. Altunbas and Marqués (2008) acknowledge that size itself matters in European mergers, and Carletti, Hartmann, and Spagnolo (2007) show how large mergers increase liquidity needs in financial systems. The survey by DeYoung, Evanoff, and Molyneux acknowledges that achieving TBTF status is a motive for banks contemplating mergers, and Ongena and Penas (2009) find that expectations of a government bailout have been an important motive for banks' bondholders. Carow, Kane, and Narayanan (2005) show that TBTF status leads to less responsiveness in the loan market, especially for smaller borrowers; and Jones and Nguyen (2005) show how granting TBTF to a wider set of financial institutions compromises deposit insurance programs. Finally, Valkanov and Kleimeier (2007) argue that big banks overcapitalize to avoid excessive regulatory attention.

This skepticism filters through an academic literature that continues to approach the study of mergers as an exercise in whether financial institutions whose activities center on classically defined banking activities—deposit-taking and loan-making—can increase shareholders' returns or operating efficiency through M&As. This chapter has argued that understanding bank M&As requires a broader lens, one which encompasses both the macro-structures that define banks' opportunity sets, and geo-economic factors that can facilitate banks' deposit inflows and underwrite their risk-taking. Taking these factors into explicit account helps to clarify why, when, and where bank M&As have occurred for different kinds of institutions in the past 30 years. Further integration between the use of established empirical methods and the analysis of strategic and macro-structural factors should lead to still deeper insights into both the causes and consequences of these combinations.

These insights are needed because of the profound confusion that currently exists over the post-crisis financial condition of banks—especially megabanks—in the US, UK, and Europe. The crisis of budget-cutting and national solvency that emerged in Europe pushed questions of banking reform there to the back-burner. In the UK, the implications of partial nationalization are still being sorted out; and in the US, banks have been pushing back against the 2010 financial reforms. In consequence, the value of securitized and formerly securitized assets that megabanks continue to hold on their books remains uncertain, and may yet plunge and force many megabanks into a further round of insolvencies.

But more profound still is confusion about what banking and banking guarantees are today. Banks have been defined for years as institutions whose primary activities consist of deposit-taking and loan-making; adding investment banks to this list, securities-underwriting and long-term financing would be included. Most banks below the megabank level continue to pursue these primary banking activities; experiments with alternative financial instruments and strategies have mostly led to failure, when banks at this level have tried them. High rates of failure have also been experienced by megabanks, especially in the post-regulation era. But those that have survived have been given renewed guarantees of their possible immortality through TARP subsidies, Federal Reserve credit facilities, and the conferring of BHC status.

Indeed, the granting of BHC status has further muddied the waters. Thanks to actions taken in the heat of the 2008 crisis, the protections associated with TBTF status have been intermixed with BHC status; and now some institutions that have BHC status are not primarily banks. Consider Goldman Sachs' CEO Lloyd Blankfein's statement to the Financial Crisis Investigation Commission in early 2010:

> In our market-making function, we are a principal. We represent the other side of what people want to do. We are not a fiduciary. We are not an agent. Of course, we have an obligation to fully disclose what an instrument is and to be honest in our dealings, but we are not managing somebody else's money. (FCIC, 2010: 27)

This Goldman Sachs banker is stating reality as investment banks understand it. The fact that Goldman and other former investment banks have aggressively resisted limits on their pay and on their firms' activities is, further, consistent with the eat-or-be-eaten approach that has come to define contemporary investment banking.[11] It is not surprising that these institutions used the "emergency conditions" of late 2008 to avail themselves of geo-economic advantages. But these are institutions whose philosophy of market action is only sustainable if they face real enterprise risk, wherein failure is a possibility.

If institutions which neither behave as depositories nor have depositories' balance sheets are given protections previously reserved to depositories, while those doing the work of depositories face rising failure rates and stagnant local economies, then banking has emerged into a through-the-looking-glass world, where nothing is as it appears. Whether such a state of affairs can persist, and even serve as the basis for new rounds of bank consolidation, depends on many factors, including how uncertainty about bank regulation is resolved in Europe and on how the the scope of banking activity, risk, and guarantees is defined in the emerging mega-economies of China, India, and Brazil. As Casey Stengel might have put it, most of our future lies ahead of us.

ENDNOTES

1. The framework set out here further develops an analysis presented in Dymski (2002).
2. The emergence of the super-regionals is related to the extensive losses and failures of money-center banks due to non-performing oil-patch and Latin American loans. For example, Continental Illinois and Manufacturers Hanovers Bank failed in the 1980s, and Bank of America and Citibank barely survived.
3. "Top 1000 World Banks," *The Banker*, July 2000, page 161.
4. See the Federal Reserve Press Release dated September 23, 1998, at http://www.federalreserve.gov/boarddocs/press/bhc/1998/19980923/.
5. Appropriately for the post-regulation era, these insurance contracts (offered most notoriously by AIG, as Lewis (2010) has documented) were not regulated as insurance, but instead were treated as derivatives subject to the 2000 Act (and thus left effectively unregulated).
6. These statistics were generated using the 2004 and 2010 *Fortune 2000* lists of large global companies and *The Banker*'s 2000 and 2010 listing of the 1,000 largest banks in the world.
7. One unresolved issue about the 2008 subprime crisis is precisely how much of what was done was necessary to get through the crisis. The rhetoric used in the heat of the moment, well described by Sorkin (2009), was of "saving" the US economic and banking systems. Boyer (2010) and Dymski (2010b) further develop analyses of power in finance.
8. This deal was approved by the Federal Reserve on November 26, 2008.

9. WaMu's $307 billion in assets (Sidel, Enrich, and Fitzpatrick 2008) would have made it the eighth largest US bank holding company at that time.

10. These two entities worked together closely in this period, with some analysis provided by staff borrowed from Wall Street megabanks (Sorkin 2009). The Federal Reserve also aggressively used quantitative easing to maintain liquidity in the US and global financial systems. At its peak in December 2008, the Federal Reserve had $1.5 trillion in credit outstanding on its balance sheet (Chan and McGinty 2010).

11. On Wall Street megabanks' resistance to restrictive regulations under the 2010 US reforms, see Harper (2010) and Guerrera and Braithwaite (2010). On the evolution of investment banking, see Cassidy (2010). European banks' resistance to taking write-downs on the sovereign debt they hold from distressed EU nations provides a parallel example.

References

Altunbas, Y., & Marqués, D. (2008). "Mergers and Acquisitions and Bank Performance in Europe: The Role of Strategic Similarities." *Journal of Economics and Business*, 60: 204–22.

Barth, J. R., Caprio, G., Jr., & Levine, R. (2004). "Bank Regulation and Supervision: What Works Best?" *Journal of Financial Intermediation*, 13/2: 205–48.

Beck, T., Demirgüç-Kunt, A., and Levine, R. (2006). "Bank Concentration and Fragility. Impact and Mechanics," in M. Carey and R. M. Stulz (eds.), *The Risks of Financial Institutions*. Chicago: University of Chicago Press, 193–34.

Berger, A. N. (1995). "The Profit-Structure Relationship in Banking—Tests of Market-Power and Efficient-Structure Hypotheses." *Journal of Money, Credit and Banking*, 27/2: 404–31.

——Demirgüç-Kunt, A., Levine, R., & Haubrich, J. G. (2004). "Bank Concentration and Competition: An Evolution in the Making." *Journal of Money, Credit, and Banking*, 36/3, part 2: 433–52.

Board of Governors of the Federal Reserve System (2008). "Order Approving Formation of Bank Holding Companies," September 28. Accessed at <http://www.federalreserve.gov/newsevents/press/orders/20080922a.htm>.

Boyd, J. H., Graham, S. L., & Hewitt, S. R. (1993). "Bank Holding Company Mergers with Non-bank Financial Firms: Effects on the Risk of Failure." *Journal of Banking and Finance*, 17: 43–63.

Boyer, R. (2010). "Capitalismes, Finance, Pouvoir: Leçons d'une Crise." September. Mimeo.

Braithwaite, T., & Guerrera, F. (2010). "Financial Regulation: A Garden to Tame," *Financial Times*, November 14.

——— & Baer, J. (2010). "Financial Regulation: A Line is Drawn," *Financial Times*, June 30.

Brock, W. A. (1983). "Contestable Markets and the Theory of Industry Structure: A Review Article." *Journal of Political Economy*, 91/6: 1055–66.

Buch, C. M., & DeLong, G. L. (2004). "Cross-Border Bank Mergers: What Lures the Rare Animal?" *Journal of Banking and Finance*, 28: 2077–102.

——— (2008). "Banking Globalization: International Consolidation and Mergers in Banking," IAW-Diskussionspapiere Discussion Paper 38, Institut für Angewandte Wirtschaftsforschung, Tübingen, January.

Cabral, I., Dierick, F., & Vesala, J. (2002). "Banking Integration in the Euro Area." European Central Bank Occasional Paper Series No. 6, December.

Carletti, E., Hartmann, P., & Spagnolo, G. (2007). "Bank Mergers, Competition, and Liquidity." *Journal of Money, Credit and Banking*, 39/5: 1067–105.

Carow, K. A., Kane, E. J., & Narayanan, R. P. (2005). "How Have Borrowers Fared in Banking Mega-mergers?" Working paper 2005–09. Federal Reserve Bank of San Francisco, March.

Cassidy, J. (2010). "What Good Is Wall Street?" *The New Yorker*, November 29.

Chan, S., & McGinty, J. Craven (2010). "Fed Documents Breadth of Emergency Measures." *New York Times*, December 2: A1.

Cornett, M. M., McNutt, J. J., & Tehranian, H. (2006). "Performance Changes around Bank Mergers: Revenue Enhancements versus Cost Reductions." *Journal of Money, Credit, and Banking*, 38/4: 1013–50.

Crotty, J., & Dymski, G. A. (1998). "Can the Global Neoliberal Regime Survive Victory in Asia? The Political Economy of the Asian Crisis." *International Papers in Political Economy*, 5/2: 1–47.

Degryse, H., Masschelein, N., & Mitchell, J. (2004). "SMEs and Bank Lending Relationships: The Impact of Mergers," NBB Working Paper No. 46. National Bank of Belgium, May.

DeLong, G. (2003). "Does the Long-Term Performance of Mergers Match Market Expectations? Evidence from the US Banking Industry." *Financial Management*, 32/2: 5–25.

—— & DeYoung, R. (2007). "Learning by Observing: Information Spillovers in the Execution and Valuation of Commercial Bank M&As." *Journal of Finance*, 62/1: 181–216.

Demirgüç-Kunt, A., & Levine, R. (eds). (2004). *Financial Structure and Economic Growth: A Cross-Country Comparison of Banks, Markets, and Development*. Cambridge, MA: MIT Press.

DeYoung, R., Evanoff, D. D., & Molyneux, P. (2009). "Mergers and Acquisitions of Financial Institutions: A Review of the Post-2000 Literature." *Journal of Financial Services Research*, 36: 87–110.

Dymski, G. A. (1999). *The Bank Merger Wave: The Economic Causes and Social Consequences of Financial Consolidation*. Armonk, NY: M.E. Sharpe, Inc.

—— (2002). "The Global Bank Merger Wave: Implications for Developing Countries." *The Developing Economies*, 40/4: 435–66.

—— (2006). "La Crise des Banques Coréennes après la Crise." ("The Post-Crisis Korean Banking Crisis"). *Revue de Tier Monde*, 186: 361–84.

—— (2010a). "Understanding the Subprime Crisis: Institutional Evolution and Theoretical Views." Kirwan Institute for the Study of Race and Ethnicity, Ohio State University, March. Available at <http://kirwaninstitute.org/research/projects/future-of-fair-housing.php>.

—— (2010b). "The Global Crisis and the Governance of Power in Finance," in Philip Arestis, Rogério Sobreira, & José Luis Oreiro (eds.), *The Financial Crisis: Origins and Implications*. London: Palgrave-Macmillan, 63–26.

Economic Commission on Latin America and the Caribbean (ECLAC) (2001). *Foreign Investment in Latin America and the Caribbean – 2000 Report*. Santiago: Chile.

Financial Crisis Inquiry Commission (FCIC) (2010). *The Official Transcript: First Public Hearing of the Financial Crisis Inquiry Commission*. Washington, DC. January 13. Accessed at <http://www.fcic.gov/hearings/pdfs/2010-0113-Transcript.pdf>.

Fraser, D. R., and Zhang, H. (2009). "Mergers and Long-Term Corporate Performance: Evidence from Cross-Border Bank Acquisitions." *Journal of Money, Credit and Banking*, 41: 1503–13.

Gilbert, A. (1984). "Bank Market Structure and Competition: A Survey." *Journal of Money, Credit, and Banking*, 16: 617–56.

Guerrera, F., & Braithwaite, T. (2010). "Goldman Lobbies against Fiduciary Reform." *Financial Times*, May 12.

Hannan, T. (1991). "Foundations of the Structure-Conduct-Performance Paradigm in Banking." *Journal of Money, Credit, and Banking*, 23: 68–84.

Harper, C. (2010). "Out of Lehman's Ashes Wall Street Gets Most of What It Wants." *Bloomberg News*, December 28. Accessed at <http://www.bloomberg.com/news/2010-12-28/out-of-lehman-s-ashes-wall-street-gets-what-it-wants-as-government-obliges.html>.

Harvard Business Review (1999). "Building Consumer Banking Internationally." *Harvard Business Review*, 77/2, March–April: 169.

Hyun, H.-J., & Kim, H. H. (2010). "The Determinants of Cross-Border M&As: The Role of Institutions and Financial Development in the Gravity Model." *The World Economy*, 33/2: 292–310.

Jones, K. D., & Nguyen, C. (2005). "Increased Concentration in Banking: Megabanks and their Implications for Deposit Insurance," *Financial Markets, Institutions & Instruments*, 14/1: 1–42.

Kane, E. J. (1989). "The High Cost of Incompletely Funding the FSLIC Shortage of Explicit Capital." *Journal of Economic Perspectives*, 3/4, Fall: 31–48.

Kaufman, G. G. (1995). "The U.S. Banking Debacle of the 1980s: A Lesson in Government Mismanagement." *The Freeman: Ideas on Liberty*, 45/4, April: 254–9.

—— & Benston, G. J. (eds.) (1990). *Restructuring the American Financial System*. Norwell, MA: Kluwer Academic.

Lewis, M. (2010). *The Big Short: Inside the Doomsday Machine*. New York: W.W. Norton.

Liang, N., & Rhoades, S. A. (1988). "Geographic Diversification and Risk in Banking," *Journal of Economics and Business*, 40: 271–84.

Méon, P.-G., & Weill, L. (2005). "Can Mergers in Europe Help Banks Hedge against Macroeconomic Risk?" *Applied Financial Economics*, 15/5: 315–26.

Montoriol-Garriga, J. (2008). "Bank Mergers and Lending Relationships." Working Paper Series No. 934, September. European Central Bank.

Mullineux, A. (2006). "Financial Sector Convergence and Corporate Governance." Birmingham Business School, University of Birmingham, June.

Ongena, S., & Penas, M. F. (2009). "Bondholders' Wealth Effects in Domestic and Cross-Border Bank Mergers." *Journal of Financial Stability*, 5: 256–71.

Pozzolo, A. F. (2008). "Bank Cross-Border Mergers and Acquisitions (Causes, Consequences, and Recent Trends)." MoFiR Working Paper No. 9. Money and Finance Research Group, Università degli Studi del Molise, November.

Parker, G., Croft, J., & Tait, N. (2009). "EU Ruling Threatens Lloyds' Branches." *Financial Times*, September 25.

Rose, P. S. (1989). *The Interstate Banking Revolution: Benefits, Risks, and Tradeoffs for Bankers and Customers*. Westport, CT: Greenwood Press.

Scott, J. A., & Dunkelberg, W. C. (2003). "Bank Mergers and Small Firm Financing." *Journal of Money, Credit and Banking*, 35/6, part 1: 999–1017.

Sidel, R., Enrich, D., & Fitzpatrick, D. (2008). "WaMu is Seized, Sold off to J.P. Morgan, in Largest Failure in U.S. Banking History." *Wall Street Journal*, September 26: A1.

Smaghi, L. B. (2009). "Europe Cannot Ignore its Financial Trilemma." *Financial Times*, June 21.

Sorkin, A. R. (2009). *Too Big to Fail*. New York: Viking.

Stiglitz, J. E., & Uy, M. (1996). "Financial Markets, Public Policy, and the East Asian Miracle." *World Bank Research Observer*, 11/2: 249–76.

Valkanov, E., & Kleimeier, S. (2007). "The Role of Regulatory Capital in International Bank Mergers and Acquisitions." *Research in International Business and Finance*, 21: 50–68.

CHAPTER 24

MERGERS BETWEEN PROFESSIONAL SERVICE FIRMS

How the "Big Eight" Became the "Big Five"

NICHOLAS C. FAIRCLOUGH AND
SAMANTHA FAIRCLOUGH

INTRODUCTION

This chapter examines the motivations for, and some of the issues surrounding, merger and acquisition activity between professional service firms (PSFs). In particular, we discuss how and why professional firms choose to merge with, or acquire the assets of, another firm, and develop a typology of rationales for merger, based on a historical analysis of the merger and acquisition activities of firms in the global accounting sector. The intention of our discussion is to build upon and expand the small amount of research which has considered the form, operation, and outcomes of mergers and acquisitions between professional firms, and to draw some conclusions about how and why M&A activity occurs between them. Our starting point is to outline the defining characteristics of PSFs, paying particular attention to the nature of their work and the professional human resources they deploy. Having established a working definition of what they are and how they operate, we argue that PSFs' characteristics raise distinctive managerial challenges which shape the kinds of organizational arrangements that are appropriate to professional activity. Our focus then turns to an examination of the evolution of a significant transnational professional industry—accountancy—during a period of intense consolidation, in order to identify the factors which motivate PSFs to integrate their activities with partners. We use our analysis of this industry to develop a typology of merger motivations for PSFs, and conclude with a discussion of the issues raised by our examination, and potential avenues for further research.

Why Look at PSFs?

Professional service firms are important organizations in an economy in that they provide particular, value-added, advice and services to businesses and government. They are composed primarily of professional individuals, that is to say, individuals holding a designated professional qualification (e.g. a lawyer), or having specific high value skills or expertise (e.g. a management consultant). The term PSF has thus been applied to, inter alia, accounting firms, law firms, management consulting firms, engineering firms, architectural practices, and investment banks.

There is considerable support for the assertion that PSFs constitute a distinct category of organization (e.g. Abbott 1988; Greenwood et al. 2005; Malhotra et al. 2006), with organizational and contextual characteristics which make them extremely challenging to manage. For Lowendahl (2000: 31) they are "substantially different from ... traditional manufacturing firms." Maister (1993, p. xvi) maintains that PSFs are so different that to apply theories from other forms of organizations is "not only inapplicable ... but may be dangerously wrong." These assumptions are not unreasonable given that studies have confirmed PSFs use particular organizational and governance arrangements which differ from those of other organizations (e.g. Greenwood and Empson 2003; Malhotra et al. 2006). Despite these acknowledged distinctions, the majority of research and theorization in the mergers and acquisitions literature has largely failed to recognize that PSFs differ in unique and consistent ways from traditional organizations such as manufacturing firms, and other labor- or capital-intensive organizations.

There are other good reasons to look at PSFs in detail. They are significant in the modern economy because they facilitate commercial exchange and the application of expert knowledge for business (Lorsch and Tierney 2002; Greenwood et al. 2006). A number of the largest European and North American PSFs in the legal, accounting, consulting, and investment banking sectors have transformed themselves into multinational practices by way of organic growth, and mergers and acquisitions. As a result, many have become "mega-firms" which have established an industry-dominant position in a global context (Lowendahl 2000). These "global PSFs" employ 5.6 million people and generate annual fees of US$795 billion (Managing Partners Forum 2010), and some are amongst the world's biggest and most geographically complex business enterprises. PricewaterhouseCoopers, the largest accounting firm[1] in the world, has over 146,000 employees and generates US$25.2 billion in revenue. Table 24.1 illustrates the size and scope of some of these leviathans in five sectors. Moreover, as exceptional forms of knowledge-intensive organization, PSFs are seen as firms of the future: exemplars for the structural and management issues which may soon confront other types of organization in a knowledge-based economy (e.g. Empson 2007; Gardner et al. 2008; Lowendahl 2000).

Table 24.1 Largest firms in selected professional service sectors*

Sector	Largest Firms	Turnover ($US million)	Employees (000s)	Geographical Scope Countries	Offices
Accounting	1. PWC	25,200	146	150	766
	2. Deloitte & Touche	23,100	155	140	700
	3. Ernst & Young	21,100	130	130	700
Engineering	1. URS	3,900	56	34	370
	2. SNC-Lavalin	2,860	13.3	34	350
	3. Atkins	3,200	16.8	25	150
Law	1. Clifford Chance	2,040	7.4	21	28
	2. Linklaters International	2,200	3.0[†]	23	30
	3. Skadden, Aarps, Slate, Meagher & Flom	2,170	4.5	13	23
Management Consulting	1. IBM Global Services	47,400	190	170	300
	2. Accenture	22,400	178	49	110
	3. Cap Gemini	12,005	83	36	N/A

Note: [†] Total number of lawyers. Total employees not given.
* *Source*: Firms' websites.

Distinctive Task and Resource Characteristics

Given their size and significance, there is a growing interest in how PSFs function (e.g. Greenwood et al. 2006; Lorsch and Tierney 2002; Morris and Empson 1998). This work frequently implies that professional firms share distinctive task and resource character-istics which shape their organizational arrangements, including their governance struc-tures and decision-making processes. In particular, researchers and commentators have noted that professionals are hard to direct because they enjoy high levels of autonomy within their working environment, which allows them wide discretion in the manner in which they carry out their tasks, manage their work, and develop their client relation-ships (DeLong and Nanda 2003; Greenwood and Empson 2003; Lorsch and Tierney 2002). In the largest firms, traditional authority and reward systems have become more problematic: these firms may have many hundreds of owner-partners, meaning that col-lective decision-making has become virtually impossible and the delegation of authority to designated professionals, committees, and task forces has become inevitable. In these firms, managing professional human resources has been described as "cat herding" (von Nordenflycht 2010: 160; Lowendahl 2000).

One of the distinctive characteristics of PSFs is that they are critically dependent on their ability to recruit, motivate, and retain a highly educated (professional) workforce in order to ensure their survival and growth (Lorsch and Tierney 2002; Scott 1998). These professionals are critical assets; they embody, operate, and translate the knowledge and expertise inherent in the firm's output. However, as individuals they are also highly mobile: although they are repositories of the firm's expert knowledge and social capital, professionals can easily leave the firm and exploit their knowledge assets elsewhere (e.g. Levinthal and Fichman 1988; Broschak 2004). Disruptions to a PSF's structure, culture, or management—such as those which occur during a merger or acquisition—can cause mass employee defections, increase turnover rates, and decrease levels of employee satisfaction and morale (Ashkanasy and Holmes 1995; Empson 2000; Greenwood et al. 1994). Thus, a significant challenge for the managers of PSFs is to not only pursue and secure client work and the professionals who will perform it, but also secure the ongoing commitment and direction of their staff. Balancing the needs and demands of highly educated professionals with a firm's requirements for growth and efficiency is a complex task (Teece 2003). In particular, managers of PSFs must recruit professional staff of appropriate quality, provide incentives for them to perform well, and satisfy their need for developmental and promotional opportunities.

PSFs have also been increasingly subject to a variety of pressures over the past two decades (Greenwood and Suddaby 2006). Deregulation, technological advances, growing global competition, and, especially, the increasing globalization of client firms, have all been significant forces in transforming PSFs into multinational organizations. Insurance, advertising, law, and consulting firms have all responded to clients' demands that they become international organizations, and provide a consistent and coordinated global service (Aharoni 1999; Aharoni and Nachum 2000). Together, these resource and contextual characteristics raise important managerial challenges which are not typically found in non-professional organizations.

Organizational Form

Researchers and theorists argue that one of the most significant responses by PSFs to the unique challenges they face is their adoption of "partnership" as a dominant organizational form (e.g. Gilson and Mnookin 1989; Greenwood and Empson 2003; Maister 1993). Partnerships emphasize collegial forms of governance rather than more formal systems such as those observed in corporations of equivalent size and complexity. Although not universally used, partnerships remain dominant in some professional sectors—notably law and accounting—and are proposed as an appropriate governance mechanism for delivering the necessary degree of autonomy required to motivate professionals (Tolbert and Stern 1991; Greenwood et al. 1990).

A partnership is a specific kind of organization, where ownership is vested in a group of professionals who are also managers and practitioners within the firm (i.e. the "partners"). Each partner shares in the profits of the firm but is also responsible for its business debts, taxes, and other legal liabilities, including the misdemeanors of other partners in the firm. Unlike a company, a partnership does not have limited liability, it does not have shareholders, and it is not subject to the kinds of reporting requirements that companies have to meet (such as publishing annual accounts).[2]

The partnership form is highly institutionalized in several PSF sectors, not least because it is a governance mechanism which encourages partners to maintain the quality standards of the collective whole, since each partner is at risk for the actions of any other partner that exposes the firm to financial or legal liability (Greenwood and Empson 2003).[3] Professional partnership structures embody notions of peer control and bonding between owner-employees, which establish strong social norms of mutual support and sanction, and discourage free riding or the maximization of individual interests (Empson 2007). The challenge of retaining valuable human resources and providing them with incentives to stay and perform well is also addressed by offering individuals the prospect of becoming a partner and therefore of sharing in the firm's profits (Gilson and Mnookin 1989; Starbuck 1992; Sherer 1995).

It would be an oversimplification to assume that all professional firms are the same and use the same organizational arrangements. In recent years, for example, many PSFs have grown exponentially in size and complexity, resulting in the abandonment of traditional partnership structures, which imply unrestricted personal liability on the part of the partners, in favor of limited liability partnerships (Empson 2007). The conversion means that members of the firm are able to restrict their personal liability to their capital contribution to the business, whilst still being organized as a traditional partnership.

For some PSF sectors, such as consulting and architecture, there are no legal or regulatory requirements to be constituted as a partnership, and firms have tended to be organized as companies, either private (e.g. McKinsey & Co.) or publicly quoted companies (e.g. Accenture), with limited liability (McKenna 2006; Winch and Schneider 1993). Despite these differences, however, research has found that these firms often imitate the cultural and governance structures of traditional partnership forms in order to address the managerial challenges associated with knowledge-intensive inputs and outputs (Empson and Chapman 2006). Further, there is anecdotal evidence to suggest they retain the "ethos" of a partnership in their internal and external relationships, and still embrace the values of peer control and professional self-monitoring (Empson 2007). The implications of this for our discussion are that professionals—whether as partners or employees—are frequently able to exercise their preference for autonomy and are often prepared to oppose decisions which attempt to merge or otherwise reorganize the firm, and may do so even if their opposition will have negative consequences for them by undermining the firm's ability to increase profits (Morris et al. 2010).

It is also important to note at this stage how differently partnerships can approach a merger or an acquisition when compared with companies. An incorporated institution, usually referred to as a company or a corporation, is owned by its shareholders, but managed by its directors. Companies, especially listed companies, are heavily regulated and in many countries, whenever a public or listed company becomes involved in a merger or acquisition transaction, they must abide by strict reporting requirements. For example, if the company is listed, it must adhere to its particular stock exchange rules on takeovers and mergers; it will have to comply with any other regulator-mandated takeover rules, take extreme care with any public announcements, and follow strict timetables and informational requirements. Further, because of the complex legal and valuation issues associated with mergers and takeovers, there will be the significant cost of advisers (investment banks, lawyers, etc.), who will need to be paid whether the proposal is successful or not, and the expense of sending information, and possibly prospectuses and voting papers, to shareholders. Finally, there will be the actual cost of the takeover or merger itself (cash, share issuance, etc.). Companies are also potentially subject to hostile takeovers by other companies, and significant costs can be incurred if a company decides to try and fight off such a move.

In contrast, partnerships are managed and owned by the same individuals; there are no shareholders. Further, there are no regulations that apply to mergers or acquisitions between such firms (except competition or antitrust regulations, if relevant). There are no public valuation issues, no need for expensive financial and legal advice, no strict timetables to abide by, and no possibility of hostile takeovers. Therefore the picture is far more straightforward, and the process much less expensive. Of course costs will be incurred, but they need only be a fraction of those associated with the acquisition of one listed company by another. This means that partnerships can enter into, and indeed break off, merger discussions more easily, and without regard to the considerations and consequences that would occupy the minds of the directors of a listed, possibly international company.

PSF MERGERS AND ACQUISITIONS— PRIOR RESEARCH

Despite the growth of research into the organizational arrangements of PSFs (e.g. Nelson 1988; Greenwood et al. 1990; Lowendahl 1997; Leicht and Fennel 2001), there is only a limited understanding of why and how mergers and acquisitions are undertaken between these firms. Previous investigations have found that PSFs often face difficulties in harmonizing the direction and culture of a newly created organizational context during the post-merger integration process (e.g. Empson 2000; Greenwood et al. 1994). In particular, the merging partnerships face a number of troublesome integration issues as a result of the inherent and unique structural and ownership characteristics of PSFs. Given that these firms are populated by strong-willed and individualistic professionals, studies find that the key challenge of the integration process is to negotiate issues of organizational fit and status differences. For example, Greenwood and his colleagues (1994) found that members of merging firms were frustrated by differences in beliefs and values between them, resulting in increased turnover rates and resistance by partners to new procedures and integration measures. Similarly, Empson (2000) found resistance to integration amongst professionals within a merged corporation, who refused to share knowledge and expertise with their new colleagues because they did not believe they would receive knowledge of equal or greater value in return.

Whilst these studies illuminate the culture clashes and dissatisfaction of partners and staff which can result from PSF mergers, their human focus fails to consider the economic or strategic reasons for joining with, or acquiring, another professional firm, and it is this aspect of PSF M&A activity which is of concern in this chapter.

M&A Activity in the Accounting Industry, 1980s to 1998: From The "Big Eight" to the "Big Five"

Having established that PSFs have distinctive managerial challenges and organizational arrangements, our discussion adopts an historic lens in order to assess how changes in the wider business, social, and political environment over the last 30 years have impacted the professional services sector. The aim is to discern the kinds of forces that have brought about changes in the merger and acquisition behaviors of PSFs. In particular, we note the effect of forces for globalization and transnational growth, which have opened up new international markets, resulting in more complex financial markets and the rise of a new generation of knowledge- and technology-intensive industries. In the face of such changes, the very largest PSFs have had to adapt, growing rapidly in both the scale and scope of services they offer, in order to keep pace with clients' demands (Aharoni and Nachum 2000).

Whilst these pressures for growth have been felt across a range of professional service contexts, we have chosen to examine PSFs' impetus for merger by analyzing the evolution of international accounting firms during the years 1985–98, a period during which there was a significant amount of industry consolidation to reduce the so-called "Big Eight" accounting firms (Arthur Andersen; Arthur Young & Co.; Coopers & Lybrand; Ernst & Whinney; Deloitte Haskins and Sells; Peat Marwick; Price Waterhouse; and Touche Ross) down to the "Big Five" (Ernst & Young; Deloitte & Touche; PricewaterhouseCoopers; Arthur Andersen; and KPMG). These organizations were amongst the very largest PSFs in the world, their consolidation illustrating the effect of client-driven changes on a significant professional service industry.

Along with law firms, accounting firms have been described as "classic PSFs" that demonstrate the "archetypal view of the professions" (von Nordenflycht 2010: 165). In particular, we note that, because of regulatory or legal requirements, accounting firms are almost always constituted as partnerships (with unlimited liability, or as limited liability partnerships), and as such exhibit many of the traditional features of PSFs described earlier. We consider these "Big Eight" firms to be exemplar organizations, and their behavior to be illustrative of the kinds of issues and responses typical of PSFs more broadly.

We propose that the story of how a series of mergers at the elite end of the accounting industry reduced the "Big Eight" to the "Big Five" is one that illustrates many of the rationales driving merger behavior between PSFs. Our analysis of this period of consolidation also demonstrates how merger and acquisition behavior responded to adjustments in the industry environment, particularly in respect of the changing demands of an increasingly international client base.

The 1980s: The "Big Eight" and KMG

During the 1980s, the accountancy field was dominated by an oligopoly of eight large, multinational firms with Anglo-American roots; all were the product of a steady series of mergers dating back to the late 19th century (Wootton et al. 2003; Allen and McDermott 1993; Jones 1995). Arguably, however, one might also add a ninth firm, Klynveld Main Goerdeler (KMG). Founded in 1979 from the merger of a number of leading firms in several major European countries, and firms in the US, UK, and Australia, its creation was an attempt to resist the encroachment of the "Big Eight" into Europe and to preserve the blue-chip client lists of its original constituent firms (Cypert 1991). Although perhaps left out of the prevailing nomenclature due to its relatively small presence in North America, it was "the only alternative comparable in overall strength to the US-dominated Big Eight firms... [and]... the largest international organization outside the United States" (McKinsey Report 1985, cited in Cypert 1991).

The 1980s was a watershed for the accounting industry. International trade flourished, financial markets became more integrated, emergent economies began to take advantage of the liberalization of international trade, and companies became far more global in their strategic thinking as they looked to take advantage of new markets and possibilities (Ghemawat 2007, 2008). As recently as the 1970s, accounting firms provided only a handful of products—auditing, tax advice, estate planning, and management consulting—and a cartel-like camaraderie had prevailed amongst the leading firms. However, thrust into a new era of competition, firms began to branch out into new products and jurisdictions beyond their regular audit work, cutting fees and sometimes even stealing clients from one another. As the senior partner of Deloitte Haskins & Sells noted in 1985, "[before the 1980s] most firms wouldn't be caught dead swiping a competitor's client... five years ago if a client of another firm came to me and complained about the service, I would have immediately warned the other firm's chief executive... Today, I try to take away his client" (*Wall Street Journal* 1985a).

This emerging context presented the "Big Eight" with a number of specific challenges, and in part shaped their responses. In particular, they faced: (i) pressures for international expansion due to the globalization of their clients, requiring that they establish a global presence in order to service them appropriately; (ii) concern that heightened M&A activities around the globe could result in fewer clients, given that each merger or acquisition meant the loss of an actual or potential audit client; (iii) the lure of new opportunities resulting from "Big Bang"[4] and the deregulation of many financial services activities; (iv) the prospect of entering new markets in Japan and the Pacific Rim as these economies became more significant on the world stage; (v) increasing income streams from consulting and other non-audit services; (vi) rampant growth in revenues amongst the largest firms, which created expectations of, and pressure for, continued growth; (vii) moves by the largest firms to increase capacity and geographic spread by "hoovering up" smaller accounting firms (between 1982 and 1985 the eight largest US accounting firms merged with 50 smaller accounting firms, whilst the next largest eight saw over 100 mergers (Wootton et al. 2003)); and (viii) an awareness of the increasing importance of the European market after 1992, prompting the need for a credible European presence.

It was predominantly this last point which made KMG such an attractive target, and led ultimately to the formation of KPMG in 1987. However, for the "Big Eight," each of these factors contributed to a greater or lesser degree to the drive for growth, increased profits, and the desire to remain in the top tier of the profession (for a timeline of consolidation through merger between 1985 and 1998, see Figure 24.1).

Peat Marwick International and KMG

The first significant alliance/merger amongst the elite firms was that of Peat Marwick, an Anglo-US firm with a strong presence in North America, and KMG, whose strong European credentials made it *sui generis* amongst the leading international firms. Although it engaged in preliminary talks with six different members of the Big Eight in 1985, KMG ultimately settled into serious discussions with Peat Marwick. Although those talks failed, the firms began negotiations again in mid-1987 which led, ultimately, to formal agreement to merge later that year (*Financial Times* 1987). The merger made strong strategic sense to both firms. Over two-thirds of Peat's worldwide revenues were from US operations, whilst only 23% of KMG's revenues came from the US. Moreover, Main Hurdman, KMG's US member firm, was falling further behind its rivals in the Big Eight, was only the tenth largest firm in the US by revenues, and was losing traction in the race for recognition (McKinsey Report 1985, cited in Cypert 1991). The organization which resulted from the merger—KPMG—immediately became the largest accounting firm in the world, with revenues close to 30% higher than the next largest firm. Although an increase in size was important for both merger partners, the rationale for the union seems to have been largely driven by strategic "synergistic" reasons rather than purely size-orientated factors. As Arthur Bowman, editor of the *Public Accounting Report* noted, "size is a big attraction to audit clients these days, but these two firms also seem to mesh well in strengths and weaknesses," (*Wall Street Journal* 1985b).

Between 1987 and 1990, KPMG acquired a number of prestigious clients and increased its revenues by 44%, despite the fact that the new firm had 127 fewer offices and 510 fewer partners. Although the merger process was not without its problems, the new firm was a success and was the spur for the wave of merger activity which was to follow. The merger drew attention to some of the smaller firms in the "Big Eight," whose revenues, size, and coverage now appeared less impressive when compared with KPMG. Whereas previously there had been some proximity in the size and global revenues of the "Big Eight," the merger pushed KPMG far ahead of the pack, thus changing the field's dynamics irreversibly. The rest of the "Big Eight" became increasingly aware of the competitive pressures within the accounting industry and of the advantages in merging. As the managing partner of Arthur Andersen remarked, "the hurdles of combining two big firms' cultures are great, but if two that fit could do it, they could reap the benefits beyond size alone" (*Wall Street Journal* 1985b).

The birth of KPMG demonstrated several important dynamics to other members of the "Big Eight," and revealed that a successful fusion of two large international accounting firms was possible. In particular, the union confirmed that combined firms could gain access to clients that neither alone could get (e.g. ICI and Bertlesmann (*Wall Street Journal* 1989b; Cypert 1991)), and could reap economies of scale and other cost efficiencies that would make the merged firm a more formidable competitor. It also demonstrated that success was possible despite the fact that member firms in some countries did not ultimately join the combined organization (e.g. KMG's French firm, and Peat Marwick's Japanese firm). Given the increasing level of competition within the accounting industry, especially in audit work (Wootton et al. 2003), the merger was a savvy strategic move that demonstrated how a firm could lower its costs, increase the quality of its services, and become more attractive to its clients worldwide.

1989: Merger Frenzy

The "Big Eight" were only too aware that a merger between their number would propel the resulting firm into a dominant position (in terms of partners, professionals, offices, fees, and, arguably, prestige), alongside or even surpassing KPMG at the head of the field. Moreover, any merger would reduce the number of potential partners from within the "Big Eight" by two. This likely scarcity suggested the need to explore the potential for merger with others sooner rather than later. By 1989, the question was not whether there would be another merger between the "Big Eight," but rather who would merge with whom? As the trade journal *Public Accounting Report* (1989) asked, "Big Eight? Big Five? Final Four?" It was becoming clear that the elite firms were now only looking amongst their own number for partners, since these were the candidates who offered the best combination of size, geographic coverage, and reputation.

Ernst & Whinney and Arthur Young

Industry watchers and participants were thus unsurprised when, in May 1989, Ernst and Whinney (E&W) and Arthur Young (AY) confirmed their merger. Although the senior partners of the two firms were at pains to stress that size for its own sake was not an objective, and that the primary motive was to increase the firm's ability to serve clients (*Accountancy Age* 1989a), commentators and competitors firmly believed that the rationale behind the merger was "the belief that bigger is better" (ibid.). Indeed, the merged firm would be the biggest in Europe, North America, and the Pacific, and would be amongst the top three firms in the sector in all major trading countries. The merger announcement created media speculation about the future structure of the industry, with claims that "other large firms would have to merge to keep in touch" (ibid.) and that membership of the elite was contingent on size: "When there was just one really big firm it was possible for the others to survive. Now there are almost two…I guess the other firms will need to merge to keep up" (Jim Butler, Senior Partner at KPMG UK: *Accountancy* 1989a).

Industry experts stressed the difficulties of merging such large organizations due to differences in management and cultural styles. In particular, E&W had a strong top-down governance style, whilst AY was considered to be more decentralized in its management decisions: "the challenges to achieving and implementing any Big Eight merger are formidable and daunting and painful; that's because of the differences in firms' cultures, client positions and the differing growth patterns" (Touche Ross executive, *Wall Street Journal* 1989a). In addition, divergence in the firms' *profits per partner* (PPP) could create problems if the firm with the higher PPP feared dilution. Nevertheless, both found a significant degree of complementarity: E&W was strong in manufacturing and commercial banking, whilst AY was a force in high-tech and investment banking. Internationally, the combined firm would hold the top audit and tax position in most countries (Wootton et al. 2003), and would become the second largest firm worldwide in terms of consulting services.

Deloitte Haskins & Sells and Touche Ross

The merger to produce Ernst & Young (E&Y) was swiftly followed by the announcement of a union between the seventh and eighth largest firms, Deloitte Haskins & Sells (DHS) and Touche Ross (TR). The two appeared to be a good fit, with similar revenues, earnings, and PPP, and both had been looking for a merger in order to strengthen their position in the elite group and within the US market. There were thus several important rationales for pursuing the merger: the relative weakness of the two firms compared to their peers; the weaknesses of the two firms in the US; and the exacerbating factor presented by the E&Y merger, which meant that these two firms would trail the pack by an even greater margin. Further, the similarity of the two would make the integration process more palatable to the partnership: many partners wanted to avoid the repercussions seen at KPMG, where there had been "a sizeable exodus of former [KMG] partners" due to the fact that it had been "over-partnered in relation to Peat Marwick" (*Wall Street Journal* 1989a). Importantly, the mooted merger would be one between firms with similar PPP figures, unlike the apparent "shotgun wedding" that produced E&Y.

Although the Deloitte & Touche merger was a success in terms of logistics and competitive dynamics, the process proved to be far from straightforward. In several countries—notably the UK, Canada, Australia, and the Netherlands—the corresponding member firms did not merge. These "failures" indicate the difficulties inherent in trying to combine organizations made up of individual member firms, where direction can be recommended but not mandated. The union was also pursued and negotiated against the backdrop of merger talks between Arthur Andersen and Price Waterhouse, a combination which would have created the largest accounting firm in the world, surpassing

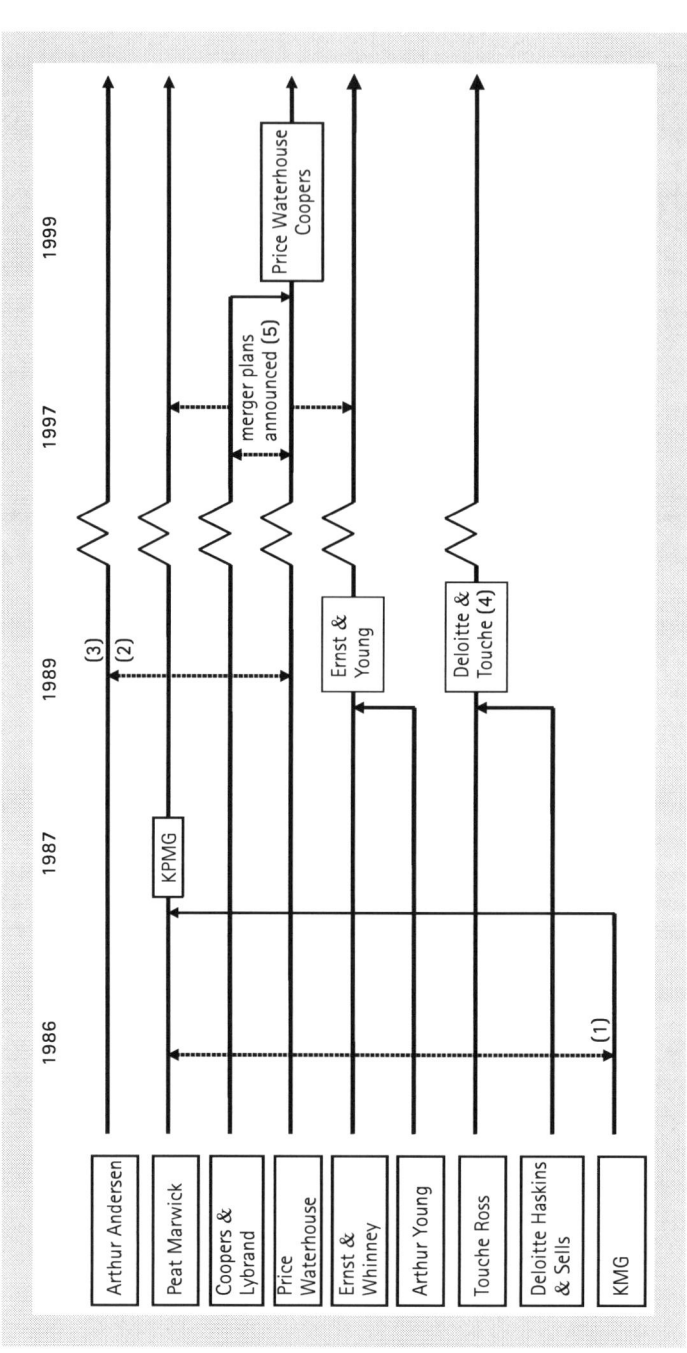

FIG. 24.1 From the Big Nine to the Big Five: 1986 to 1999

Notes: (1) and (2) Failed merger talks.

(3) Arthur Andersen and Andersen Consulting split up within Arthur Worldwide S.C. organization.

(4) In UK, Deloitte firm merged with Coopers & Lybrand to form Coopers & Lybrand Deloitte in 1989.

(5) Ernst & Young and KPMG merger, which would have created world's largest accounting and consulting firm (exceeding PwC by $5 billion), rejected by competition authorities in EU in late 1997.

both Ernst & Young, and KPMG. Failing to achieve a successful merger would have left DHS and TR even further behind the pack, and the consequences of this were no doubt prominent in the minds of senior management as the two firms made every effort to agree protocols and terms for the merger.

Arthur Andersen and Price Waterhouse

The impetus to merge because of a fear of being left out or left behind was perhaps best typified by the merger negotiations between Arthur Andersen (AA) and Price Waterhouse (PW). Observers and industry participants alike were surprised by the move: "It would be difficult to find two firms of such wildly differing cultures as PW and AA" (*Accountancy* 1989b). The fact that the firms entered into negotiations indicated how concerned they both were by recent merger activity and how that would impact their relative positions in the industry. AA's status as the largest firm in the US would be lost once the E&Y merger took effect, with the potential to lose both status and clients to the new mega-firm. The KPMG merger had already demonstrated that clients could be impressed enough by a firm's international coverage to switch their loyalties.

AA was also beset by internal problems, whereby its consulting partners were pushing for a greater share of global profits and increased representation within the firm's management structure given that the consulting practice was vastly outperforming more traditional audit work. Although the smallest by personnel numbers of the "Big Eight," AA and PW were ranked first and second respectively when measured by revenues per partner. Not only would a merger of the two produce the largest firm in the world, it would also instantly create a far more impressive and prestigious audit function than currently existed in either firm, and would help AA to counter-balance the growing unrest in its consultancy division.

However, the AA/PW discussions did not progress because of client conflicts, problems in the way the respective firms funded their partner retirement plans, and disagreements about how to combine their respective consulting businesses. At the end of September 1989, they announced that their talks had ended owing to mutual incompatibilities. Moreover, the possibility of further mergers within the accounting industry had drawn the attention of antitrust regulators in the US, and it seemed increasingly unlikely that the industry would be able to accommodate a consolidation to create fewer than five elite firms.

Coopers & Lybrand

During the height of the merger frenzy of 1989, Coopers & Lybrand (C&L) faced the possibility that it might be the only member of the "Big Eight" without a partner. Had all three merger plans come to fruition, it would have become a distant fifth amongst the "Big Five" in terms of both North American and global revenues. According to C&L's UK Chairman, the firm was not interested in a merger, and was critical of the rationales behind those enacted by its competitors: "you don't make a Mike Tyson by putting two middleweights together" (*Accountancy Age* 1989b). Nevertheless, rumors still circulated that C&L were engaged in preliminary discussions with KPMG, which was itself faced with the prospect of losing its crown to Ernst & Young as the world's largest accounting firm (*Wall Street Journal* 1989b). C&L were also linked with Spicer & Oppenheim International, the ninth-ranked firm globally and the 15th largest firm in the US, which indicated that it was also willing to consider a partner from outside the elite group (*Accountancy* 1989b). Ultimately, however, these discussions failed to gather sufficient momentum, suggesting perhaps that the issue of status was important, in terms of both how C&L members might accept a partner of lesser status, and how the merger might be perceived by clients and industry analysts. Given the recent frenzy of mega-mergers in the field, a union with Spicer & Oppenheim International could only be perceived as a weakening of C&L's capabilities as compared to its peers, and a dilution of its talent. Perhaps for these reasons C&L decided to go it alone, choosing to remain in last place amongst the "Big Six" rather than accept an unsuitable merger.[5]

The Quiet Years

The years from 1991 to 1996 were relatively quiet in terms of accounting mergers. Following the excitement of 1989, the various marriages were consummated as each new firm resolved local issues and amalgamated their offices, operations, and people. The beginning of the 1990s also saw an end to merger activity in the wider global economy, as more austere economic conditions set in and a global recession began to bite. Far from looking for growth, many accounting firms were looking to economize and were cutting their workforces. In addition, some were facing the real costs of the merger process. As *Accountancy Age* (1991) reported:

> At first it appeared as though the Ernst & Whinney takeover of Arthur Young had been well executed. But now...it seems certain that the deal has turned sour. An honest senior partner would admit that stitching together these mega-deals is harder than anticipated in terms of time, people and money...It has proved to be more expensive than was ever envisaged for all the mega-mergers—from accommodation to equalizing partners' drawings—and costs have just spiraled out of control.

It would be several years before the elite firms began to look for merger partners again.

1997 to 1999—The End Game

In September 1997, Coopers & Lybrand and Price Waterhouse announced formal plans to merge to create the world's largest accountancy firm. Outwardly premised on the notion that only a truly global firm could deliver the services required by international clients, C&L's Chairman, Nicholas Moore, envisaged a new business model providing "seamless global support," to be achieved through "global reach and global strength" (*Accountancy Age* 1997a). Both firms believed the merger was a near perfect fit—where one was weak, the merger backers claimed, the other was strong. Although C&L had previously criticized the "King Kong" philosophy behind the creation of Deloitte & Touche and Ernst & Young (ibid.), that same philosophy seemed to be at the heart of the C&L/PW plans to create an organization to dominate the profession like never before.

The plan raised antitrust issues. Regulation and competition authorities in the US, the UK, Australia, and the European Union quickly announced that they would be investigating the proposed merger. In the UK, for example, the new firm would audit 45 of the FTSE 100 companies, and in the US, 26% of all public firms (*Accountancy* 1997; *Wall Street Journal* 1997a).

The initial response from the rest of the "Big Six" was to downplay any suggestion that they might themselves entertain the idea of a merger, but within four weeks of the C&L/ PW announcement, KPMG and Ernst & Young proclaimed their own intentions to merge. This merged firm would form an even larger presence, accounting for over a quarter of the total annual revenues of the "Big" firms, and would further reduce the number of potential alliance partners for those remaining. The two firms left out of the equation, Arthur Andersen and Deloitte & Touche, would be left as the distant third and fourth largest firms if the proposed mergers went ahead.

Opinion was that the sheer size of the proposed mergers would provoke full-blown enquiries into the accounting profession, both in North America and Europe, and some even suggested that the E&Y/KPMG plans had been initiated to spoil the C&L/PW proposal by having the competition authorities reject both plans (*Accountancy Age* 1997b). *Accountancy Age* referred to the two proposed mega-firms as "the would-be Big Two" (1998a), and described the KPMG/Ernst &Young proposal as "a merger too far" (1997c). As 1997 drew to a close, both parties to the merger began to hesitate. For example, despite being touted as a "merger of equals," it became clear that the PW/C&L union would place PW in control of the most important parts of the combined organization, despite the fact that C&L earned larger revenues than PW. A senior partner in Cooper's consulting division sent a memo to his 1,300 consulting partners stating, "this is not a merger, it's a Price Waterhouse takeover of Coopers & Lybrand" (*Wall Street Journal* 1997b). In addition, the mergers of PW and C&L, and of KPMG and Ernst & Young, became subject to the scrutiny of the European Commission and the US Department of Justice, given that "the four combined firms would audit more than half of the 11,600 publicly traded US companies and 88 of Britain's Financial Times-Stock Exchange 100" (*Wall Street Journal* 1998). On another front, Deloitte & Touche went on the attack, running an aggressive advertising campaign which claimed that the planned mergers would cause irreparable competitive damage, and hiring antitrust experts to advise them on a strategy to oppose industry consolidation.

E&Y and KPMG called off their plans to merge on February 14, 1998, citing increasing regulatory pressure and considerable costs as reasons for terminating the arrangement. E&Y's senior partner claimed that there had been problems in reconciling the divergent cultures of the two firms, saying that the clash "became more noticeable as the regulatory review took longer" (*Wall Street Journal* 1998). KPMG said they believed that the planned union could have been a success in spite of the various regulatory and client issues, but a spokesman confirmed that "we didn't need to merge, we can grow alone" (*Wall Street Journal* 1998).

Following the demise of the KPMG/Ernst & Young merger, regulators became more favorably inclined toward the PW/C&L combination, which was finally approved by both the US Department of Justice and the European Commission during March 1998. By the end of the year, the new firm of PricewaterhouseCoopers (PwC) had emerged as a true global giant of 140,000 staff in 152 countries, and was hailed as "the benchmark against which rival firms are measured" (*Accountancy Age* 1999).

DEVELOPING A TYPOLOGY OF RATIONALES FOR M&A BEHAVIOR OF PROFESSIONAL SERVICE FIRMS

Having discussed the consolidation, through merger and maneuver, at the elite end of the accounting industry between the mid-1980s and 1998, we are now in a position to identify and characterize the underlying rationales for the merger and acquisition behavior of these firms. The following is a list of reasons why mergers are sought, and the benefits of these strategies.

Global Reach: Provision of Services to International Clients In New Countries

As client businesses look to overseas markets as a source of new revenues and other expansion opportunities, so PSFs are compelled to respond to the needs of these clients. In 1985, the European Union announced measures that would, by 1992, allow the free movement of goods, services, and capital between member states and harmonize their various fiscal, legal, and administrative systems. It was clear to the "Big Eight" that this new market provided significant opportunities for client growth, and they would need to prepare for those new demands. As an industry commentator noted at the time, "accountancy firms have realized they need a well-planned European strategy to cope with the fierce competition for new work ... [they need to be] positioned to meet clients' needs in individual member states and on a pan-European and international basis" (*Accountancy Age* 1988).

In the main, companies move into foreign markets either by creating a subsidiary in the new market, acquiring a local company, or teaming up with a local venture. For PSFs, a merger with a local firm, or with an existing international firm with a local presence, offered the best way to keep pace with the growing global reach of their own clients. In 1987, KMG was the largest European accounting firm, with over 1,200 partners in its EU offices (the next largest being C&L's 722: *Accountancy* 1989c), a string of blue-chip European clients, and unequalled European roots and credentials. These characteristics made it a hugely attractive partner to all the "Big Eight," and resulted in it having merger discussions with six members of that group during 1985 and 1986. Ultimately, however, Peat Marwick (PM) gained the prize.

The KPMG merger was a success in terms of its revenue and growth. Soon after the merger, KPMG's British firm gained ICI as a client from Price Waterhouse. As an ICI spokesman commented, "we manufacture in more than 40 countries and sell in 150, and after its merger, KPMG had a more complete international organization that served as a second intelligence source for us on taxes and business decisions...it's a great advantage to have your auditor with such a global presence" (Cypert 1991: 207). KPMG also acquired Bertlesmann, the German media giant, as a client following that company's purchase of US publishers Bantam and Doubleday. A spokesman for Bertelsmann commented that "we feel that [PM's] merger with KMG was a major reason for our decision to hire Peat...[the] recent merger of Peat in Germany with [KMG Germany], will give it our West German audit business too, meaning that it will be auditing 70% of our world-wide net sales...we couldn't be more delighted" (*Wall Street Journal* 1989b). In the year following the merger, KPMG posted revenues of $3.9 billion, a 20% increase on the previous year.

Need for Size and Scope to Service Client Needs

As clients become larger, so larger numbers of professionals are required to service their needs, but the necessary growth in professionals cannot always be achieved by recruitment and organic growth of the firm. Further, as clients begin to demand more varied or sophisticated advice—in the form of tax, management, human resources, and technology consulting—so firms need to be able to provide those services. Our analysis also reveals that accounting firms were increasingly providing corporate finance advice, and in so doing were encroaching into an area which was traditionally the preserve of investment and merchant banks. The biggest accounting firms recognized that their future growth lay in non-audit services. Also important was the fact that these firms were gaining consultancy business from organizations who were not existing audit clients. As the Chairman of C&L noted, "[management consultancy] is no longer just an optional add-on to the audit base. In many ways it is free standing and we are competing in an open market" (*Accountancy Age* 1989c).

The merger of E&W and AY illustrates how two firms can justify their decision to merge on the basis of a strong complementary fit: E&W had a stronger banking-audit practice, whereas AY had a stronger investment banking and brokerage firm practice. E&W also had the largest market share of hospital and nursing home audits, whilst AY had a strong practice in high-technology companies such as Apple and Unisys. Further, during the preceding five years, E&W's consulting practice had grown faster than its audit and tax practices, whilst at AY the opposite was true. William Gladstone, AY's Chief Executive, said, "being the biggest in size didn't drive us to consummate this merger as much as the synergism we hope to generate by bringing two strong quality firms together" (*Wall Street Journal* 1989a).

A Need to Remain in the "Big League"—Not Being Left Behind

For all leading PSF firms, there is a strong need and desire to remain amongst the elite, and firms will take whatever steps they can to ensure they do not fall out of that nomenclature. Elite firms in all the PSF fields can look to attract the biggest and most valuable clients, and can expect to charge the highest fees. They can look to attract the brightest and most talented to come and work for them, either as graduate recruits because they offer the best training and brightest prospects, or as lateral hires because they can offer lucrative salaries and the most prestigious and challenging work. Our story indicates that the "Big Eight" all felt a pressure to be at the forefront of the elite group—whether in terms of revenues, partners, professionals, or offices—and not be merely one of the pack. Although referred to as a collective group, at various times during the period there were substantial size differences between the eight firms. For example in Europe, following the creation of KPMG, the firm was more than double the size of the second placed firm, Coopers (*Accountancy* 1989c).

The formation of KPMG made the firm *primus inter pares* amongst the elite. This successful merger demonstrated that a "super-firm" was possible, and others felt the need to keep up with the rest of the pack. This was the prevailing sentiment following the E&W/AY merger announcement in 1989; industry players and watchers speculated that the other large firms would have to merge to keep in touch. As E&W's then UK Senior Partner said, "to be a leading firm you have to be in the top three" (*Accountancy Age* 1989a).

The AA/PW merger discussions in 1989 were undoubtedly a response to the proposed mergers of E&W/AY, and DHS/TR. After the E&W/AY announcement, AA's UK Senior Partner said that AA would consider a merger with any of the "Big Eight" (*Accountancy Age* 1989a). However, the choice of PW as a potential partner suggested that size, above any other single criterion, was the primary consideration for AA because, as industry insiders explained, the firms appeared to have more differences than similarities in their structures, strategy, and cultures: "there are some serious conflicts between the cultures of Price Waterhouse and Arthur Andersen . . . they are opposites, and more different from one another than from any of their other competitors" (*Public Accounting Report* 1989). Another likened the proposed merger to "trying to merge the Beefeaters into the Marine Corp" (*Accountancy* 1989b). Nevertheless, their combined worldwide fee income was estimated at $5,000 million, which was significantly higher than their nearest competitors, E&Y ($4,244m), and KPMG ($3,900m), and it was their desire and need to stay with the frontrunners in the field that played strongly in their move (Jones 1995).

As a Bulwark against Expanding Competitors—Strength in Numbers

PSFs continually face threats from competitors. These threats can come in the form of the loss of clients to a rival, or where a competitor has the ability to offer a unique service or a wider variety of services to a client. When two competitors merge, the new firm might have larger numbers of professionals to work for a client, or be able to provide better geographical reach. Further, because PSFs are critically dependent on their ability to motivate and retain their highly educated and skilled workforce, the loss of individuals or client teams to competitors can be catastrophic. Thus, firms will try to grow—and damage each other—by poaching talented individuals or groups from others through offers of more money, better prospects, or more challenging or prestigious work. By the mid-1980s, KMG was a firm facing up to the growth and competitive ambitions of the "Big Eight" as they looked to Europe as the next battleground. KMG's leadership began to question whether it could continue to hold out against this growing threat.

KMG was essentially "a loosely knit collection of international firms," who were so independent that the organization had never developed a formal international strategy (Cypert 1991). By 1985, KMG's leadership had become so concerned about the future that it hired consultants McKinsey & Co. to help it develop a plan to continue as a major firm. In both the UK and the US, KMG's member firms trailed well behind the "Big Eight"; further, McKinsey found that Wall Street banks actively steered international clients away from Main Hurdman, KMG's US firm (Cypert 1991). Despite some in the organization believing that KMG could remain independent and successful, others thought that its future lay in a merger with one of the "Big Eight." Industry experts also believed that KMG had to find a partner if it was to remain successful.

In 1986 KMG lost its Canadian firm, Thorne Riddell, to E&Y, and its Japanese firm, Sanwa Audit, to Tohmatsu. The loss of these two firms severely damaged KMG's network and its international credentials. The defections were blamed on the fact that these firms had been enthusiastic supporters of the merger discussions with Peat Marwick during 1985, and both had become disillusioned when those talks failed: "[the losses were] the clear result of not getting [merger discussions] on the road last September" (KMG's Chairman: *Accountancy Age* 1986). The twin threats of aggressive competition from the "Big Eight" and the possible loss of further members of the network were critical. However, in agreeing to merge with Peat Marwick in 1987, KMG's partners managed to secure their future as members of what was to be the world's preeminent firm.

Remaining Viable—for example, Spicer & Oppenheim in the UK Switching Allegiances

The story of Spicer & Oppenheim (S&O), the ninth largest firm in the UK in 1990, illustrates how firms can look to a merger to ensure their ongoing viability in the face of

severe, potentially terminal, difficulties. S&O was a "second-tier" firm with a strong reputation in London, and a client list which included many leading investment banks and
law firms. During the early 1980s it had been very successful in gaining business from
the development of the capital markets and financial sector in London. However, it
began to lose clients to the "Big Eight" after "Big Bang" in 1986, and then its fee income
slumped sharply following the stock market crash in 1987. In 1990 it became involved in
two of the biggest financial collapses of the decade, Barlow Clowes and Atlantic
Computers. In the latter case alone, S&O faced potential damages of up to $1.5 billion,
which was vastly in excess of the firm's insurance coverage, leaving the possibility of
plaintiffs chasing the firm's individual partners (*Financial Times* 1990).

The firm had been approached by "Big Eight" firms several times during the late 1980s,
but had opted to remain a member firm of Spicer & Oppenheim International (SOI), an
organization headquartered in New York. However, SOI had shed 20% of its partners
following the 1987 crash, and by 1990 there were rumors that it had serious cash-flow
issues (*New York Times* 1990). In July 1990, facing a bleak and uncertain future, the partners of S&O voted to resign from SOI and join the UK firm of Touche Ross, thus preserving the firm's business and client list. The urgency behind S&O's move to find a
partner is demonstrated by the fact that the terms on which the merger was agreed were
viewed by the industry as less a merger and more a takeover by Touche Ross (*Accountancy
Age* 1990).

"Spoiling"—An Oligopolistic Option

The idea of proposing a merger as a "spoiling" maneuver was demonstrated in the
announcement made by KPMG and E&Y in October 1997, which followed hard on the
heels of the PW/C&L merger announcement in September. By 1997 the elite group was
down to six firms and it was believed that only one further merger was possible before
the competition authorities stepped in. PW/C&L appeared to have beaten the field to
the punch, and the merger would create the world's biggest firm by some distance.

However, the subsequent KPMG/E&Y announcement put both proposed mergers
into question, since it was unlikely that both would be permitted, and a KPMG/E&Y
deal would completely dominate the global accounting field. Unsurprisingly, at the end
of October, the EU announced that an investigation would look to see if the proposals
breached competition rules. In the US, the Department of Justice had already begun
looking at the PW/C&L plans to see if an investigation was needed, but following the
KPMG/E&Y announcement it hinted that the effect of a "Big Four" would certainly lead
to an investigation (*Accountancy Age* 1997b). PW and C&L, and even some industry-
watchers, suggested that KPMG/E&Y were not really serious about a merger and were
only looking to frustrate the PW/C&L plans by forcing a full-blown inquiry by competition authorities into a contracting oligopolistic market (ibid.).

In February 1998 KPMG and E&Y called off their "marriage," declaring problems with
costs and client hostility, and competition issues, thus increasing the likelihood of the

PW/C&L proposal going ahead. The trade press had referred to the KPMG/E&Y plans as having been merely a "grand spoiler" (*Accountancy Age* 1997b). However, if the move had been a plan to ultimately derail both bids, then it was surely "one of the most expensive spoilers on record" (*Accountancy Age* 1998b).

Access to Capital

As the leading PSFs have increased in size over the last 30 years, in terms of partners, number of offices, and revenues, they have been able to leverage their growing financial muscle to negotiate better commercial terms with banks to finance their growth and activities. With annual revenues in the billions of dollars, the leading firms became comparable in size to some of the world's largest companies, and lenders were willing to compete for their business. When lending to traditional industries, banks can look to protect their interests by taking security over property, machinery, or products until the loan is repaid. However, PSFs do not possess tangible assets so the situation is different. The value in a PSF lies in the size of its revenue stream from client work, and also in the "pockets" of its partners. Therefore the larger the PSF, the more likely it is to be able to negotiate better commercial terms for its borrowing.

The size of the sums involved and the high regard in which the leading accounting firms were held by the banks is illustrated by the fact that, just days before the Enron scandal erupted in 2001, Arthur Andersen had arranged loans with Citibank and other leading banks totaling $700 million "on terms extended to only the most credit-worthy customers" (*Wall Street Journal* 2002a). Therefore, for two merging firms, the size and revenues of the combined entity would have real implications for the costs of borrowing to finance the firms' operations. For a small firm considering joining a much larger organization, the ability to access highly competitive borrowing terms would be a huge incentive, and could offer significant savings.

Insurance/insuring Capabilities

PSFs sell their services to clients on the basis of their skills and expertise, and the engagements concerned can involve tens of millions of dollars. Since there is always a risk that a client or third party may seek redress because of what they consider to be poor service or advice, PSFs will look to insure themselves against potential claims. However, during the 1980s and 1990s, a disconnect developed between the size of fees gained from the work being performed and the potential liabilities that might arise from doing that work. With mounting corporate failures and an increasingly litigious market environment, firms found it difficult to find insurance coverage, especially for high-value engagements and activities involving higher risks, such as corporate finance advisory work. The cost of insurance rocketed for firms, and in some cases, insurers were unwilling to provide coverage for certain matters, or capped their exposure in the event of a claim.

For accounting firms in particular, where the ultimate liability would fall on the partners, this was a significant problem.

A solution developed by Arthur Andersen was to create an insurance company in Bermuda that was owned by its member firms, and provided insurance coverage to AA firms (*Wall Street Journal* 2002b). This allowed AA to make substantial savings on the costs of insurance to protect it against liabilities to multinationals. Therefore for firms who might consider merging with AA, the ability to access significant savings on their insurance costs would be a major benefit.

Conclusions and Opportunities for Further Research

The specific issues and characteristics of professional service firms are underrepresented in the mergers and acquisitions literature. Even when researchers have addressed the subject of merger between PSFs, they have, in the main, looked at issues of integration and assimilation, and the problems arising from differences in cultures and status. In this chapter, our aim was to build upon the small amount of research which has considered the form, operation, and outcomes of mergers and acquisitions between PSFs, by developing an understanding of the rationales underpinning merger and acquisition decisions and strategies in the sector. Further, due to the fact that non-corporate, knowledge-intensive organizations have specific characteristics and considerations, and because they operate under particular environmental and regulatory conditions, our aim was to demonstrate that the rationales underpinning mainstream corporate M&A decisions and activity do not necessarily apply to these particular kinds of organizations.

The period from 1985 to 1998 saw huge changes at the elite end of the accounting industry which were driven by changes in the wider international economic, political, and social environment. Our examination of the merger and acquisition activity between the premier accounting firms during this time illustrates the kind of issues germane to professional service firms in general, and demonstrates the kind of factors that underpin their decisions to seek merger.

However, we do not purport to suggest that the rationales for merger developed above are exhaustive; indeed further examination of merger activity in the PSF sphere, perhaps in other industries, may help to further define and refine these rationales and justifications. Other opportunities for research may lie in an examination of the differing mechanisms by which PSFs actually consummate their union, and the rationales and justifications which underpin the choice of mechanism—we found suggestions that several methods are used. Further, when PSFs analyze the merits of mergers and acquisitions, it would be helpful to establish and understand what are deemed to be the important considerations and relevant time frames, and to what extent these are different from those seen in mainstream companies and industries.

Professional service firms constitute an important and valuable part of national economies, and make an incalculable contribution to the functioning of the global economy. However, our understanding of how these firms think and behave when considering and undertaking merger and acquisitions activity is relatively underdeveloped. Extant research has tended to focus on the human and cultural aspects of merger, to the detriment of developing an understanding of the motivations and justifications underpinning M&A activity; but on the basis that law firms, accounting firms, strategy consultants, and investment banks play key advisory roles in mainstream merger activity, it would indeed be instructive to develop a more comprehensive understanding of how these firms rationalize and justify their own behavior to their professionals and owners.

EndNotes

1. We refer to PricewaterhouseCoopers as an accounting firm, even though it provides a range of non-accounting services.
2. In the last 15 years, in many jurisdictions partnerships can now become limited liability partnerships; essentially these organizations have the same characteristics as partnerships but the partners do not face unlimited liability.
3. However, many PSFs, notably legal and accounting firms, are restricted to the use of a partnership or LLP structure by legal and regulatory constraints.
4. "Big Bang" refers to the reform of the London Stock Exchange and the deregulation of the financial markets in the United Kingdom in 1986, resulting in a rapid expansion in economic and capital market activity.
5. However, by October 1989, C&L had agreed a merger with the UK member firm of DHS, a firm which had refused to merge with the UK Touche Ross firm as part of the larger global merger of DHS and TR. The move helped C&L to become the largest firm in the UK in terms of number of partners, fee income, and markets (audit, tax, insolvency, and consulting).

References

Abbott, A. (1988). *The System of Professions*. Chicago: Chicago University Press.
Accountancy (1989a). "Medium-Sized Accountancy Firms Live in Hope." July 1.
—— (1989b). "Merger Mania—Will Coopers be the Next to Fall?" August 1.
—— (1989c). "Analysis of the Structure of the Auditing Profession." February 1.
—— (1997). "Regulators Expected to Look Closely at Mergers." November 19.
Accountancy Age (1986). "Analysis: The Proposed Merger of KMG and Peat Marwick." September 11.
—— (1988). "The Opportunities that 1992 Holds and How Firms are Gearing up to Meet the Challenge of the Single European Market." June 16.
—— (1989a). "Ernst and Whinney and Arthur Young—Trying Marriage for Size" (by Nick Speechly). May 25.
—— (1989b). "Accountancy Mergers—The Domino Effect that may Leave Some Standing." July 13.

Accountancy Age (1989c). "Accountancy Firms Get Flexible to Cope with Life after the Boom." June 8.

—— (1990). "Spicer and Oppenheim International Trawls for UK Replacement Firm." July 19.

—— (1991). "Painful Cost of Accountancy Mega-mergers becomes Clear." March 7.

—— (1997a). "The Global Imperative—Coopers & Lybrand and Price Waterhouse Merger" (by Jon Bunn & John Stokdyk). September 25.

—— (1997b). "Deals Face EU Probe." October 23.

—— (1997c). "A Merger Too Far." October 23.

—— (1998a). "Leader—Andersens—Back to the Future." January 22.

—— (1998b). "When Two into One Doesn't Go." February 19.

—— (1999). "BIG FIVE—PwC and All That." June 24.

Aharoni, Y. (1999). "Internationalization of Professional Services: Implications for Accounting Firms," in D. M. Brock, M. Powell, & C. R. Hinings (eds.), *Restructuring the Professional Organization: Accounting, Health Care and Law.* London: Routledge.

—— & Nachum, L. (2000). *Globalization of Services: Some Implications for Theory and Practice.* London: Routledge.

Allen, D. G, & McDermott, K. (1993). *Accounting for Success: A History of Price Waterhouse in America, 1890–1990.* Boston, MA: Harvard Business School Press.

Ashkanasy, N. M., & Holmes, S. (1995). "Perceptions of Organizational Ideology Following Merger: A Longitudinal Study of Merging Accounting Firms." *Accounting, Organizations and Society,* 20/1: 19–34.

Broschak, J. P. (2004). "Managers' Mobility and Market Interface: The Effect of Managers' Career Mobility on the Dissolution of Market Ties." *Administrative Science Quarterly,* 49: 608–40.

Cypert, S. A. (1991). *Following the Money: The Inside Story of Accounting's First Mega-Merger.* New York: AMACOM.

DeLong, T., & Nanda, A. (2003). *Professional Services: Text and Cases.* Boston, MA: McGraw-Hill Irwin.

Empson, L. (2000). "Mergers between Professional Service Firms: Exploring an Undirected Process of Integration." *Advances in Mergers and Acquisitions,* 1: 205–37.

—— (2007). "Surviving and Thriving in a Changing World: The Special Nature of Partnership," in L. Empson (ed.), *Managing the Modern Law Firm.* Oxford: Oxford University Press, 10–36.

—— & Chapman, C. (2006). "Partnership versus Corporation: Implications of Alternative Forms of Governance in Professional Service Firms," in R. Greenwood & R. Suddaby (eds.), *Research in the Sociology of Organizations: Professional Service Organizations,* vol. 24. Greenwich, CT: JAI Press, 139–70.

Financial Times (1987). "Accountants Cost the Pros and Cons of the Megamerger Game: How Leading Accountancy Firms are Operating within an Increasingly Polarised Profession." July 13.

—— (1990). "Survey of Accountancy: Focus on the Four Fs—Profile of Spicer and Oppenheim." December 1.

Gardner, H. K., Anand, N., & Morris, T. (2008). "Chartering New Territory: Diversification, Legitimacy, and Practice Area Creation in Professional Service Firms." *Journal of Organizational Behavior,* 29: 1101–21.

Ghemawat, P. (2007). *Redefining Global Strategy: Crossing Borders in a World Where Differences Still Matter.* Boston, MA: Harvard Business School Press.

—— (2008). "Reconceptualizing International Strategy and Organization." *Strategic Organization*, 6/2: 195–206.

Gilson, R. J., & Mnookin, R. H (1989). "Coming of Age in a Corporate Law Firm: The Economics of Associate Career Patterns." *Stanford Law Review*, 41/3: 576–95.

Greenwood, R., & Empson, L. (2003). "The Professional Partnership: Relic or Exemplary Form of Governance?" *Organization Studies*, 24/6: 909–33.

—— Hinings, C. R., & Brown, J. (1990). "'P²-form' Strategic Management: Corporate Practices in Professional Partnerships." *Academy of Management Journal*, 33/4: 725–55.

—— —— —— (1994). "Merging Professional Service Firms." *Organizational Science*, 5/2: 239–57.

—— Li, S., Prakash, R., & Deephouse, D. (2005). "Reputation, Diversification and Organizational Explanations of Performance in Professional Service Firms." *Organization Science*, 16/6: 661–73.

—— & Suddaby, R. (2006). "Institutional Entrepreneurship in Mature Fields: The Big Five Accounting Firms." *Academy of Management Journal*, 49/1: 1–21.

—— —— & McDougald, M. (2006). "Introduction," in R. Greenwood & R. Suddaby (eds.), *Research in the Sociology of Organizations: Professional Service Firms*, vol. 24. Oxford: Elsevier JAI Press, 1–16.

Jones, E. (1995). *True and Fair. A History of Price Waterhouse*. London: Hamish Hamilton Ltd.

Leicht, K. T., & Fennel, M. (2001). *Professional Work: A Sociological Approach*. Oxford: Blackwell.

Levinthal, D. A., & Fichman, M. (1988). "Dynamics of Interorganizational Attachments: Auditor-Client Relationships." *Administrative Science Quarterly*, 33/3: 345–69.

Lorsch, J., & Tierney, T. (2002). *Aligning the Stars: How to Succeed When Professionals Drive Results*. Boston, MA: Harvard Business School Press.

Lowendahl, B. R. (1997). *Strategic Management of Professional Service Firms*. Copenhagen: Copenhagen Business School Press.

—— (2000). *Strategic Management of Professional Service Firms* (2nd ed.). Copenhagen: Copenhagen Business School Press.

Maister, D. (1993). *Managing the Professional Service Firm*. New York: Free Press.

Malhotra, N., Morris, T. & Hinings, C. R. (2006). "Variation in Organizational Form among Professional Service Organizations," in R. Greenwood & R. Suddaby (eds.), *Research in the Sociology of Organizations: Professional Service Firms*, vol. 24. Oxford: Elsevier JAI Press, 171–202.

Managing Partners' Forum (2010). *Global 500 Annual Report 2010*. Available at <http://www.mpfglobal.com/system/file.aspx?fn=MPFGlobal5002010.pdf> (accessed October 27, 2010).

McKenna, C. D. (2006). *The World's Newest Profession: Management Consulting in the Twentieth Century*. New York: Cambridge University Press.

Morris, T., & Empson, L. (1998). "Organization and Expertise: An Exploration of Knowledge Bases and the Management of Accounting and Consulting Firms." *Accounting, Organizations and Society*, 23/5: 609–24.

—— Greenwood, R. & Fairclough, S. (2010). "Decision Making in Professional Service Firms," in P. C. Nutt & D. C. Wilson (eds.), *Handbook of Decision Making*. Chichester: John Wiley, 275–306.

Nelson, R. (1988). *Partners with Power: The Social Transformation of the Large Law Firm*. Berkeley, CA: University of California Press.

New York Times (1990). "Auditors Adjust to Desperate Times." November 5.

Public Accounting Report (1989). "Big Eight? Big Five? Final Four?" 12/19, October 1.

Scott, W. R. (1998). *The Intellect Industry: Profiting and Learning from Professional Service Firms.* New York: Wiley.

Sherer, P. (1995). "Leveraging Human Assets in Law Firms: Human Capital Structures and Organizational Capabilities." *Industrial and Labor Relations Review,* 48/4: 671–91.

Starbuck, W. H. (1992). "Learning by Knowledge Intensive Firms." *Journal of Management Studies,* 29/6: 713–40.

Teece, D. J. (2003). "Expert Talent and the Design of (Professional Service) Firms." *Industrial and Corporate Change,* 12/4: 895–916.

Tolbert, P. S., & Stern, R. N. (1991). "Organizations of Professionals: Governance Structures in Large Law Firms." *Research in the Sociology of Organizations: Organizations and Occupations,* 8: 97–117.

von Nordenflycht, A. (2010). "What is a Professional Service Firm? Toward a Theory and Taxonomy of Knowledge-Intensive Firms." *Academy of Management Review,* 35/1: 155–74.

Wall Street Journal (1985a). "Total War: CPA Firms Diversify, Cut Fees, Steal Clients in Battle for Business" (by Lee Berton). September 20.

——(1985b). "Peat Marwick and KMG Main Hurdman are Holding Preliminary Merger Talks" (by Lee Berton). September 23.

——(1989a). "Arthur Young and Ernst Firm Plan to Merge—Combination Will Create Top Accounting Firm in U.S., World-Wide" (by Lee Berton). May 19.

——(1989b). "Bottom Line: Peat Experience Shows Why Accountants are Rushing to Merge" (by Lee Berton). July 17.

——(1997a). "Levitt Says Wave of Accounting Mergers Could Affect Independence of Auditors." October 21.

——(1997b). "Coopers, Price Waterhouse Begin Vote on Merger, amid Concerns of Big Clients." November 10.

——(1998). "Ernst Blamed for Collapse of Merger." February 17.

——(2002a). "Andersen: Called to Account: Citigroup, Other Banks Set Credit Line for Andersen on Eve of Probe Disclosure." March 29.

——(2002b). "Arthur Andersen Insurer is Rendered Insolvent—Funds from Bermuda Firm Were Going to be Used to Settle Host of Claims." April 1.

Winch, G., & Schneider, E. (1993). "Managing the Knowledge-Based Organization: The Case of Architectural Practice." *Journal of Management Studies,* 30: 923–37.

Wootton, C. W., Wolk, C. M., & Normand, C. (2003). "An Historical Perspective on Mergers and Acquisitions by Major US Accounting Firms." *Accounting History,* 8/1: 25–60.

CHAPTER 25

EXAMINING RESOURCE AND EXPECTATIONAL AMBIGUITY IN TECHNOLOGY M&A INTEGRATION

ANNETTE L. RANFT, ADELAIDE WILCOX KING, AND JENNIFER C. SEXTON

> In short, managers of acquisitions face an ironic situation: ambiguity is useful—if not essential—during negotiations. Yet the very ambiguity that aids negotiating sows the seeds of later post-acquisition problems.
>
> (Jemison and Sitkin 1986b: 114)

The pace of globalization and technological change places significant pressures on firms to adapt (Agarwal and Helfat 2009). Technology acquisitions, acquisitions that take place in high-technology industries, represent one way in which firms can respond to the demands of their competitive environments. Acquisitions of technology-intensive firms are a significant portion of all acquisition activity in both number of deals and value of deals. For example, during 2006–10, approximately 14,000 acquisitions of US based high-tech firms were reported by Securities Data Corporation (SDC). Approximately 34% of all acquired US firms occurred in high-technology industries (SDC Database), with over $400 billion dollars spent on these deals during the same time period. In addition to being an important way that firms can respond to increasing competition and demands for innovation (Makri et al. 2010), these acquisitions can be an effective way for firms to gain valuable resources, technologies, and capabilities, and initiate strategic renewal (Graebner et al. 2010; Ranft and Lord 2002).

Knowledge as a resource has become increasingly important in today's competitive environment (Grant 1996; Makri et al. 2010). Through technology acquisitions, firms can access important knowledge, processes, and capabilities that may help in their own innovation and R&D processes (Makri et al. 2010). The acquisition of knowledge through technology acquisitions has become an important topic for both practitioners and scholars; a search of recent literature within the last five years resulted in over 100 articles written on the topics of knowledge transfer and technology acquisitions.

The process of acquiring another firm is fraught with ambiguities, however, as managers evaluate acquisition targets, define objectives, and pursue performance outcomes during acquisition integration (Jemison and Sitkin 1986a, 1986b). Exacerbating the ambiguity inherent in any acquisition process is the fact that many technology firms are acquisition targets precisely because they contain valuable firm-specific resources and technologies that are not otherwise easily imitated or developed internally (Capron et al. 1998; Dierickx and Cool 1989; Ranft and Lord 2002). Intrinsic characteristics of a firm's technologies and characteristics that obscure the link between these resources and firm performance (King and Zeithaml 2001; Reed and DeFillippi 1990) frequently contribute to the ambiguity faced by managers making strategic decisions during acquisition integration.

Reducing ambiguity about a target firm's resources is a key objective as managers pursue potential acquisition targets, conduct due diligence of the target, value the target accordingly, and then redeploy resources post-acquisition (Jemison and Sitkin 1986b). Although a major objective of the due-diligence phase of an acquisition is to reduce ambiguity about the target's resources, efforts to facilitate the completion of the acquisition may, in fact, prevent ambiguity reduction (Jemison and Sitkin 1986a; Pablo 1994; Pablo et al. 1996). Specifically, during acquisitions, ambiguity may (1) be embedded in a target firm's resources and the linkages among its resources, capabilities, and competitive advantage (King and Zeithaml 2001) or (2) arise as part of the acquisition process (Jemison and Sitkin 1986a).

In this chapter, we argue that (1) resource-based ambiguity surrounding the technologies and capabilities of the acquired firm, and (2) expectational ambiguity arising from the acquisition process itself have a direct influence on the pace of post-acquisition integration. Ambiguity arising from the nature of acquired resources and their impact on performance is difficult to reduce prior to the closing of an acquisition, particularly in the case of valuable technology-based resources and capabilities that may be a primary motivation for the acquisition (Ahuja and Katila 2001; Ranft and Lord 2000, 2002). Resource-based ambiguity, therefore, can generate expectational ambiguity through compromises made during the acquisition due-diligence process itself, as decision makers agree to hold off on articulating exactly how technologies and capabilities will be integrated post-acquisition in order facilitate the closing of the deal (Jemison and Sitkin 1986a). Expectational ambiguity arises as decision makers agree on higher-order objectives for value creation post-acquisition, but do not specify how objectives will be achieved *prior* to the closing of the deal.

By integrating our knowledge of resource-based ambiguity with our knowledge of expectational ambiguity that can arise during the acquisition process, we hope to contribute to two classic discussions in the literature regarding acquisitions of technology-intensive firms. First, we hope to contribute to the literature examining performance outcomes of acquisitions. Despite the preponderance of continued acquisition activity, traditional financial, strategic, and organizational perspectives of mergers and acquisitions have failed to explain disappointing value creation in these corporate events (King et al. 2004; Larsson and Finkelstein 1999; Pablo et al. 1996). Scholars have increasingly emphasized the importance of the post-acquisition integration process, where "the actions of management, and the process of integration, determine the extent to which potential benefits of the acquisition are realized" (Birkinshaw et al. 2000: 397). Indeed, it is during the acquisition integration process that *potential* synergy in an acquisition is *realized* (Larsson and Finkelstein 1999). Our first contribution is to examine acquisition performance outcomes by focusing on the acquisition integration process of technology-intensive firms through the lens of managing ambiguity.

Our second contribution is to isolate a specific dimension of the acquisition integration process—the speed, or pace, of the integration process. Several dimensions of the acquisition integration process have been identified in the literature. Haspeslagh and Jemison (1991) first identified the primary, yet competing, dimensions of (1) the need for strategic interdependence and (2) the need for autonomy post-acquisition. The need for strategic interdependence creates pressure to combine resources and break down organizational boundaries to create new value with the newly merged firm. The need for autonomy creates a potentially opposing pressure to spend time learning about the acquired firm and its resources and operations prior to combining resources and organizations. In addition to these two primary dimensions of post-acquisition integration, other authors have emphasized the importance of communications (Marks and Mirvis 2001; Schweiger and DeNisi 1991), target reputation (Saxton and Dollinger 2004), and the retention of key employees (Ranft and Lord 2000, 2002) as resources are transferred and shared during integration (Capron et al. 1998). There is general agreement in the literature on the importance of these dimensions of the integration process. Differing perspectives exist, however, among academics and practitioners alike, regarding how rapidly changes should be made in the newly acquired firm and how rapidly acquired resources should be integrated with the acquirer (Cording et al. 2008; Puranam et al. 2006).

Much practitioner advice, along with early academic research, indicates that rapid integration of an acquired firm and its resources is essential to realizing the expected value creation in an acquisition (Ashkenas et al. 1998; Kitching 1967). Yet in acquisitions of technology firms, slower and purposeful pacing of acquisition integration may be necessary to protect resources and create an opportunity for learning between the merging firms (Bower 2001; Cording et al. 2008; Haspeslagh and Jemison 1991; Ranft and Lord 2002; Véry and Schweiger 2001). These authors argue that a period of learning may be necessary before changes are made in the acquired firm, particularly when acquiring firms gain access to new technologies, knowledge, or capabilities (Chaudhuri and Tabrizi 1999; Ranft and Lord 2002; Véry and Schweiger 2001). Building on this logic, others have warned that "integration takes time, and pushing it too quickly can result in frustration or failure" (Goh 2001: 153). Time is necessary for learning and in an acquisition context, allows for reduction of ambiguity about the acquired firm's resource base and value creation.

In the next sections, we discuss these two specific types of ambiguity in an acquisition context. We first review the literature that examines resource-based ambiguity—ambiguity arising from technologies and capabilities. Next, we integrate resource-based ambiguity literature with literature examining ambiguity that arises more generally from the acquisition process. Finally, we develop propositions regarding ambiguity in a technology acquisition, the temporal pacing of the acquisition process, and performance outcomes.

AMBIGUITY IN ACQUISITIONS

Resource Ambiguity

Ambiguity has been described as "uncertainty about uncertainties" (Einhorn and Hogarth 1986). Factors that affect ambiguity include the amount of relevant data, the reliability and consistency of evidence, and clarity about the causal processes that generate outcomes (Einhorn and Hogarth 1986: S227; Ellsberg 1961). In the psychology literature, ambiguity encompasses not only the "random influences that affect outcomes from a well-defined process . . . but [extends] to uncertainty about the underlying data generating process itself" (Einhorn and Hogarth 1986: S227). In the strategy literature, scholars describe ambiguity as a cognitive construct that describes decision makers' understanding of the relationship between a resource, or set of resources, and its performance outcomes (e.g. Reed and DeFillippi 1990). Resource-based theory refines the notion of ambiguity by examining the sources of ambiguity—those factors that may contribute to the inability of one to fully understand the details of a cause-effect relationship between resources and firm success. The resource-based literature suggests two key sources of resource-based ambiguity (King and Zeithaml 2001).

First, ambiguity about a resource is generated by the characteristics inherent in a resource itself (Ambrosini and Bowman 2002; King and Zeithaml 2001). Resource characteristics such as tacitness, complexity, and asset specificity generate ambiguity that cannot be completely reduced, creating challenges for competitors to imitate and making these resources valuable assets for a firm (Reed and DeFillippi 1990). Because of their organizational embeddedness, these characteristics may even contribute to making the firm an attractive acquisition target (Ahuja and Katila 2001; Ranft and Lord 2002). For example, a high degree of tacitness, which describes the non-codifiable accumulation of knowledge and skills often gained from practice, tends to increase the difficulty in identifying and understanding a resource (Reed and DeFillippi 1990; Simonin 1999; Szulanski 1996). High resource complexity—where the resource involves a large number of interrelated technologies, resources, and individuals—imbues a resource with ambiguity (Mosakowski 1997; Reed and DeFillippi 1990; Simonin 1999; Zollo and Winter 2002). Second, the link between a resource and firm performance may be a source of resource-based ambiguity (Ambrosini and Bowman 2002; King and Zeithaml 2001).

The strategic value of a resource may be unclear because of attributes of the relationship, or link, between a resource and its outcomes.

In summary, one pertinent type of ambiguity in acquisitions is *resource ambiguity*. Resource-based theorists suggest that there are two sources of ambiguity: (1) the characteristics of the resource, or characteristic ambiguity, and (2) the characteristics of the relationship between the resource and firm performance, or linkage ambiguity. In other words, how does the resource contribute to a firm's competitive advantage? These two forms of resource ambiguity will be hereafter studied in this chapter.

Expectational Ambiguity

In addition to resource-based ambiguity in an acquisition context, there is *expectational* ambiguity inherent in the acquisition process itself (Jemison and Sitkin 1986a). Jemison and Sitkin (1986a) first described *expectational ambiguity* that can be created during an acquisition process as ambiguity about the means to achieve an acquisition's higher-order goals, performance expectations, and timing. This ambiguity may build during the pre-acquisition stages of due diligence and valuation. Managers make predictions and have expectations regarding value creation in an acquisition as they construct the deal. At times, to reduce the potential for disagreement and to speed the process of closing a deal, managers will agree to disagree or leave some issues unresolved until after the acquisition is closed (Jemison and Sitkin 1986a; Pablo et al. 1996). Although this practice helps speed the process of pre-acquisition activities, it creates ambiguity in the acquisition process—*expectational ambiguity* about how the newly merged firm will combine resources and create value during the post-acquisition integration phase. Due to the complex and often socially embedded nature of technologies and capabilities in high-tech firms (Ranft and Lord 2002), we argue that resource and expectational ambiguity may be particularly high in acquisitions of these firms.

A Model of Ambiguity, Pacing, and Performance in Acquisitions of Technology Firms

Due diligence is designed to reduce resource ambiguity in a target firm and to define the expected value created by merging the resources of two distinct organizations. The traditional logic of acquisitions is that effective due diligence allows the acquiring firm to price the target firm appropriately for the expected value creation of the organizational combination (Pablo 1994). This approach to acquisitions points to the due-diligence stage as the point in time that all ambiguity can be eliminated and valuation of the deal will be appropriately determined (Marks and Mirvis 2001). Within this traditional logic, resource-based ambiguity is resolved without generating ambiguity surrounding expectations. Managers at the acquiring firm have identified and clearly understand the target firm's key resources, as well as the target firm's ability to perform by leveraging these resources. In addition, expectations regarding how the acquirer and target firms' resources will be combined to create new value are clearly understood and agreed upon. In this case, the integration phase can move quickly and determinately. Expectations are clear; mutual goals are set; and a timetable for implementation is followed in subsequent stages of the acquisition process. Marks and Mirvis state: "successful acquirers know what they are looking for and conduct a thorough due diligence to ensure that they get what they want" from a particular acquisition (2001: 83). It follows from this process that the integration phase is the point at which the expected value of an acquisition is realized through resource reconfiguration and sharing (Capron et al. 1998).

In many situations, resource-based ambiguity can indeed be reduced during effective due diligence to facilitate valuation of the deal (Duhaime and Schwenk 1985). For example, during due diligence, resource-based ambiguity may be reduced through the process of gathering explicit information about the target firm, such as its financial and market positions. An acquiring firm needs explicit knowledge of the factors that contribute to a target firm's performance to facilitate learning about and integration of the target firm post-acquisition. This interfirm information is often concrete and codified once it is accessed.

As ambiguity regarding resources and their value within the combined organization is reduced during the pre-acquisition phase of due diligence, decision-making momentum builds, resulting in rapid decision making and resource integration post-acquisition. In cases where little residual ambiguity remains after due diligence, acquisition integration can proceed quickly. Traditional models of acquisitions rely on the pre-acquisition reducibility of ambiguity in target firm resources and the value-creation potential in their combination with the parent firm. Based on this logic, our first two propositions are the following:

P1: Ambiguity reduction during due diligence builds momentum, resulting in rapid acquisition integration.

P2: When post-acquisition ambiguity is low, rapid acquisition integration is associated with higher performance.

This traditional logic, which assumes that the due-diligence process largely eliminates ambiguity, provides the premise for our proposed relationships among ambiguity reduction in acquisitions, the speed of acquisition integration, and performance. Although reducing ambiguity in an acquired firm is a primary objective of the acquisition process, we suggest that this process is particularly difficult when acquiring technology firms due to the nature of the knowledge and technologies being acquired. In these cases, we expect expectational ambiguity, which interacts with resource ambiguity, to arise and ultimately influence the pace of the merger integration. As shown in Figure 25.1, we refine the traditional approach by distinguishing two types of ambiguity that arise in acquisitions of technology firms: (1) resource ambiguity and (2) expectational ambiguity arising from the acquisition process.

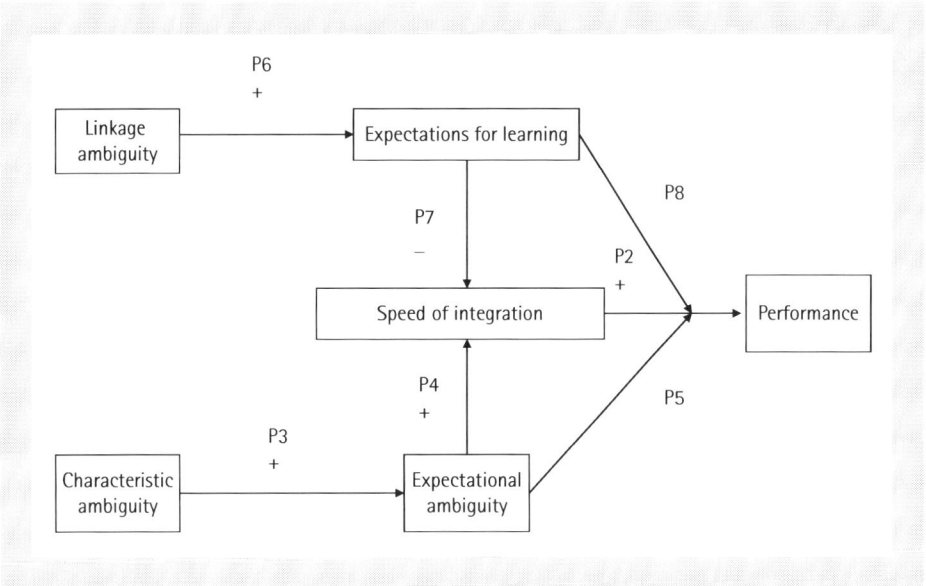

FIG. 25.1 Impact of types of ambiguity on speed of acquisition integration

Some resources, such as technological and knowledge-based resources, are less amenable to ambiguity reduction prior to the acquisition close. Recent research on acquisitions points to the notion that some of the most attractive acquisition targets are attractive because of the complex and experiential nature of their resources (Ahuja and Katila 2001; Coff 1999; Ranft and Lord 2000, 2002; Saxton and Dollinger 2004). These resources are attractive precisely because of their inherent ambiguity that contributes to protecting competitive advantage.

Early efforts to reduce ambiguity during due diligence and the compromises made about defining how to achieve expected outcomes are not independent from the sources of resource ambiguity in the target firm—characteristic and linkage ambiguity. As discussed, *characteristic ambiguity* is inherent in less tangible, more knowledge-intensive types of resources, capabilities, technologies, and human capital. *Linkage ambiguity* surrounds how a firm leverages its set of resources and capabilities to achieve its performance levels. These forms of ambiguity may be irreducible prior to the acquisition closing.

As managers attempt to define goals, timetables, and sources of value creation in the acquisition, they face difficulty when evaluating a target firm that has unique resources that are less tangible. Fully understanding the sources of competitive advantage in a firm from outside the firm is difficult. Managers of the acquiring firm may recognize linkage ambiguity in a potential target firm. As an outside observer, managers of the acquiring firm are unable to observe the overall bundle of resources leveraged for competitive advantage in a potential target and are unable to observe the temporal contiguity of leveraging those resources and ultimate competitive advantage of the target.

It is likely that *characteristic* ambiguity of a potential target firm's resources may exist both for external observers and internal organizational members. A firm's resources, particularly knowledge-based or technology-intensive, complex resources, by their very nature, exhibit ambiguity not only to outside observers but also to internal organizational members. Prior research has pointed out the knowledge barriers that exist in certain resources (Miller and Shamsie 1996) contributing to such characteristic ambiguity. When firms are acquired to leverage their competitive advantage based on such knowledge-based and often intangible resources, the characteristic ambiguity of these resources may not be reduced during the due-diligence process. From an acquirer's perspective, a target firm's resources imbued with highly ambiguous characteristics are more difficult to identify through thin communication methods and explicit data gathering typically used in the pre-acquisition stage. These types of resources require rich media, including regular face-to-face interactions, to gain a full appreciation of a resource's value to the acquirer (Graebner 2004; Ranft and Lord 2002). As a result, characteristic ambiguity must be reduced over time and managed post-acquisition.

In these situations, decisions and analysis are deferred to the post-acquisition integration stage rather than the due-diligence stage, rather such rich face-to-face communication between experts can only occur post-acquisition (Jemison and Sitkin 1986a). When faced with resource-based characteristic ambiguity during due diligence, therefore, managers may make compromises and defer critical decisions to post-acquisition integration (Saxton and Dollinger 2004) in order to close the deal (Jemison and Sitkin 1986b: 114).

Pressures to complete the due-diligence process and close the acquisition deal will more likely lead to expectational ambiguity in the presence of characteristic ambiguity that cannot be reduced by outside decision makers in the parent firm. Conversely, if the target firm is built around physical assets such as land, equipment, and capital, greater understanding of how to manage these assets and combine them with the parent's resources can be achieved during due diligence. In this case, expectational ambiguity is not generated during due diligence. Our next proposition, then, is the following:

P3: Characteristic resource-based ambiguity that is irreducible during due diligence creates expectational ambiguity.

Prior research has pointed to the potential for momentum building in pursuing an acquisition (Jemison and Sitkin 1986a; Pablo et al. 1996). The escalating momentum of decision making during the due-diligence stage results from pressures to close the deal quickly and may create over-commitment to the acquisition despite objective information (Haunschild et al. 1994; Jemison and Sitkin 1986a). This escalating momentum can lead to additional sources of ambiguity in the acquisition process, in the form of ambiguous expectations about how the acquisition will be managed.

If managers first focus on reducing tangible, codifiable resource-based ambiguity, they will anchor subsequent decision making on the reducibility of that initial ambiguity, given that individuals use cognitive strategies that anchor their decision making to the initial levels of ambiguity that they face (Einhorn and Hogarth 1985). The speed at which decisions can be made regarding reducible ambiguity is then transferred to subsequent decisions regarding resources that are more ambiguous. To continue the pace and perceived progress of the acquisition process, managers may leave critical factors undefined and allow expectational ambiguity to build (Jemison and Sitkin 1986a). This expectational ambiguity creates additional pressures in the acquisition process to proceed quickly, and momentum continues to build through acquisition integration. During acquisition integration, then, expectational ambiguities create pressure to rapidly integrate an acquired firm to reduce expectational ambiguities and create value. The momentum built from making compromises and agreeing to hold off on defining details of integration creates an action-biased trajectory to rapidly integrate the resource scenario of the two firms and quickly create value.

P4: Expectational ambiguity creates momentum for rapid acquisition integration.

Due to the expectational ambiguity created during due diligence in the presence of characteristic resource-based ambiguity, however, problems of resource exchange during integration are likely to occur after the deal is closed (Jemison and Sitkin 1986a). The pace of decision making created during due diligence is increased by compromises to hold off on articulating detail regarding resource exchange post-acquisition. This lack of specificity facilitates closing the acquisition deal and building expectational ambiguity and decision-making momentum. For purposes of closing the deal, this expectational ambiguity is considered to be functional by accelerating the pace of the acquisition process (Jemison and Sitkin 1986a).

This acceleration can become dysfunctional, however, when the decision-making momentum carries over to the post-acquisition integration process. Paradoxically, the characteristic ambiguity of resources that contributed to building expectational ambiguity and increasing the momentum of the due-diligence process also makes these resources particularly vulnerable to rapid organizational change (Nelson and Winter 1982). These resources are often tacit and socially embedded in the human capital and complex technological and management systems of the firm (Ahuja and Katila 2001; Coff 1999; Ranft and Lord 2000, 2002; Saxton and Dollinger 2004), so any disruption to these systems may alter or damage the resource (Nelson and Winter 1982). Therefore, although expectational ambiguity increases the speed of closing the deal, it also facilitates building a decision-making momentum that carries over to post-acquisition integration. Rapid decision making regarding resource exchange and organizational changes surrounding resources that are imbued with characteristic ambiguity may damage or alter the acquired resources and prevent desired performance outcomes despite rapid integration. Our next proposition, therefore, is the following:

P5: Expectational ambiguity moderates the relationship between rapid integration and performance outcomes of the acquisition.

To this point, we have discussed the impact of characteristic ambiguity on the creation of expectational ambiguity that can build during the acquisition process. However, differing conditions of characteristic ambiguity and linkage ambiguity may exist: the two sources of resource ambiguity may or may not act in parallel on the overall level of ambiguity present about a particular acquisition target. For example, managers may recognize a potential acquisition target's competitive advantage but not be able to understand how concrete resources are leveraged in a particular context to achieve that advantage.

Linkage ambiguity among competitors contributes to a focal firm's ability to sustain a competitive advantage by prohibiting a competitor's ability to copy a firm's competencies (Barney 1991). For instance, linkage ambiguity may be higher for decision makers at competitive firms than for decision makers at the focal firm who have full access to information about temporal order. In situations in which the resources of a target firm are relatively codifiable but their contribution to performance is not completely understood outside the firm, an explicit learning objective may drive the acquisition (Haspeslagh and Jemison 1991). In this case, the due-diligence process may proceed slowly to reduce ambiguity surrounding which resources and in what combination resources contribute to the potential value of the acquired firm. As managers step through the process of acquiring a firm that has reducible characteristic ambiguity and irreducible linkage ambiguity, they may tend to step through the integration phase more slowly so as not to disrupt the performance of the target firm. In these cases, acquiring managers know they don't know how to leverage resources in the acquired firm for competitive advantage and grant the acquired firm autonomy to facilitate a period of learning about the acquired firm's performance (Haspeslagh and Jemison 1991; Ranft and Lord 2002). A firm's resource base is acquired and time is spent learning from acquired management how to leverage resources for advantage and ultimately reduce linkage ambiguity over time (Saxton and Dollinger 2004).

Prior research has shown that when firms enter new markets, for example, a high need for autonomy of the newly acquired firm exists (Haspeslagh and Jemison 1991; Ranft and Lord 2002). Ambiguity about how an acquired firm leverages its resources in a new market is less understood than the set of resources the acquired firm owns, such as land, equipment, and location. Characteristic ambiguity may be reduced fairly early and quickly in these acquisitions, yet linkage ambiguity may take time to reduce in a new market context. In these cases, expectational ambiguity remains low as managers pursue the explicit objective of learning over time (Haspeslagh and Jemison 1991). Understanding how a firm has a competitive advantage in a new international market, for example, may require that the firm remain relatively autonomous with regard to human resources, procurement, and marketing management in the host country, because of unique local market knowledge that is critical to success (Lord and Ranft 2000). Some integration of common physical resources, supply-chain management, or infrastructure may occur, however, after the period of learning is achieved, leading to performance advantages in the longer term. As such, we propose the following:

P6: Linkage ambiguity is associated with expectations for post-acquisition learning.
P7: Expectations for learning slow the post-acquisition integration process.
P8: Expectations for learning moderate the relationship between rapid integration and performance outcomes of the acquisition.

Based on our model, it is possible that countervailing forces affect the speed of integration. When linkage ambiguity is recognized and exists prior to the closing of the deal, we predict an expectation for learning to slow down the integration process. However, despite an expectation for learning that may arise from the presence of linkage ambiguity, the creation of expectational ambiguity may arise due to the nature of the resource being acquired. This expectational ambiguity builds decision-making momentum that increases pressures on the speed of integration. In the presence of expectational ambiguity, pressures intensify during integration to meet higher-order goals set and to recoup premiums paid for an acquired firm (Jemison and Sitkin 1986a). These pressures build momentum and can lead to a "speed trap" in managerial decision making regarding the acquisition (Perlow et al. 2002), despite the existence of an explicit learning objective.

P9: Expectational ambiguity builds momentum for rapid post-acquisition integration that overrides slow post-acquisition integration associated with expectations for learning.

DISCUSSION

This chapter set out to examine the relationships among ambiguity and the pace of acquisition integration in the context of technology acquisitions. Ambiguity reduction regarding the target firm and its technologies and resources is a primary objective during due diligence and the overall acquisition process. As ambiguity is reduced, the target firm can be valued and performance goals can be set. After that, an articulation of how to achieve these goals through resource reconfiguration can be stated and then pursued during post-acquisition integration. In this chapter, however, we have developed a more nuanced understanding of ambiguity in acquisitions that reveals different patterns of the pacing of firms' post-acquisition integration efforts and potential performance effects. As we have shown, the pace of post-acquisition integration is, in part, dictated by resource-based ambiguity surrounding the acquired firm's resources, and expectational ambiguity rooted in the due-diligence process of an acquisition. In our model, two primary types of ambiguity in acquisitions are distinguished—resource-based and expectational ambiguity; both are expected to lead to unique challenges in acquisitions of technology-intensive firms.

Figure 25.2 depicts varying levels of the sources of resource-based ambiguity—characteristic and linkage ambiguity surrounding a target firm's resources—resulting in four scenarios. These scenarios highlight the interplay among resource-based and expectational ambiguity in the acquisition process, their potential impact on the speed of post-acquisition integration, and ultimately the performance outcomes of the acquisition. The first scenario describes the "traditional logic" argument as presented in our first two propositions. This scenario illustrates that as ambiguity is reduced, momentum builds and speed is functional to post-merger integration success. The other three scenarios reveal systematic patterns in characteristic, linkage, and expectational ambiguity that build momentum from early stages of the acquisition process—momentum that may *not* be functional, particularly in high-tech acquisitions. We suggest that the insights generated by recognizing the roles that ambiguity and pacing play in the acquisition integration process can help shed light on heretofore unresolved prescriptions regarding the speed of the acquisition integration process and acquisition performance, particularly in technology-intensive acquisitions. Each of these scenarios is discussed below.

	Reducible Linkage Ambiguity (many cues to causality)	Irreducible Linkage Ambiguity (limited cues to causality)
Reducible Characteristic Ambiguity (e.g. physical assets, codified knowledge)	TRADITIONAL LOGIC *Stage I:* Resource-based ambiguity is reduced, and no expectational ambiguity is created during due diligence, increasing the momentum of decision making *Stage II:* Rapid integration of resources *Stage III:* Performance outcome positive	LET A GOOD PERFORMER PERFORM *Stage I:* Characteristic ambiguity is reduced, and linkage ambiguity remains during due diligence. Little expectational ambiguity and momentum building *Stage II:* Slower and selective integration of resources due to defined goal of learning *Stage III:* Performance outcome positive in long run but neutral in short run
Irreducible Characteristic Ambiguity (e.g. high levels of tacitness)	SPEED TRAP *Stage I:* Linkage ambiguity is reduced, and expectational ambiguity is created during due diligence, increasing the momentum of decision making *Stage II:* Rapid integration of resources despite remaining characteristic ambiguity *Stage III:* Performance outcome questionable due to fragile nature of resources and potential serendipitous value creation	PRESSING FOR RESULTS FROM UNCERTAINTY *Stage I:* Resource-based ambiguity is not reduced, and high expectational ambiguity is created increasing momentum of decision making *Stage II:* Rapid integration pressures to reduce resource and process ambiguity *Stage III:* Performance outcome negative

FIG. 25.2 Ambiguity and speed of integration

Traditional Logic Scenario

Although some authors point to the importance of rapid integration, they also articulate the importance of reducing ambiguity. GE Capital tends to acquire firms and assets in the financial services sector that, in most cases, broaden its own operations in financial services. Resources are codifiable, and the competitive advantage of acquired firms is unambiguous. Resources that are relatively codifiable and clearly linked to firm performance are most readily understood and integrated during post acquisition integration. Given that managers can make decisions regarding these resource combinations during due diligence fairly rapidly, momentum builds and rapid decision making continues throughout the integration process effectively (Perlow et al. 2002). We expect this situation to be characteristic of acquisitions of low-tech firms, and, as such, we expect the traditional logic scenario in Figure 25.2 to be appropriate.

Pressing for Results from Uncertainty Scenario

At the other extreme in high-tech firms, irreducible resource-based (characteristic and linkage) ambiguity is present. In these firms, the nature of the resources themselves, and the need to observe their causal linkages more fully, presents challenges to reducing ambiguity prior to closing the deal. In pursuing ambiguity reduction to facilitate the acquisition closing, compromises are made to defer detailed decisions and understanding regarding how value will be created (Jemison and Sitkin 1986a). As a result, high expectational ambiguity is created, a price is set for the acquired firm, and value must be created to recoup the cost of the acquisition. These pressures create a momentum to rapidly integrate the firm to generate value as well as finding the expected sources of value creation. The momentum built from generating expectational ambiguity that allows efficient closing of the deal may override any explicit recognition for learning about new technologies and capabilities that could potentially slow down integration. In these cases, managers expect to find serendipitous value (Graebner 2004) and to identify new sources of value creation during the integration phase as they increase their understanding of the acquired resources and the target firm's source of advantage.

A case in point may be the AOL Time Warner merger, one of the costliest and least successful technology-intensive mergers in history. During due diligence, huge premiums were placed on the value to be created by merging an "old economy" and a "new economy" firm. The sources of this value were not articulated, but rather dubbed "transformational synergies", in which resources and capabilities were to be combined and reconfigured in ways that could not possibly be articulated prior to the closing of the merger. These transformational synergies depended upon serendipitous value creation after the deal was closed and created high levels of expectational ambiguity.

The process of serendipitous value creation, however, depends upon face-to-face interaction and integrating key human capital in a firm (Graebner 2004; Ranft and Lord 2002). This very process may, in fact, damage resources high in characteristic ambiguity, such as the knowledge and capabilities of the acquired firm, and prevent effective value creation (Coff 1999). It is precisely in this case that a period of learning is necessary to preserve acquired, highly ambiguous resources, while beginning to understand their relationship with performance and value creation. Yet, it is also true, in this case of irreducible characteristic and linkage ambiguity, that the potential exists for expectational ambiguities and momentum building in the process to be the greatest. This momentum building in the early stages of an acquisition carries over as managers begin to integrate the two firms, searching for sources of serendipitous value creation and recoupment of the cost of the deal.

Speed Trap Scenario

In this scenario, expectational ambiguity is again built and may be common to high tech acquisitions. As managers of an acquiring firm gain understanding about how a configuration of resources contributes to the acquired firm's performance, linkage ambiguity is lowered. If, however, these resources are based on sophisticated technologies or socially complex knowledge shared by a team of experts, they are dependent upon the human capital of the firm and potentially quite fragile (Coff 1999; Ranft and Lord 2002). These types of resources are inherently socially complex and often dependent upon knowledge-workers who, in the organizational chaos and uncertainty of an acquisition, may choose to leave the firm and take much of the social capital and technological knowledge that supports these ambiguous resources with them (Coff 1999; Dess and Shaw 2001; Ranft and Lord 2000).

When firms are acquired to leverage their competitive advantage based on technological resources, the ambiguity inherent in their resources and capabilities may not be reduced during the due-diligence process, even if the link between these resources and competitive advantage can be understood. From an acquirer's perspective, a target firm's resources imbued with highly ambiguous characteristics are more difficult to identify through the thin communication methods typically used in the pre-acquisition stage. These types of resources require rich media, including regular face-to-face interactions, to gain a full appreciation of a resource's value to the acquirer (Graebner 2004; Ranft and Lord 2002). As a result, characteristic ambiguity must be reduced over time and managed post-acquisition.

In the case of irreducible characteristic ambiguity and reducible linkage ambiguity, managers may become overly confident of their understanding of the acquired firm (Jemison and Sitkin 1986a). Their ability to relatively rapidly understand the relationship between resources and performance outcomes of the acquired firm, due to reducible linkage ambiguity, may increase their decision-making momentum during the acquisition process, despite the ambiguity surrounding the acquired resources. This can lead to a "*speed trap*" in acquisitions, where rapid decision making and rapid resource integration of an acquired firm lead to the deterioration of the acquired resources themselves (Perlow, et al. 2002; Ranft and Lord 2002).

Pressures to integrate an acquired firm, despite significant inherent ambiguity surrounding its resources, arise from momentum built during due diligence, when linkage ambiguity is reduced and expectational ambiguity is built. Managers may understand how resources combine to create advantage in the target firm, but they lack knowledge of *how to protect and manage* these resources. As such, they set targets and goals without fully understanding how to manage resources that are characteristically ambiguous. Expectational ambiguity in this case arises not from lack of clarity of goals, but from lack of clarity about how to preserve the resources and manage the organization to reach defined goals. Compromises may occur to agree to disagree on critical management implementation decisions, as acquiring managers know what they hope to achieve with acquired resources. Pressures intensify during integration to meet defined targets and goals and to recoup potentially high premiums paid for an acquired firm (Jemison and Sitkin 1986a). These pressures build momentum and can lead to a "speed trap" in managerial decision making regarding the acquisition (Perlow et al. 2002).

Momentum builds, then, in acquisitions with irreducible characteristic ambiguity and reducible linkage ambiguity, to rapidly integrate the acquired firm. Performance outcomes are uncertain in this case, however. Efforts to reach defined value-creation goals may damage some acquired resources. For example, a pharmaceutical firm's acquisition of a biotech firm may have clearly defined goals for new drug introduction and screening. However, as managers attempt to facilitate meeting these goals, they may make a simple decision to relocate the acquired biotech firm. This relocation may undermine scientists' commitment to the firm and facilitate their departure. These scientists may have critical knowledge and skills, as well as leadership abilities in the ranks of the scientists in the lab, that are critical to the success of the acquired biotech firm. On the other hand, relocating the biotech firm may facilitate serendipitous value creation (Graebner 2004) as managers from the acquired and parent firms interact and discover new ways to integrate resources and capitalize on benefits not uncovered in the due-diligence and deal-construction phase of the acquisition.

Let Good Performers Perform Scenario

Managers may recognize a potential acquisition target's competitive advantage, but not be able to understand how resources are leveraged in a particular context to achieve that advantage. Linkage ambiguity among competitors contributes to a focal firm's ability to sustain a competitive advantage by prohibiting a competitor's ability to copy a firm's competencies (Barney 1991). As mentioned previously, the due-diligence process to reduce ambiguity proceeds more slowly when the contribution of the target firm's resources to performance is not completely understood outside the firm. As managers go through the process of acquiring a firm that has reducible characteristic ambiguity and irreducible linkage ambiguity, they may tend to *"let good performers perform"* and move through the integration phase more slowly. In these cases, acquiring managers, because they don't know how to leverage resources in the acquired firm for competitive advantage, learn from acquired management how to leverage resources for advantage and ultimately reduce linkage ambiguity over time (Haspeslagh and Jemison 1991).

Prior research has shown that when firms enter new markets, for example, a high need for autonomy of the newly acquired firm exists (Haspeslagh and Jemison 1991). Ambiguity is often associated with how to leverage acquired resources rather than the set of resources the acquired firm owns. While characteristic ambiguity may be resolved fairly quickly and early in these acquisitions, linkage ambiguity may take more time to reduce in a new market context. In these cases, expectational ambiguity remains low as managers pursue the explicit objective of learning over time (Haspeslagh and Jemison 1991). Understanding how a firm has a competitive advantage in a new international market, for example, may require that the firm remain relatively autonomous with regard to human resources, procurement, and marketing management in the host country, because of unique local market knowledge that is critical to success (Lord and Ranft 2000). Some integration of common physical resources, supply-chain management, or infrastructure may occur, however, after the period of learning is completed, leading to performance advantages in the longer term.

Future research should empirically examine the propositions and acquisition scenarios developed in this chapter. Empirical assessment of the scenarios developed here is necessary for validation. In particular for acquisitions of technology firms, future research should examine the emergence of expectational ambiguity during due diligence and the likelihood of the various scenarios. The theorizing presented here predicts that expectational ambiguity will be highest in high-tech firms with complex and sophisticated resources. In addition, the impact of this expectational ambiguity on post-acquisition integration momentum and decisions should be examined, since our theorizing predicts that this momentum can lead to a speed trap or pressing for results from uncertainty in acquisition integration. Further investigation into the concept of "serendipitous value creation" (Graebner 2004) in acquisitions of high-tech firms would be advantageous. The relationship between expectational ambiguity created during due diligence and the role of acquired managers in facilitating unexpected value creation would seem to be particularly relevant to acquisitions of high-tech firms where resources are inherently ambiguous. Again, future empirical research is needed to test these assertions.

CONCLUSION

Starting from Bower's (2001) concept that "not all acquisitions are alike," we have begun to explore the underlying concept of ambiguity in integrating acquisitions. Because of the inherent nature of resources in technology-intensive acquisition targets, ambiguity is expected to be high in these cases. Three specific types of ambiguity, characteristic and linkage ambiguity inherent in the resources themselves, and expectational ambiguity that can build during due diligence, are examined for their influence on the acquisition integration process.

There are several managerial implications of our research. First, managers must recognize that, in some cases, not all ambiguity is reducible during due diligence. Second, managers must recognize the need for a period of learning at some point during the acquisition process. If not all ambiguity is reducible during due diligence, then a period of learning is necessary during post-acquisition integration, obviously increasing the time necessary to create value in an acquisition. This is the crux of why some acquisition integration processes can effectively move quickly and others must move more slowly. The third implication, then, for managers, is that performance targets may be more long term in nature for acquisitions that require learning during acquisition integration. In addition, managers must be aware of the potential for expectational ambiguities to build, increasing the momentum of the overall process of acquisitions. If momentum builds and high expectational ambiguities are created, it is likely that rushing the integration process will be at the expense of preserving resources.

References

Agarwal, R., & Helfat, C. (2009). "Strategic Renewal of Organizations." *Organization Science*, 20/2: 281–93.

Ahuja, G., & Katila, R. (2001). "Technological Acquisitions and the Innovation Performance of Acquiring Firms: A Longitudinal Study." *Strategic Management Journal*, 22: 197–220.

Ambrosini, V., & Bowman, C. (2002). "Causal Ambiguity: Some Empirical and Conceptual Developments." Presented at the Annual Academy of Management Meeting, Denver, August.

Ashkenas, R. N., DeMonaco, L. J., & Francis, S. C. (1998). "Making the Deal Real: How GE Capital Integrates Acquisitions." *Harvard Business Review*, 76: 165–78.

Barney, J. (1991). "Firm Resources and Sustained Competitive Advantage." *Journal of Management*, 17: 99–121.

Birkinshaw, J., Bresman, H., & Hakanson, L. (2000). "Managing the Post-acquisition Integration Process: How the Human Integration and Task Integration Processes Interact to Foster Value Creation." *Journal of Management Studies*, 37: 395–425.

Bower, J. L. (2001). "Not All M&As Are Alike—And That Matters." *Harvard Business Review*, 79: 93–101.

Capron, L., Dussuage P., & Mitchell, W. (1998). Resource Deployment Following Horizontal Acquisitions in Europe and North America, 1988–1992." *Strategic Management Journal*, 22: 817–44.

Chaudhuri, S., & Tabrizi, B. (1999). "Capturing the Real Value in High-Tech Acquisitions." *Harvard Business Review*, 77: 123–30.

Coff, R. W. (1999). "How Buyers Cope with Uncertainty When Acquiring Firms in Knowledge-Intensive Industries: Caveat Emptor." *Organization Science*, 10: 144–61.

Cording, M., Christmann, P., & King, D. (2008). "Reducing Causal Ambiguity in Acquisition Integration: Intermediate Goals as Mediators of Integration Decisions and Acquisition Performance." *Academy of Management Journal*, 51: 744–67.

Dess, G. G., & Shaw, J. D. (2001). "Voluntary Turnover, Social Capital, and Firm Organizational Performance." *Academy of Management Review*, 26: 446–56.

Dierickx, I., & Cool, K. (1989). "Asset Stock Accumulation and Sustainability of Competitive Advantage." *Management Science*, 35: 1504–14.

Duhaime, I. M., & Schwenk, C. R. (1985). "Conjectures on Cognitive Simplification in Acquisition and Divestment Decision Making." *Academy of Management Review*, 10: 287–95.

Einhorn, H. J., & Hogarth, R. M. (1985). "Ambiguity and Uncertainty in Probabilistic Inference." *Psychological Review*, 92: 433–61.

—— —— (1986). "Decision Making under Ambiguity." *Journal of Business*, 59: 225–50.

Ellsberg, D. (1961). "Risk, Ambiguity, and the Savage Axioms." *Quarterly Journal of Economics*, 75: 643–9.

Goh, S. C. (2001). "Management Strategies for Successful Post-Acquisition Integration." *Academy of Management Executive*, 15: 152–3.

Grant, R. M. (1996). "Toward a Knowledge-Based View of the Firm." *Strategic Management Journal*, 17, Winter Special Issue: 109–22.

Graebner, M. E. (2004). "Momentum and Serendipity: How Acquired Leaders Create Value in the Integration of Technology Firms." *Strategic Management Journal*, 25: 751–77.

—— Eisenhardt, K. M., & Roundy, P. T. (2010). "Success and Failure in Technology Acquisitions: Lessons for Buyers and Sellers." *Academy of Management Perspectives*, 24/3: 73–92.

Haspeslagh, P. C., & Jemison, D. B. (1991). *Managing Acquisitions: Creating Value through Corporate Renewal*. New York: The Free Press.

Haunschild, P. R., Davis-Blake, A., & Fichman, M. (1994). "Managerial Overcommitment in Corporate Acquisition Processes." *Organization Science*, 5: 528–40.

Jemison, D. G., & Sitkin, S. B. (1986a). "Corporate Acquisitions: A Process Perspective." *Academy of Management Review*, 11: 145–63.

—— —— (1986b). "Acquisitions: The Process Can Be a Problem." *Harvard Business Review*, 64: 107–16.

King, A. W., & Zeithaml, C. P. (2001). "Competencies and Firm Performance: Examining in the Causal Ambiguity Paradox." *Strategic Management Journal*, 22: 75–99.

King, D. R., Dalton, D. R., Daily, C. M., & Covin, J. G. (2004). "Meta-Analysis of Post-acquisition Performance: Indications of Unidentified Moderators." *Strategic Management Journal*, 25: 187–200.

Kitching, J. (1967). "Why Do Mergers Miscarry?" *Harvard Business Review*, 45: 84–101.

Larsson, R., & Finkelstein, S. (1999). "Integrating Strategic, Organizational, and Human Resource Perspectives on Mergers and Acquisitions: A Case Survey of Synergy Realization." *Organization Science*, 10: 1–26.

Lord, M., & Ranft, A. (2000). "Entering Emerging International Markets: Sharing Local Knowledge within the Firm." *Journal of International Business Studies*, 31: 573–89.

Makri, M., Hitt, M. A., & Lane, P. J. (2010). "Complementary Technologies, Knowledge Relatedness, and Invention Outcomes in High Technology Mergers and Acquisitions." *Strategic Management Journal*, 31/6: 602–28.

Marks, M. L., & Mirvis, P. H. (2001). "Making Mergers and Acquisitions Work: Strategic and Psychological Preparation." *Academy of Management Executive*, 15: 80–93.

Miller, D., & Shamsie, J. (1996). "The Resource-Based View of the Firm in Two Environments: The Hollywood Film Studios from 1936 to 1965." *Academy of Management Journal*, 39: 519–53.

Mosakowski, E. (1997). "Strategy Making under Causal Ambiguity: Conceptual Issues and Empirical Evidence." *Organizational Science*, 8: 414–42.

Nelson, R. R., & Winter, S. G. (1982). *An Evolutionary Theory of Economic Change*. Cambridge, MA: Harvard University Press.

Pablo, A. (1994). "Determinants of Acquisition Integration Level: A Decision-Making Perspective." *Academy of Management Journal*, 37: 803–36.

—— Sitkin, S., & Jemison, D. (1996). "Acquisition Decision-Making Processes: The Central Role of Risk." *Journal of Management*, 22: 723–46.

Perlow, L. A., Okhuysen, G. O., & Repenning, N. P. (2002). "The Speed Trap: Exploring the Relationship between Decision Making and Temporal Context." *Academy of Management Journal*, 45: 931–55.

Puranam, P., Singh, H., & Zollo, M. (2006). "Organizing for Innovation: Managing the Coordination-Autonomy Dilemma in Technology Acquisitions." *Academy of Management Journal*, 49: 263–80.

Ranft, A. L. & Lord, M. D. (2000). "Acquiring New Knowledge: The Role of Retaining Human Capital in Acquisitions of High-Tech Firms." *Journal of High Technology Management Research*, 11: 295–319.

————(2002). "Acquiring New Technologies and Capabilities: A Grounded Model of Acquisition Implementation." *Organization Science*, 13: 420–41.

Reed, R., & DeFillippi, R. J. (1990). "Causal Ambiguity, Barriers to Imitation, and Sustainable Competitive Advantage." *Academy of Management Review*, 15: 88–102.

Saxton, T., & Dollinger, M. (2004). "Target Reputation and Appropriability: Picking and Deploying Resources in Acquisitions." *Journal of Management*, 30: 123–47.

Schweiger, D. M., & DeNisi, A. S. (1991). "Communication with Employees Following a Merger: A Longitudinal Field Experiment." *Academy of Management Journal*, 34: 110–35.

Simonin, B. L. (1999). "Ambiguity and the Process of Knowledge Transfer in Strategic Alliances." *Strategic Management Journal*, 20: 595–624.

Szulanski, G. (1996). "Exploring Internal Stickiness: Impediments to the Transfer of Best Practice within the Firm." *Strategic Management Journal*, 17, Winter Special Issue: 27–43.

Véry, P., & Schweiger, D. M. (2001). "The Acquisition Process as a Learning Process: Evidence from a Study of Critical Problems and Solutions in Domestic and Cross-Border Deals." *Journal of World Business*, 36: 11–31.

Zollo, M., & Winter, S. (2002). "Deliberate Learning and the Evolution of Dynamic Capabilities." *Organization Science*, 13: 339–51.

CHAPTER 26

CHARACTERISTICS OF BIOTECHNOLOGY MERGERS AND ACQUISITIONS

LARS SCHWEIZER

INTRODUCTION

This chapter deals with mergers and acquisitions (M&As) involving biotechnology companies, the number of which has increased steadily since the beginning of the 1990s. M&As have been a popular strategy for firms because they offer various advantages such as immediate access to technologies, products, distribution channels, and desirable market positions. Moreover, they can provide access to knowledge and bring into a company capabilities that are hard to develop. However, there is considerable evidence that many M&As have not been successful and have failed to achieve their objectives due to questionable acquisition motives, problems regarding valuation and premiums paid, and, particularly, difficulties in the post-acquisition integration process (Agrawal and Jaffe 2000; Datta et al. 1992; Sirower 1997).

The desire to obtain valuable resources, including know-how, technologies, and capabilities possessed by target firms has always been a driver of M&A activities (Ahuja and Katila 2001; Chaudhuri and Tabrizi 1999). It seems that this motive has increased in importance in the most recent wave of acquisition activity (Bower 2001) because in industries characterized by rapid innovation, technological complexity, and highly specialized skills and know-how, the pace and magnitude of technological change may not allow firms to internally develop all the necessary technologies and capabilities to remain competitive. Thus, the number of acquisitions during the 1990s rose dramatically in high-technology sectors such as biotechnology (*BioCentury* 2007; Goldman Sachs 2001; Inkpen et al. 2000). Start-up companies in this research-intensive high-technology industry face a high risk of failure during the first few years of their existence. It is a challenging task for start-up company managers to build up a valuable resource platform in order to gain competitive advantage, because the development of complex new (bio-)technologies requires not only substantial financial resources, but also competencies in different scientific and technological fields (Jones et al. 2001). Although at least 50–100 M&A transactions are announced on average in the biotech industry every year (*BioCentury* 2003), with 75 biotech acquisitions in 2006 (*BioCentury* 2007), there is very little scientific research devoted to the M&A activities of biotechnology firms (Bower 2001; Patzelt et al. 2007; Schweizer 2005). Table 26.1 (based on DealSearchOnline.com) provides an overview of biotechnology mergers and acquisitions from 2000 to 2009.

An analysis from Business Insights (2008) showed that US companies accounted for 42% of acquiring companies and 41% of targets in global biotech M&A deals over the 2003–8 period. Of the 378 M&As analyzed by Business Insights (2008) and for which values are known during that five-year period, companies based in the US were the most active acquirers, accounting for 186 of the deals, followed by the UK (41), India (28), Canada (23), Australia (13), Switzerland (11), Germany (10), China (8), Ireland (8), and Japan (7). While the average values of US deals are generally higher than most, the average values for both Canada and India registered a sharp upward trend in 2006.

In general, M&As are a possible strategy for overcoming a lack of knowledge, reducing R&D costs, increasing the number of potential products in a pipeline, and closing an earnings gap (Ahuja and Katila 2001; Ranft and Lord 2002). Several contributions (e.g. Arora and Gambardella 1990; Graebner 2004; Haspeslagh and Jemison 1991; Hitt et al. 1996) have pointed to the important role that M&As can play as an external source of innovation. Yet, the management and the integration of such acquisitions might pose some problems because acquisitions can lead to high levels of stress (Cartwright and

Table 26.1 Biotechnology M&A, 2000–2009

Year	US$ committed	Number of deals
2009	$47,523,349,040	193
2008	$93,879,257,347	148
2007	$42,105,127,700	145
2006	$36,407,170,500	115
2005	$23,196,902,050	113
2004	$6,764,873,000	96
2003	$16,681,231,200	128
2002	$3,274,727,708	96
2001	$20,150,840,000	85
2000	$5,076,797,094	52

Source: Based on DealSearchOnline.com.

Cooper 1992) and increased turnover (Hambrick and Canella 1993), which will hinder the successful realization of innovations following an acquisition. Especially in the biotechnology industry, M&A deals are an essential element of the "business development" activities of a company as biotechnology companies increasingly use acquisitions as part of their R&D strategy (Bower 2001).

This chapter proceeds in the following manner. First, I briefly describe the development of the biotechnology industry from scientific and organizational perspectives. This analysis leads to the conclusion that a strategic consolidation in the biotechnology industry will take place. Second, I analyze the major strategic reasons for biotechnology M&A activities, as well as the challenges and recommendations for the successful post-acquisition integration. Finally, I summarize the major issues, establish a link to other chapters in this *Handbook*, and identify future research questions. Following prior research (e.g. Haleblian et al. 2009; King et al. 2004), I have used the terms merger and acquisition interchangeably in this chapter, although empirically M&A transactions in the biotechnology sector are mainly acquisitions.

DEVELOPMENT OF THE BIOTECHNOLOGY INDUSTRY AND THE NEED FOR M&A

This section deals with the analysis of the development of the biotechnology industry from scientific and organizational perspectives. These perspectives reveal the need for a strategic consolidation in the biotechnology industry and present the challenges for a successful post-acquisition integration of acquired biotech firms that will be discussed below.

The Development of the Biotechnology Industry from a Scientific Perspective and the Challenges for the Post-acquisition Integration Process

The roots of modern biotechnology, the so-called "first generation of biotechnology," lie in the fermentation of foods and drinks, industries spanning almost every society and evolving over centuries (Sharp 1991; Kenney 1986). They include techniques as old as Western civilization itself (such as e.g. the cultivation of micro-organisms for brewing). "Second-generation biotechnology" developed as an outgrowth of traditional fermentation. The discovery of penicillin and the subsequent development of the antibiotic industry is one of its major milestones. "Third-generation biotechnology"—also called "new" biotechnology—resulted from discoveries in the early 1970s, such as the use of recombinant DNA and cell fusion techniques as well as bioprocessing technology to make or modify products.

Wirth (1994) has characterized the development of "new biotechnology" in four phases. The first phase, the so-called research phase, lasted from 1970–80 and was dominated by two path-breaking discoveries: the discovery of recombinant DNA (rDNA) and monoclonal antibodies (MABs). In this phase, universities and research institutes played a critical role in biotech's emergence, not only as the places where young scientists were educated, but, particularly, as the sources of breakthrough discoveries and techniques fostering scientific and technological innovation (Powell 1996). As a result, most biotechnology firms have been started by scientists with the help of either venture capitalists or ex-pharmaceutical executives, while pharmaceutical companies have applied a "wait-and-see approach."

The second phase, from 1980–5, is considered to be the pioneering phase. The first product of a biotech company made by recombinant DNA, human insulin, was launched in 1982. In 1983, the first experiments with genetically modified micro-organisms were allowed to be carried out in the US and in 1985 the first genetically produced hepatitis B viral antigens were introduced.

The third phase, from 1984–90, is considered to be the first prosperous phase of biotechnology. There had been strong indications that the real "take-off" point for the large corporations came in the years 1984–5, because big-firm investment in commercial biotechnology in the US increased dramatically (Office of Technology Assessment 1988).

The fourth phase, from 1990–6, is perceived as the prosperous phase of biotechnology. The first experiment to treat ADA deficiency genetically took place and the US Trade Office worked out new rules for biotechnology as well as genetic engineering. Moreover, the market share of biotechnology drugs and diagnostic methods increased steadily. By the end of 1994, more than two dozen biotech drugs and vaccines had been approved by the FDA, and more than 200 medicines were at various stages of clinical testing (Powell 1996).

The fifth phase, starting in 1997, has been characterized by discussion about necessary consolidation activities and the future "dream" about the never-ending benefits of biotechnology. On the one hand, biotechnology companies are considered to be the "innovative engine" for the pharmaceutical and biotechnology industry. On the other hand, however, institutional investors are not motivated by biotechnology's past performance and are looking for new areas to invest (Purcell 1998). Moreover, with the launch of the Human Genome Project in 1990, there was a growing perception that drug discovery was to undergo radical changes. Along with that, growing awareness of the innovation deficit at pharmaceutical companies made them look for alternatives, namely biotechnology. Overall, the convergence of genomics and informatics not only heralds a new era of biomedical research, but it will also foster M&A activities in the biotechnology sector.

Teitelman (1989) describes Wall Street's initial attitude toward biotechnology as "biomania." In 1980/1, biotechnology investments in the US were attracting nearly $100 million of venture capital (Hacking 1986). However, Wall Street's overall relationship with biotechnology has been extremely variable. In its early enthusiasm for the technology, Wall Street ensured that many new biotechnology firms enjoyed substantial funding.

Large, established pharmaceutical companies have generally been slow to become involved in biotechnology, but, over time, have been devoting considerable resources to it. In addition, many have also acquired biotechnology firms.

The technological frontier of biotechnology is advancing with a knowledge, skill, and competence base fundamentally different from prior know-how (Patzelt and Brenner 2008; Powell 1996). Therefore, biotechnology and pharmaceutical firms face the need to constantly search for new knowledge worldwide immediately after they are established. In line with that specific M&A reason, Hoskisson et al. (1994) suggest that an acquirer should search for target firms that will complement R&D projects and/or enhance the acquirer's core competence. However, it is not enough for an acquirer to simply "buy" a technology or know-how, because, to create value and generate innovations, the knowledge must be integrated throughout the post-acquisition integration process (Larsson and Finkelstein, 1999)—despite all the problems that frequently come up during this phase.

Haspeslagh and Jemison (1991) distinguish between three clear choices regarding post-acquisition integration approaches. (1) Preservation reflects the need for low interdependence and high autonomy so that the acquired company is only integrated to a modest degree and preserves its way of doing business. (2) Symbiotic acquisitions reflect high interdependence and at the same time a high need for organizational autonomy. (3) In an absorption acquisition, the acquirer absorbs the acquired business directly and assimilates it into its culture. However, there will often be situations where no clear choice is possible. The subject of M&A, especially in the context of biotechnology, is by nature a multi-level and multi-stage construct that cannot be captured by single-level and single-stage approaches which would be too narrowly focused and would fail to capture the dynamic and complex nature of the subject (Javidan et al. 2004). Furthermore, the organic nature of biotech products and technologies makes them far more difficult to integrate than computer or chip components that benefit from the modularity of IT design (Bower 2001).

The aim of gaining access to knowledge and innovative capabilities through acquisitions is a clear case of neither internal (Zander and Kogut 1995) nor external (Lane and Lubatkin 1998) knowledge transfer. Even after the closing of the deal, the two companies are still far from being a united entity in terms of organization and culture. Thus, accomplishing the transfer of knowledge and capabilities is particularly complex and difficult in the context of transitional organizational conditions as created by acquisitions (Capron 1999; Ranft and Lord 2002). Especially in the biotechnology sector, this highly specific knowledge (DeCarolis and Deeds 1999; Powell 1993) is harder to transmit because fewer parties other than the innovator can benefit from its application (Henderson and Cockburn 1994; McEvily and Chakravarthy 2002).

In industries with long development cycles, as in biotechnology, it is of crucial importance that a smooth and quick post-acquisition integration and knowledge transfer takes place so that increased innovation results. Moreover, the duration of the (protected) patent heavily influences the profit situation of the newly combined companies. Being more innovative and, therefore, being able to more rapidly file a patent and to develop a new product will significantly enhance the competitive position of the combined entity. Thus, the question is what can be done to speed up and ease the post-acquisition integration process of knowledge in the "M&A as R&D" type of acquisition (Bower 2001).

The Development of the Biotech Industry from an Organizational Perspective and the Challenges for the Post-acquisition Integration Process

University laboratories have played a critical role in developing the scientific fundamentals of biotechnology during the first phase of the development of the "new biotechnology." However, it was the dedicated biotechnology firms that commercially exploited the results of the research. The scientific breakthroughs of biotechnology constituted a radical change from previously dominant technologies in the pharmaceutical sector. Hence, "biotechnology is a dramatic case of a competence-destroying innovation" (Powell and Brantley 1992: 368). This particular radical technological change builds on a scientific basis that differs significantly from the knowledge base of the established pharmaceutical industry (Powell 1993, 1996).

Usually, biotechnology firms are organized flexibly in overlapping interdisciplinary project teams with minimal hierarchy in order to create a lean and effective organization for drug discovery and commercial development (Powell 1996). Employees often have a significant ownership stake in the firm, so that they have very strong incentives to quickly develop new technologies at the lowest costs and are driven by an entrepreneurial spirit. These unique organizational characteristics are a source of key strategic and inventive capabilities (Barney 1991), as they form the foundation for the innovative research results of the entrepreneurial biotech firms. Small biotechnology firms require large financial support and regulatory knowledge, while larger pharmaceutical companies desire access to the research capabilities of smaller companies. It is usually the case that the full range of relevant skills needed to develop therapeutic drugs is not readily available under a single roof. The necessary basic and research skills to create a new product are found either in universities, research institutes, or small biotechnology companies, whereas the cash needed for product development, clinical trials, and worldwide marketing is located in large pharmaceutical companies. Hence, the players in this field have turned to numerous forms of collaboration, such as joint ventures, research agreements, or licensing agreements (Goldman Sachs 2001).

The pattern of interfirm collaboration in biotechnology is probably more extensive than in any other industry (Arora and Gambardella 1990; Barley and Freeman 1992; Powell 1993; Powell and Brantley 1992). Moreover, the biotechnology industry is characterized by a social network structure so that a prerequisite for success is a shift from coordinating the internal activities of the firm through a command and control structure to providing organizational support for internal as well as external exchanges. Greis et al. (1995) distinguish four different types of partnership agreements: (1) research contracts or minority investments, (2) licensing and marketing agreements, (3) corporate alliances such as joint ventures, and (4) mergers and acquisitions, the latter being the focus of that chapter.

From an organizational point of view, most acquisitions fail during the complex post-acquisition integration process (Larsson and Finkelstein 1999; Schweiger and Lippert 2005). Nonetheless, in order to profit from the know-how, knowledge, and capabilities of the acquired firms, these companies have to be integrated as value creation takes place after an acquisition (Haspeslagh and Jemison 1991; Pablo 1994). To trigger innovation after an acquisition in know-how and technology-intensive industries, such as biotechnology, knowledge transfer must take place between the acquirer and the target following the acquisition. As a consequence of that, acquirers must integrate the target firms in order to further develop and commercialize their technologies, while at the same time preserving organizational autonomy for the acquired firms in order to avoid harming their innovative capabilities (Puranam et al. 2006; Ranft and Lord 2002; Schweizer 2005). However, existing integration approaches and typologies (Buono and Bowditch 1989; Haspeslagh and Jemison 1991; Marks and Mirvis 1998; Nahavandi and Malekzadeh 1988; Napier 1989) fail to address the complexity of the post-acquisition integration process as they tend to offer a "one-size-fits-all" solution—that may partly explain why so many M&A transactions fail (Sirower 1997). Puranam et al. (2006) suggest that acquirers can resolve the coordination-autonomy dilemma by recognizing that the effect of structural form on innovation outcomes depends on the developmental stage of the acquired firms' innovation trajectories (Dosi et al. 1988). Given the difficulty of determining the appropriate post-acquisition integration approach, it will also be difficult for the acquirer to exactly determine the developmental stage of the acquired firm's innovation trajectory right after the acquisition of a firm without any prior "inside knowledge" of the target firm.

Realizing Biotechnology M&A Activities

The last section contained a short description of the development and challenges of the biotechnology industry. It has been argued that this industry is undergoing radical changes and that it faces a host of difficulties, thus making M&A a very likely strategic, yet implementation-wise challenging option.

Strategic Reasons for Biotechnology M&A Activities

The analysis of Schweizer (2005, 2009) has come to the conclusion that M&A activities in the biotechnology industry are driven by the motive to internationalize research and development, to take part in the industry's development process, as well as to realize the biotech firm's growth strategy. This is to a large extent in line with the conclusion of Oviatt and McDougall (1997) and Zahra et al. (2000) that international expansion positively influences new ventures' survival, profitability, and growth. However, a more detailed differentiation is required. The first two main motives for biotech firms to enter into M&A transactions with pharmaceutical companies are (1) securing the future survival of the company by getting access to financial resources and (2) support of the entrepreneurial firm's growth strategy in order to expand their R&D activities. While these two motives are going hand in hand and are short-term oriented, the third motive of (3) bringing their drug to the market refers to their "raison d'être" and is long-term oriented.

When analyzing further articles and reports on biotech M&A activities (e.g. Arnold et al. 1999; *BioCentury* 2003; Van Brunt 2005; Webber 1999; Patzelt et al. 2007), the following further reasons and motives for merger and acquisition activities in the biotechnology industry can be identified:

- Some venture capitalists prefer M&A activities over initial public offerings (IPOs) which become increasingly difficult in order to cash in their investments.
- M&As can add revenue and profit to the newly combined biotech firm, since too many biotech stocks have greatly underperformed and need money.
- Some biotech companies acquire others in order to position themselves as integrated product developers, thus becoming a more fully integrated drug discovery company, or service providers or to complete their existing intellectual property portfolio.
- The acquisition of a biotech company can provide access to local or regional networks and to necessary management skills.
- Patent expiration in the pharmaceutical industry will force pharmaceutical firms to acquire biotechnology firms in order to develop new blockbusters.
- M&A is a possible strategy for overcoming lack of biotechnology knowledge, reducing R&D costs, increasing the number of potential products in the pipeline, and closing any earnings gap (Ahuja and Katila 2001; Higgins and Rodriguez 2003; Ranft and Lord 2002).
- By internalizing a whole body of laboratory or product development capabilities, pharmaceutical companies try to create internally a research environment that fosters the kind of innovation and discovery necessary to survive in the long run (Powell and Brantley 1992; Powell 1993).

All these reasons and motives appear to be in place for a major increase in M&As in the biotechnology industry over the coming years. Taking a closer look at two further important reasons for M&A activities in the biotechnology sector, one can first identify the financial necessities from the point of view of the biotechnology companies. The financing environment for biotechnology offerings has not been robust in recent years and most of the companies are only in the early stages of development of products and will face significant challenges to stay solvent. Thus, one biotech company may acquire another merely for its fat bank account in order to ensure their future survival. Second, biotech acquisitions are driven by the desire to get access to promising drug candidates (i.e. fill up the pipeline), enabling technologies or intellectual property in order to achieve a critical mass and improve their competitive position.

Major pharmaceutical companies have always had a big interest in biotechnology firms, primarily to secure access to new technologies and products. However, these companies have more commonly operated through licensing agreements rather than outright takeovers. In the meantime, the valuations of biotech firms have been adjusted downwards, making acquisitions more attractive and cheaper. Thus, pharmaceutical companies are now seeing the potential to acquire broad-based technologies more cheaply than they could have acquired them before and than they can build internally. Schweizer (2005) showed in his study that biotech acquisitions are driven by multiple motives. The motives behind the biotech acquisitions were very similar: they were a desire to fill up the R&D pipeline, to gain access to potential blockbusters, and to acquire valuable biotech know-how and technologies that would enhance the acquirer's growth strategy. Moreover, these motives turned out to be divided between short- and long-term motives. Although the long-term rationale behind the acquisitions was largely identical in the analyzed acquisitions (support of the pharmaceutical firms' growth strategy by acquiring valuable biotech know-how and technologies), some of the short-term drivers for the acquisitions differed substantially (e.g. improvement of market position; getting a blockbuster and filling up R&D pipelines; acquiring patent rights; increasing efficiency).

The total valuations of mergers and acquisitions which involved biotechnology companies have increased steadily from $3.3 billion in 1997, to over $8.9 billion in 1998 and $13.7 billion in 1999, and up to $19.0 billion in 2000. Apart from that, the average valuation attached to the acquisition of a biotechnology company has also increased from $129 million in 1998 to over $191 million in 1999 and up to $202 million in 2000 (Goldman Sachs 2000, 2001). However, Bower (2001: 99–100) pointed out that "many of the pharmaceuticals' R&D acquisitions have yet to pay off" because biotech products and technologies are organic and far more difficult to integrate than computer or chip components. Intangible assets like know-how and intellectual property do not passively translate into tangible revenue.

Bernstein (2003) emphasizes five key questions concerning biotech M&As:

- Does the acquisition strengthen the balance sheet?
- Does the acquisition strengthen the intellectual property?
- Does the acquisition fill the pipeline?
- Does the acquisition provide any technological synergies?
- Does the acquisition add key people?

These key questions correspond also to the main benefits Patzelt et al. (2007) identify in their empirical study concerning the acquisition of German biotechnology companies. They show that M&As provide an important opportunity for biotech start-ups to acquire financial resources as they give a clear signal to investors that the companies are willing to reduce costs and to restructure their project portfolio. Moreover, a merger with a foreign company may be a way for biotech start-ups to escape the hostile financing environment of their home country. Furthermore, Patzelt et al. (2007) demonstrate that

M&As are an opportunity for biotech start-ups to expand their pipeline of clinical products and that the integration of new technologies can save time and costs in comparison with building up the resources internally. Finally, they show that managerial benefits can be achieved through M&As, if one company is lacking management experience which the other company offers.

Knyphausen et al. (2006) analyze the M&A and diversification strategies of venture capital firms and their portfolio companies in the biotech sector. They argue that in an economic downturn there should be a rationale for venture capital firms to merge some of their portfolio companies in order to make the best of their biotech investments. They call this a "flagship strategy." Haeussler (2007) analyzes firm characteristics and external firm linkages as determinants of M&A activities in the biotechnology industry. She finds that firms with interfirm collaborations are generally more likely to engage in M&A activities than firms that lack such connections. The results of her study do not support the view that financial distress is a factor that influences the propensity to engage in M&As. Based on this finding, she concludes that M&As in the biotechnology industry are proactively carried out rather than reactively enforced.

In conclusion, there is a need to distinguish between two different layers (or types) of M&A activities. The first layer deals with M&A activities between biotechnology companies, whereas the second layer concerns M&A activities between pharmaceutical and biotechnology companies. Thus, the specific type of M&A depends on the strategic reason to enter into the M&A transaction. For example, M&A activities between biotech companies, or the acquisition by a pharmaceutical company, may provide a viable solution to get access to new capital. Nonetheless, products are considered as the primary motive for biotech M&A deals, since every company needs to fill up its pipeline.

Challenges and Recommendations for the Successful Post-acquisition Integrations of Biotechnology M&As

In the following, I will discuss the different aspects of a successful post-acquisition integration of biotechnology M&A deals along the dimension of culture, people, and organizational integration. The latter, in particular, deals with the experience effect, knowledge transfer, and the question of how to measure M&A success.

Issue of Culture

Buono and Bowditch (1989) consider cultural differences to be one of the major reasons why mergers and acquisitions fail. Cultural differences are associated with lower commitment by acquired employees, diminished relative standing (Hambrick and Canella 1993), and increased turnover of acquired top managers (Walsh 1989). In addition, cultural clashes are likely to be more prominent in cross-border M&A activities than in domestic ones (Véry et al. 1993). While Hitt and Pisano (2002: 50) emphasize that "post-merger integration is likely to be more difficult to achieve between firms with home bases in different countries," Barkema et al. (1996) call for a double-layered acculturation process comprising national and organizational cultural differences. Schweizer (2005, 2009) showed that differences in terms of national cultures, as extensively analyzed by Hofstede (1980), do not play a major role in the successful post-acquisition integration of acquired biotechnology firms. Either national cultural differences did not really turn out to be a problem, or they could be solved quite quickly and easily. His analysis showed that people working in the pharmaceutical and biotechnology R&D field have very often undergone the same training and are used to working in international teams, reducing the cultural gap in terms of communication. This might be explained with the help of Levitt's (1983) globalization thesis. Moreover, it supports the statement of Van Brunt (2000) that the pharmaceutical and biotech industry are considered to be global high-tech industries, and that biotechnology firms are born globals (Oviatt and McDougall 1994).

With regard to the double-layered acculturation process (Barkema et al. 1996), a second level needs to be considered. Organizational culture tends to be unique to a particular organization and it is a powerful determinant of individual and group behavior. Schweizer (2009) showed that organizational cultural differences between small, entrepreneurial-driven and high-risk-taking biotech firms and large, rather slow pharmaceutical firms constituted a source of problems when pursuing an M&A strategy. These differences in terms of entrepreneurial spirit, risk-taking, and thinking endangered successful post-acquisition integration. The culture of the Biotech-Style is entrepreneurial, risk-taking, highly participative, team-oriented, informal, and decentralized, whereas the culture of the Pharma-Style can be characterized as market-oriented, discovery-focused, hierarchical, directive, formal, and centralized. Due to the combination of both firms, their cultures get mixed. This leads to a cultural change in biotechnology firms, which developed from an entrepreneurial and risk-taking culture to a more research- and discovery-oriented culture.

Al-Laham et al. (2010) show that a biotech-specific dominant logic exists when acquiring another biotech company. That is, when remaining in the same industry sector, the acquirer can rely on his experience with the general nature of biotech companies that have similar management styles (Larsson and Finkelstein 1999) and that follow the same biotech-specific dominant logic (Prahalad and Bettis 1986). As a result, the acquirer is able to strengthen his core competencies by rapidly integrating the target due to reduced organizational, human resources, and cultural-related problems (Hoskisson et al. 1994). In that way, the post-acquisition integration process can be speeded up.

Issue of People

Buono and Bowditch (1989) argue that the human side of M&A is frequently neglected as M&As may lead to a disruption of culture (Nahavandi and Malekzadeh 1988) and increased levels of stress (Cartwright and Cooper 1993). Increased turnover among key managers (Hambrick and Canella 1993) or key R&D personnel (Ranft and Lord 2000) following an acquisition results in the loss of their knowledge and expertise, which, in turn, limits knowledge transfer and the opportunities for value creation. Ranft and Lord (2000) argue that the retention of valuable human capital is critical for the post-merger integration and, thus, for merger success as value creation takes place after the merger (Haspeslagh and Jemison 1991). Especially in biotechnology M&As, the integration process creates value by preserving, transferring, and applying the tacit knowledge and know-how of employees from the biotech start-up (Schweizer 2005, 2009). Many of the key employees are not top managers, but can be found at different levels and in different functions throughout the organization. Very often, important organizational capabilities are embedded in relationships between individuals or in the broader social and organizational context of the organization (Kogut and Zander 1992), i.e. within the specific organizational culture.

Schweizer (2005, 2009) found that most top managers leave biotech firms after the acquisition. This can be explained by the fact that these firms lost their entrepreneurial and risk-taking spirit when pursuing their M&A strategy. This conclusion is in line with Walsh (1989) and supports the statement of Stevenson and Gumpert (1985), who noted that a manager with an entrepreneurial focus will favor a flat organizational structure with informal networks, whereas a manager with a rather administrative or conservative focus will prefer an organizational structure with clearly defined authority, responsibility, and formal hierarchy. When comparing this with the two organizational cultural styles identified in the previous section, one can conclude that an entrepreneurial-oriented manager in the biotechnology industry will prefer a firm that provides a biotech-style-oriented organizational culture. Thus, it is not surprising that most of the top managers of the biotechnology firms decided to leave.

Schweizer (2005, 2009) found much less turnover of R&D people. In line with Ranft and Lord (2000), he argues that it is more important to retain the R&D people than top management, because the former know how to apply the technologies. For them, the merger provides some advantages because they get access to more resources, enabling them to continue with their research under stable conditions.

A lack of stock option programs had an impact on the increase in turnover after the acquisition. Consequently, biotechnology firms had some difficulty attracting and retaining employees after an acquisition by a pharmaceutical company that has limited access to stock options. This observation is in line with the results of Inkpen et al. (2000), analyzing the issue of stock options in cross-border acquisition of US technology assets located in the Silicon Valley. Moreover, this supports the few studies dealing with rewards and payment of entrepreneurial firms (Balkin and Logan 1988; Zahra 1991), arguing that start-up firms need different incentive systems than traditional firms. In order to moderate this negative effect of a lack of stock option programs, special incentives and additional bonus programs are required in order to make some of the people stay.

Issue of Organizational Integration

Experience Effect and Knowledge Transfer Given the fundamental importance of know-how and knowledge for innovative success in the biotechnology industry, firms who access and exploit external knowledge by acquisitions will be able to increase their patenting speed. Frequent acquirers are more likely to make subsequent acquisitions because they have the opportunity to learn from their past acquisitions (Haleblian et al. 2006). Vermeulen and Barkema (2001) argue that acquiring organizations tend to be exposed to a large variety of events and ideas, causing them to develop richer knowledge structures (Levinthal and March 1993; March 1991), thus making these firms more flexible and adaptable to new and changing circumstances (Hitt et al. 1998).

Al-Laham et al. (2010) show that prior acquisition experience will have a positive effect on the post-acquisition patent rate, since these firms have already built up integrative and combinatory capabilities regarding the integration of acquired companies. Furthermore, in the highly sensitive biotechnology context, direct pre-acquisition alliances, as well as sector familiarity between the acquirer and the target, are very important because this facilitates and speeds up the post-acquisition organizational integration. Prior alliances allow the acquirer to gain inside information on the quality of the target and/or potential problems related to their technologies. Al-Laham et al. (2010) argue that especially the integration of knowledge during the post-acquisition integration phase is a very complex task so that the incorporation of such specific knowledge is facilitated when prior acquisition experience, direct alliance experience, as well as sector familiarity prevail.

Organizational Issues and Knowledge Transfer From an organizational perspective, acquirers need to integrate target firms in order to further develop and commercialize their technologies, while at the same time preserving the organizational autonomy of the acquired firms in order to avoid harming their innovative capabilities (Puranam et al. 2006; Ranft and Lord 2002; Schweizer 2005). Existing integration approaches and typologies (Buono and Bowditch 1989; Haspeslagh and Jemison 1991; Marks and Mirvis 1998) mostly fail to address the complexity of the post-acquisition integration process. In view of the high failure rate of M&As, there is a need to go beyond single integration approaches (Puranam et al. 2006; Schweizer 2005). Given the big differences in terms of organizational structure and culture between pharmaceutical and biotech companies (Powell 1996), existing post-acquisition integration typologies (Haspeslagh and Jemison 1991) would suggest granting the acquired biotech companies a high degree of autonomy (Datta and Grant 1990). However, the analysis of Schweizer (2005) has revealed that different integration strategies with different degrees of autonomy have to be used, suggesting a more complex process, since the realization of some of the short-term motives called for the immediate absorption of the acquired biotech company, while the long-term motives could only be realized with a preservation approach.

When acquiring biotech companies, pharmaceutical companies face the need to make hybrid organizational arrangements (Borys and Jemison 1989) in order to integrate biotech companies in some way and, at the same time, preserving the autonomy of the latter so as not to endanger the future existence of the desired capabilities. Schweizer (2005) develops a post-acquisition integration framework that calls for a hybrid integration approach with simultaneous short- and long-term orientations and segmentation across different functions and value-chain components. There is a clear need for cooperation between biotech and pharmaceutical companies after the acquisition in order to create value (Haspeslagh and Jemison 1991). This raises the problem of how to coordinate and combine the organizations (Birkinshaw et al. 2000), as well as how to allocate control among those firms after the acquisition (Borys and Jemison 1989). Schweizer (2005) has found that the integration of acquired biotech firms requires the simultaneous application of two distinct integration approaches concerning R&D and non-R&D-related portions. The reason for this is that pharmaceutical companies pursue different motives, which in turn require different integration approaches depending on the know-how and competencies of the acquired biotech firms.

For a successful post-acquisition integration of acquired biotech companies, it is necessary to protect the acquired firms' competencies by applying a slow preservation approach concerning R&D-related areas, granting the acquired biotech companies a high degree of autonomy (Datta and Grant 1990). Highly specific know-how, such as that in the biotech context (Powell 1993), is hard to transmit because fewer parties other than the innovator can benefit from its application (Henderson and Cockburn 1994; McEvily and Chakravarthy 2002). However, as far as clinical trials, regulatory affairs, and sales and marketing are concerned, a rapid integration is possible as they belong to the core competencies of the pharmaceutical company (or of a large biotech firm).

The acquisition and subsequent integration of biotech companies is a multidimensional and multifaceted phenomenon (Javidan et al. 2004), driven by different motives (Bower 2001; Steiner 1975). This is due to the fact that pharmaceutical companies pursue different motives, especially the desire to acquire specific technological know-how and technologies (Ahuja and Katila 2001). Thus, pharmaceutical companies usually pursue a hybrid acquisition strategy when approaching biotech companies. On the one hand, they pursue the short-term strategy of improving their market positions by filling their R&D pipelines and gaining potential blockbusters. On the other hand, they pursue the long-term strategy of supporting their overall growth strategies by accessing biotechnology know-how and technologies. Thus, Schweizer (2005) suggests that the right organizational integration approach for clinical trials, regulatory affairs, and sales and marketing is a rapid absorption approach in which the pharmaceutical company takes over control. In order to realize this, the pharmaceutical companies need to receive the necessary "biotech knowledge," so that they are enabled to bring the drug to market. Furthermore, the supporting functions (finance, HR, IT) are carried out by the pharmaceutical companies because they usually have more elaborate systems. In contrast to this, the existing biotech know-how and technologies are to support the growth strategy of the pharmaceutical, so that their competencies need to be protected by applying a slow preservation approach, granting the acquired biotech company a high degree of autonomy.

According to Ernst & Young (2004) and the findings of Patzelt et al. (2007), there might be hurdles that prevent successful M&A activities between biotech companies. These hurdles have their roots in the attitudes of the investors and the management. With regard to investors, they may not be willing to sell or merge their companies cheaply in hostile financing environments, when valuations of private companies are low. Besides the egos of biotech CEOs, brokering an agreement among all parties to an M&A transaction is a major hurdle that is often complicated by a lack of relevant M&A experience vis-à-vis both management and investors.

Measuring M&A Success in Biotechnology M&As Given the fact that so far there is no consensus on a common way of measuring M&A success (Javidan et al. 2004; King et al. 2004; Larsson and Finkelstein 1999) and that the race to patent innovations is a crucial aspect of competitive strategy in the biotechnology industry, the post-acquisition patent rate can be used as an appropriate measure for acquisition success in the biotech context. This is in line with Haleblian et al. (2009), who emphasize the need for a match between acquisition performance measures, the subjects of analyses, and the questions of interest in order to effectively measure acquisition performance. In the context of biotechnology M&A activities, the post-acquisition patent rate seems to be the most appropriate measure for acquisition performance because researchers want to analyze the success of this "M&A as R&D" strategy, as carried out by Al-Laham et al. (2010). Patents are not only used to establish property rights, but also to facilitate licensing, and are used as "bargaining chips" in negotiations (Von Hippel 1988). A biotech firm with intellectual property protection is more likely to find willing partners to support commercialization activities (Lerner 1994; Powell and Brantley 1992).

SUMMARY AND FUTURE RESEARCH QUESTIONS

The biotechnology industry has witnessed a continuous increase in M&A activities during the last decade. In an industry context where developing a successful product is no guarantee that it will ever happen again, firms will frequently have to look outside for new products in order to fill up their pipeline. Moreover, drug discovery and development is about getting the right teams of people with the necessary skills, know-how, as well as capabilities together, and it is often cheaper and more effective to buy these teams than to build them internally.

However, the acquiring company needs to make sure that these people and teams also stay within the company and that they do not decide to leave. Even if a deal seems to put the merged entity on a new growth curve, it will take a lot of time to finally realize the intended synergies because the development cycles in biotech companies are very long. This makes it difficult to measure the success of such a biotech merger; whilst the logic of M&As in the biotech sector is a long-term one, many investors expect results in the short term. Thus, the post-acquisition patent rate might be an appropriate success measure for M&A activities in the biotechnology industry. The following major research questions that may guide research for M&As in the biotech sector can be identified:

- When do biotech companies make the decision to look for M&A partners?
- How do biotech firms compare M&As with other strategic options like alliances or licensing agreements and what criteria do they use?

- What pitfalls does the due-diligence process provide?
- How can the acquirer make sure that top researchers remain with the new entity?
- How do biotech firms calculate the expected synergies of the deal?
- What further success measures could be used in biotech M&A activities?

Following Hagedoorn and Duysters (2002), pharmaceutical companies have three potential strategies to gain access to biotechnological know-how. In so doing, they seek to fill up their R&D pipeline and remain competitive in the long run. These three strategies are: first, organic growth, in which pharmaceutical companies build this know-how on their own; second, strategic alliances with biotech firms; and, third, M&A to integrate companies with know-how and capabilities. In the field of biotechnology, the technological frontier is advanced with a knowledge, skill, and competence base fundamentally different from prior know-how (Powell 1993), so that it is not enough for an acquirer to simply "buy" a technology, because, to create value, this technology must be nurtured and integrated throughout the post-acquisition integration process (Larsson and Finkelstein 1999). However, considering the big differences in culture and organizational styles between pharmaceutical and biotech companies, the challenge of gaining access to the desired capabilities becomes even more obvious and highlights the importance of the "absorptive capabilities" (Cohen and Levinthal 1990), as well as the importance of keeping key R&D talent from the acquired biotech company. Moreover, in view of the complexity and multifaceted nature of M&As, pharmaceutical companies need to apply a hybrid post-acquisition integration approach, with simultaneous short- and long-term motives/orientations and segmentation at a different pace across different value-chain components. Future research on M&A activities between pharmaceutical and biotechnology companies might focus on the following questions:

- What can a pharmaceutical company do in order to retain key R&D talent/teams from the acquired biotech company?
- How can a pharmaceutical company protect the specific research culture of the acquired biotech firm in the long run?
- Do pharmaceutical companies have a different success measure for biotech acquisitions than biotech firms?

This section has identified key questions that may provide some guidance for future research concerning M&A activities in the biotechnology and pharmaceutical sectors. I encourage researchers to keep these questions in mind as they pursue future studies.

REFERENCES

Agrawal, A., & Jaffe, J. F. (2000). "The Post-merger Performance Puzzle," in C. Cooper & A. Gregory (eds.), *Advances in Mergers and Acquisitions*. New York: Elsevier Science, 7–42.

Ahuja, G. & Katila, R. (2001). "Technological Acquisitions and the Innovation Performance of Acquiring Firms." *Strategic Management Journal*, 22: 197–220.

Al-Laham, A., Schweizer, L., & Amburgey, T. (2010). "Analyzing the Influence of Acquisition Experience, Direct Alliance Experience and Sector Familiarity on Acquisition Success in the "M&A as R&D" Type of Acquisition in the Biotechnology Industry." *Scandinavian Journal of Management*, 26: 25–37.

Arnold, R., Grindley, J., & Smart, S. (1999). "Honorable Disposals as Planned Exit Route." *Nature Biotechnology*, 17/Supplement: BE6–BE7.

Arora, A., & Gambardella, A. (1990). "Complementarity and External Linkages. The Strategies of Large Firms in Biotechnology." *Journal of Industrial Economics*, 38/4: 361–79.

Balkin, D. B., & Logan, J. W. (1988). "Reward Policies that Support Entrepreneurship." *Compensation and Benefits Review*, 20/1: 18–25.

Barkema, H. G., Bell, J. H., & Pennings, J. M. (1996). "Foreign Entry, Cultural Barriers, and Learnings." *Strategic Management Journal*, 17: 151–66.

Barley, S., & Freeman, J. (1992). "Strategic Alliances in Commercial Biotechnology," in N. Nohria and R. Eccles (eds.), *Networks and Organizations*. Boston, MA: Harvard Business School Press, 311–47.

Barney, J. B. (1991). "Firm Resources and Sustained Competitive Advantage." *Journal of Management*, 17: 99–120.

Bernstein, K. (2003). "Modeling Deals." *BioCentury*, 11/38: A19.

Biocentury (2003). "Back-to-School Issue: The M&A Game." *BioCentury*, 11/38: A1–A18.

——(2007). M&A upside. *BioCentury*, 15/1: A1–A7.

Birkinshaw, J., Bresman, H., & Hakanson, L. (2000). "Managing the Post-Acquisition Integration Process: How the Human Integration and Task Integration Processes Interact to Foster Value Creation." *Journal of Management Studies*, 37: 395–425.

Borys, B., & Jemison, D. B. (1989). "Hybrid Arrangements as Strategic Alliances: Theoretical Issues in Organizational Combinations." *Academy of Management Review*, 14: 234–49.

Bower, J. L. (2001). "Not All M&As are Alike—And That Matters." *Harvard Business Review*, 79/2: 93–101.

Business Insights (2008). *Biotech M&A Strategies: Deal Assessments, Trends and Future Prospects*. London: Business Insights.

Buono, A. F., & Bowditch, J. L. (1989). *The Human Side of Mergers and Acquisitions. Managing Collisions between People, Cultures and Organizations*. San Francisco: Jossey-Bass.

Capron, L. (1999). "The Long-Term Performance of Horizontal Acquisitions." *Strategic Management Journal*, 20: 987–1016.

Cartwright, S., & Cooper, C.L. 1992. *Mergers and Acquisitions: The Human Factor*. Oxford, UK: Butterworth-Heinemann.

————(1993). "The Role of Culture Compatibility in Successful Organizational Marriage." *Academy of Management Executive*, 7: 57–70.

Chaudhuri, S., & Tabrizi, B. (1999). "Capturing the Real Value in High-Tech Acquisitions." *Harvard Business Review*, 77/5: 123–30.

Cohen, W., & Levinthal, D. (1990). "Absorptive Capacity: A New Perspective on Learning and Innovation." *Administrative Science Quarterly*, 35: 128–52.

Datta, D. K., & Grant, J. H. (1990). "Relationships Between Type of Acquisitions, The Autonomy Given to the Acquired Firm, and Acquisition Success: An Empirical Analysis." *Journal of Management*, 16: 29–44.

——Pinches, G. E., & Narayanan, V. K. (1992). "Factors Influencing Wealth Creation from Mergers and Acquisitions: A Meta-Analysis." *Strategic Management Journal*, 13: 67–84.

DeCarolis, D. M. & Deeds, D. L. (1999). "The Impact of Stocks and Flows of Organizational Knowledge on Firm Performance: An Empirical Investigation of the Biotechnology Industry." *Strategic Management Journal*, 20/10: 953–68.

Dosi, G., Freeman, C., Nelson, R., Silverberg, G., & Soete, L. (1988). *Technical Change and Economic Theory*. London: Pinter Publishers.

Ernst & Young (2004), *Per Aspera Ad Astra: "Der steinige Weg zu den Sternen." Deutscher Biotechnologie-Report 2004 [The stony way to the stars: German biotechnology report 2004]*. Mannheim: Ernst & Young.

Goldman Sachs (2000). *Strategic Alliances in Biotechnology*. New York: Goldman Sachs.

—— (2001). *Strategic Alliances in Biotechnology*. New York: Goldman Sachs.

Graebner, M. (2004). "Momentum and Serendipity: How Acquired Leaders Create Value in the Integration of Technology Firms." *Strategic Management Journal*, 25: 751–77.

Greis, N., Dibner, M., & Bean, A. (1995). "External Partnering as a Response to Innovation Barriers and Global Competition in Biotechnology." *Research Policy*, 24: 609–30.

Hacking, A. (1986). *Economic Aspects of Biotechnology*. Cambridge: University Press.

Haeussler, C. (2007). "Proactive versus Reactive M&A Activities in the Biotechnology Industry." *Journal of High Technology Management Research*, 17/2: 109–23.

Hagedoorn, J., & Duysters, G. (2002). "External Sources of Innovative Capabilities: The Preference for Strategic Alliances or Mergers and Acquisitions." *Journal of Management Studies*, 39: 167–88.

Haleblian, J., Devers, C. A., McNamara, G., Carpenter, M. A., & Davison, R. B. (2009). "Taking Stock of What We Know about Mergers and Acquisitions: A Review and Research Agenda." *Journal of Management*, 35: 469–502.

—— Kim, J., & Rajagopalan, N.(2006). "The Influence of Acquisition and Performance on Acquisition Behavior: Evidence from the U.S. Commercial Banking Industry." *Academy of Management Journal*, 49: 357–70.

Hambrick, D. C., & Canella, A. A. (1993). "Relative Standing: A Framework for Understanding Departures of Acquired Executives." *Academy of Management Journal*, 36: 733–62.

Haspeslagh, P. C., & Jemison, D. B. (1991). *Managing Acquisitions: Creating Value through Corporate Renewal*. New York: Free Press.

Henderson, R., & Cockburn, I. (1994). "Measuring Competence? Exploring Firm Effects in Pharmaceutical Research." *Strategic Management Journal*, 15: 63–84.

Higgins, M. J., & Rodriguez, D. (2003). "The Outsourcing of R&D through Acquisitions in the Pharmaceutical Industry." *Emory Economics Paper Series*, 0324.

Hitt, M. A., Harrison, J. S., Ireland, R. D., & Best, A. (1998). "Attributes of Successful and Unsuccessful Acquisitions of US Firms." *British Journal of Management*, 2: 91–114.

—— Hoskisson, R. E., Johnson, R. A., & Moesel, D. D. (1996). "The Market for Corporate Control and Firm Innovation." *Academy of Management Journal*, 39: 1084–119.

—— & Pisano, V. (2002). "Cross-Border Mergers and Acquisitions: Challenges and Opportunities," in A. Pablo and M. Javidan (eds.), *Mergers and Acquisitions: Creating Integrative Knowledge*. Oxford, UK: Blackwell, 45–59.

Hofstede, G. (1980). *Culture's Consequences: International Differences in Work-Related Values*. Beverly Hills, CA: Sage.

Hoskisson, R. E., Hitt, M. A., & Ireland, R. D. (1994). "The Effect of Acquisitions and Restructuring (Strategic Refocusing) Strategies on Innovation," in G. von Krogh, A. Sinatra, and H. Singh (eds.), *The Management of Corporate Acquisitions*. Basingstoke, UK: Macmillan, 144–69.

Inkpen, A. C., Sundaram, A. K., & Rockwood, K. (2000). "Cross-Border Acquisitions of U.S. Technology Assets." *California Management Review*, 42/3: 50–71.

Javidan, M., Pablo, A., Singh, H., Hitt, M., & Jemison, D. (2004). "Where We've Been and Where We're Going," in A. Pablo and M. Javidan (eds.), *Mergers and Acquisitions: Creating Integrative Knowledge*. Oxford, UK: Blackwell, 245–61.

Jones, G. K., Lanctot, A., & Teegen, H. J. (2001). "Determinants and Performance of External Technology Acquisition." *Journal of Business Venturing*, 16/3: 255–83.

Kenney, M. (1986). *Biotechnology: The University-Industrial Complex*. New Haven, CT: Yale University Press.

King, D. R., Dalton, D. R., Daily, C. M., & Covin, J. G. (2004). "Meta-analyses of Post-Acquisition Performance: Indications of Unidentified Moderators." *Strategic Management Journal*, 25: 187–200.

Knyphausen-Aufseß, D. zu, Zaby, A., & Kind, S. (2006). "M&A and Diversification Strategies of VC-Backed Firms in the Biotechnology Industry: Towards Understanding The Perspectives of Venture Capitalists and their Portfolio Companies," in J. Butler, A. Lockett, & D. Ucbasaran (eds.) *Venture Capital in the Changing World of Entrepreneurship*. Greenwich, CT: Information Age Publishing.

Kogut, B., & Zander, U. (1992). "Knowledge of the Firm, Combinative Capabilities and the Replication of Technology." *Organization Science*, 3: 383–97.

Lane, P. J., & Lubatkin, M. (1998). "Relative Absorptive Capacity and Interorganizational Learning." *Strategic Management Journal*, 19: 461–77.

Larsson, R., & Finkelstein, S. (1999). "Integrating Strategic, Organizational, and Human Resource Perspectives on Mergers and Acquisitions: A Case Survey of Synergy Realization." *Organization Science*, 10: 1–26.

Lerner, J. (1994). "Venture Capitalists and the Decision to Go Public." *Journal of Finance*, 49: 293–316.

Levinthal, D., & March, J. G. (1993). "The Myopia of Learning." *Strategic Management Journal*, 14: 95–112.

Levitt, T. (1983). "The Globalization of Markets." *Harvard Business Review*, 61/3: 92–102.

March, J. G. (1991). "Exploration and Exploitation in Organizational Learning." *Organization Science*, 2: 71–87.

Marks, M. L., & Mirvis, P. H. (1998). *Joining Forces: Making One Plus One Equal Three in Mergers, Acquisitions And Alliances*. Chichester, UK: Wiley.

McEvily, S., & Chakravarthy, B. (2002). "The Persistence of Knowledge-Based Advantage: An Empirical Test for Product Performance and Technological Knowledge." *Strategic Management Journal*, 23: 285–305.

Nahavandi, A., & Malekzadeh, A. R. (1988). "Acculturation in Mergers and Acquisition." *Academy of Management Review*, 13: 79–90.

Napier, N. K. (1989). "Mergers and Acquisitions: Human Resource Issues and Outcomes. A Review and Suggested Typology." *Journal of Management Studies*, 26: 271–89.

Office of Technology Assessment (1988). *New Developments in Biotechnology: U.S. Investment in Biotechnology—Special Report OTA-BA-360*. Washington, DC: U.S. Government Printing Office.

Oviatt, B. M., & McDougall, P. P. (1994). "Toward a Theory of International New Ventures." *Journal of International Business Studies*, 3: 30–44.

—— —— (1997). "Challenges for Internationalization Process Theory: The Case of International New Ventures." *Management International Review*, 37: 85–99.

Pablo, A. (1994). "Determination of Acquisition Integration Level: A Decision-Making Perspective." *Academy of Management Journal*, 37: 803–39.

Patzelt, H., & Brenner, T. (2008). "Introduction to the Handbook of Bioentrepreneurship," in H. Patzelt & T. Brenner (eds.), *Handbook of Bioentrepreneurship*. New York: Springer, 1–6.

——Schweizer, L., & Knyphausen-Aufseß, D. zu (2007). "Mergers and Acquisitions of German Biotechnology Startups." *International Journal of Biotechnology*, 9/1: 1–19.

Powell, W. (1993). "The Social Construction of an Organizational Field: The Case of Biotechnology." Working Paper. Tucson, AZ: Department of Sociology, University of Arizona.

——(1996). "Inter-organizational Collaboration in the Biotechnology Industry." *Journal of Institutional and Theoretical Economics*, 152/1: 197–215.

——& Brantley, P. (1992). "Competitive Cooperation in Biotechnology: Learning through Networks?", in N. Nohria and R. Eccles (eds.), *Networks and Organizations*. Boston, MA: Harvard Business School Press, 366–94.

Prahalad, C. K., & Bettis, R. A. (1986). "The Dominant Logic: A New Linkage between Diversity and Performance." *Strategic Management Journal*, 7: 485–501.

Puranam, P., Singh, H., & Zollo, M. (2006). "Organizing for Innovation: Managing the Coordination-Autonomy Dilemma in Technology Acquisitions." *Academy of Management Journal*, 49: 263–80.

Purcell, D. J. (1998). "Navigating Biotechnology's New Fiscal Opportunities." *Nature Biotechnology*, 16/Supplement: 51.

Ranft, A. L., & Lord, M. D. (2000). "Acquiring New Knowledge: The Role of Retaining Human Capital in Acquisition of High-Tech Firms." *Journal of High Technology Management Research*, 11: 295–319.

—— ——(2002). "Acquiring New Technologies and Capabilities: A Grounded Model of Acquisition Implementation." *Organization Science*, 13: 420–41.

Schweiger, D. M., & Lippert, R. L. (2005). "Integration: The Critical Link in M&A Value Creation," in G. K. Stahl & M. E. Mendenhall (eds.), *Mergers and Acquisitions: Managing Culture and Human Resources*. Stanford, CA: Stanford University Press, 17–45.

Schweizer, L. (2005). "Organizational Integration of Acquired Biotechnology Companies into Pharmaceutical Companies: The Need for a Hybrid Approach." *Academy of Management Journal*, 48/6: 1051–74.

——(2009). "Post-merger Integration of International Biotechnology Start-Ups: The Relationship between Entrepreneurial Strategy, Culture and Human Resources." *Zeitschrift für Betriebswirtschaft*, ZfB—Special Issue International Entrepreneurship, 61/1: 133–53.

Sharp, M. (1991). "Technological Trajectories and the Corporate Strategies in the Diffusion of Biotechnology," in E. Deiaco, E. Hornell, and G. Vickery (eds.), *Technology and Investment: Crucial Issues for the 1990s*. London: Pinter Publishers, 93–114.

Sirower, M. L. (1997). *The Synergy Trap: How Companies Lose the Acquisition Game*. New York: Free Press.

Steiner, P. O. (1975). *Mergers: Motives, Effects, Policies*. Ann Arbor, MI: University of Michigan Press.

Stevenson, H. H., & Gumpert, D. E. (1985). "The Heart of Entrepreneurship." *Harvard Business Review*, 63/3: 85–94.

Teitelman, R. (1989). *Gene Dreams: Wall Street, Academia, and the Rise of Biotechnology*. New York: Basic Books.

Van Brunt, J. (2000). "Borderless Biotech." *Signals Magazine*, December 13. Available at <http://www.signalsmag.com>.

—— (2005). "Biotech's Old Soldiers." *Signals Magazine*, May 10. Available at <http://www.signalsmag.com>.

Vermeulen, F., & Barkema, H. (2001). "Learning through Acquisitions." *Academy of Management Journal*, 44: 457–76.

Véry, P., Calori, R. & Lubatkin, M. (1993). "An Investigation of National and Organizational Cultural Influences in Recent European Mergers," in P. Shrivastav, A. Hiff, and J. Dutton (eds.), *Advances in Strategic Management* (9th ed.). Greenwich, CT: JAI Press, 323–46.

Von Hippel, E. (1988). *The Sources of Innovation*. New York: Oxford University Press.

Walsh, J. P. (1989). "Doing a Deal: Merger and Acquisition Negotiations and their Impact upon Target Company Top Management." *Strategic Management Journal*, 10: 307–22.

Webber, D. (1999). "Economic Darwinism versus Financial Tooth Fairies." *Nature Biotechnology*, 17/Supplement: BE14–BE15.

Wirth, P. (1994). "Biotechnologie/Biomedizin: Stand und Perspektiven [Biotechnology/Biomedicine: State of the Art and Perspectives]," in C. P. Hollenberg and V. Hempel (eds.), *Biotec: Technologieforum [Biotech: Technology forum]*. Düsseldorf: Rudolf Stehle, 53–65.

Zahra, S. A. (1991). "Predictors and Financial Outcomes of Corporate Entrepreneurship: An Exploratory Study." *Journal of Business Venturing*, 6: 259–85.

—— Ireland, R. D., & Hitt, M. A. (2000). "International Expansion by New Venture Firms: International Diversity, Mode of Market Entry, Technological Learning, and Performance." *Academy of Management Journal*, 43/5: 925–50.

Zander, U., & Kogut, B. (1995). "Knowledge and the Speed of the Transfer and Imitation of Organizational Capabilities. An Empirical Test." *Organization Science*, 6: 76–92.

PART V

SYNTHESIS

CHAPTER 27

....

MERGERS AND ACQUISITIONS

A Synthesis

....

SATU TEERIKANGAS, RICHARD J. JOSEPH,
AND DAVID FAULKNER

INTRODUCTION

....

Despite decades of scholarly attention, the study of M&A has been criticized for its inability to provide "robust" theories to explain the underlying dynamics and value-creation mechanisms of this organizational encounter called a "merger" or an "acquisition" (Schweiger and Goulet 2000; King et al. 2004; Haleblian et al. 2009). In this *Handbook*, we have attempted to provide a response to this prevailing chasm. Our principal aim has been to synthesize the hitherto separately practiced and studied disciplines of finance, strategy, and human relations (which we term "sociocultural" later in the chapter), as they relate to, and impact, the decision to merge, the execution of the merger process, and the transaction's long-term consequences.

With this objective in mind, throughout this *Handbook*, we have viewed M&A through strategic, financial, sociocultural, and sectorial lenses. We have given voice to prominent and emerging scholars in their respective domains of expertise. To our knowledge, in the practice and study of M&A, this integrative approach based on key disciplines is the first of its kind (see also Haleblian et al. 2009). The tendency so far has been toward a disciplinary divide visible across the practice and study of M&A. Textbooks tend to focus primarily on the financial or sociocultural aspects of M&A, with few intersections. M&A practitioners and consultants generally focus on pre-deal valuation, post-deal integration, or change management. A conceptual gulf places M&A academics into disciplinary silos ranging from finance, to strategy, organizational behavior, international management, and beyond, to the disciplines of psychology, history, and sociology (Haleblian et al. 2009; Mirc et al. 2010).

Having completed this examination, we are now in a position to answer the fundamental question: where does a comprehensive review of the financial, strategic, and sociocultural dimensions of M&A activity lead us? An overview of the chapters in this *Handbook* reinforces the view of M&A as an activity with multiple drivers, disciplines, contexts, levels, phases, and actors; an activity that spans the merging parties' histories and shapes their long-term constitution and performance; an activity that impacts a variety of stakeholders, evolves over time, assumes various forms depending on the deal type, firms, and sectors involved; an activity that is shaped by an array of shifting local, national, and global drivers, as is evident from the history of M&A since the end of the 19th century.

This complexity explains why M&A has largely eluded simplistic definitions and typologies (see Chapter 3) and is difficult to categorize, much less operationalize and evaluate (see Chapters 3, 4, 5, 8, and 16). It might also explain why Cartwright (see Chapter 15) soberly concludes that the fate of the average acquirer has changed little over time (as confirmed by the reviews of M&A performance; see Chapters 4 and 5).

For M&A scholars, this complexity highlights the need to take a multidimensional and long-term look at M&A that might better relate its seemingly disparate activities, facilitate strategic, financial, and managerial decision-making, and capture the subtle dynamics underlying the entire process. Forging this view undoubtedly requires the involvement and contribution of a multiplicity of actors engaged in the practice or the study of M&A, who can grasp its "multi-dimensional heterogeneity" (Zollo and Singh 2004).

The following sections purport to critique and synthesize the various findings of the current M&A literature, so as to better integrate and reconcile their strategic, financial, and sociocultural foci. We first proceed to a critical review of the changing landscape of M&A scholarship across disciplines, as well as the methodological lenses through which these endeavors have been pursued. Whilst the field has, overall, advanced to more nuanced and fine-tuned analyses of M&A, serious gaps in the literature remain. This chapter will identify these gaps and thus pave the way for future research.

In this dynamic synthesis, we attempt to capture and convey the multifaceted nature of M&A activity. We portray M&A in terms of (1) its changing features, as well as the drivers that have propelled it forward since the end of the 19th century, (2) the ways in which its component parts differ from one another, and (3) a phase-based conceptual framework intended to convey the richness, complexity, and interdependence of its underlying processes. To better illustrate our dynamic synthesis, we conclude by presenting a three-dimensional model that integrates the financial, strategic, and sociocultural aspects of M&A. This model has served as the structural backbone of this *Handbook* and depicts its scholarly contribution. By laying the foundation for this multidimensional approach, we purport to "re-root" the study of M&A, thus enabling more effective practice and enlightened research into this significant transactional form, and organizational encounter.

THE STUDY OF M&A—DISCIPLINARY AND METHODOLOGICAL FOCI

Shifting Disciplinary Orientations

The formal study of M&A emerged in the 1950s, when economists and business historians became interested in the financial and economic aspects of M&A activity (Stigler 1950; Navin and Sears 1955). Their ranks were soon joined by strategy scholars, who saw M&A as a means of improving a firm's competitive advantage in specific markets (Ansoff 1965; see Chapter 3). Somewhat later, the interest of strategists shifted to the organizational fit, market complementarities, and operational synergies of the merging firms (Salter and Weinhold 1979; see Chapter 3). The question of whether M&A improves firm performance, and further, what explains M&A performance has been at the forefront of strategy and finance research since the 1970s (Jensen and Ruback 1983), with an increasing rate, breadth, and finesse of scholarly efforts (see Chapters 4 and 5). Finance researchers have been interested in refining pre-acquisition valuation methods, pricing models, financing means, transactional structures, and measures intended to create shareholder value (see Chapter 8).

Whilst early mentions of the identity challenges in mergers date back to the 1920s (McKinsey 1929), it was only in the 1960s and 1970s that scholars made the first research strides in the areas of post-merger integration management (Mace and Montgomery 1962; Howell 1970). The 1980s marked the advent of a growing interest in the management and human aspects of M&A (Marks 1982; Jemison and Sitkin 1986). This interest led to the development of phase and process perspectives on M&A (Haspeslagh and Jemison 1991), as well as an appreciation of the ways in which the human dimension of M&A manifests itself (Napier 1989; Cartwright and Cooper 1990; see Chapter 15). Whilst the cultural clash (Buono et al. 1985) and acculturation challenges (Nahavandi and Malekzadeh 1988) of merger integration were highlighted in the 1980s, the rise of cross-border M&A activity in Europe in the 1990s was paralleled by a plethora of research on acquisitions as a means of market entry (Barkema and Bell 1996). It was also accompanied by queries into the impact of clashing national and organizational cultures on M&A performance (for reviews, see Stahl and Voigt 2008; Teerikangas and Véry 2006; Chapter 16). Since the early 21st century, scholarly research into the human side of M&A has gravitated toward an analysis of the process of identification in the aftermath of the deal. Much of this research has been conducted by social psychologists (see Chapter 19). Despite major research advances, many areas of M&A remain unexplored, thus leaving an intellectual void in the literature. At the end of this chapter, we shall point out these hitherto unaddressed themes.

In synthesis, the study of M&A began with isolated research efforts in the various disciplines. Research streams in strategy and finance emerged in the 1970s. Parallel streams in organizational behavior and management arose in the 1980s. These streams focused on specific aspects of M&A, such as integration, human relations, culture, and identity. Whilst these intellectual developments have broadened our understanding of M&A, they have also contributed to the "silo" effect so characteristic of M&A scholarship today. Indeed, whilst every major discipline has succeeded in capturing the essence of part of the phenomenon (Haleblian et al. 2009), because there has been little cross-fertilization and mutual cooperation (Mirc et al. 2010), few, if any, have captured the essence of the phenomenon as a whole.

As a result, M&A scholarship has been virtually segregated into (1) temporal *phases*, with finance scholars focusing primarily on pre-deal valuation, whilst strategy and human relations scholars focus mainly on post-deal management; and (2) topical *themes*, under the implicit assumption that the phenomenon of M&A can be accurately viewed and adequately comprehended with the aid of financial, strategic, human, cultural, or identity lenses, without considering a priori the ways in which these thematic lenses might be positioned, aligned, or combined. We argue that a lack of scholarly dialogue, reinforced by rigid disciplinary structures and pre-defined career paths, have impeded the advancement toward more enlightened and relevant theories of M&A.

Realist Methodological Underpinnings

In terms of methodology, the field of M&A has been biased toward a rational discourse. Placing the study of M&A on the seminal two-by-two matrix designed by Burrell and Morgan (1979), we note that significant scholarly work on M&A can be positioned in the "functionalist" quadrant, i.e. founded on an objective approach to the scientific endeavor, a realist ontology, and a non-critical perspective. This positioning is attributable in part to the long-standing and predominant nature of finance and strategy M&A studies, both imbued with a positivistic attitude and largely based on quantitative methods. It is surprising, perhaps, to note that the sociocultural dimensions of M&A (i.e. the integration, human, cultural, identity, knowledge sides) have also veered toward this methodological bias.

It is only since the late 1990s and the early 2000s that scholarship inspired by a more subjective epistemology has emerged. This scholarship adopts an interpretive, constructionist approach to M&A. It offers more nuanced ways to explore institutional cultures (Risberg 1997; Vaara 1999, 2000; Riad 2005), employee reactions (Risberg 2001), integration management (Vaara, 2003), and identity dynamics in M&A (Vaara et al. 2003).

In the literature, critical perspectives on M&A remain rare. We note how M&A scholars have practically avoided a critical approach to the study of the phenomenon. This posture is manifest in the ways in which, for example, the management of M&A has been examined. In the study of culture in M&A, Risberg (1997) and Riad (2005) have advocated more critical approaches, instead of merely assuming "culture" to matter. The review of M&A from a power and politics perspective reveals a lack of explicit treatment of power issues. Tienari and Vaara (see Chapter 20) find power and politics to be an important aspect of

M&A, yet both have received scant attention. In other words, the study of M&A to date has embodied an uncritical and seemingly monolithic approach that fails to acknowledge the less visible undercurrents of the phenomenon, including power, politics, and complex cultural dynamics.

Furthermore, the absence of a critical stance is visible with respect to ways in which the linkages between M&A as a phenomenon and its regulatory and financial drivers have been treated. Two *Handbook* chapters touch on the more vulnerable and questionable dimensions of M&A activity. In Chapter 13, Ryan paints a critical picture of the rise of shareholder value-driven capital markets dominated by numerous, shifting investors seeking short-term profits. In such an environment, Ryan asks, has M&A become the vehicle for growth merely for the sake of growth? Is it time to question the wisdom of using M&A as a vehicle for growth? Furthermore, is it time to question the shareholder-driven rationale of the entire financial system? In Chapter 23, Dymski traces the historical development of merger activity in the banking sector worldwide. Dymski regards the expansion of M&A activity in this sector since the 1980s as attributable to easing regulations, and the ultimate "collapse" of regulated banking activity. On this view, these developments have practically left the sector to its own devices—animated by the pursuit of short-term profits and devoid of concern for broader societal interests. To some extent, M&A has galvanized the internationalization of the banking sector in the context of deregulation and a "Wild West"-type of financial innovation. From a critical perspective, this outcome begs the question—is M&A a neutral vehicle in this sad saga? What role has M&A played in recurring financial crises? Looking forward, one can only hope that the current unsettled state of financial affairs will lead to new ways of operating, running, and organizing global capital markets, thus bearing on the look and shape of future M&A activity.

The M&A Phenomenon—Historical and Definitional Complexity

A Historical Overview of the M&A Phenomenon

Since the end of the 19th century, scholars have identified six waves of intense M&A activity (see Chapters 2 and 8). Each wave is characterized by a particular type of activity. These types are mirrored, in turn, in the various scholarly approaches to M&A.

As Chapter 2 highlights, the waves are characterized by varying company rationales for pursuing acquisitions, differing acquisition types (in terms of degree of relatedness, friendly vs. hostile takeovers, and the profile of buyers involved), and differing ways to finance the deal (cash vs. stock). Occurring at different moments in history, each wave was driven by a distinct set of drivers, including technological, legislative, and regulatory reforms; the expansion of capital markets, and rapid globalization. Hence,

M&A activity is context dependent; that is, it must be placed in a broader economic and societal setting.

Not surprisingly, the peculiarities of each wave are reflected in the performance of the participating companies. Across the waves, regardless of acquisition, deal, and financing type, the acquired firm has largely benefited. By contrast, the fate of the acquiring firm has varied from one wave to another, being largely positive in the first wave, negative in the second, mixed in the third, positive for acquirers of related acquisitions in the fourth, and negative in the fifth (see Chapter 2).

The shift toward related company acquisitions, i.e. acquisitions in the same industry, is noteworthy in the fourth wave, which occurred in the 1980s. Paralleling this development has been a scholarly emphasis on post-merger integration, human relations, and the cultural aspects of M&A since the 1980s. Earlier waves were characterized largely by horizontal consolidations (first wave), the creation of oligopolies (second wave), and unrelated diversification, i.e. acquisitions of firms in unrelated industries (third wave).

Whilst the first two M&A waves (end 1890s and 1920s) occurred predominantly in the United States, from the third wave onward (1960s), the trend moved increasingly toward Europe. Since the fourth wave (1990s), Asian activity (initially, Japan) has noticeably increased, propelled in the sixth wave in the early 21st century by the entry of the emerging economies of India, China, Brazil, and Russia into the fray. The shifting transactional nature and national focus of this phenomenon is mirrored, somewhat retrospectively, in the study of M&A, conducted principally by North American scholars who, until the late 1980s, focused mainly on US deals. Interestingly enough, the scholarly review of cross-border M&A gained momentum during the fourth M&A wave, in the 1990s, even though European cross-border activity had accelerated since the 1960s. This development is reflected in the in-depth analyses of cross-border transactions by European academics in the 1990s (Cartwright 1998). Since the beginning of the New Millennium, scholarly interest in emerging market M&A has dawned (Chapter 22).

Since the 1980s, deregulation and financial innovation have given rise to a new breed of acquisitions, including hostile takeovers, purchases of bankrupt and distressed firms, and leveraged buyouts. In the latter type of transaction, banks, private equity firms, hedge funds, and/or target managers acquire an investment stake in the target. Correspondingly, these M&A activities are mirrored in the study of hostile takeovers (see Chapter 11), leveraged buyouts (see Chapter 12), and acquisitions of bankrupt and distressed firms (see Chapter 10).

More recent M&A waves have witnessed sector-specific activity. With the gradual easing of bank regulations, the number and value of M&A deals in the financial sector surged in the 1980s (see Chapter 23). Increasing globalization and the advent of the European Union led to a series of mega-mergers among international professional service firms (see Chapter 24). Technology developments and a growing realization of the criticality of innovation for firm survival have catalyzed technology acquisitions since the 1980s (see Chapter 25). Developments in specific sectors, e.g. biotechnology, have fueled M&A activity in these sectors since the 1990s (see Chapter 26). In sum, sector-specific M&A activity over the years has been galvanized by a variety of regulatory, competitive, legislative, and technological factors (see Chapter 2).

The relative strength of the corporate parties to a merger has also noticeably changed. Until recently, OECD-based firms dominated the M&A scene, generally through the acquisition of firms in other advanced economies or in emerging markets. Typically, in these deals, the parties to the merger were relatively equal in terms of financial strength or market position; alternatively, the acquiring firm was clearly dominant. As a result, the acquired firm became the "learning party," and integration, takeover, or merger modes of execution were adopted. This pattern is gradually changing in the 21st century with the rise of emerging market multinationals (see Chapter 22). The latter now play a more prominent role in the M&A game, with the result that the acquiring firm has become the "learning party." This phenomenon partly explains why these firms adopt a seemingly "non-conventional" integration strategy, seeking to partner as opposed to integrate.

In synthesis, we highlight the shifting patterns of M&A activity over the past 120 years in terms of drivers, acquisition types, countries, and sectors. In general, these patterns are mirrored in the themes, approaches, and methodologies of the contemporaneous academic literature.

Uncovering M&A Diversity

This historical overview of the waves of M&A activity sheds light on the changing nature of the phenomenon since the 1890s. In a sense, this overview contextualizes a key challenge in the practice and study of M&A: what *are* M&A transactions? A review of the chapter findings leads to a definition of a merger or acquisition that assumes many forms, depending on the context (see also Haleblian et al. 2009).

To begin with, many M&A scholars do not explicitly distinguish between the object of their study: merger or acquisition. Indeed, they use the terms interchangeably, examine both, focus on acquisitions but label their work "M&A," or vice versa. The use of the all-encompassing, and somewhat vague, term "M&A" might be at the core of the confusing findings and conclusions of M&A research (see also Haleblian et al. 2009). As Stahl and Voigt (2008) adroitly note, there is a danger that M&A researchers are comparing "apples and oranges." Often, after reviewing M&A articles, one has difficulty discerning which of the two deal types has been the object of the research: merger or acquisition. How, then, can we expect comparable and consistent results across studies?

Whilst the terms "merger" and "acquisition" are often used interchangeably, this terminology masks the fact that in form and in substance a merger is different from an acquisition, and moreover, both types of transactional structure and organizational encounter can be differentiated in numerous ways (see Appendix 1). Further, from the perspective of power politics, notwithstanding how the parties characterize a transaction publicly, mergers often *are* acquisitions (see Appendix 1). In the following discussion, with the aim of synthesizing the findings set forth in this *Handbook's* chapters, we will summarize ways in which mergers and acquisitions can differ. In so doing, we propose, as a potential solution to this dire state of affairs, that the umbrella concept "M&A" be used to refer to a portfolio of transactional types. The various dimensions of this portfolio are presented below:

- Target type:
  - Degree of internationality: is the deal domestic or cross-border? (Chapter 4)
  - Target's nationality (Chapters 4, 16, 17, 22)
  - Target's industry (Chapters 2, 23, 24, 25, 26)
  - Relative size: is the target smaller, similar, or larger in size than the buyer? (Chapter 4)
  - Ownership: is the target in public or private ownership? (Chapters 10, 12)
  - Financial health: is the target healthy, distressed, or bankrupt? (Chapter 10)
  - Strategic rationale of seller: why is the seller willing to sell? (Chapter 4)
  - Divestment: is the target a divested business or a privately owned one? (Chapters 4, 5)
- Buyer type and approach:
  - Degree of friendliness: is the deal friendly or hostile? (Chapter 11)
  - Buyer type: is the buyer an industrial buyer, a private equity firm, or a hedge fund? (Chapter 12)
  - Strategic rationale of buyer: increase geographical presence, enhance product portfolio, enlarge customer base, gain technological/professional know-how, gain operational efficiencies and cut costs, create mutual synergies, grow in size and scope, buy off competitor... (Chapters 15, 18; Appendix 1)
  - Integration strategy: what degree(s) of integration is sought post-deal across the involved firms' operations? (Chapters 14, 15, 17)
  - Buyer's degree of previous acquisition experience and its acquisition capability? (Chapters 4, 5, 6)
  - Buyer's nationality and industry (Chapters 2, 17, 22, 23, 24, 25, 26)
- Timing:
  - Does the deal take place in a period of growth or recession? (Chapters 2, 8)
  - Does the deal take place in a period of intense M&A activity (i.e. wave)? (Chapters 2, 8)
  - Where in the buying firm acquisition program is the deal positioned? (Chapters 6, 8)
  - Within what time frame are short- and long-term results expected? (Chapters 4, 5, 14)
- Deal structure:
  - Method of payment: stock or cash? (Chapters 4, 8, 9)
  - Means and source of financing: is the deal financed with cash, stock, and/or debt? (Chapters 8, 12)
  - Size of premium (Chapters 4, 8)
- Relative fit:

- Degree of firm relatedness (Chapters 4, 14)
- Degree of strategic fit between the buyer and target (Chapter 14)
- Degree of organizational fit between the buyer and target (Chapter 14)
- Relative competence level: who learns from whom? (Chapter 22)

In synthesis, the various dimensions of M&A, as well as the subtle structural differences between mergers and acquisitions, could explain why it is difficult to provide once-off answers to M&A performance and success, let alone offer a useful comparison of M&A studies. Thus far, calls for all-encompassing frameworks have been made (Haleblian et al. 2009; see Chapters 4 and 5), with insufficient responses. The extensive review by Haleblian et al. (2009) that reconciles findings in the M&A management, economics, and finance literature is a notable exception. However, the latter review focuses primarily on M&A outcomes, antecedents, and moderators and pays scanter attention to the process of M&A execution.

CONTEXTUAL FRAMEWORK FOR APPROACHING M&A

The preceding chapters have brought us to the realization that the phenomenon of M&A is complex in terms of approaches and methods, form and substance, historical evolution, nature and drivers, and basic definitions. Whilst the analysis thus far has enabled us to grasp this fundamental complexity, it has also fostered an image of M&A as, at worst, inherently unmanageable. In the final analysis, we might claim that each deal is unique, and thus spare ourselves the aggravation of meta-level synthesis. Doing so, however, would be contrary to reason, as well as our central purpose. Our review of the various chapters in this *Handbook* leads us to the conclusion that, however complex, the phenomenon of M&A can be comprehended intuitively and simplified conceptually. With this conclusion in mind, we will next attempt to provide a contextual framework for understanding the process of M&A execution.

A contextual overview of phase-based M&A execution is illustrated in Figure 27.1. This overview casts M&A as occurring, shaping, and being shaped by factors at several levels of understanding: (1) the changing global and societal landscape; (2) the merging firms' evolving strategic and organizational contexts; (3) the pre- and post-deal execution of a transaction from decision-making to successful integration; and (4) the internal and external actors involved in M&A. We argue that at all these levels, the foregoing factors exert a dual influence; specifically, they are all at once active drivers of M&A activity, whilst passively bearing the consequences of M&A. What is more, this M&A execution framework will assume different forms, depending on deal type (see previous section).

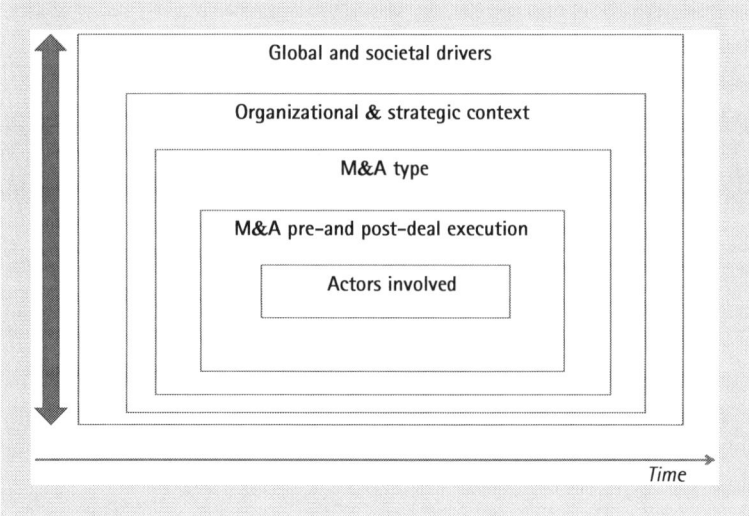

Time

FIG. 27.1 A contextual framework of M&A execution

M&A is Set in Evolving and Continuously Changing Global and Societal Landscapes

The historical review of M&A (see Chapters 2, 3, 4, 8, 13, 23), together with the preceding overview of M&A across sectors (see Chapters 22–26), highlights the need to examine the phenomenon not in an isolated vacuum arising in neutral intra-organizational zones, but rather in the context of a continuously evolving set of global and societal drivers ranging from globalization, technological innovation, geo-economic evolution, to regional/national regulation and legislation. M&A activity is neither spontaneous nor self-generating, but rather propelled by, and contingent on, a myriad of external factors. The existence of these factors, and changes within them, influence the relative strength of M&A activity, as is evident from the rise and fall of M&A in cyclical waves throughout the centuries (see Chapter 2). The variety of M&A transactional structures and organizational forms partly explains why it is so difficult to encapsulate the essence of the phenomenon. Indeed, the object of the analysis is constantly shifting and transforming itself. It is as hard to grasp the true nature of this continuously evolving phenomenon, as it is unwise to generalize from one historical context to another. In synthesis, this leads us to propose:

> Proposition 1a: M&A transactions are not isolated events occurring in a vacuum, but rather are set in a broader, continuously evolving global and societal landscape.

More importantly, the increasing velocity of M&A activity since the late 1980s should be viewed in the context of financial deregulation (Chapters 13, 23), as well as an obsessive concern for the creation of shareholder value (see Chapter 13). To some extent, before the 2008 financial crisis, M&A had become a vehicle for business growth in a world dominated by a supposedly innovative financial sector guided unwittingly by its own "invisible hand" (see Chapter 23). This begs the question—why are M&A transactions undertaken? Is growth for the sake of growth the most wise and sustainable business approach? Earlier, we highlighted the relative paucity of critical perspectives in the practice and study of M&A. This growth-based, shareholder-oriented, financial innovation-driven strategy—or should we say "ritual"—has rarely been questioned or debated. Yet, critically speaking, through acquiescence, M&A practitioners and academics have let the "beast enjoy its feast." It is time for M&A scholars to cast a critical eye over this phenomenon. It is time for them to carefully scrutinize the corporate governance and capital market drivers that have propelled it forward. In synthesis, we state:

> Proposition 1b: M&A activity has come to be embedded in the logic of ongoing growth, short-term shareholder gains, and lax financial regulation.

M&A Transactions are Set in the Merging Firms' Evolving Strategic and Organizational Contexts

Scholars should place M&A not only in a broad institutional context, but also in the merging firms' strategic and organizational contexts, which remain in a state of evolution and flux. In this regard, calls have been made to shift attention from the execution of individual transactions to the acquiring firm's long-term corporate strategy and acquisition program (see Chapter 6; also Chapters 4, 5, and 8). For example, the performance of an acquisition has been found to differ, depending on its position in an acquiring firm's acquisitive cycle (Barkema and Schijven 2008; Chapter 6). Serial acquirers have developed not only acquisition-related capabilities, but also acquisition program-level capabilities (Laamanen and Keil 2008).

Whilst M&A discourse often emphasizes M&A strategies, a look at the "silent forces" that shape M&A activity (see Chapter 21) highlights the challenge of pre- and post-deal execution. According to this view, the magnitude of this challenge is linked to the merging firms' organizational histories and their mutual relationships. Thus, for example, one might postulate that engaging in a merger is more difficult for long-standing competitors than for partners with years of alliance and shared experience (see Chapter 15).

As a result, the challenge and consequences of post-deal integration should be placed in a long-term context. For example, the degree of integration impacts the involved firms' long-term constitutions (Barkema and Schijven 2008), in terms of organizational structures, cultures, and identities (see Chapter 21). This revelation parallels the insight that post-deal integration spans numerous years. In fact, the process is estimated to continue five to twelve years after conclusion of the deal (Barkema and Schijven 2008). In acquisitions, a key challenge for managers is not only absorbing the acquired firm into the acquiring firm's organizational and operational structure, but also, recognizing that if this structure consists of an amalgamation of non-homogeneous units acquired over time, each unit is likely to react differently to the news of a newly acquired unit (see Chapter 21). By implication, acquiring firms that have expanded through acquisitions must be able to coordinate and manage a set of diverse organizational backgrounds (Barkema and Schijven 2008; Chapter 21). Firms that have grown piecemeal through acquisitions, rather than organically, encounter this modern organizational challenge. Thus, we are led to propose:

> Proposition 2: M&A transactions are not isolated events occurring in a vacuum, but rather are set in continuously evolving strategic and organizational landscapes.

Dynamics of M&A Execution

Scholars have cited the challenges of M&A throughout the four sections of this *Handbook*. In this section, we will attempt to provide a dynamic synthesis of their findings as they relate to M&A execution. We will focus on events spanning the pre- and post-deal phases, from decision-making to successful integration. In this synthesis, we aim to integrate the strategic, financial, and sociocultural perspectives on M&A presented in the various *Handbook* chapters, as they relate to M&A execution.

Pre-deal Execution Dynamics

Since the 1960s, a conception of M&A as a set of sequential phases spanning the pre- and post-deal phases has prevailed in the academic literature. The process-based perspectives formulated in the 1980s and 1990s in scholarly works such as Jemison and Sitkin (1986) and Haspeslagh and Jemison (1991) fostered a view of the pre- and post-deal phases as interrelated, the former bearing heavily on the latter.

An overview of the pre-deal era (see Chapters 3, 7, 8, and 9) suggests a multiplicity of pre-deal activities, ranging from acquisition planning to candidate search, valuation, due diligence, negotiations, structuring the deal, and closing. Critically speaking, our understanding of pre-deal execution is weak relative to that of post-deal execution. To date, there has been relatively little discussion, debate, and criticism of scholarly views relating to the pre-acquisition phases. What exactly are these phases? How are they defined? How are they related? What are their underlying temporal dynamics (see Chapters 3, 7, 8, 14)? What are the pre-deal negotiation dynamics that bear upon the firms' relationship, the impending deal, and the post-deal regime (see Chapters 3, 7, 8). Moreover, how do events in the pre-deal phase affect considerations in the post-deal phase (see Chapters 7, 8, 14, 21)? A reason for these deficiencies might relate to the fact that filling this intellectual void likely requires simultaneously dealing with the strategic, financial, and sociocultural perspectives pre- and post-deal.

As synthesizing these perspectives has been the underlying goal of this *Handbook*, based on its readings, we propose a few important pointers. The quality and strength of the interpersonal relationships forged before the deal has been found to enhance the ease of post-deal integration (see Chapters 7, 14, and 21). The outcome of negotiations will undoubtedly impact the post-deal regime; yet the negotiation process itself might be subject to biased, undisclosed motives on both sides (see Chapters 3, 7, and 8). The thoroughness of pre-deal due diligence will have an effect on the number and nature of post-deal surprises likely to be encountered, as well as the prospect of achieving the desired synergies from the deal (Chapters 7, 8, 9, and 21).

The meticulousness of pre-deal valuation and the soundness of the methodology used will influence the price and premium paid for the acquisition—the higher the latter variables, the greater will be the pressure on managers to deliver in the post-deal phase (Chapter 8). That being the case, valuation itself is more of an art than a science. Often, the models used in the process are inherently flawed, thus distorting price and premium. Moreover, various psychological biases might interfere with rational executive decision-making, adversely impacting the decision to acquire, the method of payment, and the price to be paid (Chapter 8). What is more, the accounting methods used to determine target market and asset value are in part flawed, in that they fail to adequately account for the value of intangibles, i.e. human capital, know-how, technology, and innovative potential (see Chapter 9). Yet it is precisely these factors that represent the "crown jewels" of target companies in today's knowledge-based industries. One can poignantly ask, is the pre-deal undervaluation or zero-valuation of human capital implicitly mirrored in the oft-observed underestimation of the human element in post-M&A integration (see Chapters 14–21)?

To complicate matters still further, underlying the pre-deal phase are human dynamics propelled by factors ranging from acquiring firm managerial hubris and overconfidence (see Chapter 8) to the hidden agendas on both sides of the negotiation table (see Chapters 3, 7, 8, and 9). Both warrant attention. The tendency in the academic literature is to regard behavioral dynamics as characteristic of the post-deal phase only. This attitude neglects the fact that behaviors also impact the progress and outcome of the pre-deal phase and bear heavily on decisions, price, and information, on the basis of which the post-deal phase must deliver. It is time to remove the mask of rationality that hides the irrational aspects of the financially driven pre-deal phase.

In summary, the "outcome" of the pre-deal phase is, more or less, a subjective assessment of the target based on due diligence, a strategic aim for the target, and a decision to buy, possibly based on management biases and hubris. If such is in fact the case, the ultimate result will be a distorted bid price and premium, calculated with little regard for the human aspect of M&A or the intangible values inherent in the acquired enterprise—all this flowing from a, more or less, well-executed pre-deal phase plan, formulated in terms of a myriad of non-rational behaviors. The post-deal phase does not emerge in a void. In synthesis:

> Proposition 3a: Assumptions, decisions, and behavioral dynamics shaping the pre-deal phase will ultimately impact execution in the post-deal phase, and by implication, long-term value creation.

Post-deal Execution Dynamics

Since the 1960s, post-deal integration has been identified as the most challenging phase in the M&A process and as critical to the success of the deal (Mace and Montgomery 1962). As the previous sections emphasize, this phase should not be viewed in isolation. It is influenced by deal type, societal and organizational contexts, and the dynamics and outcome of the pre-deal phase. The managerial challenge of this phase stems from a myriad of factors, including integration management, employee motivation and retention, organizational change and sensitivity to cultural differences, unfolding identification processes, and underlying power and politics; all this placed in an increasingly competitive "shareholder pressurized" context.

Whilst the pre-deal era is demarcated by phases or activities undertaken prior to deal conclusion and closing, stages in the post-deal era are less well-defined (see Chapter 14). It is generally accepted that the challenge and nature of integration will depend on the strategy adopted, which in turn will depend on the buyer's nationality, the rationale for the acquisition, and firm relatedness. Integration is conducted at various levels, from technical, administrative, systems, to organization and culture (Shristava 1986). Recent work suggests that these levels are interconnected. Cultural changes are catalyzed by structural changes (Teerikangas and Laamanen 2006). Integration best practices relate to planning, the use of integration teams, starting the process early, communicating effectively, fair attitudes, and allowing for autonomy and target firm involvement. Scholars have also stressed the importance of positive attitudes fostering cooperation (see Chapters 14, 21).

Finance scholars have called into question the non-recognition of certain types of intangibles, including human capital, in M&A accounting (see Chapter 9). Management scholars have observed a similar neglect of the human aspect of M&A in the post-deal phase. Since the 1980s, this deficiency has led academics to advocate greater research in this area (see Chapter 15). The literature has generally viewed the human consequences of M&A with pessimism. It has typically characterized employee reactions to integration efforts in negative terms. Drawing a parallel with recent developments in psychology (Cameron et al. 2003), where notions of positive human behavior and leadership have emerged to counter the pessimistic view of human nature, one might ask—what role can positive psychology play in the study of M&A? Indeed, is it possible to view the sociocultural aspects of M&A in a positive light? By discounting and partly neglecting the role of the human spirit in M&A, have researchers practically dehumanized the entire process?

The cultural shock, assimilation, and change following M&A are characteristic of the post-deal phase. This finding is based primarily on research relating to domestic mergers. Significantly, relatively few insights into this aspect of M&A have been derived from studies of cross-border M&A (see Chapters 15, 16). What is more, the cultural complexity inherent in M&A has been conceptualized primarily in terms of the merger of one homogeneous nationally based organizational culture into another one. Whilst this conceptualization creates a valid ideal-typical construct for the analysis of some underlying phenomena, this construct is flawed in that it departs significantly from salient features of other widespread phenomena. Indeed, many mergers today involve combinations of non-homogenous organizational cultures dispersed across national boundaries (see Chapters 14, 16, and 17).

All the while, scholars have devoted considerable effort to trying to discern whether and how cultural differences impact M&A performance. They observe that differences in organizational culture contribute to performance deficiencies more than do differences in national culture. They attribute this result to the fact that the latter differences create greater opportunities for learning, perhaps by making employees more conscious of the national identity of "the other side" (see Chapter 16). More recent studies of identity highlight the long-term nature of post-deal identification. Regardless of the progress made by managers in instilling in employees a new sense of identity, pre-deal identifications generally endure for years. Scholars have cited the creation of a common identity as critical in avoiding negative group dynamics (see Chapter 19).

As Chapter 14 highlights, the types of models and frameworks that M&A scholars have developed over the years foster a linear, rational, prescriptive view of post-merger integration. Chapter 3 notes that many M&A integration typologies are rooted in the "process" school of strategy. Furthermore, the organizations involved in M&A are generally seen as "singular monoliths" (see Chapters 14, 16), evidencing little micro-complexity. There is little consideration of the power and politics involved (Chapter 20). This view contrasts sharply with more recent theories in strategy, organizational behavior, and change management that embody notions of practice, emergence, ambidexterity, uncertainty, and unpredictability (Lynch 2006; Burnes 2009). Indeed, there is ample room in business scholarship for a reinvention of M&A management. In the 21st century, what would an emergent, ambidextrous, practice-driven view of M&A integration depict? To summarize, we posit:

> Proposition 3b: M&A integration is an intertwined, multi-layered, long-term process that demands talent, time, and resources to adequately address the managerial, human, cultural, identity, and power issues at stake.

The Actors Shaping and Enduring M&A Activity

In this section, we focus on the internal and external actors involved in the M&A process, across hierarchical levels. These actors play two roles: first, they drive M&A activity, and second, they endure its consequences. In contrast to the considerable attention paid to the strategic, financial, and managerial aspects of M&A, scholars have paid relatively little attention to the roles critical for M&A. This explains Angwin's (see Chapter 3) call for more "strategy as practice"-based research on M&A. What do we really know about the individuals who drive the M&A process, or are driven by it?

In the pre-deal phase, a key question relates to actors' motives and incentives. As has been pointed out, miscalculations of bid prices and post-deal operating costs are often attributable to the over-optimism of the senior managers who execute the deal, and in some instances, to the fact that CEO compensation might be linked to consolidated operating results. Other "irrational" motives underlying M&A frenzy (see Chapter 8) include personal biases and management hubris. Furthermore, institutionalized financial incentives might drive M&A activity not toward quality, but rather toward size and quantity.

In the post-deal literature, emphasis has been placed on deal movers, be they transformation team members, integration managers, or target firm directors who implement integration. Further emphasis has been placed on the roles of senior managers, human resource advisors, and other mid-level personnel who drive acquisition performance (see Chapters 14, 15, 19, 21). To some extent, this focus suggests a managerial bias in the study of M&A, with insufficient attention paid to the rank and file; specifically, the role played by research and operations engineers, analysts across functions, the sales and marketing force, "blue-collar" workers, and administrative and support staff in pursuing integration objectives (see Chapter 21). In the literature, the latter have often been depicted as wrought with negative stamina, i.e. as passive victims of these organizational upheavals, and at worst, as "justifiably" made redundant (see Chapter 15). The extraordinary difficulty of transitioning from a pre-merger to a post-merger phase could well explain their "anti-social" behavior. Perhaps we should view M&A as the merging of two cultures or social systems, i.e. a people encounter, the success of which depends on the daily interactions of the individuals involved (see Chapter 21).

Furthermore, in the literature, greater emphasis has been placed on the acquiring firm's interests (see Chapters 4, 14) relative to those of the selling side (Graebner and Eisenhardt 2004), or target firm managers (Graebner 2004). Likewise, greater emphasis has been placed on the interests of internal actors, relative to those of external stakeholders (see Haleblian et al. 2009). This leads one to ask: how do local constituencies, institutions, customers, suppliers, or competitors react to M&A? How have M&A waves impacted social structures—as typically smaller family-owned businesses have become owned by "faceless" multinationals, as industrial communities have become depopulated, as multinationals seem to neglect social welfare in their drive to augment shareholder value? All the while, the patrons and beneficiaries of this activity, i.e. banks, private equity firms, hedge funds, and serial acquirers, seem to remain unscathed. Critically speaking, one might ask, have scholars approached the study of M&A with a management bias that virtually neglects the interests of other key stakeholders? Are M&A practitioners guilty of the same bias? To summarize, we propose:

> Proposition 4: M&A activity is set in the context of organizations involving a multiplicity of internal and external stakeholders, each with differing motivations, expectations, incentives, and leverage to influence the transactional outcome.

Succeeding in M&A—A Three-Dimensional Typology

As mentioned in the introduction, scholars have historically viewed M&A primarily through the prism of their respective disciplines. Thus, for example, finance scholars have focused on an analysis of bid premiums, transactional structures, acquisition financing, operating performance, and value creation. Strategy scholars have empha-sized takeover strategies, post-merger integration, and institutional synergies, whilst human relations scholars have paid attention to the human aspect of M&A.

Few, if any, scholars have succeeded in aligning the prisms, synthesizing the various perspectives, or identifying key overlapping elements—hence, the perceived "silo effect" of the current literature on M&A. This unsatisfactory state of affairs has led the editors to ask, "How can the 'silos' be broken down to achieve a dynamic synthesis of the various perspectives, a broader understanding of this universally recognized phenomenon?" Based on the analysis presented in this chapter, we are now in a position to synthesize the strategic, financial, and sociocultural dimensions of M&A.

A Three-Dimensional Typology

Perspectives on M&A may be said to "intersect" at three different levels: strategic, finan-cial, and sociocultural. Each level presents a unique proposition. Success in M&A requires a careful balancing and integration of all three dimensions (see Figure 27.2). On

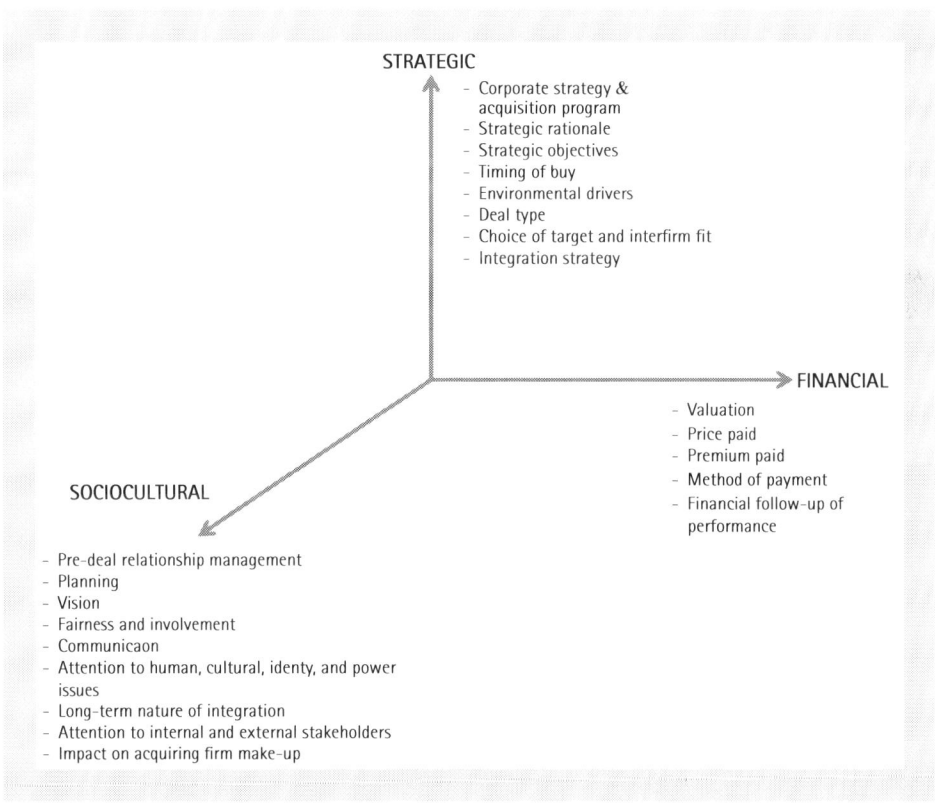

STRATEGIC
- Corporate strategy & acquisition program
- Strategic rationale
- Strategic objectives
- Timing of buy
- Environmental drivers
- Deal type
- Choice of target and interfirm fit
- Integration strategy

FINANCIAL
- Valuation
- Price paid
- Premium paid
- Method of payment
- Financial follow-up of performance

SOCIOCULTURAL
- Pre-deal relationship management
- Planning
- Vision
- Fairness and involvement
- Communicaon
- Attention to human, cultural, identy, and power issues
- Long-term nature of integration
- Attention to internal and external stakeholders
- Impact on acquiring firm make-up

FIG. 27.2 Three-dimensional M&A success typology

a strategic level, the key question is, "How do the strategic decisions of managers affect shareholder value?" On a financial level, the essential proposition is, "How does the subjective pursuit of M&A by corporations affect the costs incurred by, and benefits accruing to society?" On a sociocultural level, the question becomes, "How does the pre-merger process affect the post-merger outcome for all involved?"

Strategic Considerations Underlying Successful M&A

Regarding the first question, Sudi Sudarsanam (Chapter 8) insightfully points out that the ability of managers to create value depends on the robustness of the strategy that drives the acquisition. If this strategy is somehow flawed, management implementation ultimately erodes shareholder value. If it is inherently sound, such implementation effectively enhances this value. Because managers formulate M&A strategy with imperfect knowledge, sometimes communicate it to stakeholders ineffectively, occasionally encounter obstacles in the way of implementation, and often are motivated by considerations that are not necessarily rational relative to desired ends, their strategic decisions frequently misstate shareholder value. Prospectively, such misstatements translate into an overestimation of revenue growth, profit margins, return on investment, and company worth. Retrospectively, they result in a gross mispricing of the deal.

From a strategy perspective, the ultimate aim should be to ensure that the decision to acquire and the choice of target are consistent with the acquiring firm's long-term goals and perspectives. This means that the rationale for the deal should be sound, closely related to the corporate strategy, and reflect the company's acquisition program. Moreover, key questions should be addressed, such as what type of an acquisition should be pursued, and what is the degree of fit between the firms? Short- and long-term objectives for value creation should be defined. An effective M&A strategy requires a thorough assessment of the global, societal, competitive, and regulatory contexts in which the deal occurs. Moreover, timing is crucial—at what juncture in an M&A wave, economic cycle, and the firm's acquisition program does the deal occur? Once the target has been identified, an appropriate integration regime should be designed. In synthesis, we propose the following "M&A strategy checklist":

- Assess what environmental drivers incentivize M&A activity—is the deal necessary and timely?
- Ensure the deal relates to corporate strategy and the relevant acquisition program;
- Avoid buying an enterprise that is too large;
- Avoid buying at the peak of a business cycle;
- Acquisitions of related companies are likely to outperform acquisitions of unrelated ones;
- Design an integration strategy that best fits the firms and deal in question;
- Be mindful of strategic synergies;
- Consider how competitive advantage might be achieved.

Financial Considerations Underlying Successful M&A

Concluding a financially sound deal requires relative precision in valuation (i.e. taking into account all the relevant financial and economic variables and utilizing a sophisticated model), setting a market-based price and premium for the target (i.e. ideally based on comparables), carefully structuring the deal, analyzing the tax consequences in light of the consideration used, and procuring acquisition financing at a reasonable cost. Ultimately, the strategic rationale for, and objectives of, the deal translate into financial measures that track the progress of the acquisition in later years.

One must bear in mind that from a financial perspective, the subjective pursuit of M&A gains may be "rational" in terms of short-term business goals, but "irrational" in terms of long-term economic effect. For *private* costs and benefits are not necessarily synonymous with *public* costs and benefits, nor are *real* costs and benefits synonymous with *opportunity* costs and benefits. Ultimately, the inexorable drive to merge could result in "zero-sum" gains, or even substantial losses in the public domain because of unforeseen, hidden, or immeasurable externalities, not to mention forgone opportunities and benefits. Indeed, the increased efficiency, higher productivity, and greater profitability accruing to private enterprise could be more than offset by increased unemployment, lower productivity, and heavier welfare burdens for society as a whole. In a capitalist world, it is perhaps unreasonable to expect corporate executives to serve as guardians of the public interest, especially when shareholder wealth is at stake. Nonetheless, this interest must be safeguarded if M&A are to play a constructive role in the creation of social wealth. In synthesis, we propose the following "M&A finance checklist":

- Ensure that the deal's financial drivers are linked to the deal strategy;
- Beware of managerial overconfidence and hubris;
- Be careful not to understate the value intangibles;
- Be careful in forecasting future cash flows; no method can flawlessly predict their occurrence or magnitude;
- Be cognizant that in some jurisdictions, the use of cash (as opposed to stock) as consideration is likely to have tax consequences.

Sociocultural Considerations Underlying Successful M&A

From a sociocultural standpoint, effective pre- and post-deal execution requires relationship building throughout the pre-deal phase. For one, constructive working relationships will positively affect the ease and speed of post-deal integration. Moreover, the adequacy of pre-merger planning will ultimately impact the costs associated with integration. If such planning is thorough, methodical, and sound, these costs are likely to be minimized. If it is flawed, hurried, or motivated by factors irrational relative to desired ends, they are likely to be excessive. The nature and magnitude of these costs will ultimately depend on the organizational, operational, cultural, and human challenges posed by the post-merger process. To the extent that managers can foresee these challenges, estimate with reasonable accuracy the means and expenditures required to tackle them, and adequately provide for post-merger contingencies in the pre-merger planning phase, they will succeed at increasing efficiency, improving productivity, and enhancing the overall financial performance of the merged enterprise. From a managerial perspective, appropriate consideration should be given to internal and external stakeholders related to, involved in, and affected by the deal, at all hierarchical levels and across organizational boundaries. In synthesis, we propose the following "sociocultural checklist for M&A execution":

- Aim to create a working relationship with the target in the pre-deal phase;
- Plan the integration as early as possible;
- Provide a compelling vision for the future;
- Treat employees fairly and communicate transparently;
- Strive to involve key parties in decision-making;
- Be sensitive to the emotional casualties of the deal;
- Recognize the long-term nature of cultural change and identification;
- Accept that change will raise the power stakes and political games in both firms;
- Identify in advance issues of cultural clash and develop a contingency plan for addressing them.

Alternative M&A Success Scenarios

Based on this threefold typology of M&A linking its strategic, financial, and sociocultural dimensions (see Figure 27.3), we postulate three scenarios relating to M&A results:

1. A "worst-case" scenario, characterized by inadequate strategic planning, poor financial performance, and weak sociocultural execution. In this scenario, the acquisition is unlikely to create value.
2. A series of "medium-case scenarios," characterized by adequate, but suboptimal, strategic planning, financial performance, and sociocultural execution (see Table 27.1). Underlying these scenarios are the following considerations: if the strategy is flawed, regardless of its financial and sociocultural merits, the deal is unlikely to add significant value to the acquiring firm's business. On the other hand, if the strategy is sound, but the financial and sociocultural aspects of the deal are flawed, the deal still might add value if management errors are rectified promptly. In the latter case, the acquiring firm might have made the right decision, but have either based it on faulty financial data or poor execution. Finally, to the extent that this strategy is based on reliable financial data, takes into account the sociocultural costs associated with post-merger integration, and is executed efficiently and expeditiously, shareholder value is likely to be augmented.
3. A "best-case" scenario, characterized by optimal strategic planning, financial performance, and sociocultural execution. Where the strategy is sound, financial considerations are weighed carefully, and sociocultural issues are adequately addressed, the acquisition is highly likely to create value.

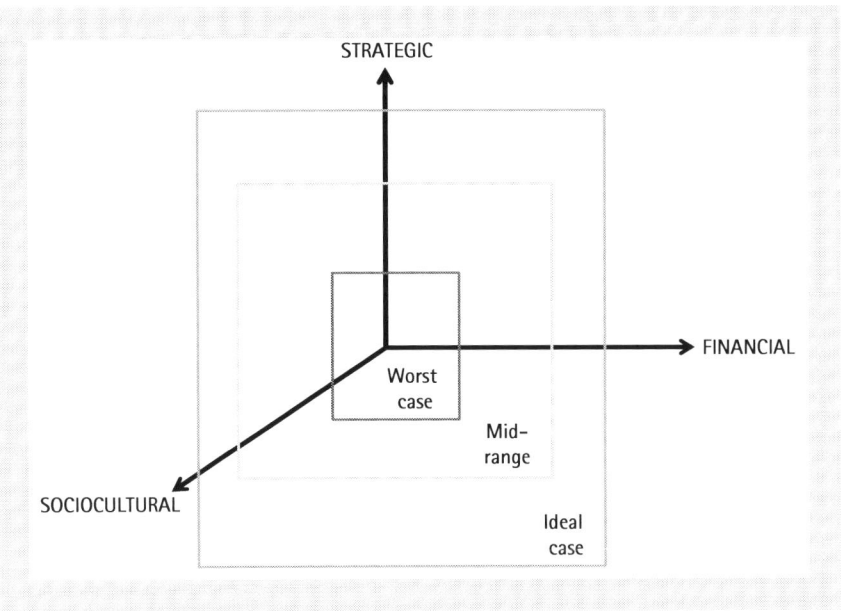

FIG. 27.3 Alternative M&A success scenarios

Table 27.1 Overview of the alternative M&A success scenarios

STRATEGIC	FINANCIAL	SOCIOCULTURAL	SUCCESS SCENARIO
+	+	+	(1) Ideal case
+	+	−	(2) Difficult execution
+	−	−	(2) Right strategy
+	−	+	(2) Poor finance considerations
−	+	+	(2) Wrong strategy, sound execution
−	+	−	(2) Sound finance, poor strategy and execution
−	−	+	(2) Sound execution, poor strategy
−	−	−	(3) Worst case

LOOKING FORWARD

These findings portend major trends in the New Millennium. Fuelled by cycles of easy credit and abundant equity (yet constrained by the financial crisis since 2008), cross-border M&A activity is nevertheless expected to surge in the decades ahead. It may catalyze the consolidation of a global market for goods and services and also pave the way for a gradual dismantling of institutional barriers to free trade and capital flows. As an indirect consequence, this activity is likely to continue rendering national markets more interdependent and the global economy more vulnerable to crisis, thus highlighting the need to institute an international framework for regulating cross-border transactions. To the extent that M&A erodes sovereign powers, disrupts local economies, displaces social strata, and reduces cultural distinctions, it may well contribute to sharp nationalistic, socialistic, or fundamentalist counter-reactions along its tumultuous path.

Within this long-term trend, the proportion of US-led deals is likely to decrease relative to those of EU, Chinese, Japanese, and Indian-led deals. As European and Asian markets consolidate, the terms of trade will shift increasingly toward emerging economies. Major exporters will accumulate foreign currency reserves vast enough to upset the Old World monetary order, and new powers will emerge on the international stage, soon to discover the acquisition potential of their new-found wealth. As Gary Dymski insightfully points out in Chapter 23, rather than seek to penetrate national markets by tearing down trade barriers, multinationals are likely to attempt to do so circuitously by acquiring major players within those markets.

On a global scale, these trends are likely to lead to a convergence of public policies, as governments take defensive measures to minimize the disruptive effects of M&A upon their national economies. Principal among these measures will be tougher antitrust laws, tighter foreign investment restrictions, more stringent bank regulations, more aggressive tax laws, and more flexible accounting standards. Their ultimate aim will be to regulate cross-border mergers, without necessarily impeding them.

In terms of future research directions, a key challenge is how to forge an interdisciplinary view of M&A, as well as a scholarly means of comparing and contrasting research findings across disciplines. In addition, scholars should endeavor to assemble data on transactions and trends that are more comprehensive, more accurate, and more detailed than those currently available. Such data might be disaggregated to shed light on the number of domestic and cross-border transactions, transactional values, deal structures, sources of financing, proportions of debt and equity, company valuations, premiums paid, industry comparisons, and historical trends. Finally, the issues of what accounts for M&A performance and how M&A transactions create value should be further addressed. Our understanding of particular types of acquisitions remains weak, as regards e.g. leveraged buyouts, acquisitions of bankrupt and distressed concerns, divestments, or takeovers.

Regarding M&A financial research, much remains to be done. Specifically, accounting scholars might devote considerably more attention to developing sound methodologies for valuing company intangibles. Such methodologies could bridge the gap between perceptions of external market value and internal asset values, thus providing greater insight into a key motive for company acquisitions. Finance scholars might strive to elucidate the essential linkages between strategic decision-making, managerial behavior, and value creation. The results of their research could broaden our understanding of the tight interdependence between pre-merger planning and post-merger operating performance. Finance scholars might also explore the vast array of innovations in financial instruments, investment vehicles, loan terms, and sources of financing. To date, mezzanine financing, high-yield bonds, and private equity have played a major role in the rise of M&A. What types of financial innovation could fuel this activity in the future?

With respect to M&A execution, important gaps in the literature remain. Scholars should devote considerably more attention to execution dynamics in the pre-deal phase. They should address questions, including: what happens in the pre-deal phase? What types of behavioral dynamics are manifest? How do developments in this phase impact those in the post-deal phase? In addition, qualitative assessments of integration microdynamics, especially in cross-border M&A are needed. To date, scholarly attempts to define how post-deal change processes are interrelated have largely been unsuccessful. Or, are these processes in fact independent? Furthermore, how does integration management differ from one sector to another, from one country to another?

The related research streams of management, culture, employee reactions, and identity have lived rather separate lives. For example, attempts to relate cultural integration and post-merger identification with integration management are few and far between. Moreover, only a handful of studies in the realm of integration, culture, or identity are qualitative or longitudinal in nature; there are even fewer studies of cross-border deals, in the domain of identity, for example. Rigorous qualitative research as regards M&A micro-dynamics, integration progress, cultural, identity, or power dynamics, and the way in which M&A execution affects M&A value creation is needed. Active, innovative, and courageous research efforts spanning countries and disciplines are called for to gradually make sense of this multifaceted phenomenon, M&A.

For years, the phenomenon of M&A has remained an unfolding mystery, that is difficult to grasp, professionally challenging, intellectually stimulating. To some extent, this mystery stems from the manner in which the phenomenon has been characterized, the analytical tools used to examine it, the concepts through which it has been understood, and the lenses through which it has been viewed. Until recently, these lenses have been narrowly focused. They have been crafted by M&A experts within the confines of their respective disciplines. The purpose of this *Handbook* has been to combine, align, and refocus these lenses so as to create a new intellectual paradigm based on a dynamic synthesis of the strategic, financial, and sociocultural dimensions of M&A. This synthesis has been based on the findings of the outstanding scholars who have contributed to this *Handbook*. It creates a legacy that, hopefully, others will follow, and upon which they will build to expand our knowledge.

References

Ansoff, H. I. (1965). *The Concept of Corporate Strategy*. Homewood, IL: Dow-Jones Irwin.

Barkema, H. G., & Bell, H. J. (1996). "Foreign Entry, Cultural Barriers, and Learning." *Strategic Management Journal*, 17: 151–66.

—— & Schijven, M. (2008)."Toward Unlocking the Full Potential of Acquisitions: The Role of Organizational Restructuring." *Academy of Management Journal*, 51/4: 696–722.

Buono, A. F., Bowditch, J. L., & Lewis, J. W. (1985). "When Cultures Collide: The Anatomy of a Merger." *Human Relations*, 38/5: 477–500.

Burnes, B. (2009). *Managing Change* (4th ed.). Harlow: Pearson.

Burrell, G., and Morgan, G. (1979). *Sociological Paradigms and Organisational Analysis*. Aldershot: Ashgate.

Cameron, K., Dutton, J. E., & Quinn, R. E. (2003). *Positive Organizational Scholarship*. San Francisco: Berrett-Koehler.

Cartwright, S. (1998). "International Mergers and Acquisitions: the Issues and Challenges," in M. Gertsen, A.-M. Söderberg, & J. E. Torp (eds.), *Cultural Dimensions of International Mergers and Acquisitions*. Berlin: De Gruyter, 5–16.

—— & Cooper, C. L. (1990). "The Impact of Mergers and Acquisitions on People at Work: Existing Research and Issues." *British Journal of Management*, 1: 65–76.

Graebner, M. E. (2004). "Momentum and Serendipity: How Acquired Firm Leaders Create Value in the Integration of Technology Firms." *Strategic Management Journal*, 25/8–9: 751–77.

—— & Eisenhardt, K. M. (2004). "The Seller's Side of the Story: Acquisition as Courtship and Governance as Syndicate in Entrepreneurial Firms." *Administrative Science Quarterly*, 49: 366–403.

Haleblian, J., Devers, C. E., McNamara, G., Carpenter, M. A., & Davison, R. B. (2009). "Taking Stock of What We Know About Mergers and Acquisitions: A Review and Research Agenda." *Journal of Management*, 35: 469–502.

Haspeslagh, P. C., & Jemison, D. B. (1991). *Managing Acquisitions: Creating Value through Corporate Renewal*. New York: The Free Press.

Howell, R. A. (1970). "Plan to Integrate your Acquisitions." *Harvard Business Review*, 48/6: 66–76.

Jemison, D. B., & Sitkin, S. B. (1986). "Corporate Acquisitions: A Process Perspective." *Academy of Management Review*, 11/1: 145–63.

Jensen, M. C., & Ruback, R. S. (1983). "The Market for Corporate Control." *Journal of Financial Economics*, 11/1–4: 5–50.

King, D. R., Dalton, D. R., Daily, C. M., & Covin, J. G. (2004). "Meta-analyses of Post-acquisition Performance: Indications of Unidentified Moderators." *Strategic Management Journal*, 25/2: 187–200.

Laamanen, T., & Keil, T. (2008). "The Performance of Serial Acquirers: Toward an Acquisition Program Perspective." *Strategic Management Journal*, 29: 663–72.

Lynch, R. (2006). *Corporate Strategy* (4th ed.). Harlow: Prentice Hall.

Mace, M. L., & Montgomery, G. (1962). *Management Problems of Corporate Acquisitions*. Cambridge, MA: Harvard University Press.

Marks, M. L. (1982). "Merging Human Resources: A Review of the Literature." *Mergers and Acquisitions*, 16, Summer: 38–44.

McKinsey, J. O. (1929). "Effect of Mergers on Marketing, Production, and Administrative Problems." *The Journal of Business of the University of Chicago*, 2: 326–37.

Mirc, N., Rouzies, A., Teerikangas, S., and Tarba, S. (2010). "The M&A Community: Myth or Reality? A Social Network Analysis of M&A Scholars." Paper presented at the Annual Conference of the European Academy of Management, Rome, May 19–22.

Nahavandi, A., & Malekzadeh, A. R. (1988). "Acculturation in Mergers and Acquisitions." *Academy of Management Review*, 13/1: 79–90.

Napier, N. K. (1989). "Mergers and Acquisitions, Human Resource Issues and Outcomes: A Review and Suggested Typology." *Journal of Management Studies*, 26/3: 271–89.

Navin, T. R., & Sears, M. V. (1955). "The Rise of a Market for Industrial Securities, 1877–1902." *Business History Review*, 29:105–38.

Riad, S. (2005). "'The Power of 'Organizational Culture' as a Discursive Formation in Merger Integration." *Organization Studies*, 26/10: 1529–54.

Risberg, A. (1997). "Ambiguity and Communication in Cross-Cultural Acquisitions: Towards A Conceptual Framework." *Leadership and Organization Development Journal*, 18/5: 257–66.

——(2001). "Employee Experiences of Acquisition Processes." *Journal of World Business*, 36/1: 58–84.

Salter, M. S., & Weinhold, W. A. (1979). *Diversification through Acquisition*. New York: The Free Press.

Schweiger, D. M., & Goulet, P. K. (2000). "Integrating Mergers and Acquisitions: An International Research Review," in C. Cooper and A. Gregory (eds.), *Advances in Mergers and Acquisitions*, vol. 1. Amsterdam: JAI Press, 61–91.

Shristava, P. (1986). "Postmerger Integration." *Journal of Business Strategy*, 7/1: 65–76.

Stahl, G. K., & Voigt, A. (2008). "Do Cultural Differences Matter in Mergers and Acquisitions? A Tentative Model and Examination." *Organization Science*, 19/1: 160–76.

Stigler, G. (1950). "Monopoly and Oligopoly Power by Merger." *American Economic Review*, 40: 23–34.

Teerikangas, S. (2006). "Silent Forces in Cross-Border Acquisitions: An Integrative Perspective on Post-acquisition Integration." Helsinki: Helsinki University of Technology, Institute of Strategy and International Business, Doctoral Dissertation Series, 1/2006.

——& Laamanen, T. (2006). "Cultural and Structural Dynamics of Post-acquisition Integration." Paper presented in the IM Division of the Academy of Management Annual Conference, Atlanta, USA, August 11–16.

——& Véry, P. (2006). "The Culture-Performance Relationship in M&A: From Yes/No to How." *British Journal of Management*, 17/S1: 31–48.

Vaara, E. (1999). "Cultural Differences and Post-merger Problems: Misconceptions and Cognitive Simplifications." *Organisasjonsstudier*, 1/2, 59–88.

——(2000). "Constructions of Cultural Differences in Post-merger Change Processes: A Sense-Making Perspective on Finnish-Swedish cases." *Management*, 3/3: 81–110.

——(2003). "Post-acquisition Integration as Sense-making: Glimpses of Ambiguity, Confusion, Hypocrisy, and Politicization." *Journal of Management Studies*, 40/4: 859–94.

—— Tienari, J., & Säntti, R. (2003). "The International Match: Metaphors as Vehicles of Social Identity Building in Cross-Border Mergers." *Human Relations*, 56/4: 419–51.

Zollo, M., & Singh, H. (2004). "Deliberate Learning in Corporate Acquisitions: Post-acquisition Strategies and Integration Capability in U.S. Bank Mergers." *Strategic Management Journal*, 25: 1233–56.

M&A MOTIVES, DEFINITIONS, AND DEFINING CHARACTERISTICS

In the following sections, we review some of the fundamentals in the study of M&A. We start with an overview of motives for undertaking M&A. We continue by defining M&A, identifying various types of M&A, and how M&A relate to other forms of interfirm or interorganizational activity.

Motives for Undertaking M&A

Why do firms engage in M&A activity? A host of motives have been identified, ranging from financial and strategic motives to unstated managerial ones (Halpern 1983; Napier 1989). In terms of classical financial motives, firms engage in M&A activity as a means of maximizing firm value, either by increased synergies through the deal (e.g. via economies of scale or scope) or through increased sales or asset growth (Halpern 1983). Synergies can also be reached through sharing knowledge across the firms (Jensen and Ruback 1983). A financially driven acquisition can further aim to control the target firm's management and board in order to have an impact on the firm's future performance. Strategic motives relate to pursuing related diversification as a means of enlarging the firm's portfolio and reach, increasing a firm's competitive strength and position nationally or internationally, and limiting risk if a firm operates in a variety of sectors (Lynch 2006).

Much of the financial and strategic motivation guiding M&A relates to reducing uncertainty in the external environment (Pfeffer 1972). Paralleling these stated motivations are unstated managerial motives, including fear of obsolescence on the part of the managers concerned (Levinson 1970), finding excitement through a "new game to play" (Hunt 1988), an increase in managers' prestige or power (Rhoades 1983), or managerial hubris seeking managerial rather than corporate gains from the deal (Marris 1964; Berkovitch and Narayanan 1993). Alternatively, the hubris hypothesis (Roll 1986) argues that, as managers undertake acquisitions, they make mistakes in evaluating target firms, resulting in a premium paid that reflects a random error.

Whilst it is helpful to understand the variety of other M&A motives, it has been noted that we lack sufficient understanding of the way in which stated M&A motives are carried out, how they affect performance, and what parallel performance effects they might have, e.g. on employee reactions, employee turnover, or customer retention (Napier 1989). As Chapter 2 highlights, motives for conducting M&A have been influenced by the changing economic and institutional contexts over the last century, resulting in a set of five subsequent waves (and a recent sixth) of M&A activity. External conditions that have given rise to increased M&A activity since the end of the 19th century relate to the easing of legislation and regulations, the increase in international trade, and technological advances. These factors have resulted in intensified global competition and increased company interdependence, as firms attempt to cope with "complex, indivisible problems" (Aldrich and Pfeffer 1976).

DEFINING MERGERS AND ACQUISITIONS

The practice and literature on M&A tends to use the term "M&A" or "merger" or "acquisition" to denote either of the two transaction types. As the following overview will point out, however, not all deals are alike. Moreover, one must bear in mind that though in terms of value the largest mergers get a wealth of media attention and are clearly significant, numerically, about 97% of all deals are declared to be acquisitions (Buckley and Ghauri 2002).

To begin with, the differences and similarities between the terms merger vs. acquisition need to be clarified. A "merger" refers to the merging of two previously separate organizations and their operations into one. Typically this change is paralleled by the creation of a new joint identity, as in the example of the DaimlerChrysler merger. What the term "merger" masks, however, is that there tends to be a buying party in most mergers, i.e. one firm buying out a majority stake or all shares in the target firm. Consequently, most mergers, though organizationally termed "mergers," are actually, in economic terms, "acquisitions." This economic dominance of one party over the other typically becomes visible in the post-merger years, as many mergers end up resembling acquisitions. It is also the case that some major M&A events are classified as "mergers" to spare the feelings employees might have about being "acquired" and thus reduced to a subsidiary and perhaps submissive position, prompting them to look for another job, as e.g. in the case of DaimlerChrysler. This metaphoric use of the term does not necessarily reflect the acquiring firm's long-term aims with regard to the buyout. In synthesis, we see that, all too often, a merger is a metaphoric tool to mask what is essentially an acquisition, or the aim to acquire and dominate the acquired party.

It should be emphasized, however, that this is not always the case, and that there are genuine mergers where the value chains (Porter 1985) and management teams of two companies are jointly seen to provide a potential competitive advantage, where the individual value chains of either partner alone failed to do so, and the post-merger management team is composed of the key members from the top management teams of both partners. Indeed one of the editors, Professor Faulkner has been involved in just such a merger, when Magna Carta College, Oxford merged with the West London School of Management and Technology. This was and is a genuine merger, instead of a disguised acquisition.

In contrast, an "acquisition" refers to a transaction in which an "acquiring firm" uses capital (e.g. stock, debt or cash) to buy another company. In acquisitions, the acquiring party tends to be larger or "more important" than the target in terms of market share or going-concern value, this being reflected in the term "acquisition." When the acquiring and target parties, or some of their businesses, are of roughly equal size or position, the term "merger" is often used instead. There are also reverse takeovers when a smaller company buys a larger one. The acquisition some years back by Royal Bank of Scotland of National Westminster Bank is an example of just such a case.

In addition to vagueness and similarities of meaning, what complicates the study of M&A further is that there are a variety of M&A types and several distinct typologies. First, a distinction needs to be made between friendly and hostile takeovers (Schweiger et al. 1987; Hunt 1990; see also Chapter 11).

Second, M&A types can be distinguished from one another on the basis of the strategic motive for the transaction. In one of the earliest scholarly studies of M&A, Kitching (1967) introduced the following typology: (1) horizontal acquisitions, referring to acquisitions conducted within the acquiring firm's industry; (2) vertical acquisitions, referring to acquisitions, where the target is a supplier or a customer within the acquiring firm's industry; (3) concentric acquisitions, when the firms engaged in the acquisition either share the same technology, but have different customers, or share the same customers, but have different technologies; (4) conglomerate acquisitions (also termed unrelated acquisitions) which refer to situations where the customers and technology of the acquiring and target firms differ. This typology is useful as it helps to set the broad scene of acquisition types. Whilst Kitching's (1967) typology has been influential in the M&A literature, since the 1960s the shift in the practice of M&A at least in the West has been from unrelated toward a variety of related acquisitions (see Chapter 2).

To capture the diversity of related acquisitions the more recent categorization by Bower (2001), for example, can prove helpful. He classified M&A strategies into: (1) overcapacity M&A, with the aim of reducing capacity within an industry; (2) geographic roll-up M&A, with the aim of expanding geographical presence; (3) product or market extension M&A, with the aim of expanding a firm's product line or international presence; (4) M&A as research and development, with the aim of strengthening the firm's R&D capability; and (5) industry-convergence M&A, where the acquiring firm is aiming to establish itself in a new, emerging, industry by acquiring firms from the various converging industries.

Having completed the transaction, the acquiring firm can then decide the extent to which it wishes to integrate target firm operations into its own operations. As Chapters 3 and 14 point out, acquiring firms have a variety of options for achieving this end, ranging from providing the target firm with full autonomy, to absorbing it into their operations, or aiming to synergistically combine the two (for an overview, see e.g. Haspeslagh and Jemison 1991). Significantly, not all acquisitions are alike in their approach to integration. Consummating an acquisition is not synonymous with integration, implementation difficulties, or indeed uniformity of approach (Haspeslagh and Jemison 1991; Child et al. 2001).

M&A vs. Other Forms of Interfirm Associations

Given the relative conceptual similarity between M&A and other forms of interorganizational associations, we shall next briefly aim to situate M&A in this broader realm. Interorganizational arrangements, in their various forms—including mergers, acquisitions, alliances, joint ventures, franchising, licensing, partnerships, outsourcing, and contracting arrangements—have been ongoing for the last century at an increasing pace and have increased in frequency since 1990 as globalization has gained pace. They represent forms of interfirm cooperation in an increasingly competitive global landscape (Buckley and Casson 1988; Beamish and Killing 1996).

The term "hybrid" was introduced in 1989 to denote these various forms of interorganizational encounters (Borys and Jemison 1989). This new term was paralleled by a call for more cross-fertilization of work across these hitherto separate fields of study. In the next few sections, we will examine these various forms of "hybrids" and analyze their similarities and differences. Table A.1 summarizes the discussion.

The fundamental difference between various forms of M&A and other forms of "hybrids" relates mainly to ownership. In M&A transactions, a transfer of ownership occurs. In contrast, with some other forms of "hybrids," a shorter-term perspective may be taken and sometimes no change of ownership takes place. An "alliance," for example, refers to two organizations opting to cooperate for a certain period of time with regard to specified joint objectives, be these related to winning new market share in a geographical market, conducting joint product development, or developing a joint technology platform. In other words, in alliances, only parts of both organizations cooperate, and sometimes only for a limited period of time. In many cases, such arrangements are accompanied by a limited purchase of each other's shares, often largely to demonstrate commitment, as in the examples of Rover/Honda and RBS/Santander. The interorganizational interface in alliances is thus more limited than it is in a merger or an acquisition, where by definition every person is somewhat affected. The managerial challenges in forging alliances relate to the difficulty in finding the right partner, negotiating suitable terms, and managing the interfirm interface during cooperation (Hamel 1991; Parkhe 1991; Reuer et al. 2002). Entering into an alliance partnership can at times be a precursor to a merger or an acquisition (Bleeke and Ernst 1993), a means of getting to know the other party better before engaging in a decision to buy a full stake in it.

Table A.1. Comparing and bridging forms of interfirm associations

	Definition	Types	Link to M&A
Acquisition	One firm buys another	Acquisitions differ depending on e.g.: • Strategic rationale behind the deal • Related/unrelated • Friendly or hostile • Domestic or cross-border • Degree of integration	Some acquisitions are termed mergers to mark their inherent or desired equity
Merger	Two firms merge to create a joint new entity	Mergers differ depending on: • Strategic rationale behind the deal • Related/unrelated • Degree of integration • Friendly or hostile • Domestic or cross-border	A way of masking an acquisition?
	Despite aims, economically one is the buyer		
	Often a friendly metaphor masking an acquisition		
Alliance	Two firms cooperating over a period of time on a certain objective		Can be a precursor to an M&A
Joint venture	The most common form of alliance, leading to the creation of a new organizational entity, termed a joint venture		Can be a precursor to an M&A
Licensing	A firm sells rights to manufacture/sell to another company in exchange for royalty payments		Can be a precursor to an M&A
Franchising	A firm sells its corporate concept to another company in exchange for royalty payments		Can be a precursor to an M&A
Relationship/ partnership	A (non)-contractual partnership between two firms		How to maintain relationships with key stakeholders after an M&A?
Outsourcing	An agreement to have a third party operate part of a company's operations		Can be a precursor to a divestment
Divestment	A company sells off parts of its operations		Mirror process to M&A for the selling firm Another acquisition for the target

Closely related to the logic of an alliance, a "joint venture"—the most popular sub-set within the alliance category—refers to a separately set-up organization that is jointly owned by two or more firms. The association might be formalized through written contract, or informally observed through a verbal understanding. This might apply in the case of a manufacturing site in Shanghai jointly owned by an American manufacturer and a local Chinese player. Both bring their own expertise to the deal. The key managerial issues in a joint venture relate to finding the right partner, negotiating suitable terms, and the post-deal governance of the newly founded firm (Barkema et al. 1997; Yan and Zeng 1999). A joint venture might also be based on the financial logic behind a merger, as in the case of the Nokia Siemens Networks merger, which financially was a joint venture between Nokia and Siemens, but in practice is a merger, and only time will tell whether it will turn out to be an acquisition by the majority owner.

Licensing and franchising are yet other forms of interfirm association (Lynch 2006). Both modes of operation are typically used when a firm seeks to increase its geographical reach by partnering with other firms. In licensing, a firm sells to another firm the rights to manufacture and/or sell its products in a certain market. This is often a relatively low-risk entry strategy to a new market, in which the licensor gets a guaranteed royalty on the percentage of sales and the licensee gets a fast track with an established brand name to a new market. In franchising, a firm sells the license to operate its firm concept to a "franchisee," in return for a royalty on the profits. The concept of McDonald's operating its outlets worldwide is a prime example of franchising. Linking back to M&A, it should be noted that both licensing and franchising can be precursors to an acquisition.

Another related mode of interfirm encounters is outsourcing. In this arrangement, a firm outsources parts of its operations or activities to another firm. Outsourced activities typically relate to non-core, non-strategic activities of the firm, outsourced to an organization that is considered to be more cost-effective at delivering these services, as they relate to its core activity.

One can also regard various form of partnering in the context of building relationships with one's suppliers and customers. This follows the logic of relationship marketing and relationship building (Christopher et al. 2002; Grönroos 2007), whereby a firm's long-term profitability depends on its ability to retain its customers, this in turn depending on its ability to develop enriching relationships with them.

Taking the reverse perspective, having undertaken an acquisition or a merger, the acquiring firm can, after a certain period of time, decide to sell or divest part or all of the target firm (Porter 1987). The divestment process represents the mirror-image of an acquisition process; yet for the acquired firm, or the target firm, a divestment is the start of a new acquisition by a new acquiring firm (Brauer 2006). Many firms' subsidiaries have undergone many acquisitions, and just as many divestitures, from their previous owners to their current ones.

Bridging these various forms of interfirm encounters with corporate-level strategies (Lynch 2006) of stability, growth, or retrenchment, we find the same pattern for all kinds of interfirm encounters. As Table A.2 highlights, they are all used when a firm seeks to grow, expand, or escape a potential predator. They are avoided when a firm aims to maintain stability, to limit its risk, and to make only small incremental strategic moves.

Table A.2 Linking interfirm associations with firm strategies

Type of interfirm association	Stability strategy	Growth strategy	Retrenchment strategy
Acquisition	• No acquisitions	• Industry concentration through horizontal integration (buying off a related firm) • Vertical integration to gain control of the supply chain (buying off a supplier, distributor ...) • Portfolio extension to gain access to new related and unrelated business areas • Geographical extension to gain access to new markets	• Avoid acquisitions
Merger	• No mergers	• Industry concentration through horizontal integration (buying off a related firm) • Vertical integration to gain control of the supply chain (buying off a supplier, distributor ...)	• Avoid acquisitions

Alliance	• Maintain current alliances	• Portfolio extension to gain access to new related and unrelated business areas • Geographical extension to gain access to new markets • Seek potential alliance partners	• Review viability of current alliances
Joint venture	• Maintain current joint ventures	• Seek potential joint venture partners	• Review viability of current joint ventures
Licensing	• Maintain current licensing agreements	• Seek potential licensing partners	• Review viability of current licensing agreements
Franchising	• Maintain current franchising agreements	• Seek potential franchising partners	• Review viability of current franchising agreements
Relationship/ partnership	• Maintain current partnerships and relationships	• Actively seek to expand business through the firm's relationships	• Review viability of firm's relationships
Outsourcing	• No changes in outsourcing strategy	• Seek outsourcing opportunities if that supports the firm's growth strategy	• Seek outsourcing opportunities
Divestment	• No divestments	• Seek to divest parts of one's business that do not help the firm to grow	• Seek to divest parts of firm's businesses

REFERENCES

Aldrich, H., & Pfeffer, J. (1976). "Environments of Organizations." *Annual Review of Sociology*, 2/1: 79–105.

Barkema, H. G., Shenkar, O., Vermeulen, F., & Bell, J. H. J. (1997). "Working Abroad, Working with Others: How Firms Learn to Operate International Joint Ventures." *Academy of Management Journal*, 40/2: 426–42.

Beamish, P., & Killing, P. (1996). "Introduction: Global Perspectives on Cooperative Strategies." *Journal of International Business Studies*, 27/5: iv–ix.

Berkovitch, E., & Narayanan, M. P. (1993). "Motives for Takeovers: An Empirical Investigation." *Journal of Finance and Quantitative Analysis*, 28: 347–62.

Bleeke, J., & Ernst, D. (1993). *Collaborating to Compete* (eds). New York: John Wiley & Sons.

Borys, B., & Jemison, D. (1989). "Hybrid Arrangements as Strategic Alliances: Theoretical Issues in Organizational Combinations." *The Academy of Management Review*, 14/22: 234–49.

Bower, J. L. (2001). "Not All M&As are Alike—And That Matters." *Harvard Business Review*, 79/3: 93–101.

Brauer, M. (2006). "What Have we Acquired and What Should We Acquire in Divestiture Research? A Review and Research Agenda." *Journal of Management*, 32: 751–85.

Buckley, P. J., & Casson, M. (1988). "A Theory of Cooperation in International Business," in F. Contractor & P. Lorange (eds.), *Cooperative Strategies in International Business*. Toronto: Lexington Books, 31–53.

—— & Ghauri, P. N. (2002). *International Mergers and Acquisitions: A Reader*. London: Thomson.

Child, J., Faulkner, D., & Pitkethly, R. (2001). *The Management of International Acquisitions*. Oxford: Oxford University Press.

Christopher, M., Payne, A., & Ballantyne, D. (2002). *Relationship Marketing: Creating Stakeholder Value*. Oxford: Butterworth Heinemann.

Grönroos, C. (2007). *Service Management and Marketing: Customer Management in Services*. Chichester: John Wiley and Sons.

Halpern, P. (1983). "Corporate Acquisitions: A Theory of Special Cases? A Review of Event Studies Applied to Acquisitions." *Journal of Finance*, 38/2: 297–317.

Hamel, G. (1991). "Competition for Competence and Inter-partner Learning within International Strategic Alliances." *Strategic Management Journal*, 12: 83–103.

Haspeslagh, P. C., & Jemison, D. B. (1991). *Managing Acquisitions: Creating Value through Corporate Renewal*. New York: The Free Press.

Hunt, J. (1988). "Managing the Successful Acquisition: A People Question." *London Business School Journal*, 12/1: 2–15.

—— (1990). "Changing Patterns of Acquisition Behaviour in Takeovers and the Consequences for Acquisition Processes." *Strategic Management Journal*, 11: 69–77.

Jensen, M. C., & Ruback, R. S. (1983). "The Market for Corporate Control." *Journal of Financial Economics*, 11/1–4: 5–50.

Kitching, J. (1967). "Why Do Mergers Miscarry?" *Harvard Business Review*, 45, November–December: 84–100.

Levinson, H. (1970). "A Psychologist Diagnoses Merger Failures." *Harvard Business Review*, 44/2: 139–42.

Lynch, R. (2006). *Corporate Strategy* (4th ed.). Harlow: Prentice Hall.

Marris, R. (1964). *The Economic Theory of Managerial Capitalism*. London: Macmillan.

Napier, N. K. (1989). "Mergers and Acquisitions, Human Resource Issues and Outcomes: A Review and Suggested Typology." *Journal of Management Studies*, 26/3: 271–89.

Parkhe, A. (1991). "Interfirm Diversity, Organisational Learning, and Longevity in Global Strategic Alliances." *Journal of International Business Studies*, 22, fourth quarter: 579–601.

Pfeffer, J. (1972). "Interorganizational Influence and Managerial Attitudes." *Academy of Management Journal*, 15: 317–30.

Porter, M. E. (1985). *Competitive Advantage*. New York: The Free Press.

—— (1987). "From Competitive Advantage to Corporate Strategy." *Harvard Business Review*, 65/3: 43–59.

Reuer, J. J., Zollo, M., & Singh, H. (2002). "Post-formation Dynamics in Strategic Alliances." *Strategic Management Journal*, 23: 135–51.

Rhoades, S. A. (1983). *Power, Empire-Building, and Mergers*. Lexington, MA: Lexington Books.

Roll, R. (1986). "The Hubris Hypothesis of Corporate Takeovers." *Journal of Business*, 12: 371–86.

Schweiger, D. M., Ivancevich, J. M., & Power, F. R. (1987). "Executive Actions for Managing Human Resources before and after Acquisition." *Academy of Management Executive*, 1/2: 127–38.

Yan, A., & Zeng, M. (1999). "International Joint Venture Instability: A Critique of Previous Research, a Reconceptualization, and Directions for Future Research." *Journal of International Business Studies*, 30/2: 397–414.

INDEX OF AUTHORS

SUBJECT INDEX

16003803R00448

Printed in Great Britain
by Amazon